Organizational Behavior 5e

Securing Competitive Advantage

John A. Wagner III
Michigan State University

John R. Hollenbeck
Michigan State University

THOMSON

SOUTH-WESTERN

Australia · Canada · Mexico · Singapore · Spain · United Kingdom · United States

Organizational Behavior: Securing Competitive Advantage, 5/e

John A. Wagner III & John R. Hollenbeck

VP/Editorial Director:
Jack W. Calhoun

VP/Editor-in-Chief:
Michael P. Roche

Senior Publisher:
Melissa S. Acuña

Acquisitions Editor:
Joseph A. Sabatino

Developmental Editor:
Emma Guttler

Marketing Manager:
Jacque Carrillo

Production Editor:
Margaret M. Bril

Media Developmental Editor:
Kristen Meere

Media Production Editor:
Karen Schaffer

Manufacturing Coordinator:
Rhonda Utley

Production House:
Lachina Publishing Services

Printer:
Quebecor World
Taunton, Massachusetts

Senior Design Project Manager:
Michael H. Stratton

Cover and Internal Designer:
Michael H. Stratton

Cover Images:
Artville/Marco Prozzo

For more information
contact South-Western,
5191 Natorp Boulevard,
Mason, Ohio 45040.
Or you can visit our Internet site at:
http://www.swlearning.com

To Mary Jane, Allison, Jillian, and Andrew Wagner

To Patty, Jennifer, Marie, Tim, and Jeff Hollenbeck

BRIEF CONTENTS

Preface   xvii

About the Authors   xxiii

PART 1   INTRODUCTION

CHAPTER 1   ORGANIZATIONAL BEHAVIOR   3

CHAPTER 2   MANAGEMENT AND MANAGERS   15

PART 2   MICRO ORGANIZATIONAL BEHAVIOR

CHAPTER 3   MANAGING DIVERSITY AND INDIVIDUAL
DIFFERENCES   43

CHAPTER 4   PERCEPTION, DECISION MAKING, AND CREATIVITY   71

CHAPTER 5   WORK MOTIVATION AND PERFORMANCE   103

CHAPTER 6   SATISFACTION AND STRESS   135

Case 2-1 Freida Mae Jones   163

Case 2-2 Precision Machine Tool   166

Case 2-3 Denver Department Stores   169

Case 2-4 Chancellor State University   173

Case 2-5 Connors Freight Lines   175

Case 2-6 Cameran Mutual Insurance Company   182

PART 3   MESO ORGANIZATIONAL BEHAVIOR

CHAPTER 7   EFFICIENCY, MOTIVATION, AND QUALITY
IN WORK DESIGN   187

CHAPTER 8   INTERDEPENDENCE AND ROLE RELATIONSHIPS   215

CHAPTER 9   GROUP DYNAMICS AND TEAM EFFECTIVENESS   249

CHAPTER 10 LEADERSHIP OF GROUPS AND ORGANIZATIONS   279

Case 3-1 The Lordstown Plant of General Motors   307

Case 3-2 Beta Bureau   314

Case 3-3 Nurse Ross   318

Case 3-4 Executive Retreat: A Case of Group Failure   323

Case 3-5 Bob Collins   329

Case 3-6 The Case of Dick Spencer   333

PART 4   MACRO ORGANIZATIONAL BEHAVIOR

CHAPTER 11   POWER, POLITICS, AND CONFLICT   343

CHAPTER 12   STRUCTURING THE ORGANIZATION   373

CHAPTER 13   TECHNOLOGY, ENVIRONMENT, AND ORGANIZATION DESIGN   405

CHAPTER 14   CULTURE, CHANGE, AND ORGANIZATION DEVELOPMENT   435

Case 4-1 City National Bank   465

Case 4-2 Newcomer-Willson Hospital   467

Case 4-3 O Canada   472

Case 4-4 Dumas Public Library   478

Case 4-5 L. J. Summers Company   495

Case 4-6 Consolidated Life: Caught between Two Corporate Cultures   499

Case 4-7 World International Airlines, Inc.   502

PART 5   CONCLUSION

CHAPTER 15   INTERNATIONAL ORGANIZATIONAL BEHAVIOR   509

CHAPTER 16   CRITICAL THINKING AND CONTINUOUS LEARNING   531

Endnotes   557

Glossary   G-1

Index   I-1

CONTENTS

Preface   xvii

About the Authors   xxiii

PART 1   INTRODUCTION

CHAPTER 1   ORGANIZATIONAL BEHAVIOR   3

Defining Organizational Behavior   5
*Micro Organizational Behavior 7, Meso Organizational
Behavior 7, Macro Organizational Behavior 7*

Contemporary Issues   8
*Workforce Diversity 8, Team Productivity 8,
Organizational Adaptability 8, International Growth
and Development 8*

Putting Organizational Behavior Knowledge
to Work   9
*Diagnosis 9, Solution 10, Action 10, Evaluation 10,
Becoming an Active Problem Solver 11*

Overview of This Book   11

Summary   13

Review Questions   13

CHAPTER 2   MANAGEMENT AND MANAGERS   15

Defining Management   16
*Three Attributes of Organizations 16, Formal
Definition 17*

What Managers Do   21
*Managerial Jobs 21, Managerial Skills 23, Managerial
Roles 24, The Nature of Managerial Work 26*

A Framework of Management Perspectives   27
*1890–1940: The Scientific Management Perspective 28,
1900–1950: The Administrative Principles Perspective 30,
1930–1970: The Human Relations Perspective 32,
1960–Present: The Open Systems Perspective 36,
A Contingency Framework 38*

Summary   39

Review Questions   39

PART 2   MICRO ORGANIZATIONAL BEHAVIOR

CHAPTER 3   MANAGING DIVERSITY AND INDIVIDUAL DIFFERENCES   43

Capitalizing on Diversity   45
Selection 45, Training 46, Reengineering 47

Diversity in Personality: Five Critical Factors   48
The Big Five Framework 48, Making Personality Tests More Effective 51

Diversity in Cognitive Abilities: Four Critical Factors   52
General and Specific Aspects of Cognitive Ability 52, Validity of Cognitive Ability Tests 53

Diversity in Physical Abilities: Three Critical Factors   55

Diversity in Experience: Two Critical Factors   56
Broadening Demographic Experience: Political Aspects 58, Broadening Demographic Experience: Competitive Aspects 59, Broadening Cultural Experience 62

Adaptability: Flexibility in the Face of Diversity   64

Summary   65

Review Questions   65

Learning Through Experience   66

CHAPTER 4   PERCEPTION, DECISION MAKING, AND CREATIVITY   71

Perceptual Processes   73
Attention 74, Organization 75, Recall 77, Reducing Perceptual Problems 78

Decision-Making Processes   80
The Rational Decision-Making Model 80, The Administrative Decision-Making Model 90, Reducing Decision-Making Errors 91

Creativity in Decision Making   92
The Creative Process 93, Creative People 94, Creativity-Inducing Situations 95

Summary   96

Review Questions   96

Learning Through Experience   97

CHAPTER 5   WORK MOTIVATION AND PERFORMANCE   103

A Model of Motivation and Performance   106
*Expectancy Theory   106, Supplemental
Theories   107, Overview of the Model   107*

Valence: Need Theories   108
*Maslow's Need Hierarchy   109, Murray's Theory
of Manifest Needs   110*

Instrumentality: Learning Theories   111
Reinforcement Theory   113, Social Learning   117

Expectancy: Self-Efficacy Theory   118
*Self-Efficacy and Behavior   118, Sources
of Self-Efficacy   118*

Accuracy of Role Perceptions:
Goal-Setting Theory   119
*Important Goal Attributes   120, Goal Commitment
and Participation   121, Goals and Strategies   122*

Ability and Experience Revisited   123
*Nonmotivational Determinants of Performance   123,
Experience and Cyclical Effects   124*

High-Performance Work Systems   126
*Merit-Pay and Incentive Systems   127,
Profit-Sharing and Cost-Savings Plans   128*

Summary   129

Review Questions   130

Learning Through Experience   130

CHAPTER 6   SATISFACTION AND STRESS   135

Defining Satisfaction and Stress   138
*Satisfaction   138, Stress   138, Measuring
Satisfaction and Stress   140*

Organizational Costs of Dissatisfaction
and Stress   141

Performance at the Individual and Organizational Level 141, Health Care Costs 142, Absenteeism and Turnover 143, Low Organizational Commitment and Citizenship 143, Workplace Violence and Sabotage 144

Sources of Dissatisfaction and Stress   146
Physical and Social Environment 146, Personal Dispositions 147, Organizational Tasks 148, Organization Roles 149

Eliminating and Coping
with Dissatisfaction and Stress   152
Identifying Symptoms of Dissatisfaction and Stress 152, Eliminating Dissatisfying and Stressful Conditions 152, Managing Symptoms of Dissatisfaction and Stress 153

Summary   155

Review Questions   155

Learning Through Experience   156

Case 2-1 **Freida Mae Jones**   **163**
Case 2-2 **Precision Machine Tool**   **166**
Case 2-3 **Denver Department Stores**   **169**
Case 2-4 **Chancellor State University**   **173**
Case 2-5 **Connors Freight Lines**   **175**
Case 2-6 **Cameran Mutual Insurance Company**   **182**

PART 3   MESO ORGANIZATIONAL BEHAVIOR

CHAPTER 7   **EFFICIENCY, MOTIVATION, AND QUALITY IN WORK DESIGN**   **187**

The Efficiency Perspective   188
Methods Engineering 188, Work Measurement: Motion and Time Studies 192, Evaluating Industrial Engineering and the Efficiency Perspective 192

The Motivational Perspective   193
Horizontal Job Enlargement 193, Vertical Job Enrichment 194, Comprehensive Job Enrichment 197, Sociotechnical Enrichment 200, Evaluating the Motivational Perspective 202

The Quality Perspective   203
*Quality Circles 204, Self-Managing Teams 206,
Automation and Robotics 206, Evaluating the
Quality Perspective 207*

Summary   208

Review Questions   208

Learning Through Experience   209

**CHAPTER 8   INTERDEPENDENCE AND ROLE
RELATIONSHIPS   215**

Patterns of Interdependence and
Organizational Roles   217
*Types of Interdependence 217, Implications of
Interdependence 218, Role Taking and Role Making
219, Norms and Role Episodes 220*

Communication Processes in
Interdependent Relationships   223
*Communication Messages and Media 223, Barriers
to Effective Communication 225*

Socialization to New Roles   227
*Socialization Goals and Tactics 230, Designing
Socialization Programs 232*

Quality of Interpersonal Role Relationships 233
*Equity and Social Comparisons 233, Distributive,
Procedural, and Interactive Justice 234, Responses
to Inequity 236, Managing Inequitable Situations 238*

Summary   240

Review Questions   240

Learning Through Experience   241

**CHAPTER 9   GROUP DYNAMICS AND TEAM
EFFECTIVENESS   249**

Formation and Development of Groups   251
Group Formation 252, Group Development 255

Group versus Individual Productivity   256
*Process Loss 256, Group Synergy 258, Groups
versus Teams 259*

Keys to Team Effectiveness: Setting
the Stage   260
Task Structure 260, Communication Structure 261,
Group Size 263, Group Composition 263

Keys to Team Effectiveness: Managing
the Process   267
Motivation in Groups 267, Group
Cohesiveness 270, Group Conflict 272

Summary   273

Review Questions   273

Learning Through Experience   274

**CHAPTER 10   LEADERSHIP OF GROUPS AND
              ORGANIZATIONS   279**

The Integrated Leadership Model   281

Universal Approaches to Leadership   284
Leader Traits 285, Leader Decision-Making
Styles 285, Leader Behaviors 287, Transformational
Leadership 288, Leader Irrelevance 289

Characteristics of Followers and Situations   291
The Leadership Motivation Pattern 291, Vertical
Dyad Linkage 292, Life-Cycle Model 293,
Substitutes for Leadership 294

Comprehensive Theories of Leadership   295
Fiedler's Contingency Theory 296, Vroom–Yetton
Decision Tree Model 297, Path–Goal Theory 300

The Integrated Leadership Model Revisited   301

Summary   302

Review Questions   303

Learning Through Experience   303

Case 3-1 **The Lordstown Plant of General Motors**   307
Case 3-2 **Beta Bureau**   314
Case 3-3 **Nurse Ross**   318
Case 3-4 **Executive Retreat: A Case of Group Failure** 323
Case 3-5 **Bob Collins**   329
Case 3-6 **The Case of Dick Spencer**   333

PART 4   MACRO ORGANIZATIONAL BEHAVIOR

CHAPTER 11 POWER, POLITICS, AND CONFLICT   343

Power in Organizations   344
*Interpersonal Sources of Power   345, Conformity
Responses to Interpersonal Power   347, A Model of
Interpersonal Power: Assessment   348, Structural
Sources of Power   349, The Critical Contingencies
Model: Assessment   351*

Politics and Political Processes   352
*Personality and Politics   353, Conditions That
Stimulate Politics   354, Political Tactics   354,
Managing Destructive Politics   356*

Conflict in Organizations   357
*Is Conflict Necessarily Bad?   357, Conditions That
Stimulate Conflict   358, Effects of Conflict   360*

Negotiation and Restructuring   360
*Managing Diverging Interests   360, Managing
Structural Interdependence   362*

Summary   366
Review Questions   366
Learning Through Experience   367

CHAPTER 12 STRUCTURING THE ORGANIZATION   373

Structural Coordination   374
*Basic Coordination Mechanisms   375, Choosing
among the Mechanisms   378*

Departmentation   381
Hierarchy and Centralization   383
Types of Organization Structure   385
*Prebureaucratic Structures   385, Bureaucratic
Structures   387, Postbureaucratic Structures   393*

Summary   394
Review Questions   395
Learning Through Experience   395

**CHAPTER 13 TECHNOLOGY, ENVIRONMENT, AND
ORGANIZATION DESIGN**   **405**

An Adaptive Model
of Organization Design   406
*Organizational Effectiveness   407, Structural
Alternatives   408, Structural Contingencies   410*

Lifecycle Contingencies: Age and Stage
of Development   410

Inception Contingencies   413

Formalization and Elaboration
Contingencies   414
*Core Technology   414, The External
Environment   419*

Transformation Contingencies   425
*Environmental Turbulence   426, Transaction
Costs   426, Final Considerations   428*

Summary   429

Review Questions   429

Learning Through Experience   430

**CHAPTER 14 CULTURE, CHANGE, AND
ORGANIZATION DEVELOPMENT**   **435**

Organization Culture   436
*Elements of Organization Culture   437, Managing
Organization Culture   440*

Change and Organization Development   442
Resistance to Change   443, Action Research   446

Organization Development Interventions   448
*Interpersonal Interventions   449, Group
Interventions   451, Intergroup Interventions   453,
Organizational Interventions   455*

Evaluating Change and Development   457

Summary   459

Review Questions   459

Learning Through Experience   460

Case 4-1 **City National Bank**   **465**
Case 4-2 **Newcomer-Willson Hospital**   **467**
Case 4-3 **O Canada**   **472**
Case 4-4 **Dumas Public Library**   **478**
Case 4-5 **L. J. Summers Company**   **495**
Case 4-6 **Consolidated Life: Caught between Two
          Corporate Cultures**   **499**
Case 4-7 **World International Airlines, Inc.**   **502**

PART 5   CONCLUSION

**CHAPTER 15 INTERNATIONAL ORGANIZATIONAL
             BEHAVIOR**   **509**

International Dimensions   510
*Uncertainty Avoidance 510, Masculinity–Femininity
511, Individualism–Collectivism 512, Power Distance
513, Short-Term/Long-Term Orientation 513*

Effects on Organizational Behavior   514
*Cultural Trends: Four Scenarios 514, Organizational
Effects 517, Cross-Cultural Differences 518*

Managing International Differences   522

Summary   525

Review Questions   525

Learning Through Experience   526

**CHAPTER 16 CRITICAL THINKING AND
             CONTINUOUS LEARNING**   **531**

Critical Thinking and the Scientific Process   534
*Ways of Knowing 534, The Purposes of
Science 536, The Interplay of Theory and
Data 537, Characteristics of Good Theories and
Good Data 538*

Causal Inferences   540
*Criteria for Inferring Cause 541, Designing
Observations to Infer Cause 545*

Generalizing Research Results   549
*Sample, Setting, and Time   549, Facilitating
Generalization   550*

Linking Organizational Behavior Science
and Practice   551

Summary   554

Review Questions   555

Endnotes   557
Glossary   G-1
Index   I-1

COMPETING FOR ADVANTAGE

In today's business environment, competition arises when other organizations seek to do what your company does, only better. Advantage is gained when you can do something your competitors find difficult to duplicate. Competitive advantage is further secured when competitors cannot duplicate your company's special ability at all.

We contend—based on solid research evidence—that an especially strong source of competitive advantage rests in the hands of the people who make up your organization. One of the most effective ways to secure competitive advantage is to make the best use of the knowledge, skills, and other human assets possessed by your company's employees. No other firm has the same people as yours. Therefore, no other company can duplicate the range of products and services requiring the particular capabilities of the members of your firm. Managing organizational behavior is thus essential to the process of gaining and sustaining competitive advantage. This statement is a central theme of our book.

COMMON SENSE OR VALUABLE INSIGHT?

Over the years, we have taught courses on management and organizational behavior, and we have also talked regularly with others who have taught similar courses in companies, schools, and universities throughout the world. In our experiences and conversations, we've noticed a recurring lament: Although the management of organizational behavior is a topic whose importance should be evident, students often don't take courses on organizational behavior that seriously. One typical student reaction is to argue that organizational behavior is little more than common sense. Another is to suggest that management and organizational behavior are soft subjects, lacking much in the way of hard facts and figures. A third is to claim that organizational behavior is nothing but theory and research and not at all about anything real or practical.

All three of these reactions are mistaken. When sufficiently understood, the field of organizational behavior is a valuable source of practical insight that managers can use to improve the workings of their own firms and to thrive where others might fail. Nonetheless, in trying to determine the reason for the existence of such negative reactions, we've found that they *are* reasonably accurate reactions of the way organizational behavior is treated in many contemporary textbooks. In some instances, textbook authors have avoided deep coverage. In others, they have failed to build any sense of challenge. In yet others, authors have resisted making the appropriate connection between theory and practice. All of these failings have driven down the substance, factuality, and utility of textbooks. All have contributed to the false perception that organizational behavior is simplistic and of little use.

Despite this trend, we know through personal experience that students *do* have the ability to excel when challenged to learn something meaningful. We know that properly presented materials can motivate exceptional student performance. Thus, we have developed a textbook that requires students to think and take seriously what it has to say. This challenge, we believe, is the key to reversing the all-too-prevalent tendency to underestimate the importance of understanding how to manage organizational behavior.

DISTINGUISHING PEDAGOGICAL FEATURES

As in earlier editions, our writing of the fifth edition was guided by two primary goals: first, to cover the field of organizational behavior thoroughly and accurately, and second, to offer you, the student, solid guidance in using the theories and concepts that we discuss. With these two objectives before us, we created a set of tools that will help you acquire the skills and expertise you'll need to be an effective manager in the complex work world.

In addition to the thoroughly updated and revised information presented in each chapter, we have redesigned the feature set to provide both student and instructor with up-to-date information about current topics in organizational behavior. Each box features real companies and real situations, providing students with concrete examples of the material presented in the text.

Securing Competitive Advantage

This boxed feature provides insight into the competitive advantages provided by organizational behavior. Each box pinpoints an issue and explores the climate surrounding the competitive advantage as discussed in the box.

Cutting-Edge Research

Current topics in organizational behavior are discussed in these boxes, and areas of ongoing research are presented.

Ethics and Social Responsibility

Each box considers an ethical dilemma faced by various individuals or organizations, and the outcome of their decisions.

End-of-Chapter Materials

To reinforce the real world applications of the text's theories and concepts, students will find a variety of examples using real people and familiar companies. This reinforces text material, and makes the concepts easier to grasp. Each chapter also includes end-of-chapter summary material and review questions designed to help you understand and remember what you've learned while reading our book.

Cases and Experiential Exercises

Instructors and students demand comprehensive textbooks. For this reason, in preparing the fifth edition we've integrated experiential exercises and cases into the central chapters of our book. Along with the diagnostic questions that accompany these chapters and the summary models presented at various points, the exercises and cases included in the fifth edition afford students the opportunity to use what they have learned from our book to solve realistic business problems in a classroom setting. The cases also provide an opportunity to develop useful skills that will help them succeed as managers outside the classroom. As cases can be applicable to any number of topics, they are grouped at the end of each part to provide flexibility of usage.

Tasks that were once accomplished by individuals working alone, coordinated by massive hierarchies, today are performed increasingly by self-managed groups connected by computerized information systems. The implications of this change are immense, and they are considered carefully in our book. As a result, the fifth edition presents a thoroughly contemporary overview of the field of organizational behavior.

SUPPLEMENTARY MATERIALS

The fifth edition's ancillary package is loaded with powerful resources for students and instructor alike. This expansive collection of supplemental teaching materials offers support to instructors—from the novice to the most seasoned professor. Completely integrated with the text, this comprehensive package continues to lead the market with its innovative and real-world management application.

Instructor's Manual

Designed to provide support for instructors new to the course, as well as innovative materials for more experienced professors, the *Instructor's Manual* contains chapter outlines, detailed lecture outlines, answers to the end-of-chapter questions, teaching notes, and answers to the exercises and supplementary case materials.

Test Bank

Scrutinized for accuracy, the *Test Bank* includes more than 1500 true/false, multiple choice, and discussion questions.

ExamView®

ExamView® contains all of the questions in the printed test bank. This program is an easy-to-use test creation software compatible with Microsoft Windows. Instructors can add or edit questions, instructions, and answers, and can select questions (randomly or numerically) by previewing them on the screen. Instructors can also create and administer quizzes online, whether over the Internet, a local area network (LAN), or a wide area network (WAN).

PowerPoint Lecture Presentation

Available on the Instructor's Resource CD-ROM and the web site, the PowerPoint Lecture Presentation enables instructors to customize their own multimedia classroom presentation. Containing approximately 200 slides, the package includes figures and tables from the text as well as outside materials to supplement chapter concepts. Material is organized by chapter and can be modified or expanded for individual classroom use. PowerPoint slides are also easily printed to create customized Transparency Masters.

Instructor's CD-ROM

Key instructor ancillaries (*Instructor's Manual, Test Bank,* ExamView and PowerPoint slides) are provided on CD-ROM, giving instructors the ultimate tool for customizing lectures and presentations.

Videos

A complete set of videos shows students how organizations are dealing with issues such as diversity in the workforce, the importance of individuals in the larger organization, motivation, communication, teamwork, organizational structure, and organizational change.

Web Site (http://wagner.swlearning.com)

The Wagner/Hollenbeck web site is a comprehensive, resource rich location for both instructors and students to find pertinent information. The Instructor Resource center includes an Instructors Manual download, as well as the Test Bank and PowerPoint Lecture Presentation, and a PDF file of one chapter. The Interactive Study Center contains a complete text glossary and key end of chapter materials for online reference.

InfoTrac® College Edition

Free with the purchase of each textbook, this online database of articles gives students access to full-text articles from hundreds of scholarly and popular periodicals such as *Newsweek, Time,* and *USA Today.* Updated daily, this tool allows students to research topics pertinent to classroom discussion and to keep up with current events.

TextChoice: Management Exercises and Cases

TextChoice is the home of Thomson Learning's online digital content. TextChoice provides the fastest, easiest way for you to create your own learning materials. South-Western's Management Exercises and Cases database includes a variety of experiential exercises, classroom activities, management in film exercises, and cases to enhance any management course. Choose as many exercises as you like and even add your own material to create a supplement tailor-fitted to your course. Contact your South-Western/Thomson Learning sales representative for more information.

eCoursepacks

Create a tailor-fitted, easy-to-use online companion for any course with eCoursepacks, from Thomson companies South-Western and Gale. The eCoursepacks tools give educators access to content from thousands of current popular, professional, and academic periodicals, as well as NACRA and Darden cases, and business and industry information from Gale. In addition, instructors can easily add their own material with the option of even collecting a royalty. Permissions for all eCoursepack content are already secured, saving instructors the time and worry with securing rights.

The eCoursepacks online publishing tools also save time and energy by allowing instructors to quickly search the databases to make selections, organize all the content, and publish the final online product in a clean, uniform, full-color format. The eCoursepacks system is the best way to provide current information quickly and inexpensively. To learn more, visit: **http://ecoursepacks.swlearning.com.**

AN INVITATION

By reading this book, you are committing yourself to learn how to manage organizational behavior. We can't think of anything more important for you to understand. In return for this commitment, we extend a special invitation to you, our newest student. We want to know how you like our book and how you feel about the field of organizational behavior.

We encourage you to contact us with your ideas, especially your suggestions for making improvements to future editions. Please write to us at:

Michigan State University
Eli Broad Graduate School of Management
Department of Management
East Lansing, Michigan 48824-1122

John A. Wagner III
John R. Hollenbeck

JOHN A. WAGNER III is professor and chair of the department of management in the Eli Broad College of Business and Graduate School of Management at Michigan State University. Professor Wagner received his Ph.D. degree in business administration from the University of Illinois at Urbana–Champaign in 1982. He has taught undergraduate and graduate courses in management, organizational behavior, and organization theory.

Professor Wagner is a member of the review board of *Administrative Science Quarterly* and past member of the board of *Academy of Management Review*. He is also series editor of *Qualitative Organizational Research*. In 1989 Professor Wagner was co-recipient of the Scholarly Achievement Award conferred by the Human Resources Division of the Academy of Management. In 1993 he received the Research Methods Division's Walter de Gruyter Best Paper Award. He is a member of the Academy of Management and the American Psychological Association.

Professor Wagner's research is in the fields of organizational behavior and organization theory. His publications have examined the efficacy of participatory decision making, the effects of individualism-collectivism on cooperation and performance, the effects of size on the performance of groups and organizations, and the long-term effects of incentive payment on group productivity.

JOHN R. HOLLENBECK received his Ph.D. degree in management from New York University in 1984, and he is currently the Eli Broad Professor of Management at the Eli Broad Graduate School of Business Administration at Michigan State University. He teaches graduate courses in organizational behavior and research methods.

Professor Hollenbeck served as the acting editor at *Organizational Behavior and Human Decision Processes* in 1995, served as the editor of *Personnel Psychology* from 1996 to 2002, and currently serves as the associate editor of *Decision Sciences*. Prior to serving as editor, he served on the editorial boards of these journals, as well as the boards of the *Academy of Management Journal,* the *Journal of Applied Psychology,* and the *Journal of Management*. He was the APA Program chair in 1996 and the SIOP Program Chair in 1997.

Professor Hollenbeck has published more than sixty articles and book chapters on the topics of team decision making and work motivation. He was the first recipient of the Ernest J. McCormick award for early contributions to the field of industrial and organizational psychology in 1992, and is a fellow of the American Psychological Association.

1

Introduction

Chapter 1 Organizational Behavior

Chapter 2 Management and Managers

CHAPTER

1

Defining Organizational Behavior
Micro Organizational Behavior
Meso Organizational Behavior
Macro Organizational Behavior

Contemporary Issues
Workforce Diversity
Team Productivity
Organizational Adaptability
International Growth and Development

Putting Organizational Behavior Knowledge to Work
Diagnosis
Solution
Action
Evaluation
Becoming an Active Problem Solver

Overview of This Book
Summary
Review Questions

Organizational Behavior

Throughout the world, workplace productivity has grown steadily for more than a decade, allowing standards of living to rise significantly without the threat of significant economic inflation. With recent technological advancements in such areas as information systems, manufacturing processes, inventory management, and service delivery, the current trend of increasing productivity may extend well into the future. Nonetheless, individual companies sometimes run into productivity problems. Consider Ford Motor Company, one of the North American "Big Three" automotive manufacturers. Headquartered in Detroit, Michigan, and with operations around the world, Ford and its subsidiaries build cars ranging from the economical Ford Focus and sporty Ford Mustang to the fashionable Land Rover SUV and luxury-market Jaguar X-type. Competition in the automotive manufacturing industry is fierce, involving aggressive discounting by domestic producers Daimler-Chrysler and General Motors (GM) as well as attractive pricing by international competitors including Toyota, Volkswagen, Honda, and BMW. CEO William Clay "Bill" Ford Jr. faces the daunting task of cutting up to $4.5 billion in expenses while updating aging product lines and shoring up falling quality. Although company projections indicate that Ford will capture greater market share and increase profitability over the next several years, its current production costs per vehicle trail well behind those of GM and DaimlerChrysler, and may continue to do so even after the pending closings of four U.S. manufacturing plants and loss of up to 15,000 jobs. In the absence of higher workforce productivity, Ford may be unable to live up to the expectations of its management, stockholders, and customers.[1]

What would you do if you were a manager in a company like Ford Motor Company? How would you improve employee productivity in the face of unacceptably high production costs? Suppose that initial assessments indicate that productivity lapses in your company are due to poor employee motivation and your boss tells you to solve this problem. Your future with the company—and possibly the future of the company itself—depends on whether you can find a way to improve employee motivation. To help you decide what to do, you call in four highly recommended management consultants.

After analyzing your company's situation, the first consultant states that many of today's jobs are so simple, monotonous, and uninteresting that they dampen employee motivation and fulfillment. As a result, employees become so bored and resentful that productivity falls off. The consultant recommends that you redesign your firm's jobs in order to make them more complex, stimulating, and fulfilling. Employees challenged by these new jobs will feel motivated to improve performance, leading to higher workforce productivity and reduced production costs.

The second consultant performs her own assessment of your company. As she reviews her findings, she agrees that monotonous work can reduce employee motivation. She says, however, that the absence of clear, challenging goals is an even greater threat to motivation and productivity at your firm. Such goals provide performance targets that draw attention to the work to be done and focus employee effort on achieving success. The second consultant advises you to solve your company's productivity problem by implementing a program of formal goal setting.

The third consultant conducts an investigation and concedes that both job design and goal setting can improve employee motivation. She suggests, however, that you consider establishing a contingent payment program. Contingent payment means paying employees according to their performance instead of giving them fixed salaries or hourly wages. For instance, salespeople may be paid commissions on their sales, production employees may be paid piece-rate wages according to their productivity, and executives may be paid bonuses based on the firm's profitability. The consultant points out that contingent payment programs change the way wages are *distributed* but not necessarily the *amount* of wages paid to the workforce as a whole.

Finally, the fourth consultant examines your situation and agrees that any of the other three approaches might work, but describes another technique that is often used to deal with motivational problems—allowing employees to participate in decision making. He suggests that such participation gives employees a sense of belonging or ownership that energizes productivity. To support his recommendation, he recites an impressive list of companies—among them, General Motors, IBM, and General Electric—that have established well-known participatory programs.

Later, alone in your office, you consider the four consultants' reports and conclude that you should probably recommend all four alternatives—just in case one or more of the consultants are wrong. Unfortunately, you also realize that your company can afford the time and money needed to implement only one of the recommendations. What should you do? Which alternative should you choose?

According to contemporary research comparing the effectiveness of these alternatives, if you choose the first option, job redesign, productivity would probably rise by 9 percent.[2] An increase of this size would save your job, keep your company in business, and probably earn you the company president's lasting gratitude. If you choose the second alternative, goal setting, productivity would probably increase by 16 percent.[3] This outcome would save your job and your company, and it might even put you in the running for a promotion. If you choose the third alternative, contingent payment, productivity could be expected to increase by approximately 30 percent.[4] A gain of this magnitude would ensure your place in the company's executive suites for the rest of your career.

But what about the fourth alternative, employee participation in decision making? How might this approach affect productivity, where low performance is attributable to poor motivation? Knowing that managers are choosing participatory programs at an increasing rate to solve motivation problems, you might think that this alternative should work at least as well as the other three. Surprisingly, participation usually has no effect on productivity problems caused by poor motivation. Despite the fourth consultant's suggestion, employee participation is likely to improve motivation and performance only when combined with one or more of the other three alternatives.[5] If you choose participation, then, you and the other members of your firm might soon be looking for new jobs. Perhaps your choice might even cost your company its existence.

How realistic is this story? In fact, the predicament it portrays is an everyday problem. Besides our example of Ford, experts throughout the world have pointed out many other instances of low organizational productivity, often identifying "people problems" as an important factor in causing these situations.[6] Solving such problems is critical to company survival and growth in today's competitive environment. As suggested in the Securing Competitive Advantage box, problems associated with the management of people may grow even more pressing in the future as the supply of skilled workers diminishes throughout the world. Knowing which solutions to choose and how to implement them will differentiate organizations that succeed and thrive from those that fail.

More generally, competitive success depends on the ability to produce some product or service that is perceived as valuable by some group of consumers, and to do so in a way that no one else can duplicate.[7] At first glance, there appear to be many ways to accomplish this feat. Most experts agree, however, that an organization's employees are its foremost source of competitive advantage. If your company employs the best people and is able to hold on to them, it enjoys a competitive edge not easily duplicated by other firms. If your company also has the "know-how" to properly manage its employees, it has an advantage that can be sustained and even strengthened over time.[8]

In the case of our opening example, the know-how needed to solve motivational productivity problems like those encountered at the Ford Motor Company and similar firms can be found in the field of organizational behavior. Without this knowledge, managers have no solid basis for accepting any one consultant's advice or for choosing one particular way to solve people problems instead of another. With it, managers have the guidance needed to avoid costly or even catastrophic mistakes and instead make effective choices. *The management of people through the application of knowledge from the field of organizational behavior is a primary means through which competitive advantage can be created and sustained.*

DEFINING ORGANIZATIONAL BEHAVIOR

Organizational behavior is a field of study that endeavors to understand, explain, predict, and change human behavior as it occurs in the organizational context. Underlying this definition are three important considerations:

1. Organizational behavior focuses on observable behaviors, such as talking in a meeting, running production equipment, or writing a report. It also deals with

SECURING COMPETITIVE ADVANTAGE

HOW WILL COMPANIES COPE WITH WORKER SHORTAGES?

Demographic trends in developed countries throughout the world suggest that human capital will become increasingly difficult to attract and retain. In Japan and Western Europe, the depressed birthrates of today mean that fewer able-bodied workers will be available for employment in the coming decades. Although immigration rates in the United States will shore up its population, current trends in college graduation make it probable that highly skilled employees will be in short supply. Given that a company's strongest competitive advantage rests in its workforce, today's "people problems" seem likely to take on even greater importance in the future. Effectiveness in the management of organizational behavior will become increasingly crucial to the success of tomorrow's companies.

Even now, skilled workers are hard to attract and retain in many parts of the United States. For example, human resource managers at the 15,000-employee New York Presbyterian Hospital found it necessary to award ultrasound and X-ray technicians two raises in a single year, totaling 7 percent of their $50,000-per-year pay, in addition to annual merit pay increases. The hospital also increased employee tuition assistance from $2,000 to $10,000, hoping that lesser-skilled employees would use the opportunity to develop the abilities needed to move up to skilled positions. According to hospital spokespeople, such changes are due to the loss of employees to other hospitals and pharmacies in the region who

have mounted aggressive campaigns aimed at stealing skilled workers away from current employers. The hospital feels it has no choice but to become equally aggressive in its efforts to retain existing skilled employees and "grow" newly skilled workers out of its pool of general labor.

What else will companies do to cope with such problems? One recommended solution is to offer more flexible working hours, to allow the parents of young children the opportunity to keep their jobs and fulfill childcare and other parental roles. Another possibility is to induce older workers to put off retirement or return to work (an option that also reduces retirement costs). A third alternative is to hike spending on training and education—as done by the hospital—to broaden the supply of skilled workers. A fourth approach is to offer rewards such as stock options or direct company ownership as a way to build up loyalty.

Implemented alone, none of these options will be able to solve the problems caused by chronic labor shortages, whether current or pending. In fact, companies will find it necessary to continue to look for additional approaches, and to combine them in multifaceted programs intended to create and retain the necessary skilled workforce. In this endeavor, knowledge derived from the field of organizational behavior will provide the guidance needed to attract or train highly prized workers and secure continued competitive advantage through their retention.

Sources: A. Bernstein, "Too Many Workers? Not For Long," *Business Week,* May 20, 2002, pp. 126–130; J. Ewing, K. Carlisle, and K. Capell, "Help Wanted," *Business Week,* September 17, 2001, pp. 52–53; G. Smith, "Is the Magic Starting to Fade?" *Business Week,* August 6, 2002, pp. 42–43.

the internal states, such as thinking, perceiving, and deciding, that accompany visible actions.
2. Organizational behavior involves the analysis of how people behave both as individuals and as members of groups and organizations.
3. Organizational behavior also assesses the "behavior" of groups and organizations per se. Neither groups nor organizations "behave" in the same sense that people do. Nevertheless, some events occur in organizations that cannot be explained in terms of individual behavior. These events must be examined in terms of group or organizational processes.

The field of organizational behavior traces its roots to the late 1940s, when researchers in psychology, sociology, political science, economics, and other social sciences joined together in an effort to develop a comprehensive body of organizational research.[9] Despite the intentions of its founders, however, the field has re-

TABLE 1-1
Subfields of
Organizational
Behavior

Subfield	Focus	Origins
Micro organizational behavior	Individuals	Experimental, clinical, and organizational psychology
Meso organizational behavior	Groups	Communication, social psychology, and interactionist sociology, plus the origins of the other two subfields
Macro organizational behavior	Organizations	Sociology, political science, anthropology, and economics

sisted unification. It is now divided into the three distinct subfields, delineated in Table 1-1: micro organizational behavior, meso organizational behavior, and macro organizational behavior.

Micro Organizational Behavior

Micro organizational behavior is concerned mainly with the behaviors of individuals working alone.[10] Three subfields of psychology were the principal contributors to the beginnings of micro organizational behavior. *Experimental psychology* provided theories of learning, motivation, perception, and stress. *Clinical psychology* furnished models of personality and human development. *Industrial psychology* offered theories of employee selection, workplace attitudes, and performance assessment. Owing to this heritage, micro organizational behavior has a distinctly psychological orientation. Among the questions it examines are the following: How do differences in ability affect employee productivity? What motivates employees to perform their jobs? How do employees develop perceptions of their workplace, and how do these perceptions in turn influence their behavior?

Meso Organizational Behavior

Meso organizational behavior is a middle ground, bridging the other two subfields of organizational behavior.[11] It focuses primarily on understanding the behaviors of people working together in teams and groups. In addition to sharing the origins of the other two subfields, meso organizational behavior grew out of research in the fields of *communication, social psychology,* and *interactionist sociology,* which provided theories on such topics as socialization, leadership, and group dynamics. Meso organizational behavior seeks answers to questions such as the following: What forms of socialization encourage co-workers to cooperate? What mix of skills among team members increases team performance? How can managers determine which prospective leader will be the most effective?

Macro Organizational Behavior

Macro organizational behavior focuses on understanding the "behaviors" of entire organizations.[12] The origins of macro organizational behavior can be traced to four disciplines. *Sociology* provided theories of structure, social status, and institutional relations. *Political science* offered theories of power, conflict, bargaining, and control. *Anthropology* contributed theories of symbolism, cultural influence, and comparative analysis. *Economics* furnished theories of competition and efficiency. Research on macro organizational behavior considers questions such as the following: How is power acquired and retained? How can conflicts be resolved? What mechanisms can be used to coordinate work activities? How should an organization be structured to best cope with its surrounding environment?

CONTEMPORARY ISSUES

Considered both individually and collectively, the three subfields of organizational behavior offer valuable information, insights, and advice to managers facing the challenge of understanding and reacting to a broad range of contemporary management issues. According to a variety of sources, today's managers find four of these issues especially important: workforce diversity, team productivity, organizational adaptability, and international growth and development.

Workforce Diversity

Within the societal cultures of the United States and Canada, subcultural differences once ignored by many managers now command significant attention and sensitivity. Historically, the North American workforce has consisted primarily of white males. Today, however, white males make up only about 15 percent of business new hires in the United States, whereas women and African American, Hispanic, and Asian men account for increasingly large segments of the U.S. workforce.[13] It is becoming—and will continue to become—even more important for managers to know about and be ready to respond to the challenges deriving from individual differences in abilities, personalities, and motives. Knowledge about the workplace consequences of these differences, drawn from the subfield of micro organizational behavior, can provide managers with help in this regard.

Team Productivity

Management is becoming less of a process relying on top-down command and control, where managers have all the power and nonmanagerial employees have little say in what they do.[14] For various reasons organizations now use greater amounts of *empowerment*—the delegation to nonmanagers of the authority to make significant decisions on their jobs. Often, empowerment is accomplished by grouping employees into teams, then giving those teams responsibility for self-management activities such as hiring, firing, and training members; setting production targets; and assessing output quality. Guidance from meso organizational behavior precepts can help managers establish realistic expectations about the implementation difficulties and probable effects of team-based empowerment.

Organizational Adaptability

In today's business world, emphasis is shifting from the mass production of low-cost, interchangeable commodities to the production of high-quality goods and services, made individually or in small batches and geared to meet the specific demands of small groups of consumers. This shift requires greater flexibility than ever before and necessitates that quality receive greater emphasis than it has in the past. Companies are reacting by implementing programs that require new ways of dividing an organization's work into jobs and coordinating the efforts of many employees.[15] Implementations of this sort benefit from insights derived from macro organizational behavior.

International Growth and Development

Fewer firms today limit their operations to a single national or cultural region than was once the case. Instead, multinationalism or even statelessness has become the norm. The resulting globalization is changing the way business is conducted, and it promises to continue to do so at an increasing pace.[16] Managers facing this massive change must develop increased sensitivity to international cultural differences. All three subfields of organizational behavior have valuable advice to offer managers confronted with this challenge.

PUTTING ORGANIZATIONAL BEHAVIOR KNOWLEDGE TO WORK

Putting theoretical knowledge from the field of organizational behavior to practical use requires that managers develop skills in using such knowledge to identify and solve problems in an effective manner. To develop your own managerial skills and learn how to put them to work, it is important that you understand the process of problem solving and become proficient at experimenting with ways of becoming a better problem solver. The process of problem solving can be simplified and made more effective by breaking it into the four stages described in Table 1-2: diagnosis, solution, action, and evaluation.[17]

Diagnosis

Problem solving begins with **diagnosis,** a procedure in which managers gather information about a troublesome situation and try to summarize it in a *problem statement.* Information gathering may require direct observation of events in or around an organization. Consultants often praise the practice of "managing by wandering around," in part because it provides a rich source of firsthand information that can be used during problem-solving procedures.[18]

Managers may also conduct interviews to gather facts and opinions, or administer questionnaires to collect others' views. Both approaches lack the immediacy of personal observation, but enable the collection of diverse information and opinions.

Summarizing information in a problem statement requires that managers use the mix of theories, experience, and intuition they have amassed to construct a statement of what is wrong. Often the information placed before a manager looks much like the kind of data that a medical doctor uses to identify the source of an illness. Just as the doctor may have to consider evidence of fever, body pain, and nausea to diagnose a case of influenza, the manager may have to interpret the meanings of several *symptoms* to formulate a problem statement.

For example, when the Buick Motor Division of General Motors dropped Plumley Companies as a supplier of hoses and other rubber parts, citing poor product quality, company owner Michael A. Plumley discovered that workers wanted to produce good parts but lacked the knowledge and skills necessary to perform their jobs correctly. After stepping up worker training, the company improved its situation

TABLE 1-2
Four Stages of Problem Solving

Stage	Description
Diagnosis	Collection of information about a troubling organizational situation and summarization of this information in a problem statement.
Solution	Identification of ways to resolve the problem identified during diagnosis.
Action	Stipulation of the activities needed to solve the problem and oversight of the implementation of these activities. Also, identification of the indicators to be used to measure success and collection of data reflecting these measures.
Evaluation	Determination of the extent to which the actions taken to solve the problem had the intended effect, using the indicators and data collected during the action stage.

substantially and now holds quality awards from GM, Nissan, Ford, and Chrysler.[19] The manager, acting as a diagnostician, often must take responsibility for analyzing the individual symptoms and learning how they fit together to point toward the larger problem.

Solution

Solution is the process of identifying ways to resolve the problem identified during the diagnosis phase. Organizational problems are often multifaceted, and usually more than one way to solve a given problem exists. Effective managers consider several reasonable alternatives before choosing one. In the case of Plumley Companies, Michael Plumley considered but ruled out poor supervision, equipment deficiencies, raw material defects, and employee motivation, and also considered a variety of training approaches before making a final choice. More generally, managers prescribing solutions must resist the urge to *satisfice*—to choose the first alternative that seems workable—and must instead push themselves to consider several potential solutions and choose the best available alternative.[20]

Action

Action is setting a proposed solution into motion. In this stage, managers must first stipulate the specific activities they believe are needed to solve a particular problem, then oversee the implementation of these activities. Sometimes it is possible to implement a step-by-step program that was developed earlier to solve a similar problem encountered previously or in another organization. General Motors used this approach when it adopted product quality and customer service programs first developed in its Saturn Division throughout its other automotive divisions. In other cases it is necessary to start from scratch, creating a new sequence of activities to be implemented for the first time. IBM forced the developers of its first personal computer to use this approach by isolating them from the rest of the company's operations. Because of their isolation, staff members could not solve problems by simply referring to procedures used elsewhere in the company. The innovation and creativity stimulated by this approach, and the subsequent success of IBM's personal computer, led many other companies to emulate IBM's strategy—patterned after earlier programs at Lockheed Aircraft (now Lockheed Martin Corporation)—of creating a "skunkworks" for new product development.

Evaluation

Problem solving concludes with **evaluation,** the process of determining whether actions taken to solve the problem had the intended effect. To evaluate their solutions properly, managers must identify in advance the indicators they will use to measure success and collect measures of these indicators as the action stage proceeds. For instance, to evaluate a program intended to improve productivity, managers must decide what kinds of measures to use—for example, counts of items produced, questionnaire indices of customer satisfaction, dollar volume of sales, or similar measures. They must then decide how to collect this information and what value or cutoff amount to use as an indication of success (for example, a 5 percent increase in sales, measured as booked transactions).

The evaluation process highlights any differences between the intended results of a particular solution and the actual results. Sometimes the chosen course of action completely resolves the problem. Often, however, additional problems are uncovered and further problem solving becomes necessary. At this point, managers use evaluation information as diagnostic data and the process of problem solving begins again.[21]

Becoming an Active Problem Solver

As you read this book, you will find yourself thinking about how you might use textbook information to solve real-world problems. To sharpen your skills as a problem solver, we suggest that you study each theory presented in this book to develop a basic understanding of the variables and relationships it describes. Next, practice using these theories as tools to help work through the exercises at the end of each chapter and define problems in the cases also included in this book. As you grow more comfortable applying the theories, try combining them to develop more comprehensive management tools. For example, you might blend theories of employee motivation, leadership, and job design to develop an enriched explanation of the causes of poor employee performance.

To help you study and learn, we have included sets of diagnostic questions at the ends of Chapters 3–15. These questions provide a useful application-oriented review of chapter materials. In addition, you can use them as you work on the exercises or analyze cases, ensuring that you apply all relevant theories in the most appropriate way. In the near term, the personalized theories that you develop as you use these questions will help you solve the exercises and cases more effectively. Over the long run, the diagnostic questions and the personal theories they stimulate will provide the basic insights required to help you excel as a problem solver in everyday managerial situations.

You should also practice following the theories applied during problem definition to their logical conclusions. For instance, the same theory of employee motivation that you use to diagnose a productivity problem in a case may also suggest the actions needed to reduce or eliminate the problem. Similarly, a theory of leadership that helps you begin an exercise on the distribution of power may also provide guidance about how power should be managed later in the exercise. At the same time, you should work on applying several theories simultaneously as you diagnose problems and search for solutions. The more theories you apply during diagnosis, the more comprehensive your final solution is likely to be. As you become a more skillful problem solver, the solutions you devise are likely to become increasingly thorough and more effective.

As part of the process of learning how to apply the material in this book, you should also practice specifying the actions required to implement and assess your proposed solution. Your action plan should include a sequence of steps that indicate what needs to be done, who will do it, and when it will be done. Your evaluation procedure should indicate how you plan to measure the effectiveness of your actions as well as what you expect to do if the evaluation reveals shortcomings in your solution (see the Ethics and Social Responsibility box).

OVERVIEW OF THIS BOOK

As we have indicated in this chapter, our book focuses on providing conceptual frameworks that will prove helpful in the future as you solve problems and manage behaviors in organizations. What you learn now will serve later as a valuable source of competitive advantage for you and your firm.

The book consists of five parts. Part 1 includes two introductory chapters, this one on organizational behavior and a second one on management, that provide a conceptual foundation for later chapters. Part 2, on micro organizational behavior, consists of four chapters on diversity and individual differences, decision making and creativity, motivation and work performance, and satisfaction and stress at work. These chapters provide information useful for the management of people as individuals in organizations.

ETHICS AND SOCIAL RESPONSIBILITY

WHO IS RESPONSIBLE FOR ETHICS TRAINING?

Evaluation, central to problem solving, is inherently a process of applying values. Thus, it is subject to ethical concerns. Whose values should guide the evaluation process? Will this process provide benefit for the greatest number of people? Will it provide greatest benefit to those individuals who are least advantaged by the status quo? Will it provide undue benefit to those who serve as evaluators? All of these questions reflect matters of *ethics*, or socially accepted standards of responsibility and conduct. It follows that ethical behavior is central to effective management.

Given the importance of ethics, the question arises as to who should be held accountable for the ethical training of current and future managers. One approach is to place responsibility for such training in the hands of the business schools that educate management students. As suggested by Jennifer Merritt, most undergraduate business schools and nearly all MBA programs have added coursework in business ethics, partly in response to pressures to do so that have mounted in the aftermath of ethical scandals in such companies as Enron, Global Crossing, and Arthur Andersen. Such reforms are welcome, according to Merritt, but run the danger of fading away like other recent educational fads. To avoid this danger, business school programs must consider engaging in the following: (1) Invest in the study of business ethics. Ethics and ethicality are seldom the focus of the business cases used in many programs to teach managerial behavior. In addition, studies of ethics seldom appear in academic journals that publish research in the area of management and organizational behavior. Commentators such as Merritt suggest that such trends fly in the face of the growing practical importance of ethics training, and must be reversed so that business educators can integrate such training into their curricula. (2) Use ethicality as a selection criterion. Business programs use grades and aptitude tests as entrance criteria; why not also require application essays or focused interviews that allow programs to screen for ethicality? The alternative of expelling students who lie on their application or cheat once admitted to the program is more painful, and the possibility that unethical graduates will tarnish their program's reputation is sobering. (3) Seek corporate support. Companies can influence business school programs and students. Why not use this influence to institutionalize training and research in the area of ethics? Identifying ethics as an important focus of the recruitment process would have a profound effect on the way ethicality training is viewed by educators and students. At the same time, the importance of business ethicality would be further reinforced.

Another approach is to suggest that businesses should educate their trainees and young managers to engage in ethical behavior. Marvin Bower, managing director of consultant McKinsey & Company from 1950 to 1967, was legendary in his assertion that values mattered more than money. Stories are still recounted among McKinsey employees about Bower's contention that consulting was not a business but a profession, and one in which the company's consultants should put the interests of their clients above all others. Bower also insisted that McKinsey's success brought personal obligations. Partners found themselves responding to his question, "What are you going to do to give something back?" by joining public school boards, helping to plan urban redevelopment, or reviewing welfare programming costs and effectiveness. Today, Bower's legend serves as the foundation for training used in the firm to encourage ethicality and social responsibility among developing employees. Such training is intended to provide future partners with the ethical perspective needed to succeed as a consultant on McKinsey's terms.

In truth, both approaches are probably necessary. Inquiry into ethical behavior should begin during formal education, and employers should reinforce the importance of ethics over the course of the business career. Throughout this book, we will raise ethical issues where appropriate to encourage you to reflect on your own system of values and the kinds of dilemmas likely to confront you in the future. Our aim is to encourage your interest in ethics, with the hope that this interest will be further reinforced as you progress as a student and employee in the coming years.

Sources: J. A. Byrne, "Goodbye to an Ethicist," *Business Week,* February 10, 2003, p. 38; J. Merritt, "Why Ethics Is Also B-School Business," *Business Week,* January 27, 2003, p. 105.

Part 3, on meso organizational behavior, includes four chapters dealing with work design, socialization and other interpersonal processes, group and team effectiveness, and leadership in groups and organizations. These chapters furnish the information needed to manage interpersonal relations and group processes in organizations. Part 4, on macro organizational behavior, consists of four chapters on the topics of power and conflict, organization structure, organizational design, and culture and organizational development. The information in these chapters concerns organization-level problems and the management of related processes and procedures. Finally, Part 5 includes two chapters on topics that span the three subfields of organizational behavior. One chapter covers international organizational behavior, and the other focuses on research methods and critical thinking. Both provide information that will help you apply what you've learned elsewhere in the book to a wide variety of situations.

SUMMARY

Organizational behavior is a field of research that helps predict, explain, and understand behaviors occurring in and among organizations. Organizational behavior's three subfields—micro organizational behavior, meso organizational behavior, and macro organizational behavior—reflect differences among the scientific disciplines that contributed to the founding of the field. As a consequence, each focuses on a different aspect of organizational behavior. *Micro organizational behavior* is concerned primarily with the attributes and performance of individuals in organizations. *Meso organizational behavior* focuses on the characteristics of groups and the behaviors of people in teams. *Macro organizational behavior* addresses the "behaviors" of organizations as entities.

Effective managers use knowledge from the three subfields during problem solving, which is the process of diagnosis, solution, action, and evaluation. *Diagnosis* involves interpreting symptoms and identifying the problem. *Solution* occurs when one or more ways of resolving the problem are formulated. In *action*, specific activities are enacted and a solution is implemented. *Evaluation*, the final phase of problem solving, involves assessing the effectiveness of the implemented solution and can serve as an input for further problem solving, if required.

REVIEW QUESTIONS

1. Define the field of organizational behavior. What kinds of behavior does it examine? Why is knowledge drawn from the field of organizational behavior so important for managers?

2. What are the three subfields of organizational behavior? Why have they developed separately? What kinds of organizational problems does each subfield help managers solve?

3. What are the four stages of the problem-solving process? How can knowing about them help you become a better manager?

4. Why should you refer to textbook theories during the process of problem solving? How will using this textbook make you a better manager?

Defining Management
Three Attributes of Organizations
Formal Definition

What Managers Do
Managerial Jobs
Managerial Skills
Managerial Roles
The Nature of Managerial Work

A Framework of Management Perspectives
1890–1940: The Scientific Management Perspective
1900–1950: The Administrative Principles Perspective
1930–1970: The Human Relations Perspective
1960–Present: The Open Systems Perspective
A Contingency Framework

Summary
Review Questions

Management and Managers

You've probably watched professional sporting events hundreds of times without thinking about the management and managers behind them. In order for such events to take place, however, managers must plan, organize, and oversee the players, arenas, and league operations that make up professional sports. In the National Basketball Association (NBA), for example, Commissioner David Stern negotiates the league's television contract, providing a large percentage of the billions of dollars needed to meet the salary requirements of current players. Simultaneously, NBA team owners such as Mark Cuban of the Dallas Mavericks run the franchise operations required to attract talented players and build the coaching staff needed to turn those players into a team. The commissioner of the National Hockey League (NHL), Gary Bettman, seeks ways to control the growing costs of player recruitment and league operations, in order to reverse trends that threaten to bankrupt several NHL teams. In the National Football League (NFL), Commissioner Paul Tagliabue negotiates the labor agreements that keep players on the field, and works with team owners and cities to update the stadiums that host the league's games. In Major League Baseball (MLB), Commissioner Bud Selig coordinates the national schedules of baseball's two divisions, the American and National Leagues, and franchise owners such as the Florida Marlins' Jeffrey Loria develop promotions to attract greater numbers of fans. And for every professional team, a staff of managers and coaches perform the day-to-day management activities needed to field a competitive lineup—ranging from coordinating daily training exercises to making sure that game-day uniforms are clean. Management and managers are thus an essential, albeit sometimes underappreciated, part of professional sports.[1]

Although managers like Stern, Tagliabue, and colleagues are well known and widely respected, few people really understand what they and other managers do as part of their jobs. Could you tell someone what management is? What skills and abilities managers need to succeed in their work? How today's management practices have developed? Modern societies depend on the well-being of organizations ranging from industrial giants like General Electric and IBM to local businesses like the corner grocery store. In turn, all of these businesses depend on the expertise of managers. It is therefore important that members of modern societies, including you, know what management is, what managers do, and how contemporary practices have developed.

This chapter introduces management theory and practice. It begins by defining the concept of management in terms of the various functions that managers perform in organizations. Next, it describes the job of a manager in greater detail, focusing on the skills managers use and the roles they fill as they perform their jobs every day. The chapter then examines how modern management theory has evolved, discussing four schools of thought about management and managers that have developed between the late 1800s and the present.

DEFINING MANAGEMENT

Management, defined most simply, is the process of influencing behavior in organizations such that common purposes are identified, worked toward, and achieved. To define management in greater detail, we must consider a closely related question: What is an organization?

Three Attributes of Organizations

An **organization** is a collection of people and materials brought together to accomplish purposes not achievable through the efforts of individuals working alone. Three attributes enable an organization to achieve this feat: a mission, division of labor, and a hierarchy of authority.

Mission Each organization works toward a specific **mission,** which is its purpose or reason for being. As illustrated in Table 2-1, a mission statement identifies the primary goods or services that the organization is intended to produce and the markets that it hopes to serve. An organization's mission helps hold it together by giving members a shared sense of direction.

Division of Labor In every organization, difficult work is broken into smaller tasks. This **division of labor** can enhance *efficiency* by simplifying tasks and making them easier to perform. A classic example of this effect can be seen in the following analysis of the pin-making process by the eighteenth-century Scottish economist Adam Smith:

One man draws out the wire, another straightens it, a third cuts it, a fourth points it, a fifth grinds it at the top for receiving a head. To make the head requires two or three more operations. [Using a division of labor such as this,] ten persons could make among them upward of forty-eight thousand pins a day. But if they had all wrought separately and independently they certainly could not each of them have made twenty; perhaps not one pin in a day.[2]

TABLE 2-1
Sample
Mission
Statements

Company	Mission
Hershey Foods	Hershey Foods' basic business mission is to become a major, diversified food company. . . . A basic principle that Hershey will continue to embrace is to attract and hold customers with products and services of consistently superior quality and value.
Polaroid	Polaroid designs, manufactures, and markets worldwide a variety of products based on its inventions, primarily in the photographic field. These products include instant photographic cameras and films, light-polarizing filters and lenses, and diversified chemical, optical, and commercial products. The principal products of the company are used in amateur and professional photography, industry, science, medicine, and education.

Source: Excerpted from recent annual stockholder reports.

The division of labor enables organized groups of people to accomplish tasks that would be beyond their physical or mental capacities as individuals. Few people can build a car by themselves, yet companies like Nissan turn out thousands of cars each year by dividing the complex job of building a car into a series of simple assembly line tasks.

Hierarchy of Authority   The **hierarchy of authority** is another common organizational attribute. In very small organizations, all members of the organization may share equally the authority to make decisions and initiate actions. In contrast, in larger organizations authority is more often distributed in a pyramidal hierarchical pattern like that shown in Figure 2-1. At the top of this hierarchy, the chief executive officer (CEO) has the authority to issue orders to every other member of the organization and to expect these orders to be obeyed. At successively lower levels, managers direct the activities of people beneath them and are constrained by the authority of managers above them.

Formal Definition

The three attributes of organizations just described help clarify the role of management in organizational life. In a sense, the first two attributes are discordant, as the mission assumes the integration of effort whereas the division of labor produces a differentiation of effort. As a result, an organization's members are simultaneously pushed together and pulled apart. Managerial influence, derived partly from the third attribute of hierarchical authority, reconciles this conflict and balances the two opposing attributes. This balancing act is what managers do and what management is all about.

Management is thus a process of planning, organizing, directing, and controlling organizational behaviors to accomplish a mission through the division of labor. This definition incorporates several important ideas. First, management is a process—an ongoing flow of activities—rather than something that can be accomplished once and for all. Second, managerial activities affect the behaviors of an organization's members *and* the organization itself. Third, to accomplish a firm's mission requires organization. If the mission could be accomplished by individuals working alone, neither the firm nor its management would be necessary. Fourth, the process of

FIGURE 2-1 Briggs & Stratton Organization Chart

An organization chart is a graphic representation of a firm's hierarchy of authority. The organization chart in this figure shows the top and middle management of Briggs & Stratton, a manufacturer of small gasoline engines used in lawn mowers, snow blowers, and similar equipment. Note that the company is divided horizontally into various functional departments—such as manufacturing and sales—whose efforts are unified through authority relations that extend vertically between vice presidents and the CEO.

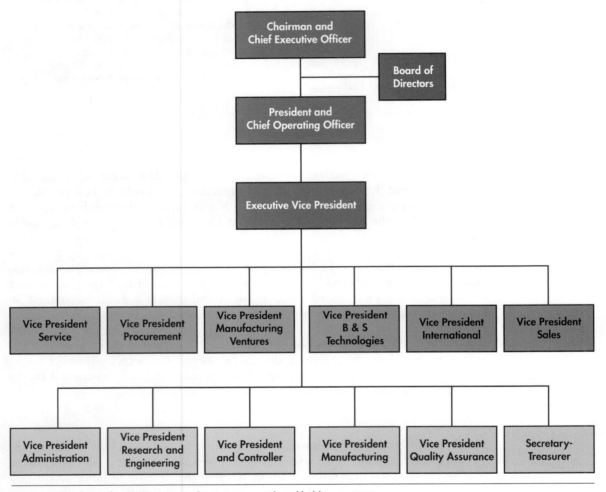

Source: Based on information contained in recent annual stockholder reports.

management can be further divided into the four functions shown in Figure 2-2: planning, organizing, directing, and controlling.

Planning is a forward-looking process of deciding what to do. Managers who plan try to anticipate the future, setting goals and objectives for a firm's performance and identifying the actions required to attain these goals and objectives. For example, when Michael Eisner meets with other Walt Disney Company executives to develop specifications for the attractions and concessions at theme parks under construction, he is engaged in planning. In planning, managers set three types of goals and objectives:

1. *Strategic goals* are the outcomes that the organization as a whole expects to achieve by pursuing its mission.

FIGURE 2-2   The Four Management Functions

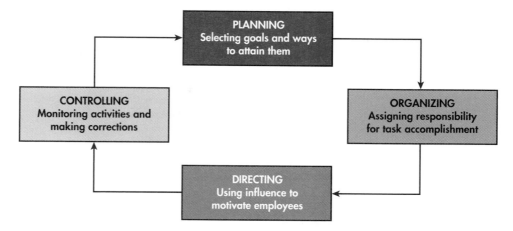

2. *Functional or divisional objectives* are the outcomes that units within the firm are expected to achieve.
3. *Operational objectives* are the specific, measurable results that the members of an organizational unit are expected to accomplish.[3]

As shown in Figure 2-3, these three types of goals and objectives are linked together. The focus of lower-order objectives is shaped by the content of higher-level goals, and achieving higher-level goals depends on the fulfillment of lower-level objectives.

Goals and objectives are performance targets that the members of an organization seek to fulfill by working together—for instance, gaining control over 15 percent of the firm's market, or manufacturing less than one defective product for every thousand produced. Setting such goals and objectives helps managers plan and implement a sequence of actions that will lead to their attainment. For example, financial objectives growing out of Eisner's planning meetings at Disney become targets that newly opened theme parks are expected to meet or exceed during their first few years in operation. Goals and objectives also serve as benchmarks of the success or failure of organizational behavior. When they review past performance, managers can judge the company's effectiveness by assessing its goal attainment. For example, Disney theme park managers can assess the success of their operations by comparing actual revenue and cost data with corporate profitability goals.

As part of the **organizing** function, managers develop a structure of interrelated tasks and allocate people and resources within this structure. Organizing begins when managers divide an organization's labor and design tasks that will lead to the achievement of organizational goals and objectives. In companies such as Whirlpool, Boeing, and IBM, assembly operations are devised and built during this phase. Next, managers decide who will perform these tasks. To make this determination, they analyze the tasks to identify the knowledge, skills, and abilities needed to perform them successfully. They can then select qualified employees or train other employees who lack the necessary qualifications to carry out these tasks.

Grouping tasks and the people who perform them into *organizational units* is another step in the organizing process. One type of organizational unit, a *department,* includes people who perform the same type of work. For instance, all employees who market an organization's goods or services can be brought together in a marketing department. Another type of unit, a *division,* includes people who do the

FIGURE 2-3   The Hierarchy of Goals and Objectives

An organization's strategic goals set boundaries within which functional objectives are established. In turn, functional objectives shape the objectives of operational units. Accomplishing operational objectives therefore contributes to the attainment of functional objectives and strategic goals.

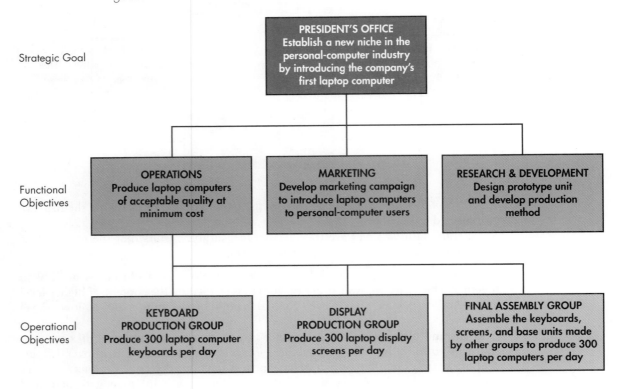

company's work in the same geographic territory, who work with similar kinds of clients, or who make or provide the same type of goods or services. For example, Coca-Cola has a European division that does business in Europe. General Electric's financial services division markets only financial services.

The **directing** function encourages member effort and guides it toward the attainment of organizational goals and objectives. Directing is partly a process of communicating goals and objectives to members. Managers must announce, clarify, and promote targets toward which effort should be directed. For example, Jeff Bezos is directing when he meets with other top managers at Amazon.com to announce yearly sales objectives. Directing is also a process of learning employees' desires and interests and of ensuring that these desires and interests are satisfied in return for successful goal-oriented performance. In addition, directing may require managers to use personal expertise or charisma to inspire employees to overcome obstacles that might appear insurmountable. Apple Computer's Steve Jobs relies heavily on charisma to keep employees in his company excited about new products and market opportunities. In sum, directing is a process in which managers *lead* their subordinates, influencing them to work together to achieve organizational goals and related objectives.

Controlling means evaluating the performance of the organization and its units to see whether the firm is progressing in the desired direction. In a typical evaluation, managers compare an organization's actual results with the desired results as described in its goals and objectives. For example, Capital One executives might compare the actual profitability of their Visa card operations with the profitability objectives set during previous planning sessions. To perform this kind of evaluation, members of the organization must collect and assess performance information. A firm's accounting personnel might gather data about the costs and revenues of organizational activities. Marketing representatives might provide additional data about sales volume or the organization's position in the marketplace. Finance specialists might then appraise the firm's organizational performance by determining whether the ratio of costs to revenues meets or surpasses the company's target level.

If the evaluation reveals a significant difference between goals and actual performance, the control process enters a phase of *correction*. In this phase, managers return to the planning stage and redevelop their goals and objectives, indicating how differences between goals and outcomes can be reduced. The process of management then continues anew, as managers engage in additional organizing, directing, and controlling.

WHAT MANAGERS DO

Managers are the people who plan, organize, direct, and control so as to manage organizations and organizational units. Managers establish the directions to be pursued; allocate people and resources among tasks; supervise individual, group, and organizational performance; and assess progress toward goals and objectives. To succeed in these functions, they perform specific jobs, use a variety of skills, and fill particular roles.

Managerial Jobs

Although all managers are responsible for fulfilling the same four functions, not all of them perform exactly the same jobs. Instead, most organizations have three types of managers: top managers, middle managers, and supervisory managers. The Cutting-Edge Research box reports on recent research that has examined how managers advance from one type or level of management to the next. Figure 2-4 illustrates the distinctive combination of planning, organizing, directing, and controlling performed by each type of manager.[4]

Top Managers Top managers, who are responsible for managing the entire organization, include individuals with the title of *chairperson, president, chief executive officer, executive vice president, vice president,* or *chief operating officer.* For these managers, their job consists mainly of performing the planning activities needed to develop the organization's mission and strategic goals. Top managers also carry out organizing and controlling activities as determined by strategic planning. As part of the controlling function, they assess the firm's progress toward attainment of its strategic goals by monitoring information about activities both within the firm and in its surrounding environment. Top management's responsibilities include adjusting the organization's overall direction on the basis of information reviewed in the controlling procedures. Because strategic planning, organizing, and controlling require a great deal of time, top managers have little time to spend in directing subordinates' activities. Typically, they delegate responsibility for such direction to middle managers lower in the hierarchy of authority.

Middle Managers Middle managers are usually responsible for managing the performance of a particular organizational unit and for implementing top managers'

CUTTING-EDGE RESEARCH

WHAT PREDICTS MANAGERIAL ADVANCEMENT?

What factors affect whether managers will be promoted? A recent study by Phyllis Tharenou sought to answer this question by examining the effects of personal characteristics and social support on the careers of male and female managers.

Research prior to Tharenou's had indicated that education, technical knowledge, and work-related skills help employees gain entry into supervisory management, and that interpersonal networks and social support have greater effects on promotions to middle and top management. Tharenou sought to further examine the differential effects of personal characteristics and social factors by assessing the influence of two personal traits and two types of social support. The personal characteristics were managerial aspirations, defined as the extent to which an employee wants to advance into management or progress in the managerial ranks, and masculinity, or the degree to which the individual focuses on getting the job done or problem solved. The two types of social support were career encouragement provided by mentors, and hierarchical support provided by the organization's management hierarchy.

An analysis of questionnaire data collected from 1,593 female and 1,841 male employees in Australia indicated that managerial aspirations and masculinity predicted advancing in management versus staying at the same level for all types of managers. In addition, career encouragement from mentors predicted advancement for women more than men when advancing from supervisory to middle management or from middle management upward. Finally, hierarchical support predicted advancement for men more than women into supervisory or middle-management jobs.

Emerging from Tharenou's study and prior research is a complex model of how personal and social variables influence managerial advancement. Personal characteristics seem to affect advancement irrespective of the level of management being considered, whether the employee is male or female. Social support, however, appears more bounded in influence, having different effects depending on the gender of the employee and the level of management under consideration. Tharenou concluded that her results offer a partial explanation for the relative absence of female managers, since she found that management hierarchies tend to facilitate the promotion of men more than women. However, she also indicated that mentorship targeted toward women, especially when received early in their careers, might be able to reverse this trend.

Source: P. Tharenou, "Going Up? Do Traits and Informal Social Processes Predict Advancing in Management?" *Academy of Management Journal* 44 (2001), 1005–1017.

strategic plans. As they work to transform these strategies into programs that can be implemented at lower levels of the company, middle managers help establish functional or divisional objectives that will guide unit performance toward attainment of the firm's strategic goals. For instance, middle managers in a company's marketing department might transform the strategic goal of attaining control of 35 percent of the company's market into objectives specifying the level of sales to be achieved in each of the company's twelve sales districts. Middle managers are also responsible for ensuring that the managers beneath them implement the unit goals and appropriately direct employees toward their attainment. Terms such as *director* or *manager* are usually a part of a middle manager's title—for example, *director of human resources* or *western regional manager*.

Supervisory Managers   Supervisory managers, often called *superintendents, supervisors,* or *foremen,* are charged with overseeing the nonsupervisory employees who perform the organization's basic work. Of the three types of managers, supervisory managers spend the greatest amount of time actually directing employees. Except for making small, on-the-job adjustments, they seldom perform planning and organizing activities. Instead, supervisory managers initiate the upward flow of infor-

FIGURE 2-4   Managerial Functions and Types of Managers
Planning is the most important function of top managers. Middle managers fulfill all four manage-ment functions about equally. Directing is the most important function of supervisory managers.

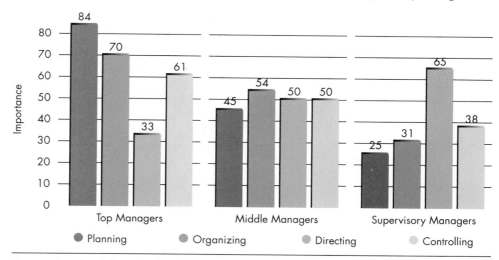

Source: Based on information from L. Gomez-Mejia, J. E. McCann, and R. C. Page, "The Structure of Managerial Behaviors and Rewards," *Industrial Relations* 24 (1985), 147–154.

mation that middle and top managers use to control organizational behavior. They may also distribute many of the rewards or punishments used to influence non-supervisory employees' behaviors. Their ability to control subordinates' activities is limited, however, to the authority delegated to them by middle management.

Managerial Skills

Not surprisingly, the skills that managers use to succeed in their jobs are largely determined by the combination of planning, organizing, directing, and controlling functions that they must perform. As shown in Figure 2-5, each level of manage-ment has its own skill requirements.[5]

Conceptual skills include the ability to perceive an organization or organizational unit as a whole, to understand how its labor is divided into tasks and reintegrated by the pursuit of common goals or objectives, and to recognize important relation-ships between the organization or unit and the environment that surrounds it. Con-ceptual skills involve a manager's ability to *think* and are most closely associated with planning and organizing. These skills are used most frequently by top man-agers, who take responsibility for organization-wide strategic endeavors.

Included in **human skills** is the ability to work effectively as a group member and build cooperation among the members of an organization or unit. Managers with well-developed human skills can create an atmosphere of trust and security in which people can express themselves without fear of punishment or humiliation. Such managers, who are adept at sensing the aspirations, interests, and viewpoints of oth-ers, can often foresee others' likely reactions to prospective courses of action. Because all management functions require that managers interact with other employees to acquire information, make decisions, implement changes, and assess results, it is not surprising that top, middle, and supervisory managers all put human skills to use.

FIGURE 2-5 Managerial Skills

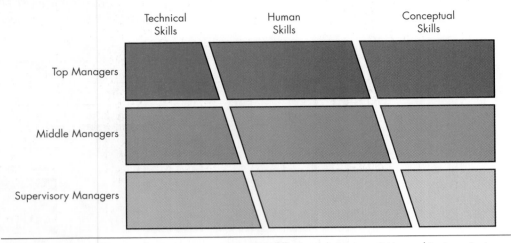

Source: Based on information from R. L. Katz, "Skills of an Effective Administrator," *Harvard Business Review* 52 (1974), 90–102.

Technical skills involve understanding the specific knowledge, procedures, and tools required to make the goods or services produced by an organization or unit. For example, members of a company's sales force must have skills in selling. Accountants have bookkeeping or auditing skills. Maintenance mechanics may need to have welding skills. For managers at the top or middle of an organization's hierarchy of authority, who are far removed from day-to-day production activities, technical skills are the least important of the three types of skills to have. Such skills are more critical to the success of supervisory managers overseeing employees who use technical skills in performing their jobs.

Managerial Roles

Like skill requirements, **managerial roles** vary from one kind of manager to another. Indeed, the same manager may play more than one role at the same time. As shown in Table 2-2, these roles cluster together in three general categories: interpersonal, informational, and decisional roles.[6]

Interpersonal Roles   In fulfilling interpersonal roles, managers create and maintain interpersonal relationships to ensure the well-being of their organizations or units. They represent their organizations or units to other people in the *figurehead role,* which can include such ceremonial and symbolic activities as greeting visitors, attending awards banquets, and cutting ribbons to open new facilities. Managers also function as figureheads when they perform public service duties, including such activities as chairing the yearly fund drive for the United Way or serving on the board of the local Urban League. In the *leader role,* they motivate and guide employees by performing such activities as issuing orders, setting performance goals, and training subordinates. Managers create and maintain links between their organizations or units and others in the *liaison role.* For example, a company president may meet with the presidents of other companies at an industry conference.

Informational Roles   Because they serve as the primary authority figures for the organizations or units they supervise, managers have unique access to internal and

TABLE 2-2
Ten Roles of
Managers

Role	Description
Interpersonal Roles	
Figurehead	Representing the organization or unit in ceremonial and symbolic activities
Leader	Guiding and motivating employee performance
Liaison	Linking the organization or unit with others
Informational Roles	
Monitor	Scanning the environment for information that can enhance organizational or unit performance
Disseminator	Providing information to subordinates
Spokesperson	Distributing information to people outside the organization or unit
Decisional Roles	
Entrepreneur	Initiating changes that improve the organization or unit
Disturbance handler	Adapting the organization or unit to changing conditions
Resource allocator	Distributing resources within the organization or unit
Negotiator	Bargaining or negotiating to sustain organizational or unit survival

Source: Based on information presented in H. Mintzberg, *The Nature of Managerial Work* (Englewood Cliffs, NJ: Prentice Hall, 1980).

external information networks. In informational roles they receive and transmit information within these networks. In the *monitor role,* managers scan the environment surrounding their organizations or units, seeking information to enhance performance. Such activities can range from reading periodicals and reports to trading rumors with managers in other firms or units. In the *disseminator role,* managers pass information to subordinates who would otherwise have no access to it. To share information with subordinates, they may hold meetings, write memoranda, make telephone calls, and so forth. In the *spokesperson role,* managers distribute information to people outside their organizations or units through annual stockholder reports, speeches, memos, and various other means.

Decisional Roles In decisional roles, managers determine the direction to be taken by their organizations or units. In the *entrepreneur role,* they make decisions about improvements in the organizations or units for which they are responsible. Such decisions often entail initiating change. For example, a manager who hears about a new product opportunity may commit the firm to producing it. She may also delegate the responsibility for managing the resulting project to others. The *disturbance handler role* also requires making change-oriented decisions. Managers acting in this role must often try to adapt to change beyond their personal control. For example, they may have to handle such problems as conflicts among subordinates, the loss of an important customer, or damage to the firm's building or plant.

In the *resource allocator role,* managers decide which resources will be acquired and who will receive them. Such decisions often demand difficult trade-offs. For instance, if a manager decides to acquire personal computers for sales clerks, he may have to deny manufacturing department employees a piece of production equipment. As part of the resource allocation process, priorities may be set, budgets established, and schedules devised. In the *negotiator role,* managers engage in formal bargaining or negotiations to acquire the resources needed for the survival of

FIGURE 2-6   Managers' Jobs and the Roles They Fill

When researchers asked top, middle, and supervisory managers about the importance of the roles they perform, their answers provided the data illustrated graphically here. Note that the roles of figurehead, entrepreneur, and negotiator were not included in this survey.

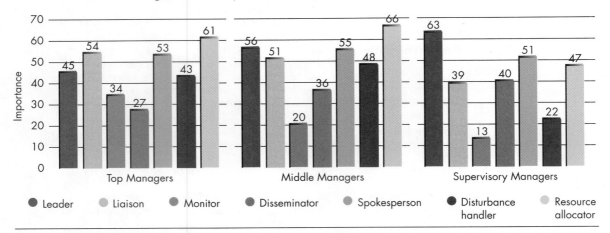

Source: Based on information from A. I. Kraut, P. R. Pedigo, D. D. McKenna, and M. D. Dunnette, "The Role of the Manager: What's Really Important in Different Management Jobs," *Academy of Management Executive* 3 (1989), 286–293.

their organizations or units. For example, they may negotiate with suppliers about delivery dates or bargain with union representatives about employee wages and hours.

Differences among Managers   Just as the functions managers perform and the skills they use differ from one managerial job to another, so do the roles managers fill. In Figure 2-6, the roles of liaison, spokesperson, and resource allocator are shown as being most important in the jobs of top managers, reflecting top management's responsibilities for planning, organizing, and controlling the strategic direction of the firm. In addition, monitoring activities are more important for top managers than for other types of managers because they must scan the environment for pertinent information.

For middle managers, the leader, liaison, disturbance handler, and resource allocator roles are the most important. These roles reflect the importance of middle management's job of organizing, directing, and controlling the functional or divisional units of the firm. The role of disseminator is also important in middle managers' jobs, as these managers must explain and implement the strategic plans formulated by top management.

For supervisory managers, the leader role is the most important, as they spend most of their time directing nonsupervisory personnel. They also act as spokespeople who disseminate information within their groups and serve as liaisons who connect their groups with the rest of the organization. In addition, they acquire and distribute the resources that their subordinates need to carry out their jobs.

The Nature of Managerial Work

To further analyze the classification of managerial roles just discussed, Henry Mintzberg observed a group of top managers at work for several weeks. After listing these managers' major activities and monitoring the time it took to perform them, Mintzberg found that the managers spent by far the most time in scheduled meetings. When combined with unscheduled meetings, this activity accounted for

TABLE 2-3
Distribution of
Managerial
Activities

Managerial Activity	Percentage of Workday Consumed	Average Duration
Scheduled meetings	59%	61 minutes
Desk work	22%	11 minutes
Unscheduled meetings	10%	12 minutes
Telephone calls	6%	6 minutes
Tours	3%	15 minutes

Source: Based on information presented in H. Mintzberg, *The Nature of Managerial Work* (Englewood Cliffs, NJ: Prentice Hall, 1980).

almost 70 percent of the managers' time. As Table 2-3 shows, the managers were left with barely a fifth of the day for desk work, and about a tenth for telephone calls and tours—walking around the company to see what was going on.

Mintzberg also recorded the amount of time consumed by each instance of each activity. As indicated in Table 2-3, scheduled meetings averaged a little more than an hour in length and ranged from less than 10 minutes to more than 2 hours. Unscheduled meetings were generally shorter, lasting from a few minutes to about an hour and averaging approximately 12 minutes each. Periods of desk work and tours to inspect the company averaged from 11 to 15 minutes each and were fitted in between scheduled meetings and unscheduled interruptions. Telephone calls were almost always quite short, averaging about 6 minutes each.

Based on his observations, Mintzberg concluded that managers' roles often require them to work in short bursts rather than in long, uninterrupted sessions. Such individuals frequently lack the time to complete rigorous planning, organizing, directing, and controlling. Rather than taking the form of a routine, well-planned course of action, managing can involve making nonroutine *incremental adjustments*.[7] Clearly, managing is a fast-paced, active profession.

A FRAMEWORK OF MANAGEMENT PERSPECTIVES

The definitions of *management* and *manager* introduced in this chapter are products of the North American culture and differ from the definitions used in other regions of the world. Nonetheless, our discussions thus far have been based on management thoughts and practices developed all over the world, many of which are thousands of years old. Consider the following:

1. As early as 3000 B.C., the Sumerians formulated missions and goals for government and commercial enterprises.
2. Between 3000 and 1000 B.C., the Egyptians successfully organized the efforts of thousands of workers to build the pyramids.
3. Between 800 B.C. and about 300 A.D., the Romans perfected the use of hierarchical authority.
4. Between 450 A.D. and the late 1400s, Venetian merchants developed commercial laws and invented double-entry bookkeeping.
5. In the early 1500s, Niccolo Machiavelli prepared an analysis of power that is still widely read.
6. At about the same time, the Catholic Church perfected a governance structure built upon the use of standardized procedures.

Truly modern management practices did not begin to develop until the Industrial Revolution of the 1700s and 1800s. Inventions such as James Watt's steam engine and Eli Whitney's cotton gin created new forms of mass production that made existing modes of organization obsolete. Mass-assembly operations accelerated the pace of production dramatically and required the employment of large numbers of workers, overwhelming the small administrative staffs then employed by most companies. In addition, expertise became important to maintain production equipment, even though managers had little time to develop this expertise themselves. The field of industrial engineering, which first emerged because of the need to invent and improve workplace machinery, began to address the selection, instruction, and coordination of industrial employees. Toward the end of the Industrial Revolution, managers and engineers throughout North America and Europe focused on developing general theories of management.

1890–1940: The Scientific Management Perspective

Management theories initially took the form of *management principles* intended to provide managers with practical advice about managing their firms. Most of these principles were written by practicing managers or others closely associated with the management profession. Among the first principles to be widely read were those of the **scientific management perspective.**

All principles of scientific management reflected the idea that through proper management an organization could achieve profitability and survive over the long term in the competitive world of business. Theorists sharing the scientific management perspective devoted their attention to describing proper management and determining the best way to achieve it.

Frederick W. Taylor   The founder of scientific management, Frederick W. Taylor (1856–1915), developed his principles of scientific management as he rose from the position of laborer to chief engineer at the Midvale Steel Works in Philadelphia, Pennsylvania. These principles, which appear in Table 2-4, focused on increasing the efficiency of the workplace by differentiating managers from nonsupervisory workers and systematizing the jobs of both types of employees.

According to Taylor, an organization's profitability could be ensured only by finding the "one best way" to perform each job. Managers were charged with teaching workers this technique and implementing a system of rewards and punishments

TABLE 2-4
Frederick W. Taylor's Principles of Scientific Management

1. *Assign all responsibility to managers rather than workers.* Managers should do all the thinking related to the planning and design of work, leaving workers the task of carrying it out.
2. *Use scientific methods to determine the one best way of performing each task.* Managers should design each worker's job accordingly, specifying a set of standard methods for completing the task in the right way.
3. *Select the person most suited to each job to perform that job.* Managers should match the abilities of each worker to the demands of each job.
4. *Train the worker to perform the job correctly.* Managers should train workers to use the standard methods devised for their jobs.
5. *Monitor work performance to ensure that specified work procedures are followed correctly and that appropriate results are achieved.* Managers should exercise the control necessary to guarantee that workers under their supervision always perform their jobs in the one best way.
6. *Provide further support by planning work assignments and eliminating interruptions.* Managers can help their workers continue to produce at a high level by shielding them from distractions that interfere with job performance.

Source: Based on information presented in F. W. Taylor, *The Principles of Scientific Management* (New York: Norton, 1911), pp. 34–40.

to encourage its use. For example, Taylor reported that he used this approach to improve the productivity of coal shovelers at the Bethlehem Steel Company. As he observed these workers, he discovered that a shovel load of coal could range from 4 to 30 pounds, depending on the density of the coal. By experimenting with a group of workers, Taylor discovered that shovelers could move the most coal in one day without suffering undue fatigue if each load of coal weighed 21 pounds. He then developed a variety of shovels, each of which would hold approximately 21 pounds of coal of a particular density. After Taylor taught workers how to use these shovels, each shoveler's daily yield rose from 16 tons to 59 tons. At the same time, the average wage per worker increased from $1.15 to $1.88 per day. Bethlehem Steel was able to reduce the number of shovelers in its yard from about 500 to 150, saving the firm about $80,000 per year.[8]

Taylor's ideas influenced management around the world. In a 1918 article for the newspaper *Pravda,* the founder of the Russian Communist Party, Vladimir Lenin, recommended that Taylor's scientific management be used throughout the Soviet Union. In the United States, Taylor's principles had such a dramatic effect on management that in 1912 he was called to testify before a special committee of the House of Representatives. Unions and employers both objected to Taylor's idea that employers and employees should share the economic gains of scientific management and wanted Congress to do something about it.

Nevertheless, with the newspaper publicity he gained from his appearance, Taylor found even wider support for his ideas and was soon joined in his work by other specialists.

Other Contributors   The husband-and-wife team of Frank (1868–1924) and Lillian (1878–1972) Gilbreth followed in Taylor's footsteps in pursuing the "one best way" to perform any job. The Gilbreths are probably best known for their invention of *motion study,* a procedure in which jobs are reduced to their most basic movements. Table 2-5 lists some of these basic movements, each of which is called a *therblig* ("Gilbreth" spelled backward without inverting the *th*).The Gilbreths also invented the microchronometer, a clock with a hand capable of measuring time to 1/2000 of a second. Using this instrument, analysts could perform time-and-motion studies to determine the time required by each movement needed to perform a job.

Another contributor to scientific management, Henry Gantt (1861–1919), developed a task-and-bonus wage plan that paid workers a bonus besides their regular wages if they completed their work in an assigned amount of time. Gantt's plan also provided bonuses for supervisors, determined by the number of subordinates who met deadlines.[9] In addition, Gantt invented the Gantt chart, a bar chart used by managers to compare actual with planned performance.[10] Present-day scheduling methods such as the program evaluation and review technique (PERT) are based on this invention.

Harrington Emerson (1853–1931), a third contributor to scientific management, applied his own list of twelve principles to the railroad industry in the early 1900s.[11] Among Emerson's principles were recommendations to establish clear objectives, seek advice from competent individuals, manage with justice and fairness, standardize procedures, reduce waste, and reward workers for efficiency. Late in his life,

TABLE 2-5
Therblig
Motions

Search	Transport empty	Transport loaded	Inspect
Find	Position	Disassemble	Assemble
Select	Rest	Preposition	Plan
Grasp	Use	Release load	Avoidable delay

Emerson became interested in the selection and training of employees, stressing the importance of explaining scientific management to employees during their initial training. He reasoned that sound management practices could succeed only if every member of the firm understood them.

1900–1950: The Administrative Principles Perspective

At about the same time that Taylor and his colleagues were formulating their principles of scientific management, another group of theorists was developing the **administrative principles perspective.** In contrast to scientific management's emphasis on reducing the costs of production activities, this perspective focused on increasing the efficiency of administrative procedures.

Henri Fayol   Considered the father of modern management thought, Henri Fayol (1841–1925) developed his principles of administration in the early 1900s while serving as chief executive of a French mining and metallurgy firm, Commentry-Fourchambault-Decazeville, known as "Comambault." Fayol was the first to identify the four functions of management we have already discussed: planning, organizing, directing, and controlling.[12] He also formulated the fourteen principles shown in Table 2-6 to help administrators perform their jobs.

Fayol believed that the number of management principles that might help improve an organization's operation is potentially limitless. He considered his principles to be flexible and adaptable, labeling them principles rather than laws or rules

. . . to avoid any idea of rigidity, as there is nothing rigid or absolute in [management] matters; everything is a question of degree. The same principle is hardly ever applied twice in exactly the same way, because we have to allow for different and changing circumstances, for human beings who are equally different and changeable, and for many other variable elements. The principles, too, are flexible, and can be adapted to meet every need; it is just a question of knowing how to use them.[13]

For Fayol, management involved more than mechanically following rules. It required that managers exercise intuition and engage in skillful behavior in deciding how, when, and why to put management principles into action.

Max Weber   Max Weber (1864–1920) was a German sociologist who, although neither a manager nor a management consultant, had a major effect on management thought. Like Fayol, he was interested in the efficiency of different kinds of administrative arrangements. To figure out what makes organizations efficient, Weber analyzed the Egyptian Empire, the Prussian army, the Roman Catholic Church, and other large organizations that had functioned efficiently over long periods of time. Based on the results of these analyses, he developed his model of **bureaucracy,** an idealized description of an efficient organization that is summarized in Table 2-7.

Weber's bureaucratic model provides for both the differentiation (through the division of labor and task specialization) and the integration (by the hierarchy of authority and written rules and regulations) necessary to get a specific job done. Weber believed that any organization with bureaucratic characteristics would be efficient. He noted, however, that work in a bureaucracy could become so simple and undemanding that employees might grow dissatisfied and, as a result, less productive.[14] Subsequent experience has also indicated that bureaucratic efficiency can be undermined by the very rules and regulations that are a basic feature of bureaucratic organizations, as discussed in the Securing Competitive Advantage box on page 33.

TABLE 2-6   Fayol's Fourteen Principles of Management

Principle	Description
Division of work	A firm's work should be divided into specialized, simplified tasks. Matching task demands with workforce skills and abilities will improve productivity. The management of work should be separated from its performance.
Authority and responsibility	Authority is the right to give orders, and responsibility is the obligation to accept the consequences of using authority. No one should possess one without having the other as well.
Discipline	Discipline is performing a task with obedience and dedication. It can be expected only when a firm's managers and subordinates agree on the specific behaviors that subordinates will perform.
Unity of command	Each subordinate should receive orders from only one hierarchical superior. The confusion created by having two or more superiors will undermine authority, discipline, order, and stability.
Unity of direction	Each group of activities directed toward the same objective should have only one manager and only one plan.
Individual versus general interests	The interests of individuals and the whole organization must be treated with equal respect. Neither can be allowed to supersede the other.
Remuneration of personnel	The pay received by employees must be fair and satisfactory to both them and the firm. Pay should be distributed in proportion to personal performance, but employees' general welfare must not be threatened by unfair incentive-payment schemes.
Centralization	Centralization is the retention of authority by managers, to be used when managers desire greater control. Decentralization should be used if subordinates' opinions, counsel, and experience are needed.
Scalar chain	The scalar chain is a hierarchical string extending from the uppermost manager to the lowest subordinate. The line of authority follows this chain and is the proper route for organizational communications.
Order	Order, or "everything in its place," should be instilled whenever possible because it reduces wasted materials and efforts. Jobs should be designed and staffed with order in mind.
Equity	Equity means enforcing established rules with a sense of fair play, kindliness, and justice. It should be guaranteed by management, as it increases members' loyalty, devotion, and satisfaction.
Stability of tenure	Properly selected employees should be given the time needed to learn and adjust to their jobs. The absence of such stability undermines organizational performance.
Initiative	Staff members should be given the opportunity to think for themselves. This approach improves the distribution of information and adds to the organization's pool of talent.
Esprit de corps	Managers should harmonize the interests of members by resisting the urge to split up successful teams. They should rely on face-to-face communication to detect and correct misunderstandings immediately.

Other Contributors   A number of other management experts have contributed to the administrative principles perspective. James Mooney (1884–1957) was vice president and director of General Motors and president of General Motors Overseas Corporation during the late 1920s, when he espoused his principles of organization.[15] Mooney's *coordinative principle* highlighted the importance of organizing the tasks and functions in a firm into a coordinated whole. He defined coordination as the orderly arrangement of group effort to provide unity of action in the pursuit of a common mission. His *scalar principle* identified the importance of scalar—hierarchical—chains of superiors and subordinates as a means of integrating the work

TABLE 2-7
Features of
Bureaucratic
Organizations

Feature	Description
Selection and promotion	Expertise is the primary criterion. Friendship criteria or other favoritism is explicitly rejected.
Hierarchy of authority	Superiors have the authority to direct subordinates' actions. They must ensure that these actions serve the bureaucracy's best interests.
Rules and regulations	Unchanging regulations provide the bureaucracy's members with consistent, impartial guidance.
Division of labor	Work is divided into tasks that can be performed by the bureaucracy's members in an efficient, productive manner.
Written documentation	Records provide consistency and a basis for evaluating bureaucratic procedures.
Separate ownership	Members cannot gain unfair or undeserved advantage through ownership.

Source: Based on information presented in H. H. Gerth and C. W. Mills, trans., *From Max Weber: Essays in Sociology* (New York: Oxford University Press, 1946).

of different employees. Finally, Mooney's *functional principle* stressed the importance of functional differences, such as marketing, manufacturing, and accounting. He noted how work in each functional area both differs from and interlocks with the work of other areas as well as how the success of the larger firm requires coordination and scalar linkages among its different functional parts.

Lyndall Urwick (1891–1983), another contributor to the administrative principles perspective, was a British military officer and director of the International Management Institute in Geneva, Switzerland. Urwick made his mark by consolidating the ideas of Fayol and Mooney with those of Taylor.[16] From Taylor, Urwick adopted the idea that systematic, rigorous investigation should inform and support the management of employees. He also used Fayol's fourteen principles to guide managerial planning and control, and Mooney's three principles of organization to structure his discussion of organizing. In this way, Urwick's synthesis bridged Taylor's scientific management and the administrative principles approach, and it integrated the work of others within the framework of the four functions of management identified by Fayol.

Mary Parker Follett (1868–1933), who became interested in industrial management in the 1920s, was among the first proponents of what later became known as *industrial democracy*. In her writings on administrative principles, Follett proposed that every employee should have an ownership interest in his or her company, which would encourage attention to a company's overall mission and goals.[17] In promoting cooperation in the workplace, her work foreshadowed the human relations perspective, which is described next. Follett also suggested that organizational problems tend to resist simple solutions, because they typically stem from a variety of interdependent factors. Here again she anticipated later theorists, contributing to the contingency approach discussed later in this chapter.

1930–1970: The Human Relations Perspective

Although members of the scientific management and administrative principles perspectives advocated the scientific study of management, they rarely evaluated their ideas in any formal way. This omission was corrected in the mid-1920s, when university researchers began to use scientific methods to test existing management thought.

SECURING COMPETITIVE ADVANTAGE

BUSTING BUREAUCRACY TO ENHANCE COMPETITIVENESS

General Motors (GM), once the dominant player in the North American automotive industry but subsequently challenged by competition from abroad, has regained a position of prominence through market incentives made possible by aggressive cost cutting within the firm. Through attrition and buyouts, GM has eliminated nearly 11,000 jobs in two years; current plans are to cut its white-collar workforce by another 3 to 7 percent within the next 18 months. Savings have been plowed back into low-interest loans and customer rebates intended to increase the company's market share, presently just above 28 percent. Despite a tepid market, GM has reemerged as leader in the light truck segment and is gaining elsewhere in the market.

Whether GM's current success will continue is subject to question, however. Beyond the issue of whether the costs of incentive-based marketing can continue to be absorbed lie questions concerning GM's product line. Simply put, bureaucratic rules, regulations, and procedures that have flourished for many years now stifle the process of new product development. Under a system developed during the 1980s, a concept for a new product would go from a designer to the marketing staff, which would then try to adapt it to consumer tastes. Then it would go to engineers who would try to figure out how to produce it, and then on to separate groups that would work with suppliers and factories on their individual parts of the project, all without significant interaction—bureaucratic procedures were supposed to provide the needed intergroup coordination.

Unfortunately, these procedures—"red tape"—bogged down the process to the point where product development took years, and the results were sometimes off the mark. The Pontiac Aztec, which

went to market in 2000 as a misplaced combination of SUV and minivan five years after designers first envisioned it as a racy entry aimed at younger drivers, serves as a case in point.

To reverse this situation, current CEO Rick Wagoner went outside GM—a company where promotion from within is a strongly held norm—and hired Robert A. Lutz as head of product development. Lutz, a classic "car guy" who ran Chrysler before its merger with Daimler-Benz, had overseen the development of the Dodge Viper and Ram pickup as well as Chrysler's PT Cruiser. Wagoner also eliminated the design-by-committee approach that often took four or more years to produce new products, and implemented a procedure designed to cut new car development to 20 months. Now, Lutz and other top managers decide what goes from the design studio to Wagoner's Automotive Strategy Board for approval. For approved vehicles, 75 percent of the engineering work is done before project management is set in motion to build the car. Product champions such as Lutz oversee the coordination once accomplished through bureaucracy. As a result, new products progress from design table to market more rapidly, and at lower cost.

The success of GM's product line, and of the firm itself, depends on whether this new approach can produce vehicles viewed by consumers as exciting, "have to own" cars and trucks. Early products such as the Chevrolet SSR, a combination pickup truck and hot rod, and the resurrected Pontiac GTO, famous muscle car of the 1960s, suggest that bureaucracy slashing will pay off, and that GM will grow increasingly competitive in the North American automotive market.

Sources: J. Porretto, "Ford, GM Step Up Cost Cutting," *Lansing State Journal*, April 8, 2003, p. D1; D. Welch and K. Kerwin, "Rick Wagoner's Game Plan," *Business Week*, February 10, 2003, pp. 53–60.

The Hawthorne Studies The *Hawthorne studies*, which began in 1924 at Western Electric's Hawthorne plant near Chicago, Illinois, were among the earliest attempts to use scientific techniques to examine human behavior at work.[18] As summarized in Table 2-8, a three-stage series of experiments assessed the effects of varying physical conditions and management practices on workplace efficiency. The first experiment examined the effects of workplace lighting on productivity; it produced the unexpected findings that changes in lighting had little effect but that changes in social conditions seemed to explain significant increases in group productivity.

TABLE 2-8
The Hawthorne
Studies

Experiment	Major Changes	Results
Stage I		
Illumination study	Lighting conditions	Improved productivity at nearly all levels of illumination
Stage II		
First relay-assembly test	Job simplification, shorter work hours, rest breaks, friendly supervision, incentive pay	30 percent productivity improvement
Second relay-assembly test	Incentive pay	12 percent productivity improvement
Mica-splitting test	Shorter work hours, rest breaks, friendly supervision	15 percent productivity improvement
Stage III		
Interview program	—	Discovery of presence of informal productivity norms
Bank-wiring-room test	Incentive pay	Emergence of productivity norms

Additional experiments led the researchers to conclude that social factors—in particular, workers' desires to satisfy needs for companionship and support at work—explained the results observed across all of the Hawthorne studies.

Later reanalyses of the Hawthorne experiments not only found weaknesses in the studies' methods and techniques, but also suggested that changes in incentive pay, tasks being performed, rest periods, and working hours led to the productivity improvements attributed by researchers to the effects of social factors.[19] Nonetheless, the Hawthorne studies raised serious questions about the efficiency-oriented focus of the scientific management and administrative principles perspectives. In so doing, they stimulated debate about the importance of human satisfaction and personal development at work. The **human relations perspective** of management thought that grew out of this debate redirected attention away from improving efficiency and toward increasing employee growth, development, and satisfaction.[20]

Douglas McGregor   Douglas McGregor (1906–1964) played a key role in promoting this redirection, through his efforts at sharpening the philosophical contrast between the human relations approach and the scientific management and administrative principles perspectives.[21] McGregor used the term **Theory X** to describe his key assumptions about human nature, which appear in Table 2-9. He suggested that theorists and managers holding these assumptions would describe management as follows:

1. Managers are responsible for organizing the elements of productive enterprise—money, materials, equipment, people—solely in the interest of economic efficiency.
2. The manager's function is to motivate workers, direct their efforts, control their actions, and modify their behavior to fit the organization's needs.

TABLE 2-9
Theory X and
Theory Y
Assumptions

Theory X Assumptions
1. The average person has an inherent dislike of work and will avoid it if possible.
2. Because they dislike work, most people must be coerced, controlled, directed, or threatened with punishment before they will put forth effort toward the achievement of organizational objectives.
3. The average person prefers to be directed, wishes to avoid responsibility, has relatively little ambition, and desires security above all.

Theory Y Assumptions
1. Expanding physical and mental effort at work is as natural as play and rest. The average person does not inherently dislike work.
2. External control and the threat of punishment are not the only way to direct effort toward organizational objectives. People will exercise self-direction and self-control in the service of objectives to which they feel committed.
3. Commitment to objectives is a function of the rewards associated with their achievement. The most significant rewards—the satisfaction of ego and self-actualization needs—can be direct products of effort directed toward organizational objectives.
4. Avoidance of responsibility, lack of ambition, and emphasis on security are not inherent human characteristics. Under proper conditions, the average person learns not only to accept but also to seek responsibility.
5. Imagination, ingenuity, creativity, and the ability to use these qualities to solve organizational problems are widely distributed among people.

Source: Based on information presented in D. McGregor, *The Human Side of Enterprise* (New York: McGraw-Hill, 1960), pp. 33–34, 47–48.

3. Without such active intervention by managers, people would be passive or even resistant to organizational needs. They must therefore be persuaded, rewarded, and punished for the good of the organization.[22]

According to McGregor, the scientific management and administrative principles perspectives promoted a "hard" version of Theory X. Both perspectives favored overcoming employees' resistance to organizational needs through strict discipline and economic rewards or punishments. McGregor added that a "soft" version of Theory X seemed to underlie the Hawthorne studies, as the Hawthorne researchers appeared to regard satisfaction and social relations mainly as being rewards for employees who followed orders.

Theory Y, a contrasting philosophy of management that McGregor attributed to theorists, researchers, and managers holding the human relations perspective, is based on the second set of assumptions shown in Table 2-9. According to McGregor, individuals holding Theory Y assumptions would view the task of management as follows:

1. Managers are responsible for organizing the elements of productive enterprise—money, materials, equipment, people—in the interest of economic ends.
2. Because people are motivated to perform, have potential for development, can assume responsibility, and are willing to work toward organizational goals, managers are responsible for enabling people to recognize and develop these basic capacities.
3. The essential task of management is to arrange organizational conditions and methods of operation so that working toward organizational objectives is also the best way for people to achieve their own personal goals.[23]

Unlike Theory X managers, who try to control their employees, Theory Y managers try to help employees learn how to manage themselves.

Other Contributors   Many management theorists, including Abraham Maslow and Frederick Herzberg, embraced the point of view embodied in McGregor's Theory Y and speculated about ways in which personal autonomy and group participation might encourage employee growth, development, and satisfaction. The works of these contributors also served as benchmark theories during the early development of research on micro and meso organizational behavior, as described later in this book.

1960–Present: The Open Systems Perspective

With the emergence in the 1960s of the **open systems perspective,** human relations concerns related to employee satisfaction and development broadened to include a focus on organizational growth and survival. According to the open systems perspective, every organization is a *system*—a unified structure of interrelated subsystems—and it is *open*—subject to the influence of the surrounding environment. Together, these two ideas form the central tenet of the open systems approach, which states that organizations whose subsystems can cope with the surrounding environment can continue to do business, whereas organizations whose subsystems cannot cope will not survive.

Daniel Katz and Robert L. Kahn   In one of the seminal works on the open systems perspective, Daniel Katz and Robert Kahn identified the process shown in Figure 2-7 as essential to organizational growth and survival.[24] This process consists of the following sequence of events:

1. Every organization imports *inputs,* such as raw materials, production equipment, human resources, and technical know-how from the surrounding environment. For instance, Shell Oil Company hires employees and, from sources around the world, acquires unrefined oil, refinery equipment, and knowledge about how to refine petroleum products.
2. Some of the inputs are used to transform other inputs during a process of *throughput.* At Shell, employees use refinery equipment and their own know-how to transform unrefined oil into petroleum products such as gasoline, kerosene, and diesel fuel.
3. The transformed resources are exported as *outputs*—saleable goods or services— to the environment. Petroleum products from Shell's refineries are loaded into tankers and transported to service stations throughout North America.
4. Outputs are exchanged for new inputs, and the cycle repeats. Shell sells its products and uses the resulting revenues to pay its employees and purchase additional oil, equipment, and know-how.

FIGURE 2-7   The Open Systems Perspective

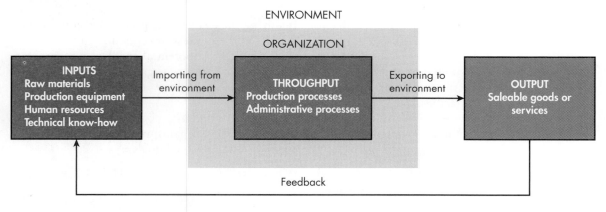

According to Katz and Kahn, organizations will continue to grow and survive only as long as they import more material and energy from the environment than they expend in producing the outputs exported back to the environment. *Information inputs* that signal how the environment and organization are functioning can help determine whether the organization will continue to survive. *Negative feedback* indicates a potential for failure and the need to change the way things are being done.

Fred Emery and Eric Trist   In Katz and Kahn's model, the environment surrounding an organization is both the source of needed resources and the recipient of transformed products. Accordingly, organizational survival depends on sensing that environment and adjusting to its demands. Describing environments and their associated demands so as to improve this sensing and adjustment process was the goal of Fred Emery and Eric Trist, two early theorists of the open systems perspective.[25]

After noting that every organization's environment is itself composed of a collection of more or less interconnected organizations—supplier companies, competitors, and customer firms—Emery and Trist proposed the existence of four basic kinds of environments. The first kind, which they labeled the *placid random environment,* is loosely interconnected and relatively unchanging. Organizations in such environments operate independently of one another, and one firm's decision to change the way it does business has little effect on its rivals. These organizations are usually small—for example, landscape maintenance companies, construction firms, and industrial job shops—and can usually ignore each other and still stay in business by catering to local customers.

Placid clustered environments are more tightly interconnected. Under these conditions, firms are grouped together into stable industries. Environments of this sort require organizations to cope with the actions of a *market*—a fairly constant group of suppliers, competitors, and customers. As a result, companies in placid clustered environments develop strategic moves and countermoves that correspond to competitors' actions. Grocery stores in the same geographic region often do business in this type of environment, using coupon discounts, in-store specials, and similar promotions to lure customers away from other stores.

Disturbed reactive environments are as tightly interconnected as placid clustered environments, but are considerably less stable. Changes that occur in the environment itself have forceful effects on every organization. For instance, new competitors from overseas, by increasing automation, and changing consumer tastes in the U.S. automobile market, revolutionized the domestic auto industry in the 1970s and 1980s. In response, GM and Ford had to change their way of doing business, Chrysler ultimately merged with Germany's Daimler-Benz to become Daimler-Chrysler, and a fourth long-time manufacturer, American Motors, ceased to exist. In such circumstances, organizations must respond not only to competitors' actions but also to changes in the environment itself. Due to their unpredictability, it is difficult to plan how to respond to these changes.

Turbulent fields are extremely complex and dynamic environments. Companies operate in multiple markets. Public and governmental actions can alter the nature of an industry virtually overnight. Technologies advance at lightning speed. The amount of information needed to stay abreast of industrial trends is overwhelming. As a result, it is virtually impossible for organizations to do business in any consistent way. Instead, they must remain flexible in the face of such uncertainty, staying poised to adapt themselves to whatever circumstances unfold. Today's computer and communications industries exemplify this sort of environment. Technological change and corporate mergers are creating and destroying entire categories of companies at ever-increasing rates.

Other Contributors   Emery and Trist suggested that organizations must respond in different ways to different environmental conditions. Tighter environmental interconnections require greater awareness about environmental conditions, and more sweeping environmental change necessitates greater flexibility and adaptability. Other open systems theorists, including Paul Lawrence, Robert Duncan, and Jay Galbraith, have similarly stressed the need for organizations to adjust to their environments. Their ideas, and those of other open systems theorists, form the basis of several current models of macro organizational behavior, described in later chapters of this book.

A Contingency Framework

Of the four management perspectives just described, none tells the whole story about management and managers. Instead, as indicated in Figure 2-8, each contributes valuable insights that supplement the others' contributions. The scientific management perspective focuses on making a profit in the *external* world by increasing the *efficiency* of production activities. The administrative principles perspective emphasizes improving *internal* operations by increasing the *efficiency* of administration. The human relations perspective stresses the importance of developing the *flexibility* to respond to the individual needs of members *inside* the organization. The open systems perspective focuses on developing the *flexibility* to respond to changes in the *external* environment.[26]

Similarities are readily evident among the four perspectives. For example, the scientific management and administrative behavior perspectives both promote attention to efficiency and stability. The human relations and open systems perspectives share a common emphasis on flexibility and change. The administrative principles and human relations perspectives focus on procedures within the organization. The

FIGURE 2-8   Contingency Framework

The four management perspectives differ in terms of their emphasis on flexibility or efficiency, and on internal operations or the external environment. Depending on the situation faced by a manager, one or more of the perspectives may provide useful guidance. This contingency relationship is summarized in the form of a simple matrix.

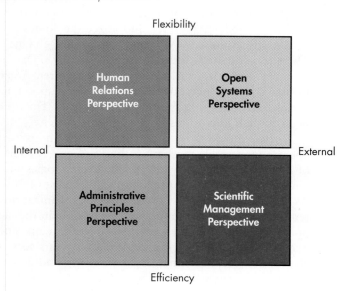

open systems and scientific management perspectives emphasize the importance of dealing with demands on the organization from external sources.

Each perspective also has an opposite, however. The human relations perspective, with its emphasis on human growth and satisfaction, stands in stark contrast to the scientific management perspective's emphasis on employee efficiency and task simplification. The open systems perspective's focus on adapting to environmental circumstances contrasts sharply with the administrative principles perspective's concern with developing stable, internally efficient operations.

These differences reflect dilemmas that managers face every day. Is it more important to stimulate task performance or employee satisfaction? Should the organization be structured to promote efficiency or flexibility? Should jobs be designed to encourage satisfaction or to maximize profitability? We will address these and other issues in the remaining chapters of this book. For now, we conclude our discussion of management and managers by repeating a key idea: *In dealing with management dilemmas, no single approach is either always right or always wrong.* In recommending this approach, we advocate a **contingency approach** to management—the view that no single theory, procedure, or set of rules is applicable to every situation.[27] Managers must make difficult choices, but the insights offered by all four perspectives can help them weigh the alternatives and decide what to do.

SUMMARY

Management is a process of *planning, organizing, directing,* and *controlling* the behavior of others that makes it possible for an *organization* using a *division of labor* and a *hierarchy of authority* to accomplish a *mission* that would not be achievable through the efforts of individuals working alone. *Managers* differ in terms of where they fit in the organization's hierarchy. These differences influence their use of *conceptual, human,* and *technical skills* and shape the *managerial roles* they fill. The fast-paced job of manager allows little uninterrupted time to devote to any single activity.

Over the years, four perspectives have developed to explain and improve management practices. Supporters of the *scientific management perspective* have tried to increase the efficiency of production processes so as to enhance marketplace profitability. Proponents of the *administrative principles perspective* have focused on enhancing the efficiency of administrative procedures. Researchers in the *human relations perspective* have emphasized nurturing the growth and satisfaction of organization members. Theorists working in the *open systems perspective* have highlighted the importance of coping with the surrounding environment. According to the *contingency approach,* these four perspectives form a framework of alternative ways to view the process of management. This framework provides managers with useful guidance as they manage organizational behavior.

REVIEW QUESTIONS

1. How does an organization enable its members to accomplish a goal that might not be achievable by individuals working alone? Why aren't organizations formed to achieve purposes that people can accomplish individually?

2. What is an organization's mission? Its division of labor? Its hierarchy of authority? How do these three organizational attributes fit together to define the nature of management?

3. Describe the work of a manager in performing each of the four basic management functions: planning, organizing, directing, and controlling. How does planning affect organizing? How does organizing affect directing? How does directing affect controlling? How does controlling affect later planning?

4. What are the three kinds of managers? How do hierarchical differences affect the job of being a manager?

5. What kinds of skills do all managers use to perform their jobs? Which skill becomes more important as they move up the hierarchy of authority? Which one stays about the same? Which one loses importance?

6. What roles do managers perform? How do hierarchical differences affect the roles of managers?

7. What is the central idea underlying the scientific management perspective? What advice would an expert in this perspective give managers? Give an example of the kind of change that an expert in scientific management might recommend if he or she were asked to improve the efficiency of your class.

8. How does the administrative principles perspective differ from the scientific management perspective? What is a management principle? How does it differ from a law or rule? What is a bureaucracy? Give an example of an organization that is extremely bureaucratic. Give an example of an organization that is not very bureaucratic.

9. On what does the human relations perspective focus attention? According to McGregor, what view do holders of this perspective have on management? In what important respect did the Hawthorne researchers differ from other proponents of the human relations perspective?

10. What are the two key ideas underlying the open systems perspective? What central principle do they support? Explain the cycle of events described by Katz and Kahn's open systems model. Why is it important for managers to be able to diagnose environmental conditions and adapt their organizations to environmental changes as they occur?

11. Explain the contingency model constructed from the four perspectives of management thought described in this chapter. If you were a manager having problems with employee satisfaction, which perspective would you consult for advice? If you were concerned about efficiency, which perspectives could probably help you?

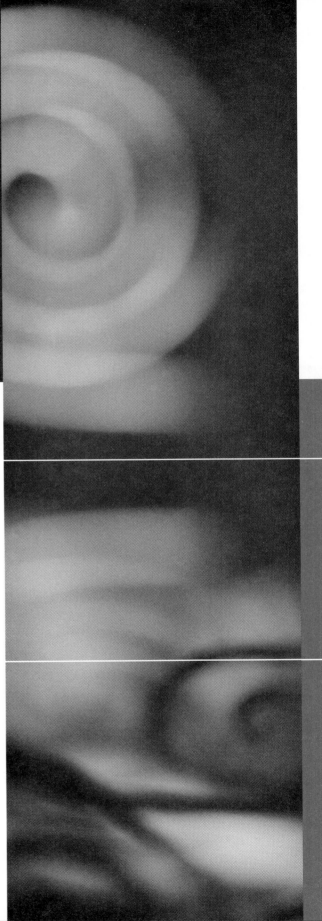

2

Micro Organizational Behavior

Chapter 3 Managing Diversity and Individual Differences

Chapter 4 Perception, Decision Making, and Creativity

Chapter 5 Work Motivation and Performance

Chapter 6 Satisfaction and Stress

Cases

CHAPTER

3

Capitalizing on Diversity
Selection
Training
Reegineering

Diversity in Personality: Five Critical Factors
The Big Five Framework
Making Personality Tests More Effective

Diversity in Cognitive Abilities: Four Critical Factors
General and Specific Aspects of Cognitive Ability
Validity of Cognitive Ability Tests

Diversity in Physical Abilities: Three Critical Factors

Diversity in Experience: Two Critical Factors
Broadening Demographic Experience: Political Aspects
Broadening Demographic Experience: Competitive Aspects
Broadening Cultural Experience

Adaptability: Flexibility in the Face of Diversity

Summary
Review Questions

Learning Through Experience
Diagnostic Questions 3-1: Diversity and Individual Differences
Exercise 3-1: Individual Similarities and Differences

Managing Diversity and Individual Differences

America's Best Carpet Care Company hired Jerrol Glenn Woods for the job of in-home cleaner. Although America's Best made a large number of hiring decisions in their history, this was one that they were to never forget.

Woods was sent out by America's Best to clean the carpet of Kerry Spooner-Dean. Spooner-Dean complained after he left that the work was shoddy and demanded that America's Best send him back to try again. The company, ever mindful of generating satisfied customers, agreed to this request; however, when Woods showed up, instead of redoing his work, he robbed and fatally stabbed Spooner-Dean. Woods eventually pleaded guilty to first-degree murder, and the Spooner-Dean family promptly sued America's Best.

America's Best tried to defend itself by arguing that it was not liable for Woods's actions and that it was impossible for them to know he was a dangerous person. However, closer inspection revealed that despite being more than 30 years old, Woods had listed only one previous job on his employment application—carpet cleaner for Sears, Roebuck & Company. Had America's Best even bothered to call Sears, they could have learned that Woods was terminated from Sears because he was caught stealing from the company. Had they bothered to take this even a step further and conduct a background check, they would have learned that Woods was on parole following a twelve-year prison sentence for armed bank robbery. Finally, even if all they did was listen to their own employees, America's Best could have learned of Woods's past, because he had told other employees he had been in prison on more than one occasion. When one employee mentioned this to management, he was told it didn't really matter.[1]

A jury of the Alameda Superior Court did not share this opinion; they ordered the company to pay $11.5 million in damages. The award threatened to push the *entire organization into bankruptcy, and it would not be the first time that a single bad hiring decision put a company out of business. Trusted Health Resources filed for bankruptcy after it was ordered to pay more than $26.5 million because one of its home health care workers who had a previous prison record murdered a customer at home. Indeed, the average award in a negligent-hiring suit is roughly $900,000, and if this sum is not sufficient to knock out an organization for good, it is the type of body blow that sets up the organization's demise due to the loss of business that quickly follows from such an announcement.*[2]

In order to avoid this type of life-threatening outcome, employers are increasingly trying to learn more about their prospective employees before hiring them. In some cases this involves standard tests of ability and measures of personality, but in more cases employers are also turning to private investigators or security firms to get a glimpse of the person's past record. According to past audits, 44 percent of all resumes submitted for executive positions contain some type of inaccuracy. This may be as slight as a volunteer position listed that was never held, or something as major as lying about a past educational degree or former job.[3]

The cost of a comprehensive background check is often in the $100–$200 range, and that would typically include an examination of criminal, employment, and educational records. Although many employers may balk at this cost, this attitude may be pennywise but dollar foolish—especially for jobs that involve managing money or unmonitored employee-customer contact. Indeed, many organizations now advertise the amount of money they spend on background checks and employee testing as a reason why someone should use their services rather than those of their competitors. Thus, the extra time, effort, and care they put into the selection of their workforce is used as a means of distinguishing themselves and gaining competitive advantage in the consumer market.[4]

When it comes to building and leading organizations, inexperienced managers often make one of two critical mistakes when it comes to individual differences. On the one hand, some new managers fall victim to the "mirror image fallacy" and presume that all other people are "just like me." In one sense, this is a comforting bias, because if it were true, it would make managing people very easy. For example, if owners of a firm believe that everyone in their company shares their abilities, interests, beliefs, and values, they will consider it an easy task to organize and encourage their employees to pursue a common goal. Because the **mirror image fallacy** *is* a fallacy, however, the owners soon find that the myriad differences among the people they employ will make their task far from easy. While few readers of this book would ever commit fraud or acts of violence like the one described in the opening vignette, this does not mean that you may not come in contact with others who cannot be trusted. Because of this, managers need to take steps to ensure that those they hire can contribute to the organization and not place the group at risk.

On the other hand, some managers fail because they hold prejudicial stereotypes about people based on sex or membership in a racial, ethnic, or age group. That is, they assume that all women, or all older workers, or all members of various minority groups are "all alike." They then employ these prejudicial misperceptions in making decisions regarding organizational membership and rewards that harm members of these groups and limit organizational effectiveness. For example, managers may mistakenly assume that all Arab Muslims are violent fanatics, and then take steps to remove them from the organization in order to promote security. In fact, on most dimensions of ability and personality, there is wide variation within groups (among Arabs) and these differences are often much more important than the sometimes trivial differences between groups (Arabs versus Hispanics versus African Americans). Managers who fail to pay attention to differences between people *within these groups* inevitably damage their employees, their companies, and their own careers.

Ralph Waldo Emerson once wrote that "the wise man shows his wisdom in separation, in gradation, and his scale of creatures and of merits is as wide as nature. . . .The foolish have no range in their scale, but suppose that every man is as every other man." That statement captures the essence of this chapter. It seeks to familiarize you with some of the major occupationally relevant dimensions on which humans vary and to describe the means by which you can use this information to secure a competitive advantage for your organization.

The first section of the chapter discusses how information about individual differences can be used to generate added value and competitive advantage. Next, we describe ten critical dimensions on which people vary. Although these dimensions are hardly the *only* ways in which people can vary (indeed, later chapters will explore others), they serve as a useful starting point for considering the bases of diversity. A manager needs to treat each person as a unique configuration of these ten characteristics rather than simply categorizing workers by surface characteristics such as race, sex, age, or culture. Managers who think in terms of these characteristics will be able to capitalize on individual differences in a way that promotes the competitiveness of their organizations, while at the same time avoiding the mirror image fallacy and prejudicial stereotypes.

CAPITALIZING ON DIVERSITY

Even the most tolerant manager might sometimes wish that individual differences would just go away. If all supervisors, colleagues, and subordinates were alike, managing would be a much easier task. Of course, such homogeneity is highly unlikely to happen. Consequently, successful organizations must try to capitalize on differences in a way that advances their competitiveness. Indeed, research on how firms gain sustainable competitive advantage consistently identifies selectivity in hiring and an emphasis on training as two central characteristics of successful companies.[5] The findings from this research are supported by the practices of highly successful managers who immerse themselves in the process of selecting new organizational members. For example, Larry Bossidy, chairman of Honeywell, was famous for his ability to turn around floundering organizations. He attributed much of his success to hiring the right people, and devoted 30 to 40 percent of his time to hiring and developing future leaders of the organization. Bossidy notes, "I personally interviewed many of the 300 new MBAs we hired. I knew that the standard I set would be followed by the rest of the organization: You hire a talented person, and they will hire a talented person."[6] As shown in Figure 3-1, we can derive benefits from individual differences in organizational behavior through selection, training, and reengineering.

Selection

Selection and placement programs enable managers to assess people and jobs, and then try to match up the two in a way that maximizes the fit between the abilities and traits of the individual and the abilities and traits required for the job. This type

FIGURE 3-1   Three Ways to Capitalize on Individual Differences

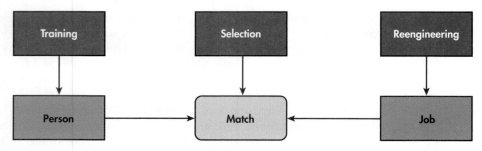

of matching allows us to take advantage of individual differences without changing either the person or the job. Personnel selection is the process of choosing some applicants and rejecting others for particular positions.

Effective selection is especially critical for carrying out certain business strategies. For example, part of 3M's competitive advantage derives from its business strategy of growing talent and innovation within the organization. At the same time, 3M definitely does not want valuable people to leave the company, taking its ideas or secrets with them. Thus 3M's goal is to create a company of employees with long-term service to the firm.

As Richard Listad, a manager at 3M, notes, "When you promote from within the way we do, you want to make sure that you're recruiting high-quality people." To make sure that the organization will have a reliable pool of talent on which to draw, 3M has established close ties to a small number of midwestern universities. By forming long-term relationships with the targeted schools, 3M gets to know the people (faculty) who are in a good position to know the people (students) whom the company is likely to hire. This knowledge, along with an expansive internship program that gives 3M direct experience working with soon-to-be-graduates, helps to ensure that any hiring decision will turn out to be a good one for both 3M and the applicant. In fact, 3M has an annual attrition rate of less than 3 percent among salaried staff—highly in line with its chosen strategy for competing in its industry.[7]

Training

A second way to benefit from knowledge of individual differences is to train people so as to compensate for any job-related deficiencies in their current profile of traits or abilities. The beginning of the twenty-first century has been marked by widespread labor shortages in some U.S. industries. Much of this problem can be traced not so much to the scarcity of workers, but rather to shortcomings in the skill levels of those workers who are available. According to surveys conducted by the National Association of Manufacturers, five of six applicants for manufacturing jobs are currently rejected because of gaps between their skills and the job requirements. Of those rejected, two out of five are rejected specifically for lack of basic proficiency in reading and arithmetic.[8] In fact, research has documented that the illiteracy rates associated with the growing segments of the U.S. labor market (young people and immigrants) are among the highest among industrialized nations.[9]

Some organizations have responded to this crisis by trying to upgrade the skills of the new, highly diverse entrants into the labor pool. The Aetna Institute for Corporate Education, which was founded by the Aetna Life and Casualty Corporation, represents a $42 million response to this problem. The institute is housed in a building containing both hotel rooms and fifty-six classrooms, where a sixty-member full-time faculty teaches as many as 400 "students" each day. This effort is the centerpiece of Aetna's ongoing reorganization scheme aimed at keeping the company competitive. Aetna plans to rewrite all of its job descriptions to emphasize general competencies rather than job-specific skills. Individual employees will then be assessed on these competencies and assigned to the institute to master whatever abilities they lack. The institute will also help employees develop the competencies needed for upper-level jobs as part of Aetna's promotion-from-within policy.[10]

Training can also be directed at changing people's personality styles. At Chemical Bank, many accountants with excellent technical skills cannot be promoted to managerial levels because of their weaknesses in dealing with other people. For example, as one manager notes, when the bank values an asset one way and the client values it another way, a lack of agreeableness on the part of the accountant can make discussions "more contentious than they need to be." Accountants also struggle sometimes when they must work in cross-functional teams. Training programs aimed at enhancing their skills in getting along with others can help reduce these problems. When armed with both technical skills and interpersonal skills, Chemical Bank officers find that not only are the right decisions made, but the implementation of these decisions is also facilitated.[11]

Selecting for an attribute and training for an attribute can be equally effective strategies, as demonstrated in a recent study of 210 resort-hotel employees. In this study, high levels of performance were found in employees who either were high in conscientiousness or had attended a training program aimed at increasing their level of self-directed leadership. Thus one could choose to take advantage of existing differences in people's levels of conscientiousness or, alternatively, use training to change the level of conscientiousness. Both approaches yielded positive results. In contrast, performance in contexts where neither selective hiring nor training took place was very low.[12]

Reengineering

Assessing individual differences is clearly critical for training purposes, because the intent is to change the person. A different approach is to assess individual differences and then respond to any mismatch between person and job by changing the *job* or reengineering work processes. For example, the Americans with Disabilities Act (ADA) of 1990 requires that employers make "reasonable accommodations" in an effort to employ the disabled. Such accommodations often mean deleting, changing, or moving a job requirement to a different job, so that the lack of a particular ability no longer disqualifies some disabled worker from being considered for a certain position.

A good example of such a program can be seen at Samsonite Corporation in Denver, where many jobs have been changed so that they can be performed by deaf people. The accommodations required are often very simple—for example, the company now uses lights on forklifts in the production area rather than the traditional beepers to alert people to the presence of a moving vehicle. Even so, such accommodations have proved effective in eliminating the need for an ability that some people might not have.[13]

As another example, Nordstrom's, working in conjunction with the United Cerebral Palsy Association, has attempted to isolate all the tasks in its job descriptions that can be performed by someone with cerebral palsy. These tasks (such as sorting hangers) are then removed from the job, freeing up the original worker to do other things, and given to a worker who has cerebral palsy. The program provides Nordstrom's

FIGURE 3-2   Ten Critical Dimensions of Individual Differences

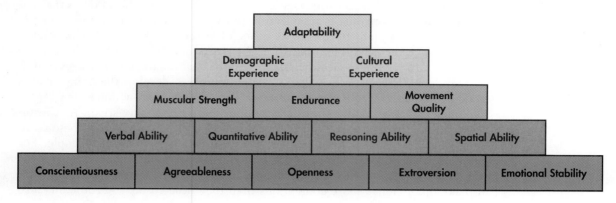

with a means of incorporating people with disabilities into the workforce in a meaningful and productive way.[14]

Successful managers strive to put each worker in a position that best taps his or her own talents, often informally shifting or trading tasks between two people working under the same job title.[15] This type of informal job redesign allows the manager to take advantage of each person's unique blend of strengths and weaknesses. Of course, accommodating the different abilities and traits of different workers need not be limited to meeting the legislative requirements set forth in the ADA.

In a perfect world, all managers would work with people who had all strengths and no weaknesses. In the real world, however, they rarely get this opportunity. The next best option is for managers to become aware of the strengths and weaknesses of their various workers, and then through selection, training, or job design create a situation that plays to their employees' strengths and leans away from their weaknesses. Given the many possible dimensions on which people might differ, which are the most critical for a manager to target? The next section of this chapter lays out a framework that attempts to answer this question by isolating ten specific dimensions on which managers need to focus. We will use the model shown in Figure 3-2 to organize our discussion into five personality traits, four cognitive abilities, three physical abilities, two aspects of experience, and finally an overarching characteristic we will label "adaptability."

DIVERSITY IN PERSONALITY: FIVE CRITICAL FACTORS

Given the vast number of personality characteristics that are described in the scientific literature, we need some type of classification scheme before we can understand both the characteristics and their interrelationships. Fortunately, a great deal of research has been conducted on the dimensionality of personality, which has helped clarify the structure of human traits. Indeed, the current personality literature tends to focus on a consensus group of five dimensions of personality, known as the "Big Five."[16]

The Big Five Framework

The Big Five personality characteristics home in on a person's social reputation, in the sense that they describe what the person is like when viewed by other people. The five characteristics (Table 3-1) can be used to comprehensively capture what people are like. Because work organizations are social institutions, the fact that

TABLE 3-1
The Five
Dimensions of
Personality

1. Extroversion
   Sociable, gregarious, assertive, talkative, expressive
2. Emotional adjustment
   Emotionally stable, nondepressed, secure, content
3. Agreeableness
   Courteous, trusting, good natured, tolerant, cooperative, forgiving
4. Conscientiousness
   Dependable, organized, persevering, thorough, achievement oriented
5. Openness to experience
   Curious, imaginative, artistic, sensitive, broad minded, playful

Source: M. R. Barrick and M. K. Mount, "The Big Five Personality Dimensions and Job Performance: A Meta-Analysis," *Personnel Psychology* 44 (1991), 1–26.

these characteristics are expressed in terms of a person's social reputation makes them highly relevant in understanding organizational behavior. The Big Five traits include **extroversion, emotional stability, agreeableness, conscientiousness,** and **openness to experience.**[17]

Many companies, including General Motors, American Cyanamid, JCPenney, and Westinghouse, rely heavily on personality assessment programs to evaluate and promote employees. Many other firms use such programs as screens for initial hiring.[18] Despite their widespread adoption by industry, however, the usefulness of such personality measures in explaining and predicting human behavior has been criticized on several counts.

Traditionally, the most significant criticism deals with the validity of these measures for actually predicting future job success. Although it is possible to find reliable, commercially available measures of each of the traits shown in Table 3-1, some have suggested that the evidence for their validity and generalizability has traditionally been only mixed.[19] Conscientiousness is the only dimension of personality that seems to display any validity across a number of different job categories.[20] Indeed, conscientiousness is not only a valid predictor of job performance, it is also a predictor of employee theft[21] and white-collar crime.[22] Extroversion is relevant to a few types of jobs such as sales and management, but the level of predictability is low[23] and contingent upon other factors such as the amount of freedom inherent in the job.[24] In contrast to this traditional view, a great deal of the more recent research is painting a more positive picture of the usefulness of personality testing for a wide range of organizational behavior. Indeed, as the Cutting-Edge Research box shows, improved statistical techniques are revealing new findings regarding the relevancy and utility of these kinds of measures.

In addition, because companies are increasingly competing on the dimension of quality of service, the importance of the personalities of the people who provide that service has never been more important. These customer-contact people make up one of the fastest-growing segments of the U.S. workforce, and they serve at the front-line in the battle among organizations striving for competitive advantage. Many of the most successful firms therefore take great care when hiring people for these jobs.

For example, at Marriott Hotels, applicants take a computerized, self-administered questionnaire as part of the hiring process. The items on this questionnaire tap into dimensions such as conscientiousness and agreeableness. Marriott rejects 90 percent of all would-be guest service associates based on these kinds of tests and interviews, and this selectivity enhances the level of its service quality. Manager Richard Bell-Irvine notes, "When someone leaves, it messes up your employee teams, messes up your productivity, and messes up the service you provide." Whereas nearly 50 percent of Marriott's new employees once left after their first three

CUTTING-EDGE RESEARCH

CUMULATING KNOWLEDGE ABOUT THE BIG FIVE FACTORS OF PERSONALITY

One advantage of conceptualizing personality traits using the Big Five framework is that it helps provide a structure for adding together all the results from a wide variety of studies that examined the role of personality in organizational behavior. Even if the original investigators did not use the specific name for the trait that is employed by the Big Five, the comprehensive nature of this categorization scheme allows all traits to be placed into one factor or another, and then the results from disparate studies can be added up via a technique called meta-analysis. This often reveals relationships and patterns of findings that could not be picked up in the original set of studies when examined in isolation.

In the two years prior to the publication of this book, no less than four such analyses were conducted, revealing a great deal of new knowledge regarding how these traits relate to critical areas of organizational behavior such as leadership, motivation, job satisfaction, and balancing the need to both "get ahead" and "get along" in the workplace. Taken together, these four meta-analyses summarized the results from more than 350 samples and more than 45,000 people, and in many ways implied that the role that personality plays in these outcomes and processes has been underestimated in the past.

For example, although many have questioned the value of leadership traits, when all the evidence is added together at least three traits emerge as useful predictors. The strongest predictor of leadership is extroversion, followed by conscientiousness and openness to experience. Extroversion and conscientiousness seemed to be particularly good predictors of leadership emergence, whereas openness to experience was a better predictor of leadership effectiveness. When it comes to either leader emergence or effectiveness, neither agreeableness nor emotional stability seemed to matter one way or the other. In fact, one can probably think of many leaders who were either high or low on these traits.

With respect to work motivation, two of the traits that were relevant for predicting leadership, extroversion and conscientiousness, were also valid precursors to motivation. However, emotional stability, which seems to play a less prominent role in leadership, seems to be a very strong predictor of individual work motivation. People who were emotionally stable were found to set higher goals, show higher levels of confidence and self-efficacy, and persist longer in the face of failure relative to emotionally unstable individuals. People who were highly agreeable tended to display high levels of confidence, but this was offset by the fact that they set low goals, resulting in no overall effect one way or the other for motivation. The same three traits that were related to how motivated people would be at work were also valid when it came to trying to predict job satisfaction. People who were low in emotional stability tended to be dissatisfied with their jobs, and this was also true of people who were introverted and who were low in conscientiousness.

Finally, it has often been argued that to succeed in organizations, individuals need to both strive to "get ahead" (that is, to stand out from others and obtain recognition), but at the same time, work to "get along" (that is, to collaborate with others and be viewed as a team player). At some points, these two behavioral goals may come in conflict; thus people need a complex set of assets to achieve the highest level of success. Research on how this dilemma can be resolved via the Big Five framework suggests that extroversion is critical for getting ahead, whereas emotional stability is critical for getting along. Interestingly, conscientiousness plays a close second to pursuing both of these goals, in the sense that people high on this characteristic seem to be in the best position to achieve both goals.

Sources: T. A. Judge, J. E. Bono, R. Ilies, and M. Gerhardt, "Personality and Leadership: A Qualitative and Quantitative Review," *Journal of Applied Psychology* 87 (2002), 765–780; T. A. Judge and R. Ilies, "Relationship of Personality to Performance Motivation: A Meta-Analytic Review," *Journal of Applied Psychology* 87 (2002), 797–807; T. A. Judge, D. Heller, and M. K. Mount, "Five-Factor Model of Personality and Job Satisfaction: A Meta-Analysis," *Journal of Applied Psychology* 87 (2002), 530–541; J. Hogan and B. Holland, "Using Theory to Evaluate Personality and Job Performance Relations: A Socioanalytic Perspective," *Journal of Applied Psychology* 88 (2003), 100–112.

months on the job, this sort of testing has cut the attrition rate to closer to 10 percent. Another Marriott manager, Chris Kerbow, notes, "We're willing to be patient. It's so critical to the success of the hotels that our associates be committed and enthusiastic."[25]

The fact that many personality characteristics are described in everyday language—for example, aggressiveness, sociability, and impulsiveness—is both good news and bad news for the study of organizational behavior. It is good news because most people can readily perceive individual differences in these qualities and can see how such variations might affect particular situations. It is bad news because terms adopted from everyday language are usually imprecise. This vagueness can create considerable difficulty in understanding, communicating, and using information obtained from scientific measures of personality. We will next focus on ways to increase the usefulness of measuring these characteristics in organizational contexts.

Making Personality Tests More Effective

Although the validity of personality tests may never exceed that of ability tests, organizations can nevertheless take concrete steps to more successfully capitalize on individual differences in personality. First, in many cases, the effects of some trait on performance are revealed only when the person is also high in ability. That is, it is not so much the trait itself, but rather how the trait interacts with ability. For example, in a study of 203 workers at Weyerhaeuser, researchers found little correlation between conscientiousness and supervisory ratings of performance. However, for workers who were high in cognitive ability, there was a strong positive relationship between this aspect of personality and performance.[26] Thus, conscientiousness, in the absence of ability, is not much of an asset, but when conscientiousness and ability both reside in the same person, the results can be dramatic.

Second, any one trait by itself may not be as important as how the trait interacts with other traits. For example, although it is important for workers to be high in conscientiousness, some people who are high on this trait can be abrasive and interpersonally difficult. Thus, the relationship between conscientiousness and performance—especially when measured by supervisory ratings—might be particularly high when the highly conscientious person is also high on agreeableness. This is the precise finding of a recent study conducted in five different samples of workers across a wide variety of occupations.[27]

Third, the relationship between the trait and performance could be a function of the specific demands of the job. Again turning to agreeableness, although it is nice to be around co-workers who are trusting, tolerant, and cooperative, the nature of some jobs demands just the opposite approach. For example, David Duncan, an auditor for Arthur Andersen, was arrested for his part in the Enron disaster. Duncan's job was to monitor Enron's accounting practices to make sure they conformed to the rules laid down by Arthur Andersen. However, many who know him well attribute his downfall to the fact that he was an overly agreeable person who hated conflict and would do anything to keep his clients happy. In fact, he not only avoided conflict with his clients by approving some very questionable practices, he even avoided conflict with his co-workers who disapproved of Enron's practices. In fact, in a memo that proved significant in his trial, he responded to a concerned co-worker by noting "on your point (i.e., the whole thing is a bad idea), I really couldn't agree more."[28] In this instance, being trusting, tolerant, and cooperative ran counter to actually getting the job done.

Fourth, the relationship between the trait and performance may be a function of whether the job is stable or unstable. For example, many jobs experience changes in technology that radically alter the nature of the work on a routine basis. This may weaken the ability of some traits to manifest consistent relationships with performance. On the other hand, this kind of dynamic environment enhances the role played by a trait such as openness to experience. Indeed, research has shown that in contexts where new technologies are being introduced, people who are high in openness perform much better than those who are low in this characteristic.[29]

Finally, obtaining information about the job applicant's personality is also an area where one can take steps to improve the predictive validity of such tests. Unstructured interviews conducted by untrained personnel are unlikely to provide much in the way of valuable information about someone's personality. Moreover, the direct and sometimes obvious nature of self-report surveys often leads to either conscious faking on the part of applicants or inaccurate responses due to lack of self-insight. Fortunately, research suggests that structured interviews constructed in the form of situational interviews and judgment tests can often provide much more useful information when making hiring decisions based on personality and interpersonal skills.[30] With a situational interview, applicants are asked to relate how they would respond to either hypothetical events that are likely to occur on the job or actual past experiences they had responding to similar issues in prior jobs. Trained evaluators, often armed with standardized grading forms, then rate the answers provided in terms of what they suggest about the person's personality traits or interpersonal skills. Because of the vast amount of research evidence supporting the validity of situational judgment tests, these are quickly supplanting the use of traditional, unstructured interviews in most organizational hiring contexts.[31]

DIVERSITY IN COGNITIVE ABILITIES: FOUR CRITICAL FACTORS

Although mental abilities are not one-dimensional, we do generally find positive relationships between people's performances on different kinds of mental tests. To emphasize the positive relationships among the facets of mental ability while still recognizing their unique features, we will discuss each aspect separately.

General and Specific Aspects of Cognitive Ability

Because scores across different types of mental tests are related, they are often summed and treated as an index of general intelligence. Specialists tend to prefer the term **general cognitive ability** to *intelligence*, because the former term is more precise, and because it conjures up less controversy over such issues as the role of genetic factors in mental ability. The term *intelligence* is used imprecisely in the lay community, where the high social value placed on it complicates discussions of things such as age, sex, and racial differences.

Although cognitive abilities all share some features, some facets of mental ability are sufficiently distinctive so that they are worth assessing in their own right. Because specific jobs may require more of one type of mental ability than of the other types, we may want to home in on gathering data on this particular ability.

In this section, we will focus our attention on four facets of cognitive or mental ability that stand out in terms of both their generality and their usefulness as predictors of performance in the real world.[32] Table 3-2 defines these abilities, and Figure 3-3 displays sample test items that assess each ability.

The first two dimensions are probably the most familiar to college students who have taken many standardized tests throughout their academic careers. **Verbal ability** reflects the degree to which a person can understand and use written and spoken

TABLE 3-2
The Four
Dimensions of
Cognitive
Ability

1. Verbal ability
   The ability to understand and effectively use written and spoken language
2. Quantitative ability
   The ability to quickly and accurately solve arithmetic problems of all kinds, including addition, subtraction, multiplication, and division, as well as applying mathematical rules
3. Reasoning ability
   The ability to think inductively and deductively to invent solutions to novel problems
4. Spatial ability
   The ability to accurately detect the spatial arrangement of objects with respect to one's own body

Source: J. C. Nunnally, *Psychometric Theory* (New York: McGraw-Hill, 1978), pp. 59–61.

language. **Quantitative ability** reflects a person's ability to perform all kinds of arithmetic problems—not only problems dealing with addition, subtraction, multiplication, and division, but also those involving square roots, rounding procedures, and the multiplication of positive and negative values.

A different kind of analytical skill is associated with the third dimension of mental ability. **Reasoning ability** is the ability to invent solutions to many different types of problems. Although tests of reasoning ability sometimes employ numbers, they should not be confused with simple measures of quantitative ability. At the heart of a reasoning problem is the need to create a solution or grasp a principle, not a need to make computations.

The last dimension of mental ability we will examine is **spatial ability,** which reflects a person's ability to imagine how an object would look if we changed its position in space. It also reflects the ability to make an accurate determination of the spatial arrangement of objects with respect to one's own body. This dimension is important, for example, to an airplane pilot, who should be able to detect changes in a plane's position just by looking at changes in the horizon seen through the cockpit window. Engineers, physical scientists, and artists also need high levels of this ability.

Validity of Cognitive Ability Tests

The usefulness of cognitive ability tests in predicting task performance has been investigated in both academic and organizational contexts. In academic settings, researchers have found high correlations between tests like the Scholastic Aptitude Test (SAT) and both a person's first-year-college grade-point average (correlations in the .50s) and his or her overall class rank (correlations in the .60s).[33] The predictive value of these tests is greater for students in the physical sciences or math than it is for students in the humanities or social sciences. The tests are less predictive of success in graduate school (correlations in the .30s), because most applicants for graduate school score relatively high in mental ability and therefore represent a somewhat homogeneous group.

A great deal of evidence suggests that general cognitive ability is also predictive of success in the work world.[34] Research has shown that in virtually any job where planning, judgment, and memory are used in day-to-day performance, individuals high in general cognitive ability will generally outperform those who are low in this ability. Other research has shown that the strength of the relationship between general cognitive ability and job performance increases as the job becomes more complex in terms of decision making, planning, problem solving, and analyzing information.[35]

FIGURE 3-3 Sample Items That Test Specific Dimensions of Cognitive Ability

1. Verbal Ability

    Which of the following words means most nearly *the same* as ABERRATION:
    (a) conception, (b) discussion, (c) abhorrence, (d) deviation, (e) humiliation.
    Which of the following words means most nearly *the opposite* of AMICABLE:
    (a) nauseous, (b) unfriendly, (c) obscene, (d) penetrating, (e) fondness.

2. Quantitative Ability

    Mrs. Jones deposits $700.00 in a bank that pays 3 percent interest per year. How much money will she have by the end of the year?
    (a) $21.00 (b) $679.00 (c) $702.10 (d) $721.00 (e) $910.00
    What is the value of r after it has been decreased by 16 2/3 percent?
    (a) 1/6 r (b) 1/3 r (c) 5/6 r (d) 6/7 r (e) 7/6 r

3. Reasoning Ability

    _____ is to Prison as Smithsonian is to _____
    (a) Alcatraz—Museum (b) Guard—Washington, D.C.
    (c) Warden—Warhol (d) Criminal–Washington, D.C.
    (e) Guard—Museum
    Which design belongs in E—a, b, c, d, or e?

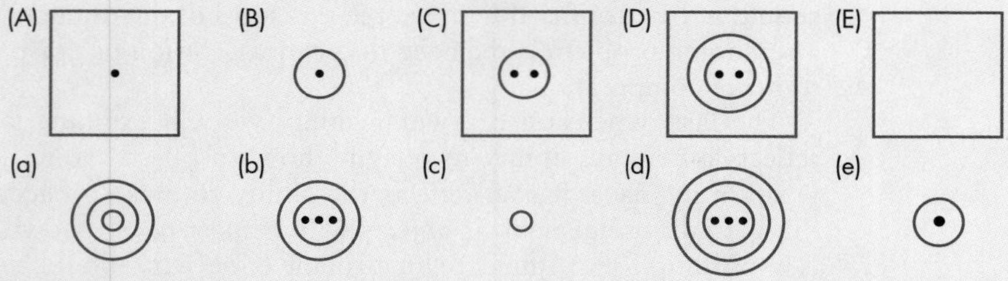

4. Spatial Ability

    Place a check next to every alternative that can be obtained by a rotation of the first figure.

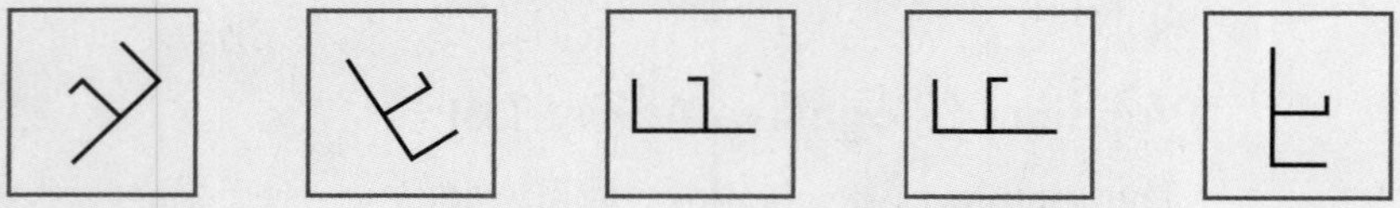

General cognitive ability is important even for jobs that lack such complexity if these positions require the worker to learn something new. Individuals high in general cognitive ability will learn the job more quickly than their low-ability counterparts. In low-complexity jobs, experience over time often wipes out this initial difference between high- and low-ability individuals, as Figure 3-4 demonstrates.[36] As months on the job increase, the initial performance differences attributable to discrepancies in ability decrease. Thus general cognitive ability is important in two respects: in learning the job and in performing the job when the job requires the person to deal continually with new situations.

For certain jobs, tests of specific mental ability can add significantly to the predictive power of tests of general intelligence.[37] For example, spatial visualization is critical for drafters and individuals in technical positions, and it is an important characteristic in jobs that require mechanical skills, such as machinist, forklift operator, and warehouse worker. Verbal ability and reasoning ability are critical to suc-

FIGURE 3-4   General Cognitive Ability and Experience on the Job as Determinants of Performance

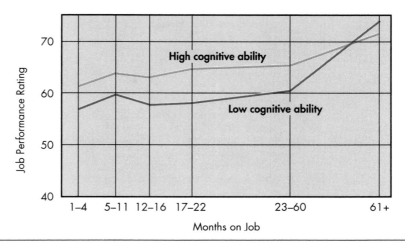

Source: From "Joint Relation of Experience and Ability with Job Performance" by F.L. Schmidt, J.E. Hunter, A. N. Outerbridge and S. Goff in *Journal of Applied Psychology* 73 (1998), p. 54. Copyright © 1988 by the American Psychological Association. Adapted with permission.

cess in executive, administrative, and professional positions. Quantitative ability is important in jobs such as accountant, payroll clerk, and salesperson and in many types of supervisory positions. Whereas general mental ability tests have relevance for a wide variety of jobs, specific mental ability tests are useful for more job-specific evaluations.

General cognitive ability influences both how quickly a person can learn a job and how readily he or she can adapt to changing circumstances when on the job. The more complex the job in terms of decision making, planning, and judgment, the more learning and improvising required. With complex jobs, a great deal of job experience is beneficial only if it is accompanied by general cognitive ability, which helps one benefit from experience. In simple jobs, the key is mastering a few specific tasks; general cognitive ability is therefore less important. While general cognitive ability will almost always be relevant to one's work, the importance of specific abilities can be determined only through a detailed job analysis.

DIVERSITY IN PHYSICAL ABILITIES: THREE CRITICAL FACTORS

Although more recent research has tended to focus on cognitive abilities, a great deal of the early research in the area of organizational behavior examined physical abilities. Edwin Fleishman was one of the first researchers to systematically analyze the structure of human physical abilities, and much of the research on this topic in the last forty years represents a refinement and extension of his early work.[38] More recently, the emphasis in this field has moved slightly, from evaluating physical fitness to predicting job performance. Occupation-oriented studies, taken together with human physiology studies, provide us with a solid foundation for understanding the structure of physical performance (Table 3-3).[39]

As noted in Table 3-3, physical ability consists of three major dimensions: muscular strength, endurance, and movement quality. Muscular strength comes in three

TABLE 3-3
The Three
Dimensions of
Physical Ability

1. Muscular strength
    Ability to exert muscular force against objects in terms of pushing, pulling, lifting, carrying, or lowering them (muscular tension)
    Exerting muscular force in quick bursts (muscular power)
    Exerting muscular force continuously over time while resisting fatigue (muscular endurance)
2. Endurance
    Ability to sustain physical activity that results in increased heart rates for a long period
3. Movement quality
    Ability to flex and extend body limbs to work in awkward or contorted positions (flexibility)
    Ability to maintain the body in a stable position and resist forces that cause loss of stability (balance)
    Ability to sequence movement of the fingers, arms, legs, or body to result in skilled action (coordination)

Source: J. Hogan, "Structure of Physical Performance in Occupational Tasks," *Journal of Applied Psychology* 76 (1991), 495–507.

slightly different varieties (tension, power, and endurance); the same is true for movement quality (flexibility, balance, and coordination).

Although a thorough analysis of a job is needed to determine whether it requires a particular physical capacity, the abilities listed in Table 3-3 tend to be needed most frequently in two types of jobs: the protective services, such as police departments, fire departments, and correctional facilities; and construction and other physically demanding industries. If personnel in these industries lack the necessary physical abilities, they or the people they seek to protect may be injured.[40]

Testing for the kinds of physical abilities listed in Table 3-3 is much more common now than in the past, when height and weight criteria were often substituted for specific abilities. Because height and weight measures are considered to discriminate unfairly against women and members of some minority groups, they are rarely used today.

Physical ability tests are also used to select employees for work such as construction, where jobs require both physical strength and agility. Such tests can predict not only a person's level of job performance, but also his or her risk of job-related injuries. For instance, research has shown that the incidence of lower-back injury can be predicted by tests of physical strength.[41] This finding is significant because back-related disability claims have been rising at fourteen times the rate of population growth over the last ten years. Because many employers pick up the bill for employees' medical costs (and because lower-back pain is such a widespread and recurring affliction), tests that predict health problems for a job applicant can prove extremely cost-effective. General Dynamics Corporation's electric boat unit has actually developed specific physical examinations designed to screen out individuals at risk for back-pain problems.

DIVERSITY IN EXPERIENCE: TWO CRITICAL FACTORS

Recent trends related to the labor supply have heightened managers' awareness of individual differences found among workers. Most of this awareness has focused less on differences in physical abilities, cognitive abilities, and personality traits, and more on diversity related to demographic and cultural characteristics. Much of the current concern about managing demographic diversity can be traced to studies

SECURING COMPETITIVE ADVANTAGE

ORGANIZATIONS PUT ON THE FULL-COURT PRESS IN THEIR HUNT FOR TALENT

At first glance, it might not appear that Yao Ming and Luo Ying have much in common, other than their Chinese ancestry. Yao Ming is the 7′5″ center for the Houston Rockets professional basketball team, whereas Luo Ying is a 5′5″ Ph.D. trained expert in biomedical science and engineering. Moreover, Yao Ming was recruited away from China to work in the United States, whereas Luo Ying went in the opposite direction, recruited away from the United States to work in China. However, both became millionaires as a result of their moves, and in a very real way, both personify the global search for talent, as well as the global desire to expand into new markets. Taken together, a study of their migratory behavior reveals a great deal about how industries and nations compete in today's global economy, where jobs and people move across borders with an ease that has never been experienced in prior human history.

Yao Ming is representative of a growing number of players in the National Basketball Association (NBA) that hail from outside the United States. Other prominent NBA immigrants include Dirk Nowitzki (Germany), Eduardo Najero (Mexico), Hedo Turkoglu (Turkey), Pau Gasol (Spain), Tony Parker (France), Andre Kirilenko (Russia), Nene Hilario (Brazil), and Peja Stojakovic (Serbia). In fact, with sixty-five players (16 percent of all NBA rosters) representing thirty-five different countries in its midst, the NBA is improving its product—and its marketing base—with the introduction of all this international talent.

In terms of the product, international players bring both size and speed to a league that is already well known for these attributes. Beyond this, however, sportswriters and fans are beginning to appreciate the different and unique contributions these international players bring to the game. Many fans have often complained that NBA games too often become one-on-one isolation games where a single person tries to take over the game while his teammates look on as little more than interested observers. However, most Europeans play a much more team-oriented style with an emphasis on defense, passing, and outside shooting, rather than purely physical play. "Foreign players have added the skill factor back into the game," notes Rick Adelman, the coach of the Sacramento Kings, "and in the process brought back a lot of fans."

These same foreign players have also served as a vehicle through which the league is trying to reach out and expand into global markets. NBA Commissioner David Stern has been purposively and consciously building the league into a national brand. Currently, more than 20 percent of NBA merchandising revenue comes from outside the United States and 15 percent of its television revenues can be traced to 148 broadcasting partners in 212 different countries. Thanks to Yao Ming, sales of NBA-related products in China have increased 44 percent since the new rookie entered the league.

Although not up to Yao Ming in terms of physical stature, Luo Ying's talents in biomedical engineering also make him a hot commodity for countries that seek to develop marketable products from bioengineering. In this case, however, he migrated from the United States to China, lured by more than $3 million in venture capital funding. Indeed, this was just a tiny fraction of the $420 million spent by China to reverse the "brain drain" that the country has experienced over the last twenty years. In that time, close to 500,000 students left China for opportunities in the United States and never returned. The number of Chinese who are returning has doubled twice in the last four years, however, as internal changes in Chinese politics have added increasing pressure to expand the country's global competitive position.

The hope is that U.S.-trained scientists like Luo Ying will work with the local base of Chinese-trained scientists to develop pharmaceutical products that could be sold in the lucrative U.S. market. Thus, just like the NBA, the idea is not only to pursue talent to improve products, but to market them as well. In addition to the enhanced access to venture capital, Ying was also interested in returning to China because of the opportunities it offered him to run his own company that he felt would never materialize in the United States. He notes, "In the U.S., there is a glass ceiling in corporations for Chinese people . . . I wouldn't call it discrimination, but the higher you go, the more political it is and it is difficult for outsiders to merge into business at the top level." In the global competition for talent, this kind of prejudice against certain groups will surely hurt U.S. companies, who would do well to model the more aggressive and assimilating to international talent taken by the NBA.

Sources: F. Balfour, "Is Your Job Next: A New Round of Globalization Is Sending Upscale Jobs Offshore," *Business Week,* February 3, 2003, pp. 50–60; C. B. Thomas, "The NBA's Global Game Plan," *Time,* March 17, 2003, pp. 61–63; J. Kaufman, "China Reforms Bring Back Executives Schooled in U.S.," *Wall Street Journal Online,* March 6, 2003, pp. 1–2.

indicating that 60 percent of new entrants into the labor pool by 2005 will be women, minorities, or immigrants. Interest in managing cultural diversity also reflects the trend toward globalization, as many corporations begin rapidly expanding operations to foreign locales. Indeed, as shown in the Securing Competitive Advantage box, in an effort to both secure the best talent and to market products globally, organizations, industries, and entire nations are often looking across national boundaries when making hiring decisions.

Both developments have forced companies that were once predominantly staffed by white males to rethink their hiring policies.[42] Specifically, the experiences of white males are now seen as too homogeneous to enable them to effectively manage a diverse workforce or to effectively exploit opportunities in the global market. Instead, organizations are looking to either hire people with different experiences (that is, people from different demographic groups or cultures) or provide their current managers with more diverse demographic or cultural experiences to broaden their perspectives. In general, we will use the term **demographic experience** to discuss the variability between people in terms of how much exposure they have had in working with people from different demographic groups (race, sex, age) and the term **cultural experience** to describe the variability between people in terms of how much exposure they have had in working with people from different nations and cultures.

Broadening Demographic Experience: Political Aspects

In the past, political forces, particularly civil rights activists who tried to increase opportunities for women and minorities in the workplace, drove integration of the workforce. The motivation to level the playing field for women and minorities still exists today, and there are still clear vestiges of discrimination in our culture. For example, a recent study that sent out identical résumés of hypothetical job applicants showed that those that came from people with "white-sounding" names, such as Neil, Brett, Emily, or Anne, were 50 percent more likely to be asked for an interview relative to those that came from people with "black-sounding" names, such as Ebony, Tamika, Rasheed, or Khirese.[43] Moreover, when it come to advancement, a recent class-action suit has been filed at Wal-Mart on behalf of 500,000 women who allege that even though 66 percent of Wal-Mart employees are women, less than 25 percent ever get the opportunity to advance to middle-management positions.[44]

These political forces are still alive today, but relative to twenty years ago the strength and breadth of these motivations have waned for several reasons. First, to some extent, many of the affirmative action programs instituted in the 1970s and 1980s have achieved some measure of success. The number of African Americans enrolled in colleges and universities has increased 500 percent since 1965, and over the last twenty-five years the share of black families earning more than $50,000 a year rose from 8 percent to 20 percent. In the last five years alone, the ranks of black managers and professionals have increased 30 percent. Within these occupations, the pay gap between college-educated African Americans employed as executives, administrators, and professionals was 86 percent relative to their white peers, and the remaining difference is largely attributed to seniority differences. Indeed, college-educated African American women actually earned 10 percent more than comparable white women.[45]

Second, whereas existing affirmative action programs have failed to completely wipe out discrimination or all the differences between races in outcomes, the perception is that these programs no longer target the groups who need the most support. That is, a growing core of poor inner-city black youths are most often the victims of the international competitive forces that are driving down wages and employment levels for low-skilled workers. Manufacturing jobs that used to support this group are increasingly moving overseas, and the types of benefits that come out of current affirmative action programs benefit affluent, middle-class black workers, rather than those in the inner cities who need the support more desperately.[46]

Finally, the 1990s witnessed an increase in backlash against affirmative action and other remedial programs aimed at minorities, especially by white males who see such programs as giving preferential treatment to other groups at their expense.[47] Moreover, this backlash is particularly strong among younger, Generation X whites who grew up having no experience with the segregation that drove early civil rights initiatives. The tolerance that many older white workers had with race-based remedial programs, partially fueled by guilt and direct experience, simply does not exist among younger people who group up in less segregated schools and neighborhoods.

Broadening Demographic Experience: Competitive Aspects

Hiring Issues   Rather than being motivated by a sense of social justice or fear of litigation, affirmative action programs in the twenty-first century are part of a larger strategy that seeks to leverage diverse experience into competitive advantage.[48] As Mark Jennings, a top-level executive at Gannett News, notes, "Diversity is important in every company, and certainly in the news and information business. A diverse workforce is more innovative and creative. The whole point of this is getting a competitive edge from the people who work for you."[49] The same theme is echoed by IBM's CEO, Louis Gerstner, who notes, "Our marketplace is made up of all races, religions, and sexual orientations, and therefore it is vital to our financial success that our workforce also be diverse."[50]

Cosmetics manufacturer Maybelline provides a dramatic example of how an organization can use diversity as a means of leveraging competitive advantage. Minority women in the firm were the first to recognize that an untapped market existed for cosmetics developed specifically for women with darker skin hues. This discovery led to the launch of the "Shades of You" line of products aimed specifically at minority women. Thanks to the early recognition of this untapped market, Maybelline now claims 35 percent of a market worth $100 million per year (and still growing).[51]

Similarly, Pat Nichols, a district manager for DuPont Chemicals Ag-Products Division, notes, "There is a vital need to develop different foods for different cultures, and companies need a diverse workforce to do that."[52] To attract such a labor force, DuPont runs an aggressive college recruiting campaign aimed directly at women and minorities, who have historically shown little interest in agricultural careers. In a similar outreach effort, Gaylord Container Corporation, in conjunction with the Los Angeles County Health Department, has created a program to help low-income, inner-city youths overcome barriers to employment. Its program provides practical work experience, interpersonal communication training, and mentoring to help participants make the transition into the working world.[53]

Successfully creating a diverse workforce can also enhance a firm's bottom line and hence its standing in the financial markets. The literature on capital budgeting indicates that valuable investments increase a firm's stock price. A recent study suggests that financial markets view successful diversity management as just such an investment. In this study, researchers examined the stock prices for firms that had won the U.S. Department of Labor's Exemplary Efforts Award for Affirmative Action Programs, comparing these prices to the stock prices of a sample of control firms matched for size and industry. They also examined the stock prices of firms that were publicly cited for discriminatory practices. Stock prices for award-winning firms were found to increase relative to control firms after the announcement of the awards, whereas stock prices for firms that were cited for violations declined.[54] Indeed, given the financial benefits that seem to accrue from affirmative action programs, it is not surprising that when the government recently challenged the legality of such a program at the University of Michigan, more than thirty of the country's largest companies, including Microsoft, General Motors, Bank One, and Steelcase, wrote a letter supporting the university's policy.[55]

Retention Issues Once minority workers are hired, firms that value diversity also need to ensure that they can retain the services of members of these groups. Turnover rates among minorities at the managerial level are often two to three times higher than the rates for white males, with the difference often attributable to a perceived lack of opportunities for promotions. Figure 3-5 shows the disparity in upper-level jobs for varying groups. Lawrence Perlman, CEO of Ceridian Corporation of Minneapolis, states, "The combination of women and people of color dropping out is really discouraging . . . it just isn't good business." To prevent this exodus, Ceridian set diversity goals for promotions and career-enhancing experiences, and similar steps are being taken at Polaroid, Ameritech, Texaco, and Dow Chemical.[56]

Other companies provide training programs to help with this problem. For example, Corning found that African American and female professionals left the company at roughly twice the rate of white men. A diversity-training program for managers helped reduce attrition rates for both groups. Avon encourages employees to organize into African American, Hispanic American, and Asian American networks by granting them official recognition and providing senior mentors to act as advisors to the groups. The cosmetics company once operated a similar network for women, but disbanded it after the program achieved its objective (today women hold 79 percent of the management positions at Avon). As Avon's chief of human

FIGURE 3-5 Percentage of Executive and Managerial Jobs Held by Various Subgroups

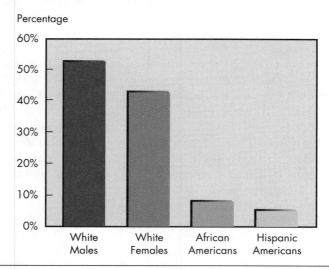

Source: Based on data from M. Galen, "Diversity: Beyond the Numbers Game," *Business Week*, August 14, 1995, pp. 60–61.

resources told a reporter, "My objective is to create an organization where people don't feel a need for a black network, a Hispanic network, or an Asian network, just as women decided they didn't need their network."[57]

Retention of minority representation is also enhanced by establishing programs that promote mentoring relationships between new minority employees and more established organizational members.[58] In fact, one recent study suggests that the real key in such programs is linking up women and minority members with white male mentors. The benefits that accrue from these cross-race and cross-gender pairings for the new worker seem to be much larger than those realized by women and minorities who have mentors with the same demographic characteristics.[59]

Of course, beyond these factors, diversity programs must receive top managerial support if they are to be successful.[60] Indeed, a recent study involving approximately 800 managers pointed to this factor as the single most important characteristic in predicting the success of these programs. The second most critical factor was the organization's ability to channel this top-level enthusiasm down the hierarchy. The best way to ensure that the effects trickle down is to formally appraise and reward middle- and lower-level managers for creating, maintaining, and profiting from diversity.[61] For managers of operating units at Colgate-Palmolive, the link between measurement and achievement is created by annual pay raises determined through the company's Executive Incentive Compensation Plan. Similar programs can be found at Corning and at Quaker Oats, where the ability to manage diversity is one of the major factors considered during managers' annual performance reviews. Indeed, recent surveys indicate that 53 percent of all Fortune 500 companies have initiated incentives for executives to enhance their skills in this area.[62]

Although people generally think of race and sex as the major workforce diversity issues, one of the more sweeping demographic forces with which many organizations are attempting to come to grips is the aging of the workforce. The majority of the 76 million baby boomers born between 1946 and 1960 are now, or will soon be, fifty years old. Because of the "baby bust" that occurred between 1965 and 1976, many have predicted that organizations will eventually face major labor shortages. Some firms are seeking to turn these trends into a competitive advantage by hiring and retraining older workers.[63]

For example, McDonald's Corporation has recently struggled to find the young workers who once dominated the ranks of its employees. To deal with this problem, the company initiated the ReHIREment Program, which attempts to entice older individuals to work in its restaurants. As part of this program, McDonald's developed specific recruiting materials geared toward the older generation. Whereas its recruiting brochures for young candidates emphasize the learning opportunities and long-term career benefits of McDonald's jobs, the brochures in the ReHIREment Program stress the scheduling flexibility and the fact that part-time earnings do not threaten Social Security earnings.[64]

Of course, attracting older workers is just one part of the age-diversity problem. The organization must also strive to ensure that existing stereotypes held by younger workers do not destroy the older worker's chances to contribute to the company.[65] A substantial body of data from scientific studies refutes many of the negative stereotypes that color perceptions of older workers.[66] Organizations that hire older workers need to work hard to dispel these myths.

For example, the Home Shopping Network (HSN), the Clearwater, Florida–based cable network, operates a program for older employees similar to that used at McDonald's. Located in an area well populated by retirees, HSN uses older workers on a part-time basis to answer telephones and take orders for merchandise advertised on its shows. It also maintains a sensitivity program for its managers that gives them valid information about what is fact and what is fiction in the area of aging and job performance.[67]

Broadening Cultural Experience

Just as creating a workforce with diverse demographic experience can help in penetrating developing and fragmented markets, creating a workforce with diverse international and cultural experience can help firms move into global product markets. For example, Starbucks Coffee brings employees from China to its training facilities in Tacoma, Washington, to teach them the secrets of brewing dozens of exotic coffees and to indoctrinate them in Starbucks' unique corporate culture. The Chinese workers, in turn, educate Starbucks management about some of the idiosyncratic aspects of Chinese culture that this company needs to respect as it launches its new joint venture into the Chinese marketplace—Beijing Mei Da Coffee Company.[68]

Many organizations have also attempted to broaden the cultural experience of their current employees by sending them on international assignments. A recent survey of nearly 200 multinational corporations found that more than half of these organizations had as many as fifty top-level managers on expatriate assignments and that this number was expected to grow over the next five years.[69] Many managers struggle with this experience and terminate their assignments early, especially employees who are low in agreeableness, emotional stability, and extroversion.[70]

In addition to competing in product markets, because of the labor shortage that has marked the beginning of the twenty-first century, firms have moved into international labor markets to bring in the type of talent they need to compete both domestically and abroad.[71]

One aspect of this trend can be seen in the high-skill end of the economy, where U.S. organizations have been forced to search more widely for skilled technicians and engineers. In the aerospace industry, for example, executive David Williams notes, "Every major space contractor who wants to be cost-effective and competitive has to be thinking about relations with Russian partners."[72] Alliances are now common between small Russian firms and many large Western corporations within this industry, including Rockwell, McDonnell-Douglas, Boeing, Pratt and Whitney, and Rolls-Royce. The mathematical and technical abilities of Russian scientists and technicians are astounding those who staff Western companies. The fact that all this talent can be had at bargain prices (many Russian Ph.D.'s currently work for less than $5,000 per year) creates a virtual treasure, often scattered and hidden throughout regions (such as Novosibirsk and Yekatarinburg) with names that Americans can barely pronounce, let alone find on a map. In other industries, such as software development, engineering, and pharmaceuticals, high-ability/low-cost talent is being mined increasingly in India, Taiwan, Singapore, China, and South Korea.

At the low end of the skill range, an influx of international workers has also entered the United States to perform low-paying jobs that most Americans are unwilling to do—for example, dishwashers, hotel maids, janitors, and construction workers.[73] This labor shortage is especially acute in the summer months, because American teens have recently been avoiding the traditional low-skill summer jobs in amusement parks and other recreational areas. As Gene Kijowski, president of Century Pool Management, notes, "There is so much affluence in this whole region, it is hard to find young people who want to hustle." Indeed, to stay in business, Century Pool had to bring in 100 teenagers from Prague to work as lifeguards.[74] Likewise, across the United States a large segment of the workforce at amusement parks and recreational areas now comes from eastern Europe.[75]

ETHICS AND SOCIAL RESPONSIBILITY

BALANCING SECURITY, PRIVACY, AND FAIRNESS IN AN AGE OF TERRORISM

In the aftermath of the 9/11 terrorist attacks and the war in Iraq, it does not serve one well to have "Osama" for a first name or "Hussein" for a last name—especially if you are working in the transportation industry. Osama Sweilan was born in Egypt, but had been working at the Federal Express sorting center at Newark Airport for over a year when he was pulled aside and asked questions about his religious and political beliefs. Apparently investigators were not pleased with his answers and confiscated his employee ID, ending his employment with the firm. Mohammed Hussein, who was born in Fiji, had had a similar experience working for Trans State Airlines as a pilot. Indeed, according to the Equal Employment Opportunity Commission (EEOC), in the last few years, the number of employment discrimination complaints lodged by Arab Americans has exploded.

Part of this can be traced to a general unease among Americans regarding U.S.–Arab relations, but in addition to this, the 2001 Aviation and Transportation Security (ATS) Act has enhanced the chances for distrust and misunderstandings between employers and employees. The act was passed in the wake of 9/11 and authorizes the Transportation Security Administration (TSA) to bar anyone from flying or working in the industry if he or she poses a threat to national security. Although no one could argue with the need for protecting national security, a unique feature of the ATS Act was that the TSA does not have to disclose the evidence it uses to arrive at its judgments.

The unusual secrecy with which these types of decisions are being made has infuriated many pilots' groups and unions that represent some of the affected workers. However, the government defends its actions by noting that "disclosing such information could jeopardize sources and methods of the intelligence community, possibly giving a terrorist organization or other group a roadmap of the course of an investigation." Thus, when two pilots from Saudi Arabia had their licenses revoked in 2003, they had no way to challenge the rulings. When they tried to appeal to the National Transportation and Safety Board, the chief administrative-law judge simply noted that he had to "assume the truth of the government's assertion that the men are security threats."

While the lack of due process inherent in this procedure might strike fear in civil libertarians and Arabs, many other Americans may feel that this is not a relevant concern to them. However, concerns with security have pushed many employers to do background checks on not just would-be hires, but current employees as well. At Eli Lilly, Kim Kelly was fired when a background check revealed that she had bounced a check for $60 to a refrigerator rental company. Another employee, Chris Lochard, was fired when it was discovered that ten years ago—when he was eighteen years old—he stole a guitar from his high school music room. Indeed, even employees with perfect past histories were caught up in the Lilly sweep. Sandy Snodgrass was fired from Lilly when a background check uncovered a conviction for misdemeanor shoplifting and battery. Snodgrass was clueless about the charges until he realized that the convictions belonged to his twenty-seven-year-old nephew, who shared his first and last name. Although they rectified the case of mistaken opportunity, Lilly defended all their other actions noting, "We make 60 percent to 70 percent of the world's insulin. We need to know who's on our property."

Clearly, because of recent events, U.S. employers need to be increasingly vigilant about who has access to sensitive areas of commerce, and one of the main points embodied in this chapter is that organizations need to know a great deal about the people they hire. Employers can be held liable for negligent hiring, and are therefore responsible for the acts of their workers. At the same time, the ethics of firing workers because they are Arabs or Muslims or have long past violations that may now seem minor and unrepresentative of who they are also have to be examined. Employers need to take a balanced approach to protecting themselves, while at the same time respecting the rights of employees and applicants. At the very least, affected employees need some recourse when secret evidence is used to make sure that cases of mistaken identity have been ruled out.

Sources: M. Conlin, "Taking Precautions—or Harassing Workers?" *Business Week*, December 3, 2001, p. 84; S. Black, "Federal Officials Say Pilot Fired Because He Is Muslim," *USA Today*, February 5, 2003, p. D1; S. Power, "U.S. Bars 2 Saudi Pilots, Says They Posed a Security Threat," *Wall Street Journal Online*, February 14, 2003, pp. 1–3; A. Davis, "Firms Dig Deep into Workers' Pasts amid Post–September 11 Security Anxiety," *Wall Street Journal Online*, March 12, 2002, pp. 1–4.

Although there have been failed legislative attempts aimed at curtailing the inevitable flow of human ability across borders,[76] the real barrier to effectively integrating this talent is the cultural differences between people, as manifested in different personalities and working styles. Many of the companies that tap global talent create cross-functional work teams (often virtual teams linked via technology). The key to developing a new drug, for instance, often depends as much on group chemistry as pharmaceutical knowledge. McDonnell-Douglas's southern California managers often grow impatient with what they perceive as a lack of conscientiousness among Russian workers. As one manager notes, "World practice is that we agree on a price and if they run over, it's their problem . . . But in Russia, if they run out of money, they just stop working."[77] In addition to different work styles, certain prejudices and stereotypes may also exist regarding members of certain groups that lead to a lack of trust. One area where this can be clearly perceived in most recent times is how employers in the United States deal with Arab and Muslim workers. As the Ethics and Social Responsibility box shows, firms need to somehow strike a balance between the need for security and the need to treat all workers fairly.

The ability to overcome the problems wrought by individual differences is a critical skill for today's managers. Consequently, many organizations are trying to train their workers to raise their cultural sensitivity to these kinds of issues.[78] When sensitivity training programs work well, they are able to dispel the mirror image fallacy, yet avoid fostering prejudicial stereotypes about various groups. They achieve their success by helping managers focus on individuals as individuals, each of whom can be seen as a unique constellation of physical abilities, cognitive abilities, personality traits, and experiences. Each personal profile of abilities, traits, and experiences is idiosyncratic, and their differences transcend simple categorization schemes based solely on sex, race, age, or culture.

ADAPTABILITY: FLEXIBILITY IN THE FACE OF DIVERSITY

The preceding sections of this chapter have focused on many different facets of diversity. They also noted the many changes taking place in the cultural, technological, political, and competitive contexts within which contemporary organizations operate. Given the complex and dynamic nature of this environment, perhaps the most critical aspect of human variability in the twenty-first century (shown at the top of Figure 3-2) will be **adaptability**.

Most traditional treatments of individual differences have relied on static conceptions of these traits, with the idea that firms will match people to their work and co-workers. More recent research on individual differences, however, has examined individuals' abilities to display flexibility and versatility in their behavior at different times and in different situations.[79] Someone who is adaptive can display one trait in one situation (for example, being agreeable with a customer who has a valid complaint) and the opposite trait in a different situation (for example, being disagreeable with a supplier who is reneging on an established contract). Someone who is adaptive might also be a natural introvert, but can act like an extrovert if the situation demands this latter trait.

Highly adaptable people can handle emergencies and deal effectively with uncertain and unpredictable situations. They also tend to be creative problem solvers and quickly learn new tasks, technologies, and procedures. Finally, they demonstrate a sensitivity to interpersonal and cultural differences, and they can work effectively in many different types of groups.

Clearly, adaptability is similar to some of the traits and abilities discussed earlier in this chapter, and research has shown that both general cognitive ability and openness to experience are related to adaptability.[80] Direct measures of this characteristic have been developed, however, and the dynamic nature of this aspect of human variability makes it worth singling out at the top of our model. Given the changing nature of both work and the workforce, future managers will need this trait, perhaps more than any other.

SUMMARY

Individuals differ on a number of dimensions. Taking advantage of this fact—that is, diversity—is essential to effective control of organizational behavior. Individuals differ in personality characteristics, which often spill over into job-performance differences. The Big Five framework, which focuses on *extroversion, agreeableness, emotional stability, conscientiousness,* and *openness to experience,* can be used to organize these traits and suggest how each might be related to job performance.

General cognitive ability, another characteristic on which individuals differ, has important implications for a wide variety of jobs. Indeed, this characteristic is relevant for any job that requires planning and complex decision making on a daily basis. General cognitive ability also affects both a person's ability to learn the job and his or her ability to adapt to new situations. Four specific facets of cognitive ability are *verbal ability, quantitative ability, reasoning ability,* and *spatial ability.* These characteristics supplement general cognitive ability in affecting performance on certain types of jobs.

Individuals also differ in three primary physical abilities: *muscular strength, endurance,* and *movement quality.* In many job situations, people who lack the necessary physical abilities may perform poorly and put themselves and others at risk for injuries.

Changes in product markets and the composition of the labor force have made organizations aware of the need for having a workforce with diverse *demographic experience* and *cultural experience.*

Given the increased complexity and dynamic nature of both work and the workforce, individual *adaptability* will likely be the preeminent requirement for future managers. Successful organizations are casting aside stereotypes held about different groups of people and seeking ways to convert workforce diversity into a source of sustainable competitive advantage.

REVIEW QUESTIONS

1. Is the mirror image fallacy more likely to affect our assessments of others' abilities or our assessments of their personalities? Are particular dimensions of ability or classes of personality characteristics especially susceptible to this kind of mistaken perception? Explain.

2. Think of someone you know who is highly successful in his or her chosen field. What were the important personal characteristics that led to this person's success? Now think of what would have happened if that person had chosen a different line of work. Do you think this person would have been successful in any field, or can you imagine lines of work for which the person was poorly suited?

How does your answer to this question relate to the selection-versus-placement distinction?

3. Imagine someone who is turned down for a job because of (a) his or her performance on a paper-and-pencil cognitive ability test, (b) an interviewer's assessment of the person's intelligence and conscientiousness, or (c) his or her responses to a personality inventory. What differential reactions would you expect from this person? Explain your answer.

4. One firm hands out several different kinds of tests to prospective employees but never actually scores them before making employment decisions. What message is indirectly sent to applicants by firms that employ rigorous selection testing, and how might the intention to send such a message explain this company's behavior?

5. Some nations, such as Japan, control education through federal mandates, which results in educational standardization. Such nations also promote a clear hierarchy of primary schools, secondary schools, and universities, arranged in order of their prestige and quality. Other nations, including the United States, leave control over education to state and local authorities. How might this difference in educational policies lead to different employer needs in the area of personnel testing?

LEARNING THROUGH EXPERIENCE

DIAGNOSTIC QUESTIONS 3-1

Diversity and Individual Differences

In managing individual differences and their effects on organizational behavior, it may help to ask the following diagnostic questions:

1. Do any features of this job require certain types of personality traits, such as agreeableness or extroversion? Does the holder of this job possess those traits?

2. What motives seem to drive this person, and is he or she likely to be conscientious on the job?

3. Are there any signs of emotional maladjustments that may hinder this person's ability to concentrate his or her effort on the task?

4. Do any features of this job require specific facets of mental ability? Does the jobholder possess these abilities?

5. How much general cognitive ability does the jobholder have? How will this ability influence the speed with which he or she will learn the job?

6. How complex is the job? If it is highly complex, does the jobholder have enough cognitive ability to handle this complexity?

7. Do any special features of this job call for high levels of specific physical abilities? Does the jobholder possess these abilities?

8. How much varied demographic experience is represented in the work group?

9. How much varied cultural experience is represented in the work group?

10. How much improvising and adapting will the person have to do on this job?

EXERCISE 3-1 **Individual Similarities and Differences**

Spence Tower, Deborah Winters, and John Wagner,
Michigan State University

Individual differences reflect the way people think, feel, and behave at work. Among these differences are four that parallel the kinds of international differences identified by Geert Hofstede in his study of forty national cultures: uncertainty avoidance, masculinity–femininity, individualism–collectivism, and power distance. In this exercise, after assessing yourself in terms of these four differences, you will meet with class members who have assessed themselves as being similar to you. You will share your self-perceptions and learn how the four differences can be related to people's satisfaction and performance in organizations. Then you will meet with students who have assessed themselves as being different from you and learn how similarities and differences in these characteristics can affect the way people work together.

Step One: Pre-Class Preparation

To prepare for class, read the entire exercise. Next, find out where you stand on the four behavioral dimensions by completing the Individual Differences Questionnaire (Exhibit 3-1). As you respond to the questions, keep in mind that this instrument measures personal characteristics, not ability or knowledge. There are no right or wrong answers, so just respond as honestly as you can.

EXHIBIT 3-1 Individual Differences Questionnaire

Indicate whether you agree with each of the following statements by circling the appropriate number:
1 = Strongly Disagree, 2 = Disagree, 3 = Slightly Disagree, 4 = Neither Agree nor Disagree,
5 = Slightly Agree, 6 = Agree, 7 = Strongly Agree.

1. I enjoy going to new and unfamiliar places . . . . [1] [2] [3] [4] [5] [6] [7]
2. I would feel comfortable socializing with my instructors outside
   of class . . . . [1] [2] [3] [4] [5] [6] [7]
3. People are more likely to succeed in life if they are dominant
   and aggressive . . . . [1] [2] [3] [4] [5] [6] [7]
4. I prefer to participate in team sports or activities rather than in
   individual sports or activities . . . . [1] [2] [3] [4] [5] [6] [7]
5. I would thrive in a cooperative work setting more than one emphasizing
   competitiveness . . . . [1] [2] [3] [4] [5] [6] [7]
6. I prefer it when my grade is based on my personal performance and
   not on the performance of a group that I am working in . . . . [1] [2] [3] [4] [5] [6] [7]
7. One of the reasons a college degree appeals to me is the added
   prestige it will provide . . . . [1] [2] [3] [4] [5] [6] [7]
8. Safety and security are the most important things in life . . . . [1] [2] [3] [4] [5] [6] [7]
9. I am more proud when I achieve things as an individual than when I
   accomplish things while working with others in a group . . . . [1] [2] [3] [4] [5] [6] [7]
10. People are more likely to succeed in their lives if they are
    compassionate and understanding . . . . [1] [2] [3] [4] [5] [6] [7]
11. Not knowing what is going to happen next makes me feel anxious
    and uncomfortable . . . . [1] [2] [3] [4] [5] [6] [7]
12. Status and responsibility distinctions between students and instructors
    are barriers to effectiveness in the classroom . . . . [1] [2] [3] [4] [5] [6] [7]
13. I admire people who are aggressive and dominant . . . . [1] [2] [3] [4] [5] [6] [7]
14. I prefer for instructors to make all the decisions about how the courses
    I take will be structured and conducted . . . . [1] [2] [3] [4] [5] [6] [7]
15. Given the choice, I would prefer working on a group paper instead of
    working on an individual paper . . . . [1] [2] [3] [4] [5] [6] [7]
16. I like not knowing what will happen tomorrow . . . . [1] [2] [3] [4] [5] [6] [7]

Reprinted with authors' permission.

When you have completed the questionnaire, score your answers using the key at the end of this exercise. Do not be concerned about your actual scores on the four dimensions. It is neither good nor bad to be high on one or low on another. The focus in this exercise is on how people who are either alike or different from each other interact and work together, not on the personal characteristics of any one individual.

Step Two: Discussions in Similar Groups

The class session will begin by dividing into groups of people who have similar scores on the Individual Differences Questionnaire. Your instructor will set up four types of groups—one type to represent each of the four dimensions. You will probably join a group for the dimension on which you get the highest total. Thus, if your highest score is on power distance, you will join a power distance group. Suppose, however, that you have two or more high scores—say, individualism–collectivism and power distance—that are about the same. In this case, you would join either a power distance or an individualism–collectivism group, depending on which one needs another member. In general, each group should have between four and six members.

After forming, each group should work to answer the following questions:

1. What terms best describe the way we think, act, and feel? How do we differ from others?

2. Since our dimension actually has two extremes, how might people who scored extremely low on our dimension think and behave? What might they do in their spare time? What kinds of jobs would they be best suited for?

3. How does having our group's defining characteristic affect our behavior in the group? Our satisfaction with the group?

4. How might our group's defining characteristic serve as an advantage in the workplace? As a disadvantage?

Step Three: Discussions in Dissimilar Groups

Now the class should divide into new groups of four to six members in which each of the four dimensions is represented by at least one high-scoring member. These groups should begin by having each member report the results of the Step Two discussions. After everyone in the group understands all four dimensions and their corresponding advantages and disadvantages, the group should answer the following questions:

1. Which dimensions seem to be in conflict with one another? How might these conflicts be managed?

2. Which seem to complement each other? Do some dimensions' advantages make up for other dimensions' disadvantages?

3. What kinds of tasks would probably be performed best by groups whose members are dissimilar? Similar? Why?

4. In general, are effective groups more likely to be made up of people who are similar or different from one another? What sort of group—similar or dissimilar membership—would you rather be in for the rest of this course? Why?

The group should select a spokesperson to present a five-minute summary of these answers to the rest of the class.

Step Four: Group Reports and Class Discussion

In this last step, the spokespeople will present their summaries, and the class should look for similarities and differences among the conclusions that the various Step Three groups have reached. Your instructor will then share his or her personal observations of how the members of the similar and dissimilar groups worked together. Finally, the class should discuss how the individual differences examined in this exercise may affect organizational behavior. Here are some questions to consider in this discussion:

1. Did you see the advantages and disadvantages you associated with the different dimensions actually influence work in the groups created in Step Three? What positive things happened? What negative things occurred?

2. What might be done to help people with different characteristics, attitudes, and beliefs work together? In what ways might the four dimensions examined here influence the management of organizational behavior?

Conclusion

Knowledge of individual differences such as those examined in this exercise can help human resource specialists improve selection and placement practices. Intelligently applied, it can also help managers reduce absenteeism and turnover, and it can strengthen communication, motivation, and cooperation in organizations. Nonetheless, managers must always bear in mind that many factors influence attitudes and performance at work: General and specific abilities, intelligence, job knowledge, and motivation also have important effects on organizational behavior.

Scoring Key

1. For questionnaire items 1, 2, 4, 5, 10, 12, 15, and 16, subtract the number you circled from 8; the result is your score on each of these items. For example, if you circled the number (5) on item 1, your score for that item is 3. For questionnaire items 3, 6, 7, 8, 9, 11, 13, and 14, the number you circled is your item score.

2. Add your scores for items 1, 8, 11, and 16 and write the total here: _____.This is your score on *uncertainty avoidance* (UA).

3. Add your scores together for items 3, 5, 10, and 13 and write the total here: _____. This is your score on *masculinity–femininity* (MF).

4. Add your scores together for items 4, 6, 9, and 15 and write the total here: _____. This is your score on *individualism–collectivism* (IC).

5. Add your scores together for items 2, 7, 12, and 14 and write the total here: _____. This is your score on *power distance* (PD).

Perceptual Processes
Attention
Organization
Recall
Reducing Perceptual Problems

Decision-Making Processes
The Rational Decision-Making Model
The Administrative Decision-Making Model
Reducing Decision-Making Errors

Creativity in Decision Making
The Creative Process
Creative People
Creativity-Inducing Situations

Summary
Review Questions

Learning Through Experience
Diagnostic Questions 4-1: Perception and Judgment
Exercise 4-1: Judgment, Heuristics, and Biases

Perception, Decision Making, and Creativity

On April 18, 2002, the president of the United States and his team of advisors had to make a critical decision. Specifically, the administration became aware of some tenuous intelligence information suggesting that a suicide bomber was planning to set off explosives at a bank along the East Coast—perhaps the next day. With so little lead time to react, the administration's options were somewhat limited, and the question became whether they should issue a public warning to all the banks and/or to the public at large. FBI Director Robert Mueller and Attorney General John Ashcroft were advising the president to issue the warning, but Homeland Security Advisor Tom Ridge and Treasury Secretary Paul O'Neill were advising against such an action.

On the one hand, al-Qaeda leaders had always made it clear that they liked to target financial institutions, so the target was right.[1] Second, officials have also known that terrorist groups have wanted to conduct suicide bombing in the United States to create an association between these attacks and those conducted in Israel, so the method was right. Third, financial ministers from the World Bank were meeting that day in the nation's capital. The World Bank has always been a target of protestors, so this made the timing right. Finally, when all of this was taking place, information regarding potential intelligence that might have prevented the 9/11 attacks was in all the papers, prompting many to second-guess the president and ask, "What did he know and when did he know it?"[2] Thus, the context was right for action.

On the other hand, President Bush and his staff had no desire to create mass panic by issuing such an alert, if they were not 100 percent sure that the threat was actually going to materialize. The economy was very fragile at this point, and consumers had enough to worry about without having to consider any problems in the banking industry. Moreover, disinformation campaigns by terrorists—or weapons of mass disruption, as the administration called them—also served the terrorists' aims. Finally, just days before, on Sunday, April 14, an anonymous caller said that there was going to be a bomb at a bank in Washington, D.C. The local police, without waiting for federal guidance, warned the banks, and more than 150 of them were closed on Monday. It turned out that the call was actually from a thirteen-year-old boy in the Netherlands, who was later arrested by Dutch police. Indeed, in the previous eight months, the administration had issued a dozen warnings, all for naught, and Tom Ridge was the butt of running jokes on many talk shows. In this context, Ridge argued for patience, and the group decided to take no action that day, agreeing to "sleep on it."

While they slept, hundreds of miles away, a CIA agent who was interrogating captured al-Qaeda official Abu Zabayda jotted down in his electronic notebook that Zabayda mentioned that a plot was in the works to blow up a bank in an eastern city. This was posted electronically and the next morning, Ashcroft received this data as part of a regular, ongoing threat matrix briefing. Ashcroft reported it to the administration, emphasizing, "This is heavy information." When this information was shared with Ridge and O'Neill, it tipped the balance of the decision-making debate. The nation's color-coded warning system was raised from yellow to orange and banks were issued a warning that most of them heeded by closing down—the second time that week for many.[3]

In the end, there was no attack on any banks. Was this because the warnings prevented the threats or was it simply a case of sounding a false alarm? We may never know the truth, but because of the proximity to the earlier false alarm associated with banks initiated by the Dutch youth's prank call, most observers perceived this as a decision-making error made by a jittery administration. One also wonders how this affects the credibility of future warnings and how it might influence future decision making in the administration.

Perception is the process by which individuals select, organize, store, and retrieve information. *Decision making* is the process whereby this perceived information is used to evaluate and choose among possible courses of action. As this opening story about the decision to raise the nation's color-coded threat level makes clear, in many high-stakes environments, choosing among alternatives is never a simple process, and arguments for and against taking certain actions have to be carefully weighed. This is particularly true in complex and dynamic environments, where the opportunity to be second-guessed after the fact by outsiders remains an ever-present danger.[4] In addition to having accurate perceptions of the present conditions, decision makers need to be able to envision the future and use their vision to generate *innovative and creative* options.

These three topics—perception, decision making, and creativity—are examined in this chapter. The first section explores the process of human perception and discusses the keys to developing accurate beliefs about oneself and one's environment. Translating these accurate beliefs into decisions that are rational—or at least satisfactory—is the focus of the second section. Finally, the third section, on creativity, examines the process of going beyond the traditional decision options to uncover new and innovative alternatives. As Raymond Smith, CEO of Bell Atlantic, has noted, "Leadership in the late twentieth century is all about making decisions in the midst of complexity. This requires a different kind of corporate manager: flexible,

FIGURE 4-1   The Processes of Perception and Decision Making

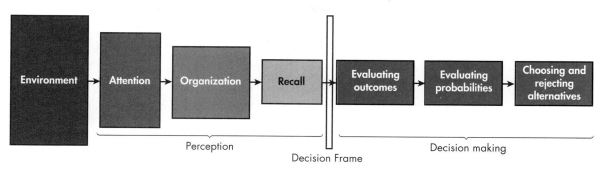

rigorous, and highly tolerant of ambiguity—one who can revisit decisions constantly and reverse course, even at the risk of personal embarrassment and exposure."[5] The material presented in this chapter should help the reader become just such a manager.

Figure 4-1 provides an overview of the processes of perception and decision making; it will serve as a road map for the first two sections. Specifically, we start at the left of Figure 4-1, which shows the environment in which the individual is embedded. Through the perceptual process, the individual uses some portion of the information that exists in that environment to make decisions. The process of perception will be broken down into three stages: attention, organization, and recall. In Figure 4-1, the boxes become smaller as we move from left to right, indicating that some information is lost at each stage.

At the end of the perceptual process, the decision is "framed"; that is, the decision maker finishes the process of collecting information and states the decision-making problem in specific terms. At this point, the decision-making process begins. The information collected in the perceptual process is evaluated in terms of what outcomes may result from various decisions and what odds are associated with various outcomes. Using the combined assessment of outcomes and probabilities, the decision maker chooses those alternatives that are most likely to lead to good outcomes and rejects those alternatives that are either unlikely to lead to good outcomes or likely to lead to bad outcomes.

We will explore each substage of the perception and decision-making processes more closely in the sections that follow.

PERCEPTUAL PROCESSES

Humans have five senses through which we experience the world: sight, hearing, touch, smell, and taste. Most of us "trust our senses," but sometimes this blind faith can lead us to believe that our perceptions are a perfect reflection of reality. People react to what they perceive, and their perceptions do not always reflect objective reality. This discrepancy can create major problems, because as the difference between perceived and objective reality increases, so too does the opportunity for misunderstanding, frustration, and conflict.

You can begin to appreciate the vast possibilities for perceptual distortion by considering some well-known illusions (Figure 4-2). Obviously, if we can misperceive something as objective as size, shape, and length, then our likelihood of misperceiving something more subjective, such as the intentions or thoughts of other people,

FIGURE 4-2 Four Common Perceptual Illusions

A. Are there two or three prongs on this object?

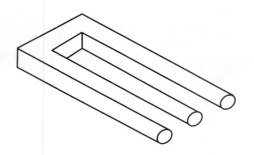

B. Ignoring the arrows, which vertical line is longer?

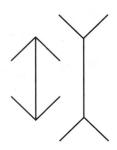

C. Are the four lines of the inner square straight lines?

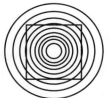

D. Which dotted circle is larger?

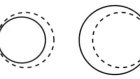

is high. For example, the data displayed in Table 4-1 show differences in perceptions between managers and subordinates regarding the manager's behavior as identified in a famous study conducted by Rensis Likert. These kinds of perceptual differences within a work group can lead to trouble and frustration for both the manager and the people with whom that manager works. Consequently, a great deal of research over the past forty years has focused on reducing the gap between the perceptions of managers and subordinates. By enhancing your understanding of the perception process, you can avoid situations in which your perceptions become as out of touch with reality as those reported for the managers in Table 4-1.

Attention

At any given moment in time, our five senses are bombarded with information of all sorts. In the **attention stage,** most of this available information is filtered so that some enters the system but other information does not. The attention stage is obviously critical, because any piece of information that is ignored at this stage can never figure into decision making. For this reason, you should appreciate how characteristics of the perceiver affect the way in which attention is directed.

For example, the perceiver's expectations of an object will often influence his or her evaluation of that object.[6] This reaction occurs partly because a person's attention is more easily drawn to objects that confirm the individual's expectations. Indeed, in the performance appraisal context, supervisors who are led to anticipate that one group of workers is likely to perform better than another tend to rate subordinates in a way that reflects these expectations, even when the subordinates perform at exactly the same objective level.[7]

The effects of needs and interests on perceptions can also be seen in the area of race relations at work. Research by Madeline Heilman has shown that affirmative

TABLE 4-1 Supervisors' and Subordinates' Views of Supervisors' Praise for Good Work

Form of Recognition	Frequency with Which Supervisors Say They Give Recognition "Very Often"	Frequency with Which Employees Say Supervisors Give Recognition "Very Often"
"A pat on the back"	82%	13%
Sincere and thorough praise	80	14
Training for a better job	64	9
Special privileges	52	14
More interesting work	51	5
Added responsibility	48	10

Source: Adapted from R. Likert, *New Patterns in Management* (New York: McGraw-Hill, 1961), p. 71.

action programs designed to help advance minorities often cause misperceptions on the part of all involved. Heilman found that nonminorities who feel that their interests are not served by such programs tend to discount the accomplishments of minorities who take advantage of such programs.[8] Table 4-2 lists other important differences in perceptions between African Americans and whites.[9] Clearly, marked differences occur in the way the two subgroups in Table 4-2 perceived and judged current opportunities for African Americans in the United States. These variations are probably best explained by the fact that each group is attending to different things. Given the differing perceptual inputs, it is not surprising that the two sides would come to markedly different judgments. Working out these kinds of perceptual differences may be essential before true progress can be made in race relations on and off the job.

Organization

Although much information is automatically filtered out at the attention stage, the remaining information is still too abundant and too complex to be easily understood and stored. Because human perceivers can process only a few bits of information at a time, in the **organization stage** they further simplify and organize incoming sensory data. For example, humans "chunk" several discrete pieces of information into a single piece of information that can be processed more easily.

To see how effective this kind of chunking can be, imagine your reaction if someone asked you to memorize a string of forty numbers. You might doubt your capacity to

TABLE 4-2 Perceptual Differences Regarding Affirmative Action Programs on a Five-Point Agree/Disagree Scale

	African Americans	Whites
African Americans are routinely discriminated against in most organizations	4.03	3.26
I personally have been discriminated against because of my race or sex	2.49	1.68
Affirmative action programs give unfair advantages to women and minorities	1.25	1.58
Affirmative action programs hire women and minorities, even if they are less qualified than men	2.64	3.14

Source: D. A. Kravitz and S. L. Klineberg, "Reactions to Two Versions of Affirmative Action among Whites, Blacks, and Hispanics," *Journal of Applied Psychology* 85 (2000), 597–611.

memorize so many numbers regardless of how much time you had. Your doubts are probably misplaced, however. If asked to do so, you could probably write down (a) your Social Security number, (b) your telephone number with area code, (c) your license plate number, (d) the month, date, and year of your birth, (e) your current ZIP code, and (f) your height and weight. You might say, "Well, yes, but these are only six numbers." Note, however, that (a) and (b) have nine digits each, (c) and (d) have six digits, and (e) and (f) probably have five; together, the data include a grand total of forty digits. The fact that humans think of these bits of information as six numbers rather than forty digits shows how we mentally chunk things together. In fact, using the chunking process, you can memorize many more than forty numbers (think of all the telephone numbers, ZIP codes, and birthdays that you can recall), which attests to the efficiency of this type of organizing process.

When chunking nonnumerical information, the chunks are called schemas. **Schemas** are cognitive structures that group discrete bits of perceptual information in an organized fashion.[10] Two types of schemas are particularly important to understanding the processing of social–interpersonal information: scripts and prototypes.

Schemas that involve sequences of actions are called **scripts** because they resemble the material from movies or plays. Clearly, numerous events in organizations can be conceived of as scripts, such as "taking a client to lunch," "preparing a written report," or "disciplining a subordinate." Each script involves certain sequences of behavior. Thus a request to take a client to lunch is actually a request to engage in hundreds of sequenced behaviors. Although this shorthand is clearly an efficient way of communicating, not everyone will define a script in the same way, with the exact same specific behaviors. For example, some organizations may have informal norms that discourage drinking alcohol at business lunches. A new employee who is told to "take a client to lunch" may not be aware of this specific part of the script.

Thus, while the kind of simplification provided by scripts is vital for efficient information processing, their use may lead to adding things that never took place or deleting things that did happen. Clarifying these scripts is essential to ensure perceptual accuracy. This consideration is especially important in team contexts. The term **shared mental model** has been used to differentiate between teams that have a common set of scripts and teams that do not have such a shared understanding. Teams that share the same mental model both with respect to the task and other team members tend to perform better because they enjoy enhanced coordination, communication, and cooperation.[11]

While some schemas focus on simplifying descriptions of events, others seek to simplify the descriptions of people. **Prototypes** are schemas that enable us to chunk information about people's characteristics. For example, if one manager asks another manager what a new employee is like, the second person may report that the new hire is spirited, exuberant, outgoing, boisterous, and warm. The manager might then say, "You mean she's an extrovert." In this example, multiple bits of information are chunked into one word that is meant to provide a detailed description of a person. Like scripts, however, prototypes sometimes carry excess baggage and thus may not reflect the person accurately—especially if two people hold different beliefs about the meaning of the word *extrovert*.

In the area of organizational behavior, the "leader" prototype is an important one. Most managers want others to perceive them as leaders. What characteristics are likely to cause people to categorize someone in this way? According to research conducted by Robert Lord, the leader prototype consists of the twelve characteristics shown in Table 4-3. People who exhibit most of these characteristics will be seen as leaders. In today's more collaborative organizational contexts, it is also critical to

TABLE 4-3
Major
Characteristics
of the Leader
Prototype
(in Descending
Order of
Importance)

1. Intelligent	5. Aggressive	9. Decisive
2. Outgoing	6. Determined	10. Dedicated
3. Understanding	7. Industrious	11. Educated
4. Articulate	8. Caring	12. Well dressed

Source: Adapted from R. G. Lord, R. J. Foti, and D. DeVader, "A Test of Leadership Categorization Theory: Internal Structure, Information Processing, and Leadership Perceptions," *Organizational Behavior and Human Performance* 34 (1984), 343–378.

be perceived as flexible, adaptable, and able to bring about change—three characteristics that some have argued favor female leaders over their male counterparts.[12] Indeed, the percentage of senior executive positions held by women reached 11 percent in 2000. Although much of this increase in female leadership occurred in the high-tech sector, large gains were also witnessed in manufacturing sectors of the economy that were formerly hostile to female leaders.[13]

Not all prototypes are useful. A **stereotype** is a prototype organized around a person's race, sex, age, ethnic origin, socioeconomic group, or other sociocultural characteristics—for example, African Americans, women, the elderly, Hispanic Americans, blue-collar workers, and homosexuals. In one study, business students displayed a clear stereotype of the elderly.[14] Among other things, they described this group as less creative, less able to do physically demanding work, and less able to change or be innovative. These perceptions led the students to make other negative judgments about elderly workers. For instance, they expressed the belief that these workers would be less likely than younger workers to benefit from training and development. Given the increasing age of our national workforce, such stereotypes need to be reconsidered.[15]

Recall

After information is organized, it next must be stored in memory for later retrieval. Just as raw information is sometimes lost when it is organized into scripts and prototypes, so too information can be lost in the storage and retrieval process.

To see how this loss can create illusions and lead to decision-making errors, consider the following problem: In a typical passage of English prose, does the letter *k* occur more often as the first or the third letter in a word? When confronted with this problem, twice as many people choose first letter as choose third letter, even though *k* appears in the third spot almost twice as often as in the first. This phenomenon can be explained in terms of the **availability bias,** which means that people tend to judge the likelihood that something will happen by the ease with which they can call examples of it to mind. Most people assume that *k* is more common at the beginning of words simply because humans store words in memory by their first letters—not their third letters. For this reason, it is easier to retrieve and remember words beginning with *k* than words that have *k* as their third letter. This kind of availability bias was illustrated in our opening story when John Ashcroft implied that the most recently received evidence from the interview of Abu Zabayda was "heavier" than the rest of the information the group was weighing in its deliberations. The availability bias also manifests itself in a tendency for people to overgeneralize from the recent past to make assumptions about what is going to happen next. This too is well illustrated in our opening story, in the sense that the group was concerned that the World Bank was meeting in Washington, and violent acts had been directed toward World Bank meetings in the recent past, thus increasing the perceived likelihood that they would be a target again.

You can see the availability bias at work by considering the way that people think about death, illness, and disasters. In general, people vastly overestimate the number of deaths caused by spectacular events such as airplane crashes and underestimate the number of deaths caused by illnesses such as emphysema or heart disease. Deaths caused by sudden disasters are more easily called to mind because they are so vivid and public, often making the front pages of newspapers across the country. Death caused by illness, on the other hand, is generally private and thus less likely to be recalled. The tendency to confuse the probability that something will happen with the ease with which one can remember it is especially a problem for decision makers who are inexperienced or low in cognitive ability.[16]

Another problem that can arise at the recall stage is hindsight bias. **Hindsight bias** occurs when people feel that they would have predicted the outcome to events better than they actually did or better than they actually would have if they had been asked to make a forecast. For example, a group of students might be asked to read a case that sets up an important decision, such as whether a person should invest in a risky "dot.com" stock. The students would be asked to state the probability of getting a 20 percent return on investment. After the passage of time, the same individuals are told that the company either went out of business or gave a 40 percent return on investment, and they are asked to recall their original probabilities. People who are told about positive outcomes tend to recall their probabilities of reaching the 20 percent return on investment goal as being much higher than they really were. People who are told that the company failed, on the other hand, tend to recall their probabilities of reaching a 20 percent return as being much lower than they really were.[17] Clearly, as depicted in our opening story, the president and his advisors were ultimately the victim of this kind of hindsight bias, in that when it became clear that there was not going to be a terrorist attack on banks, people outside the group concluded that they were too jittery and overly alarmist, even though when the decision was made, there were good arguments for both sides.

Reducing Perceptual Problems

Clearly, there are many ways that a human observer can fail to portray the environment accurately. Fortunately, one can take many steps to avoid these problems.

First, accuracy can be improved by increasing the frequency of observations. That is, the observer can be exposed more often to whatever needs to be observed. By making more observations, an observer can gather more information and thus heighten the accuracy of his or her perceptions.[18]

Second, taking care in how and when observations are made can ensure the representativeness of the information. That is, the manner in which observations are obtained should be thoughtfully considered. Random sampling will increase the probability that the resulting observations are accurate. If a supervisor observes a group of workers only at a given time on a given day or only when problems develop, the observations may not reflect the group's true behavior. In addition, because the very act of observing someone can cause him or her to alter the normal behavior (and thus destroy representativeness), it is important to make observations as unobtrusively as possible.

The opportunities to observe employee work behaviors frequently, randomly, and unobtrusively have increased rapidly with technological developments in the field of surveillance. In fact, they have grown so dramatically that some monitoring practices have raised ethical questions. DuPont now uses hidden long-distance cameras to monitor its loading docks. At Delta Airlines, computers track which salespeople write the most reservations. At Management Recruiters, Inc., in Chicago, supervisors surreptitiously watch computerized schedules to see which interviewers talk to the most job candidates. Supervisors at the Internal Revenue Service can tap into telephone conversations between IRS agents and taxpayers calling for information.

The increased use of computerized employee monitoring has been a product of two forces. First, the need to observe employees' work behaviors has long existed, and recent developments in surveillance technology have simply made this endeavor easier and less obtrusive. Second, an increasing number of court cases have dealt with "negligent hiring," where employers are held liable for the mistakes or crimes of employees. These two developments have seriously eroded employees' right to privacy. Finding the right balance between employees' rights and the rights and responsibilities of employers to monitor workers will be difficult to achieve.[19] One critical feature that predicts how employees will react to this kind of monitoring is the degree to which they are given advance notice about the practice. People who are given advance warning feel much more positive about the practice and are less likely to turn over than people who learn of it on their own.[20]

Third, the accuracy of perceptions can be improved by obtaining observations from different people and different perspectives. Having multiple points of view is especially valuable when it comes to self-perceptions of upper-level managers, who often overestimate their interpersonal effectiveness when their perceptions go unchecked.[21] This kind of misperception is based more on ignorance than arrogance, because few people are eager to give their boss negative feedback—even if he or she directly asks for it.[22] In order to overcome these problems, organizations have increasingly turned to 360-degree feedback programs where managers receive anonymous survey feedback on their strengths and weaknesses from supervisors, peers, and subordinates, and then compare the perceptions of these people to their own self-rated strengths and weaknesses. Managers who tend to over-estimate their strengths and underestimate their weaknesses typically perform the worst when it comes to external performance indices, and the purpose of these kinds of feedback programs is to bring perceptions more in line with reality.[23]

Fourth, because observers tend to ignore information that does not match their expectations, it is often a good idea to actively seek out information that is inconsistent with or contradicts one's current beliefs.[24] For example, Bell Atlantic uses a team of managers to play the "devil's advocate" role in organizational decision making. This group is explicitly assigned the role of challenging and disputing the key assumptions on which decisions are being made. People are often reluctant to assume this role on their own because they want to be seen as a "team player" rather than a "heretic." By explicitly saying that someone's role on the team is that of a heretic, Bell Atlantic ensures that the role is covered and no one becomes alienated from the team.

When a person must work with social groups that differ from his or her own, a fifth method for ensuring perceptual accuracy is to increase that individual's exposure to different social groups in an effort to develop more accurate prototypes. Research shows that experts in all kinds of domains differ from novices not because they ignore prototypes, but because they develop more complex, detailed prototypes that are more accurate.[25] As people develop experience with unfamiliar people and situations, their processes of organization become more complex and better able to reflect the underlying reality.

For example, Park Kwang Moo, a twenty-eight-year-old employee at Samsung Company, spent a year in Russia living, eating, and drinking with the people there in an effort to help his organization learn what was needed to expand into this market. He learned how bribes smooth the way for everything from airplane tickets to gasoline. He also learned what it felt like to stand in line for ten hours waiting for a flight that never took off—at that moment, he noted, "I felt strength in their misery,

I felt like a Russian."[26] As part of the same program, Samsung sent 400 other young executives on similar assignments in Europe, Australia, Africa, and the United States. Despite an average cost of $80,000 per executive, Samsung believes that the program will more than pay for itself. In the long run, such programs allow the firm to perceive things in the same way as consumers within the target market.

DECISION-MAKING PROCESSES

At the end of the process of perception depicted in Figure 4-1, the decision has been framed. That is, the decision maker has collected and discarded various pieces of information to arrive at the final set of information that will be used in making the final decision. From this point on, this set of information will be further processed in an effort to choose which course of action to accept and which alternatives to reject. Two general models are employed in understanding the decision-making process: the rational model and the administrative model.

The Rational Decision-Making Model

The rational decision-making model is sometimes referred to as the rational-economic model, reflecting its ties to classic theories of economic behavior. As originally developed, this model included a primary assumption of economic rationality—that is, the notion that people attempt to maximize their individual *economic* outcomes. The system of values consistent with this assumption assesses outcomes based on their current or prospective monetary worth. Values of this type are used in business situations whenever managers weigh alternatives in terms of profitability or loss. They then choose one of the alternatives and implement it as the preferred solution or decision. This choice is determined through a process of utility maximization, in which the alternative with the highest expected worth is selected as the preferred alternative. The expected worth of a particular alternative consists of the sum of the expected values of the costs and benefits of all outcomes associated with that alternative.

Ideally, observers would use this information in a rational way to reach their final decisions. Such is not always the case, however. Our earlier discussion used perceptual illusions to show that perception is not nearly as straightforward as it seems. Here, we will use "decision-making illusions" to show how things can go wrong in the decision-making process.[27]

Evaluating Outcomes   As a prelude to this discussion, read the paragraph in Table 4-4 and decide what strategy you would choose if you were the sales executive faced with the situation described. If you perceive strategy one (save the 200 accounts for sure) to be the best approach, you are not alone. Research shows that managers and nonmanagers alike perceive this choice as preferable to strategy two by a margin of roughly three to one.

Now turn to a similar decision situation, shown in Table 4-5, and decide which strategy is preferable under these circumstances. If you judge strategy two as being the best option, again you are not alone. Research shows that this choice is preferred by a margin of roughly four to one over strategy one.

The surprising thing about these results is that the problems described are virtually identical. Reread the paragraphs in Tables 4-4 and 4-5. Strategy one is the same in both tables. The only difference is that in Table 4-4 it is expressed in terms of accounts *saved* (200 out of 600), whereas in Table 4-5 it is expressed in terms of accounts *lost*

TABLE 4-4
Two Strategies
for Handling an
Environmental
Threat

> The development of a new technology by a competitor threatens the viability of your organization which manages 600 accounts. You have two available strategies to counter this new technology. Your advisors make it clear that if you choose strategy one, 200 of the 600 accounts will be saved. If you choose strategy two, there is a one-third chance that all of the 600 accounts will be saved and a two-thirds chance that none will be saved.
> Which strategy will you choose?

Source: Adapted from A. Tversky and D. Kahneman, "The Framing of Decisions and the Psychology of Choice," *Science* 211 (1981), 453–458.

(400 out of 600). Clearly, if 200 accounts are saved, 400 accounts are lost, and vice versa. Why is strategy one preferred in the situation described in Table 4-4 and strategy two preferred in the situation outlined in Table 4-5?

Research by Nobel Prize–winning scientist Daniel Kahneman and his colleague Amos Tverskey indicates that in general, people have a slight preference for sure outcomes as opposed to risky ones. However, this research also shows that people hate losing.[28] This **loss-aversion bias** affects their decision making even more strongly than their preference for nonrisky situations. When given a choice between a sure gain and a risky gain, most people will take the sure thing and avoid the risk. When given a choice between a sure loss and a risky loss, however, most people will avoid the sure loss and take a chance on not losing anything.

A real-world example of this can be seen in Arthur Andersen's risky decisions regarding aggressive accounting practices that it employed as part of its work with Enron. Over the last decade, Arthur Andersen increasingly derived more of its revenue growth from its consulting contracts as compared to its auditing business. Wanting a larger share of its own success, the consulting side of the business, which brought in close to $10 billion a year in revenue, sought independence. An arbitrator granted them this freedom (creating a new company called Accenture) in return for a one-time $1 billion payment to the parent company. Faced with this huge loss of revenue, Arthur Andersen became highly aggressive in trying to rebuild its consulting business, and many have speculated that unwarranted level of risk seeking made it overlook problems that were being caused by one of its best-paying new clients—Enron. Former Federal Reserve Chairman Paul Volcker stated bluntly, "There is no doubt in my mind that Andersen took its eye off the ball by basing what was acceptable practice on how much revenue it could generate."[29]

In addition to people's asymmetric treatment of losses and gains, evaluating outcomes is also complicated by the fact that often multiple outcomes need to be met, and these may be at odds with each other. For example, we may want decisions to be both timely and correct, but in many contexts, speed and accuracy of decision making are negatively related to each other, and respond differently to managerial actions.[30] Research shows that putting workers in competition with each other generally makes

TABLE 4-5
Two More
Strategies for
Handling an
Environmental
Threat

> The development of a new technology by a competitor threatens the viability of your organization which manages 600 accounts. You have two available strategies to counter this new technology. Your advisors make it clear that if you choose strategy one, 400 of the 600 accounts will be lost. If you choose strategy two, there is a one-third chance that no accounts will be lost and a two-thirds chance that all will be lost.
> Which strategy will you choose?

Source: Adapted from A. Tversky and D. Kahneman, "The Framing of Decisions and the Psychology of Choice," *Science* 211 (1981), 453–458.

TABLE 4-6
Identifying a
Hit-and-Run
Driver

A cab is involved in a hit-and-run accident.
    Two taxicab companies serve the city. The Green Company operates 85 percent of the cabs, and the Blue Company operates the remaining 15 percent.
    A witness describes the hit-and-run cab as blue. When the court tests the witness's reliability under circumstances similar to those on the night of the accident, the witness correctly identifies the color of a cab 80 percent of the time and misidentifies it 20 percent of the time.
    Which cab company was most probably involved in the hit-and-run accident?

Source: Adapted from A. Tversky and D. Kahneman, "The Framing of Decisions and the Psychology of Choice," *Science* 211 (1981), 453–458.

them work faster, but with less accuracy, whereas promoting cooperation among workers increases their accuracy but slows them down.[31] Moreover, once a group or organization commits itself to competing on speed or accuracy, this initial decision often persists and forces the group to maintain its current emphasis into the future, even when it might make more sense to change.[32]

Evaluating Probabilities   Irrationality can also enter into the decision-making process through errors made in evaluating the probabilities associated with various outcomes. For example, consider the decision-making problem described in Table 4-6. Most people would conclude that the hit-and-run driver was in the blue cab. In fact, the odds are much better that the cab was green.

That is, if 100 cabs operated in the city, 85 would be green and 15 would be blue. This base rate represents the initial probability given no other piece of information. Using the premise established in Table 4-6, which says that the witness (who provides an additional piece of information over and above the base rate) would be right 80 percent of the time, we can analyze what would happen in each possible scenario. If the cab in the accident was actually blue, the witness would identify it correctly as a blue cab 12 times (.80 × 15 = 12) and would incorrectly identify it as a green cab 3 times (.20 × 15 = 3). If the vehicle was a green cab, however, the witness would correctly identify it 68 times (.80 × 85 = 68) and misidentify it 17 times (.20 × 85 = 17). Thus the odds are much greater that the witness's identification of the cab as blue was a misidentification of a green cab (which happens 17 out of 100 times) than a correct identification of a blue cab (which happens only 12 out of 100 times).

The reason why virtually everyone who approaches this problem naively gets it wrong is the tendency to give too much weight to the evidence provided by the witness and not enough weight to the evidence provided by the base rate. Because of **base rate bias,** people tend to ignore the background information in this sort of case and feel that they are dealing with something unique. In this example, decision makers will discount the evidence regarding how few cars are actually blue, and instead put more confidence in human judgment about the color of the car. Ignoring the base rate can lead to irrational decisions.

The problem of misplaced confidence is particularly pronounced when more than one probabilistic event is involved. Not surprisingly, actual business ventures frequently face such situations. Suppose, for example, that a house builder contracts to have a house completed by the end of the year. Assume also that the chances of accomplishing four specific tasks in time to meet this deadline are as follows:

Get permits	Excellent (90%)
Get financing	Very good (80%)
Get materials	Excellent (90%)
Get subcontractors	Very good (80%)

Reviewing these data, the builder might well conclude that there is a good to excellent chance that the project can be completed in the time specified in the contract. In fact, the odds of this outcome are only 50-50. Multiplying the four probabilities together ($.9 \times .8 \times .9 \times .8 = .52$) gives slightly more than 50 percent—hardly a good to excellent chance. The axiom known as Murphy's law states that "anything that can go wrong, will go wrong." This view may be a tad pessimistic, but in a long series of probabilistic events, the odds are quite good that any one event will go wrong, and sometimes a single mishap can destroy an entire venture. Any business executive who is putting together a deal where the ultimate outcome depends on a series of discrete events, none of which is a sure thing, must keep this fact in mind.

Dynamic Influences   The rational model assumes that each decision is made independently of other decisions—that is, each decision is examined on its own merits in terms of outcomes and probabilities. Irrationality can creep into the process, however, because in reality people often see decisions as being related, and because past decisions may "reach forward" and affect future decisions in irrational ways.

For example, in a bias referred to as **escalation of commitment,** people invest more and more heavily in an apparently losing course of action so as to justify their earlier decisions. Usually the investments made once this process gets started are disproportionate to any gain that could conceivably be realized, and the level of irrationality becomes particularly pronounced when the project nears completion.[33]

Even when costs clearly outstrip benefits, a decision maker may feel many different kinds of pressure to continue to act in accord with a particular decision.[34] For psychological reasons, the decision maker may not want to appear inconsistent by changing course; that is, the person may not want to admit to an earlier mistake. Moreover, particularly where feedback is ambiguous or complex, perceptual distortions such as the expectation effect can make the picture appear more hopeful than is really the case. Because decision makers cannot make perfect predictions regarding future outcomes, there is always the hope that staying the course will pay off. Moreover, many people have been rewarded in past situations for sticking it out. Although rare, such experiences are usually quite memorable (the availability bias). The experience of giving up when it is the appropriate choice often goes unrewarded, at least in the short run, and thus is something people like to forget. Finally, sometimes cost-benefit analyses are abandoned in favor of a win-at-any-cost mentality. The quest to prove oneself takes over, and obsession overcomes better judgment.

Factors Limiting Rational Decision-Making Models   As the decision-making illusions previously described show, the complexity of real-world decision situations often makes rationality impossible to achieve. This can often lead some decision makers to "freeze up" and attempt to avoid making a decision at all costs. We saw this in our opening story when the president and his group of advisors chose "to sleep on it" rather than make a decision. As the Cutting-Edge Research box shows, this is a common response to complex decision-making problems and has to be managed carefully. Herbert A. Simon, a cognitive scientist and Nobel laureate in economics, has remarked that "the capacity of the human mind for formulating and solving complex problems is very small compared with the size of the problems whose solution is required for objectively rational behavior in the real world."[35] Simon's comment on the limits of human intelligence does not seek to condemn humans, but rather acknowledge the complexity of the environment in which they must operate. Indeed, according to Simon and to others who have followed his lead, the complexity of the real world often overwhelms the decision maker at each step of the rational decision-making process, making complete rationality an impossibility.

CUTTING-EDGE RESEARCH

DECIDING NOT TO DECIDE: THE ORIGINS AND COSTS OF DECISION AVOIDANCE

Imagine that you just returned from a weekend business conference that brought together many different companies working in your industry. At the conference, you met someone from another organization that seemed interested in hiring you away from your current employer, implying that she has a job for you that is more meaningful than your current job, and pays better as well. This person tells you to call her next week if you are interested. It is now Friday, and with telephone number in hand you pick up the phone, fingers raised to punch out the numbers that could connect you to, perhaps, a better future.

You hesitate, however, because although it would be nice to get a better job, the person you spoke with did not guarantee you anything other than an interview to "explore this option at greater length." Moreover, although it does seem to be a better job in terms of pay and the nature of the work, maybe you would not like the people who work there. You really like your current boss, and she has hinted that you may be in line for a promotion if the company starts to grow. After all, it's a pretty small industry, and if your boss hears about you "exploring other options," she may misinterpret this as disloyalty, which would quash any hopes you have of getting promoted. Of course, there is certainly no guarantee that your company is going to grow, so that is a rather "iffy" proposition as well, and given the rumors you have heard, who is to say you won't get laid off next month if the company has to downsize? You stand poised and ready to dial, but are frozen—hating the thought of dialing; hating the thought of not dialing. After a long minute, the weight of the phone becomes unbearable, and you put it down, just like you did Thursday, Wednesday, and every other day this week. Perhaps you will think about it more over the weekend.

This situation depicts a recurring problem in many decision-making contexts, where when confronted with a decision-making opportunity that has both positive and negative features, the person who needs to make up his or her mind decides not to decide. In some situations, this may be acceptable, especially if in the interim more information relevant to the decision is likely to come in and if there are no costs to delay. However, in many cases, such as this one, the information that is likely to come in while you wait will not be decisive, and by not getting back in a timely fashion, your contact may infer that you are not interested and then pursue another candidate—leaving you high and dry. Indeed, in many cases, this type of decision avoidance creates a great many difficulties, and we have all met people for whom the inability to pull the trigger on any decision, no matter how trivial, borders on pathology.

Fortunately, there has been a great deal of research on the topic of decision avoidance, which was all recently summarized by Christopher Anderson, who analyzed the results of more than fifty studies on this topic. What one learns from this research is that in this type of context, beyond the cold calculation of expected probabilities and outcomes associated with various options, people also struggle with two additional aversive emotional states: anticipated regret associated with making a bad decision that cannot be reversed, and fear that others may ridicule or think less of them for making such a bad decision. Both regret and fear of failure can be temporarily be avoided by either sticking with the status quo, taking no action, or otherwise just deciding to decide later.

If you are managing someone who seems to have this kind of problem, research suggests that you can engage in several behaviors to help this person become more decisive. First, ask the person exactly what new information he or she is waiting for, and why the person expects this is going to be decisive. If the person cannot precisely specify exactly what he or she is waiting for, then perhaps there is no benefit in waiting. Second, describe the costs of waiting so that they figure into the cold and calculated part of the equation. Note concretely how decision avoidance may lead to a lost opportunity or how other people may interpret this as reflecting something you do not intend (such as lack of interest). Third, minimize the sense of regret by framing the positive features of each decision option as a "win-win opportunity" (for example, one way or the other, you will either raise your odds of getting promoted because of your loyalty or you'll raise the odds of getting a new and better job with someone else). Avoid a focus on the negative sides of each option; if the person keeps bringing up negatives, even a "damned if you do; damned if you don't" frame may reduce anticipated regret by implying that regret is unavoidable. Fourth, if there are a large number of both positive and negative features associated with each alternative, simplify the problem by focusing on the number one reason, or the top three reasons (going with the alternative that wins two out of three) in terms of the degree to which they are convincing.

Finally, setting a deadline to force the decision maker's hand will ensure timely results; however, this will often cause a great deal of suffering on the part of the decision maker, and the high level of emotionality it generates may lead to a bad decision. Thus, in order to reduce fear, deadlines need to be accompanied by a statement on the leader's part that you will support the decision even if it turns out

badly, as long as the person can justify the *process* he or she went through to make the decision. You have to commit to the person, stating explicitly that if the person makes it clear that he or she engaged in a conscientious and reasonable process, and did not make the decision without thought or reflection, you will support the person. If the person knows you will take his or her side against anyone who, with the benefit of hindsight bias, tries to second-guess the decision, this may enhance the accuracy and timeliness of decisions, as well as your ability to justify them.

Sources: C. J. Anderson, "The Psychology of Doing Nothing: Forms of Decision Avoidance Result from Reason and Emotion," *Psychological Bulletin* 129 (2003), 139–167; R. Dhar and S. J. Sherman, "The Effect of Common and Unique Features in Consumer Choice," *Journal of Consumer Research* 23 (1996), 193–203; M. F. Luce, "Choosing to Avoid: Coping with Negatively Emotion-Laden Consumer Decisions, *Journal of Consumer Research* 24 (1998), 409–433.

One issue that may undermine the rational decision-making model is the fact that rational models work only if there is general agreement on the definitions of problems, decisions, and decision-making goals that are framed at the outset. Especially in large organizations, such consensus is difficult to achieve. Different individuals, work groups, and departments are likely to rank outcomes in different ways. Indeed, in large, complex organizations, the only problem definitions likely to be widely shared are those so vague as to be almost meaningless. As an example, Table 4-7 shows a generic formula that seems to be the source of most organizations' "vision statements."[36] Whereas such vision statements may be generally palatable, they provide little in the way of guidance for day-to-day decision making.[37]

Another problem for the rational decision-making model is the difficulty inherent in trying to generate an exhaustive list of alternatives and then select the most promising one. Managers often cannot anticipate which actions will lead to which consequences. Because, as Simon points out, most real-world decisions are characterized by uncertainty, managers cannot even speculate on the odds. Under these conditions, they cannot compute expected values, and thus they lack a common measure with which to compare various alternatives. This problem is especially common with nonprogrammed decisions—that is, decisions that are required only infrequently. In making these kinds of decisions, no one ever develops enough experience to easily assess the odds associated with any alternative.[38]

For example, in 2003 Boeing was faced with the decision of either developing its first all-new jetliner in nine years, the 7E7, or hunkering down and just trying to cautiously weather the airline's worst downturn ever. Some members of Boeing's board felt that the $10 billion cost for designing the new plane was too high, and that the market for large passenger planes was too volatile. They sought to diversify

TABLE 4-7
Generic Corporate Vision Generator

To generate your corporate vision, just circle one entry in each set of brackets.
TO BE A [premier, leading, growing, world-class] COMPANY THAT PROVIDES [innovative, cost-effective, diversified, high-quality] [products, services, products and services] TO [create shareholder value, serve the global marketplace, delight our customers, satisfy our stakeholders] IN THE RAPIDLY CHANGING [information solution, business solution, financial solution, consumer solution] INDUSTRY

the company and look for minor evolutionary changes that would allow them to derive small incremental profit improvements from existing lines of business. Others on the board wanted to risk a revolutionary redesign of its passenger aircraft in order to make up for ground lost to Europe's Airbus. These individuals were afraid that Boeing was going to face the same fate of the failed McDonnell-Douglas organization, which, in their words, "frittered away a pretty solid market position by not taking risks."[39] The one-time, highly idiosyncratic nature of this decision precluded any opportunity to calculate any kind of expected value that is required by rational decision-making models.

In addition, managers are not free to choose among all the choices they may generate. The term **bounded discretion,** first suggested by Simon, refers to the fact that the list of alternatives generated by any decision maker is restricted by social, legal, and moral norms. As Figure 4-3 indicates, the discretionary area containing acceptable choices is bounded on many sides. The boundaries between each set of limitations and the discretionary area are not clear-cut. As a result, decision makers do not always know whether an alternative is in or out of bounds.

In some cases, social norms and traditions may limit one's options, and the "rational decision" may conflict with these customs. For example, in the high-tech industry, it was customary to offer clients and customers rather large incentives for their businesses. One of the well known incentives was referred to as "Friends and Family IPO Stock Options," a tradition that often led to initial IPO stock prices that were much too low relative to what rational reasoning would demand. Specifically, friends-and-family programs allowed companies that were going public for the first time to distribute as much as 5 percent of their offerings early to whomever they chose. These individuals got to purchase the stock at the original IPO price, whereas everyone else had to wait a day. At one point, tech stocks were jumping an average of 65 percent on their first day of trading, guaranteeing a huge payoff to those who were part of the friends-and-family programs, but a rather large disadvantage to shareholders who were outside the loop. As one commentator noted, "If it weren't for friends and family programs company executives would have pushed for a

FIGURE 4-3   The Concept of Bounded Discretion

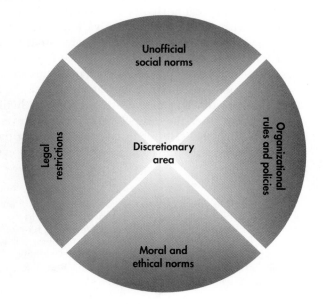

SECURING COMPETITIVE ADVANTAGE

POLITICS AND CULTURAL DECISION-MAKING CONSTRAINTS: WHY GERMANY CONTINUES TO SLIDE

Jennifer Knoblach is a twenty-four-year-old journalism major who will graduate from a Bavarian university in June 2003. Her prospects for getting a job in her native Germany after college do not look good, and she is not alone. "All the people I know are at the end of their studies and don't know what to do. It's a catastrophe." Like many of her young friends, she has decided to look for work outside Germany, even though she is saddened by the thought of leaving all her family behind.

The cause of Jennifer's problems can be traced to the stagnant national economy. Of the fifteen largest industrial countries in Europe, Germany ranks last in growth, and its stock market, as reflected in the DAX 30, was the worst-performing market in all of the developed world in 2002. The unemployment rate is among the highest of industrialized nations, and even domestically oriented companies such as Deutsche Post invest more money abroad than they do at home. Indeed, those companies in Germany that are expanding are doing so by opening up facilities outside the country. For example, drug producer Schering and software developer SAP have shifted most of their research and development activities to the United States.

From a purely analytic perspective, both the causes and solutions to Germany's problems are well known. Unfortunately, a host of political and cultural forces conspire against those who would make the necessary changes. One of the primary drags on the German economy is the concept of *Kundigungsschutz*, which refers to the culturally ingrained notion that jobs are to be protected at all costs. Backed by powerful unions, the laws make it difficult if not impossible for employers to lay off workers. For example, when entrepreneur Arndt Rautenberg merged his company with another, the government would not allow him to lay off any of the worst performers in the merged business, creating huge inefficiencies. Rautenberg learned his lesson, and now when demand for his product grows, rather than hire any new local German workers, he instead farms the work out to outsourcing companies in India.

In addition to the cultural constraints posed by Kundigungsschutz, employers also are limited in what they can do by politicians. Taxes in Germany are among the highest in the industrialized world, and where this once was a mixed blessing, offset by a well-funded, high-quality health care system and university system, this is no longer the case. Increasingly, instead of going to public goods, the largest share of the high tax burden winds up as transfer payments going from the western region of the country to the less well developed eastern portion of the country. Indeed, integrating the former East Germany into the rest of the country has proven prohibitively expensive, but at this point, there are so many voters in the eastern region that any politician who would try to stop this runaway welfare system would be voted out of office. In the words of one German executive, "I do not think the government will have the courage to go for fundamental reforms."

If the problems confronting Germany affected only Jennifer Knoblach and other Germans, the situation would be bad enough. However, the failure to make and implement the necessary decisions threatens not only Germany's future, but also the futures of the other nations that recently signed on to partner with Germany as part of the European Union. Other European nations such as Ireland, Finland, Spain, Britain, and the Netherlands have growth rates that are two to four times as high as Germany's. Even France, whose growth rates are close to the bottom of those in the EU, have rates that are a full percentage point higher than Germany's. Indeed, one French government official went so far as to state that "Germany has neither economic power nor political vision anymore, so it's a waste of time to make an alliance with it." This is the kind of public rebuke that may help create a climate conducive to the needed reforms, but well-entrenched cultural and political habits are often difficult to change, regardless of how obvious the changes are from a strictly rational perspective.

Sources: J. Ewing, "The Decline of Germany," *Business Week,* February 17, 2003, pp. 44–53; J. Ewing, "This 'Super Minister' Is Gunning for Reform," *Business Week,* February 17, 2003, pp. 50–51; J. Rossant, "How Germany's Fall from Grace Harms Europe," *Business Week,* February 17, 2003, p. 53.

ETHICS AND SOCIAL RESPONSIBILITY

THE DECISION TO BECOME A WHISTLE-BLOWER: MULTIPLE PATHS TO AN ETHICAL END

Often, the only thing that stands between unethical individuals, groups, and organizations and your physical and financial security is a whistle-blower. Whistle-blowers are organizational insiders who observe unethical or illegal behavior and then, rather than go along with the crowd, report the activity to authorities. Whistle-blowers put themselves at great risk. Many are undermined or humiliated within their organization and are even threatened with physical violence. Many not only lose their jobs, but also become blackballed from their industry, thus ending their entire career. Many lose their homes and their marriages break up under the unrelenting financial and social pressures that result from making such a choice. Given the potential costs associated with informing on one's own organization like this, what goes into the decision to take this path?

Although there are often multiple reasons for a single decision, for the most part whistle-blowers tend to fall into three distinct categories. First, there are the "outsiders," that is, people who for one reason or another do not fit into the organizational culture. Indeed, in some cases the very beliefs that make them an outsider make them more likely to detect and report unethical transgressions. For example, Cowleen Rowley was simply a midlevel lawyer at a field office in the midwest, far from the FBI's center of power in Washington, D.C. Moreover, she was a woman in a very hierarchical, political, secretive, and male-dominated culture where the primary value was loyalty to the system.

Thus, when she heard the director of the FBI, Robert Mueller, speaking on national television about the airliner attacks of 9/11, say that "there were no warning signs that I am aware of that would indicate this type of operation in the country," she knew it was untrue, and was torn about what to do next. In fact, for weeks she was on the trail of Zacharias Moussaoui, and knew he was a suspected terrorist who was receiving flight training to fly a 747. She repeatedly noted that this was a worrisome development, but could not receive permission to examine the case more closely. In the end, she sent a memo to higher authorities, which eventually leaked to the press, leading to congressional investigations and a major shake-up at the bureau. In commenting on the culture at the FBI, Rowley noted, "Loyalty to whoever you work for is extremely

important. The only problem is, it is not *the* most important thing. And when it comes to not admitting mistakes or covering up or not rectifying things only to save face, that's a problem."

In addition to the "outsiders," some whistle-blowers fall into the "by the books" category. These individuals tend to be professionally or technically trained specialists who recoil whenever others fail to follow the prescribed rules for performing critical tasks—especially if there are good reasons for the rules and poor reasons for the deviations away from those rules. For example, Randy Robarge was a nuclear power plant supervisor at ComEd's Zion power plant on Lake Michigan. Robarge was a technical junkie and relentlessly studied industry protocols for managing hazardous waste. Far from being an outsider, Robarge was a twenty-year veteran at the plant who was so respected when it came to safety issues that the organization used him as the narrator on their training videos. However, when the organization, for financial reasons, began violating safety rules for containment of radiation, Robarge simply could not stop himself from speaking out. He was harassed, then fired and then blackballed from the industry and the technical work that he loved. He was later vindicated by a federal investigation that proved that Zion's procedures were in fact violating the law and threatening the safety of both workers and citizens of the local community.

Finally, Doug Durand, a new sales director for TAP Pharmaceutical Products, exemplifies yet a third type of whistle-blower—the "self-protectors." TAP produced Lupron, one of the leading drugs used to treat prostate cancer, but a competing product that entered the market threatened that lead. In a conference call about how to respond to the threat, Durand was shocked to hear the sales staff openly discussing how to bribe doctors to prescribe the drug. The plan, which apparently had worked in the past, was to give doctors a secret discount price for Lupron, and then support the doctors who would charge Medicare or Medicaid the full price for the drug. When one of the callers asked what would happen if they got caught, another quipped, "How do you think Doug would look in stripes?" Durand recalls how that conversation "scared the heck out of me . . . I felt really vulnerable." It led him to work undercover with the government to root out the problem. In the end, TAP pleaded guilty of robbing the government and U.S. taxpayers and was fined $875 million. Like Cowley and Robarge, Durand has a hard time seeing himself as a hero, and recoils at the very word *whistle-blower*. In the end, these were ordinary people who just happened to find themselves in extraordinary situations, and then responded in a manner that we all hope we ourselves would respond.

Sources: P. Dwyer, "Year of the Whistleblower," *Business Week*, December 16, 2002, pp. 107–110; A. Ripley and M. Sieger, "The Special Agent," *Time*, December 30, 2002, pp. 35–40; C. Daniels, "It's a Living Hell," *Fortune*, April 15, 2002, pp. 367–368; C. Haddad, "A Whistleblower Rocks an Industry," *Business Week*, June 24, 2002, pp. 126–130.

higher price offering," and this cost these companies more than $60 billion.[40] Although this example shows how the customs of a company or industry can harm the larger society, in other cases, the customs and traditions of the larger society can work to harm the interests of companies and industries. An example of this is depicted in the Securing Competitive Advantage box, which documents the difficulties that German companies face in trying to turn around their struggling industries and how this is related to national customs.

When organizational decision makers choose alternatives that fall outside the legal or ethical boundaries, this often triggers whistle-blowers to go public with information that can be highly damaging to the company. As the Ethics and Social Responsibility box shows, many different factors may motivate such whistle-blowers, but regardless of the motivation, the negative publicity and legal costs associated with organizations that are guilty of these kinds of breaches is significant. Indeed, the passage of the new Sarbanes-Oxley Corporate Reform Act seeks to protect these kinds of whistle-blowers, making it illegal for companies to threaten or harass them. This act requires organizations to establish internal procedures for hearing whistle-blower complaints, and any executive who is found to retaliate against a whistle-blower can be sentenced to up to ten years in a federal prison.[41]

Finally, the rational decision-making model assumes that one can evaluate the implemented alternative by checking the actual outcome against the initial intentions. In many contexts, this assumption simply does not hold. Most business situations are complex, and many factors other than the chosen alternative can influence the ultimate outcome. Thus the "right" choice may not invariably lead to the desired outcome. Such decision-making contexts, in which the link between actions and outcomes is tenuous and difficult to predict, are sometimes called noisy environments.

In noisy environments, we can make sense of action–outcome links only by making many observations of the same outcomes after the same actions. If one makes the same decision numerous times, noisy influences factor themselves out, and the true nature of the action–outcome link becomes clearer. Unfortunately, most decision makers in noisy environments fail to stick with one action long enough to sort out the effects of the chosen action from the effects of random influences. This lack of consistency in decision making means that the person moves from one action to another without ever learning much about the action–outcome link associated with any one specific action.[42]

Thus the rational decision-making model can provide helpful guidance in only a limited number of places. It may suggest how to structure routine decision making where everyone agrees on the desired outcomes and the best methods for attaining those outcomes, and where few outcomes and alternatives must be considered. Because the various factors may render the rational decision-making model less useful in many contexts, however, alternatives to the model have been suggested.

The Administrative Decision-Making Model

One of the most influential alternatives to the rational decision-making model is Herbert Simon's administrative decision-making model (Figure 4-4). Simon's model is intended to paint a more realistic picture of the way managers make most decisions.[43] According to Simon, the rational decision-making model may outline what managers *should* do, but the administrative model provides a better picture of what effective managers *actually* do when strict rationality is impossible. Simon's model differs from the rational model in several important ways.

One difference has to do with satisficing versus optimizing. According to Simon, *optimal* solutions require that the final decision be better than all other possible alternatives. For all the reasons discussed earlier, such optimality is simply not possible most of the time. Instead of striving for this impossible goal, organizations may try to find **satisficing** solutions to their problems. Satisficing means settling for the first alternative that seems to meet some minimum level of acceptability. Needless to say, it is much easier to achieve this goal than to strive for an optimal solution;

FIGURE 4-4 The Administrative Decision-Making Model

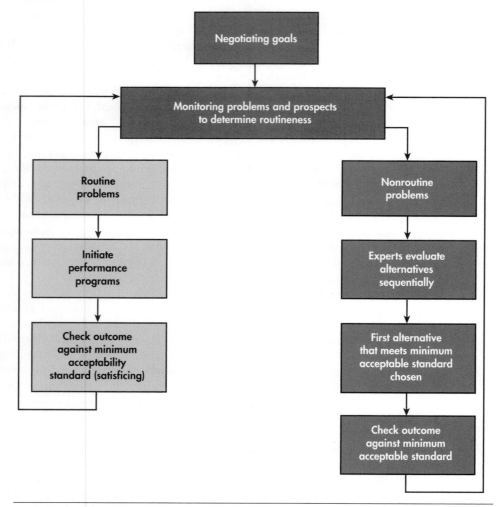

Source: Based on J. G. March and H.A. Simon, *Organizations* (New York: Wiley, 1958).

indeed, Simon evokes the comparison between finding a needle in a haystack (satisficing) and finding the biggest, sharpest needle in the haystack (optimizing).

In searching for satisficing solutions, managers further simplify the process by considering alternatives sequentially rather than simultaneously. Instead of first generating a list of all possible alternatives and then comparing and contrasting each alternative with all the others, the decision makers evaluate each alternative, one at a time, against the criteria for a satisficing outcome. The first satisfactory alternative identified in this way is chosen, and the manager moves on to other problems.

For example, a firm that needs to downsize by reducing its total number of employees faces more than a dozen options for accomplishing this objective. Rather than compare the expected results for every possible downsizing means with every other possible means, the firm's managers may simply consider initiating an early retirement program. If management implements such a program and it achieves the desired results, no further alternatives need be considered. If the plan does not work, some other reasonable alternative, like a hiring freeze, may be tried as well. If this course of action fails, it may be followed by yet another downsizing attempt, such as laying employees off according to seniority.

Reducing Decision-Making Errors

Given our knowledge about the limits to rationality, it is possible to identify many different means of reducing errors in decision making.

First, the main problem inherent in many decision-making biases (for example, loss aversion, availability bias, and base rate bias) is that the judges oversimplify information processing and take decision-making shortcuts. One good means of eliminating this problem is to provide decision makers with aids that will force them to ask all the right questions, get all the right information, and then process this information in all the right ways.

Computerized expert systems represent one excellent decision aid. These systems are typically developed by asking a team of experts, "How would you go about making such a decision?" and then recording every piece of information they request as well as the way in which they process those data. The interview findings are then turned into a computer program that performs the same function for a relatively naive decision maker, who is prompted to ask the right questions by the program itself. An expert system turns what was formerly a qualitative, subjective process into a more mechanical, objective process that has higher validity for making personnel selection decisions, for example.[44] The use of these kinds of systems is growing in organizations almost as fast as the adoption of computer technology itself. Although they will never replace the human decision maker, such systems may be instrumental in helping people overcome built-in judgment biases.

For example, Home Depot was having a difficult time fairly evaluating female candidates for traditionally masculine jobs. To solve this problem, the company developed an automated hiring and promotion system that helped managers ask the right questions and make decisions that had less adverse impact on women. Now when a Home Depot manager needs to make a hiring or promotion decision, the program offers a list of prescreened candidates as well as a set of interview questions, preferred answers, and advice to give the job seeker if that person lacks the right qualifications. This system has helped Home Depot develop a much more integrated workforce. Since its inception, the number of female managers has increased by 30 percent and the time required for managers to make such decisions has decreased. Similar types of expert systems for personnel selection and promotion have been developed at Target, Publix Supermarkets, and Hollywood Video.[45]

Even though expert systems may help simplify routine decision making, uncertainty in the environment makes it impossible to develop perfectly detailed scripts that will be applicable everywhere. At the highest level of any field, a need for discretion, or individual authority on the part of decision makers, persists. Consequently, organizations also need to hire or develop specialized areas of expertise that can be managed by one or more specialized staff members. The range of discretion of such experts tends to be limited to tightly defined areas, and the experts become the decision makers or internal consultants for different subareas. Using experts in decision making enables people with special expertise in an area to devise more accurate and more detailed scripts. In this way, complexity can be handled more effectively by being broken up into discrete, manageable chunks—jobs—that can be tackled by individuals working alone. The holder of an individual job typically focuses on one very narrow area of organizational problem solving. Of course, as we saw in our opening story, these experts may often disagree, as was the case when President Bush was receiving conflicting advice from the head of the Justice Department and the head of Homeland Security. The ability of the leader to accurately weigh different sources of information when rendering the group's judgment has repeatedly been found to be a critical factor in determining group decision-making accuracy.[46]

As noted earlier in the discussion of the perceptual process, chunking (breaking up jobs into small parts) reduces the burden on any one individual. Of course, each person's contribution must then be integrated with everyone else's contribution. Chunking does not change the fact that organization members are interdependent, and it is unrealistic to think that one expert can operate unaffected by others or that one set of programs can be activated independently of others. In integrating groups, the complexity of planning is greatly simplified by **loosely coupling** the different parts—that is, by weakening the effect that one subgroup has on another so that each subgroup can plan and operate almost as if the other were not present.

With respect to dynamic influences on decision making, one means of trying to minimize judgment errors caused by escalating commitment is to develop separate project development and project evaluation teams.[47] Because the evaluation team likely will not share the sense of ownership felt by the development team, this structure can eliminate many of the forces that can lead to feelings of psychological entrapment. It is also a good idea to initially set up goals, timetables, and reevaluation parameters that spell out under what conditions the project will be terminated. Establishing these parameters early makes later judgments more rational and coldly calculated. Once a project is begun, however, sunk costs may entice workers to inappropriately reevaluate the level of loss they are willing to risk.

CREATIVITY IN DECISION MAKING

One elusive quality essential to all decision making is creativity. Creative decisions consist of choices that are new and unusual but effective. Neither the rational nor the administrative decision-making model deals with the issue of producing creative decisions, nor does guarding against errors in group decision making necessarily guarantee that creativity will result. Indeed, some aspects of everything discussed in this chapter so far will make the generation of creative solutions to problems less—rather than more—likely. For example, strictly adhering to the demands of expert systems will rarely result in innovation. In this last section of the chapter, we emphasize the creativity process and describe how organizations can enhance creativity by selecting appropriate people or by managing in the appropriate fashion.

FIGURE 4-5 Steps in the Creative Decision-Making Process

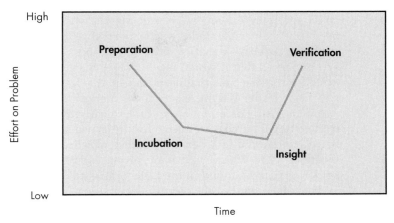

The Creative Process

Studies of people engaged in the creative process and examinations of the decision-making processes of people who are famous for their creativity suggest that a discernible pattern of events leads up to most innovative solutions. Most creative episodes can be broken down into four distinct stages: preparation, incubation, insight, and verification (Figure 4-5).

Contrary to what most people think, creative solutions to problems rarely come out of the blue.[48] More often than not, innovations are first sparked by a problem or perceived need. For example, despite having a Ph.D. from the California Institute of Technology, Henry Yuen struggled to program his videocassette recorder (VCR). During one of these struggles, Yuen realized that telephones would never have become so popular if a person had to type in a name, address, city, and state every time he or she needed to make a call. So why not develop a system for VCRs that was more like dialing a telephone? Along with Daniel Kwoh, Yuen invented a computer program that generated unique code numbers for television programs. Their software forms the core of the VCR Plus technology, and today the numbers generated by this program appear beside each listing in every *TV Guide* and television section of the newspaper.[49]

Because creative decision making resembles other decision-making processes in this way, it should not surprise you to learn that preparation, the first stage in the creative process, requires assembling materials. Analogous to the rational model's stage of generating alternatives, preparation is characterized by plain, old-fashioned hard work. In attempting to solve the problem, the creative person immerses himself or herself in existing solutions to the problem, usually to the point of saturation.

The second stage of creativity, incubation, differs greatly from steps in other decision-making models. Rather than reaching a decision immediately after assembling and evaluating relevant materials, creative decision makers enter a period during which they seem not to expend any visible effort on the problem. Sometimes out of frustration or sheer exhaustion they may stop working on the problem temporarily and turn to other things. Indeed, some have argued that if such a stage does not evolve naturally, it should be forced on decision-making groups if the goal is to arrive at a creative solution.[50]

After a person spends some time in the incubation stage, the solution to the problem typically manifests itself in a flash of inspiration, or insight. Usually, the person is engaged in some other task when this insight comes. For example, Howard

Wright invented a whistle that would work under water. After building three or four whistles for his skin-diving friends, Wright gave up on his invention because he could not figure out any large-scale market where it could be sold (since few people need to whistle while under water). Several years later, while being trained in emergency procedures on a cruise ship, Wright looked down at the whistle he was issued and remarked that it would never work once it got wet. At that moment, he recognized for the first time that his invention was less an underwater whistle than an all-weather whistle. Wright analyzed the market for whistles and found that the U.S. Army and Air Force alone purchased nearly 500,000 whistles per year. When he tracked down purchasing agents for the armed services, all reported that they would be very interested in a new all-weather whistle. Today, Wright's company, the All-Weather Safety Whistle Company, produces 10,000 whistles per week that retail for $5.95 and can be found in the L. L. Bean catalog.[51]

The fourth stage of the creative decision-making process is solution verification. In this step, the solution formulated in the insight stage is tested more rigorously to determine its usefulness for solving the problem. This stage in creative decision making closely resembles the rational decision-making model's evaluation stage. Typically, the verification process takes a long time. In fact, it resembles the preparation stage in the amount of hard work it requires. People often resist change, particularly if they have a large investment in traditional ideas and methods. They must be convinced, which is rarely possible without independent verification of the new approach.

Creative People

Certain characteristics of individuals seem to be associated with creative endeavors. First, a modest relationship appears to exist between creativity, general cognitive ability, and the specific capacities of reasoning and deduction. Indeed, some minimum threshold of intelligence seems to be necessary for creative work. Once that minimum threshold is reached, general intelligence becomes less critical and hard work is probably more important.

Personal characteristics such as interests, attitudes, and motivation are more important than intelligence in distinguishing creative people from the general population. Creative people generally set high goals for themselves, which may make them dissatisfied with the status quo and current solutions to problems. Indeed, dissatisfaction seems to be a general precursor to creative activity in that people are much more likely to be creative when they are in a bad mood, relative to a good mood.[52] Their high levels of aspiration may also explain why creative people often do not seem to feel loyalty to a particular employer but instead remain highly mobile, moving from company to company.[53] Like most valued commodities, creative talent is highly sought after. Thus a company may find it difficult to hold on to its creative people.

Some have suggested that the creative person is unusually persistent and has a high energy level. These characteristics are probably particularly useful in the stages of preparation and verification, which demand hard work carried out over long periods of time. Persistent people will stick with something despite encountering obstacles and setbacks, and people with a lot of energy can continue to work diligently for extended periods. This persistence is often fueled by strong perceptions of creative self-efficacy, and recent research has produced a new measure that specifically taps individual differences in this critical trait.[54]

Finally, age seems to be related to creativity. In a seminal study of people recognized for their creativity, one consistent finding was that regardless of the field in which the person did his or her work (the fields studied included mathematics, physics, biology, chemistry, medicine, music, painting, and sculpture), creativity peaked between ages 30 and 40.[55]

Creativity-Inducing Situations

Selecting people who have characteristics that seem to be related to creativity is not the only option for organizations that seek to increase their innovativeness. Providing specific and difficult goals and firm deadlines actually seems to stimulate creative achievement, as long as the deadlines are far enough into the future. If the deadlines are set too short, this can create time pressure that stifles creativity as people begin to look for the simplest and quickest solution rather than a more complex and creative solution.[56] In general, difficult goals seem to motivate people to think of non-traditional solutions, and lack of time pressure allows them to convert that motivation into effective action.[57]

Some firms even set goals for creativity. For instance, 3M has set a goal that 35 percent of its total revenues should come from new products developed in the past four years. Of course, focusing people on coming up with innovative techniques, as opposed to cranking out products with the existing technologies, sometimes comes at the expense of short-term productivity. For example, one of 3M's rules is that each employee should devote 15 percent of his or her time to reading and learning about recent developments that have nothing to do with the employee's primary project.[58]

In setting goals for creativity, the way in which these goals are framed is also important, in terms of whether one sets goals for incremental improvements or major revolutions. For example, John Pepper, CEO of Procter and Gamble (P&G), has recently argued that too much of P&G's money and scientific talent has been wasted on making minor improvements in existing products based on findings from focus groups and consumer surveys. Tide detergent has been "new and improved" more than sixty times. Most of these changes are not even truly improvements, but rather minor tailorings of products to specific market segments. Pepper notes, "If we spend our time working on small modifications to something, we won't have time to work on big new stuff." Pepper is interested in developing a smaller number of big-ticket innovations with a greater upside for growth. One such project is P&G's patented Olestra, a chemical ingredient that looks, tastes, and fries like a fat, albeit without the calories of a fat.[59]

Certain characteristics of organizational culture (see Chapter 14) may also be related to creativity.[60] First, the degree to which organizations recognize and reward creativity is of paramount importance. Many organizations, either unwittingly or knowingly, place more emphasis on following existing written rules and procedures than on experimenting with new procedures. A culture that promotes creativity must ensure not only that innovativeness is reinforced, but that experimentation leading to failure is not punished. Executives in these companies, like James Burke, CEO of Johnson & Johnson, attempt to create a climate where the risks of innovation are minimized. Burke, in fact, has even told his employees, "We won't grow unless you take risks. Any successful company is riddled with failures. There's just no other way to do it."[61]

Although they need not reward every failure, companies that seek to encourage innovation must lower the cost of conducting a "failed experiment." Employees need to know that risk taking is perceived as being worth making a few mistakes—especially if the size of the mistake is small and the damage can be contained. In addition, the importance of supportive leadership that does not overcontrol employees seems to be a key factor in translating creative talent into innovative products.[62]

Because much creativity comes out of collaborative efforts carried out by different individuals, organizations should promote internal diversity and work environments that enhance the opportunity to exchange ideas.[63] If all members of a group share the same interests, experiences, strengths, and weaknesses, they will be less likely to generate new ideas than if they have divergent backgrounds and capabilities.[64] For example, Lockheed's Skunk Works R&D subsidiary, which is famous for making several aerospace technological breakthroughs (such as the U-2 "Blackbird" spy planes and the F117A Stealth fighter plane), takes a team-based approach to production. Each team is headed by a manager with wide latitude in recruiting in-house specialists from an array of scientific and engineering backgrounds. The teams are isolated from Lockheed's sprawling bureaucracy but can have direct contact with their "customer" (the U.S. Department of Defense). In a time of shrinking defense budgets, the Skunk Works plant remains one of Lockheed's most profitable units. It achieves this goal only by continuously pushing the envelope of technological innovation.

Finally, because different organizations do different things in different places, exposing people to varying kinds of experiences, such as foreign assignments, professional development seminars, or extended leaves, may help shake up overly routine decision-making processes. The notion that difference and variety encourage creative thinking receives some support from the finding that organizations that emphasize external recruiting seem to be more innovative than firms that promote from within.[65] Of course, organizations should not completely abandon promote-from-within policies. They should, however, recognize that mixing new and long-tenured employees can foster a climate of creativity.

SUMMARY

A thorough understanding of the perceptual process by which people encode and make sense out of the complex world around them is critical to those who would manage organizational behavior. The very existence of perceptual illusions proves that what we perceive is not always a very close approximation of objective reality. At the *attention stage* of the perceptual process, we select a small subset of all information available for subsequent processing. The degree to which any stimulus attracts our attention is a complex function of characteristics of the object and of ourselves. At the *organization stage* of the information-processing cycle, information is simplified. We convert complex behavioral sequences into *scripts* and represent people by *prototypes*. A number of biases, including *stereotyping*, can creep into this complex process.

In the decision-making process, we use the information from the perceptual process to evaluate an object, person, or event. This evaluation, once made, affects our decisions, behaviors, and subsequent perceptions. Many features of people and situations need to be considered when trying to increase the accuracy and creativity of decision making.

REVIEW QUESTIONS

1. List a set of traits that would make up the prototype for a terrorist, a hippie, an absent-minded professor, and a card-carrying member of the American Civil Liberties Union. Recalling Chapter 3, is your list dominated by ability or personality characteristics? What kinds of abilities or personality characteristics are most heavily represented? What does this exercise tell you about how prototypes are developed and in what ways they are most likely to be accurate?

2. Sometimes the same behavioral episode in an organization—for example, a fight among co-workers, a botched work assignment, or an ineffective meeting—can be organized perceptually along the lines of either a script or a prototype. How might the choice of schema affect what occurs later in the process of interpretation or judgment?

3. Escalation of commitment to a failing course of action has been widely researched, and it is easy to think of many examples of this kind of mistake. The flip side of this mistake, however, is giving up too soon, which has not been studied as much and for which it is more difficult to think of examples. Why can't we recall such events? How might researchers in this area be victims of availability bias?

4. Compare and contrast the decision-making process associated with rational decision making, administrative decision making, and creative decision making. At what points do these three descriptions of decision making diverge most? What implications does this divergence have for decision makers who attempt to follow the wrong model?

5. Suppose that managerial jobs can be distinguished by the kinds of decision-making processes required. For example, some jobs call for rational decision making, others require administrative decision making, and still others require creative decision making. If you were a recruiter, what personal characteristics would you seek when staffing each kind of position? Do you think one individual could be equally adept at all three kinds of processes? If so, what characteristics would this person display?

LEARNING THROUGH EXPERIENCE

DIAGNOSTIC QUESTIONS 4-1

Perception and Judgment

The following questions are designed to help you diagnose perceptual problems in analyzing both the case studies in this book and on-the-job problems now or in the future.

1. On whose perceptions do you rely to describe and diagnose organizational problems? How might the choice of this person affect the description and diagnosis provided?

2. What kinds of expectations do you have for people or objects that you need to evaluate? How might these expectations affect your judgment?

3. What are some major events in your organization that you think of in terms of scripts? How might your version of these scripts differ from others' views?

4. What are some major prototypes that exist for people in the organization? How accurate are these prototypes?

5. What stereotypes do you hold of people from particular social groups in the organization? Are these stereotypes accurate?

6. Do you keep external records of important past events, or do you rely exclusively on your own memory for important information?

7. Do you take the point of view of a judge or of a witness when evaluating others? How might each view affect your judgments?

8. How are your present judgments influenced by judgments that you or others have made in the past?

9. Which of the many ways to manage perceptual problems and increase perceptual accuracy are most practical for the organization?

10. Does the organization have clear goals and objectives, so that analytical solutions can be developed? Or is the organization characterized by a lack of goal consensus, thus requiring a bargaining solution?

11. When deciding on a course of action, does the organization tend to rely more on past practice or on experimentation?

12. Does the organization employ experts? Does it use them successfully, through loose coupling, and integrate them with other members of its own staff?

EXERCISE 4-1   **Judgment, Heuristics, and Biases**

Ariel S. Levi, Wayne State University
Larry E. Mainstone, University of Michigan, Flint

Managers often work under complex, changing circumstances that require rapid and accurate judgment. They must constantly process information, diagnose problems, think creatively, and develop solutions under conditions of substantial uncertainty. Technical aids like computerized information systems and visual planning charts can be helpful, but they cannot substitute for human judgment.

In making judgments of all kinds, managers often violate some fundamental laws of logic and probability. This violation occurs because humans use heuristics—mental strategies—for processing information and reaching judgments. Heuristics are really rules of thumb. For example, a common heuristic is, When it is cloudy, carry an umbrella. Heuristics can produce accurate results. If it rains, you will be glad you have the umbrella. On the other hand, they can also bias judgment processes. If you carry an umbrella and it does not rain, you will not be quite so happy. The biases discussed in this chapter—loss aversion, availability, and base rate—are all rooted in the use of heuristics.

This exercise focuses on judgment processes in which people collect and mentally combine information to make estimates and evaluations of people, objects, and events. To make you more aware of heuristic biases and to stimulate class discussion about how to control their effects, we will show you how several heuristics work and how they influence human judgment processes.

Step One: Pre-Class Preparation

To prepare for class, read this entire exercise and then write down your responses to the four problems that follow. Try your hardest to come up with the best answer to each one. The first problem will be familiar to you, as it was discussed in this chapter.

1. A cab company was involved in a hit-and-run accident at night. Two cab companies, the Green Company and the Blue Company, operate in the city. You have the following information:
   a. Eighty-five percent of the cabs in the city are Green and 15 percent are Blue.

Adapted from "A Group-Based Procedure for Revealing Judgmental Heuristics and Biases" by Arial S. Levi and L. E. Mainstone in *Organizational Behavior Teaching Review*, 10 (1985), 9–24. Reprinted by permission of the author.

   b. A witness identified the vehicle as a Blue cab. The court tested her ability to identify cabs under night visibility conditions. When presented with a sample of cabs (half Blue and half Green), the witness made correct identifications in 80 percent of the cases and erred in 20 percent.

   Question: The probability that a Blue cab was involved in the accident is _____ percent.

2. Bill is 34 years old. He is intelligent, compulsive, unimaginative, and sedentary. In school, he was strong in mathematics but weak in science and social studies. Rank the following statements in order of their probability of being correct, using 1 for the most probable and 8 for the least probable.
   __ a. Bill is a physician who plays poker for a hobby.
   __ b. Bill is an architect.
   __ c. Bill is an accountant.
   __ d. Bill plays jazz for a hobby.
   __ e. Bill surfs for a hobby.
   __ f. Bill is a television reporter.
   __ g. Bill is an accountant who plays jazz for a hobby.
   __ h. Bill climbs mountains for a hobby.

3. In an average year in the United States, do more people die of fire or drowning? Circle the letter that indicates your answer:
   a. Fire
   b. Drowning
   c. About the same

4. Many professional athletes believe that to be pictured on the cover of *Sports Illustrated* is bad luck because the athlete's performance is likely to decline during the weeks and months afterward. Do you think there is any basis for this belief? If so, what is it?

   _____

   _____

   _____

Step Two: Comparing Individual and Group Answers

The class should divide into groups containing four to six members. If you have previously formed permanent groups, you should assemble in those same groups. In each group, begin by discussing the four problems just presented and reach agreement on an answer for each one. Next, compare your group's answers with those you and other members reached working alone. Select a spokesperson to compile this information and prepare a brief presentation for the entire class. The spokesperson should discuss similarities and differences among individual responses to each question, the group's response to each question, and the way the group reached agreement. For example, did the group take a majority vote or was it persuaded by one dominant individual?

Step Three: Group Presentations and Discussion

The spokespeople should take no more than five minutes each to report their groups' results. The class should try to uncover reasons for any differences between individual responses and group agreements and for any dissimilarities among different groups' responses.

Next, your instructor will reveal the best answers for the four questions and discuss the heuristics and biases that the problems illustrate.

Step Four: Group Judgment Tasks

Once everyone understands the heuristics and biases discussed in Step Three, the judgment groups should reconvene and choose the best answer to each of the following four problems.

1. As of 1985, approximately what percentage of the male working-age population in Japan was guaranteed lifetime employment? _____ percent

2. Film critics have noted that sequels like *Home Alone II* or *Star Wars: Episode I* are usually of lower quality than their predecessor films. Sequels are usually financially less successful as well. Critics sometimes accuse the film studios of trying to "milk" a good idea. Do you think this criticism is valid and, if so, how do you explain the phenomenon?

   _____

   _____

3. A panel of psychologists has interviewed and administered personality tests to thirty engineers and seventy lawyers, all successful in their fields. The following is one of the descriptions written about these 100 people, based on the results of the tests.

   Joan is a forty-five-year-old woman. She is married and has four children. She is generally conservative, careful, and ambitious. She shows no interest in political or social issues and spends most of her time on her many hobbies, which include camping, sailing, and mathematical puzzles.

   Question: The probability that Joan is an engineer is _____ percent.

4. Rank the following events in order of their probability of occurrence this year, using 1 for the most probable and 4 for the least probable.
   __ a. The industrial midwest will gain in economic strength.
   __ b. The industrial midwest will decline in economic strength.
   __ c. The fortunes of the major U.S. automakers will improve.
   __ d. While the fortunes of the major U.S. automakers will improve, the industrial midwest will decline in economic strength because of the continued exodus of companies to the Sun Belt.

   After reaching agreement on how to answer the four problems, each group should appoint a spokesperson to report the group's four answers and describe how they were reached.

Step Five: Group Reports and Class Discussion

After each spokesperson has presented his or her report and the class has discussed similarities and differences between the groups' answers, your instructor will reveal the best answers and discuss relevant heuristics and biases. The class should then discuss the problems raised by heuristics and biases, paying special attention to the following questions:

1. Some people will not admit they have biases. Others react defensively when their biases are pointed out. Are biases a sign of abnormality? Of low intelligence? Of not trying hard enough to reach an accurate judgment?

2. Are group judgments generally more accurate than individual judgments? Or can groups impair accuracy? What factors might determine whether groups improve or impair accuracy?

3. What real-world organizational examples illustrate each of the biases you learned about in this exercise? Do any of these examples show the effects of more than one bias?

4. Businesses sometimes make monumental errors, as exemplified by NASA's decisions to launch *Challenger* despite warnings from the space shuttle's designer and to orbit the Hubble Space Telescope without adequately checking the focus of its mirrors. Based on what you have learned from this exercise, what advice would you give to organizations like NASA to help avoid similar mistakes in the future?

Conclusion

Managers need to learn about heuristics and biases for several reasons. First, heuristic-based biases are pervasive. They affect many organizational phenomena, ranging from performance appraisal to strategic planning. Second, because these biases often operate unconsciously, neither intelligence, expertise, or motivation to be accurate can protect us against them. Once we become aware of these biases, however, we can learn to step back each time and ask ourselves whether one or more biases have led us to misdiagnose a problem, make a poor decision, or fail to respond effectively to a crisis or opportunity. As management tasks become more complicated and challenging, bias-free managerial judgment becomes increasingly important.

CHAPTER 5

A Model of Motivation and Performance
Expectancy Theory
Supplemental Theories
Overview of the Model

Valence: Need Theories
Maslow's Need Hierarchy
Murray's Theory of Manifest Needs

Instrumentality: Learning Theories
Reinforcement Theory
Social Learning

Expectancy: Self-Efficacy Theory
Self-Efficacy and Behavior
Sources of Self-Efficacy

Accuracy of Role Perceptions: Goal-Setting Theory
Important Goal Attributes
Goal Commitment and Participation
Goals and Strategies

Ability and Experience Revisited
Nonmotivational Determinants of Performance
Experience and Cyclical Effects

High-Performance Work Systems
Merit-Pay and Incentive Systems
Profit-Sharing and Cost-Savings Plans

Work Motivation and Performance

Summary
Review Questions

Learning through Experience
Diagnostic Questions 5-1: Diagnosing Situations Where Motivation Is a Problem
Exercise 5-1: Motivation through Pay Raise Allocation

It seemed like such a simple idea. In order to motivate people to work harder and direct their efforts in the interests of shareholders, why not tie their outcomes to the outcomes of shareholders via stock options? In a traditional stock option plan, an anniversary date is established and the price of the company's stock on that day (for example, $25) is recorded. The employee is then given the option to buy the stock at that price in the future. If the stock price rises over time (for example, it goes up to $30), then the employee can purchase it at the old price, thus deriving an immediate payoff that is directly attributed to the organization's good fortune. Scott McNealy, CEO of Sun Microsystems, was speaking for many when he stated, "Stock options are an incredible mechanism to get employees, management, and shareholders all aligned."[1] What could possibly be wrong with this simple idea? Turns out: plenty.

The 1990s witnessed an explosion of stock options programs, and when the economy went bust at the end of the decade, many wound up laying some of the blame at this type of compensation practice, especially when it became clear that they played such a large role in many of the scandals at companies such as Enron, Qwest, and Global Crossing. Many politicians thought that laws should be passed to eliminate, restrict, or otherwise amend these kinds of programs in order to protect shareholders, employees, and the economic health of the society at large. As one commentator put it, "Stock options seem to have replaced money itself, as 'the root of all evil.'"[2] Given the apparent simplicity of this motivational scheme, what went so wrong that the U.S. Congress felt they might have to step in and halt this practice?

First, many critics felt that the goal associated with most stock option plans was too easily met, in that it usually required only that the stock value go up for recipients to derive value from the option. This meant that if the stock market rose across the board, everyone got rich, even if in a relative sense the stock of the organization in question rose less than that of all of the competing companies in its own industry. In addition, some companies engaged in "repricing," which meant if the stock went down, the price of the option was lowered also, which meant that people were not punished in any way if performance was poor.[3]

Second, in addition to companies' using repricing to limit the downside risk, many people held options, but no actual stock in the company they worked for, and thus did not share the pain of investors if the organization fared poorly. For example, although Apple Computer's Steve Jobs owns $22 million worth of options, he owns only two shares of the company, and a similar situation exists with many other top executives. Since an option, unlike a real share, requires no investment on the part of the holder, this means that unlike real shareholders, the option holder does not have any of his or her own money on the line.[4]

Third, in addition to options' being too easy and risk-free, many felt that organizations distributed options poorly, granting too many options to a few select people at the top, and not sufficiently distributing them among the rank and file. For example, research has established that 30 percent of all stock options granted by U.S. corporations went to the top five executives at each company, and that 65 percent of the remaining options were held by 5 percent of the employees, all of whom were top-level executives. This means that the rank and file holds only 5 percent of the options. This is problematic because research has established a clear link between lower-level employee ownership and shareholder returns, whereas the evidence for the link between shareholder returns and the level of CEO pay is equivocal at best.[5]

Fourth, probably because options did not have to be treated as a normal expense like salary, organizations simply gave away too many options, well beyond what might be needed to motivate anyone. For example, Oracle's Larry Ellison was awarded $10 million in options in order to "more closely align his compensation with the company's stock performance." However, unlike Jobs, Ellison owned real shares of his company, and had as much as $10 billion worth of his own money tied to the stock's performance already.[6] Given his standing with real shares, was his day-to-day motivation level really likely to be affected by the options, or was the board of directors simply giving these away without a great deal of reflection?

Finally, and perhaps most pointedly, because of the large value associated with stock options, it simply became too tempting for those at the top to "cook the books" and manipulate the short-term value of the stock price for their own benefit. In many ways, the outcomes of powerful option holders were not truly aligned *because the option holders had control over operations, and inside knowledge about when it would be advantageous to sell. Enron's Ken Lay, Global Crossing's Gary Winnick, and Qwest Communications' Joe Nacchio sold stock and executed options worth millions of dollars just weeks before their companies collapsed.[7] They sold this tainted stock to regular shareholders who did not share this kind of inside information about the stock's immediate future. Shareholders' portfolios were crushed when these companies failed, but the top management team escaped unscathed—totally discrediting the argument that their interests were "aligned" with the shareholders.*

One way for an organization to gain a competitive advantage over its rivals is to generate a more motivated workforce. **Motivation** refers to the energy a person is willing to devote to a task. A person who is highly motivated will start work sooner and leave work later relative to someone is unmotivated. While engaged at work, a highly motivated person will work faster, take fewer breaks, and be less easily distracted relative to someone who is motivated. A person who is highly motivated will go out of his or her way to learn new things to improve future performance and help co-workers when the workload within the group gets unbalanced. Managers who can create high levels of motivation can get more work out of five people than their less inspiring counterparts can get out of ten, and this is a form of competitive advantage that is hard to deny.

One way to try to create motivation is through rewards. Perhaps the easiest thing to say to a manager, *in theory,* is that he or she should "pay for performance" or "link rewards to accomplishment." Perhaps the most difficult thing to do, *in practice,* is to implement this advice in a manner that does not backfire. As we saw in the opening story, although it might seem at first glance that stock options are a means of "paying for performance," when put into practice, this simple idea often results in a number of complicated and unexpected side effects that result in outcomes that are almost diametrically opposed to what was originally intended. Instead of aligning the interests of workers and shareholders, these kinds of programs became a way for a subset of workers in top management positions to rob shareholders and damage the reputations and prospects of all the other workers in the organization.

We will return to this example from time to time in this chapter to illustrate certain points regarding the motivation process and how it can go wrong, even by those who start out with the best intentions. Although the problems with stock options may seem like a new and unique case of a motivation system gone bad, in fact, the history of management is littered with motivational interventions that sound good and simple in theory, but then get "gamed" by experienced and sophisticated employees who do not always have the best interests of shareholders, co-workers, or management at heart.

The purpose of this chapter is to introduce and discuss the topic of worker motivation and performance. Given the centrality of creating and maintaining high levels of motivation, it should come as no surprise that many, many theories deal with this topic. Indeed, the sheer number of theories of motivation that exist can sometimes obscure rather than promote understanding and application. Indeed, the complexity of this issue sometimes drives confused managers toward, rather than away from, fads and overly simplistic approaches that promise so much and then deliver so little.

We will try to avoid this problem in two ways. First, rather than try to comprehensively cover every theory of motivation, we will focus our attention on a subset of five theories: expectancy theory, need theory, learning theory, self-efficacy theory, and goal-setting theory. Second, we will develop an overarching model to clarify how the theories relate to each other and to show how each specific theory is best for describing a certain aspect of the overall motivation process. This model describes four concrete steps that need to be taken in order to motivate people, and thus specifically addresses how to apply what we have learned from research on these theories in real organizational contexts. Managers who learn and apply this model can take four steps forward in their attempts to gain competitive advantage in product and labor markets.

A MODEL OF MOTIVATION AND PERFORMANCE

Expectancy Theory

The model of motivation developed in this chapter is an elaboration of Vroom's *expectancy theory,* particularly as it was extended by Porter and Lawler.[8] Expectancy theory is a broad theory of motivation that attempts to explain the determinants of workplace attitudes and behaviors.[9] Three major components underlie expectancy theory: the concepts of *v*alence, *i*nstrumentality, and *e*xpectancy (sometimes collectively known as *VIE* theory).

The concept of **valence** is based on the assumption that at any given time, a person prefers certain outcomes to others. Valence measures the attraction that a given outcome holds for an individual, or the satisfaction that the person anticipates receiving from a particular outcome. Outcomes can have positive, negative, or zero valence. An outcome has a positive valence when a person would rather attain it than not attain it. When a person is indifferent to attaining an outcome, that outcome is assigned a valence of zero. If a person prefers *not* to attain the outcome, the outcome is said to have a negative valence. For example, in the opening vignette, raising the stock price of the company was something that had a great deal of valence to many top executives who were holding large quantities of options, and this motivated their behavior in a number of directions, not all of which were in the best long-term interests of shareholders.

From a motivational perspective, it is important to distinguish between valence and value. *Valence* refers to *anticipated* satisfaction. *Value* represents the *actual* satisfaction a person experiences from attaining a desired outcome. With experience, someone might discover that a discrepancy exists between the anticipated satisfaction from an outcome (its valence) and the actual satisfaction that it provides (its value).[10] When this disparity occurs, a reward may eventually lose its motivational value. For example, if a person comes to believe that "money cannot buy happiness," then the motivational values of financial incentives may quickly wane.

Instrumentality is a person's belief about the relationship between performing an action and experiencing an outcome. It is sometimes referred to as a *performance-outcome expectation*. Determining a person's instrumentalities is important because that individual will likely have a strong desire to perform a particular action only when both valence and instrumentality are perceived as high. Thus, to understand motivation, we need to know more than the satisfaction an individual expects as the consequence of attaining a particular outcome—we need to know what the person believes he or she must do to obtain or avoid that outcome. If a corporate executive believes that fraudulent accounting practices will raise the price of the stock, he or she may become motivated to engaging in this type of behavior. On the other hand, if this same person believes that he or she will be arrested and placed in prison for this action, then he or she may search for other means of raising the stock price.

The third element of expectancy theory is the concept for which the theory is named: expectancy. **Expectancies** are beliefs about the link between making an effort and actually performing well. Whereas knowledge about valences and instrumentalities tells us what an individual *wants to do,* we cannot anticipate what the individual will *try to do* without knowing the person's expectancies. For example, even if a middle manager in a large corporation is holding a large set of options, this person may not believe that extra levels of effort on his or her part are likely to affect something as distant as the stock price. That is, even though there is a clear *performance–outcome linkage* (instrumentality) between raising the stock price and enhancing the value of his or her personal portfolio, the manager may not believe that he or she can do anything that will affect the stock price. This means that there is a weak *effort–performance linkage* (expectancy). Even if the manager came in and did extra work on the weekend fifty-two times a year, would this really impact the company's stock price? If the answer to this question is no, then the motivational value of the stock options for this person is not very strong.

Thus expectancy theory defines motivation in terms of desire and effort, whereby the achievement of desired outcomes results from the interaction of valences, instrumentalities, and expectancies. Desire arises only when both valence and instrumentality are high, and effort comes about only when all three aspects are high.

Supplemental Theories

Two primary reasons explain why, to build a model of motivation and performance, we need to supplement expectancy theory with other motivation theories.

First, a number of other theories deal in much more detail with certain specific components of motivation. As a consequence, they help to elaborate on expectancy theory. *Need theories* provide important insights into how valences develop and how they can change over time. *Learning theories* explain how perceptions of instrumentality arise. *Self-efficacy theory* describes the origins of effort–performance expectancies and the ways in which they are maintained.

Second, expectancy theory must be extended to explain outcomes other than desire and effort. To predict performance, expectancy theory requires information about human ability, goals, and strategies.

For these reasons, along with expectancy theory, our model will incorporate ideas from the need, learning, self-efficacy, and goal-setting theories.

Overview of the Model

The model of motivation and performance built in this chapter consists of *five components* put together in *four steps* to explain *three outcomes.* Figure 5-1 presents this model graphically; it serves as a road map for the remainder of this chapter.

One component (abilities) was explained in Chapter 3 and will be touched on only briefly here. Three other components are valence, instrumentality, and expectancy. These have already been defined, but we will elaborate on each using need, learning, and self-efficacy theories. The final component is accuracy of role perceptions, particularly as described via goal-setting theory.

FIGURE 5-1   A Diagnostic Model of Motivation and Performance

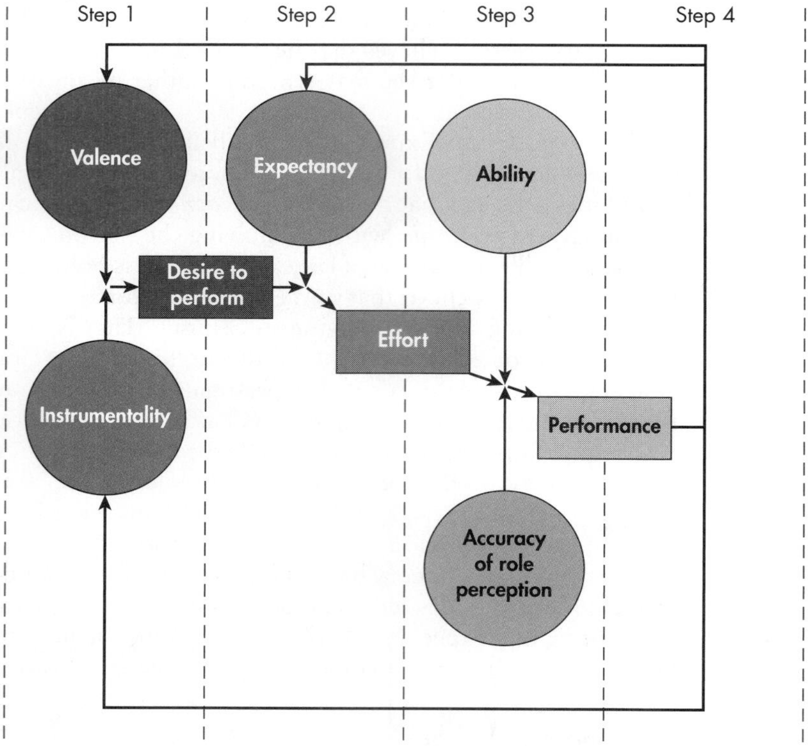

VALENCE: NEED THEORIES

People differ greatly in their personal preferences. For example, a recent study of MBAs found that the relationship between changing jobs and getting higher salaries was strong and positive among white males, but close to zero among women and minorities.[11] White males tended to place a high value on pay and would change employers only if some higher level of compensation was offered. In contrast, women and minorities were more likely to change employers for other reasons; they did not use pay as the single overarching factor driving their mobility. Thus the different valences of these groups can help explain their different behaviors.

The goal for employers is to find exactly what drives each employee and then, as far as possible, build reward systems around these drives, taking advantage of each person's unique sets of interest and values. In fact, this process is getting so sophisticated that new statistical modeling software is available to track and exploit the different values people have, so that employers can tailor the money spent on human resources in ways that maximize their motivational value. For example, one worker may prefer to receive compensation in the form of retirement support, whereas another may prefer health care coverage; innovative software programs are available that support organizational efforts at customizing their reward systems to the idiosyncratic value systems of each employee.[12] When it comes to understanding how valences originate and why they differ among people, need theories can prove especially informative.

FIGURE 5-2   Maslow's Need Hierarchy

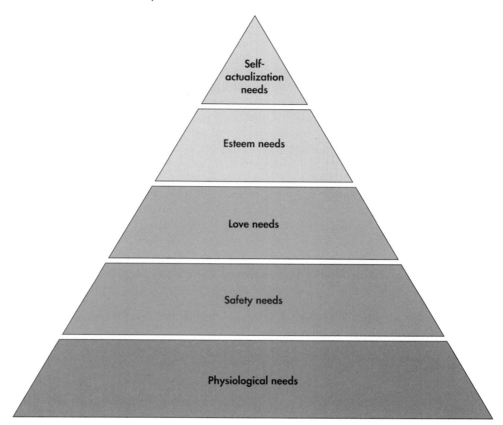

Maslow's Need Hierarchy

Abraham Maslow was a clinical psychologist and a pioneer in the development of need theories. In Maslow's day, little existed in the way of empirical, scientific studies of motivation. He based his own theory on twenty-five years of experience in treating individuals with varying degrees of psychological health. Based on this experience, Maslow's need theory proposed the existence of five distinct types of needs: physiological, safety, love, esteem, and self-actualization. These needs, according to Maslow, are genetically based and characteristic of all humans. Moreover, he argued, these five needs are arranged in the hierarchy shown in Figure 5-2 and influence motivation on the basis of need **prepotency.** Prepotency means that needs residing higher in the hierarchy can influence motivation only if needs residing lower in the hierarchy are already largely satisfied.

At the lowest level of Maslow's need hierarchy are physiological needs such as hunger and thirst. According to Maslow, these physiological needs possess the greatest initial prepotency. Once these needs have been mostly gratified, however, they no longer serve as strong motivating elements. Under these conditions, second-level safety needs increase in importance. Safety needs relate to the acquisition of objects and relationships that protect their possessor from future threats, especially threats to the person's ability to satisfy his or her physiological needs.

If both physiological and safety needs are mostly fulfilled, love needs become prepotent. Maslow used the term *love* in a broad sense to refer to preferences for affection from others as well as a sense of community or belongingness. The need for friends, family, and colleagues falls within this category.

At the fourth level in Maslow's need hierarchy are esteem needs. Maslow grouped two distinct kinds of esteem within this category. Social esteem consists of the respect, recognition, attention, and appreciation of others. Self-esteem reflects an individual's own feelings of personal adequacy. Consequently, esteem needs can be satisfied partly from external sources and partly from internal sources.

The last set of needs, at the top of Maslow's hierarchy, comprises self-actualization needs. According to Maslow, if all needs beneath self-actualization are fulfilled, a person can be considered generally satisfied. In Maslow's words, self-actualization "might be phrased as the desire to become more and more what one is, to become everything that one is capable of becoming."[13] Unlike all the other needs identified by Maslow, self-actualization needs can never be fully satisfied. Hence, the picture of human motivation drawn by this theory emphasizes constant striving as well as constant deprivation of one sort or another.

Perhaps owing to its simplicity, Maslow's need theory has gained wide acceptance among managers and management educators. Maslow failed to provide researchers with clear-cut measures of his concepts, however, and his theory has not received much empirical support.[14] It holds interest for us primarily because of its place in history as one of the earliest motivation models and as a precursor to more modern theories of motivation.

Murray's Theory of Manifest Needs

Henry Murray's theory of manifest needs defines needs as recurrent concerns for particular goals or end states.[15] Each need consists of two components: the object toward which the need is directed (for example, achievement or autonomy) and the intensity or strength of the need for that particular object (for example, strong versus weak). Murray proposed more than twenty needs, several of which are described in Table 5-1.

Because Murray's needs are not arranged in any hierarchical fashion, the theory offers considerable flexibility. Unlike Maslow, Murray held that an individual could be motivated by more than one need simultaneously, and he also suggested that needs could sometimes conflict with each other. Also unlike Maslow, who viewed needs as innate and genetically determined, Murray regarded needs as something people learned from interacting with their environment.

Other researchers later extended and expanded Murray's work on need theories. Most notably, David McClelland developed a theory of motivation that focused particularly on the need for achievement.[16] According to McClelland, people can be characterized as either high or low on the need for achievement (nAch). Those who are high in nAch prefer situations in which they have the opportunity to take personal responsibility. These individuals also prefer to receive personal credit for the consequences of their actions and clear and unambiguous feedback about personal performance. According to McClelland, the key to workplace motivation is to find high-nAch individuals (or raise the levels of low-nAch individuals through training) and expose them to situations conducive to fulfilling the need for achievement.

For example, Microsoft is well known for selecting individuals who have high intelligence and a high need for achievement. To make this strategy truly effective, however, the company must tie the person's perceptions of self-worth and achievement to task accomplishment—often expressed in terms of creating marketable products. As one insider notes, "Creativity is highly regarded at Microsoft for a

TABLE 5-1
Some of
Murray's
Manifest
Needs

Achievement	To do one's best, to be successful, to accomplish tasks requiring skill and effort, to be a recognized authority, to accomplish something important, to do a difficult job well
Deference	To get suggestions from others, to find out what others think, to follow instructions and do what is expected, to praise others, to accept leadership of others, to conform to custom
Order	To keep things neat and orderly, to make advance plans, to organize details of work, to have things arranged so they run smoothly without change
Autonomy	To be able to come and go as desired, to say what one thinks about things, to be independent of others in making decisions, to do things without regard for what others may think
Affiliation	To be loyal to friends, to participate in friendly groups, to form strong attachments, to share things with friends, to write letters to friends, to make as many friends as possible
Dominance	To argue for one's point of view, to be a leader in groups to which one belongs, to persuade and influence others, to supervise and direct the actions of others
Nurturance	To help friends when they are in trouble, to treat others with kindness and sympathy, to forgive others and do favors for them, to show affection and have others confide in one
Change	To do new and different things, to travel, to meet new people, to have novelty and change in daily routine, to try new and different jobs, to participate in new fads and fashions
Endurance	To keep at a job until it is finished, to work hard at a task, to work at a single job before taking on others, to stick to a problem even though no apparent progress is being made
Aggression	To attack contrary points of view, to tell others off, to get revenge for insults, to blame others when things go wrong, to criticize others publicly, to read accounts of violence

Source: Based on H. A. Murray, *Explorations in Personality* (New York: Oxford University Press, 1938), pp. 152–205.

short period of time, but that is not how people really rank each other. The primary thing is to ship a product. Until you have done that—you're suspect. It involves taking this passion of yours and running it through a humiliating, exhausting process."[17] When people who rate high in their need for achievement are personally challenged in this fashion, they are no longer being driven by the money, but instead are driven by more intrinsic rewards and punishments. The ability to shift away from purely financial inducements is particularly important in an economy where money is tight. Indeed, as the Securing Competitive Advantage Box shows, employers are increasingly trying to lower their labor costs, which in turn restricts the degree to which they can reward top performers with pay raises. Organizations risk losing their top performers if they cannot come up with alternatives to pay as a means of motivating their workforce.[18]

INSTRUMENTALITY: LEARNING THEORIES

The understanding of valence contributed by need theories provides only one piece of the motivational puzzle—what people want. To understand behavior, we need to know not just what people want, but what they believe will lead to the attainment of what they want. As noted earlier, these beliefs are referred to as *instrumentalities*. Learning theories help clarify how relationships between behaviors and rewards

SECURING COMPETITIVE ADVANTAGE

A NEW REWARD FOR TOP PERFORMERS: PINK SLIPS

Like a trip to the principal's office, when your boss tells you to come to an emergency meeting first thing in the morning, it can be a little disconcerting. This is especially the case when you know that your company is experiencing some financial problems. Thus, Robert Wood, a veteran salesperson at the Circuit City store in Jensen Beach, Florida, was reassured to see that he was not the only person called in, but instead was part of a group that included all the top salespeople at the Jensen Beach store. His relief was short-lived, however, when he and the rest of the group were fired in the span of five minutes. The reason for their dismissal was not poor attendance or poor performance or any deficiency in their work. They were also not part of a wider downsizing effort; in fact, the company intended to replace them that day. The reason they were fired is simply that they were the highest-paid employees of the store, and all of those had to go. The irony was that Circuit City had relied heavily on commissions up to that point, and thus the reason these individuals were the highest-paid employees was that they were also the highest performers. Said Woods: "We didn't see that coming."

Perhaps they should have. Exchanging expensive labor with lower-paid workers is becoming an increasingly common practice. This is especially true in the retail industry, where the pressure to reduce prices in order to stay competitive is high, but unlike the manufacturing industry, there are few opportunities to automate the work or move jobs overseas. Since most retailers are not unionized, there is no collective bargaining unit to protect them, and the approach is generally legal, because there is no law written to protect high-wage workers. Moreover, in a weak economy and slow labor market, there was no shortage of people who were willing to do the job Woods was doing for $40,000 for roughly half of that. Circuit City expected to save $130 million by the move, desperately hoping that it could make them more competitive. Circuit City, which once had annual revenues that were twice as large as Best Buy, recently saw that lead erode to the point where it had annual revenues that were half of those of Best Buy. Unlike Circuit City, Best Buy employed a strategy of using a noncommissioned sales force.

Although labor swapping is one means of reducing costs, organizations have also begun using another unprecedented tactic—yearly wage cuts. Historically, most workers looked forward to end-of-year raises, and although there was sometimes variation between individuals based upon performance, even the lowest performers achieved some small gains. Tod Raphaely, the European sales manager for Ralton Electronics, epitomizes the new two-way traffic when it comes to pay adjustments. Raphaely took a 10 percent pay cut in the fall of 2001, and then another 10 percent cut that spring. He was hoping to just weather the storm, but then in the fall of 2002, he had to take yet another cut of 20 percent. This is far from an isolated example; across the U.S. economy, median weekly earnings adjusted for inflation fell 1.5 percent in the first three months of 2003—the biggest drop in more than twelve years. In the words of one contemporary manager, "When you can show me you are more productive and can deliver a higher level of service, the raises will be there, but they will not be automatic."

Another alternative in the race to the bottom for labor costs is to keep pay constant but increase the number of hours people work for the same salary. This is a common practice in workplaces where there is a downsizing of labor, but no reduction in the work that needs to done. Those lucky enough to avoid the layoff are often reclassified from hourly workers into salaried employees, who are ineligible for overtime pay (a move that under some conditions is illegal). This is not exactly that promotion to management that most workers are looking for. As a result of this type of reclassification and the general push to do more with less, the percentage of professional white-collar workers who reported working more than fifty hours a week reached nearly 20 percent in 2002, the highest figure ever recorded by the Bureau of Labor Statistics.

In an increasingly global economy, where labor and products move seamlessly across borders, low costs are going to be a key to organizational survival and competitiveness. Because employee pay is a substantial portion of costs, these changes in the competitive landscape mean that there is going to be a continued downward pressure on wages that is unlike anything U.S. workers have experienced in the nation's history. For employers, this means finding means other than pay to motivate workers. SAS Institute, for example, tries to make workers happier and more productive by helping them meet nonwork needs with concierge services, on-site health care, on-site child care and private schools, an on-site grocers market, and an on-site gym. CEO Jeff Chambers, whose firm boasts a 97 percent employee retention rate despite paying salaries lower than the industry's average, notes, "When the economy turns around, we'll be poised to execute because we've got all the talent we need." Time will tell if the same is true for Circuit City.

Sources: C. Tejada and G. McWilliams, "New Recipe for Cost Savings: Replace Highly Paid Workers," *Wall Street Journal Online*, June 11, 2003, pp. 1–4; D. Kadlec, "Where Did My Raise Go?" *Time*, May 26, 2003, pp. 44–54; M. Conlin, "The Big Squeeze on Workers," *Business Week*, May 13, 2002, pp. 96–97; J. Rawe, "A Homey Cubicle Helps," *Time*, May 26, 2003, p. 5.

come to be perceived. They also provide information that allows us to estimate the character, permanence, and strength of these relationships.

The notion that people generally behave so as to maximize pleasure and minimize pain was first formulated by the ancient Greek philosophers and captured in the concept of **hedonism.** Virtually all modern theories of motivation incorporate this concept. It is especially conspicuous in learning theories, all of which attempt to explain behavior in terms of the associations that people use to link some behavior and some outcome. Two types of learning theories are discussed here: operant learning (reinforcement theory) and social learning.

Reinforcement Theory

Reinforcement theory proposes that a person engages in a specific behavior because that behavior has been reinforced by a specific outcome. A simple example of positive reinforcement can be seen in a recent study that examined ways to reduce absenteeism. In this study, several locations of a garment factory that had been experiencing attendance problems served as the backdrop for an intervention that was designed around public recognition. The idea was to give positive attention to workers who were absent less than three days each quarter. Employees who managed this were given (a) personal attention in the form of a letter from the CEO thanking them for their diligence, (b) a public celebration party where they were wined and dined along with other winners, and (c) small symbolic mementos (a gold necklace for women and a gold penknife for men) to highlight their accomplishments. Within a year, plants that had adopted the recognition program experienced a 50 percent reduction in absenteeism compared to control plants.[19]

A more complex example of how to link organizational strategy, technological advances, and positive reinforcement can be seen with MBNA, a company that produces Visa and Mastercard credit cards. MBNA's strategy is to market credit cards to "affinity groups," that is, groups with strong loyalties. Thus, they produce cards that incorporate anything from the Dallas Cowboys logo to personal pet photos (for Ralston Purina). Members of these affinity groups are lucrative customers, with incomes 20 percent above the national average and balances close to $2,000 above the industry average. Not surprisingly, however, these high-profile customers also demand high levels of service, and above all, they hate to wait.

To make sure that service is provided, MBNA relies heavily on an integrated system of technology and incentives. For example, one goal they have is to make sure that 98.5 percent of phone calls get picked up on fewer than two rings. They measure this electronically, and at any moment on a given day, it is possible to get a reading that shows that employees are achieving "two-ring pickup" 98.4 percent of the time, and to show that this is 1.2 percent higher than average, a 1 percent fall-off from the previous day, and 0.1 percent shy of the goal. Results for this and 14 other goals (such as processing a request to increase a credit line in fifteen minutes or less) are then posted daily on sixty scoreboards at MBNA facilities around the country.

Incentives are then wrapped around these electronic measures. For example, every day the 98.5 percent standard is met, money is thrown into an employee pool. Money from this pool is then handed out in regular intervals—as much as $1,000 per employee—depending on the percentage of times the goal is met. Similar incentives are tied to the other 14 goals. The effect on employees is evident in the words of manager Janine Marrone, who notes, "If you're an MBNA employee and go to a restaurant and hear a phone ring more than twice, it drives you nuts—you have to stop yourself from going behind the counter and answer it."[20] Indeed, the term *operant learning* derives from the fact that the person must perform some *operation* to receive the reinforcing outcome.

Operant learning is especially good for reinforcing simple or well-learned responses. In some cases, however, managers may want to encourage a complex behavior that might not occur on its own. In this instance, the process of shaping can be helpful. **Shaping** means rewarding successive approximations to a desired behavior, so that "getting close counts." For example, someone who has never played golf is highly unlikely to pick up a club and execute a perfect drive with his or her first swing. Left alone to try repeatedly with no instruction, a novice golfer probably will never exhibit the correct behavior.

In shaping, rather than waiting for the correct behavior to occur on its own, close approximations win rewards. Over time, rewards are held back until the person more closely approaches the right behavior. Thus a golf instructor might at first praise a novice golfer for holding the club with the right grip. To obtain a second reward, the novice may be required not only to display the correct grip, but also to stand at the appropriate distance from the ball. To obtain additional rewards, the novice may have to do both of these things and execute the backswing correctly, and so on. In this way, simple initial behaviors become shaped into a complex desired behavior.

Extinction is a second form of reinforcement. In extinction, a weakened response occurs because the desired outcome is no longer paired with some positive reinforcer. Indeed, one problem with reinforcement systems is that they often focus attention so exclusively on the reinforced behavior that other nonreinforced behaviors languish. For example, in attempting to process a credit application more quickly, an employee may sacrifice quality (and perhaps issue credit to a poor risk) if no reinforcement exists for making good decisions as well as fast ones.

Negative reinforcement and punishment are two other types of reinforcement used to influence behavior. In **negative reinforcement,** the likelihood that a person will engage in a particular behavior increases because the behavior is followed by the removal of something the person dislikes. In **punishment,** the likelihood of a given behavior decreases because it is followed by something that the person dislikes. Figure 5-3 illustrates the distinctions drawn among positive reinforcement, extinction, negative reinforcement, and punishment. As shown in the figure, reinforcement theory can both promote and inhibit behaviors, as well as predict the effects of both positive and negative rewards.

Managers in organizations sometimes contend that they cannot use reinforcement theory because they do not have enough resources to give positive reinforcements. For example, they cannot always raise salaries or award bonuses as they might like. As the Cutting-Edge Research box shows, behavioral management programs that rely on positive reinforcement often need to go beyond money to truly be effective. Moreover, as Figure 5-3 makes clear, positive reinforcement is merely one of a number of possible ways to increase the frequency of a desired behavior.

CUTTING-EDGE RESEARCH

LEARNING THE ABCs OF BEHAVIORAL MANAGEMENT: GETTING BEYOND MONEY

Behavioral-management approaches to motivation focus on the relationship between performance and rewards, and generally propose that contingent positive reinforcement promotes effective organizational behavior. To apply behavioral management, the person who is trying to motivate someone else needs to determine (a) the *antecedent conditions* where one would like to see the behavior take place, (b) the precise *behavior* one would like to see, and (c) the *consequences* that can be made contingent on performance of the behavior. This antecedent-behavior-consequences linkage (ABC) forms the core of this model of motivation, and a number of research studies in many different contexts support the utility of this approach for sustaining and changing behavior.

What has never been clear, however, is what type of reward works best in terms of motivating employees. Of course, financial compensation is often commonly considered the most salient form of reward since most people derive the majority of their income from the job. However, some have speculated that paying people to do something specific can undermine their own intrinsic interest in the task. In addition, others have contended that the process of defining one or two specific behaviors that will be rewarded focuses the employees too much on this narrow set of behaviors at the expense of many other critical behaviors, such as teamwork or citizenship. Moreover, some managers do not have control or access to discretionary financial resources, and hence are limited in the degree to which they can use money as a reinforcement. Given these concerns and limitations, the question becomes, what other incentives can managers use and how do these stack up compared to money in terms of their ability to motivate performance?

A recent meta-analysis on this topic has, for the first time, gone a long way toward clarifying the answer to this question. Summarizing the findings of seventy-two studies that took a behavioral-management approach, Stajkovic and Luthans found that beyond money, the two most widely used reinforcements employed in these types of programs have been feedback and social recognition. *Feedback* refers to specific information regarding either process or outcomes that allows the employee to know where he or she stands in relative position to others doing similar work.

Social recognition refers to verbal or symbolic distinctions that are directed to the employee as a consequence of performing some behavior. Feedback appeals to the competitive spirit in the person and his or her needs for growth and esteem, whereas social recognition appeals to the person's need for affiliation and esteem. Both feedback and social recognition are less costly to employ than money, but what does the scientific evidence say regarding their effectiveness?

According to the accumulated evidence, behavior management with money as the sole reinforcement led to an increase in performance of 23 percent on average across all the studies. Social recognition, by itself, was associated with a 17 percent increase, and feedback alone resulted in a 10 percent gain. Although one might expect that programs that employed both social recognition and feedback might combine to lead to a 27 percent gain (the sum of their individual effects), in reality, the effects of the two reinforcers were redundant. That is, their combined effect was virtually identical to the effect for recognition alone (that is, 17 percent). This suggests that even in conditions where managers do not have the ability or interest to employ money as a motivator, the use of social recognition alone can go a long way toward improving performance.

Because the effects of social recognition and feedback are not as strong as those of money, some managers that *do* have the ability and interest to employ financial reinforcement may feel they can ignore the other types of rewards. Before dismissing them altogether, however, one should consider a few studies that were analyzed as part of this research that used all three possible reinforcements at once; the results of these programs were extremely impressive. Studies that used a behavioral-management intervention that incorporated money, social recognition, and feedback produced a 45 percent increase in performance—almost twice the effect of money alone. Thus, even if managers do have the ability and interest to use financial rewards, these results make it clear that they should not overlook the value of social recognition and feedback as important supplements to their reward system. Getting beyond money is thus important for both those who do and do not control this important type of resource.

Sources: E. L. Deci, "Effects of Externally Mediated Rewards on Intrinsic Motivation," *Journal of Personality and Social Psychology* 18 (1971), 105–115; A. Kohn, *Punished by Rewards* (Boston: Houghton Mifflin, 1993); A. D. Stajkovic and F. Luthans, "Behavioral Management and Task Performance in Organizations: Conceptual Background, Meta-Analysis, and Test of Alternative Models," *Personnel Psychology* 56 (2003), 155–194.

FIGURE 5-3 Effects of Methods of Reinforcement on Behavioral Response

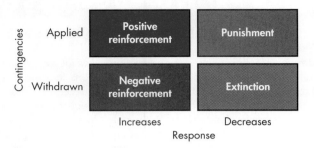

For instance, managers can employ negative reinforcement to increase a response. They can find something about the job that people do not like and, when employees engage in desired behaviors, remove it. A sales manager who wants to increase sales and who knows that salespeople hate to complete paperwork associated with their work, for example, might offer to shift the responsibility for completing paperwork to others if these employees increase their productivity. The sales force's enthusiasm for selling might increase noticeably as a result.

Although coming up with ideas for rewards is sometimes difficult, most organizations can easily envision a wide variety of ways to punish people. Indeed, managers often instinctively react in this manner when confronted with a behavior that they wish to eliminate. This is somewhat problematic because research shows that when approached the right way, people can learn a great deal from their errors, and in some training contexts, the *best* way for people to learn is to force them to make certain types of errors.[21] If the errors occur in a supportive training context that minimizes the negative emotional reactions that come with failure, this promotes both learning and risk taking.[22] As Figure 5-3 shows, however, by itself, punishment can only suppress undesired behaviors, but not promote desired behaviors. In many instances, some other undesirable behavior may simply spring up in place of the old, bad behavior. For example, taking away access to the Internet may simply transform a cyberslacker into a slacker. Moreover, punishment tends to have short-lived effects, and it can produce side effects such as negative emotional reactions among those who are punished.[23]

Despite these dangers, many organizations continue to mete out punishment, because some behaviors are so damaging to the firm that stopping them is crucial. Moreover, failure to take action may imply acceptance of the offending behavior, and the organization may be held liable for the employee's actions. For example, if a cyberslacking employee downloads and transmits pornography over the company's Internet connection, this practice could be viewed as creating a hostile work environment—opening up the organization to sexual harassment charges. Thus, rather than eliminating punishment altogether, organizations need to strive to punish employees more effectively. A company can take several steps to move in this direction.

First, effective discipline programs are *progressive*—that is, they move in incremental steps. A program might start with a simple oral warning, followed by a written formal notice, then some actual disciplinary action that falls short of termination (such as suspension). Second, punishment should be *immediate* rather than delayed. This characteristic maximizes the perceived contingency between the offending behavior and the punishment, and it minimizes the perception that the offending behavior represents a pretext to punish the person for something else. Third, punishment should be *consistent,* so that the punishment is the same no matter who commits the offense. Fourth, punishment should be *impersonal*—that is, directed at the behavior, rather than at the individual as a person. Finally, punishment should be *documented* to construct a "paper trail" of physical evidence that supports the contention that the punishment meted out was progressive, immediate, consistent, and impersonal.

In addition to implementing these five steps, in organizations that employ self-managing teams, it is important to have team members join in this decision. As individuals, group members are often more lenient than hierarchical supervisors. When allowed to discuss the offense as a group and reach consensus, however, the group as a whole tends to show much less leniency.[24] Indeed, group-based decisions regarding discipline often resemble the decision that would be made by supervisors working alone. Recognition of this fact is important, because supervisors armed with the support of the work group they represent enjoy a much stronger position when it comes to doling out punishment.

Although the steps described previously may seem like simple and rational procedures that do not need to be spelled out, this perception is not always accurate. The types of offenses that call for punishment often generate strong emotional reactions from managers that short-circuit rationality. Indeed, these disciplinary procedures may seem excruciatingly slow to the offended manager, and they may frustrate his or her need for quick and satisfying retribution. Managers need to be assured that the process is slow but sure. In the end, if the problem employee must be fired, the procedures ensure that the company can prove the action was justified. Otherwise, the company might be sued for "wrongful discharge" and be unable to terminate the offending party.[25]

Social Learning

Social learning theory, as proposed by Albert Bandura, encompasses a theory of observational learning that holds that most people learn behaviors by observing others and then *modeling* the behaviors perceived as being effective. Such observational learning is in marked contrast to the process of learning through direct reinforcement, and it better explains how people learn complex behavioral sequences.

For example, suppose a worker observes a colleague who, after giving bad news to their manager, is punished. Strict reinforcement theory would suggest that when confronted with the same task, the observing worker will be neither more nor less prone to be the bearer of bad tidings because that person has not personally been reinforced. Social learning theory suggests otherwise. Although the worker may not have directly experienced the fate of a colleague, he or she will nonetheless learn by observation that this manager "shoots the messenger." The employee will probably conclude that the best response in such situations is to keep quiet. Even though the manager might not agree that problems should be covered up, his or her behavior may send precisely this message. Indeed, "fearing the boss more than the competition" has been cited as one of the top ten reasons companies fail.[26]

Besides focusing on learning by observation, social-learning theory proposes that people can reinforce or punish their own behaviors; that is, they can engage in *self-reinforcement*. According to Bandura, a self-reinforcing event occurs when (1) tangible rewards are readily available for the taking, (2) people deny themselves free access to those rewards, and (3) they allow themselves to acquire the rewards only after achieving difficult self-set goals.[27] For example, many successful writers, once alone and seated at their workstations, refuse to take a break until they have written a certain number of pages. Obviously, the writers can leave any time they wish. They deny themselves the reward of a rest, however, until they have accomplished

FIGURE 5-4   Step 1. The Desire to Perform as a Function of Valence and Instrumentality

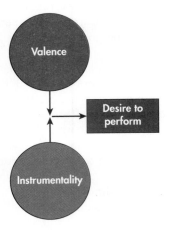

their self-set goals.[28] Research indicates that this type of self-reinforcement can be used to help people stop smoking, overcome drug addiction, cure obesity, improve study habits, enhance scholastic achievement, and reduce absenteeism.[29]

   Valence and instrumentality, the first two parts of our model of motivation, combine to influence the desire to perform (Figure 5-4). People will be motivated to perform at a high level as long as they perceive that receiving high-valence outcomes is contingent upon giving a strong personal performance. Our understanding of the process depicted in Figure 5-4 partly depends on need theories, which explain which outcomes individuals will perceive as having positive valences. In addition, reinforcement theories explain how people learn about contingencies, so they provide insight into the process that makes people want to perform.

EXPECTANCY: SELF-EFFICACY THEORY

Self-Efficacy and Behavior

Although actually part of Bandura's social-learning theory, self-efficacy constitutes an important topic in its own right. **Self-efficacy** refers to the judgments that people make about their ability to execute courses of action required to deal with prospective situations.[30] Individuals high in self-efficacy believe that they can master (or have mastered) some specific task. Self-efficacy determines how much effort people will expend and how long they will persist in the face of obstacles or stressful experiences.[31] When beset with difficulties, people who entertain serious doubts about their capabilities tend to slacken their efforts or give up altogether. In contrast, those who have a strong sense of efficacy tend to exert greater effort to master the challenges. Indeed, if high levels of self-efficacy have a downside, it is the fact that these people will often confidently persist even in the face of consistent feedback indicating that they should change their tactics or lower their self-image.[32] This overconfidence effect associated with self-efficacy needs to be managed in certain contexts;[33] however, for the most part, the positive aspects of high self-efficacy outweigh these negative side effects.[34]

Sources of Self-Efficacy

Given that feelings of self-efficacy can greatly influence behavior, it is important to identify the sources of those feelings. Bandura identified four sources of self-efficacy beliefs.

FIGURE 5-5 Step 2. Level of Effort as a Function of Desire and Expectancy

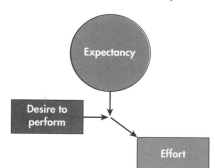

First, self-efficacy can reflect a person's *past accomplishments*. Past instances of successful behavior increase personal feelings of self-efficacy, especially when these successes seem attributable to unchanging factors such as personal ability or a manageable level of task difficulty.[35]

The link between self-efficacy theory and social-learning theory is made clear in Bandura's second source of self-efficacy beliefs: *observation of others*. Merely watching someone else perform successfully on a task may increase an individual's sense of self-efficacy with respect to the same task. Note, however, that characteristics of the observer and model can influence the effects of observation on feelings of self-efficacy. For instance, the observer must judge the model to be both credible and similar to the observer (in terms of personal characteristics such as ability and experience) if the observation is to influence the individual's efficacy perceptions.

A third source of self-efficacy is *verbal persuasion*. Convincing people that they can master a behavior will, under some circumstances, increase their perceptions of self-efficacy. The characteristics of the source and the target of the communication, however, can affect how the verbal persuasion influences self-efficacy perceptions. Again, people who are perceived as credible and trustworthy are most able to influence others' self-efficacy perceptions in this manner.

Logical verification is another source of self-efficacy perceptions. With logical verification, people can generate perceptions of self-efficacy at a new task by perceiving a systematic relationship between the new task and an already-mastered task. For example, if an experienced employee is apprehensive about his or her ability to learn some new software program, the manager should emphasize how many other changes in work procedures this person has successfully managed in the past, and then argue that there is no logical reason why learning this new program will be any different.

Self-efficacy theory is particularly useful for explaining how expectancies are formed and suggesting how they might be changed. Of course, as Figure 5-5 suggests, a person's beliefs will not necessarily translate into motivation unless the person truly desires to excel. Similarly, simply wanting to excel will not bring about high levels of effort unless the person has some belief that such performance is possible.

ACCURACY OF ROLE PERCEPTIONS: GOAL-SETTING THEORY

Role perceptions are people's beliefs about what they are supposed to accomplish on the job and how they should achieve those goals. When these beliefs are accurate, people facing a task know what needs to be done, how much needs to be accomplished, and who will have the responsibility to carry out the task at hand. Such role accuracy guarantees that the energy devoted to task accomplishment will be directed toward the right activities and outcomes. At the same time, it decreases the amount of energy wasted on unimportant goals and activities. Goal-setting theory can help us understand how to enhance the accuracy of role perceptions.

Important Goal Attributes

Employees are often told, "Do your best." Although this axiom is intended to guide job performance in everyday situations, research has consistently demonstrated that such vague instructions can actually undermine personal performance. In contrast, more than 100 studies support the assertion that performance is enhanced by goals that are both *specific and difficult*.[36] Indeed, setting specific goals has improved performance in a wide variety of jobs (Table 5-2). Moreover, goal setting works most effectively when teamed with feedback (so that progress can be monitored) and incentives (so that goal accomplishment takes on meaning).[37] Specific and difficult goals are especially effective when incorporated into a continuous improvement cycle in which future goals consist of reasonable increments on past goals.[38] Specific and difficult goals appear to promote greater effort and to enhance persistence. They also encourage people to develop effective task strategies and sharpen their mental focus on the task.[39] Their primary virtue, however, is that they direct attention to specific desired results, clarifying perceptions of both what is important and what level of performance is needed.[40]

Many of the problems that were seen in our opening story regarding stock option programs can be traced to the fact that in many cases the goal—increase the stock price—was simply too easy to meet in many economic cycles. That is, in a bull market, even people at companies that perform poorly relative to their competitors (for example, the average stock price in the industry goes up 20 percent but the stock for one specific company only goes up 5 percent) experience a reward. Many compensation specialists have argued that this creates a need for different types of options. With an indexed option, for example, executives have to beat some type of industry average before they can cash out stock options. Another alternative is premium-priced options, where the stock has to rise above a certain threshold set above the current price. This type of option only reinforces executives for what would be considered unusual returns on the investment. Yet another alternative is performance-vested options, which kick in only when the organization meets other non-stock-price-related goals (such as an increase in profits or a reduction in operating costs).

In other instances, the problems can be traced to goals that are simply too difficult. For example, Bernard Ebbers, CEO of WorldCom, stated, "Our goal is not to capture market share or be global, but instead, our goal is to be the Number 1 stock on Wall Street." Of course, achieving the latter goal was going to be very difficult if one ignored the first two goals, and Ebbers tried to achieve this by acquiring more

TABLE 5-2
Jobholders Who Have Improved Performance in Goal-Setting Programs

Telephone servicepersons	Loggers
Baggage handlers	Marine recruits
Typists	Union bargaining representatives
Salespersons	Bank managers
Truck loaders	Assembly line workers
College students	Animal trappers
Sewing machine operators	Maintenance technicians
Engineering researchers	Dockworkers
Scientists	Die casters

and more unrelated businesses.[41] This made it look like the company was experiencing ever greater revenues in the short term, but without the knowledge of how to achieve market share or expand their markets, this could not be sustained over the long term—resulting in one of the largest bankruptcies ever recorded in U.S. history.[42] Thus, although the motivational power of goals is often impressive, one has to be very careful of exactly how goals are expressed, how difficult they will be to achieve, and what exact behaviors they will motivate.

Goal Commitment and Participation

The extent to which a person feels committed to a goal can also affect performance. As depicted in Figure 5-6, specific and difficult goals tend to lead to increased performance only when there is high goal commitment.[43] The requirement that people be committed to goals means that goals must be set carefully because when they are too difficult, they are typically met with less commitment. People may view a goal that is set too high as impossible; thus, they reject it altogether.

Fortunately, research has examined several ways to increase commitment to difficult goals. One important factor is the degree to which the goals are public rather than private. In one study, students for whom difficult goals for GPA were made public (posted on bulletin boards) showed higher levels of commitment to those goals relative to students with private goals. This study also found a significant positive relationship between need for achievement and goal commitment. Moreover, the positive relationship between need for achievement and goal commitment was especially strong when the goals were set by the students themselves, as opposed to being assigned by an outside party.[44] If the employee is not allowed to set his or her own goals, the next best thing for instilling commitment is to at least let the employee participate in the goal-setting process. Participation promotes commitment, especially in certain cultures (low power distance). We will have more to say about cultural differences in Chapter 15, but for now we will simply note that in some cultures (high power distance), people do not expect to participate, and hence will often show more commitment to assigned goals than those they set for themselves.[45]

FIGURE 5-6 Conceptual Interactive Relationship between Goal Difficulty and Goal Commitment

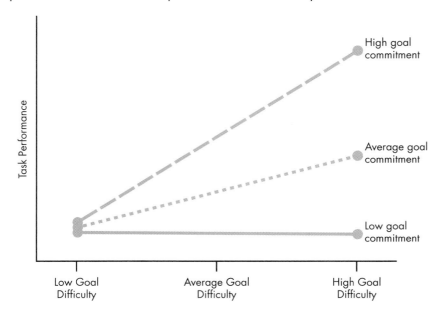

Goals and Strategies

As shown in Table 5-2, goal setting can increase performance on a variety of jobs. Nevertheless, most early research on goal setting consisted of studies that focused attention on relatively simple tasks. More recent research has extended goal-setting theory into more complex task domains. In these situations, however, the links between goals, effort, and performance are less clear. A review of these studies indicates that while goals have positive effects on all tasks, the magnitude of the effect is stronger for simple tasks than for complex tasks.[46] Figure 5-7 illustrates how the effect of goal difficulty on performance decreases as task complexity increases.

For complex tasks, the *task strategies* (that is, the plans of action devised) greatly influence the outcome of those efforts. This impact can obscure and, in some rare cases, even eliminate the effects of goal setting. Research on goal setting and task strategies suggests that whereas setting specific and difficult goals may increase strategy development, the resulting strategies are not guaranteed to be effective.[47] Moreover, because developing strategies consumes time that might otherwise be devoted to task performance, goals may actually hinder performance in some situations.[48]

In fact, focusing on narrow goals related to performance may discourage people from experimenting with new strategies and developing new skills.[49] A performance drop-off often occurs when people switch from well-learned strategies to new and different ones. For example, if a person has gained a great deal of proficiency with one word-processing program, that individual may express reluctance to upgrade to a new and improved program; while learning the new program, the employee fears that he or she will not work as quickly as was possible with the old program. Indeed, even if the worker is convinced that in the long run he or she will be able to work

FIGURE 5-7   Goal Difficulty, Task Complexity, and Performance

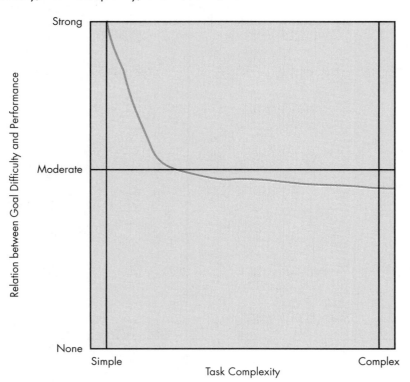

more rapidly with the new program, the employee may still be unwilling to pay the short-term performance costs of learning the new program.

The term **goal orientation** has been coined to distinguish between people who approach a task with the goal of learning how to improve themselves and people whose goals focus strictly on performing at a certain level.[50] Although people with a strict performance orientation often perform best on simple, stable, short-term tasks, people with a learning orientation often perform better on complex, dynamic, long-term tasks.[51] Thus the objectives of any managerially inspired goal-setting program must account for the need to perform at a high level as well as the need to create enough slack in the system to allow people to experiment with new and potentially improved task strategies. This seems to be particularly the case for workers who are high in intelligence, and hence derive more from potential learning experiences.[52]

Although research on performance strategies has yielded findings that sometimes conflict with the results of other goal-setting studies, it is nevertheless helpful in delineating the specific, role-clarifying effects of goals. In simple tasks, where the *means* to perform a task are clear, specific and difficult goals lead to higher performance because they clarify the *ends* toward which task effort should be directed. In complex tasks, however, the means are not clear. Individuals performing such tasks do not know how to proceed in the best way, so merely clarifying the ends sought is unlikely to enhance performance.

ABILITY AND EXPERIENCE REVISITED

Nonmotivational Determinants of Performance

Although this chapter has focused primarily on motivation, task performance is also contingent on the worker's abilities. Chapter 3 discussed abilities at great length, so here we will narrow the focus to how individual differences interact with goal setting and task strategies.

Two things are worth noting with respect to nonmotivational determinants of performance. First, people lacking the requisite abilities cannot perform a complex task even under the most favorable goal-related circumstances.

Second, some subtle relationships exist among goal setting, attention, and cognitive capacity that affect task performance. As you will recall, one way that goal setting affects performance is by directing attention to the kinds of desired results. Kanfer and Ackerman have developed a model that recognizes that different people bring varying amounts of cognitive ability to bear on a task, and that this restriction limits how much they can attend to at any one time.[53] Because it diverts attention from the task to the goal, goal setting may be particularly damaging to people who have low ability or who are still learning the task. Such people need to devote all their attention to the task, and goal setting is unlikely to enhance their performance.

Thus, although motivation is critical to performance, we should not forget the lessons learned in Chapter 3 about the importance of ability. For all but the simplest tasks, there is no substitute for ability.

In this third step of building our overall motivation model, we can see how motivation and other factors combine to determine performance (Figure 5-8). Specifically, performance will be high when a person puts forth significant effort, directs this effort toward the right outcomes, and has the ability to execute the behaviors necessary for bringing about those outcomes.

FIGURE 5-8   Step 3. Performance as a Function of Effort, Accuracy of Role Perception and Ability

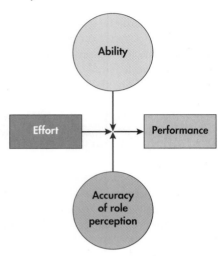

Experience and Cyclical Effects

The fourth and final step needed to complete our motivation and performance model deals with the links that make the model dynamic over time. Figure 5-1 includes three arrows that head back left. First, a feedback loop goes from performance to valence. Recall that valence, as a construct, deals with *anticipated* satisfaction, not realized satisfaction. The feedback loop allows for the possibility that an outcome received for performing some task might not bring much real satisfaction to the person when it is actually received. Valence for such an outcome would then decrease relative to its value at an earlier time.

Another link in Figure 5-1 goes from performance to instrumentalities. This loop implies that the outcomes received for performing at some level at one time will affect the person's perceived instrumentalities at later times. If no reward follows high performance, extinction of the performance response could take place, lowering the perceived instrumentality of high performance.

Finally, an arrow goes from performance to expectancy in Figure 5-1. This loop affirms that expectancies and self-efficacy are based at least partially on prior performance. All else being equal, successful performance strengthens self-efficacy and leads to high expectancies. Failing at a task, however, generally leads to lower levels of self-efficacy. Clearly, feedback is central to the motivational process for a number of different reasons, and as the Ethics and Social Responsibility box shows, the ability to monitor employees and provide feedback on what they are doing has expanded a great deal with modern technologies—often creating ethical dilemmas regarding how much one should monitor.

These three dynamic links in our motivation model suggest that motivation can change over time. For example, Figure 5-1 suggests that even highly motivated people might lose motivation for any of three reasons. First, individuals who start out with high expectancies might discover during job performance that they cannot perform nearly as well as they anticipated. Decreased self-efficacy would lead to reduced expectancy perceptions, and lower motivation would probably result. Second, individuals might discover that performing well on a job does not lead to the desirable outcomes they expected. Motivation could then diminish as projected instrumentalities fail

ETHICS AND SOCIAL RESPONSIBILITY

PRIVACY VERSUS PRODUCTIVITY IN A HIGH-TECH WORLD

A truck driver, needing a break, gets off the highway to catch a quick nap prior to starting to the next leg of the delivery. What was intended as a twenty-minute "power nap" turns into a two-hour, REM-inducing deep sleep that is rudely interrupted by a message from the trucking company's manager to get back to work. The message was delivered via an Internet-based alarm installed on the truck, and the manager was alerted to the driver's behavior because of a global positioning system installed in the trucks that allows them to be monitored from afar. How far? In this case, the manager, Skip Coghill, was on a cruise off the coast of Acapulco. According to Coghill, "I was drinking a piña colada, sitting in my swimsuit, having a total ball."

Although there has always been a need to monitor employees to ensure that their efforts are being aimed in the right direction, as this example shows, there has been a radical revolution in the ability to monitor people, and this has changed the way many companies are doing business. At British Airways, for example, managers use Web-enabled employee performance software to make sure that customer service representatives' time in the breakroom or time spent on personal calls does not count as "company time" when it comes to calculating paychecks. The software also calculates ticket sales and customer complaint records, and uses this information to provide performance-based bonuses to deserving representatives. Annual performance reviews, which were once ambiguous and hard-to-defend subjective judgments, are being transformed into highly precise, objective indicators of behavior that can be used to justify wide pay differentials between star performers and struggling novices working at the same job. Steven Pruneau, a British Airways manager, notes, "We knew how many hours our planes were on the ground or in the air—the productivity of our capital—but we didn't have a fraction of that kind of information about the productivity of our other assets—our human capital."

This revolution is transforming labor from a fixed cost to a variable cost, and has the potential to increase organizational efficiency. However, as with any revolution, some fear this can go too far. This is especially the case when employers feel it is necessary to monitor e-mail usage or Internet activity of their employees. On the one hand, one can imagine legitimate business reasons for monitoring e-mail—for example, to ensure that people are not giving away proprietary information or spending a great deal of time sending and receiving personal messages on company time and equipment. Similarly, if an employee is surfing the Net all day, hogging bandwidth by downloading music or video and not doing any meaningful or productive work, the organization has a right to know this as well.

For example, Sapphire Technologies, a Massachusetts-based IT placement firm, uses a program called Message Inspector that automatically examines all transmitted files, searching for certain words. If it detects something that it is programmed to catch (such as pornographic or shopping Web sites), it forwards a message to the head of cybersecurity, who can then try to steer the employee back to more conventional methods of accomplishing business objectives. The demand for products such as this is on the rise, in that the market for software that monitors employees was estimated at $100 million in 2001, but is expected to top $2 billion by 2005.

Whereas the lure of productivity enhancements attributable to this technology is a powerful force, some have argued that this type of snooping represents an Orwellian violation of the individual's right to privacy. In fact, new low-priced cameras can be attached to most computers that allow cost-effective means of literally watching employees as they go about their work. As one manager puts it, "The proposed policy tells our 30,000 dedicated employees that we trust them so little we must monitor all their communications. How did we get to such a draconian policy?" Indeed, beyond the moral question of whether this is right or wrong, the question becomes, at what point does surveillance such as this create the kind of business environment that will chase away many high-skilled employees who have other, less intrusive and degrading employment options? This would destroy the very argument—increased productivity—that motivated the use of the technology in the first place. Clearly, organizations are going to have to walk a fine line in using these technologies to support both organizational objectives and employee rights.

Sources: J. Spencer, "Shirk Ethic: How to Fake a Hard Day at the Office," *Wall Street Journal Online,* May 15, 2003, pp. 1–3; M. Conlin, "The Software Says You're Just Average," *Business Week,* February 25, 2002, p. 126; E. Zimmerman, "HR Must Know When Employee Surveillance Crosses the Line," *Workforce,* February 2002, pp. 38–44.

to materialize. Third, experience with the rewards received from performing a job might lead someone to discover faults with the initial valences. That is, the rewards expected to yield satisfaction might not do so.

HIGH-PERFORMANCE WORK SYSTEMS

As we noted at the outset of this chapter, in theoretical terms, one of the least controversial statements one can make about paying workers is that it is important to tie pay to job performance. In reality, the implementation of programs to bring about such a relationship often proves quite difficult. To get a feeling for some of the dilemmas involved, consider the following issues that arise when pay-for-performance programs are contemplated.

First, should pay increases be based on outcomes that occur at the individual level (that is, performance of individual workers), the group level (performance of different teams), or the organizational level (performance of the entire business)? If the individual level is used as the standard, the organization may create competition among co-workers and destroy team morale. When pay-for-performance occurs at the group and organizational levels, individuals may find it difficult to see how their own performance relates to group or organizational performance and outcomes.[54] In expectancy theory terms, these kinds of conditions lower instrumentality.

Second, if the firm decides to pay at the individual level, should it establish the rules for payment in advance (for example, telling workers that they will receive $5 per widget produced)? This plan may sound like a good idea, but prevents the company from accurately forecasting its labor costs; that is, the firm cannot anticipate exactly how many widgets will be produced. Moreover, because the price of the product sold or service rendered cannot be known in advance, the organization may not be able to anticipate its revenues. On the other hand, if the firm waits until the end of the year to see how much money is available for merit pay, people will not know in advance exactly how their performance relates to their pay. Moreover, if the organization engages in pay secrecy to protect people's privacy, how can anyone actually know whether the merit system is fair?

Third, how large should incentives be, and how much variability should exist within and between job categories? Research suggests that incentives that are less than 5 percent of the regular salary have little motivational value; thus the company may want to aim for larger incentives.[55] If the overall amount of compensation is fixed, however, larger incentives imply that fewer rewards will be handed out, which can lead to wide variability of pay within the same job category. Such systems tend to engender resentment among workers and hinder collaboration and teamwork.[56]

Fourth, if the company decides to keep incentives at an organizational level, should it base the rewards on cost savings and distribute them yearly, or base them on profits and distribute them on a deferred basis? The calculations and accounting procedures required by cost-savings plans are enormous and complex, but rewards are distributed quickly. Profit-sharing plans are much easier to handle from an accounting perspective. Because the rewards are distributed on a deferred basis, however, they are less motivating than cost-savings plans.

These questions highlight the complexity inherent in putting into practice the seemingly simple theoretical concept of "paying for performance." Covering all the complexities of these issues is well beyond the scope of this chapter. We will examine, however, the distinguishing features of four kinds of pay-for-performance programs: merit-based plans, incentive plans, cost-savings plans, and profit-sharing plans.

Merit-Pay and Incentive Systems

Individual pay-for-performance plans base financial compensation, at least in part, on the accomplishments of individual workers. Two types of individual programs exist: those based on merit and those based on incentives.

Merit-based pay plans are by far the easiest to administer and control. These programs assess performance at the end of the fiscal year via subjective ratings of employees made by supervisors. Also at the end of the year, a fixed sum of money is allocated to wage increases. This sum is distributed to individuals in amounts proportional to their performance ratings.

In designing merit-based programs, three major considerations arise. First, what will the average performer receive? Many firms try to ensure that the pay of average performers at least keeps up with inflation. As a result, the midpoint of the rating scale is often tied to the consumer price index (CPI).

Second, what will a poor performer receive? Companies rarely *lower* an employee's wages; however, raises that fail to cover the CPI are actually wage decreases in terms of buying power. Is it in the firm's best interests to allow the wage increases of poor performers to slip below the inflation level? If so, how much damage does the organization wish to inflict on low performers? How easily replaced are these people if they respond by quitting?

Third, how much will high performers receive? Will high performers at the top of a pay grade receive the same raise as those at the bottom of a higher wage grade? Paying for performance could cause top performers in jobs lower in the hierarchy to surpass (through yearly raises) low performers in upper-level jobs over time. Indeed, to prevent this type of compression, many companies have adopted the practice of *broad banding*. Broad banding simply means reducing the number of hierarchical distinctions between jobs. For example, General Electric has tried to move away from length of service and rank as pay determinants. To do so, it cut the levels of salary grades from 29 to 6. As a result, people now have more opportunities to get a raise without a promotion.[57]

Although supervisors have traditionally given the performance ratings that determine merit pay, this practice is now changing. In the services sector of the economy, high-performance work systems have eliminated the "middle man" (the supervisor). In such companies, merit-pay raises are tied directly to customer service ratings obtained from surveys. For example, at GTE customer ratings are weighted 35 percent when making annual merit-pay decisions for certain managerial groups.[58]

In general, although many organizations continue to rely partially on merit systems, throughout the 1990s raises lost favor while other forms of pay for performance gained in popularity. Some of the latter deal with incentive systems. Incentive systems differ from merit-based systems in two ways. First, incentive programs stipulate the rules by which payment will be made in advance, so that the worker can calculate exactly how much money will be earned if a certain level of performance is achieved. Second, rewards in an incentive program are based on objective measures of performance.

Simple *piecework plans* establish a standard of productivity per time interval, and any productivity beyond that standard is rewarded with a set amount per unit. This type of plan is easy for the worker to understand, and it creates an obvious performance–outcome expectancy. On the other hand, the standard must often be adjusted. If it is initially set too low, labor costs can get out of hand. If it is set too high, workers will reject it when they discover that the standard cannot be reached, even with harder work. If the standard is flexible, gradual increases in the standard may be viewed as a manipulative management trick, whereas decreases will cause some workers to try to manipulate the system by lowering output. Furthermore, without built-in safeguards, these programs may lead workers to achieve quantity at the price of quality or ethical violations.[59]

For example, U.S. government regulations specify a limit on the percentage of salary that can be paid out in the form of commissions in an insurance agency (55 percent). This ceiling was established to prevent the practice of "churning"—that is, selling unsophisticated customers insurance policies that they do not need, financed with cash value drained out of their existing coverage. Insurers are lobbying to end these restrictions because they must increasingly compete with non-insurance companies (for example, brokerage houses) in the area of retirement planning services. The government restrictions on how to pay employees hinders the ability of the insurance companies to compete with the unregulated, non–insurance companies, illustrating the important link between motivational systems and competitive advantage.[60]

In addition to creating ethical difficulties, individual-based incentives can hinder cooperation within the organization. That is, individuals may become so focused on achieving their own goals and rewards that they lose their concern for the overall health of the organization or their co-workers. For example, Lantech, a small manufacturer of packaging material in Louisville, Kentucky, implemented a bonus-type incentive system built around cost containment. The competition within the organization to get the bonus grew heated, and each person tried to assign costs to others. At one point, the competition became so petty that a manager tried to pass off the cost of his toilet paper to a different division. Pat Lancaster, CEO at Lantech, noted, "I was spending 95 percent of my time on conflict resolution instead of on how to serve our customers."[61] To eliminate these types of problems, Lantech, like many other organizations, eventually scuttled its individual-based plan, replacing it with an organization-level plan.

Profit-Sharing and Cost-Savings Plans

Whereas merit-based plans and incentive plans tie pay to performance at the individual level, profit-sharing and cost-savings plans tie pay to performance at a broader level.

Profit-sharing plans distribute organizational profits to employees. According to recent estimates, 20 percent of U.S. firms have such plans in place, and the popularity of these plans is growing.[62] Cash distribution plans provide full payment soon after profits have been determined (annually or quarterly). To reap tax advantages, most plans—indeed, as many as 80 percent—provide deferred payments.[63] In these plans, current profits accumulate in employee accounts, and a cash payment is made only when a worker becomes disabled, leaves the organization, retires, or dies. Of course, not all the company's profits are redistributed. Research suggests that the share of profits distributed may range from a low of 14 percent to a high of 33 percent.[64]

As we saw earlier with another form of organizational-level plan, stock options, one problem with profit-sharing plans is that employees often find it difficult to see the connection between their activities and their company's profits. This issue is especially apparent when something uncontrollable, such as an overall downturn in the economy, totally eliminates any hope of the organization making a profit in the short term.[65] Similarly, with respect to profit-sharing plans, when multiple businesses are involved, people may struggle to see the link between their efforts and corporate profits. For these reasons, the day-to-day motivational value of these kinds of programs may be questionable. Would a worker who might otherwise quit work an hour early really stop for fear of how it might affect the company's profits?

FIGURE 5-9 Deciding among Alternative Pay-for-Performance Programs

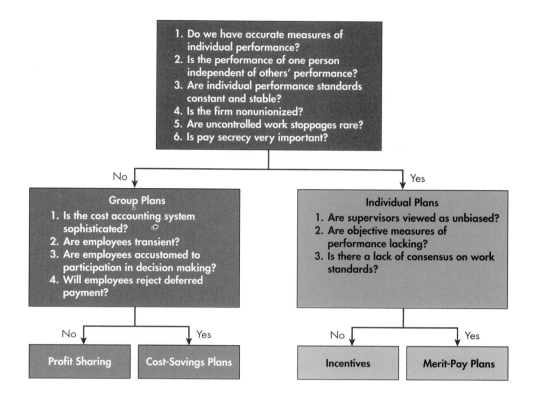

To eliminate this problem, some organizations have adopted cost-savings plans that pay workers bonuses out of the money the company has saved through increased efficiency of its operations. Workers often have more control over the costs of doing business than the company's stock price or profits, so it is easier for them to see the connection between their own work and cost reductions.[66]

We have sampled only a few of the many pay-for-performance programs currently in use. As you can see, some of these programs are highly complex. You should, however, have some feel for the kinds of issues raised by such programs. Figure 5-9 provides guidance on choosing a suitable plan. It explains under what circumstances an individual or a group plan is appropriate and in what situations specific individual or group plans are most effective.

SUMMARY

Our model of motivation and performance is based on *expectancy theory* and incorporates concepts from five other theories of motivation: *need theory, learning theory, self-efficacy theory,* and *goal-setting theory.* The model focuses on explaining three outcomes. The first, desire to perform, is a function of *valences* and *instrumentalities.* A person's desire to perform well will be high when valence rewards are associated with high performance. The second outcome, effort, is a function of desire to perform and *expectancy.* Effort will be forthcoming only when individuals want to perform well and when they believe they can do so. The third outcome, performance, is a function of effort, *accurate role perceptions,* and *ability.* Performance will be high only when individuals with the requisite abilities and knowledge of desired goals and strategies put forth their best effort.

The dynamic nature of the motivation process is revealed in the way present levels of performance affect future levels of valence, instrumentality, and expectancy. The complexity of the motivational process can be seen in high-performance work systems and the many issues that must be considered when one attempts to "pay for performance."

REVIEW QUESTIONS

1. Recent research suggests that individual needs may be determined more by genetic factors than previously thought. Take each of the need theories described in this chapter and discuss whether this new evidence supports, contradicts, or is irrelevant to that theory.

2. Specific, difficult goals have been suggested to enhance performance, but researchers have also shown that performance will be high only when expectancies are high. You might think that as goals become increasingly difficult, expectations for accomplishing them would decrease. Can you resolve this apparent contradiction between goal-setting theory and expectancy theory?

3. Analyst Daniel Shore once called motivation researchers "servants of power" because the results of their research were often used to manipulate lower-level workers. Is trying to motivate people necessarily exploitative? Under what conditions might providing external motivation be exploitative? Which theories of motivation do you feel are exploitative? Which ones are not?

4. Imagine two pharmaceutical companies that employ the same job categories but different business strategies. One tries to increase its market share through innovation (developing new and better drugs). The other sticks to established products and tries to increase its market share by lowering costs. Why might the two firms wind up with dramatically different pay-for-performance programs? What types of programs might be most and least suitable to each organization?

LEARNING THROUGH EXPERIENCE

DIAGNOSTIC QUESTIONS 5-1

Diagnosing Situations Where Motivation Is a Problem

When you are trying to diagnose a situation in which motivation may be a problem, the following questions can help guide your inquiry:

1. What are the most important needs of the person I am trying to motivate?

2. What contingencies has this person learned over the course of his or her reinforcement history?

3. How can I make the receipt of positive-valence outcomes contingent upon this person performing at a high level?

4. What negative-valence outcomes can I remove, contingent upon the person performing at a high level?

5. Does the person I am trying to motivate believe that he or she can perform well? If not, how can I increase the person's self-efficacy perceptions?

6. Does the person I am trying to motivate actually have the ability to accomplish the tasks that he or she is attempting to perform?

7. Does the person I am trying to motivate have specific, difficult performance goals in mind?

8. Is the person I am trying to motivate committed to these goals?

9. Does the person I am trying to motivate know the best strategies for accomplishing these goals?

10. If the person I am trying to motivate was initially higher in motivation than he or she is at present, which of the three feedback loops in the diagnostic model might account for the loss in motivation?

11. How does the firm reward employees for their performance? If it uses pay as a reward, is a merit or incentive plan most appropriate?

12. How does the organization reward people for organizational performance? If it uses pay, would a cost-savings or a profit-sharing approach be most appropriate?

EXERCISE 5-1:   **Motivation through Pay Raise Allocation**

Edward E. Lawler III, University of Southern California

Although piece-rate, commission, or other fixed-ratio reinforcement plans provide rewards to employees that are highly motivating, many organizations can only pay fixed salaries and make yearly salary adjustments. Thus an annual pay raise is the only indicator that employees of such firms have of how the organization views their performance. Making salary decisions under these circumstances is a critically important, but immensely difficult task. In this exercise you will experience the demands of this task firsthand.

Step One: Pre-Class Preparation

Read the instructions to the Employee Profile Sheet (Exhibit 5-1) and then decide on a pay increase for each of the eight employees. Be prepared to explain your decisions in class.

Step Two: Group Discussion

The class should divide into groups containing four to six members (if you have already formed permanent groups, reassemble in those same groups). Each member should share the recommendations he or she made in Step One and explain his or her reasons for making those decisions. After all members have reported, the group should analyze and try to explain differences among everyone's recommendations. The group should then develop a set of recommendations on which it can agree. A spokesperson should be appointed to present the group's recommendations to the class.

Step Three: Class Discussion

Your instructor will reassemble the class so that the group spokespersons can present their reports. As each group's recommendations are presented, the instructor will record them on a blackboard, flip chart, or overhead projector. After the reports

EXHIBIT 5-1 Employee Profile Sheet

You must make salary increase recommendations for eight managers whom you supervise. All of the managers have just completed their first year with the company and are ready to be considered for their first annual raise. Keep in mind that you may be setting precedents that will shape future expectations and that you must stay within your salary budget. Otherwise, no formal company policies restrict you in deciding how to allocate raises. Write the raise you would give each manager in the space to the left of each name. You have a total of $26,000 in your budget for pay raises.

$__   a. J. Adams. Adams is not, as far as you can tell, a good performer. You have discussed your opinion with others and they agree completely. Adams, however, has one of the toughest work groups to manage. Adams's subordinates have low skill levels, and their work is dirty and difficult. If you lose Adams, you are not sure that you could find an adequate replacement. *Current salary: $30,000.*

$__   b. K. Berger. Berger is single and seems to lead the life of a carefree swinger. In general, you feel that Berger's job performance is not up to par, and some of Berger's "goofs" are well known to other employees. *Current salary: $33,750.*

$__   c. C. Carter. You consider Carter to be one of your best subordinates, but other people obviously don't agree. Carter has married into wealth and, as far as you know, doesn't need any more money. *Current salary: $37,000.*

$__   d. L. Davis. From your personal relationship with Davis, you know that this manager badly needs more money because of certain personal problems. Davis also happens to be one of your best managers. For some reason, your enthusiasm is not shared by your other subordinates and you have heard them make joking remarks about Davis's performance. *Current salary: $34,000.*

$__   e. J. Ellis. You believe that Ellis just isn't cutting the mustard. Surprisingly enough, however, when you check with others to see how they feel, you find that Ellis is very highly regarded. You also know that Ellis badly needs a raise. Ellis was recently divorced and is finding it extremely difficult to support a young family of four as a single parent. *Current salary: $30,750.*

$__   f. M. Foster. Foster has turned out to be a very pleasant surprise, has done an excellent job, and is seen by peers as one of the best people in your group of managers. You are surprised because Foster is generally frivolous and doesn't seem to care very much about money or promotions. *Current salary: $32,700.*

$__   g. K. Green. Green has been very successful so far. You are particularly impressed by this performance because Green has one of the most difficult jobs in your company. Green needs money more than many of your other subordinates and is respected for good performance. *Current salary: $35,250.*

$__   h. A. Hunt. You know Hunt personally. This employee seems to squander money continually. Hunt has a fairly easy job assignment, and your own view is that Hunt doesn't do it especially well. You are therefore surprised to find that several of the other new managers think that Hunt is the best of the new group. *Current salary: $31,500.*

are completed, the class should look for similarities and differences among the recommendations of different groups and consider the following questions:

1. What kinds of differences could you detect among the eight managers described on the Employee Profile Sheet? Which differences influenced your pay raise decisions?

2. What were the reasons for basing pay raises on these factors? Why did you choose to concentrate on some differences among the eight supervisors and to ignore others?

3. If the recommendations made by different groups were not the same, how can you explain the discrepancies? If there are similarities, what caused them?

"Motivation through Compensation" by Edward E. Lawler III. Reprinted by permission of the author.

4. What would probably happen if you implemented the recommendations made by your class? How would each manager react? How would these reactions affect the performance of the company?

Conclusion

Using rewards to motivate employees requires that the receipt of rewards be tied as closely as possible to instances of successful performance. Performance–reward instrumentalities are certainly strongest when companies implement piece-rate or commission plans. If companies have no choice except to pay yearly salaries, a limited degree of contingency can still be established by tying yearly raises directly to employee performance.

As you have learned in this exercise, maintaining a tight connection between employee performance and yearly raises can be more challenging than it sounds, sometimes requiring you to make difficult decisions. At some point in your future role as manager, you may have to make such decisions and explain them to your subordinates. Base your decisions on sound information about employee performance, and make sure that your explanations are clearly understood.

CHAPTER

6

Defining Satisfaction and Stress
Satisfaction
Stress
Measuring Satisfaction and Stress

Organizational Costs of Dissatisfaction and Stress
Performance at the Individual and Organizational Level
Health Care Costs
Absenteeism and Turnover
Low Organizational Commitment and Citizenship
Workplace Violence and Sabotage

Sources of Dissatisfaction and Stress
Physical and Social Environment
Personal Dispositions
Organizational Tasks
Organization Roles

Eliminating and Coping with Dissatisfaction and Stress
Identifying Symptoms of Dissatisfaction and Stress
Eliminating Dissatisfying and Stressful Conditions
Managing Symptoms of Dissatisfaction and Stress

Summary
Review Questions

Learning Through Experience
Diagnostic Questions 6-1: Evaluating an Organization to Determine Where
    and When Dissatisfaction and Stress May Occur
Exercise 6-1: Understanding Roles as Sources of Stress

Satisfaction and Stress

In the spring of 2002, Argenbright Security was the #1 provider of airport security in the United States, controlling a full 40 percent of a $2 billion industry. The organization employed close to 10,000 screeners at thirty-five airports, and derived half of its total revenue from aviation security contracts. A mere one year later, Argenbright had to completely withdraw from the aviation services market, and many were speculating that the impact this would have on their profits would more than likely put them out of business.[1] There were many factors that caused this drastic turn of events, but at the heart of the problem was that people were very dissatisfied with working as Argenbright screeners, and this led to high levels of employee turnover, which in turn resulted in an excessive number of highly visible performance failures.

At Logan International Airport, for example, the turnover rate among baggage screeners was roughly 300 percent, and it was rare to find an employee on the job who had been working there for as long as one year. The high level of inexperience of these workers led to many errors in the screening process, including those that led to the 9/11 terrorist attacks. Although one could perhaps pass this off, and note that those attacks took many by surprise, the remarkable feature of Argenbright's problems were that they persisted even after 9/11. At this point, one might think the harsh spotlight of public opinion would have resulted in tightened operations, but instead, on November 3, a heavily armed man slipped by an Argenbright checkpoint at Chicago's O'Hare Airport, and then two weeks later, an Argenbright employee left a concourse door open and unattended at Logan.[2]

The incidents at Logan and O'Hare led to lost contracts at both of those airports, but a more devastating blow came a few months later, when the Department of Transportation announced that it would not do any business with Argenbright.[3] The problem in this case was that the dissatisfying nature of Argenbright Security jobs, coupled with intensive pressures to hire more and more workers to offset the turnover, made it difficult to recruit new workers. In order to meet hiring quotas, Argenbright relaxed hiring standards and wound up placing a large number of convicted felons at critical security posts at Philadelphia's airport. Since the Department of Transportation (DOT) had recently taken over airport security, their unwillingness to work with Argenbright was a deathblow. The DOT was going to either hire its own personnel or subcontract to private agencies, and announcing that it would not work with Argenbright because of hiring fiascoes meant that Argenbright could no longer do this type of work.

An analysis of the screener's job as designed by Argenbright and many other private companies provides a number of clues as to why so many people were dissatisfied with this work. First, the pay for the job was very low, often less than six dollars an hour. Airport employees working at fast-food restaurants often made more money. Second, these were all dead-end jobs, and there was no hope that anyone who performed well could, with time, eventually progress and work their way up to some better-paying management position. Third, the work was boring and monotonous, requiring the worker to stay in the same spot all day and do the same things over and over again. Fourth, the jobs were very low in status, and many of the people who flew looked down on the workers and often made derogatory comments toward them if they were delayed in any way. Finally, the job was very insecure in that a person could be fired for a single mistake, and mistakes were easy to make because the company pressured the workers to keep traffic moving quickly during peak departure periods.[4]

The Transportation Security Administration (TSA), the arm of the DOT that has taken over airport security, has vowed to turn this situation around.[5] They have raised the pay for security personnel and created career tracks that can lead one from low-level screening positions to management positions based on performance and seniority. The TSA has also enhanced the status and professionalism of the units, with new uniforms, expanded training, and standardization of operations. Workers now rotate through various jobs to break up the monotony and work in teams that are designed to provided social support as well as backup behaviors in emergency situations. Although it is too early to tell if these changes will lead to higher satisfaction and retention of personnel, it is clearly too late for Argenbright to try to rectify the problems they experienced along these lines.

Most organizations are not in the "job satisfaction business." For that reason, sometimes managers find it difficult to see the importance of understanding and enhancing employees' attitudes and feelings about their work. Those attitudes and feelings can have important effects on the organization, however, as can be seen in our opening story regarding Argenbright Security, which basically went out of the aviation security business for failing to manage employee satisfaction and turnover problems, as well as the side effects of recruiting difficulties and performance failures. Indeed, given the recently documented links between employee retention and the retention of customers and investors, these attitudes must be considered critical even by managers who are interested only in financial profits.

For example, sales agents at State Farm Insurance stay with the company on average eighteen to twenty years, or two to three times the average tenure in the insurance industry. This lengthy tenure allows the average State Farm agent to learn the job and develop long-term relationships with customers that cannot be matched by competitors that may lose half of their sales staff each year. State Farm also benefits from having such an experienced staff; the company is able to systematically survey its agents to get their views about where customer satisfaction is high, where it is low, and what can be done to improve service.[6] The result in terms of the bottom line is clear: State Farm agents achieve 40 percent higher sales per agent than their competition. In addition, as an indicator of quality of service, the retention rates among State Farm customers exceed 95 percent.

Another example of this can be seen at SAS Institute, which has been rated by *Fortune* magazine among the top twenty companies to work for in America each of the last six years.[7] The SAS Institute is a privately held statistical software producer that manages and analyzes databases for more than 30,000 customer sites in more than 120 countries. The programming work at SAS deals with taking data from old and incompatible systems at the user's site and integrating it into the SAS system, where it can be analyzed for patterns and trends. Because each user's needs are unique and idiosyncratic, the only way to provide service that is of high quality but also efficient is to establish a long-term relationship with the customer. Turnover among programmers can destroy this long-term relationship, and the high demand for computer programmers means that SAS must constantly battle other employers bent on stealing away their best employees.

Realizing this, James Goodnight, the company's CEO and majority owner, has designed a retention strategy built around employee satisfaction. Located on a spacious 200-acre campus, the company headquarters boasts ergonomically designed private offices for each employee, a free clinic staffed by two doctors and six nurse practitioners, and a 55,000-square-foot recreation facility. The facilities host breakrooms that are stocked with free soft drinks, fruit, and candy, and the lunchroom includes a pianist who entertains daily. The company helps subsidize an excellent private school for the children of employees, and also offers country club memberships to all who are interested. These amenities have produced positive employee attitudes and have promoted retention. SAS has been able to experience a 4 percent rate of annual turnover in an industry where the norm is 20 percent. This has been estimated to save the company $75 million a year in labor costs, and has been instrumental in helping the company grow from a three-person operation in 1976 to a company estimated to be worth $5 billion today.[8]

Firms that take advantage of the employee retention–customer retention link remain in the minority, however. Indeed, the massive restructurings and downsizing efforts that took place in many organizations in the 1990s have left many organizations in the 2000s filled with dissatisfied, stressed, and insecure workers who are ready to abandon their current jobs for new opportunities at a moment's notice.[9] Thus, creating a stable and satisfied workforce serves as another opportunity for one firm to gain a competitive advantage over others in their industry.

This chapter focuses on the key attitudes and emotions that people experience in the workplace. We begin by defining job satisfaction and job stress. Then, to underline the importance of job satisfaction, we examine the consequences of dissatisfaction and stress, both in human terms and in terms of financial loss. Next, we review the major sources of dissatisfaction and stress in work environments. The chapter ends by discussing methods to manage dissatisfaction and stress in the workplace (see Figure 6-1 for an overview).

FIGURE 6-1 Chapter Overview

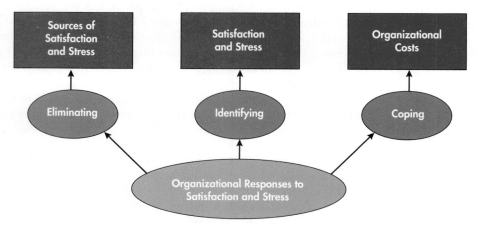

DEFINING SATISFACTION AND STRESS

Satisfaction

Job satisfaction is "a pleasurable feeling that results from the perception that one's job fulfills or allows for the fulfillment of one's important job values."[10] Our definition of job satisfaction includes three key components: values, importance of values, and perception.

Job satisfaction is a function of values. In his review of the topic, Edwin Locke defined *values* in terms of "what a person consciously or unconsciously desires to obtain." Locke distinguished between values and needs, suggesting that needs are best thought of as "objective requirements" of the body that are essential for maintaining life, such as the needs for oxygen and for water. Values, on the other hand, are "subjective requirements" that exist in the person's mind.

The second component of job satisfaction is the *importance* of those values. People differ not only in the values they hold, but also in the weights they give to those values, and these differences critically influence the degree of their job satisfaction. One person may value job security above all else. Another may be most concerned with the opportunity to travel. Yet another person may be primarily interested in doing work that is fun or that helps others. Although the first person may be satisfied by long-term employment, the other two may find little satisfaction in a permanent employment relationship.

The final component of our definition of job satisfaction is *perception*. Satisfaction reflects our perception of the present situation and our values. Recall that perceptions may not be completely accurate reflections of objective reality. When they are not perfect, we must look at the individual's perception of the situation—not the actual situation—to understand his or her personal reactions.

Stress

Stress is an unpleasant emotional state that results when someone is uncertain of his or her capacity to resolve a perceived challenge to an important value.[11] As in the case of satisfaction, we may find it easier to understand the nature of stress if we decompose this definition into three key components.

The first component, *perceived challenge*, emphasizes that stress arises from the interaction between people and their perceptions of the environment (not necessarily reality). For example, unfounded rumors about a factory closing will create stress among employees, even if no real threat exists.

The second component of this definition, *importance of values*, is critical for the same reason as was noted in our definition of satisfaction. Unless a challenge threatens some important value, it will not cause stress. For example, the rumored plant closing may not create stress for a worker who is already preparing to retire.

The third component, *uncertainty of resolution*, emphasizes that the person interprets the situation in terms of the perceived probability of successfully coping with the challenge. Obviously, if people believe that they can readily cope with the challenge, they will not experience stress. Perhaps surprisingly, experienced stress is also low if the person sees no possible chance that the problem can be resolved. Under these conditions, a person tends to accept his or her fate with little emotional reaction. Stress is actually highest when the perceived difficulty of the challenge closely matches the person's perceived capacity to meet the demand. Why? As the difficulty level and the ability level approach one another, the outcome becomes increasingly uncertain. This uncertainty about meeting the challenge creates the stress, rather than the fear of a negative outcome.[12]

The body's physiological reaction to this type of threat once had great survival value. When threatened, the human body produces chemicals that cause blood pressure to rise and divert blood from the skin and digestive organs to the muscles. Blood fats are then released, providing a burst of energy and enhancing blood clotting in case of injury. When the individual faces a prolonged threat, other changes begin that prepare the body for a long battle. For example, the body begins to conserve resources by retaining water and salts. Extra gastric acid is produced to increase the efficiency of digestion in the absence of blood (which has been diverted away from internal organs).[13]

Although these physiological changes probably had adaptive value ages ago, when they readied the person either to physically fight or to flee some threat, the same changes continue to occur today in response to threats, regardless of whether the increased physical capacity they produce is adaptive. For example, workers who hold jobs characterized by many demands over which the employees have little control are three times more likely to suffer from high blood pressure than other workers. The increased physical capacity gained through higher blood pressure will not, however, help these workers cope with the demands they face.

Hans Selye, a prominent physician and researcher, proposed that the **general adaptation syndrome** can explain the relationship between stress and these physical–physiological symptoms. According to Selye, the body's reaction to chronic stress occurs in three stages (Figure 6-2). In the *alarm stage*, the person identifies the threat. Whether this threat is physical (a threat of bodily injury) or psychological (the threat of losing one's job), the physiological changes described previously ensue. In the *resistance stage*, the person becomes resilient to the pressures created by the original threat. The symptoms that occurred in the alarm stage disappear, even though the stressor remains in place. Resistance seems to rely on increased levels of hormones secreted by the pituitary gland and the adrenal cortex.

If exposure to the threatening stressor continues, the person reaches the *exhaustion stage*. Pituitary gland and adrenal cortex activity slows down, and the person can no longer adapt to the continuing stress. Many of the physiological symptoms that originally appeared in the alarm stage now recur. If stress continues unabated, individuals may suffer **burnout**, which can lead to severe physical damage, including death via coronary failure or heart disease.[14]

FIGURE 6-2　The General Adaptation Syndrome

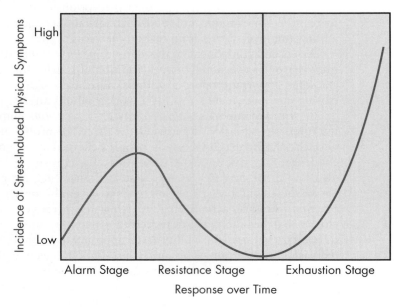

Measuring Satisfaction and Stress

Most attempts made to measure worker satisfaction rely on self-reports. A vast amount of data has been gathered on the reliability and validity of many existing scales, and a wealth of data is available on companies that have used these scales in the past, which allows for comparisons across firms. Established scales are excellent starting points when employers seek to assess the satisfaction levels of their employees. An employer would be foolish to "reinvent the wheel" by generating its own versions of measures of these broad constructs. Of course, in some cases, an organization may want to measure its employees' satisfaction with aspects of their work that are specific to that organization (for example, satisfaction with one health plan versus another health plan). In these situations, the organization may need to create its own scales. This scenario will be the exception rather than the rule, however.

Regardless of which measures are used or how many facets of satisfaction are assessed, a systematic, ongoing program of employee survey research should be a prominent component of any retention strategy for a number of reasons. First, it allows the company to monitor trends over time, thereby enabling the firm to prevent problems in the area of voluntary turnover before they happen. Indeed, one of the most critical trends to watch is the percentage of people who comply by filling out such surveys, because employees who are not willing to be surveyed often have the most negative attitudes.[15]

Second, an ongoing program of survey research provides a means of empirically assessing the effects of changes in policy (such as the introduction of a new performance appraisal system) or personnel (such as the introduction of a new CEO) on worker attitudes. Moreover, when these surveys incorporate standardized scales, they often allow the company to compare itself with others in its industry along the same dimensions. If the firm detects major differences between the organization and the industry as a whole (for example, in satisfaction with pay levels), the company might be able to react and change its policies before it experiences a mass exodus of people moving to the competition.

Finally, with the advent of increased networking capacity in many organizations, the cost of conducting online surveys has never been lower. Computerized versions of many scales perform as well, if not better, when administered over a company's intranet.[16] In addition, the results can be calculated more quickly. Some programs even allow the worker to see where he or she stands relative to co-workers immediately after filling out the survey.

ORGANIZATIONAL COSTS OF DISSATISFACTION AND STRESS

The previous section focused on the effects of dissatisfaction and stress as measured in terms of human physiology. In this section, we examine the costs of dissatisfaction and stress from an organizational effectiveness perspective. That is, even if we coldly ignore the human costs, important financial reasons exist for monitoring and managing the satisfaction and stress levels of employees.

Performance at the Individual and Organizational Level

Although it was once believed that job satisfaction and job performance were not strongly related, a recent comprehensive analysis of studies that involved 312 organizations and 54,417 employees has revealed a significant, positive correlation between these two variables.[17] Thus, the problems we saw in our opening story with Argenbright Security were not idiosyncratic to that one company, but instead generalize to most employers. Employees who are highly engaged with their work put in longer hours and generally see work as its own reward, creating less of a need to set up financial incentives, which as we saw in our last chapter can often backfire.[18] The satisfaction–performance link is especially strong in the service industry where employees have direct, face-to-face contact with customers.[19] In service contexts, there seems to be a direct transfer of attitudes from employees to customers.[20]

For example, at Southwest Airlines, airline staff were always encouraged to tell jokes onboard the aircraft in order to lighten the spirits of passengers. After 9/11 the company feared this was no longer such a good idea, and told the staff to lay off the humor. Loyal customers came to expect the lighthearted approach to air travel, however, and the management was deluged with letters asking for a return to the earlier practices. Thus, on a recent flight, one steward responded by telling passengers, "If you smoke on this airplane, the FAA will fine you $2,000, and at those prices, you might as well fly Delta."[21]

One might wonder whether the relationship between the attitudes of individual workers and their own performance actually translates to higher levels of organizational performance as measured via traditional financial performance indicators, and the evidence is clear that it often does. A recent study by *Fortune* magazine compared the financial performance of the "100 Best Companies to Work For" with a closely matched set of firms that were the same size and in the same industry. In terms of operational performance, the results of this study showed that between 1995 and 2000 the return on assets for the 100 best was 9.3 percent versus 7.3 percent for the control firms. In terms of stock market perceptions, the market-to-book ratio for the 100 best firms was 4.5 versus 2.0 for the controls, suggesting that investors appreciate the competitive value inherent in having a stable and satisfied workforce.[22] Although some have suggested that the link between employee attitudes and firm performance may be such that performance causes attitudes, in fact, as the Cutting-Edge Research box documents, it is increasingly clear that attitudes are the cause, not the effect in this relationship.

CUTTING-EDGE RESEARCH

EMPLOYEE SATISFACTION AND ORGANIZATIONAL OUTCOMES: CAUSE OR EFFECT?

Most managers recognize the critical need to generate customer satisfaction and organizational profitability, but in the aggressive pursuit of these desired goals, they often disregard employee satisfaction. For some, this oversight is based on the belief that employee satisfaction and the other two outcomes—customer satisfaction and profitability—are unrelated. For others, it is based on the belief that even though there may be a relationship between employee satisfaction and organizational outcomes, the nature of this relationship is such that organizational effectiveness is the cause, and employee satisfaction is the effect. That is, if the organization performs well, it will generate more profits, which in turn allows the company to treat employees better, which in turn leads to higher employee satisfaction. Both of these beliefs imply that satisfaction does not causally drive effectiveness, and according to the most recent research evidence on the topic, both of these beliefs are flat wrong.

First, with respect to whether there is any relationship between attitudes and outcomes, a recent meta-analysis summarized findings from 2,940 business units that employed 198,514 employees. This study employed a widely used measure of satisfaction, and found significant correlations between aggregated scores on employee satisfaction on the one hand, and customer satisfaction and profitability on the other. The size of these correlations (in the .10 to .20 range) was not large in an absolute sense, and in terms of percentage of improvement in profitability, the impact was only modest. That is, firms that were above the median in employee satisfaction had profits that were 2 to 3 percent higher than firms that were below the median. However, the size of many of these companies meant that small increases in profit percentages often resulted in large gains in terms of absolute dollars, with firms above the median reporting profits that were roughly $1 million per year higher than those below the median.

Any suspicion that employee satisfaction is the result of firm performance and not the cause was refuted in a second recent study that longitudinally examined data from 28 units of a regional restaurant chain. This study collected attitudinal data, profitability data, and customer satisfaction over several years, and analyses indicated that while there were significant relationships between measures of employee satisfaction in the previous year and both profits and customer satisfaction in the next year, there was no relationship between profits and customer satisfaction in the previous year and employee satisfaction in the next year.

In both of these studies, although there were effects of current employee attitudes on both future profits and future customer satisfaction, the relationships tended to be stronger for customer satisfaction. Thus, the potential competitive advantage that can be created by cultivating high levels of satisfaction may be particularly pronounced in the service sector of the economy, where there is a more direct, face-to-face relationship between employees and customers. In these contexts, the positive feelings experienced by workers may spill over to customers, and the longer tenure associated with satisfied employees allows them to build more personal, long-term relationships with customers.

Sources: J. K. Harter, F. L. Schmidt, and T. L. Hayes, "Business-Unit-Level Relationship between Employee Satisfaction, Employee Engagement, and Business Outcomes: A Meta-Analysis," *Journal of Applied Psychology* 87 (2002), 268–279; D. J. Koys, "The Effects of Employee Satisfaction, Organizational Citizenship Behavior, and Turnover on Organizational Effectiveness: A Unit-Level, Longitudinal Study," *Personnel Psychology* 54 (2001), 101–114; R. Batt, "Managing Customer Services: Human Resource Practices, Quit Rates, and Sales Growth," *Academy of Management Journal* 45 (2002), 587–597.

Health Care Costs

As noted earlier, work-related stress has the potential to greatly affect a person's health and well-being. A fact of current organizational life is that employing organizations bear much of the cost for employee health care. Although wages have risen during the last thirty years, spiraling medical fees and hospital room-and-board charges have increased the cost of patient insurance by three times as much as wage increases over the same period. Indeed, medical insurance and claims costs currently constitute a full 10 percent of payroll for U.S. companies.[23]

Besides paying for general health insurance, employers are increasingly finding themselves held liable for specific incidents of stress-related illness. The Occupational Safety and Health Act of 1970 (OSHA) and many state laws hold employing organizations accountable "for all diseases arising out of and in the course of employment."[24] A study conducted at Boeing Company found that dissatisfied employees were more than twice as likely to file back-injury claims as were satisfied workers.[25] Similarly, research has shown a strong link between stress and mental disorders, making it possible for an overworked advertising executive who was the victim of a nervous breakdown to successfully sue his employer.[26] Stress and dissatisfaction have also been linked to problem drinking by employees, which can result in direct costs associated with treating these problems, as well as indirect costs associated with increased absenteeism and reduced safety levels associated with problem drinkers at work.[27]

Absenteeism and Turnover

Dissatisfaction and stress not only create direct costs for organizations (that is, health care programs expenditures), but also are the source of indirect costs—most notably in the form of absenteeism and turnover. Dissatisfaction is a major reason for absenteeism, a very costly organizational problem.[28]

Dissatisfaction also triggers organizational turnover. Replacing workers who leave the organization voluntarily is a costly undertaking. For example, one high-tech company, Hewlett-Packard, estimates the cost of replacing one middle-level manager at $40,000.[29] When workers depart from these jobs, companies lose the investment they have made in employee development. In the worst cases, disgruntled, experienced employees may take jobs with competitors. A company's investment in employee development is then not only lost, but actually winds up as a bonus for a competing firm that gains access to a great deal of knowledge about the competition's operations.[30]

Low Organizational Commitment and Citizenship

Dissatisfaction also contributes to declining organizational commitment. **Organizational commitment** is the degree to which people identify with the organization that employs them. It implies a willingness on the employee's part to put forth a substantial effort on the organization's behalf and his or her intention to stay with the organization for a long time.

The subject of organizational commitment has recently attracted a great deal of attention. Many employers fear that the downsizing policies pursued so aggressively in the 1990s may have killed company loyalty in the new millennium.[31] Evidence provided by surveys of U.S. workers bolsters this claim. When asked if employees today are more loyal or less loyal to their companies compared with ten years ago, 63 percent said less loyal, and only 22 percent said more loyal. A full 50 percent of those responding reported that they would likely change employers in the next five years.[32] Thus, just when U.S. businesses are trying to inculcate a new sense of worker participation and involvement, many of their employees are seeking to reduce their levels of commitment and dependency.

Although formal performance evaluation systems may often prevent someone who is dissatisfied from expressing his or her unhappiness directly (that is, through poor job performance), dissatisfaction may nevertheless have a negative effect on **organizational citizenship behaviors** (OCBs).[33] OCBs are acts that promote the organization's interest, but are not formally a part of any person's documented job requirements. They include behaviors such as volunteering for assignments, going out of one's way to welcome new employees, helping others who need assistance, staying late to finish a task, or voicing one's opinion on critical organizational issues.[34]

OCBs tend to make the organization run more smoothly, but dissatisfied employees rarely engage in them. Instead, employees seem to take a reciprocating approach to these kinds of behaviors; that is, they show a willingness to engage in them only if they feel that the employer goes out of its way as well. For example, one recent study conducted at Fel-Pro, an engine gasket manufacturing firm in the Midwest, showed that OCBs were high, but only among employees who believed that the company's work–life benefits program helped them and their families.[35] Another study showed that OCBs declined when workers became emotionally exhausted due to an increase in the number of hours worked, suggesting a quality–quantity trade-off when it comes to stretching workers too far.[36]

Workplace Violence and Sabotage

In the last fifteen years, violence in the workplace has developed into a major organizational problem. Workplace homicide is the fastest-growing form of murder in the United States. It is especially a problem for women, for whom workplace homicide is the leading cause of death in the workplace.[37] Moreover, homicide is merely the most extreme example of workplace violence—other forms of work-related violence are also proliferating. In any given year, 2 million employees are physically attacked, 6 million are threatened with physical attack, and 16 million suffer from some form of harassment. One of the most infamous employers in this regard is the U.S. Postal Service: During one eighteen-month period, it experienced 500 cases of employee violence directed toward a manager, and 200 cases of violence by a manager directed at an employee.[38]

Most violence that involves organizational insiders is triggered by extreme levels of dissatisfaction and stress on the part of the attacker.[39] To come to grips with its problems in this area, the U.S. Postal Service has launched an intense initiative to improve the agency's work environment. Managers and supervisors now go through a series of training sessions that deal with such issues as employee empowerment, conflict resolution, and positive reinforcement. The Postal Service is also working with unions to improve the grievance process and has launched a regular series of employee attitude surveys intended to measure and monitor employee satisfaction levels. In addition, cross-functional intervention teams of employees and managers have been created that can step in and try to change the environment in regions where levels of dissatisfaction or stress seem dangerously high.[40]

Organizational sabotage is violence directed at property rather than people. Dissatisfied workers may either consciously or subconsciously produce faulty products, and as the Securing Competitive Advantage box shows, this can have disastrous effects for both consumers and the company.

Although traditionally organizational sabotage was seen as dealing with vandalism or theft, it is now increasingly being directed at computer information systems. These systems, while protected from external tampering, remain highly vulnerable to manipulation by insiders. For example, Omega Engineering suffered $10 million in losses after one very dissatisfied employee unleashed a software program (a "logic bomb") that deleted critical computer files.[41] Erecting technical barriers to this kind of act, while simultaneously fostering the widespread use of technology within an organization, can be difficult. Often, the only way to prevent such acts is to monitor and eliminate the dissatisfaction that motivates the behavior in the first place.

SECURING COMPETITIVE ADVANTAGE

JOB SATISFACTION AND SAFETY: WHERE THE RUBBER MEETS THE ROAD

Marisa Rodriguez was forty years old when the doctor told her that she would need to use a wheelchair the rest of her life. She was injured when the tread on the right rear tire of her Ford Explorer separated from the rest of the tire, causing the SUV to fly off the road and flip over several times before finally coming to rest in a ditch off a Texas highway. Unfortunately, this was not an isolated incident for the specific tire that was on her car, the Firestone Wilderness AT. Indeed, according to the National Highway Transportation Safety Administration, tread separation problems associated with these specific tires were a contributing factor in 119 deaths, more than 500 injuries, and at least 3,500 complaints to the agency.

What first looked like a problem in tire design, however, is now appearing to be a case of disgruntled workers and confrontational managers at a single plant, who apparently lost focus on the production process during a time of labor strife. As the following chart shows, rather than being a general problem with the AT Wilderness Tire, tread separation problems were primarily an issue with tires produced in one plant at one specific time. That is, the data on "fatalities per million miles produced" indicates that during 1994–1996, when the plant was in a labor dispute, fatalities associated with tires produced at the Decatur, Illinois, plants were more than twenty times those in either the Wilson, North Carolina, plant or the plant in Joliette, Quebec, despite the fact that they were using the same tire design. In fact, the fatality rate for the Decatur plant during this period was more than thirty times the rate for the Decatur plant itself, before and after 1994–1996. As one analyst noted, "It appears likely to us that something about the chemistry between the replacement workers and the recalled strikers created conditions that led to the production of many defective tires."

Workers in the Decatur plant during this time period were very upset, because management was pressing for wage cuts and a change to twelve-hour shifts. The workers went on strike, and management responded by hiring strikebreakers to take their jobs.

Many, but not all, of the workers capitulated a year later, and grudgingly went to back to work on the new shifts at the new lower rate, working side by side with people they considered to be scabs. According to testimony from both workers and management, work practices during this time period began to deteriorate. For example, the tires in question had steel belts, and the steel needed to be kept in a climate-controlled room to prevent corrosion and rust, which makes it difficult for the steel to adhere to the rubber. The published work procedures demanded that even if the steel was left out for as little as thirty minutes, it had to be reprocessed, but this was difficult and time-consuming, and the unhappy workers, who were pushed by management to go faster and faster, often failed to follow through on this policy. As one worker noted, "The bottom line was to get the tires out."

The cost of these safety breakdowns in terms of human life and suffering are incalculable, but the financial repercussions of these failures for Firestone can be well documented. The company was eventually forced to pay out more than $40 million in lawsuits and lost more than 60 percent of its customer base to competing firms—including the Ford Motor Company, a huge demander of tires that had a long-term, steady relationship with Firestone prior to the Decatur incident. The Decatur plant was eventually closed down, putting strikers, strikebreakers, and managers out of their jobs. Clearly, the inability to keep the workforce satisfied severely damaged Firestone's competitive position in the industry, and some have speculated that the organization may never return to its former status in this industry.

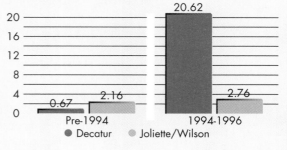

Sources: C. Yancho, "Driver Testifies in Firestone Lawsuit," *CNN.com*, August 15, 2001, p. 1; E. Ahlberg, "Court Blocks Search for Class Action in Bridgestone Case," *Wall Street Journal Online*, June 23, 2003, p. 1; D. Wessel, "The Hidden Cost of Labor Strife," *Wall Street Journal Online*, January 20, 2002, pp. 1–2; E. Garsten, "Firestone CEO, Former Workers Answer Questions in Tire Lawsuits," *CNN.com*, October 27, 2000, pp. 1–3; E. Ahlberg, "U.S. Government Won't Reopen Probe of Bridgestone/Firestone Tires," *Wall Street Journal Online*, June 16, 2003, pp. 1–2.

SOURCES OF DISSATISFACTION AND STRESS

Certain inherent features of organizations can cause dissatisfaction and stress. In this section, we focus on the physical and social environment, the person, the task, and the role.

Physical and Social Environment

A wealth of evidence shows that some physical features of the workplace can stimulate negative emotional reactions in workers. For example, studies have shown that *extremes in temperatures* can affect job attitudes as well as performance and decision making.[42] In addition, different optimal *lighting requirements* appear to exist for different tasks, and perceived darkness has been found to correlate significantly with job dissatisfaction.[43] Moreover, research on how people perceive tasks has shown that physical features of the environment, such as *cleanliness, working outdoors,* and *health hazards,* are very important in the way people perceive their tasks.[44]

Recent studies have focused on some very subtle characteristics of the physical environment. Researchers have coined the term *sick-building syndrome* to describe physical structures whose indoor air is contaminated by invisible pollutants. Today, many new buildings are constructed with windows that do not open, which means that workers in these buildings breathe a great deal of recycled air. This air can contain a mixture of carbon monoxide sucked into a building from air intake vents that overhang parking lots; ozone discharged from office printers; chemicals that are emitted by paint, carpet, or new furniture; and even bacteria funneled through heating, ventilation, and cooling systems. This problem has gotten so bad that the U.S. Environmental Protection Agency recently ranked indoor air as one of the top five environmental health risks of our time.[45]

In terms of the social environment, supervisors and co-workers serve as the two primary sources of satisfaction or frustration for the employee. The employee may be satisfied with a supervisor or co-workers because they help the employee attain some valued outcome, or because they share similar values, attitudes, or philosophy. The greatest degree of satisfaction with supervisors and co-workers occurs where both kinds of attraction exist, although the negative outcomes associated with abusive supervisors (that is, lack of commitment and turnover) are particularly pronounced.[46] In fact, data from exit interviews show that 75 percent of the reasons cited for leaving a job can be directly tied to the actions or decisions of the direct supervisor.[47]

Social support is the active provision of sympathy and caring. Many researchers have suggested that social support from supervisors and co-workers can buffer employees from stress. Figure 6-3 illustrates the notion behind **buffering.** As shown in the figure, the presence of people who are supportive can lower the incidence of stress-related symptoms under conditions of high stress. Evidence for this effect has come largely from research in medical contexts, which shows that recovery and rehabilitation from illness proceed better when the patient is surrounded by caring friends and family.[48] The same seems true for work-related stress—for example, a study of nurses working in stressful units showed that those who received social support were much better able to perform their jobs.[49]

The physical and social aspects of work converge to create the behavior setting. Two important and interrelated aspects of the behavior setting are social density and privacy. **Social density,** a measure of crowding, is calculated by dividing the number of people in a given area by the number of square feet in that area. **Privacy** is the freedom to work without observation or unnecessary interruption.

FIGURE 6-3   How Social Support May Buffer Stress

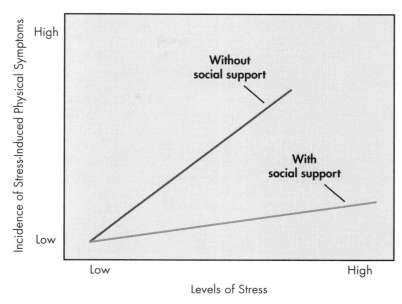

Research with clerical workers has shown that job satisfaction decreases as social density increases.[50] Social density is a particular problem when it becomes compounded by lack of privacy (for example, when work stations are not enclosed by walls or partitions).[51] In fact, turnover is exceptionally high when workers are both crowded and lack privacy.[52]

Personal Dispositions

Because both stress and dissatisfaction ultimately reside within a person, many researchers who have studied these outcomes have focused on individual differences. The term **negative affectivity** describes a dispositional dimension of subjective distress that includes such unpleasant mood states as anger, contempt, disgust, guilt, fear, and nervousness.[53] Negative affectivity is similar to the construct of emotional stability (discussed in Chapter 3) and tends to remain quite stable over time. In fact, recent research has shown that the work attitudes of adults can be predicted from measures of emotional stability and negative affectivity collected when those individuals were children.[54]

People who are generally high in negative affectivity tend to focus on both their own negative qualities and those of others. Such people are also more likely to experience significantly higher levels of distress than are individuals who rate low on this dimension. This consideration needs to be taken into account when conducting surveys regarding satisfaction or stress levels attributed to organizational practices.[55] It highlights the fact that some people bring stress and dissatisfaction with them to work, and that these workers may remain relatively dissatisfied regardless of what steps are taken by the organization or the manager.[56]

At the extreme, negative affectivity can turn into clinical depression, which is responsible for the loss of more than 200 million working days in the United States each year. More than 3,000 psychiatric claims are filed annually with the Equal

Employment Opportunity Commission, making this category the single largest type of claim brought under the Americans with Disabilities Act.[57] Managers facing this type of problem need to work with mental health professionals (in employee assistance programs, for example) to help make the kinds of accommodations necessary to get their employees back into a healthy and productive mode.[58]

A second critical individual-difference variable is the Type A behavior pattern.[59] People with Type A personalities are characterized as being aggressive and competitive, as setting high standards for themselves and others, and as putting themselves under constant time pressure.[60] People with Type B personalities, on the other hand, lack such feelings of urgency. The unrealistic expectations of the impatient, ambitious, and overly aggressive Type A person render him or her particularly susceptible to dissatisfaction and stress. This susceptibility may also account for the fact that the Type A person has two times the risk, as compared with the Type B person, for developing coronary heart disease.

Organizational Tasks

Although we cannot entirely discount the influence of dispositional traits and nonwork experiences, nothing predicts a person's level of workplace satisfaction or stress better than the nature of the work itself. Table 6-1 lists some of the most and least stressful jobs. Innumerable aspects of tasks have been linked to dissatisfaction and stress. In general, the key factors that determine satisfaction and stress are task complexity, physical strain, and task meaningfulness.

Task Complexity   Although in extreme cases tasks can become overly complex, research generally shows a positive relationship between task complexity and satisfaction.[61] The boredom generated by simple, repetitive jobs that are not mentally challenging has been consistently found to frustrate most workers.[62] This frustration, in turn, manifests itself as dissatisfaction, stress, and ultimately tardiness, absenteeism, and turnover. In some cases, external interventions can alleviate the boredom inherent in these kinds of jobs. For example, research suggests that, for some simple jobs, allowing employees to use personal stereos increases both performance and satisfaction.[63]

Boredom created by lack of task complexity can also hinder performance on certain types of jobs. For example, airport security personnel, air traffic controllers, operators in nuclear power stations, medical technicians, and inspectors on production floors all belong in a class of jobs that require *vigilance*. Such workers must continually monitor equipment and be prepared to respond to critical events. Because such events are rare, however, these jobs are exceedingly boring and hence workers are vulnerable to poor concentration.[64] Ultimately, this inattention may result in performance breakdowns of often serious dimensions.

Physical Strain   Another important determinant of work satisfaction is the amount of physical strain and exertion involved in the job. This factor is sometimes over-

TABLE 6-1
Jobs Characterized as High and Low in Stress

High-Stress Jobs	Low-Stress Jobs
Manager	Farm laborer
Supervisor	Craft worker
Nurse	Stock handler
Waitress	College professor
Air traffic controller	Heavy-equipment operator

looked in the present age of technology, where much of the physical strain associated with jobs has been removed by automation. Indeed, the very fact that technology continues to advance highlights the degree to which physical strain is universally considered an undesirable work characteristic. Many jobs, however, can still be characterized as physically demanding, and this is especially the case overseas, where worker rights are not always respected at the same level one might experience in Western nations. Indeed, as the Ethics and Social Responsibility box shows, some countries that serve as sub-contractors to Western companies employ a system of debt bondage that forces foreign workers into something that closely resembles slavery in terms of both physical working conditions and the ability to freely quit the job.

Task Meaningfulness   It is also important for the worker to believe that his or her work is meaningful and has value. For example, the Peace Corps recruits applicants by describing its work as "the toughest job you'll ever love." At the opposite of the spectrum, after 9/11 many investment brokers in New York City quit their jobs despite the high pay. In the words of one Goldman Sachs employee, "It got to the point where everybody wound up working only for the money, and after 9/11, I was in search of more soulful work."[65]

Recently, the term *empowerment* has been used to define work that is not only meaningful, but also characterized by autonomy. Empowered workers feel that they can display their competence and make a positive impact on the world—or at least their little corner of it. This belief, in turn, creates a high level of intrinsic motivation that results in high job performance and organizational commitment.[66]

For example, at Marriott Hotels, the "First 10 Program" is the label attached to the company's strategy of making a lasting impression on the guest in the first ten minutes of the service encounter, beginning when the guest steps out of the car or taxi. At this point, one employee is personally responsible for the entire encounter, including greeting the guest, handling check-in, helping with luggage, and escorting the person to the room. Prior to this program, guests were shuffled through these tasks by four different people. The program has markedly improved consumer satisfaction while simultaneously making the task more meaningful and interesting for the employee.[67]

Because empowerment often entails a delegation of authority from supervisors to subordinates, the positive effects of empowering workers tend to be culturally specific. Some countries, such as the United States, are relatively low in power distance (that is, low in terms of accepting status differences between people). In these cultures, empowerment leads to high satisfaction with supervision. On the other hand, in cultures that are high in power distance, such as India, such a program is seen as an abdication of responsibility and leads to dissatisfaction with supervision.[68] We will have much more to say about power distance in Chapter 15, when we deal with international issues.

Organization Roles

The person and the social environment converge in the form of an **organization role**. The person's role in the organization can be defined as the total set of expectations of the person held by both the person and others who make up the social environment. These expectations of behavior include both the formal aspects of the job and the informal expectations of co-workers, supervisors, clients, and customers. They greatly influence how the person responds to the work. Three of the most heavily researched aspects of roles are role ambiguity, role conflict, and role scope.

Role Ambiguity   Role ambiguity comprises the uncertainty or lack of clarity surrounding expectations about a person's role in the organization. It indicates that the

ETHICS AND SOCIAL RESPONSIBILITY

CUTTING COSTS THE OLD-FASHIONED WAY: DEBT BONDAGE

Although the price of cell phone service is hardly a bargain, when one considers the small price of a cell phone itself—often a giveaway item when one purchases the service—it is truly remarkable. The price for a low-cost cell phone, however, tends to get paid by workers who are the modern version of slaves. Although slavery per se is illegal in most industrialized countries, many of the workers who produce cell phones are victims of a practice called debt bondage, which winds up looking and acting a lot like slavery. Although many U.S. companies have responded to societal pressures to improve overseas factory conditions, many are just becoming aware of the problems associated with debt bondage. This would include Pia Gideon, vice-president of external relations for Ericcson, who, when told about the use of debt bondage among subcontractors in Taiwan, noted, "I wasn't aware of this at all."

Debt bondage starts with workers in countries like Vietnam, Thailand, and the Philippines who are desperate to find jobs, but cannot locate work in their own country. Second, it is fueled by countries such as Taiwan, South Korea, and Malaysia, which have relatively high labor costs for Asia and are in desperate competition with China, which boasts of an incredibly large supply of low-wage workers. Third, labor brokers, who bring the two parties together—identifying, transporting, and writing contracts for the relocated workers—facilitate it. In theory, one might examine this exchange and think it could work out for all sides. Poor countries reduce their unemployment rate, wealthy countries secure inexpensive labor, workers find jobs, and you and I get cheap cell phones. The only problem is that the workers are powerless, the labor contractors are often unethical, and the companies and consumers are typically unaware of the terms of the contracts—which make virtual slaves out of the workers.

In most debt bondage cases, the worker starts with no money, which is why he or she is looking to move in the first place. In order to pay the labor contractor for moving and re-establishing the worker in the new country, the worker has to take out a loan with the labor contractor, who will deduct payments

from the worker's future wages. The workers often sign contracts written not in their own language, but in the language of the country they are moving to, which means they cannot read it. The terms of the contracts, which are legally enforceable in the countries to which they are moving, are usually so skewed to the contractor that the debt can never be paid off. In fact, the debt is sometimes then extended to family members and can be passed down to future generations.

For example, one worker at a Motorola subsidiary in Taiwan took out a $2,400 loan to a labor contractor to help her move from the Philippines. The job paid $460 a month, which was five times what she could earn in her own country if she could find a job at all. The interest on the loan was 10 percent a *month,* however. Once she was settled in Taiwan, she soon realized that after taxes, room and board, and "runaway insurance" (money paid into a monthly escrow that is returned to her only if she completes the three-year contract), the money she had left was not enough to pay off the interest, let alone the original loan. This leads to a need for more loans and an ever-increasing cycle of dependence that eventually turns into slavery. At one shelter for the poor run by Catholic Relief Services, a counselor noted, "We have workers come to the center that have been working in Taiwan for six months and never seen any Taiwanese money."

One employer that is ahead of the curve on debt bondage is The Gap. Negative publicity due to poor working conditions at factories left the company sadder but wiser when it comes to dealing with overseas contractors. Gap routinely evaluates how it treats foreign workers, weighing this along with product quality and safety standards when evaluating contractor fitness. Gap requires that factory managers let all foreign workers control their own travel documents and wages. It also makes the factory owners agree to assume the worker's debt bond and travel costs if the worker decides to leave for any reason. Time will tell if other companies such as Motorola and Ericcson will follow this lead.

Sources: N. Stein, "No Way Out," *Fortune,* January 20, 2003, pp. 102–108; K. Bales, "The Social Psychology of Modern Slavery," *Scientific American,* April 2002, pp. 22–25; D. Jones, "Unilever, Watchdog Groups to Discuss Child Labor," *Wall Street Journal Online,* May 5, 2003, pp. 1–3.

worker does not have enough information about what is expected. Role ambiguity can also stem from a lack of information about the rewards for performing well and the punishments for failing. For example, imagine that your college instructor has assigned a term paper but neglected to tell you (1) what topics are pertinent, (2) how long the paper should be, (3) when it is due, (4) how it will be evaluated, and (5) how much it is worth toward the final course grade. Clearly, most people would feel stress under these circumstances, a reaction that can be directly attributed to role ambiguity.

Role Conflict   **Role conflict** is the recognition of incompatible or contradictory demands that face the person who occupies a role. It can take many different forms.

Intersender role conflict occurs when two or more people in the social environment convey mutually exclusive expectations. For example, a middle manager may find that upper management wants to institute severe reprimands for worker absenteeism, whereas the workers expect greater consideration of their needs and personal problems.

Intrasender role conflict occurs when one person in the social environment holds two competing expectations. For example, a research assistant for a magazine editor may be asked to write a brief but detailed summary of a complex and lengthy article from another source. In attempting to accomplish this task, the assistant may experience considerable distress when trying to decide what to include and what to leave out of the summary.

A third form of role conflict is *interrole conflict.* Most people occupy multiple roles, and the expectations for our different roles may sometimes clash. A parent who has a business trip scheduled during a daughter's first piano recital, for example, is likely to feel torn between the demands of two roles.

Earlier in this chapter, we noted the relative higher level of financial performance associated with companies that were part of the top 100 best companies to work for as rated by *Fortune* magazine. In terms of how one gets into the top 100, it is instructive to see how many of them directly support their workers in terms of helping them manage role conflict that spills over from life to work. Of the top 100, 26 offer on-site day care and 29 offer concierge service.[69] Thirty-one percent of these companies offer fully paid sabbaticals, in recognition of the fact that time off for renewal is a major aspiration for many of today's most talented workers.[70]

Role Scope   **Role scope** refers to the absolute number of expectations that exist for the person occupying a role. In *role overload,* too many expectations or demands are placed on the role occupant. In *role underload,* the opposite problem occurs. Because researchers have traditionally focused on jobs with high role scope, they have tended to look at the negative consequences of jobs that are too challenging. Two aspects of modern U.S. workplaces have created problems in the area of role scope. First, layoffs and reductions in the labor force have often left fewer people to do more work in many large companies. Second, telecommunications advancements have made it easier for people to take their work home with them. Thus, whereas much of the rest of the developed world has cut back on the number of hours worked per person per year, the United States has gone in the other direction, actually increasing the number of hours worked per year. In addition, in 2002 the average U.S. worker took twelve vacation days, which is half of that taken by Japanese and British workers, one-third of that taken by workers in France and Germany, and one-fourth of that taken by Italians—world leaders in vacation time among industrialized nations.[71] Some are concerned that this is taking a toll on people in terms of stress and health, and have argued that U.S. firms need to strike a better balance between the work and nonwork lives of employees.

ELIMINATING AND COPING WITH DISSATISFACTION AND STRESS

Because the costs associated with employee dissatisfaction and stress can be high, identifying these factors should be a major part of the job description of every manager. Once identified, interventions should target the source of the stress. If it is impossible to eliminate the stressor for some reason, then the manager should at least help employees manage and cope with the stress. In this section, we discuss how to identify, eliminate, and manage dissatisfaction and stress in the workplace.

Identifying Symptoms of Dissatisfaction and Stress

In some cases, employees themselves report problems in these areas. Many others, however, are afraid to admit that they cannot overcome some problem associated with their work. Workers who are dissatisfied with some facet of their job may not speak out to avoid sounding like chronic complainers. In other cases, the attitudes of some workers may have become so bad that they view reporting dissatisfaction as a waste of time. For this reason, as noted earlier, it is critical for managers to monitor the kinds of attitudes via a regular, systematic employee survey program.

Conducting an organizational opinion survey is not a task that should be taken lightly, because such surveys often raise expectations. For this reason, the organization conducting the survey should be prepared to act on the results. For example, at Doctor's Hospital in Manteca, California, a survey of employees' opinions revealed dissatisfaction in several areas (defined as an "unfavorable" rating by at least 35 percent of the employees).When these results were fed back to employees, each problem area was accompanied by a corresponding action plan so that the workers could see how the organization intended to address the problem.

For example, in the area of career development, the survey indicated that even though the hospital reimbursed 100 percent of employee expenses for tuition, it did so at the end of the semester; the inability to obtain the money up front therefore prevented many workers from using this benefit. The hospital now provides tuition up-front, along with loans to help defray other nontuition costs associated with taking a class (for example, childcare expenses). In this way, a source of dissatisfaction for employees has been transformed into a plus.[72]

In the process of using employee surveys to monitor employee satisfaction, service organizations can benefit by using those surveys to also monitor employees' perceptions of customer satisfaction. Front-line employees of service organizations have a great deal of information on what makes customers satisfied or dissatisfied, and organizations that tap this resource consistently outperform other firms in terms of customer satisfaction ratings.[73] In addition to closely observing employees and conducting surveys, managers should be aware of well-known sources of dissatisfaction and stress and be prepared to eliminate, or at the very least help employees cope with, the source of dissatisfaction and stress. Had the managers at Argenbright Security been more concerned about these kinds of issues within its workforce, the problems depicted in our opening story might have been avoided.

Eliminating Dissatisfying and Stressful Conditions

Because the nature of the task influences dissatisfaction and stress so strongly, some of the most effective means of reducing negative reactions to work focus on the task. Job enrichment methods include many techniques designed to add complexity and meaning to a person's work. As the term *enrichment* suggests, this kind of intervention targets jobs that are boring because of their repetitive nature or low scope.

Although enrichment cannot always improve all employees' reactions to work, it can prove very useful. This topic will be covered in more depth in Chapter 7 on work design.

Role problems rank immediately behind job problems in terms of creating distress. The role analysis technique is designed to clarify role expectations for a jobholder by improving communication between the person and his or her supervisors, co-workers, subordinates, and perhaps even customers. In role analysis, both the jobholder and the role set members write down their expectations. These people then gather together to review their lists. Writing down all expectations ensures that ambiguities can be removed and conflicts identified. Where conflicts arise, the group as a whole (perhaps with the assistance of a group facilitator) tries to decide how to resolve these problems. When this kind of analysis is done throughout an organization, instances of overload and underload may be discovered and role requirements may be traded off, allowing for the development of more balanced roles.

Skills training is a means of trying to help the employee change a dissatisfying or stressful condition. For example, training in time management and goal prioritization has successfully reduced managers' physiological stress symptoms such as rapid pulse rate and high blood pressure.[74] With this type of training, participants decide on their most important work values. They then learn how to pinpoint goals, identify roadblocks to successful goal accomplishment, and seek the collaboration of co-workers in achieving these goals.

Skills training also gives job incumbents the ability to better predict, understand, and control events occurring on the job, which in turn reduces stress. That is, being able to understand and control these events weakens the effect of perceived stress on job satisfaction.[75] As Jerry Lee, managing director of Texas Instruments' Malaysian operation, notes, "The key to employee loyalty lies not in offering higher wages or better amenities, but in giving workers more control over their jobs."[76]

A person's ability to handle dissatisfying or stressful work experiences is also enhanced when the worker has an opportunity to air any problems and grievances.[77] The formal opportunity to complain to the organization about one's work situation has been referred to as **voice.** Having voice provides employees with an active, constructive outlet for their work frustrations.[78] Research with nurses, for example, shows that the provision of voice mechanisms such as grievance procedures, employee attitude surveys, and question-and-answer sessions between employees and management can all lead to better worker attitudes and less turnover.[79]

One step beyond voicing opinions is the chance to take action or make decisions based on one's opinions. *Participation in decision making* (PDM) provides opportunities for workers to have input into important organizational decisions that involve their work and has been found to reduce role conflict and ambiguity. In fact, research has shown that simply holding participatory meetings twice per month can reduce stress, which in turn lowers absenteeism and turnover.[80]

Managing Symptoms of Dissatisfaction and Stress

In some situations, neither roles, tasks, nor individual capacities can be altered sufficiently to reduce dissatisfaction and stress. Here interventions must be aimed at the symptoms of stress. Although not as desirable as eliminating the stressors themselves, eliminating the symptoms is better than no action at all. Some interventions that fall into this category focus exclusively on physiological reactions to stress.

Physical conditioning, particularly in the form of *aerobic exercise,* helps make a person more resistant to the physiological changes, such as high blood pressure, that accompany stress reactions. Tenneco, a diversified manufacturing company, even provides its employees with a free, 25,000-square-foot gym containing basketball and racquetball courts, a workout area, a glass-enclosed running track with piped-in music, and $200,000 worth of exercise and bodybuilding equipment. Tenneco chairman James Ketelsen believes that the $3 million required to run the center is well worth the expense. He comments, "Our testing process discovered problems that could have been fatal. I'm sure we've saved some lives. How do you put a value on that?"[81]

Another approach to treating stress symptoms is to employ *relaxation techniques*. Under a severe amount of stress (as when preparing a fight-or-flight response), many of the body's muscles tighten. Relaxation programs focus on eliminating tenseness in most of the major muscle groups, including the hand, forearm, back, neck, face, foot, and ankle. Relaxing these muscle groups lowers blood pressure and pulse rate and reduces other physiological stress manifestations. One experiment that dealt with relaxation therapy in a social service agency found that people who were randomly assigned to such therapy reported less stress and manifested reduced absenteeism as compared with people who did not receive the therapy.[82]

At one time, it was thought that people had no voluntary control over their physiological responses. **Biofeedback** machines, which allow a person to monitor his or her own physiological reactions, have since changed that perception. Indeed, with the appropriate feedback, some people can learn to control brain waves, muscle tension, heart rate, and even body temperature. Biofeedback training teaches people to recognize when these physiological reactions are taking place as well as how to ameliorate these responses when under stress. A biofeedback program set up by Equitable Life Insurance, for example, led to an 80 percent reduction in visits to the company's health center for stress-related problems.[83]

Because a supportive environment can reduce stress, many organizations encourage employees to participate in team sports both at work and in their off hours. Ideally, softball and bowling leagues will increase group cohesiveness and support for individual group members through socializing and team effort. Although management certainly cannot ensure that every stressed employee will develop friends, it can make it easier for employees to interact on a casual footing.

Other means of coping with stress that cannot be eliminated at the source focus on allowing the person time away from the stressful environment. Although a person may not feel capable of handling the stress or dealing with the dissatisfying aspects of a particular job indefinitely, it is often possible to do so temporarily. Many employers employ **job rotation**—that is, moving workers from one job to another temporarily—in an effort to give workers a break from stress.

Job rotation can do more than simply spread out the stressful aspects of a particular job. It can increase the complexity of the work and provide valuable cross-training in jobs, so that any one person eventually comes to understand many different tasks. For example, at Rhino Foods, a producer of frozen desserts, employees spend as many as five hours per week in positions that bear no relationship to their own job description. This endeavor allows employees to familiarize themselves with a variety of functions within the company, leading to a more knowledgeable and flexible workforce.[84]

Finally, if the company cannot change the negative aspects of a job, managers should be honest with prospective jobholders about the nature of the work. Many companies hesitate to mention the undesirable aspects of a job when trying to recruit workers, for fear that no one will take the job. Fooling someone into taking a job in which he or she would not otherwise be interested, however, is not good for the company or the person. The ultimate result is increased turnover. *Realistic job previews* (RJPs) lower expectations and are likely to attract workers whose values more closely match the actual job situation. RJPs are especially important for applicants who lack work experience.[85]

SUMMARY

Among the great variety of attitudes and emotions generated in the workplace, the most important are *job satisfaction* and occupational *stress*. Job satisfaction is a pleasurable emotional state resulting from the perception that a job helps the worker attain his or her valued outcomes. Occupational stress, an unpleasant emotional state, arises from the perceived uncertainty that a person can meet the demands of a job. Multiple responses to stress are possible, including physiological responses, behavioral responses, and cognitive reactions. These stress reactions have important consequences for organizations, particularly in terms of the financial costs of health care, absenteeism, turnover, and performance failures.

Dissatisfaction and stress originate from several sources: the *physical* and *social environment*, the *person*, the *organizational task*, and the *organization role*. A number of different intervention programs can be implemented to eliminate the stress-inducing event, enable the person to avoid or cope with the stressor, or, failing these efforts, at least eliminate the symptoms of stress. These measures include *job enrichment, skills training, biofeedback, job rotation,* and *realistic job previews.*

REVIEW QUESTIONS

1. Recall from Chapter 1 some of the many roles that a manager must play. Which of these roles do you think create the most stress? Which are probably the least stressful? From which role do you think most managers derive their greatest satisfaction? Compare your answers to these three questions and speculate on the relationship between satisfaction and stress for managerial employees.

2. Organizational turnover is generally considered a negative outcome, and many organizations spend a great deal of time, money, and effort trying to reduce it. Can you think of any situations in which an increase in turnover might be just what an organization needs? What are some steps organizations might take to enhance functional types of turnover? Do you think mass firings of ineffective workers are likely to enhance overall organization effectiveness, or do you think that they would have deleterious effects on the firm's ability to recruit the most desirable applicants?

3. Characteristics like negative affectivity and the Type A behavior pattern are associated with aversive emotional states including dissatisfaction and stress. Do you think these tendencies are learned or genetically determined? If they are learned, from a reinforcement theory perspective, what reinforcers might sustain the behaviors associated with them?

4. If off-the-job stress begins to spill over and create on-the-job problems, what do you think are the rights and responsibilities of managers in helping employees overcome these problems? If employees are engaged in unhealthy, off-the-job behavior patterns such as smoking, overeating, or alcohol abuse, what are the rights and responsibilities of the employer to change these behaviors? Are such efforts an

invasion of privacy? Or do they simply constitute a prudent financial step taken to protect the firm's well-being?

LEARNING THROUGH EXPERIENCE

DIAGNOSTIC QUESTIONS 6-1

Evaluating an Organization to Determine Where and When Dissatisfaction and Stress May Occur

In evaluating an organization to determine where and when dissatisfaction and stress may be problems and how to go about resolving these problems, the following diagnostic questions may prove a useful start.

1. Why might the organization be concerned about dissatisfaction and stress? What costly health-related or behavioral problems linked to stress are evident?

2. Are the values that the organization expects its members to uphold consistent with the members' own values and needs?

3. Do any aspects of the physical environment (such as noise, darkness, or hazards) cause stress among organizational members?

4. Do any aspects of the social environment (such as hostile co-workers or supervisors) cause stress among organizational members?

5. Do any aspects of the behavioral settings (such as crowding or lack of privacy) cause stress among organizational members?

6. Do certain characteristics of organization members contribute to stress problems at work (such as negative affectivity or the Type A behavior pattern)?

7. How can the jobs that need to be performed by organization members be described in terms of complexity, meaning, and physical demand? How might characteristics of the jobs relate to dissatisfaction and stress?

8. How clear and unambiguous are the role expectations being sent to various organization members? How might the ambiguity of some expectations relate to stress?

9. Is the organization most interested in eliminating the sources of stress, or is it willing (or forced) to deal only with stress-related symptoms?

10. How can overly simple jobs in the organization be enriched? How can jobs characterized by too many conflicting role requirements be simplified?

11. Do employees have outlets for registering complaints? Do they have any influence in decisions that affect how they conduct their jobs?

12. What other types of programs would be most useful in handling stress-related physiological symptoms that arise in this organization?

EXERCISE 6-1

Understanding Roles as Sources of Stress

Patrick Doyle, St. Lawrence College

All of us fulfill various roles in our lives. Each of these roles comprises a set of expectations about good or appropriate behaviors that people hold for us because we

Adapted from J. William Pfeiffer, *The 1986 Annual: Developing Human Resources* (San Diego, CA: University Associates, Inc., 1986). Reprinted by permission of John Wiley & Sons, Inc.

EXHIBIT 6-1   The Role Set of an Employed Student-Parent

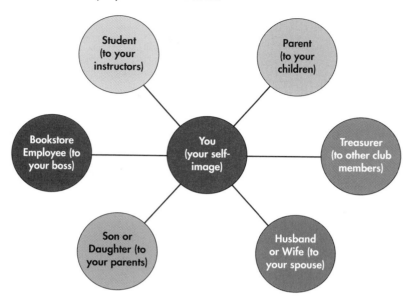

occupy a specific social position. When these expectations conflict with the way we see ourselves in that role, or when the expectations associated with one role conflict with the expectations associated with another that we must also fulfill, we tend to experience stress.

To reduce this stress we must first recognize its causes. To do so, we must identify the different roles we hold and recognize the expectations associated with each one. Suppose, for example, that you are a student in the business school, and that you are married and have several children. You are treasurer of your school's management club and a part-time employee in the campus bookstore. All of these roles and the people with expectations about your role performance could be diagrammed as shown in Exhibit 6-1. Starting at the upper-left side of this diagram, your instructors will expect you to attend class and do your homework. Your boss at the bookstore will expect you to be at your job on time and to perform the tasks you are assigned. Your parents will expect you to telephone them occasionally and to do well in school. Your spouse will expect you to be a companion and help support the family. The members of your club will expect you to keep accurate records of club revenues and expenses. Your children will expect you to spend time with them and to show an interest in their activities. You can readily imagine the potential for conflicts among these varying role expectations. One such conflict could be expressed as shown in Exhibit 6-2.

Group discussions can often help identify ways of resolving such conflicts. For example, a family discussion might lead to the suggestion that you plan to take part in family activities earlier in the term, when schoolwork demands are somewhat lighter, then focus more energy on coursework as the term progresses and you have projects to complete and final exams to take.

Reducing role-related stress requires you not only to identify the causes of stress, but also to modify role expectations and resolve conflicts among your different roles. This exercise gives you the opportunity to develop these kinds of skills, which you can then use to manage the stress in your life.

EXHIBIT 6-2   Conflicting Role Expectations

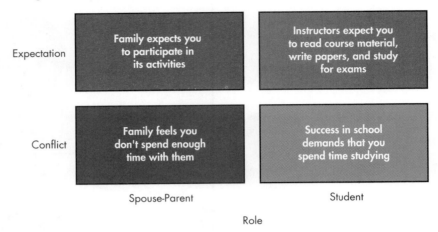

Step One: Pre-Class Preparation

In class you will discuss the roles you actually occupy and consider how to reduce any stress that you feel as a result of conflicting role expectations. To prepare for this discussion, begin by completing the Roles Diversity Sheet in Exhibit 6-3. Identify *at least* four different roles. Next, fill in the Roles Characteristics Sheet in Exhibit 6-4, listing each role you identified in the Roles Diversity Sheet and, for each role, identifying the people who provide you with role expectations and the expectations themselves. Think about which pairs of expectations might conflict. List these pairs, putting one on each side of the top portion of the Roles Conflict-Resolution Sheet in Exhibit 6-5. In the bottom portion of the sheet, list any ways that you might be able to cope with these conflicts or resolve them.

EXHIBIT 6-3   Roles Diversity Sheet
Instructions: Use this sheet to identify four to six roles that you fill.

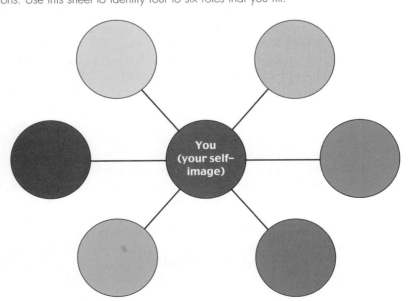

EXHIBIT 6-4   Roles Characteristics Sheet

Use the roles you have identified as follows: First, list these roles in descending order, according to how comfortable you feel in them—the most comfortable first, the least comfortable last. Then, for each role, list the people who provide you with expectations for that role and describe those expectations.

Roles	Expectations

EXHIBIT 6-5   Roles Conflict-Resolution Sheet

Given the roles that you have listed, what expectations are likely to conflict?	
Expectations That Conflict	

What are some potential ways to resolve these conflicts?
Potential Resolutions

Step Two: Group Discussion

The class should divide into groups of four to six members each (if you formed permanent groups in an earlier exercise, reassemble in those same groups). Each group member should begin by describing one of the conflicts identified in Step One, being sure to include descriptions of the roles involved, the people holding expectations for those roles, and the expectations themselves.

After every group member has described a conflict, the group should discuss potential ways to reduce the stress caused by each conflict identified. To begin this discussion, members should refer to potential solutions identified during Step One and provide one another with feedback about those solutions. The group should then search for additional ways to solve the role conflicts of its members.

If time permits, group members may describe other conflicts and ask the group to consider how to solve them. Throughout Step Two, a spokesperson should take notes and be prepared to summarize the group's discussion for the class as a whole.

Step Three: Class Discussion

The instructor should convene the entire class. As each group spokesperson summarizes a group's discussion, the instructor should list all role conflicts and potential solutions that the group finds acceptable on a blackboard, flip chart, or overhead projector. The class should look for similarities and contrasts among the results of Step Two, being sure to discuss the following questions:

1. What is the most common type of role-related stress experienced by members of this class? The second most common type? The third most common type? What expectations cause each kind of stress? From whom do these expectations originate?

2. For each type of stress, what seem to be the most effective methods of stress reduction? Did any approaches seem promising initially but fail ultimately to be useful?

3. What kind of support might you need from others around you to implement the stress reduction approaches identified? What obstacles stand in your way? What are the benefits of adopting one or more of these approaches? How might they change your life?

Conclusion

Stress originating in conflicts among role expectations is ever-present in modern organizations and everyday life. It is important, therefore, that you have the skills needed to identify role conflicts and to decide what to do about them. The process of charting roles, recognizing expectations, and identifying potential conflicts and solutions might seem overly complicated and time-consuming. The costs of failing to deal with role conflict, however, are even greater: Prolonged stress can cause severe physical and psychological illness, limiting your ability to lead a satisfying and productive life.

PART 2 CASES

Case 2-1 Freida Mae Jones

Case 2-2 Precision Machine Tool

Case 2-3 Denver Department Stores

Case 2-4 Chancellor State University

Case 2-5 Connors Freight Lines

Case 2-6 Cameran Mutual Insurance Company

CASE 2-1 / FREIDA MAE JONES

Martin R. Moser, University of Lowell

Freida Mae Jones was born in her grandmother's Georgia farmhouse on June 1, 1969. She was the sixth of George and Ella Jones's ten children. Mr. and Mrs. Jones moved to New York City when Freida was four because they felt that the educational and career opportunities for their children would be better in the North. With the help of some cousins, they settled in a five-room apartment in the Bronx. George worked as a janitor at Lincoln Memorial Hospital and Ella was a part-time housekeeper in a nearby neighborhood. George and Ella were conservative, strict parents. They kept a close watch on their children's activities and demanded that they be home by a certain hour. The Joneses believed that because they were black, the children would have to perform and behave better than their peers to be successful. They believed that their children's education would be the most important factor in their success as adults.

Freida entered Memorial High School, a racially integrated public school, in September 1983. Seventy percent of the student body was Caucasian, 20 percent black, and 10 percent Hispanic. About 60 percent of the graduates went on to college. Of this 60 percent, 4 percent were black and Hispanic and all were male. In the middle of her senior year, Freida was the top student in her class. Following school regulations, Freida met with her guidance counselor to discuss her plans upon graduation. The counselor advised her to consider training in a "practical" field such as housekeeping, cooking, or sewing, so that she could find a job.

George and Ella Jones were furious when Freida told them what the counselor had advised. Ella said, "Don't they see what they are doing? Freida is the top-rated student in her whole class and they are telling her to become a manual worker. She showed that she has a fine mind and can work better than any of her classmates and still she is told not to become anybody in this world. It's really not any different in the North than back home in Georgia, except that they don't try to hide it down

South. They want her to throw away her fine mind because she is a black girl and not a white boy. I'm going to go up to her school tomorrow and talk to the principal." As a result of Mrs. Jones's visit to the principal, Freida was assisted in applying to ten Eastern colleges, each of which offered her full scholarships. In September 1986, Freida entered Werbley College, an exclusive private women's college in Massachusetts. In 1990, Freida graduated summa cum laude with a degree in history. She decided to return to New York to teach grade school in the city's public school system. Freida was unable to obtain a full-time position, so she substituted. She also enrolled as a part-time student in Columbia University's Graduate School of Education. In 1995 she had attained her master of arts degree in teaching from Columbia but could not find a permanent teaching job. New York City was laying off teachers and had instituted a hiring freeze because of the city's financial problems.

Feeling frustrated about her future as a teacher, Freida decided to get an MBA. She thought that there was more opportunity in business than in education. Churchill Business School, a small, prestigious school located in upstate New York, accepted Freida into its MBA program. Freida completed her MBA in 1997 and accepted an entry-level position at the Industrialist World Bank of Boston in a fast-track management development program. The three-year program introduced her to all facets of bank operations, from telling to loan training and operations management. She was rotated to branch offices throughout New England. After completing the program she became an assistant manager for branch operations in the West Springfield branch office.

During her second year in the program, Freida had met James Walker, a black doctoral student in business administration at the University of Massachusetts. Her assignment to West Springfield precipitated their decision to get married. They originally anticipated that they would marry when James finished his doctorate and could move to Boston. Instead, they decided he would pursue a job in the Springfield–Hartford area.

Freida was not only the first black woman but also the first woman to hold an executive position in the West Springfield branch office. Throughout the training program Freida felt somewhat uneasy, although she did very well. There were six other black employees in the program, five men and one woman, and she found support and comfort in sharing her feelings with them. The group spent much of their free time together. Freida had hoped that she would be located near one or more of the group when she went out into the "real world." She felt that although she was able to share her feelings about work with James, he did not have the full appreciation or understanding of her co-workers. However, the nearest group member was located 100 miles away.

Freida's boss in Springfield was Stan Luboda, a 55-year-old native New Englander. Freida felt that he treated her differently than he did the other trainees. He always tried to help her and took a lot of time (too much, according to Freida) explaining things to her. Freida felt that he was treating her like a child and not like an intelligent and able professional.

"I'm really getting frustrated and angry about what is happening at the bank," Freida said to her husband. "The people don't even realize it, but their prejudice comes through all the time. I feel as if I have to fight all the time just to start off even. Luboda gives Paul Koehn more responsibility than me and we both started at the same time, with the same amount of training. He's meeting customers alone and Luboda has accompanied me to each meeting I've had with a customer."

"I run into the same thing at school," said James. "The people don't even know that they are doing it. The other day I met with a professor on my dissertation committee. I've known and worked with him for over three years. He said he wanted to talk with me about a memo he had received. I asked him what it was about and he said that the records office wanted to know about my absence during the spring semester. He said that I had to sign some forms. He had me confused with Martin Jordan, another black student. Then he realized that it wasn't me, but Jordan he wanted. All I could think was that we all must look alike to him. I was angry. Maybe it was an honest mistake on his part, but whenever something like that happens, and it happens often, it gets me really angry."

"Something like that happened to me," said Freida. "I was using the copy machine, and Luboda's secretary was talking to someone in the hall. She had just gotten a haircut and was saying that her hair was now like Freida's—short and kinky—and that she would have to talk to me about how to take care of it. Luckily, my back was to her. I bit my lip and went on with my business. Maybe she was trying to be cute, because I know she saw me standing there, but comments like that are not cute, they are racist."

"I don't know what to do," said James. "I try to keep things in perspective. Unless people interfere with my progress, I try to let it slide. I only have so much energy and it doesn't make sense to waste it on people who don't matter. But that doesn't make it any easier to function in a racist environment. People don't realize that they are being racist. But a lot of times their expectations of black people or women, or whatever, are different because of skin color or gender. They expect you to be different, although if you were to ask them they would say that they don't. In fact, they would be highly offended if you implied that they were racist or sexist. They don't see themselves that way."

"Luboda is interfering with my progress," said Freida. "The kinds of experiences I have now will have a direct effect on my career advancement. If decisions are being made because I am black or a woman, then they are racially and sexually biased. It's the same kind of attitude that the guidance counselor had when I was in high school, although not as blatant."

In September 2000, Freida decided to speak to Luboda about his treatment of her. She met with him in his office.

"Mr. Luboda, there is something that I would like to discuss with you, and I feel a little uncomfortable because I'm not sure how you will respond to what I am going to say."

"I want you to feel that you can trust me," said Luboda. "I am anxious to help you in any way I can."

"I feel that you treat me differently than you treat the other people around here," said Freida. "I feel that you are overcautious with me, that you always try to help me, and never let me do anything on my own."

"I always try to help the new people around here," answered Luboda. "I'm not treating you any differently than I treat any other person. I think that you are being a little too sensitive. Do you think that I treat you differently because you are black?"

"The thought had occurred to me," said Freida. "Paul Koehn started here the same time that I did and he has much more responsibility than I do." (Koehn was already handling accounts on his own, while Freida had not yet been given that responsibility.)

"Freida, I know you are not a naive person," said Luboda. "You know the way the world works. There are some things that need to be taken more slowly than others. There are some assignments for which Koehn has been given more responsibility than you, and there are some assignments for which you are given more responsibility than Koehn. I try to put you where you do the most good."

"What you are saying is that Koehn gets the more visible, customer contact assignments and I get the behind-the-scenes running of the operations assignments," said

Freida. "I'm not naive, but I'm also not stupid either. Your decisions are unfair. Koehn's career will advance more quickly than mine because of the assignments that he gets."

"Freida, that is not true," said Luboda. "Your career will not be hurt because you are getting different responsibilities than Koehn. You both need the different kinds of experiences you are getting. And you have to face the reality of the banking business. We are in a conservative business. When we speak to customers, we need to gain their confidence, and we put the best people for the job in the positions to achieve that end. If we don't get their confidence, they can go down the street to our competitors and do business with them. Their services are no different than ours. It's a competitive business in which you need every edge you have. It's going to take time for people to change some of their attitudes about whom they borrow money from or where they put their money. I can't change the way people feel. I am running a business, but believe me I won't make any decisions that are detrimental to you or to the bank. There is an important place for you here at the bank. Remember, you have to use your skills to the best advantage of the bank as well as your career."

"So what you are saying is that all things being equal, except my gender and my race, Koehn will get different treatment than me in terms of assignments," said Freida.

"You're making it sound like I am making a racist and sexist decision," said Luboda. "I'm making a business decision utilizing the resources at my disposal and the market situation in which I must operate. You know exactly what I am talking about. What would you do if you were in my position?"

When you have read this case, review the diagnostic questions included at the end(s) of the chapter(s) you are using to analyze this case, and choose the ones that seem applicable. Then use those questions to begin working on your case analysis.

CASE 2-2 PRECISION MACHINE TOOL

Janet Barnard, Rochester Institute of Technology

John Garner, president of Precision Machine Tool, watched the elegantly tailored Mr. Wang leave the office after making his disturbing proposition. Of course, John had known that his own production people were working with Suzuki Machines on developing specifications for a machining center that would help solve Precision's nagging quality problems. Negotiations were winding down and the Japanese firm's price quotation was expected. Ako Wang's name on today's appointment calendar, therefore, was no surprise. From past dealings with Asian firms, John had expected the traditional old-world formalities that precede the closing of a sale for a major piece of capital equipment. In fact, he had braced himself for the usual rich combination of urbane courtesy and sharp technology. The U.S. machine tool industry has a strong bias to "buy American," and Precision was no exception.

This morning Wang had performed as expected, but this time Suzuki wasn't intent on making a sale. True, the proposal on John's desk contained a purchase document, but it wasn't a quotation for a $250,000 heavy-duty machining center. Instead, it was a formal invitation to discuss the purchase of Precision Machine Tool by Suzuki Machines.

"Lorraine," John spoke into the intercom on his desk, "see if you can find Tom and ask him to come up." While waiting for his partner, John stood by the window that overlooked a big machining bay on the floor below. Even through the heavy insulated glass he could hear the ceaseless clamor of the big machines that were making high-precision parts for the lathes that Precision produced and sold to the automobile industry to use in their factories. John watched as an operator checked the control panel of a new cobalt-blue lathe that stood among the aging machines on the shop floor. The hulking lathe was state-of-the-art machine technology, precise and sophisticated—with a manufacturer's nameplate that read, "Suzuki/Made in Japan." The machine tool industry is unique in that it uses its own products to make its own products, and much of Precision's old equipment was becoming dulled by decades of use. In a desperate move to stem customer complaints about quality, the company had bought the computer-controlled Japanese lathe to use for making parts for the machines it produced. To buy foreign-made machinery went against the grain, but many domestic toolmakers were buying imported machines because they were more efficient to operate, gave a higher quality of output, and were cheaper than American-made equipment. For some toolmakers it was the alternative to joining the 20 percent of the nation's machine tool companies that had gone out of business recently.

John turned away from the window and took a sales printout from a desk drawer. His company was in better shape than many of the medium-sized toolmakers, but that wasn't saying a lot. Sales were down 30 percent. Booked orders were weak, and quality rejects due to the aging and long-used equipment ate into profits. Precision was a victim of recession in the automobile industry. Like many other machine tool-makers, it had never fully recovered. John looked up as his partner entered the office.

Tom Avery flung himself into the chair that had been occupied by Ako Wang. Precision's works manager was a big man, blunt and outspoken, and a first-class tool design engineer. Tom ran the manufacturing and materials management end of the business and, with John, had founded Precision Machine Tool. His reaction to John's news about Wang's proposition was expressed in a single word that was short, direct, and explosively negative.

Despite excess capacity in American plants, Japan's share of the American machine tool market was increasing and was hotly resented by the domestic industry. The fire was currently being fueled by Japan's determination to increase exports of cars to the United States now that the voluntary quota system had expired. There was no corresponding assurance that there would be any increase in the trickle of American goods that were allowed to enter Japan. As a result, the decrease in American market share could be significant in an industry linked so closely with automobiles and steel. Employment would be hard hit as well, and Precision's 312 employees were already down 22 percent.

"That was my first reaction, too, Tom. But I think we should think this through." John held up his hand to silence his partner as Tom leaned forward, scowling. "Let me go on for a minute. Our industry is in its worst crisis since the depression. Sure, Precision's done better than some, but our sales are down to sixteen million dollars and you know what the reject rate is doing to costs. Orders have softened steadily, Tom, and that's what worries me most. We've had a reputation for top-quality machine tools from the time we opened our shop.

"Precision Machine Tool has always been synonymous with precision quality. We're losing that, Tom." John went over to the bay window. "Sixty percent of our equipment is old, some of it more than twenty years. Accuracy of these machines is unreliable; they're expensive to operate, and not worth any more rebuilding. We're in a spiral, Tom. Without profits, we can't afford to modernize the plant. And with obsolete machines, we can't compete with foreign imports, not in price and not in quality."

The late 1980s were the apex of the domestic machine tool industry. There was a record backlog in orders that couldn't be filled because of inadequate production capacity. Industrial customers waited two years for machine tool orders they needed today. The domestic industry was too busy to notice that several years before, Japan had identified machine tools as a growth industry and started subsidizing modern factories. Now was the time to cash in. American manufacturers were turning overseas for fast delivery of high-quality, inexpensive machines and machine tools to use in their production processes. During the 1991–1992 recession, American tool firms had little capital for investment. When the economy recovered, they were left behind in the marketplace. Lately, subsidiaries of big Japanese toolmakers had begun to appear in the United States, along with an occasional Japanese acquisition of a domestic firm.

"What are you telling me, John? That you want to sell out?" Tom's voice was tight. "This is the most exciting industry around right now. We've got the wonders of automation to sell these days, the futuristic manufacturing systems. You want them all to be Japanese, John? Or West German, or Korean, or everything but American? You want to get out of the race just when we've survived the cash crunch from buying the new equipment we do have? That Japanese lathe, for starters." It had taken Tom a long time to accept the idea of using an imported machine in their own production process, but the harshness in his voice was gone as he said, "Listen, John. You're a financial expert, but I know that yesterday's production gives us yesterday's dollars. Why not get rid of this patch-and-mend philosophy and shop for some real capital to modernize the plant? The U.S. capabilities for producing the computer software that meshes the tools together are superior to anybody's. We've got access to that, John, and all Precision needs is modern machines to get the edge we need to stay in the race."

Tom waited. He knew that John was a financial conservative, dedicated to financing capital improvements from profits. John turned from the window and sat down in the chair across from his partner. Tom knew as well as he did that it wasn't a matter of catching up with the competition; it would be necessary to leapfrog over a moving target. A big capital investment meant a big debt, and interest rates would tend to be high for a firm in the troubled machine tool industry. Precision would become highly leveraged and could risk ruin. There were too many "ifs." What if there was a downturn in the economy . . . or if too many customers were irrevocably lost during the transition . . . or if foreign toolmakers slashed prices to protect their market share. . . or if software companies outside the machine tool industry won important orders in the area of software expertise where American toolmakers had the edge? It was ironic, but John knew that Tom would infinitely prefer bankruptcy to selling out to foreign competition.

"All right, Tom," John took a deep breath. "Look at *this* scenario, and think about it for a minute. If we wanted to go the retrenchment route, maybe it makes sense to sell a line of imports to help us finance some new equipment. I don't like the idea any better than you do, but it would be temporary, Tom, and it's profitable. They wouldn't have to be Asian. The dollar's strong, and we might be able to buy West German machine tools at a price that would give us a good markup." John stopped, expecting Tom's outburst, which was as vehement as his response to the Wang proposition.

Both men, especially Tom, had always been severely critical of the strategy of some of the hard-up domestic toolmakers that acted as distributors of imported machines and machine tools, or that bought imported products and customized them for special-order customers. John had to agree with the tone of derision and contempt in Tom's words. Selling imported machine tools in direct competition with your own industry was quite different from using a couple of pieces of imported equipment to beef up your own production process in a crisis. Not only could the practice spell doom for the domestic industry, but the knife cut a lot deeper. One of the opportunity costs of selling foreign goods is that while a manufacturer is doing it, the firm tends not to improve its own technology and capabilities. The machine tool industry is at the core of modern manufacturing, and the country that controls state-of-the art machines and machine tools has the advantage of being able to make better cars and aircraft and drilling equipment—and ballistic missiles.

It was inconsistent that an industry that had spent so much time and resources trying to get the federal government to provide protection from foreign competition by limiting imports was itself buying those same imports. Buying foreign was repugnant, John knew that, but it was a trade-off. Was it worth it?

"What are our options, Tom?" John's voice was quiet. "Is it better to commit ourselves to a debt that could wipe us out? Is it better to fold? Whatever we do, we've both got to buy into it, right? We always have." Tom smiled, and John knew that they were both remembering the early days of Precision Machine Tool, when they operated on a shoestring and sat down together every Thursday to decide which bills they could afford to pay.

Things seemed more complex now, and even more uncertain. During the life of Precision, its industry had experienced a revolutionary change in products, and the past ten years had been either feast or famine for domestic machine tools. Now the race to build the factories of the future would be won by the nation that had the most efficient computerized operations to produce the cheapest, most reliable products. For the owners of Precision Machine Tool, the price paid for falling behind was high, and the risks in trying to stay in the race were great.

Precision's key executives had to take a number of complex variables into account in making their decision. Important economic and political factors impacted Precision's ability to compete in its industry. Foreign competition and foreign technologies posed a serious threat both to the machine tool industry and to the future of domestic manufacturing. Personal attitudes and values as well influenced John and Tom in their task.

Lorraine sent out for sandwiches and coffee, and as the afternoon passed the two men examined the future of their industry and their place in it. When they parted late that night, their decision had been made—and they agreed to meet in John's office the next morning at ten for his telephone call to Ako Wang.

When you have read this case, review the diagnostic questions included at the end(s) of the chapter(s) you are using to analyze this case, and choose the ones that seem applicable. Then use those questions to begin working on your case analysis.

CASE 2-3 / DENVER DEPARTMENT STORES

J. B. Ritchie and Paul H. Thompson, Brigham Young University

In the early spring of 1991, Jim Barton was evaluating the decline in sales volume experienced by the four departments he supervised in the main store of Denver Department Stores, a Colorado retail chain. Mr. Barton was at a loss as to how to

---

improve sales. He attributed the slowdown in sales to the current economic down-turn affecting the entire nation.

However, Mr. Barton's supervisor, Mr. Cornwall, pointed out that some of the other departments in the store had experienced a 15 percent gain over the previous year. Mr. Cornwall added that Mr. Barton was expected to have his departments up to par with the others in a short period of time.

BACKGROUND

Jim Barton had been supervisor of the sporting goods, hardware, housewares, and toy departments in the main store of Denver Department Stores for three of the ten years he had worked for the chain. The four departments were situated adjacent to each other on the ground floor of the store. Each department had a head sales clerk who reported to Mr. Barton on merchandise storage and presentation, special orders, and general department upkeep (see Case Exhibit 2-1).

The head sales clerks were all full-time, long-term employees of Denver Department Stores, having an average of about eight years' experience with the chain. The head clerks were also expected to train the people in the department they supervised. The rest of the staff in each department was made up of part-time employees who lived in or near Denver. Most of the part-time people were students at nearby universities who worked to finance their education. In addition, two or three housewives worked about ten hours per week in the evenings.

All sales personnel at Denver Department Stores were paid strictly on an hourly basis. Beginning pay was just slightly over the minimum wage, and raises were given based on length of employment and work performance evaluations. The salespeople in the housewares and sporting goods departments were paid about $0.40 per hour more than the clerks in the other departments, because it was thought that

CASE EXHIBIT 2-1   Denver Department Stores Organization Chart

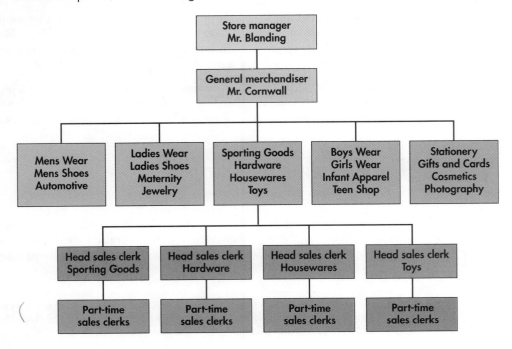

more sales ability and experience were needed in dealing with the people who shopped for items found in those departments.

As a general rule the head sales clerk in each department did not actively sell, but kept the department well stocked and presentable, and trained and evaluated sales personnel. The part-time employees did most of the clerk and sales work. The role of the sales clerk was seen as one of answering customer questions and ringing up the sale rather than actively selling the merchandise, except in the two departments previously mentioned where a little more active selling was done.

The sales clerks in Mr. Barton's departments seemed to get along well with one another. The four department heads usually ate lunch together. If business was brisk in one department and slow in another, the salespeople in the slower area would assist in the busy department. Male clerks often helped female clerks unload heavy merchandise carts. Store procedure was that whenever a cash register was low on change, a clerk would go to a master till in the stationery department to get more. Mr. Barton's departments, however, usually supplied each other with change, thus avoiding the longer walk to the master till.

Mr. Barton's immediate supervisor, Mr. Cornwall, had the reputation of being a skilled merchandiser and in the past had initiated many ideas to increase the sales volume of the store. Some longer-term employees said that Mr. Cornwall was very impatient and that he sometimes was rude to his subordinates while discussing merchandising problems with them. The store manager, Mr. Blanding, had been with Denver Department Stores for twenty years and would be retiring in a few years. Earlier in his career Mr. Blanding had taken an active part in the merchandising aspect of the store, but recently he had delegated most of the merchandising and sales responsibilities to Mr. Cornwall.

SITUATION

Because of Mr. Cornwall's concern, Mr. Barton consulted with his department supervisors about the reason for the declining sales volume. The consensus reached was that the level of customer traffic had not been adequate to allow the departments to achieve a high sales volume. When Mr. Barton presented his problem to Mr. Cornwall, Cornwall concluded that since customer traffic could not be controlled and since the departments had been adequately stocked throughout the year, the improvement in sales would have to be a result of increased effort on the part of the clerks in each department. Cornwall added that if sales didn't improve soon, the hours of both the full- and part-time sales clerks would have to be cut back. Later Mr. Barton found out that Mr. Cornwall had sent a letter to each department informing employees of the possibility of fewer hours if sales didn't improve.

A few days after Mr. Barton received the assignment to increase sales in his department, Mr. Cornwall called him into his office again and suggested that each salesperson carry a personal tally card to record daily sales. Each clerk would record his or her sales. At the end of the day, each personal sales tally card would be totaled. Mr. Cornwall said that reviewing the cards over a period of time would enable him to determine who were the "dead wood" and who were the real producers. The clerks were to be told about the purpose of the tally card and informed that clerks who had low sales tallies would have their hours cut back.

Mr. Barton told Mr. Cornwall he wanted to consider this program and discuss it with the head salespeople before implementing it. He told Mr. Cornwall that the next day was his day off, but that when he returned to work he would discuss this proposal with the head sales clerks.

Upon returning to the store after his day off, Mr. Barton was surprised to see each of his salespeople carrying a daily tally sheet. When he asked Mr. Cornwall why the program had been adopted so quickly, Mr. Cornwall replied that when it came to improvement of sales, no delay could be tolerated. Mr. Barton wondered what effect the new program would have on the personnel in each of his departments.

When Mr. Cornwall issued the tally cards to Mr. Barton's salespeople, the head sales clerks failed to fill them out. Two of the head clerks had lost their tally cards when Mr. Cornwall came by later in the day to see how the program was progressing. Mr. Cornwall issued the two head clerks new cards and told them that if they didn't "shape up" he would see some "new faces" in the departments. The part-time salespeople filled out the cards completely, writing down every sale. The rumor that clerks who had low sales tallies would have their hours cut spread rapidly.

Soon the clerks became much more active and aggressive in their sales efforts. Customers were often approached more than once by different clerks in each department. One elderly lady complained that while making her way to the restroom in the back of the hardware department, she was asked by four clerks if she needed assistance in making a selection.

When Mr. Barton returned the day after the institution of the program, the head sales clerks asked him about the new program. Mr. Barton replied that they had no alternative but to follow Mr. Cornwall's orders or quit. Later that afternoon the head clerks were seen discussing the situation on their regular break. After the break the head clerks began waiting on customers and filling out their sales tally cards.

Not long after the adoption of the program, the stock rooms began to look cluttered. Unloaded carts lined the aisles of these rooms. The shelves on the sales floor were slowly emptied and remained poorly stocked. Sales of items that had a large retail value were especially sought after, and the head sales clerks were often seen dusting and rearranging these more expensive items. The head clerks' tally sheets always had the greatest amount of sales when the clerks compared sheets at the end of each day. (Mr. Barton collected them daily and delivered them to Mr. Cornwall.) The friendly conversations among salespeople and between clerks and customers were shortened, and sales were rung up on the cash register and completed in a much shorter time. Breaks were no longer taken as groups; when they were taken, they seemed to be much shorter than before.

When sales activity was slow in one department, clerks would migrate to other departments where there were more customers. Sometimes conflicts between clerks arose because of competition for sales. In one instance, the head clerk of the hardware department interrupted a part-time clerk from the toy department who was demonstrating a large and expensive table saw to a customer. The head clerk of the hardware department introduced himself as the hardware specialist and sent the toy clerk back to his own department.

Often customers asked for items that were not on the shelves of the sales floor. When the clerk looked for the item, it was typically found on the carts that jammed the stock room aisles. Some customers were told the item they desired wasn't in stock, only to have the clerk later find it on a cart in the stock room.

When Mr. Barton reported his observations of the foregoing situations to Mr. Cornwall, he was told that it was a result of the clerks' adjusting to the new program and to not worry about it. Mr. Cornwall pointed out, however, that sales volume had still not improved. He further noted that the sum of all sales reported on the tally sheets was often $500 to $600 more than total department sales according to the cash register.

A few weeks after the instigation of the tally card system, Mr. Cornwall walked through the hardware department and stopped beside three carts of merchandise left in the aisle of the stock room from the day before. He talked to the head clerk in an impatient tone and asked him why the carts weren't unloaded. The clerk replied that if Mr. Cornwall had any questions about the department, he should ask Mr. Barton. Mr. Cornwall picked up the telephone and angrily dialed Mr. Barton's office. Mr. Barton told him that the handling of merchandise had been preempted by the emphasis on the tally card system of recording sales. Mr. Cornwall slammed down the receiver and stormed out of the department.

That afternoon, at Mr. Barton's request, Mr. Blanding, Mr. Cornwall, and Mr. Barton visited the four departments. After talking with some of the salespeople, Mr. Blanding sent a memo announcing that the tally card program would be discontinued immediately.

After the program was terminated, sales clerks still took their breaks separately and conversations seemed to be limited to only the essential topics needed to run the department. Mr. Barton and the head sales clerk didn't talk as freely as they had before, and some head clerks said that Mr. Barton had failed to represent their best interests to Mr. Cornwall. Some clerks said they thought the tally card system was Mr. Barton's idea. The part-time people resumed the major portion of the sales and clerking jobs, and the head clerks returned to merchandising. Sales volume in the department didn't improve.

When you have read this case, review the diagnostic questions included at the end(s) of the chapter(s) you are using to analyze this case, and choose the ones that seem applicable. Then use those questions to begin working on your case analysis.

CASE 2-4 ⟋ CHANCELLOR STATE UNIVERSITY

Thomas R. Miller, Memphis State University

THE SETTING

Chancellor State University is a large, urban university in the Midwest. Although the university had experienced rapid growth for several years, overall enrollment has since stabilized. The School of Business Administration, however, continued to grow, drawing students away from programs in the School of Education and the College of Arts and Sciences as well as attracting new students concerned with future vocational opportunities. The faculty and administration of the business school were pleased to see the enrollment growth, as it signaled acceptance of their degree programs, but the enrollment expansion also created strong pressure to expand the business faculty.

Under normal circumstances, faculty expansion would simply have meant an active recruitment effort by school administrators. But the situation at Chancellor State was representative of a national phenomenon of enrollment growth in business schools that had resulted in a strong demand for doctorally qualified faculty in the face of a relatively short supply. Thus faculty recruitment at many business schools had become a priority activity, rather than merely one of the many administrative responsibilities of deans and department heads.

At Chancellor State, Fred Kennedy, chairman of the Management Department, had been actively seeking new faculty members for his staff, which had the heaviest course load in the school. As is often customary in academia, the faculty in the Department of Management participated in recruitment, spending considerable time meeting with the faculty candidates in an effort to evaluate their candidacy for a faculty position. Faculty members could then make recommendations as to whether the prospect should be tendered an offer to join the staff.

THE CONFERENCE

It was late in February, and several prospective faculty members had visited Chancellor State for campus job interviews. Early one Friday morning, Kennedy was in his office reviewing the job files of prospective faculty members. He looked up as he heard the voice of Larry Gordon, an assistant professor of management who was now in his third year at Chancellor State.

"Good morning, Fred," said Larry, as he walked into the department office. "Do you have a couple of minutes? I want to talk with you about something."

Fred gestured to him to come into his office. "Sure, Larry, what's on your mind?"

After entering Fred's office, Larry closed the door, indicating to Fred that this was not to be just a casual, friendly conversation.

"Fred," Larry began, "I was wondering what you thought about the prospective faculty member we had in here for an interview last week. I've been talking with a couple of other faculty members about him, and they're not really all that impressed. He seems to be okay, I guess, but we may be able to do better. Are we going to make him an offer? If we do, he's sure not worth top dollar in my opinion."

"Well, I've received some of the written evaluations back from the faculty, and they seem to be fairly positive," replied Fred. "They're not as favorable as they could be, but the other faculty seem to think that he would be acceptable and that he could work out pretty well on our staff. His academic credentials are not bad, and he has had some good experience. Given the state of the market for business faculty in his specialty, I expect that we'll extend an offer to him. By the way, I know that he already has a couple of offers in hand from our competition." Fred could readily see that Larry was not pleased to hear all of this. From their earlier conversations, Fred could anticipate Larry's next comment.

"Yeah, okay, I can see that we could use him, but what kind of money are we offering in these new positions?" questioned Larry. "I don't mean to pry into somebody else's business, but what sort of salary is the department offering our new faculty?"

Fred winced at this question. In the past he had made no secret about general salary ranges for new faculty members. In fact, this information was generally known throughout the school. But this had become a very sensitive issue in the last few years, given the rapid increases in starting salaries for new business faculty members.

"Well, Larry, I guess you know that we're paying competitively for our new faculty. With our enrollment increase we've got to increase our teaching staff, and to do that we're probably going to have to meet the market," Fred responded.

Larry was obviously not satisfied with this response and was becoming irritated with the conversation. "Fred, I assume that by 'meeting the market' you mean that we're going to offer this guy two or three thousand dollars more than some of us who have been here for several years are now making. This new guy has not yet finished his doctorate, has very little teaching experience, has no publications, and, in my opinion, is not as good as a lot of our current faculty. How much can you justify paying for an unknown quantity? I think it's just unfair to the present faculty to offer him more money than many of us are making. When is somebody going to do something for us? Fred, I'm not unhappy in this department, but I'm sure going to keep my eyes open for other opportunities. I feel certain that I could move to another school at a higher rank and increase my salary significantly. You may think I'm wrong and maybe I shouldn't feel this way, but this situation is just not fair!"

Fred sighed and tried to calm Larry down. "Larry, I know what you're concerned about, and I'm certainly sympathetic to the problem. After all, this salary compression issue affects me in the same way it does you. I can assure you that I have reservations about paying the kind of money we are for new faculty in light of our existing faculty salaries, but I don't believe that we can attract the kind of faculty we want by paying less than competitive rates. Although this seems to create some internal inequities, I hope that we'll have sufficient salary increase money to make some adjustments to reduce these discrepancies. Certainly I want to be able to reward and retain our productive people . . ."

Larry, feeling a little embarrassed by his earlier emotional statement, interjected, "I know you've got other problems, Fred, and I didn't mean to lash out at you. I know it's not really your fault, but a lot of the other faculty are talking about this salary issue. It surely doesn't help morale any when a new, inexperienced assistant professor is hired for more than some of the associate professors are making."

"Yes, I'm well aware of this issue, Larry, and I'm making the dean aware of it, too. We're certainly going to do what we can to try to resolve this salary compression problem," Fred responded.

As Larry moved toward the door, he continued to make his point: "I hope you can do something soon because it's most inequitable at the present time. People are pretty upset about it, and it's likely to cause the department some turnover problems in the future. No one likes to be treated unfairly. I'll see you later, Fred. I've got to run to class. Maybe we can talk about it again later."

As Larry walked out of his office, Fred reflected on their conversation. It reminded him of other discussions in which he had engaged previously with several other faculty members. In fact, Larry had hinted at his dissatisfaction before, but had not been so outspoken about it. Yes, the salary compression problem was reaching a crisis. No longer was it a matter of the "new hires" nearing the salaries of some present faculty—it was a matter of their exceeding them. Never in his experience had Fred recalled a labor market for faculty that was this chaotic. Fred had puzzled over this dilemma before, but he had not been able to come up with a solution for the problem. He wondered if, in fact, some solution would enable him to hire the new personnel he wanted without offending some of the present staff. "Maybe it is just one of those 'no win' administrative situations," he mused. Perhaps this was something that could be discussed with the other department chairs and the dean, as some of them had basically the same problem. Perhaps he would then have a better idea of how to deal with the situation. He certainly hoped so!

When you have read this case, review the diagnostic questions included at the end(s) of the chapter(s) you are using to analyze this case, and choose the ones that seem applicable. Then use those questions to begin working on your case analysis.

CASE 2-5   CONNORS FREIGHT LINES

Richard Peterson, University of Washington

Connors Freight Lines is a large, interstate trucking concern serving the north, central, and western states. Its head office is in Fargo, North Dakota, and it has forty-three terminals, with Chicago at one extreme and Los Angeles at the other. The La Crosse, Wisconsin, terminal has been in existence for sixty of the company's seventy-five years and enjoys a fair reputation competitively.

The technical organization of the La Crosse plant consists of a fleet of twenty-seven pickup trucks, ten town-tractors, two forklifts, and a cart line hookup track to facilitate loading. This branch is housed at a typical freight terminal, which is superior to that of most other trucking firms from a technical standpoint, although considered only adequate from the standpoint of its social organization. Since the plant is located well away from the business district, most drivers and dock workers bring their lunches, and a small lunchroom is provided for their convenience, where they can also buy coffee or milk. This lunchroom is furnished with long tables and benches, measures approximately fifteen by twenty feet, and will comfortably seat about twenty-four workers.

The formal organization of the company, which employs approximately 180 people, consists of the terminal manager, Ralph Preston, and his assistant terminal manager, Jason Hobbs. Case Exhibit 2-2 shows the company organizational structure. Although Connors appears successful enough in solving its external problems, the high rate of absenteeism, the generally low morale among the truckers, and their relatively short tenure of employment are puzzling internal problems that have vexed management for the past several years. The truck drivers at Connors are strongly union-oriented, which results in feelings of mixed loyalties. To some extent, therefore, an undercurrent of conflict is felt in this area by the company as well as by the workers.

It is part of the company's policy to select its supervisors from the ranks of the drivers. This approach assures the firm of selecting people who are experienced with the specific job and its problems. In theory, at least, it also rewards the employee with the advancement from a job at worker level to a position within the organization. Upon becoming a supervisor, the employee is no longer a union member, so he or she works overtime without any pay and forfeits his or her seniority standing. The new supervisor is now salaried, with a base income slightly higher than that which he or she had earned as a driver on straight time. This person no longer wears work clothes, as the job is considered a "clean" one, and it would seem that some increase in prestige should also accompany this advancement.

Workers of supervisory caliber at Connors have not been too plentiful among the ranks of truck drivers, and the high rate of turnover aggravates this problem further. The drivers fall mainly into three categories: (1) family-minded individuals in their thirties and forties who are settled in their jobs and, because of various circumstances, have decided to make a career of it; (2) drivers in their twenties who have a few years of college and must earn money to continue toward a degree; and (3) young individuals for whom it is simply "a job," and who in time will probably make up the bulk of the first group or drift on to other employment elsewhere.

Chuck Fletcher would belong in the second of these categories. At twenty-five, he had three years of college but was still uncertain about his field of interest, so he decided to work a while, keep his eyes open, and do some thinking. The son of parents who were both college graduates, Fletcher was well above average in intelligence. Other truckers on his shift both liked and respected him, as did the members of management who had come to know him. He had worked for Connors for two years, spending half his shift on the dock doing loading, and the other half as a driver.

Because of the nature of the freighting business, there is a great need for overtime help, since prompt movement of freight is a large part of the "product" that the company sells. Fletcher maintained a good attitude about this added workload, which was lightened somewhat by his paychecks, reflecting the regular union demand for

CASE EXHIBIT 2-2   Organization Structure of Connors Freight Lines

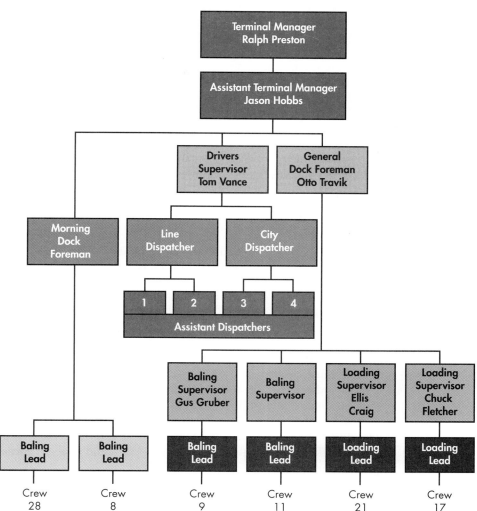

overtime pay. Not all workers showed an equally good attitude toward this overtime work even with the added pay, and several among the top 5 percent in seniority who were given a choice as to overtime work flatly refused any work other than the regular eight-hour shift, regardless of compensation.

There is a fairly intricate technique involved in correctly loading trucks and trailers so that the weight is kept under the maximum allowed in highway regulations and is distributed evenly and correctly. The more fragile or perishable items must be given special attention and the merchandise loaded with logic in respect to the order of its being unloaded at the delivery point. Fletcher caught on quickly to these loading techniques and soon attracted the attention of the dock foreman, Otto Travik. In a conversation with Chuck's loading supervisor, Ellis Craig, Travik suggested that Craig "keep his eye on" Fletcher, with the idea of possibly bringing him into management in the future when an opening might occur within the organization. Craig, who was aware of Fletcher's ability to get along well with other workers and knew him as a hard worker, agreed that he was worth watching.

In January 1995, at one of the regular Wednesday morning staff meetings, Hobbs, the assistant terminal manager, mentioned that a sales job would soon open up and that the company planned to move Al Johnson into this spot. Johnson's move to sales would then leave a supervisor's job open on the loading dock. Preston, the terminal manager, asked for suggestions as to who might best fill this spot. Thomas Vance, the drivers' supervisor, suggested Ford Wheeler, who had been working on day shift and who was thirty-five years old and a former schoolteacher. Preston agreed that Wheeler was a good prospect, but Travik and Craig suggested that they consider Fletcher for the position. The qualifications of both men were then compared and discussed, and the decision was left open, pending more thought on the two candidates and the actual job opening.

At about this time, Craig said to Fletcher: "I know you like the shift you're on, but would you consider cancelling your bid on it and taking the St. Paul loading job that's driving me crazy? I know the late-night shift is a crummy one, but this would be the chance you've wanted to learn to drive the heavy-duty trucks. Vance is our official qualifier, and he's on that shift, so I'm sure by coming to work early you could qualify inside of a month. I'll help expedite the whole thing if you'll help me out on this. After all, the annual bids come up in five months, so if you don't like the job, you can always rebid. And keep this under your hat—there's going to be a supervisor's job open before too long, and if you make good on this job I think your chances for it would be excellent."

Fletcher thought about the St. Paul loading job. He didn't like the night shift, and the job was an especially dirty one, but he took it for two reasons: He had been hoping for a chance at supervision, and he also wanted time to learn to drive the heavy-duty rigs both because of the increased pay that diesel drivers drew and because it offered him a challenge.

At a staff meeting in June 1998, after other articles of business were out of the way, the conversation ran something like this:

Preston: "There is now a definite need for a new supervisor, and I hope you have all been keeping this situation in mind and giving it earnest thought. What are your suggestions?"

Vance: "I still think Ford Wheeler is your boy."

Preston: "Yes, I've been seriously considering him. Checked into his background from his job application and I was really quite impressed. Do the rest of the workers respect him? Would they work for him?"

Craig: "I don't feel he has any of the workers' respect! For one thing he's lazy, and we'll be setting the poor example that all you have to do to get ahead in the organization is do nothing. On the other hand, there's Fletcher, who really is liked by the other workers, and respected, too. In the time he has worked for me he has shown himself a hard worker, often doing more than is required. For a couple of months he's been coming to work an hour early to practice driving heavy-duty trucks on his own time and hoping to get qualified—and by the way, Vance, he's been ready for his test for some time. He shows a great desire to do a thorough job and accepts more than his share of responsibility. To me, this adds up to material for a good company man."

Vance: "Heck! He's a union boy straight down the line. Don't you remember how he initiated two valid grievances against us last year? There has even been some talk of his being named shop steward. But Wheeler, now, has a college degree as a schoolteacher. He can hardly wait to shake loose from the union."

Preston remembered seeing Fletcher many times, and in all kinds of weather, out practicing driving the diesel rig in the loading zones before his shift time. In checking over Fletcher's job application, he found it to be almost as good as Wheeler's, considering the differences in their ages.

After some further discussion Preston decided in favor of Fletcher. The supervisory position was offered to him on the usual ninety-day provision, which would allow either him or the company to terminate the arrangement at the end of that time, with no loss of status or seniority on his part.

After a few days of consideration, Fletcher accepted the new assignment and went to work as a supervisor of the same crew with which he had been working previously.

Preston gave Fletcher a short "welcoming" talk before his first day in the new job. In it he covered three main points. He first suggested that Fletcher try to be tactful in his initiation of ideas, maybe even to the point of making his cooperating supervisors sometimes think that the idea came from them. Second, he stressed the importance of demanding respect from his crew. "If the occasion demands a reprimand, see that it's done in some private place where others can't see or hear you. Otherwise, you both lose face. It must be kept private between you and your person." That led to the third point—not being too familiar with the workers on the crew. "It's not really any of our business what you do off the job, but it'd be best if you don't hobnob with your crew," Preston had said.

Soon afterward, at Craig's invitation, Fletcher joined the bowling team, of which both Preston and Vance were members. He and Craig, with whom he had always had a good relationship, were becoming close friends since he had been made supervisor. They would usually go somewhere for a couple of beers together on the nights after bowling.

One night Fletcher was off his game. After some ribbing from Vance and Preston, he mentioned to Craig how tired he was from so much overtime; "tired and disgusted" was the way he put it. He told Craig that earlier that day he had overheard Preston "chewing out old Gus Gruber" down in the steel bay, and the incident had both embarrassed and disappointed Fletcher. Craig, at that time, was planning a vacation to the East Coast with his family and invited Fletcher to come with them. Fletcher said he knew he needed a rest and a change of scenery, but he was short of funds. Last year he had gone to Canada with some of the men from his crew, but that was when he was getting paid for overtime.

Craig previously had included Fletcher on a couple of family outings and at one time, when the men were alone, they got to talking shop as usual. Fletcher seemed discouraged about the attitude of his crew. "We have always gotten along so well before, but now there's no more kidding. No one hardly cracks a smile and I keep getting jibes like 'Gettin' rich on your overtime, Chuck?' or 'How do you like your new raise by now?'" Part of Fletcher's interest in taking the supervising job was that he hoped he would find ways of easing the obvious friction between management and labor. This development was really discouraging.

The weekly staff meetings, which were attended by all management personnel, were the occasions when affairs concerning the company's technical and social organization and welfare were brought up for discussion. A variety of issues were constantly being introduced, listened to, and considered, and many were acted upon promptly. At his third staff meeting Fletcher made the suggestion that the company might see fit to supply work aprons to the workers, adding that these were not expensive items when bought in quantity, and that the gesture of goodwill on the part of the company might help to improve the rather poor relations between it and the workers. This suggestion was listened to but not acted upon.

Fletcher made another suggestion within the next few weeks: switching lunch-rooms between the workers and supervisors. The lunchroom reserved for the twelve supervisors was twice the size of the one into which forty-five drivers were crowded at peak times to have their lunches, and this necessitated several of them sitting on the floor or standing to eat. This suggestion, too, was not acted upon, although Craig and Travik both thought it was "worth considering." Within a short space of time, however, the company was gratified by the outcome of two other suggestions that Fletcher made in work operations. One resulted in substantial savings to the company, and the second produced a greater profit. The first was accomplished by Fletcher's simplifying of a certain loading procedure and organizing it in such a way that two men from another crew, ordinarily required for extra help at this time, were no longer needed. Dispensing with this usual short-handing of the second crew enabled it to finish its own loading on schedule, resulting in more efficient moving of freight on the two jobs and less need for overtime on both.

At about this time, two company officials from Fargo were visiting the terminal and Preston took them on a tour of the docks. As they passed the loading area, Fletcher looked up and nodded. Farther on, as they circled the dock, one of the officials said, "Where is this new supervisor, Fletcher, that you've mentioned a few times lately?" Preston replied, "Oh, he's the fellow in the red shirt we just passed down there at the north end. I'll introduce him to you at coffee break if he comes up."

The second instance in which Fletcher's suggestion worked to the company's advantage took place toward the end of the ninety-day trial period. It was not presented at the staff meeting but to Hobbs in person one day when he happened to be out on the dock as Fletcher came on shift. Fletcher's attitude, which had always been friendly and respectful, seemed to have changed in recent weeks. Hobbs, who had become confident that Fletcher was proving to be good supervisory material, was a little puzzled by his apparently growing coolness.

Hobbs: "Good morning, Fletcher."

Fletcher: "Good morning, Mr. Hobbs. May I speak to you a minute when you have the time?"

Hobbs: "Sure. Right now is as good a time as any."

Fletcher: "It's about the St. Paul run. While I was on the St. Paul loading job, I realized that on the last schedule to St. Paul at night there was always more freight moving from La Crosse to St. Paul than returned from St. Paul to La Crosse. We'd always need a "double" heading east and then have to haul back one "empty." A college friend of mine is the son of a truck farmer over east of the Mississippi, and I was talking to him the other day. I think we could arrange for a full load of produce to be picked up near Winona. Then we'd have a full paying load in both directions. I've already said something to Vance about it yesterday but didn't hear anything from him, so I thought I'd let you know. The arrangements could be made easily. I'll give you the farmer's name, if you're interested. It's all up to you, of course."

Hobbs thought Fletcher seemed a bit abrupt, but the suggestion pleased and impressed him, just as it did Preston when he was told about it later in the day.

On Thursday of the last week of the ninety-day trial period, Fletcher came into the office of the assistant manager and told Hobbs that he was going to exercise his option and ask to be returned to worker status the following Monday.

Hobbs was surprised by this unexpected turn of events, but said, "Well, we'll live up to our side of the bargain. I'm sure Mr. Preston will want to hear your reasons for this decision, though. He has some free time at two o'clock. Could you come in and see him then?"

In Preston's office later, the following conversation took place:

Preston: "What's this I hear about your request to be returned to your old job as trucker?"

Fletcher: "Yes, I've decided to hang it up. The long hours are getting me down."

Preston: "Well, you knew what the hours were like when you took the job. Aren't they the same ones you worked as a driver?"

Fletcher: "Yes. I thought perhaps I could expedite a few things and maybe shorten them a little, I guess."

Preston: "Are you sure you gave this 'expediting' your best efforts?"

Fletcher: "Yes, sir I did. Until I got to the point where I felt I was knocking my head against a stone wall."

Preston: "Are you sure it's the long hours, or are there some other reasons?"

Fletcher: "The money and the shift, coupled with the long hours."

Preston: "We think you were doing a fine job, and we are already taking steps in these areas you're dissatisfied with. In two weeks we hope to add one new supervisor and possibly two to cut down hours worked by the supervisors."

Fletcher: "Well, that would make it a lot easier all right . . ."

Preston: "And there will be an opening in Dispatch in the not-too-distant future that would be a day-shift job rather than a night one."

Fletcher: "That would be a real improvement . . ."

Preston: "So that just leaves the problem of money. How much more would you say you'd need to make it worth your while to stay on?"

Fletcher: "A hundred dollars a month, sir."

Preston: "I think we can probably make some kind of arrangements that will make you more contented. I'll check with the head office and let you know on Monday."

Fletcher: "Fine. You can let me know."

After Fletcher left his office, Preston said to Hobbs, "I think the head office will go for an eighty-five dollar raise anyway, which will probably be enough to hold Fletcher here. Put a note in his locker-box stating we will meet his demands, but don't mention a definite amount of money. I have to talk to the head office first."

Hobbs: "That's still a lot of money. Do you realize that would make him the sixth-highest-paid person in this terminal? He'll be jumping over eight people."

Preston: "Fletcher has already saved the company more than he'll make in a year on that produce haul alone, and he has come up with quite a number of ideas that have helped us out. He's a thinking boy and that's the kind we need. He has a bright future and I want to keep him with us."

The Monday morning mail contained the following note addressed to Preston:

Dear Mr. Preston: Please accept this notice of my resignation from the company, to be effective in two weeks. I have thought it over carefully and this is the only possible solution. Thank you for your generous offer, even though I cannot accept it.

Sincerely,

Charles S. Fletcher

When you have read this case, review the diagnostic questions included at the end(s) of the chapter(s) you are using to analyze this case, and choose the ones that seem applicable. Then use those questions to begin working on your case analysis.

CASE 2-6 CAMERAN MUTUAL INSURANCE COMPANY

Robert J. Cox, Salt Lake Community College

Cameran Mutual Insurance Company is a large national insurance company that has been in business since the early 1900s. The company is best known for its loss prevention service and for its workers compensation policies. The company also takes pride in personal sales and service to its industrial insurance accounts.

Recently, Mrs. Kay was referred to a local insurance office in Salt Lake City, Utah, where she had applied for a job. She had a college degree in sociology, some business background, five years' experience with public relations-type jobs, and an excellent reputation at her previous jobs for being reliable, dependable, and a hard worker. She was well qualified for the job except for her lack of technical knowledge about the insurance business. However, she typed up a résumé and made an appointment for a job interview.

The job interview was long and intense. First, the potential supervisor, Mrs. Perry, interviewed her for thirty minutes. She was then required to fill out an application form. After completing the form, she was called back into the office to talk with the district sales manager, Mr. Landers. At the conclusion of this interview, she was asked to fill out a more in-depth questionnaire that required far more detailed information. Finally, she was asked to come into the office for a third interview. While Mrs. Kay was a bit overwhelmed by the length of interviews and the personal data required on the forms, she was nevertheless flattered by the personal attention and felt that the extra time and depth of concern was a good omen for her chances of securing the job for which she applied. In this final interview, both Mrs. Perry and Mr. Landers asked, "What is your major goal in life? If you had a chance to do anything over again in your life, what would it be? Do you have any objections to working with people who smoke? If you get this job, what do you think you would dislike the most?" Such questions caught her off guard, but somehow she felt she responded favorably in the eyes of the interrogators.

The job was described in the interview as being the "right-hand" assistant to the sales manager, Mr. Landers. It would be Mrs. Kay's job to fill in whenever he was out of the office: to prepare rates as specified by the underwriters, prepare reports, collect data for policies, handle phone calls, file, type, and perform other duties assigned by the sales manager and the supervisor of sales assistance. She would even handle some duties assigned by the district sales manager and underwriters. Since she would need to be licensed by the state to sell policies, the company would pay for the on-the-job training and the cost of the license fee.

Early that afternoon, Mrs. Kay was informed that, provided her references and other job information checked out, she would have the job and would start her job training the following Monday. She would be working very closely with the woman whom she would be replacing, Mrs. Mone. Mrs. Mone had agreed to stay on for the next three weeks to help with the orientation process.

Mrs. Kay arrived at work early Monday morning so she could become oriented to the office. She met Mr. Johnson, the claims manager; Mr. Metts, the loss prevention manager; and several other workers in the office. When Mr. Landers arrived, Mrs. Kay was asked to fill out additional legal and administrative forms, including government licensing forms, a bonding contract, and insurance forms. She was then oriented to many of the company policies and benefits. She learned that raises were to be based upon the quality and quantity of work she performed, not on seniority. There was a mandatory probation period of three months, and then she would be eligible for insurance and sick leave benefits. There were also educational benefits, which included full financial reimbursement for all classes dealing with insurance and reimbursement for half the price of the books used. There were also many other benefits offered.

After a rather formal introduction to most of the workers in the office, Mrs. Kay was shown to her desk and told to start "on-the-job reading" of manuals in a prescribed manner. She started her studies in insurance with an introduction to and description of the loss prevention program. Because this particular office served Utah, Wyoming, and Montana, it was necessary for some members of the staff to be out of the office much of the time, leaving a large amount of clerical work to be done by those who stayed in the office, including Mrs. Mone (who handled both technical assistance and routine clerical responsibilities).

During the course of the day, there was time for Mrs. Kay to observe office functions and procedures. She also watched, with growing interest, the relationship between Mr. Landers and Mrs. Mone. Mrs. Kay was rather surprised at the behavior of Mr. Landers. Without any apparent provocation except for a minor mistake, Mr. Landers burst into a fit of rage, belittling Mrs. Mone in front of the other workers. Mrs. Mone was apparently accustomed to her supervisor's behavior because she put up with his temper tantrum and did not get upset over the incident.

Later that day, Mrs. Kay talked briefly with Mrs. Mone about Mr. Landers. Mrs. Mone said, "Well, you see, everybody in the company below the level of executive vice president has two or more bosses. For example, you will have Mr. Landers and Mrs. Perry as your main supervisors. Later on, you'll learn that the handling of many of your accounts and your bosses' accounts will be subject to the judgment and releases of the underwriting department. In a sense, you'll be taking on a third boss." She talked further about Mr. Landers. "Mr. Landers tends to get angry without regard to who is at fault. You'll also find out that there will be occasions where Mrs. Perry will direct you to do one thing, and Mr. Landers will tell you to do almost the complete opposite. There will also be occasions when they will both direct you to do the same chore, but they will use different terminology for the specific tasks they want you to accomplish. I've tried to find assigned tasks in the procedural manuals, but many times I've found that I've had to ask either Mr. Landers or Mrs. Perry for directions to complete the task, only to find that Mr. Landers gets angry and Mrs. Perry is out of her office. Just don't let him bully you around. If you are right (and you'd better be sure you are), stick to your guns and you'll come out okay."

Reflecting on the day's activities caused Mrs. Kay to feel good about the people she'd be working with, but she still felt a little apprehensive about Mr. Landers. Getting into her car, she immediately sensed the day's accumulation of the cigarette smoke that had adhered to her clothes and hair. It was soon apparent that the smoking of the other employees made her physically ill. This surprised her a bit since she had smoked up until four years before.

The next day, accustomed to arriving a few minutes early for work, Mrs. Kay arrived at 8:15 A.M., just 15 minutes before work was to begin. She straightened out her desk and then pondered over the events of the previous day. When the clock reached 8:30 A.M., she started immediately into her studies. She later talked to the claims manager, Mr. Johnson, who informed her of his departmental functions. This discussion helped her grasp how she fit into the picture of this office.

Mr. Landers instructed Mrs. Mone to spend at least an hour per day teaching Mrs. Kay the clerical duties. No specific hour was mentioned, however. At three o'clock that afternoon, Mr. Landers again verbally assaulted Mrs. Mone because she hadn't instructed Mrs. Kay on the clerical duties. Twenty other people in the office looked on and listened to the argument. Mrs. Kay felt sympathetic toward Mrs. Mone and wondered if this was the way that she would be treated by Mr. Landers. She talked with another technical-clerical person, Sherry Olsen, who told Mrs. Kay that every time that Mrs. Mone stood up to Mr. Landers, she felt like applauding. She added, "If he ever yells at you, don't feel embarrassed because all of the staff knows how he reacts and we're all used to it."

At the end of the day, Mrs. Kay put on her coat and prepared to go home. The instant she sat in the car, the nauseating smell of stale tobacco recaptured her attention. The odor became very strong and almost overwhelmed her. This problem added to the anxiety that she already felt. There were several heavy smokers in the office, and the office had very little ventilation. It was quite easy to accumulate smoke in her clothes.

When she arrived home, suppressed feelings rose to the surface and she became very temperamental, even hostile. This reaction was contrary to her nature, but she supposed that the anxieties in acquiring a new job, the irritating physical effects of the office smoke, and the problems of working with a very temperamental boss had finally taken their toll. Family members unfortunately were most convenient and subject to the venting of her frustrations.

That night she pondered the events of the past two days. She tried to weigh the benefits and drawbacks of her new job. Could she do it? She would receive a fair salary with good benefits, undergo on-the-job training, and have opportunities for advancement. However, there were obvious complications. Much would be expected of her: a much heavier workload than most new employees carry, the "pool hall" working conditions, and a very temperamental boss. Could she expect to have much impact on working conditions or her boss? Would there be a way of implementing new office procedures or practices?

When you have read this case, review the diagnostic questions included at the end(s) of the chapter(s) you are using to analyze this case, and choose the ones that seem applicable. Then use those questions to begin working on your case analysis.

3

Meso Organizational Behavior

Chapter 7 Efficiency, Motivation, and Quality in Work Design

Chapter 8 Interdependence and Role Relationships

Chapter 9 Group Dynamics and Team Effectiveness

Chapter 10 Leadership of Groups and Organizations

Cases

The Efficiency Perspective
Methods Engineering
Work Measurement: Motion and Time Studies
Evaluating Industrial Engineering and the Efficiency Perspective

The Motivational Perspective
Horizontal Job Enlargement
Vertical Job Enrichment
Comprehensive Job Enrichment
Sociotechnical Enrichment
Evaluating the Motivational Perspective

The Quality Perspective
Quality Circles
Self-Managing Teams
Automation and Robotics
Evaluating the Quality Perspective

Summary
Review Questions

Learning Through Experience
Diagnostic Questions 7-1: Work Design
Exercise 7-1: Redesigning a Simplified Job

Efficiency, Motivation, and Quality in Work Design

I stand in one spot, about a two- or three-foot area, all night. . . . We do about 32 [welding] jobs per car, per unit. Forty-eight units an hour, eight hours a day. Thirty-two times forty-eight times eight. Figure it out. That's how many times I push that button. . . . You dream, you think of things you've done. I drift back continuously to when I was a kid and what me and my brothers did. . . . [Y]ou're nothing more than a machine. They give better care to that machine than they will to you. They'll have more respect, give more attention to that machine. . . . Somehow you get the feeling that the machine is better than you are.[1]

The other day when I was proofreading [insurance policy] endorsements I noticed some guy had insured his store for $165,000 against vandalism and $5,000 against fire. Now that's bound to be a mistake. They probably got it backwards. . . . I was just about to show it to [my supervisor] when I figured, wait a minute! I'm not supposed to read these forms. I'm just supposed to check one column against another. And they do check. . . . They don't explain this stuff to me. I'm not supposed to understand it. I'm just supposed to check one column against the other. . . . If they're gonna give me a robot's job to do, I'm gonna do it like a robot! Anyway, it just lowers my production record to get up and point out someone else's error.[2]

Few people can build a car by themselves, but companies like Ford, Toyota, and Volkswagen turn out thousands of cars each year by dividing car building into simple assembly line jobs. Likewise, insurance policies cannot be underwritten by individuals working alone, but companies like Allstate, State Farm, and Prudential succeed by breaking down policy preparation into a number of less complicated clerical tasks. As described in Chapter 2, the *division of labor,* in which difficult work is broken into smaller tasks, enables organized groups of people to accomplish tasks that would otherwise be beyond their physical or mental capacities as individuals.

When utilized effectively, the division of labor can lead to the creation of jobs that contribute to satisfaction, success, and significant competitive advantage. Sometimes, however, it leads to the creation of jobs that are monotonous and unchallenging, like the welding and proofreading jobs just described. Why do managers design jobs that are so unappealing? What do they expect to gain by simplifying work so drastically? What can be done to counteract the negative effects of oversimplified work—outcomes like the welder's detached daydreaming or the proofreader's alienation? Can oversimplification be avoided completely?

This chapter seeks answers to these questions by examining theories and methods of **work design,** the formal process of dividing an organization's total stock of work into jobs and tasks that its members can perform. The chapter begins by describing one approach to work design, the *efficiency perspective,* which originated in the work on scientific management described in Chapter 2. Today this approach is widely used to economize on the costs of production activities. Next, the chapter turns to the *motivational perspective,* a second approach that arose largely in reaction to problems with the efficiency perspective. This perspective, which is based on ideas about human motivation and satisfaction like those discussed in Chapters 5 and 6, highlights the importance of designing jobs that encourage employee growth and fulfillment. The chapter then describes a third approach, the *quality perspective,* which combines key elements of the efficiency and motivational perspectives. Growing out of the total quality management movement, this perspective focuses primarily on improving innovation and quality through the use of self-managed teams and advanced production technologies.

THE EFFICIENCY PERSPECTIVE

To achieve *efficiency,* companies minimize the resources consumed in providing a product or service. Thus, the **efficiency perspective** on work design is concerned with creating jobs that conserve time, human energy, raw materials, and other productive resources. It is the foundation of the field of **industrial engineering,** which focuses on maximizing the efficiency of the methods, facilities, and materials used to produce commercial products. Methods engineering and work measurement are two areas of industrial engineering that have had especially noticeable effects on the division of labor in modern organizations.

Methods Engineering

Methods engineering is an area of industrial engineering that originated in Frederick Winslow Taylor's work on scientific management (described in Chapter 2). It attempts to improve the methods used to perform work by incorporating two related endeavors—process engineering and human factors engineering.

Process engineering assesses the sequence of tasks required to produce a particular product or service and analyzes the way those tasks fit together into an integrated job. It also examines tasks to see which should be performed by people and which should be carried out by machines, trying to determine how workers can perform their jobs most efficiently.

Process engineers study the product or service to be produced and decide what role, if any, humans should play in its production. They also determine whether some employees should act as managers, directing and controlling the flow of work, and they differentiate the resulting managerial jobs from those of nonmanagerial workers. Process engineers specify the procedures for employees to follow, the equipment they should use, and the physical layout of offices, workstations, and materials-storage facilities.

Consider the job of selling women's shoes. The process chart in Figure 7-1 details the job as originally carried out. The large circles in the figure denote activities

FIGURE 7-1 Process Chart of Selling Women's Shoes, Original Method

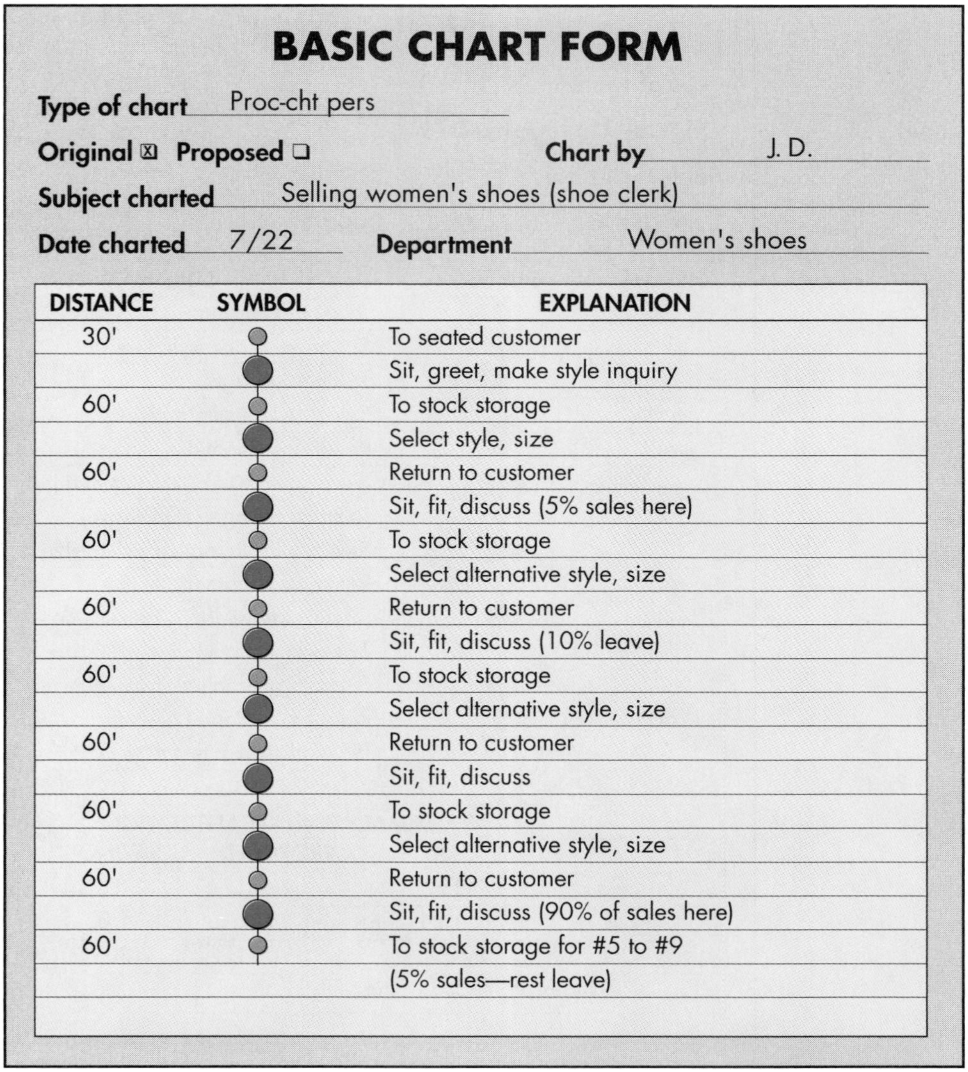

BASIC CHART FORM

Type of chart __Proc-cht pers__

Original ☒ Proposed ☐   Chart by _____ J. D. _____

Subject charted __Selling women's shoes (shoe clerk)__

Date charted __7/22__   Department __Women's shoes__

DISTANCE	SYMBOL	EXPLANATION
30'	●	To seated customer
	⬤	Sit, greet, make style inquiry
60'	●	To stock storage
	⬤	Select style, size
60'	●	Return to customer
	⬤	Sit, fit, discuss (5% sales here)
60'	●	To stock storage
	⬤	Select alternative style, size
60'	●	Return to customer
	⬤	Sit, fit, discuss (10% leave)
60'	●	To stock storage
	⬤	Select alternative style, size
60'	●	Return to customer
	⬤	Sit, fit, discuss
60'	●	To stock storage
	⬤	Select alternative style, size
60'	●	Return to customer
	⬤	Sit, fit, discuss (90% of sales here)
60'	●	To stock storage for #5 to #9
		(5% sales—rest leave)

Source: From *Motion and Time Study: Improving Productivity,* 7th edition by M. E. Mundel and D. L. Danner, p. 228. Copyright © 1994. Reprinted by permission of Pearson Education, Inc., Upper Saddle River, NJ 07458.

performed at a fixed location. The small circles indicate movements by which the jobholder moves toward an object or changes an object's location. As shown in the figure, before redesign, clerks regularly performed nineteen different work activities and walked a distance of 870 feet to complete a sale in which the customer decided to try on nine styles of shoes, one at a time. Figure 7-2 shows the same job after the completion of process engineering. The new method reduces the job of selling women's shoes by thirteen activities and saves clerks 480 feet of walking.

In contrast to the process engineer's focus on improving work processes, experts in **human factors engineering** (sometimes called **ergonomics**) design machines and work environments so that they better match human capacities and limitations. Table 7-1 summarizes some of the most important areas of study of human factors engineering.

FIGURE 7-2   Process Chart of Selling Women's Shoes, Improved Method

BASIC CHART FORM

Type of chart   Proc-cht pers

Original ☐   **Proposed** ☒   **Chart by**   J. D.

Subject charted   Selling women's shoes (shoe clerk)

Date charted   7/23   **Department**   Women's shoes

DISTANCE	SYMBOL	EXPLANATION
30'	○	To seated customer
	●	Sit, greet, make style inquiry
60'	○	To stock storage
	●	Select style + alternative, size
60'	○	Return to customer
	●	Sit, fit, discuss (10% sales here)
60'	○	To stock storage (10% leave)
	●	Select two alternative styles, size
60'	○	Return to customer
	●	Sit, fit, discuss (85% of sales here)
60'	○	To stock storage
	●	Select 5 alternative styles, size
60'	○	Return to customer
		(5% sales—rest leave)

SUMMARY AND RECAPITULATION

SYMBOL	ORIG	PROPOSED	SAVING
●	19*	6	13
○	15*	7	8
Dist	870'*	390'	480'

*Includes 5th through 9th style

Source: From *Motion and Time Study: Improving Productivity,* 7th edition by M. E. Mundel and D. L. Danner, p. 230. Copyright © 1994. Reprinted by permission of Pearson Education, Inc., Upper Saddle River, NJ 07458.

TABLE 7-1   Human Factors Engineering

Area of Study	Examples
Physical aspects of the user–machine interface	Size, shape, color, texture, and method of operation of controls for cars, home appliances, and industrial and commercial equipment.
Cognitive aspects of the user–machine interface	Human understanding of instructions and other information. Style of information exchange between computer and user.
Workplace design and workspace layout	Layout of offices, factories, kitchens, and other places where people work. Design of relationships between furniture and equipment and between different equipment components.
Physical environment	Effects of climate, noise and vibration, illumination, and chemical or biological contaminants on human performance and health.

When people make mistakes at work, human factors engineers investigate whether the equipment being used is partially to blame for these mistakes. Are mistakes made when workers use certain kinds of equipment but not others? Can equipment be redesigned so as to minimize or even eliminate human error? In most cases, the effects of human fallibility and carelessness can be substantially decreased by minimizing the error-provoking features of jobs and equipment. For example, shape-coded controls like those shown in Figure 7-3 can be used to reduce aircraft accidents caused when pilots activate the wrong control. To help pilots differentiate among control levers without looking at them, two general rules were followed during the design process: (1) the shape of a control should suggest its purpose, and (2) the shape should be distinguishable even when gloves are worn.[3]

FIGURE 7-3   Shape-Coding to Reduce Flying Errors

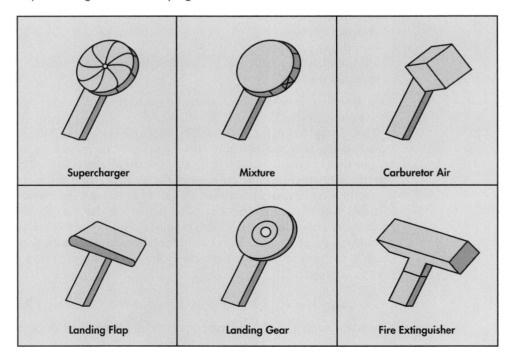

Work Measurement: Motion and Time Studies

Besides designing job methods, industrial engineers sometimes examine the motions and time required to complete each job. Although such work can be traced to Taylor's work on scientific management, it is more directly the product of research by Frank and Lillian Gilbreth, who set out to find the "one best way" to do any job. In the course of this pursuit, the Gilbreths developed motion study, a procedure that reduces jobs to their most basic movements. As noted in Chapter 2, each of these basic movements is called a *therblig* (a near reversal of the name *Gilbreth*) and consists of motions such as "search," "grasp," and "assemble." The Gilbreths also developed procedures to specify in advance the time required for each of the movements needed to perform a job. These procedures gave rise to **work measurement,** an area of industrial engineering concerned with measuring the amount of work accomplished and developing standards for performing work of an acceptable quantity and quality. Work measurement includes both micromotion analysis and time-study procedures.

In **micromotion analysis,** industrial engineers analyze the hand and body movements required to do a job. This technique is a direct descendant of the motion-study methods devised by the Gilbreths, whose therbligs continue to be used in current micromotion procedures. Industrial engineers usually conduct micromotion analysis by using a slow-speed film or videotape of a person performing his or her job. They then analyze the movements performed in the task and try to improve efficiency by means of principles such as the following:

1. Try to have both hands doing the same thing at the same time or to balance the work of the two hands.
2. Avoid using the hands simply for holding. Use specialized jigs, vises, or clamps instead.
3. Keep all work inside a work area bounded by the worker's reach.
4. Relieve the hands of work wherever possible.
5. Eliminate as many therbligs or as much of a therblig as possible, and combine therbligs when possible.
6. Arrange therbligs in the most convenient order. Each therblig should flow smoothly into the next.
7. Standardize the method of performing the job in the manner that promotes the quickest learning.[4]

As is apparent from these principles, jobs designed by means of micromotion analysis are characterized by economy of motion.

Time-study techniques are used to measure the time actually consumed by job performance; they are also sometimes employed to specify the time that a particular job should take to complete. In **stopwatch time analysis,** an analyst uses a stopwatch (or microchronometer) to time the sequence of motions needed to complete a job. In **standard time analysis,** the analyst matches the results of micromotion analysis with standard time charts to determine the average time that should be required to perform a job. When combined with micromotion analyses, the results of either type of time analysis can be used to create descriptions that identify the therblig motions required to perform a job and the length of time that the job should take to complete.

Evaluating Industrial Engineering and the Efficiency Perspective

Consistent with the efficiency perspective that underlies them, all industrial engineering methods attempt to enhance productivity by simplifying jobs. Often, use of these methods can improve productivity dramatically.[5] There is, however, a danger that simplification will be carried too far, leading to the creation of oversimplified jobs like those of the welder and proofreader described at the beginning of this chapter.

Workers performing oversimplified, routine jobs often become bored, resentful, and dissatisfied—attitudes that contribute to problems with workforce absenteeism and turnover. Employees who choose to remain on their jobs may slow down their work pace or resort to sabotage to compensate for the lack of challenge and interest in their work. Performance quantity and quality are likely to suffer as a consequence.

Oversimplification can also have dire health consequences. According to U.S. government sources, far more than 50 percent of all workplace illnesses are attributable to the adverse effects of repetitive stress caused by doing routine jobs again and again. Repetitive stress injuries (RSIs) accounted for 117,000 instances of job-related illness in 1989 and for another 185,000 reported cases in 1990. Workers compensation claims and other expenses related to such injuries cost U.S. employers as much as $20 billion per year, according to estimates made by insurer Aetna Life and Casualty. To deal with this problem, businesses such as DaimlerChrysler Corporation have begun to rotate workers among tasks to break up repetition over the course of each working day. DaimlerChrysler has also redesigned many jobs and developed special tools to reduce or eliminate repetitive stress.[6] In summary, *the simplification intended to enhance the efficiency of work processes may actually reduce that efficiency, if carried to an extreme.*

THE MOTIVATIONAL PERSPECTIVE

What can be done to counteract the effects of oversimplification, or to make sure that jobs are not oversimplified from the beginning? The answer to this question, offered initially by Lillian Gilbreth, is that *jobs should be designed in such a way that performing them creates feelings of fulfillment and satisfaction in their holders.*[7] This idea forms the central tenet of the **motivational perspective** on work design, which suggests that fitting the characteristics of jobs to the needs and interests of the people who perform them provides the opportunity for satisfaction at work.[8] Table 7-2 contrasts this approach with the efficiency perspective discussed in the previous section, and the Cutting-Edge Research box describes recent research that examined some of the trade-offs highlighted in this table. The methods of work design developed with the motivational perspective in mind include horizontal job enlargement, vertical job enrichment, comprehensive job enrichment, and sociotechnical enrichment.

Horizontal Job Enlargement

To counteract oversimplification, managers sometimes attempt to boost the complexity of work by increasing the number of task activities entailed in a job. This approach is based on the idea that increasing **job range,** or the number of tasks that a jobholder performs, will reduce the repetitive nature of the job and thus eliminate worker boredom.[9] Increasing job range in this manner is called **horizontal job enlargement**—so named because the job is created out of tasks from the same horizontal "slice" of an organization's hierarchy.

Some horizontal job enlargement programs rely on **job extension,** an approach in which several simplified jobs are combined to form a single new job. For example,

TABLE 7-2 Two Perspectives on Work Design

Efficiency Perspective	Motivational Perspective
Tasks are shaped mainly by technology and organizational needs.	Tasks are shaped at least partly by workers' personal needs.
Tasks are repetitive and narrow.	Tasks are varied and complex.
Tasks require little or no skill and are easy to learn and perform.	Tasks require well-developed skills and are difficult to learn and perform.
The management and performance of work are separated into different jobs.	The management and performance of work are merged in the same jobs.
It is assumed that only one best way to do each job exists.	It is assumed that each job can be performed in several ways.
Tools and methods are developed by staff specialists.	Tools and methods are often developed by the people who use them.
Workers are an extension of their equipment and perform according to its requirements. The pace of work is often set by a machine.	Workers use equipment but are not regulated by it. The pace of work is set by people rather than machines.
Extrinsic rewards (incentive wages) are used to motivate performance.	Intrinsic rewards (task achievements) are used along with extrinsic rewards to motivate performance.
Social interaction is limited or discouraged.	Social interaction is encouraged and, in some cases, required.
Efficiency and productivity are the ultimate goals of work design.	Satisfaction and fulfillment are important goals of work design.

the insurance clerk job described at the beginning of this chapter, which consists solely of proofreading, might be extended by adding filing and telephone-answering tasks to it. Similarly, the welder's job might be extended by adding other assembly operations to it.

Organizations as diverse as Maytag, AT&T, and the U.S. Civil Service have all implemented job extension programs. When a number of simple, readily mastered tasks are combined, however, workers may view job extension as giving them more of the same routine, boring work to do. Although the initial efforts seemed promising, most research has suggested that job extension rarely succeeds in reversing oversimplification sufficiently to strengthen employee motivation and satisfaction.[10]

In **job rotation,** workers switch jobs in a structured, predefined manner. Rotation of this sort creates horizontal enlargement without combining or otherwise redesigning a firm's jobs. For instance, a supermarket employee might run a checkout lane for a specified period of time and then, after switching jobs with another employee, restock shelves for another set period of time. As workers rotate, they perform a wider variety of tasks than they would if limited to a single job. As with job extension, however, critics have observed that job rotation often achieves little more than having people perform several boring, routine jobs rather than the same one. Thus, although companies such as Ford Motor Company and Western Electric have tried job rotation, it has generally failed to improve worker motivation or satisfaction (although it can help solve RSI and similar health problems).[11]

Vertical Job Enrichment

The failure of horizontal job enlargement to counteract the undesirable effects of oversimplification has led managers to try a variety of alternative approaches. Many such trials involve attempts to increase **job depth**—that is, the amount of discretion a jobholder has to choose his or her job activities and outcomes. This approach, called **vertical job enrichment,** is based on the work of Frederick Herzberg, an industrial psychologist who studied the sources of employee satisfaction and dissatisfaction at work.[12]

CUTTING-EDGE RESEARCH

CAN TRADE-OFFS BETWEEN EFFICIENCY-ORIENTED AND MOTIVATIONAL WORK DESIGN BE MANAGED?

Do the efficiency and motivational approaches to work design necessarily incur trade-offs between job simplification and employee satisfaction, as seems to be suggested by Table 7-2? This question was the focus of a longitudinal (long-term) investigation of the redesign of computer information system jobs in a large pharmaceutical company, published recently by Frederick P. Morgeson and Michael A. Campion.

At the time of Morgeson and Campion's study, prior research on work design appeared to provide evidence of a trade-off. However, all such research consisted of short-term studies that failed to assess long-lasting effects. In addition, these studies examined efficiency programs *or* motivational programs, but none looked at both types of programs at the same time. To correct these research deficiencies, Morgeson and Campion opted for a longer-term analysis of *both* efficiency-oriented and motivational work designs. In particular, their study was designed to run for two years, and involved three groups of jobs: one, in which work was redesigned in accordance with the efficiency perspective; a second, in which jobs were reshaped by the motivational approach; and a third, in which both efficiency and motivational changes were made.

For jobs redesigned along the lines of the efficiency perspective alone, Morgeson and Campion refocused employee efforts on the core tasks of their job and eliminated tasks that were unrelated to the core. Thus, the jobs were simplified and made easier to perform. For jobs redesigned in accordance with the motivational perspective alone, the researchers increased the range of task activities, thereby increasing satisfaction by reducing repetition and boredom. For jobs redesigned in the manner of both perspectives combined, Morgeson and Campion centralized into a single job a variety of tasks once performed by numerous employees. The centralization created specialized jobs, and therefore greater efficiency. At the same time, however, each of the jobs required

use of a broader range of skills and abilities, thereby increasing motivational effects.

Morgeson and Campion hypothesized that efficiency-oriented redesign would lead employees to see their jobs as easier to learn and simpler to perform, while motivational redesign would cause employees to report greater satisfaction with their work. The researchers also predicted that redesign incorporating both efficiency and motivational components would lead to increased satisfaction without serious dropoffs in perceived simplicity. Results of their study confirmed these expectations, indicating that, in instances where jobs were redesigned in accordance with the motivational approach alone, employees expressed increased overall satisfaction, and that training requirements (that is, the amount of training required to perform successfully) also increased while work simplification decreased. For jobs redesigned in the manner of the efficiency perspective alone, the study showed evidence of greater simplicity and lower needs for training. Finally, jobs redesigned along both efficiency and motivational lines were accompanied by increased employee satisfaction but no meaningful changes in training requirements or job simplification.

The first two findings are consistent with the idea that each perspective has its own distinctive effects, as indicated in Figure 7-2. The third finding, however, indicates that the trade-off implied by Table 7-2 can be lessened when a combination of the two perspectives is used—that is, that satisfaction can be enhanced without significant sacrifices in efficiency. Thus, in answer to the question posed in this box, the trade-off between efficiency and motivation can be reduced by applying both perspectives during the process of work design. It is worth noting that this conclusion foreshadows the underlying principles and effects of the quality perspective on work design, as described later in this chapter.

Source: F. P. Morgeson and M. A. Campion, "Minimizing Tradeoffs When Redesigning Work: Evidence from a Longitudinal Quasi-Experiment," *Personnel Psychology* 55 (2002), 589–612. Reprinted by permission of Personnel Psychology.

Herzberg, who began his research in the mid-1950s, started out by interviewing 200 engineers and accountants in nine companies, asking them to describe incidents at work that made them feel "exceptionally good" or "exceptionally bad" about their jobs. From these interviews, Herzberg concluded that satisfaction (feeling good) and dissatisfaction (feeling bad) should be considered independent concepts, rather than opposite extremes on a single continuum as traditional views had held.

This approach suggests that a person might feel more satisfied with his or her job without feeling less dissatisfied, more dissatisfied without feeling less satisfied, and so forth.

As he dug further into his interview data, Herzberg also found that certain characteristics of the work situation seemed to influence employee satisfaction, whereas other characteristics appeared to affect employee dissatisfaction. **Motivator factors,** such as achievement or recognition, increased satisfaction. Their absence produced a lack of satisfaction but not active dissatisfaction. In contrast, **hygiene factors,** such as company policy or employees' relationships with their supervisors, usually led to serious dissatisfaction and rarely contributed to a gain in satisfaction.

Armed with this distinction, Herzberg then noticed that only the motivator factors identified in his research seemed able to increase the incentive to work. Hygiene factors, he said, could help maintain motivation but would more often contribute to a decrease in motivation. As indicated in Figure 7-4, many of Herzberg's hygiene factors are the very same work characteristics emphasized by the efficiency perspective on work design. In fact, Herzberg contended that following the principles advocated by Taylor, the Gilbreths, and later specialists in industrial engineering would create oversimplified jobs that could only dissatisfy and demotivate workers. Consequently, he suggested that managers should pay less attention to issues such

FIGURE 7-4 Herzberg's Motivator Factors and Hygiene Factors

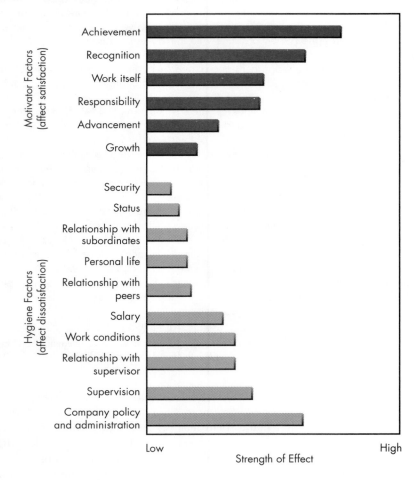

as working conditions and salary and instead design jobs that incorporated opportunities for growth, achievement, and recognition.

Over the years, many critics have attacked Herzberg's ideas.[13] Among the most serious criticisms are the following:

1. The *critical-incident technique* that Herzberg used, in which he asked people to recall earlier feelings and experiences, is a questionable research method subject to errors in perception or memory and to subconscious biases. Its use leaves the validity of his conclusions open to question.
2. All of Herzberg's interviewees—engineers and accountants—were male members of professional, white-collar occupational groups (few women were engineers or accountants in Herzberg's day). Women, minorities, and members of other occupational groups, such as salespeople or industrial laborers, might have answered Herzberg's questions differently.
3. Other studies have failed to replicate Herzberg's results. As will be discussed in Chapter 16, which covers research methods, such failure casts grave doubts on the merits of research findings.
4. Work design programs based on Herzberg's model almost always fail to stimulate workforce satisfaction of lasting significance.

Because of these questions about its validity, Herzberg's two-factor theory is not a useful guide for managerial actions.[14] Nonetheless, it remains widely known among managers and continues to stimulate interest in questions of motivation, satisfaction, and work design. In addition, it has influenced more recent ideas about work design by highlighting the importance of designing jobs that satisfy *higher-order* desires for growth, achievement, and recognition.

Comprehensive Job Enrichment

Although neither horizontal job enlargement nor vertical job enrichment can counteract oversimplification when implemented separately, **comprehensive job enrichment** programs that combine both horizontal and vertical loading improvements are usually more successful in stimulating motivation and satisfaction. Many such programs are based on the model of work design developed by J. Richard Hackman and Greg Oldham, shown in Figure 7-5.[15]

The Hackman–Oldham Model   According to Hackman and Oldham, jobs that are likely to motivate performance and contribute to employee satisfaction exhibit the following five **core job characteristics:**

1. *Skill variety.* The degree to which a jobholder must carry out a variety of activities and use a number of different personal skills in performing the job.
2. *Task identity.* The degree to which performing a job results in the completion of a whole and identifiable piece of work and a visible outcome that can be recognized as the result of personal performance.
3. *Task significance.* The degree to which a job has a significant effect on the lives of other people, whether those people are co-workers in the same firm or other individuals in the surrounding environment.
4. *Autonomy.* The degree to which the jobholder has the freedom, independence, and discretion necessary to schedule work and to decide which procedures to use in carrying out that work.
5. *Feedback.* The degree to which performing the activities required by the job provides the worker with direct and clear information about the effectiveness of his or her performance.

FIGURE 7-5 The Hackman–Oldham Job Characteristics Model

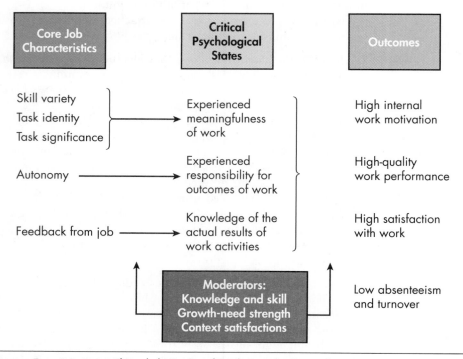

Source: From "Motivation Through the Design of Work: Test of a Theory" by J. R. Hackman and G. R. Oldham in *Organizational Behavior and Human Performance,* (1976), 256. Copyright © 1976. Reprinted with permission from Elsevier.

In turn, these five core job characteristics influence the extent to which employees experience three **critical psychological states,** or personal, internal reactions to their jobs. The first state, *experienced meaningfulness of work,* refers to the degree to which a worker sees his or her job as having an outcome that is useful and valuable to the worker, the company, and the surrounding environment. The second psychological state, *experienced responsibility for work outcomes,* concerns the degree to which the worker feels personally accountable and responsible for the results of work. The third state, *knowledge of results,* reflects the degree to which the worker maintains an awareness of the effectiveness of his or her work.[16]

As indicated in Figure 7-5, each job characteristic influences a particular psychological state. Specifically, skill variety, task identity, and task significance affect the experienced meaningfulness of work. Thus jobholders should feel that their jobs are meaningful if they must use a variety of activities and skills to produce an identifiable piece of work that influences the lives of others. Autonomy, on the other hand, influences the jobholder's experienced responsibility for work outcomes. Consequently, workers who have the discretion to determine their work procedures and outcomes should feel responsible for the results of that work. Finally, feedback determines whether a worker will have knowledge of the results of his or her work. Through information about performance effectiveness that comes from the job itself, the jobholder can maintain an awareness of how effectively he or she is performing.

According to the Hackman–Oldham model, if workers experience all three states simultaneously, four kinds of work and personal outcomes are likely to result. First, workers will tend to view their jobs as interesting, challenging, and important, and they may be motivated to perform them simply because they are so stimulating, challenging, and enjoyable. *High internal work motivation,* or being "turned on" to job performance by its personal consequences, is therefore one possible outcome. Second, experiencing the three critical psychological states and the internal, or intrinsic, motivation they arouse can encourage *high-quality work performance* (and, in some instances, a higher quantity of production as well).[17] Third, workers who experience the three psychological states do so because their work provides them with opportunities for personal learning, growth, and development. As discussed in Chapter 6, these kinds of experiences generally promote *high satisfaction with work.* Fourth, work that stimulates all three psychological states also tends to lead to *lower absenteeism* and *turnover.*

The Hackman–Oldham model proposes that several individual differences determine whether the core job characteristics will actually trigger the critical psychological states, leading to the four outcomes just described. The first of these differences is the worker's *knowledge and skill.* To succeed on a job characterized by high levels of the five core job characteristics, a worker must have the knowledge and skill required to perform the job successfully. People who cannot perform a job because they lack the necessary knowledge or skill will merely feel frustrated by their failure, not encouraged. The motivational aims of comprehensive job enrichment will thus be thwarted.

Growth-need strength, or the strength of a worker's need for personal growth, is a second individual difference that moderates the effects of the Hackman–Oldham model. Workers who have strong growth needs are attracted to enriched work because it offers the opportunity for growth. In contrast, workers with weak growth needs are likely to feel overburdened by the opportunities offered them. As a consequence, they will try to avoid enriched work and will not derive personal benefit if required to perform it.

Finally, *context satisfactions* can influence the Hackman–Oldham model's applicability. Hackman and Oldham identified several context satisfactions—satisfaction with pay, with job security, with co-workers, and with supervisors. Workers who feel exploited and dissatisfied because they are poorly paid, feel insecure about their jobs, or have abusive co-workers or unfair supervision are likely to view job enrichment as just one more type of exploitation. Context dissatisfaction can thus negate the expected benefits of comprehensive job enrichment.

Implementation   To put their model to use, Hackman and Oldham developed the **Job Diagnostic Survey** (JDS). This questionnaire measures workers' perceptions of the five core job characteristics, the three critical psychological states, and certain moderating factors (the Task Diagnostic Questionnaire in Exercise 7-1 is an abbreviated version of the JDS, created specifically for classroom use).

The deficiencies identified by a JDS analysis of a particular job can be corrected in several ways. To enhance skill variety and task identity, oversimplified jobs can be *combined* to form enlarged modules of work. For example, the production of a toaster could be redesigned so that the entire appliance is constructed by a single employee working alone rather than by a dozen or more people working on an assembly line. *Natural units of work* can be created by clustering similar tasks into logical or inherently meaningful groups. For instance, a data-entry clerk who formerly selected work orders randomly from a stack might be given sole responsibility for the work orders of an entire department or division. This intervention is intended to strengthen both task identity and task significance for the clerk.

To increase task variety, autonomy, and feedback, a firm can give workers the responsibility for *establishing and managing client relationships.* At John Deere &

Company, for example, assembly line workers take stints as traveling salespeople, getting to know their customers' needs and complaints.[18] To increase autonomy, managerial duties can be designed into a particular job through *vertical loading*. Finally, to increase feedback, *feedback channels* can be opened by adding to a job such things as quality-control responsibilities and computerized feedback mechanisms.

Sociotechnical Enrichment

The Hackman–Oldham model focuses on designing individualized units of work, each performed by a single employee. Therefore, it is not appropriate for jobs that must be performed by closely interacting groups of workers. To counteract the negative effects of oversimplified *group work*, managers can instead use a **sociotechnical enrichment** approach.

Sociotechnical enrichment originated in the early 1950s, when researchers from England's Tavistock Institute set out to correct faults in the processes used to mine coal in Great Britain.[19] Historically, coal had been excavated by teams of miners working closely with each other to pool efforts, coordinate activities, and cope with the physical threats of mining. With the advent of powered coal-digging equipment in the 1930s and 1940s, however, coal mining changed drastically. Teams were split up, and miners often found themselves working alone along the long walls of exposed coal created by the equipment. Mining—which is normally a hazardous, physically demanding occupation—grew even more unbearable due to the changes stimulated by the new technology. Miners expressed their dissatisfaction with these circumstances through disobedience, absenteeism, and occasional violence.

The Tavistock researchers soon concluded that the roots of the miners' dissatisfaction lay in the loss of the social interaction that mining teams had provided, which had made the dangerous, demanding job of mining more tolerable. According to the researchers, the technology had been allowed to supersede important social factors. Performance in the mine could be improved only by redressing this balance. Indeed, after small teams were formed to operate and provide support for clusters of powered equipment, production rose substantially.

This finding, along with similar results found at other research sites, led the Tavistock researchers to make the general suggestion that workforce productivity could be hurt when either social or technical factors alone were allowed to shape work processes. They further suggested that work designs that sought to balance social and technological factors—*sociotechnical designs*—would encourage both performance and satisfaction in the workplace.

Stated differently, researchers suggested that employees should work in groups that allowed them to talk with each other about their work as they performed their duties. These work groups should include the people whose frequent interaction is required by the production technology being used. For instance, salespeople, register clerks, and stock clerks, who must often interact with each other to serve customers in a department store, should be grouped together to facilitate communication about work. Salespeople and clerks from other departments should not be included in the group, because they do not share job-related interdependencies with the group's members.

In the course of conducting their studies, the Tavistock sociotechnical researchers identified the following psychological requirements as critical to worker motivation and satisfaction:

1. The content of each job must be reasonably demanding or challenging and provide some variety, although not necessarily novelty.

2. Performing the job must have perceivable, desirable consequences. Workers should be able to identify the products of their efforts.
3. Workers should be able to see how the lives of other people are affected by the production processes they use and the things they produce.
4. Workers must have decision-making authority in some areas.
5. Workers must be able to learn from the job and go on learning. This requirement implies having appropriate performance standards and adequate feedback.
6. Workers need the opportunity to give and receive help and to have their work be recognized by others in the workplace.[20]

This list of required job characteristics was developed independently of the work of Hackman and Oldham, as the Tavistock group did its research mainly in England and Norway and Hackman and Oldham worked only in the United States. Nonetheless, items 1 through 5 of the Tavistock list are similar to the five core job characteristics of the Hackman–Oldham model. Only item 6 differs from the latter model, and it reflects the emphasis placed by sociotechnical enrichment on the importance of satisfying social needs at work.

Contemporary sociotechnical designs normally create **semiautonomous groups.** These groups must respond to the management direction needed to ensure adherence to organizational policies, but they are otherwise responsible for managing group activities. Within each such group,

. . . Individuals must move about within the group spontaneously and without being ordered to do so, because it is necessary to the efficient functioning of the [group] . . . If we observe the group in action, we will see movements of individuals between different jobs. When an especially heavy load materializes at one work station and another is clear for the moment, we will see the person at the latter spontaneously move to help out at the former. . . . It is a natural and continuous give and take within a group of people, the object being to attain an established production target. . . . The group members are not merely carrying out a certain number of tasks. They are also working together, on a continuing basis, to coordinate different tasks, bearing responsibility, and taking whatever measures are necessary to cope with the work of the entire unit.[21]

As they work together in this manner, the members of a semiautonomous group are able to do the following:

1. Rotate in and out of tasks to enhance skill variety
2. Work together on a group product that is a whole, identifiable piece of work
3. Influence the lives of other members of the group and the lives of those who consume the group's output
4. Decide as a group who will belong to the group and what tasks the group members will perform
5. Obtain feedback from group members about task performance
6. Count on the help and support of other group members if it is needed

When it proceeds in this manner, the work of semiautonomous groups is rich in the psychological requirements identified by sociotechnical researchers as enhancing workforce motivation and satisfaction.

Implementation Figure 7-6 contrasts a traditional assembly line with semiautonomous groups. As shown in the figure, the decision to adopt sociotechnical design principles has important implications for shop floor operations. In both panels of the figure, workers are assembling truck engines. In the upper panel, each worker

FIGURE 7-6 Comparison of an Assembly Line and Semiautonomous Groups

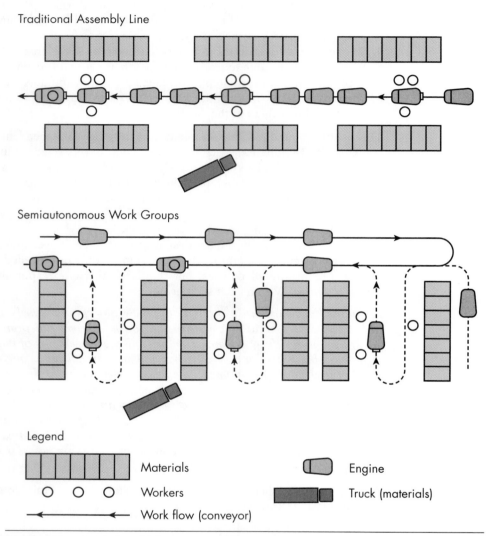

Source: Adapted with the publisher's permission from J. P. Norstedt and S. Aguren, *The Saab-Scania Report* (Stockholm: Swedish Employers' Confederation, 1973), pp. 35, 37.

performs a simplified job that consists of taking a part from a storage bin and attaching it to a partially completed truck engine as it moves along a conveyor. In the lower panel, workers are clustered into semiautonomous groups, each of which removes a bare engine block from a conveyor loop, assembles a complete truck engine from parts in surrounding storage bins, and returns the finished engines to the conveyor loop for transportation to other truck assembly operations. As suggested by this example, sociotechnical work designs typically eliminate traditional assembly line operations.

Evaluating the Motivational Perspective

Consistent with the motivational perspective that underlies them, all enlargement and enrichment techniques are aimed at designing jobs that satisfy the needs and interests of their holders. As noted earlier, methods that consist solely of horizontal job enlargement or vertical job enrichment have largely failed to achieve this goal. Methods of work design that incorporate *both* horizontal enlargement and vertical enrichment, however, have proved more effective in stimulating workforce motivation and satisfaction in a wide variety of situations.[22]

Some doubts have been raised about the validity of the Hackman–Oldham model. Studies of this model have sometimes failed to verify the existence of the five distinct job characteristics proposed by these researchers.[23] It is also unclear whether JDS questionnaire items measure objective, stable job characteristics or subjective, changing worker opinions.[24] Some researchers have even questioned whether job characteristics like those identified by Hackman and Oldham truly influence motivation and satisfaction. They suggest that employees' feelings about themselves and their work might instead be affected more profoundly by the opinions of other people in the surrounding social context.[25] This idea will be considered further in Chapter 14, when we discuss *social information processing* and organizational culture. Finally, some disagreement exists as to whether the moderators identified by Hackman and Oldham actually influence the model's applicability.[26]

Nonetheless, the Hackman–Oldham model has served as the basis of successful work design programs implemented at many well-respected companies, including Texas Instruments, AT&T, Motorola, and Xerox. Such programs are not without their drawbacks. In particular, they are usually incompatible with assembly line production processes. To enrich jobs using the Hackman–Oldham approach, a firm must almost always abandon the sort of simplified, repetitive tasks that serve as the foundation of assembly lines. Consequently, companies with substantial investments in modernized assembly lines are often reluctant to try Hackman–Oldham enrichment. In addition, 5 to 15 percent of the workforce typically lacks the skills, growth needs, or context satisfactions needed to realize the benefits of such work; those workers are likely to be "overstretched" by enriched work. Therefore, a cluster of unenriched jobs must be maintained if the firm wants to avoid displacing a significant number of its employees.

The sociotechnical enrichment approach was first implemented in Europe, where it influenced the design of jobs in firms such as Norsk Hydro, Volvo, Saab-Scania, and the Orrefors Glass Works. Since then, U.S. companies including Xerox, Cummins Engine, IBM, Polaroid, and General Electric have also experimented with sociotechnical work design, and investigation has shown that this approach yields virtually the same outcomes stimulated by the Hackman–Oldham method.[27] Sociotechnical work designs do not always improve productivity or reduce absenteeism and turnover, but they do strengthen motivation, satisfaction, and similar workplace attitudes.[28] In addition, as is true for programs based on the Hackman–Oldham model, experience suggests that a small but significant number of workers are likely to resist sociotechnical enrichment. Consequently, either a few jobs must be left unchanged or managers must be prepared to deal with the overstretching problem.

THE QUALITY PERSPECTIVE

Within the last twenty-five years, a third perspective on work design has emerged as researchers and managers have sought new ways to improve the quality of goods and services produced in North America. Founders of the **quality perspective** include W. Edwards Deming, Philip B. Crosby, and Joseph M. Juran, three U.S. quality experts who have inspired widespread adoption of an approach known as Total Quality Management (TQM).[29] TQM is guided by an overarching emphasis on making *continuous* improvements in quality throughout the process of planning objectives, organizing work, designing products, undertaking production, and monitoring results.[30] Reflecting this emphasis, TQM advocates recommend the use of self-management, teamwork, and technology to stimulate innovation and flexibility, so that companies can produce high-quality products and respond effectively to changing customer demands (see the Securing Competitive Advantage box).[31] As part of the TQM movement, quality circles, self-managed teams, and automation and robotics have been introduced throughout North America and have significantly affected the way work is designed.

Quality Circles

Quality circles (QCs) are small groups of employees, ranging in size from roughly three to thirty members, who meet on company time to identify and resolve job-related problems. Although usually thought of as a Japanese management technique, QCs were actually invented in the United States and exported to Japan by Deming and Juran during the Allied occupation that followed World War II.[32] In North America, companies such as Westinghouse, Eastman Kodak, Procter and Gamble, General Motors, Ford, and DaimlerChrysler have implemented QCs to achieve the following goals:

1. Reduce assembly errors and enhance product quality
2. Inspire more effective teamwork and cooperation in everyday work groups
3. Promote a greater sense of job involvement and commitment
4. Increase employee motivation
5. Create greater decision-making capacity
6. Substitute problem prevention for problem solving
7. Improve communication in and between work groups
8. Develop harmonious relations between management and employees
9. Promote leadership development among nonmanagerial employees[33]

Ordinarily, QC membership is voluntary and remains stable over time. The amount of time spent in QC activities can range from one hour per month to a few hours every week. Topics of discussion can include quality control, cost reduction, improvement of production techniques, production planning, and even long-term product design.[34] Over the course of many meetings, the activities of a typical QC proceed through a series of steps:

1. Members of the QC raise issues about their work and workplace in a group discussion coordinated by their supervisor or a specially trained facilitator. Often, the facilitator is an internal change agent with expertise in micro organization development.
2. QC members examine these concerns and look for ways to collapse or integrate them into specific projects. For instance, concerns about production speed and raw-material quality may be grouped together in a production methods project. Concerns about workplace safety and worker health may be combined into a work environment project.
3. Members perform initial analyses of their QC's projects using various group decision making techniques and tools, including data gathering, graphs, checklists, or charts.
4. QC members reach consensus decisions about the feasibility and importance of different projects, deciding which ones to abandon and which ones to pursue.
5. Representatives from the QC make a presentation or recommendation to management that summarizes the work of their group.
6. Management reviews the recommendation and makes a decision. Often, the decision is that QC members will have the opportunity to implement and assess their own recommendations.[35]

SECURING COMPETITIVE ADVANTAGE

DESIGNING INFORMATION TECHNOLOGY INTO JOBS TO INCREASE FLEXIBILITY

Organizational success and survival in the twenty-first century require increasingly high levels of flexibility. Companies that cannot adapt to change now find it difficult to do business, while firms that are "change friendly" are able to gain significant competitive advantage. Information technology provides the ability to recognize and adapt to changing conditions, if integrated into jobs during the process of work design. As a result, the most recent focus in work design has been on building information technology into a wide variety of jobs, in order to enhance responsiveness to change.

At Krispy Kreme, for example, franchise holders can visit the company's customized Web portal to obtain weather news in order to forecast how many doughnuts to make—since more people buy coffee and doughnuts when the weather turns inclement. Also included at the same site is a virtual help desk where employees can view streaming videos that show how to calibrate a coffee grinder or fix a deep fryer. The company's site offers architectural blueprints for franchisees planning on expansion and access to a central source of supplies and doughnut mix. Inventory updating that used to take hours can now be completed in fifteen minutes, and managers report that this change alone has led to increases in profitability of 2 to 3 percent.

At U.S. Fleet, which refuels vehicles for customers such as Nabisco and Coca-Cola, each fuel truck now carries mobile devices and wireless connections to the corporate intranet. This enables managers at the company's central terminals to check each driver's location online and rearrange service routes on the fly, increasing the average number of daily deliveries per truck from six to seven. As soon as drivers fill an order the information is scanned into handheld computers and entered into the company's network. This allows customers to check deliveries immediately on U.S. Fleet's Web site, two days faster than before

the system was installed. The $1.5 million system—less than a quarter of the cost of similar systems three years earlier—has increased efficiency and customer satisfaction well beyond initial expectations.

Finally, at Volvo, where car design was once a matter of sculpting clay models and building wood and metal prototypes, design work is increasingly done on computer laptops using software called Alias. When networked, designers in Detroit, home of Volvo's owner Ford Motor, can collaborate in real time with their Swedish counterparts in Volvo's own studios, saving time and clarifying communication. As a design progresses, designers can perform a "walkthrough" by donning virtual-reality glasses and projecting images in the company's VR theater. Some senior designers accustomed to the "smell of clay" find computer-based design lacking in important tactile respects. However, younger designers value being able to do their jobs anywhere they can flip open their laptops.

Building in flexibility by enriching the information technology incorporated in jobs—as in all three illustrations—is a natural offshoot of the quality perspective on work design, since flexibility is a requirement of high-quality work systems. Yet in many instances today so much attention is paid to flexibility, in the absence of overt concerns about quality, that a new perspective on work design—the adaptability perspective—may be emerging.

It is worth noting that greater information technology in a job may improve the job's motivational profile, by increasing the variety of skills required to perform the job. It may also increase efficiency, by automating various information processing tasks that might otherwise reduce the time available for productive activities. Thus, the adaptability approach, if actually gaining the influence needed to qualify as a true perspective on work design, may grow to integrate and supplant the three perspectives that preceded its development.

Sources: C. Skipp, "Hot Bytes, by the Dozen," *Newsweek,* April 28, 2003, p. 42; H. Green, "Winging into Wireless," *Business* Week, February 18, 2002, p. EB8; K. Naughton, "Modeling with Digital Clay," *Newsweek,* April 28, 2003, pp. 46–47.

Many companies that suffer the negative consequences of job oversimplification are unable or unwilling to modify production equipment or methods to the extent required by the Hackman–Oldham and sociotechnical models. In some of these firms, managers have attempted to use QCs to counteract the negative effects of overzealous job specialization and simplification. QCs fight oversimplification by giving employees the opportunity to participate in the management of their jobs, and they do not require the modification of existing work technologies. For example, employees who work on an assembly line for thirty-nine hours each week might meet as a QC group during the fortieth hour to evaluate the assembly line's performance and prepare for the following week's work. They might also meet in an extended session on a monthly basis to discuss more complicated issues and resolve more difficult problems.

Such monthly sessions offer an opportunity for QC members to engage in more managerial activity, group autonomy, and information exchange than allowed by the regular QC meetings. To the extent that QC meetings focus workers' attention on the outputs of the entire assembly line, they may also reinforce task identity and task significance.

Self-Managing Teams

Self-managing teams take the general orientation of QCs a step further, by grouping employees together into *permanent* teams and empowering each team with the authority to manage itself.[36] Such teams resemble the semiautonomous groups investigated in Tavistock's sociotechnical research, except that self-managing teams have greater autonomy.[37] This difference is attributable to the recent emergence of computer networks, which provide self-managing groups with the ability to interact with one another and exchange information about company goals, job assignments, and ongoing production progress without the assistance of an intervening hierarchy of managers.[38]

Among the management responsibilities allotted to each self-managing team is the duty of continually assessing the work of the team and redesigning the jobs of the team's members. To enable teams to fulfill this responsibility, team members receive training in how to design jobs and assess performance quality and efficiency. Techniques taught to team members include many of the industrial engineering procedures described earlier in this chapter.

For example, the members of self-managing teams might analyze each of the team's jobs by performing stopwatch time studies, micromotion analyses, ergonomic equipment assessments, or similar investigations, all in an effort to improve each job's efficiency. Inefficient jobs are either eliminated or redesigned by the team. The newly designed jobs are then retested, assessed, and, if successful, adopted throughout the plant.

Automation and Robotics

Automation is a third approach available to managers who seek to improve quality. Like other TQM approaches, it also has implications for the design of jobs. For many years, automation in the form of assembly line manufacturing created some of the most oversimplified and demotivating jobs in industry. Today, however, with the invention of automated technologies that can totally replace people in production processes, automation is sometimes used instead to eliminate repetitive, physically demanding, mistake-prone work.[39] Such jobs frequently utilize **industrial robots,** or machines that can be programmed to repeat the same sequence of movements over and over again with extreme precision. Robots have been introduced throughout the automotive industry, taking over various painting and parts installation jobs. In fact, the welding job described at the beginning of this chapter is currently performed by robots on many North American automotive assembly lines. Robots have also moved from the factory floor to the operating room, performing such functions as precision hip replacement and cancerous tumor radiation.[40]

Robots are not without their flaws. At General Motors, for example, employees regularly tell stories of one robot busily smashing the windshields installed by another robot or a group of robots painting each other instead of the cars passing by them on the assembly line. Proper programming is obviously a critical aspect of introducing robots into the workplace,[41] and careful planning, implementation, and adjustment is essential. In addition, experience has shown that building a robot capable of performing anything more than the simplest of jobs is often cost-prohibitive. Consequently, the U.S. population of robots is far less than the hundreds of thousands once predicted. Nonetheless, robots provide an effective way to cope with many repetitive jobs that people do not want or cannot perform well.[42]

Computer-integrated manufacturing in the form of *flexible manufacturing cells* is another type of automated technology introduced in the name of TQM, albeit one that focuses on adaptability rather than robotic repetitiveness. Products made in such cells include gearboxes, cylinder heads, brake components, and similar machined-metal components used in the automotive, aviation, and construction-equipment industries. Companies throughout Europe, Japan, and North America are also experimenting with using flexible manufacturing cells to manufacture items out of sheet metal.[43]

Each flexible manufacturing cell consists of a collection of automated production machines that cut, shape, drill, and fasten metal components together. These machines are connected to each other by convertible conveyor grids that allow for quick rerouting to accommodate changes from one product to another. It is possible, for instance, to produce a small batch of automotive door locks, then switch over to fabricate and finish a separate batch of crankshafts for automotive air-conditioner compressors. The conversion simply involves turning some machines on and others off, then activating those conveyors that interconnect the machines that are in use— and operations of this sort are normally computer-controlled. When employed in this manner, the same collection of machines can manufacture a wide variety of products without substantial human involvement and without major alteration of the cell.[44]

Workers in a flexible manufacturing cell need never touch the product being manufactured, nor must they perform simple, repetitive production tasks. Instead, their jobs focus on the surveillance and decision making required to initialize different cell configurations and oversee equipment operations. Often, a cell's workforce forms a self-managing team to accommodate the sizable amount of mutual adjustment that must occur to manage occasional crises and keep production flowing smoothly. Under such circumstances, employees in a flexible manufacturing cell have enriched jobs that allow them to exercise expertise in teamwork, problem solving, and self-management.[45]

Evaluating the Quality Perspective

In many respects, the quality perspective represents a hybrid of the efficiency and motivational perspectives on work design. For instance, quality circles allow employees to enjoy at least modest satisfaction under conditions in which work processes are shaped mainly by concerns about productive efficiency. Self-managed teams enable their members to satisfy needs for social- and growth-oriented outcomes partly by requiring them to work together to apply many of the work design methods conforming to the efficiency perspective. Automation—perhaps the peak of mechanical efficiency—releases employees from jobs devoid of satisfying elements.

What effects does this "middle ground" approach have on performance and satisfaction in the workplace? Evidence identifying the effects of QCs as a form of job enrichment is sketchy. The information that is available suggests that QCs have little effect on productivity but can enhance feelings of satisfaction and involvement significantly.[46] The magnitude of such effects is usually smaller than the results produced by job enrichment programs based on the Hackman–Oldham model or the

Tavistock sociotechnical model. This discrepancy is understandable, however, because workers who participate in QCs must still perform unenriched jobs during most of their time spent at work.

Evidence concerning the job enrichment effects of self-managing groups is even more meager. Extrapolation from research on semiautonomous groups and QCs suggests that self-management should improve team members' satisfaction and perhaps performance, and anecdotal accounts seem to support this contention.[47] Researchers have also noted that the quality standards developed and then observed in TQM teams can severely limit autonomy, which in turn reduces potential motivational gains, but workers who are able to alternate between adhering to existing standards and working to create new ones report significant satisfaction with their jobs.[48]

Research on the work design effects of automation is similarly lacking. At its core, automation represents a return to the efficiency perspective of industrial engineering. Some jobs resist enrichment, and it is more effective to turn them over to machines than to attempt to convert them into interesting, enjoyable work for people. Among both the old jobs that remain and the new ones that are created by adoption of innovation, the danger exists that human satisfaction may be ignored during the job design process. Nevertheless, research suggests that employees in flexible manufacturing cells do show signs of increased motivation, satisfaction, and improved performance if the tasks they perform provide greater autonomy than was available before the introduction of automation.[49]

To summarize, the relevant evidence seems to support the conclusion that work design implementations stimulated by the quality perspective may have positive effects on workforce motivation, satisfaction, and productivity. This evidence is far from conclusive, and additional information is needed to prove the true benefits of TQM and the quality perspective.[50]

SUMMARY

Contemporary work design began with Frederick Taylor, Frank and Lillian Gilbreth, and other experts whose work on *industrial engineering* served as the foundations of the *efficiency perspective* on work design. Within this perspective, *methods engineering* attempts to improve the methods used to perform work, and *work measurement* examines the motions and time required to complete each job. A second approach to work design was first developed when Frederick Herzberg differentiated between *motivator* and *hygiene factors*. Other specialists later extended this perspective by introducing early models of *horizontal job enlargement* and *vertical job enrichment*. The *motivational perspective* emerged as work progressed on *comprehensive job enrichment programs* and on *sociotechnical job enrichment*. A third approach, the *quality perspective*, then emerged as experience with *Total Quality Management* programs indicated that *quality circles, self-managing teams,* and *automation* could be used as alternatives to traditional job assignments during the process of work design. Incorporated in this third perspective were elements of both the efficiency and motivational perspectives that preceded its development.

REVIEW QUESTIONS

1. Explain how following Taylor's principles of scientific management can simplify the jobs in an organization. What are some positive effects of this simplification? What negative effects might occur?

2. What do the fields of process engineering and human factors engineering have in common? How do they differ from one another? Are they more likely to enhance satisfaction or efficiency? Why?

3. How do motion and time studies affect the design of jobs? What type of work measurement would you use to analyze the job of installing engines on an automobile assembly line? What type would you use to analyze the time required to sort and shelve library books?

4. Why do horizontal job enlargement programs, such as job extension and job rotation, often fail to stimulate employee satisfaction?

5. How do work design programs based on the Hackman–Oldham job characteristics model differ from programs based on Herzberg's motivator–hygiene model? Of the two types of programs, which is most likely to produce significant improvements in employee motivation and satisfaction?

6. In what ways is the sociotechnical model of work design similar to the Hackman–Oldham model? In what ways do the two models differ? Which would you use if you were designing the job of a postal carrier? Which would you use to design the job of a surgical team?

7. How does the quality perspective differ from the efficiency and motivational perspectives? What similarities does it share with each of the other two? How do concerns about quality affect the design of jobs?

8. The quality perspective includes quality circles, self-managed groups, and automation. Which of these approaches would you select to enrich jobs in a newly built assembly line? Which would you use to design jobs that resist all attempts at enrichment?

LEARNING THROUGH EXPERIENCE

DIAGNOSTIC QUESTIONS 7-1

Work Design

Differences among the three perspectives on work design invite confusion, requiring managers to consider carefully the various alternatives before choosing one to use in solving the specific work design problems faced by their organizations. The following diagnostic questions are provided to help guide this consideration:

1. Does the design of the organization's current jobs reflect the efficiency perspective or the motivational perspective? Are most jobs simplified, or have attempts been made to alter job range or depth? Does the quality perspective and a balance between efficiency and motivation seem evident instead?

2. If the efficiency perspective dominates the environment, do productivity and satisfaction data support the idea that jobs have not been oversimplified? Or does faltering productivity and conspicuous dissatisfaction indicate that oversimplification may be a problem?

3. Can the firm's current technology be changed to the degree required by job enrichment methods? Are jobs mainly individualized, indicating the appropriateness of Hackman–Oldham enrichment? Or are jobs often performed by groups of people working together closely, suggesting the sociotechnical approach?

4. If technological considerations prohibit job enrichment, might quality circles provide enough relief to restore motivation and satisfaction? If not, can you eliminate the troublesome jobs through automation?

5. If the motivational perspective dominates the environment, do productivity and satisfaction data suggest that jobs have been enriched without creating overdemanding work? Or do falling productivity and satisfaction indicate that workers are being overstretched and asked to do more than they can?

6. If you are facing an overenrichment problem, do the results of work measurement procedures suggest ways to simplify jobs enough to facilitate successful performance while still retaining opportunities for growth, achievement, and recognition? Could self-managing teams solve this problem instead?

7. If work measurement fails to reveal a remedy, can methods engineering be used to create new jobs that are both feasible and capable of adequate enrichment? If not, can you eliminate the troublesome jobs through automation?

8. Is your company having problems coordinating its work that can be traced to poor information sharing? Can work be restructured in a manner such that technological means can be used to mollify these problems?

EXERCISE 7-1   **Redesigning a Simplified Job**

John Wagner, Michigan State University

The drive toward efficiency in modern organizations sometimes results in the creation of oversimplified jobs that fail to challenge or involve the worker. People in these jobs often express strong dissatisfaction as product quality falls and both absenteeism and turnover increase. Comprehensive job enrichment is intended to counteract this situation. This technique changes job content in several ways. For instance, it combines tasks and forms natural work units so as to increase skill variety, task identity, and task significance. It also gives each worker more autonomy on the job, and it opens up channels for immediate feedback to the worker. In this exercise you will diagnose a job and suggest how it might be enriched, thereby experiencing the initial steps of job redesign.

Step One: Pre-Class Preparation

In Step Two of this exercise, you will work in groups to diagnose one of the following jobs:

1. A job your group has observed and discussed before class. If your instructor assigns this option, you should meet as a group, decide which job you want to observe, verify with your instructor that your choice is appropriate, and meet on site and observe the jobholder as he or she performs the job. Be sure to take notes to refresh your memory as you perform the rest of the exercise.

2. A job that has been performed by a member of your class. If your instructor assigns this option, he or she will ask for volunteers from class to serve as interviewees. In this role, the jobholders will describe in depth a job they have performed. Depending on the number of volunteers, each group may have a volun-

The questionnaire in this exercise was adapted with permission from the Job Diagnostic Survey developed by J. Richard Hackman and Greg R. Oldham.

teer to interview, several groups may combine to interview the same volunteer, or the class as a whole may conduct a single interview. Depending on your instructor's preference, interviews may be conducted before or during class.

3. A videotaped job. If your instructor assigns this option, he or she will show a videotape of a job being performed and you will diagnose the job based on what you see. Your instructor will supply the videotape and show it at the beginning of class.

Read the remainder of the exercise and prepare for the next step as necessary, depending on the option your instructor has chosen.

Step Two: Completing the Task Diagnostic Questionnaire

The class should divide into groups containing four to six members. If you have already formed permanent groups, you should reassemble in those groups. If your instructor assigned the task of observing a job before coming to class, the groups you form for this step of the exercise should match those that you formed to observe the job. The members of each group should work together to fill out the Task Diagnostic Questionnaire (TDQ) shown in Exhibit 7-1. The group should reach consensus on its response to each item. Note any significant disagreements next to the relevant item on the TDQ.

EXHIBIT 7-1   Task Diagnostic Questionnaire

This questionnaire contains statements with which you may agree or disagree. It is intended to reveal how people perceive different kinds of jobs. It is not intended to measure how much someone likes or dislikes a job, but rather to elicit as accurate and objective a description as possible. To be useful, the respondent must fill out the questionnaire honestly.

In the blank next to each statement, write the number that represents how accurate you think the statement is in describing the job: 1 = very inaccurate; 2 = mostly inaccurate; 3 = slightly inaccurate; 4 = uncertain; 5 = slightly accurate; 6 = mostly accurate; 7 = very accurate.

__ 1. The job requires the worker to use a number of complex, high-level skills.
__ 2. The way the job is structured, the worker does not have the opportunity to do a complete piece of work from beginning to end.
__ 3. Just doing the job provides the worker with many chances to figure out how well he or she is doing.
__ 4. The job is quite simple and repetitive.
__ 5. In this job, many other people can be affected by how well the work is done.
__ 6. The job does not give the worker any chance to use his or her personal initiative or judgment in carrying out the work.
__ 7. The job allows the worker to completely finish every piece of work he or she begins.
__ 8. The job itself provides very few clues about whether the worker is performing well.
__ 9. The job gives the worker considerable independence and freedom in the way he or she does the work.
__ 10. The job is not very significant or important in the overall work of the organization.
__ 11. The job permits the worker to decide for himself or herself what needs to be done.
__ 12. The job is merely one small part of an overall piece of work that is finished by other people or by automated machines.
__ 13. The job requires the worker to do many different things, using a variety of skills and talents.
__ 14. The results of the job have a significant effect on the lives and well-being of other people.
__ 15. The job itself provides clues about how well the worker is doing; feedback from co-workers or supervisors is not needed.

Step Three: Scoring and Discussing the TDQ

To score your group's evaluations on the TDQ for the job you're examining, do the following:

1. For items 2, 4, 6, 8, 10, and 12, subtract the number you circled from 8. The result is your score for each of these items. For items 1, 3, 5, 7, 9, 11, 13, 14, and 15, the number you circled is the correct score.

2. Add your scores for items 1, 4, and 13, divide the sum by 3, and write the result here:

   _____. This is the job's score on *skill variety*.

3. Add your scores for items 2, 7, and 12, divide the sum by 3, and write the result here:

   _____. This is the job's score on *task identity*.

4. Add your scores for items 5, 10, and 14, divide the sum by 3, and write the result here:

   _____. This is the job's score on *task significance*.

5. Add your scores for items 6, 9, and 11, divide the sum by 3, and write the result here:

   _____. This is the job's score on *autonomy*.

6. Add your scores for items 3, 8, and 15, divide the sum by 3, and write the result here:

   _____. This is the job's score on *feedback*.

Next, calculate a motivational summary score, or MSS (similar to the motivation potential score discussed in Chapter 7), using the following formula:

$$MSS = \frac{(\text{skill variety} + \text{task identity} + \text{task significance})}{3} \times \text{autonomy} \times \text{feedback}$$

Your group should discuss the meaning of the scores it has derived and the results of its diagnosis. Next, appoint a spokesperson to present a report to the class. This report should include information about the kind of job that the group diagnosed, the group's scores on each of the five dimensions, significant disagreements among group members, and the MSS calculated by the group. The spokesperson should also show a diagram of the job profile developed by the group on a blackboard, flip chart, or overhead projector.

Step Four: Developing a Job Enrichment Strategy

The class should convene, and all spokespeople should give their reports. After discussing the different jobs analyzed by the class, members should return to their groups. Each group should then develop a strategy to enrich the job it has diagnosed. The following points should be considered during this step:

1. Which specific job characteristics need enrichment? Which, if any, are good enough as is? What specific actions should be taken to enrich the job along the dimensions that need further help?

2. Before redesigning the job, should additional data be collected? What kind? From whom?

3. Who in the organization will be responsible for developing the work design strategy if additional refinement is needed? Who will be responsible for implementing it? How will the effectiveness of the implementation be measured? Who will perform this evaluation?

4. What are some likely sources of resistance to the strategy you have developed? How should the organization deal with them?

The group spokesperson should prepare an overview of the group's strategy for presentation to the class.

Step Five: Strategy Reports and Class Discussion

The class should reconvene, and each spokesperson should report on the results of Step Four. Class members should ask any questions necessary to understand each strategic plan. The entire class should then compare, contrast, and critique the strategies developed by the groups, being sure to address the following points:

1. To what extent did each strategy emphasize employee involvement? Changes in the job itself? Changes in the context surrounding the job? Does the strategy appear workable?

2. What consequences would the strategy have for the structure of the organization? For current policies? For the distribution of power in the firm?

3. For each strategy, what positive and negative indirect effects might it have on those individuals who are not directly involved in it? How might these individuals act as forces for or against change?

Conclusion

This exercise has introduced some of the factors underlying the nature of work and highlighted the complexity of issues involved in trying to redesign jobs. Job redesign programs can be applied to jobs in the consumer products industry, jobs in service industries, white collar jobs, blue-collar jobs—any place where work has been oversimplified to the point of reducing worker satisfaction and productivity.

Patterns of Interdependence and Organizational Roles
Types of Interdependence
Implications of Interdependence
Role Taking and Role Making
Norms and Role Episodes

Communication Processes in Interdependent Relationships
Communication Messages and Media
Barriers to Effective Communication

Socialization to New Roles
Socialization Goals and Tactics
Designing Socialization Programs

Quality of Interpersonal Role Relationships
Equity and Social Comparisons
Distributive, Procedural, and Interactive Justice
Responses to Inequity
Managing Inequitable Situations

Summary
Review Questions

Learning Through Experience
Diagnostic Questions 8-1: Interdependence and Role Relationships
Exercise 8-1: The Admissions Committee: A Consensus-Seeking Task

Interdependence and Role Relationships

On Wednesday, April 16, 2003, the unionized employees of American Airlines voted in favor of one of the most painful wage concession plans in the history of U.S. labor. Flight attendants, ground workers, and pilots agreed to work up to 20 percent more days for up to 40 percent less pay in an effort to ward off bankruptcy. CEO Don Carty had convinced labor leaders that the airline could not survive without the pay cuts, and heralded the new agreement as part of a new openness in labor management relations and evidence of the "shared sacrifice" between union and management.[1]

However, on Thursday, April 17, the union learned that American had granted forty-five of its officers a special supplemental retirement bonus that would be out of reach if the company went bankrupt. It also offered cash retention bonuses to the top six executives that also would be in effect regardless of whether the firm went under. All of a sudden, the notion of "shared sacrifice" became a little suspect, and many of the workers—especially those in the flight attendant unit—wanted to rescind their approval of the wage cuts. Failure to obtain the wage cuts would more than likely force the company into bankruptcy, but at this point, Carty had zero credibility with the union members, who were no longer willing to talk to him.

The union leaders were especially adamant about this, because Carty had destroyed not only his own credibility, but theirs as well, making them look like fools who had been duped and cheated. "Every union member—those who voted for the agreement and those that voted against it—[is] outraged by this action," noted John Ward, president of the Association of Professional Flight Attendants.[2] A date was set for new elections, and the prospect of recovering the wage concessions looked dubious.

Carty desperately tried to mend the damage by abruptly canceling the bonus program. He also sent a public letter of apology to the union members. He tried to defend the bonus program by noting that it had been initiated almost a year earlier, after several key executives left the airline following the 9/11 incidents. He also noted that the packages were much less lucrative relative to those that were put in place by Delta Airlines, one of American's key competitors. Still he noted that the bonuses were a "big mistake" and that although the timing was awful, he would hope the unions would stand by their previous ratification vote.³

In the scramble to salvage the wage concessions, a new negotiation process began to take place, but regardless of whatever else came out of this wrangling, one undeniable demand was clear—Don Carty's reign as CEO at American was over. On Thursday, April 25, one week after the disclosures, Carty announced his resignation, and Gerard Arpey became the new CEO of American. Arpey tried to undo the damage caused by his predecessor, and noted at his first public opportunity that "none of American's turnaround initiatives can fully succeed until we build trust and teamwork back into the company."⁴ Arpey apologized to the employees, praised them for American's solid operational performance, and opened the company's books to union leaders in an unprecedented action.

Only time will tell if American, which as of this writing is still losing close to $1 million a day, will survive for much longer. But there is a new spirit of hope that Arpey can create a new culture of collaboration, cooperation, and trust. In the words of one employee, "I think he understands the employee relationship problem we have here and the impact this has on the bottom line."⁵

Our last chapter dealt with jobs and how they can be designed to enhance the fit between tasks and individual people. Jobs and the individuals that hold these jobs do not exist in a vacuum, however. Rather, in organizations, jobs and individuals are linked to each other, and much of the competitive success of an organization can be traced to how well the relationships between jobs and individuals are managed. Thus, managers need to know about various factors that affect people as they *work together*.

We begin this chapter by identifying several different patterns of *interdependence* that develop among people and connect them as they work with one another. For example, in our opening story, the union workers and management at American Airlines were dependent on each other in the sense that neither side could operate the airline without the other. Moreover, to avoid bankruptcy, the two sides needed to work together to come up with a more viable business model.

Next we note that people occupy specific *roles* in the networks of interdependence they share with others, and we examine the process of *communication*, which is the glue that holds role occupants together. Thus, the union leaders had the role of representing the interests of their members, and the membership expected them to be well informed on the financial status of the airline. The union leaders, in turn, had expectations that the management was being open with them when they stated publicly that there was a need for "shared sacrifice" on both sides. At no time is this communication more important than when people are first introduced into their organizational roles, and thus, we will pay particular attention to *socialization* processes through which individuals learn about the roles they are expected to fill.

Finally, we conclude the chapter by examining *equity theory* as a framework for judging and enhancing the quality of relationships between individuals and organizations in terms of fairness. If people feel that they are being treated fairly in their organizational relationships, the quality of relationships will be high, and over time, this can lead to trust and a long-term focus on well-coordinated efforts. However, if this trust is violated, as was the case at American Airlines, then workers will try to "get even" or terminate the relationship. Don Carty eventually lost the top job at American because he violated the role expectations of the union leaders and members, and once he lost their trust, the relationship had to be terminated.

PATTERNS OF INTERDEPENDENCE AND ORGANIZATIONAL ROLES

People in organizations share a rich variety of connections. Their work may require them to associate with one another as a regular part of job performance. They may band together to share resources, such as access to valuable equipment or financial resources, even when their work does not require direct contact between individuals. Such connections make interpersonal relations a very important aspect of organizational life. Among both individuals and groups, these relationships take the form of patterns or networks of interdependence.

Types of Interdependence

In the workplace, interdependence typically takes one of the four forms diagrammed in Figure 8-1: pooled, sequential, reciprocal, or comprehensive interdependence.

Pooled interdependence occurs when people draw resources from a shared source but have little else in common. Resources pooled together in this manner might include money, equipment, raw materials, information, or expertise. As the simplest form of interdependence, pooled interdependence requires little or no interpersonal interaction. In a company like Metropolitan Life Insurance, for example, individual data-entry specialists draw off a common pool of work that must be entered into the firm's computers. Each data-entry person works alone to perform the task of entering information, however. That is, the task itself requires little interaction with other employees.

FIGURE 8-1   Types of Interdependence

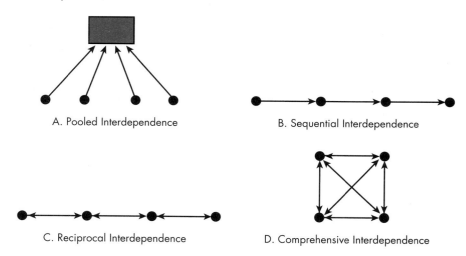

A. Pooled Interdependence

B. Sequential Interdependence

C. Reciprocal Interdependence

D. Comprehensive Interdependence

Sequential interdependence comprises a chain of one-way interactions in which people depend on those individuals who precede them in the chain. People earlier in the chain, however, remain independent of those who follow them. Thus sequentially interdependent relationships are said to be *asymmetric,* meaning that some people depend on others who do not in turn depend on them. For example, employees at Steelcase who work on an assembly line manufacturing office furniture are connected by sequential interdependence. Workers earlier in the line produce partial assemblies, which workers later in the line complete. By its very nature, sequential interdependence prevents people at the end of the chain from performing their jobs unless people at the head of the chain have already carried out their tasks. On the other hand, people at the head of the chain can complete their tasks no matter what people at the other end do. Research shows that sequential systems like this are very sensitive to differences either between people in their performance (two workers who operate at different speeds) or between the same person at different times (a worker who operates faster in the morning than in the afternoon). Performance variability can "starve" workers down the line if the work moves too slow or "block" the line if it moves faster than the next person can handle it.[6]

In reciprocal interdependence, a network of two-way relationships ties a collection of people together. A good example of this kind of interdependence is the relationship between a sales force and a clerical staff. Sales representatives rely on clerks to complete invoices and process credit card receipts, and clerks depend on salespeople to generate sales. Reciprocal interdependence also occurs among the members of a hospital staff. Doctors depend on nurses to check patients periodically, administer medications, and report alarming symptoms. Nurses, in turn, depend on doctors to prescribe medications and to specify the nature of symptoms associated with potential complications.

Reciprocal interdependence always involves some sort of direct interaction, such as face-to-face communication, telephone conversations, or written instructions. As a result, people who are reciprocally interdependent are more tightly interconnected than are individuals who are interconnected by either pooled or sequential interdependence. Reciprocal interdependence incorporates symmetric, two-way interactions in which each person depends on the person who depends on him or her.

Comprehensive interdependence develops in a tight network of reciprocal interdependence. It is the most complex form of interdependence, because everyone involved is reciprocally interdependent with one another. As in reciprocal interdependence, people who depend on one another interact directly. In comprehensive interdependence, however, these interactions tend to be more frequent, more intense, and of greater duration than in any other type of interdependence.

For example, in the brand-management groups that oversee the development of new products at firms such as Colgate-Palmolive and Procter & Gamble, product designers, market researchers, production engineers, and sales representatives are all linked by a completely connected network of two-way relationships. The product designers interact with the market researchers, product engineers, and sales representatives. The market researchers also interact with the product engineers and the sales staff, who in turn interact with each other.

Implications of Interdependence

The type of interdependence that connects people together in interpersonal relationships has several important managerial implications. First, a greater potential for conflict arises as the complexity of the interdependence grows in moving from pooled to comprehensive interdependence. Sharing a greater number of interconnections and being more tightly connected increase the likelihood that differences in opinions, goals, or outcomes will be noticed and disputed.

Second, the loss of individuals due to turnover becomes more important as the intensity of the interdependence increases. One person's departure requires that few relationships be rebuilt under conditions of pooled or sequential interdependence. In situations characterized by reciprocal or comprehensive interdependence, however, many more relationships must be redeveloped if a new individual is introduced into the system. In some cases of extreme interdependence, the loss of even a single person can make everyone else perform below par.

Third, comprehensive interdependence can stimulate greater flexibility and enable groups of people to adapt more quickly to changing environments than groups unified by less complex forms of interdependence. As discussed more fully in Chapter 9, this flexibility requires that greater attention be paid to maintaining continued interdependence, and it can contribute to *process loss* and reduced productivity if managed unwisely.

Fourth, the type of interdependence has implications for the design of motivational systems. Group-level goals and group-level feedback are associated with high performance in organizations utilizing sequential, reciprocal, or comprehensive interdependence, but individual-level goals and performance feedback work best for people connected via pooled interdependence.[7]

Role Taking and Role Making

As interdependent people associate with one another and gain experience with interpersonal relations, they come to expect other individuals to behave in specific ways. These expectations may be based partially on the formal job descriptions that each person has, but typically go well beyond this. For example, the union leaders expected that the management at American Airlines was going to do all it could to avoid bankruptcy, since both management and workers were in the same boat. Hence, when it became clear that the managers were going to be well compensated regardless of whether the firm went under, this was a violation of the workers' expectations.

Expectations such as these, and the behaviors they presuppose, form the **roles** that individuals occupy in interpersonal relations.[8] Chapter 6 introduced the concept of work-related roles, which were described there as a source of dissatisfaction and stress. This chapter will elaborate on the concept of a role, using it as a framework for understanding how interpersonal relationships develop and sometimes break down.

As indicated in Table 8-1, the behavioral expectations that make up such roles can include formal *established task elements* that are generally determined by a company's management as well as many other informal *emergent task elements* that evolve over time as interpersonal relations develop and mature.[9]

TABLE 8-1 Elements of Work Roles

Established Task Elements	Emergent Task Elements
1. Created by managers or specialists, independently of the role incumbent	1. Created by everyone who has a stake in how the role is performed, including the role incumbent
2. Characterized by elements that are objective, that are formally documented, and about which there is considerable consensus	2. Characterized by elements that are subjective, not formally documented, and open to negotiation
3. Static and relatively constant	3. Constantly changing and developing

Established task elements are the parts of a role that arise because the role occupant is expected to perform a particular *job*. A job is a formal position, often accompanied by a written statement of the tasks it entails. Such written statements, called *job descriptions,* are generally prepared by managers or specialists with expertise in job analysis and description. When such descriptions exist, a fair amount of agreement usually exists at the outset regarding what constitutes the established task elements of a role.

Because job descriptions are prepared before the fact by people who do not actually perform the job, they are often incomplete. Moreover, most do not account for job incumbents' personal characteristics or the complex and dynamic environments in which jobs must be performed. Thus, as a person begins to do a job, it often becomes clear that tasks omitted from the written job description must be performed to successfully fulfill the role. These added-on tasks are referred to as **emergent task elements.**

For instance, secretarial workers are increasingly being asked to perform duties other than typing, filing, and answering telephones. As business has grown more complex and executives' time has become more precious, some secretaries have expanded their roles. Many of today's executive secretaries have assumed some of the burdens of middle management, according to Nancy Shuman, vice president of a New York placement firm called Career Blazers. Kay Kilpatrick, assistant to Richard Smith, chairperson of Harcourt General, Inc., finds herself doing tasks that her job description never mentioned. She runs the company's employee matching gift program and charitable corporate gift program. Kilpatrick also evaluates stock portfolios and handles distributions from various trusts.[10]

Established and emergent task elements can be combined in different ways. At one extreme is the *bureaucratic prototype,* in which the role occupant performs few duties other than those written in the job description. When people move into these highly prescribed roles, they engage in role taking. Many low-level jobs in automated, assembly line factories are of this type. At the other extreme is the *loose-cannon prototype,* in which emergent elements greatly outnumber the few established elements. When people move into this kind of loosely defined role, they engage in role making—a term that highlights the degree to which the role occupant "builds or constructs" his or her own role.

Organizations are structured in terms of roles, rather than in terms of the unique acts of specific individuals. Consequently, they can remain stable despite persistent turnover of personnel. For this reason, roles are of crucial importance to organizations and a central concern for those charged with managing organizational behavior.

Norms and Role Episodes

As indicated in Figure 8-2, the expectations that make up roles and give shape to interpersonal relations are called **norms.** Norms develop over time through repeated interaction; in many instances, group members may not even be aware that they exist.[11] For example, in your class norms direct students to sit down and wait for the instructor to begin the day's activities. Norms may also direct students to participate in class discussions and exercises and to contribute to group case discussions. Without such norms, each class meeting would require your instructor to reestablish the basic rules of behavior and set an agenda for the day. You would therefore have much less time available to pursue the learning activities on the schedule.

In organizations, norms exist for both the job's formal requirements, or its established task elements, and the job's generally agreed-upon informal rules, or emer-

FIGURE 8-2 The Role-Taking Process

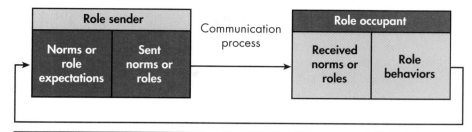

Source: Adapted from D. Katz and R. L. Kahn, *The Social Psychology of Organizations* (New York: Wiley, 1978), p. 112.

gent task elements.[12] Either type may evolve from a variety of sources.[13] Sometimes *precedents* that are established in early exchanges simply persist over time and become norms. For example, students take certain seats on the first day of class and, even though the instructor may not establish a formal seating arrangement, the students may tend to return to the same seats for each session. Norms may also be *carryovers* from other situations. In such instances, people may generalize from what they have done in the past in other, similar situations. For instance, a person may stand when making a presentation at a meeting because he or she was required to stand in prior meetings. Sometimes norms reflect *explicit statements from others*. A part-time summer worker, for instance, may be told by more experienced workers to "slow down and save some work for tomorrow."

Finally, some *critical historical event* may influence norms. Suppose, for example, that a secretary leaks important company secrets to a competitor. In response to this incident, a norm may evolve that requires all sensitive information to be typed by managers, not delegated to the secretarial staff. This new norm may even be written into job descriptions, thus taking what was once an informal, emergent element and converting it to a formal, established element. If this occurs over and over again, the organization can become full of written rules and procedures, which makes it very rigid and bureaucratic. Thus, what starts out as an adaptive process (formalizing norms), if left unchecked, can become a maladaptive process (excessive formalization). Because of this, it is critical to distinguish pivotal norms from peripheral norms.

Adherence to the first type of norms, **pivotal norms,** is an absolute requirement if interpersonal relations are to persist and work is to be performed without major interruption. Failure to adopt such norms threatens the survival of existing interpersonal relations and continued interdependence.[14] For example, the management of American Airlines must negotiate with the duly elected members of the unions that represent the workers because there are federal laws that require them to do so. This is a pivotal norm, and management does not have the discretion to just lower wages or increase hours without first negotiating such changes. In contrast, adherence to the second kind of norm, **peripheral norms,** is more discretionary. Although the nature of these norms (and their violation) can strongly influence the character of the interpersonal relations, they are not formally required. For example, in the labor negotiations at American, it is not necessary for the management to totally open up the books, and share with the union leaders every piece of financial data they have. However, as we saw in our opening story, this is exactly what American's new CEO, Gerard Arpey, did, hoping that this kind of transparency would help regain lost trust caused by excessive secrecy in the past.

Indeed, many other organizations have already adopted this kind of "open-book management" culture because it has been shown to promote employee trust and willingness to cooperate.[15] In the wake of the recent corporate scandals, some CEOs have moved in this direction voluntarily.[16] In other cases, union leaders and shareholders have pressed for it more directly.[17] In still other cases, the government has threatened to demand it, suggesting that there may be a need for laws that would convert this from a peripheral norm to a pivotal norm. Indeed, this was a major theme echoed by President Bush in a national address to the nation in the wake of these scandals, when he noted, "At this moment, America's greatest economic need is higher standards for financial disclosure, standards enforced by strict laws."[18]

Whether interdependent individuals adopt pivotal and peripheral norms has important consequences for their behaviors and performance as members of groups and organizations. As Table 8-2 indicates, *individual adjustment,* or the acceptance or rejection of these norms, leads to four basic behavior patterns: conformity, subversive rebellion, open revolution, and creative individualism.

When role occupants choose to accept both pivotal and peripheral norms, the resulting **conformity** is marked by a tendency to try to fit in with others in a loyal but uncreative way. People who conform to all norms become caretakers of the past. So long as tasks remain unchanged and the work situation is stable, conformity can facilitate productivity and performance. Conversely, it can endanger the organization's long-term survival if tasks or the surrounding situation changes significantly.

When individuals accept peripheral norms but reject pivotal ones, the result is **subversive rebellion.** That is, people conceal their rejection of norms that are critical to the survival of existing interpersonal relations by acting in accordance with less important ones. This outward show of conformity may make it possible for rebellious members to continue occupying important roles. If their number is large, however, their failure to adhere to important pivotal norms may jeopardize the survival of ongoing interpersonal relations.

Open revolution may break out if role occupants reject both pivotal and peripheral norms. If only a few individuals revolt, they may be pressured to conform or asked to leave. Interpersonal relations dominated by open revolution, however, may simply fall apart.

In **creative individualism,** individuals accept pivotal norms but reject peripheral ones. This behavior ensures continued productivity and survival. It also opens the door to the individual creativity needed to develop new ways of doing things. Creative individualism is, therefore, especially desirable when dealing with change in tasks or work situations. It ensures that individuals have the freedom to invent new responses to changing conditions. This type of creativity is often sought because norms do not always remain effective over time. For example, most organizations have a norm where people sit down for meetings, even though research shows that meetings where people stand up are generally faster and equally—if not more—productive.[19]

TABLE 8-2
Norms and Individual Adjustment

| | | Pivotal Norms | |
		Accept	Reject
Peripheral Norms	ACCEPT	Conformity	Subversive rebellion
	REJECT	Creative individualism	Open revolution

Source: From *Organization Psychology,* 3rd ed. by E.H. Schein, p. 100. Copyright © 1980. Reprinted by permission of Pearson Education, Inc. Upper Saddle River, NJ.

Norms develop through a series of role episodes. A **role set** comprises a collection of people who interact with a role occupant and serve as the source of the norms that influence that person's behaviors (see Figure 8-2). A typical role set includes such people as an employee's supervisor and subordinates, other members of the employee's functional unit, and members of adjacent functional units that share tasks, clients, or customers. Members of the role set communicate norms to the role occupant via *role-sending messages.*

Some role-sending messages are informational, telling the role occupant what is going on. Others attempt to influence the role occupant (for example, by letting him or her know what punishments will follow if the individual disregards norms). Some of these messages may be directed toward accomplishing organizational objectives. Others may be unrelated to, or even contrary to, official requirements.

As long as the role occupant complies with these expectations, role senders will attend to their own jobs. If the role occupant begins to deviate from expectations, however, the role senders, their expectations, and their means of enforcing compliance will become quite visible. The part-time summer worker who fails to heed the warnings of more experienced personnel may soon become the victim of derision, practical jokes, or isolation. Indeed, recent research shows that peers can be the most accurate and discriminating source in terms of monitoring norm-related activity.[20]

Although the members of the organization communicate the do's and don'ts associated with a role through the *sent role,* the *received role* actually has the most immediate influence on the behavior of the role occupant. As discussed later in this chapter, factors that influence the process of communication may distort a message or cause it to be misunderstood. Even when messages are communicated effectively, role occupants often fail to meet senders' role expectations. Several types of role conflict (as discussed in Chapter 6) can prevent a role receiver from meeting the expectations of a sender.

First, *intersender role conflict* may place competing, mutually exclusive demands on the role occupant. A person who meets one sender's expectations may violate the expectations of another. In addition, the role occupant may experience *person–role conflict* and have some ideas about how the role should be performed that conflict with the role sender's demands. Finally, *interrole conflict,* caused by occupying two roles at once (for example, being a manager and a parent), can create stress both at home and at work. Thus, role making and taking is a process characterized not by unilateral demands and forced acceptance but instead by flexibility and give-and-take negotiation.

COMMUNICATION PROCESSES IN INTERDEPENDENT RELATIONSHIPS

In Figure 8-2, a straight line was drawn between the sent role and the received role to denote the communication of a message between members of the role set and the role occupant. A more detailed representation of the process of communication breaks it into three general stages: encoding information into a message, transmitting the message via a medium, and decoding information from the received message.[21] Because problems can develop at any one of these stages, it is important to understand what happens at each stage, and how this might translate into barriers to effective communication.

Communication Messages and Media

Encoding is the process by which a communicator's abstract idea is translated into the symbols of language and thus into a message that can be transmitted to someone else. The idea is subjective and known only to the communicator. Because it employs a common system of symbols, the message can be understood by other people who know the communicator's language.

The *medium,* or the carrier of the message, exists outside the communicator and can be perceived by everyone. We can characterize media by the human senses on which they rely: oral speech, which uses hearing; written documentation, which uses vision or touch (Braille); and nonverbal communication, which may use at least four of the five basic senses.

Nowhere is technology having a greater effect on the workplace than in the area of communication media.[22] Facsimile (fax), electronic mail (e-mail), and cellular phones all decrease the need for travel among executives and professional workers, yet make these workers more efficient when they must travel. The menu of options in terms of finding the best medium for each message has never been larger or more varied.[23] Many of these new media choices, such as e-mail, are so new that researchers are only beginning to document their advantages and disadvantages.[24]

New wireless technology is also being increasingly employed by service personnel and repair workers. For example, all copy machine repair workers at Pitney Bowes, Inc., carry wireless data terminals that allow them to tap into a database while they are servicing remote repair jobs. The database gives the location of the worker's next assignment, and it provides information about the make and model of the machine used there, the date and nature of its last service, and the person to consult upon arrival. If parts must be ordered, the employee can make the request from the remote location, drastically reducing delivery times. Pitney Bowes estimates that the system has improved productivity by 15 percent and simultaneously increased customer satisfaction.[25]

Oral communication relies predominantly on the sense of hearing; its symbols are based on sounds and consist of spoken language. Face-to-face conversations, meetings, and telephone calls are the most commonly used forms of communication in organizations. As you will recall from Chapter 1, as much as 75 percent of a manager's time is devoted to meetings and telephone calls.[26] Oral communications offer the advantage of speed. One can encode information quickly, and the feedback cycle is rapid. If receivers are unclear about the message, they can immediately ask for clarification. Presenting a proposal orally, for example, provides much more opportunity for answering questions than does preparing a written report. Oral messages are generally efficient in handling the day-to-day problems that arise in groups and organizations, although individuals vary widely in terms of how effectively they use this medium.[27]

Sometimes *written communication* is preferred over oral communication. Although written messages are more slowly encoded, they allow the communicator to use more precise language. A sentence in a labor contract, for example, can be rewritten many times to ensure that everyone involved knows exactly what it means. The aim is to minimize the possibility of any future confusion or argument over interpretation. Written materials also provide a permanent copy of the communication that can be stored and retrieved for later purposes. For example, a supervisor may write a formal memo to an employee, noting that she has been late for work ten of the last eleven days and warning that failure to arrive on time will result in her dismissal. If the behavior continues, the supervisor has documentary evidence that the employee received fair warning.

Indeed, one of the problems caused by new communication media such as e-mail is that people get confused regarding the strengths and weaknesses of the media. For example, most people treat e-mail as if it is a form of oral communication, ignoring grammar, writing style, and form, in return for quick and informal communication. Many e-mails are "zipped off" in a hurry, without a great deal of planning and forethought as to their content and expression. However, e-mail is in fact a written form of communication that leaves a paper trail, providing written documentation of ideas that one may later regret. Thus, when Merrill Lynch stock analyst Henry Blodgett told his clients in a formal letter to "accumulate" a certain stock, and then a day later turned around and told a friend in an e-mail that the same stock "was a piece of crap," this set the stage for a $100 million conflict-of-interest lawsuit.[28] Indeed, recovered e-mails are more often than not the "smoking gun" evidence that form the basis for many of the legal actions brought against unethical organizations, including suits where the charge is destruction of e-mail evidence.[29]

To complete the communication process, the message sent must be subjected to decoding, a process in which the message is translated in the mind of the receiver. When all works well, the resulting idea or mental image corresponds closely to the sender's idea or mental image. Unfortunately, myriad things can go wrong and render communication ineffective. The term **noise** refers to the factors that can distort a message. Noise can occur at any stage of the process, but is particularly problematic when two people are from different cultures.[30]

Barriers to Effective Communication

A variety of organizational, interpersonal, and individual factors can hinder communication within groups or organizations. For instance, the nature of the physical space occupied by jobholders inevitably affects patterns of communication. If an organization wants to promote the development of interpersonal relations, it must place people in close physical proximity. People who work closely together have more opportunities to interact and are more likely to form lasting relationships than are people who are physically distant from one another. Apparently, whether you are a clerk, a college professor, or a member of a bomber crew, the nearer you work to other people, the more often you will communicate with them.[31]

Whether the purpose of the communication is to inform or persuade, the *credibility* of the source will largely determine whether the role occupant internalizes the message. Credibility refers to the degree to which the information provided by the source is believable, and it is a function of three factors:

- Expertise, or the source's knowledge of the topic at hand
- Trustworthiness, or the degree to which the recipient believes the communicator has no hidden motives
- Consistency between words and actions

Credibility is low whenever the source of the communication is uninformed, is untrustworthy, or acts in a way that contradicts the individual's words. In the case of American Airlines, CEO Don Carty was forced to resign because he was perceived as untrustworthy, but it should be noted that ill intent does not have to be established to harm one's credibility. For example, after the war with Iraq, the failure of the United States to immediately uncover weapons of mass destruction led many to question the Bush administration's credibility, because this was one of the primary justifications for the war. This perception was particularly acute when it became clear that some of the evidence that the president mentioned in a nationally televised speech to the nation was based on forged documents.[32] Although few believed that the president knew that the evidence was forged, and therefore deliberately misled the public, the fact that he was uninformed because of failure within the intelligence community still harmed his credibility. As seen in the Securing Competitive Advantage box, if a manager is perceived as credible, this can make a huge difference in how people respond to potential crises.

SECURING COMPETITIVE ADVANTAGE

COMMUNICATION CAMPAIGNS: THE CURE FOR SARS-RELATED RUMORS

According to the Chinese government, the Chinese National Health Minister and the mayor of the city of Beijing conspired to keep the severe acute respiratory syndrome (SARS) epidemic a secret for as long as they could. Fearing a public panic and a loss of face for their regions and country, the two bureaucrats tried to hide data on the number of SARS-related deaths. However, it was clear to anyone who lived and worked in the Chinese capital that the number of people getting seriously ill with flulike symptoms was highly unusual. This fact, combined with new information regarding a new form of virus that was emerging in the southern region of the country, fed a rumor mill that more than filled in for the communication vacuum created by many official political and business organizations. The rumors were so terrifying that 10 million workers who migrated from rural areas to the cities to work in urban jobs abandoned those employers to retreat to the safety of their farms at the height of the crisis.

In this environment, it was a very difficult task for employers to keep their workers at their posts, and clearly those that could achieve this objective enjoyed a substantial competitive advantage over those who could not. One success story that emerged out of this crisis was Flextronic International, a multinational manufacturer that employed close to 12,000 workers at a 150-acre factory complex in Zhuhai. Flextronic generates more than $1 billion annually and its most well-known product is the console for Microsoft's Xbox. Indeed if you have ever played an Xbox game, the odds are that your console was assembled in one of Flextronic's South China plants.

Like most Chinese manufacturers, many of the workers assembling the Xbox consoles were uneducated rural migrants, and when two of their co-workers who lived in the company dormitory died the same day from a respiratory illness, rumors spread like wildfire, prompting plans for a mass exodus back to the farms. Flextronic officials had to move quickly to create an information campaign that would prevent this short-term disaster, as well as create a climate of trust and security that would help stave off future problems.

The first step Flextronic took was to bring in medical professionals to lecture the employees on the facts and myths of SARS, with special attention directed toward the ten-day incubation period, the method of transmission, and the early symptoms that mark the disease. This information was critical because it reinforced the value of the other steps the company was about to take. The second step in their information campaign was to quickly issue a statement, including the official medical forms, indicating that the workers that died did not have SARS. Third, the thirty workers who lived in the same dormitory as the deceased workers were quarantined and publicly removed from the plant. Fourth, the company initiated a testing center that took the temperature of visitors and employees who had been outside the plant for ten days. In addition, newly hired employees were forced to eat in a separate section of the cafeteria for the first ten days of their employment. Fifth, new work rules were instantiated that required workers to wash their hands twice a day, and maintenance personnel went around the plant disinfecting all the doorknobs and other objects that people might touch. Finally, the company worked with local hospitals that issued daily memos to certify that there were no Flextronic employees at the hospitals that were being treated for SARS.

Tim Didwiddle, the plant manager who designed and implemented the communication campaign, noted that in the last four years he has dealt with fires, typhoons, and the Y2K bug, but "they all paled in comparison to this." Thanks to his efforts, however, while the rest of China was seething with secrecy, rumors, speculation, and worker flight, Flextronic's communication campaign was successful in calming the fears of the employees. Although in early April, half of the workers took advantage of the free surgical masks the company offered, by mid-May, virtually no one in the plant was wearing a mask anymore, and an air of normalcy dominated the plant. Production was unaffected, and the company was able to fulfill all of its orders to Microsoft on time.

Sources: D. Roberts, "SARS: An Amazing About-Face in Beijing," *Business Week*, May 5, 2003, p. 48; D. Jones, "China's Economy Is Expected to Grow 8% in Spite of SARS," *Wall Street Journal Online*, July 2, 2003, p. 1; D. Henninger, "The Fabulous World of Fact, Factoid and SARS," *Wall Street Journal Online*, May 23, 2003, pp. 1–3; M. Clifford, "Standing Guard: How a Big Factory is Keeping SARS Out," *Business Week*, May 5, 2003, pp. 46–48.

A *power imbalance* between a role sender and a role occupant can also impede communication. For example, *upward communication* flows from people low in the organizational hierarchy to people above them. Because people at upper levels of the hierarchy have a great deal of power to reward and punish employees at lower levels, the latter are sometimes inhibited in their upward communication. Insecure lower-level workers may tend to forget about losses and exaggerate gains when reporting information upward, leaving managers at upper levels with a distorted sense of reality. Similarly, lower-level employees who are unsure about how to perform their jobs may be reluctant to ask for assistance, fearing to appear less than knowledgeable.[33] Upper-level managers may also get a distorted view of the competencies and capabilities of those who serve under them from this situation.

Some leaders unwittingly contribute to this problem, by "shooting the messenger" or surrounding themselves with "yes people." In this context, the manager receives only positive feedback on his or her personal performance or the performance of the organization, setting the manager up for future failure. The pervasiveness of this problem has led many top leaders to turn to executive coaches, who provide an external and often painful assessment of the manager's weaknesses in the realm of interpersonal relations. As one such executive coach has noted, "CEOs get hired for their skills but fired for their personalities."[34] The research evidence suggests that this kind of coaching can have modest effects in terms of improving the manager's receptivity to negative feedback, which in turn enhances his or her performance.[35]

Finally, distortion can occur because of jargon. **Jargon** is an informal language shared by long-tenured, central members of units. Within a small closed group, it can be extremely useful. It maximizes information exchange with a minimum of time and symbols by taking advantage of the shared training and experience of its users. On the other hand, because jargon is likely to confuse anyone lacking the same training and experience, it can create a barrier to communication with new members or between different groups. Often technical specialists use jargon unconsciously and may find it difficult to express themselves in any other terms. This habit can become a permanent disability, greatly reducing people's career opportunities outside their own small groups.

SOCIALIZATION TO NEW ROLES

Although effective communication is always important within organizations, perhaps at no time is it more critical than when a person assumes a new role. **Socialization** is the procedure through which people acquire the social knowledge and skills necessary to correctly assume new roles in a group or an organization.[36] This process of "learning the ropes" entails much more than simply learning the technical requirements associated with one's job. It also deals with learning about the group or organization, its values, its culture, its past history, its potential, and the role occupant's position in the overall scheme.

Although most people think of socialization only in terms of someone joining a group or organization for the first time, in fact socialization is an ongoing process. It occurs whenever an individual moves into a new role within the group or organization. A role can be considered "new" for an individual as long as it differs from the previous role on any one of three dimensions: functional, hierarchical, or inclusionary.[37]

The *functional* dimension reflects differences in the tasks performed by members of a group or an organization. Figure 8-3A shows the typical functional groupings

FIGURE 8-3   The Functional Dimension of Organizations

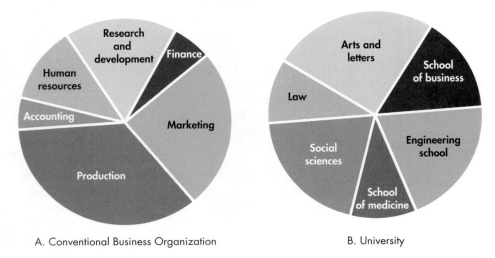

A. Conventional Business Organization   B. University

of a conventional business organization: marketing, production, accounting, human resources, research and development, and finance. Similarly, Figure 8-3B depicts the functional groupings common to many universities: the schools of business, engineering, medicine, social sciences, law, and arts and letters. The roles performed in each group are quite distinct, because the jobholders are trying to accomplish different aspects of the organization's overall mission.

The *hierarchical* dimension concerns the distribution of rank and authority in a group or an organization. As you will recall from Chapter 1, a hierarchy establishes who is officially responsible for the actions of whom. In traditional organizations, this dimension takes the shape of a pyramid, in which fewer people occupy the highest ranks. The roles performed by people higher in the pyramid differ from the roles assumed by individuals lower in the pyramid largely in that the former have greater authority and power. In a highly centralized organization, this triangle is often rather steep. Figure 8-4A depicts one such pyramid, representing the hierarchical structure of a hypothetical military organization. In a more decentralized organization, fewer levels of authority exist and the hierarchical pyramid looks flatter. As indicated in Figure 8-4B, city police departments usually have fewer levels of hierarchy than an army. Most employees are arresting officers, the highest rank is captain, and only two genuine levels of hierarchy separate the top and the bottom.

The *inclusionary* dimension reflects the degree to which an employee of an organization finds himself or herself at the center or on the periphery of things. As shown in Figure 8-5, a person may move from being an outsider, beyond the organization's periphery, to being an informal leader, at the center of the organization. A job applicant, or outsider, joins the organization and becomes a newcomer, just inside the periphery. For this employee to move further along the radial dimension shown in Figure 8-5, others must accept the newcomer as a full member of the organization. This move can be accomplished only by proving that the individual shares the same assumptions as others about what is important and what is not. Usually, newcomers must first be tested—formally or informally—as to their abilities, motives, and values before they are granted inclusionary rights and privileges. Women and minorities often find it particularly difficult to advance along this dimension in traditional organizations.[38]

FIGURE 8-4   The Hierarchical Dimension of Organizations

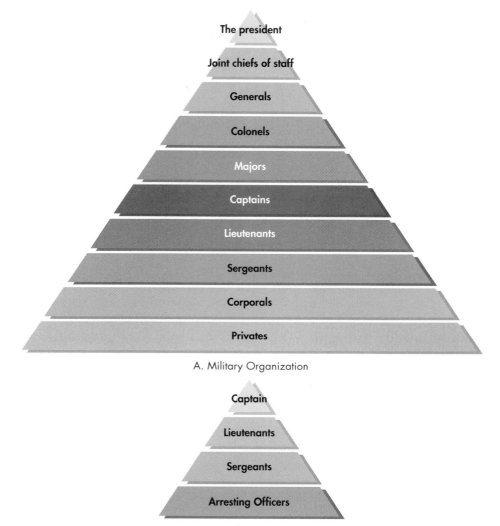

A. Military Organization

B. City Police Department

Socialization occurs whenever an individual crosses boundaries in any of the three dimensions—for instance, transferring between functional departments or being promoted to a position of higher authority. When moving across functional boundaries, the key concern is the person–job fit, and the major attributes considered during this transition are the person's knowledge, skills, and abilities. For the hierarchical and inclusionary boundaries, the person's values and personality traits seem to become more relevant concerns.[39]

Socialization is likely to be particularly intense when a person crosses all three boundaries at once. When a person joins a new organization, he or she crosses the inclusionary boundary, moving from nonmember to member status, and crosses functional and hierarchical boundaries by joining a particular functional unit, such as the advertising department, at a specific hierarchical level, such as account executive. It is at this time that the organization has the most instructing and persuading

FIGURE 8-5 The Inclusionary Dimension of Organizations

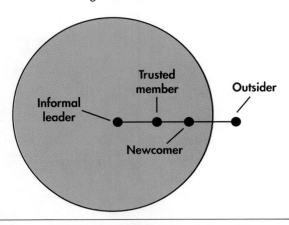

Source: Adapted from D. Katz and R. L. Kahn, *The Social Psychology of Organizations* (New York: Wiley, 1978), p. 112.

to accomplish. It is also the time when a person may have the least accurate expectations, and therefore, is most susceptible to being taught and influenced.[40] If handled well, this instruction can lead to increased commitment to the role.[41]

Socialization Goals and Tactics

Although instructing individuals about their roles is part of all socialization programs, different firms may seek to accomplish different goals in this process. Some organizations may pursue a **role custodianship** response. Here, recipients of socialization take a caretaker's stance toward their roles. They do not question the status quo but instead conform to it. A popular expression in the U.S. Marine Corps, paraphrased from Tennyson's "Charge of the Light Brigade," is "Ours is not to question why; ours is but to do or die."

When an organization hopes instead that recipients of socialization will change either the way their roles are performed or the ends sought through role performance, it may have **role innovation** as a goal. For example, businesses that live and die by identifying changes in consumer needs, such as Colgate-Palmolive or Procter & Gamble, may find it especially desirable to encourage market researchers to come up with innovative ways of identifying new products and measuring consumer reactions.[42]

Firms can use any of several tactics in socializing new members, each of which has different effects. As shown in Figure 8-6, we can classify these strategies along four critical dimensions to help understand their likely consequences: collective–individual, sequential–random, serial–disjunctive, and divestiture–investiture. The first alternative in each pair brings about a custodianship response from the new member. The second alternative of each pair leads the recipient toward role innovation.

In *collective socialization,* recipients are put in groups and go through socialization experiences together. This method is characteristic of military boot camps, fraternities, sororities, and management-training courses. In collective processes, the recruits accomplish much of the socialization themselves. For example, Marine Corps recruits may abuse one another verbally or even physically in a way that the formal institution never could.

In *individual socialization,* the second alternative in this pair, new members are taken one at a time and put through unique experiences. This treatment is charac-

FIGURE 8-6   The Custodianship–Innovation Continuum and Its Socialization Techniques

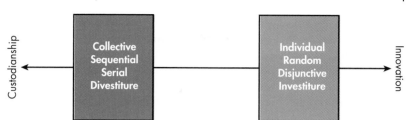

teristic of apprenticeship programs or on-the-job learning. It yields much more variable results than collective socialization does, and its success depends heavily on the qualities of the individual recruit.

In the second dimension of socialization, the alternative of *sequential socialization* takes new members through a set sequence of discrete and identifiable steps leading to the target role. A physician's training, for example, includes several observable steps: the undergraduate premed program, medical school, an internship, and a residency. A person must complete all of these steps before taking specialist board examinations. Usually, in sequential processes, each stage builds on the prior stage. The algebra teacher socializing the student to the world of math, for example, notes that geometry will be easy if the person understands algebra. The geometry teacher, in turn, explains that trigonometry will be painless if the student appreciates geometry. This type of presentation helps recruits stay focused on the current stage. It minimizes the discouragement that comes with the knowledge that they have a long journey to reach the ultimate goal.

At the other end of the second dimension are *random socialization* processes, in which learning experiences have no apparent logic or structure. Steps of the socialization process are unknown, ambiguous, or continually changing. Training for a general manager, for example, tends to be much less rigorously specified than that for a medical professional. Some managers rise from lower ranks, some come from other organizations, and some come straight from business school programs.

Socialization strategies also differ along a third dimension that concerns the amount of help and guidance provided to new members as they learn their new roles. In *serial socialization,* experienced members of the organization teach individuals about the roles they will assume. The more experienced employees serve as role models or mentors for the new members. Observing and discussing issues with these role models is the primary means by which newcomers gather information.[43] In police departments, for example, rookies are assigned as partners to older, veteran officers. Some observers have suggested that this practice creates a remarkable degree of intergenerational stability in the behaviors of police officers. This method of socialization also allows recruits to see into the future—that is, to get a glimpse of their future role. This knowledge can be good or bad, depending on the person doing the socialization. For this reason, organizations need to take great care in assigning mentors to new members.

In *disjunctive socialization,* new members must learn by themselves how to handle a new role. For example, the first woman partner in a conservative law firm may find few people (if any) who have faced her unique problems. She may be completely on her own in coping with the challenges of her new position. Disjunctive socialization is sometimes created when organizations "clean house"—that is, sweep out the older members of the organization and replace them with new personnel. Such a shakeup causes almost all employees of the firm to relearn their roles. Typically the organization hopes that the result will bring more creativity in problem solving, as this kind of move eliminates individuals who might have taught others the established way of doing things.

The fourth dimension of socialization deals with the degree to which a socialization process confirms or denies the value of an individual's personal identity. *Divestiture socialization* ignores or denies the value of the individual's personal characteristics. The organization wants to tear new members down to nothing and then rebuild them as completely new and different individuals. Some organizations require either explicitly or implicitly that recruits sever old relationships, undergo intense harassment from experienced members, and engage in the dirty work of the trade (work that is associated with low pay and low status) for long periods.

In contrast, *investiture socialization* affirms the value to the organization of the recruit's particular personal characteristics. The organization says, in effect, "We like you just the way you are." It implies that, rather than changing the new member, the organization hopes that the recruit will change the organization. Under these conditions, the organization may try to make the recruit's transition process as smooth and painless as possible.

Designing Socialization Programs

The strategy employed in designing a socialization program depends on the goals of that program. If the intention is to foster a custodianship response, a group or an organization is best served by a strategy that is collective, sequential, and serial and that involves divestiture. In this way, every socialization recipient will start with the same "clean slate" and receive the same experiences in the same order.

For example, the French Foreign Legion is an organization with a 150-year history of competitive excellence in an industry where success is measured in terms of life and death rather than dollars and cents. Much of its achievement can be attributed to its socialization practices, which clearly aim to instill a custodianship response in new members.[44] The socialization task confronting the Foreign Legion is formidable. Recruits come from more than 100 different countries and must be assembled into a cohesive unit in which members are willing to risk their lives for strangers. Far from being the "cream of the crop," most applicants are fugitive criminals, ex-convicts, dishonorably discharged members of regular armies, ex-mercenaries, and other men running from their past for some reason.

For this applicant pool, one major attraction of the Foreign Legion is the fact that it is probably the only employer in the world that does not request any formal proof of identification before hiring. Indeed, the first step of the socialization program is to assign new names and nationalities to all recruits. Along with their former identities, most recruits must also say goodbye to their native tongue, because multilingualism is not appreciated. This organization has one official language: French. New recruits are then whisked off to train in exotic locales—the jungles of French Guiana or the deserts of Chad—far from their homes, families, and friends. Their training includes many of the task-specific fighting skills that one would imagine, but the standards for proficiency are much higher than those of NATO armies. Many individuals cannot stand up to the hardships of this training and drop out, leaving only a small core of the most committed members.[45]

While few businesses may want to emulate all of the socialization tactics practiced by the Foreign Legion, its example does offer some lessons for organizations whose socialization goals are to instill change in recruits. Changing recruits into conforming organizational members requires sacrificing old identities and behavior patterns and assuming new identities and behavior patterns. This change is instilled by disconnecting new members from their pasts and challenging them to realize a new future.

If the goal is to not change the individual, but rather to help the individual change the organization, the opposite tactics should be employed. That is, to promote innovation, a group or organization is better served by a strategy that provides a unique and individualized program for each recipient and places value on each recipient's particular personality, characteristics, and style.[46] In this alternative type of socialization program, individuals need to proactively seek feedback and build relationships, and this is enhanced when they are high on the traits of extraversion and openness to experience.[47] Research indicates that two different types of networks need to be established in building these relationships: first, a small and dense set of relationships with people who work directly with the newcomer, and second, a broader, more superficial network with people from different departments and levels of the organization. The first network is critical for learning one's current job and role, and the latter is instrumental for planning for one's future roles in the organization.[48]

Regardless of its goals and strategies, and the degree to which it allows individuals to proactively socialize themselves, a good socialization program will teach new role occupants about the history, values, people, language, and culture of the group or organization in which membership is sought. If conducted properly, it will enhance the understanding of the person's role and increase his or her commitment to the organization's goals.[49]

QUALITY OF INTERPERSONAL ROLE RELATIONSHIPS

Given the importance of role relationships within organizations, it is critical to have a framework whereby the quality of these relationships can be judged and enhanced. Equity theory is a theory of social exchange that focuses on the "give and take" of various relationships, such as supervisors and subordinates.[50] It describes the process by which people determine whether they have received fair treatment in their relationships.

Equity and Social Comparisons

As shown in Figure 8-7, equity theory holds that people make judgments about relational fairness by forming a ratio of their perceived investments (or inputs, I) and perceived rewards (or outcomes, O). They then compare this ratio to a similar ratio reflecting the perceived costs and benefits of some other person. Equity theory does not require that outcomes or inputs be equal for equity to exist. Individuals who receive fewer desirable outcomes than someone else may still feel fairly treated if they see themselves contributing fewer inputs than the other person. Thus, a new entry-level employee may not feel that it is unfair if the CEO is paid more because there is a corresponding perception that CEO brings more to the relationship. At some point, however, this ratio may be perceived as getting out of alignment. For example, in 1980, the ratio of CEO pay to hourly worker pay was roughly 40 to 1. In 2003, the same ratio was 400 to 1, and many objected to this, arguing that it was unfair.[51]

FIGURE 8-7 Algebraic Expression of How People Make Equity Comparisons

$$\frac{I \text{ person}}{O \text{ person}} = \frac{I \text{ reference person}}{O \text{ reference person}}$$

TABLE 8-3
Inputs and
Outcomes in
Equity Theory

Inputs	Outcomes
Education	Pay
Intelligence	Satisfying supervision
Experience	Seniority benefits
Training	Fringe benefits
Skill	Status symbols
Social status	Job perquisites
Job effort	Working conditions
Personal appearance	
Health	
Possession of tools	

Table 8-3 lists other possible inputs and outcomes that might be incorporated in equity comparisons in work organizations.

Distributive, Procedural, and Interactive Justice

Equity theory provides a simple framework for understanding how people decide whether they are being treated fairly in their relationships. Even with this simple framework, however, it can prove difficult to achieve widespread perceptions of justice in organizations for several reasons.

First, equity judgments are based on individual *perceptions* of inputs and outcomes, and perceptions of the same inputs or outcomes may differ markedly from one person to the next. There can also be cultural differences in how different groups weigh their own inputs and outputs. For example, one study found that people from individualistic cultures like the United States were much more likely to overestimate their own personal inputs (in order to "stand out") relative to people from collectivist cultures like Japan, where people tend to underestimate their own personal inputs (in order to "blend in"). This can make it very difficult to see eye to eye on what is fair, thus leading to many more impasses and fewer negotiated settlements that are accepted by each side.[52]

Second, it is difficult to predict who will be chosen as the reference person. As a consequence, a change in policy that targets one group may inadvertently spill over and create perceived inequity in another group. For example, in our opening story, Don Carty thought the retention bonuses that American Airlines was issuing to executives were fair because he was comparing them to what similar executives received at Delta Airlines, and realized that they were less than what Delta executives were getting. The union workers, however, were comparing the executive bonuses, which were in effect even if the company went bankrupt, to their own outcomes, which were highly contingent on the organization's survival.

Third, in addition to outcomes and inputs, people are keenly sensitive to the procedures through which allocation decisions are made and the manner in which these decisions are communicated. We can distinguish between three kinds of justice perceptions. **Distributional justice** refers to the judgments that people make with respect to the input/outcome ratios they experience relative to the ratios experienced by others with whom they identify (that is, reference persons). The degree to which perceptions of distributional justice translate into the type of anger and resentment that might harm or sever the relationship, however, depends at least partially on perceptions of procedural and interactional justice.[53] In some instances, managers can maintain perception of fairness and trust even in the face of some pretty negative outcomes, if they carefully manage these "non-distributional" aspects of justice.[54]

TABLE 8-4
Six Deter-
minants of
Procedural
Justice

1. **Consistency:** The procedures are applied consistently across time and other people.
2. **Bias Suppression:** The procedures are applied by a person who has no vested interest in the outcome or prior prejudices regarding the individual.
3. **Information Accuracy:** The procedure is based on information that is perceived to be true.
4. **Correctability:** The procedure has built-in safeguards that allow for appealing mistakes or bad decisions.
5. **Representativeness:** The procedure is informed by the concerns of all groups or stakeholders (co-workers, customers, owners) affected by the decision, including the individual who is being harmed.
6. **Ethicality:** The procedure is consistent with prevailing moral standards as they pertain to issues such as invasion of privacy or deception.

Whereas distributive justice focuses on "ends," procedural and interactional justice focus on "means." If the methods and procedures used to arrive at and implement decisions that affect the employee negatively are seen as fair, the reaction is likely to be much more positive than otherwise. Table 8-4 details the factors that determine whether **procedural justice** will be applied. Even if someone experiences a decision that may harm him or her in an outcome sense (for example, by being passed over for a promotion), the organization can minimize the amount of anger and resentment felt by the employee by focusing on the procedures used to make the decision and showing that they were consistent, unbiased, accurate, correctable, representative, and ethical. Allowing people to participate in the decision-making process may also increase perceptions of procedural justice.[55]

Promoting perceptions of procedural justice among employees is important for a number of other reasons. Workers who feel that organizational procedures are just are much more likely to engage in organizational citizenship behaviors (OCBs) relative to other workers.[56] Indeed, this can have a trickle-down effect, in that if managers experience procedural justice, they will often engage in citizenship behaviors toward their subordinates, who in turn will reciprocate with more OCBs directed toward management—creating a positive, self-reinforcing cycle.[57] This can help establish a climate of procedural justice throughout the work unit, which has been shown to promote group performance and reduce absenteeism.[58] This is especially the case in organizations that are structured in a mechanistic fashion and rely a great deal on formalized rules and procedures to promote coordination[59] (see Chapter 12 for a discussion of organizational structures).

Whereas procedural justice deals with the manner in which a decision was reached, **interactional justice** focuses on the interpersonal nature of the implementation of the outcomes. Table 8-5 lists the four key determinants of interactional justice. When the decision is explained well and implemented in a fashion that is socially sensitive, considerate, and empathetic, this approach may help diffuse some of the resentment produced by a decision that, in an outcome sense, might be seen as unfair to a particular employee.[60]

Over time, if a relationship is characterized as being high on all three dimensions of justice, then trust will develop. In a trusting relationship, each member of the exchange has faith in the other, knowing that he or she will be judged fairly and act in accordance with the other's needs.[61] Developing trust is critical, because it ensures that the two people need not constantly direct their attention and effort at negotiating the short-term inputs and outputs of their relationship. It is especially crucial in today's decentralized, networked organizations that rely on teams, because trust replaces formal, hierarchical authority as a control mechanism.[62]

TABLE 8-5
Four Determinants of Interactional Justice

1. **Explanation:** Emphasizes aspects of procedural fairness that justify the decision.
2. **Social Sensitivity:** Treats the person with dignity and respect.
3. **Consideration:** Listens to the person's concerns.
4. **Empathy:** Identifies with the person's feelings.

Instead, in a trusting relationship, people take a long-term focus, where the expectation of fair treatment in the long run precludes the necessity of frequent "equity checks." People in trusting relationships spend less time and attention on maintaining the relationship, which means that they can direct their effort and attention toward working together productively to meet their interdependence needs. Thus a much stronger relationship between motivation and performance exists in groups characterized by trust.[63] A trusting culture arises where the level of trust is high across all relationships within a group. Groups with this kind of culture show high levels of group cohesion and spontaneous, helping behavior relative to low-trust groups.[64] Figure 8-8 depicts the relationships between the three types of justice, trust, and work outcomes.

Responses to Inequity

Perceptions of inequity create unpleasant emotions. When people feel that they are receiving a greater share of outcomes than they deserve, they may feel guilty. In contrast, perceiving oneself as coming up short in the equity comparison results in anger—a much stronger emotion than guilt. Such anger could make a person want to retaliate against the partner in the relationship, especially if the person is low in agreeableness or negative affectivity.[65] Indeed, the tension associated with inequity may motivate the person to take any of several actions in response.

First, the individual might *alter his or her personal inputs*. For example, in decision-making teams, if one team member perceives that his or her opinion is not being given any weight, he or she may cease contributing to the group's discussion.[66]

A second possible response to inequity is to try to *alter personal outcomes*. For example, individuals who feel that they are relatively underpaid may demand raises, threaten to leave or strike, steal from the employer, or sabotage operations.[67] Sabotage is an especially likely response to perceived injustice when the individual feels powerless to affect change in any other more legitimate form.[68] As the Ethics and

FIGURE 8-8 The Relationship between Justice, Trust, and Work Outcomes

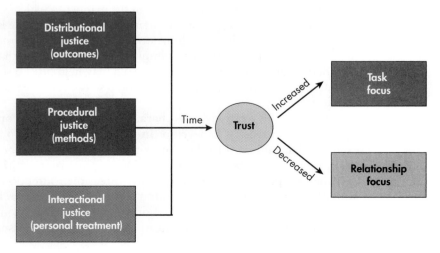

ETHICS AND SOCIAL RESPONSIBILITY

FREE SPEECH OR TRESPASSING? THE ETHICS OF MASS E-MAILING

Kourish Hamidi was fired from Intel after a work-injury dispute. Although most people react negatively to this kind of news, Hamidi's response was definitely novel: the ex-engineer wrote a series of e-mail letters critical of the company and sent them to all 30,000 Intel employees. Prior to an injunction issued by the Third Court of Appeals, lawyers for Intel estimate that Hamidi sent close to a half million such messages to the chipmaker's employees, and the company's records indicated that most employees did open and read the messages.

Since these messages were being distributed via Intel's internal e-mail system, the company tried to find some technical means to block them, but most of these interventions had side effects that were more damaging to the business than the messages themselves. Therefore, the company sought and received a court injunction that made it illegal for Hamidi to send the messages. Intel argued that it was forced to spend a great deal of time and resources to block the messages, and that in effect Hamidi was trespassing on Intel's private property. They argued that his actions were the equivalent of intruding into the mailroom of a private business, commandeering the mail cart, and then dropping off unwanted verbal attacks of the company on 30,000 desks.

But is intruding on computer servers really the same as trespassing on private property? Moreover, is it appropriate to treat cyberspace like physical space, such that some of it can be sealed off and treated as private property? Finally, isn't blocking Hamidi's messages a violation of his right to free speech guaranteed by the Constitution?

In May 2003, the California Supreme Court attempted to answer all of these questions, and in a controversial 4–3 split decision, sided with Hamidi. In doing so, the court reversed the ruling of the appeals court and overturned the injunction. The state supreme court decided that laws regarding trespassing "do not encompass, and should not be extended to encompass electronic intrusions that do not damage the recipient's computer systems nor impairs its functioning." In addition, the court rejected Intel's claim that the time that employees spent reading the messages caused economic damage, because it was clear that the employees could drop themselves from the list if they so chose. Finally the court argued that Intel's chief concern was not really the volume of the messages, but their content, and that this is the kind of content that is explicitly protected by the First Amendment.

One of the dissenting judges on the court noted, "Intel should not be helpless in the face of repeated and threatened abuse and contamination of its private computer system." Another judge who disagreed with the ruling went further, stating that "those who have contempt for grubby commerce and reverence for the rarified heights of intellectual discourse may applaud this ruling, but even the flow of ideas will be curtailed if the right to exclude is denied." Indeed, the California ruling may not prove to be the last word on mass e-mailing, free speech, and trespassing, as Intel is planning on appealing the decision to the U.S. Supreme Court.

Hamidi's plans are clear. When asked if he is going to renew his mass e-mailing to Intel employees, he vowed, "I'm going to do it to the max."

Sources: P. Desmaris, "California Supreme Court Says Anti-Intel E-Mail Not Trespassing," *USA Today,* July 7, 2003, p. 1; C. Mallard, "E-Mails Criticizing Former Employer Is Protected Speech," *CNN.com,* July 1, 2003, p. 1; D. Clark, "California High Court Rules Against Intel in E-Mail Case," *Wall Street Journal Online,* July 1, 2003, pp. 1–2.

Social Responsibility box shows, attempts aimed at harming the employer may even persist long after the employee is gone.

A third way of responding to inequity is to use *cognitive distortion*—that is, to rationalize the results of one's comparisons. For example, people can distort their perceptions of outcomes. In one study, people who were underpaid for a particular task justified this underpayment by stating that their task was more enjoyable than the task performed by people who were overpaid—even though the tasks were identical. This type of overjustification effect has been documented in a number of contexts.[69] Another means of eliminating inequity via cognitive distortion is to change the reference person. A salesperson who brings in less revenue than others in his or her department may claim, "You can't compare me with them because I have a different territory." By this statement, the salesperson seeks to disqualify his or her peers as reference persons.

A fourth way to restore equity is to take some action that will *change the behavior of the reference person*. Workers who, according to their peers, perform too well on piece-rate systems often earn the derogatory title of "rate buster." Research has shown that if such name calling fails to constrain personal productivity, more direct tactics may be invoked. In one study, researchers coined the term "binging" to refer to a practice in which workers periodically punched suspected rate busters in the arm until they reduced their level of effort.

Finally, if all else fails, equity can be secured by *leaving an inequitable situation*. Turnover and absenteeism are common means of dealing with perceptions of unfairness in the workplace. Although organizations concerned about retention frequently focus on pay and benefits, exit interviews of employees who leave companies often reveal that the driving factor was either a poor relationship between the individual and his or her supervisor[70] or lack of supporting relationships among co-workers.[71]

Managing Inequitable Situations

In a perfect world, managers would be able to ensure that every employee felt equitably treated at all times. Given the wide variety of inputs and outputs that employees might consider relevant and the many reference people who might be called on in comparisons, however, there will inevitably be situations in which the manager is confronted with an employee who is angry and feels that he or she has been treated unfairly. In these circumstances, the manager's first step should be to try to change the actual source of the inequity. For example, the manager might seek to increase the outcomes the aggrieved individual receives (for example, through a pay raise) or decrease the inputs that the aggrieved individual must contribute (for example, by reduced responsibilities).

If true change cannot be initiated, the manager's second step might be to change the aggrieved person's perceptions of the situation, by persuading the worker to focus on outcomes of which he or she might be unaware (for example, the added chances of being promoted given those responsibilities) or inputs the worker takes for granted (for example, not being asked to travel or work weekends). The manager can also try to switch the reference person being utilized by the aggrieved individual to someone in an even worse position (for example, by noting how many people with similar jobs have been laid off).

As a last resort, if a manager cannot change either the conditions or the perceptions of the angry individual, he or she may be left with only excuses and apologies. With an excuse, the manager basically admits that the person was treated unfairly, but implies that the problem was beyond the manager's control. With an apology, the manager admits both harm and responsibility, but shows remorse and denies that the inequity is truly representative of the past and future of the relationship. A successful apology is usually accompanied by some form of compensation that, at least symbolically, restores equity in the relationship. In today's increasingly litigious society, these kinds of apologies are increasingly rare, since they may be seen as an admission of guilt by parties who may be interested in suing their employer. This is unfortunate because a good sincere apology is often a cheap, fast, and effective way to eliminate the problems caused with a specific perceived injustice.

For example, on July 12, 2002, Joette Schmidt, vice president of America West Airlines, went on the *Today* show and was confronted with a passenger, Sheryl Cole, who was thrown off a recent America West flight for making a joke about security.

CUTTING-EDGE RESEARCH

ONE KIND OF JUSTICE FOR ALL OR THREE KINDS OF JUSTICE FOR SOME?

Although the concept of justice has been around since antiquity, empirical scientific approaches to this topic began only in the last part of the twentieth century. Much of this research took place in organizational contexts and was directed at three questions: (1) What does justice mean as a scientific construct, (2) what determines perceptions of justice, and (3) what outcomes result from justice judgments? A recent review of this research evidence shows just how far social and behavioral scientists have come in terms of answering these questions. Jason Colquitt and his colleagues published a review that covered all the studies published at the end of the century (1975 to 2000) in the major scientific outlets for this type of research. This review encompassed more than 180 separate studies that involved more than 33,000 people, and provides a definitive base for addressing the questions such as those posed here.

First, in terms of what justice means as a scientific construct, debate has raged among researchers as to whether it reflects a single overall judgment or is best conceived as three separate judgments regarding fairness of outcomes (distributive justice), fairness of rules for determining outcomes (procedural justice), and the fairness with which outcomes were administered interpersonally (interactional justice). On the one hand, it has been argued that if someone experiences a bad outcome, he or she is very likely to feel that the rules that led to that outcome were bad, and that the style in which it was administered was also bad, thus suggesting there is one single overall judgment. On the other hand, it has also been argued that people can discriminate between the three judgments, and recognize that even though they may have received a very bad outcome, the rules by which this was determined were very fair, and the style in which it was administered was somewhat fair.

In terms of the evidence, Colquitt and his colleagues found significant correlations among the various types of justice (well into the .50 range), indicating that they share a common core. However, the three components of justice still had enough unique aspects that there was some conceptual value in making the distinctions.

Second, in terms of factors that lead people to conclude that they have been fairly treated, a key factor is the degree to which they have some control over the procedures employed. However, beyond this, many of the factors shown in Table 8-4 were also important predictors, almost doubling the amount of variance that the researchers could explain in perceptions of justice. Moreover, when one examines the overlap between the three types of justice judgments, perceptions of distributive justice had a much stronger impact on perceptions of procedural justice than did perceptions of interactional justice.

Finally, in terms of the outcomes of the justice determination process, Colquitt and his colleagues concluded that for *affective reactions* (such as overall job satisfaction) and the behaviors they generate (such as turnover), perceptions of distributive justice dominate how people will respond—appearing to be more important than the other types of justice perceptions. Procedural justice, on the other hand, related more strongly to *calculative reactions*, predicting people's performance and commitment to a higher degree relative to the other types of judgments. Finally, interactional justice showed the weakest effects, primarily being a major determinant of only a single outcome—evaluation of the manager. Of course, since this is a book on how to be a successful manager, this one outcome is still important, thus supporting the need for our readers to manage all three types of justice perceptions.

Sources: J. S. Adams, "Inequity in Social Exchange," in L. Berkowitz, ed., *Advances in Experimental Social Psychology* (New York: Academic Press, 1965), pp. 267–269; J. Thibaut and L. Walker, "Procedural Justice: A Psychological Perspective" (Hillsdale, NJ: Erlbaum, 1975); M. L. Ambrose, "Contemporary Justice Research: A New Look at Familiar Questions," *Organizational Behavior and Human Decision Processes* 89 (2002), 803–812; J. A. Colquitt, D. E. Conlon, M. J. Wesson, C. O. Porter, and K. Y. Ng, "Justice at the Millennium: A Meta-Analysis of 25 Years of Organizational Justice Research," *Journal of Applied Psychology* 86 (2001), 425–445.

Instead of trying to defend the company, Schmidt looked directly into the camera and stated, "I'm here primarily to apologize to Ms. Cole. We overreacted." Cole, who had spent her first few minutes on camera harshly criticizing the airline, was visibly caught off guard, and immediately softened her stance, responding, "I appreciate the apology, and I am sympathetic to America West right now, knowing that they are going through a tough time."[72]

This shows the power of simple apologies to restore equity, although in general apologies work best when there is a base level of trust to start with, which may explain why Don Carty's apology fell on deaf ears at American Airlines. Clearly, if an employee's first move is to turn to a lawyer rather than someone in the organization to redress some perceived inequity, this is already a sign of lack of trust. Thus, again we see that building trust is truly the key to developing sustainable and effective long-term relationships, and this is why, as the Cutting-Edge Research box (on page 239) illustrates, there has been so much research devoted to this topic.

SUMMARY

This chapter discussed the three key ingredients of all interpersonal relations: interdependence, roles, and communication.

Different types of interdependence form among people who are joined together in interpersonal relations. *Pooled interdependence* is the simplest of these forms; increasingly more complex forms are *sequential, reciprocal,* and *comprehensive interdependence.*

Roles form among interdependent individuals to guide their behaviors as they interact with one another. They capture the expectations that members of a *role set* have for the person occupying a given work role. Roles can be differentiated along *functional, hierarchical,* and *inclusionary* dimensions. *Socialization* is the process through which individuals learn about their roles. Depending on the goal of socialization, different communicators, using different tactics, may be required to strengthen *custodianship* or *innovation* expectations.

Just as socialized roles form the building blocks of interpersonal relations, *communication* is the cement that holds these blocks together. It involves the encoding, transmission, and decoding of information sent from one person to another via a communication medium.

Equity theory is a theoretical framework that helps explain how people judge the fairness of their relationships. This theory provides a great deal of practical guidance in terms of managing perceptions of *distributional, procedural,* and *interactional justice.*

REVIEW QUESTIONS

1. Of the four types of interdependence discussed in this chapter, which type is most adversely affected by turnover among organizational members? Which type of interdependence is most adversely affected by turnover in group leadership? How might the nature of the turnover process affect the kind of interdependence built into groups?

2. Socialization refers to the effect that the group or organization has on the individual. This effect tends to be greatest when the individual is moving through more than one dimension simultaneously (for example, functional and hierarchical). In contrast, when is the individual most likely to have the greatest effect on the organization? (Are there honeymoon periods? Do lame ducks have any influence?) How might your answer depend on the tactics of socialization initially employed to bring the individual into the group or organization?

3. What role do ceremonies play in the socialization process of someone crossing an important organizational boundary? In terms of the three kinds of boundaries that a person can traverse, where are ceremonies most frequently encountered, and why? What role do ceremonies play in the motivation of group members who are not crossing a boundary but are merely observers at the affair?

4. In communication, it has been said that "the medium is the message." What factors should be considered when choosing a medium for one's communication? Some of the greatest leaders of all time actually wrote very little. What might explain why people who are perceived as strong leaders avoid leaving a paper trail? When might writing be used to enhance leadership?

LEARNING THROUGH EXPERIENCE

DIAGNOSTIC QUESTIONS 8-1

Interdependence and Role Relationships

When you are confronting problems of communication or socialization or attempting to deal with difficulties that arise in interpersonal relations, the following questions may prove useful.

1. What type of interdependence unites people in the interpersonal relations you are diagnosing? What sorts of problems might this interdependence cause?

2. What important components of the work roles of interdependent individuals are not part of their job descriptions? Are they consistent with the formal job requirements?

3. What are some of the important functional, hierarchical, and inclusionary dimensions in the group or organization? Do current problems seem attributable to recent passage across boundaries on one or more of these dimensions?

4. For a particular individual, who are the members of the relevant role set? What are their expectations for the role occupant? How do they communicate these expectations to the occupant?

5. What are the occupant's own expectations? How do these expectations compare with those of the role set? How should any discrepancies be handled?

6. Do group members demonstrate the adherence to pivotal norms necessary for group or organizational survival? If the group or organization must cope with a changing work situation, is there evidence that it can adapt by selectively ignoring peripheral norms?

7. Is custodianship or innovation the goal of socialization processes? How should the socialization program be designed to promote this goal?

8. What means of communication (oral, written, or nonverbal) are used to accomplish the goals of the group or organization? Do these media seem to be the best choices? Why?

9. How do individuals perceive each other's influence and credibility? How do these perceptions affect the communications they exchange with one another?

10. What are some of the major values, beliefs, and frames of reference of the individuals involved in interpersonal relations? How might these affect their interpretations of communications received from others?

11. What are the major inputs that people give to this organization, what outcomes do they receive in return for these inputs, and how does this ratio compare with the ratios of their peers in terms of fairness?

12. Are people angry about the way in which they are treated? Can this situation be managed by changing inputs, outcomes, perceptions, or reference persons, or is it excusable for some other reason?

EXERCISE 8-1

The Admissions Committee: A Consensus-Seeking Task

William J. Heisler, Wake Forest University

In *consensus acceptance,* all members of a group agree to support a group decision. Everyone in the group is actively involved in reaching consensus acceptance. Everyone discusses the issues, and all members' ideas are incorporated into the group's ultimate decision. This method of decision making pools the knowledge and experience of all of the group's members and gains each individual's personal support.

Consensus, however, is difficult to attain. Moreover, achieving it takes more time than other methods of decision making, such as majority rule or autocratic imposition of one or only a few members. To achieve consensus agreement in a group, all members of the group must do the following:

1. Before meeting with the group, they must consider and be ready to state their personal positions to the group. They must also keep in mind that the decision-making process is incomplete until everyone has explained his or her own ideas and the group as a whole has reached a decision.

2. They must recognize their obligation to explain their own opinions fully, so that the group can benefit from each member's thinking.

3. They must accept the obligation to listen to the opinions of all other group members, and they must be able to modify their own positions on the basis of logic and improved understanding.

4. Realizing that differences of opinion are normal and helpful, they must not resort to conflict-reducing techniques like voting, compromising, or giving in to others. They must believe that in exploring differences, they will arrive at the best course of action.

In this exercise you will first work alone to make several college admissions decisions. You will then join a group and reach a consensus about the same set of admissions decisions. As you work together, remember that consensus is difficult to attain and that not every decision made during the admissions task may meet with everyone's unqualified approval. Nevertheless, there should be a general feeling of support from all members before a group decision is finalized. Take the time to listen, to consider *all* members' views, and to make your own view known. Be reasonable in arriving at a group decision.

Step One: Pre-Class Preparation

Read the entire exercise, then record your own admissions judgments in the "Personal Ranking" column of the Admissions Committee Decision Worksheet in Exhibit 8-1. Be sure to bring your answers to class.

Adapted from J. William Pfeiffer and John E. Jones, eds., *The 1978 Annual Handbook for Group Facilitators* (San Diego, CA: University Associates, Inc., 1978). Used by permission of William J. Heisler.

EXHIBIT 8-1
Admissions
Committee
Decision
Worksheet

Use this worksheet to record your personal decisions and the consensus decisions reached by your group. Then compare these decisions with the students' actual performance ranking (supplied by your instructor) and compute the total scores as indicated.

Applicant	(1) Personal Ranking	(2) Committee Ranking	(3) Actual Performance Ranking	(4) Difference between (1) and (3)	(5) Difference between (2) and (3)
S. Dameon					
S. Green					
L. Hutch					
E. Jakes					
J. Lorain					
T. Miller					
R. Morris					
A. Wen					

Individual   Group
Score   Score

Note: The total score for each column is the sum of the differences between the "correct" rank for each applicant (column 3) and the rank attributed to each applicant (column 1 or 2). In computing these scores, all differences should be considered positive, regardless of their actual sign. The lower the score, the better.

The Central Business School Admissions Committee

You are a faculty member of the Central Business School, located on the campus of Lake State University. In addition to your research and teaching responsibilities, you are a member of the admissions committee that screens applications for admission to your program. The committee must review each application for admission and decide whether to admit or reject the applicant as well as whether to extend an offer of financial aid. The committee meets every other week to review applications received between meetings and to rank applicants on the basis of their potential for success in Central's program. It is your policy to review applicant profiles before each meeting and to arrive at your own ranking of applicants. These profiles, which are prepared and distributed to each committee member, provide information concerning the applicant's prior grade-point average (A = 4.0, B = 3.0, C = 2.0, D = 1.0), admission test scores, records of extracurricular activities, work experience, recommendations, and other general data.

Pressures for academic achievement at Central appear to be moderate but can be expected to increase, as your business school moves toward greater national prominence. Approximately 40 percent of all applicants are accepted, and 60 to 70 percent of those accepted ultimately enroll at Central. Nearly 90 percent of your school's faculty hold doctoral degrees in their areas of teaching specialization. The student–faculty ratio is about 12:1. Central's admissions policy reflects a desire to develop a quality student body with a diversity of interests and backgrounds. Maturity, motivation, and intellectual ability are all judged to be important, as all contribute to the success of students in your program.

During the last two weeks you received the eight applicant profiles that follow. Tomorrow the admissions committee will meet to consider the applications. As is always the case, you have decided to work alone to reach your own conclusions before meeting with the rest of the committee. Read the eight profiles and record your decisions in the first column of Exhibit 8-1 before meeting with your group.

Admissions
Committee
Applicant
Profiles

Sam Dameon
Sam is a graduate of a small, private, church-affiliated institution in the southern United States.
Educational record: Cumulative GPA: 2.3
                      GPA last two years: 2.5
                      Rank in class: 340/551
Admissions test scores: Total: 487 (55%ile)
                         Verbal: 32 (70%ile)
                         Quantitative: 24 (30%ile)
Best subject: Psychology
Major activities: Social organization memberships (chairperson of one), R.O.T.C.
Work experience: Summer work as construction laborer; part-time employment as a sand-wich sales business operator
Recommendations: None provided
Personal data: U.S. citizen: yes
                 Father's occupation: certified public accountant
                 Mother's occupation: newspaper editor
                 Hobbies: fishing, golf, painting
Additional information: None

Sarah Green
Sarah attended a small midwestern school for two years before transferring to a school located in a large eastern metropolitan area.
Educational record: Cumulative GPA: 2.2
                      GPA last two years: 2.4
                      Rank in class: not available
Admissions test scores: Total: 486 (54%ile)
                         Verbal: 32 (70%ile)
                         Quantitative: 22 (23%ile)
Best subject: Business
Major activities: Social organization memberships (president of one), Accounting Club (treasurer)
Work experience: Summer work at a textile plant and as a junior auditor
Recommendations: Two excellent, one average
Personal data: U.S. citizen: yes
                 Father's occupation: accountant
                 Mother's occupation: legal secretary
                 Hobbies: flying, stamp collecting, soccer, reading
Additional information: None

Larry Hutch
Larry attended a medium-size school in the upper Midwest.
Educational record: Cumulative GPA: 2.7
                      GPA last two years: 2.7
                      Rank in class: not available
Admissions test scores: Total: 476 (51%ile)
                         Verbal: 23 (30%ile)
                         Quantitative: 34 (74%ile)
Best subject: Biology
Major activities: Theater (publicity manager), student government
Work experience: Summer work on a farm, in a hospital, and as a student laborer
Recommendations: One good, one average

Admissions
Committee
Applicant
Profiles
(continued)

Personal data: U.S. citizen: yes
                   Father's occupation: farmer
                   Mother's occupation: roadside produce business
                   Hobbies: skiing, canoeing
Additional information: None

Edward Jakes
Ed is a graduate of an inner-city school in the East that serves predominantly minority students.
Educational record: Cumulative GPA: 3.1
                        GPA last two years: 3.0
                        Rank in class: 31/437
Admissions test scores: Total: 283 (4%ile)
                            Verbal: 14 (7%ile)
                            Quantitative: 13 (2%ile)
Best subject: Politics
Major activities: Student government (vice president), political science club
Work experience: Full-time work as an insurance salesman, part-time employment as a
                     sales clerk, restaurant worker, and legislative assistant for a state
                     senator
Recommendations: Two good
Personal data: U.S. citizen: yes
                   Father's occupation: deceased
                   Mother's occupation: teacher
                   Hobbies: reading
Additional information: None

Jennifer Lorain
Jennifer is a graduate of a very small, private, church-affiliated school in the Southwest.
Educational record: Cumulative GPA: 2.7
                        GPA last two years: 3.2
                        Rank in class: not available
Admissions test scores: Total: 410 (27%ile)
                            Verbal: 23 (30%ile)
                            Quantitative: 22 (23%ile)
Best subjects: Economics, business
Major activities: Student government (committee chair), intramural sports
Work experience: Management intern for a large corporation
Recommendations: Two good
Personal data: U.S. citizen: yes
                   Father's occupation: doctor
                   Mother's occupation: volunteer worker, homemaker
                   Hobbies: sports
Additional information: None

Tim Miller
Tim is a graduate of a large school in the Northwest.
Educational record: Cumulative GPA: 2.3
                        GPA last two years: 2.6
                        Rank in class: 1,542/2,117
Admissions test scores: Total: 534 (72%ile)
                            Verbal: 31 (66%ile)
                            Quantitative: 33 (70%ile)
Best subject: Physics
Major activities: Student government (representative), varsity sports
Work experience: Summer work as a store clerk, U.S. Army Second Lieutenant
Recommendations: One excellent, one good
Personal data: U.S. citizen: yes
                   Father's occupation: research chemist
                   Mother's occupation: TV program director
                   Hobbies: reading, ham radio
Additional information: Granted full fellowship by U.S. Army

Admissions
Committee
Applicant
Profiles
(continued)

Richard Morris
Richard is a graduate of a very small school in the South that serves predominantly minority
  students.
Educational record: Cumulative GPA: 3.3
                       GPA last two years: 3.2
                       Rank in class: 11/216
Admissions test scores: Total: 398 (21%ile)
                           Verbal: 20 (17%ile)
                           Quantitative: 24 (28%ile)
Best subject: Business, economics
Major activities: Student government (treasurer), Business Club (president)
Work experience: Accountant intern (summer)
Recommendations: None provided
Personal data: U.S. citizen: yes
                  Father's occupation: auto mechanic
                  Mother's occupation: nurse
                  Hobbies: reading, listening to jazz
Additional information: None

Anne Chek Wen
Anne is currently attending the Cheng-Kung University in the Republic of China but wants to
  transfer to a U.S. school.
Educational record: Cumulative GPA: 3.0 (approximate)
                       GPA last two years: 3.5 (approximate)
                       Rank in class: not available
Admissions test scores: Total: 357 (14%ile)
                           Verbal: 12 (5%ile)
                           Quantitative: 27 (45%ile)
Best subject: Business, math
Major activities: Sports teams (swimming, basketball)
Work experience: Part-time assistant to professors
Recommendations: Two good
Personal data: U.S. citizen: no
                  Father's occupation: schoolteacher
                  Mother's occupation: homemaker
                  Hobbies: reading, travel, camping, sports
Additional information: TOEFL (Test of English as a Foreign Language) score of 578 (500
is an average TOEFL score)

Step Two: Consensus Seeking in Groups

The class should divide into groups of four to six members each (if you have formed permanent groups, reassemble in those groups). Your group should then seek consensus decisions about each of the eight applicants. Record these decisions in the column of the Admissions Committee Decision Worksheet labeled "Committee Ranking." After all groups have reached a consensus, your instructor will inform you of the actual performance ranking of the eight applicants following their completion of college. This information should be entered in the "Actual Performance Ranking" column of the Admissions Committee Decision Worksheet.

To complete Step Two, your group should determine the differences requested in the fourth and fifth columns, and you should calculate individual scores for each group member (the sum of the differences in column 4, where all differences are considered positive regardless of their actual sign; a small sum indicates greater accuracy) and a single committee score for the group as a whole (the sum of the differences in column 5, interpreted the same way as column 4). Appoint a spokesperson to report on the results of Steps One and Two to the entire class.

Step Three: Class Discussion

Your instructor will reconvene the class and call on each spokesperson to report the range of individual scores in the group (lowest, highest), the average of individual scores, and the group's overall score on the exercise. As the spokespeople make their reports, the instructor will list the scores on a blackboard, flip chart, or overhead projector:

Outcome	Group 1	Group 2	Group 3 . . .
Range of individual scores (low–high)			
Average of individual scores			
Group score			

After all groups have reported, class members should discuss the consensus-seeking procedures they used in their groups and consider the following questions:

1. What specific behaviors promoted consensus in your group? What behaviors hindered consensus? What rules could be set up to encourage helpful behaviors and discourage harmful ones?

2. Did groups with wider ranges of individual scores have a more difficult time reaching consensus than groups whose individual scores were more similar? What effects, if any, did differences among the opinions of individual members have on your group's ability to reach consensus?

3. How do interpersonal processes help or impede reaching consensus in groups? How might a group use socialization to improve its ability to reach group consensus? How might having clearly defined roles help the members of a group reach consensus more rapidly?

Conclusion

Requiring consensus acceptance increases the time it takes to make decisions and solve problems. It also enables every member to influence the decisions that are made and encourages acceptance of those decisions. Whether consensus should be sought depends on a variety of factors. The need for speedy decisions will argue against it. If decision acceptance and commitment are important, or if group members have uncommon abilities or insights that can be shared in consensus-building discussions, it would seem worthwhile to pursue consensus. The size and communication structure of the group will also affect the decision to seek consensus, with larger size and less complete structuring working against the use of such techniques. As you have learned in this exercise, consensus can be very desirable, but it can also be challenging to achieve.

CHAPTER 9

Formation and Development of Groups
Group Formation
Group Development

Group Versus Individual Productivity
Process Loss
Group Synergy
Groups versus Teams

Keys to Team Effectiveness: Setting the Stage
Task Structure
Communication Structure
Group Size
Group Composition

Keys to Team Effectiveness: Managing the Process
Motivation in Groups
Group Cohesiveness
Group Conflict

Summary
Review Questions

Learning Through Experience
Diagnostic Questions 9-1: Managing Group Effectiveness and Productivity
Exercise 9-1: Recyclers, Inc.: A Nominal Group Exercise

Group Dynamics and Team Effectiveness

Twenty years ago, when it became clear that a virus was wreaking havoc on certain subgroups of the population, scientists went to work to uncover the source of the trouble. It took them two years to isolate the virus, now known as HIV (AIDS); several more years after that to map out its gene structure; and almost fifteen years to develop effective treatments for those afflicted with the virus.

Jump ahead to 2003. A new virus was discovered that was causing death and illness throughout southern China, and rapidly spreading to places as far away as Toronto. In this case, however, it took scientists only two months to isolate and unravel the genetic code of this new virus—SARS. Two months after that, the World Health Organization (WHO) declared victory over the disease when it took Taiwan, the last city on the list, off the register of SARS-infected areas.[1]

The difference in these two cases can be traced to technological developments that allowed researchers from different disciplines working on three different continents to bring their expertise together with an ease that was historically unprecedented. The project started in earnest in mid-March, when WHO learned from a cell phone call that a doctor on a Singapore Airlines flight—still in the air—had the virus. Klaus Stohr, the manager of the WHO team assigned to this project, led a contentious meeting where his staff argued about whether to downplay the news and keep it quiet or quarantine everyone on the plane and issue a world travel alert. The group decided to go public, and eliminating the need for secrecy gave Stohr the freedom to begin setting up a worldwide network of laboratories. He established a password-controlled Web site and held twice-a-day videoconference calls so that collaborators from twelve different labs could exchange information and opinions.

The impact this had on speed was tremendous. Five minutes after the first electron microscope picture of the virus was taken in a Hong Kong lab, all the other labs had it. Hours later, a lab in the Netherlands recognized the similarity between this virus and another they had worked with; via overnight courier they sent all the other labs kits for detecting this family of virus. Within one day of extracting fluids from the infected Singapore doctor, all twelve labs had samples, and within weeks, three different labs in Great Britain, the United States, and Canada had worked together to map the genetic structure of the virus, which was posted that day on the Web.

Beyond the technology, however, one of the biggest challenges was to get these twelve laboratories, which traditionally competed against one another for funding and scientific prestige, to work together. As Stohr noted, "We needed people to share data and set aside Nobel Prize interests or their desire to publish articles in Nature *[a scientific journal] for the common goal of saving lives."[2] Much of the wrangling on this topic dealt primarily with what labs would and would not be on the team, and negotiating the membership was a highly sensitive affair. Indeed, the Netherlands lab that first recognized the virus from the electron microscope picture was the last lab to be chosen to be part of the select group.*

This same kind of virtual team that saved so many lives in the case of the SARS breakout is also being employed in business organizations to create new collaborative units that bring together the best people on important projects regardless of their location. Increasingly, organizations are even ignoring their own boundaries when assembling these teams, forming alliances with other organizations so that each contributes what it does best to a larger project. For example, Affitech, a Norwegian company that specializes in discovering human antibodies, formed a coalition with Viventia, a Canadian firm that specializes in developing biotechnology treatments, to form a new team that will look into developing cures for cancer.[3] As another example, Lockheed Martin, which recently won the contract to produce the new Joint Strike Fighter aircraft, will form a team of people to work on that project that spans more than fifty different companies. As program manager Mark Peden asserts, "We're getting the best people from wherever we need them; it's a true virtual connection."[4]

A single person working alone cannot accomplish very much, and the relative success of the human species on this planet can be traced to a large part on the ability of people to work together and coordinate their efforts in a way that is qualitatively different from other species. As our opening story shows, if one can get the right people together, and place aside their own self-interests to work for the common goal of the team, incredible feats can be accomplished. Contemporary organizations are recognizing the power of work teams, and are increasingly structuring themselves around flexible project teams that are temporally bound rather than fixed, individual jobs that exist in isolation on the organization chart. For example, 3M (Minnesota Mining and Manufacturing Company), which is headquartered in St. Paul, Minnesota, also turned to teams to solve its problems. Although once famous for its new product developments (such as surgical staples and Post-it Notes), by the mid-1990s 3M's introduction of new products had slowed to a trickle and its annual sales growth had fallen to a sluggish 2 percent. Against this backdrop, chief executive L. D. "Desi" DeSimone vowed to reinvigorate product development and slash the time required to introduce new products by half, to less than three years on average.

To accomplish this ambitious goal, DeSimone first encouraged closer teamwork among researchers and marketers, who had previously worked independently on product design and market introduction. Next, he ordered teams to scour 3M's research libraries for existing materials that might be adapted to emerging customer needs. Thanks to this effort, 3M was able to launch a special film for laptop computer screens that enhances brightness while conserving energy. The film, made of microscopic reflective prisms, had originally been developed in the mid-1980s for decorative signs on buildings. As a consequence of this single innovation, the battery life of laptops has been extended almost 50 percent.

Because product developers work directly with marketers, 3M's scientists know more about its customers and its sales force has ready access to the company's vast storehouse of materials and technologies. New product development time has declined considerably, approaching the three-year target set by DeSimone. At the same time, such innovative products as Never Rust Wool Soap Pads, manufactured from recycled plastic bottles and marketed as competitors to Clorox Company's S.O.S. brand, are propelling sales growth on the order of 6 percent per year.[5]

Clearly, team building is a very popular trend in contemporary organizations both large[6] and small.[7] Whereas a team-based approach did wonders at 3M, however, in other contexts, the introduction of team-based work has had disastrous results. For example, at Levi's, workers who once worked by themselves on a piece-rate system were assembled into groups, and decision-making authority was decentralized and based on establishing consensus in the team.[8] The shift to teamwork did not have the intended result, however, as efficiency dropped to 77 percent of preteam levels, and the cost to assemble a pair of Dockers increased by 33 percent. Instead of workers being happier, morale actually went down as skilled and experienced workers who had done well under the old individually based piece-rate system fought bitterly with new and inexperienced workers who were holding the team back from reaching its team-based incentives. The conflict here and elsewhere in the organization resulted in stagnation, because in the words of former CFO George James, "Unless you could convince everyone to agree with your idea, you didn't have authority to make a decision."[9] As team building gains greater favor in organizations (some might call it a fad), managers need to keep in mind that teams are often the solution to one set of problems, but the source of a second set of problems.

This chapter discusses the management of group and team performance. We begin by examining how groups are formally constituted in organizations and by exploring the processes within groups that give rise to a sense of group identity and purpose. After laying this groundwork, we identify several critical factors that can influence the decision to have individuals work alone or work in groups. Next, we identify the special type of group called a team, discussing how to "set the stage" and then "manage the process" so as to derive the benefits of teamwork while avoiding some of the potential pitfalls associated with teams.

FORMATION AND DEVELOPMENT OF GROUPS

A *group* is a collection of two or more people who interact with one another in a way such that each person influences and is influenced by the others.[10] The members of a group draw important psychological distinctions between themselves and people who are not group members. For example, in our opening story, one of the most controversial aspects of putting the WHO SARS team together was the decision regarding who would and would not be in the group. Since group membership says a great deal about who the group really is, in many groups, membership is often granted very selectively, and in some cases, the higher the selectivity, the stronger the psychological identification with the group. Generally, group members share ten characteristics:

1. They define themselves as members.
2. They are defined by others as members.
3. They identify with one another.
4. They engage in frequent interaction.
5. They participate in a system of interlocking roles.
6. They share common norms.
7. They pursue shared, interdependent goals.
8. They feel that their membership in the group is rewarding.
9. They have a collective perception of unity.
10. They stick together in any confrontation with other groups.[11]

These distinctions provide the group with boundaries and a sense of permanence. They lend it a distinct identity and separate it from other people and other groups.[12] They also contribute to **group effectiveness,** the ultimate aim of group activities. A group is effective when it satisfies three important criteria:

1. *Production output.* The product of the group's work must meet or exceed standards of quantity and quality defined by the organization. *Group productivity* is a measure of this product.
2. *Member satisfaction.* Membership in the group must provide people with short-term satisfaction and facilitate their long-term growth and development. If it does not, members will leave and the group will cease to exist.
3. *Capacity for continued cooperation.* The interpersonal processes that the group uses to complete a task should maintain or enhance members' capacity to work together. Groups that do not cooperate cannot remain viable.[13]

Thus, an effective group is able to satisfy immediate demands for performance and member satisfaction, while making provisions for long-term survival. These three criteria are all slightly different from each other, and in some cases, a manager needs to be careful not to promote one goal in the short term (productivity) and unwittingly harm another one in the long term (long-term continuity). Over the long term, the three tend to come together, however. For example, a recent study of basketball teams in the National Basketball Association showed that the longer a group stayed together, the better they performed, because team members were better able to learn and exploit subtle differences in each player's strengths and weaknesses. This kind of "tacit knowledge" did not develop in teams that were constantly changing their membership, and this put them at a severe competitive disadvantage.[14]

Group Formation

In most organizations, groups are formed based on similarities either in what people do or in what they make.[15] To illustrate these two contrasting approaches to **group formation,** imagine a company that makes wooden desks, bookshelves, and chairs. To produce each product, four basic activities are required:

1. A receiver must unpack and stock the raw materials required for the product.
2. A fabricator must shape and assemble the raw materials into a partially completed product.
3. A finisher must complete the assembly operation by painting and packaging the product.
4. A shipper must dispatch the finished products to the organization's customers.

Also imagine that the company's manufacturing workforce consists of twelve employees, who are organized into three assembly lines consisting of four employees each. One employee on each line performs each of the four basic work activities.

The company must decide whether to group the twelve employees by the tasks they perform, called **functional grouping,** or by the flow of work from initiation to completion, called **work flow grouping.** Each alternative offers significant advantages and disadvantages.

Consider first what functional grouping, or grouping by the means of production, can offer the firm. The upper panel of Figure 9-1 shows how the four tasks from each assembly line can be grouped together so that the four resulting work groups consist of people with the same sets of abilities, knowledge, and skills.

Functional work groups help integrate and coordinate employees who perform similar tasks. Employees in such groups can exchange information about task procedures, sharpening their knowledge and skills. They can also help one another out when necessary. This sort of cooperation can greatly enhance productivity.

In addition, functional grouping can allow the organization to take advantage of other cost savings. Suppose that the receivers for all three assembly lines in Figure 9-1 need only five hours per day to complete their work; they remain idle for the remaining three hours. If receiving is handled in a single work group, the firm can economize by employing two receivers instead of three. The third receiver can be moved elsewhere in the company to perform a more productive job, and the company can derive substantial benefit from improved efficiency in the use of human resources.

FIGURE 9-1   Group Formation by Function or Work Flow

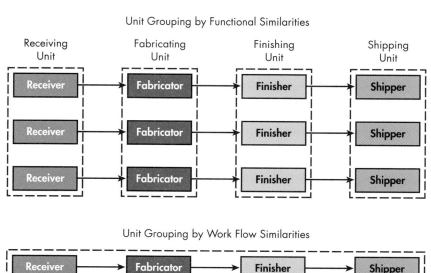

On the negative side, functional grouping separates people performing different tasks along the same flow of work. This differentiation can encourage slowdowns that block the flow, thereby reducing productivity. For instance, suppose the finisher on the desk assembly line has nothing to do and wants the desk fabricator to speed up so as to provide more work. Because of functional grouping, the two people are members of different groups, and no simple way exists for them to communicate with each other directly.

Instead, the desk finisher must rely on hierarchical communication linkages between the fabricating and finishing groups. The finisher must tell the supervisor of the finishing group about the problem. The finishing supervisor must notify the superintendent overseeing all manufacturing operations. The manufacturing superintendent must talk with the supervisor of the fabricating group. Finally, the fabricating supervisor must tell the desk fabricator to work more quickly. Meanwhile, productivity suffers because of the absence of direct communication along the flow of work. 3M was trying to solve this type of problem when it created cross-functional teams composed of research, marketing, and production personnel.

Now consider what happens if work groups are created on the basis of work flow. In the furniture company example, a different flow of work is associated with each of its three product lines (desks, bookshelves, and chairs). The lower panel of Figure 9-1 illustrates the results of choosing this approach.

The primary strengths of work flow grouping relate to the fact that this approach integrates all activities required to manufacture a product or provide a service. Each separate work flow is completely enclosed within a single group. If employees who fill different functions along the assembly line need to coordinate with each other to maintain the flow of work, they can do so without difficulty.

Owing to its encouragement of integration, work flow grouping also enhances organizational adaptability. Operations on any of the furniture company's three assembly lines can be halted or stopped without affecting the rest of the company. Suppose, for example, that the desk assembly line in the company is shut down because of poor sales. To simulate this situation, cover the upper assembly line in the bottom panel of Figure 9-1 with a piece of paper. You can see that neither of the remaining two groups will be affected in any major way. Under functional grouping, however, the firm would not enjoy the same degree of flexibility. If you cover the upper assembly line in the top panel of Figure 9-1, you will note that all four of the groups created by functional grouping would be affected by the interruption in desk production.

Despite its strengths, work flow grouping does not permit the scale economies associated with functional grouping. In work flow grouping people who perform the same function cannot help or substitute for one another. In addition, they will inevitably duplicate one another's work, adding to the firm's overall costs. Moreover, it becomes very difficult for people who perform the same task to trade information about issues such as more efficient work procedures and ways to improve task skills. Just as functional grouping does not allow the adaptability of work flow grouping, work flow grouping does not produce the economic efficiency of functional grouping. The alternative structures also place different demands on managers, in the sense that managing a unit grouped around work flow is often a more complex job where the manager has a high degree of autonomy, whereas the manager of a unit grouped around functional similarity is s simpler task but one where the manager is more interdependent on other managers. For this reason, managers of groups organized around work flow often need to be higher in cognitive ability than managers of groups organized around functional similarities.[16] Thus, although many different types of groups are possible, each type inevitably has its own set of strengths and weaknesses.

Group Development

In most organizations, choices between functional and work flow grouping are made by managers who must decide whether efficiency or adaptability should be given a higher priority. Group formation is, therefore, a process of determining the formal, established characteristics of groups.

A second process, *group development,* allows informal aspects of groups to emerge. As groups develop, members modify formally prescribed group tasks, clarify personal roles, and negotiate group norms. Research indicates that these developmental processes tend to advance through the four stages shown in Figure 9-2: initiation, differentiation, integration, and maturity.[17]

The first stage of group development, **initiation,** is characterized by uncertainty and anxiety. Potential members focus on getting to know each other's personal views and abilities.[18] In the beginning, they often discuss neutral topics, such as the weather and local news, that have little bearing on the group's purpose. As they gain familiarity with one another and begin to feel more comfortable, members begin discussing general work issues and each person's likely relationship to the formally prescribed task of the group. Attention now concentrates on determining which behaviors should be considered appropriate and what sorts of contributions people should be expected to make to the group. As ideas are exchanged and discussed, people who have the option may decide whether to join or leave the group.

When a group enters the second stage of development, **differentiation,** conflicts may erupt as members try to reach agreement on the purpose, goals, and objectives of the group. Strong differences of opinion may emerge as members try to achieve consensus on exactly how they will accomplish the group's formally prescribed task. Sorting out who will do what when, where, why, and how and what reward members will receive for their performance often proves to be extremely difficult. Sometimes disagreements about members' roles in the group become violent enough to threaten the group's very existence. If successful, however, differentiation creates a structure of roles and norms that allows the group to accomplish missions that its members could not accomplish by working alone.

Having weathered the differentiation stage, group members must resolve conflicts over other crucial issues in the third stage of group development, **integration.** Integration focuses on reestablishing the central purpose of the group in light of the structure of roles developed during differentiation. Members may define the task of the group in informal terms that modify the group's formal purpose and reflect their own experiences and opinions. Reaching a consensus about the group's purpose

FIGURE 9-2 Stages in Group Development

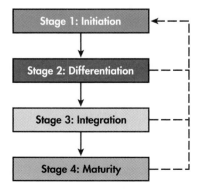

helps develop a sense of group identity among members and promotes cohesiveness within the group. It also provides the foundation for the development of additional rules, norms, and procedures to help coordinate interactions among members and facilitate the pursuit of group goals.

In the final stage of group development, **maturity,** members fulfill their roles and work toward attaining group goals. Many of the agreements reached about goals, roles, and norms may take on formal significance, being adopted by management and documented in writing. Formalizing these agreements helps to ensure that people joining the group at this stage will understand the group's purpose and way of functioning.

Even at this late stage, a group may be confronted with new tasks or new requirements for performance. Changes in the group's environment or in its members may make it necessary to return to an earlier stage and reenter the development process. Thus group development is a dynamic, continuous process in which informal understandings support or sometimes displace the formal characteristics of the group and its task.

Not every group passes through all four stages of development in a predictable, stepwise manner. Moreover, the process of passing between stages may be more erratic than smooth.[19] For example, many project-based groups experience what has been referred to as a **punctuated equilibrium** near the halfway point of the project. The halfway point is significant because it is easy for the group members to estimate their final progress by simply multiplying what they have accomplished at the point by two. In most cases this projection terrifies the members, who have often gotten stuck somewhere between stage two and stage three in terms of their overall development. This causes an abrupt change in the group's motivation and willingness to compromise with others, and thus helps accelerate the group's move to stage four.[20]

GROUP VERSUS INDIVIDUAL PRODUCTIVITY

Are people necessarily more productive when they work in groups than when they work alone? Based on the growing prevalence of groups and teams in organizations, it appears that many people believe the answer to this question is "yes."[21] A large body of research, however, indicates that groups of individuals working together are sometimes less productive than the same number of people working alone.[22] In addition, it often takes longer to make decisions in a group—especially if one must arrive at consensus—and the resulting decisions are not guaranteed to always be better than the decision made by the group's best member. Several reasons explain why groups sometimes falter in this fashion.

Process Loss

Adding more people to a group increases the human resources that the group can put to productive use. Thus, as depicted in Figure 9-3, the *theoretical* productivity of a group should rise in direct proportion to the size of the group. In reality, after an initial rise, the group's *actual productivity* falls as its size continues to increase. The difference between what a group actually produces and what it might theoretically produce constitutes **process loss.**[23] It results from the existence of obstacles to group productivity, the most influential of which are production blocking, group maintenance activities, and social loafing.

Production blocking occurs when people get in each other's way as they try to perform a group task[24]—for example, when one member of a moving-van crew car-

FIGURE 9-3 Group Size and Process Loss

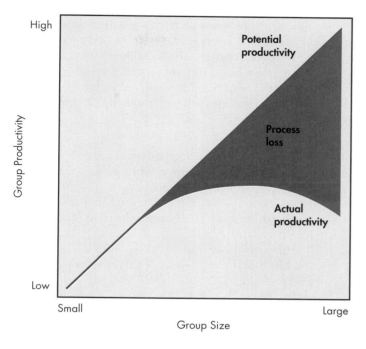

ries a chair through a doorway and another member waits to carry a box of clothing through the same doorway. In large groups, one form of production blocking is caused by the fact that only one person can effectively talk at once, and in this context, it may be difficult for some members to get their ideas discussed. Good ideas may never be introduced simply because of this limitation.

In addition, for a group to function effectively over time, its members must fulfill the requirements of several **group maintenance roles.** Each of these roles helps to ensure the group's continued existence by building and preserving strong interpersonal relations among its members. These roles include the following:

- *Encouragers,* who enhance feelings of warmth and solidarity within the group by praising, agreeing with, and accepting the ideas of others
- *Harmonizers,* who attempt to minimize the negative effects of conflicts among the group's members by resolving disagreements fairly, quickly, and openly and by relieving interpersonal tension
- *Standard setters,* who raise questions about group goals and goal attainment and who set achievement standards against which group members can evaluate their performance.[25]

Although group maintenance activities support and facilitate a group's continued functioning, they can also interfere with productive activity. For instance, members of a management team who disagree about a proposal must spend time not only on improving the proposal, but also on harmonizing among themselves, diverting valuable time and effort and reducing the group's productivity.

Process loss can also result from **social loafing,** the choice by some members of a group to take advantage of others by doing less work, working more slowly, or in other ways decreasing their own contributions to group productivity.[26] According to economists, social loafing—also called *free riding*—makes sense from a loafer's perspective if the rewards that his or her group receives for productivity are shared more or less equally among all group members.[27] A loafer can gain the same rewards bestowed on everyone else without having to expend personal effort.

Unless someone else in the group takes up the slack, even one person's loafing may lower the entire group's productivity. In the worst-case scenario, the other team members who witness the social loafer may feel that they are being taken advantage of, and then begin to reduce their level of effort as well. If this happens, the group as a whole begins to look more and more like its worst member, and unless this is managed, it creates a huge amount of process loss.[28]

Group Synergy

Whereas process loss focuses on the reduction of productivity attributed to putting people into groups as opposed to leaving them alone, the concept of **group synergy** deals with the opposite phenomenon—productivity of a group that exceeds the expectation, based on the potential individual contributions. Figure 9-4 shows the relationship between group productivity and group size under conditions of group synergy.

Although process loss is the more common outcome, group synergy is possible, and much of the remainder of this chapter is devoted to identifying those conditions where synergy happens more frequently. Indeed, for each of the three factors that results in process loss, a corresponding factor exists that might be able to account for group synergy. For example, whereas in production blocking individuals get in one another's way, **social facilitation** may allow the presence of others to increase an individual's performance.

The presence of others can be facilitating for a number of reasons. Perhaps most important, in a group context, one person who is unskilled or inexperienced can model his or her behavior on the behavior of others in the group who are more skilled and experienced. As we saw in our opening story on SARS, when people

FIGURE 9-4 Group Size and Synergy

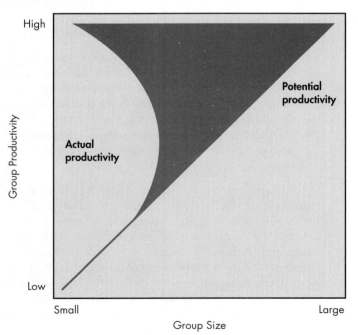

bring different types of skills or experiences to the group, this mixture creates many opportunities for people to learn from one another and improve over time.

Similarly, although it takes time to build and maintain interpersonal relationships in the group, under many conditions the presence of close interpersonal relationships will help create the very behaviors that are essential for success. For example, Chapter 8 mentioned emergent task elements, such as volunteering, helping, correcting other people's errors, making personal sacrifices, and so on. Although not part of any one person's job description, these behaviors are essential for organizational functioning, and they tend to be seen only in trusting groups that have successfully developed and maintained their relationships.

Finally, although some people will respond to working in groups by social loafing, the within-group competition aspect of group tasks motivates other people to work harder than they would have if left on their own. Research shows that some amount of within-group competition can increase the speed of individual members, and that this effects is particularly pronounced on the group's worst member (the potential social loafer).[29] Indeed, some tasks may be so boring or monotonous that the only way to inspire workers is by creating a competition out of the situation. Although this type of within-group competition must be monitored so that it does not interfere with larger group goals, the fact that it can work in certain situations shows that forming groups can increase or decrease individuals' efforts.

Groups versus Teams

Although the previous sections make it clear that it is not always beneficial to form groups or teams, under some circumstances one has no alternative. To understand these circumstances, it is worth drawing a distinction between work groups and teams, because the choice to form groups is often more discretionary than the decision to form teams.

Teams are a special subset of groups. They share all ten characteristics of groups noted earlier in the chapter, plus three additional distinguishing features:

1. The members of teams are highly interdependent, typically being connected via comprehensive interdependence (recall Chapter 8's discussion of the types of interdependence).
2. Teams are formed using work flow grouping, so the members of a team are responsible for performing several functions.
3. Skills, knowledge, expertise, and information are often distributed unequally among the members of a team, owing to differences in their backgrounds, training, abilities, and access to resources. Thus the members are not interchangeable.

The last feature on this list explains why managers often have less discretion when forming teams than when creating groups. Specifically, some tasks are so large and require so many different skills that no single individual could perform them by working alone. Any type of complex surgery, for example, requires at least a surgeon, an anesthesiologist, and a surgical nurse. In this instance, it makes no sense to question whether those three individuals could perform more operations working alone versus working together. The skill set required of each person is so complex that no person could perform an operation by himself or herself.

As we saw in our opening story, organizations like Lockheed and Viventia are increasingly structuring themselves around these kinds of teams. That is, the best people are all brought together to work on a specific project for a set period of time, and then disassembled when the project is complete, perhaps being assigned to a different project with a different team after that.

These team-based structures offer two primary advantages over traditional hierarchical structures. First, they enable organizations to bring products to market faster than would be possible in systems in which experts work sequentially—for instance, designers handing over drawings to engineers, who then hand over specifications to manufacturers, who then deliver a product to marketers. If the designers envision a project that will be too difficult to produce or too challenging to market, this problem is spotted early by teams, when it is easier to rectify.

Second, team-based structures eliminate the need for having multiple levels of middle management, giving workers autonomy over decisions that were previously the province of managers. Autonomy has a powerful, positive effect on workforce motivation, as indicated in Chapter 5, and trimming the number of managers reduces administrative overhead. Indeed, when autonomous team-based structures are combined with the motivational force of employee ownership, firms can gain a great deal of competitive advantage over their traditionally structured rivals. For example, W. L. Gore, maker of Gore-Tex waterproof fabric, has no fixed hierarchy, no fixed job titles, and no formal job descriptions. Instead, this employee-owned company is organized around flexible teams that move from project to project depending on the swings in demand for various products. This flexibility means the firm can produce more fabric than its competitors with fewer people, and the saved labor costs are then reinvested in the company, increasing its value for the employee owners.[30]

Of course, to derive this sort of benefit from teams, the organization must avoid the types of problems that can arise in group or team contexts. For example, as we noted earlier, it is critical that the right people are brought in to the team because this will create interdependence among the group members who can be harmed by others who may lack conscientiousness or integrity. For example, New Balance Shoes created a partnership with a Chinese company that was supposed to help the U.S. sneaker manufacturer increase production. After learning the secrets of the New Balance manufacturing process, however, the Chinese company began producing lower-priced clones of New Balance shoes that they sold on the world market for half the price—drastically cutting into New Balance's profit margins.[31] Similar horror stories of firms that entered into teams where they were subsequently ripped off by their supposed team members are not uncommon, and show again that teams can help or hurt competitiveness, depending upon how they are managed.[32] The remainder of this chapter will focus on ways to maximize group and team effectiveness. First, we will examine decisions that are made prior to the group actually going to work (that is, "setting the stage"). We will then discuss factors that become relevant once the group begins its work (that is, "managing the process").

KEYS TO TEAM EFFECTIVENESS: SETTING THE STAGE

Task Structure

In the initial stage of group formation, a decision must be made with respect to whether the group will employ functional grouping or work flow grouping (reexamine Figure 9-1). This decision is important because it is a primary determinant of how much task interdependence the group will experience. The level of task interdependence is related to performance on both cognitive and behavioral tasks[33] as well as commitment to the team.[34] Task interdependence refers to the degree to which team members interact cooperatively and work interactively to complete tasks. When task interdependence is high, two other aspects of structuring the team can promote coordination and performance. First, structures that rotate members through different roles via cross-training help create shared mental models among team members, which in turn promotes coordination and mutual support.[35] Indeed, this kind of "within-person" functional diversity (where one person has varied experiences) seems to be even more important than "cross-unit" functional diversity (where different people each bring a unique experience) in terms of promoting effective team performance.[36] Second, in self-managed teams, rotating the leadership position is also instrumental in promoting cooperation and participation among members, because all team members get a "big picture" appreciation of how all the parts sum to the whole.[37]

In addition to directly affecting group performance and commitment to the group, interdependence influences the relationship between member attributes and group performance. For example, a highly useful typology for classifying group tasks breaks them down into additive, disjunctive, and conjunctive tasks.[38]

In an **additive task,** each group member contributes to group performance in proportion to his or her ability, so that the sum of the individual team members' abilities equals the team performance. Shoveling snow is an example of an additive task—the amount of snow shoveled by a group of people is the sum of the amounts that each group member could shovel alone. Additive tasks are low in interdependence.

A **disjunctive task** is structured such that one person could perform it effectively alone as long as he or she had the requisite resources (information, cognitive ability, and so on). Solving an algebra problem is an example of disjunctive task, in the sense that the solution to such a problem depends on the most capable group member—once one person solves the problem, the team's task is complete (this type of task is sometimes referred to as a eureka task). Disjunctive tasks are moderately high in task interdependence, because the people who do not solve the task are dependent on the one person who can solve the task; the person who solves the task, however, is not really dependent on the others.

In a **conjunctive task,** in contrast, the group's level of performance depends on the resources that the least able group member brings to the task. For example, the speed with which a team of mountain climbers can reach the top of a cliff is a close function of how fast the slowest, weakest member can climb. A common expression in team contexts is that "a chain is only as strong as its weakest link"; this saying indicates how teams are often characterized as performing conjunctive tasks.[39] The unique skills that each person brings to the task and their lack of interchangeability mean that if one team member fails to perform his or her role, then the entire team will fail because no one else is equipped to carry out those duties.

Communication Structure

Once a decision on task structure is made and roles have been designed, the next question becomes who within the team can talk to whom. This issue deals with **communication structure.** If the members of a group cannot exchange information about their work, the group cannot function effectively. A viable communication structure is, therefore, crucial to group productivity. For managers, it is important to know about the different kinds of group communication structures and to be able to implement those that encourage the greatest productivity.

In research on group communication and productivity, five structures have received considerable attention: the wheel, Y, chain, circle, and completely connected communication network (Figure 9-5). The first three of these networks are the most centralized, in that a central member can control information flows in the group. In contrast, in the decentralized circle and completely connected networks, all members are equally able to send and receive messages.

FIGURE 9-5 Group Communication Structures and Group Effectiveness

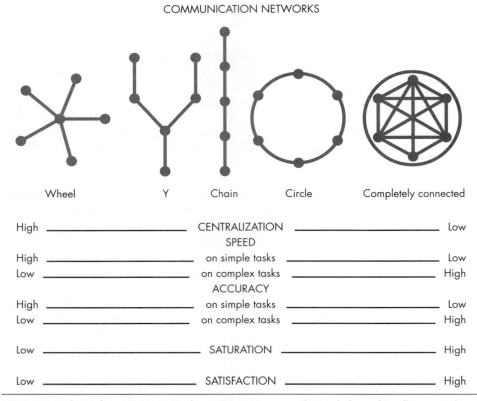

COMMUNICATION NETWORKS

Wheel	Y	Chain	Circle	Completely connected

High	————————	CENTRALIZATION	————————	Low
		SPEED		
High	————————	on simple tasks	————————	Low
Low	————————	on complex tasks	————————	High
		ACCURACY		
High	————————	on simple tasks	————————	Low
Low	————————	on complex tasks	————————	High
Low	————————	SATURATION	————————	High
Low	————————	SATISFACTION	————————	High

Source: Based on information in M. E. Shaw, *Group Dynamics: The Psychology of Small Group Behavior* (New York: McGraw-Hill, 1976), pp. 262–314.

The five communication networks differ in several ways:

- The *speed* at which information can be transmitted
- The *accuracy* with which information is transmitted
- The degree of *saturation,* which is high when information is distributed evenly in a group and low when some members have significantly more information than others
- The *satisfaction* of members with communication processes and the group in general[40]

As indicated in Figure 9-5, communication speed and accuracy in a group are affected both by the nature of the group's communication network and by the relative complexity of the group's task. Group tasks can range from *simple* tasks, which involve physical demands but little mental effort or need for communication among co-workers, to *complex* tasks, which require greater mental effort, less physical exertion, and significant communication.[41]

When a task is simple and communication networks are centralized, both speed and accuracy are higher. Centralization facilitates the minimal communication required to succeed at simple tasks. When tasks are simple and communication networks are decentralized, however, speed and accuracy are lower because extra people are involved in communication.

In contrast, when tasks are relatively complex, centralized communication networks lower both speed and accuracy because people serving as network hubs succumb to **information overload.** Overload and its effects are less likely to occur in decentralized networks, as more people process information and share responsibilities for communication.

Both network saturation and member satisfaction are generally higher in decentralized networks. Everyone is informed and fully involved in the communication process and the task. (The exception to this rule involves centralized networks, where the one person located at the hub of the network is usually very satisfied.) Task complexity does not appear to affect saturation or satisfaction in groups.

To summarize, centralization increases the productivity of groups in performing simple tasks that require little or no communication but generally reduces member satisfaction. In contrast, decentralization increases not only the productivity of groups in performing complex tasks that require much communication, but also member satisfaction and perceptions of group potency.[42] The decentralized network therefore provides an efficient *and* effective way of organizing communication when the group must tackle complex tasks. Indeed, as the Cutting-Edge Research box shows, changes in communication media have allowed organizations to increasingly employ decentralized communication networks; however, questions have been raised regarding the degree to which computer-mediated communication can substitute for face-to-face communication.

Group Size

The basic "infrastructure" of the group is established by making decisions about task structure and communication structure of the team. Once the infrastructure is in place, another issue crops up: staffing the team with people. Here, the first consideration relates to group size. That is, how many people should the group include?

Because of the wide variability in tasks that groups might be asked to perform, it is impossible to answer this question with a precise number that will apply to all cases. A good general principle is that a group should be as small as possible. That is, if one must err in putting together a group, it is far better to create a group that is too small than one that is too big.

On average, people working in smaller groups are more productive than people in larger groups.[43] As suggested by Figure 9-6, this relationship can be traced to several factors. First, small groups simply have fewer members who might get in each other's way. Clearly, production blocking caused by *physical constraints* is less likely to occur in small groups than in large ones. Second, group size influences productivity by affecting the amount of *social distraction* that people experience when they work in a group. The smaller the group, the less likely that group members will distract one another and interrupt behavioral sequences that are important to the task. Third, smaller groups have lower *coordination requirements.* The fewer the members that a group has, the fewer the interdependencies that must be formed and maintained. Fourth, group size is related to the incidence of *behavioral masking.* The behaviors of a group member may be masked or hidden by the simple presence of other members.[44] The smaller the group, the easier it is to observe each member's behavior, and this visibility in turn affects the frequency of social loafing.[45] Finally, group size influences the *diffusion of responsibility*—the sense that responsibility is shared broadly rather than shouldered personally. In a small group, each person is more apt to feel personally responsible for group performance and effectiveness.

Group Composition

After establishing the number of people to include in the group, the next staffing decision involves the identities of those people. Having the appropriate level of expertise in the right positions helps ensure that the team can accomplish its tasks and

CUTTING-EDGE RESEARCH

FACING THE FACTS: COMPUTER-MEDIATED COMMUNICATION AND TEAM EFFECTIVENESS

From the earliest days of our hunter-gatherer ancestors until the latter part of the twentieth century, groups of people met face-to-face (FTF) to make joint decisions and produce team products. Within the last twenty years, however, revolutionary changes in communication technology have allowed people who are distant from each other in space or time to work together without the need to travel. This has allowed the creation of new kinds of teams working in new kinds of ways, and not surprisingly, social scientists have devoted a great deal of effort toward learning whether computer-mediated communication (CMC) promotes or hinders group processes and outcomes relative to FTF communication.

Some have suggested that the status differences between group members become less salient when working via CMC, and this might enhance more openness and equality in participation rates. Similarly, interpersonal styles (such as assertiveness and extroversion) are also reduced as factors that affect participation rates, and this too could lead to more widespread participation. Equality of participation could in turn lead to higher satisfaction and performance by the group. Alternatively, others have suggested that the lack of nonverbal cues and the fact that information and opinions have to be written, as opposed to simply uttered, could frustrate work groups, which in turn could lead to low satisfaction and performance.

A recent meta-analytic study by Boris Baltes and his colleagues sought to answer these kinds of questions by summarizing the extant research, aggregating the results of twenty-seven separate studies on the topic that involved more than 3,000 individuals. Most of these studies contrasted FTF groups with a special type of CMC, which most closely resembles "chat" groups (synchronous written communication). Several important findings emerged from this analysis.

First, there was a major effect for timing in that CMC groups, not surprisingly, took much longer to complete tasks relative to FTF groups. Second, CMC groups generally performed worse than FTF groups, but this was neutralized if the team members were anonymous. This implies that there are positive aspects to anonymity (such as openness) that make up for some of the other liabilities of CMC (such as lack of nonverbal cues). Third, there were also no differences in performance between FTF and CMC teams when there were no time constraints, suggesting that the lack of speed associated with CMC teams played a role in their performance deficiencies. Finally, in terms of satisfaction, although anonymous CMC groups performed as well as FTF groups, they were highly dissatisfied with the experience, whereas the lower-performing, nonanonymous CMC groups were actually equally satisfied with FTF groups.

Although these initial results are intriguing, this will not be the last word on CMC for a number of reasons. First, currently, more organizations use "e-mail-types" of asynchronous technologies more than they use "chat-types" of technology, and hence these results may underestimate the negative effects of CMC as actually operationalized in organizations. Second, technologies are changing rapidly, and recent developments in the area of videoconferencing create opportunities to reintroduce nonverbal exchanges as part of CMC. This technology may make "chat" irrelevant. Finally, there are age differences in the familiarity with new technologies, and for many young people, sharing information via a computer, whether by e-mail, chat, or file sharing, has become the norm rather than the exception. This group of people may show fewer negative side effects of CMC, but only time and more future research will be able to confirm this.

Sources: P. S. Weisband, "Group Discussion and First Advocacy Effects in Computer-Mediated and Face-to-Face Groups," *Organizational Behavior and Human Decision Processes* 83 (2000), 352–380; B. B. Baltes, M. W. Dickson, M. P. Sherman, C. C. Bauer, and J. S. LaGanke, "Computer-Mediated Communication and Group Decision-Making: A Meta-Analysis," *Organizational Behavior and Human Decision Processes* 87 (2002), 156–179; P. Lewis, "Apple Puts the Eye in IM," *Fortune*, July 21, 2003, pp. 159–160.

subgoals. Clearly, having individuals with the right skills, abilities, knowledge, or dispositions is critical for all jobs—whether they are part of a team or not—but it is especially critical for teams because of the interdependence that exists among team members. Under such circumstances, the effective execution of one person's role becomes a critical resource needed by others so that they can in turn execute their

FIGURE 9-6 How Group Size Affects Group Productivity

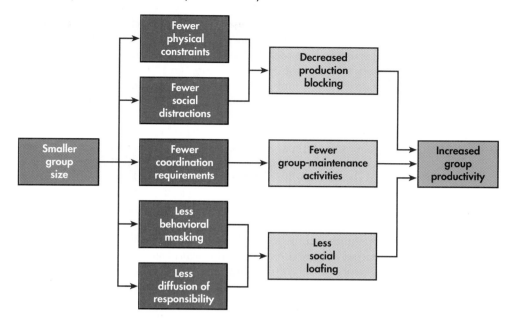

own roles. This consideration is also critical with conjunctive tasks, because the team will be only as good as its weakest member.

In addition to considering each team member's standing on critical abilities, traits, and characteristics, in team contexts one must decide whether to construct the team so that the members are heterogeneous (all different) or homogeneous (all the same) on these characteristics. We will consider the homogeneity–heterogeneity issue with respect to three factors: function, personality, and demography/culture.

Functional heterogeneity means that different people in the team have different skills or functions (as in a cross-functional team). A large body of evidence indicates that on complex tasks, heterogeneity on this characteristic is highly valuable—especially if people with different skills can communicate effectively and manage the debate that is likely to ensue from their different backgrounds and experiences.[46] The group also benefits when team members are aware of the different skills represented by each member, and they respect the training that the others have received.[47] This again points to the value of structures that support cross-training, rotated leadership, and educational experiences that expand people's understanding beyond their own narrow job.[48]

Turning to personality traits, the degree to which homogeneity or heterogeneity is desired depends on the trait in question.[49] With certain traits such as conscientiousness, all members should have the same level of this characteristic. If some members rate very high on it, but others rate very low, this discrepancy may create the type of social loafing situation that starts fights and destroys group cohesiveness. Moreover, because they feel like the other members are taking advantage of them, highly conscientious team members may withhold effort; ultimately, they may resemble low-conscientiousness members. Another virtue of highly conscientious team members deals with propensity to seek and offer help or support to other members. People who are high in conscientiousness are often the first to provide assistance to others when it is needed, and they are the least likely to ask for help from others when it is not needed.[50]

With other traits, such as extroversion, it is best to build in heterogeneity. If all members are high on extroversion, a power struggle will arise as everyone tries to dominate the group. Alternatively, if everyone in the group is low on this trait, no leadership will emerge and the group will flounder. Consequently, heterogeneity is preferred so that the group includes some people who are comfortable leading and others who are comfortable following. Heterogeneity in characteristics such as personality, values, and interests is often referred to as "deep-level psychological diversity" and although this sometimes creates short-term problems in the group formation differentiation stage, it has generally been found to have long-term value in terms of team viability and performance.[51]

Given the increased frequency of international joint ventures, it is also important to consider the role of demographic and cultural diversity in groups. Although this kind of diversity has great potential to lead to new ideas and insights, group composition issues can often thwart this potential.[52] In terms of cultural diversity, a more complex pattern emerges relative to what is seen with diversity along functional lines or personality traits.

To understand how cultural heterogeneity works, you must recognize that the eventual culture adopted by the team, referred to as a "hybrid culture," represents a mixture of the cultures brought by individual team members. If all members of the team come from the same culture (for example, four Americans), the hybrid culture naturally closely resembles the culture they all share, and this type of convergence can lead to high performance. When all of the members come from different cultures (for example, one American, one German, one Chinese, and one South African), no culture dominates, and the members must jointly construct a hybrid culture that is unique and idiosyncratic to that team. Although these teams may struggle initially, they eventually arrive at a hybrid culture. Indeed, teams can perform quite well under these conditions.

When one subset of group members share a dominant culture, and the others do not share this culture (for example, two Americans, one German, and one Chinese), then a struggle will ensue, and the team often fails to arrive at a hybrid culture. In teams with this type of "moderate" homogeneity, the dominant group (in this example, the two Americans) is not strong enough to assert the primacy of its particular culture, but still strong enough to resist adopting a new, unique, and idiosyncratic culture. Under these conditions, teams often perform poorly. Research suggests that culture is an all-or-nothing proposition: Highly homogeneous or heterogeneous teams can be effective, but teams with moderate levels of heterogeneity tend to struggle.[53] In contrast, research on gender diversity in teams seems to imply that it only takes the introduction of one member of the opposite sex to have a significant and positive impact on group processes and outcomes of an otherwise homogeneous group.[54]

Regardless of whether the team members differ on skills, traits, or culture, the critical consideration is their ability to arrive at a shared mental model about each other and the task at hand. Teams with shared mental models enjoy a great deal of coordination with a minimum of communication. Although it might seem that good teams should communicate more often than poor teams, research indicates just the opposite. The mutual understanding embodied in the best teams makes substantial talk unnecessary. Typically, too much communication is a sign of trouble and indicates that the team is struggling with organization and coordination issues.[55]

Sharing mental models yields benefits beyond coordination. First, high levels of mutual understanding create the conditions necessary for supporting and backing up other team members. If one team member knows another's responsibilities and is aware of extenuating circumstances that might prohibit this person from meeting them, he or she may fill in and assist the beleaguered teammate. The mutual understanding that arises via shared mental models also helps the team diagnose problems with a member who, for one reason or another, is not meeting the expectations of the team. This type of mutual understanding among team members provides a system of checks and balances that is especially critical given the interdependence and specialization that characterize teams.[56]

Because team members depend so heavily on one another, one practice that is becoming more widespread is the involvement of team members in personnel selection decisions. This practice reinforces the idea that members must get along with each other and work together to succeed as a team. One needs to be careful with such practices, however, because left to their own devices people may create groups that are homogeneous along all dimensions because they fear the type of conflict or unpredictability that accompanies heterogeneity.[57] The old saying that "opposites attract" has been largely refuted by empirical research, which instead suggests that people, left to their own devices, are attracted mainly to people who are similar to themselves on most dimensions.[58]

KEYS TO TEAM EFFECTIVENESS: MANAGING THE PROCESS

Motivation in Groups

Member motivation is an important factor that affects group productivity and must be managed to minimize process loss and maximize synergy. A major aspect of motivation in team contexts is getting people to sacrifice their own self-interests for the overall good of the collective. We saw this in our opening story with the WHO SARS team, whose leader needed to get labs that used to compete against each other for funding and prestige to put aside their own personal considerations in order to pursue the larger goal of saving lives as quickly as possible.

As is true for research on individuals, studies of group performance have substantiated that setting specific, difficult group goals has a strong positive effect on group productivity. One early study compared members of groups with clear, specific goals and members of groups with vague and ambiguous goals. The members of groups with specific goals were more attracted to their groups' tasks and conformed more to their groups' expectations; these factors enhanced group performance.[59] Specific and difficult goals appear to work especially well in group contexts when they are paired with feedback and incentives.[60]

Research has also begun to highlight the specific processes through which group goals influence performance. In one study in which students participated in a managerial simulation, groups with specific, difficult goals outperformed groups with vague, "do-your-best" goals. The groups with specific and difficult goals surpassed the other groups in planning how to meet those goals.[61] Groups confronted with difficult goals also seem to put forth more effort.[62] Employing challenging temporal deadlines for when the work needs to be completed can also induce increased levels of group effort.[63]

Rewards contingent on specific achievement help to motivate groups. Two fundamentally different types of group rewards exist: cooperative and competitive. **Cooperative group rewards** are distributed *equally* among the members of a group. That is, the group is rewarded *as a group* for its successful performance, and each member receives exactly the same reward.[64] This compensation technique does not recognize individual differences in effort or performance, but rather rewards employees' efforts to coordinate their work activities and to rely on one another. As a result, the cooperative reward system ignores the possibility that some members will make greater contributions to group task performance than others. As discussed in Chapter 8, the inequity caused by this type of reward distribution can demotivate group members who are high performers.

Under the **competitive group rewards** system, group members are rewarded for successful performance *as individuals in a group*. They receive *equitable* rewards that vary based on their individual performance. This system, which relies on the idea that high group performance requires all members to perform at their highest capacity, rewards individuals who accomplish more than their peers. It provides a strong incentive to individual effort, thereby enhancing individual productivity. Unfortunately, it can also pit group members against one another in a struggle for greater personal rewards. In such a case, the cooperation and coordination needed to perform group tasks may never develop, and group performance may suffer. An extreme form of this can be seen in organizations that employ "forced ranking systems" and while many tout the advantages of this type of system for encouraging continuous improvement, as the Ethics and Social Responsibility box shows, others have questioned both the efficacy and ethics of these kinds of ranking systems.

Which of these two approaches is likely to ensure the highest group productivity? The answer depends on the degree of task interdependence.[65] Higher levels of task interdependence require group members to work closely together. For this reason, cooperative rewards, which encourage cooperation and coordination, promote group productivity when paired with high task interdependence. In contrast, lower task interdependence—either complete independence or pooled interdependence—enables the members of a group to work independently. In this case, competitive rewards motivate high personal performance and lead to increased group productivity, as depicted in Figure 9-7.

The nature of the team members' personalities also affects the choice of which structure to employ. Research shows that people who are interpersonally skilled—that

FIGURE 9-7 Effects of Task Interdependence and Type of Reward on Group Productivity

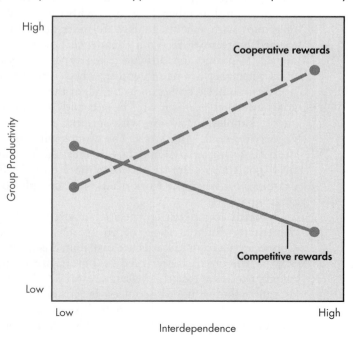

ETHICS AND SOCIAL RESPONSIBILITY

THROWING TEAM MEMBERS A CURVE: THE ETHICS OF FORCE RANKING SYSTEMS

Garrison Keillor has always described the mythical town of Lake Wobegon, Minnesota, as a place where "all the men are handsome, all the women are strong, and all the children are above average." Although that last part was meant to be funny, if one examines the performance evaluation systems in place in many organizations, one might think they are in Lake Wobegon, where all the employees are above average on performance, as well. Many managers who have little in the way of objective evidence regarding performance, and who would just as soon avoid a great deal of interpersonal conflict, respond by rating all their employees high on all aspects of performance. In the face of uniformly positive ratings, organizations struggle to make decisions about raises and promotions, and this creates a culture where the status quo is always seen as "good enough." In order to overcome this tendency, many firms turn to forced ranking systems that require an obligatory rating structure where some set percentage of employees are mandated to fall into "A" (high), "B" (medium), and "C" (low) categories.

There are many different names for such systems (vitality curves, topgrading, bell curve ratings, differentiation cells, rank-and-yank judgments) and an infinite number of ways to construct them. However, at the heart of all forced distribution systems is the notion that a fixed percentage of employees must receive a "C" rating, and be told to either "shape up or ship out" if it happens repeatedly. The manager is not given the option of saying that all the workers are great and should be retained, but instead is given the option of saying what workers should not be retained, knowing full well that some will be let go. As Jack Welch, CEO of GE and a champion of the process, notes, "This is hard stuff. No leader enjoys making the tough decisions. We constantly faced severe resistance from even the best people in the organization. Still, more than any other process, the system creates and sustains a high-performance, high talent culture." Many other organizations have embraced this philosophy, and the evidence suggests that at least 25 percent of Fortune 500 companies have some sort of forced ranking system in place.

Others have questioned the ethics of such systems, however, such as Robert Shoemake, director of the Center for Ethical Business Practices. "I personally think it's horrible. If you don't give people what they need to perform well and expect them to succeed; if you set a measure to which people should perform and don't give them the tools they need to do it, then it's abusive and unethical." Many victims of this procedure agree, noting that there is no evidence that true employee performance levels in all units are distributed via a normal curve or any other mathematical distribution that the organization may rally around. Short of this evidence, this means that the ratings that come out are inaccurate, and that errors are made due to (1) lack of objective evidence for performance, (2) subtle differences between jobs that make some more difficult than others, (3) political pressures directed at keeping popular or well-networked individuals, or (4) bias due to factors such as sex, race, culture, or age.

Moreover, the culture that is created by the extensive use of such systems over time fosters a high degree of competitiveness among employees, especially after the first few cycles, when all the obvious poor performers have been eliminated. After this, former "A" employees start to slip down to the "B" category, and some of the former "B" employees slide into the "C" category. In this kind of culture, there is little motivation for teamwork, and there really is no good reason for one person to help his or her own team members. Instead, there may even be motivation to sabotage or harm the efforts of co-workers so that the bell curve tolls for them. Ethicist Michael Josephson takes this tack and concludes, "My instinct is that it hurts morale, pits employees against each other when you really need to be creating teamwork. What we really ought to have is pressure on managers to make honest evaluations." Indeed, if more managers lived up to their ethical responsibility to make honest and forthright evaluations, there would be no need for arbitrary forced distributions of unknown accuracy.

Sources: M. Boyle, "Performance Reviews: Perilous Curves Ahead," *Fortune*, May 28, 2001, pp. 187–188; A. Meisler, "Dead Man's Curve," *Workforce Management*, July 2003, pp. 44–49; A. Meisler, "It's Tough, but Is It Fair? Ethics of Forced Ranking," *Workforce Management*, July 2003, p. 49.

is, high in extroversion and agreeableness—respond well to cooperative rewards and prefer to work toward group-based bonuses. In contrast, people who are introverted and disagreeable prefer to work alone, and resent group-based compensation plans that link their pay to the accomplishments of others.[66] If one has to assemble a group of introverted and disagreeable members into a single group, research suggests it is better to have them go through a process of simply identifying who the best member is and go with that one person's judgment. On the other hand, if the members are interpersonally skilled it is better to have them go through a process where they try to pool their inputs and arrive at a consensus decision.[67]

Group Cohesiveness

A group's **cohesiveness** reflects the degree to which a group sticks together. In a cohesive group, members feel attracted to one another and to the group as a whole.[68] A variety of factors encourage group cohesiveness:

1. *Shared personal attitudes, values, or interests.* People who share the same attitudes, values, or interests are likely to be attracted to one another.
2. *Agreement on group goals.* Shared group goals encourage members to work together. When members participate in determining their purpose and goals, they get to know and influence one another.
3. *Frequency of interaction.* Frequent interaction and the physical closeness afforded by it encourage members to develop the mutual understanding and intimacy that characterize cohesiveness.
4. *Group size.* Smaller groups are more likely to be cohesive than larger groups, because physical proximity makes it easier for their members to interact.
5. *Group rewards.* Cooperative group rewards that encourage interaction can stimulate cohesiveness, especially when members must perform interdependent tasks.
6. *Favorable evaluation.* Recognition given a group for effective performance can reinforce feelings of pride in group membership and group performance.
7. *External threats.* Threats to a group's well-being that originate from outside the group can strengthen its cohesiveness by providing a common enemy that motivates a unified response. That is, conflict between groups can promote cohesion within groups.
8. *Isolation.* Being cut off from other groups can reinforce members' sense of sharing a common fate, again motivating a unified response.

As the Securing Competitive Advantage box shows, the last two of these factors, external threats and isolation, can be particularly strong factors that bind otherwise incompatible people together into a tight cohesive unit. Group cohesiveness is a potential source of competitive advantage because cohesive groups need to spend less energy on group maintenance activities, and can instead focus all their effort on alternative activities. Cohesiveness is not always an unmixed blessing, however.

First, cohesiveness does affect the degree to which the members of a group *agree* on productivity norms, but it does not ensure that the group will adopt *high* productivity norms.[69] If a highly cohesive group has adopted norms favoring high productivity, its productivity will be high, because everyone agrees that working productively is the right thing to do (see the upper-right cell in Figure 9-8). Such groups also tend to be persistent and are more likely to struggle through barriers to goal accomplishment.[70] In contrast, the productivity of highly cohesive groups adopting norms that favor low productivity tends to be quite low, because everyone agrees that working productively is *not* the objective (see the lower-right cell in Figure 9-8).

Second, cohesiveness can also increase the probability that the group will come to premature consensus when making difficult decisions, and this has sometimes

SECURING COMPETITIVE ADVANTAGE

MAINTAINING GROUP COHESIVENESS: LESSONS FROM AL-QAEDA

The stereotype one conjures up when thinking of al-Qaeda is a group of cohesive members, united by religion and politics. In reality, however, documents and computer files that became available in 2002, after the war in Afghanistan, are beginning to make it clear that this is instead a fractious collective of individuals who struggled at times to keep it all together. The external events and internal moves that went into keeping this collective together before and after the war illuminate many of the determinants of group cohesiveness—especially the need to invoke a common enemy and a sense of isolation.

For example, the first crisis within this group took place in 1998 when the Saudi government, infuriated by Osama bin Laden's criticism of their country, asked Muhammad Omar, the religious leader of the Taliban government, to hand over the ex-Saudi dissident. Omar was ready to do this because the relationship between him and bin Laden had always been a resentful one, full of anger, disappointment, and petty slights directed both ways. Omar, a quiet town cleric, always had felt that bin Laden was an arrogant showman, avidly seeking publicity and issuing religious fatwas against foreign powers for which he had no legitimate authority. In his words, bin Laden had "caught the disease of TV screens, flashes and applause." In turn, bin Laden felt that Omar was too poorly educated to run the country, noting to a colleague that Omar "did not have the ability to grasp contemporary reality, politics and management." Going further, he even questioned the Mullah's religious qualifications, suggesting that because he could not read Arabic, he could not truly appreciate the Qur'an and could relate to Islam only in an "emotional" way. This further infuriated Omar, who started working with Islamic scholars to formulate a justification for expelling bin Laden from the country.

All of this changed, however, when President Clinton, trying to deflect much of the attention that was focused on the Monica Lewinsky affair, launched seventy-nine cruise missiles into Afghanistan and Sudan in alleged retribution for the bombing of the U.S. embassies in East Africa. This external threat provided a common enemy that brought the two sides together, and bin Laden learned quickly that provoking the United States to strike at Islamic targets in sovereign Arab countries was the perfect way to hold together the otherwise mixed set of al-Qaeda's religious and political subgroups. It was also at this point that bin Laden started his use of issuing videotapes; in the first one, he declared that Americans were "too cowardly to meet the young people of Islam face-to-face" and flattered Mullah Omar as the "new caliph" who would lead a pure Islamic state that would encompass all of central Asia. This message was a magnet that attracted thousands of disenchanted and disenfranchised young Muslims to the al-Qaeda cause.

Perhaps due to issues related to groupthink, however, bin Laden and his associates severely misjudged reaction to the 9/11 attacks. In a letter to Omar, bin Laden predicted that "even if the Americans did strike, they would quickly retreat, just like the Soviet Red Army in the 1980s." Having this set up as the expectation, bin Laden's followers were shocked by the speed and lethality of the American response, which killed many al-Qaeda members and scattered the rest. In addition to this, bin Laden miscalculated the Arab reaction to the 9/11 attacks, in that many Arabs were appalled by what they considered the indiscriminant mass murder of innocent civilians—some of whom were Muslims.

The collective vision of a united Islamic state that held al-Qaeda together was crushed, and negative Muslim reaction to the 9/11 murders made it difficult to hold and attract new members. In order to overcome this second crisis, bin Laden, having already established one common enemy, invoked a new one—one he knew Arabs would find hard to resist: Israel. Historically, bin Laden's sole concern was what he considered to be infidels living in Saudi Arabia, the home of Islam. Except for one missive that claimed that Yasser Arafat was a traitor, one can find no references to the Palestinian–Israeli conflict in bin Laden's tapes or writings prior to the war in Afghanistan. However, after the war, bin Laden continually claimed that the purpose of al-Qaeda was to champion the Palestinian cause, and many Arab Muslims, incensed by what they perceived as Israel's harsh treatment of the Palestinians, again rallied to al-Qaeda and its leader. These new members brought innovative tactics and strategies to the terrorist organization, which scored new successes, thus showing the power of invoking a common external enemy to maintain internal group cohesiveness.

Sources: A. Cullison and A. Higgens, "A Once-Stormy Terror Alliance Was Solidified by Cruise Missiles," *Wall Street Journal Online*, August 2, 2002, pp. 1–5; A. Cullison and A. Higgens, "One Acolyte of Many Vows to Die for al Qaeda," *Wall Street Journal Online*, December, 30, 2002, pp. 1–5; L. Lopez and J. McBeth, "How Police Turned the Bali Blast into a Win in War on Terrorism," *Wall Street Journal Online*, July 2, 2003, pp. 1–4.

FIGURE 9-8 How Cohesiveness and Productivity Norms Affect Group Productivity

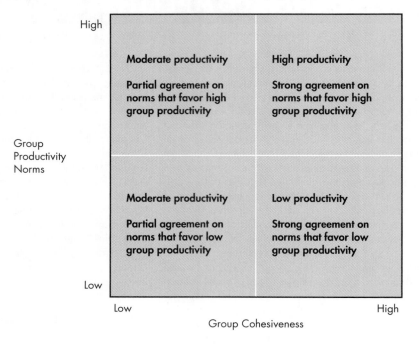

been referred to as "groupthink."[71] That is, rather than argue and hash out the positive and negative features of various alternatives, highly cohesive groups sometimes agree too quickly on the first idea that is offered up. This is especially the case if the group is isolated from outside sources of influence and the leader is the person who came up with the first idea. Dissenting opinions are either directly squelched or not shared with the team by members who self-censor their own misgivings. This flawed and incomplete process often leads to disastrous outcomes that outsiders, in the light of hindsight bias, severely criticize.

Group Conflict

Groups that lack cohesiveness often experience a great deal of within-team conflict. Just as cohesiveness is not always an unmixed blessing when it comes to group performance, so too conflict is not always undesirable. Groups may experience two types of conflict: cognitive and mixed motive.

In **cognitive conflict,** all group members agree on the goals sought, but differ in their views on how those goals can be best met. With this type of conflict, members can still cooperate and do not necessarily compete.[72] This type of conflict focuses on task procedures rather than on the people involved.[73]

Cognitive conflict within groups can lead to effective debate, and it often generates well-thought-out, highly effective decisions.[74] Some groups try to build in this type of conflict structurally by creating the role of "devil's advocate," that is, a team member whose primary job is to question and critique the team's ideas. Although this kind of "contrived dissent" is better than nothing when it comes to preventing premature consensus, it is not nearly as potent as genuine dissent that comes from team members who truly believe the group is heading down the wrong track.[75]

Alternatively, groups can experience **mixed motive conflict.** In these situations, group members may not agree on the goals being sought, and this type of conflict can prove difficult to overcome. Because mixed motive conflict often hinges on differences in values, and given the centrality of values to people, this kind of conflict can quickly become personal and emotional. Unlike in cognitive conflict, where the best ideas for approaching the problem may win out in a group discussion, such discussions rarely persuade people to change their values. Rather, a formal leader may have to make a unilateral decision or create some type of political compromise or voting procedure to overcome the inability to reach group consensus. We will have more to say about this type of conflict and ways to manage it in Chapter 10 (on leadership) and Chapter 11 (power, politics, and conflict). For now, suffice it to say that it is critical to distinguish between cognitive conflict, which can be beneficial to groups, and mixed motive conflict, which is almost always destructive.

SUMMARY

Groups in organizations are formed on the basis of *functional grouping*, which favors efficiency, or *work flow grouping*, which enhances flexibility. Informal characteristics emerge during the process of *group development* as groups pass through the four stages of *initiation, differentiation, integration,* and *maturity*.

Due to *process loss*, groups are usually less productive than individuals working alone. Process loss can be traced to the effects of production blocking, group maintenance activities, and social loafing. Due to *group synergy*, groups can sometimes be more productive than individuals working alone; this gain can be traced to social facilitation, the need for affiliation, and within-group competition.

Teams are a special type of group characterized by high levels of interdependence, work flow grouping, and differentiated knowledge, skills, and abilities possessed by team members. Because teams are not always more effective than individuals working alone, managers need to pay particular attention to the group's *task and communication structure, size and composition, goals and incentives,* and *cohesiveness and conflict*.

REVIEW QUESTIONS

1. What are the three criteria of group effectiveness? Why is group effectiveness assessed in terms of all three criteria instead of being measured solely by group productivity?

2. Why is work flow grouping more flexible than functional grouping? If your company sold pencils, pens, and notebook paper, which type of grouping would provide the greatest benefit? Why?

3. What is process loss? How do production blocking and social loafing contribute to its presence? How does a group's size affect its productivity? What factors explain this relationship?

4. What influence do group goals have on member motivation? What effects do group rewards have on motivation? What implications do your answers have for managers who must motivate individuals to perform productively in groups?

5. Explain why the following statement is not necessarily correct: "Highly cohesive groups are more productive than groups that are not cohesive." What specific things might you do as a manager to ensure that high cohesion actually leads to high productivity?

6. Explain why centralized communication structures enhance the productivity of groups performing simple tasks but depress the performance of groups performing complex jobs. What sort of structure would you recommend for a group of accountants who are auditing the books of a large manufacturing firm? Why?

7. In the United States, television ratings make it clear that many more people are interested in watching professional football games than major league baseball games. One major exception to this rule, however, involves the all-star games of each sport—baseball's all-star game is much more popular than football's all-star game (which is not televised by any of the three major networks). Most people believe that baseball's all-star game is exciting and filled with great plays, whereas football's all-star game is dull and filled with major miscues. Although no one could question the skills of individual players in either of these all-star games, why might one sport surpass the other in terms of generating effective all-star teams?

LEARNING THROUGH EXPERIENCE

DIAGNOSTIC QUESTIONS 9-1

Managing Group Effectiveness and Productivity

Managing group effectiveness in general, and group and team productivity in particular, requires careful analysis. The following questions can help guide this analysis.

1. Was the group formed using functional grouping or work flow grouping? Does its formation seem to match its purpose in the organization? Does the group's formation seem to match the mission and purpose of the organization as a whole?

2. In what stage of development is the group? Can ineffectiveness, such as poor productivity or member dissatisfaction, be traced to its current level of development?

3. Do you see evidence that the group suffers from serious process loss? Is production blocking a problem? Are maintenance activities overwhelming productive resources? Is social loafing a problem?

4. Can group size be manipulated to solve productivity problems? If so, does available evidence suggest that this manipulation will enhance productivity?

5. Can you trace productivity problems to poor group member motivation? Does the group have specific and difficult individual *and* group performance goals? Are performance-contingent rewards used? Does the type of reward match the level of task interdependence?

6. Is the group cohesive? If so, do group norms support productive activities?

7. Can the group's communication structure cope with the information required to perform its task?

8. Can this group be considered a team? If so, does it have the resources necessary to accomplish its mission?

9. Does each team member have the necessary specialized skills and abilities? Do the specialists have a shared mental model of how they should coordinate their activities?

10. Are team members committed to team goals, or is each team member driven by his or her own self-interest?

EXERCISE 9-1 **Recycler, Inc.: A Nominal Group Exercise**

John Wagner, Michigan State University

Of the various roles filled by managers, decision-making roles are among the most important. Such roles may require managers to make entrepreneurial decisions about how to improve the productivity of a group or an organization, how to adapt to changing business conditions, or how to allocate resources. Decision-making roles may also demand that managers act as negotiators, seeking to strike bargains that will sustain the survival of their group or organization.

Sometimes managers are able to fulfill decision-making roles by working alone. At other times, they find it necessary to involve others in decision-making processes. For instance, a manager might involve groups of subordinates in making decisions about their group's work, or groups of other managers in making decisions about company policies. Making decisions in groups can produce benefits, but it can also complicate decision-making processes. In this exercise, you will learn about some of these benefits and complications as you work in a group to reach a management decision.

Step One: Pre-Class Preparation

To prepare for class, read the entire exercise and make sure you understand the decision- making procedure that will be used in your group. Review the Recyclers, Inc., case that appears below and think about how to state the company's problem most simply. Write your problem statement here:_____

_____.

Step Two: Forming Nominal Groups

The class should divide into groups of four to six members each. If you formed permanent groups in a prior session, you should reassemble in those groups. Each group should begin by discussing the problem statements identified by its members, arriving at a single statement with which everyone agrees. Next, each group should appoint a spokesperson to lead the decision-making process within the group and to report back to the class at the conclusion of the activities.

Recyclers, Inc.

> For five years you have owned and operated Recyclers, Inc., a small recycling facility located in the suburbs of a large metropolitan area. Your company has contracted with several nearby communities to provide residents with recycling services. Each residence has received a plastic container that can hold about three cubic feet of material as well as printed instructions describing how to select and prepare material for recycling.
>
> Companies like Recyclers, Inc., make money by charging residents (or communities) for picking up materials and by selling these materials to end-use companies that use them as raw materials in subsequent manufacturing processes. Recyclers, Inc., has been especially effective in recruiting residents and communities to provide materials for pickup. Your company has failed to enlist enough end-use companies to absorb the materials it is collecting, however, and competition from other recyclers makes it unlikely that you will be able to resolve this problem in the near term by recruiting additional manufacturers. Thus, if you want to continue operating, you may need to develop a new business of your own that will convert recycled materials into finished products that can be sold in wholesale or retail markets.
>
> An audit of your facility has shown that most of the materials processed by your company are paper goods (newspapers, magazines, office refuse) and plastic (mainly soda bottles and milk jugs). You are having trouble disposing of both kinds of materials. You also collect aluminum (soda bottles) and steel (food cans), but you can sell metal materials without difficulty. You already have enough employees to expand operations, and your company can spend about $250,000 to set up one or more new businesses. What should you do?

Step Three: Idea Generation

Working alone, each member of your group should generate as many solutions as possible for the problem statement identified by your group. As you work alone, you should emphasize the *quantity* of ideas you generate and ignore concerns you might have about the *quality* of these ideas. An idea that might seem silly at first could potentially lead to the discovery of another idea that proves to be the best one identified by your group. Write your ideas down, but do not show them to other group members during this step.

Step Four: Group Discussion

The spokesperson should begin group discussion by asking each member to state one of his or her ideas. As ideas are presented, the spokesperson should write them on a piece of paper visible to all group members. The process should continue, circling the group, until all members have had the opportunity to report all of their ideas.

Next, the spokesperson should ask whether any members can think of additional ideas, triggered by the ones already presented. These ideas should be added to the master list. During this step, members can ask each other questions for clarification, to ensure that everyone understands all ideas. Criticism is not allowed, and disagreements should not be voiced. As in Step Three, the focus is on producing the largest *quantity* of ideas without regard for their *quality*.

After the group feels satisfied with the number of ideas generated, the spokesperson should lead an "idea structuring" discussion in which members look for similarities and differences among the group's ideas to identify categories into which the ideas can be sorted. During this discussion, three to five categories will usually emerge that can accommodate most of the group's ideas. These categories help synthesize and summarize the group's thinking at this point in the decision-making process. If members suggest additional ideas at this point, add them to the group's list.

Step Five: Idea Ranking

Working as individuals, group members should identify the five ideas they like best, and rank these ideas from 1 (the least favored idea of the five) to 5 (the most preferred idea of the five). Favored ideas and rankings should be written down privately.

Step Six: Selection of the Preferred Alternative

The group should reconvene, and each member should report his or her rankings. The spokesperson should record all rankings on the list of ideas generated by the group in Step Four. After all members have reported their rankings, the spokesperson should determine which idea has received the greatest support by adding together the number of points received by each idea. The idea with the greatest total number of points is the one designated as the group's preferred solution to the problem stated in Step Two.

Step Seven: Class Discussion

The class should reconvene, and each group's spokesperson should make a short presentation describing the problem statement and most preferred solution identified by the group. If time permits, spokespeople should report four to five other ideas that received strong support. After all spokespeople have completed their reports, the class should look for similarities and differences among the problems and solutions identified by the various groups. Discussing the following questions may prove help-ful during this process:

1. Did all of the groups identify the same problem? If so, how do you explain this out-come? If not, what differences are apparent among the various problems? What might explain these differences?

2. What variations do you see in the solutions identified by the groups? How well are these variations explained by differences in the problem statements? What other factors might explain these differences?

3. Comparing the nominal group decision-making technique used in this exercise with the way groups normally make decisions (or, if applicable, with the way your group has made decisions during prior exercises), which approach seems more able to produce higher-quality decisions? Which appears better at stimulating cohesion and agreement among group members?

Conclusion

Decision making is an important activity performed by every manager, and manag-ing groups engaged in decision making is a challenge with which all managers must deal. The nominal group technique introduced in this exercise can prove especially helpful if the group must generate a large number of alternatives before selecting a final choice. The benefits of this technique are gained by controlling the amount of interaction that occurs among group members during decision making. Offsetting this benefit are costs in the form of reduced cohesion among group members or dis-agreements about the final choice. With this trade-off in mind, the nominal group technique should be considered whenever groups are used to make decisions.

CHAPTER 10

The Integrated Leadership Model

Universal Approaches to Leadership
Leader Traits
Leader Decision-Making Styles
Leader Behaviors
Transformational Leadership
Leader Irrelevance

Characteristics of Followers and Situations
The Leadership Motivation Pattern
Vertical Dyad Linkage
Life-Cycle Model
Substitutes for Leadership

Comprehensive Theories of Leadership
Fiedler's Contingency Theory
Vroom–Yetton Decision Tree Model
Path–Goal Theory

The Integrated Leadership Model Revisited
Summary
Review Questions

Learning Through Experience
Diagnostic Questions 10-1: Applying the Integrated Leadership Model in
    Performing Diagnostic Analyses
Exercise 10-1: Choosing a Leadership Style: Sharing Influence

Leadership of Groups and Organizations

For years, Home Depot was the undisputed leader in the growing home improvement industry, renowned for its customer service. However, this leadership position has recently been challenged by its archrival, Lowe's. In contrast to Home Depot, Lowe's competes on cost, and its disciplined operations have allowed it to chip away at much of Home Depot's traditional base. In addition, Lowe's has shown a willingness to expand the market by catering to nontraditional hardware customers—especially women—whereas Home Depot has on more than one occasion faced discrimination charges from female employees who have been denied jobs on the sales floor. Needing to turn this situation around, Home Depot looked for new leadership, and their search took them to a place where many others before them have gone—General Electric.[1]

Robert Nardelli was one of the top leaders at General Electric (GE), overseeing all the complex operations at the large GE Power Systems unit. When Home Depot brought in the ex-GE executive as its new leader, it was hailed by many as a coup. Unfortunately, like many of his other GE alumni, Nardelli has found it difficult to replicate the success he experienced at GE in his new venue. No two organizations are exactly alike, and in this case, Nardelli was trying to make the transition from a manufacturing operation to a retail unit. In Nardelli's first two years as CEO, Lowe's beat Home Depot in sales every quarter and shareholders saw the stock price drop by 50 percent in his short tenure. Recently, one analyst went so far as to say, "I think there are people on Wall Street who are questioning his ability to make the change and run a retail organization."[2]

Nardelli's moves to increase the efficiency of the ever-expanding Home Depot empire came straight from the GE playbook, and on paper, the plays looked great. For example, he centralized purchasing operations that used to take place at nine different regional centers into one single location in Atlanta. This allowed the firm to increase its clout at the negotiating table and coordinate nationwide buys with nationwide store displays. He lowered labor costs by hiring more part-time workers and limited merit raises that were once locally administered, but which he felt were handed out too frequently to mediocre performers. In order to further promote centralized control, Nardelli instituted new "manufacturing-like" processes aimed at reducing inventory, along with new monitoring systems and measures such as "inventory velocity." The "velocity" metric was totally foreign to the old store managers, and it generally restricted the number of different products that they could place on the shelf.

However, what worked at GE did not seem to work in this new context. Whereas GE employees were naturally competitive and were attracted to the idea of climbing its traditional hierarchical structure, Home Depot employees were more like craftspeople. They were attracted to working at Home Depot because of the freedom they were given. One of Home Depot's founders noted, "We hire people who couldn't work for anybody else, who might otherwise be well suited to being self-employed or running their own shop." These store managers bristled at the new leadership, and one longtime employee observed, "After Mr. Nardelli arrived, things weren't presented to you, they were told to you." Indeed, it soon became clear that many differences between purchasing decisions at the old regional centers reflected important geographic and cultural differences that the local managers understood better than the people in Atlanta.

In addition, GE's turbine customers were large in size, but small in number, and most of them had similar needs and preferences. However, Home Depot's customers were a highly variable group of idiosyncratic, small-time buyers. The well-skilled professional craftspeople that formerly came to the store because of its wide inventory reacted negatively to the reduced choices they encountered. In contrast, the weekend amateurs who came to the store because of the advice they could get found that the part-time employees often knew less than they did about home improvement.

Nardelli has admitted that he went overboard on the number of part-time employees and is developing new software that will make it easier for regional store managers to provide input on local needs so that purchasing decisions can be tailored more specifically. This kind of adaptability is perhaps the best sign that Home Depot will get back on the right track. In the words of Bernie Marcus, Home Depot co-founder, "this guy has made some errors, but when he makes an error, he backs off of it, and he isn't ashamed to say, 'I made a mistake,' and he learns from it."[3]

As noted in Chapter 8, few important tasks or goals can be accomplished by one person working alone. Indeed, this fact largely explains why so many organizations exist in our society. Nevertheless, few groups or organizations can accomplish much without the help of a single individual acting as a leader. Leadership is the force that energizes and directs groups. Many have suggested that the pool of available leaders is smaller today than it has ever been.[4] Nearly 20 percent of the CEOs at Fortune 500 companies are two years or less from retirement, and the available pool of executives who might replace these leaders is not growing nearly fast enough.[5]

Given the centrality of leadership to the behavior of people in groups and to organizational achievement, it is important that we understand how leaders emerge and what qualities make them effective. This chapter focuses on this topic, showing how leadership is a complex function involving a leader, followers, and situations. All too often, people who want to learn about leadership focus too much on the leader and not enough on the followers and the situation. As we can see from the Robert Nardelli example that opened this chapter, however, the same person who was successful in one organization may struggle to lead in a different organization because the nature of the followers or situation is different.

Strategies that worked at GE did not work at Home Depot, and other GE executives have had to learn the same lesson when they took their act on the road. For example, Gary Wendt, former head of GE's Capital, took over as CEO of Conseco in June 2000, but was forced to resign in September 2002 after playing a large role in driving the company into bankruptcy.[6] W. James McNearney, an eighteen-year veteran at GE, became the first outsider to run 3M Corporation in its 100-year history, and he too has struggled to make the various processes he learned at GE work in his new venue. 3M employees were accustomed to a decentralized organization where individual departments had free rein to pursue and commercialize technological advancements. These departments and their unit heads reacted negatively to McNearney's more top-down approach, and he soon learned the key roles of followers, noting that "you can't order change; after all, there's only one of me and 75,000 of them."[7]

Because of its centrality to organizational effectiveness, you should not be surprised to learn that a large number of theories have been proposed about leadership. Trying to explain them all might leave you more confused about the topic than when you started. Conversely, ignoring important approaches so as to simplify our discussion might give you a false impression about the real subtlety and complexity of the leadership process. If leadership were a simple process, everyone would be a great leader—which is hardly the case. In fact, in the wake of the recent business scandals involving many CEOs, workers have lamented the lack of leadership in much of corporate America. A survey taken in September 2002 indicated that 83 percent of those questioned felt there was a leadership vacuum in their organization.[8] Given this state of affairs, superior leadership processes serve as another area where one firm can gain competitive advantage over another.

To facilitate the process of learning about the many different theories of leadership, this chapter begins by presenting a single conceptual framework, *the integrated leadership model*, that encompasses all of the other theories. The model reflects our emphasis on the three elements that go into leadership: *the leader; the followers and the situation;* and the three factors that characterize the leader, that is, his or her *traits, behaviors and decision-making styles.* Our general approach to leadership will assert that no one trait, behavior, or decision-making style is always going to result in leadership success, but instead, certain followers or situations require one set of traits, behaviors, and styles, whereas other followers or situations may demand an alternative set of traits, behaviors, and styles. With this framework in place, we then examine individual theories, fitting them into a single overall scheme. This model is comprehensive in reflecting the many ingredients that contribute to effective leadership, but concise in classifying these ingredients and showing how they can be applied in different organizational situations.

THE INTEGRATED LEADERSHIP MODEL

Most people have a difficult time expressing exactly what the word *leadership* means. Indeed, even experts offer conflicting definitions of this term. Nevertheless, when asked to name strong leaders throughout history, people respond in a remarkably consistent way. Table 10-1 lists a number of people who are almost always cited as strong leaders. This list should give you an idea of how difficult it is to develop a definition of leadership that is specific enough to be useful, yet broad enough to include people who differ so greatly from one another. What traits do the people in the table share in common?

One characteristic shared by the people listed in Table 10-1 is their *ability to influence others.* The use of influence certainly should be paramount in any definition of leadership. Influence is not the only piece of the leadership puzzle, however. For example, would you consider an armed robber who enters a subway train and induces passengers to hand over their personal belongings to be a leader? Most people would recognize this person's influence, but would not consider this act one of leadership. Instead, a leader's influence must to some degree be *sanctioned by followers*. In some situations, a person may be compelled to lead; in other cases, a leader may be merely tolerated for a short time. Whatever the circumstances, the idea that followers voluntarily surrender control over their own behavior to someone else forms an integral part of any definition of leadership.

Finally, a complete definition of leadership must describe the context in which leadership occurs and the symbolism captured in the leader. Leadership occurs in *goal-oriented* group contexts. This statement does not mean that moving the group toward its goal is a leader's only function. Leaders also serve an important *symbolic* function for both group members and outsiders. Thus, when Home Depot went outside of its organization to hire its new leader, it was sending a symbolic message to the rest of the organization that there was going to be a change in goals, and the hope was that by hiring a famous ex-GE executive, Home Depot employees would recognize and sanction the influence this new leader was bringing to the firm.

This type of symbolism is important, because every employee cannot possibly understand all that goes on in the organization. As noted in Chapter 4, when the complexity of a stimulus exceeds a person's cognitive capacity, the individual attempts to simplify the stimulus. In the organizational context, the leader provides the means for much of this simplification. The leader offers a logically compelling and emotionally satisfying focal point for people who are trying to understand the causes and consequences of organized activity. Focusing on the leader reduces organizational complexities to simple terms that people can more readily understand and communicate.[9] As the Ethics and Social Responsibility box shows, this simplifying aspect of leadership can often be dysfunctional, and therefore we need to resist the temptation to need to resort to such unsophisticated descriptions of the leadership process.

With these points in mind, we will define **leadership** as the use of noncoercive and symbolic influence to direct and coordinate the activities of the members of an organized group toward the accomplishment of group objectives.[10] In defining leadership, it is important to distinguish between leaders and managers. Recall from Mintzberg's overview of managerial roles (see Chapter 2) that the role of leader is just one of ten roles commonly occupied by managers. Leadership, according to Mintzberg,

TABLE 10-1 Conventional Examples of Strong Leaders		
	Adolf Hitler	Martin Luther King, Jr.
	Mahatma Gandhi	Napoleon Bonaparte
	Mao Tse-Tung	Moses
	Franklin D. Roosevelt	Abraham Lincoln
	Winston Churchill	Golda Meir
	John F. Kennedy	Mikhail Gorbachev

ETHICS AND SOCIAL RESPONSIBILITY

THE DARK SIDE OF CHARISMATIC LEADERSHIP

Charismatic leaders influence others by providing a vision of the future that compels followers to transcend or sacrifice their own self-interests for the sake of collective goals. The word *charisma* was derived from the religious term *charisms*, which, according to biblical scriptures, meant "gifts of the Holy Spirit." Prior to the 1980s it was not a term that was commonly attributed to business leaders, who instead reigned in a world driven by cold, rational economic models, objective financial performance metrics, and strategies that had to be sold based on a well-reasoned logic to a skeptical set of professional investment bankers. CEOs were "organization men" who slowly and quietly climbed the hierarchical ladder, and most were unheralded and largely unheard of. However, much of that changed in the 1980s.

During the long economic recession that occurred during that period, insulated and inflexible corporate insiders were viewed as a large part of the problem, and increasingly boards of directors looked for outsiders to come in and overhaul the systems that were in place. Also at this time, ordinary American citizens were increasingly holding stock, and this rise of "populist capitalism" created a subtle shift in the language used to describe organizational requirements. Instead of traditional financial and economic indicators, the business press began to rely on more accessible, religious-like, spiritual terms such as "visions," "missions," "values," and "messiahs." The complexity associated with the performance determinants of large organizations was increasingly boiled down to the personality of various "star-CEOs" who were rare and took on celebrity status. Indeed, whereas only 7 percent of CEOs were outside hires in the period between 1980 and 1982, in 2000–2002 50 percent of CEOs were external hires, and one of the most important assets these new hires were seen bringing to their new organization was their charisma.

Unfortunately, as author Rakesh Khurana notes, "'charismatic authority' has always been the worst kind of authority," and the rush to assign all the credit or blame to a single leader, although perhaps satisfying some primitive urge, has a number of unfortunate side effects in business contexts. First, rather than basing arguments on logical analysis, past historical trends, or critical discussions, the cult of personality approach to business leadership overly simplifies and distorts the process. Thus, rather than facing the large myriad of real and difficult problems that face the firm, the board of directors can instead just "fire the manager" and act as if they have discharged their responsibility. Indeed, today, controlling for firm performance, CEOs are three times more likely to be fired than they were in the 1980s, and much of this is unwarranted given the CEO's role in most cases.

A second problem with emphasis on charisma is that it creates a perceived shortage of talent for CEOs. Boards of directors, after firing the old CEO, need to find a new one and they face a dilemma. On the one hand, they need to find a charismatic figure who will radically change the organization; however, given the elusive, hard-to-define nature of charisma, they are often uncertain regarding who has it and who doesn't. In order to play it safe and not be second-guessed, boards often turn to well-recognized figures who have been wildly successful in the past, but who are few and far between. This creates a severe labor shortage and drives up the price they have to pay for executive talent. This may explain why the salaries of the top ten CEOs has risen 4,300 percent since 1980.

Finally, charismatic leaders, through either their own direct influence or due to the nature of those who are attracted toward them, tend to be surrounded by compliant "yes people." The individuals follow not because they have been convinced by a set of rational arguments about what is best or what is right, but instead by the blind belief that simply doing what they are told by their near supernatural leader will lead to the outcomes they desire. They will often dispense with their own set of moral guidelines, and hence are much more likely to engage in unethical behaviors than those who are more critically and skeptically examining the words and acts of less charismatic leaders. Indeed, leaders who recognize their own limits and liabilities are much more likely to build systems that can sustain success long after they are gone, and as James Collins has noted, when one examines the top CEOs evaluated by this benchmark, it is clear that "much depended on them, but was never *about* them."

Sources: R. Khurana, "Good Charisma, Bad Business," *New York Times,* September 13, 2002, p. D1; J. Useem, "Kill Your Career with Charisma," *Fortune,* September 16, 2002, p. 40; J. Sonnenfeld & R. Khurana, "Fishing for CEOs in Your Own Backyard," *Wall Street Journal,* July 3, 2002, p. B2; R. Khurana, "The Curse of the Superstar CEO," *Harvard Business Review,* September 2002, pp. 21–29; C. Grossman, "In the Name of God," *USA Today,* July 17, 2003, pp. 1–2; J. Collins, "The Ten Greatest CEOs of All Time," *Fortune,* July 21, 2003, pp. 54–68.

FIGURE 10-1 The Integrated Model of Leadership

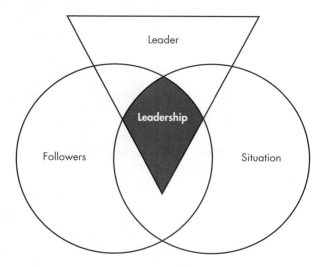

deals explicitly with guiding and motivating employees.[11] From this point of view, leadership is merely one of many managerial tasks.

Edward Hollander has suggested that the leadership process is best understood as the occurrence of mutually satisfying interactions among leaders and followers within a particular situational context.[12] As Figure 10-1 indicates, the *locus of leadership* appears where these three forces—*leaders, followers,* and *situations*—come together. In Hollander's view, we can understand leadership only by gaining an appreciation of the important characteristics of these three forces and the ways in which they interact.

To better appreciate the influence of followers on leadership, return to Table 10-1 and ask yourself the following questions. Could a person with Hitler's totalitarian characteristics rise to power in the United States following the Vietnam War, where opposing almost any government act was virtually a national pastime? Could Martin Luther King, Jr.'s peaceful, patient approach to civil rights have worked for central European Muslims in their recent opposition to the Serbians, who seemed to seek nothing less than the extermination of the Muslims? Can anyone establish a position of leadership with a group of intellectuals who reject the very idea that they need to be led?[13]

Turning to the characteristics of the situation, would Mahatma Gandhi's program of civil disobedience have been successful if he had been opposing the Nazis instead of the British? Could Saddam Hussein have remained in power in Iraq if that country had been a constitutional democracy? These questions underline the complex nature of leadership and the contribution of the situation in making a leader successful.

UNIVERSAL APPROACHES TO LEADERSHIP

Not all theories about leadership emphasize the three-dimensional character of the leadership process as proposed by Hollander. The earliest probes into the nature of leadership focused almost exclusively on leader characteristics (rather than on followers or situations). These *universal theories* emphasized the traits and abilities, typical behaviors, and decision-making styles that made leaders different from nonleaders.

Leader Traits

The earliest approaches to leadership held that leaders were born, not made. In 1869, Sir Francis Galton argued that the traits of great leaders were inherited. Studies of the physical characteristics of leaders have yielded weak but consistent relationships between a person's *energy level* and the ability to rise to positions of leadership.[14] Large-scale research projects involving hundreds of leaders and thousands of followers suggest that the perceived amount of time and energy that the leader devotes to the job is a major determinant of follower ratings of leader effectiveness.[15] Certainly, anecdotal reports support the notion that many leaders simply work harder than average individuals. Bill Gates, founder and CEO of Microsoft, is famous for working 80 to 90 hours per week.[16] Similar workweeks have been reported for CEOs of many other companies.

Weaker and less consistent results have been found in examining leader characteristics such as height or gender (see the Cutting-Edge Research box). Oddly, we tend to think of leaders as being tall people, even though many are not. Consider the leaders listed in Table 10-1. No more than half could have been considered tall or physically imposing people. Research on mental abilities has produced few substantial predictors of leadership quality and effectiveness, although some findings have been reported consistently. *General cognitive ability* seems to be one of the best overall predictors of leadership ability.[17] Specific *technical skills* and *knowledge about a group's task* also show modest relationships with success in leadership.[18]

In terms of personality traits, the evidence suggests that there are weak but consistent relationships between four of the five characteristics identified by the Five-Factor Model (see Chapter 3), suggesting that leaders are generally extroverted, conscientious, emotionally stable, and open to experience.[19] Agreeableness is the one trait that is not associated with leadership, because, as you may suspect, it is more important in describing followers. In general, however, as we will see, the effects of these traits tend to depend on characteristics of the situation or the followers.[20]

The weak magnitude and contingent nature of the relationships between leadership and the personal traits of leaders ultimately prompted researchers to explore other approaches to understanding this important concept.

Leader Decision-Making Styles

Whereas the research discussed previously dealt with leader traits, other early research in the area of leadership focused more specifically on how leaders make decisions and how these styles affect subordinates' rates of productivity and general satisfaction. Research in this tradition has examined three decision-making styles: authoritarian, democratic, and laissez-faire. The **authoritarian leader** makes virtually all decisions by himself or herself. The **democratic leader** works with the group to help members come to their own decisions. The **laissez-faire leader** leaves the group alone to do whatever it wants.

Results of studies on leader decision styles suggest that most groups prefer a democratic leader. Members of groups led by authoritarian leaders tend to be either extremely submissive or extremely aggressive in interacting with one another. They are also the most likely to quit the organization. Authoritarian groups are highly productive, but only when members are closely supervised. When left alone, these groups tend to stop working. At the time of their publication, these results were considered interesting and provocative.[21] As with the leader trait, however, the studies revealed only modest correlations between leader style and follower behavior. Subsequent research has indicated that democratic and participative leadership is not always the

CUTTING-EDGE RESEARCH

HE LED, SHE LED: THE IMPACT OF GENDER ON LEADERSHIP STYLE

Ask anyone you meet if men and women have different leadership styles, and you are bound to get an opinion—often a very emotional one. Women have broken into middle management ranks in droves over the last twenty years, and now occupy close to half (46 percent) of these jobs. So at this point, most people have now had some limited experience working for both male and female leaders, and have no reservations pronouncing their verdicts based on their encounters. Moreover, although few women have broken into the very top spots of large companies (only 1 percent of the CEOs of the Fortune 500 companies are women), the exploits of those who have accomplished this feat have been extremely well publicized. Many women are routinely featured in business magazines, and some, like Carly Fiorina, CEO at Hewlett-Packard (HP), tend to contradict widely held stereotypes. For example, although the stereotype might be that a female CEO is more nurturing, consensus-oriented, and pro work-life balance, none of these characteristics are descriptive of Fiorina. She has laid off more than 16,000 employees, has ditched HP's participative culture, and routinely demands that employees put in sixty-hour work weeks.

Some have suggested that female leaders face a double standard, and that due to discrimination they have to perform much better than male leaders to obtain and hold the same position of authority. In contrast, others have suggested that women are the beneficiaries of affirmative action, and this has boosted their status more than is warranted based on their objective accomplishments. Against this backdrop, any scientific evidence regarding male versus female differences in leadership style and effectiveness would be welcome; fortunately, a recent meta-analysis published by Alice Eagly and her colleagues has shed some much needed light on a topic that more often than not, just generates heat.

Eagly and her team analyzed the results of forty-five different scientific studies of gender effects in the area of leadership, and together, the studies involved more than 30,000 people working in a wide variety of contexts. The results indicated several differences in terms of both style and outcomes associated with male versus female leaders. First, in terms of style, female leaders were more likely than male leaders to (1) appeal to workers' pride and need for respect, (2) rely on emotional appeals to inspire motivation, (3) provide more of an intellectual basis for their decisions, (4) give more individual consideration to employees (as opposed to relying on policies), and (5) apply performance-contingent rewards and bonuses. Male leaders, on the other hand, were much less active leaders, and were more likely to (1) lead by exception, that is, step in only when something went wrong, or (2) demonstrate laissez-faire tactics or a hands-off approach to management. In terms of results, the more active role of the female leaders led to employees who (1) were more likely to report putting forth extra effort, (2) were more satisfied with their leader, and (3) were more effective in terms of meeting work goals.

Although this evidence would seem to support the double standard argument, as the authors of this study note, the size of the effects for gender across all the different styles and outcomes were very small. The largest effect was for individual consideration and effectiveness, and in both of these cases, the advantage held by female leaders was roughly one-fifth of one standard deviation. In lay terms, this means that if one looked at all the groups that were above the average in individualized consideration and effectiveness and called them the "top teams," 52.5 percent of these teams would be led by women and 47.5 would be led by men. The other differences were smaller than this, and suggest that when it comes to leadership, neither sex holds a strong monopoly on the keys to success. Instead of arguing about gender, most of those looking for organizational leaders would be better off focusing on the traits and behaviors of individuals, and the degree to which they match the needs of followers and situations.

Sources: U.S. Bureau of Labor Statistics, "Monthly Household Data from the Current Population Survey," 2002, p. 343; S. Caudron, "Don't Mess with Carly," *Workforce Management*, July 2003, pp. 29–33; A. Eagly, M. Johannesen-Schmidt, and M. von Engen, "Transformational, Transactional, and Laissez-Faire Leadership Styles: A Meta-Analysis Comparing Men and Women," *Psychological Bulletin*, July 2003, pp. 569–591.

single best approach for *all* followers. For example, research on cross-cultural differences suggests that Russian workers perform very poorly under participative leaders.[22]

The nature of required decision-making style is also affected by the size and maturity of the organization. For example, Microsoft leader Bill Gates had a very autocratic decision-making style that was highly effective as the organization grew from a small operation to a larger one. Gates involved himself in almost all significant organizational decisions. However, the complexity and scope of operation made it increasingly difficult for him to lead this way, especially when the organization was under attack by the Justice Department for antitrust violations. He ceded much of the authority for day-to-day operational decisions to Steve Ballmer, but together, the two men still made a majority of the firm's decisions. Although attempts have been made to further decentralize the decision-making process, there have been a series of failed attempts to interject new leaders in organization, and as one employee noted, "it's always been the Bill and Steve show, and its still the Bill and Steve show."[23]

Leader Behaviors

A third school of early leadership research focused on the behaviors exhibited by leaders. Based on interviews with supervisors and clerical workers at the Prudential Insurance Company, researchers concluded that two general classes of supervisory behavior exist: **employee-oriented behavior,** which aims to meet the social and emotional needs of group members, and **job-oriented behavior,** which focuses on careful supervision of employees' work methods and task accomplishment.[24] Early studies indicated that work attitudes were better and productivity was higher in the groups led by supervisors who displayed employee-oriented behaviors.[25]

Another set of early studies that relied on questionnaires rather than interviews reached similar conclusions about leader behavior. After analyzing workers' responses to a questionnaire through a sophisticated statistical procedure called factor analysis, researchers concluded that most supervisory behaviors could be assigned to one of two dimensions: **consideration** or **initiating structure.**[26] Table 10-2 shows some items from the Leadership Behavior Description Questionnaire (LBDQ) that evolved from these original studies. The consideration dimension closely resembles the employee-centered orientation, in that both dimensions address the individual and social needs of workers. Similarly, the initiating-structure dimension resembles the job-centered orientation, in that both are concerned with the clarification of work processes and expectations. Rather than being mutually exclusive (that is, if a person is high on one dimension, he or she must be low on the other), these two dimensions are somewhat independent (that is, a person can be high on one dimension, and high, medium, or low on the other). If anything, a small positive correlation exists between the two dimensions, in that leaders who are considerate also seem to rate slightly higher on initiating structure.[27]

Based on this early research, Blake and Mouton developed the notion of the managerial grid, proposing that a leader needs to rate highly in terms of both concern for people and concern for production to be truly effective.[28] This approach was suggested to be "the one best way" to lead (that is, regardless of followers or situations). Blake and Mouton subsequently developed an elaborate training program to move managers in that direction. Managers find the program appealing because it points to two specific sets of behaviors—consideration and initiating structure—in which they can engage to enhance the attitudes and performance of their group. Despite its appeal, however, the managerial grid approach lacks support from rigorous scientific studies. In fact, some investigators have even labeled the whole idea a myth.[29]

TABLE 10-2
Items Similar to Those in the Leader Behavior Description Questionnaire

Consideration Items

1. Is easy to get along with
2. Puts ideas generated by the group into operation
3. Treats everyone the same
4. Lets followers know of upcoming changes
5. Explains actions to all group members

Initiating-Structure Items

1. Tells group members what is expected
2. Promotes the use of standardized procedures
3. Makes decisions about work methods
4. Clarifies role relationship among group members
5. Sets specific goals and monitors performance closely

Transformational Leadership

Perhaps because of the weaknesses associated with universal approaches that emphasize only traits, or behaviors, or decision-making styles, subsequent universal approaches were developed that incorporated all three aspects of leadership simultaneously. Among these are theories of **transformational leadership,** which emphasize the ability of the leader to communicate new visions of an organization to followers.[30] Transformational leaders can be characterized by their traits, behaviors, and decision-making styles. In terms of traits, transformational leaders are often called *charismatic leaders* because of the centrality of this trait to their effectiveness, as well as their tendency to rely on moralistic emotional appeals rather than calculative, instrumental, or financial appeals, which tend to be employed more by transactional leaders.[31] In terms of behaviors, transformational leaders raise followers' awareness of the importance and value of group goals, often getting people to transcend their own interests in the pursuit of new goals.[32] They also "raise the stakes" of organizational performance by convincing subordinates of the importance of the leader's vision and the dangers of not adopting this vision.[33]

This vision and emphasis on change distinguishes transformational leaders from more ordinary leaders, according to this theory, and for the most part charismatic leaders tend to be autocratic because they are the ones that best understand the vision.[34] However, although decisions are often arrived at autocratically, these leaders are experts at getting subordinates to commit and implement these decisions because the followers deeply trust the leader.[35] Transformational leaders accomplish this by creating a strong identification between the leader and the follower, as well as increasing the strength of the bond among the followers themselves, thus enhancing group cohesiveness[36] and collective self-efficacy.[37] Indeed, the social and value-oriented nature of charismatic leadership is best revealed by research that shows that perceptions of charisma spread much faster among people who are in the same social network (friends), as opposed to the same physical location or task network.[38] Still, many transformational leaders also engage in behaviors that most would characterize as transactional, and the two styles are often complementary and not mutually exclusive.[39]

Although charisma may seem hard to capture operationally, standardized measures of charisma have been developed recently, and these have been found to relate to leader effectiveness.[40] However, again we see that this depends on the nature of the situation and followers. For example, research indicates that with respect to followers, charismatic leadership is more effective with followers who are collectivistic rather than individualistic.[41] In terms of situations, it also seems to be more effective when there is direct contact between the leader and the followers, as opposed to when the relationship is indirect.[42] Charismatic leadership also seems to be more effective in nonprofit organizations, as compared to for-profit organizations.[43] Finally, charismatic leadership also seems to be less important in contexts where people perceive high levels of procedural justice, suggesting that trust in procedures can serve as a substitute for the role of a charismatic leader.[44]

We will discuss the concept of substitutes for leadership in more detail in a later section of this chapter. For now, we will merely assert that as these findings suggest, the evidence argues against the notion that there is any "one best way" of leading, regardless of followers and situations. The primary problem of all the approaches we have discussed is that they specify one best way to lead (for example, be extroverted or initiate structure, or use a democratic leadership style) regardless of the characteristics of followers and situations. This led to weak results in terms of predicting or explaining leader emergence and effectiveness, and started many people wondering just how critical leadership really was to large organizations. As we will see in our next section, some began to argue that leadership might be irrelevant.

Leader Irrelevance

Advocates of leader irrelevance, a situation-based approach to understanding leadership, emphasize that situations are much more important determinants of events than leader characteristics, for several reasons.[45] First, factors outside the leader's control tend to affect profits and other critical elements in the business context more than anything a leader might do. For example, as the Securing Competitive Advantage box shows, many aspects of the situation that are outside the control of a new leader will affect that person's success, including characteristics of the previous leader.

Second, even leaders at relatively high levels tend to have unilateral control over only a few resources. The discretionary use of any set of resources is constrained by the leader's accountability to other people both inside and outside the organization. Even the CEO of a major corporation must answer to shareholders, consumers, and government regulators.

Finally, the selection process through which all leaders must go filters people such that those in leadership positions tend to act in similar ways. For example, the process used to select the president of the United States makes it impossible for some types of people (for example, illiterates, introverts, extremists of either the left or right) to rise to that position. The people who make it through screening procedures of this kind tend to be alike in more ways than they are different. "Homogenizing" leaders in this way reduces the effect that any change in leadership has on an organization's outcomes.

The failure to find robust direct relationships between leader traits, behaviors, and decision-making styles promoted this kind of antileadership sentiment. In fact, it can be quite useful to remember that leaders are often victims of their environments rather than masters of their domain. Even so, research on leadership continued, and more contemporary approaches maintained that leadership did provide some value. These approaches suggested, however, that the value of leadership was a highly contingent phenomenon that could not be captured by "one best way" approaches that dominated the early research in this area. Thus, in our opening story regarding Home Depot, the idea to centralize all purchasing operations was a good one at GE because of the small number of homogeneous customers that purchased turbine engines. However, the same idea was less than effective at Home Depot, where there were important regional differences in what customers wanted.

SECURING COMPETITIVE ADVANTAGE

IN THE WAKE OF A LEGEND: NEW SOUTHWEST AIRLINES LEADER FACES TURBULENCE

Founder and longtime CEO of Southwest Airlines Herb Kelleher is a leadership legend. Famous for his hard drinking, chain smoking, and fun-loving antics, he created a culture of camaraderie at Southwest Airlines that epitomized the ability to gain and sustain competitive advantage from people. Costs at the airline are 20 percent to 50 percent less than those of other carriers and the firm has posted thirty consecutive years of profits. Shareholders have watched the stock soar continuously. In fact, the stock price increased more than 1,000-fold—that's right—1,000-fold since 1972. Since the organization runs a profit-sharing and stock purchase program for employees, it has made millionaires out of its mechanics and flight attendants, and not just the CEO and other top executives as is the case at so many other airlines. Its unionized but loyal employees look everywhere to cut costs and improve service, and are rewarded with a commitment from management, which has never laid off a worker in more than thirty years of operation.

Kelleher stepped down as CEO in June 2001, however, and after two years some strain is beginning to show at the airline as its new leader, James F. Parker, tries to continue the firm's success. Parker's southern drawl and penchant for quiet, behind-the-scenes diplomacy stands in stark contrast to Kelleher's manic energy and constant presence. More important, the challenges that face the carrier in 2003 differ from those that characterized its rise from small, underdog upstart thirty years ago to the recognized leader in the industry.

For one, Southwest has turned from the hunter to the hunted, in the sense that both new and older airlines are specifically developing strategies to offset Southwest's advantages. For example, Jet Blue airlines has emulated Southwest on many dimensions, but has been attracting a large number of customers by offering assigned seating and televisions in the seatbacks of all its planes. Moreover, older, more traditional airlines have used the threat of bankruptcy to force their unions into wage concessions that to some degree offset Southwest's former advantage in this area. Beyond this, however, the mood of the air traveler has changed in the wake of the 9/11 terrorist attacks, and Southwest's once widespread use of humor and practical jokes as a means of increasing customer satisfaction has had to be cut back. A memo from headquarters directly told the staff, "It is evident that the usual Southwest humor should temporarily play a lesser role in our lives," although no alternative for enhancing customer satisfaction was suggested.

Second, the past growth of the airline, combined with its reduced potential for more growth, created some problems of its own. The past growth meant that the organization has hired an army of new employees, and not all of these new recruits fully appreciated the nature of the culture, leading to some conflicts between the "old guard" and the recent hires. It also makes it more difficult for the top managers to create a one-on-one relationship with the company's 35,000 workers as it could in the "good old days." Moreover, the reduced potential for future growth meant that the steady stream of promotions that people experienced as the organization constantly grew over time began to taper off. Historically, the airline opened operations in two new cities a year, but has not expanded to a single new location in more than two years. The restricted promotion opportunities combined with the lower levels of profits and stock price increases have eroded many of the powerful incentives that formerly fueled its hardworking employees.

Finally, there may be limits in the degree to which one can keep leveraging enhanced employee work efforts as the primary source of competitive advantage. In July 2003, flight attendants balked when management wanted to increase their standard workday from ten to thirteen hours, while at the same time eliminating their customary meal break. Karen Amos, a twenty-five-year veteran, protested, "We have been there for them, but there comes a time when it becomes too much." Indeed, in an unprecedented event, forty flight attendants actually picketed Southwest's Dallas headquarters, handing out cards to travelers asking to "give our flight attendants a break."

Parker has responded by rewriting the contract with the flight attendants and slowly introducing humor back into the work protocols. He also took the cash grants that the federal government gave all the airlines to prop up the industry and distributed them directly to employees, even though this was not really a "profit," and therefore not contractually required. He has teamed up with Colleen Barrett, the company's president, who brings a little bit more of the "Kelleher style" back to the management team. Parker recognizes the fine line he has to walk as Southwest's new leader, observing, "There are two kinds of traps you can fall into. One is to have an ego-driven desire to leave your mark and to try and change things. The other is to be too passive and fail to recognize the need for change." Time will tell if Parker can find the right balance for Southwest.

Sources: S. McCartney, "Secret to Southwest's Success May Lie in Its Labor Contracts," *Wall Street Journal Online,* September 17, 2002, pp. 1–3; R. Suskind, "Humor Has Returned to Southwest Airlines," *Wall Street Journal Online,* January 13, 2003, pp. 1–3; M. Trottman, "Inside Southwest Airlines, Storied Culture Feels Strains," *Wall Street Journal Online,* July 13, 2003, pp. 1–5; W. Zellner, "Holding Steady: As Rivals Sputter, Can Southwest Stay on Top?" *Business Week,* February 3, 2003, pp. 66–68.

Similarly, the idea of cutting costs by using part-time workers made sense at GE because these were manufacturing jobs where the worker did not have direct contact with the customers. However, at Home Depot, the need for knowledgeable staff that could work with both seasoned professional contractors and naive do-it-yourself amateurs made the same decision look ineffective. The theories discussed next all acknowledge these types of leader–follower–situation interactions.

CHARACTERISTICS OF FOLLOWERS AND SITUATIONS

The Leadership Motivation Pattern

The theory behind the leadership motivation pattern (LMP), an early interaction theory, grew out of David McClelland's research on characteristics of the leader. This theory focuses most squarely on the interaction between the traits of the leader and the characteristics of the situation. In terms of traits, McClelland proposed that leaders must either have a high need for achievement (see Chapter 7) or display the leadership motivation pattern. The leadership motivation pattern is a composite of three specific characteristics: a high need for power, a low need for affiliation with others, and a high degree of self-control.

McClelland also suggested that two types of leadership situations exist. The *entrepreneurial situation* occurs in small organizations or in small technical units in large organizations where a few key people do most of the work themselves. The *bureaucratic situation* is found in the context of large, formalized, tightly structured organizations. According to McClelland's theory, the need for achievement is critical to leaders in entrepreneurial situations and the leadership motivation pattern is essential for success in bureaucratic situations. That is, people high in the need for achievement are primarily interested in their own progress and much less interested in influencing and encouraging others. As a result, although the need for achievement is useful in small groups or technical groups where one person's progress readily spills over into group progress, it is less important for leadership success in large organizations.

In contrast, in large, bureaucratic organizations, the three-characteristic configuration of the leadership motivation pattern has much more utility. A person who has a strong need for power also has an interest in influencing and controlling others, a prerequisite for leading a group of people. Having a low need for affiliation enables a leader to make difficult decisions without worrying about being unpopular. Finally, high self-control makes it possible for a person to wield his or her power so as to get things done within the organizational rules of the game.

How do these predictions play out in the real world? One study of 246 AT&T managers who were followed for sixteen years tested McClelland's theory. The theory predicted that high LMP scorers would be successful in nontechnical areas, which were generally bureaucratic in organizations, but not in technical ones, which tended to be more entrepreneurial. The results of the study showed that this scenario was exactly what had happened. Nontechnical managers who had high LMP scores had a 75 percent rate of promotions, whereas managers in technical units with high LMP scores had only a 25 percent promotion rate. The key to success for the latter group of managers was the need for achievement. In fact, the correlation between need for achievement and success was twice as strong in technical areas as in nontechnical ones.[46]

These findings strongly suggest that the effect of a set of leader characteristics on a leader's success depends on the situation in which the leader is performing. Entrepreneurial situations call for leaders high in the need for achievement, whereas bureaucratic situations call for a leader high in the leadership motivation pattern.

Vertical Dyad Linkage

An approach to leadership that emphasizes the characteristics of followers is the *vertical dyad linkage* (VDL) theory of leadership. Also, rather than focusing on leader traits, this approach places more emphasis on leader behaviors. A **vertical dyad** consists of two persons who are linked hierarchically, such as a supervisor and a subordinate. Most studies that involve measurements of leader consideration or initiating structure average subordinates' ratings of leaders. VDL proponents, however, argue that there is no such thing as an "average" leadership score. Instead, they insist, each supervisor–subordinate relationship is unique. A supervisor may be considerate toward one person but not another. Similarly, the leader may initiate structure for some workers but not others.

The importance of distinguishing dyadic from average scores has received broad research support. For example, Figure 10-2 compares the strength of the relationship between (1) leader consideration and follower satisfaction and (2) leader initiating structure and follower role clarity as measured by both dyadic scores and average scores.[47] As shown in the figure, the relationships based on dyadic scores were much stronger than the relationships based on average scores. This finding suggests that leaders do behave differently with different subordinates and that these differences spill over into worker reactions.[48]

FIGURE 10-2 Measuring the Relationship between Leader Behaviors and Follower Outcomes by Dyadic Ratings and Average Group Ratings

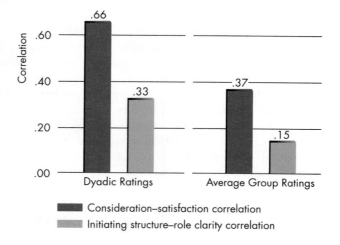

The vertical dyad linkage approach also suggests that leaders tend to classify subordinates as either in-group members or out-group members. According to this theory, *in-group members* are willing and able to do more than the tasks outlined in a formal job description. Once they have been identified, the leader gives these people more latitude, authority, and consideration.[49] *Out-group members*, on the other hand, either cannot or will not expand their roles beyond formal requirements. Leaders assign these individuals more routine tasks, give them less consideration, and communicate less often with them.[50]

Whether distinguishing among subordinates in this manner improves a leader's effectiveness depends on the leader's reasons for placing some people in the in-group and others in the out-group. Research shows that performance is not always the reason for separating members into in-groups and out-groups; indeed, if these kinds of distinctions are based on non-performance-related information, then this classification can interfere with leader effectiveness.[51] Highly competent and committed workers might differ from their supervisors but could excel if given in-group status and support. On the other hand, when leaders differentially weigh the opinions of their followers based on their competence, highly effective results often follow.[52]

Life-Cycle Model

Whereas the previous two interactive approaches focused on leader traits and behaviors, the next approach features the leader's decision-making style, emphasizing how it combines with characteristics of the followers to determine leadership effectiveness. According to the lifecycle model developed by Paul Hersey and Kenneth Blanchard, the effectiveness of a leader's decision-making style depends largely on followers' level of maturity, job experience, and emotional maturity.[53] This model proposes two basic dimensions on which decision-making style may vary: task orientation and relationship orientation.

The life-cycle model suggests that these two dimensions combine to form four distinct types of decision styles: telling, selling, participating, and delegating. The *telling style* is characterized by high task orientation and low relationship orientation—the leader simply tells the follower what to do. The *selling style* is characterized by both high task and high relationship orientations, in that the leader tries to convince subordinates that the decision is appropriate. The *participating style* is marked by a high relationship orientation but a low task orientation. The leader who uses this style of decision making includes subordinates in discussions so that decisions are made by consensus. Finally, in the *delegating style*, which is low on both task and relationship orientations, the leader actually turns things over to followers and lets them make their own decisions.

According to Hersey and Blanchard, the type of decision-making style that a leader should adopt depends on the level of maturity of the followers (Figure 10-3). It suggests that for followers at very low levels of maturity, telling is the most effective leadership decision style. As followers move from very low to moderately low levels of maturity, a selling style becomes more effective. That is, the leader in this case should act as an opinion leader.[54] When followers show a moderately high level of maturity, participating is the most effective style. At the very highest levels of follower maturity, the delegating style leaves followers essentially on their own.

Although empirical research has not supported this model completely, the notion that performance will be higher in matched situations is supported at one level of maturity—the lowest. That is, with workers at low levels of maturity, the telling style is slightly more effective in eliciting good performance than the other styles. A good example of this can be seen at Yahoo! Inc. New CEO Terry Semel came into a situation where the playful, egalitarian, and loosely structured culture among talented

FIGURE 10-3 The Life-Cycle Model of Leadership in Four Dimensions

Three of this model's four dimensions are easily seen. Relationship orientation may be low (bottom half of the rectangular box model) or high (top half). Task orientation may also be low (left half of the model) or high (right half). Follower maturity ranges from very low (front of the model) to very high (back). The fourth dimension, leader effectiveness, is represented by the highlighted cell at each follower-maturity level. For example, at the high-maturity level, the highlighting of the cell for the participating leader style—which is high on relationship orientation and low on task orientation—indicates that at this level this style should be the most effective.

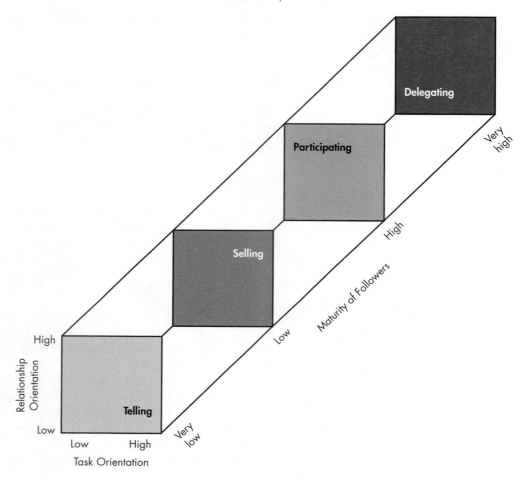

but young and inexperienced software designers had resulted in chronic performance problems at the firm. Most analysts thought that Yahoo would go the way of other failed dot-coms, but the sixty-year-old Semel came in and autocratically restructured work processes and decisions, and generally brought a much needed dose of control and maturity to the firm. In eighteen months, Semel had helped quadruple Yahoo sales and doubled the stock price. In the process, he eventually won over the hearts and minds of the younger designers, who were at first very leery of a leader that they considered too old and too staid to be successful in the high-tech industry.[55]

Substitutes for Leadership

Whereas the VDL approach to leadership places a great deal of weight on leader behaviors and the characteristics of followers, the **substitutes for leadership** theory

FIGURE 10-4 How a Situational Characteristic Can Substitute for Leader Behavior

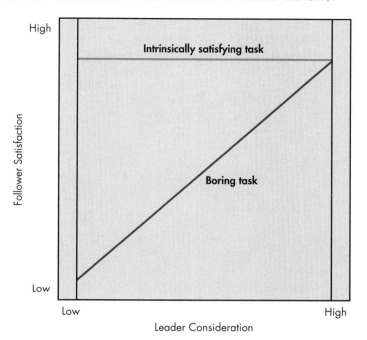

emphasizes leader behaviors and the situation. Although not as extreme as the antileadership approaches, this theory argues that traditional leader behaviors, such as initiating structure and consideration, are sometimes made irrelevant by certain characteristics of situations.[56] That is, characteristics of situations can act to *substitute* for leader behavior. Figure 10-4 illustrates the effect of a substitute. Here consideration leads to follower satisfaction when boring tasks must be performed. When tasks are intrinsically satisfying, however, the satisfying nature of the task substitutes for leader behavior; leader consideration has no effect in this case, because satisfaction is already high.

One review of the scientific literature on this topic suggests that the most powerful substitutes for leadership relate to both characteristics of the task and the organization as a whole. In general, leadership tends to be neutralized in situations where tasks are intrinsically satisfying and good objective feedback about task performance is provided. Leadership is also neutralized in organizations that are highly formalized (that is, organizations that develop written rules and procedures for most jobs) and lacking in flexibility.[57]

COMPREHENSIVE THEORIES OF LEADERSHIP

Whereas all four of the interactive approaches discussed earlier deal with two of the three forces identified in the transactional model of leadership (leader–follower–situation), the comprehensive leadership theories discussed in this section account for all three simultaneously. The three comprehensive theories that we will examine differ only in that each tends to focus on a particular leader characteristic—either a personal characteristic, a behavioral orientation, or a decision-making style.

Fiedler's Contingency Theory

Think for a moment of someone with whom you dislike to work. In fact, considering all of your co-workers in the past, whom do you remember as being the worst? Now rate this person on the qualities listed in the scale shown in Table 10-3. If you described your *least preferred co-worker* (LPC) in relatively harsh terms, then contingency theory would suggest that you are most likely to take a *task orientation* toward leadership. Task-oriented leaders emphasize completing tasks successfully, even at the expense of interpersonal relations. A task-oriented leader finds it difficult to overlook the negative traits of a poorly performing subordinate. On the other hand, if you described your least preferred co-worker in relatively positive terms, you are likely to take a *relationship orientation* toward leadership. Relationship-oriented leaders, according to this theory, are permissive, considerate leaders who can maintain good interpersonal relationships even with workers who are not contributing to group accomplishment.

The leader's orientation toward either tasks or relationships is the central piece of this complex and controversial theory of leadership that was proposed by Fred Fiedler. Fiedler's model is called a contingency theory of leadership because it holds that the effectiveness of a leader's orientation depends on both the followers *and* the situation. A leadership situation can be placed along a continuum of favorability, depending on three factors.

First, **leader–follower relations** are considered good if followers trust and respect the leader.[58] Good relations are obviously more favorable for leader effectiveness than poor relations. Second, **task structure** is high when a group has clear goals and a clear means for achieving these goals. High task structure is more favorable for the leader than low task structure. Third, **position power** is the ability to reward or punish subordinates for their behavior.

Clearly, the more power possessed by a leader, the more favorable the situation is from the leader's perspective.[59] A good example of a leader who is in an unfavorable situation is Muhammad Dahlan, who in the summer of 2003 was the new national security administrator for the Palestinian Authority in the Middle East. Dahlan's job was to prevent fellow Palestinian militant groups like Hamas and the al-Aqsa Martyrs' Brigade from making attacks on Israelis as part of President Bush's "roadmap for peace" in the Middle East. Unfortunately, Dahlan had poor leader–follower relations, in the sense that he was trusted by neither Palestinians, who felt he sold out to Israel, or Israel, who claimed he was a former terrorist involved in the bombing of a school bus. Task structure was poor because no one knew how to stop the terrorists, who were often a loosely structured set of individuals who moved in and out of various terrorist cells and were sometimes under no one's direct control. Finally, position power was weak, in the sense that most of the Palestinian infrastructure was destroyed by the Israelis and the Palestinian Authority had little in the

TABLE 10-3   Items Similar to Those on the Least Preferred Co-Worker Scale

Agreeable	8	7	6	5	4	3	2	1	Disagreeable
Closed-minded	1	2	3	4	5	6	7	8	Open-minded
Courteous	8	7	6	5	4	3	2	1	Rude
Agitated	1	2	3	4	5	6	7	8	Calm
Dull	1	2	3	4	5	6	7	8	Fascinating

ways of guns or money to fight the terrorist groups, who were instead well supported by many external sources.[60]

Fiedler's analysis of a number of studies that used the least preferred co-worker scale suggested that task-oriented leaders are most effective in situations that are either extremely favorable or extremely unfavorable. Relationship-oriented leaders, on the other hand, achieve their greatest success in situations of moderate favorability. Returning to our example, this would imply that the new leader of the Palestinian Authority, because of the highly unfavorable nature of the situation, would need to employ a very task-oriented approach.

One offshoot of this work is the leader training program called Leader Match, which attempts to translate contingency theory into managerial practice. Fiedler has commented that it is easier to change almost anything in the job situation than personality and leadership style, and Leader Match training reflects this belief in the immutability of people.[61] This self-paced, programmed text tells leaders not to change their styles but instead to try to manipulate the situation. For example, if leader–follower relations are poor, the leader might try to raise morale by giving bonuses or time off. If a task is unstructured, a leader might break it down into simpler subtasks. If position power is low, a leader might try to increase his or her authority by ensuring that workers channel all information through the leader.

Both the contingency theory and Leader Match training have been subject to considerable criticism. The theory has been criticized as "too data-driven." According to his critics, Fiedler started with a set of results that he tried to explain, rather than with a logical, deductive theory. In addition, the LPC measure itself has aroused controversy. Critics have questioned what the scale actually measures and how well it measures this variable.[62] Likewise, the Leader Match training program has been criticized for using questionable measures of performance and for failing to control for rater expectation biases and the so-called Hawthorne effect.[63]

Vroom–Yetton Decision Tree Model

Fiedler's comprehensive model focused on personality characteristics of the leader. In contrast, the *decision tree model of leadership* developed by Victor Vroom and his colleagues emphasizes the fact that leaders achieve success through effective decision making.[64] Vroom's model recognizes four general styles of leadership decision making: *authoritarian, consultative, delegation,* and *group-based.* These alternatives are then broken down into seven specific decision styles: three that are appropriate to both individual and group decisions, two that are appropriate only to decisions involving individual followers, and two that are appropriate only to decisions that involve an entire group of followers (see Table 10-4).

Like all comprehensive theories of leadership, the decision tree model proposes that the most effective leadership style depends on characteristics of both the situation and the followers. Specifically, the model asks eight questions—three about the situation and five about the followers—to determine which of the seven leadership styles outlined in Table 10-4 is best. The decision tree presented in Figure 10-5 makes the question-and-answer process easy.[65] Responding to questions A through H leads to one of eighteen answers, each of which identifies one or more decision-making styles that are appropriate to the problem confronted. To choose among two or more styles, the leader must decide whether to maximize the speed of decision making or the personal development of subordinates. Autocratic approaches favor speed, whereas consultative or group approaches favor employee growth.

For example, suppose that you are a corporate vice president who has just been given the responsibility for starting up a new plant in a developing country, and you must choose a plant manager. Should it be one of your five current and highly

TABLE 10-4
The Seven
Decision
Styles in the
Vroom–Yetton
Decision Tree
Model of
Leadership

For All Problems

AI   You solve the problem or make the decision yourself, using information available to you at the time.

AII   You obtain any necessary information from subordinates, then decide on the solution to the problem yourself. You may or may not tell subordinates what the problem is in getting the information from them. The role played by your subordinates in making the decision is clearly one of providing specific information that you request, rather than one of generating or evaluating solutions.

CI   You share the problem with the relevant subordinates individually, getting their ideas and suggestions without bringing them together as a group. Then *you* make the decision. This decision may or may not reflect your subordinates' influence.

For Individual Problems

GI   You share the problem with one of your subordinates, and together you analyze the problem and arrive at a mutually satisfactory solution in an atmosphere of free and open exchange of information and ideas. You both contribute to the resolution of the problem, with the relative contribution of each being dependent on knowledge rather than formal authority.

DI   You delegate the problem to one of your subordinates, providing any relevant information that you possess, but giving your subordinate responsibility for solving the problem independently. Any solution that the person reaches will receive your support.

For Group Problems

CII   You share the problem with your subordinates in a group meeting. In this meeting you obtain their ideas and suggestions. Then *you* make the decision, which may or may not reflect your subordinates' influence.

GII   You share the problem with your subordinates as a group. Together you generate and evaluate alternatives and attempt to reach agreement (consensus) on a solution. Your role is much like that of chairperson, coordinating the discussion, keeping it focused on the problem, and making sure that the critical issues are discussed. You do not try to influence the group to adopt "your" solution and are willing to accept and implement any solution that has support of the entire group.

Note: A stands for authoritarian, C for consultative, D for delegative, and G for group-based.

experienced plant managers? Should it be someone from outside the firm who has had experience working overseas? Should it be a citizen of the target country? As vice president, you might move through the decision tree as follows:

Question A: Yes. Some managers may be better suited than others.

Question B: No. You, the vice president, may not know all the interests or past experience that would be relevant to the assignment.

Question C: No. This problem is a new one for the company, and thus no clear guidelines dictate what steps to take.

Question D: Yes. Your current managers could all find good jobs with other firms in their own country if they refused the overseas job.

Question E: No. The decision will have too large an effect on subordinates' lives.

Question F: Yes. They have been with the company a long time and are committed to the organization.

Question H: No. Only you, the vice president, know about many details of the assignment.

FIGURE 10-5 The Vroom–Yetton Decision Tree Model of Leadership

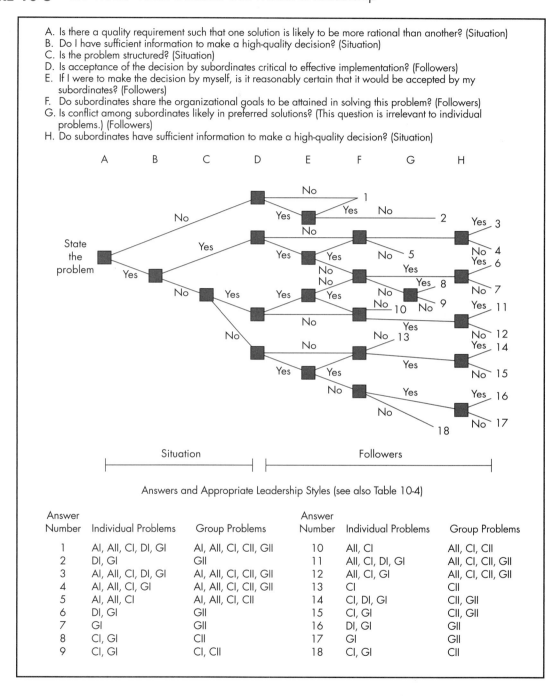

A. Is there a quality requirement such that one solution is likely to be more rational than another? (Situation)
B. Do I have sufficient information to make a high-quality decision? (Situation)
C. Is the problem structured? (Situation)
D. Is acceptance of the decision by subordinates critical to effective implementation? (Followers)
E. If I were to make the decision by myself, is it reasonably certain that it would be accepted by my subordinates? (Followers)
F. Do subordinates share the organizational goals to be attained in solving this problem? (Followers)
G. Is conflict among subordinates likely in preferred solutions? (This question is irrelevant to individual problems.) (Followers)
H. Do subordinates have sufficient information to make a high-quality decision? (Situation)

Answers and Appropriate Leadership Styles (see also Table 10-4)

Answer Number	Individual Problems	Group Problems	Answer Number	Individual Problems	Group Problems
1	AI, AII, CI, DI, GI	AI, AII, CI, CII, GII	10	AII, CI	AII, CI, CII
2	DI, GI	GII	11	AII, CI, DI, GI	AII, CI, CII, GII
3	AI, AII, CI, DI, GI	AI, AII, CI, CII, GII	12	AII, CI, GI	AII, CI, CII, GII
4	AI, AII, CI, GI	AI, AII, CI, CII, GII	13	CI	CII
5	AI, AII, CI	AI, AII, CI, CII	14	CI, DI, GI	CII, GII
6	DI, GI	GII	15	CI, GI	CII, GII
7	GI	GII	16	DI, GI	GII
8	CI, GI	CII	17	GI	GII
9	CI, GI	CI, CII	18	CI, GI	CII

The "no" response to question H leads to answer number 17. This answer, applied to a group problem, eliminates both autocratic and consultative styles and recommends the GII, group-based decision-making style.

Early studies of the model's usefulness asked managers to think about past decisions that were effective or ineffective and had them trace their decision processes back to see whether they had followed the model's prescriptions. When the managers' decision-making processes were consistent with the model, 68 percent of decisions were effective, compared to only 22 percent when decisions violated the model.[66] Research also indicates that most managers' natural decision-making processes seem to violate the model's prescriptions. In particular, managers tend to overuse the consultative CII style and underutilize the group-based GII style.[67] The difference between these two styles is subtle but critical; the leader retains ultimate decision-making responsibility in the first but not the second. Giving up this ultimate responsibility is difficult for many leaders, because they know they may ultimately be blamed for the employees' mistakes. For example, although we may never know the truth of exactly what went on at Enron, CEO Ken Lay always portrayed himself as a leader who "empowered" his employees, and delegated huge responsibilities to them, refusing to micromanage or second-guess their decisions. When evidence of fraud was uncovered, he suggested that his hands-off leadership style made him a victim of the crimes, rather than the perpetrator—a claim that fell on deaf ears at the U.S. Department of Justice.[68]

Path–Goal Theory

The most comprehensive theory of leadership to date and the theory that best exemplifies all aspects of the transactional model is the *path–goal theory of leadership*.[69] At the heart of the path–goal theory is the notion that the leader's primary purpose is to motivate followers by clarifying goals and identifying the best paths to achieve those goals. Because motivation is essential to the leader role, this approach is based on the expectancy theory of motivation (described in Chapter 5) and emphasizes the three motivational variables that leaders may influence through their behaviors or decision-making styles: valences, instrumentalities, and expectancies.

The job of the leader, according to the path–goal theory, is to manipulate these three factors in desirable ways. Correspondingly, the theory's proponents recommend that leaders fulfill three major roles. First, leaders need to *manipulate follower valences* by recognizing or arousing needs for outcomes that the leader can control. Second, leaders must *manipulate follower instrumentalities* by ensuring that high performance results in satisfying outcomes for followers. Third, leaders need to *manipulate follower expectancies* by reducing frustrating barriers to performance.[70]

The path–goal theory proposes that four behavioral styles can enable leaders to manipulate the three motivational variables: directive, supportive, participative, and achievement-oriented leadership. As described in Table 10-5, these styles are composed of both behaviors, such as initiating structure, and decision-making styles, such as the authoritarian approach. In each case, the leader's effectiveness depends on follower and situation characteristics. Much like the substitutes for leadership

TABLE 10-5
The Path–Goal Theory's Four Behavioral Styles

Directive leadership	The leader is authoritarian. Subordinates know exactly what is expected of them, and the leader gives specific directions. Subordinates do not participate in decision making.
Supportive leadership	The leader is friendly and approachable and shows a genuine concern for subordinates.
Participative leadership	The leader asks for and uses suggestions from subordinates but still makes the decisions.
Achievement-oriented leadership	The leader sets challenging goals for subordinates and shows confidence that they will attain these goals.

approach, the path–goal theory recognizes that situational characteristics may make leader behavior unnecessary or impossible.[71]

Researchers have tested small parts of the path–goal model. Some of their findings are as follows:

Leader participative behavior results in satisfaction in *situations* where the task is nonroutine, but only for *followers* who are nonauthoritarian.[72]

Leader directive behavior produces high satisfaction and high performance, but only among *followers* who have high needs for clarity.[73]

Leader supportive behavior results in *follower* satisfaction, but only in *situations* where the task is highly structured.[74]

Leader achievement-oriented behavior results in improved performance, but only when *followers* are committed to goals.[75]

Perhaps because the theory is so complex, no one has yet undertaken a comprehensive study of the path–goal theory that tests every variable. The theoretical framework provided by the path–goal theory, however, is an excellent one for generating, testing, and understanding the complexities of the leadership process. Moreover, its tie to the expectancy theory of motivation makes it particularly suitable for leadership as conceptualized by Mintzberg—that is, the leader as a group motivator.

THE INTEGRATED LEADERSHIP MODEL REVISITED

This chapter began with a discussion of an integrated model of leadership and expressed a view of leadership as a complex interaction involving characteristics of the leader, the followers, and the situation. These ideas provided a framework for our discussion of several theories of leadership that vary in breadth and emphasis.

Figure 10-6 depicts the dynamic relationships among the elements of these several theories as they fit together in an *integrated model of leadership.* At the core of this model is the notion that the purpose of leaders is to meet the performance and satisfaction needs of individual group members. Through their abilities and personality characteristics, their behaviors, and their decision-making styles, leaders must affect their followers' valences, instrumentalities, and expectancies.

The first key to applying this model to your own leadership situation is to engage in self-assessment to learn your standing on various traits (for example, LMP or LPC), behavioral tendencies (on dimensions such as consideration and initiating structure), and decision-making style (autocratic, consultative, participative, delegative).[76] High levels of self-awareness are critical for leadership effectiveness and can often be raised through 360-degree feedback interventions like those discussed earlier in Chapter 4.[77]

Leaders must recognize that these phenomena are affected by a variety of follower characteristics. A trait, behavior, or decision style that works well with one group of followers is unlikely to work well with another group. Thus, the second key to applying this model to your own leadership situation is to make a critical assessment of those people who are following you, in terms of their maturity, competence, and cohesiveness, to determine the degree of match between their characteristics and yours.

Finally, the situation that leaders find themselves in will also affect the relationship between the leaders' traits, behaviors, and decision styles on the one hand, and group effectiveness on the other. Thus, the third key to applying this model is leaders

FIGURE 10-6 The Fully Articulated Integrated Model of Leadership

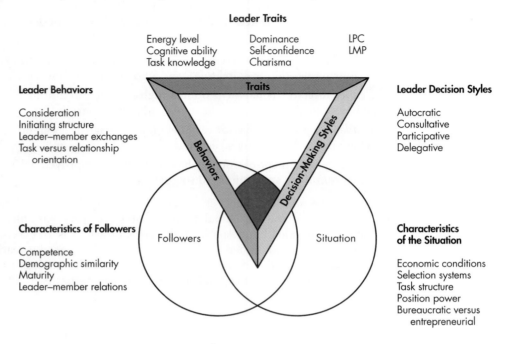

Leader Traits

Energy level   Dominance   LPC
Cognitive ability   Self-confidence   LMP
Task knowledge   Charisma

Leader Behaviors

Consideration
Initiating structure
Leader–member exchanges
Task versus relationship
   orientation

Leader Decision Styles

Autocratic
Consultative
Participative
Delegative

Characteristics of Followers

Competence
Demographic similarity
Maturity
Leader–member relations

**Characteristics
of the Situation**

Economic conditions
Selection systems
Task structure
Position power
Bureaucratic versus
   entrepreneurial

need to study the situation they are in (for example, in terms of task structure or the leader's power to change certain conditions like the overall economy) to determine what kinds of leadership will be most effective with this specific configuration of followers and situation. Effective leadership requires careful analysis of and reaction to the three forces—leader, followers, and situation—highlighted in the integrated framework you have learned about in this chapter. Although this may seem overly complex, it will help ward off the common problem we saw in our opening story on Home Depot, where a potential leader simply assumes that what worked well for one group of followers in one situation is likely for work for all followers in all situations.

SUMMARY

Many theories and a great deal of research have focused on the topic of leadership. Leadership differs from management in that leading is merely one task of managerial work. The emergence and continued success of a *leader* is a complex function of personal characteristics, characteristics of the *followers,* and characteristics of the *situation.* Important personal characteristics of a leader seem to include high intelligence, extroversion, and agreeableness. Important dimensions of leader behavior include *consideration* of employee needs (sometimes referred to as a *relationship orientation* or concern for people), *initiating structure* (sometimes referred to as a *task orientation* or concern for production), and leader–member exchange behaviors that separate subordinates into in-groups and out-groups.

Leaders also differ in terms of their decision-making styles. *Authoritarian* leaders make all decisions for their followers. Leaders who take a *laissez-faire* approach leave followers to do as they please. Leaders may also take a *democratic* approach, working actively with followers to ensure that all group members have a chance to contribute to a task.

According to the *integrated model of leadership*, the effectiveness of these different behaviors and decision-making styles is contingent on characteristics of the followers and of the situation. Followers differ along several important dimensions. They may be highly knowledgeable, mature, professional, and committed to the organization and its mission, or they may be quite the opposite. Different leadership styles will be required to work effectively with followers with different characteristics. The situation in which the leader and followers find themselves also affects the relationship between leader characteristics, behaviors, and decision-making styles on the one hand, and leader effectiveness on the other hand. Where the leader has great *position power, leader task structure* is high, and *leader–follower relations* are characterized by trust and respect, one set of behaviors or decision styles may be warranted. In situations where the opposite conditions hold, a different kind of leader or leader style may be needed.

REVIEW QUESTIONS

1. Theories of leadership differ in terms of how adaptable they suggest the leader can be. Of the theories discussed in this chapter, choose two that suggest the leader is inflexible and two that suggest the leader is readily adaptable. Which of these two conflicting perspectives seems most likely to be true? Are leaders born or are they made?

2. Most of the early research on leadership involved leaders who were almost exclusively white and male. Demographic research suggests that increasingly fewer of the new entrants in the labor force will be white males. Which theories of leadership may need to be seriously reexamined because of this change? Which do you feel will generalize well to the new workforce?

3. This chapter discussed the least preferred co-worker scale. Although no such instrument exists, what if there were a least preferred leader scale? Who would be your least preferred leader? Why? Can you think of followers other than yourself, or situations other than the one you face, for which this person might be an excellent leader?

4. Although we can think of a few exceptions, in general people who achieve preeminence as leaders in business organizations do not achieve success as political leaders. What are some characteristics of leaders, followers, or situations that make this kind of transition difficult?

5. The list of often-cited leaders in Table 10-1 clearly includes both saints and sinners. Why does the general moral character of the leader apparently play no consistent role in a leader's emergence or continuation in power?

LEARNING THROUGH EXPERIENCE

DIAGNOSTIC QUESTIONS 10-1

Applying the Integrated Leadership Model in Performing Diagnostic Analyses

We have attempted to develop and describe a model of the leadership process that will help you diagnose organizational problems attributed to poor leadership. The following questions should help you apply the integrated leadership model in performing diagnostic analyses.

1. Compared to other aspects of managerial work, how important to you is the specific process of leadership?

2. Which of the five components of follower motivation—valence, instrumentality, expectancy, accuracy of role perceptions, and rewards—seems most lacking in your setting?

3. What abilities related to leadership (for example, general cognitive ability, task knowledge, supervisory skills) do you or your managers have? How do these abilities relate to the five components of motivation?

4. What personality characteristics that are related to leadership (for example, self-esteem, need for power, charisma) do you or your managers have? How do these characteristics relate to the five components of motivation?

5. How readily do you think your abilities and characteristics or the abilities and characteristics of your managers can be changed?

6. What leader behaviors (for example, consideration, initiating structure, contingent rewarding and punishing) do you or you managers typically employ? How do these behaviors relate to the five components of motivation?

7. Do you and your managers tailor your behaviors to different followers?

8. How do you or your managers determine in-group versus out-group status for group members? For example, do you base your selection on competence or on demographic similarity?

9. What kind of decision-making styles (autocratic, participating, delegating) do you or your managers typically employ?

10. How should this decision-making style be tailored to your followers? Should you match it to their level of maturity? Their commitment to goals? The situation?

11. What are some of the major characteristics of the followers or of the situation you confront that might substitute for leader behaviors or neutralize them?

12. How favorable is the situation for the leader in terms of leader task structure, position power, and leader–member relations? What can be done to make this situation more favorable?

EXERCISE 10-1   **Choosing a Leadership Style: Sharing Influence**

Stephan H. Putnam, University of North Carolina at Chapel Hill

We tend to think of leaders as using their influence unilaterally to help people achieve stated goals. Leaders, however, may choose a number of ways in which to share influence with others in pursuing a given mission or purpose. When a leader chooses the *autocratic* mode, he or she decides what to do without sharing any influence at all. If the leader chooses the *consultative* mode, he or she will share a modest amount of influence by asking others for their opinions before making a decision himself or herself. If the leader chooses the *group-based* mode, he or she will share influence, encouraging others in the group to participate equally in the decision making. If the leader chooses the *delegation* mode, he or she will transfer all of the leader's influence to others. This exercise will give you the opportunity to consider trade-offs among these four modes of influence sharing as you decide which to use in dealing with a typical management problem.

Step One: Pre-Class Preparation

In the class before the one in which you will perform this exercise, your instructor will divide the class into groups of four to six people (if your class has formed permanent groups, you should reassemble in those groups). The instructor will then assign each group member the role of representative of one of six departments of a manufacturing business. That is, you will be a representative of either sales and marketing, accounting and finance, manufacturing and operations, purchasing and legal affairs, research and development, or human resource management. Write the name of your role in the space provided in the Task Role and Agenda Sheet in Exhibit 10-1. Then read the task role and agenda description, and prepare to follow it in the next class.

Step Two: Group Decision Making

At the beginning of class, each group should meet and immediately elect or appoint a leader. In each group, every member should write his or her role on a piece of paper and display it so that everyone else will know which department he or she represents. When the groups have completed these tasks, the instructor will give a large paper circle to each group leader. This "pie" represents all of the decision-making power in the group, and it can be divided and distributed among the group's members as the leader sees fit. Once the leader gives the pie or any part of it to another person, power travels with that part by percentage. For instance, if the leader cuts the pie into four equal pieces and gives three to other individuals, keeping one for himself or herself, each of those four members has equal decision-making power in the group and the remaining members have none.

After the pie has been distributed and everyone understands how decision-making power is to be shared in this task, each group will have thirty minutes to reach the decision outlined in Exhibit 10-1. As group members work on the task, the group can further subdivide pieces of the pie if this course of action seems desirable. A spokesperson should be appointed to keep a record of group activities and to report back to the class afterward.

Step Three: Class Discussion

After thirty minutes the instructor will assemble the entire class, and spokespeople should report on the activities of their group. The class should then discuss its

EXHIBIT 10-1
Task Role and
Agenda Sheet

You are a member of a central steering committee composed of the heads of the departments in an industrial plant. The departments represented are sales and marketing, accounting and finance, manufacturing and operations, purchasing and legal affairs, research and development, and human resources management. Leadership of your committee rotates among the department representatives every six months.

Today's meeting has been called to allocate $100,000 that has come from company headquarters. This money must be spent within the next 60 days or be lost to taxes. The only restriction on your decision is that the money must be used to benefit the employees of your plant and to raise their morale. Your committee has thirty minutes to decide how the money will be spent.

You are the representative of the _____ department. Before the class in which your group will make its decision on this matter, think about your role and do whatever research is necessary to understand what functions are performed by departments such as yours. You will be expected to fulfill your assigned role convincingly and to display the expertise that one might expect of a department head.

experience in allocating influence among the members of a group. Be sure to address the following questions:

1. For each group, which of the four influence-sharing modes was the group's original choice? Which other modes did the group try out subsequently? Which mode seemed to work best? Which seemed least useful? Why?

2. Was it easy or difficult to move from one mode to another? How might rough transitions be smoothed?

3. If you had to repeat this exercise, would you want your group to use the same influence-sharing modes? What changes, if any, would you make? Which things would you want to stay the same?

4. What aspects of a decision and the surrounding situation are most likely to influence the usefulness of a particular mode?

5. In a real organization, what mechanisms might take the place of the "influence pie" in the regulation of sharing? In your future job, how much say do you expect to have over who will have influence and who will not? Do you think you will find this division of power acceptable?

Conclusion

The process of sharing influence and reaching a decision is complicated and requires great managerial insight. Leading a group through decision-making procedures can involve paying as much attention to *how* to decide as *what* to decide. No single mode of influence sharing and decision making is suitable for every situation. Instead, to perform effectively, managers must adopt the contingency approach, diagnosing each situation to determine which mode to employ.

Adapted from J. William Pfeiffer, *The 1977 Annual Handbook for Group Facilitators*. Reprinted by permission of John Wiley & Sons, Inc.

PART 3 CASES

Case 3-1 The Lordstown Plant of General Motors

Case 3-2 Beta Bureau

Case 3-3 Nurse Ross

Case 3-4 Executive Retreat: A Case of Group Failure

Case 3-5 Bob Collins

Case 3-6 The Case of Dick Spencer

CASE 3-1 THE LORDSTOWN PLANT OF GENERAL MOTORS

Hak-Chong Lee, Yonsei University

Although the events described in this case took place more than twenty years ago, the case remains a classic example of certain kinds of problems that managers and employees face in modern industrial workplaces. Today, companies throughout the United States continue to wrestle with exactly the same predicaments as those that confronted General Motors in its Lordstown plant in the early 1970s.

INTRODUCTION

In December 1971, the management of the Lordstown plant was very much concerned with an unusually high rate of defective Vegas coming off the assembly line. For the previous several weeks, the lot with a capacity of 2,000 cars had been filled with Vegas that were waiting for rework before they could be shipped out to the dealers around the country.

The management was particularly disturbed by the fact that many of the defects were not the kinds of quality deficiencies normally expected in an assembly production of automobiles. There was a countless number of Vegas with their windshields broken, upholstery slashed, ignition keys broken, signal levers bent, rearview mirrors broken, or carburetors clogged with washers. There were cases in which, as the plant manager put it, "the whole engine blocks passed by forty men without any work done on them." Since then, the incident in the Lordstown plant has been much publicized in news media, drawing public interest. It has also been frequently discussed

Reprinted by permission of Hak-Chong Lee, Professor Management, Graduate School of International Studies, Yonsei University, Seoul, Korea.

in the classroom and in the academic circles. While some people viewed the event as "young worker revolt," others reacted to it as a simple "labor problem." Some viewed it as "worker sabotage," and others called it "industrial Woodstock." This case describes some background and important incidents leading to this much publicized and discussed industrial event.

The General Motors Corporation is the nation's largest manufacturer. The company is a leading example of an industrial organization that has achieved organizational growth and success through decentralization. The philosophy of decentralization has been one of the most valued traditions in General Motors from the days of Alfred Sloan in the 1930s, through the management of Charles Wilson and Harlow Curtice in the 1950s, and up to recent years. Under decentralized management, each of the company's car divisions—Cadillac, Buick, Oldsmobile, Pontiac, and Chevrolet—was given maximum autonomy in the management of its manufacturing and marketing operations. The assembly operations were no exception, with each division managing its own assembly work. The car bodies built by Fisher Body were assembled in various locations under maximum control and coordination between Fisher Body and each car division.

In the mid-1960s, however, the decentralization in divisional assembly operations was subject to a critical review. At the divisional level, the company was experiencing serious problems of worker absenteeism and increasing cost with declines in quality and productivity. They were reflected in the overall profit margins, which were declining from 10 percent to 7 percent in the late 1960s. The autonomy in the divided management of the body manufacturing and assembly operations, in separate locations in many cases, became questionable under the declining profit situation.

In light of these developments, General Motors began to consolidate in some instances the divided management of body and chassis assembly operations into a single management unit under the already existing General Motors Assembly Division (GMAD) to better coordinate the two operations. GMAD was given an overall responsibility to integrate the two operations in these instances and to see that the numerous parts and components going into car assembly got to the right places in the right amounts at the right times.

THE GENERAL MOTORS ASSEMBLY DIVISION

GMAD was originally established in the mid-1930s, when the company needed an additional assembly plant to meet the increasing demands for Buick, Oldsmobile, and Pontiac automobiles. The demand for these cars was growing so far beyond the available capacity at the time that the company began, for the first time, to build an assembly plant on the West Coast that could turn out all three lines of cars rather than an individual line. As this novel approach became successful, similar plants turning out multiple lines of cars were built in seven other locations in the East, South, and Midwest. In the 1960s, the demand for Chevrolet production also increased, and some Buick–Oldsmobile–Pontiac plants began to assemble Chevrolet products. Accordingly, the name of the division was changed to GMAD in 1965.

To improve quality and productivity, GMAD increased its control over the operations of body manufacturing and assembly. It reorganized jobs, launched programs to improve efficiency, and reduced the causes of defects that required repairs and rework. With many positive results attained under the GMAD management, the company extended the single-management concept to six more assembly locations in 1968, which had previously been run by the Fisher Body and Chevrolet Divisions.

In 1971, GM further extended the concept to four additional Chevrolet–Fisher Body assembly facilities, consolidating the separate management under which the body and chassis assembly had been operating. One of these plants was the Lordstown plant. The series of consolidations brought to eighteen the number of assembly plants operated by GMAD. In terms of total production, they were producing about 75 percent of all cars and 67 percent of trucks built by GM. Also in 1971, one of the plants under the GMAD administration began building certain Cadillac models, thus involving GMAD in the production of automobiles for each of GM's five domestic car divisions as well as trucks for Chevrolet, GMC Trucks, and GM's Coach Division.

THE LORDSTOWN COMPLEX

The Lordstown complex is located in Trumbull County in Ohio, about fifteen miles west of Youngstown and thirty miles east of Akron. It consists of the Vega assembly plant, the van–truck assembly plant, and Fisher Body metal fabricating plant, occupying about 1,000 acres of land. GMAD, which operates the Vega and van–truck assembly plants, is also located in the Lordstown complex. The three plants are in the heart of the heavy industrial triangle of Youngstown, Akron, and Cleveland. With Youngstown as a center of steel production, Akron as the home of rubber industries, and Cleveland as a major center for heavy manufacturing, the Lordstown complex commands a good strategic and logistic location for automobile assembly.

The original assembly plant was built in 1964–1966 to assemble Chevrolet Impalas. In 1970, it was converted into Vega assembly through extensive redesign. The van–truck assembly plant was constructed in 1969, and the Fisher Body metal fabricating plant was added in 1970 to carry out stamping operations to produce sheet-metal components used in Vega and van assemblies. In October 1971, the Chevrolet Vega and van–assembly plants and the Fisher Body Vega assembly plants, which had been operating under separate management, were merged into a single jurisdiction of GMAD.

WORKFORCE AT THE LORDSTOWN PLANT

More than 11,400 employees were working in the Lordstown plant [as of 1973]. Approximately 6,000 people, of whom 5,500 were on hourly payroll, worked in the Vega assembly plant. About 2,600 workers, 2,100 of them paid hourly, worked in van–truck assembly. As members of the United Auto Workers Union, Local 1112, the workers commanded good wages and benefits. They started out on the line at about $5.00 per hour, got a 10¢ per hour increase within 30 days, and received another 10¢ per hour raise after 90 days. Benefits came to $2.50 per hour. The supplemental unemployment benefits virtually guaranteed the workers' wages throughout the year. A worker who was laid off got more than 90 percent of his or her wages for 52 weeks. The worker was also eligible for up to six weeks for holidays, excused absence, or bereavement, and up to four weeks of vacation time.

The workforce at the plant was almost entirely made up of local people, with 92 percent coming from the immediate area of a twenty-mile radius. Lordstown itself was a small rural town of about 500 residents. The sizable city closest to the plant was Warren, five miles away, which together with Youngstown supplied about two-thirds of the workforce. The majority of the workers (57.5 percent) were married, 7.6 percent were homeowners, and 20.2 percent were buying their homes. Of those who did not own their homes (72 percent), more than half were still living with their parents. The rest lived in rented houses or apartments.

The workers in the plant were generally young. Although various news media reported the average worker age as twenty-four years old, and in some parts of the plant as twenty-two years old, company records showed that the overall average worker age was slightly higher than twenty-nine years as of 1971–1972. The national average worker age was forty-two years. The workforce at Lordstown was the second-youngest among GM's twenty-five assembly plants around the country. The fact that the Lordstown plant was GM's newest assembly plant may partly explain the relatively young workforce.

The educational profile of the Lordstown workers indicated that only 22.2 percent had less than a high school education. Nearly two-thirds (62 percent) were high school graduates, and 16 percent were either college graduates or had attended college. Another 26 percent had attended trade school. The average education of 13.2 years made the Lordstown workers among the best educated in GM's assembly plants.

THE VEGA ASSEMBLY LINE

Conceived as a major competitive product against the increasing influx of foreign cars, which were being produced with labor costs as low as one-fourth of the U.S. labor rate, the Vega was specifically designed with a maximum production efficiency and economy in mind. From the initial stages of planning, the Vega was designed by a special task team with the most sophisticated techniques, using computers in designing the outer skin of the car and making the tapes that form the dies. Computers were also used to match up parts, measure the stack tolerances, measure safety performance under head-on collision, and make all necessary corrections before the first 1971 model car was ever built. The 2300-cubic-centimeter, all-aluminum, four-cylinder engine was designed to give gas economy comparable to the foreign imports.

The Vega was also designed with the plant and the people in mind. As GM's newest plant, the Vega assembly plant was known as the "super plant" with the most modern and sophisticated designs to maximize efficiency. It featured the newest engineering techniques and a variety of new power tools and automatic devices to eliminate much of the heavy lifting and physical labor. The line gave the workers easier access to the car body, reducing the amount of bending and crawling in and out as compared with other plants around the country. The unitized body in large components such as prefab housing made the assembly easier and lighter with greater body integrity. Most difficult and tedious tasks were eliminated or simplified, on-the-line variations of the job were minimized, and the most modern tooling and mechanization were used to the highest possible degree of reliability.

The Vega production line was also the fastest-moving assembly line in the industry. The average time per assembly job was 36 seconds, with a maximum of 100 cars rolling off the assembly line per hour, giving a daily production of 1,600 cars from two-shift operations.

The time cycle per job in other assembly plants averaged about 55 seconds. Although the high speed of the line did not necessarily imply greater workload or job requirements, it was part of GM's attempt to maximize economy in Vega assembly. The fact that the Vega was designed to have 43 percent fewer parts than a full-size car also helped the high-speed line and economy.

IMPACT OF GMAD AND REORGANIZATION IN THE LORDSTOWN PLANT

As stated previously, the assembly operations at Lordstown had originally been run by Fisher Body and Chevrolet as two plants. There were two organizations, two plant managers, two unions, and two service organizations. The consolidation of the two organizations into a single operating system under GMAD in October 1971 required the difficult task of reorganization and dealing with the consequences of workforce reduction, such as work slowdowns, worker discipline, grievances, and so forth.

As duplicate units such as production, maintenance, inspection, and personnel were consolidated, the problem of selecting the personnel to manage the new organization arose. Chief inspectors, personnel directors, and production superintendents as well as production and service workers were displaced or reassigned. The unions that had been representing the respective plants also had to go through reorganization. Union elections were held to merge the separate union committees at Fisher Body and Chevrolet in a single union bargaining committee. This eliminated one full local union shop committee.

At the same time, GMAD launched an effort to improve production efficiency to bring it more in line with that in other assembly plants. This effort included increasing job efficiency through reorganization and better coordination between the body and chassis assembly, and improving controls over product quality and worker absenteeism. It also coincided with adjustments in line balance and work methods. Like other assembly plants, the Vega assembly plant was going through an initial period of diseconomy caused by suboptimal operations, imbalance in the assembly line, and a somewhat redundant workforce. According to management, line adjustments and work changes were part of a normal process in accelerating the assembly operation to the peak performance for which the plant had been designed after the initial break-in and start-up period.

As for job efficiency, GMAD initiated changes in those work sequences and work methods that were not well coordinated under the divided managements of body and chassis assembly.

For example, prior to GMAD control, Fisher Body had been delivering the car body complete with interior trim to the final assembly lines, where the workers often soiled the front seats as they did further assembly operations. GMAD changed this practice so that the seats were installed as one of the last operations in building the car. Fisher Body also had been delivering the car body with a complete panel instrument frame, which made it extremely difficult for the assembly workers to reach behind the frame in installing the instrument panels. GMAD improved the job method so that the box containing the entire instrument panel was installed on the assembly line. Such improvements in job sequences and job methods resulted in savings in time and the number of workers required. Consequently, in some jobs the assembly time was cut down and/or the number of workers was reduced.

GMAD also put more strict control over worker absenteeism and the causes for defective work; the reduction in absenteeism was expected to require fewer relief workers, and the improvements in quality and the smaller amount of repair work were expected to require fewer repairpeople. In implementing these changes, GMAD instituted a strong policy of dealing with worker slowdowns via strict disciplinary measures, including dismissal. It was rumored that the inspectors and supervisors passing defective cars would be fired on the spot.

Many workers were laid off as a result of the reorganization and job changes. The union claimed that as many as 700 workers were laid off. Management, on the other hand, put the layoff figure at 375, to which the union later conceded. Although management claimed that the changes in job sequences and methods in some assembly work did not bring a substantial change in the overall speed or pace of the assembly line, the workers perceived the job change as "tightening" the assembly line. The union charged that GMAD brought a return of an old-fashioned line speedup and a "sweatshop style" of management reminiscent of the 1930s, making the workers do more work at the same pay. The workers blamed the "tightened" assembly line for the drastic increase in quality defects. As one worker commented, "That's the fastest line in the world. We have about forty seconds to do our job. The company adds one more thing and it can kill us. We can't get the stuff done on time and a car goes by. The company then blames us for sabotage and shoddy work."

The number of worker grievances also increased drastically. Before GMAD took over, there were about 100 grievances in the plant. After GMAD's entry, grievances increased to 5,000, of which 1,000 were related to the charge that too much work had been added to each job. Worker resentment was particularly great in the "towveyor" assembly and seat subassembly areas. The "towveyor" is the area where engines and transmissions are assembled. As in seat subassembly, it involves a large concentration of workers working together in close proximity. Also, these jobs are typically performed by beginning assemblers, who are younger and better educated.

The workers in the plant were particularly resentful of the company's strict policy in implementing the changes. They stated that the tougher the company became, the more they would stiffen their resistance, even though other jobs were scarce in the market. One worker said, "In some of the other plants where the GMAD did the same thing, the workers were older and they took this. But I've got twenty-five years ahead of me in this plant." Another worker commented, "I saw a woman running to keep pace with the fast line. I'm not going to run for anybody. There ain't anyone in that plant who is going to tell me to run." One supervisor said, "The problem with the workers here is not so much that they don't want to work, but that they just don't want to take orders. They don't believe in any kind of authority." While the workers were resisting management orders, there were some indications that the first-line supervisors had not been adequately trained to perform satisfactory supervisory roles. The average supervisor at the time had less than three years of experience, and 20 percent of the supervisors had less than one year of experience. Typically, they were young, somewhat lacking in knowledge of the provisions of the union contract and other supervisory duties, and less than adequately trained to handle the workers in the threatening and hostile environment that was developing.

Another significant fact was that the strong reactions of the workers were not entirely related to the organizational and job changes brought about by GMAD. Management felt that the intense resentment was particularly due to the nature of the workforce in Lordstown. The plant workforce not only was made up of young people, but also reflected the characteristics of "tough labor" in the steel, coal, and rubber industries in the surrounding communities. Many of the workers, in fact, came from families who made their living working in these industries. Management also noted that the worker resistance had been much greater in the Lordstown plant than in other plants where similar changes had been made.

A good part of the young workers' resentment also seemed to be related to the unskilled and repetitive nature of the assembly work. One management official admitted that the company was facing a difficult task in getting workers to "take pride" in the product they were assembling. Many of them were participating in the company's tuition assistance plan, which was supporting their college education in the evening. With this educated background, obviously assembly work was not fulfilling their high work expectations. Also, the job market was tight at the time, and they could neither find any meaningful jobs elsewhere nor, even if they found such work, afford to give up the good money and fringe benefits they were earning on their assembly line jobs. This frustrated them, according to company officials.

Many industrial engineers were questioning whether management could continue simplifying assembly line work. As the jobs became easier, simpler, and repetitive, requiring less physical effort, there were fewer traces of skill and increased monotony. Worker unrest indicated that employees not only wanted to go back to the work pace prior to the "speedup" (the pre-October pace), but also wanted the company to do something about the boring and meaningless assembly work. One worker commented, "The company has got to do something to change the job so that a guy can take an interest in the job. A guy can't do the same thing eight hours a day year after year. And it's got to be more than the company just saying to a guy, 'Okay, instead of six spots on the weld, you'll do five spots.'"

As worker resentment mounted, the UAW Local 1112 decided in early January 1972 to consider possible authorization of a strike against the Lordstown plant in a fight against the job changes. In the meantime, the union and management bargaining teams worked hard on worker grievances; they reduced the number of grievances from 5,000 to a few hundred, and management even indicated that it would restore some of the eliminated jobs. However, the bargaining failed to produce accord on the issues of seniority rights and shift preference, which were related to wider issues of job changes and layoff.

A vote was held in early February 1972. Nearly 90 percent of the workers came out to vote in the heaviest turnout in the history of Local 1112. With 97 percent of the votes supporting the move, the workers went out on strike in early March.

In March 1972, with the strike in effect, the management of the Lordstown plant was assessing the impact of the GMAD reorganization and the resultant strike in the plant. It was estimated that the work disruption because of the worker resentment and slowdown had already cost the company 12,000 Vegas and 4,000 trucks, amounting to $45 million. There had been repeated closedowns of assembly lines since December 1971, because of the worker slowdowns and the cars passing down the line without all necessary operations performed on them. The car lot was full, with 2,000 cars waiting for repair work.

There had also been an amazing number of complaints from Chevrolet dealers—6,000 complaints in November alone—about the quality of the Vegas shipped to them. This was more than the combined complaints from all of the other assembly plants.

The strike in the Lordstown plant was expected to affect other plants. The plants at Tonawanda, New York, and Buffalo, New York, were supplying parts for Vega. Despite the costly impact of the worker resistance and the strike, management felt that the job changes and cost reductions were essential if the Vega was to return a profit to the company. The plant had to be operating at about 90 percent capacity to break even, because its highly automated features cost twice as much as had been estimated.

While the company had to do something to increase the production efficiency in the Lordstown plant, the management was wondering whether it could not have planned and implemented the organizational and job changes differently in view of the costly disruption of operations that the plant had been experiencing.

When you have read this case, review the diagnostic questions included at the end(s) of the chapter(s) you are using to analyze this case, and choose the ones that seem applicable. Then use those questions to begin working on your case analysis.

CASE 3-2 BETA BUREAU

Donald Austin Woolf, University of Oklahoma

PART A

The Sigma Agency is a large division of the Epsilon Department, a cabinet-level department of the federal government. It has primary responsibility for the administration of a law providing a variety of services to a large number of citizens. In general terms, the agency is organized in terms of operating bureaus, an administrative and staff services bureau, and a bureau providing support services. Each of the operating bureaus administers or assists in administering a separate portion of the law. Beta Bureau operates regional claims-processing centers for the Sigma Agency.

Claims are filed by applicants at widely dispersed branch offices, each of which is administered by a branch office bureau. Routine claims may be authorized by representatives at the branch offices. All others—about half of the total workload—are forwarded to Beta Bureau processing centers along with the record of actions taken on those claims authorized at the branch office. The processing center reviews all actions taken at the branch level, processes initial claims not authorized by branches, reviews or authorizes changes in eligibility of existing claimants (post-entitlement), and initiates recovery action in cases where claimants have received services in excess of that permitted by law, rule, or regulation.

Claim files are physically maintained at and by the processing centers. Finally, information on all actions taken is transmitted to the central data storage and retrieval system, located at headquarters near Washington, D.C. Central Data operates as a separate service bureau and provides this service to all operating bureaus. Each of the centers employs about 2,000 people. Most of the bureaus—including Beta Bureau—have been organized along "functional" lines, or relatively large sections of people in which all do the same or very similar work. Accordingly, processing centers have had an intake unit, which receives and sends correspondence, records, claims, and files; a records unit; and two kinds of claims units, each constituting several sections, which are devoted to initial claims and post-entitlement claims, respectively.

Records assembles various documents relating to a given case, places them in a folder, and routes the folder to the appropriate section. Accordingly, queuing occurs at Records, and at each of the subsequent sections to which the file is sent. Because of the magnitude of the records, they formerly were moved from place to place in large canvas "tubs" mounted on casters, with about 11,000 folders in each tub.

Folders frequently failed to have all information necessary to complete processing, so they were often rerouted to other sections or even other centers, where queuing occurred again. In the past, it has taken from one to two weeks for a given case to move through a queue. As queues multiplied, the time necessary for processing sometimes extended to several months.

Authorizers processing initial claims held the most prestigious professional jobs, with post-entitlement authorizers holding a lesser grade and pay status. The sections were relatively large, having as many as sixty kinds of cases. This specialization was formal in some instances and informal in others. Since all authorizers were evaluated in terms of number of cases processed and the accuracy thereof, there was a tendency for difficult cases to be rerouted, ostensibly for more documentation, or because another authorizer was deemed to have superior expertise in the problem associated with the case. Given the queuing phenomenon associated with functional organization, Beta Bureau experienced a chronic problem with aged cases.

Unsurprisingly, claimants were likely to file complaints, sometimes with Sigma Agency, frequently with congressional representatives, and occasionally with the executive office of the president. Sigma Agency maintained a special headquarters unit to process these complaints and to continue communication with the claimant, the elected official referring the complaint, and the bureau responsible for the claim. Meanwhile, the claim, most likely in transit, could prove exceedingly difficult to track down. Accordingly, processing centers developed "freeze lists" of aged claims. All claims on the freeze list were to be assigned highest priority until located and processed.

By the early 1990s, processing time, error rates, employee morale, turnover, and service to clients had reached unacceptable levels. Documentation of cases became critical in several areas, especially in "unassociated material"—that is, documents needed to complete a claims case that, for one reason or another, never found their way to the claims folder for that case. Efforts were made to improve the existing system by upgrading the data storage and retrieval system and by tightening controls. A somewhat higher proportion of new claims were authorized at the branch office, enabling the same official to follow a new claim through from start to finish. Numerous additional changes in equipment and procedure were authorized to expedite processing and to improve control. Although there is little hard evidence to suggest that firmer discipline was exercised, awards for exceptional service were increased and publicized.

Results of these efforts were disappointing, serving mainly to slow the decline in service, rather than to reverse it. Accordingly, bureau top management decided that the basic structure itself would have to be revised. A special staff was authorized to design and experiment with organizational structures to identify a system that would enhance service to the clientele and improve case control as well as productivity. Among things to be considered were job enlargement and enrichment, physical layout, composition of the work group, and supervision.

PART B

Because of increasing problems of administration under the existing structure, the top management of Beta Bureau of the Sigma Agency initiated a study of alternative forms of organization utilizing its in-house special staff. After initial research and planning at headquarters, the special staff conducted field research at a processing center. Interviews and meetings were held with all levels of management, professional and support personnel, and union representatives. Results of the research indicated that it would be appropriate to conduct a pilot study to determine further the feasibility of work units organized along different lines from the traditional functional organization.

The Bureau Director, working with special staff and relevant line managers, proposed a concept of a "processing center within a processing center." Accordingly, the kinds of work to be done in such a unit, optimum size, positions, support staff, equipment, and facilities had to be determined as well as the appropriate grades and pay rates for new positions created.

After some discussion, it was decided to call the new type of work group a "module," and the concept "modular organization." A number of combinations and variations in size, composition, work flow support equipment, span of control, chain of command, and support services were tried. Experimentation with and evaluation of two pilot work units over a period of two years produced a viable structure, although not one considered by staff to be "optimum." Top management determined that the problems leading to the experimentation were of such urgency that further study and experimentation were precluded. Also, in the interim, a number of new buildings had been built to house existing centers and it was felt that moving from existing facilities to the new ones could be combined with the change in organizational structure.

Matters were further complicated by a number of major, new amendments to the law relating to the programs being administered. New positions were created, necessitating authorization by the Civil Service Commission, which proved more difficult than had been anticipated. All of these events placed a massive burden on the existing training staff as well as on management from the first-line level to the top. Rank-and-file employees were also obviously affected by the rapid rate of change. Concurrent adoption of new technologies of case handling further complicated matters. The result was a kind of "future shock" felt by all concerned. Finally, during the latter stages of phasing in modularization, a massive reorganization of top management took place following the retirement of the bureau director who had initiated the original study.

Interviews with employees produced responses such as "I wish the world would just stop for about six months so I could catch up," "We might just be able to do a professional job on this program if Congress would quit making special exceptions for left-handed Eskimo veterans of the Korean War," and "If management *really* knew what it was doing, we wouldn't have procedural changes every fifteen minutes." The modules that emerged from this process contained about fifty employees each, supervised by a module manager and two assistant managers. A technical adviser served as a resource for professionals in the module. The latter position tended to be of a "rotating" nature in some locations; that is, different rank-and-file professionals were temporarily assigned to the position rather than having it as a permanent assignment. Case records were specifically assigned to and physically located in each module. Accordingly, at the time a case was assigned an identification number, it was determined which of the more than 200 modules would have virtually absolute responsibility for any future claim related to the case. Each time a folder was moved, information as to location change was fed into a central computer through a network terminal. For the most part, individual authorizers followed through on a single case until it was completed. Queuing was reduced to a minimum.

Two years after the initial installation of this system, a "faculty fellow" from a state university was assigned to attempt evaluation. Most of his efforts were directed toward job satisfaction. Initially, productivity was determined to be extremely difficult to measure because of the massive changes in the law, increased mechanization of some activities, difficulty in evaluating increased complexities in the program and their resulting impact on processing, and a number of changes in databases. Realignment of the workload between branch offices, processing centers, and headquarters combined to make precise evaluation of productivity impossible. Nevertheless, some useful baseline data were obtained.

Two years later, a follow-up study was commissioned almost immediately after the conversion to modular organization was completed. In addition to job satisfaction, aggregate measures of productivity, turnover, absenteeism, processing time, control, and relative costs were obtained. From the initiation of modular organization, massive change was a continuous phenomenon. In addition to the change in the form of organization, a substantial revision of relevant legislation was passed, creating a number of new programs. In general, the new laws tended to make all but purely routine cases more difficult to process. Estimates of the level of increased difficulty were in the range of 15 percent. During the second study, Beta Bureau was engaged in a project to upgrade data-processing equipment such that each module had complete access to the master data file at headquarters. Accordingly, given the variety of changes, it was difficult to measure the precise impact of reorganization.

Nevertheless, a variety of findings were obtained. In comparison with other operating bureaus doing comparable work, both absenteeism and turnover declined. Cost of administration as a proportion of total cost declined. "Freeze lists" declined by 85 percent or more, demonstrating a marked improvement in control. Average processing time declined slightly where the new remote terminals had not been installed, and markedly where they were installed.

Job satisfaction for the modules studied improved in four out of five categories measured; however, there were significant differences in perceived job satisfaction among different classes of employees. In general, lower-level clerical workers liked the change to modular organization, while professionals and first-line supervisors exhibited considerable variance in their opinion. Of the total number surveyed, about 80 percent preferred modules to functional organization. Few, if any, changes in quality control were demonstrated, but a decline attributable to the massive change in procedures as well as the law would not have been unexpected. Such a decline did not take place.

In the early stages, union representatives expressed substantial reservations about the proposed reorganization. This initial reluctance declined in most of the processing centers, although one local continued to maintain an official attitude of opposition. The attitude change was attributable in part to a modest net increase in pay-grade level resulting from the reorganization.

Summing up results of the studies, there appeared to be few, if any, problems with the structural configuration of modules. They seemed to work in this kind of service operation. Nevertheless, problems remained with the operation of the centers as a whole. A few of these were structural, but most appeared to be procedural or managerial in nature.

In the process of abolishing sections of people, all of whom were doing about the same thing, and substituting modules of people doing different things, a number of one-of-a-kind positions were created. For example, some of the specialized sections merged into modules had only a few dozen people in them. This resulted in each module having only a single specialist in that category after reorganization. Accordingly, if the incumbent was promoted or left the job, the function served went uncovered. Although other professionals could be temporarily assigned to the function, they did not like it, and such occurrences were disruptive. Meanwhile, support functions such as recruiting and training were geared to the old-style sections, and would allow vacancies to accumulate in substantial numbers before selecting new candidates.

Job enlargement was also found to be a mixed blessing. Professionals and indeed entire sections had tended to specialize in particular kinds of cases under the functional pattern of organization. With modularization, it became necessary to become proficient in all kinds.

This latter kind of problem was intensified for module managers. Previously, they needed to have detailed technical knowledge about only a single phase of the processing operation and the way in which it interfaced with other parts; under the new scheme of organization, it became necessary to be familiar with all parts of the operation.

Among the most visible signs of this problem was a substantial exodus of former section heads destined to become—or who had become—module managers. Although headway was being made, the highest proportionate number of vacancies in modules was at the managerial level, with up to one-third of the modules systemwide operating either with "acting" (temporary) managers or without the usual complement of a manager and two assistant managers in each module. Estimates were that as many as one-third of the former supervisors had retired or transferred to other jobs in the federal government. On a brighter note, the remaining managers and a number of newer appointees appeared to be more flexible and more knowledgeable and to consider the new position more of a challenge.

A continuing problem was that of substantial variation in productivity between individuals and between modules. Moreover, marginal personnel were at least benignly tolerated, so that an employee could be producing up to four times as much as his or her neighbor doing the same work, yet receive identical pay. The result of this system amounted to rewarding poor performance rather than excellence. Predictably, policy was applied inconsistently because of relatively poor intermodular communication in some instances.

In viewing the physical arrangement of modules, it was noteworthy that barriers, such as files, tables, and coat racks, were placed so as to impede movement between the modules. In part, this was done so that anyone entering or leaving a module would have to pass in view of the manager, a form of control. On the other hand, it discouraged professionals and others from seeking counsel from their peers in other modules. Professionals also aired complaints about inequitable distribution of the workload.

A substantial minority of professionals perceived a loss of status when they were physically located with lower-level personnel. By contrast, the overwhelming majority of all personnel approved of the opportunity to observe all phases of the work as well as the integration of it.

Good producers were very pleased with the increased accountability found in the modules, but not as pleased with what they viewed as inadequate management response to poor work.

In summation, the movement of an organization of this size from a traditional, functional mode to a form not previously tried on a large scale in service organizations during a period marked by a new construction, new law, and new procedures was an accomplishment of considerable magnitude in itself. Improvements in relative cost, case control, processing time (which means improved service to clientele), absenteeism, turnover, and job satisfaction were observed. Remaining problems include interfacing staff support and service to the modular structure, intermodular communication, consistent application of policy, and improving performance of some low producers. These problems would not appear to be insurmountable.

When you have read this case, review the diagnostic questions included at the end(s) of the chapter(s) you are using to analyze this case, and choose the ones that seem applicable. Then use those questions to begin working on your case analysis.

CASE 3-3   ## NURSE ROSS

William M. Fox, University of Florida

The following situation was reported by Miss Jackson, who had known Miss Evelyn Ross for several years and had also worked in some of the same hospitals as Miss Ross on different occasions.

Miss Ross, a registered nurse, began working at Benton Hospital when she was thirty-one years old. This hospital was an industrial hospital in a fairly large city on the West Coast. The bed capacity of the hospital was about 150, but 50 to 100 patients received treatment daily through the hospital's clinic facilities. The hospital was built and operated by a large shipbuilding concern. All the employees of the company's shipyards and their dependents could receive medical care through the company's hospitalization plan.

The nursing staff was headed by a director of nurses, who had two assistants. One was in charge of nursing services in the hospital, and the other was in charge of the clinic nursing services. However, the two departments operated as a coordinated unit, and personnel were exchanged between them in the event that the workload became too heavy in either place.

The medical director of the hospital, Dr. Peake, was energetic and his manner was usually quite brusque. Although he was a stickler for discipline and efficiency, he was fair in his treatment of the staff, and they respected him and cooperated well. Dr. Peake had many progressive ideas and had helped to build the hospital up from 75 to 150 beds. The new ideas he had were discussed in staff conferences. Any people or heads of departments who might be affected by proposed changes participated in these conferences.

Miss Ross worked as a head nurse, both in the hospital and in the clinic, during her employment there. (Miss Jackson at that time was employed as assistant head nurse in the clinic.) Miss Ross resigned her position to enter the Army Nurse Corps as a first lieutenant. She served in the Army for two and a half years, most of which entailed duty in the South Pacific. During the time she was overseas, she was promoted to captain. She was transferred to reserve status upon leaving the corps. Shortly afterward, she took a three-month course in operating room supervision.

In the meantime, Miss Jackson had moved to the East Coast and was employed at Hughes Hospital, a large industrial hospital in a relatively small New England city. The two nurses had corresponded during this time, and Miss Jackson wrote that the position of operating room supervisor would soon be open at the hospital and that Miss Ross had a good chance of getting the position if she wanted to move to the East Coast. Miss Ross applied to the director of nursing at the hospital and was accepted for the position. She began working soon thereafter at Hughes. Hughes Hospital was set up much like Benton Hospital. It took care of the medical needs of most of the community in addition to serving the employees of the Hughes Steel Company, the city's principal employer. It had clinic facilities for emergency and outpatient care. The bed capacity was 250, and the clinic staff treated more than 100 patients daily, although often a complete record of the number of patients was not kept.

The organization of the nursing department was quite similar to that of Benton Hospital, with one important exception: The hospital department and the clinic department operated as two completely separate units. The clinic was in a building separate from the hospital building; thus moving a stretcher case from the clinic to the hospital was an extreme ordeal.

Besides the lack of proper equipment for moving patients, there was a shortage of male orderlies, and nurses' aides had to be utilized for this arduous task. This shortage of personnel and equipment was especially acute when emergency cases and accident victims came into the clinic and had to be moved to the hospital with a minimum loss of time and disturbance.

The director of nurses, Miss McHaffey, was about forty-five years old; she had been at the hospital three years. Miss Linden had been the hospital supervisor for six months, and Miss Hartman had been employed as a clinic supervisor for over a year. There were twenty-four graduate nurses employed in the hospital wards, thirty aides, and ten maids. The staff under Miss Hartman in the clinic consisted of five graduate nurses, four aides, and two maids. The orderly personnel numbered only six for all three shifts. One was utilized throughout the hospital on the evening shift, one on the night shift, and during the day shift one worked in the clinic, one in the operating room (O.R.), and one in each of the two men's wards in the hospital. Miss Ross, as supervisor of the O.R., had a staff of four nurses, three aides, and the one orderly. The nurses in the O.R. rotated turns, being "on call" each night for any emergency surgery cases.

Miss Ross found that the work was quite strenuous and often entailed long hours, but she was deeply interested in it and never seemed to object. She frequently stayed to help in emergency surgery cases, as a number of rather serious accidents occurred from time to time in the steel plants that the hospital served. Miss McHaffey praised her highly for increasing the efficiency and cleanliness in the operating rooms.

Dr. McMillan, the medical director of the hospital, was nearly sixty-five years old. He had been employed as a company doctor for the Hughes Steel Company for more than twenty years. Dr. McMillan would usually arrive at his offices in the hospital about nine in the morning, dictate answers to his correspondence, make sporadic rounds of some of the hospital wards (very rarely did he put in an appearance at the clinic), leave for lunch promptly at noon, and only two or three times a week return to the hospital for a few hours after lunch.

On his occasional ward rounds, he would stop at the floor nurse's desk, inquire if everything was going all right, then say, "Fine! Fine!" and go on his way.

When Dr. McMillan suffered a heart attack severe enough to prevent him from retaining his position at the hospital, a new medical director had to be found. The president of the steel company was familiar with the West Coast shipbuilding concern and knew that Dr. Peake had been at Benton. He contacted Dr. Peake to see whether he would be interested in the position as the hospital medical director. Dr. Peake accepted the job. He entered the new situation with his usual brusque and energetic manner and made complete daily rounds in the clinic and hospital.

He often spent considerable time talking to patients, nurses, aides, and staff physicians. After nearly a month of concentrated observation of the clinic and hospital routines, Dr. Peake had a conference with Miss McHaffey and the nursing supervisors. He criticized the "unprofessional attitude" of several nurses, and said he had received complaints from many of the patients about the care they were receiving. He asked why so many of the nurses seemed to be away from their wards when he made morning rounds. Miss McHaffey said the nurses were permitted to leave the wards at intervals between nine and eleven to have coffee in the hospital dining room. The time for this was not rigidly enforced. Dr. Peake also talked to Dr. Albright, the staff physician in charge of the clinic, and to the clinic nurses to ascertain why the clinic patients often had to wait so long to see a doctor in the clinic. (The gist of these conferences was given by Miss Jackson, who was assistant supervisor of the clinic.) The clinic staff agreed that there was definitely a "bottleneck" in the clinic, but they felt that it was due primarily to a shortage of personnel when needed most, the inconvenience of having to transport the patients the distance to the hospital, and the lack of satisfactory laboratory facilities in the clinic itself. Dr. Peake told the staff that the new additions being built onto the hospital would be used for clinic facilities. In the meantime, he said, he would try to help them find some way to ease the situation.

During the second week of August of that year, Miss McHaffey asked Miss Ross to come into her office.

Miss McHaffey: "Miss Ross, Dr. Peake tells me that you worked with him at Benton Hospital. I knew that he had been at Benton at one time, but didn't realize that it was during the same time you were there. He said that you are familiar with the clinic–hospital arrangement there and told me to relieve you of your present position so that you may help to coordinate the clinic and hospital units here."

Miss Ross: "I'm sorry to hear that. I have been very happy with my present position. Will I be working in the clinic or in the hospital?"

Miss McHaffey: "Both. I want you to know that I consider Miss Linden a very capable supervisor, and I don't want her to be hurt in this new arrangement. Also, I want to know everything that is going on down there. I expect you to report to me at least once a day. I don't know what Dr. Peake expects you to do that hasn't already been done. He should hire more people if he expects to make this a model hospital. He comes in here and all he does is criticize."

Miss Ross: "I'll do the best I can. I am familiar with the setup that Dr. Peake had at Benton. Maybe I can help put it into operation here."

A few hours later Dr. Peake entered Miss Ross's office in the O.R. unit.

Dr. Peake: "Hello, Rossie, I have a new job for you."

Miss Ross: "Miss McHaffey has told me about it."

Dr. Peake: "You know how things were at Benton. I want the units to be set up in exactly that way here. During the past few months I have arranged for another physician to help out in the clinic during their busy hours, and we've hired a couple more aides, but there doesn't seem to be too much improvement. Maybe you can help me find out what the trouble is there. Our new building program has been started, and when it is finished I want the two units to be operating as one integrated unit. I don't like to take you away from the surgery—you've been doing a fine job here—but I feel you can help me get the clinic and hospital units functioning better together."

Miss Ross: "I can try, Dr. Peake."

Dr. Peake: "Good! Now, I don't want you to go through anybody—if you have any problems, come right to me!"

Miss Ross—knowing the strained relationship between Dr. Peake and Miss McHaffey—was especially dubious about bypassing her immediate supervisor, the director of nurses. She decided at that time it would be best to observe the regular channels of communications.

Miss Ross reported for her new job and discussed Dr. Peake's plans and ideas for integrating the two units with both Miss Linden and Miss Hartman. She also told them that the reason he picked her for the job was because she had worked at Benton under him. They had known that both she and Miss Jackson had worked at Benton for a time while Dr. Peake was there. Neither of the supervisors seemed very surprised. Miss Linden remarked that it sounded like another of Dr. Peake's "wild ideas." Both Miss Linden and Miss Hartman seemed concerned over the shortage of adequate staff members and said that any changes that would improve the situation would be welcomed.

Personnel problems were especially acute in the hospital at that time. Several staff members were off duty because of illness and there were more patients than usual. The clinic was open Saturday and Sunday for emergencies only. One nurse and two aides were on duty weekends, but were not too busy. Miss Ross arranged to transfer the two aides to the hospital for the weekends. Miss Linden was elated with the additional help. On the following Wednesday, the clinic was far behind in its work because of an emergency that had arisen.

Miss Ross went to Miss Linden to see if someone could go over for the afternoon to help. The following conversation ensued:

Miss Ross: "Miss Hartman is swamped. She had an emergency to take care of and the other patients are not being seen. Have you anyone you can send to help?"

Miss Linden: "I am not going to send anyone to that clinic. They have enough help! We are too short here."

Miss Ross went over to one of the wards and found two of the aides in the ward kitchen drinking coffee. She asked if they were slack right then.

One of them said, "Oh, sure. We haven't had very much to do all afternoon." Miss Ross returned to Miss Linden and told her of the episode. She asked that one of them be sent to help out in the clinic. Miss Linden complied reluctantly.

Shortly after this incident, Miss Linden went on vacation for two weeks. Miss McHaffey asked Miss Ross to take charge of the hospital unit until her return. Thus Miss Ross was faced with the problem of making out time schedules for all the nurses, aides, orderlies, and maids employed in the hospital unit. Dr. Peake had also asked her to initiate a study to determine the personnel needs in the various hospital wards and the clinic departments, and to help with the plans for the layout of new equipment in the building additions. During the two weeks of Miss Linden's absence, Miss Ross found that one ward had more nurses than another one, although the workloads were the same. Also, she discovered that maids were not doing the cleaning assigned to them; some were not even aware of what their duties were.

With the cooperation of Miss Hartman and the approval and permission of Miss McHaffey, Miss Ross arranged to reallocate the nursing personnel so that all wards would have equal coverage in relation to their workloads. She made out schedules to provide available clinic help as relief in the hospital on weekends and instructed the maids as to their duties.

There seemed to be a gradual improvement in the amount and quality of patient care, and most of the employees seemed to be more satisfied when they were placed in jobs where they were kept busy and understood their duties. Several patients commented on the improved care they received after the changes had been made. Dr. Peake praised Miss Ross and Miss McHaffey for the success of the new program.

Two days after Miss Linden returned from her vacation, Miss Ross was called to the office of the director of nurses.

Miss McHaffey: "Miss Ross, Miss Linden has requested a transfer to the operating room, because she doesn't think you and she will get along. She is doing a good job in the hospital and I don't want to lose her. Hereafter, you will not interfere with the operation of the hospital unit and its personnel. Miss Linden will take care of everything over there."

Miss Ross: "I don't understand, Miss McHaffey. Do you mean that my job is finished?"

Miss McHaffey: "No. You are to continue working in the clinic and help set up new departments there as the building program continues. I really don't know what made Dr. Peake think you would be able to do anything to improve the situation. He will just have to realize that we haven't sufficient personnel."

Miss Ross left the interview feeling very confused as to her exact status, because she knew that Dr. Peake would expect her to continue to try to coordinate the two units.

When you have read this case, review the diagnostic questions included at the end(s) of the chapter(s) you are using to analyze this case, and choose the ones that seem applicable. Then use those questions to begin working on your case analysis.

CASE 3-4   EXECUTIVE RETREAT: A CASE OF GROUP FAILURE
Donald D. White, University of Arkansas

John Matthews was a young executive at the divisional level of a large corporation. John, like a number of other young executives throughout the United States, had been selected by his manager to attend a two-and-a-half-week executive development retreat. The retreat was held at a remote camp in northern Minnesota. Although all of the necessary facilities for an enjoyable vacation were present, the structure and demands of the retreat left little time for relaxing and enjoying the surroundings. John was among sixty male executives who were registered to attend the retreat. They would spend fifteen days living, working, and competing with one another.

ORGANIZATION AND ACTIVITIES

The sixty participants were broken down into five groups of twelve. Each group was provided with a group leader. This leader was a senior corporate executive who had previously attended the retreat. For fifteen days, the men were involved in a variety of academic and athletic activities. Selected sessions of the retreat were designated for "educational activities." The men participated in seminar sessions designed to deepen their understanding of central management decision making. These sessions involved a limited amount of lecture by either the group leader or a visitor. However, the majority of time devoted to academic pursuits was spent in case studies and a business game. A good deal of the men's time was spent in physical fitness training and athletic competition. Finally, a few sessions were conducted along the lines of sensitivity training.

Although a considerable amount of time was spent in intragroup activities, intergroup competition was also fostered. In particular, groups competed athletically and through the business game. The remaining portions of this case represent the reflections of John Matthews on his experiences at the executive retreat.

Modified and reprinted with the author's permission.

FIRST IMPRESSIONS

It is hard to express the emotions or thoughts that were going through my mind, let alone the minds of others, when I first met the members of my group. Until now, I had been working with business acquaintances in my company's San Francisco office. When I learned of my selection for the retreat and the manner in which it would be conducted, I wondered what my new associates would be like. Would we all remain for the full two and one-half weeks of the retreat? Would I be able to take the criticisms of others? How would our group do athletically and academically? And would the other members of my group resent the fact that I could not partici-pate in the sporting events due to an old knee injury? Subconsciously, I had been establishing the criteria by which I would accept others and they would accept me.

During the first group meeting, I tried to learn the backgrounds of others who were with me. I went through the following process. I tried to find out where the others were from, what their education was, and the kind of experience they had accu-mulated. I discovered that the level at which one had worked within a firm together with whether he had held down a "home office" job were important because they cre-ated identification and solidarity between individuals; that is, financial officers inter-acted with other financial officers, production managers with production managers, marketing people with others from marketing departments, and so forth. Our group leader made sure that he allowed enough time for all of us to meet each other before he walked in the door.

The group leader was the faculty member who had overall responsibility for administrative functions in the group. He also graded papers and presentations, conducted all of our counseling sessions, and was the all-around nursemaid for the group. Our leader, Mark, was a top-level corporate executive out of New York. This posed an immediate threat to some in the group when they first met him. After a few minutes of informal chitchat, Mark called everyone into a seminar room.

Mark made a low-key introduction of himself and the retreat. He emphasized that to be a success individually at "the camp," everyone had to cooperate and func-tion as a group. He explained that no group always dominated intellectually or ath-letically. He related that his last group was not especially great in academics or athletics, yet their cumulative scores in both tests and games enabled them to become the top group at the retreat. This allowed certain privileges over other groups. The point Mark kept trying to make was that the men could no longer think of them-selves as individuals. "The school theme," he said, "is 'Think—Communicate—Cooperate,' and I suggest that you, too, adopt it as your guiding principle while you are here."

GROUP MEMBERS

The following are my recollections of the other members in our group.

Wally was an older member of the group and became the group student leader. He was a middle-level manager in a large company and had no formal technical training. This may have made him reluctant to assume a leadership role in the group. He appeared to be afraid of hurting other people's feelings even though his actions usually were justified.

Dave also did not have formal technical training; however, he was one of the few who had experience as a corporate president. He was an average student and speaker and above average in his writing ability. He appeared to be obsessed with sex. He called his wife every night, "studied" *The Art of Sensual Response,* and occasionally sniffed some musk oil that he had bought for his wife.

Jim was a financial analyst. He was one of two bachelors and was considered to be the playboy of the group. His goal was just to finish the retreat and get back to his home office.

Bob was a manager of production and operations for a leading producer of men's apparel. He, too, was a bachelor and considered himself to be a "ladykiller." To most of us he appeared conceited and boisterous. He claimed to be an authority on most subjects. He was also suspected of cheating in the 25-Mile Jogging Club (cheating on anything was strictly forbidden).

Larry was a director of public relations for a major steel producer. He had a liberal arts background and turned out to be our only distinguished graduate. Although he participated in everything, he never really assumed a leadership role and his contribution to the section was minimal. He was the only one (with the exception of me) who was not able to run a mile and a half in twelve minutes. He was a good speaker but a below-average writer.

Rich was an internal financial consultant. He attended Harvard Business School and was later considered one of the better executive prospects at the retreat. He was a good speaker and writer. Although he was very outspoken, he did make a lot of sense. He assumed the leader's role in two major exercises; however, he never did maintain his hold as leader over the group.

Wayne was a personnel director. He was an average student, writer, and speaker. He never did assume a leader's role, possibly because he was the most naive member of the group.

Ollie was a marketing manager and was considered the "country boy" of the group. He was an average student, good speaker, and good writer. He performed many odd jobs for us and was successful in leading us to two victories in athletics.

Gary was an executive vice president for a pipeline supplier whom I thought, at the beginning, would emerge as the leader of the group. He was poor academically, an average writer, and a good speaker. His additional duty was that of athletic chairman. Although he encouraged everyone to run twenty-five miles (25-Mile Jogging Club) during this period, he himself failed to achieve this goal.

Burrell was a personnel and public relations manager. He also was considered to be among the more promising men at the retreat. He was a fair speaker and an average writer. His additional duties were academic chairman and basketball coach. He was the type of guy that, if something were to go wrong, he would be in the middle of it.

Paul was manager of engineering for an electronics manufacturer. He had to spend three days of the first week of the retreat in the infirmary with a virus. This may have been one of the reasons why he was always trying to promote group functions when he got back. One thing I remember in particular about Paul is that he was always complaining about the "developmental rotation" program in his company. The program placed technically trained managers in functional areas other than their own for as long as six months to provide them with career broadening. He saw the program as a threat to his own career, but failed to see it as a threat to "general managers with no technical expertise." Overall, Paul was an average speaker, writer, and student.

I, John, did not have formal education for my job as division director of industrial relations. I was an average student and writer and above-average speaker. I considered myself a harmonizer of the group. I was the only member who was excused from sports because of an injury. Although I disagreed many times with decisions that were made, I usually went along with the group to the end.

The group members lived in three locations during the school. Living in Cabin I were Dave, Wally, Jim, Bob, John, and Larry. Wayne, Burrell, and Paul lived in Cabin II, while Ollie, Rich, and Gary lived in Cabin III. Bob and John generally walked to seminar sessions together, as did Wally and Larry; Wayne, Burrell, and Paul; and Ollie, Rich, and Gary. Dave and Jim walked separately to the sessions. Rich and Burrell studied together regularly. Larry, Rich, and Paul generally studied together.

GROUP ORGANIZATION AND ACTIVITIES

For convenience, Mark arranged the seating alphabetically around the table (see Case Exhibit 3-1).There was only one exception; Wally, the designated leader by virtue of age and experience, sat near the front. Following some brief introductions and a few administrative actions, goals of the group were established.

After much haggling about the goals, which ranged from totally idealistic to extremely pragmatic, the group decided on the following goals:

1. Everyone in the group would strive to complete the program and would seek to ensure that our group was ranked first among various competing groups.

CASE EXHIBIT 3-1   Seating Arrangement, First Day

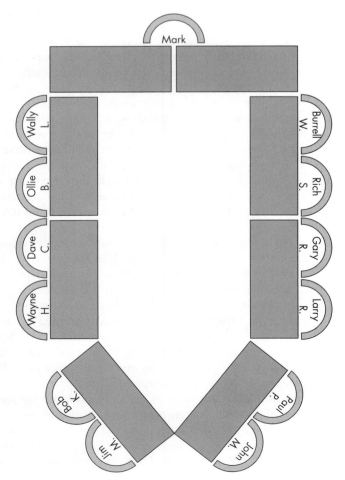

2. We would strive to be the best in sports.
3. Everyone would run at least twenty-five miles.
4. We would strive to maintain a harmonious atmosphere in the group.

Of immediate importance to the group was developing athletically rather than academically. (In final group ratings, athletics ranked a very close second to academics in total possible points that could be scored.) In fact, it wasn't until the latter part of the school that the section would come together in academics.

A couple of incidents that occurred during the retreat illustrated the extent of the group's success. Toward the end of the first week, an entire afternoon was set aside for self-evaluation. The session resembled a sensitivity-training group session. Most groups had lunch followed with a little beer drinking to "loosen things up. "After our loosening up, we started our discussion. Several comments were made that should have provoked a fiery discussion, but for some reason they never did.

I don't believe we were open that afternoon. We looked at our leadership in academics, but none of us was willing to tell Burrell that he had a weak academic program. None of us would tell Gary that our athletics program was bad and that our group looked worse than most other groups with whom we competed. We all knew these things, but were unwilling to place the blame on anyone. Our group leader must have been totally frustrated at the end of the day. How could a group that had such high goals and such mediocre results have allowed such an opportunity to pass by?

A few days later another group project was scheduled. An obstacle course, intriguingly called "Project X," consisted of a series of tasks to be performed by six people at a time. It was supposed to test the group's ability to recognize the problem, decide on a solution, and carry it out in a fifteen-minute period. During the break, we tallied our score, 0 for 5. Mark seemed very upset. It was the first time he got upset with the entire group. Larry commented on the episode: "We didn't see 'Project X' or even the rest of the retreat as a life-or-death situation. In a retreat where no one fails to graduate, it can hardly be considered as a threat to anyone's career if these group goals go unaccomplished."

Personally, I saw us as a group of individuals in search of a real leader. We were all strong in our own individual specialties in our own organizations, but couldn't muster up the same vitality and enthusiasm to carry forth this synthetically designed group toward goal achievement. Although we wouldn't openly admit it, we were not committed to our goals. Yet, even though we lacked this commitment, we still maintained the goals. Going back to the afternoon encounter session, someone suggested that we revise our goals in light of our successes and failures to date. Even though it was impossible to achieve the original goals set, they still were unchanged!

The seating as depicted in Case Exhibit 3-2 was the arrangement for the last few days.

GROUP PERFORMANCE

Our group finished the two-and-one-half-week session having accomplished the following: Out of twelve individuals, one finished as a distinguished graduate and three finished in the top third of the class. Ollie observed, "Lacking strong leadership in education, we each went our separate ways in trying to wade through all the material." Our second goal also met with defeat. At the beginning of the program it was felt that our group had a chance to do well in sports. During practice sessions, we appeared relatively good. However, practice sessions reflected one characteristic of the group. Generally, we were disorganized, and there was always a lot of joking going on. I believed this carried over to the games and resulted in less than full

CASE EXHIBIT 3-2

Seating Arrangement, Last Few Days

1. These individuals finished in the top third of the class.
2. These individuals never changed their seats.
3. Gary and John sat next to each other during the last seven days.
4. Wally never did assume the leader's position at the end of the table except when he led the two seminars.

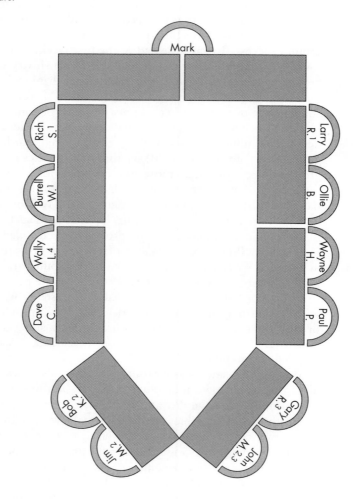

commitment to winning. Gary would get frustrated and try to motivate the team at times, but his sudden surge of spirit usually was short lived.

The third goal also fell short of being successfully accomplished. Only six of the members of our group actually finished the twenty-five miles. Another important factor regarding the 25-Mile Jogging Club centered on the ethics of one individual. Bob had been suspected of not running all the miles that he logged. At first Wally and Larry had suspected this, as later all the group members living around Bob did. One member noted, "We all felt that Wally should have confronted him with our suspicions." However, because the evidence against Bob was circumstantial, Wally didn't formally say anything to Bob about the incident. One change that did develop out of the episode was that the entire group ceased to listen to or trust Bob once they suspected his cheating.

The group came closest to achieving the final goal, which involved the maintenance of harmonious relationships between one another. An example of this was our mutual respect for each other's territory. As one member stated it, "When Paul went to the hospital, his seat remained vacant even though we didn't have permanently assigned seats. When he returned, everyone made a special effort to make him feel a part of the group. Even when we suspected Bob of not really completing his running, we tried not to make too big a deal out of it."

Personally, I think I got a lot out of the retreat. I learned a lot in the academic sessions and even discovered some things about myself that I hadn't realized before. But, truthfully, I never figured out our group. Sometimes I think it was a near disaster.

When you have read this case, review the diagnostic questions included at the end(s) of the chapter(s) you are using to analyze this case, and choose the ones that seem applicable. Then use those questions to begin working on your case analysis.

CASE 3-5 · BOB COLLINS

Richard E. Dutton and Rodney C. Sherman, University of South Florida

Bob Collins was employed by the Mansen Company, a division of Sanford, Barnes, Inc., a diversified company engaged mainly in the manufacture and sale of men's and women's apparel. The Miami plant of the Mansen Company was the largest of the nineteen manufacturing locations and had, in its organization, an industrial engineering unit.

As department head of industrial engineering in the Miami plant, Jim Douglas also had the responsibility for all industrial engineering functions in the Florida region. This included three smaller plants within a 275-mile radius of Miami. Jim reported to the Miami plant manager, Mr. Scott, for local projects and to the Florida regional manager, Mr. Glenn, for projects of a regional nature. Mr. Glenn had been regional manager for many years, but only for the previous twenty-three months had this been his sole responsibility. Prior to this time, he was also the manager of the Miami plant, and he was still a dominant personality in the plant, partially because of Mr. Scott's indecisiveness.

Assisting Jim in Miami were two other industrial engineers, Bob Collins and Mark Douglas (see Case Exhibit 3-3). Mark was hired in September 1992, soon after his release from the Army, and had been with Mansen about 27 months. Bob had been with the company for about 21 months since leaving his last position because of a conflict there regarding a heavy workload and a schedule requiring some night work. Bob had freely given this information during his preemployment interview, but no effort had been made to uncover the past employer's version of the situation.

Jim held an associate degree in industrial engineering from a two-year technical school, while both Bob and Mark had bachelor's degrees, in history and business, respectively. All three men were army veterans. Jim and Mark served as enlisted men for nine and two years, respectively, with Jim becoming a staff sergeant and Mark a sergeant. Bob served as an officer for four years, reaching the rank of captain. Bob had displayed a talent for creative and imaginative thinking in regard to mechanical development and was assigned a majority of the projects that delved into the creation, installation, and improvement of mechanical innovations and devices. In addition, he and the local head of mechanical development, Ned Larson, worked together on many of their own original ideas, both in the planning and development.

CASE EXHIBIT 3-3

Partial Organization Chart—The Mansen Company

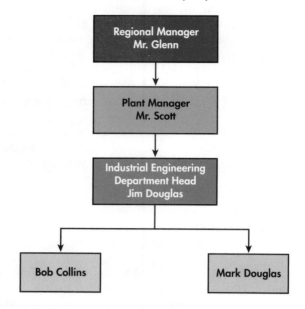

THE CURRENT SITUATION

One day Bob came upon an interoffice memo in Jim's incoming mailbox containing a question from Mr. Glenn about a mechanical project on which Bob was working. Feeling that he could save time for Jim, he picked up the memo, read it, and proceeded to Mr. Glenn's office to answer the question. When he returned, he simply put the memo back in Jim's mailbox and went on with other work.

Later in the day Jim returned to the office to answer his mail and came upon Mr. Glenn's memo. Jim sought out Bob and the following conversation ensued:

Jim: "Bob, I've got a short note here from Mr. Glenn asking about the status of the cuff machine project I gave you. Where do we stand on that now?"

Bob: "Well, as I mentioned before, all we have to build is the automatic stacking device and then we should have the machine about ready to go. Some of the parts won't be in until the first of the next week, but it should only take a day after that to finish."

Jim: "Okay, that's good. How about answering this memo to Mr. Glenn and we'll have him up to date on this thing?"

Bob: "I already have. I saw the memo earlier and went on in and brought him up on how the project stands."

Jim: "Did you get a copy of this too?"

Bob: "No, I saw yours and decided to save you time so I went ahead and answered his question."

Jim: "You mean you got this out of my box?"

Bob: "Yeah, I saw it as I was coming to my desk and decided to go ahead and get it out of the way."

Jim: "Oh well, I'll just hold on to this for a while then."

Several days later, Jim and Bob were discussing one of Bob's new ideas, and the discussion became very heated when Jim rejected the idea as too expensive, in both time and money.

Jim: "And another thing, Bob, I don't want you going through my mailbox again. What's in there is none of your business unless I assign it to you."

Bob: "I was just trying to do you a favor and get the memo answered. If you don't want me to do that, then I won't."

Jim: "You would have answered eventually, but I don't want you to do these things unless I tell you to. I'm in charge of the department, and I have to know what's going on. That reminds me of another thing. From now on, you tell me about all of the projects you're working on. I don't want any more secret projects being worked on without my knowing it. I feel pretty stupid when Mr. Scott or Mr. Glenn asks me a question about something I've never even heard of. From now on, you tell me about your ideas, and if we can work it into the schedule we will; otherwise, it will have to wait until we can get to it. This also means not going to Mr. Glenn with your ideas first, and then telling me that he thinks it's a good idea and should be developed. I'll approve the ideas first, and then we'll check with him if necessary."

Bob: "I know you're talking about the new sleeve hemming stacker. I just happened to mention it to Mr. Glenn this morning at coffee break, and he wanted to know more about it. I had to tell him about it when he asked."

Jim: "That's right. In that case you couldn't have done anything else, but from now on make sure you've cleared these ideas with me before going to him."

Mark came into the office, and the discussion was ended.

The following day, Bob and Mark were leaving the office together, and Bob told Mark about his discussion with Jim.

Bob: "Mark, I'm so mad at Jim I'd like to quit and walk out of here right now. I know darn well I could make more money somewhere else and wouldn't have to put up with Jim. You know, what really gets me down is the thousands of dollars that I can prove I've saved the company, and I can't get a decent raise. I know Jim is making about thirty-six thousand dollars, and I feel I'm worth as much as he is, but I do realize that they have to pay him more because he's a department head. However, he's not worth the amount of difference in our salaries. I feel I should be able to get at least a thousand dollars a year more than I'm getting now, but the "Book" won't allow that much of a raise at one time. And besides that, I'd feel more like putting out more for the company. As it is, I want to do my best, but it's hard to feel that way when you aren't fairly paid for your work."

Mark: "You know what chances you've got of getting *that* kind of a raise! What started all of this anyway?"

Bob: "Well, I was telling Jim about my idea for the fronts presser and he turned it down, just like he's done most of my ideas."

Mark: "Did he tell you *why* he turned it down?"

Bob: "Said it would be too expensive and would take too much time. Mark, it would save us a penny a dozen, which would be about $5,000 a year; they're just time studies to try to satisfy some operator who doesn't really want to work."

Mark: "I know. My projects are like that, too, and he turned down my idea for revamping the boxing department. You know what a bottleneck that has been. My first estimate, which was conservative, was savings of $50,000 a year in addition to being able to get out our weekly production. We're not anywhere near that now and spending twice the amount of money we need to. This would also allow the warehouse to have half of the present boxing area. But Jim says it can't be done because there would have to be too much coordination between departments, and that it would take someone with more authority than we have to make it work. I told him if we were to work up the proposal and send it to Mr. Scott, he couldn't pass up those savings on a system that's workable. Of course, you know how Scott hates to make decisions, but if Mr. Glenn knew about it, it would be our main project until it was installed. You know how he likes those dollar signs."

Bob: "Yeah, I know. Jim doesn't seem to understand that these little projects don't save us any money and yet he turns down ideas that will save us thousands of dollars a year. You know he doesn't know anything about mechanical development. And besides that, when you try to explain something to him and he doesn't understand it, he says it won't work. But I know that he takes some of these ideas and mentions them to Mr. Scott and Mr. Glenn and takes credit for them. I don't like that one little bit, and I'm going to tell him so one of these days. Then, after telling me my idea for the fronts presser wasn't any good, he chewed me out for going through his mailbox. That happened a couple of days ago. When I tried to do him a favor by answering a question Mr. Glenn had asked in a memo, he got all upset. He didn't know anything about it anyway, so what's the difference?"

Mark: "Do you think it was right to go through his mail?"

Bob: "I just happened to see the subject of the memo and I knew it was concerned with my project, so I went ahead and answered the question. I didn't go through his mail; the memo was right on top, and I just happened to see it on my way to my desk."

Mark: "Yes, but you *did* get into his personal mailbox and went ahead without him knowing about it. Do you see what I mean, Bob? I mean he *is* the head of the department, and he needs to know what goes on within the department."

Bob: "But he doesn't have to know *everything* I'm working on. It's none of his business. Most of the things Ned and I do are our own ideas, and he doesn't have a thing to do with them—he doesn't even understand them. Anyway, he told me he didn't want me working on any "secret" projects, that I was to tell him about all of my ideas before I did anything with them. Well, I'll tell you, I'm going ahead and doing the projects he assigns me, but I'm *still* going to work on my own ideas whenever I get a chance. Here comes Mr. Scott, I'll see you later."

After closing hours that night and after Bob had left, Jim and Mark were still in the office.

Jim: "Mark, did Bob tell you about our little discussion yesterday afternoon?"

Mark: "He said you had a few words."

Jim: "Bob's just getting too big for his own britches. If he doesn't like something I say or do, he acts like a little child. Goes around pouting and gloomy for two or three days. He's just going to have to learn that he's not running the department, although I'm sure he feels he could do a better job than I'm doing. But the thing is that he can't take any criticism. Some of his ideas are good, but others are just too far out and we don't have the time for them.

"He's going to have to realize that we have other things to do besides mechanical development. I know a lot of our projects cost us more to carry out than can be saved in terms of dollars, but if we can show an operator what is being done is right or, if it's wrong, admit the error and correct the situation, then that can be worth as much as saving several thousand dollars a year. Although we are becoming increasingly automated, we have to remember that people are still our main source of production and that without their cooperation, we're out of business. Besides, mechanical development isn't even his job, but because he has had some good ideas, I've let him work with Ned on them. I know he's sensitive, and that he is worth a lot to the company because some of his ideas are worthwhile, but if he doesn't change his ways, I'm going to have to talk to Mr. Glenn about letting him go. I've got to run this department, and we can't do our best when he acts up like he does."

When you have read this case, review the diagnostic questions included at the end(s) of the chapter(s) you are using to analyze this case, and choose the ones that seem applicable. Then use those questions to begin working on your case analysis.

CASE 3-6 THE CASE OF DICK SPENCER

Margaret P. Fenn, University of Washington

After the usual banter when old friends meet for cocktails, the conversation between a couple of university professors and Dick Spencer, a former student who was now a successful businessman, turned to Dick's life as a vice president of a large manufacturing firm.

"I've made a lot of mistakes, most of which I could live with, but this one series of incidents was so frustrating that I could have cried at the time," Dick said in response to a question. "I really have to laugh at how ridiculous it is now, but at the time I blew my cork." Dick was plant manager of Modrow Company, a Canadian branch of the Tri-American Corporation. Tri-American was a major producer of primary aluminum, with integrated operations ranging from the mining of bauxite through the processing and fabrication of aluminum into a variety of products. The company also made and sold refractories and industrial chemicals. The parent company had wholly owned subsidiaries in five separate U.S. locations and had foreign affiliates in fifteen different countries.

Tri-American mined bauxite in the Jamaican West Indies and shipped the raw material by commercial vessels to two plants in Louisiana, where it was processed into alumina. The alumina was then shipped to reduction plants in one of three locations for conversion into primary aluminum. Most of the primary aluminum was then moved to the companies' fabricating plants for further processing. Fabricated aluminum items included sheet, flat, coil, and corrugated products; siding; and roofing.

Tri-American employed approximately 22,000 employees in the total organization. The company was governed by a board of directors that included the chairman,

---

vice chairman, president, and twelve vice presidents. However, each of the subsidiaries and branches functioned as an independent unit. The board set the general policy, which was then interpreted and applied by the various plant managers. In a sense, the various plants competed with one another as though they were independent companies. This decentralization in organizational structure increased the freedom and authority of the plant managers, but also increased the pressure for profitability. The Modrow branch was located in a border town in Canada. The total workforce in Modrow was 1,000. This Canadian subsidiary was primarily a fabricating unit. Its main products were foil and building products such as roofing and siding. Aluminum products were gaining in importance in architectural plans, and increased sales were predicted for this branch. Its location and its stable workforce were the most important advantages it possessed.

In anticipation of estimated increases in building product sales, Modrow had recently completed a modernization and expansion project. At the same time, its research and art departments combined their talents in developing a series of twelve new patterns of siding that were being introduced to the market. Modernization and pattern development had been costly undertakings, but the expected return on investment made the project feasible. However, the plant manager, who was a Tri-American vice president, had instituted a campaign to cut expenses wherever possible. In his introductory notice of the campaign, he emphasized that cost reduction would be the personal aim of every employee at Modrow.

SALESMAN

The plant manager of Modrow, Dick Spencer, was an American who had been transferred to this Canadian branch two years previously, after the start of the modernization plan. Dick had been with the Tri-American Company for fourteen years, and his progress within the organization was considered spectacular by those who knew him well. Dick had received a master's degree in business administration from a well-known university at age twenty-two. Upon graduation he had accepted a job as salesman for Tri-American. During his first year as a salesman, he succeeded in landing a single, large contract that put him near the top of the sales-volume leaders. In discussing this phenomenal rise in the sales volume, several of his fellow salesmen concluded that his looks, charm, and ability on the golf course contributed as much to his success as his knowledge of the business or his ability to sell the products.

The second year of his sales career, Dick continued to set a fast pace. Although his record set difficult goals for the other salesmen, he was considered a "regular guy" by them, and both he and they seemed to enjoy the few occasions when they socialized. However, by the end of the second year of constant traveling and selling, Dick began to experience some doubt about his future.

His constant involvement in business affairs disrupted his marital life, and his wife divorced him during the second year with Tri-American. Dick resented her action at first, but gradually seemed to recognize that his career at present depended on his freedom to travel unencumbered. During that second year, he ranged far and wide in his sales territory, and successfully closed several large contracts. None of them was as large as his first year's major sale, but in total volume he again was near the top salesmen for the year. Dick's name became well known in the corporate headquarters, and he was spoken of as "the boy to watch." Dick had met the president of Tri-American during his first year as a salesman at a company conference. After three days of golfing and socializing, they developed a relaxed camaraderie considered unusual by those who observed the developing friendship. Although their contacts were infrequent after the conference, their easy relationship seemed to blossom the few times they did meet. Dick's friends kidded him about his ability to use his new friendship to promote himself in the company, but Dick brushed aside their jibes and insisted that he'd make it on his own abilities, not someone's coattail.

By the time he was twenty-five, Dick began to suspect that he did not look forward to a life as a salesman for the rest of his career. He talked about his unrest with his friends, and they suggested that he groom himself for sales manager. "You won't make the kind of money you're making from commissions," he was told, "but you will have a foot in the door from an administrative standpoint, and you won't have to travel quite as much as you do now." Dick took their suggestions lightly and continued to sell the product, but was aware that he did not seem to get the same satisfaction out of his job that he had once enjoyed.

By the end of his third year with the company, Dick was convinced that he wanted a change in direction. As usual, he and the president spent quite a bit of time on the golf course during the annual company sales conference. After their match one day, the president kidded Dick about his game. The conversion drifted back to business, and the president, who seemed to be in a jovial mood, started to kid Dick about his sales ability. In a joking way, he implied that anyone could sell a product as good as Tri-American's, but that it took real "guts and know-how" to make the products. The conversation drifted to other things, but the remark stuck with Dick. Sometime later, Dick approached the president formally with a request for transfer out of the sales division. The president was surprised and hesitant about this change in career direction for Dick. He recognized the superior sales ability that Dick seemed to possess, but was unsure that Dick was willing or able to assume responsibility in any other division of the organization.

Dick sensed the hesitancy, but continued to push his request. He later remarked that it seemed that the initial hesitancy of the president convinced Dick that he needed an opportunity to prove himself in a field other than sales.

TROUBLESHOOTER

Dick was finally transferred back to the home office of the organization and indoctrinated into production and administration roles in the company as a special assistant to the senior vice president of production. As a special assistant, Dick was assigned several troubleshooting jobs. He acquitted himself well in this role, but in the process succeeded in gaining a reputation as a ruthless headhunter among the branches where he had performed a series of amputations.

His reputation as an amiable, genial, easygoing guy from the sales department was the antithesis of the reputation of a cold, calculating headhunter that he earned in his troubleshooter role. The vice president, who was Dick's boss, was aware of the reputation that Dick had earned but was pleased with the results. The faltering departments in which Dick had worked seemed to bloom with new life and energy from Dick's recommended amputations. As a result, the vice president began to sing Dick's praises, and the president began to accept Dick in his new role in the company.

MANAGEMENT RESPONSIBILITY

About three years after Dick's switch from sales, he was given an assignment as assistant plant manager of an English branch of the company. Dick, who had remarried, moved his wife and family to London, and they attempted to adapt to their new routine. The plant manager was English, as were most of the other employees. Dick and his family were accepted with reservations into the community life as well as into the plant life. The difference between British and American philosophy and performance within the plant was marked for Dick, who was imbued with modern managerial concepts and methods. Dick's directives from headquarters were to update and upgrade performance in this branch. However, his power and authority were less than those of his superior, so he constantly found himself in the position of having to soft-pedal or withhold suggestions that he would have liked to make, or innovations that he would have liked to introduce. After a frustrating year and a half, Dick was suddenly made plant manager of an old British company that had just been purchased by Tri-American. He left his first English assignment with mixed feelings and moved from London to Birmingham.

As the new plant manager, Dick operated much as he had in his troubleshooting job for the first couple of years of his change from sales to administration. Training and reeducation programs were instituted for all supervisors and managers who survived the initial purge. Methods were studied and then simplified or redesigned whenever possible, and new attention was directed toward production that better met the needs of the sales organization. A strong controller helped straighten out the profit picture through stringent cost control.

By the end of the third year, the company showed a small profit for the first time in many years. Because he felt that this battle was won, Dick requested transfer back to the United States. This request was partially granted when nine months later he was awarded a junior vice president title and was made manager of a subsidiary Canadian plant, Modrow.

MODROW MANAGER

Prior to Dick's appointment as plant manager at Modrow, extensive plans for plant expansion and improvement had been approved and started. Although he had not been in on the original discussions and plans, he inherited all the problems that accompany large-scale changes in any organization. Construction was slower in completion than originally planned, equipment arrived before the building was finished, employees were upset about the extent of change expected in their work routines with the installation of additional machinery, and, in general, morale was at a low ebb.

Various versions of Dick's former activities had preceded him, and on his arrival he was viewed with dubious eyes. The first few months after his arrival were spent in a frenzy of catching up. This entailed constant conferences and meetings, volumes of reading of past reports, events to become acquainted with the civic leaders of the area, and a plethora of dispatches to and from the home office. Costs continued to climb unabated.

By the end of his first year at Modrow, the building program had been completed, although behind schedule; the new equipment had been installed; and some revamping of cost procedures had been incorporated. The financial picture at this time showed a substantial loss, but since it had been budgeted as a loss, this result was not surprising. All managers of the various divisions had worked closely with their supervisors and accountants in planning the budget for the following year, and Dick began to emphasize his personal interest in cost reduction.

As he worked through his first year as plant manager, Dick developed the habit of strolling around the organization. He was apt to leave his office and appear anywhere on the plant floor, in the design office, at the desk of a purchasing agent or accountant, in the plant cafeteria rather than the executive dining room, or wherever there was activity concerned with Modrow. During his strolls he looked, listened, and became acquainted. If he observed activities that he wanted to talk about, or heard remarks that gave him clues to future action, he did not reveal these at the time. Rather he had a nod, a wave, and a smile for the people near him, but a mental note to talk to his supervisors, managers, and foremen in the future.

At first his presence disturbed those who noted him coming and going, but after several exposures to him without any noticeable effect, the workers came to accept his presence and continue their usual activities. Supervisors, managers, and foremen, however, did not feel as comfortable when they saw him in the area. Their feelings were aptly expressed by the manager of the siding department one day when he was talking to one of his foremen: "I wish he'd stay up in the front office where he belongs. Whoever heard of a plant manager who had time to wander around the plant all the time? Why doesn't he tend to his paperwork and let us tend to our business?"

"Don't let him get you down," joked the foreman. "Nothing ever comes of his visits. Maybe he's just lonesome and looking for a friend. You know how these Americans are."

"Well, you may feel that nothing ever comes of his visits, but I don't. I've been called into his office on three separate items within the last two months. The heat must really be on from the head office. You know these conferences we have every month where he reviews our financial progress, our building progress, our design progress, et cetera? Well, we're not really progressing as fast as we should be. If you ask me, we're in for continuing trouble."

In recalling his first year at Modrow, Dick had felt constantly pressured and badgered. He always sensed that the Canadians he worked with resented his presence since he was brought in over the heads of the operating staff. At the same time he felt this subtle resistance from his Canadian workforce, he believed that the president and his friends in the home office were constantly on the alert, waiting for Dick to prove himself or fall flat on his face. Because of the constant pressures and demands of the work, he had literally dumped his family into a new community and had withdrawn into the plant. In the process, he built up a wall of resistance toward the demands of his wife and children, who, in turn, felt as though he were abandoning them.

During the course of the conversation with his university friends, he began to recall a series of incidents that probably had resulted from the conflicting pressures. When describing some of these incidents, he continued to emphasize the fact that his attempt to be relaxed and casual had backfired. Laughingly, Dick said, "As you know, both human relations and accounting were my weakest subjects during the master's program, and yet they are two fields I felt I needed the most at Modrow at this time." He described some of the cost procedures that he would have liked to incorporate. However, without the support and knowledge furnished by his former controller, he busied himself with details that were unnecessary. One day, as he described it, he overheard a conversation between two of the accounting staff members with whom he had been working very closely. One of them commented to the other, "For a guy who's a vice president, he sure spends a lot of time breathing down our necks. Why doesn't he simply tell us the kind of systems he would like to try, and let us do the experiments and work out the budget? "Without commenting on the conversation he overheard, Dick then described himself as attempting to spend less time and be less directive in the accounting department.

Another incident he described that apparently had real meaning for him was one in which he had called a staff conference with his top-level managers. They had been going "hammer and tongs" for better than an hour in his private office, and in the process of heated conversation had loosened ties, taken off coats, and really rolled up their sleeves. Dick himself had slipped out of his shoes. In the midst of this, his secretary reminded him of an appointment with public officials. Dick had rapidly finished up his conference with his managers, straightened his tie, donned his coat, and had wandered out into the main office in his stocking feet.

Dick fully described several incidents when he had disappointed, frustrated, or confused his wife and family by forgetting birthdays, appointments, dinner engagements, and so on. He seemed to be describing a pattern of behavior that resulted from continuing pressure and frustration. He was setting the scene to describe his baffling and humiliating position in the siding department. In looking back and recalling his activities during this first year, Dick commented on the fact that his frequent wanderings throughout the plant had resulted in a nodding acquaintance with the workers, but probably had also resulted in supervisors spending more time getting ready for his visits and reading meaning into them afterward than attending to their specific duties. His attempts to know in detail the accounting procedures being used required long hours of concentration and detailed conversations with the accounting staff, which were time-consuming and very frustrating for him as well as for them. His lack of attention to his family life resulted in continued pressure from both his wife and family.

THE SIDING DEPARTMENT INCIDENT

Siding was the product that had been budgeted as a large profit item of Modrow. Aluminum siding was popular with both architects and builders because of its possibilities in both decorative and practical uses. Panel sheets of siding were shipped in standard sizes on order; large sheets of the coated siding were cut to specifications in the trim department, packed, and shipped. The trim shop was located near the loading platforms, and Dick often cut through the trim shop on his wanderings through the plant. On one of his frequent trips through the area, he suddenly became aware of the fact that several workers responsible for the disposal function were spending countless hours at high-speed saws cutting scraps into specified lengths to fit into scrap barrels. The narrow bands of scrap that resulted from the trim process varied in length from 7 to 27 feet and had to be reduced in size to fit into the disposal barrels.

Dick, in his concentration on cost reduction, picked up one of the thin strips, bent it several times and fitted it into the barrel. He tried this with another piece and it bent very easily. After assuring himself that bending was possible, he walked over to a worker at the saw and asked why he was using the saw when material could easily be bent and fitted into the barrels, resulting in saving time and equipment. The worker's response was, "We've never done it that way, sir. We've always cut it." Following his plan of not commenting or discussing matters on the floor, but distressed by the reply, Dick returned to his office and asked the manager of the siding department if he could speak to the foreman of the scrap division. The manager said, "Of course, I'll send him up to you in just a minute."

After a short time, the foreman, very agitated at being called to the plant manager's office, appeared. Dick began questioning him about the scrap disposal process and received the standard answer: "We've always done it that way." Dick then proceeded to review cost-cutting objectives. He talked about the pliability of the strips of scrap. He called for a few pieces of scrap to demonstrate the ease with which it could be bent, and ended what he thought was a satisfactory conversation by requesting the foreman to order heavy-duty gloves for his workers and use the bending process for a trial period of two weeks to check the cost-saving possibilities. The foreman listened throughout the most of this hour's conference, offered several reasons why it would not work, raised some questions about the record-keeping process for cost purposes, and finally left the office with the forced agreement to try the suggested new method of bending, rather than cutting, for disposal.

Although Dick was immersed in many other problems, his request was forcibly brought home one day as he cut through the scrap area. The workers were using power saws to cut scraps. He called the manager of the siding department and questioned him about the process. The manager explained that each foreman was responsible for his own processes, and since Dick had already talked to the foreman, perhaps he had better talk to him again. When the foreman arrived, Dick began to question him. He received a series of excuses, and some explanations of the kind of problems they were meeting by attempting to bend the scrap metal. "I don't care what the problems are," Dick nearly shouted, "when I request a cost-reduction program instituted, I want to see it carried through." Dick was furious. When the foreman left, Dick phoned the maintenance department and ordered the removal of the power saws from the scrap area immediately.

A short time later the foreman of the scrap department knocked on Dick's door, reporting his astonishment at having maintenance men step into his area and physically remove the saws. Dick reminded the foreman of his request for a trial at cost reduction to no avail, and ended the conversation by saying that the power saws were gone and would not be returned, and the foreman had better learn to get along without them. After a stormy exit by the foreman, Dick congratulated himself on having solved a problem and turned his attention to other matters.

A few days later Dick cut through the trim department and literally stopped to stare. As he described it, he was completely nonplussed to discover gloved workmen using hand shears to cut each piece of scrap.

When you have read this case, review the diagnostic questions included at the end(s) of the chapter(s) you are using to analyze this case, and choose the ones that seem applicable. Then use those questions to begin working on your case analysis.

4

Macro Organizational Behavior

Chapter 11 Power, Politics, and Conflict

Chapter 12 Structuring the Organization

Chapter 13 Technology, Environment, and Organization Design

Chapter 14 Culture, Change, and Organization Development

Cases

CHAPTER 11

Power in Organizations
Interpersonal Sources of Power
Conformity Responses to Interpersonal Power
A Model of Interpersonal Power: Assessment
Structural Sources of Power
The Critical Contingencies Model: Assessment

Politics and Political Processes
Personality and Politics
Conditions That Stimulate Politics
Political Tactics
Managing Destructive Politics

Conflict in Organizations
Is Conflict Necessarily Bad?
Conditions That Stimulate Conflict
Effects of Conflict

Negotiation and Restructuring
Managing Diverging Interests
Managing Structural Interdependence

Summary
Review Questions

Learning Through Experience
Diagnostic Questions 11-1: Power, Politics, and Conflict
Exercise 11-1: Building Customer Lists: Cooperate or Compete?

Power, Politics, and Conflict

Early one morning in May 2000, G. Richard Thoman, then CEO of Xerox, arrived at his office to find an urgent message from Paul A. Allaire, Xerox chairman of the board, requesting him to meet with Allaire in his office next door. The meeting was not pleasant. Allaire opened by saying that Thoman's colleagues had lost confidence in him and that the board was planning to announce his resignation the following day. After a lengthy conversation and despite feelings of betrayal, Thoman obliged and agreed to resign.

Thirty hours later, Thoman sat alone in a Xerox conference room and fielded questions from the press. Publicly, he indicated that his activities as an outsider brought in to stimulate change had proved destabilizing and that the board now felt that a team of Xerox insiders could better implement the company's strategy. Privately, however, he could only guess at why he had been asked to step down, since he had not been asked to attend the board's meeting and had not been allowed to provide evidence in his own defense.[1]

Two years later, in August 2002, Frederick G. Steingraber, former CEO of consulting firm A. T. Kearney Inc., sat in a conference room in the firm's Chicago office. Also present in the room were lawyers for Electronic Data Systems (EDS), Kearney's parent company. A week earlier, they had asked for the meeting with Steingraber in order to discuss an employee's misconduct. Left out of their request was the fact that the employee to be discussed was none other than Steingraber.

During the meeting, EDS's lawyers accused Steingraber of submitting $100,000 in phony expenses while serving as Kearney's top executive. Steingraber denied all charges. Nonetheless, EDS filed a suit alleging fraudulent behavior, and Steingraber was fired as Kearney's chairman emeritus a day later.[2]

Far from being exceptions to the rule, Xerox and A. T. Kearney are merely two among many companies that have suffered through significant management strife and turnover. Similar "palace revolts" have led to the ouster of top executives in such firms as Coca-Cola, DaimlerChrysler, and Time Warner.[3] Rather than fading away, these kinds of political processes can be expected to continue to influence business organizations in the future.

Power, politics, and conflict in firms can increase productivity and efficiency—or reduce them substantially. Political processes can even determine the existence and strategic direction of entire organizations. Restructuring, often stimulated as much by internal power struggles as by external market conditions, is prompting executives to search out new strategic directions for their firms. In the process, political considerations are altering the careers of thousands of employees—both managers and nonmanagers. At the same time that these events are creating opportunities for some, they are costing many others their jobs.[4]

Understanding power, politics, and conflict is critical to managerial success—and survival—in today's business organizations. For this reason, this chapter begins with a discussion of the nature, sources, and consequence of power. Next, it turns to the closely related topic of organizational politics, the process through which people acquire and use power to get their way. Finally, it examines conflict, describing the origins, results, and resolution of political confrontation in organizations.

POWER IN ORGANIZATIONS

When asked to define *power,* many people recall master politicians like Great Britain's wartime prime minister Winston Churchill or former U.S. president Bill Clinton, describing power as the ability to influence the behaviors of others and persuade them to do things they would not otherwise do.[5] For other people, images of the less powerful come to mind, leading them to define power as the ability to avoid others' attempts to influence their behavior. In truth, both of these views are correct. That is, **power** is the ability both to influence the conduct of others and to resist unwanted influence in return.[6]

According to David McClelland, people are driven to gain and use power by a need for power—which he called *nPow*—that is learned during childhood and adolescence.[7] This need for power can have several different effects on the way people think and behave. Generally speaking, people with high nPow are competitive, aggressive, prestige-conscious, action oriented, and prone to join groups. They are likely to be effective managers if, in addition to pursuing power, they also do the following:

Use power to accomplish organizational goals instead of using it to satisfy personal interests.

Coach subordinates and use participatory management techniques rather than autocratic, authoritarian methods.

Remain aware of the importance of managing interpersonal relations but avoid developing close relationships with subordinates.[8]

McClelland's research has suggested that seeking power and using it to influence others are not activities to be shunned or avoided in and of themselves. In fact, the process of management *requires* that power be put to appropriate use—where appro-

ETHICS AND SOCIAL RESPONSIBILITY

THE ETHICS OF POWER

How should power holders determine whether the use of power is appropriate? One approach is to adopt the *utilitarianist* perspective and judge the appropriateness of the use of power in terms of the consequences of this use. Does using power provide the greatest good for the greatest number of people? If the answer to this question is "yes," then the utilitarian perspective would suggest that power is being used appropriately.

A second perspective, derived from the theory of *moral rights*, suggests that power is used appropriately only when no one's personal rights or freedoms are sacrificed. It is certainly possible for many people to derive great satisfaction from the use of power to accomplish some purpose, thus satisfying utilitarian criteria, while simultaneously causing the rights of a few individuals to be abridged. According to the theory of moral rights, the latter effect is an indication of inappropriateness. Power holders seeking to use their power appropriately must therefore re-

spect the rights and interests of the minority as well as look after the well-being of the majority.

A third perspective, drawn from various theories of *social justice*, suggests that even having respect for the rights of everyone in an organization may not be enough to fully justify the use of power. In addition, those using power must treat people equitably, ensuring that people who are similar in relevant respects are treated similarly whereas people who are different are treated differently in proportion to those differences. Power holders must also be accountable for injuries caused by their use of power and must be prepared to provide compensation for these injuries.

Obviously, the three perspectives offer conflicting criteria, suggesting that no simple answers exist for questions concerning the appropriateness of using power. Instead, as power holders, managers must seek to balance efficiency, entitlement, and equity concerns as they attempt to influence the behaviors of others.

Sources: G. F. Cavanagh, D. Moberg, and M. Velasquez, "The Ethics of Organizational Politics," *Academy of Management Review* 6 (1981), 363–374; D. Vrendenburgh and Y. Brender, "The Hierarchical Abuse of Power in Work Organizations," *Journal of Business Ethics* 17 (1998), 1337–1347.

priateness is determined on the basis of several competing ethical perspectives such as those described in the Ethics and Social Responsibility box.

Interpersonal Sources of Power

If management requires the use of power, then what is the source of a manager's power? In their pioneering research, John French and Bertram Raven sought to answer this question by identifying the major bases, or sources, of power in organizations.[9] As indicated in Table 11-1, they discovered five types of power: reward, coercive, legitimate, referent, and expert power.

Reward power is based on the ability to allocate desirable outcomes—either the receipt of positive things or the elimination of negative things. Praise, promotions,

TABLE 11-1
Five Types of Power and Their Sources

Type of Power	Source of Power
Reward	Control over rewarding outcomes
Coercive	Control over punishing outcomes
Legitimate	Occupation of legitimate position of authority
Referent	Attractiveness, charisma
Expert	Expertise, knowledge, talent

Source: Based on J. R. P. French, Jr., and B. Raven, "The Bases of Social Power," in D. Cartwright, ed., *Studies in Social Power* (Ann Arbor: Institute for Social Research, University of Michigan, 1959), pp. 150–165.

raises, desirable job assignments, and time off from work are outcomes that managers often control. If they can make decisions about the distribution of such rewards, managers can use them to acquire and maintain reward power. Similarly, eliminating unwanted outcomes, such as unpleasant working conditions or mandatory overtime, can be used to reward employees. For instance, police officers who receive clerical support to help complete crime reports generally look at this reduction of paperwork as rewarding.

Whereas reward power controls the allocation of desirable outcomes, **coercive power** is based on the distribution of undesirable outcomes—either the receipt of something negative or the removal of something positive. People who control punishing outcomes can get others to conform to their wishes by threatening to penalize them in some way. That is, coercive power exploits fear. To influence subordinates' behaviors, managers may resort to punishments such as public scoldings, assignment of undesirable tasks, loss of pay, or, taken to the extreme, layoffs, demotions, or dismissals.

Legitimate power is based on norms, values, and beliefs that teach that particular people have the legitimate right to govern or influence others. From childhood, people learn to accept the commands of authority figures—first parents, then teachers, and finally bosses. This well-learned lesson gives people with authority the power to influence other people's attitudes and behaviors. In most organizations, authority is distributed in the form of a hierarchy (Chapter 2). People who hold positions of hierarchical authority are accorded legitimate power by virtue of the fact that they are office holders. For example, the vice president of marketing at a firm such as Philip Morris issues orders and expects people in subordinate positions to obey them because of the clout that being a vice president affords.

Have you ever admired a teacher, a student leader, or someone else whose personality, way of interacting with other people, values, goals, or other characteristics were exceptionally attractive? If so, you probably wanted to develop and maintain a close, continuing relationship with that person. This desire can provide this individual with **referent power.** Someone you hold in such esteem is likely to influence you through his or her attitudes and behaviors. In time you may come to identify with the admired person to such an extent that you begin to think and act alike. Referent power is also called *charismatic power.*

Famous religious leaders and political figures often develop and use referent power. Mahatma Gandhi, John F. Kennedy, Martin Luther King, Jr., and Nelson Mandela, for example, have all used personal charisma to profoundly influence the thoughts and behaviors of others. Of course, referent power can also be put to more prosaic use. Consider advertising's use of famous athletes and actors to help sell products. Athletic shoe manufacturers such as Nike, Reebok, and Adidas, for example, employ sports celebrities as spokespeople in an effort to influence consumers to buy their products. Similarly, movie producers try to ensure the success of their films by including well-known stars in the cast.

Expert power derives from the possession of expertise, knowledge, and talent. People who are seen as experts in a particular area can influence others in two ways. First, they can provide other people with knowledge that enables or causes those individuals to change their attitudes or behavior. For example, media critics provide reviews that shape people's attitudes about new books, movies, music, and television shows. Second, experts can demand conformity to their wishes as the price for sharing their knowledge. For instance, doctors, lawyers, and accountants provide advice that influences their clients' choices. Auto mechanics, plumbers, and electricians also exert a great deal of influence over customers who are not themselves talented craftspeople.

TABLE 11-2
Three
Responses to
Interpersonal
Power

Level	Description
Compliance	Conformity based on desire to gain rewards or avoid punishment. Continues as long as rewards are received or punishment is withheld.
Identification	Conformity based on attractiveness of the influencer. Continues as long as a relationship with the influencer can be maintained.
Internalization	Conformity based on the intrinsically satisfying nature of adopted attitudes or behaviors. Continues as long as satisfaction continues.

Source: Based on H. C. Kelman, "Compliance, Identification, and Internalization: Three Processes of Attitude Change," *Journal of Conflict Resolution* 2 (1958), 51–60.

Conformity Responses to Interpersonal Power

How do employees respond when managers use the different kinds of power identified by French and Raven? According to Herbert Kelman, three distinctly different types of reactions are likely to occur as people respond to attempts to influence their behavior. As indicated in Table 11-2, they are compliance, identification, and internalization.[10]

Compliance ensues when people conform to the wishes or directives of others so as to acquire favorable outcomes for themselves in return. They adopt new attitudes and behaviors not because these choices are agreeable or personally fulfilling, but rather because they lead to specific rewards and approval or head off specific punishments and disapproval. People are likely to continue to display such behaviors only as long as the favorable outcomes remain contingent on conformity.

Of the various types of power identified by French and Raven, reward and coercive power are the most likely to stimulate compliance, because both are based on linking employee performance with the receipt of positive or negative outcomes. Employees who work harder because a supervisor with reward power has promised them incentive payments are displaying compliance behavior. Similarly, employees who work harder to avoid punishments administered by a supervisor with coercive power are likely to continue doing so only while the threat of punishment remains salient.

Identification occurs when people accept the direction or influence of others because they identify with the power holders and seek to maintain relationships with them—not because they value or even agree with what they have been asked to do. French and Raven's concept of referent power is based on the same sort of personal attractiveness as is identification. Consequently, referent power and identification are likely to be closely associated with each other. Charismatic leaders are able to continue influencing other people's behaviors for as long as identification continues.

Finally, through *internalization*, people may adopt others' attitudes and behaviors because this course of action satisfies their personal needs, or because they find those attitudes and behaviors to be congruent with their own personal values. In either case, they accept the power holders' influence wholeheartedly. Both legitimate and expert power can stimulate internalization, as these forms of power rely on personal credibility—the extent to which a person is perceived as truly possessing authority or expertise. This credibility can be used to convince people of the intrinsic importance of the attitudes and behaviors they are being asked to adopt.

Internalization leads people to find newly adopted attitudes and behaviors personally rewarding and self-reinforcing. A supervisor who can use her expertise to convince colleagues to use consultative leadership (see Chapter 10) can expect the other managers to continue consulting with their subordinates long after she has withdrawn from the situation. Likewise, a manager whose legitimate power lends credibility to the orders he issues can expect his subordinates to follow those orders even in the absence of rewards, punishments, or charismatic attraction.

A Model of Interpersonal Power: Assessment

French and Raven describe the different kinds of interpersonal power used in organizations, and Kelman identifies how people respond to this use. Although valuable as a tool for understanding power and its consequences, the model integrating these ideas, shown in Figure 11-1, is not entirely without fault. Questions arise as to whether the five bases of power are completely independent, as proposed by French and Raven, or whether they are so closely interrelated as to be virtually indistinguishable from one another. The idea that reward, coercive, and legitimate power often derive from company policies and procedures, for instance, has led some researchers to subsume these three types of power in a single category labeled **organizational power.** Similarly, because expert and referent power are both based on personal expertise or charisma, they have sometimes been lumped together into the category of **personal power.**

In fact, French and Raven's five bases of power may be even more closely interrelated than this categorization would suggest. In their study of two paper mills, Charles Greene and Philip Podsakoff found that changing just one source of managerial power affected employees' perceptions of three other types of power.[11] Initially, both paper mills used an incentive payment plan in which supervisors' monthly performance appraisals determined the employees' pay. At one mill, the incentive plan was changed to an hourly wage system in which seniority determined an employee's rate of pay. The existing incentive plan was left in place at the other mill. Following this change, the researchers found that employees at the first mill perceived their supervisors as having significantly less reward power—as we might expect. Surprisingly, however, they also saw significant changes in their supervisors' punishment, legitimate, and referent power. As shown in Figure 11-2, they attrib-

FIGURE 11-1 A Model of Interpersonal Power

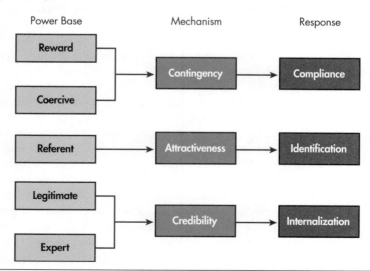

Source: Based on H. C. Kelman, "Compliance, Identification, and Internalization: Three Processes of Attitude Change," *Journal of Conflict Resolution* 2 (1958), 51–60; M. Sussmann and R. P. Vecchio, "A Social Influence Interpretation of Worker Motivation," *Academy of Management Review* 7 (1982), 177–186.

FIGURE 11-2 Effects of a Change in Method of Payment on Perceived Bases of Power

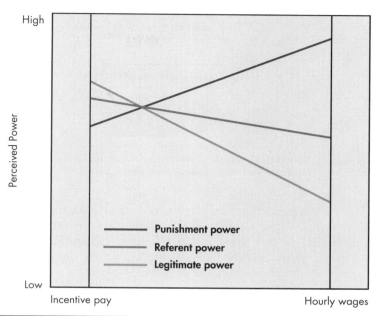

Source: Based on C. N. Greene and P. M. Podsakoff, "Effects of Withdrawal of a Performance-Contingent Reward on Supervisory Influence and Power," *Academy of Management Journal* 24 (1981), 527–542.

uted significantly more punishment power, a little less referent power, and substantially less legitimate power to their supervisors.

In contrast, employees in the second mill, where the incentive plan remained unchanged, reported no significant changes in their perceptions of their supervisors' reward, punishment, legitimate, and referent power. Because all other conditions were held constant in both mills, employees' changed perceptions in the first mill could not be attributed to other unknown factors. Instead, their perceptions of reward, coercive, legitimate, and referent power proved to be closely interrelated. This finding suggests that four of the five types of power identified by French and Raven appear virtually indistinguishable to interested observers.[12]

Despite this limitation, the model created by joining French and Raven's classification scheme with Kelman's theory is useful in analyzing social influence and *interpersonal* power in organizations. Managers can use this model to help predict how subordinates will conform to directives based on a particular type of power. For example, is the use of expertise likely to result in long-term changes in subordinates' behavior? Since the model shown in Figure 11-1 indicates that internalization is stimulated by the use of expert power, long-term behavioral changes are quite probable. Alternatively, subordinates may find the model useful as a means of understanding—and perhaps influencing—the behaviors of their superiors. For instance, an employee interested in influencing his boss to permanently change her style of management would be well advised to try using personal expertise.

Structural Sources of Power

In addition to the interpersonal sources discussed so far, power also derives from the *structure* of patterned work activities and flows of information found in every

FIGURE 11-3   The Critical Contingencies Model of Power

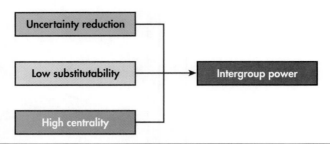

Source: Based on D. J. Hickson, C. R. Hinings, C. A. Lee, R. H. Schneck, and J. M. Pennings, "A Strategic Contingencies Theory of Intraorganizational Power," *Administrative Science Quarterly* 16 (1971), 216–229.

organization. Chapter 12 will examine the topic of organizational structure in detail. The discussion here will, therefore, be limited to those characteristics of organizations that shape power relations—uncertainty reduction, substitutability, and centrality. As depicted in Figure 11-3, these three variables combine to form the critical contingencies model of power.[13]

Uncertainty Reduction   **Critical contingencies** are the things that an organization and its various parts need to accomplish organizational goals and continue surviving. The raw materials needed by a company to manufacture goods are critical contingencies. So, too, are the employees who make these goods, the customers who buy them, and the banks that provide loans to buy inventory and equipment. Information can also be a critical contingency.

Consider the financial data used by banks to decide whether to grant loans, or the mailing lists employed by catalog merchandisers to locate prospective customers. Uncertainty about the continued availability of such critical contingencies can threaten the organization's well-being. If a purchasing manager cannot be certain that she can buy raw materials at reasonable prices, then her organization's ability to start or continue productive work is compromised. Similarly, when a marketing department reports shifting consumer tastes, the firm's ability to sell what it has produced is threatened. Thus, as explained by Gerald Salancik and Jeffrey Pfeffer, the critical contingencies model of power is based on the principle that "those [individuals or groups] most able to cope with [their] organization's critical problems and uncertainties acquire power"[14] by trading *uncertainty reduction* for whatever they want in return.

One way to reduce uncertainty is by gaining *resource control*—that is, by acquiring and maintaining access to those resources that might otherwise be difficult to obtain.[15] A human resources management department may be able to reduce an important source of uncertainty in an organization that has experienced problems in attracting qualified employees if it can hire and retain a productive workforce. Similarly, a purchasing department that can negotiate discounts on raw materials can help reduce uncertainty related to whether the firm can afford to continue to produce its line of goods. Each of these departments, by delivering crucial resources and thereby reducing success-threatening uncertainty, can gain power.[16]

Information control offers another way to reduce uncertainty in organizations. Providing information about critical contingencies is particularly useful when such information can be used to predict or prevent threats to organizational operations.[17] Suppose, for example, that a telecommunication company's legal department learns of impending legislation that will restrict the company's ability to buy additional television stations unless it divests itself of the stations it already owns. By alerting management and recommending ways to form subsidiary companies to allow continued growth, the firm's legal department may eliminate much uncertainty for the firm.

A third way to reduce uncertainty is to acquire *decision-making control*—that is, to have input into the initial decisions about what sorts of resources will be critical contingencies. At any time, events may conspire to give certain groups power over others. This power, in turn, allows its possessors to determine the rules of the game or to decide such basic issues as what the company will produce, to whom it will market the product, and what kinds of materials, skills, and procedures will be needed. In the process, those already in power can make the contingencies they manage even more important to organizational well-being. In this manner, power can be used to acquire power of even greater magnitude—"the rich get richer."[18]

Substitutability   Whether individuals or groups gain power as a result of their success in reducing uncertainty depends partly on their **substitutability.** If others can serve as substitutes and reduce the same sort of uncertainty, then individuals or departments that need help in coping with uncertainty can turn to a variety of sources for aid. Hence no single source is likely to acquire much power under such a scenario. For example, a legal department's ability to interpret laws and regulations is unlikely to yield power for the department if legal specialists working in other departments can fulfill the same function. When substitutes are readily available, other departments can ignore the pressures of any particular group, so each group's ability to amass power is undermined.

If others can get help in coping with uncertainty only from the target person or group, however, this person or group is clearly in a position to barter uncertainty reduction for desired outcomes. For example, a research and development group that serves as a company's sole source of new product ideas can threaten to reduce the flow of innovation if the firm does not provide the desired resources. The less substitutability present in a situation, the more likely that a particular person or group will be able to amass power.[19]

Centrality   The ability of a person or a group to acquire power is also influenced by its **centrality,** or its position within the flow of work in the organization.[20] The ability to reduce uncertainty is unlikely to affect a group's power if no one outside the group knows that it has this ability and no one inside the group recognizes the importance of the ability. Simply because few other people know of its existence, a clerical staff located on the periphery of a company is unlikely to amass much power, even if its typing and filing activities bring it in direct contact with critically important information. When uncertainty emerges that the staff could help resolve, it is likely to be ignored because no one is aware of the knowledge and abilities possessed by the staff members.

The Critical Contingencies Model: Assessment

Despite a few criticisms,[21] research strongly supports the critical contingencies model's suggestion that power is a function of uncertainty reduction, substitutability, and centrality. An analysis of British manufacturing firms in business during the first half of the twentieth century confirms this idea.[22] The analysis revealed that accounting departments dominated organizational decision making in the Great Depression era preceding World War II, because they kept costs down at a time when money was scarce. After the war ended, power shifted to purchasing departments as money became more readily available and strong consumer demand made access to plentiful supplies of raw materials more important. During the 1950s, demand dropped so precipitously that marketing became the most important problem facing British firms. As a result (and as predicted by the model), marketing and sales departments that succeeded in increasing company sales gained power over important decision-making processes.

In another study, researchers examined twenty-nine departments of the University of Illinois, looking at the departments' national reputations, teaching loads, and financial receipts from outside contracts and grants.[23] Their results indicated that each department's ability to influence university decision making was directly related to its reputation, teaching load, and grant contributions.

In addition, the amount of contract and grant money brought in from outside sources had an especially strong effect on departmental power. Contracts and grants provide operating funds critical to the survival of a public institution such as the University of Illinois. Thus, as predicted by the critical contingencies model, the power of each department in the university was directly related to its ability to contribute to the management of critical contingencies.

An even more intriguing piece of evidence supporting the critical contingencies model was discovered by Michel Crozier, a French sociologist who studied a government-owned tobacco company located just outside Paris.[24] As described by Crozier, maintenance mechanics in the tobacco company sought control over their working lives by refusing to share knowledge needed to repair crucial production equipment. The mechanics memorized repair manuals and then threw them away so that no one else could refer to them. In addition, they refused to let production employees or supervisors watch as they repaired the company's machines. They also trained their replacements in a closely guarded apprenticeship process, thereby ensuring that outsiders could not learn what they knew. Some mechanics even altered equipment so completely that the original manufacturer could not figure out how it worked. In this manner, the tobacco company's maintenance mechanics retained absolute control over the information and skill required to repair production equipment. In essence, the maintenance personnel ran the production facility as a result of the information they alone possessed about its equipment.

Crozier's account of the tobacco factory mechanics illustrates the usefulness of the critical contingencies model in explaining why people who have hierarchical authority and formal power sometimes lack the influence needed to manage workplace activities. If subordinates have the knowledge, skills, or abilities required to manage critical contingencies, thereby reducing troublesome uncertainties, they may gain enough power to disobey their hierarchical superiors. In turn, as long as superiors must depend on subordinates to manage such contingencies, it will be the subordinates—not the superiors—who determine which orders will be followed and which will be ignored.[25]

In sum, the critical contingencies model appears to describe the structural bases of power quite accurately. Its utility for contemporary managers lies in the observation that the roots of power lie in the ability to solve crucial organizational problems. Managers must understand and exploit this simple premise, because such knowledge can help them acquire and keep the power needed to do their jobs.

POLITICS AND POLITICAL PROCESSES

Politics can be defined as activities in which individuals or groups engage so as to acquire and use power to advance their own interests. In essence, politics is power in action.[26] Although political behavior can be disruptive, it is not necessarily bad. The unsanctioned, unanticipated changes wrought by politics can, in fact, enhance

CUTTING-EDGE RESEARCH

SOME CONSEQUENCES OF ABUSIVE SUPERVISION

What happens when people with power use it in abusive ways? Bennett J. Tepper sought answers to this question in a study of 362 individuals employed in service, retailing, manufacturing, small business, government, and education organizations.

Tepper focused his study on a particular type of power abuse, abusive supervision, which he defined as the extent to which supervisors are perceived to engage in *the sustained display of hostile verbal and nonverbal behaviors, excluding physical contact.* Drawing from prior research on supervisory behaviors and perceived fairness, Tepper hypothesized that the degree to which supervisors were seen by their subordinates as abusive would affect subordinates' perceptions of organizational justice (that is, the extent to which procedures and outcomes in an organization are seen as fair), which would then shape their propensities to quit as well as reported levels of job satisfaction, life satisfaction, organizational commitment, psychological distress, and conflict between work and family life. He also theorized that greater employee mobility—ability to find other work—as perceived by the employee would lessen the effects of supervisory abuse.

Results of Tepper's study confirmed these predictions. In particular, subordinates who perceived their supervisors as abusive reported higher turnover; less favorable attitudes toward their jobs, lives, and organizations; greater conflict between work and fam-

ily obligations; and greater psychological distress. In addition, effects for job satisfaction, life satisfaction, work-family conflict, depression, and emotional exhaustion were stronger for employees who reported lower levels of job mobility. Thus, supervisory abuse had more profound effects when subordinates saw no means of escape. Finally, perceived organizational fairness exerted mediating effects of various amounts on all outcome variables (partial mediation with respect to anxiety and emotional exhaustion and full mediation with regard to job satisfaction, life satisfaction, decision to quit, organizational commitment, work-life conflict, and depression). This suggests that observed effects of supervisory abuse could be explained in terms of reduced perceptions of organizational justice.

Tepper summarized these findings by suggesting that they indicate that "employees regard abusive supervision as a source of injustice that, in turn, has implications for their attitudes and well-being . . . The links between abusive supervision and the various indexes of psychological distress are troubling because even the milder manifestations may engender significant social and financial costs to organizations" (p. 186). He also suggested that future research should focus on determining the incidence and seriousness of abusive supervision, so as to develop a better understanding of the true impact of this negative use of power.

Source: From "Consequences of Abusive Supervision," by B.J. Tepper in *Academy of Management Journal* 43 2000, 178–190. Copyright © 2000 by Academy of Management. Reproduced with permission of Academy of Management via copyright clearance center.

organizational well-being by ridding companies of familiar but dysfunctional ways of doing things.[27] Nonetheless, because politics has a negative connotation, political behavior is seldom discussed openly in organizations. In fact, managers and employees may even deny that politics influences organizational activities. Research indicates, however, that politicking *does* occur and that it has measurable effects on organizational behavior (see the Cutting-Edge Research box).[28]

Personality and Politics

Why do people engage in politics? As with power in general, certain personal characteristics predispose people to exhibit political behaviors. For example, some people have a need for power (nPow), as identified by McClelland and discussed previously. Just as nPow drives people to seek out influence over others, it also motivates them to use this power for political gain.

Other researchers have suggested that people who exhibit the personality characteristic of **Machiavellianism**—the tendency to seek to control other people through opportunistic, manipulative behaviors—may also be inclined toward politics. In addition, studies have indicated that self-conscious people may be less likely than others to become involved in office politics because they fear being singled out as a focus of public attention and being evaluated negatively for engaging in politics. This fear keeps them from seeking power and using it for personal gain.[29]

Conditions That Stimulate Politics

In addition to personality characteristics such as nPow and Machiavellianism, certain conditions encourage political activity in organizations (see Figure 11-4). One such condition is *uncertainty* that can be traced to ambiguity and change (see Table 11-3). Uncertainty can hide or disguise people's behaviors, enabling them to engage in political activities that would otherwise be detected and prohibited. It can also trigger political behavior, because it gives people a reason to be political—they may resort to politics in efforts to find ways to reduce uncertainty that provide them with added power and other personal benefits.

Besides uncertainty, other conditions that may encourage political behavior include *organizational size, hierarchical level, membership heterogeneity,* and *decision importance.* Politicking is more prevalent in larger organizations than in smaller ones. The presence of a greater number of people is more likely to hide the behaviors of any one person, enabling him or her to engage in political behaviors with less fear of discovery. Politics is also more common among middle and upper managers, because the power required to engage in politics is usually concentrated among managers at these levels. In heterogeneous organizations, members share few interests and values and therefore see things very differently. Under such circumstances, political processes are likely to emerge as members compete to decide whose interests will be satisfied and whose will not. Finally, important decisions stimulate more politics than unimportant decisions do simply because less important issues attract less interest and attention.

Political Tactics

When personal characteristics and surrounding conditions favor them, a variety of political tactics may surface. Each tactic is intended to increase the power of one person or group relative to others. When power increases, so does the likelihood that the person or group will be able to seek out and acquire self-interested gains.[30]

Acquiring Interpersonal Power: Forming Affiliations Forming **coalitions** or political affiliations with each other represents an important way for people to increase their power and pursue political gain beyond their individual grasp.[31] By banding

FIGURE 11-4 A Model of the Emergence of Politics

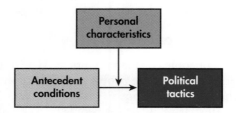

Source: Based on G. R. Ferris, G. S. Russ, and P. M. Fandt, "Politics in Organizations," in R. A. Glacalone and P. Rosenfield, eds., *Impression Management in the Organization* (Hillsdale, NJ: Erlbaum, 1989), pp. 143–170.

TABLE 11-3
Types of
Uncertainty
That Encourage
Politics

- Interruptions in the availability of critical resources or of information about these resources.
- Ambiguity (no clear meaning) or equivocality (more than one possible meaning) in the information that is available
- Poorly defined goals, objectives, work roles, or performance measures
- Unclear rules for such things as who should make decisions, how decisions should be reached, or when decision making should occur
- Change of any type—for example, reorganization, budgetary reallocations, or procedural modifications
- Dependence on other individuals or groups, especially when that dependence is accompanied by competitiveness or hostility

Source: Based on D. R. Beman and T. W. Sharkey, "The Use and Abuse of Corporate Politics," *Business Horizons* 30 (1987), 26–30; A. Raia, "Power, Politics, and the Human Resource Professional," *Human Resource Planning* 8 (1985), 198–209; J. P. Kotter, "Power, Dependence, and Effective Management," *Harvard Business Review* 53 (1977), 125–136.

together, people can share their collective control over rewards or punishments. They can also combine their expertise, legitimacy, and charisma. For instance, collective bargaining enables union members to obtain wages and conditions far superior to those that they could demand as individuals. Conversely, companies form trade associations so as to exchange information about collective bargaining and union agreements.

As part of the process of forming political affiliations, favors may be used to create a sense of indebtedness. People who pursue this tactic can increase the dependence of others by building up a bank of favors that are owed them. In the U.S. Congress, for instance, representatives from industrial regions will vote for bills providing farm subsidies with the understanding that farm-state representatives will reciprocate by supporting bills that secure industrial assistance grants.

Besides exchanging favors, people engaging in politics sometimes use cooptation to preserve their interests in the face of adversity. In **cooptation,** former rivals become transformed into allies, often by involving them in planning and decision-making processes.[32] Colleges and universities often use this tactic during periods of campus unrest, inviting student protesters to join university representatives on administrative committees. Making opponents part of the team often silences their objections, but carries the risk of making major changes in plans and decisions.

Finally, ingratiation and impression management can be used to build and maintain political relationships. *Ingratiation* is the use of praise and compliments to gain the favor or acceptance of others. Similarly, *impression management* involves behaving in ways intended to build a positive image. Both can increase personal attractiveness, thereby raising the likelihood that others will seek a close relationship.[33]

Acquiring Structural Power: Controlling Critical Resources As suggested by the critical contingencies model of power, controlling the supply of a critical resource gives people power over those whose success or survival depends on having that resource. A warehouse manager, for example, can decide which orders will be filled immediately and which will be delayed. As a political tool, power of this sort can be used to ensure that personal interests are satisfied. Similarly, controlling access to information sources provides power over those who need that information to reduce uncertainty. Political players often attempt to control access to the people who are sources of important information or expertise. Managers, for instance, may shield the staff specialists who advise them from others in their firm. Engineers who are working on new product development are often sequestered from other employees; cost accountants may be separated from other members of a company's accounting department. Such employees are an important resource because they possess critical information that is unavailable elsewhere.

To succeed as a political tactic, controlling access to important resources, information, or people requires eliminating substitutes for these critical resources and discrediting alternative definitions of what is critical. The presence of substitutes counteracts attempts to gain power by controlling critical resources because it neutralizes political efforts. In addition, successful control of critical resources requires that people have at least the centrality needed to identify which resources are critical and which are not.

Negative Politics   If all else fails, a person may sometimes gain the political upper hand by attacking or blaming others, or making them *scapegoats* for failures.[34] Another tactic is to denigrate or belittle others' accomplishments. Either approach involves a direct attack on the interpersonal sources of power that others might possess in an attempt to weaken their political positions, thereby creating doubt about their ability to control rewards and punishments or reducing their credibility, legitimacy, or attractiveness. Negative politicking can also justify the creation of substitute sources of critical resources or information or reduction of the degree of centrality enjoyed by a person or group. After all, who would want an incompetent individual or group in charge of something that is critically important to organizational survival?

Managing Destructive Politics

You can easily imagine some of the consequences when people band together, hoard resources, or belittle each other for no other reason than to get their own way. Morale may suffer; battle lines between contending individuals or groups may impede important interactions; energy that should go into productive activities may instead be spent on planning attacks and counterattacks if politicking is left uncontrolled. For this reason, controlling political behavior is a major part of every manager's job.[35]

Set an Example   One way to manage destructive politics is to set an example. Managers who do not tolerate deceit and dirty tricks and who refuse to engage in negative politics themselves make it clear that such political tactics are inappropriate. Subordinates are thus discouraged from engaging in destructive political activities. In contrast, managers who engage in negative politics—blaming their mistakes on others, keeping critical information from others—convey the message that politics is acceptable. Little wonder, then, that subordinates in such situations are themselves prone to politicking.

Communicate Openly   Sharing all relevant information with co-workers and colleagues can thwart the effects of destructive politics. Managers who communicate openly with their peers, superiors, and subordinates eliminate the political advantage of withholding information or blocking access to important people. Information that everyone already knows cannot be hoarded or hidden. In addition, open communication ensures that everyone understands and accepts resource allocations. Such understanding eliminates the attractiveness of political maneuvers intended to bias distribution procedures. Shrinking the potential benefits of destructive politicking lessens the incidence of political behaviors.

Reduce Uncertainty   A third way to minimize destructive political behavior is to reduce uncertainty. Clarifying goals, tasks, and responsibilities makes it easier to assess people's behaviors and brings politics out into the open. Expanding decision-making processes by consulting with subordinates or involving them in participatory decision-making processes helps make the resulting decisions understandable and discourages undercover politicking.

Manage Informal Coalitions and Cliques Managing informal coalitions and cliques can also help reduce destructive politics. Influencing the norms and beliefs that steer group behaviors can ensure that employees continue to serve organizational interests. When cliques resist less severe techniques, job reassignment becomes a viable option. Group politicking is thereby abolished by eliminating the group.

Confront Political Game Players A fifth approach to managing politics is to confront political game players about their activities. When people engage in politics despite initial attempts to discourage them from this course of action, a private meeting between superior and subordinate may be enough to curb the subordinate's political pursuits. If not, disciplinary measures may become necessary. Punishments such as a public reprimand or a period of layoff without pay ensure that the costs of politicking outweigh its benefits. If this approach does not work, managers who must cope with damaging politics may have no choice except to dismiss political game players.

Anticipate the Emergence of Damaging Politics In any effort intended to control political behavior, awareness and anticipation are critical. If managers are aware that circumstances are conducive to politicking, they can try to prevent the emergence of politics. Detection of any of the personal characteristics or favorable conditions discussed earlier should be interpreted as a signal indicating the need for management intervention *before* destructive politics crop up.

CONFLICT IN ORGANIZATIONS

Conflict—a process of opposition and confrontation that can occur in organizations between either individuals or groups—occurs when parties exercise power in the pursuit of valued goals or objectives and obstruct the progress of other parties.[36] Key to this definition is the idea that conflict involves the use of power in confrontation, or disputes over clashing interests. Also important is the notion that conflict is a process—something that takes time to unfold, rather than an event that occurs in an instant and then disappears. Finally, to the extent that obstructing progress threatens effectiveness and performance, the definition implies that conflict is a problem that managers must be able to control.

Is Conflict Necessarily Bad?

Conflict might seem inherently undesirable. In fact, many of the models of organization and management discussed in Chapter 2 support this view. Classic theorists often likened organizations to machines and portrayed conflict as symptomatic of breakdown of these machines. Managers in the days of Henri Fayol and Frederick Taylor concerned themselves with discovering ways either to avoid conflict or to suppress it as quickly and forcefully as possible.

In contrast, contemporary theorists argue that conflict is not necessarily bad.[37] To be sure, they say, *dysfunctional* conflict—confrontation that hinders progress toward desired goals—does occur. For example, protracted labor strikes leave both managers and employees with bad feelings, cost companies lost revenues and customers, and cost employees lost wages and benefits. Current research, however, suggests that conflict is often *functional,* having positive effects such as the following:

- Conflict can lessen social tensions, helping to stabilize and integrate relationships. If resolved in a way that allows for the discussion and dissipation of disagreements, it can serve as a safety valve that vents pressures built up over time.
- Conflict lets opposing parties express rival claims and provides the opportunity to readjust the allocation of valued resources. Resource pools may thus be consumed more effectively due to conflict-induced changes.
- Conflict helps maintain the level of stimulation or activation required to function innovatively. In so doing, it can serve as a source of motivation to seek adaptive change.
- Conflict supplies feedback about the state of interdependencies and power distributions in an organization's structure. The distribution of power required to coordinate work activities then becomes more clearly apparent and readily understood.
- Conflict can help provide a sense of identity and purpose by clarifying differences and boundaries between individuals or groups. Such outcomes are discussed in greater detail later in this chapter.[38]

At the very least, conflict can serve as a red flag signaling the need for change. Believing that conflict can have positive effects, contemporary managers try to manage or resolve disagreements rather than avoiding or suppressing them.

Conditions That Stimulate Conflict

For conflict to occur, three key conditions must exist: interdependence, political indeterminism, and divergence. *Interdependence* is found where individuals, groups, or organizations depend on each other for assistance, information, feedback, or other coordinative relations.[39] As indicated in Chapter 8, four types of interdependence—pooled, sequential, reciprocal, and comprehensive—can link parties together. Any such linkages can serve as sources of conflict. For example, two groups that share a pool of funds may fight over who will receive money to buy new office equipment. Similarly, employees organized along a sequential assembly process may disagree about the pace of work. In the absence of interdependence, however, parties have nothing to fight about and, in fact, may not even know of each other's existence.

The emergence of conflict also requires *political indeterminism,* which means that the political pecking order among individuals or groups is unclear and subject to question. If power relations are unambiguous and stable, and if they are accepted as valid by all parties, appeals to authority will replace conflict, and differences will be resolved in favor of the most powerful. Only a party whose power is uncertain will gamble on winning through conflict rather than by appealing to power and authority. For this reason, individuals and groups in a newly reorganized company are much more likely to engage in conflict than are parties in an organization with a stable hierarchy of authority.

Finally, for conflict to emerge, there must be *divergence,* or differences or disagreements deemed worth fighting over.[40] For example, differences in the functions they perform may lead individuals or groups to have *varying goals.* Table 11-4 describes some differences in the goal orientations of marketing and manufacturing groups. In this example, each group's approach reflects its particular orientation—marketing's focus on customer service, manufacturing's concern with efficient production runs. In such situations, conflicts may occur over whose goals to pursue and whose to ignore.

TABLE 11-4   Differences in Goal Orientations: Marketing and Manufacturing

Goal Focus	Marketing Approach	Manufacturing Approach
Product variety	Customers demand variety	Variety causes short, often uneconomical production runs
Capacity limits	Manufacturing capacity limits productivity	Inaccurate sales forecasts limit productivity
Product quality	Reasonable quality should be achievable at a cost that is affordable to customers	Offering options that are difficult to manufacture undermines quality
New products	New products are the firm's lifeblood	Unnecessary design changes are costly
Cost control	High cost undermines the firm's competitive position	Broad variety, fast delivery, high quality, and rapid responsiveness are not possible at low cost

Source: Based on information presented in B. S. Shapiro, "Can Marketing and Manufacturing Coexist?" *Harvard Business Review* 55 (September–October 1977), 104–114.

Individuals and groups may also have different *time orientations*. For example, tasks like making a sale to a regular customer require only short-term planning and can be initiated or altered quite easily. In contrast, tasks like traditional assembly-line manufacturing operations necessitate a longer time frame, because such activities require extensive preplanning and cannot be changed easily once they have begun. Certain tasks, such as the strategic planning activities that plot an organization's future, may even require time frames of several decades. When parties in a firm have different time orientations, conflicts may develop regarding which orientation should regulate task planning and performance.

Often, *resource allocations* among individuals or groups are unequal. Such differences usually stem from the fact that parties must compete with each other to get a share of their organization's resources. When the production department gets new personal computers to help schedule weekly activities, the sales department may find itself forced to do without the new computers it wants for market research. In such instances, someone wins and someone loses, laying the groundwork for additional rounds of conflict.

Another source of conflict may be the practices used to *evaluate* and *reward* groups and their members. Consider, for example, that manufacturing groups are often rewarded for their efficiency, which is achieved by minimizing the quantity of raw materials consumed in production activities. Sales groups, on the other hand, tend to be rewarded for their flexibility, which sometimes sacrifices efficiency. Conflict often arises in such situations as each group tries to meet its own performance criteria or tries to force others to adopt the same criteria.

In addition, *status discrepancies* invite conflict over stature and position. Although the status of a person or group is generally determined by its position in the organization's hierarchy of authority—with parties higher in the hierarchy having higher status—sometimes other criteria influence status.[41] For instance, a group might argue that its status should depend on the knowledge possessed by its members or that status should be conferred on the basis of such factors as loyalty, seniority, or visibility.

Conflict can emerge in *jurisdictional disputes* when it is unclear who has responsibility for something. For example, if the personnel and employing departments both interview a prospective employee, the two groups may dispute which has the ultimate right to offer employment and which must take the blame if mistakes are made.

Finally, individuals and groups can differ in the *values, assumptions,* and *general perceptions* that guide their performance. Values held by the members of a production group, which stress easy assembly, for instance, may differ from the values held by the research and development staff, which favor complex product designs. These values can clash, leading to conflict, whenever researchers must fight for demanding product specifications that production personnel dismiss as unnecessarily complicated.

Effects of Conflict

Conflict affects relationships among people and groups in many ways. Especially when conflict occurs between groups, several important effects can be predicted to occur within the opposing groups.[42]

First, as noted in Chapter 9, external threats such as intergroup conflict bring about *increased group cohesiveness*. As a result, groups engaged in conflict become more attractive and important to their own members. Ongoing conflict also stimulates an *emphasis on task performance*. All efforts within each conflicting group are directed toward meeting the challenge posed by other groups, and concerns about individual members' satisfaction diminish in importance. A sense of urgency surrounds task performance; defeating the enemy becomes uppermost, and much less loafing occurs.

In addition, when a group faces conflict, otherwise reluctant members will often submit to *autocratic leadership* to manage the crisis, because they perceive participatory decision making as slow and weak. Strong, authoritarian leaders often emerge as a result of this shift. A group in such circumstances is also likely to place much more emphasis on standard procedures and centralized control. As a result, it becomes characterized by *structural rigidity*. By adhering to established rules and creating and strictly enforcing new ones, the group seeks to eliminate any conflicts that might develop among its members and to ensure that it can succeed repeatedly at its task.

Other changes may occur in the relations between conflicting groups. Hostility often surfaces in the form of hardened *"we–they" attitudes*. Each group sees itself as virtuous and the other groups as enemies. Intense dislike often accompanies these negative attitudes. As attitudes within each group become more negative, group members may develop *distorted perceptions* of opposing groups. The resulting negative stereotyping can create even greater differences between groups and further strengthen the cohesiveness within each group.

Eventually, negative attitudes and perceptions of group members may lead to a *decrease in communication* among conflicting groups. The isolation that results merely adds to the conflict, making resolution even more difficult to achieve. At the same time, conflicting groups often engage in *increased surveillance* intended to provide information about the attitudes, weaknesses, and likely behaviors of other groups.

NEGOTIATION AND RESTRUCTURING

A variety of conflict-management techniques have been developed to help resolve conflicts and deal with the kinds of negative effects just described. In general, these techniques are of two types: bargaining and negotiation procedures that focus on managing *divergence* among the interests of conflicting parties, and restructuring techniques that focus on managing *interdependence* between conflicting individuals and groups.

Managing Diverging Interests

Bargaining and negotiation are two closely associated processes that are often employed to work out the differences in interests and concerns that generate conflict. **Bargaining** between conflicting parties consists of offers, counteroffers, and concessions exchanged in a search for some mutually acceptable resolution. **Negotiation,** in turn, is the process in which the parties decide what each will give and take in this exchange.[43]

In the business world, relations between management and labor are often the focus of bargaining and negotiation. Both processes also occur elsewhere in organizations, however, as people and groups try to satisfy their own desires and control the extent to which they must sacrifice so as to satisfy others. In tight economies, for example, groups of secretaries who are dependent on the same supply budget may have to bargain with each other to see who will get new office equipment and who will have to make do with existing equipment. A company's sales force may try to negotiate favorable delivery dates for its best clients by offering manufacturing personnel leeway in meeting deadlines for other customers' orders.

In deciding which conflicting interests will be satisfied, parties engaged in bargaining and negotiation can choose the degree to which they will assert themselves and look after their own interests. They can also decide whether they will cooperate with their adversary and put its interests ahead of their own. As Figure 11-5 shows, five general approaches to managing divergent interests exist that are characterized by different mixes of assertiveness and cooperativeness:[44]

1. *Competition* (assertive, uncooperative) means overpowering other parties in the conflict and promoting one's own concerns at the other parties' expense. One way to accomplish this aim is by resorting to authority to satisfy one's own concerns. Thus the head of a group of account executives may appeal to the director of advertising to protect the group's turf from intrusions by other account execs.
2. *Accommodation* (unassertive, cooperative) allows other parties to satisfy their own concerns at the expense of one's own interests. Differences are smoothed over to maintain superficial harmony. A purchasing department that fails to meet budgetary guidelines because it deliberately overspends on raw materials in an effort to satisfy the demands of production groups is trying to use accommodation to cope with conflict.

FIGURE 11-5 Managing Divergence

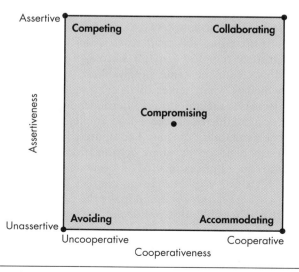

Source: From "Support for a Two-Dimensional Model of Conflict Behavior," by T. L. Ruble and K. Thomas in *Organizational Behavior and Human Performance* 1976, p. 145. Copyright © 1976. Reprinted with permission from Elsevier.

3. *Avoidance* (unassertive, uncooperative) requires staying neutral at all costs or refusing to take an active role in conflict resolution procedures. The finance department that "sticks its head in the sand," hoping that dissension about budgetary allocations will simply blow over, is exhibiting avoidance.

4. *Collaboration* (assertive, cooperative) attempts to satisfy everyone by working through differences and seeking solutions in which everyone gains. A marketing department and a manufacturing department that meet on a regular basis to plan mutually acceptable production schedules are collaborating.

5. *Compromise* (midrange assertive, cooperative) seeks partial satisfaction of everyone through exchange and sacrifice, settling for acceptable rather than optimal resolution. Contract bargaining between union representatives and management typically involves significant compromise by both sides.

As indicated in Table 11-5, the appropriateness of each of these approaches depends on the situation and, in many cases, on the time pressure for a negotiated settlement. Beyond these general alternatives, experts on organizational development have devised an assortment of more specific techniques for conflict management that are based on structured sessions of bargaining and negotiation. Several of these techniques will be described in detail in Chapter 14, which deals with culture, change, and organizational development.

Managing Structural Interdependence

In addition to divergence in interests, conflict requires interdependence. It can therefore be managed or resolved by restructuring the connections that tie conflicting parties together.[45] One way to accomplish this goal is to *develop superordinate goals,* identifying and pursuing a set of performance targets that conflicting parties can achieve only by working together. Sharing a common goal requires the parties to look beyond their differences and learn to cooperate with each other. In the automobile industry, for instance, unions and management, fearing plant closures, have forgone adversarial relations to strengthen the competitiveness of automotive firms. In many companies, teamwork has replaced conflict in the pursuit of the superordinate goal of producing high-quality products for today's world markets.

Expanding the supply of critical resources is another way to restructure. This strategy removes a major source of conflict between individuals and groups that draw from the same supply. Pools of critical resources are not easily enlarged— which is what makes them critical, of course. When this method is successful, it decreases the amount of interdependence between parties, which then compete less for available resources. For example, one way to eliminate interoffice conflicts over the availability of shared computers is to buy a network of personal computers for every department. Some organizations purchase large quantities of used computers at reduced prices instead of a few new ones at full retail.

A third way to manage conflict by restructuring interdependence is to *clarify existing relationships* and make the political position of each party readily apparent. If it is feasible, this political clarification affects interdependence by strengthening everyone's understanding of how and why they are connected. It also reduces the political indeterminism that must exist for conflict to occur.

A fourth approach is to *modify existing structural relationships*. This strategy includes a number of mechanisms that either uncouple conflicting parties or modify the structural linkage between them.[46] Two such mechanisms—the **decoupling mech-**

TABLE 11-5
The Application of Different Styles of Managing Divergence

Style	Application
Competing	When quick, decisive action is required; to cope with crises.
	On important issues where unpopular solutions must be implemented, such as cost cutting or employee discipline.
	On issues vital to organizational welfare when your group is certain that its position is correct.
	Against groups who take advantage of noncompetitive behavior.
Accommodating	When your group is wrong and wants both to show reasonableness and to encourage the expression of a more appropriate view.
	When issues are more important to groups other than yours, to satisfy others and maintain cooperation.
	To build credits or bank favors for later issues.
	To minimize losses when your group is outmatched and losing.
	When harmony and stability are especially important.
Avoiding	When a conflict is trivial or more important conflicts are pressing.
	When there is no chance that your group will satisfy its own needs.
	When the costs of potential disruption outweigh the benefits of resolution.
	To let groups cool down and gain perspective.
	When others can resolve the conflict more effectively.
Collaborating	To find an integrative solution when conflicting concerns are too important to be compromised.
	When the most important objective is to learn.
	To combine the ideas of people with different perspectives.
	To gain commitment through the development of consensus.
	To work through conflicting feelings in individuals and between groups.
Compromising	When group concerns are important but not worth the disruption associated with more assertive styles.
	When equally powerful groups are committed to pursuing mutually exclusive concerns.
	To achieve temporary or transitional settlements.
	To arrive at expedient resolutions under time pressure.
	As a backup when neither competing nor problem-solving styles are successful.

Source: Adapted from "Toward Multidimensional Values in Teaching: The Example of Conflict Behaviors," by K. W. Thomas in *Academy of Management Review* 2 (1977), 487. Copyright © 1977 by Academy of Mangement. Reproduced with permission of Academy of Management via copyright clearance center.

anisms of slack resources and self-contained tasks—manage conflict by eliminating the interdependence that must exist for conflict to occur.

Slack resources help decouple otherwise interconnected individuals and groups by creating buffers that lessen the ability of one party to affect the activities of another. Suppose one person assembles telephone handsets, and another person connects finished handsets to telephone bodies to form fully assembled units. The two employees are sequentially interdependent, because the second person's ability to perform the work is contingent on the first person's ability to complete the task. The second employee cannot work if the first employee stops producing. If a buffer inventory is created—a supply of finished handsets—on which the second worker can draw when the first worker is not producing anything, we have (at least temporarily) decoupled the two individuals.

In contrast, the creation of *self-contained tasks* involves combining the work of two or more interdependent parties and then assigning this work to several independent parties. If the original parties are groups, then the self-contained groups are usually staffed by employees drawn from each of the interdependent groups. For example, engineering and drafting groups might have problems coordinating engineering specifications and the drawings produced by the drafting group. These two groups might be re-formed into several independent engineering–drafting groups. After this restructuring, the original two groups would no longer exist. Key interdependencies that lie outside the original groups are contained within redesigned groups and can be managed without crossing group boundaries or involving outside managers.

Sometimes concerns about minimizing inventory costs rule out the use of slack resources. Among U.S. manufacturers, for instance, the cost of carrying excessive inventory is a major concern and has stimulated increasing interest in just-in-time (JIT) procedures. Using JIT, inventory is acquired only as needed, eliminating the cost of having unused items lying around. In addition, work often cannot be divided into self-contained tasks. For example, the task of producing the parts required to make a car and assembling them into a final product is so immense that many individuals and groups (in fact, many companies) must be involved. In such cases, existing structural relationships may be modified instead by means of various **unit-linking mechanisms.**

Network information systems are one such mechanism. These systems consist of mainframe computers with remote terminals or network servers connected to personal computers that can be used to input and exchange information about organizational performance. If you have taken courses in computer science, you have probably worked with a computer network similar to the *intranets* now used in businesses. Managers use such systems to communicate among themselves and to store information for later review. The networks facilitate the transfer of large amounts of information up and down an organization's hierarchy of authority. In addition, they support lateral exchanges among interdependent individuals and groups. In the process, they facilitate communication that might otherwise develop into misunderstandings and lead to conflict. The fact that many organizations have recently added the corporate position of chief information officer (CIO) reflects the growing use of network information systems to manage interdependent, potentially conflictful relationships.[47]

A second type of unit-linking mechanism consists of several *lateral linkage devices* that managers can use to strengthen communication between interdependent parties. In one of these, an employee may be assigned a *liaison position* in which he or she is responsible for seeing that communications flow directly and freely between interdependent groups. The liaison position represents an alternative to hierarchical communication channels. It reduces both the time needed to communicate between groups and the amount of information distortion likely to occur. The person occupying a liaison position has no authority to issue direct orders, but rather serves as a neutral third party and relies on negotiation, bargaining, and persuasion. This person is called on to mediate between groups if conflict actually emerges, resolving differences and moving the groups toward voluntary intergroup coordination.[48]

The liaison position is the least costly of the lateral linkage devices. Because one person handles the task of coordination, minimal resources are diverted from the primary task of production. In addition, because the position has no formal authority, it is the least disruptive of normal hierarchical relationships. Sometimes, however, a liaison position is not strong enough to manage interdependence relations. Managers then have the option of turning to another type of lateral linkage device, *representative groups,* to coordinate activities among interdependent parties. Representative groups consist of people who represent the interdependent individuals or groups, and who meet to coordinate the interdependent activities.

Two kinds of representative groups exist. One, called a *task force,* is formed to complete a specific task or project and then disbanded. Representatives get together, talk out the differences among the parties they represent, and resolve conflicts before they become manifest. For this reason, companies such as Colgate-Palmolive & Procter and Gamble form product task groups by drawing together members from advertising, marketing, manufacturing, and product research departments. Each product task group identifies consumer needs, designs new products that respond to these needs, and manages their market introduction. Once a new product is successfully launched, the product task group responsible for its introduction is dissolved, and its members return to their former jobs.

The other type of representative group is a more or less permanent structure. Like the members of the task force, the members of this group, called a *standing committee,* represent interdependent parties, but they meet on a regular basis to discuss and resolve ongoing problems. The standing committee is not assigned a specific task, nor is it expected to disband at any particular time. An example of a standing committee is a factory's Monday morning production meeting. At that meeting, representatives from production control, purchasing, quality assurance, shipping, and various assembly groups overview the week's production schedule and try to anticipate problems.

Like task forces, standing committees use face-to-face communication to manage interdependence problems and resolve conflict-related differences. Despite their usefulness in this regard, both of these linkage devices are more costly than the liaison position. Through process loss, their group meetings inevitably consume otherwise productive resources. In addition, because representative groups (especially task forces) are sometimes designed to operate outside customary hierarchical channels, they can prove quite disruptive to normal management procedures.

When neither liaison positions nor representative groups solve intergroup conflict problems, the company may use a third type of lateral linkage device, called an *integrating manager.* Like the liaison position, the integrating manager mediates between interdependent parties. Unlike the liaison position, however, this individual has the formal authority to issue orders and expect obedience. He or she can tell interdependent parties what to do to resolve conflict. Project managers at companies such as Rockwell International and Lockheed fill the role of integrating manager. They oversee the progress of a project by ensuring that the various planning, designing, assembling, and testing groups work together successfully.

Normally, when coordinating the efforts of groups, an integrating manager issues orders only to group supervisors. Giving orders to the people who report to these supervisors might confuse employees, as employees might feel that they were being asked to report to two supervisors. Because an integrating manager disrupts normal hierarchical relationships by short-circuiting the relationships between the group supervisors and their usual superior, this device is used much less often than either the liaison position or representative groups.

Occasionally, even integrating managers cannot provide the guidance needed to manage conflict through structural means. In these rare instances, a fourth type of lateral linkage device, called the *matrix organization structure,* is sometimes employed. Matrix structures are the most complicated of the mechanisms used to coordinate group activities and resolve intergroup conflicts, and they are extremely costly to sustain.[49] The matrix organization structure will be discussed in greater detail in Chapter 12, which covers organization structure, because it is both a conflict resolution device and a specific type of structure. For now, we conclude by suggesting that matrix structures are appropriate only when all other intergroup mechanisms have proved ineffective.

SUMMARY

Power is the ability to influence others and to resist their influence in return. Compliance, identification, and internalization are outcomes that may result from the use of five types of interpersonal power—*reward, coercive, legitimate, referent,* and *expert* power. Power also grows out of uncertainty surrounding the continued availability of *critical contingencies*. It is therefore based on the ability to *reduce this uncertainty* and is enhanced by low *substitutability* and high *centrality*.

Politics is a process through which a person acquires power and uses it to advance the individual's self-interests. It is stimulated by a combination of personal characteristics and antecedent conditions and can involve a variety of tactics, ranging from controlling supplies of critical resources to attacking or blaming others. Several techniques are employed to manage politicking, including setting an example and confronting political game players.

Conflict is a process of opposition and confrontation that requires the presence of interdependence, political indeterminism, and divergence. It can be managed through *bargaining* and *negotiation,* or it can be resolved by restructuring interdependence relations through the use of various *decoupling* or *unit-linking mechanisms*.

REVIEW QUESTIONS

1. Is power being exercised when a manager orders a subordinate to do something the subordinate would do even without being ordered? When a subordinate successfully refuses to follow orders? When a manager's orders are followed despite the subordinate's reluctance?

2. What is the difference between reward power and coercive power? What do these two types of power have in common? How are they similar to legitimate power? How do they differ from both expert and referent power?

3. Why must uncertainty reduction, high centrality, and low substitutability *all* be present for power to be acquired? Explain how a group's power might be reduced by increasing its substitutability.

4. How does uncertainty encourage politics? What can managers do to control this antecedent condition?

5. What is a coalition? What is gained by forming one? Explain how political tactics such as impression management and doing favors can make it easier to form a coalition.

6. How can controlling information serve as a political tactic? How can managers guard against this tactic?

7. Why does intergroup conflict require interdependence? How does political indeterminism influence whether this sort of conflict will occur? Based on your answers to these two questions, how can managers resolve intergroup conflicts without attempting to reduce divergence?

8. How does an integrating manager differ from a liaison position? Which of the two is more likely to prove successful in resolving a longstanding conflict? Given your answer, why isn't this "stronger" approach the only option used in organizations?

9. Why is accommodation unlikely to succeed as a conflict management technique in most instances? Under what specific conditions is it most useful?

LEARNING THROUGH EXPERIENCE

DIAGNOSTIC QUESTIONS 11-1

Power, Politics, and Conflict

Considered together, power, politics, and conflict form a complex collection of political processes. If they take a dysfunctional turn, these processes can undermine the productivity and satisfaction of individuals and groups, thereby jeopardizing organizational performance. Asking the following diagnostic questions can help manage the political face of organizations.

1. Do individuals and groups in the organization have the power needed so that they can function productively and interact effectively?

2. Which types of interpersonal power are currently in use? Are these types of interpersonal power likely to generate the compliance, identification, or internalization needed to energize appropriate behaviors? Might other types of interpersonal power be more effective?

3. If power inadequacies exist, can they be traced to limitations in the ability to reduce uncertainty? To high substitutability? To low centrality? What actions can be taken to correct these deficiencies?

4. Is politics undermining satisfaction or performance in the organization? Can you eliminate antecedent conditions that promote politics?

5. Are managers controlling politics by setting an example, encouraging open communications, managing coalitions, confronting game players, and anticipating future occurrences?

6. Do antecedent conditions—interdependence, political indeterminism, divergence—favor the emergence of conflict? Is there evidence that dysfunctional conflict is brewing? Can you modify any of the antecedent conditions to resolve the conflict before it manifests itself?

7. Is there evidence of ongoing conflict? Do the dysfunctional, destructive effects of this conflict outweigh its functional benefits? Can you modify any of the antecedent conditions to resolve the conflict?

8. If interdependence or political indeterminism can be modified, which of the approaches to managing interdependence seems most suitable?

9. If divergence can be modified, which style of bargaining and negotiation best fits the conflict situation?

EXERCISE 11-1

Building Customer Lists: Cooperate or Compete?

John Wagner, Michigan State University

Working in organizations means depending on others and having them depend on you. This interdependence can often stimulate conflict because individuals and groups have different needs and viewpoints. Although conflict is normal, it sometimes has harmful effects. Managers must therefore be able to guide and resolve conflict, when necessary. The purpose of this exercise is to give you a chance to observe and experience the feelings generated by conflict and competition and to examine strategies for developing cooperation among individuals and groups before conflict occurs.

Step One: Pre-Class Preparation

To prepare for this exercise, familiarize yourself with the set of rules described next, then read the rest of the exercise.

Customer List Exercise Rules   The Customer List Exercise involves two groups that must make a series of decisions about whether to cooperate or compete with one another. For each set of two groups, one individual should be selected from another group in the class to assist the instructor and act as a referee. Both groups are small catalog sales forces that are collecting lists of customers to add to their mailing lists, with the ultimate goal of broadening the distribution of their catalogs and increasing resulting sales. The two groups sell the same products: baseball cards and sports memorabilia. Past experience indicates that a household that places an order with one group is unlikely to order from the other.

Decisions and Outcomes   Your group already has a list of 1,000 names, but needs a total of 5,000 names to ensure that it can sell enough to remain in business. The other group is in exactly the same position: it has 1,000 names but needs 5,000. The objective of both groups is to remain in business by acquiring the necessary 5,000 names.

Customer lists come in lists of 1,000 names, and circumstances require that lists be purchased one at a time. To acquire the necessary number of names, your group must take part in a series of purchase transactions. For each transaction, your group does not have the money on hand to buy a list by itself; the same is true for the other group. If the two groups decide to *cooperate* and pool their money, however, they can buy a list and divide it in half so that each group receives 500 names.

Alternatively, one or both groups can decide to *compete* by refusing to cooperate. If one group chooses to cooperate and give its money to the other group, but the other group decides to compete and keep its money for itself, the competing group can buy a list and keep all 1,000 names, while the cooperating group does not receive any names for its use. If both groups decide to compete, neither can buy the list and both must do without additional names. In fact, each group loses 200 names to other competitors that have taken advantage of the fact that both groups have spent time and effort deciding what to do.

In summary, for your group to reach its objective of 5,000 names, you must engage in a series of transactions in which you decide to cooperate or compete with the other group to acquire lists of 1,000 names. For each purchase transaction, the results of different decisions are as follows:

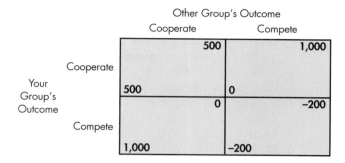

Member Roles At the start of Step Two, each group will have five minutes to review the instructions for the exercise and plan a group strategy. You must also select people to fill three specialized roles. No person can fill more than one role at the same time, and the roles can be reassigned at any time by a majority vote of the group (each role holder will also participate with everyone else in the group in making group decisions).The roles are as follows:

- *A group representative.* The representative will inform the referee of group decisions about whether to cooperate or compete, and whether to call for negotiations with the other group. All such communications must take place in writing. The referee will not acknowledge messages in any other form nor will he or she accept messages from any other group member.
- *A spokesperson.* The spokesperson records group decisions and outcomes on a piece of paper. The record must include the decision made by the group (cooperate or compete) during each transaction, the number of names gained or lost by the team during the transaction, and the total number of names owned by the team at the end of each transaction. The spokesperson should also note who initiates decision making and how the group makes its decisions.
- *A negotiator.* One group member will serve as a negotiator. This role is explained below.

Exercise Procedure The exercise will consist of a number of sets of transactions, completed according to the following instructions:

1. Sets of transactions
   a. As many sets as possible will be completed in the time available. A set consists of a series of transactions. It ends when either group has collected lists totaling 5,000 names or when either group has forfeited its entire list and has no names left.
   b. Each group has two minutes to decide whether to cooperate or to compete. If a group fails to reach a decision in the allotted time, it is assumed to have made the same decision as the one indicated during the previous transaction (if it is early in the set and a team has not reached a prior decision, a decision of "compete" will be assumed). In addition, during each transaction the group must decide whether to initiate negotiations with the other group (see next section). You must communicate your decision to the referee in writing during the two-minute period.

2. Negotiations
   a. Between transactions your group will have the opportunity to communicate with the other group through negotiations.

b. You may call for negotiations when making your decision about whether to cooperate or compete. You must request negotiations in writing, as part of your written decision about whether to cooperate or to compete. No other means of requesting negotiations is allowed. After you have submitted your request to the referee, the referee will notify the other group. That group may then accept or reject your request. Negotiations can last no longer than two minutes, and must take place between transactions.

c. Following negotiations, the next two-minute transaction period will start immediately after the negotiators have rejoined their groups.

d. Negotiators may say whatever is necessary to most benefit their group. In addition, a group is not necessarily bound by agreements made by its negotiator.

e. Negotiators *must* meet after the second transaction.

Notes to Referee   While managing the exercise, keep the following tips in mind:

1. Keep the pairs of groups separated, so that neither group can hear the other's conversations.

2. Be strict about timing the length of transaction periods and negotiations. Allow no exceptions.

3. You must not assist either team.

Step Two: Exercise Sets

The class should divide into groups of four to six members each (if you have already formed permanent groups, reassemble in those groups). Your instructor will pair up groups and select extra members to serve as referees. Each pair of groups should then be assigned a referee and should immediately begin the exercise.

Step Three: Class Discussion

Your instructor will notify all groups when the exercise is over. Each group should make sure that its record of results (kept by the spokesperson) is complete and should calculate its final outcome. Next, the class should reconvene. Each spokesperson should then report briefly on group activities. Finally, the class should discuss the following questions:

1. How did each group interpret the goal of this exercise? Did the groups become aware of the need to collaborate with each other and the advantages of doing so? What part did trust between groups play in this exercise?

2. If you were to go through the exercise again, would you do anything differently?

3. If one of the groups in an analogous real-world situation were the manufacturing department and the other were the marketing department of an industrial company, what recommendations would you make to the two departments based on the results of this exercise?

Conclusion

As you have learned in this exercise, looking after the interests of your own group and ignoring or even subverting the interests of another group can stimulate disagreements. These disagreements, when coupled with mistrust and opportunism, can lead to intergroup conflict. Such conflict occurs when interdependent groups lack other means of resolving differences among themselves. For this reason, groups that must work together should develop trust and the ability to handle differences in constructive ways.

CHAPTER 12

Structural Coordination
Basic Coordination Mechanisms
Choosing among the Mechanisms

Departmentation
Hierarchy and Centralization

Types of Organization Structure
Prebureaucratic Structures
Bureaucratic Structures
Postbureaucratic Structures

Summary
Review Questions

Learning Through Experience
Diagnostic Questions 12-1: Organization Structure
Exercise 12-1: Restructuring a University

Structuring the Organization

Faced with growing competition and increasing performance expectations, organizations of the twenty-first century are restructuring themselves to improve the way they do business. At Hewlett-Packard (HP), producer of personal computers and ink-jet printers, CEO Carleton S. "Carly" Fiorina has responded to disappointing earnings by reshaping the company in a series of steps. To begin, she regrouped the company's eighty-three formerly independent units into four groups: consumer products, consumer sales, business products, and business marketing. In support of this change, Fiorina argued that simplifying company operations would aid in decision-making and make it easier for employees in the larger groups to share valuable information.

Next, Fiorina led a successful effort to acquire Compaq Computer in order to broaden HP's product line and strengthen the company's position in the personal computer (PC) market. At the time, many saw Compaq's acquisition as a test of Fiorina's political mettle, since she faced the opposition of Walter B. Hewlett, son of founder Bill Hewlett, and the Hewlett Trust, owner of more than 10 percent of HP's stock. In fact, Fiorina and Hewlett took their fight to HP's shareholders and, in the process, created something of a public spectacle. Through last-minute politicking, the $19 billion acquisition was approved by a slim margin, and Fiorina and company set about the task of integrating Compaq's products—including a new tablet PC—into existing lines of HP hardware.

Most recently, Fiorina has expanded company operations in high-tech services, pitting HP against IBM and Electronic Data Systems (EDS) in a highly competitive industry segment. Customers including Procter & Gamble, Ericsson, and the Bank of Ireland have signed service agreements with HP totaling nearly $4.6 billion, on top of the $12.4 billion in contracts already in effect. Ann M. Livermore, executive *vice president of HP services, presides over a staff of 65,000, acquired in part from Compaq. Company insiders see growth in the services area as critical to company survival.*

Fiorina now manages a company much larger than the one she directed at the beginning of her tenure as CEO. Decisions once made in a labyrinth of decentralized committees are now the purview of top management. Product lines have grown in size even as the number of company divisions has decreased. All the while, through aggressive organizational restructuring, Fiorina and her management team have sought to increase profitability and strengthen HP's position in an increasingly competitive industry.[1]

Whether it is as well known as Hewlett-Packard or as anonymous as a locally owned convenience store, every organization is composed of a system of interrelated jobs. This **organization structure** comprises a relatively stable network of interconnections or interdependencies among the different people and tasks that make up an organization.[2] Like the steel framework of a building or the skeletal system of the human body, an organization's structure differentiates among its parts even as it helps to keep those parts interconnected. In so doing, it creates and reinforces relationships of interdependence among the people and groups within it. Balancing this structural *integration* and *differentiation* is an important challenge facing current-day managers. The ability to create a workable balance between the two can determine whether a company succeeds in organizing work activities in a way that allows something meaningful to be accomplished.[3]

An organization's structure enables the people within it to work together, thereby accomplishing things beyond the abilities of unorganized individuals. To help their employees achieve this feat in the most effective manner, managers must know how to structure their organization in a way that will enhance employee performance, control the costs of doing business, and keep the organization abreast of changes in the surrounding environment. They must therefore understand the basic design and specific features of the various types of structures they might choose to implement in their company, and they must be aware of the likely advantages and disadvantages of each structural type.

To cultivate this understanding and awareness, this chapter introduces the basic elements of an organization's structure—how coordination is established among interdependent people and jobs, how teams and groups are formed through departmentation and joined together in a hierarchy, and how information and decision-making are distributed within this hierarchy so as to stimulate continued coordination and maintain effective interdependence. Using these basic elements, the chapter then describes the possible types of structure that an organization might adopt, and it examines some of the strengths and weaknesses of each structural type. After studying this chapter, you should be able to recognize a wide range of structural features and organization structures, and you should understand the most important advantages and disadvantages of each of the different types.

STRUCTURAL COORDINATION

Achieving structural integration is an important challenge facing all managers, requiring them to make decisions about how to coordinate relationships among the interdependent people and groups they manage. *Coordination* is a process through which otherwise disorganized actions become integrated so as to produce a desired result. For example, if appropriately coordinated, different parts of the human body work together to produce complex behaviors. The arms follow a trajectory plotted by the eyes so as to catch a ball. The hands manipulate a car's steering wheel at the same time that the foot depresses the accelerator pedal. It would be very difficult— if not impossible—to catch a ball without first seeing it and judging its path. It would be dangerous to accelerate or even move the car without being able to coordinate the control of its direction.

In a similar manner, through coordination the members of an organization are able to work together to accomplish outcomes that would otherwise be beyond the abilities of any one person working alone. The primary means by which organizational activities are integrated—the **basic coordination mechanisms** of mutual adjustment, direct supervision, and standardization—enable the organization to perform complex activities by bringing together the efforts of many individuals.[4]

Basic Coordination Mechanisms

Mutual adjustment is coordination accomplished through person-to-person communication processes in which co-workers share job-related information.[5] The simplest of the three basic coordination mechanisms, it consists of the exchange among co-workers of knowledge about how a job should be done and who should do it. A group of factory maintenance mechanics examining service manuals and discussing how to fix a broken conveyor belt is coordinating job efforts by means of mutual adjustment. Similarly, sales managers meeting together to discuss their company's market position are using mutual adjustment to coordinate among themselves. In both of these examples, information is exchanged among people who can exercise at least partial control over the tasks they are discussing. Unless the co-workers doing the communicating possess this control, they cannot successfully coordinate their activities with mutual adjustment.

Until fairly recently, virtually all of the mutual adjustment in an organization occurred via face-to-face communication among neighboring co-workers. This situation has changed, however, with the advent of local area networks (LANs) and *intranets,* or Internet-like communication networks within organizations. Within company intranets, employees can use *electronic conferencing* and *chat rooms* to coordinate work activities even though they might be separated by great distance. Both are real-time procedures that require participation at the same point in time but not necessarily in the same physical location. Thus, instead of having to limit mutual adjustment to their colleagues in close physical proximity, intranet-connected co-workers can work together to determine what must be done and decide how to do it without succumbing to the deleterious effects of significant geographic separation.

In addition, time need not stand in the way of coordinating via mutual adjustment. Intranet mechanisms such as *e-mail* and *electronic bulletin boards* (EBBs) are asynchronous communication devices, meaning that people need not be in the same place or work at the same time to "talk" with one another. Thus, e-mail or bulletin board postings can accomplish the same coordination among employees who work at different times or on different shifts that otherwise would require coordination by other means.

With intranet-mediated mutual adjustment, employees who need to communicate with one another to coordinate work activities can send and receive e-mail messages without physically meeting. Workers who need information about a particular product, customer, or technology to determine how to perform their tasks can

SECURING COMPETITIVE ADVANTAGE

INCREASED FLEXIBILITY THROUGH ELECTRONIC MUTUAL ADJUSTMENT

Mutual adjustment among proximate co-workers enhances flexibility by allowing them to modify how they interact at the point in time where such modification is necessary, without the added complication of hierarchical communications or standardized procedures. Mutual adjustment among workers separated by time and space, made possible by recently developed information technologies, allows even greater flexibility since physical proximity is no longer necessary.

At FedEx, for example, overnight packages sent across the North American continent will be scanned an average of twelve times between pickup and delivery. Couriers carry handheld PowerPads—developed by FedEx, Motorola, and AT&T—that provide real-time, online information about shipping rates, custom clearance, and so on, and that communicate with a printer on the courier's waistbelt to prepare bar-coded shipping labels. Tracking information is transmitted by the PowerPad on pickup, before the courier even gets back to the truck. In this manner, the company is able to track—instantly—the positions of all couriers and packages and coordinate operations as needed to ensure overnight delivery.

Similarly, at Lockheed Martin managers face the challenge of coordinating more than eighty suppliers working at 187 locations to build components of the Joint Strike Fighter, the United States' next-generation supersonic stealth fighter plane. Lockheed and partners are using a system of ninety web software tools to share designs, track the exchange of documents, and measure progress against performance targets. The company's net-collaboration technologies enable people separated by oceans to coordinate among themselves as though all were at the same location.

As indicated in both examples, time that might otherwise be used tracking down orders or looking for people can be used instead for productive purposes. At the same time, coordination can occur on an "as needed" basis and is tailored to the specific problem at hand. Companies that might otherwise find it difficult to integrate the activities of various parts and partners are able to combine efforts and work toward common goals. In this way, mutual adjustment by electronic means can offer an important source of competitive advantage.

Sources: E. Yellin, "Squeezing Out Seconds," *Newsweek,* April 28, 2003, p. 48; F. Keenan and S. E. Ante, "The New Teamwork," *Business Week,* February 8, 2002, pp. EB12–EB16.

consult EBBs on the company intranet. In electronic conference rooms, employees can communicate with one another about job problems and fixes without ever meeting face to face. Interdependence that might otherwise prove difficult or impossible to coordinate can be organized effectively and maintained with relatively little effort.[6] Companies can gain significant competitive advantage through these means, as indicated in the Securing Competitive Advantage box.

Direct supervision, a second type of coordination mechanism, occurs when one person takes responsibility for the work of a group of others.[7] As part of this responsibility, a direct supervisor acquires the authority to decide which tasks must be performed, who will perform them, and how they will be linked to produce the desired result. A direct supervisor may then issue orders to subordinates, verify that these orders have been followed, and redirect subordinates as needed to fulfill additional work requirements. The owner of a grocery store is functioning as a direct supervisor when, having instructed an employee to restock the shelves, she finds that the clerk has completed the job and directs him next to change the signs advertising the week's specials. In this example, as in every instance of direct supervision, an individual with the authority to issue direct orders is able to coordinate activities by telling subordinates what to do.

Standardization, a third type of coordination mechanism, is itself a collection of four different mechanisms that coordinate work by providing employees with standards and procedures that help them determine how to perform their tasks, thereby alleviating their need to communicate with one another or consult their supervisor to find out what to do. Coordination via standardization requires that standards be set and procedures designed—in the process of *formalization,* or the development of formal, written specifications—before the work is actually undertaken.[8] So long as formalized, "drawing-board" plans are followed and the work situation remains essentially unchanged, interdependent relationships can be reproduced repeatedly, and coordination can be maintained.

One form of standardization, *behavioral standardization,* involves specification of the precise behaviors or work processes in which employees must engage to accomplish their jobs. Some of these behaviors link each job with other jobs in the organization, such as the requirement that the holder of an assembly line job place finished work on a conveyor that transports it to other employees for packing and shipping. In this way, the need for other types of coordination among jobs is reduced. Behavioral standardization originates in the process of *formalization by job,* also called *job analysis,* in which the sequence of steps required to perform each job is identified and documented in writing. The written documentation is referred to as a *job description.* At the corporate offices of Burger King, for example, job analysts develop procedures manuals containing job descriptions that specify how long company employees should cook each type of food served, what condiments should be used to flavor the food, and how workers should package the food for the customer.

Output standardization, a second type of standardization, involves the formal designation of output targets or performance goals. So long as everyone coordinated by output standardization accomplishes his or her goals, the work that is handed off from one employee to the next remains consistent and no one needs to engage in further coordination. The process of establishing written targets and goals is sometimes called *formalization by work flow,* because it produces standards that coordinate interdependence by directing and stabilizing the flow of work in a firm—as exemplified by the set of standards for display-screen brightness, keyboard responsiveness, and exterior appearance prepared for workers who assemble notebook computers.

Unlike employees working under behavioral standardization, people coordinated by output standardization are free to decide for themselves *how* to attain their goals. For instance, posted monthly sales goals indicate levels of performance that insurance sales representatives are expected to achieve, but do not specify particular behaviors required to achieve them.

Consequently, output standardization allows a degree of autonomy not permitted by behavioral standardization. As indicated in Chapters 5 through 7, this difference is important because autonomy can have favorable effects on employee motivation, satisfaction, and success at work.

A third type of standardization, *skill standardization,* relies on the specification of skills, knowledge, and abilities needed to perform tasks competently. Skilled employees seldom need to communicate with one another to figure out what to do, and they can usually predict with reasonable accuracy what other similarly skilled employees will do. Consequently, on jobs staffed by such employees, there may be much less need to coordinate in other ways among people and jobs.

Skill standardization can be implemented in either of two ways: by hiring professionals from outside the organization, or by training employees already working within the firm. As part of their education, *professionals* learn a generalized code of conduct that shapes their behavior on the job, enriching or in some cases replacing the local rules and regulations of the employing firm. As a result, professionals can be brought into a firm to perform work for which useful written specifications do not exist or cannot be prepared.[9] In contrast, in *training* the knowledge and skills needed to perform the work of an organization are acquired within the organization itself. Such training, as provided by the employing organization, is purposely organization-specific and often job-specific.

Because skill standardization is aimed at regulating characteristics of people rather than jobs, it is used most often in situations where neither behaviors nor output standards can be easily specified. Few experts agree, for example, on the precise behaviors in which high school teachers should engage while teaching. In addition, general consensus exists that the output indicators for the job of teaching, such as course grades and standardized test scores, have questionable validity as measures of teaching success: grades can be artificially inflated and test scores can be influenced by pretest coaching. For this reason, instead of specifying expected behaviors or outputs, school districts often mandate that their teachers be certified by a state agency. Achieving such certification typically requires that teachers not only hold certain educational degrees, but also provide evidence of having acquired specific knowledge and skills. As a result, all teachers hired by a school district that requires state certification should possess a more or less standardized set of job qualifications or skills and be similarly able to perform their jobs.

Finally, *norm standardization* is present when the members of a group or organization share a set of beliefs about the acceptability of particular types of behavior, leading them to behave in ways that are generally approved. At DaimlerChrysler, for example, corporate norms promote the importance of producing high-quality automobiles, as embodied in Daimler's Mercedes-Benz vehicles. Workers on Chrysler's U.S. lines who adopt these norms as their own do not need to be directed by a supervisor to produce high-quality products. Instead, the norms of the larger company influence them to behave in ways that enhance product quality. Accepting shared norms and behaving accordingly reduce the need to coordinate activities in other ways, because they increase the likelihood that people will behave appropriately and consistently over time.

As described in Chapter 8, organizations use *socialization* to teach important behavioral norms to employees, particularly newcomers. To the extent that these norms regulate activities required to coordinate the flow of work, coordination by norm standardization can be enacted without formalized written rules and procedures. This approach lies at the heart of the system of coordination used in many companies in Japan and South Korea. Asian companies use practices such as reciting company mottos before beginning work each day or singing company songs during social outings after work to constantly remind employees of the firms' norms and to ensure compliance with these norms. In less obvious forms, norm standardization is cropping up with increasing frequency in North American organizations. For instance, at Hewlett-Packard employees learn the history of their company. Along the way, they hear stories about the company's founders and early management that illustrate which behaviors are presently considered appropriate at Hewlett-Packard and which are not. In addition to being entertaining, these stories promote important company norms.

Choosing among the Mechanisms

Managers charged with managing an organization's structure continually confront the need to make choices among the basic coordination mechanisms summarized in Table 12-1. Most of the time, two or more of these mechanisms are used concurrently to integrate work activities in and among the groups in an organization. In

TABLE 12-1
Basic
Coordination
Mechanisms

Mechanism	Definition
Mutual adjustment	Face-to-face communication in which co-workers exchange information about work procedures
Direct supervision	Direction and coordination of the work of a group by one person who issues direct orders to the group's members
Standardization	Planning and implementation of standards and procedures that regulate work performance
Behavior standardization	Specification of sequences of task behaviors or work processes
Output standardization	Establishment of goals or desired end results of task performance
Skill standardization	Specification of the abilities, knowledge, and skills required by a particular task
Norm standardization	Encouragement of attitudes and beliefs that lead to desired behaviors

such instances, one serves as the primary mechanism used to solve most coordination problems. The others, if present, serve as secondary mechanisms that supplement the primary mechanism, backing it up in case it fails to provide enough integration.

Managers must decide which mechanism will serve as the primary means of coordination and which (if any) will act as secondary mechanisms. In general, two factors influence such choices: the number of people whose efforts must be coordinated to ensure the successful performance of interdependent tasks, and the relative stability of the situation in which the tasks must be performed.[10] In small groups, containing twelve or fewer people, coordination is often accomplished by everyone doing what comes naturally. Employees communicate face to face, using mutual adjustment to fit their individual task behaviors into the group's overall network of interdependence. No other coordination mechanism is needed, and none is used. Family farms and neighborhood restaurants are often organized around this type of coordination.

Suppose, however, that a group includes more than twelve people—as many as twenty, thirty, or even forty—who use mutual adjustment alone to coordinate their activities. As depicted in Figure 12-1, the number of needed communication links rises geometrically as the number of individuals rises arithmetically; that is, although two people need only one link, three people need three links, six people need fifteen links, and so on. Clearly, the members of larger groups must spend so much time communicating with one another that very little time is left for task completion. This sort of *process loss* (discussed in Chapter 9) diminishes group productivity in such instances.

For this reason, direct supervision is typically employed instead of mutual adjustment in larger groups as the primary means of coordinating group activities. In communicating information to subordinates, the direct supervisor acts as a proxy for the group as a whole. To use an analogy, the direct supervisor functions like a switching mechanism that routes telephone messages from callers to receivers. The supervisor originates direct orders and collects performance feedback, while channeling information from one interdependent group member to another.

In such situations, mutual adjustment serves as a supplementary coordination mechanism: When the direct supervisor is unavailable or does not know how to solve a particular problem, employees communicate among themselves to try to figure out what to do and how to do it. Besides clarifying how direct supervision functions as

FIGURE 12-1   Group Size and Mutual Adjustment Links

Number of People	Number of Links	Group Configuration
2	1	
3	3	
4	6	
5	10	
6	15	

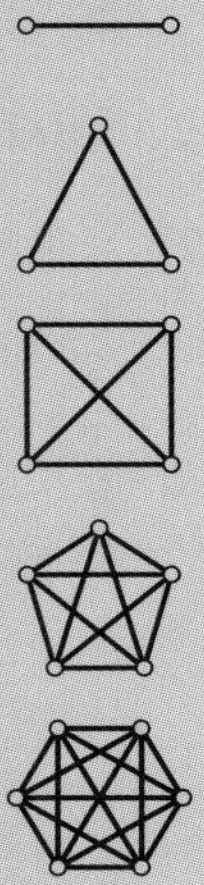

a basic coordination mechanism, the telephone-switching analogy helps to explain the failure of direct supervision to coordinate the activities of members in even larger groups (for example, groups containing fifty or more individuals). Just as a switching mechanism can become overloaded by an avalanche of telephone calls, in successively larger groups the direct supervisor becomes increasingly burdened by the need to obtain information and channel it to the appropriate people. Ultimately, he or she will succumb to information overload, failing to keep up with subordinates' demands for information and coordination.

At this point, standardization is likely to replace supervision as the primary means of coordination. Coordination by standardization can prevent information overload by greatly reducing or eliminating the amount of communication needed for effective coordination. In this type of system, workers perform specified task behaviors, produce specified task outputs, use specified task skills, or conform to specified workplace norms. Thanks to the guidance provided by such standardization, members of very large groups can complete complex, interdependent networks of task activities with little or no need for further coordination.

Where standardization serves as the primary means of coordination, direct supervision and mutual adjustment remain available for use as secondary coordination mechanisms. On an assembly line, for instance, direct supervision may be used to ensure that workers adhere to formal behavioral standards. Mutual adjustment may also be employed on the assembly line to cope with machine breakdowns, power outages, or other temporary situations in which standard operating procedures are ineffective and direct supervision proves insufficient.

Standardization requires stability. If the conditions envisioned during the planning of a particular standardization program change, the program's utility may be lost. For example, behavioral specifications that detail computerized check-in procedures are likely to offer few benefits to hotel-registration personnel who face a long line of guests and a dead computer screen. Mutual adjustment often reemerges in such instances, assuming the role of the primary basic coordination device. The

FIGURE 12-2   Continuum of Coordination Mechanisms

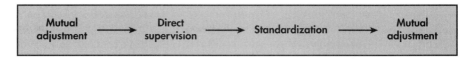

process loss associated with mutual adjustment in these situations is simply toler-ated as a necessary cost of staying in business.

The three means of coordination form a continuum, as depicted in Figure 12-2.[11] As coordination needs progress from left to right along the continuum, mechanisms to the left are not completely abandoned. All the way to the right end of the con-tinuum, standardization, direct supervision, and secondary mutual adjustment remain available to supplement the mutual adjustment that serves as the primary means of coordination.

A critical trade-off exists between the *costs* of using a particular mechanism and the *flexibility* it permits. Mutual adjustment, especially through face-to-face com-munication, requires neither extensive planning nor the hierarchical differentiation of an organization's membership into supervisors and subordinates. Therefore, it affords a high degree of flexibility. Although each new use of mutual adjustment gen-erates new coordination costs that tend to be modest initially, over time these costs can add up and become quite significant. They may take the form of time, effort, and similar resources that are consumed by communication activities and thus must be diverted away from task-related endeavors.

In contrast, the initial costs of standardization are quite high. The process of developing standards and procedures often requires the services of highly paid spe-cialists, and otherwise-productive resources must be diverted toward the design and implementation of standardization programs. Yet, once designed and implemented, such programs no longer consume resources of major significance. The large initial costs of standardization can therefore be amortized—spread over long periods of time and across long production runs. The result is an extremely low cost per inci-dence of coordination, which is less expensive than mutual adjustment over the long run. As mentioned earlier, however, standardization requires that the work situation remain essentially unchanged, because dynamic conditions would render existing standards obsolete. Thus it lacks the flexibility of mutual adjustment.

The flexibility of direct supervision lies between the extremes associated with mutual adjustment and standardization. Because direct supervision presupposes a hierarchy of authority, it lacks the spontaneity and fluidity of mutual adjustment. Yet, because it requires much less planning than standardization, direct supervision is more flexible. Not surprisingly, its coordination costs also fall between those of mutual adjustment and standardization. Although direct supervision requires fewer costly communication links than mutual adjustment, new coordination costs are generated for every supervisory action taken.

DEPARTMENTATION

In addition to deciding how to coordinate interdependent activities, managers shap-ing an organization's structure must determine how to cluster the groups or teams produced via group formation. As indicated in Chapter 9, managers can form groups of co-workers on the basis of *functional* similarities, resulting in efficient but relatively inflexible groups of functional specialists. Alternatively, they can create groups based on *work flow* similarities, producing flexible but relatively inefficient teams that blur functional distinctions. Managers apply much the same logic to the job of linking the resulting groups together into a larger organization. The result consists of two types of **departmentation.**[12]

To illustrate these two alternatives, think of an organization that consists of four functional areas—marketing, research, manufacturing, and accounting—and three product lines—automobiles, trucks, and small gasoline engines. Figure 12-3 depicts this firm. In the figure, each box represents one of the four functions. Each of the horizontal work flows, represented by a series of arrows, stands for one of the three product lines. Dashed lines illustrate the alternative forms of departmentation.

The upper diagram in Figure 12-3 shows one type of departmentation, called *functional departmentation.* It is the equivalent of functional grouping, but rather than forming groups of individuals, the focus here is on forming groups that are themselves composed of groups.

Thus all marketing groups are combined into a single marketing department, all research groups are combined into a single research department, and so forth. As with functional grouping, the *departments* that result from functional departmentation are economically efficient. In each department, members can trade information about their functional specialty and improve their skills. Managers can also reduce overstaffing or duplication of effort by reassigning redundant employees elsewhere in the firm. Changes to any of the product lines crossing a particular department, however, require reorganization of the entire department. In other words, departments lack the flexibility to deal easily with change.

In contrast, the second type of departmentation shown in the lower diagram of Figure 12-3, called *divisional departmentation,* is equivalent to using work flow grouping to cluster groups together into larger units. Instead of being grouped into

FIGURE 12-3 Types of Departmentation

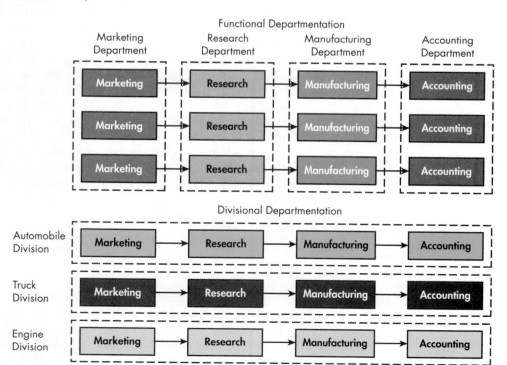

marketing, manufacturing, research, and accounting departments, the organization's activities are grouped into product divisions—an automobile division, a truck division, and a gasoline engine division. Alternatively, when an organization's clients differ more dramatically than its products, the organization's work may be grouped based on differences in the clients served. For instance, the company might include a military contracts division, a wholesale distribution division, and an aftermarket parts division. Following a third approach, an organization with operations spread throughout the world may be grouped geographically, into a North American division, an Asian division, and a European division.

Any of these alternatives offers the organization division-by-division flexibility. Each division can tailor its response to the unique demands of its own market. For example, Ford's Lincoln-Mercury division might decide to redesign its luxury market automobiles to be more conservative without worrying about the effects of this move on other Ford products and markets. Some of the economic efficiency of functional departmentation is sacrificed, however, because effort is duplicated across the organization's three product lines. Lincoln-Mercury's product design studios duplicate those of Ford, but the two divisions' studios cannot be consolidated without losing divisional flexibility. As with group formation, managers making divisional departmentation decisions face a trade-off between economy and flexibility.

By clustering related groups, departmentation of either type accentuates similarities that facilitate the management of intergroup relations. Specifically, in an organization structured around functional departmentation, groups in the same department share the same specialized knowledge, language, and ways of looking at the company's business. For instance, the members of a marketing department all share the same general marketing know-how. They discuss topics such as market segmentation and market share, and they generally agree that the best way to ensure their company's success is by appealing to customer needs. A manager charged with coordinating different groups in the marketing department can base his or her actions on this common knowledge, language, and viewpoint despite having to deal with several different groups of employees. Thus the manager can manage them using the same basic management approach.

Similarly, in an organization structured around divisional departmentation, groups in the same division share interests in the same basic line of business. Thus all employees in the truck division of a company like General Motors or Ford are concerned about doing well in the truck industry. This commonality allows the manager of a division to treat groups performing different functions—marketing, manufacturing, research, and so forth—in much the same way, without having to tailor management practices to the functional specialty of each particular group. Unfortunately, the process of clustering related groups together creates gaps or discontinuities between the resulting departments or divisions. In many instances, the kinds of conflict described in Chapter 11 may arise where these gaps occur. Unit-linking mechanisms—ranging from intranets to matrix structuring—can be deployed to manage and resolve such conflicts. In the process, departmentation is modified and the organization's structure changes.

HIERARCHY AND CENTRALIZATION

A **hierarchy** reflects the differentiation of rank that occurs as group formation processes and departmentation procedures work together to create clusters of groups and layers of managers having responsibility for the activities of particular clusters. In Figure 12-4A, each of the small squares represents an assembly line employee who works on one of the company's four lines, which are located in two separate buildings. Work groups, one per assembly line, are formed by grouping each line's workers together into a single group. In return, these groups are clustered into two larger groups, paralleling the two buildings that house assembly operations. Finally, these two "groups of groups" are themselves clustered together into a single assembly department. Figure 12-4B depicts the same pattern of clustering, but diagrams it in the familiar "organization chart" form that accentuates the presence of a hierarchy.

Once formed, a hierarchy can be used to control intergroup relations. A manager having hierarchical authority over a particular collection of groups can use this authority to issue orders that, when followed, will help coordinate activities among those groups. For instance, the manager having hierarchical authority over all manufacturing groups of the company depicted in the upper diagram in Figure 12-3 can use that authority to smooth the flow of information among groups of manufacturing employees formed through functional departmentation.

Alternatively, the manager of the automobile division shown in the lower diagram in Figure 12-3 can facilitate work flows among employees in the divisions created through divisional departmentation. In turn, interdependencies that span different departments or divisions can be coordinated by managers higher in the organization's hierarchy. For example, problems between the manufacturing department and the marketing, research, or accounting departments shown in the upper diagram can be handled by the executive responsible for overseeing the various department managers. Hierarchical authority, then, can be used to coordinate relations among groups by extending the scope of direct supervision.

The use of such a hierarchy to coordinate intergroup relations differs from one organization to the next in terms of which level of managers—top, middle, or supervisory—has the ultimate authority to make decisions and issue orders. Left to their own devices, many top managers in North America would favor **centralization,** or the concentration of authority and decision making at the top of a firm.[13] Centralization affords top managers a high degree of certainty. Because they alone make the decisions in centralized firms, they can be sure not only that decisions are made, but also that those decisions are made in accordance with their own wishes. In addition,

FIGURE 12-4 How Grouping Creates a Hierarchy

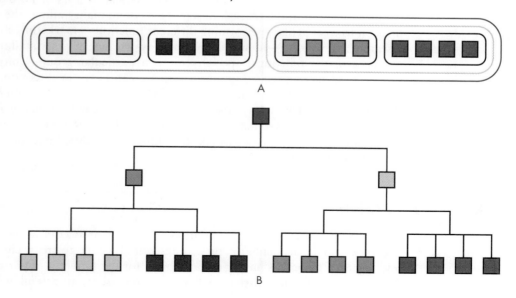

centralization can minimize the time needed to make decisions, because only an extremely limited number of people are involved in the decision-making processes.

Despite centralization's appeal to top management, **decentralization** has become increasingly common in modern organizations. In decentralized organizations, authority and decision making are dispersed downward and outward in the hierarchy of managers and employees. Several factors push otherwise reluctant top managers toward its implementation. First, some decisions require top managers to weigh a great deal of information. Managers may become overloaded by the task of processing this vast amount of information and therefore find it useful to involve more people in the decision-making process. Second, decentralization may be stimulated by a need for flexibility. If local conditions require that different parts of an organization respond differently, managers of those organizational groups must be empowered to make their own decisions. Third, decentralization may prove useful in dealing with employee motivation problems if those problems can be solved by granting employees control over workplace practices and conditions. In any of these cases, the failure to decentralize can seriously undermine attempts to coordinate intergroup relations. Fourth, decentralization and other structural modifications can strengthen a company's ethical performance, as discussed in the Ethics and Social Responsibility box.

TYPES OF ORGANIZATION STRUCTURE

The choice to emphasize standardization as a primary means of coordination leads to the creation of a bureaucratic organization structure. As noted in Chapter 2, Weber's bureaucracy is a form of organization in which rules, regulations, and standards are written down and used to govern member behaviors. In contrast, the choice to place primary emphasis on either of the other means of coordination also entails the choice to bypass bureaucracy or minimize its presence in a firm. Between complete bureaucracy and no bureaucracy lies a continuum of structures, each of which incorporates specific configurations of departmentation and centralization. These different structures are described next.

Prebureaucratic Structures

As their name suggests, **prebureaucratic structures** lack the standardization that is the defining characteristic of bureaucracies. They can be used successfully only in organizations so small in size and so simple in purpose that mutual adjustment or direct supervision provides the only coordination needed to maintain interdependence.

In one type of prebureaucratic structure, the **simple undifferentiated structure**, coordination is accomplished solely by mutual adjustment. That is, co-workers interact with one another to determine how to coordinate work among themselves. Because communicating with other people is natural for most of us, mutual adjustment is easy to initiate and relatively simple to sustain. For this reason, simple undifferentiated structures can often be established and perpetuated fairly easily.

As Figure 12-5 suggests, a simple undifferentiated structure lacks a hierarchy of authority. Such a structure is nothing more than an organization of people who decide what to do by communicating with each other as they work. No single individual has the authority to issue orders, and few, if any, written procedures guide performance. A group of friends who decide to open a small restaurant, gift shop, or similar sort of business might, at the outset, adopt this type of structure for the business.

ETHICS AND SOCIAL RESPONSIBILITY

STRUCTURING THE ETHICAL ORGANIZATION

In the wake of ethical lapses at Global Crossing, Enron, Arthur Andersen, and other companies, corporate ethics is taking on increasing importance. At Credit Suisse First Boston (CSFB), for example, CEO John J. Mack learned that regulators had uncovered e-mails showing that the company's bankers may have pressured analysts to produce positive stock recommendations for investment banking clients. To manage the situation, Mack dismantled CSFB's "star" system, in which egomaniacal traders had competed fiercely for deals, often at the expense of their clients and investors, and replaced it with close oversight by compliance officers guided by strict codes of ethics that stressed the importance of client interests. Thereafter, traders who failed to collaborate or provide clients with good advice were dismissed. Compliance, which had been the purview of a lower-level official in years prior to Mack's emergence, became the focus of a cadre of lawyers and former Securities and Exchange Commission (SEC) officials who reported directly to Mack and advised him on ethical compliance.

At Raytheon, chairman Daniel P. Burnham also faced ethical problems but opted for a different so-lution. Investigations by the SEC had uncovered evidence of financial impropriety—violations of disclosure rules and other accounting irregularities. Burnham responded by naming a lead director to the company's board. With the power to call board meetings and rally outside directors, Raytheon's lead director, former senator Warren Rudman, is a new center of power independent of management.

In both instances, company management developed structural solutions for ethical problems. By upgrading the hierarchical status of compliance officials, CSFB's Mack communicated the increasing importance of ethicality to company employees. At the same time, by decentralizing compliance activities, Mack increased the resources available to detect ethical lapses. Raytheon's Burnham used a different slant on decentralization, direct sharing of executive power, to accomplish similar aims. In both companies, power sharing allowing the involvement of a larger number of individuals strengthened programs aimed at ensuring corporate ethicality.

Sources: A. Borrus, M. McNamee, W. Symonds, N. Byrnes, and A. Park, "Reform: Business Gets Religion," *Business Week*, February 3, 2003, pp. 40–41; E. Thornton, "Can This Man Be a Wall Street Reformer?" *Business Week*, September 23, 2002, pp. 90–96.

The primary strengths of simple undifferentiated structures are their simplicity and extreme flexibility. Especially when they are organized around face-to-face communication, they can develop spontaneously and be reconfigured almost instantly. For example, just as adding another member to a small classroom discussion group is likely to cause only a momentary lapse in the group's activities, adding another worker to a family-run convenience store will have little long-term effect on coordination among the store's workers.

A major weakness of simple undifferentiated structures is their limitation to small organizations. Suppose you are a manager in an advertising firm employing twenty-five or thirty people. It would be difficult or impossible to rely on mutual adjustment alone to ensure that the firm's accounts were properly handled, because process loss would inevitably undermine the usefulness of face-to-face coordination among such a large number of individuals. So many interpersonal links would be

FIGURE 12-5 The Simple Undifferentiated Structure

| Employee 1 | Employee 2 | Employee 3 | Employee 4 |

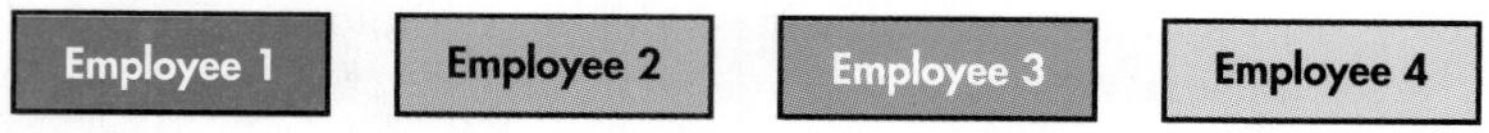

required that valuable time and effort would be lost in the struggle to maintain some degree of organization.

A related weakness is the failure of simple undifferentiated structures to provide the coordination needed to accomplish complex tasks. It is unlikely, for example, that a simple undifferentiated structure of twelve or fewer people could succeed at mass-producing automobiles. Complicated work of this sort requires a more complicated form of organization.

In the second type of prebureaucratic structure, the **simple differentiated structure,** direct supervision replaces mutual adjustment as the primary means of coordination. Organizations with simple differentiated structures are a common part of everyday life—a local grocery store or neighborhood gas station, for example. As shown in Figure 12-6, this type of structure is organized as a hierarchy with small but significant amounts of centralization.

One person (usually the firm's owner or the owner's management representative) retains the hierarchical authority needed to coordinate work activities by means of direct supervision. A secondary mechanism, mutual adjustment, is used to deal with coordination problems that direct supervision cannot resolve. For example, while the owner of a small insurance agency is at the post office retrieving the morning mail, clerks in the agency may talk among themselves to decide who will answer the telephone and who will process paperwork until the owner returns.

The simple differentiated structure can coordinate the activities of larger numbers of people than the simple differentiated structure can. By shifting to direct supervision, it eliminates some of the process loss associated with reliance on mutual adjustment alone. In addition, because its decision-making powers are centralized in the hands of a single person, an organization with a simple differentiated structure can respond rapidly to changing conditions. At the same time, this structure affords a good deal of flexibility because it avoids standardization.

The simple differentiated structure's weaknesses include its inability to coordinate the activities of more than about fifty people and its failure to provide the integration needed to accomplish complex tasks. A group of people is just as unlikely to organize itself to produce cars by using a combination of direct supervision and mutual adjustment as it is to organize itself to carry out such a task by using mutual adjustment alone. A single direct supervisor would soon be overwhelmed by the vast amount of information required to know what cars to produce, which parts to order, how to assemble them properly, and so forth.

Bureaucratic Structures

Both kinds of prebureaucratic structures are likely to be overwhelmed by the coordination requirements of complicated tasks. Some combination of standardization of behaviors, outputs, skills, or norms is required to deal with such tasks, because standardization of any type greatly reduces the amount of information that must be

FIGURE 12-6 The Simple Differentiated Structure

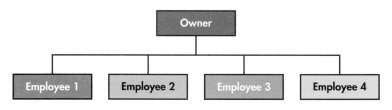

exchanged and the number of decisions that must be made as work is being performed. In the **bureaucratic structures** that arise as standardization emerges as the primary means of coordination, direct supervision and mutual adjustment are retained as secondary mechanisms that take effect when standardization fails to meet all coordination needs. This combination of coordination mechanisms allows organizations with bureaucratic structures to integrate the variety of jobs needed to perform complicated, demanding work.

The **functional structure** is a form of bureaucratic structure adopted by organizations that are larger than the fifty or so members whose activities can be coordinated via a simple differentiated structure, yet not so large that they do business in several different locations or serve widely differing groups of clientele. If your community includes locally owned banks, department stores, or manufacturing plants, chances are good that they have functional structures.

Such structures are characterized by three key attributes. First, because they are bureaucratic structures, functional structures are based on coordination by standardization. Most often they will rely on behavioral standardization, although output standardization is also used in functional structuring. Second, these structures are organized according to functional departmentation. That is, groups within them are clustered into departments that are named for the functions their members perform, such as marketing, manufacturing, or accounting. Third, functional structures are usually centralized. Most, if not all, important decisions are made by one or a few people at the tops of firms with functional structures—especially decisions related to the formation of organizational goals and objectives.

As Figure 12-7 suggests, one easy way to determine whether a particular firm has a functional structure is to examine the titles held by its vice presidents. If the firm has a bureaucratic structure and all of its vice presidents have titles that indicate what their subordinates do (for example, vice president of manufacturing, vice president of marketing, vice president of research and development), the firm has a functional structure. If one or more vice presidents have other sorts of titles (for instance, vice president of the consumer finance division or vice president of European operations), the firm has another type of structure (described later).

The primary strength of the functional structure is its economic efficiency. Standardization minimizes the long-term costs of coordination. In addition, centralization makes it possible for workers to focus their attention on their work rather than taking time out to make decisions. Functional structures, however, have a critical weakness: They lack significant flexibility. The standardization that provides so much efficiency not only takes lengthy formalization (planning and documentation) to implement, but also requires that the same standards be followed repeatedly. This inflexibility reduces the functional structure's ability to cope with instability or change. Functional departmentation adds to this rigidity, because changes to any work flow in a company organized by functional departmentation necessarily affect the other work flows in the organization.

A functional structure can coordinate the work of an organization effectively if the firm limits itself to one type of product, manufactures this product in a single geographic location, and sells to no more than a few different types of clients. Of course, many organizations produce multiple types of product, do business in several locations, or seek to serve a wide variety of clients. Such diversity of products, locations, or clients injects variety into the information that a firm needs to make managerial decisions. This variety overloads the centralized decision-making processes on which the functional structure is based. In such situations, other structures can prove more useful.

FIGURE 12-7   The Functional Structure

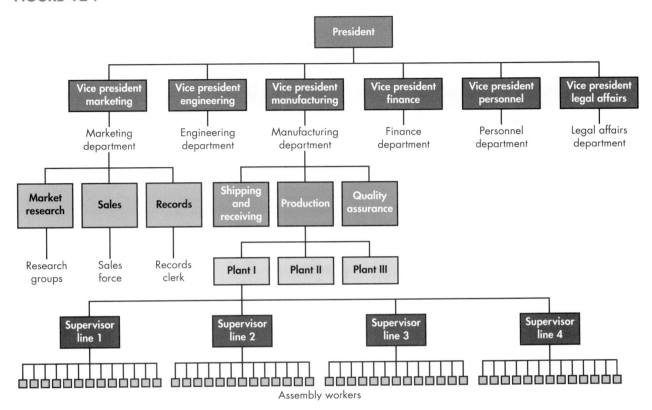

Assembly workers

The **divisional structure** is a second type of bureaucratic structure. As such, it is characterized by standardization of any of several types, most often standardization of behaviors, outputs, or skills. Unlike functional structures, however, divisional structures are moderately decentralized. Decision making is pushed downward by one or two hierarchical layers, so a company's vice presidents and sometimes their immediate subordinates share in the process of digesting information and making key decisions. Divisional departmentation is another feature that distinguishes divisional structures from functional structures. Groups in divisional structures are clustered together according to similarities in products, geographic locations, or clients. For this reason, divisional structures are sometimes called product structures, geographic structures, or market structures.

Figure 12-8 depicts three divisional structures, based on product similarities, geographic similarities, and client similarities. Each differs from the functional structure diagrammed in Figure 12-7, since in each of the structures in Figure 12-8 the vice presidential titles of *line* divisions include product, geographic, or client names. Note, however, that vice presidents of *staff* divisions in these divisional structures have titles that sound like functions—for example, vice president of legal affairs or vice president of corporate finance.

The divisional structure's departmentation scheme and moderate decentralization imbue it with a degree of flexibility not found in the functional structure.[14] Each division can react to issues concerning its own product, geographic region, or client group without disturbing the operation of other divisions. It remains securely connected to the rest of the organization, however, and is not allowed to drift away

FIGURE 12-8   Divisional Structures

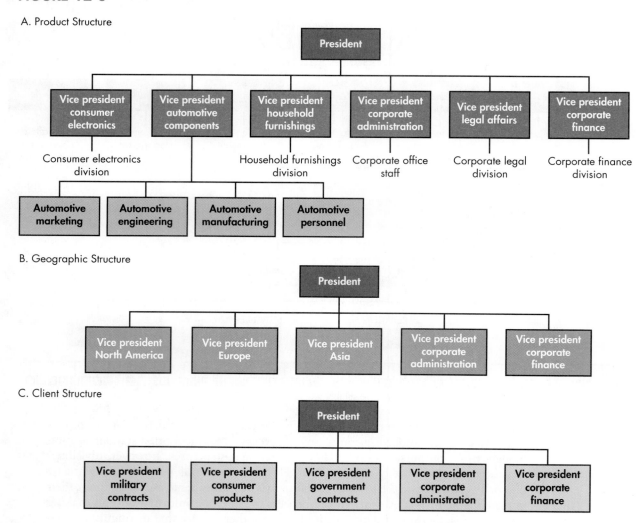

A. Product Structure

B. Geographic Structure

C. Client Structure

from the overall organization's goals and objectives. For example, the vice president of consumer electronics, shown in the upper panel of Figure 12-8, can make decisions affecting the production and sales of clock radios and steam irons without consulting with the company's president or other vice presidents, but he or she cannot decide to redirect the division into another line of products.

The limited degree of independence afforded the divisions in a divisional structure allows one to stop doing business without seriously interrupting the operations of the others. For example, the division of Boeing that fulfills military contracts could discontinue doing business without affecting work in the firm's civilian aircraft division. Remember, however, that each division in such a structure is itself organized like a functional structure, as indicated in Figure 12-8. As a result, a particular division cannot change products, locations, or clients without incurring serious interruptions in its own internal operations. Thus a decision at Boeing to service NASA contracts in its military division would require substantial reorganization of that division.

The flexibility that is the main strength of divisional structures comes at the price of increased costs arising from duplication of effort across divisions. For example, every division is likely to have a separate sales force, even though that structure means that salespeople from several different divisions may visit the same customer. The primary weakness of divisional structures is the fact that they are, at best, only moderately efficient.

Matrix structures, like divisional structures, are bureaucratic structures adopted by organizations that must integrate work activities related to a variety of products, locations, or customers. However, firms that have implemented matrix structures, such as Monsanto, Prudential Insurance, and Chase Manhattan Bank, need even more flexibility than is possible with divisional structures.[15] They try to achieve this flexibility by reintegrating functional specialists across different product, location, or customer lines. Because matrix structures use functional and divisional depart-mentation simultaneously to cluster together structural groups, they are also called *simultaneous structures.*

Figure 12-9 illustrates the matrix structure of a firm that has three divisions, each of which manufactures and sells a distinct product line. Each box or unit in the matrix represents a distinct group composed of a small hierarchy of supervisors and one or more structural groups having both functional and divisional responsibilities. For example, Unit 1 is a consumer electronics marketing group, composed of units that market televisions, radios, cellular telephones, and other electronic merchandise. Unit 2 is an automotive components engineering group, consisting of engineering units that design automobile engines, suspensions, steering assemblies, and other such items. Unit 3 is a household products manufacturing group, made up of facilities that produce furniture polishes, floor waxes, window cleaners, and other household supplies. Note that staff groups in a matrix structure are often excluded from the matrix itself. The three staff departments shown in the diagram—personnel, finance, and legal affairs—provide advice to top management but are not parts of the matrix.

Mutual adjustment is the primary means of coordination within the upper layers of a matrix structure, and decision making is decentralized among matrix managers.

FIGURE 12-9   The Matrix Structure

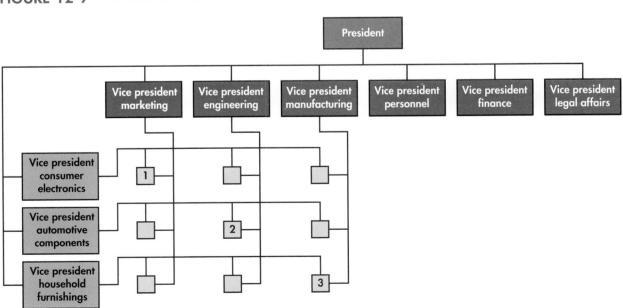

Both of these characteristics enable top managers to reconfigure relationships among the cells in the matrix, promoting extreme flexibility. Because of their dual responsibilities, each matrix cell has two bosses: a functional boss and a divisional boss. This arrangement violates Fayol's principle of unity of command (Chapter 2). Thus mutual adjustment must also be used in the upper layer of each cell to cope with conflicting orders from above.

Beneath the upper layer of each cell, standardization is used to integrate work activities. Both direct supervision and lower-level mutual adjustment serve as supplementary mechanisms that coordinate cell-level activities. For instance, once managers at the top of the matrix structure shown in Figure 12-9 have decided to manufacture a new kind of floor wax, formalization is used to develop new standards. Standardization is then used to coordinate activities in the units in the household products manufacturing cell that carry out the production of this new product. Direct supervisors help employees learn the new standards and work to correct deficiencies in the standards as they become apparent. In addition, employees engage in mutual adjustment to cope with problems that their supervisor cannot resolve.

As is apparent, a matrix structure basically consists of a simple differentiated structure designed into the upper layers of a bureaucracy—including the president and vice presidents, plus the individuals who manage each of the cells shown in Figure 12-9.This simple structure injects mutual adjustment into an otherwise bureaucratic organization so as to encourage communication, coordination, and flexibility among the managers who oversee organizational operations.

The primary strength of matrix structures derives from their extreme flexibility. They can adjust to changes that would overwhelm other bureaucratic structures. Nonetheless, matrix structures are relatively rare, because they are extremely costly to operate. In part, this costliness stems from the proliferation of managers in matrix firms, as a matrix requires two complete sets of vice presidents. Matrix structures also incorporate the same sort of duplication of effort—multiple sales forces, for instance—that make divisional structures so expensive to operate. Moreover, because employees near the top must deal with two bosses and often conflicting orders, working in a matrix can be extremely stressful. This stress can lead to absenteeism, turnover, and ultimately lower productivity and higher human resource costs.[16]

More important, matrix structures are economically inefficient because they rely on mutual adjustment as their primary coordination mechanism, despite extremely costly levels of process loss. Matrix structuring therefore represents the decision to tolerate costly coordination so as to secure high flexibility. Firms that choose matrix structures and function effectively thereafter are generally those that face radical change that would destroy them if they could not easily adapt to their dynamic environment. In effect, they choose the lesser of two evils—the inefficiency of a matrix rather than dissolution. Firms that attempt matrix organization but later abandon it tend not to face the degree of change required to justify the costs of the matrix approach.

A fourth form of bureaucratic structure, the **multiunit structure**, achieves high flexibility in extremely large organizations by decoupling the divisions of an organization rather than by further integrating divisional elements along functional lines, as in a matrix structure. A multiunit structure emerges when the divisions of a divisional structure are permitted to separate themselves from the rest of the organization and develop into autonomous, self-managed business units.[17] Each business unit is allowed to fend for itself, with little or no interference from the *holding unit* that oversees the complete firm. Companies including General Electric, Ford, Xerox, and Alco Standard have variations of this form of structure.[18]

Figure 12-10 shows a multiunit structure. All multiunit structures are organized around divisional departmentation, but each "division" is actually a self-sufficient business concern. Compared with other kinds of bureaucratic structures, multiunit structures are extremely decentralized. Unit managers several levels below the holding unit's CEO have the authority to define their unit's purpose and formulate its mission. At the same time, routine activities within each business unit are coordinated as much as possible by standardization, often involving the standardization of skills or norms to control the costs of process loss.

A major strength of the multiunit structure is its ability to provide the coordination required to manage extremely large or complex organizations, albeit in parts, without incurring the high costs of the matrix structure. Unfortunately, multiunit structures suffer from some degree of inefficiency inasmuch as their divisional departmentation means substantial duplication of effort. Another drawback is that multiunit structures are not useful when strong links are needed between the various parts of the organization. For example, it is difficult to imagine organizing a hospital as a multiunit structure. Too many transfers of patients and treatment information are required among the units of a hospital to allow any of them to operate autonomously.

Postbureaucratic Structures

Within the past 25 years, many organizations have found it necessary to be more flexible than allowed by even the most flexible form of bureaucracy. Some have grown extremely large—employing hundreds of thousands of individuals, producing a tremendous variety of goods or services, and doing business in every corner of the world. Others have found themselves competing in industries characterized by massive change occurring on a continual basis. As a result, attention has turned to forming information-rich organization structures, grounded in computerized communication networks and coordinated by mutual adjustment, that can successfully deal with extreme complexity and identify change before it threatens organizational viability. In the process, managers have begun to experiment with two new kinds of **postbureaucratic structures:** modular and virtual structures.

A **modular structure** consists of a collection of autonomous modules or cells interconnected by a computerized intranet.[19] In such structures, self-managing teams, grouped according to process, assume supervisory duties and use mutual adjustment to coordinate internal work activities. An intranet ties teams together horizontally, allowing for mutual adjustment among teams needed to manage interdependent efforts, and provides the vertical information flows required to ensure firmwide collaboration.

FIGURE 12-10   The Multiunit Structure

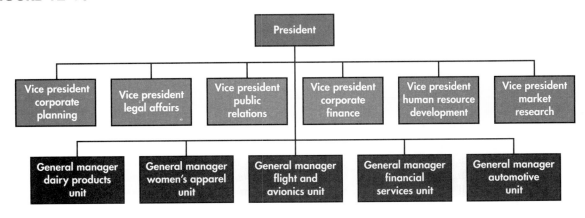

Computer-mediated networks thus supplant hierarchy and centralization as the primary means of coordinating interdependence among groups.

The modular structure can be quite flexible, as different configurations of modules can be strung together to accomplish the various tasks that might confront a firm. For example, the collection of research, production, and marketing modules assembled in a biotechnology firm to develop and distribute an influenza vaccine can be disbanded and recombined with others to perform research on cell development and market the firm's new anticancer discovery.

Modular flexibility comes at the price of significant process loss, however, due to the redirection of otherwise productive resources toward self-management activities. This loss is less than that experienced in matrix structures and is viewed as essential to organizational success and survival.

In the **virtual structure,** several organizations attain the performance capacities of a single, much larger firm while retaining extreme flexibility and significant efficiency.[20] The label *virtual structure* is patterned after the term *virtual memory,* which refers to a way of making a computer act as though it has more memory capacity than it actually possesses. Analogously, virtual structuring provides a way to make an organization act as though it has more productive capacity than it actually controls. A structure of this type develops when a company forms a network of alliances with other companies to quickly exploit a business opportunity. Thus a virtual structure is not a single organization, but rather a temporary collection of several organizations.

Levi Strauss, Atlas Industrial Door, and Dell Computer are some of the better-known companies currently implementing aspects of the virtual structuring approach.[21] In virtual structures, each firm focuses on doing the thing it does best—its core competency in design, manufacturing, marketing, or any other necessary function—and together the firms form a "best of everything" organization. During the period of its temporary existence, a virtual structure resembles a loosely coupled functional structure where each "department" is an otherwise autonomous company. Connecting the various companies together is an intranet of computerized information-processing systems that takes the place of hierarchy in coordinating interdependence relationships among companies. Such coordination is accomplished mainly by mutual adjustment through e-mail, teleconferencing, and similar electronic linkages.

The temporary nature of the virtual structure is the source of its flexibility, because companies can be added or eliminated as the situation warrants. In the face of this flexibility, the virtual structure's efficiency comes from each company's singular focus on doing what it does best. Thus it would seem that the virtual structure overcomes the efficiency-versus-flexibility trade-offs evident among the other structures just discussed. It does have some drawbacks, however. Considerable efficiency may be sacrificed by virtual structuring, due to the cost of coordinating efforts spread among several otherwise independent firms. These costs inhibit the use of virtual structures in all but the most turbulent situations.[22]

SUMMARY

An organization's *structure* is a network of interdependencies among the people and tasks that make up the organization. It is created and sustained by the *basic coordination mechanisms* of *mutual adjustment, direct supervision,* and *standardization,* all of which coordinate interdependent relationships among people and groups. Structure emerges as the groups in an organization become clustered together during *functional* or *divisional departmentation*. The resulting departments or divisions are also coordinated by means of *hierarchy* and *centralization*.

Standardization, when used as the primary means of coordination, is the hall-mark of *bureaucracy*. Depending on the mix of coordination mechanisms, departmentation, and centralization chosen by the managers of a firm, various types of *prebureaucratic*, *bureaucratic*, or *postbureaucratic* structures may be produced. These include the *simple undifferentiated structure*, the *simple differentiated structure*, the *functional structure*, the *divisional structure*, the *matrix structure*, the *multiunit structure*, the *modular structure*, and the *virtual structure*. Each structural type offers its own strengths and weaknesses, most of which involve trade-offs between efficiency and flexibility.

REVIEW QUESTIONS

1. Given that an organization's structure integrates and differentiates activities in the organization, tell which of the following structural characteristics provide integration and which produce differentiation: basic coordination mechanisms, departmentation, hierarchy, and centralization.

2. Explain why standardization requires stability. Why is mutual adjustment so much more flexible? How does direct supervision fit between the two extremes? Which mechanism(s) would you use to coordinate a television-assembly group of fifty employees? Six custom jewelry makers? A dozen door-to-door magazine salespeople? Why?

3. Explain how professionalization, training, and socialization can be used to create standardization. Based on what you have learned in other chapters, name some additional purposes that these three processes serve in organizations.

4. What kinds of departmentation can be used to cluster groups together? How do departmentation and hierarchy work together to resolve coordination problems among departments or divisions?

5. What major differences exist between prebureaucratic and bureaucratic structures? Between bureaucratic structures and postbureaucratic structures? What role do managerial choices among basic coordination mechanisms play in determining which kind of structure develops in an organization?

LEARNING THROUGH EXPERIENCE

DIAGNOSTIC
QUESTIONS 12-1

Organization Structure

You can use what you have learned in this chapter to identify the specific characteristics of an organization's structure and to gain insight into the strengths and weaknesses of that structure. The following questions are provided to assist you in this process.

1. Which of the three basic coordination mechanisms are used in and among the organization's groups? Which serves as the primary means of coordination, and what does that choice say about the importance that the firm accords to efficiency? To flexibility?

2. Which secondary coordination mechanisms back up the primary mechanisms used throughout the firm? Are activities within the organization's workgroups coordinated adequately?

3. If standardization of a particular type is present, is the appropriate amount of formalization, professionalization, training, or socialization also present?

4. Is the firm's structure based on functional or divisional departmentation? What does that choice tell you about the probable balance between efficiency and flexibility in the organization? Does this balance seem correct, given the firm's business situation?

5. Across the array of structural characteristics that you have identified, does a general profile emerge that stresses efficiency and stability, or does a profile stressing flexibility and adaptability appear instead?

6. What specific kind of structure does the organization possess? Does it appear to be the appropriate one, given the profile you have already identified?

EXERCISE 12-1   **Restructuring a University**

Eric Panitz, University of Detroit

How to cluster groups into departments or divisions is a key issue facing managers as they structure an organization. As discussed in this chapter, such departmentation is accomplished by combining groups based on either what they do or what they produce. Of course, concerns about administrative overhead can also influence choices about how to form and combine groups. Administrative overhead comprises the cost of supervising the groups and departments or divisions in a firm. It consists largely of the salaries paid to managers employed as supervisors. Sometimes it is possible to combine groups together in such a way that fewer managers are needed.

Like other organizations, universities have structures that consist of units (called departments) grouped together into large clusters (called colleges). Administrators who manage educational institutions like yours must choose what sorts of groups to form. In the process, they must often consider trade-offs affecting administrative overhead, asking themselves which sort of grouping will minimize the number of people needed to manage organizational activities. In this exercise, you will experience some of the problems and make some of the decisions faced by the management of an educational institution in this process.

Step One: Pre-Class Preparation

In class you will work with other students to restructure a university. In preparation for this session, read the following description of Midwestern State University and then familiarize yourself with the rest of the exercise. Next, list two or more structural modifications that could be made to help the university save money:

1. _____
2. _____
3. _____
4. _____
5. _____

Be prepared to explain your suggestions and describe their benefits.

Adapted with the author's permission from an exercise entitled "Restructuring the University—An Experiential Exercise." This adaptation written by John Wagner.

Midwestern State University

Midwestern State University has a student population of 14,500 undergraduates and 1,500 graduate students, divided among the university's colleges as shown in Exhibit 12-1. The university must reduce its budget. All of the "easy" actions, such as eliminating travel budgets, leaving open positions unfilled, and trimming operating expenses, have already been implemented. Now the vice president for academic affairs is considering restructuring the organization to save money. The board of regents that governs the university has made the following stipulations:

1. The number of currently employed teaching faculty must not be reduced.

2. The number of administrative personnel or staff members cannot be increased.

3. No employee can be terminated, but employees' positions and responsibilities may be changed.

4. No existing undergraduate program may be modified so extensively that it would face the loss of its accreditation.

5. Graduate programs are not to be considered during reorganization; they will be integrated into whatever organization results from restructuring the undergraduate programs.

The current structure of the university is shown in Exhibit 12-2. We will describe three colleges—the Colleges of Business Administration, Allied Health, and Natural Sciences—in some detail shortly. In addition to these three colleges, the university includes a College of Humanities and Social Sciences, a College of Education, a College of Health and Recreation, a College of Law Enforcement (which also offers first-aid courses), and a separate Graduate School. The Graduate School advises graduate students, approves theses and dissertations, and manages associated paperwork. Graduate courses are taught by faculty housed in the university's seven colleges.

Every college (including the Graduate School) is headed by a dean who receives a salary of $110,000–$250,000 depending on seniority, job responsibilities, scholarly reputation, and other factors. Each college consists of several departments, and every department is headed by a chairperson. Department chairs receive a 20 percent salary supplement (added to the salary they would normally receive as members of the teaching faculty). In addition, to give them the time needed for their managerial duties, they are relieved of all teaching responsibilities. All department chairs are former faculty members who can return to teaching when their services as chairperson are no longer required.

EXHIBIT 12-1
Student Enrollment at Midwestern State University

College	Undergraduate Students	Masters Students	Doctoral Students
Business Administration	4,500	600	29
Natural Sciences and Mathematics	1,500	125	38
Humanities and Social Sciences	1,750	25	25
Law Enforcement	2,000	65	0
Allied Health and Nursing	750	40	3
Education	2,800	405	42
Health and Recreation	1,200	85	18

EXHIBIT 12-2   Structure of Midwestern State University

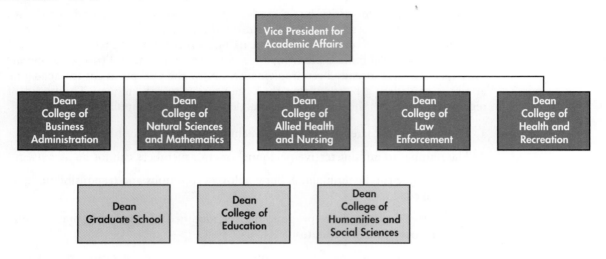

The College of Business Administration

As shown in Exhibit 12-3, the College of Business Administration consists of five departments and thirteen programs. These programs are summarized next. Not only business majors but also many students in the Colleges of Allied Health and Natural Sciences take several business courses as part of their major or minor programs. For example, Health Record Administration majors must take the Principles of Management course.

Department of Business Administration and Marketing   This department includes the management, marketing, general business, and coal mining administration programs. It has seventeen faculty: four in management, four in marketing, six in general business, and three in coal mining administration.

The *Management* program offers three majors. Business Administration trains students to become midlevel managers. Industrial Relations develops skills in human resource management, organization development, and labor relations. Operations Management develops skills in production management, quality control, inventory administration, and operations research. The *Marketing* program offers two majors. Marketing prepares students for positions in sales and sales management, retailing, market research, promotion, and advertising. Transportation qualifies students for jobs in the field of transportation and physical distribution.

The *General Business* program offers courses in law, the capstone policy course, and courses in small business administration. It also includes a major in general business for students planning to attend professional or graduate schools. Finally, the *Coal Mining Administration* program qualifies students to enter managerial positions in the coal industry, such as mine supervision and occupational safety administration. This program reflects the importance of the mining industry in the state.

Department of Finance and Business Information Systems   This department houses sixteen faculty members, four in each of four majors. The *Management Information Systems and Programming* program trains students in computer programming for business applications and in management information system development and management. The *Finance* program gives students the tools for financial decision making

EXHIBIT 12-3   Structure of the College of Business Administration

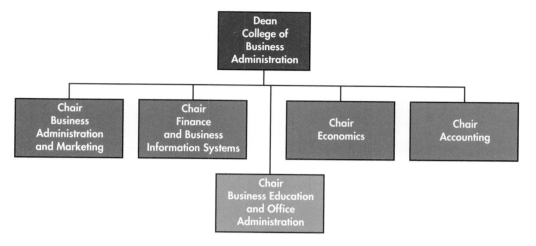

needed for careers in corporate finance, banking, or investment. The *Insurance* program provides students with the background needed for careers in the insurance industry. The *Real Estate* program develops students' capabilities in real estate management, marketing, appraisal, and property development.

Department of Economics   The economics department has eleven faculty members, who teach primarily introductory economics and business statistics courses. Advanced courses are offered to all majors in the College of Business Administration. Economics majors are offered through both the College of Business and the College of Humanities.

Department of Accounting   The accounting department includes 11 faculty members, who teach the introductory accounting course to all business majors as well as business minors from other colleges. Two majors are offered through the department. The *Accounting* program prepares students to seek CPA certification and accountancy positions in government or industry. The *Health Care Administration* program offers specific training for positions in hospital administration. This cooperative program includes faculty from the College of Allied Health.

Department of Business Education and Office Administration   This department has eight faculty members, who teach business communications courses for all majors and office management, secretarial, and business education courses to students with the following majors. The *Office Administration* program provides the skills required to fill positions as executive secretaries and administrative assistants. The *Secretarial Training* program is a two-year degree program that trains legal, medical, and other specialized secretaries in office services. The *Business Education* program prepares students to teach business subjects at the high school level.

The College of Natural Sciences and Mathematics

The College of Natural Sciences and Mathematics (Exhibit 12-4) has six departments that offer thirteen programs. Many of this college's courses are general education requirements that must be completed by all students in the university. In addition, many courses in the biology and chemistry departments serve as preparatory

EXHIBIT 12-4   Structure of the College of Natural Sciences and Mathematics

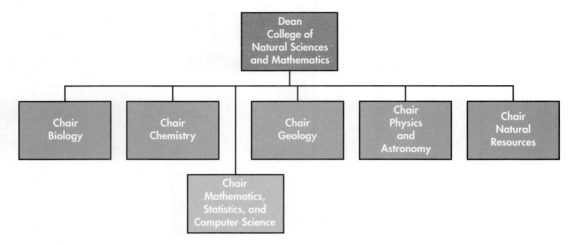

courses for students in the allied health programs (nursing, medical technology, environmental health).

Department of Biology   This department has seventeen faculty members and offers five majors. The *General Biology* program provides an overview of the biological sciences and the component fields of ecology, botany, physiology, biostatistics, entomology, vertebrate and invertebrate biology, and cell biology. The *Microbiology* program emphasizes the study of pathogenic and nonpathogenic bacteria, fungi, virology, and parasitology in clinical and nonclinical settings. The *Wildlife Biology* program focuses on the management and health of terrestrial wildlife and its environments. The *Aquatic and Fisheries Biology* program concerns the management of fisheries and their habitats, including pollution control and other aspects of marine biology. The *Environmental Resources Biology* program offers a broad view of economic and environmental aspects of biological resources.

Department of Chemistry   This department has ten faculty members and offers two majors. The *Chemistry* program includes coursework in analytical, physical, and organic chemistry and biochemistry. *Chemical Technology* is a two-year program that prepares students for positions as laboratory technicians.

Department of Geology   This department has eight faculty members and offers three majors designed to prepare students for careers in the petroleum, coal mining, and other related industries as well as for teaching assignments at the secondary level. The majors offered are *Geology, Earth Science,* and a two-year program in *Geological Engineering.*

Department of Mathematics and Computer Science   This twelve-member department offers majors in *Computer Science, Mathematics,* and *Statistics.* Most of the courses in this department are part of the general education requirement that all students must fulfill. The department has few math majors and is trying to cope with the effects of the specialized courses in statistics offered by other colleges such as Business and Law Enforcement.

Department of Natural Resources   The Department of Natural Resources has six faculty members and offers science courses for nonmajors who must take science to

EXHIBIT 12-5   Structure of the College of Allied Health and Nursing

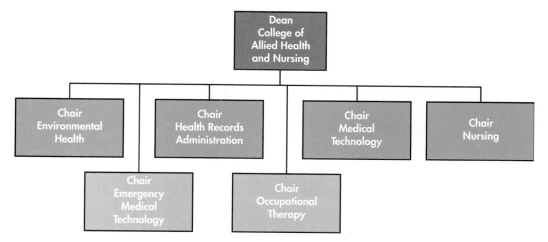

fulfill general education requirements. These courses emphasize the historical development of scientific knowledge and its effects on present-day life.

Department of Physics and Astronomy   This six-member department offers a *Physics* major and teaches courses on physics and astronomy that are listed as general education requirements.

The College of Allied Health and Nursing

The College of Allied Health and Nursing (Exhibit 12-5) has thirty-seven faculty members and offers fourteen programs through its emergency medical technology, environmental health, health records administration, medical technology, occupational therapy, and nursing departments.

Department of Emergency Medical Technology (EMT)   This three-member department offers one-year programs leading to EMT and advanced EMT certification and a two-year program leading to an *EMT Services Management* degree. Students are trained in techniques and management of ambulance services and accident management. Similar courses are offered in the College of Law Enforcement, but the law program does not include a certification or degree program in this area.

Department of Environmental Health   The Department of Environmental Health has one part-time and three full-time faculty members. It offers a program in applied biology and chemistry with emphasis on public health aspects of pollution control, disease transmission, and waste disposal. Students are trained to manage related types of public health problems.

Department of Health Records Administration   This department has three faculty members and offers four programs ranging from a one-year certification in medical transcription to a four-year degree in health record administration. The latter program is designed to train students in the effective management, storage, and retrieval of hospital records.

Department of Medical Technology   This department's seven faculty members offer a two-year medical assistant degree and four-year degrees in medical technology and medical laboratory technology. These programs are designed to train students to perform the medical testing required to support physician decision making, and to prepare students to attain the certification needed to work in hospital laboratories, clinics, or medical testing facilities. Areas of study include hematology, clinical chemistry, clinical microbiology, parasitology, and similar subjects.

Department of Occupational Therapy This department offers a four-year training program in physical therapy and has seven faculty members.

Department of Nursing The Department of Nursing is the largest department in the college, offering two programs leading to two- or four-year nursing degrees along with state RN (registered nurse) or LPN (licensed practical nurse) certification.

Step Two: Sharing Suggestions

The class should divide into groups including four to six members. If your class has already formed permanent groups, these groups should reconvene. In each group, members should describe and explain their reasons for the structural modifications they would recommend to solve Midwestern State's fiscal problems. If you think of additional modifications during these discussions, work together to describe them. Each group should combine all of the modifications proposed into a single list.

Step Three: Designing a New Structure

After the group has listed all proposed modifications, members should work together to find the combination that will create a structure that saves as much money as possible, yet remains consistent with the requirements of the board of regents. Redraw Exhibits 12-2 through 12-5 as necessary to show the changes suggested by your group. One group member should be appointed spokesperson to explain the group's proposal to the rest of the class.

Step Four: Group Reports and Discussion

Each group spokesperson should summarize the results of the group's design efforts in a five-minute presentation to the rest of the class. The list of modifications considered by the group as well as its revised structural diagrams should be presented on a chalkboard, flip chart, or overhead projector.

Step Five: Class Discussion of the Restructuring Process

The class should review the lists of modifications and structures developed by the groups, looking for similarities and differences among the ideas. If time permits, the class should try to reach consensus on one combination of modifications that will be consistent with the regents' guidelines and achieve the greatest budget reduction. The class may discuss questions such as the following during this process:

1. Which modifications seemed obvious at first but later proved to be inappropriate?

2. Which modifications came to the surface only after further consideration?

3. Which modifications, if any, conflicted with others? In the event of such conflicts, how did you decide which modification to choose?

4. In what ways is Midwestern State University similar to your school or educational program? What sort of structural modifications might the administrators of your school or program make if required to reduce costs?

5. In general, what should you do to an organization's structure to economize on administrative overhead?

Conclusion

Forming structural groups and combining them into departments or divisions involves trade-offs between the economy of functional grouping and the flexibility of divisional grouping. The costs of administrative overhead may also enter into decisions about how to form groups and cluster them together. Subtle changes in structure can sometimes save an organization a great deal of money without affecting its ability to accomplish its mission and goals.

An Adaptive Model of Organization Design
Organizational Effectiveness
Structural Alternatives
Structural Contingencies

Lifecycle Contingencies: Age and Stage of Development
Inception Contingencies

Formalization and Elaboration Contingencies
Core Technology
The External Environment

Transformation Contingencies
Environmental Turbulence
Transaction Costs
Final Considerations

Summary
Review Questions

Learning Through Experience
Diagnostic Questions 13-1: Organization Design
Exercise 13-1: Open System Planning

Technology, Environment, and Organization Design

Johnson & Johnson, well known for its Band-Aids and baby powder, is a company of 204 different businesses organized into three divisions: drugs, consumer products, and medical devices and diagnostics. In running such a complex organization, CEO William C. Weldon must balance the constant pressures for the economic efficiency and "cross talk" allowed by a unified structure with the need for the adaptability and flexibility of autonomous units. Each of the company's businesses operates as an independent enterprise, setting its own strategies and maintaining its own corporate management. This independence nurtures an entrepreneurial attitude that has kept the firm intensely competitive in an industry plagued by declining rates of innovation and creativity.

Despite this success, Weldon believes that the various parts of J&J can no longer operate in isolation. Experts assert—and Weldon agrees—that some of the most important breakthroughs in twenty-first-century medicine will come from the ability to apply scientific advances from one discipline to problems in another. Thus, while J&J has earned nearly 15 percent of its revenues over the past decade from the fifty-two businesses it acquired during the period, Weldon now sees the necessity of focusing less on growth through acquisition and more on competition through knowledge sharing throughout the company.

To move J&J in the desired direction, Weldon is creating new information systems to encourage better communication and more frequent collaboration between units. His hope is to cultivate the kind of alliances that led recently to the development of a drug-coated stent by researchers from one of the firm's drug units and individuals from the company's cardiovascular medicine business.

Synergy and convergence are now the watchwords at a company once dominated by "go it alone" individualism. Company researchers building a massive database of human genomic patterns see uses throughout the company, ranging from disease diagnosis to prediction of likely responses to experimental drugs. Weldon hopes that this and similar breakthroughs will fuel Johnson & Johnson's growth in the coming years.[1]

Organization design—the process of managing organization structure—has important implications for the competitiveness and continued survival of business organizations. Contemporary managers, whether they are maintaining existing structures or implementing new ones, need to know about the different kinds of structures as well as the key strengths and weaknesses of each structural type. In addition, they must be able to diagnose and react to the various factors that influence the effectiveness of each type of structure, and they must recognize how a particular structure matches up with their company's particular business situation.

This chapter presents an adaptive model of organization design that provides guidance to managers engaged in structuring modern organizations. It begins by discussing the concept of organizational effectiveness, which is the ultimate goal of structural management. It then examines some of the most influential contingency factors that govern the effectiveness of alternative structures. In the process, the chapter identifies which of the various structures described in Chapter 12 work best under each of several kinds of business conditions.

AN ADAPTIVE MODEL OF ORGANIZATION DESIGN

Is there a single *best* type of organizational structure? The fact that many different kinds of structures exist implies that no one type will be suitable for all organizations. Instead, each form of organization structure possesses unique strengths and weaknesses that make it appropriate for some situations but not for others. Structuring an organization involves making well-considered choices among the various alternatives available.

Organization design is the process of making these choices. In this process, managers diagnose the situation confronting their organization, then select and implement the structure that seems most appropriate. The process of organization design is consciously adaptive and is guided by the principle, illustrated in Figure 13-1, that the degree to which a particular type of *structure* will contribute to the *effectiveness* of an organization depends on *contingency factors* that impinge on the organization and shape its business.[2]

FIGURE 13-1　The Contingency Model of Organizational Design

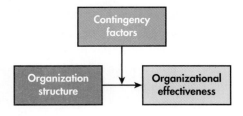

Organizational Effectiveness

Organizational effectiveness, which is the desired outcome of organization design, is a measure of an organization's success in achieving its goals and objectives. Relevant goals and objectives might include targets pertaining to profitability, growth, market share, product quality, efficiency, stability, or similar outcomes.[3] An organization that fails to accomplish its goals is ineffective because it is not fulfilling its purpose.

An effective organization must also satisfy the demands of the various **constituency groups** that provide it with the resources necessary for its survival. As suggested by Figure 13-2, if a company satisfies customers' demands for desirable goods or services, it will probably continue to enjoy its customers' patronage. If it satisfies its suppliers' demands for payment in a timely manner, the suppliers will probably continue to provide it with needed materials. If it satisfies its employees' demands for fair pay and satisfying work, it will probably be able to retain its workers and recruit new employees. If it satisfies its stockholders' demands for profitability, it will probably enjoy continued access to equity funding.[4] If a firm fails to satisfy any one of these demands, however, its effectiveness will be weakened, because the consequent loss of needed resources, such as customers or employees, will threaten its continued survival.

Effectiveness differs from **organizational productivity** in that productivity measures do not take into account whether a firm is producing the *right* goods or services.[5] A modern company producing more glass milk bottles than ever before is certainly productive, but it is also ineffective because most milk companies now sell their products in plastic containers.

Effectiveness differs from efficiency as well. **Organizational efficiency** means minimizing the raw materials and energy consumed by the production of goods and

FIGURE 13-2   Types of Constituency Groups and Their Demands

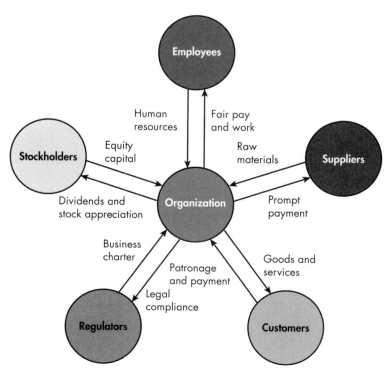

FIGURE 13-3 Tall and Flat Organizational Hierarchies

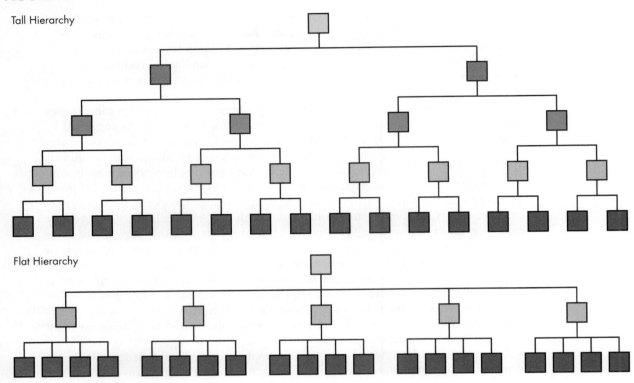

Tall Hierarchy

Flat Hierarchy

services. This parameter is often stated as the ratio of inputs consumed per units of outputs produced—for instance, the number of labor hours expended in manufacturing a bicycle.[6] Efficiency means *doing the job right,* whereas effectiveness means *doing the right job.* That is, effectiveness is a measure of whether a company is producing what it should produce in light of the goals, objectives, and constituency demands that influence its performance and justify its existence.

Structural Alternatives

The structure of an organization strongly influences its effectiveness. For each firm, one type of structure—whether simple undifferentiated, simple differentiated, functional, divisional, multiunit, matrix, modular, or virtual—will have the greatest positive effect on its ability to meet its goals and satisfy its constituencies. To clarify the fundamental differences among the various types of structures, we sometimes classify alternatives along a dimension ranging from *mechanistic* to *organic.*[7]

At one extreme on this continuum, purely **mechanistic structures** are machine-like. They permit workers to complete routine, narrowly defined tasks—designed according to the dictates of the efficiency perspective discussed in Chapter 7—in an efficient manner, but they lack flexibility. Extremely mechanistic structures are centralized, having *tall hierarchies* of vertical authority and communication relationships such as the one depicted in the upper panel of Figure 13-3. They are also characterized by large amounts of standardization, as indicated in Table 13-1.

At the other extreme on the same continuum, purely **organic structures** are analogous to living organisms in that they are flexible and able to adapt to changing conditions. In such structures, the motivational and quality perspectives on job design

TABLE 13-1   Comparison of Mechanistic and Organic Structures

Characteristics of Mechanistic Structures	Characteristics of Organic Structures
Tasks are highly specialized. It is often not clear to members how their tasks contribute to accomplishment of the organizational objectives.	Tasks are broad and interdependent. Relation of task performance to attainment of organizational objectives is emphasized.
Tasks remain rigidly defined unless they are formally altered by top management.	Tasks are continually modified and redefined by means of mutual adjustment among task holders.
Specific roles (rights, duties, technical methods) are defined for each member.	Generalized roles (acceptance of the responsibility for overall task accomplishment) are defined for each member.
Control and authority relationships are structured in a vertical hierarchy	Control and authority relationships are structured in a network characterized by both vertical and horizontal connections.
Communication is primarily vertical, between superiors and subordinates.	Communication is both vertical and horizontal, depending on where the needed information resides.
Communication mainly takes the form of instructions and decisions issued by superiors, performance feedback, and requests for decisions sent from subordinates.	Communication takes the form of information and advice.
Loyalty to the organization and obedience to superiors are mandatory.	Commitment to organizational goals is more highly valued than is loyalty or obedience.

Source: Based in part on Tom Burns and G. M. Stalker, *The Management of Innovation* (London: Tavistock Publications, 1961), pp. 120–122.

described in Chapter 7 have greater influence on the way tasks are developed and performed, which in turn allows employees more control over their work and affords the organization increased adaptability. Owing to their flexibility, however, organic structures lack the single-minded focus required to perform routine work in the most efficient manner.

The different parts of extremely organic structures are connected by decentralized networks in *flat hierarchies,* like the one shown in the lower panel of Figure 13-3. The emphasis placed on horizontal relationships means that fewer vertical layers are required to process information and manage activities. In addition, organizations with organic structures typically rely more heavily on mutual adjustment and less critically on standardization. Computerized information networks take on greater importance as modes of coordination and communication among interdependent tasks.

Of course, not all organizations represent such extreme cases. In reality, a particular type of structure may be mechanistic in some respects and organic in others. The more mechanistic the structure, the more efficient but less flexible it will be. The more organic the structure, the more flexible but less efficient it will be. These differences in efficiency and flexibility can be traced to the mechanisms used to coordinate work activities. As indicated in Chapter 12, standardization incorporates low long-term coordination costs and thus serves as the basis for mechanistic efficiency. Mutual adjustment, on the other hand, is quite flexible and therefore provides the source of organic flexibility. In this regard, the distinction between mechanistic and organic structures exactly parallels the distinction made in Chapter 12 between bureaucratic structures and both pre- and postbureaucratic alternatives.

Differences in the efficiency and flexibility of mechanistic and organic structures are also attributable to differences in centralization, a characteristic that varies independently of the degree to which a structure is bureaucratic. On the one hand, the greater centralization of mechanistic structures encourages efficient specialization, with centralized decision makers gaining ever-growing expertise in decision making. On the other hand, the greater decentralization of organic structures facilitates adaptive responsiveness, as decentralized decision makers located throughout an organization can lead its parts in several different adaptive directions at once. IBM's efforts to decentralize company operations illustrate this point quite well. As formerly organized, IBM was so centralized that decisions about the design, manufacture, and sales of personal computers were made by the same headquarters managers who also made decisions about larger mainframe computers and midsize minicomputers. With IBM's current organization, managers of IBM's personal computer lines can decide to introduce new products or enter new markets without consulting with or affecting the operations of other parts of the firm.

Structural Contingencies

In light of the contrasting strengths and weaknesses of the various types of structures, it is critically important that managers identify key **structural contingency factors** that can help determine whether a particular type of structure will function successfully in their organization.

These factors constitute the situation—both within the organization and in the surrounding environment—that managers must perceive and diagnose correctly to determine how to conduct their business most effectively. The remainder of this chapter considers some of the most important of these contingency factors and describes how each influences structural choice (see the Cutting-Edge Research box).

LIFECYCLE CONTINGENCIES: AGE AND STAGE OF DEVELOPMENT

Company age and stage of development are **lifecycle contingencies** associated with organizational growth. As organizations age and mature, they often grow out of one type of structure and into another.[8] This process can be envisioned as a series of developmental stages, as described in Table 13-2.

TABLE 13-2   Stages in Organizational Maturation

Stage	Primary Characteristics	Structural Type
Inception	Determination of firm's purpose Growth of commitment Initial planning and implementation Reliance on mutual adjustment	Prebureaucratic
Formalization	Rapid growth and change Development of routine activities Division of work into functions Systematic evaluation and rewards Formal planning and goal setting Emphasis on efficiency and stability	Bureaucratic (functional)
Elaboration	Search for new opportunities Diversification, decentralization Maturation and continued growth	Bureaucratic (divisionalized)
Transformation	Large size, either real or virtual Flattened organization hierarchy Massive change and complexity Emphasis on flexibility	Postbureaucratic

CUTTING-EDGE RESEARCH

ARE ALL TYPES OF STRUCTURAL CHANGE THE SAME?

By advocating that managers fit the structure of their organization to the demands of situational conditions, contingency models of organizational structure and design presume that shifting from one structure to another is not a major problem. Yet, research on structural contingencies has used cross-sectional designs, meaning that researchers have compared organizations having one structure with organizations having another structure in order to infer the dynamics and effects of change. No research has actually followed organizations through the process of change to determine the difficulties and challenges associated with this process.

However, in a recent study of four-person teams conducted in a behavioral laboratory, Henry Moon and colleagues examined how shifting between functional and divisional (or workflow) departmentation might affect structural effectiveness. Moon and colleagues began their study by creating teams organized along functional and divisional lines. In functionally organized teams, each of four tasks was assigned to a single team member, meaning that all members had different tasks and together performed the entire set of tasks. In divisionally organized teams, all four tasks were assigned to each member, such that every member could perform the entire set of tasks without working with others. Then the researchers created two environmental conditions, one that was stable and unchanging and another that was unstable and subject to unpredictable change. Finally, the researchers built in the requirement that functional teams shift to divisional structures, and vice versa.

Results of the study showed, first, that functionally structured teams worked most effectively under sta-
ble conditions and that divisionally structured teams worked best under conditions of unpredictable change. Second, results indicated that changing from functional structuring to divisional structuring was relatively simple, but that shifting from divisional structuring to functional structuring was not. Third, findings indicated that the reason for this difference lay in different approaches to coordination that developed in the two types of teams. In functionally structured teams, members learned to coordinate by mutual adjustment in order to ensure that individualized tasks contributed to a meaningful whole. In divisionally structured teams, however, similar coordination mechanisms were never developed since each member could do his or her job without coordinating with anyone else. Thus, when divisionally structured teams moved to functional structuring, the teams lacked appropriate coordination; in fact, prior practices of working alone impeded attempts at developing mutual adjustment. In contrast, when functionally structured teams moved to divisional structuring, previously developed coordination mechanisms were no longer needed but did not hinder productivity.

Generalizing from the activities of four-person laboratory teams to the actions of complex organizations is a tenuous proposition. Nonetheless, the study by Moon and colleagues highlights the possibility that the ease of shifting from one organization structure to another may depend on which types of structure are being initiated and left behind. Implementing the changes suggested by structural contingency models may be more challenging in some instances than in others.

Source: Henry Moon, John R. Hollenbeck, Stephen E. Humphrey, Daniel R. Ilgen, Bradley West, Aleks Ellis, and Christopher O. L. H. Porter, "Asymmetric Adaptability: Dynamic Team Structures as One-Way Streets," working paper, Goizueta Business School, Emory University, Atlanta, GA 30322.

At the *inception* stage, one person or a small group of people create an organization and identify the firm's initial purpose. As commitment to this purpose develops, initial planning and implementation bring the firm to life. If the organization proves initially successful, it may experience rapid growth. As routines emerge, workers may invent general rules to preserve these customary ways of doing things. Little, if any, formal coordination occurs, however. Mutual adjustment or direct supervision usually suffices as the primary means of unit coordination. Consequently, the organization takes on one of the prebureaucratic forms of structure—namely, either simple undifferentiated or simple differentiated, with the choice depending on the effects of other contingency considerations discussed later in this chapter.

During the second developmental stage, known as *formalization,* work becomes divided into different functional areas, the organization develops systematic evaluation and reward procedures, and its direction is determined through formal planning and goal setting. As the organization continues to grow, professional managers first supplement and then replace the firm's owners, transforming themselves into the day-to-day bosses who run the company. In addition, decision making becomes increasingly centralized. Management emphasizes efficiency and stability, and work becomes routine as tasks are designed in accordance with the efficiency perspective on job design. In the process, standardization emerges as the means by which coordination is achieved. As a consequence, the organization's structure becomes bureaucratic, and typically functional.

To adapt to changing conditions and to pursue continued growth, a firm that has progressed to the third stage, *elaboration,* seeks out new product, location, or client opportunities. As the company's business diversifies, its centralized management loses the ability to coordinate work activities, and a need develops for decentralization and divisional departmentation. If the firm continues to mature even further, continued growth and diversification might require yet more structural elaboration. Although the company's structure remains bureaucratic, management must consider reliance on mutual adjustment, no matter how costly, to cope with the firm's greater complexity or need for greater flexibility. The satisfaction and quality perspectives influence job design at this point, as standardization fades in importance and employees gain greater control over their work. Whether the specific type of structure possessed by the firm will be divisional, matrix, or multiunit depends on the effects of other contingency factors.

Finally, an organization that has advanced to the fourth developmental stage, known as *transformation,* finds itself confronted by extremes of both change and complexity in its business situation. To compete, the company enters into the process of *mass customization,* wherein it relies on skilled teams and advanced technologies to tailor mass-produced goods or services to the unique demands of different clientele.[9] The quality perspective on job design is fully apparent at this stage of development. Autonomous teams use both mutual adjustment and decentralization to manage themselves and to coordinate with one another by sharing information on computerized networks. The pyramidal hierarchy developed during the stages of formalization and elaboration becomes transformed into a flattened, horizontal structure characterized by process flows and peer relationships. These flows and relationships may be wholly contained within the organization itself, or they may extend outward and into other firms. The organization adopts a postbureaucratic structure, either modular or virtual, depending on the influence of additional contingency factors discussed later.

The four-stage developmental model just described suggests that as older organizations grow more complex, their structures and the jobs within them similarly become more complicated. Note, however, that not every organization progresses through every developmental stage. For instance, a family-owned convenience store may never grow beyond the stage of inception. Such notable companies as Apple Computer and Coca-Cola have yet to grow beyond elaboration. In addition, some companies leap over one or more stages as they develop—for example, starting out with formalization or elaboration, or moving directly from initiation to transformation. Not every company starts small, nor do all firms invest in bureaucracy. Nonetheless, the fact remains that increasing age is accompanied by a tendency to progress from prebureaucratic structures developed during the stage of inception, to bureaucratic structures developed during formalization and elaboration, and then to postbureaucratic structures developed during transformation. As an organization advances through this sequence of stages and structures, its management faces a series of new contingency factors. This progression is the focus of the remainder of this chapter.

INCEPTION CONTINGENCIES

Organizations at the developmental stage of inception are typically new, small, and fairly simple in form. Consequently, they are most likely to have prebureaucratic structures. It follows that the organization design choice confronting managers concerns which prebureaucratic structure to adopt—simple undifferentiated or simple differentiated. Both alternatives are relatively organic, despite the ownership-related direct supervision found in simple differentiated structures. Because they share this general similarity, considerations regarding trade-offs between mechanistic efficiency and organic flexibility have little relevance. Instead, the choice between the two prebureaucratic structures is influenced by the contingency factor of organization size.

Organization size can be defined in several ways:

- The number of members in an organization
- The organization's volume of sales, clients, or profits
- Its physical capacity (for example, a hospital's number of beds or a hotel's number of rooms)
- The total financial assets it controls[10]

For our purposes, size is considered to be the number of members or employees within the organization—that is, the number of people whose activities must be integrated and coordinated.

Defined in this manner, the size of an organization affects its structure mainly by determining which of the three coordination mechanisms—mutual adjustment, direct supervision, or standardization—is most appropriate as the primary means of coordination. As indicated in Chapter 12, in extremely small organizations containing twelve or fewer people, mutual adjustment alone can provide adequate coordination without incurring overwhelming process loss. If more than about a dozen people try to coordinate by means of mutual adjustment alone, however, so much process loss occurs that performance declines substantially. Thus the activities of larger numbers of people (thirty, forty, or fifty) are better coordinated by direct supervision, because such supervision reduces the number of coordination linkages that must be maintained. In even larger organizations, direct supervision succumbs to information overload. Standardization must therefore be implemented instead to reduce information processing demands and sustain coordinated efforts.

This relationship between organization size and coordination mechanism has especially strong contingency effects on choices between the two prebureaucratic structural alternatives. Simple undifferentiated structures, coordinated solely by means of mutual adjustment, can be used to effectively integrate the people and tasks that make up very small organizations. Simple differentiated structures, with their reliance on direct supervision, become the necessary choice for organizations that grow in size beyond a dozen or so individuals. For managers of small organizations who must choose among alternative prebureaucratic structures, organization size influences structural choice and effectiveness through its effects on coordination.

FORMALIZATION AND ELABORATION CONTINGENCIES

As an organization grows beyond fifty people or so, simple undifferentiated structures and simple differentiated structures become overwhelmed by coordination requirements. As the primary means of coordination, mutual adjustment becomes extremely expensive, and direct supervision is bogged down by rapidly multiplying information-processing needs. As a consequence, standardization assumes the role of primary coordination mechanism. For this reason, organizations that have progressed beyond the stage of inception and outgrown prebureaucratic structures must consider the adoption of more bureaucratic forms of structure.

Relative to prebureaucratic structures, bureaucratic structures are more mechanistic and, therefore, more standardized and often more centralized. However, the four types of bureaucratic structures also differ from one another along these same dimensions. Functional structures are the most mechanistic, due to their standardization and high level of centralization. Divisional structures are substantially less mechanistic, owing to their reduced centralization, but still quite mechanistic relative to the remaining structural alternatives. Matrix structures are even less mechanistic, and therefore more organic, due to their greater decentralization and reliance on mutual adjustment among the managers of matrix cells. Finally, multiunit structures are the least mechanistic of the four bureaucratic structures, reflecting the extreme decoupling that occurs among their parts and the high levels of decentralization that result.

Consequently, for managers trying to decide which bureaucratic structure to implement, the trade-off between mechanistic efficiency and organic flexibility plays a major role in shaping structural choices. Related to this trade-off, the most influential contingency factors at the formalization and elaboration stages of development consist of the organization's core technology and the environment that surrounds the firm.[11]

Core Technology

An organization's **technology** includes the knowledge, procedures, and equipment used to transform unprocessed resources into finished goods or services.[12] **Core technology** is a more specific term that encompasses the dominant technology used in performing work in the operational center of the organization. Core technologies are found in the assembly lines at GM, Ford, and DaimlerChrysler; in the fast-food kitchens at Burger King and Wendy's; in the employment and job-training offices in state and federal agencies; and in the reactor buildings where electricity is generated at nuclear power plants. This section introduces two contingency models that delineate basic differences in core technology: the Woodward manufacturing model and the Thompson service model. Both propose that core technology influences the effectiveness of an organization by placing certain coordination requirements on its structure.

Woodward's Manufacturing Technologies Joan Woodward, a British researcher who began studying organizations in the early 1950s, was an early proponent of the view that an organization's technology can have tremendous effects on its structural effectiveness.[13] She initially studied 100 British manufacturing firms, examining their organizational structures and their relative efficiency and success in the marketplace. While analyzing her data, Woodward discovered that not all companies with the same type of structure were equally effective. Theorizing that these differences in effectiveness might be traced to differences in core technologies, Woodward devised a classification scheme to describe the three basic types of manufacturing technology: small-batch production, mass production, and continuous process production.

Small-batch production (also called *unit production*) is a technology for the manufacture of one-of-a-kind items or small quantities of goods designed to meet unique customer specifications. Such items range from specialized electronic instruments, weather satellites, and space shuttles to hand-tailored clothing. To make this kind of product, craftspeople work alone or in small, close-knit groups. Because customer specifications change from one order to the next, the organization finds it almost impossible to predict what will be required on the next job. Thus the work in firms using small-batch technologies varies in unpredictable ways.

This unpredictability causes small-batch technologies to influence organizational structures and effectiveness. It impedes planning and therefore makes it difficult to coordinate by means of standardization. Not surprisingly, it is impossible to plan legitimate standards for use in a future that cannot be foreseen. Instead, employees must decide for themselves how to perform their jobs. When employees work alone, they are guided by their own expertise and by customer specifications. When employees work in groups, they coordinate with one another by means of mutual adjustment.

Woodward found that mutual adjustment played a pivotal role in coordinating small-batch production. In her research, she showed that among organizations using this type of technology, firms with organic structures were significantly more likely to be successful than companies with mechanistic structures. Of the four types of bureaucratic structures likely to be adopted during the developmental stages of formalization and elaboration, according to Woodward's findings, multiunit structuring would appear more likely to provide the greatest autonomy and support for technological flexibility. The matrix structure, itself a massive lateral linkage mechanism, is another suitable alternative.

The other lateral linkage mechanisms described in Chapter 11—liaison positions, representative groups, and integrating managers—can also be positioned in functional and divisional structures to increase mutual adjustment and introduce greater flexibility. In this way, otherwise mechanistic structures can be made at least modestly organic. Thus it follows that functional or divisional structures with extensive lateral linkages can prove effective when paired with small-batch technology. As with all other technology-based decisions, which one of this reduced set of structural alternatives is best suited to the needs of a particular organization becomes clearer after consideration of the environmental contingencies discussed later in this section.

In Woodward's second type of technology, *mass production* (also referred to as *large-batch production*), the same product is produced repeatedly, either in large batches or in long production runs. For instance, rather than producing a few copies of this book each time an order was received, the publisher initially printed thousands of copies in a single run and warehoused them to fill incoming orders. Other examples of mass production range from word-processing pools in which business records are transcribed in large batches to manufacturing operations in which thousands of Ford Explorers are made on an assembly line that remains virtually unchanged for several years.

As these examples suggest, work in mass-production technologies is intentionally repetitive and remains so for extended periods of time. Employees perform the same jobs over and over, knowing that the work they do tomorrow will be the same as the work done today. The existence of this stability and routine facilitates planning and formalization. As a result, a company is likely to use standardization to reduce the long-term costs of coordination. Woodward's research revealed that mass-production firms with mechanistic structures were far more likely to be effective than those with organic structures. Therefore, mechanistic structures—functional or divisional—are more apt to enhance effectiveness than are more organic alternatives.

In the third type of technology identified in Woodward's research, *continuous-process production,* automated equipment makes the same product in the same way for an indefinite period of time. For instance, at Marathon Petroleum, one refinery unit makes nothing but gasoline, another unit refines motor oil, and a third unit produces only diesel fuel. The equipment used in this type of technology is designed to produce one product and cannot readily be switched over to manufacture a different product. There is no starting and stopping once the equipment has been installed. Machines in continuous-process facilities perform the same tasks without interruption.

Of the three types of technology described by Woodward, continuous-process production involves the most routine work. Few changes, if any, occur in production processes, even over the course many years. For this reason, it seems logical to assume that organizations using continuous-process production would be most effective if structured along mechanistic lines. Interestingly, however, closer examination reveals that few of the people involved in continuous-process production perform routine, repetitive jobs. Rather, machines perform these jobs. The people act as "exception managers," monitoring production equipment by watching dials and gauges, checking machinery, inspecting finished goods, and handling the problems that arise when this equipment fails to function properly. Although some of these problems occur repeatedly and can be planned for in advance, a significant number are emergencies that have never happened before and cannot be anticipated with acceptable accuracy.

Because some of the most critical work performed by people in continuous-process production technologies is highly unpredictable, standardization is not feasible. Mutual adjustment, sometimes in conjunction with direct supervision, is therefore the dominant mode of coordination. Technicians who oversee production equipment manage unusual events by conferring with each other and devising solutions to emergencies as they arise. It is not surprising that Woodward found that firms using continuous-process production technologies were most effective when structured organically. In these circumstances, laterally linked functional or divisional structures, or matrix or multiunit structures, are the most likely to encourage effectiveness.

In the years since Woodward conducted her studies, advances in computers, robotics, and automation have led to the creation of another type of manufacturing technology, known as *flexible-cell production.* As described in Chapter 7, this type of technology is characterized by computer-controlled production machines in a group, or cell, which are connected by a flexible network of conveyors that can be rapidly reconfigured to adapt the cell for different production tasks. This technology is typically used to produce a wide variety of machined metal parts, such as pistons for car engines or parts for the lock on the front door of your home. Conceivably, however, it could be used to manufacture virtually any kind of product.

As in continuous-process production, automated equipment performs the work in flexible cells. The only people involved are technicians who monitor the equipment and handle problems. Whereas continuous-process production facilities can make only a single product, however, flexible cells can make many different things. In this respect, flexible-cell production resembles small-batch production. It is an efficient method of producing one-of-a-kind items or small quantities of similar items built to satisfy unique customer specifications.

Inasmuch as Woodward found mutual adjustment to be the most effective coordination mechanism for both continuous-process and small-batch production technologies, an organic structure would seem most suitable for a firm using flexible-cell production. Indeed, a study of 110 manufacturing firms in New Jersey revealed a significant positive relationship between organic structuring and the effectiveness of organizations with flexible cells.[14] This information updates Woodward's research, suggesting that companies employing flexible-cell technologies are likely to be more effective if they adopt laterally linked functional or divisional structures, or matrix or multiunit structures, to coordinate work activities.

Thompson's Service Technologies Because Woodward focused her research solely on manufacturing firms, her contingency model is applicable only to technologies used to produce tangible goods. Today, however, firms that provide services such as real estate sales, appliance repair, or investment planning make up an increasingly critical element of the U.S. economy as well as the economies of other countries. Another contingency model, developed by James D. Thompson, is quite useful because it examines the technologies often employed in these service organizations. These technologies, which are diagrammed in Figure 13-4, include mediating technology, long-linked technology, and intensive technology.[15] In the figure, circles represent employees, and arrows represent flows of work.

A *mediating technology* provides services that link clients together. For example, banks connect depositors who have money to invest with borrowers who need loans; insurance companies enable their clients to pool risks, permitting one person's losses to be covered by joint investments; and telephone companies provide the equipment and technical assistance that people need to talk with one another from separate locations.

When mediating technology is used to provide a service, employees usually serve each client individually. Consequently, as depicted in Figure 13-4A, bank tellers and workers in other mediating technologies normally perform their jobs without assistance from others in their organization. Assuming adequate training, a single bank

FIGURE 13-4 Thompson's Service Technologies

A. Mediating Technology

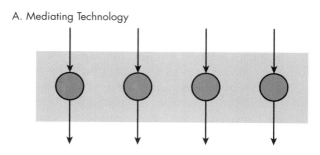

B. Long-Linked Technology

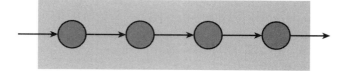

C. Intensive Technology

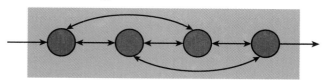

teller can handle a deposit or withdrawal without seeking help from other tellers. At the same time, however, the teller and other workers may share equipment such as the central computer that keeps track of all bank transactions.

Although individual employees work independently in a mediating technology, many perform the same job. Coordination in such firms is needed to ensure that workers provide consistently high-quality service and offer the same basic service to each client. Thus managers in service firms develop lists of the different types of clients that their organization is likely to serve and devise standard operating procedures to be followed while serving each type of client. For example, a bank teller will follow one procedure while serving a client who is making a savings account deposit, a second procedure when assisting a client who is making a loan payment, and a third procedure when helping a client open a new checking account. This standardization of behaviors means that firms using mediating technologies are most likely to be effective when structured mechanistically. Either functional or divisional structures would be suitable for such firms.

Thompson's second type of technology, *long-linked technology,* is analogous to Woodward's mass-production technology. Both refer to sequential chains of simplified tasks. A service sector example of this type of technology is the state employment agency that requires all clients to follow the same lockstep procedures. Each client moves along an "assembly line," starting with registration and progressing through assessment, counseling, training, and placement activities. Figure 13-4B diagrams the sequential movement from one station to the next that characterizes long-linked technology.

Like firms that use mass-production technology, organizations that use long-linked technology coordinate by means of standardization. According to Thompson, mechanistic structuring is likely to enhance the effectiveness of a firm using long-linked technology. This finding suggests that long-linked technology is most effectively paired with functional or divisional structures.

Intensive technology, the third type of technology in Thompson's model, consists of work processes whose configuration may change as employees receive feedback from their clients. The specific array of services to be rendered to a particular patient in a hospital, for example, depends on the patient's symptoms. A patient who enters the hospital's emergency room complaining of chest pains may be rushed to an operating room and then to a cardiac-care unit. A patient with a broken arm may be shuttled from the emergency room to the radiology lab for an X ray, then returned to the emergency room for splinting. A patient with less clear-cut symptoms may be checked into a hospital room for further observation and testing (see Figure 13-4C).

To accommodate the needs of each client, a firm using intensive technology must be able to reorganize itself again and again. Above all, it must have flexibility. Moreover, because the needs of future clients cannot be forecast accurately, the behaviors required of the workers in such a firm are too unpredictable to be successfully formalized. Both flexibility and unpredictability require the use of mutual adjustment as a coordinating mechanism. Thus, firms using intensive technology will be best served by laterally linked functional or divisional structures, or matrix or multiunit structures.

Technological Contingencies: Integration   Both the Woodward and Thompson technology models help identify which general form of organization structure is most likely to enhance the effectiveness of a firm whose primary operations incorporate a specific type of core technology. As indicated in Table 13-3, standardization and mechanistic structuring generally enhance the effectiveness of firms using core technologies that are suited to more routine work—mass-production, mediating, and long-linked technologies. Mutual adjustment and organic structuring, in contrast, promote effectiveness in firms that use core technologies suited to unpredictable, often rapidly changing requirements—small-batch, continuous process, flexible-cell, and intensive technologies.[16]

The External Environment

An organization's **environment** encompasses everything outside the organization. Suppliers, customers, and competitors are part of an organization's environment, as are the governmental bodies that regulate its business, the financial institutions and investors that provide it with funding, and the labor market that contributes its employees. In addition, general factors such as the economic, geographic, and political conditions that impinge on the firm are part of its environment. Central to this definition is the idea that the term *environment* refers to things external to the firm.[17] The internal "environment" of a firm, more appropriately called the company's culture, is distinctly different and will be discussed in Chapter 14.

As a structural contingency factor affecting organizations in the stages of formalization and elaboration, the environment influences structural effectiveness by placing certain coordination and information-processing restrictions on the firm. Five specific environmental characteristics influence structural effectiveness: change, complexity, uncertainty, receptivity, and diversity.

Environmental change concerns the extent to which conditions in an organization's environment change unpredictably. At one extreme, an environment is considered stable if it does not change at all or if it changes only in a cyclical, predictable way. An example of a stable environment is the one that surrounds many of the small firms in Amish communities throughout the midwestern United States. Amish religious beliefs require the rejection of many modern conveniences, such as automobiles, televisions, and gasoline-powered farm equipment. As a consequence, Amish blacksmiths, farmers, and livestock breeders have conducted business in much the same way for generations. Another stable environment surrounds firms that sell Christmas trees. The retail market for cut evergreen trees is predictably strong in November and December but weak at other times of the year.

At the other extreme, an environment is considered dynamic when it changes over time in an unpredictable manner. Because the type of dress deemed stylish changes

TABLE 13-3   Technological Contingencies

Industry Type	Technology	Structural Category	Structural Types	Example
Manufacturing	Small batch	Organic	Laterally linked functional or divisional, matrix	Scientific instrument fabricator
	Mass	Mechanistic	Functional, divisional	Television manufacturer
	Continuous process	Organic	Laterally linked functional or divisional, matrix	Petroleum refinery
	Flexible cell	Organic	Laterally linked functional or divisional, matrix	Auto parts supplier
Service	Mediating	Mechanistic	Functional, divisional	Bank
	Long-linked	Mechanistic	Functional, divisional	Cafeteria
	Intensive	Organic	Laterally linked functional or divisional, matrix	Hospital

so frequently in many parts of the world, the environment surrounding companies in the fashion industry is quite dynamic. Similarly, the environment surrounding companies in the consumer-electronics industry has changed dramatically in recent years. Breakthrough products such as high-definition televisions and digital cameras have created entirely new industries and markets.

Environmental change affects the structure of an organization by influencing the predictability of the firm's work and, therefore, the method of coordination used to integrate work activities.[18] Stability allows managers to complete the planning needed to formalize organizational activities. Firms operating in stable environments can use standardization as their primary coordination mechanism and will typically elect to do so to reduce long-term coordination costs. Mechanistic structures—functional or divisional—are the most likely to prove effective in such instances.

In contrast, it is difficult to establish formal rules and procedures in dynamic environments. In fact, it is useless for managers to try to plan for a future they cannot foresee. Members of an organization facing a dynamic environment must adapt to changing conditions instead of relying on inflexible, standardized operating procedures. Dynamism in the environment leaves management with little choice but to rely on mutual adjustment as a primary coordination mechanism. The organic structuring of laterally linked functional or divisional structures, or matrix or multiunit structures, is therefore appropriate.

Environmental complexity comprises the degree to which an organization's environment is complicated and therefore difficult to understand. A simple environment is composed of relatively few component parts—for example, suppliers, competitors, or types of customers—so little can affect organizational performance. A locally owned gas station does business in a relatively simple environment. It orders most of its supplies from a single petroleum distributor, does business almost exclusively with customers who want to buy gasoline or oil for their cars, and can limit its attention to the competitive activities of a fairly small number of nearby stations. On the other hand, a complex environment incorporates a large number of separable parts. The environments of aviation firms like Boeing and Airbus Industries are extremely complex, including an enormous number of suppliers and many types of customers.

Complexity influences structural effectiveness by affecting the amount of knowledge and information that people must process to understand the environment and cope with its demands.[19] To demonstrate this effect, consider an inexpensive digital watch. If you disassembled this watch, you would probably have little trouble putting it back together again, because it has very few parts—a computer chip programmed to keep time, a digital liquid-crystal face, a battery, and a case. With only a few minutes of practice or simple instructions, you could quickly learn to assemble this watch. Now suppose the pieces of a Rolex watch were spread out before you. Could you reassemble the watch? Probably not, because it includes an overwhelming number of springs, screws, gears, and other parts. Learning to assemble a Rolex properly would require extensive training and much practice.

Similarly, the organization facing a simple environment—one with few "parts"—can understand environmental events and meet the challenges they pose by using a minimal amount of knowledge and processing little new information. A local restaurant that is losing business can determine the reason for its plight simply by telephoning a few prospective customers and asking them for their comments. In contrast, organizations in complex environments—environments with many "parts"—must draw on a considerable store of knowledge and process an overwhelming amount of information to understand environmental events. For example, to find the reason for its loss of market share in the early 1980s and again in the late 1980s, Chrysler Corporation (now DaimlerChrysler) analyzed competitors' marketing strategies and performed extensive market studies of consumer preferences. To recapture market share, the company also worked with hundreds of suppliers to increase the quality and reduce the cost of the parts used to produce its cars.[20]

Environmental complexity affects organizational structures by influencing the suitability of centralized decision making. As indicated in Chapter 12, centralization is characterized by decision making that is limited to a selected group of top managers. It therefore limits the number of people available to digest information and determine its meaning. Because simple environments require little information processing, organizations operating in such environments can be centralized and function quite effectively.

Because environmental complexity requires the ability to process and understand large amounts of information, however, centralized organizations in complex environments can suffer the effects of information overload. One possible way to cope with this information overload is to invest in computerized management information systems. The usual net effect of such investment is actually to *increase* the amount of environmental information available, thereby contributing to *additional* information overload. A more successful way to handle the problem of information overload due to environmental complexity is to involve more individuals in information-processing activities. Thus organizations that are attempting to cope with complex environments often decentralize decision making. That way, they include more people—more brains—in the process of digesting and interpreting information.

In addition to pointing out distinctive environmental differences, the two environmental dimensions of change and complexity combine in the manner shown in Figure 13-5 to define yet another important environmental characteristic: **environmental uncertainty.** Uncertainty reflects a lack of information about environmental

FIGURE 13-5 Environmental Uncertainty as a Function of Change and Complexity

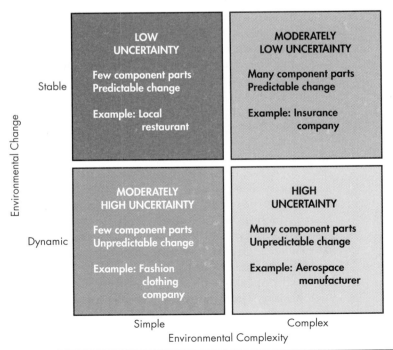

Source: Based on R. B. Duncan, "Characteristics of Perceived Environments and Perceived Environmental Uncertainty," *Administrative Science Quarterly* 17 (1972), 313–327.

factors, activities, and events.[21] It undermines an organization's ability to manage current circumstances and plan for the future. To cope with uncertainty, organizations try to find better ways of acquiring information about the environment. This effort often involves the creation of boundary-spanning positions that can strengthen the information linkage between an organization and its environment.[22]

A **boundary spanner** is a member or unit of an organization that interacts with people or firms in the organization's environment.[23] Salespeople who have contact with customers, purchasing departments that deal with suppliers of raw materials, and top managers who in their figurehead roles represent the company to outsiders are all boundary spanners. When they take on boundary-spanning roles, employees or organizational units perform several functions:

- They monitor the environment for information that is relevant to the organization.
- They serve as gatekeepers, simplifying incoming information and ensuring that it is routed to the appropriate people in the firm.
- They warn the organization of environmental threats and initiate activities that protect it from those dangers.
- They represent the organization to other individuals or firms in its environment, providing them with information about the organization.
- They negotiate with other organizations to acquire raw materials and sell finished goods or services.
- They coordinate any other activities that require the cooperation of two or more firms.[24]

When carried out successfully, these activities enable boundary spanners to provide their organization with information about its environment that can help make change and complexity more understandable.

Environmental receptivity, which ranges from munificent to hostile, is the degree to which an organization's environment supports the organization's progress toward fulfilling its purpose. In a munificent environment, a firm can acquire the raw materials, employees, technology, and capital resources needed to perform productively.[25] Such an environment enables the firm to find a receptive market for its products. The firm's competitors, if any, do not threaten its existence. Regulatory bodies do not try to impede its progress. For example, the environment surrounding the McDonald's fast-food chain at the time of its founding was munificent. Few other fast-food franchises existed, labor was plentiful in the post–Korean War era, and a convenience-minded middle class was emerging throughout North America.

In a hostile environment, the opposite situation prevails. An organization may have great difficulty acquiring, or may be unable to acquire, needed resources, employees, knowledge, or money. Customer disinterest, intense competition, or severe regulation may also threaten the firm's future. For instance, R. J. Reynolds and other members of the tobacco industry have been forced to cope with extreme hostility in North America due to widespread concerns about the health hazards of smoking. During the early 1990s, U.S. defense contractors faced similar hostility as the Cold War ended and the demand for defense weaponry diminished.[26]

Environmental hostility, though normally temporary, represents a crisis that must be handled quickly and decisively if the firm is to survive. An organization facing such hostility either finds a way to deal with it—for example, by substituting one raw material for another, marketing a new product, or lobbying against threatening regulations—or ceases to exist. For example, tobacco companies have contributed to the campaign funds of politicians known to be against the passage of antismoking laws, and defense contractors have merged with other companies to convert to peacetime manufacturing.

To deal with the crisis of a hostile environment, firms that are normally decentralized in response to environmental complexity may centralize decision making for a limited period of time.[27] This temporary centralization facilitates crisis management. Because it reduces the number of people who must be consulted to make a decision, the organization can respond to threatening conditions more quickly. It is important to emphasize that centralization established in response to a hostile environment should remain in effect only as long as the hostility persists. When the threat ends, a firm dealing with a complex environment will perform effectively again only if it reinstates decentralized decision making.

Environmental diversity refers to the number of distinct environmental sectors or domains served by an organization. A firm in a uniform environment serves a single type of customer, provides a single kind of product, and conducts its business in a single geographic location. That is, it serves only a single domain. A campus nightclub that caters to the entertainment needs of local college students, for example, operates in a uniform environment. So does a building-materials firm whose sole product is concrete, which it sells only to local contractors. In contrast, an organization in a diverse environment produces an assortment of products, serves various types of customers, or has offices or other facilities in several geographic locations. It does business in several different domains. Dell, for instance, sells computers to businesses, universities, and the general public. General Electric produces durable consumer goods, financial services, jet engines, and locomotives. Ford Motor Company markets cars in North America, South America, Europe, and Asia.

Environmental diversity affects an organization by influencing the amount of diversity that must be built into its structure.[28] In organizations with uniform environments, managers can use functional departmentation to group units together. Because firms in uniform environments face only a single domain, they must focus on only information about a single kind of environment and react to only a single set of environmental events. Functional departmentation, which facilitates this sort of unified information processing and response, is therefore sufficient in such situations. The absence of environmental diversity permits the firms to operate effectively without significant internal diversification.

In organizations with diverse environments, however, management must use divisional departmentation to gather work associated with each product, customer, or location into its own self-contained division. Companies in diverse environments face a number of distinct domains and must acquire information about each to satisfy its particular demands. Divisional departmentation allows such firms to keep track of each domain separately and to respond to the demands of one domain independently of other domains. Without this type of structure, work on one product might impede work on other products, services rendered to one type of customer might detract from services provided to other types of customers, or operations at one location might affect operations at other locations.

Environmental uniformity, then, favors functional departmentation and suggests the need for a functional structure. In contrast, environmental diversity requires divisional departmentation and either a divisional, matrix, or multiunit structure, depending on other contingency factors.

Environmental Contingencies: Integration   As just indicated, organizational environments have five distinct characteristics: change, complexity, uncertainty, receptivity, and diversity. Diagnosing the nature of a firm's environment during the process of organization design requires that managers perform five environmental analyses more or less simultaneously. The decision tree shown in Figure 13-6 can help guide this process. Each question in the figure deals with one of the environmental characteristics

FIGURE 13-6 Decision Tree: Environmental Contingency Dimensions

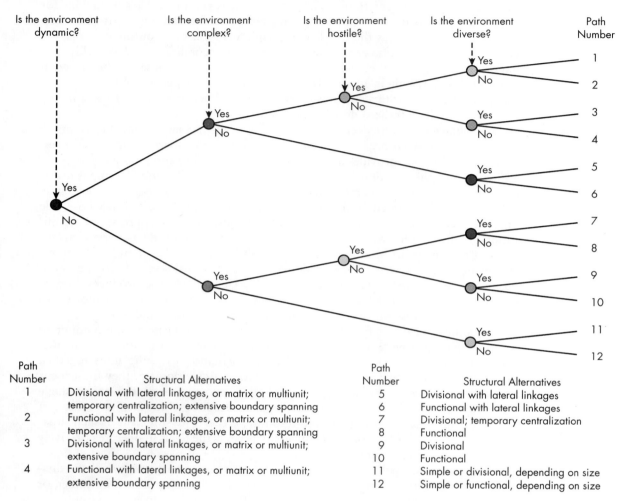

Path Number	Structural Alternatives	Path Number	Structural Alternatives
1	Divisional with lateral linkages, or matrix or multiunit; temporary centralization; extensive boundary spanning	5	Divisional with lateral linkages
		6	Functional with lateral linkages
2	Functional with lateral linkages, or matrix or multiunit; temporary centralization; extensive boundary spanning	7	Divisional; temporary centralization
		8	Functional
3	Divisional with lateral linkages, or matrix or multiunit; extensive boundary spanning	9	Divisional
		10	Functional
4	Functional with lateral linkages, or matrix or multiunit; extensive boundary spanning	11	Simple or divisional, depending on size
		12	Simple or functional, depending on size

just examined. Note that it is not necessary to ask a separate question about uncertainty, because this property is a combination of change and complexity and therefore is assessed implicitly by the answers to questions 1 and 2.

1. *Is the environment stable or dynamic?* The answer to this question identifies the amount of change in the environment and helps determine whether standardization or mutual adjustment is likely to be more effective as a coordination mechanism for the firm. Stable environments either do not change or change in a predictable, cyclical manner, thereby permitting the use of standardization. Dynamic environments change in unpredictable ways and require mutual adjustment.

2. *Is the environment simple or complex?* This answer relies on an assessment of environmental complexity and will indicate whether centralization or decentralization is more appropriate for the firm. Simple environments are more readily understood and accommodate centralization. Complex environments require a great deal of information processing and therefore exert pressure toward decentralization.

3. *Is the environment munificent or hostile?* This question is relevant only if an organization has a complex environment and decentralized decision making. How it is answered gauges environmental receptivity and indicates whether tem-

porary centralization is necessary. Munificent environments are resource-rich and allow for continued decentralization, whereas hostile environments are resource-poor and stimulate crises that mandate temporary centralization.

4. *Is the environment uniform or diverse?* To respond to this question, a manager must evaluate environmental diversity so as to determine which form of departmentation to use. Environmental uniformity supports the structural uniformity of functional departmentation. Environmental diversity requires the structural diversity of divisional departmentation.

TRANSFORMATION CONTINGENCIES

Transition beyond bureaucratic structuring occurs because the standardization intended to stimulate efficient performance can, in some instances, actually reduce efficiency and productivity. This reduction can happen for several reasons. For instance, the very existence of bureaucratic rules and procedures can encourage the practice of following them to the letter.

Some employees may interpret rules that were intended to describe minimally acceptable levels of performance as describing the maximum level of performance for which they should aim. As a result, their performance may suffer.

In addition, rigid adherence to rules and regulations can discourage workers from taking the initiative and being creative, and the organization can subsequently lose its ability to anticipate or adapt to changing conditions. During the 1980s, rules that required lengthy approval reviews for even minor design changes limited the ability of many U.S. firms then in the consumer-electronics industry to improve existing products or introduce new ones. As a result, once-dominant U.S. companies such as General Electric and Sunbeam are no longer major participants in markets for everything from hair-curling irons to stereo receivers. Forgone flexibility can cost organizations precious markets—and sometimes even their survival.

Standardization can also undermine efficiency by narrowing the scope of workplace activities to the point where employees feel bored and unchallenged. Oversimplification caused by too much standardization can contribute to serious problems of workforce motivation and, as a consequence, poor performance.[29] Groups of workers may develop informal social structures in which low productivity is the norm. Employees may even turn to dangerous horseplay or costly sabotage to break up the monotony or to "get even" with a company they perceive as insensitive and uncaring. Sometimes the job redesign and enrichment procedures described in Chapter 7 can provide sufficient relief in such circumstances. In other cases, nothing short of organizational restructuring will succeed in countering the effects of overspecialization.

In sum, the standardization that characterizes all bureaucratic structures can have important drawbacks. To the degree that these drawbacks impede efficiency, bureaucracy fails to achieve its intended purpose and can threaten the organization's success and continued well-being. Firms facing this danger have grown beyond the developmental stages of formalization and elaboration, and now find themselves entering into the stage of transformation.

Managers of organizations in the stage of transformation confront the challenge of dealing with business conditions that require the resources of a large organization but the flexibility of a small one. Global competition, technological volatility, and trends toward mass customization of products and services often contribute to this challenge.[30] Due to the drawbacks just described, bureaucratic structures often depress organizational performance under such circumstances. For this reason, entry into the stage of transformation is accompanied by the task of converting bureaucratic structures into either of two postbureaucratic alternatives, the modular structure or the virtual structure.

Both of these postbureaucratic structures are organic, meaning that they are based on decentralized decision making and mutual adjustment conducted with the assistance of computerized networks rather than on centralization and hierarchy with direct supervision or standardization (see the Securing Competitive Advantage box). As a consequence, both are quite flexible. Choices between the two involve trade-offs between completing the entire process of design, production, and distribution within the confines of a single organization, in the case of the modular structure, or relying on a network of several organizations connected together by temporary alliances, in the case of the virtual structure. At this advanced stage of growth and development, choices pertaining to organization design are influenced by two contingency factors: environmental turbulence and transaction costs.

Environmental Turbulence

The term **environmental turbulence** describes the speed and scope of change that occurs in the environment surrounding an organization. High turbulence is characterized by simultaneous and extremely high levels of environmental change, complexity (therefore uncertainty), and diversity, as well as rapid technological advances including the use of team-managed technologies. Such conditions, sometimes labeled *hypercompetitive,* require flexibility beyond the limits of bureaucracy, necessitating progression to postbureaucratic structures.[31] At the other extreme, low turbulence exists when levels of environmental change, complexity, diversity, and technological considerations are not simultaneous or less extreme in effect. The flexibility required by such conditions can be supplied in traditional bureaucratic structures by adding lateral linkages or opting for matrix or multiunit structuring, as suggested by the technological and environmental contingency models discussed earlier.

By determining the degree of flexibility and adaptability an organization must have to perform effectively, the level of environmental turbulence can also act as a contingency factor that influences choices between the two postbureaucratic alternatives. Compared with bureaucratic structures, modular structures are far more flexible.[32] For instance, General Electric's decision to allow its units to function as independent entities has enabled each of the company's businesses—consumer finance, jet engines and avionics, military contracting, and so on—to adapt itself to its own competitive situation without affecting the operations of other units.

Relying on temporary associations, as in virtual structures, allows for even greater flexibility. Such associations, in the form of short-term contracts or longer-term joint-venture relationships, are easier to modify and eliminate than are the interconnections among parts of a single firm.[33] For example, after IBM, Apple, and Motorola combined forces to design a new computer memory chip—the Power PC chip—and introduce it to computer manufacturers throughout the world, the companies disbanded joint operations, retrieved the resources they had loaned to the Power PC project, and moved on to other activities of their own.[34] In sum, whereas high levels of environmental turbulence push for the adoption of modular structures, extremely high levels encourage the use of virtual structures.

Transaction Costs

Decisions about "doing it yourself" in a modular structure versus "contracting it out" in a virtual structure also boil down to a comparison of the costs of sustaining a single organization and maintaining a unified structure, on the one hand, with the

SECURING COMPETITIVE ADVANTAGE

TECHNOLOGY ENABLES POSTBUREAUCRATIC ORGANIZATION

Collaborative technologies lie at the heart of recent advances in organizational structure and design. Consider the case of Lockheed Martin Aeronautics, manufacturer of the U.S. Defense Department's twenty-first-century combat jet. To build the Joint Strike Fighter, Lockheed must coordinate the work of the eighty suppliers working at 187 locations that design and build component parts. To accomplish this feat Lockheed relies on its tech group, which has created a system to connect manufacturing partners together, and has also developed links between these partners and end users in the U.S. Air Force, Navy, and Marines, the U.K.'s Defense Ministry, and eight other allies.

Lockheed and its partners use a system of ninety Web software tools to share designs, track documents, and measure progress against performance targets. Individuals sitting at more than 40,000 computers share the information with one another necessary for collaboration to take place. In this instance, virtual organization spans geographic distance and company boundaries to create an integrated manufacturing entity.

Or consider Microsoft Corporation and the process that led to the development of the Xbox gaming console. Working with manufacturing partner Flextronics, Microsoft used Web-based collaboration to cut about two months from the original product introduction schedule. In one instance, the bracket intended to hold the console's hard drive in place was redesigned by Microsoft engineers, who then contacted their counterparts at Flextronics by e-mail to ensure that the change would not create manufacturing problems. A copy of this message also went to Flextronics parts people, who assessed effects on the company's supply chain and confirmed their ability to deal with the change in a return e-mail message. After receiving confirmation, Microsoft engineers created a prototype and approved production of the revised design. Thus, in less than a week the two companies were able to envision, test, and implement a change in design that could have taken a month or more without the support of collaborative technology.

Once the dream of futurists, collaborative technologies are now a reality due to the advent of Web applications that enable dissimilar computers to communicate with one another, plus wireless communications protocols that allow portability and specialized software products that facilitate information sharing and collaborative modification. Using collaborative technology, General Motors can get a car into production in eighteen months, down from the forty-two months it took in the mid-1990s. Land O'Lakes Inc. saves $40,000 per month by using the Web and collaborative software to maximize loads in trucks it shares with Georgia-Pacific and other companies. United Parcel Service dockworkers have increased company productivity by 35 percent by using wireless Web-based tracking programs to enter and modify shipping information. In these and similar instances, collaborative technologies yield visible payoffs in profitability and competitive advantage.

Sources: F. Keenan and S. E. Ante, "The New Teamwork," *Business Week*, February 18, 2002, pp. EB12–EB-16; H. Green, S. Rosenbush, R. O. Crockett, and S. Holmes, "Wi-Fi Means Business," *Business Week*, April 28, 2003, pp. 86–92.

costs of writing acceptable contracts and ensuring contractual compliance, on the other. As suggested by economist Oliver Williamson, such **transaction costs** represent a second contingency factor that influences whether managers opt for the permanence of a single organization or the transience of temporary relationships.[35]

Transaction costs associated with preserving a single company or maintaining contractual relationships are affected by two important considerations. First, people are limited in the amount of information they can process, and greater complexity in a particular business situation creates a need for information processing that can prove overwhelming. This situation makes contracting out work difficult, because it increases feelings of uncertainty on the part of contractors. In turn, uncertainty increases the reluctance of prospective contractors to consign costly resources or commit to long-term relationships. Consider, for instance, the situation in which you are looking for an apartment to rent. Are you likely to sign a lease for an apartment that you have never seen, monthly payments that have yet to be specified, or a period of time that may change without notice? Or are you more likely to sign a lease when you know exactly which apartment you will live in, what your monthly payments will be, and how long the lease will last? For most people, the uncertainty of the first alternative makes it the less attractive of the two options.

In contrast, creating a single organization can help cope with human limitations in the face of complexity because it affords a sense of social stability and permanence. Containing business transactions within a single organization also allows the use of basic coordination mechanisms and makes it easier to involve many more people in decision making. All of these factors help reduce the uncertainty of work relationships. People who opt for co-ops or condominiums instead of apartments are, to some extent, buying into a permanent organization. This type of organization provides them with the greater stability of permanent ownership and unites them with other owners who share similar interests in housing quality and affordability. Items that might otherwise require a contract among co-owners can be handled through periodic meetings in which the owners discuss problems and negotiate acceptable solutions.

Second, contracting becomes more difficult and the transaction costs of contractual relationships are increased by the threat that one or more contractors will use deception and seek to profit at the expense of the others. The threat of opportunism becomes especially troublesome when few prospective contractors are available, because the low substitutability affords them power, which in turn enables them to demand special treatment (see Chapter 11). Opportunism also emerges as an issue when uncertainty hides the true intentions of contractors, blocking efforts to verify their honesty. In the absence of such verification, contractors are well advised to prepare for the worst and expect deceit. Costly surveillance should be conducted to detect opportunism before it can prove destructive.

Thus, considerations of bounded rationality and complexity drive up the transaction costs of contracting. In such situations—where uncertainty about the future undermines temporary relationships—the modular structure is favored. Likewise, concerns about opportunism increase the transaction costs of contracting and favor the modular structure. In contrast, the virtual structure is preferable when prospective contractors can negotiate good-faith contracts that are fair to all parties, honest in intention, and verifiable in every regard.[36]

Final Considerations

For large organizations that have progressed through the developmental stages of formalization and elaboration, transition to a modular structure is a matter of forming teams and giving them autonomy by decentralizing operations and reducing middle management. Transition to the virtual structure is more dramatic, requiring massive downsizing and the formation of contractual relationships. General Motors' North American operations appear headed in this direction, as GM's management is selling off the company's parts-manufacturing facilities and relying more heavily on outside contractors.

For small organizations that have jumped directly from inception or early formalization to transition, adoption of a modular structure means rapid growth through merger or internal expansion. In contrast, movement into a virtual structure requires the identification of prospective contractors and development of contractual relationships.

If successful, transitions that occur during the stage of transformation result in postbureaucratic structures that enable companies to act as both large and small entities simultaneously. Through mutual adjustment and decentralization, firms are able to realize extensive flexibility. Through large size, whether real or virtual, firms are able to control the scope of resources needed to accomplish complex tasks in an efficient manner. Key to the success of such organizations are the information-processing networks that tie their members together. In the absence of modern computer equipment and the intranets or internets it supports, postbureaucratic structures could not exist.

SUMMARY

Organization design is the process of structuring an organization to enhance its *organizational effectiveness* in the light of the *contingency factors* with which it must deal. As they develop, organizations grow through the stages of *inception, formalization, elaboration,* and *transformation.* During inception, structural effectiveness is influenced by the contingency factors of *organization size* and *ownership norms.* Managers choose between the prebureaucratic alternatives of the simple undifferentiated and simple differentiated structures. During the stages of formalization and elaboration, structural effectiveness becomes a function of the contingency factors of *core technology* and *external environment.* Managers then choose between the bureaucratic alternatives of functional, divisional, matrix, and multiunit structures. During the stage of transformation, structural effectiveness is shaped by the contingency factors of *environmental turbulence* and *transaction costs.* In this stage, managers choose between the postbureaucratic alternatives of modular and virtual structures.

REVIEW QUESTIONS

1. Name a specific business organization in your community and identify three of its most important constituency groups. What interests do each of the constituency groups expect the organization to fulfill? How does the organization's structure affect its ability to satisfy these interests? Is the company effective?

2. How do mechanistic structures differ from organic structures? What are their relative strengths and weaknesses? Which bureaucratic structure is the most mechanistic? Why? Which bureaucratic structure is the most organic? Why?

3. How does the developmental stage of an organization affect its structure? What roles do age and size play in this process?

4. Why do organizations in the inception stage usually have prebureaucratic structures? What effects do organization size and ownership norms have on organization design at this stage?

5. In which of Woodward's and Thompson's technologies is work routine and predictable? In which is work nonroutine and unpredictable? What kinds of structures are most fitting for each of the two clusters of technologies you have identified? In general terms, how does the routineness and predictability of an organization's technology affect the appropriateness of different types of structure?

6. Explain why environmental change impedes an organization's ability to coordinate by means of standardization. What sort of coordination is used instead? Why does environmental complexity push an organization toward decentralization?

7. Why is environmental receptivity an issue only for organizations that face complex environments? Under conditions of environmental complexity, why should the centralization stimulated by hostility be eliminated as the environment becomes munificent?

8. How does the developmental stage of transformation differ from the stages of formalization and elaboration? Why does this difference push the organization toward the adoption of a postbureaucratic structure? How do environmental turbulence and transaction costs affect the process of organization design at this developmental stage?

LEARNING THROUGH EXPERIENCE

DIAGNOSTIC QUESTIONS 13-1

Organization Design

The following questions should help you during the process of designing or redesigning an organization's structure by guiding you through the diagnosis of the contingency factors we have discussed.

1. What kind of structure does the organization currently have? What is its primary means of coordination? Do the titles of its line vice presidents provide evidence of one particular form of structure?

2. Does the organization's current structure match the one suggested by the firm's developmental stage and age? If the firm is young and in the inception stage, does it have a prebureaucratic structure? If it is older and in the formalization stage, does it have a bureaucratic, functional structure? If it is in the elaboration stage, does it have a bureaucratic divisional, matrix, or multiunit structure? If it has matured to the point of transformation, does it have a postbureaucratic structure?

3. If in the inception stage, is the firm's size twelve or fewer employees, suggesting the appropriateness of a simple undifferentiated structure? If larger than twelve employees, does the firm have a simple undifferentiated structure? Is the firm so large that it has actually progressed to the formalization stage and should consider adopting a bureaucratic structure?

4. If in the formalization or elaboration stage, is the organization's primary purpose to manufacture a tangible product? Does it use small-batch, continuous-process, or flexible-cell production? If it uses one of these production strategies, does the organization have an organic bureaucratic structure? Is it functional or divisional with lateral linkages, or a matrix, or multiunit structuring? Or does it use mass production? Does the organization have a mechanistic structure? Is it functional or divisional?

5. If in the formalization or elaboration stage, is the organization's primary purpose to provide a service? Does it use intensive technology? If so, does the organization have one of the organic structures mentioned earlier? Or does it use mediating technology or long-linked technology? If so, does the organization have one of the mechanistic structures mentioned earlier?

6. If in the formalization or elaboration stage, is the organization's external environment stable or dynamic? Does the organization's primary mode of coordination match the amount of change in its environment? Is the environment simple or complex? Does the degree of decentralization in the organization's structure match the amount of complexity in its environment?

7. If in the formalization or elaboration stage, is the organization's external environment uncertain? If so, do you see evidence of significant boundary-spanning activities? Is the environment munificent or hostile? If hostility exists and the environment is complex, is the organization temporarily centralized? Is the environment uniform or diverse? Does the type of departmentation used to structure the firm match the diversity of its environment?

8. If in the transformation stage, does environmental turbulence push the organization in the direction of adopting a virtual structure? Or do transaction costs push it toward adoption of a modular structure?

9. Do the various contingencies seem to mandate the same type of structure? If not, and no recent changes might explain the choice of structure, look for faulty diagnosis in one or more of your contingency analyses.

10. If the contingencies *do* seem to point toward the same type of structure, is this structure the same as the one the organization has now? If not, the structure recommended by your analysis should be implemented; structural redesign is needed. If the current structure is the one recommended by your analysis, however, structural deficiencies are not the root of the organization's problems. Look for individual or group-level problems instead.

EXERCISE 13-1

Open System Planning

Mark S. Plovnick, University of the Pacific
Ronald E. Fry, Case Western Reserve University
W. Warner Burke, Columbia University

Open system planning (OSP) is a technique that can be used to clarify an organization's mission and plan how to achieve that mission in the face of demands and expectations originating in the environment. These demands come from such constituency groups as employees, customers, and raw material suppliers. OSP is an integral part of the process of strategic planning and a useful way to improve an organization's understanding of its environment.

An OSP intervention begins with a discussion of the organization's basic goals, mission, and reason for existence. The participants in this initial OSP session then identify the constituency groups that can influence the organization's accomplishment of its goals and mission. They describe the current relations between the organization and each of its constituency groups. They assess these relations, deciding whether they satisfy both the organization and the constituency group. If this assessment uncovers dissatisfaction, participants determine how relations ought to change to achieve a good balance between organizational effectiveness and constituency satisfaction.

Next, OSP participants assess the organization's current response to each constituency group by answering several questions. What does this type of constituency want from us? What are we currently doing to respond to this demand? Is our current response moving us closer to where we want to be in relation to our organization's goals and purpose?

Finally, OSP participants decide what actions, if any, must be taken to redirect the organization toward the desired state of affairs.

Adapted with the authors' permission from M. S. Plovnick, R. E. Fry, and W. W. Burke, *Organization Development: Exercises, Cases, and Readings* (Boston: Little, Brown and Company, 1982), pp. 67–73. Copyright 1982 by Mark S. Plovnick, Ronald E. Fry, and W. Warner Burke.

This exercise will give you the opportunity to experience the OSP process first-hand as you work with other class members to assess the environment and constituency groups of a real organization.

Step One: Pre-Class Preparation

In class, you will perform parts of each phase of the OSP process. The focal organization will be the school or education program in which you are enrolled (unless your instructor specifies another organization). As preparation for class, read the entire exercise. Then think about what the basic mission or purpose of the organization should be and write a mission statement. Finally, identify five constituency groups that expect the organization to do something for them. List these groups and their demands here:

1. _____

2. _____

3. _____

4. _____

5. _____

Step Two: Defining a Mission

The class should divide into planning groups of four to six members each. If you have already established permanent groups, reassemble in those groups now. In each group, members should share the mission statements they developed before class and reach a consensus about the organization's mission. Next, your instructor will lead the entire class in developing a mission statement to be used for the rest of the exercise.

Step Three: Identifying Constituency Groups

The class as a whole should agree on the key constituency groups in the environment that place demands on the organization. If the organization being targeted is your school, examples of these groups might include students, faculty, alumni, and employees. Each planning group should be assigned one constituency group to consider in the next step of this exercise (every group should be assigned a different constituency).

Step Four: Open System Planning in Groups

To experience the OSP process, each planning group should complete the remaining phases of the process, focusing only on the constituency group assigned to it. Following is a description of the five phases you should complete:

1. *Identification of current demands.* What does the constituency group currently expect from or demand of the organization? (estimated time: 15 minutes)

2. *Current response.* For the one or two most important of these demands, what is the organization's current response? Is it a response of action or inaction? (estimated time: 10 minutes)

3. *Future demands.* Considering the current response and any changes or trends that are likely to occur over the next two years, what will the key demands from your constituency group be two years from now? (estimated time: 10 minutes)

4. *Ideal state.* Imagine two years from now. What kinds of expectations or demands would the organization like to see from your constituency group? (estimated time: 10 minutes)

5. *Identifying gaps and planning action.* Compare and contrast the results of phases 3 and 4. What gaps exist between anticipated and ideal demands? Choose one of these gaps and suggest what the organization should do to alter its current course. (estimated time: 15 minutes)

You will have 1 hour to complete these five phases, so you must manage your time carefully. A spokesperson should be ready to present a summary of the group's work in Step Five.

Step Five: Planning Group Reports and Discussion

A spokesperson from each group should take no more than 5 minutes to summarize what the group discovered, discussed, and concluded about its constituency group. Any suggestions for action should be listed on a chalkboard, overhead projector, or flip chart.

Step Six: Class Discussion of the OSP Process

The class as a whole should review the OSP process just completed and discuss the following questions:

1. Do the planning group reports reveal any potential conflicts between satisfying different constituency groups' demands? That is, will satisfying one constituency make it difficult to satisfy another? How might the organization resolve such conflicts?

2. Do the actions proposed by the planning groups fit together into a meaningful action plan? If so, describe the plan. If not, how can they be made to do so?

3. What changes, if any, would you recommend in the mission statement developed in Step Two? How does knowledge about an organization's environment affect perceptions of its mission?

4. How would you expect OSP as conducted in real organizations to differ from the process you have completed in class? In what ways might it be more complicated? Less complicated?

5. What kinds of organizations or situations do you see as likely candidates for OSP? Which ones should probably not use it?

Conclusion

Open system planning is not a panacea for all organizations. It requires a significant investment of time and energy. In addition, the OSP process may involve a great deal of ambiguity and stress. Nevertheless, it can enable organizations to manage their responses to important but often conflicting environmental demands. OSP can also be used as a method to help the members of organizations achieve consensus about organizational missions and goals.

Organization Culture
Elements of Organization Culture
Managing Organization Culture

Change and Organization Development
Resistance to Change
Action Research

Organization Development Interventions
Interpersonal Interventions
Group Interventions
Intergroup Interventions
Organizational Interventions

Evaluating Change and Development
Summary
Review Questions

Learning Through Experience
Diagnostic Questions 14-1: Culture, Change, and Organization Development
Exercise 14-1: Intergroup Mirroring

Culture, Change, and Organization Development

"We have to change our culture from the manufacturing industry to knowledge-based global culture. Kind of a reinvention of the business model itself." This statement from Nobuyuki Idei, CEO of Sony, summarizes the central challenges facing Idei and his company. Founded as the Tokyo Telecommunications Engineering Company, Sony has enjoyed great success with such products as Walkman personal radios, Trinitron televisions, and PlayStation game consoles. To survive, however, many in the company believe that Sony will have to become the home of connected entertainment in the digital age.

Idei wants to reinvent Sony, transforming it from a company that makes self-contained products shipped in boxes to one that produces an array of interconnected devices, services, and experiences, all provided through a wide-spectrum network. To begin this transformation, he has attacked and broken down the "silos" sheltering Sony's various operating companies from one another. While it was once acceptable for a unit to pursue profitability and market share without consulting elsewhere in the firm, now units are expected to communicate with each other on a regular basis.

At the same time, Idei must walk a fine line and continue to feed the loyalty of key managers accustomed to autonomy and self-sufficiency. One of these, Ken Kutaragi, creator of PlayStations 1 and 2, had run his division for many years without intervention from corporate headquarters. Recently, Idei has responded to Kutaragi's independence by assigning him broader responsibility but requiring closer coordination and control. According to Idei, "He's kind of a symbol for Sony, how the rulebreaker can survive with the rulemaker. And now, the rulebreaker has become the rulemaker."

To survive as a company in a world dominated by broadband networks, Sony will have to reinvent itself as a culture of cooperators working together in a network of information and service. "We don't want to go back to being a box company," said Kunitake Ando, keynote presenter at the 2003 Consumer Electronics Show. "If we lose our dreams [of a future in broadband networking] it's not Sony at all."[1]

Managing the organization, as an organization, is an extremely complex task. As discussed in Chapters 11 through 13, the management of macro organizational behavior requires that managers deal with issues of power, conflict, structure, and organization design. In addition, as will be discussed in this chapter, managers must consider and actively shape the culture of norms, values, and ways of thinking that influence behavior throughout the firm. In the process, they must solve problems originating in the process and outcomes of change.

For this reason, Chapter 14 discusses the topics of organizational culture, change, and development. It first focuses on organizational culture, indicating how a firm's culture affects and reflects issues of power, structure, and organization design. Next, the chapter discusses issues associated with change in organizations and introduces organization development as a process of change management. It concludes by describing organization development interventions that managers can use to initiate change aimed at resolving many of the problems identified throughout this book.

ORGANIZATION CULTURE

Every *formal* organization of prescribed jobs and structural relationships includes an *informal* organization characterized by unofficial rules, procedures, and interconnections. This informal organization arises as employees make spontaneous, unauthorized changes in the way things are done. In discussing emergent role characteristics (Chapter 8) and group development (Chapter 9), we have already discussed to some extent how such day-to-day adjustments occur in organizations. As these adjustments shape and change the formal way of doing things, a culture of attitudes and understandings emerges that is shared among co-workers. This culture is a

pattern of basic assumptions—invented, discovered, or developed [by a firm's members] to cope with problems of external adaptation and internal integration—that has worked well enough to be considered valid and, therefore, to be taught to new members as the correct way to perceive, think, and feel in relation to those problems.[2]

From this description, it follows that an organization's **culture** is an informal, shared way of perceiving life and membership in the organization that binds members together and influences what they think about themselves and their work.

In the process of helping to create a mutual understanding of organizational life, organizational culture fulfills four basic functions. First, it *gives members an organizational identity*. That is, sharing norms, values, and perceptions provides people with a sense of togetherness that promotes a feeling of common purpose. Second, it *facilitates collective commitment*. The common purpose that grows out of a shared culture tends to elicit feelings of attachment among all those who accept the culture as their own. Third, it *promotes organizational stability*. By nurturing a shared sense of identity and commitment, culture encourages lasting integration and cooperation among the members of an organization. Fourth, it shapes behavior by *helping members make sense of their surroundings.* An organization's culture serves as a source of shared meanings that explain why things occur in the way that they do.[3] By fulfilling these four basic functions, the culture of an organization serves as a sort of social glue that helps reinforce persistent, coordinated behaviors at work. In so doing, an organization's culture can enhance its performance, especially when conditions in the surrounding environment favor stability and routine.[4]

Elements of Organization Culture

Deep within the culture of every organization is a collection of fundamental norms and values that shapes members' behaviors and helps them understand the surrounding organization. In some companies, such as Polaroid, 3M, and DuPont, cultural norms and values emphasize the importance of discovering new materials or technologies and developing them into new products. In other companies, such as AT&T and Maytag Appliances, cultural norms and values focus on attaining high product quality.[5] Such fundamental norms and values serve as the ultimate source of the shared perceptions, thoughts, and feelings constituting the culture of an organization.[6]

These fundamental norms and values are expressed and passed from one person to another through *surface elements* of the culture, such as those overviewed in Table 14-1, which help employees interpret everyday organizational events.[7] One type of surface element, **ceremonies,** includes special events in which the members of a company celebrate the myths, heroes, and symbols of their culture.[8] Thus ceremonies exemplify and reinforce important cultural norms and values. In sales-focused organizations such as Mary Kay or Amway, annual ceremonies are held to recognize and reward outstanding sales representatives. Holding these ceremonies is intended to inspire sales representatives who have been less effective to adopt the norms and values of their successful colleagues. Whether they personify the "Mary Kay approach" or the "Amway philosophy," the people who are recognized and rewarded in these ceremonies greatly enhance the attractiveness of their companies' cultural underpinnings.

Often, organizational ceremonies incorporate various **rites,** or ceremonial activities meant to send particular messages or accomplish specific purposes.[9] For instance, *rites of passage* are used to initiate new members into the organization and can convey

TABLE 14-1
Surface Elements of Organization Cultures

Element	Description
Ceremonies	Special events in which organization members celebrate the myths, heroes, and symbols of their firm
Rites	Ceremonial activities meant to communicate specific ideas or accomplish particular purposes
Rituals	Actions that are repeated regularly to reinforce cultural norms and values
Stories	Accounts of past events that illustrate and transmit deeper cultural norms and values
Myths	Fictional stories that help explain activities or events that might otherwise be puzzling
Heroes	Successful people who embody the values and character of the organization and its culture
Symbols	Objects, actions, or events that have special meanings and enable organization members to exchange complex ideas and emotional messages
Language	A collection of verbal symbols that often reflect the organization's particular culture

important aspects of the culture to them. In some businesses, new recruits are required to spend considerable time talking with veteran employees and learning about cultural norms and values by listening to stories about their experiences at work. In other companies, the rite of passage consists of a brief talk about company rules and regulations delivered by a human resources staff member to newcomers during their first day at work. Little more than a formal welcoming, it does not really help newcomers learn about the culture of the firm.

When employees are transferred, demoted, or fired because of low productivity, incompatible values, or other personal failings, *rites of degradation* may draw the attention of others to the limits of acceptable behavior. Today, rites of degradation are typically deemphasized, involving little more than quiet reassignment. In the past, they were occasionally much more dramatic. In the early days of NCR, for example, executives who had incurred the founder's wrath would learn that they had lost their jobs by discovering their desks burning on the lawn in front of corporate headquarters.

Rites of enhancement also emphasize the limits of appropriate behavior, but in a positive way. These activities, which recognize increasing status or position in a firm, may range from simple promotion announcements to intricate recognition ceremonies, such as the Mary Kay and Amway ceremonies mentioned earlier.

In *rites of integration,* members of an organization become aware of the common feelings that bond them together. Official titles and hierarchical differences may be intentionally ignored in rites of this sort so that members can get to know one another as people rather than as managers, staff specialists, clerks, or laborers. At Tandem Computer, for example, a "TGIF" party is held each week, giving employees the opportunity to chat informally over pizza and drinks. Company picnics, golf outings, softball games, and holiday parties can also serve as rites of integration.

A rite that is repeated on a regular basis becomes a **ritual,** a ceremonial event that continually reinforces key norms and values. The morning coffee break, for example, is a ritual that strengthens important workplace relationships. So, too, is the annual stockholder meeting held by management to convey cultural norms and values to company shareholders. Just as routine coffee breaks enable co-workers to gossip among themselves and reaffirm important interpersonal relationships, annual stockholder meetings give the company the opportunity to strengthen connections between itself and people who would otherwise have little more than a limited financial interest in its continued well-being.

Stories are accounts of past events with which all employees are familiar and that serve as reminders of cultural values.[10] As organization members tell stories and think about the messages conveyed by the stories, the concrete examples described in this manner facilitate their later recall of the concepts presented. Stories also provide information about historical events in the development of a company that can improve employees' understanding of the present:

In one organization, employees tell a story about how the company avoided a mass layoff when almost every other company in the industry . . . felt forced to lay off employees in large numbers. The company . . . managed to avoid a layoff of 10 percent of their employees by having everyone in the company take a 10 percent cut in salary and come to work only 9 out of 10 days. This company experience is thus called the "nine-day fortnight."[11]

The story of the nine-day fortnight vividly captures a cultural value—namely, that looking after employees' well-being is the right thing to do. Present-day employees continue to tell the story because it reminds them that their company will avoid layoffs as much as possible during economic downturns.

A **myth** is a special type of story that provides a fictional but plausible explanation for an event or thing that might otherwise seem puzzling or mysterious. Ancient civilizations often created myths about gods and other supernatural forces to explain natural occurrences, such as the rising and setting of the sun, the phases of the moon, and the formation of thunderstorms.

Similarly, the members of a modern-day organization may develop fictionalized accounts of the company's founders, origins, or historical development to provide a framework for explaining current activities in their firm. In many instances, organizational myths contain at least a grain of truth. For example, myths retold throughout General Motors about the management prowess of Alfred P. Sloan, one of the company's earliest chief executives, are based in part on a study of GM's structure and procedures that Sloan performed from 1919 to 1920. This bit of truthful information makes myths sound completely true.

Heroes are people who embody the values of an organization and its culture:

Richard A. Drew, a banjo-playing college dropout working in 3M's research lab during the 1920s, [helped] some colleagues solve a problem they had with masking tape. Soon thereafter, DuPont came out with cellophane. Drew decided he could go DuPont one better and coated the cellophane with a colorless adhesive to bind things together—and Scotch tape was born. In the 3M tradition, Drew carried the ball himself by managing the development and initial production of his invention. Moving up through the ranks, he went on to become technical director of the company and showed other employees just how they could succeed in similar fashion at 3M.[12]

Heroes such as 3M's Drew serve as role models, illustrating personal performance that is not only desirable but attainable. Like stories, heroes provide concrete examples that make the guiding norms and values of a company readily apparent.

Symbols are objects, actions, or events to which people have assigned special meanings. Company logos, flags, and trade names are all familiar symbols. For example, Mercedes's three-point star logo is synonymous with quality in most people's minds, and even the youngest children know that the McDonald's arches mark the locations of fast-food restaurants. Symbols represent a conscious or unconscious association with some wider, usually more abstract, concept or meaning.[13] In organizations, they may include official titles, such as chief operating officer. Special eating facilities, official automobiles, or airplanes also may be given symbolic status. Sometimes even the size of an employee's office or its placement or furnishings have special symbolic value.[14]

Symbols mean more than might seem immediately apparent. For instance, despite the fact that a reserved parking space consists of just a few square feet of asphalt, it may symbolize its holder's superior hierarchical status or clout. It is this ability to convey a complex message in an efficient, economical manner that makes symbols so useful and important:

When two people shake hands, the action symbolizes their coming together. The handshake may also be rich in other kinds of symbolic significance. Between freemasons it reaffirms a bond of brotherhood, and loyalty to the order to which they belong. Between politicians it is often used to symbolize an intention to cooperate and work together. To members of the counter-culture of the 1960s and early 1970s, their special hand clasp and a cry of "Right On!" affirmed a set of divergent values and opposition to the system. The handshake is more than just a shaking of hands. It symbolizes a particular kind of relationship between those involved.[15]

Clearly, symbols are absolutely necessary to communication. They convey emotional messages that cannot easily be put into words. Without symbols, many of the fundamental norms and values of an organization's culture could not be shared among organizational members.

Language is another means of sharing cultural ideas and understandings. In many organizations, the language used by members reflects the organization's particular culture.[16] Dot-com companies were well known to refer to the use of loaned funding in terms of "burn rate." *Bandwidth,* a term once used in Internet firms to indicate message capacity, has now become part of the larger U.S. national culture.[17]

Managing Organization Culture

Organizational culture grows out of informal, unofficial ways of doing things. In turn, it influences the attitudes that employees hold and the behaviors in which they engage at work, thereby shaping the way that employees perceive and react to formally defined jobs and structural arrangements.[18] These relationships arise because cultural norms and values provide **social information,** which helps employees determine the meaning of their work and the organization around them.[19] For example, in a company that follows a policy of promotion from within—wherein managers are chosen from among eligible subordinates rather than being hired from outside the firm—employees tend to view their jobs as critical to personal success. By encouraging employees to perceive success as something to be valued and pursued, cultural norms stressing the importance of hard work also encourage the development of a need for achievement (see Chapter 5) and motivate high productivity. In sum, as indicated in Figure 14-1, cultural norms and values convey social information that can influence the way people choose to behave on the job. They do so by affecting the way employees perceive themselves, their work, and the organization.

Can organizational culture be managed? It might seem that the answer to this question should be "no," for the following reasons:

1. Cultures are so spontaneous, elusive, and hidden that they cannot be accurately diagnosed or intentionally changed.

FIGURE 14-1   Cultural Elements as Social Information

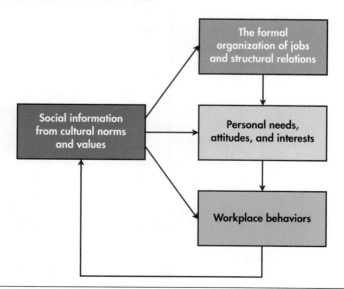

Source: Based on G. R. Salancik and J. Pfeffer, "A Social Information Processing Approach to Job Attitudes and Task Design," *Administrative Science Quarterly* 23 (1978), 224–253.

2. Considerable experience and deep personal insight are required to truly understand an organization's culture, making management infeasible in most instances.
3. Several subcultures may exist within a single organizational culture, complicating the task of managing organizational culture to the point where it becomes impossible.
4. Cultures provide organization members with continuity and stability. As a consequence, members are likely to resist even modest efforts at cultural management or change because they fear discontinuity and instability.[20]

Many experts disagree with these arguments, however, and suggest that organizational cultures can be managed by using either of two approaches.

In the first approach, **symbolic management,** managers attempt to influence deep cultural norms and values by shaping the surface cultural elements, such as symbols, stories, and ceremonies, that people use to express and transmit cultural understandings.[21] Managers can accomplish this shaping in several ways. For example, they can issue public statements about their vision for the future of the company. They can recount stories about themselves and the company. They can use and enrich the shared company language. In this way, managers not only communicate the company's central norms and key values, but also devise new ways of expressing them.

Managers who practice symbolic management realize that every managerial behavior broadcasts a message to employees about the organization's norms and values. They consciously choose to do specific things that will symbolize and strengthen a desirable culture. The fact that symbolic management involves the manipulation of symbols is apt to lead some managers to underestimate its importance. Telling stories, performing ceremonies, and anointing heroes might seem soft-headed or a waste of time to managers who do not understand the importance of managing culture. In reality, playing down the importance of symbolic management can have disastrous consequences. Managers at companies ranging from Disney to DuPont agree that managing symbols—and the culture they support—is critical to organizational success (see the Securing Competitive Advantage box).[22]

The second approach to managing the culture of an organization is to use organization development (OD) interventions. OD interventions (discussed in detail in the next two sections) can contribute to cultural management by helping the members of an organization progress through the following steps:

1. *Identifying current norms and values.* OD interventions typically require people to list the norms and values that influence their attitudes and behaviors at work. This kind of list gives members insight into the organization culture.
2. *Plotting new directions.* OD interventions often make it possible for the members of an organization to evaluate present personal, group, and organization goals and to consider whether these goals represent the objectives they truly want to achieve. Such evaluations often point out the need to plot new directions.
3. *Identifying new norms and values.* OD interventions that stimulate thinking about new directions also provide organization members with an opportunity to develop new norms and values that will promote a move toward the desirable new goals.
4. *Identifying culture gaps.* To the extent that current (step 1) and desired (step 3) norms and values are articulated, the OD process enables organization members to identify culture gaps—that is, the differences between the current and desired situations.
5. *Closing culture gaps.* OD interventions give people the opportunity to reach agreements stating that new norms and values should replace old ones and that every employee should take responsibility for managing and reinforcing these changes.[23]

SECURING COMPETITIVE ADVANTAGE

TRAGIC FAILURES CAUSED BY NASA'S OVERCONFIDENT CULTURE

How critical is an organization's culture to its success? Consider the case of NASA and the tragedies of the space shuttles Challenger and Columbia. Challenger, lost in 1986 due to failure during launch of o-ring seals in the shuttle's solid fuel boosters, was later said to have been the victim of a culture that did not permit warnings about possible failures to reach launch controllers. Columbia, lost in 2003 during reentry due to a breach in the shuttle's wing that allowed the entry of superheated gasses, was similarly said to have been the casualty of a self-censuring culture.

In both instances, investigators found that insiders had known for quite some time that the kinds of failures that caused the tragedies were likely to occur. Regarding Challenger, engineering tests had indicated that the shuttle's rubber o-rings were susceptible to the effects of low temperatures and that cold weather such as that on the day of the launch could cause the rings to harden and become ineffective. Nonetheless, launch-day warnings from engineers at the shuttle's manufacturer were summarily ignored by NASA officials. With respect to Columbia, pieces of insulating foam material like the one that broke away from the shuttle's booster and caused the hole in its wing had been observed breaking away during earlier launches. The fact that these previous flights had ended without incident was interpreted by NASA officials as evidence that Columbia would also return successfully.

According to investigators, in the period leading up to the loss of the Columbia, NASA mission managers fell into the habit of accepting significant flaws in the shuttle system as normal and tended to ignore the possibility that these problems might foreshadow tragic failures. Investigators noted that this was an "echo" of some of the root causes of the Challenger disaster nearly twenty years earlier and blamed both on cultural flaws that persisted within NASA. In particular, investigators cited "ineffective leadership" that "failed to fulfill the implicit contract to do whatever is possible to ensure the safety of the crew." In addition, investigators indicated that the broader NASA culture discouraged dissenting views on safety issues and ultimately created "blind spots" about the risks of anomalous incidents. As a result, mission managers failed to give appropriate consideration to information indicating possible catastrophes, and two crews were lost.

NASA's failures are obviously an extreme case. However, similar cultural flaws in other organizations—reflecting overconfidence, social pressure, or bureaucracy—regularly trigger tragedies ranging from workplace injuries to consumer fatalities. Investigators' concerns "that over a period of a year or two, the natural tendency of all bureaucracies, not just NASA, to morph and migrate away from the renewed attention to safety that follows an accident" seem equally applicable to the cultures of other organizations. In this respect, organizational success is very much a product of organizational culture.

Sources: D. Vaughan, "Autonomy, Interdependence, and Social Control: NASA and the Space Shuttle *Challenger*," *Administrative Science Quarterly* 35 (1990), 225–257; M. Dunn, "Report: NASA Culture Doomed Columbia," www.LSJ.com (*Lansing State Journal*), August 27, 2003; P. Recer, "NASA 'Culture' to Blame," www.ABCNews.com, August 26, 2003; R. Suriano, "Panel: NASA Culture Marked by Overconfidence, Bureaucracy," www.orlandosentinel.com, August 26, 2003.

When people engage in behaviors that are consistent with the new norms and values developed in an OD intervention, they reduce culture gaps and, in effect, change the organization's culture.

CHANGE AND ORGANIZATION DEVELOPMENT

Besides stimulating and solidifying cultural change, **organization development** entails the more general process of planning, implementing, and stabilizing the results of any type of organizational change. In addition, the OD field of research specializes in developing and assessing specific **interventions,** or change techniques.[24] As both a management process and a field of research, OD is characterized by five important features:

1. *OD emphasizes planned change.* The OD field evolved out of the need for a systematic, planned approach to managing change in organizations. OD's emphasis on planning distinguishes it from other processes of change in organizations that are more spontaneous or less methodical.

2. *OD has a pronounced social–psychological orientation.* OD interventions can stimulate change at many different levels—interpersonal, group, intergroup, or organizational. The field of OD is, therefore, neither purely psychological (focused solely on individuals) nor purely sociological (focused solely on organizations), but rather incorporates a mixture of both orientations.

3. *OD focuses primary attention on comprehensive change.* Although every OD intervention focuses on a specific organizational target, the effects on the total system are seen as equally important. No OD intervention is designed and implemented without considering its broader implications.

4. *OD is characterized by a long-range time orientation.* Change is an ongoing process that can sometimes take months—or even years—to produce the desired results. Although managers often face pressures to produce quick, short-term gains, the OD process is not intended to yield stopgap solutions.

5. *OD is guided by a change agent.* OD interventions are designed, implemented, and assessed with the help of a **change agent,** an individual who may be a specialist within the organization or a consultant brought in from outside the firm, and who serves as both a catalyst for change and a source of information about the OD process.[25]

Together, these five features suggest the following definition: *Organization development is a planned approach to interpersonal, group, intergroup, and organizational change that is comprehensive, long-term, and under the guidance of a change agent.* The Ethics and Social Responsibility box describes the founding values underlying the field, and notes the ethical basis they provide.

Resistance to Change

Change means to alter, vary, or modify existing ways of thinking or behaving. In organizations, change is both an important impetus and a primary product of OD efforts, reshaping the ways in which people and groups work together. Change in organizations is pervasive, meaning that it is a normal and necessary part of being organized.[26] Whenever managers attempt to set any change in motion, however, they must expect resistance, because people tend to reject what they perceive as a threat to the established way of doing things. The more drastic the change, the more intense the resulting resistance is likely to be.

Setting change in motion requires identifying and overcoming sources of resistance, on the one hand, and encouraging and strengthening sources of support, on the other hand. **Force field analysis** is a diagnostic method that diagrams the array of forces acting for and against a particular change in a graphic analysis. This tool is useful for managers and change agents who are attempting to visualize the situation surrounding a prospective change.

The diagram in Figure 14-2 depicts a typical force field analysis. The figure includes two lines: one representing an organization's present situation and the other representing the organization after the desired change has been implemented. Forces identified as supporting change are shown as arrows pushing in the direction of the desired change, and forces resisting change are drawn as arrows pushing in the opposite direction. The length of each arrow indicates the perceived strength of the force relative to the other forces in the force field.

ETHICS AND SOCIAL RESPONSIBILITY

ORGANIZATION DEVELOPMENT'S ETHICAL GROUNDING

Organization development is founded on a collection of norms, values, and practical guidelines that stress the importance of ethical conduct during the management of organizational change. Warren Bennis, one of the founding fathers of OD as currently practiced, suggested that OD change agents share a set of normative goals, derived from humanistic philosophy, which include the following:

1. Improvement in interpersonal competence.
2. A shift in values so that human factors and feelings come to be considered legitimate.
3. Development of increased understanding between and within working groups in order to reduce tensions.
4. Development of more effective "team management," that is, the capacity for functional groups to work more competently.
5. Development of better methods of conflict resolution. Rather than the usual bureaucratic methods, which rely mainly on suppression, compromise, and unprincipled power, more rational and open methods of conflict resolution are sought.
6. Development of organic rather than mechanical systems. This is a strong reaction against the idea of organizations as mechanisms that managers "work on," like pushing buttons.

Richard Beckhard, another founder of the field of OD, highlighted a set of assumptions intended to guide change efforts:

1. The basic building blocks of an organization are groups (teams). Therefore, the basic units of change are groups, not individuals.
2. An always relevant change goal is the reduction of inappropriate competition between parts of the organization and the development of a more collaborative condition.
3. Decision making in a healthy organization is located where the information sources are, rather than in a particular role or level of hierarchy.
4. Organizations, subunits of organizations, and individuals continuously manage their affairs against goals. Controls are interim measures, not the basis of managerial strategy.
5. One goal of a healthy organization is to develop generally open communication, mutual trust, and confidence between and across levels.

6. "People support what they help create." People affected by a change must be allowed active participation and a sense of ownership in the planning and conduct of the change.

Finally, Robert Tannenbaum and Sheldon Davis proposed a set of values intended to support and shape the practice of organization development. They listed these "values in transition" as:

1. Away from a view of people as essentially bad toward a view of people as basically good.
2. Away from avoidance of negative evaluation of individuals toward confirming them as human beings.
3. Away from a view of individuals as fixed, toward seeing them as being in process.
4. Away from resisting and fearing individual differences toward accepting and utilizing them.
5. Away from utilizing an individual primarily with reference to his or her job description toward viewing an individual as a whole person.
6. Away from walling off the expression of feelings toward making possible both appropriate expression and effective use.
7. Away from game playing toward authentic behavior.
8. Away from use of status for maintaining power and personal prestige toward use of status for organizationally relevant purposes.
9. Away from distrusting people toward trusting them.
10. Away from avoiding facing others with relevant data toward making appropriate confrontation.
11. Away from avoidance of risk taking toward willingness to risk.
12. Away from a view of process work as being unproductive effort toward seeing it as essential to effective task accomplishment.
13. Away from a primary emphasis on competition toward a much greater emphasis on collaboration.

Considered together, what emerges from these goals, assumptions, and values is a definition of ethical practice in which openness, trust, and respect for the individual are joined with participation, cooperation, open communication, and shared contribution in groups and teams. This definition prompts a critique of authoritarian, autocratic management practices and promotes a search for alternative ways to manage organizations and develop the people within them.

Sources: W. Bennis, *Organization Development: Its Nature, Origins, and Prospects* (Reading, MA: Addison-Wesley, 1969), p. 15; R. Beckhard, *Organization Development: Strategies and Models* (Reading, MA: Addison-Wesley, 1969), pp. 26–27; R. Tannenbaum and S. A. Davis, "Values, Man, and Organization," *Industrial Management Review* 10 (1969), 67–83.

The specific situation represented in the figure occurred during the early twenty-first century, when General Motors established production facilities in Lansing, Michigan, intended to produce a new line of luxury cars aimed at retaking market share recently lost to European and Asian nameplates such as Lexus, Infiniti, and BMW. Forces resisting this change included the following:

- Differing perceptions among GM's managers about the need for new products and production facilities (as opposed to continuing to sell minor modifications of existing lines)
- Differing perceptions of the importance of new products
- Concerns of employees in GM's other plants about the social disruption likely to occur as old work groups disbanded to staff the new production facilities
- Bureaucratic inertia stemming from the rules and procedures used to coordinate existing ways of doing things
- Employee fears about not being able to cope with the demands of new production technologies

Opposing these forces were others supporting change:

- U.S. consumer interests in greater sportiness in luxury automobiles
- A drive among auto manufacturers to introduce team-based production technologies and greater factory automation, so as to increase quality and control costs
- A general sense of unease in the U.S. auto industry

FIGURE 14-2 Force Field Analysis

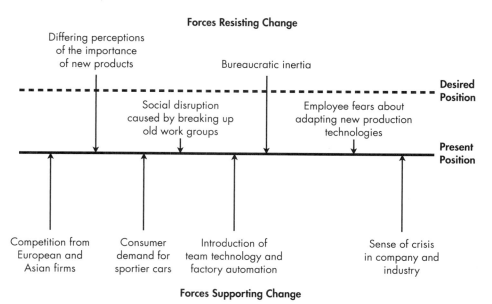

In the end, forces supporting change won out, with GM launching new Cadillac models that proved to be quite successful in the marketplace.

There is no universal, fail-safe way to overcome the resistant factors identified in a force field analysis. Of the many options available, six are used most often:

1. *Education and communication.* Information about the need and rationale for a prospective change can be disseminated through one-on-one discussions, group meetings, and written memos or reports. An educational approach is most appropriate where change is being undermined by a lack of information or where available information is inaccurate. Its strength is that, once persuaded through education, people will often help with the implementation of change. Its primary weakness is that education can be quite time-consuming if many people must be involved.

2. *Participation and involvement.* Individuals who will be affected by an intervention should be involved in its design and implementation. Thus employees should meet in special committees or task forces to participate in the decision making. Participation works well when the information required to manage change is dispersed among many people and when employees who have considerable power are likely to resist change if they are not directly involved in the initiation. This approach facilitates information exchange among people and breeds commitment among the people involved, but it can slow down the process if participants design an inappropriate change or stray from the task at hand.

3. *Facilitation and support.* Needed emotional support and training in topics related to organizational behavior should be provided through instructional meetings and counseling sessions for employees affected by a change. This method is most useful when people are resisting change because of problems with personal adjustment. Although no other method works as well with adjustment problems, facilitation efforts can consume significant amounts of time and money and still fail.

4. *Bargaining and negotiation.* Bargaining with resistant employees can provide them with incentives to change their minds. This technique is sometimes used when an individual or group with the power to block a change is likely to lose out if the change takes place. Negotiation can be a relatively easy way to avoid such resistance but can prove costly if it alerts other individuals and groups that they might be able to negotiate additional gains for themselves.

5. *Hidden persuasion.* Covert efforts can sometimes be implemented on a selective basis to persuade people to support desired changes. This approach is employed when other tactics will not work or are too costly. It can be a quick and inexpensive way to dissolve resistance, but can lead to future problems if people feel that they are treated unfairly. Covert persuasion may seem overly manipulative in retrospect, even if it leads to suitable results.

6. *Explicit and implicit coercion.* Power and threats of negative consequences may be employed to change the minds of resistant individuals. Coercion tends to be favored when speed is essential and individuals initiating change possess considerable power. It can overcome virtually any kind of resistance. Its weakness is that it can risk leaving people angry.[27]

Action Research

Organization development is a structured, multiple-step process. The **action research model** is a detailed variation of this process that promotes adherence to the scientific method (see Chapter 16) and places particular emphasis on postchange evaluation.[28] As indicated in Figure 14-3, it consists of seven stages, with the latter four forming a recurrent cycle.

FIGURE 14-3 The Action Research Model

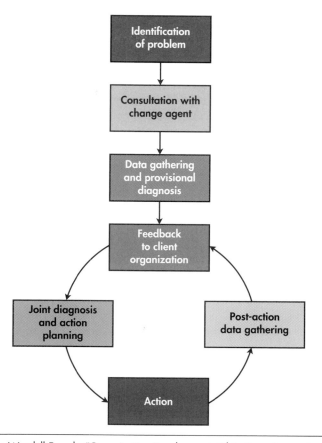

Source: Based on Wendell French, "Organization Development: Objectives, Assumptions, and Strategies," *California Management Review* 12 (1969), 26.

In the initial stage of action research, *problem identification,* someone in an organization perceives problems that might be solved with the assistance of an OD change agent. Specific problem statements can usually be formulated at this stage. Sometimes, however, problem identification cannot progress beyond an uneasy feeling that something is wrong. Consultation with a change agent may then be required to crystallize the problems.

In the second stage, *consultation,* the manager and change agent clarify the perceived problems and consider ways of dealing with them. During this discussion, they assess the degree of fit between the organization's needs and the change agent's expertise. If the agent fits the situation, action research progresses to the next stage. If not, then another change agent is sought and consultation begins anew.

In the third stage, *data gathering and provisional diagnosis,* the change agent initiates the diagnostic process by gathering data about the organization and its perceived problems. The agent observes, interviews, and questions employees and analyzes performance records. A member of the organization may assist during this process, facilitating the agent's entry into the firm and providing access to otherwise hidden or unavailable data. The change agent concludes this stage by examining the data and performing a provisional analysis and diagnosis of the situation.

Next, during the stage of *feedback to the client organization*, the change agent submits data and provisional diagnosis to the client organization's top management group. Informing top management at an early point that the OD process is under way is crucial for securing the managerial support that any OD effort must have to succeed. During the feedback presentation, the change agent must be careful to preserve the anonymity of people serving as sources of information. Identifying them could jeopardize their openness and willingness to cooperate later, especially if they possess information that might prove unflattering to management or portray the organization in negative terms.

During the fifth stage of action research, *joint diagnosis and action planning*, the change agent and the top management group discuss the meaning of the data, their implications for organizational functioning, and needs for additional data gathering and diagnosis. At this point, other people throughout the organization may also become involved in the diagnostic process. Sometimes, employees meet in feedback groups and react to the results of top management's diagnostic activities. At other times, work groups elect representatives, who then meet to exchange views and report back to their co-workers. If the firm is unionized, union representatives may be consulted as well. Throughout the action research process, the change agent must be careful not to impose any interventions on the client organization. Instead, members of the organization should deliberate jointly with the change agent and work together to develop wholly new interventions and plan specific action steps.

Next, the company puts the plan into motion and executes its action steps. In addition to the jointly designed intervention, the *action* stage may involve such activities as additional data gathering, further analysis of the problem situation, and supplementary action planning.

Because action research is a cyclical process, data are also gathered after actions have been taken during the stage of *post-action data gathering and evaluation*. Here the purpose of the activity is to monitor and assess the effectiveness of an intervention. In their evaluation, groups in the client organization review the data and decide whether they need to rediagnose the situation, perform more analyses of the situation, and develop new interventions. During this process, the change agent serves as an expert on research methods as applied to the process of development and evaluation. In filling this role, the agent may perform data analyses, summarize the results of these analyses, guide subsequent rediagnoses, and position the organization for further intervention.

ORGANIZATION DEVELOPMENT INTERVENTIONS

Many different OD interventions—perhaps hundreds—can be selected on the basis of data gathered through action research and used to facilitate the stages of joint diagnosis and action planning, action, and post-action data gathering and evaluation just described. This section overviews eight of these interventions. As indicated in Table 14-2, they differ from one another in terms of target and depth.

The **target** of an OD intervention is the aspect on which an intervention focuses. Interpersonal, group, intergroup, and organizational relations can all serve as targets of OD interventions. Associated with these targets are various kinds of problems, as shown in Table 14-2 and indicated in earlier chapters of this book.

An intervention's **depth** reflects the degree or intensity of change that the intervention is designed to stimulate.[29] A *shallow* intervention is intended mainly to provide people with information or to facilitate communication and minor change. In

TABLE 14-2 Organization Development Interventions

Target	Focal Problem	Depth	
		Shallow	Deep
Interpersonal relations	Problem fitting in with others	Role negotiation technique	Sensitivity training
Group relations and leadership	Problem with working as a group	Process consultation	Team development
Intergroup relationships	Problem with relationships between groups	Third-party peace making	Intergroup team building
Organization-wide relationships	Problem with functioning effectively	Survey feedback	Open system planning

contrast, a *deep* intervention is intended to effect massive psychological and behavioral change. An intervention of this type attacks basic beliefs, values, and norms in an attempt to bring about fundamental changes in the way people think, feel, and behave.

Interpersonal Interventions

Interpersonal interventions focus on solving problems with interpersonal relations, such as those described in Chapter 8. Depending on the particular intervention, the organization may attempt to redefine personal roles, clarify social expectations, or strengthen sensitivity to others' needs and interests.

Role Negotiation Technique The **role negotiation technique** (RNT), an interpersonal intervention of moderately shallow depth, is intended to help people form and maintain effective working relationships.[30] As indicated in Chapter 8, people at work fill specialized *roles* in which they are expected to engage in specific sorts of behavior. Often, however, they lack a clear idea of what their roles entail, or they are overburdened by role demands. RNT (as diagrammed in Figure 14-4) seeks to reduce role ambiguity and conflict by clarifying interpersonal expectations and responsibilities.

To initiate an RNT intervention, the occupant of a troublesome role contacts a change agent about his or her problem and receives instruction from the agent on the RNT procedure.

The role occupant then works alone to analyze the rationale for the role as well as its place in the organizational network of interpersonal relations. This individual tries to learn how to use his or her role in meeting personal, group, and organizational goals. Next, the role occupant discusses the results of the analysis in a meeting attended by everyone whose work is directly affected by his or her role. During this discussion, the change agent lists on a blackboard or flip chart the specific duties and behaviors of the role as identified by the role occupant.

The rest of the group suggests corrections to this list. Behaviors are added or deleted until the role occupant is satisfied that the role he or she performs is defined accurately and completely.

In the next phase of the RNT process, the change agent directs attention to the role occupant's expectations of others. To begin this step, the role occupant lists his or her expectations of those roles that are connected with his or her own. The group then discusses and modifies these expectations until everyone agrees on them. Afterward, all participants have the opportunity to modify their expectations about the person's role, in response to his or her expectations of them. Thus, as its name indicates, RNT involves a process of negotiation. The person who is the focus of the

FIGURE 14-4 Steps in the Role Negotiation Technique

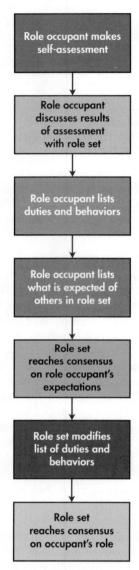

intervention can ask others to do things for him or her, and others can ask the role occupant to do something for them in return.

In the final step of the role negotiation technique, the role occupant writes a summary or profile of his or her role as it has been defined through the RNT process. This profile specifies which behaviors are required and which are discretionary. Thus it constitutes a clearly defined listing of the role-related activities that the role occupant will perform. The meeting then continues, focusing on the roles of the other RNT participants, until all relevant interpersonal relationships have been clarified.

Sensitivity Training   As a deep interpersonal intervention, **sensitivity training** focuses on developing greater sensitivity to oneself, to others, and to one's relations with others.[31] Designed to promote emotional growth and development, it typically takes place in a closed session away from work. It may involve a collection of people who do not know each other, a group of people who are well acquainted, or a combination of both. A sensitivity training session may last for a period as brief as half a day or go on for several days. It is begun by a change agent, who announces that he or she will serve solely as a nondirective resource. The change agent then lapses into silence, leaving the participants with neither a leader nor an agenda to guide interpersonal activities. Putting people in such an ambiguous situation forces them to structure relations among themselves and, in the process, question long-held assumptions about themselves, about each other, and about how to conduct interpersonal relationships.[32]

Sensitivity training participants take part in an intense exchange of ideas, opinions, beliefs, and personal philosophies as they struggle with the process of structuring interpersonal relations. Here is a description of one four-day session:

The first evening discussion began with a rather neutral opening process, which very soon led to strongly emotional expression of concern. . . . By the second day the participants had begun to express their feelings toward each other quite directly and frankly, something they had rarely done in their daily work. As the discussion progressed it became easier for them to accept criticism without becoming angry or wanting to strike back. As they began to express long-suppressed hostilities and anxieties, the "unfreezing" of old attitudes, old values, and old approaches began. From the second day onward the discussion was spontaneous and uninhibited. From early morning to long past midnight the process of self-examination and confrontation continued. They raised questions they had never felt free to ask before. Politeness and superficiality yielded to openness and emotional expression and then to more objective analysis of themselves and their relationships at work. They faced up to many conflicts and spoke of their differences. There were tense moments, as suspicion, distrust, and personal antagonisms were aired, but most issues were worked out without acrimony.[33]

By completing this process, people learn more about their own personal feelings, inclinations, and prejudices and about what other people think of them.

A word of warning: Sensitivity training is a deep intervention that can initiate profound psychological change. Participants typically engage in intensely critical assessments of themselves and others that can be both difficult and painful. Therefore, the change agent overseeing sensitivity training *must* be a trained professional who can help participants deal with criticism in a constructive manner. In the absence of expert help, participants could risk serious psychological trauma.[34]

Group Interventions

Group interventions are designed to solve problems with group or team performance and leadership, such as those identified in Chapters 7 through 10. In general, these interventions focus on helping the members of a group learn how to work together to fulfill the group's task and maintenance requirements.

Process Consultation **Process consultation** is a relatively shallow, group-level OD intervention. In a process consultation intervention, a change agent meets with a work group and helps its members examine group processes such as communication, leadership and followership, problem solving, and cooperation. The specific approach taken during this exploration, which varies from one situation to another, may include group meetings in which the following activities take place:

1. The change agent asks stimulus questions that direct attention to relationships among group members. Ensuing discussions between group members may focus

on ways to improve these relationships as well as ways that such relationships can influence group productivity and effectiveness.

2. A process analysis session is held, during which the change agent watches the group as it works. This session is followed by additional feedback sessions in which the change agent discusses his or her observations about how the group maintains itself and how it performs its task. Supplementary feedback sessions may also allow the change agent to clarify the events of earlier sessions for individual group members.

3. The change agent makes suggestions that may pertain to group membership, communication, interaction patterns, and the allocation of work duties, responsibilities, and authority.[35]

Whatever the change agent's approach in a given situation, his or her primary focus in process consultation is on making a group more effective by getting its members to pay more attention to important *process* issues—that is, to focus on *how* things are done in the group rather than *what* is to be done (the issues that normally dominate a group's attention). The ultimate goal of process consultation is to help the group improve its problem-solving skills by enhancing the ability of members to identify and correct faulty group processes.[36]

Team Development Team development is a deep, group-level extension of interpersonal sensitivity training. In a team development intervention, a group of people who work together on a daily basis meet over an extended period of time to assess and modify group processes.[37] Throughout these meetings, participants focus their efforts on achieving a balance of basic components of teamwork, such as the following:

• An understanding of, and commitment to, common goals
• Involvement of as many group members as possible, to take advantage of the complete range of skills and abilities available to the group
• Analysis and review of group processes on a regular basis, to ensure that sufficient maintenance activities are performed
• Trust and openness in communication and relationships
• A strong sense of belonging on the part of all members[38]

To begin team development, the group first engages in a lengthy diagnostic meeting, in which a change agent helps members identify group problems and map out possible solutions. The change agent asks members to observe interpersonal and group processes and to be prepared to comment on what they see. In this way, group members work on two basic issues: looking for solutions to problems of everyday functioning that have arisen in the group, and observing the way group members interact with each other during the meeting.

Based on the results of these efforts, team development then proceeds in two specific directions. First, the change agent and group implement the interventions chosen during diagnosis to solve the problems identified by the group. Second, the change agent initiates group sensitivity training to uncover additional problems that might otherwise resist detection:

As the group fails to get [the change agent] to occupy the traditional roles of teacher, seminar leader, or therapist, it will redouble its efforts until in desperation it will disown him and seek other leaders. When they too fail, they too will be disowned, often brutally. The group will then use its own brutality to try to get the [change agent] to change his task by eliciting his sympathy and care for those it has handled so roughly. If this maneuver fails, and it never completely fails, the group will tend to throw up other leaders to express its concern for its members and project its brutality onto the consultant. As rival leaders emerge it is the job of the consultant, so far as he is able, to identify what the group is trying to do and explain it. His leadership is in task performance, and the task is to understand what the group is doing "now" and to explain why it is doing it.[39]

Group sensitivity training is really an interpersonal sensitivity training intervention conducted with an intact work group. It enables co-workers to critique and adjust the interpersonal relations problems that inevitably arise during the workday. For this reason, the same cautions mentioned for interpersonal sensitivity training are also relevant to group sensitivity training. Only a change agent trained to manage the rigors and consequences of a deep intervention should take a leadership role in this type of exercise.

Intergroup Interventions

Intergroup interventions focus on solving many of the intergroup problems identified in Chapter 11. In general, these problems concern conflict and associated breakdowns in intergroup coordination. Thus OD interventions developed to manage intergroup relations involve various open communication techniques and conflict resolution methods.

Third-Party Peace Making   **Third-party peace making** is a relatively shallow intervention in which a change agent seeks to resolve intergroup misunderstandings by encouraging communication between or among groups. The change agent, who is not a member of any of the groups and is referred to as a third party, guides a meeting between the groups.[40] To be productive, the meeting must be characterized by the following attributes:

1. *Motivation:* All groups must be motivated to resolve their differences.
2. *Power:* A stable balance of power must be established between the groups.
3. *Timing:* Confrontations must be synchronized so that no one group can gain an information advantage over another.
4. *Emotional release:* People must have enough time to work through the negative thoughts and feelings that have built up between the groups. In addition, they need to recognize and express their positive feelings.
5. *Openness:* Conditions must favor openness in communication and mutual understanding.
6. *Stress:* There should be enough stress—enough pressure—on group members to motivate them to give serious attention to the problem, but not so much that the problem appears intractable.[41]

The change agent facilitates communication between the groups both directly and indirectly. He or she may interview group members before an intergroup meeting, help construct a meeting agenda, monitor the pace of communication between groups during the meeting, or actually referee the interaction. Acting in a more subtle, indirect way, the change agent may schedule the meeting at a neutral site or establish time limits for intergroup interaction.

The whole process can be as short as an afternoon, though it is more likely to last as long as several months of weekly sessions. Through these sessions, group members begin to learn things about one another and their relationships that can help them focus on common interests and begin to overcome conflictive tendencies.

Intergroup Team Building   **Intergroup team building** is a deep intervention that has three primary aims:

- To improve communication and interaction between work-related groups

- To decrease counterproductive competition between the groups
- To replace group-centered perspectives with an orientation that recognizes the necessity for various groups to work together[42]

As indicated in Figure 14-5, during the first step of intergroup team building, two groups (or their leaders) meet with an OD change agent and discuss whether relationships between the groups can be improved. If both groups agree that this goal is feasible, the change agent asks both groups to commit themselves to searching for ways to improve their relationship.

The groups then move to the second step of intergroup team building. The two groups meet in separate rooms, and each makes two lists. One list includes the group's perceptions, thoughts, and attitudes toward the other group. The other list describes their thoughts about what the other group is likely to say about them.

FIGURE 14-5 Steps in an Intergroup Team-Building Intervention

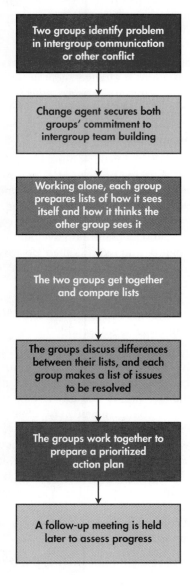

In the third step, the two groups reconvene and compare their lists. Each group can compare its view of the other group with the way the other group expects to be seen. Discrepancies uncovered during this comparison are discussed during the fourth step, when the groups meet separately. Each reacts to what it has learned about itself and the other group, then lists important issues that need to be resolved between the two groups.

During the fifth step, the two groups meet again and compare the lists of issues, setting priorities. They then work together on an action plan to resolve the issues based on their priority. They assign individual responsibilities and target dates for completion.

The final step is a follow-up meeting held later to assess progress made to date. At that time, additional actions are planned as required to ensure that intergroup cooperation will continue over the long run.

Organizational Interventions

Organizational interventions are intended to deal with structural and cultural problems, such as those identified in Chapters 12 and 13 as well as those mentioned earlier in this chapter.

Some of these interventions are directed at improving communication and coordination within the organization. Others focus on diagnosing and strengthening relations between the organization and its external environment.

Survey Feedback   The main purpose of **survey feedback** is to stimulate information sharing throughout the entire organization; planning and implementing change are of secondary importance.[43] Thus this technique is a relatively shallow, organization-level intervention.

The survey feedback procedure normally proceeds in four stages. First, under the guidance of a trained change agent, top management engages in preliminary planning, deciding such questions as who should be surveyed and what questions should be asked. Other organization members may also participate in this stage if their expertise or opinions are needed. Second, the change agent and his or her staff administer the survey questionnaire to all organization members. Depending on the kinds of questions to be asked and issues to be probed, the survey questionnaire might include any of the diagnostic questions provided in this book. Third, the change agent categorizes and summarizes the data. After presenting this information to management, he or she holds group meetings to let everyone who responded to the questionnaire know the results. Fourth, the groups that received the feedback information hold meetings to discuss the survey. The group leaders (perhaps a supervisor or an assistant vice president) help groups interpret the data—that is, diagnose the results and identify specific problems, make plans for constructive changes, and prepare to report on the data and proposed changes with groups at the next lower hierarchical level. The change agent usually acts as a process consultant during these discussions to ensure that all group members have an opportunity to contribute their opinions.

As shown in Figure 14-6, survey feedback differs dramatically from the traditional questionnaire method of gathering information. In survey feedback, not only are data collected from everyone, from the highest to the lowest level of the hierarchy, but everyone in the organization also participates in analyzing the data and in planning appropriate actions. These key characteristics of survey feedback reflect OD's basic values, which stress the criticality of participation as a means of encouraging commitment to the organization's goals and stimulating personal growth and development.

FIGURE 14-6 Two Approaches to Data Collection by Questionnaire

	Traditional Approach	Survey Feedback, or OD Approach
Data collected from:	Workers and maybe foreman	Everyone in the system or subsystem
Data reported to:	Top management, department heads, and perhaps to employees through newspaper	Everyone who participated
Implications of data worked on by:	Top management (maybe)	Everyone in work teams, with workshops starting at the top (all superiors with their subordinates)
Third-party intervention strategy:	Design and administration of questionnaire, development of report	Obtaining concurrence on total strategy, design, and administration of questionnaire, design of workshops, appropriate interventions in workshops
Action planning done by:	Top management only	Teams at all levels
Probable extent of change and improvement:	Low	High

Source: From *Organizational Development* 4th ed. by W. L. French and C. H. Bell, Jr., p. 170. Copyright © 1990. Reprinted by permission of Pearson Education Inc., Upper Saddle River, NJ 07458.

Open System Planning Open system planning is a fairly deep, organization-level intervention that is distinguished by its focus on the organization as a system open to its surrounding environment. The primary purpose of open system planning is to help the members of an organization devise ways to accomplish their firm's mission in light of the demands and constraints that originate with constituency groups in the organization's environment. As indicated in Chapter 13 (and Exercise 13-1), these groups may include raw material suppliers, potential employees, customers, government regulators, and competitors.

As shown in Figure 14-7, the intervention involves five steps:

1. *Identification of the core mission or purpose.* The members of the organization meet and, through open discussion, define the firm's basic goals, purpose, and reason for existence.
2. *Identification of important constituency groups.* Participants identify the environmental constituencies that can affect the firm's ability to accomplish its goals and purpose.
3. *"Is" and "ought" planning.* Participants describe current relationships between the organization and its constituencies. They consider each constituency separately, focusing on the importance and duration of the relationship. Other factors probed include the frequency with which the parties come in contact with one another and the organization's ability to sense and react to changes in the constituency group. Participants then determine how satisfactory the relationship *is* to both organization and constituency. If this assessment uncovers deficiencies, participants specify what the relationship *ought* to be if it is to satisfy both sides.

FIGURE 14-7 Steps in an Open System Planning Intervention

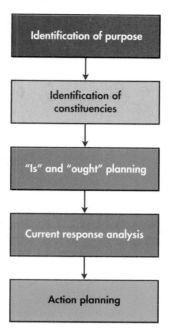

4. *Current responses to constituency groups.* Participants assess the organization's current response to each constituency group by answering these questions: What does this constituency want from us? What are we currently doing to respond to this demand? Is our current response moving us closer to where we want to be in relation to our company's goals and purpose?

5. *Action planning.* If the current situation is not what it ought to be, and if the organization's current response to its constituency groups is inadequate, participants face the final task of deciding how to redirect the firm's behavior. In planning corrective action, they usually consider these questions: What actions should be taken, and who should take them? What resource allocations are necessary? What timetable should be set? When should each action start and finish? Who will prepare a progress report, and when will it be due? How will actions be evaluated to verify that progress is proceeding in the desired direction?[44]

Unlike most other OD interventions, open system planning directs primary attention to factors *outside* the organization that can influence organizational performance. It is especially useful in providing a structured, yet participatory way to establish a firm's purpose and set the goals required to accomplish this purpose. Open system planning can also help identify critical environmental contingencies during the process of organization design. This exercise encourages the development of a better fit between an organization's structure and its environment.

EVALUATING CHANGE AND DEVELOPMENT

No matter what type of organization development intervention is used, the concluding stage of the OD process always consists of an evaluation of the technique's effectiveness. Based on the results of this evaluation, efforts may be devoted to ensuring that the newly developed attitudes, values, and behaviors become permanent fixtures

TABLE 14-3 Criteria for Evaluating Change Efforts

Criterion	Suggested Questions
Overall Results	
Desired outcomes	1. What were the intended outcomes of the intervention? How do they compare with the outcomes actually realized?
Guiding assumptions	2. How explicit were the assumptions that guided the intervention? Did experience prove them to be both valid and appropriate? Did everyone understand and agree with the intervention's purpose as a result?
Theory foundation	3. How consistent with current theories of organization behavior and organization development are these assumptions? Was everything currently known with regard to the intervention's focus and purpose incorporated in the intervention?
Phase of intervention	
Identification	4. What was the reason for starting the intervention? Who was initially involved? Was the intervention undertaken because of a broadly felt need or a narrow set of special interests?
Consultation	5. What activities were performed at the start of the intervention process? Who was involved in them? Was the intervention implemented prematurely, without adequate diagnosis? Did unnecessary resistance arise as a result?
Data gathering	6. What specific data collection and provisional diagnostic activities took place? Were they carried out fully and effectively?
Feedback and planning	7. What aspects of the organization were diagnosed to determine the target and depth of the intervention that was implemented? How was the intervention planned, and who planned it? How were resources used in this effort? How explicit and detailed were the plans that resulted?
Action	8. What was actually done? When was it done? Who did it? How do the answers to these questions compare with the action plan as initially developed?
Post-action	9. Was post-action evaluation included from the outset as part of the intervention? Were deficiencies identified during evaluation corrected through a careful, planned modification of the intervention or its action plan?
External factors	
Workforce traits	10. Were the results of the intervention affected, either positively or negatively, by workforce characteristics (such as age, gender, education, or unemployment level)?
Economy	11. What was the state of the economy and the firm's market at the time of the intervention? Did economic factors affect the success of the intervention?
Environment	12. How much did the organization's environment change over the course of the intervention? Are the intended results of the intervention still desirable given the organization's current environment?
Internal factors	
Size	13. How large is the organization? Did its size permit access to the resources required for the intervention to succeed?
Technology	14. What is the organization's primary product, and what sort of technology is used to make it? Do the results of the intervention mesh or conflict with the requirements of this technology?
Structure	15. How mechanistic or organic is the organization's structure? Do the results of the intervention mesh or conflict with this structure?
Culture	16. What are the organization's prevailing norms and values concerning change? Concerning involvement in organization development interventions?

Sources: Based on N. Tichy and J. N. Nisberg, "When Does Work Restructuring Work? Organizational Innovations at Volvo and GM," *Organizational Dynamics* (1976), 13–36; W. L. French, "A Checklist for Organizing and Implementing an OD Effort," in W. L. French, C. H. Bell, Jr., and R. A. Zawacki, eds., *Organization Development: Theory, Practice, and Research*, rev. ed. (Plano, TX: Business Publications, 1983), pp. 451–459.

in the organization. Alternatively, OD may begin anew, and additional interventions may be initiated to stimulate further change. Table 14-3 contains a checklist of questions that can prove helpful in deciding which criteria to use and how to measure them when evaluating the effectiveness of organization development.

As suggested by the checklist, resources are expended to acquire the outcomes generated by the OD process. Consequently, OD's effectiveness must be judged partly in terms of its outcomes. In addition, measuring its effectiveness requires remembering why the process was undertaken initially and assessing what took place during each stage of the OD process. This procedure guarantees that an OD effort labeled "effective" not only accomplished its intended purpose, but did so in a manner that left everyone more informed about the process of change and ways to manage it. Finally, the effects of external and internal factors, whether positive or negative, on the OD process must be examined and cataloged for subsequent reference. With this knowledge, the factors that support change can be revisited when needed again in the future, and the ones that are resistant can be anticipated and neutralized.

SUMMARY

The *culture* of an organization consists of deep-seated norms and values as well as surface expressions of these norms and values. The latter include *ceremonies, rites, rituals, stories, myths, heroes, symbols,* and *language.* Culture is a cohesive force that influences the way that the firm's members perceive the formal organization, their behaviors, and themselves. *Symbolic management* and organization development (OD) interventions can be used to manage the culture of an organization.

Organization development is both a field of research and a collection of *interventions* intended to stimulate planned change in organizations. Associated with OD is a concern about managing resistance to change and strengthening forces that favor change. *Force field analysis* is a technique that can be used to aid in the pursuit of these complementary goals. The *action research model* describes how *change agents* often manage the OD process.

OD interventions differ in terms of the types of organizational behavior that are their *targets* and the *depth* of change stimulated. The *role negotiation technique* and *sensitivity training* are interventions of increasing depth that target interpersonal problems. *Process consultation* and *team development* are group interventions of increasing depth. *Third-party peace making* and *intergroup team building* are increasingly deep intergroup interventions. *Survey feedback* and *open system planning* are organization-level interventions of increasing depth. To be considered completely successful, OD efforts should conclude with an evaluation of program effectiveness.

REVIEW QUESTIONS

1. As a manager, you face the task of reversing cultural norms that currently favor low performance. How can you accomplish this task? What role do the surface elements of culture play in your plan?

2. How do cultural norms and values act as social information? What effects does this information have on organizational behavior? Why should managers take social information into account when designing jobs and structuring the organization?

3. What differences exist between organization development and other approaches used to stimulate change in organizations? What is gained by understanding and using the action research model?

4. Suppose you were given the assignment of developing a new grading system for your class. Draw a force field analysis diagram showing the major forces for and against change that you would probably encounter while implementing your new grading system. How might you weaken the forces against change? How might you strengthen the forces for change? Is your change intervention likely to succeed?

5. Why is it important to avoid using an intervention that is deeper than needed to stimulate the required amount of change? How can you increase the likelihood that the intervention is focused on the appropriate target?

6. Which of the OD interventions described in this chapter would you choose for each of the following situations: a person who understands his or her role in a group but cannot seem to get along with co-workers; a group of people who get along with one another but are less productive than expected; an organization suffering from poor internal communication; an organization unsure about its place in the broader business environment?

7. Why is it always important to evaluate the results of an OD intervention? What kinds of information should you collect and consider during an evaluation?

LEARNING THROUGH EXPERIENCE

DIAGNOSTIC QUESTIONS 14-1

Culture, Change, and Organization Development

Managing organization culture requires knowledge about the norms and values that shape the informal side of organizational behavior. Organization development represents one way of acquiring this knowledge; it is also a general approach for the management of change that can be applied to help managers solve many of the other interpersonal, group, intergroup, and organizational problems identified in this book. The following questions offer practical guidance during such activities:

1. What cultural norms and values guide behaviors and understandings in the firm? Do surface elements reinforce these deeper elements? Do differences between surface elements and cultural norms and values suggest ongoing cultural change? Is this change desirable?

2. Does the culture hold the organization together in a way that supports the formal organization? Does it provide social information that is consistent with the firm's purpose, strategic direction, and general well-being?

3. Beyond cultural considerations, what sort of change is being contemplated? What sources of resistance to this change exist in the organization? What might you do to overcome this resistance? How successful are your efforts likely to be?

4. Based on a force field analysis, which forces in the organization favor the change? How can you strengthen them? How strong can they be made? What is the likely combined effect of the forces for and against change? Is it realistic to attempt to institute change, or should the status quo be accepted?

5. Do the depth and target of the OD intervention being implemented seem to match the problem? (Note that the shallowest intervention likely to stimulate the required amount of change is the one that should be selected for implementation.)

6. Is evaluation an integral part of the OD effort? When establishing evaluation criteria and procedures, are serious attempts made to guard against bias and distortion?

7. Is positive change likely to persist after the OD effort has ended? What can be done to ensure lasting change?

EXERCISE 14-1 **Intergroup Mirroring**

Mark S. Plovnick, University of the Pacific
Ronald E. Fry, Case Western Reserve University
W. Warner Burke, Columbia University

Intergroup mirroring is an organization development intervention used to help bring to the surface the root causes of conflict between groups. This technique is also designed to create conditions under which a win-win attitude can prevail and mutual problem solving can occur. The mirroring process involves three major phases:

1. *Imagery.* For pairs of groups, each group develops images of itself and of the other group. This first step elicits stereotypes and untested assumptions about "them" and "us." Often, simply correcting misperceptions of each other can bring groups closer together.

2. *Confrontation.* Each group acknowledges its uniqueness and its differences from the other group. The aim in this phase is to specify differences that are accepted as valid but that cause conflict. Without this clarification and labeling of just what is in conflict, meaningful resolution is unlikely. Smoothing over or avoiding the conflict is more apt to occur.

3. *Bonding.* Groups experiencing conflict that is apparently unreconcilable begin to collaborate and address problems mutually. They become more alike in their perceptions of the necessity of working together and of understanding one another.

To succeed, intergroup mirroring must occur between groups that are both motivated to improve the situation and relatively equal in the power they can bring to bear. If one group favors the current situation, it is rational for that group to avoid the changes otherwise stimulated by intergroup mirroring. Also, if one group can force the other to do things it would not otherwise consider doing, true collaboration is unlikely.

Anyone who wants to use intergroup mirroring must understand some basic assumptions underlying its design. First, the technique assumes that both groups in conflict are acting with integrity and good intentions. If the groups actually wish to harm, punish, or humiliate one another, no resolution of differences is possible. Second, the intervention assumes that both groups are responsible for the conflict occurring between them. This responsibility may be unequal, but it must be shared.

Step One: Pre-Class Preparation

The upcoming class session will give you the opportunity to experience a mirroring intervention for yourself. Prepare for it by reading the entire exercise before coming to class.

Adapted with the authors' permission from M. S. Plovnick, R. E. Fry, and W. W. Burke, *Organization Development: Exercises, Cases, and Readings* (Boston: Little, Brown, 1982), pp. 89–93. Copyright 1982 by Mark S. Plovnick, Ronald E. Fry, and W. Warner Burke.

Step Two: Generating Images—Homogeneous Groups

The class should divide into the same pairs of groups formed for Exercise 11-1 (Building Customer Lists: Cooperate or Compete?). If the class has not yet performed Exercise 11-1, it should complete Steps One and Two of that exercise before proceeding any further.

To begin Step Two of Exercise 14-1, members of each group should meet by themselves and list as many responses as possible to the three statements that follow. In filling in the blanks with as many words or phrases as you can, reflect back to the day when you performed Exercise 11-1 and think about your own group and the group that was paired with yours.

1. How we saw the other group: "We see the other group as . . ."

2. How we saw ourselves: "We see ourselves as . . ."

3. How we think the other group saw us: "The other group sees us as . . ."

As ideas are presented, they should be listed on a blackboard or flip chart so that everyone in the group can see them. Try to reach a consensus on whatever you decide to include in your group's lists. If opinion is clearly split on an item, note this disagreement next to the item. A spokesperson should be appointed to prepare a presentation for Step Three.

Step Three: Sharing Images—Heterogeneous Groups

Each pair of groups should form one discussion group. Spokespersons for each group should begin this step by reporting the results of Step Two. During these reports, listeners may ask for information that provides further clarification or understanding, but they may not debate any aspect of either report.

Step Four: Identifying Discrepancies—Homogeneous Groups

All groups should re-form, and each group should examine what it said about itself and what was said about it. Make a list (that everyone can see) of as many discrepancies as you can identify between how the group views itself, how the other group views it, and how it thought the other group would view it.

Step Five: Sharing and Prioritizing Discrepancies—Heterogeneous Groups

In this step, each pair of groups should meet again, and group spokespeople should report on the results of Step Four. Similarities in the discrepancies identified by the two groups should be noted and combined. Then each pair of groups should decide on two to four discrepancies that the pair would like to resolve.

Step Six: Problem Solving—Heterogeneous Groups

Mixed subgroups made up of members from each of the groups in the pair should discuss how to manage, neutralize, or eliminate the discrepancies identified at the end of Step Five. Each subgroup should then prepare some recommendations to be considered by the class as a whole in Step Seven. A spokesperson should be appointed to report on the discrepancies examined and actions recommended by the subgroup.

Step Seven: Class Discussion

The entire class should assemble, and all spokespeople should give their reports. As actions are recommended, class members should discuss each action's practicality and likelihood of success. The class should then create a master list of discrepancies and ways of overcoming their effects. The last part of the class should be devoted to discussing the usefulness of intergroup mirroring and should focus on the following questions:

1. With your knowledge, what would you do differently if you were required to complete Exercise 11-1 again? Would you change any of your answers to the questions at the end of Exercise 11-1?

2. When would you recommend an intergroup mirroring intervention? When would you *not* recommend one?

3. How might intergroup mirroring help interdependent task groups (such as manufacturing employees and sales personnel) set realistic performance goals? What other benefits would mirroring provide such groups?

Conclusion

Intergroup mirroring can be especially helpful in eliciting and exploring general attitudes and feelings that groups hold toward one another. This technique can also prove beneficial in identifying and solving specific procedural problems that have arisen between groups who need each other to get their work done. As you may have discovered during this exercise, it is usually easier to generate perceptions and even to identify discrepancies than to agree on how to change them. For this reason, an intervention such as intergroup mirroring can be an invaluable aid to managers who must cope with intergroup conflict and build a sense of intergroup team spirit.

PART 4 CASES

Case 4-1 City National Bank

Case 4-2 Newcomer-Willson Hospital

Case 4-3 O Canada

Case 4-4 Dumas Public Library

Case 4-5 L. J. Summers Company

Case 4-6 Consolidated Life: Caught between Two Corporate Cultures

Case 4-7 World International Airlines, Inc.

CASE 4-1 CITY NATIONAL BANK

J. B. Ritchie, Brigham Young University
Paul H. Thompson, Brigham Young University

Having worked two months during the previous summer for City National Bank, I returned again this summer to work while on my break from school. Although I would be there for only four months, the bank hired me as a full-time staff member, replacing a woman who was recently terminated. It also hired a woman just out of high school to help handle the extra workload our resort town generates in the vacation months. These additions brought our operations division up to seven women plus the assistant manager over our division (see Case Exhibit 4-1). The same day that I started, a new woman was transferred from a larger branch to our division to take over the note department. Marilyn, the new woman, was not very well liked by most of the workers in the branch, because some negative reports had preceded her arrival and because her family "owned" the town in which we worked.

City National Bank, like any other large bank with many branches, had standardized policies, procedures, and regulations. To protect customers, employees, and the corporation, these procedures have to be followed. The bank has auditors who periodically check the books and operational procedures of the branches to assure maintenance of the high standards. Our branch has relaxed several of the rules and has developed some policies unique to our branch. In part, this change stems from the informal and friendly relationships shared between customers and employees in our small town, where we know most of the customers on a first-name basis. Unlike our branch, the larger branch in which Marilyn previously worked followed procedures strictly and supposedly did everything "according to the book."

Reprinted with the publisher's permission from J. B. Ritchie and P. H. Thompson, *Organizations and People: Readings, Cases, and Exercises in Organizational Behavior*, 3rd ed. (St. Paul, MN: West Publishing Company, 1984), pp. 46–48. All rights reserved.

**CASE
EXHIBIT 4-1**   City National Bank Organization Chart

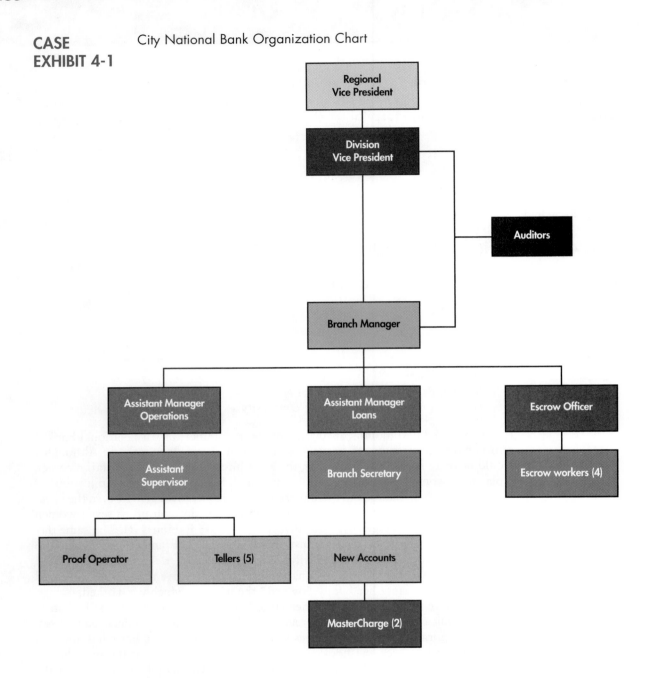

Marilyn let us know that we were inefficient and backward. Soon bad feelings developed, coming to a head in the early part of August.

In August, we were in the process of changing managers. Our assistant manager had also left on vacation, so we had a former auditor in management training and a newly promoted supervisor filling the management positions for two weeks. Their job was to sit in for people on vacations throughout our division, until each was placed in his or her own branch. The new manager and assistant manager were upset with our lax attitude toward many rules, some of which we had never even heard of, and they set out to shape up our branch. Among the things we needed to reform were the opening and closing procedures, keeping our keys with us at *all* times, always locking our cash boxes, performing balancing procedures, following the check-cashing policy, and adhering to several other regulations. Marilyn was happy with the new situation and told us "it's about time," but the rest of the branch was very defensive and uncooperative with the temporary management. During this time Marilyn changed several of her responsibilities with the temporary supervisor's permission, and when our assistant manager returned from vacation, there was a great deal of tension between them.

One afternoon while the assistant manager was out, Marilyn went around on her own, picked up three sets of keys that were lying on a table, and turned them over to the other assistant manager, saying that the "women should be taught a lesson." This event occurred after the branch had closed, and some frantic minutes were spent searching for the keys. Marilyn said nothing, and we all kept looking until someone remembered seeing Marilyn in the work area. When confronted, she merely told the women that Paul, the assistant manager, had the keys. When the whole story was put together, there was a lot of name-calling and derogatory comments, with Marilyn getting the silent treatment for almost a week.

Our management never took an official stand that was enforced. There was never a confrontation between the opposing sides. When Marilyn would approach them on a point, the managers would satisfy her by agreeing that she had a good point; when the other side brought up complaints, they would agree with them, too. A harmony between practices and policies was never reached. As the summer ended, many problems were compounded because there was no consistent authority and so many things "had changed," according to the original employees. We never knew what was expected. By Labor Day, I left to return to school and four other women had quit or transferred out of my hometown branch of City National Bank.

When you have read this case, review the diagnostic questions included at the end(s) of the chapter(s) you are using to analyze this case, and choose the ones that seem applicable. Then use those questions to begin working on your case analysis.

CASE 4-2 NEWCOMER-WILLSON HOSPITAL

Samuel M. Wilson, Temple University

The Newcomer-Willson Hospital is located in a growing and prosperous suburban community. It has grown rapidly in the last fifteen years, and with its recent expansion a total of 285 beds, 45 bassinets, and 700 rooms for different purposes are provided. It has a good rate (85 percent) of bed utilization as compared to the national average. There are 700 full-time employees, 400 medical staff members (of which 270 are courtesy members), and a nursing school of 160 students.

The policies and organization of the hospital were reviewed two years ago by Cresap, McCormick, and Paget, Management Consultants. The consultants' report covered all areas of the hospital in a rather broad way. It was generally favorable. It noted that over the past several years prime attention had been given to organization for administration purposes, but that some problem areas needed additional attention.

Case Exhibit 4-2 shows the top and middle management organization at Newcomer-Willson. The top corporate body is the board of trustees, which is composed of about

**CASE
EXHIBIT 4-2**

Basic Organization of Newcomer-Willson Hospital

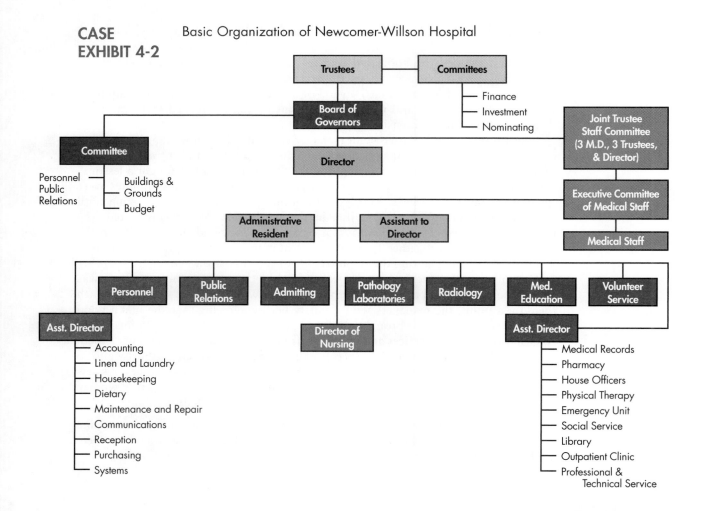

seventy volunteers (nonmedical) from a variety of fields. Most of the trustees are local citizens of some standing in the community.

The most important body in the administrative process that deals with top-level considerations and problems is the board of governors. This board includes the four corporate officers from the board of trustees and nine elected trustees. The board of governors is responsible for the general administration of the organization, and it appoints all members of the medical staff and all other key people of the hospital.

The medical staff organization is headed by an executive committee. This committee operates within the framework of the bylaws of the corporation and more specifically within its own bylaws, which were approved by the board of governors. This committee may report to either the director, Mr. Baker, or to the Joint Trustee Medical Staff Committee, depending on the situation. In the past there have been deliberate attempts at times to override the decisions of the director because of the nature of the problems. This override has not usually been achieved, however, because the director is a member of the Joint Committee.

The medical staff is composed of doctors who have private practices in the surrounding community. They use the hospital when the need arises. They serve on committees of various types (see Case Exhibit 4-3). These staff members are highly trained in their individual professional fields of medicine, and their primary concern is for their particular patients who are in the hospital. In fact, this concern causes some

**CASE
EXHIBIT 4-3** Organization of the Medical Staff

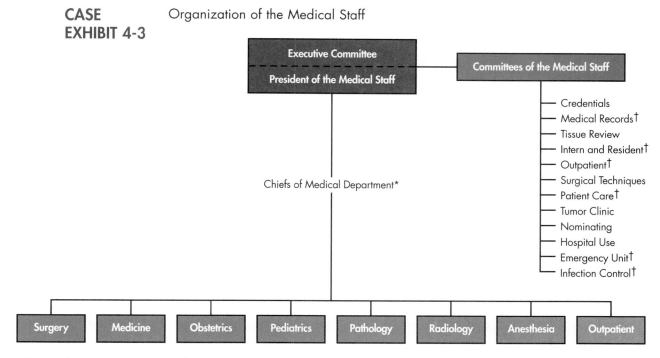

* Each medical department has several doctors.
† Administrative staff all represented on these committees.

problems for Mr. Baker, the nursing staff, and others in supervisory positions, because the hospital staff must think in terms of all of the patients, not just one or a few.

The chief full-time administrative position is that of the director, currently held by Mr. Baker. Mr. Baker has been with the hospital for several years. He is a fellow in hospital administration and has a great deal of administrative experience in several different positions with various organizations. He has been a prime mover in creating an improved administrative organization, through the establishment of committees, bylaws for the medical staff, and written descriptions of duties and responsibilities for all managers and committees. He has an excellent rapport with the medical staff doctors, the members of the board of governors, and his subordinates. Although the administrative process seems to bog down at times, the network of communications through the organization and committee structure ultimately yields satisfactory results. Mr. Baker is a member of most of the administrative committees of the hospital and spends a great deal of time with committee meetings.

Mr. Baker emphasizes the fact that the administrator's job involves many problems and believes that a study made by Charles Prall is reasonably representative of the problems encountered in a hospital. This study shows the percentage of administrators (by type) who reported one or more problems in several given categories. The summary report is presented in Case Exhibit 4-4. Mr. Baker looks upon the extensive committee structure at the trustee, board of governors, and top medical staff levels with mixed feelings. On the one hand, these committees are release valves for troublesome issues and ensure that the democratic process keeps everyone informed. On the other hand, they are very numerous, slow-acting, and time-consuming, and they reach few decisions that would not have been reached on a more timely basis by the director working directly with the executive committee of the medical staff or the board of governors.

470 Part 4 Cases

CASE EXHIBIT 4-4
Percentage of Hospital Administrators Reporting One or More Problems in Specific Categories, by Type of Administrator

Problem Areas	Percentage Reporting One or More Problems by Area		
	Laypeople	Doctors	Nurses
Working with doctors	40	41	71
Improvement of medical care	50	63	90
Business and finance	61	40	43
Public relations	50	50	50
Physical plant	33	25	50

MIDDLE MANAGEMENT ORGANIZATION

The full-time operations of the hospital are organized and conducted under the supervision of twelve people who report directly to Mr. Baker (see Case Exhibit 4-2). Nursing activities are divided into two main groups: Nursing Services and the School of Nursing. Case Exhibit 4-5 shows the internal organization for conducting these nursing activities.

The School of Nursing is largely autonomous because of its educational mission. Along with the medical staff, Nursing Services constitutes the very heart of hospital operations. The members of the nursing staff are specialized and perform their duties on a round-the-clock basis every day of the year (by shifts) in such depart-

CASE EXHIBIT 4-5   Organization of the School of Nursing and Nursing Services

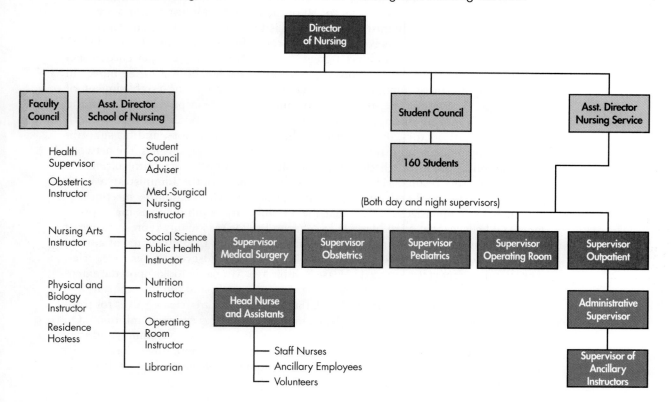

ments as Medicine, Surgery, Obstetrics, Pediatrics, and Operating Room. Theoretically, each nurse has an immediate superior (Head Nurse), but during a normal work period he or she may take instructions from several different people. This is especially the case when dealing with the individual doctors for the various patients. Nurses' work seems to run smoothly until "outsiders" create confusion and frustration by telling nurses to do things that do not constitute their job, that interfere with their primary duties, or that are against the rules or regulations of the hospital.

The medical staff organization includes the doctors who are associated with the hospital. (See Case Exhibit 4-3 for the internal organization of the medical staff.) The hospital's existence depends on the requirements for patient care as determined by the individual medical staff members. Sometimes the individual doctors do not fully realize the "public utility" nature of the hospital. While the doctor may be concerned with his or her patient, the hospital personnel are concerned with all patients. This different perspective leads to some difficulties in such activities as scheduling of operating rooms, proper use of precautionary methods, and administering the rules and regulations established by the board of governors and outside agencies.

ADMINISTRATIVE AND MEDICAL STAFF CONFLICT

Until about fifteen years ago, Newcomer-Willson had a doctor administrator. After a brief experience with a layperson administrator, it went back to a doctor. About nine years ago, it decided again to employ a nonmedical professional administrator. Since then, strides have been made in the administrative activities of the hospital. Basic problems do arise, however, which seem to indicate the need for further improvement in the organizational arrangement and/or the administrative processes. For example, the head (physician) of one of the full-time departments recently demanded "individual professional status," which he thought the medical staff members had and which he did not have. The problem became so serious that the physician threatened to resign if he did not get the status desired. After considerable discussions with various people and in several committee meetings, the board of governors decided that the current status would not be changed substantially and the issue seemed to have been settled—with no resignations. A by-product of this action was the clear evidence that the board of governors is the "governing" body of the hospital.

Another incident reflected the type of problems that Mr. Baker and the administrative supervisors face. Recently, a patient was placed on "precaution" by her doctor. Her physician, accompanied by several resident doctors, came into the patient's room without observing the precautionary rules. The staff nurse reported this incident immediately to her supervisor. The supervisor ordered all the doctors from the room, explaining the reasons to them. The physician took the patient off "precaution" on the spot and remained in the room. This change upset the nursing staff; however, the next morning the physician placed the patient back on "precaution." After discussing the problem with the director of nursing and the physician, Mr. Baker had to decide what must be done in this instance and also in the future to reduce or eliminate such situations.

Mr. Baker said, "I suppose our problem is that the nature of hospital operations makes it necessary to violate some of the essential characteristics of good organization, which authorities like Urwick emphasized. Maybe Emerson was right when he said that poor organization is the 'hookworm disease' of industry. It is a disease we haven't completely cured. Everyone seems to have too many bosses, but somehow we do get the job done."

When you have read this case, review the diagnostic questions included at the end(s) of the chapter(s) you are using to analyze this case, and choose the ones that seem applicable. Then use those questions to begin working on your case analysis.

CASE 4-3 / O CANADA

Bonnie J. Lovelace and Royston Greenwood, University of Alberta

The Public Service Commission of Canada (PSC) is responsible for the provision of a comprehensive human resources management service to the fifty-two departments and agencies of the federal public service. Initially, the commission operated through six branches. One of these, the Staff Development Branch (SDB), is the focus of the present case. The case examines the SDB after it began to experience problems of financial restraint. The SDB was responsible for the provision of:

- Regularly scheduled courses in a variety of professional, technical, and general subjects
- Regular and special courses for senior and executive managers
- Specialized, custom-designed courses on a consulting basis as needed
- A research and development service based on federal adult educational needs

Since its creation, the SDB had grown steadily. Its members were highly qualified professionals in their specific fields, and the SDB provided them with extensive training in adult education methods. The SDB served the federal government on a cost-recoverable basis. That is, it had to market courses and cover *all* of its costs, including overhead. Courses were sold to client departments at prices comparable to those charged for similar programs available on the open market. Before this case was written, SDB had enjoyed more business than it could handle. It had an excellent reputation, and there had been no lack of funds within departmental training budgets.

In prior years, the SDB had about 250 members and was organized as shown in Case Exhibit 4-6. Each of the five directorates was a cost center, responsible for forecasting its own revenues and costs. Although the SDB technically operated on a "branch break-even" basis, each directorate operated on the assumption that it should cover costs.

The two largest directorates within the branch were the Directorate of Staff Development and Training (DSDT) and the Regional Operations Directorate (ROD). These provided the bulk of the regularly scheduled courses offered by the branch. The primary division of responsibility between the DSDT and the ROD was that the DSDT serviced the Ottawa region, where the vast bulk of the public service was located, and the ROD serviced the rest of Canada. The six regional units of the ROD and the DSDT operated the same courses, but in different locations.

DIRECTORATE OF STAFF DEVELOPMENT AND TRAINING

The DSDT was organized in terms of six programs, each headed by a program manager and staffed by as many as fourteen people (including two clerks). Each program had its special field and provided a full range of courses within that field. Trainers

CASE
EXHIBIT 4-6

Staff Development Branch

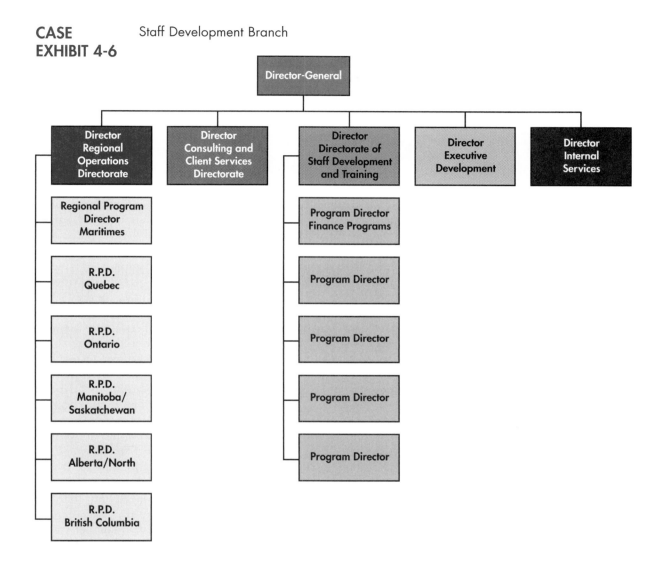

within a program did most of their own course design and teaching and would hire outside consultants only for very special courses offered on a limited basis.

The client group of the DSDT included any public servant in the Ottawa region who was not a senior manager or an executive. The latter groups were serviced through the Executive Education Directorate. The DSDT trainers worked singly or in teams, depending on the course and their experience. Each trainer generally was responsible for one or two courses that would be taught ten to fifteen times per year.

Consulting and custom design work in the Ottawa region was not handled by the DSDT. Such work would be handled through the Consulting and Client Services Directorate (CCSD). If a client department wanted a regular course to be run in-house and for itself alone (as opposed to sending participants to the DSDT's courses), the DSDT would "sell" an appropriate trainer to the CCSD. Regional units of the ROD also could use (and be charged for) DSDT trainers. Marketing and registration for Ottawa courses were handled through the Internal Services Directorate. Program units within the DSDT concentrated on providing high-quality, regularly scheduled courses in Ottawa, leasing out trainers to consulting or to regional operations when time permitted and as need demanded.

Essentially, the task facing the DSDT was reasonably straightforward: develop and teach courses in one city for a very large population. The directorate was large and operated through four levels of management providing a heavy schedule of repeated courses. Each of these levels of management had controls and pressures that affected the next.

REGIONAL OPERATIONS DIRECTORATE

The ROD had a small headquarters group in Ottawa, headed by the director. The six regional offices were located in Halifax, Montreal, Toronto, Winnipeg, Edmonton, and Vancouver. Each regional office was headed by a regional program director and staffed by two or three full-time trainers, supported by a secretary, a registry clerk, and a student from Waterloo University who administered the Open Learning Systems Correspondence courses.

Regional offices catered to federal public servants in the regions and handled most SDB business within their area. The basic role of the ROD was to provide the same spectrum of courses for the regions as was offered in Ottawa by the DSDT. However, because of the lower volume of demand, regional trainers were generalists and were required to teach and manage a variety of courses that in Ottawa were divided between the six program areas. The regional trainers were responsible for all administrative support services. They would design and advertise courses, prepare necessary materials, set up the classroom, teach, and assess the course. In addition, the regional trainers would administer, but not teach, a wide range of other courses. These courses would be taught by local consultants or Ottawa trainers (from DSDT) hired by the regional trainer.

The director and the trainers in the regions spent a considerable amount of time visiting clients, advertising programs, and putting out newsletters. The registry clerk spent most of her time contacting departmental training officers, looking for course participants. She also ensured that administrative letters and details were put out on time by the trainers. In addition, the trainers and director actively sought out consulting work, which they set up and discharged themselves.

The regions carried high overhead and travel expenses and had smaller clients with smaller budgets. The trainers were conscious that every penny counted. At the same time, quality had to be maintained. In times of trouble, most rules were set aside, and people within the regional offices worked together to generate new ideas for courses. The regional offices were small enough to encourage considerable face-to-face interaction.

Relationships between the DSDT and the regional offices of ROD had always been good. Many of the regional people had worked in the DSDT earlier in their careers. Two regional directors had worked their way up through the ranks of the Ottawa division. Minor skirmishes had often occurred over the years, generally relating to problems with a few DSDT trainers who tended to head for the regions and demand that everyone from the director down should cater to their every whim. These few were well known and avoided when possible.

The ROD deliberately sought people who preferred smaller working groups, diverse tasks, and a great deal of autonomy. In contrast, the DSDT tended more toward individuals who had a particular specialty and taught it, leaving their senior managers to handle the "paperwork." There was no question that Ottawa trainers felt strong ownership of "their" courses and, given the opportunity, wanted a say in the regions. The regional people taught "everyone's" courses, depending on the schedule, and were just as happy to find local people who could do the others with a little guidance.

FROM BOOM TO BUST

In prior years, the SDB had enjoyed a booming business. There was no lack of funding in departmental training budgets, and the branch had all the business it could handle. Although the economy seemed to be slumping, it did not appear serious. Rumors, however, were circulating about cutbacks as the full force of the economic downturn began to make itself felt. The Treasury Board demanded thorough reviews of departmental budgets, and one of the first areas cut by most departments was training. The SDB, on full cost recovery, found its market suddenly less affluent.

In June, the regional directors were in Halifax for their semiannual meeting. They usually met in one of the regions during September for a general meeting and again in January in Ottawa for a budget meeting. This year, they were meeting in June because a major educational conference was taking place for two days at Dalhousie University, at which some of the top experts in the field were featured speakers. The regional directors had agreed with their boss, George Hudson, that they would work Sunday through Wednesday to handle regular business, leaving Thursday and Friday for the conference.

On Tuesday afternoon, the group was discussing what the ensuing months might hold. "I'm worried," mused Herb Aiken of Halifax. "My registrations are dropping off, and we're looking at canceling courses. You know what that means—trainers sitting around on the overhead with nothing to do."

Sarah Wilson from Edmonton concurred. She had just received a telex from her office informing her that a three-day course set to start the next day had just suffered seven last-minute cancellations. "That leaves only eight people; we can't do it, financially or pedagogically. And we've sunk training time and administrative costs into it. I'm going to have to call and tell my staff to contact the other participants and try to postpone. This is very bad for business, though, and we can't keep it up."

She left to make her call. Thomas Russell from Vancouver picked up the ball: "The funny thing is, our clients are willing to lose the one-third late cancellation penalty, rather than pay the whole course fee. Forecasting revenues is becoming impossible, and we're barely keeping our heads above water. Where is this taking us?"

George Hudson tried to soothe everyone's fears, saying everyone in Ottawa was still doing okay and was optimistic. The directors looked at one another, each silently thinking that it was always the regions that got hit first. It was easier for the Ottawa mandarins to make cuts where the pain wasn't staring them in the face every morning. At that moment, Sarah returned and told George there was an urgent phone call for him. He left, and the others continued to discuss the future. Hudson returned about ten minutes later, his face grim. "There's very bad news," he said flatly. "Treasury Board issued a directive this morning stating that all nonessential training is to be reviewed and canceled whenever possible. The phones are ringing off the wall and everything on our books is on hold until October or November."

The situation worsened during the summer. Regional trainers were out visiting their clients constantly, trying desperately to drum up business, selling a day's consulting here, working on a problem there. It was difficult. Many clients were in offices located significant distances from the regional centers. Regional directors, however, were on the rampage over travel costs and telephone bills. But, as one Toronto trainer said to her boss one day: "A letter a day just won't do it! We need to talk to them, get them to spend whatever money they've got on our courses, rather than buying on the private market."

Alice Waters knew this was true, but she *had* to keep costs trimmed to the bone. The Treasury Board had told departments to trim training costs. Given their smaller budgets, many departments preferred to provide their own training or use consultants.

By late summer, a few courses were beginning to pick up registrants as people began to sort out their budgets. Some Ottawa courses were rescheduled, but there was still a lot of slack. One morning, Sam Wisler of Winnipeg called Vancouver: "I just had a long talk with Mike White, the Financial Management Program manager. He wants to negotiate with us about having his trainers do all the resourcing on our regional financial courses from now on. Did a lot of talking about how we should be saving branch funds by keeping the money inside wherever possible."

Thomas Russell, listening carefully, said: "Well, in the past, we could never get their trainers, unless somebody wanted to visit his relatives and made a deal with us. All the regions hire local consultants for courses we don't teach ourselves. Saves all those travel costs. However, it's worth thinking about. What did you tell him?"

Wisler replied: "Just that. We should all think about it. The way I see it, things are getting better, but we may never see those good times again. If we can get Programs to do some of our courses (which are the same ones being done in Ottawa), and for less than our local consultants can do it, we'll be helping each other. They've got a lot of trainers with expensive time on their hands, and we've got courses our own staff can't do, especially in EDP, Finance, and Personnel. Maybe we can help each other. I think I should talk it over with Hudson, and see about putting out a telex to all regions on it. We can discuss it on our next teleconference."

By November, both Ottawa and the regions had managed to reschedule most of their courses, but at drastically reduced registration levels. This meant costs were more or less the same, but revenues were way down. Even though the branch had an official policy that breakeven was calculated on the branch level, everyone knew that cost centers losing money were vulnerable. And each program, each region, was a cost center. They closed ranks. People who had worked well together for years with colleagues in the other directorate suddenly discovered negative characteristics of which they had previously been unaware. ROD jealously defended its right to hire local resources; the DSDT stubbornly insisted that course manuals were their property. Each group saw the other as untrustworthy, and open communication virtually ended. This was on everyone's mind as the regional directors held a conference by phone one morning.

George Hudson opened the discussion: "I've been getting feedback from all of you by telex on progress with Programs. My assessment so far is that they want to sell you their trainers' time to cut their overhead, and you're willing to buy it as long as charges are comparable to what it costs when you resource these programs locally. However, it appears that what they want to charge exceeds your local costs. Not only that, but each of you is negotiating separate agreements."

Thomas Russell broke in angrily: "You can say that again. Mike White wants to send me two trainers to do the four-day Fundamentals of Budget Formulation and Control course, and he wants a total of nineteen days of time plus travel costs to do it. But he offered to do it for Sarah with one trainer and fewer days of time. What's going on here?"

Sarah's reply was consistent with what everyone had been experiencing. "The month my course is scheduled is one where most of Mike's trainers are booked. He gave me whatever time was left. It seems that they want to dump all their excess time on us. Well, our budgets won't take it."

Evelyn D'Anjou in Montreal continued: "We've got to negotiate standard charges. And they must be reasonable ones, or we'll go to local, as we've always done when we had to rely on ourselves."

George Hudson, sensing that feelings were heating up and deciding that a teleconference was not the best medium for this discussion, told everyone to sit back. He promised to meet with the DSDT director, Bob Smythe, and talk things over as soon as possible.

The next day a furious Alice Waters was on the phone to George Hudson. "Things are getting totally out of hand. I phoned Mike this morning to tell him we couldn't accept the charges he wants for our next financial course, so I had hired the Jameson people to do it. He tells me that's just fine, but all those new regulations for budgeting are being worked into the course, and his people are the only ones who can do it. And he refuses to release the new course manual because he claims it's not in its final form. George, you know we can't do outdated courses in the regions. I have to have that course book. Those manuals are branch property, not DSDT property! The Programs develop them because that's part of their responsibility, but it's policy that they must be made available to the regions, because we have to offer the same course out here. Mike as much as hinted that we will all be having trouble getting manuals for the Programs from now on. He says when things were slack over the summer, they revamped many of our courses, but the changes are still being tested. We're being blackmailed!"

Alice stopped, having run out of breath. George questioned her, giving her time to cool off a bit, but he was concerned. Alice was one of his best managers, a skilled trainer herself, and one who was more than able to negotiate solid agreements with her colleagues. If her problem-solving skills were not helping, they were in trouble. "Have you considered training some of your own staff to do the more specialized courses, Alice? Maybe we can reduce our dependence on the Programs that way."

Alice was not mollified: "George, you know what our trainers do. Everything . . . teach, administer, market, consult, clean up classrooms, weekends in airports. They just don't have time for more. Besides, why train them to do a course that's only offered twice a year in their own region. . . . We have others that run frequently both on our regular schedule and on an in-house basis. But the Ottawa trainers only have their one or two little courses to think about. No marketing, no consulting. Even big training centers with everything done for them! They walk out of our classrooms on Friday night and don't clean up a thing! They say that's our job, not theirs. Well, we don't have big staffs catering to our small offices, and it's our weekend, too. But I'm getting off the topic. . . . What about those course books? I've already telexed the other regions to warn them about what's happening."

Inwardly, Hudson groaned. Every one of his directors would be up in arms by the end of the day. He promised Alice he'd go to Bob Smythe, the director of DSDT, to talk matters over, and hung up. Glancing at his telephone, he could see the lights coming on; it was starting already. Thankful it was Friday, he told his clerk to hold the calls and left to find Bob Smythe.

A half hour later, Hudson returned and dictated a telex: Everyone was to sit tight. Smythe was meeting with his managers Monday morning to discuss the matter.

The following Tuesday, Hudson picked up the teleconference phone to address his regions. He wondered how much he'd get through before the protests began. "I just had a meeting with Bob Smythe. His managers claim we're doing outdated courses and that they should be given control of course content. They also believe we should hire their resources before any consultants, to help minimize branch downtime. Smythe agrees with them, and they're tabling the matter with the director-general at the next management committee meeting."

There was silence as the six listeners digested this news, each realizing the potential consequences.

Then Sam Wisler in Winnipeg spoke angrily: "This is incredible. They want to make money at our expense! Are we working for the same place or aren't we? What is going on here? We won't let those jerks get away with this!"

Herb Aiken's language was much stronger, but the message was the same. Hudson listened to the chorus of angry voices for a while and then asked for everything in the way of financial ammunition, details of travel costs, local costs, and Programs changes. Then he ended the call.

The SDB Management Committee came to the conclusion that branch resources should be used whenever possible to teach branch courses. The regions and the Programs were instructed to work out standard charges to be used in the January budget exercise for the upcoming fiscal year. The point was noted that the regions had to provide up-to-date courses and, if that involved using the DSDT resources, that was the way things had to be.

In January, two of the regional directors came to Ottawa to meet two representatives from the DSDT. The objective was to settle standard charges for all courses. Preparation time, teaching time, travel time, and administrative responsibilities would be fixed. Ratios were to be agreed on and used as formulas for all courses in the future. Alice Waters and Sarah Wilson had canvassed the other regional directors on acceptable alternatives and had full authority from them to act. They had requested that the two DSDT representatives come with the same authority, as time was running out. The group met for a full day on Monday and, by the end of it, the two regional directors were exhausted and frustrated. The DSDT representatives were demanding costly ratios, were not giving an inch, and had to take back any proposals to their own director for his approval. And he was away until Wednesday.

That night Alice and Sarah paid a late-night visit to Hudson, venting their anger openly. The regions could not survive the charges being imposed by DSDT. It seemed that the SDB had some fundamental decisions to make about its internal affairs, decisions that were beyond the authority of Wilson and Waters. Those decisions had to be made before the new budgets were drafted.

Despite meeting again on Tuesday and Wednesday, the DSDT and ROD representatives failed to agree on standard charges. The matter was again put to the Management Committee. The committee reiterated its position that in-house resources had to be used and decided that the regions would have to live with the Program demands.

In March, the ROD tabled its budget for the upcoming fiscal year. It showed a substantial projected loss. The DSDT tabled its budget, showing a substantial projected profit.

When you have read this case, review the diagnostic questions included at the end(s) of the chapter(s) you are using to analyze this case, and choose the ones that seem applicable. Then use those questions to begin working on your case analysis.

CASE 4-4 **DUMAS PUBLIC LIBRARY**

Mark Hammer, Gary Whitney, University of San Diego

It came as a surprise when Jeff Mallet learned of the conflict between Debra Dickenson and Helen Hendricks, because he knew them both personally and regarded them both as competent administrators. Debra Dickenson, thirty-eight, was the youngest mayor in the state when she was elected three years ago, and was the first female mayor in Kimball's history. She was widely recognized for her high levels of energy and dedication. Helen Hendricks, sixty-two, had been the head librarian at

---

Dumas Public Library for fifteen years and was widely acknowledged among Kimball citizens as being primarily responsible for the high quality of the library services to the community. Dumas Public Library serves the citizens of Kimball, a town of 20,000 people in rural eastern New Mexico. Kimball is dominated by the 16,000-student state university located there, and this university presence creates a rather unique clientele for the public library. The library has enjoyed a history of solid citizen support and has until recently benefited from cordial relations between the library staff and the city's administration.

The library is housed in a modern, air-conditioned structure with carpeted floors and attractive furnishings. Approximately 35,000 volumes are on the shelves. The 1988 budget, including payroll, acquisition of new books, and building maintenance, was $195,000. The library has no formal organization. Helen Hendricks has reporting to her five full-time employees, three of whom are professional librarians. Completing the staff are ten half-time permanent employees, ten to twelve unpaid volunteers, and an occasional intern from the university.

The city is governed by an elected city council and mayor. Day-to-day administration is the responsibility of Ralph Riesen, the city supervisor, who is a permanent employee of the city. Jeff Mallet, professor of management, first learned about the existence of strained relationships between the library and the city administration from Linda Turner, adult services librarian. According to Linda, feelings of distrust and animosity toward city hall had been growing recently among the library staff. Linda was concerned about the unhealthy climate that this hostility was creating at the library.

Several weeks later, Jeff had an opportunity to talk with Debra Dickenson and Ralph Riesen. Jeff said he had heard that relations between city hall and the library were not good. Debra and Ralph confirmed that relations between the two groups had reached an intolerably low level, and they agreed something would have to be done about it. Debra and Ralph expressed bewilderment about what could be done to improve the situation. "If you have any ideas or suggestions. I'd certainly like to hear them," Debra said.

Jeff suggested that it might prove helpful to have an outsider interview members of both groups to provide some independent perspective. He volunteered his services for this purpose. Debra and Ralph readily agreed to Jeff's offer.

The next day Jeff was talking to Paul Everest, a fellow business faculty member and consultant, about the situation at the library. Jeff invited Paul to join him on the case, and Paul accepted. The next week Jeff made a series of personal visits and phone calls to the key staff members from city hall and the library. An agreement was reached to have Jeff and Paul interview both groups and make recommendations. Appointments were made for an interview with Debra Dickenson and Ralph Riesen at city hall, followed by one with Helen Hendricks, Linda Turner, and Maude Richardson (children's librarian) at the library.

THE VIEW FROM CITY HALL

Debra: "I'm really concerned about the way things have developed between us here at city hall and the library staff. There is animosity between these two groups, and the situation has been worse over the past few months. There's not nearly the level of cooperation that there should be. I'll be eager to consider any suggestions that you [professors] might have for how to improve the situation. I know that something has to be done, and I'm willing to devote some time and effort to working on it.

"The problem at the library is that I no longer have administrative control over their operations. In the past the library has reported to the mayor through the city supervisor and that has worked reasonably well. Recently, however, we discovered that legislation passed back in the 1930s makes it very clear that the library board of trustees has the legal authority for the conduct of the day-to-day operations of the library.

"My concern is that since the library is a part of the city administration, the city is legally responsible for its operations. I'm talking specifically about legal liability for such things as personnel selection, equal employment opportunity regulations, purchasing guidelines, and budgeting procedures set down by the state. In the case of lawsuits and budget overruns, it seems clear to me that the city will be liable and hence we need to have administrative control over these matters. Also, it just makes good common sense for us to coordinate certain administrative functions from city hall, such as personnel selection and budgeting. Basically the library staff agrees with us on this issue, and we have been doing many of these functions at city hall.

"One of the things that irks me most about Helen Hendricks (head librarian) and her staff is that they continue to insist on politicizing the budget-making process, even when they know or should know that this is an extremely disruptive and unfair practice. I have made it pretty clear to all the department heads within the city that the budget-making process should be one where budget requests are submitted to the city administration and to the city council along with the implications of funding increases or decreases. Based on that input, the city council then decides on the services that it wants in a non-emotional manner.

"The city council represents the citizens and that is a perfectly democratic procedure. Prior to the recent budget preparation period, the city council gave budget directives to all city departments. The library board chose to ignore these directives and submitted their own budget. Subsequently the library staff started a big political campaign to pack the council chambers at all the budget hearings with patrons of the library and other citizens who supported the library's request for more funding.

"I have tried to point out to Helen how disruptive and unfair this is. The fact is that almost every city department serves some constituency and could, if they were so inclined, rally citizen support from among their clients or constituents to bring political pressure to bear on the city council and other members of the city administration to fund their individual projects.

"It seems obvious to me that this is a chaotic way to try to prepare a city budget. Special-interest politics has no place in the preparation of the city budget, which is fair to all parties concerned. Only people who have looked at the entire city budget and have considered the total revenues available to the city and the cost-and-benefit tradeoffs made by each one of the city departments are in any position to judge whether any particular department is reasonably funded. The fact is that there are prime financial needs in all of the city departments and the library is not alone. "I support the library wholeheartedly; we all do. I'm just not one bit impressed when the librarians campaign to have a flock of citizens pack the council chambers to stand there and tell us that they support the library. That is not a helpful input to the budget-making process. Everybody supports the library.

"Following one occurrence of inappropriate political lobbying last fall, I expressed my annoyance to Walter Roy (chairperson of the library board of trustees). Subsequently the board told Helen to cease her lobbying activities. I think she got the message, but I know the lobbying did not stop. That tells me that the trustees do not have control over the library staff.

"Don't get me wrong. Helen Hendricks has done a marvelous job down there at the library, but things just haven't been the same since her husband died unexpectedly two years ago. She seems to have retreated into a womb or something. I think she uses the library staff as a personal support group. I don't know who is running the library anymore, but it certainly isn't Helen. I think the staff is running the library, to tell you the truth."

Ralph: "I, too, have noticed the worsening relations between us and the library staff. Part of the problem may be the physical isolation of the library and the fact that they don't interact much with other city personnel. (The library is three blocks from city hall.)

"If you ask me, I think there is a case of paranoia down there at the library. Some of them seem to believe that I'm out to get them. In fact, I have a definite feeling that several of the library staff members think that I'm some sort of an ogre.

"I believe many of the problems that the library staff think they have are more imaginary than real. I remember once I talked to Helen and she was complaining about some things. I asked her to make me a list of grievances that they had, ways in which they had less money or things that weren't satisfactory. Do you know, I've never gotten any list from Helen. I really don't think they have any substantial problems that aren't of their own making."

Debra: "I get the impression that the library staff feels that they are picked on and mistreated. The fact is that the library has the best working conditions of almost any other department in the city. Not only are their working conditions congenial and agreeable, but the clientele they serve are all happy and supportive of the library. It's a totally positive environment.

"That's quite a bit different from the city engineer's department, where they have to talk to irate contractors and homeowners, or the police, who have to deal with drug offenders and unhappy traffic violators.

"I'm still very confused about the proper roles of the library administration, the library board of trustees, and the city administration."

Ralph: "Lynn King (city finance director) is another player in this scenario. Lynn probably has more interaction with the library staff on a day-to-day basis than anybody else here in city hall. She deals with them on matters of auditing, purchasing procedures, and employee selection procedures. There have been disagreements and friction generated over a number of these issues. Lynn really distrusts Helen as an administrator."

Debra: "I really would like to hear from the library staff on their perceptions of what our problems are. I don't really know what they think.

"One of the areas that Helen and I have had disagreements about has been that of Helen's classification within the city administrative system. Helen seems to think that she should be classified as a department director. The trouble is that Helen's responsibilities are simply not equivalent to those of other department directors within the city. Each of the other directors has at least two major administrative functions reporting to him or her. For example, the director of public safety has both police and fire reporting to him.

"When we reorganized the city administration recently, we changed it so that Helen was reporting to the mayor through the director of public services, Jack Feldner. Helen got all bent out of shape that she wasn't reporting directly to the mayor and that she had to report through someone else. She made such a fuss about it that we finally agreed to her request.

"Ralph issued a memo of understanding to Helen to the effect that she still had direct access to us here at city hall and that we would interact with her on a direct basis.

"One of the city council members introduced a proposal to classify Helen as a department head recently, but this proposal was withdrawn at my request. I'm afraid that as a result some people are getting the impression that I am not really supportive of the library. I really am, but my concern in this matter is with equity—all the other department directors have considerably more administrative responsibility than Helen does and they wouldn't consider it fair to have Helen classified as a department director."

Ralph: "Helen keeps raising the issue of her salary level. I'm convinced that Helen is fairly paid in relation to other city employees. The trouble is that all city employees are underpaid compared to university salaries and we're *never* going to catch up. Dissatisfaction with pay is just one of those things that we have to accept and live with.

Despite what Helen says, I don't think salary is that big a problem. I remember from the supervision class that you [Jeff] taught that, according to Herzberg, pay is a hygiene factor. I don't think that we're going to solve any big problems down at the library by working on hygiene factors."

Debra: "An incident that happened recently will illustrate what I consider totally unprofessional conduct on the part of the library staff. As you know, I recently refused to reappoint Cecil Hockman to the library board of trustees after his first term expired. Now, as the mayor, I have the duty and obligation to the citizens of Kimball to appoint people to boards that I think are best qualified to do the jobs. I had my reasons for not reappointing Cecil—reasons that I consider good. Because we are making agreements with the trustees about the administration of the library, I want trustees who will work with us to try to reach a compromise. Cecil has never agreed to any compromise action and would stop library cooperative efforts.

"What happened was that somebody down at the library called a reporter and told them about my refusal to reappoint Cecil Hockman. They apparently said that I had a vendetta going against Cecil and that a reporter should look into this. The reporter did check with Mr. Hockman and got a bunch of quotes from him concerning my nonsupport for library programs. Then the reporter called me and asked me if I wanted to respond to the charges. *I was furious.* I told her, 'No, I do not want to respond.' I did explain my duties and responsibilities as mayor to the reporter, and she subsequently decided that there was no story.

"Sometimes I feel like calling Helen up here on the carpet and telling her to shape up her act or get out. It becomes clearer to me all the time that, whatever else she is, Helen is not a competent administrator.

"If the problems we're having with administration at the library can't be solved, we are going to be forced to look at the issue of regionalization of this library—that is, having the city library join the county system along with the library in Morton. However, it is apparent to me that the idea of regionalization is extremely threatening to everybody down at the library.

"This showed up recently when the capital expenditures committee recommended, among other things in its report to city council, that the feasibility of regionalization of the city's library, cemetery, and health care facil-

ities be studied. You wouldn't believe how upset the librarians became over that recommendation. They got a city council member to make a motion that the recommendation be deleted from the committee's report, and unfortunately it passed. The librarians clearly didn't even want the issue studied![22]

THE VIEW FROM THE LIBRARY

Helen: "I'm surprised and delighted to hear you [professors] report that Debra Dickenson and Ralph Riesen are really interested in improving relations with us here at the library. I feel that we have been wasting a lot of time down here because of the poor relations we have with city hall, and I wasn't at all sure how concerned they felt about it up there.

"One of the main problems that I see between us and the city administration is their general resentment toward anything involving political pressure. I sense that Debra and Ralph get upset when the community voices opinions that are contrary to their views. I sometimes get the feeling that they would like to run the city without interference from citizens. However, that's the very nature of the political process. The mayor's job is inherently a political one. You shouldn't be in that position and expect to be immune from public pressure. So I don't think it's appropriate that Debra gets upset when the citizens rally to support a program that they want.

"During the recent budget hearings, we had lots of good people come to our defense. The library board of trustees has been very supportive. The AAUW (American Association of University Women) has several members who have been strong supporters. These friends have been instrumental in helping us make the case to the mayor and the city council that the community really supports a quality program here at the library."

Linda: "We don't seem to have any problems of misunderstanding or nonsupport from either the library board of trustees or the city council. I feel good about our relations with both of these groups. When we have gone to the city council with our recommendations and proposals, they have been sympathetic and supportive. In the budget hearings, both the library board and the city council supported our proposed budget over the objections of Debra and Ralph. In effect, we bypassed the city administration and we came out better than if we had gone to them first, as they apparently wanted us to do.

"One example of a way in which we have felt 'under attack' by city hall has been the way they have acted in regard to the appointment of members of the library board of trustees."

Helen: "That's right. You probably heard that just recently Debra refused to reappoint Cecil Hockman to the board for a second term. Now Cecil has been a strong, energetic supporter of the library. He has given a great deal of his time and dedication to public service on the library board. Mr. Hockman's first term on the board has just recently expired, and for no apparent reason Debra has declined to reappoint him, even though it has been customary in the past that members serve for two terms. So Cecil Hockman is not only eligible for reappointment, but has also demonstrated in his first term that he is a dedicated and concerned public citizen.

"It seems apparent to us that Debra resents anyone who supports the library as strongly as Cecil Hockman did. You see, Cecil initiated some legal research that determined that the library board of trustees has the ultimate legislative authority for the administration of the library. Furthermore, Cecil Hockman took the initiative to argue our budget proposals before the city council. Debra did not appreciate either of these measures, I am sure, and now it seems that she is out to get him.

"In the past, I have always participated with the mayor when selecting candidates for the library board. The mayor has always been glad to have my input and opinion on which citizens would be good for the library board. None of that consultation has gone on between Debra and me recently; I just find out about her board appointments by reading the newspaper."

Linda: "Another way that we have felt attacked by the city administration has been the way we were treated in the recent reorganization of the city administrative hierarchy."

Helen: "What they did was to demote the library by changing the reporting patterns so that instead of reporting directly to the city supervisor, I was directed to report through Jack Feldner, the director of public services.

"This reassignment of the library was a serious downgrading of our status within the city. I was really upset when I learned that they expected me to report *through* Jack Feldner. Why, I have more education than Jack does. I have longer service to the city of Kimball than he does, and I supervise a *lot* of people here at the library. The very idea that the library, with its staff of professionals, should be considered subordinate to someone whose main concern is parks and recreation was an appalling idea to us over here. You see, that demotes us from one of the major functional units within the city administration to merely one of the concerns of the parks and recreation department. I don't have anything against Jack Feldner, but I don't think it's right to have the city library subordinate to him and his department.

"I was told that in the reorganization of the city administration, I was not considered an administrator (department director level) because I supervise so few people. However, Lynn King (finance director) supervises only a few people, and she doesn't have the education I do, either."

Maude: "I don't think that they regard us as professionals over here, but we *are* professionals. Each one of us has had five years of college plus additional professional training, and yet we continually get treated as if we were mere clerks."

Linda: "An incident that illustrates the library's diminished status was city hall's insistence that Helen could not retain the title of library director. The title library director is common among librarians having similar jobs to Helen's. Among the staff here at the library, it seems the logical choice of position titles. And yet the city administration insisted that Helen could not be called a director. So they suggested that we call her the library supervisor. Of course, supervisor denotes someone just above the clerical level; someone who is supervising a bunch of clerks. That seems natural to them, but the idea is considered appalling over here. We hassled back and forth over different possible titles for Helen's position and finally settled on city librarian. This title is less descriptive than library director and reflects Helen's lowered status in the city."

Maude: "I don't think Helen is regarded as an administrator by the city administration. I don't think they really know how many people she has reporting to her, or how much leadership it takes to coordinate all the volunteer help we have. Helen has a substantial administrative job to keep this library running smoothly."

Helen: "Going along with that is their resistance to paying me a salary reflecting my abilities and contribution. My salary is simply not in line with the requirements of this job, my education, and the experience I have with the city of Kimball. I know that I'm paid less than many other people in the city who have less education and less experience than I do. The city administration simply refuses to recognize the importance of my job."

Jeff: "How would your salary compare, Helen, to other library directors having similar jobs around the state?"

Helen: "Well, I would have to say that my salary today reflects some very significant adjustments upward that were made during the 1960s. At that time the university was under heavy pressure to equalize the salaries of its female professionals, and the city of Kimball also upgraded women's salaries at the same time. So I shared with some other women in some impressive gains during the 1960s.

"If you looked just at the figures, my salary wouldn't look that far off relative to other city librarians. However, the figures don't reflect the quality of education I have received, the length of my service to the city of Kimball, and the contributions that I have made to the development of this library today."

Jeff: "Could you give us an example or two of specific ways that the library's effectiveness has been impaired by the actions of members of the city administration?"

Helen: "Certainly. One good example would be the copier incident. That's a long story. Some time ago we experienced an equipment failure with the copier that we had for patrons to use. Therefore, I asked permission from the board of trustees to allocate Kimball Fund (donated) money to purchase a new copier, and they approved. I went ahead with procedures to order a new copier. The next thing that I learned was that Debra had disallowed the purchase. She said that I should have checked with her first.

"I was flabbergasted. I had never felt that I had to check with the mayor on decisions like that. Furthermore, I was angry because she had ruled on the decision without checking into what the reasons for it were. I felt 'zapped' by Debra, like I have in several other situations. It seems to me that I did the right thing by checking with my board of trustees on the decision I made. As you know, by legislation they have the responsibility for the administrative functions of the library. When they have approved a decision like this, what basis does the mayor have for interfering in our decision?

"Another way that Debra has demonstrated her lack of support for the library is by advancing the idea that the library should be regionalized to become a part of the county system. Anybody who knows anything about the library regards this as a preposterous idea.

"In the first place, to seriously consider the idea of regionalization, you would have to undertake a rather comprehensive study of the consequences. That in itself would be a major, expensive undertaking, which I don't think Debra is ready to shoulder. It is clear to me if such a study were done, the result would overwhelmingly favor the present organizational arrangement. We have very little in common with the Morton library, and nothing at all to be gained by being put in the county system. Kimball is a unique community with citizens who have very different expectations from those in the remainder of the county, which is largely rural. The whole idea of regionalization is so preposterous that it seems to me to be irresponsible to even advance the idea.

"I get the feeling that Debra is accumulating a checklist against me. I have had a fear for some time now that Debra could at any time try to have me fired. I get the feeling in talking to them that I'm not getting straight messages from them.

"At least there's one thing to be grateful for—I just passed my sixty-second birthday and can't be deprived of my pension if I am fired or forced to resign. I would like to stay on until I am sixty-five, but the way things are going between Debra and me I never know.

"I get to feeling sad and hopeless and despairing when I think about the way I'm regarded at city hall. I think it's tragic when someone like me has given many dedicated years of service and has made major contributions to building a strong program, and then finds herself spending her last few years in an atmosphere of distrust and unappreciation. I think I deserve better."

Linda: "The distrust in our relationship shows itself practically every time we have an interaction. Recently, I have taken on the duties of adult services librarian and have been out visiting members of other city departments discussing ways that the library could be of service to them. I have had really warm and friendly receptions from everybody I have visited, with the exception of Ralph Riesen. When I talked to him in the same way that I had the other people, I felt like I got a cold shoulder. He seemed very uninterested. What I would most like would be to talk straight to Debra and Ralph and get straight answers in return."

Helen: "We shouldn't overlook the fact that there have been some positive developments recently. For example, the new personnel officer, Joyce Gardner, came down and visited us last week. She was very understanding and very sympathetic about our problems. I am rather optimistic that many of our problems concerning selection, advertising, and interviewing will be better now that Joyce is here."

Linda: "The recent hiring of two part-time people with Joyce's advice and help is an example of how well things *can* be done and how we and the city administration can work together. We should find more ways to use our separate expertise cooperatively!"

Helen: "Also, I am encouraged by the cooperation I have been getting from Jack Feldner. He recently responded favorably to my request for a crew to come over here and help with moving books away from an area where we had a leaking roof. I haven't always felt that I've had Jack's complete support and cooperation, but lately I've been feeling better about that. One example of an item I'll bet is on Debra's checklist against me is the fact that the library is over its budget this year. Now the reason for this is that since the budgeting processes have been centralized in city hall, I simply haven't had access to the kind of information I need to keep track of the budget. I'm afraid that I'm going to be unjustifiably blamed for this situation. This is an example of the kind of information I should not have to ask for—they should automatically give it to me."

Linda: "I *am* concerned about the way that these crises with the city affect our morale and productivity. I have observed that when these crises come up, we on the staff cease to care about our work as much, we spend *much* time rehashing incidents to reassure ourselves, and we do not do as good a job because we do not feel secure or appreciated. I am amazed to see myself doing this, as I like my job, but I do find myself lowering the quality of my work when I feel threatened, and I see others doing it, too. So continued bad feelings are counterproductive and inefficient."

Maude: "One indicator of the kind of relationship that Debra has with us down here in the library is the reaction she gets when she comes down here. I remember a time when she was down here recently. We were all very nervous and very alert. It was like we all suspected that she was up to no good being down here, and we had to watch her every step."

INITIAL MEETINGS

After reviewing what they had learned in the meetings with city hall and the library staff, Jeff and Paul decided to recommend a series of four two-hour meetings. They formulated tentative meeting agendas and sent copies to each of the five prospective participants. After informal checks had established the agreement of each of the five to the proposed meetings, the consultants sent a confirming memo to each person, announcing the time and place for the four meetings.

Meeting 1, March 19

The agenda presented by the consultants for the first meeting included a brief introduction by the consultants, an expectations check, a sharing appreciations exercise, and a closing process check.

Following the introduction, the participants were asked to participate in an expectations check. For the first half of this exercise each person was asked to write on two separate sheets of paper (1) his or her hopes and (2) his or her fears for the upcoming series of meetings. In the second half of the exercise these hopes and fears were shared, posted on newsprint, and discussed. This exercise activity took about forty minutes.

The "sharing appreciations" exercise contained four steps. In the first step, each of the participants were given 3 × 5 cards and asked to write appreciation messages to other participants.

Each message was to be addressed to another person on a separate card and was to be unsigned. A format suggested was, "I appreciate _____ about you." Each person was asked to write at least one such message to each of the other four participants present.

In step two of the appreciations exercise, the cards were collected, sorted, and then read by one facilitator while the other wrote the appreciations on newsprint. The result was one large newsprint sheet of appreciation messages for each of the five participants.

In step three, the participants were instructed to add to their individual sheets other things for which they would like to be appreciated, or for which they felt they deserved appreciation.

Step four consisted of a series of one-on-one conferences in which each participant met individually with the other four participants for five minutes each. During these conferences each member of the pair was asked to *acknowledge* to the other person the appreciations that had been contributed by other participants, and further to acknowledge the appreciations that he or she had contributed or agreed with.

The sharing appreciations exercise took about thirty minutes.

The final activity for Meeting 1 was a process check, where participants were invited to share their feelings about the activities of the first meeting and about the upcoming meetings.

The expectations check generated a list of hopes and fears that was posted on two large sheets of newsprint. The main themes reflected in the "hopes" list included desires to improve working relations and communications between the library and the city, to clarify reporting patterns, to know others as individuals, to develop a more relaxed atmosphere among group members, to confront differences, to reduce felt threats, and to restore library staff confidence.

The list of fears included the following: that the library would become even more committed to single-issue political activity; that the meetings would result in "unpleasant repercussions" for some; that information shared in the meetings would get out and be damaging or embarrassing; that the meetings would be a waste of time; that the library would move further away from the rest of the city and become more entrenched; and that Debra and Ralph would become too busy to attend one or more of the meetings.

The general mood during the meeting was one of cautiousness. Jeff and Paul noted that the appreciations shared were quite general and that some uneasiness was sensed during the appreciation-sharing exercise. The process check at the end of the meeting revealed mildly positive reactions. Ralph seemed cool and reserved; he said that there were no dramatic gains but that he was willing to continue. Linda seconded Ralph's sentiment. Debra and Maude seemed to be more positive and appeared to feel reassured. Helen appeared to have very positive feelings about the meeting; she expressed reduced apprehensions about the meetings and increased comfort with the other participants.

Meeting 2, March 21

The meeting began with a brief introduction to the planned activities by Paul. He also apologized for having to leave early that day. Instructions were then given for the first phase of an "image exchange" exercise. Participants were told that each group was to meet in a separate room and prepare two lists. The first list was to summarize their own group's images of the other group, including thoughts, attitudes, feelings, perceptions, and behavior. The second list was to predict what the other group's images recorded in their first list would be.

After approximately thirty minutes of list preparation time, the two groups were reconvened to share the lists. During the list-sharing period, a ground rule was enforced that disallowed debate and discussion but that allowed questions for clarification.

The librarians were invited to share their list of images of the city administration first. As they did so, Jeff (Paul had left) summarized the entries on newsprint. Next, the city administration's images of the library were shared and posted. Time was allowed for clarification questions after each list had been aired.

Next, the two groups shared their predictions of the other group's list, with the librarians again going first. The time required for the sharing of the four lists was approximately forty minutes. These four lists are reproduced in Case Exhibit 4-7.

Following the image exchange period, the groups were again sent to separate rooms. This time each group was instructed to create a prioritized list of issues needing resolution. Twenty minutes was allocated for this activity.

The final activity for Meeting 2 was the sharing of the two lists of priority issues. Case Exhibit 4-8 shows the priority issues that were generated in this activity. This sharing and posting used up the remainder of the meeting time available.

CASE EXHIBIT 4-7 Image Exchange Data from Meeting 2 of City Hall and Library Administration

I. Library administration views of city hall
   1. They are suspicious of the library.
   2. They are well intentioned but inept.
   3. They are uninterested in the library program.
   4. They are protective of their own power.
   5. They are unfriendly.
   6. They want the library to accept administrative changes from city hall, but are unwilling to accept administrative changes made by the library board.
   7. They don't really want public input.
   8. They are very willing to put library staff (especially Helen) between the power play of city hall and the library board.
   9. They are personally against Helen.
II. City hall views of library administration
   1. They have limited or no respect for the administrative abilities of city hall.
   2. "Massive paranoia" exists among the library staff.
   3. The librarians have been operating a propaganda organ:
       • Internally with library staff
       • Externally with city council and public
   4. The library staff has used the library board as a separate political support group.
   5. There has been a concerted program by the librarians to establish a separate political base and become invulnerable.
   6. Library personnel operate a tight "clique."
   7. Library personnel distrust (and dislike and despise . . .) city hall.
   8. Library personnel wish to do their own thing without coordination.
   9. Library personnel don't readily accept administration assistance.
III. Library administration's predictions of city hall views of library administration
   1. They think we are paranoid.
   2. They think we are snobbish and isolated.
   3. They think we are spreading our views of the problem among staff and public.
   4. They think we are overprotective of the library.
   5. They think we are inappropriately political.
   6. They think we are encouraging the library board to move away from city hall.
IV. City hall's predictions of library administration's views of city hall
   1. They think that we believe the library is not a critical service; it is dispensable, or first to go in a crunch.
   2. They think we are nonsupportive of the library.
   3. They think we discriminate against the library.
   4. They think we impose unreasonable guidelines.
   5. They think we have a vendetta against the library.
   6. They think we are uncaring and unhelpful.
   7. They think the library gets the short end of resource allocations.
   8. They think that we are fast to control and restrict, but seldom volunteer assistance.

At the conclusion of the meeting, Jeff's impression was that there was a general sense of tension relief that this long-repressed animosity was finally out in the open. Debra appeared to feel particularly good about the meeting when she left. Jeff was impressed by the casualness and informality with which Ralph engaged in amusing conversation concerning the meeting with the three librarians for fifteen minutes after the meeting. This was the first time that Jeff could remember Ralph's being relaxed and at ease in any of the meetings concerning the library. Jeff guessed that Ralph might have felt good that some real progress had been made during this meeting.

Two days after this meeting, Linda reported to Jeff that the librarians left the meeting feeling quite discouraged.

CASE EXHIBIT 4-8   Priority Issues for Resolution: Meeting 2, City Hall and Library Administration

I. Priorities of library staff
   1. Clarify the role of the library board of trustees:
      a. Statewide
      b. Citywide
      c. Vis-à-vis the library staff
   2. Clarify the roles of the library staff, library administration, and city hall.
   3. Reach agreement regarding appropriate political activity for the library.
   4. Develop mutual respect for one another's administrative abilities.
II. Priorities of city hall
   1. (Debra) Inappropriate political activity.
   2. (Ralph) Resolve the perception that city hall is doing something "bad" to Helen—that is, the perceived vendetta.
   3. Library's impression that city hall is uninterested in the library program.
   4. Library's impression that members of city hall are being protective of their own power.

Consultants' Meeting, March 22

Jeff Mallet and Paul Everest met at Paul's house to compare notes on the progress of the meetings so far, and to discuss strategy for the upcoming meetings.

When Paul saw the two priority lists of issues for resolution that had been generated by the two groups, he had an immediate reaction. Paul noted that the items listed by the librarians appeared to reflect a willingness to compromise, collaborate, or negotiate, whereas those items listed by Debra and Ralph appeared to reflect the expectation that the library should do the changing. Jeff and Paul wondered if this difference in expectations was a pattern. They recalled other times when they had vague feelings that perhaps Debra or Ralph, or both, regarded the meetings as an opportunity to get the library to shape up. Following the meeting, Jeff had the feeling that the three librarians had seemed to take the instructions and the sessions more seriously than did Debra and Ralph. Jeff had hoped that the period for sharing the four lists would leave everyone in an introspective mood. This seemed to take place for the librarians, but not for Debra and Ralph.

After reflecting on the outcomes from Meeting 2, Jeff reported feeling overwhelmed by the pervasiveness of the issue concerning appropriate political activity. His review had led him to the conclusion that this issue was so fundamental to all the problems being experienced between the library and city hall that it was likely to be futile to work on any specific issues before addressing this major one.

As Jeff saw it, two major questions needed to be resolved. First, what is the relationship of the library board of trustees to city hall? And second, how will the diametrically opposed views expressed by the library and city hall concerning appropriate political activity be resolved? It seemed to Jeff that neither of these issues could be settled by the group that had been meeting with Jeff and Paul. Instead, it seemed more plausible that these issues needed to be referred to either the library board or the city council.

Paul agreed that there were no instant solutions in sight, and that the appropriate strategy for where to go with the present group was not at all apparent.

After some discussion, Paul and Jeff agreed on the prognosis that until the overriding issue of political activity was dealt with, administrative issues would probably be resistant to solution. They further agreed that it seemed unlikely that solutions to the political activity question could be generated from within the present group, and that action strategies to address this issue probably would have to come from the city council or the library board.

Concerning strategy for Meeting 3, Paul and Jeff agreed to begin it by reviewing for the participants the consultants' interpretations of the outcome of Meeting 2 and to invite them to join in a problem-solving session concerning appropriate action strategies. Paul and Jeff could think of two strategies that might prove fruitful:

1. Refer the issue of appropriateness of political activity to the city council, along with a request for a definitive guideline on what activities are appropriate.
2. Have Debra and Helen get together, with or without a process consultant, to work out an agreement concerning political activity.

Jeff and Paul discussed whether the issue of the newspaper reporter being called should be brought up at the next meeting. They agreed that Debra had stored up much resentment over this issue, and that if it came out it could be a "heavy" confrontation. Jeff and Paul were very uncertain about whether the issue could be constructively handled in one meeting. The uncertainties concerning the outcome of such a confrontation led Paul and Jeff to agree that they should probably try to avoid confronting this issue at the next meeting.

FURTHER DISCUSSIONS

Meeting 3, March 24

As Jeff and Paul arrived at the Savings Bank Community Room for Meeting 3, they exchanged the sentiment, "God knows what's going to happen today!" As participants entered the meeting room, they were given a three-page handout summarizing the previous meeting's outcomes. This handout contained the data generated in Meeting 2 from the image exchange exercise and the list of priority issues for resolution (Case Exhibits 4-7 and 4-8).

Jeff began by sharing some of his and Paul's reflections concerning the pervasiveness of the political issue. He raised the question about whether administration concerns could be addressed while the political issue remained unresolved. He further voiced some skepticism concerning whether the present group was the appropriate one to settle the political issue or whether it could achieve this goal.

Jeff also spent some time reflecting on the nature of the conflict over political activities. He tried to summarize the positions of the two parties to the conflict. In doing so, Jeff emphasized his understanding that each of the parties had a position that was logically defensible, internally consistent, and supportable by others.

Jeff concluded by inviting the group members to comment on the consultants' diagnosis of the problem, and to join in a problem-solving session to identify reasonable options that could be taken. The remainder of the meeting time was used for unstructured discussion, with the exception of a brief process check at the end of the meeting.

Paul served in a process observation role during this meeting. During the time that Jeff was giving an overview of the problem situation, Paul noted the reactions of the five participants. Linda, Helen, and Ralph all seemed quite attentive. Debra and Maude were observed to be staring intently at their handouts for long periods of time. This was particularly true for Maude, who hardly shifted her gaze from her handout for almost 20 minutes. Paul noted that Maude looked dejected, and that she was avoiding eye contact with others present. Because the meeting room was chilly, Maude (along with most of the others) was feeling physically cold. Maude had also mentioned that she was coming down with a cold.

After Jeff had finished his introductory remarks, Debra abruptly initiated a discussion of political activity on the part of the library staff. Debra's remarks may be paraphrased as follows:

"Politics is a fact of life now. The library staff has started something that will be very hard to stop. They have politicized the budgeting process and it will be very hard to go back to a nonpolitical procedure. What I need to know from the library staff is whether these activities will continue. If so, there will be unpleasant repercussions, which the library staff should understand.

"Two things are really bothering me. First, someone from the library called a newspaper reporter to ask that my 'vendetta' against Cecil Hockman and the library be investigated. When I got that telephone call from the reporter, I felt angry, betrayed, and nonplussed. The second issue is political activity by library staff members aimed at packing the city council chambers with citizens supporting the library. That represents a clear violation of instructions from the library board, and leads me to wonder who's running the library, anyway?"

When Debra made the point that the library staff had disregarded instructions concerning political activity, Helen pointed out that the library staff did not perceive that they had received any such instructions. Following Helen's point, discussion proceeded in another direction, with no overt evidence that Helen's comment was heard or understood.

Following Debra's expression of her feelings about the telephone call, Helen and Linda expressed consternation that the telephone call had been made. Both made it very clear that they thought such a telephone call was inappropriate. Linda said, "I didn't realize we had sunk to that low a level," and Helen seconded Linda's sentiment. During this conversation Maude was noticeably quiet, and avoided eye contact.

Ralph said, "When I come into the library, I feel hostility all around me." When Ralph made this remark, Paul intervened and asked Ralph to focus on his personal feelings when he was in this situation. Ralph's responses generally depicted his impressions of library staff members' attitudes. Paul pursued the issue by asking Ralph two more times to focus on and report his own feelings in this situation. After Ralph's responses again did not describe his own feelings, Jeff probed him by asking if he might have been feeling hurt, disliked, or disrespected. In response to this prompting, Ralph acknowledged that some of these guesses were accurate.

At this point, Paul intervened with a few observations designed to set the stage for the librarians to air some of their feelings. With a few minor exceptions, the librarians did not divulge their feelings on issues.

At one point in the conversation, Debra offered "to spend a week working in the library," if that would help to resolve some of the problems. Helen responded to this offer with apparent guardedness, citing the difficulties of time scheduling and the requirements of attending the human understanding workshops currently being conducted for all city employees.

Debra seemed annoyed that Helen's reaction to her offer was not totally positive. At this point, Maude made a pointed observation to Debra: "I have to tell you that there are some people in the library who will be pretty hostile toward you." The question of whether the library should regionalize by joining the Morton County system was then raised. Debra expressed dismay that the library staff, the library board of trustees, and several others had reacted so vehemently against the proposal that regionalization should be studied. The librarians responded to Debra's sentiment by assertively pointing out that the proposal (which had been part of a report to the city council by the capital expenditures committee) did not call for a study but called for *implementation* that was to occur by January 1, 2002. Both Debra and Ralph replied that they were sure that the wording of the capital expenditures committee report was that the January 1, 2002, date was the deadline for *completion of a study*. The librarians were equally certain that their interpretation of the report was correct. Members of both groups vowed to get a copy of the committee report to bring to the next meeting.

Discussion of the regionalization issue continued. Helen referred to a previous study concerning regionalization, which had been conducted by the League of Women Voters. This study had gathered some utilization data. Helen felt that the study supported her opinion that regionalization would be most unwise. Debra said that she had not seen or heard of the league's study, and was very interested: "That's the kind of information I need to know." At this point, one of the librarians volunteered that they had prepared a "fact sheet" concerning the regionalization issue. Debra expressed surprise at hearing about the fact sheet.

Paul noted that Debra seemed annoyed about learning about the fact sheet, and that Ralph gave the librarians a dirty look during this time.

The librarians at this point explained that the fact sheet was prepared in response to a request by a particular city council member.

Lively discussion of substantive issues was continuing when Jeff interrupted a few minutes before the end of the meeting time to ask for a process check. During this check, the general sentiment expressed was, "Whew! We really got into it today!" Linda said that she thought a lot had been accomplished, and nods of agreement from other participants were noted. Ralph acknowledged some real accomplishment for the first time. Paul and Jeff shared both surprise and relief that the issue concerning the reporter had been successfully dealt with and largely defused. In fact, they expressed the view that the whole issue of political activity had been defused at least somewhat.

Meeting 4, March 25

The meeting began with Paul and Jeff suggesting a review of the list of priority issues for resolution generated in Meeting 2. The consultants suggested that the group make an "action/no action" decision for each of the priority issues. This exercise was to provide some closure for the last of the four scheduled meetings.

During the last half of the meeting, Paul started an action list on newsprint, and he and Jeff pressed the participants for specific action commitments as the discussion approached agreement. The last ten minutes of the meeting were spent reviewing the list of hopes and fears generated at the beginning of Meeting 1.

The action list that Paul constructed on newsprint during the last half of the meeting is shown in Case Exhibit 4-9. The final issue on the action list, the perceptions of "ineptness" and "incompetence," still had not been discussed as the end of the meeting time approached. Jeff called attention to the issue, and shared the perception of the consultants that the range of specific behaviors that each group found upsetting in the other group seemed quite small—indeed, too small to support the "inept" or "incompetent" generalizations. He pointed out that feedback on specific behaviors had been constructively shared during the four meetings, but that feedback on broad evaluative generalization was difficult to respond to constructively. Jeff urged each participant to consciously avoid lapsing into the use of such evaluative stereotypes, and instead to concentrate on specific behaviors.

During the review of the hopes and fears lists, the general feeling was that most of the hopes had been either partially or fully realized, and that most of the fears had dissipated.

Concerning the fear that the meetings might prove to be a waste of time, Ralph said, "That remains to be seen." Concerning the hope that better working relations would be developed, all participants seemed to agree that this goal had been accomplished.

CASE EXHIBIT 4-9 City Hall and Library Administration Action List

Issue	Action
• Calling reporter anonymously	• Announcement at staff meeting (Helen will do; OK to break confidentially.
• Offer by Debra to spend time in library	• Helen will schedule with staff and Debra.
• Reporting relations	• Helen will draft memo to library board by May 2 asking them for direction or clarification on the following issues: • Legal liability; errors and omissions • Property • Maintenance • Reporting relations • Political activity • Debra and Ralph will review memo. • Ralph and Helen will attend May 2 meeting of library board.
• Maintaining good relations	• Debra, Ralph, Helen, Linda, and Maude will meet for brown-bag luncheons. • First luncheon: Tuesday, April 24, 12:00 to 1:00, in Ralph's office; Linda will facilitate. Participants to begin with "check-in" concerning problem issues and good news. • Facilitator and location will rotate for subsequent luncheons. • Brown-bag discussion item: exchanging of staff people. • Brown-bag luncheon "check-in" item.
• Perception that city hall is going to do something bad to Helen • Perception that city hall is "inept" • Perception that library staff is "incompetent"	• All such evaluative stereotypes were declared inoperative by Jeff, who banned their use in thought and speech.

FOLLOW-UP

A survey instrument called the Intergroup Profile was used by the consultants to measure the climate existing between city hall and the library staff. This instrument includes eight Likert-type questions concerning relationships existing between two groups. Measurements were taken in March, before the first intergroup meeting, and again in May, six weeks after the last meeting. Parallel measurements were obtained from nine separate control organizations.

Data analysis revealed that the library/city hall climate prior to the meetings was considerably worse than that existing in any of the nine control organizations ($p <$ .0001). Following the meetings, the library/city hall climate scores had improved substantially ($p <$ .001), but were still lower than the scores of any control organization.

In early August, four months after Meeting 4, a two-page written evaluation form was filled out by each of the five meeting participants. Their responses reflected general agreement that, as a result of the meetings, the climate between city hall and the library had improved, but not dramatically.

Ralph Riesen commented, "We achieved a better understanding of positions, but no real resolution of conflicts. The conflicts that exist are political rather than personal."

Debra Dickenson noted that the meetings had provided "a good chance to share concerns," and that they resulted in "better feelings for the individuals involved." She continued, "There is a period of transition that is required—just plain time to see how we all deal with the next 'challenge to authority.' Political changes have an effect. I don't feel that library personnel understand the scope of city demands and needs any better than before. In my opinion they just feel we are being nicer to them. Their anxieties are relieved a bit, so the climate is improved. There is a value to that without a doubt."

Helen Hendricks noted three specific changes that had resulted from the meetings:

1. The librarian is aware that her personal situation cannot improve, but she is not threatened by further deterioration of her position.
2. The administrative reporting pattern between the library administration, library board, and city supervisor has improved.
3. The library staff are more united and supportive than ever.

Additional comments made by Helen included the following: "I believe the library's fears and concerns were substantiated by the meetings but it was good to bring them into the open. The librarian's and city supervisor's personal contacts are slightly improved. The problems at the library stemmed from the city administration decision to regroup the city program with the resultant downgrading of the library service and personal demotion of the librarian—the view of the library. The city administration did not recognize this as the cause."

Linda Turner reported that the meetings "relieved the mayor's mind by allowing her a chance to 'let off steam.' Coming from the library, I [now] feel more relaxed in talking with the mayor and city supervisor—though not totally relaxed. The city librarian and city supervisor can now talk to each other—this is by far the most important result."

Maude Richardson concurred with Linda and Helen that the relationship between the city librarian and the city supervisor was much more comfortable. She also observed that "foul-ups at city hall are no longer seen as personally directed at the library."

When you have read this case, review the diagnostic questions included at the end(s) of the chapter(s) you are using to analyze this case, and choose the ones that seem applicable. Then use those questions to begin working on your case analysis.

CASE 4-5 L. J. SUMMERS COMPANY

J. B. Ritchie, Paul H. Thompson, Brigham Young University

Jon Reese couldn't think of a time in the history of L. J. Summers Company when there had been as much anticompany sentiment among the workers as had emerged in the past few weeks. He knew that Mr. Summers would place the blame on him for the problems with the production workers because Jon was supposed to be helping Mr. Summers's son, Blaine, become oriented to his new position. Blaine had only recently taken over as production manager of the company (see Case Exhibit 4-10). Blaine was unpopular with most of the workers, but the events of the past weeks had caused him to be resented even more. This resentment had increased to the point that several of the male workers had quit and all the women in the assembly department had refused to work. The programs that had caused the resentment among the workers were instituted by Blaine to reduce waste and lower production

---

L. J. Summers Company Organization Chart

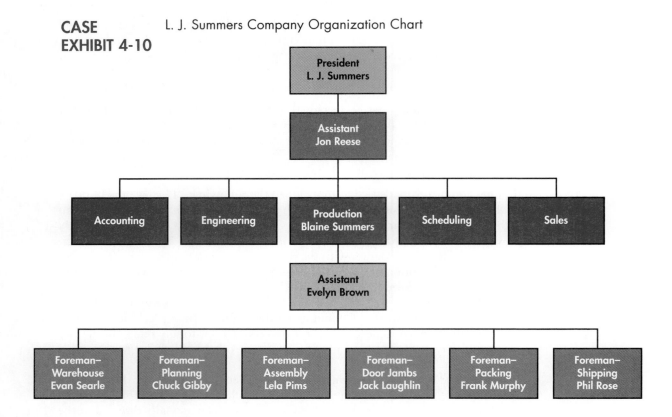

costs, but they had produced completely opposite results. Jon knew that on Monday morning he would have to explain to Mr. Summers why the workers had reacted as they did and that he would have to present a plan to resolve the employee problems, reduce waste, and decrease production costs.

COMPANY HISTORY

The L. J. Summers Company manufactured large sliding doors made of many narrow aluminum panels held together by thick rubber strips, which allowed the door to collapse as it was opened. Some of the doors were as tall as 18 feet and were used in buildings to section off large areas. The company had grown rapidly in its early years due mainly to the expansion of the building program of the firm's major customer, which accounted for nearly 90 percent of Summers' business.

When L. J. Summers began the business, his was the only firm that manufactured the large sliding doors. Recently, however, several other firms had begun to market similar doors. One firm, in particular, had been bidding to obtain business from Summers' major customer. Fearing that the competitor might be able to underbid his company, Mr. Summers began urging his assistant, Jon, to increase efficiency and cut production costs.

CONDITIONS BEFORE THE COST-REDUCTION PROGRAMS

A family-type atmosphere had existed at Summers before the cost-reduction programs were instituted. There was little direct supervision of the workers from the front office, and no pressure was put on them to meet production standards. Several of the employees worked overtime regularly without supervision. The foremen and workers often played cards together during lunchtime, and company parties after work were common and popular. Mr. Summers was generally on friendly terms with all the employees, although he was known to get angry if something displeased him. He also participated freely in the daily operations of the company.

As Mr. Summers's assistant, Jon was responsible for seeing to it that the company achieved the goals established by Mr. Summers. Jon was considered hardworking and persuasive by most of the employees and had a reputation of not giving in easily to employee complaints.

Blaine Summers had only recently become the production manager of Summers. He was in his early twenties, was married, and had a good build. Several of the workers commented that Blaine liked to show off his strength in front of others. He was known to be very meticulous about keeping the shop orderly and neat, even to the point of making sure that packing crates were stacked "his way." It was often commented among the other employees how Blaine seemed to be trying to impress his father. Many workers voiced the opinion that the only reason Blaine was production manager was that his father owned the company. They also resented his using company employees and materials to build a swingset for his children and to repair his camper.

Blaine, commenting to Jon one day that the major problem with production was the workers, added that people of such caliber as the Summers employees did not understand how important cost reduction was and that they would rather sit around and talk all day than work. Blaine rarely spoke to the workers but left most of the reprimanding and firing up to his assistant, Evelyn Brown.

Summers employed about seventy people to perform the warehousing, assembly, and doorjamb building, as well as the packing and shipping operations done on the doors. Each operation was supervised by a foreman, and crews ranged from three men in warehousing to twenty-five women in the assembly department. The foremen were usually employees with the most seniority and were responsible for quality and on-time production output. Most of the foremen had good relationships with the workers.

The majority of the work done at Summers consisted of repetitive assembly tasks requiring very little skill or training; for example, in the pinning department the workers operated a punch press, which made holes in the panels. The job consisted of punching the hole and then inserting a metal pin into it. Workers commented that it was very tiring and boring to stand at the press during the whole shift without frequent breaks.

Wages at Summers were considered low for the area. The workers griped about the low pay, but said that they tried to compensate by taking frequent breaks, working overtime, and "taking small items home at night." Most of the workers who worked overtime were in the door jamb department, the operation requiring the most skill. Several of these workers either worked very little or slept during overtime hours they reportedly worked.

The majority of the male employees were in their mid-twenties; about half of them were unmarried. There was a great turnover among the unmarried male workers. The female employees were either young and single or older married women. The twenty-five women who worked in production were all in the assembly department under Lela Pims.

THE COST-REDUCTION PROGRAMS

Shortly after Mr. Summers began stressing the need to reduce waste and increase production, Blaine called the foremen together and told them that they would be responsible for stricter discipline among the employees. Unless each foreman could reduce waste and improve production in his department, he would either be replaced or receive no pay increases.

The efforts of the foremen to make the workers eliminate wasteful activities and increase output brought immediate resistance and resentment. The employees' reactions were typified by the following comment: "What has gotten into Chuck lately? He's been chewing us out for the same old things we've always done. All he thinks about now is increasing production." Several of the foremen commented that they didn't like the front office making them the "bad guys" in the eyes of the workers. The workers didn't change their work habits as a result of the pressure put on them by the foremen, but a growing spirit of antagonism between the workers and the foremen was apparent.

After several weeks of no improvement in production, Jon called a meeting with the workers to announce that the plant would go on a four-day, ten-hour-a-day workweek to reduce operating costs. He stressed that the workers would enjoy having a three-day weekend.

This idea was greeted with enthusiasm by some of the younger employees, but several of the older women complained that the schedule would be too tiring for them and that they would rather work five days a week. The proposal was voted on and passed by a two-to-one margin. Next, Jon stated that there would be no more unsupervised overtime and that all overtime had to be approved in advance by Blaine. Overtime would be allowed only if some specific job had to be finished. Those who had been working overtime protested vigorously, saying that this would only result in lagging behind schedule, but Jon remained firm on this new rule.

Shortly after the meeting, several workers in the door jamb department made plans to stage a work slowdown so that the department would fall behind schedule and they would have to work overtime to catch up. One of the workers, who had previously been the hardest working in the department, said, "We will tell them that we are working as fast as possible and that we just can't do as much as we used to in a five-day week. The only thing they could do would be to fire us, and they would never do that." Similar tactics were devised by workers in other departments. Some workers said that if they couldn't have overtime, they would find a better-paying job elsewhere.

Blaine, observing what was going on, told Jon, "They think I can't tell that they are staging a slowdown. Well, I simply won't approve any overtime, and after Jack's department gets way behind, I'll let him have it for fouling up scheduling." After a few weeks of continued slowdown, Blaine drew up a set of specific rules, which were posted on the company bulletin board early one Monday morning (see Case Exhibit 4-11).

This move brought immediate criticism from the workers. During the next week, they continued to deliberately violate the posted rules. On Friday, two of the male employees quit because they were penalized for arriving late to work and for "lounging around" during working hours. As they left, they said they would be waiting for their foreman after work to get even with him for turning them in.

CASE EXHIBIT 4-11
Production Shop Regulations

1. Anyone reporting late to work will lose one-half hour's pay for each five minutes of lateness. The same applies to punching in after lunch.
2. No one is to leave the machine or post without the permission of the supervisor.
3. Anyone observed not working will be noted, and if sufficient occurrences are counted, the employee will be dismissed.

That same day the entire assembly department (all women) staged a stoppage to protest an action taken against Myrtle King, an employee of the company since the beginning. The action resulted from a run-in she had with Lela Pims, foreman of the assembly department. Myrtle was about sixty years old and had been turned in by Lela for resting too much. She became furious, saying she couldn't work ten hours a day. Several of her friends had organized the work stoppage after Myrtle had been sent home without pay credit for the day. The stoppage was also inspired by some talk among the workers of forming a union. The women seemed to favor this idea more than the men.

When Blaine found out about the incident, he tried joking with the women and in jest threatened to fire them if they did not begin working again. When he saw he was getting nowhere, he returned to the front office. One of the workers commented, "He thinks he can send us home and push us around, and then all he has to do is tell us to go back to work and we will. Well, this place can't operate without us." Jon soon appeared and called Lela into his office and began talking with her. Later he persuaded the women to go back to work, telling them that there would be a meeting with all the female employees on Monday morning.

Jon wondered what steps he should take to solve the problems at L. J. Summers Company. The efforts of management to increase efficiency and reduce production costs had definitely caused resentment among the workers. Even more disappointing was the fact that the company accountant had just announced that waste and costs had increased since the new programs had been instituted, and the company scheduler reported that Summers was further behind on shipments than ever before.

When you have read this case, review the diagnostic questions included at the end(s) of the chapter(s) you are using to analyze this case, and choose the ones that seem applicable. Then use those questions to begin working on your case analysis.

CASE 4-6 ## CONSOLIDATED LIFE: CAUGHT BETWEEN TWO CORPORATE CULTURES

Joseph Weiss, Bentley College
Mark Wahlstrom, Bentley College
Edward Marshall, Bentley College

It all started so positively. Three days after graduating with his degree in business administration, Mike Wilson started his first day at a prestigious insurance company—Consolidated Life. He worked in the policy issue department. The work of the department was mostly clerical and did not require a high degree of technical knowledge. Given the repetitive and mundane nature of the work, the successful worker had to be consistent and willing to grind out paperwork.

Rick Belkner was the division's vice president, "the man in charge" at the time—an actuary by training and a technical professional described in the division as "the mirror of whomever was the strongest personality around him." It was also common knowledge that Belkner made $60,000 a year while he spent his time doing crossword puzzles.

Mike was hired as a management trainee and promised a supervisory assignment within a year. However, because of a management reorganization, it was only six weeks before he was placed in charge of an eight-person unit. The reorganization was intended to streamline work flow, upgrade and combine the clerical jobs, and make greater use of the computer system. It was a drastic departure from the old way of doing things and created a great deal of animosity and anxiety among the clerical staff.

Management realized that a flexible supervisory style was necessary to pull off the reorganization without immense turnover, so the firm gave its supervisors a free hand to run their units as they saw fit. Mike used this latitude to implement group meetings and training classes in his unit. In addition, he assured all members of raises if they worked hard to attain them. By working long hours, participating in the mundane tasks with his unit, and being flexible in his management style, he was able to increase productivity, reduce errors, and reduce lost time. Things improved so dramatically that he was noticed by upper management and earned a reputation as a "superstar" despite being viewed as free-spirited and unorthodox. The feeling was that his loose, people-oriented management style could be tolerated because his results were excellent.

After a year, Mike received an offer from a different Consolidated Life division located across town. Mike was asked to manage an office in the marketing area. The pay was excellent, and the job offered an opportunity to turn around an office in disarray. The reorganization in his present division at Consolidated was almost complete, and most of his mentors and friends in management had moved on to other jobs. Mike decided to accept the offer. In his exit interview, he was assured that if he ever wanted to return, a position would be made for him. It was clear that he was held in high regard by management and staff alike. A huge party was thrown to send him off.

The new job was satisfying for a short time, but it became apparent to Mike that it did not have the long-term potential he was promised. After bringing on a new staff, computerizing the office, and auditing the books, he began looking for a position that would both challenge him and give him the autonomy he needed to be successful.

Eventually, word got back to Rick Belkner that Mike was looking for another job. Rick offered Mike a position with the same pay he was now receiving and control over a fourteen-person unit in his old division. After considering other options, Mike decided to return to his old division, feeling that he would be able to progress steadily over the next several years.

Upon his return to his old division at Consolidated Life, Mike became aware of several changes that had taken place in the six months since his departure. The most important change was the hiring of a new divisional senior vice president, Jack Greely. Greely had been given total authority to run the division. Rick Belkner now reported to Jack.

Belkner's reputation was now that he was tough but fair. It was necessary for people in Jack's division to do things his way and "get the work out." Mike also found himself reporting to one of his former peers, Kathy Miller, who had been promoted to manager during the reorganization. Mike had always "hit it off" with Miller and foresaw no problems in working with her.

After a week, Mike realized the extent of the changes that had occurred. Gone was the loose, casual atmosphere that had marked his first tour in the division. Now, a stricter, task-oriented management doctrine was practiced. Morale of the supervisory staff had decreased to an alarming level. Jack Greely was the major topic of conversation in and around the division. People joked that MBO now meant management by "oppression," not by "objectives." Mike was greeted back with comments such as, "Welcome to prison," and, "Why would you come back here? You must be desperate!" It seemed as if everyone was looking for new jobs or transfers. Their lack of desire was reflected in the poor quality of work being done.

Mike felt that a change in the management style of his boss was necessary to improve a frustrating situation. Realizing that it would be difficult to affect Greely's style directly, Mike requested permission from Belkner to form a "Supervisors' Forum" for all the managers on Mike's level in the division. Mike explained that the purpose would be to enhance the existing management training program. The forum would include weekly meetings, guest speakers, and discussions of topics relevant to the division and the industry. Mike thought the forum would show Greely that he was serious about both his job and improving morale in the division. Belkner gave the okay for an initial meeting.

The meeting took place, and ten supervisors who were Mike's peers in the company eagerly took the opportunity to "blue sky" it. There was a euphoric attitude about the group as they drafted their statement of intent. It read as follows:

TO: Rick Belkner

FROM: New Issue Services Supervisors

SUBJECT: Supervisors' Forum

On Thursday, June 11, the Supervisors' Forum held its first meeting. The objective of the meeting was to identify common areas of concern among us and to determine topics that we might be interested in pursuing.

The first area addressed was the void that we perceive exists in the management training program. As a result of conditions beyond anyone's control, many of us over the past year have held supervisory duties without the benefit of formal training or proper experience.

Therefore, we propose to use the Supervisors' Forum to enhance the existing management training program. The areas that we hope to affect with this supplemental training are (a) morale/job satisfaction, (b) quality of work and service, (c) productivity, and (d) management expertise as it relates to the life insurance industry. With these objectives in mind, we have outlined below a list of possible activities that we would like to pursue.

1. *Further use of the existing "in-house" training programs provided for manager trainees and supervisors (Introduction to Supervision, E.E.O., and Coaching and Counseling).*
2. *A series of speakers from various sections in the company. This would help expose us to the technical aspects of their departments and their managerial style.*
3. *Invitations to outside speakers to address the forum on management topics such as management development, organizational structure and behavior, business policy, and the insurance industry. Suggested speakers could be area college professors, consultants, and state insurance officials.*
4. *Outside training and visits to the field. This could include attendance at seminars concerning management theory and development relative to the insurance industry. Attached is a representative sample of a program we would like to have considered in the future.*

In conclusion, we hope that this memo clearly illustrates what we are attempting to accomplish with this program. It is our hope that the above outline will give the forum credibility and establish it as an effective tool for all levels of management within New Issue. By supplementing our on-the-job training with a series of speakers and classes, we aim to develop prospective management's role in it. Also, we would like to invite the underwriters to attend any programs at which the topic of the speaker might be of interest to them.

cc: J. Greely
Managers

The group felt that the memo accurately and diplomatically stated their dissatisfaction with the current situation. However, they pondered what the results of their actions would be and what else they could have done.

Shortly after the memo had been issued, Rick Belkner called an emergency management meeting at Jack Greely's request to address the "union" being formed by the supervisors. Four general managers, Rick Belkner, and Jack Greely were present at the meeting.

During the meeting, it was suggested that the forum be disbanded to "put them in their place." However, Rick Belkner felt that if "guided" in the proper direction, the forum could die from lack of interest. His stance was adopted, but it was common knowledge that Jack Greely was strongly opposed to the group and wanted its founders dealt with. His comment was, "It's not a democracy and they're not a union. If they don't like it here, then they can leave." A campaign was directed by the managers to determine who the main authors of the memo were so they could be dealt with.

About this time, Mike's unit had made a mistake on a case, which Jack Greely was embarrassed to admit to his boss. This embarrassment was more than Jack Greely cared to take from Mike Wilson. At the managers' staff meeting that day, Greely stormed in and declared that the next supervisor to "screw up" was out the door. He would permit no more embarrassments of his division and repeated his earlier statement about "people leaving if they didn't like it here." It was clear to Mike and everyone else present that Mike Wilson was a marked man.

Mike had always been a loose, amiable supervisor. The major reason his units had been successful was that he paid attention to each individual and how he or she interacted with the group. He had a reputation for fairness, was seen as an excellent judge of personnel for new positions, and was noted for his ability to turn around people who had been in trouble. He motivated people through a dynamic, personable style and was noted for his general lack of regard for rules. He treated rules as obstacles to management and generally used his own discretion as to what was important. His office had a sign saying, "Any fool can manage by rules. It takes an uncommon man to manage without any." It was an approach that flew in the face of company policy, but it had been overlooked in the past because of his results. However, because of Mike's actions with the Supervisors' Forum, he was now regarded as a thorn in the side, not a superstar, and his oddball style only made things worse.

Faced with the fact that he was rumored to be out the door, Mike sat down to appraise the situation.

When you have read this case, review the diagnostic questions included at the end(s) of the chapter(s) you are using to analyze this case, and choose the ones that seem applicable. Then use those questions to begin working on your case analysis.

CASE 4-7 / **WORLD INTERNATIONAL AIRLINES, INC.**

P. D. Jimerson, General Mills, Inc.
David L. Ford, University of Texas at Dallas

BACKGROUND

World International Airlines is a foreign-based multinational commercial air carrier. The corporate offices for its Western Hemisphere operations are located in New

York City. The company employs many hundreds of multilingual and multicultural employees, since its operations maintain World International terminals in South America, Central America, Mexico, the United States, and Canada, all of which make up the Western Hemisphere territory. In all of the continents the district managers, whose territory may involve several countries or, in the case of the United States, several states, are usually multilingual Europeans. The assistant managers are usually nationals of the country. The general manager of the Western Hemisphere is a native Spaniard while the personnel manager is a Spanish-American. Both the general manager and personnel manager are multilingual and multicultural.

While many air carriers in the Western Hemisphere have experienced strikes and work stoppages in the past, there is no history of strikes having ever occurred at World International Airlines. The present general manager is a man in his mid-fifties. He has worked his way up to the top of Western Hemisphere's organization. He has handpicked all of the district managers in each of the aforementioned countries. He knows more than 90 percent of the company's employees in the New York offices on a personal basis and is well liked by all of his subordinates. On one occasion when he was away attending a National Training Laboratories–sponsored workshop in California, the employees from the New York offices surprised him with a huge birthday cake, complete with decorations and even champagne.

His job performance has earned him influence and power in Spain. In addition, the present general manager's educational background is more along the classical line typical of many Spaniards in his socioeconomic class (that is, law, engineering, and so forth) as opposed to a more applied business and management education background.

CHANGE IN SENIOR PERSONNEL CREATES PROBLEMS

The company is in a state of flux. The present general manager, John Nepia, is scheduled to be transferred to Barcelona, Spain, and a new manager, Stephen Esterant, has been sent to replace him. The present general manager has had little or no input into the selection of the new general manager. However, the incoming general manager has an outstanding record in the Eastern Hemisphere, and it is rumored that he is being groomed for something big. Coupled with this impending change in senior personnel is the fact that international flights are currently in a state of flux, because a review committee is currently deliberating on a new rate structure.

John Nepia was scheduled to depart New York on April 30. Stephen Esterant arrived March 20. There was to be at least a thirty-day transition period before John's departure. Problems in setting the international rate structure became acute on or about April 20. John's departure was delayed and termed indefinite, since he was actively participating in the rate-setting negotiation with the FAA (Federal Aviation Administration).

During the transition period, Stephen was to acquaint himself with all of the district general managers as well as the rank-and-file employees. Stephen visited all of the district offices; he met and talked with district managers, sales personnel, and operations personnel; and he made comments wherever he felt that company policy was not being followed.

He seldom found anything worthy of praise if it did not comply with established company policy. The first sign of difficulty came when the corporate chauffeur in New York asked to speak to John, who had maintained a policy of being accessible to any of the company's employees. The driver explained the following: "I've been with this company for five years now. I like my work and I like my job. But I don't believe that I should get less respect because I'm a driver. I don't like the idea of having to drive Mr. Esterant's wife and her friends around on a shopping trip in downtown New York. I don't think it's part of my responsibility to walk his dog or carry his wife's packages. I realize that I work for him, but I refuse to be treated as though I were his servant. I decided that if this treatment continues on his part, I will have to find out what grievance procedure is available and file an official complaint."

John was quick to assure the driver that the matter would be looked into and he would get in touch with him as soon as he knew more about the situation.

Other rumblings came from the operations employees. They contended that Stephen Esterant was thoughtless, unappreciative, and distant in his interactions with them. They further believed that he felt and acted "too superior." For example, one of the operative employees related the following story. "Once Stephen visited the baggage-handling area at Chicago where a new computerized routing system was being tested. He had worked with a similar system before and immediately spotted some procedures that would increase the efficiency of operation. He proceeded to tell the employees that they didn't know what they were doing and questioned their intelligence." The most recent sign of major discord came when the district managers sent a plea to John begging him to implore Spain to recall the new general manager. In their opinion, morale had suffered greatly, and Stephen was the direct cause.

John and Jason DuBryne, the director of personnel, were good and longtime friends. They had survived many crises together. So John called in his trusted friend to seek advice and ponder their problem and their possible courses of action.

Many of the employees considered Jason a firm but fair administrator. He prided himself on the fact that he was always available to talk to and help his people. He was often consulted by members of the firm concerning interpersonal matters. These consultations often concerned private as well as corporate issues.

During their meeting, Jason acknowledged to John that the situation was indeed grave; however, at no point in the conversation did he indicate what his personal beliefs were concerning the problem. He stated that he did not believe that the heir apparent was technically incompetent. He also suggested the possibility that the heir apparent just did not understand the way of doing business in the Western Hemisphere. The meeting ended with John deciding that a conversation with Stephen Esterant was needed.

THE NEW GENERAL MANAGER'S VIEWPOINT

Stephen Esterant was named to head the Western Hemisphere operations of World International Airlines, Inc., as a reward for his outstanding service as a district manager in Spain. He was told that he was selected because he had been able to bring district offices into compliance with company operations policy and to maintain or increase sales volume at the same time. Stephen had served in five other district posts prior to receiving this promotion. He was thirty-two years old and married to a lovely woman who was a member of a wealthy and influential family in Spain. In fact, Stephen's wife's family was one of a few wealthy families owning a substantial portion of World International Airlines stock. Stephen was a man who knew what he wanted and he knew how to get it. He moved briskly about his affairs, asking no favors *from* anyone and giving no favors *to* anyone. He appeared to be the coming star in the organization.

Stephen Esterant received a memo from John Nepia requesting that he meet with him and Jason DuBryne, the personnel director, about a matter of apparent great importance. En route to the meeting, he pondered what might possibly be discussed. He, of course, had a few items on his own agenda. Since coming to New York, Stephen had become aware of several problems involved in his becoming the new general manager. He was displeased by the apparent lack of respect given to him by his subordinates as well as the "cocky" attitude of the hourly employees. He was sure that John and Jason were aware of the attitude problems, and yet he could not understand why they had not dealt with these matters sooner and in a stronger manner. From Stephen's point of view, there was a need to run a tight ship, as he had done in the Eastern Hemisphere. He obviously had a distaste for the hourly employees' practice of calling managers by their first names and for the lack of deference shown to those in authority, as was often apparent not only in the New York offices, but also throughout the rest of the Western Hemisphere operations. He also wanted to tell John and Jason that he needed to have them run less interference for him. Since he was soon to be general manager, he believed that he should start to handle intergroup conflict and decide about policy disputes so that the organization could easily recognize its new boss and leader. He resolved that if the opportunity arose in the meeting, he would raise these issues with John and Jason.

As he reached the door to John's office, Stephen turned the knob and jauntily entered the office to meet with John Nepia and Jason DuBryne, not really knowing what to expect.

When you have read this case, review the diagnostic questions included at the end(s) of the chapter(s) you are using to analyze this case, and choose the ones that seem applicable. Then use those questions to begin working on your case analysis.

5

Conclusion

Chapter 15 International
Organizational Behavior

Chapter 16 Critical Thinking and
Continuous Learning

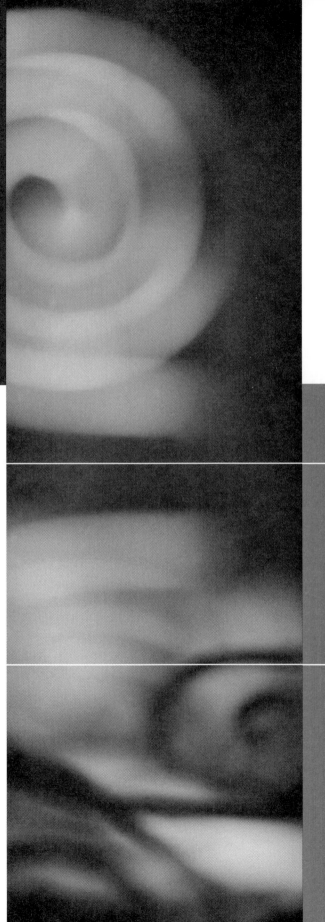

International Dimensions
Uncertainty Avoidance
Masculinity–Femininity
Individualism–Collectivism
Power Distance
Short-Term/Long-Term Orientation

Effects on Organizational Behavior
Cultural Trends: Four Scenarios
Organizational Effects
Cross-Cultural Differences

Managing International Differences
Summary
Review Questions

Learning through Experience
Diagnostic Questions 15-1: International Organizational Behavior
Exercise 15-1: Ethical Dilemmas in International Business

International Organizational Behavior

It seems like there's a Starbucks coffee shop on every street corner in the United States. The ubiquitous green-and-white circular logo is now as familiar to Americans as the red-and-white cans of Coca-Cola and the blue oval of Ford Motor Company. If entrepreneur-owner Howard Schultz has his way, soon Starbucks will become just as well known throughout the world.

In 1999, Starbucks had 281 stores outside the United States. By late 2002, that number had grown to nearly 1,200, and the company had plans for far more expansion in the future. The Starbucks name and image were tagged as one of the fastest-growing in a Business Week survey of the top 100 global brands of 2002. Why the concentration on growth abroad?

The answer, quite simply, is that sales in the United States flatlined after the terrorist attacks of September 11, 2001, and Schultz and company had to find a way to appease Wall Street analysts' demands for continued growth and profitability. Blanketing an area in the United States or Canada would do little to increase profits, and more likely would cut into the margins of other existing stores. So, about 400 of the 1,200 new stores that Starbucks opened in 2002 were located overseas, with many more expected to follow.

Global expansion poses significant risks for Starbucks. The company makes less money on each overseas store because most are operated with local partners. Added to this are problems adjusting to the cultural habits of diverse consumers and company employees. Ways of motivating workers, such as stock option programs for part-timers in U.S. stores, may not translate well to other parts of the world. It is unclear whether Starbucks will be able to succeed in its attempt to blanket the globe with successful stores without also succeeding at the task of adapting to the norms and values of its increasingly multicultural workforce.[1]

With multinationalization and globalization come differences in nationality and culture that can have major effects on micro, meso, and macro organizational behavior. These differences can complicate the jobs of contemporary managers, because they require that management practices developed in one cultural region be modified for use in other areas. Today's managers *must* take international differences seriously if they expect to compete and succeed in global markets.

This chapter describes some of the most important international differences that have been identified in organizational research, examining the effects they can have on the management of organizational behavior. It begins by introducing a five-dimensional model that is useful in identifying differences among national cultures. Next, it discusses ways in which the differences mapped by the five dimensions can affect organizations and the behavior of their members. The chapter concludes by considering the managerial implications of such international differences, focusing on a basic framework for fitting the management practices described in this book—which are primarily American in origin and cultural focus—to the job of managing people and organizations throughout the world.

INTERNATIONAL DIMENSIONS

How do cultures differ from one region of the world to another? In what ways are the **national cultures** of different countries comparable? What effects do they have on people's attitudes and behaviors in organizations? In a ground-breaking study, Dutch researcher Geert Hofstede set out to answer these questions by surveying employees who worked in IBM offices located in forty countries throughout the world. As he examined the data from 116,000 questionnaires, Hofstede discovered that most differences among national cultures were described by four cross-cultural dimensions: *uncertainty avoidance, masculinity–femininity, individualism–collectivism,* and *power distance*.[2] In later research, Canadian researcher Michael Harris Bond questioned individuals in several national cultures and uncovered a fifth dimension, *long-term/short-term orientation,* which Hofstede later added to his model.[3]

Uncertainty Avoidance

The degree to which people are comfortable with ambiguous situations and with the inability to predict future events with assurance is called **uncertainty avoidance.** At one extreme of this dimension, people with weak uncertainty avoidance feel comfortable even though they are unsure about current activities or future events. Their attitudes are expressed in the following statements:

Life is inherently uncertain and is most easily dealt with if taken one day at a time.

It is appropriate to take risks in life.

Deviation from the norm is not threatening; tolerance of differences is essential.

Conflict and competition can be managed and used constructively.

There should be as few rules as possible, and rules that cannot be kept should be changed or eliminated.[4]

At the other extreme, people characterized by strong uncertainty avoidance are most comfortable when they feel a sense of certainty about the present and future. Their attitudes about uncertainty and associated issues can be stated as follows:

The uncertainty inherent in life is threatening and must be fought continually.

Having a stable, secure life is important.

Deviant people and ideas are dangerous and should not be tolerated.

Conflict and competition can unleash aggression and must be avoided.

Written rules and regulations are needed; if people do not adhere to them, the problem is human frailty, not defects in the rules and regulations themselves.[5]

In national cultures characterized by high uncertainty avoidance, behavior is motivated at least partly by people's fear of the unknown and by attempts to cope with this fear. Often, people in such cultures try to reduce or avoid uncertainty by establishing extensive formal rules. For instance, having detailed laws about marriage and divorce diminishes uncertainty about the structure and longevity of family relationships. If uncertainty proves unavoidable, people with a cultural aversion to uncertainty may hire "experts" who seem to have the ability to apply knowledge, insight, or skill to the task of transforming something uncertain into something understandable. These experts need not actually accomplish anything, so long as they are perceived as understanding what others do not.

People with an uncertainty aversion may also engage in rituals intended to help them cope with the anxiety aroused by uncertainty. For example, they may develop extensive plans and forecasts designed to encourage speculation about the future and to make it seem more understandable and predictable. Plans and forecasts dispel anxiety, even if they prove largely invalid. For this reason, although people living in highly changeable climates often joke about the inaccuracy of local weather forecasts, many still tune into televised weather forecasts every night to plan what to wear and do the next day.

Masculinity–Femininity

Hofstede used the term *masculinity* to refer to the degree to which a culture is founded on values that emphasize independence, aggressiveness, dominance, and physical strength. According to Hofstede, people in a national culture characterized by extreme masculinity hold beliefs such as the following:

Sex roles in society should be clearly differentiated; men are intended to lead and women to follow.

Independent performance and visible accomplishments are what counts in life.

People live to work.

Ambition and assertiveness provide the motivation behind behavior.

People admire the successful achiever.[6]

Femininity, according to Hofstede, describes a society's tendency to favor such values as interdependence, compassion, empathy, and emotional openness. People in a national culture oriented toward extreme femininity hold such beliefs as the following:

Sex roles in society should be fluid and flexible; sexual equality is desirable.

The quality of life is more important than personal performance and visible accomplishments.

People work to live.

Helping others provides the motivation behind behavior.

People sympathize with the unfortunate victim.[7]

Together, the extremes of masculinity and femininity delineate the dimension of **masculinity–femininity** in Hofstede's analysis of cross-cultural differences. One important effect of the differences mapped by this dimension is the way a nation's work is divided into jobs and distributed among its citizens. In masculine national cultures, women are forced to work at lower-level jobs. Managerial work is seen as the province of men, who are portrayed as having the ambition and independence of thought required to succeed at decision making and problem solving. Women also receive less pay and recognition for their work than do their male counterparts. Only in "feminine" occupations such as teacher or nurse or in supporting roles such as secretary or clerk are women allowed to manage themselves. Even then, female supervisors must often imitate their male bosses to gain acceptance as managers.

In contrast, equality between the sexes is the norm in feminine national cultures. Neither men nor women are considered to be better managers, and no particular occupation is seen as masculine or feminine. Both sexes are equally recognized for their work, and neither is required to mimic the behavior of the other for the sake of acceptance in the workplace.

Individualism–Collectivism

According to Hofstede, **individualism–collectivism** is a dimension that traces cultural tendencies to emphasize either satisfying personal needs or looking after the needs of the group. From the viewpoint of individualism, pursuing personal interests is seen as being more important, and succeeding in the pursuit of these interests is critical to both personal and societal well-being. If each person takes care of personal interests, then everyone will be satisfied. Consistent with this perspective, the members of individualistic national cultures espouse the following attitudes:

"I" is more important than "we." People are identified by their personal traits.

Success is a personal achievement. People function most productively when working alone.

People should be free to seek autonomy, pleasure, and security through their own personal efforts.

Every member of society should take care of his or her personal well-being and the well-being of immediate family members.[8]

In contrast, the collectivist perspective emphasizes that group welfare is more important than personal interests. People who hold this view believe that only by belonging to a group and looking after its interests can they secure their own well-being and that of the broader society. For this reason, the members of collectivistic national cultures tend to ignore personal needs for the sake of their groups, ensuring group welfare even if personal hardships must be endured. They agree on the following points:

"We" is more important than "I." People are identified by the characteristics of the groups to which they belong.

Success is a group achievement. People contribute to group performance, but groups alone function productively.

People can achieve order and security and fulfill their duty to society only through group membership.

Every member of society should belong to a group that will secure members' well-being in exchange for loyalty and attention to group interests.[9]

In national cultures oriented toward the individualistic end of the dimension, membership in a group is something that can be initiated and terminated whenever convenient. A person does not necessarily have a strong feeling of commitment to any of the groups to which he or she belongs. In more collectivistic national cultures, however, changes in membership status can be traumatic. Joining and leaving a group can be likened to finding and then losing one's sense of identity. The collectivist feels a very strong, enduring sense of commitment to the group.[10]

Power Distance

Power distance is a dimension that reflects the degree to which the members of a society accept differences in power and status among themselves. In national cultures that tolerate only a small degree of power distance, norms and values specify that differences in people's ability to influence others should be minimal; instead, political equality should be encouraged. People in these cultures show a strong preference for participatory decision making and tend to distrust autocratic, hierarchical types of governance. They hold the following beliefs:

Superiors should consider subordinates "people just like me," and subordinates should regard superiors in the same way.

Superiors should be readily accessible to subordinates.

Using power is neither inherently good nor inherently evil; whether power is good or evil depends on the purposes for, and consequences of, its use.

Everyone in a society has equal rights, and these rights should be universally enforced.[11]

In contrast, national cultures characterized by a large degree of power distance support norms and values stipulating that power should be distributed hierarchically, instead of being shared more or less equally. People in these cultures favor using authority and direct supervision to coordinate people and jobs. They hold the following beliefs:

Superiors and subordinates should consider each other to be different kinds of people.

Superiors should be inaccessible to subordinates.

Power is a basic fact of society; notions of good and evil are irrelevant.

Power holders are entitled to special rights and privileges.[12]

Power distance influences attitudes and behaviors by affecting the way that a society is held together. When the members of a national culture favor only a small degree of power distance, citizens have a strong, direct voice in determining national policy. Conversely, authoritarian, autocratic government is the hallmark when societal norms and values favor larger power distance.

Short-Term/Long-Term Orientation

The dimension of **short-term/long-term orientation** reflects the extent to which the members of a national culture are oriented toward the recent past and the present versus being oriented toward the future. In national cultures characterized by a short-term orientation, individuals believe the following:

It is important to respect traditions and to remember past accomplishments.

To forget history is to risk repeating past mistakes.

Failing activities should be halted immediately.

Resources should be consumed now without worrying about the future.

Thus the short-term orientation supports immediate consumption and opposes the deferral of pleasure and satisfaction. People tend to avoid unpleasant tasks, even if they are necessary to ensure a pleasurable future. In contrast, in national cultures with a long-term orientation, people agree on the following points:

> It is important to look ahead and to envision the future.
>
> History is likely to repeat itself only if looking to the past obscures visions of the future.
>
> Perseverance in the face of adversity can overcome failure.
>
> Resources should be saved to ensure a prosperous future.[13]

A longer-term orientation favors the opposite strategy—that is, doing what is necessary now, whether pleasant or unpleasant, for the sake of future well-being. Short-term/long-term orientation thus influences people's willingness to endure hardship in the present and defer pleasurable experiences into the future.

EFFECTS ON ORGANIZATIONAL BEHAVIOR

The five-dimensional model based on the research by Hofstede and Bond does not lack for critics. For instance, a study that used the original four dimensions to assess the societal values of American, Japanese, and Taiwanese managers in Taiwan revealed problems with measurement validity and reliability (see Chapter 16 for a discussion of these kinds of problems).[14] Nonetheless, the Hofstede–Bond model is the most comprehensive cross-cultural framework currently available, and it can stimulate useful insights into ways in which organizational behavior varies from one national culture to another (see the Securing Competitive Advantage box). For this reason, it serves as the conceptual foundation of the rest of this chapter.

Cultural Trends: Four Scenarios

Table 15-1 summarizes the average scores on the five dimensions for each of the forty-four countries included in the studies by Hofstede and Bond. In the table, larger numbers signify greater amounts of uncertainty avoidance, masculinity, individualism, power distance, or longer-term orientation. The cultural distinctions quantified in this table reflect a variety of differences in the way people think and behave in different national cultures. To explore some of these differences, try using the five dimensions of the model to explain the following four scenarios.

1. *Feelings about progress.* Being modern and future-oriented is highly valued in China. From the modernist perspective, something that has existed for many years may seem old-fashioned or obsolete. In Russia, however, tradition, the status quo, and the past are more highly revered. To a traditionalist, familiar things are perceived as trustworthy, proven, and worthwhile. Which dimension explains this difference?
2. *Tendencies toward confrontation or consensus.* In Greece, it is important to smooth over differences to preserve agreement. Emphasis is placed on building consensus among co-workers and avoiding personal confrontation. In Denmark, conflict and confrontation are accepted or even encouraged. Conflict is perceived to be a signal of the need for change. How can this difference be explained?
3. *Locus of control.* The national culture of Australia instills a sense of personal responsibility for the outcomes of individual behaviors. Rewarding people for personal performance is considered a logical consequence of the value that Australians place on personal accountability.

SECURING COMPETITIVE ADVANTAGE

SENDING JOBS OFFSHORE TO INCREASE PROFITABILITY

In the early 1990s the North American Free Trade Agreement (NAFTA) became a central issue in the race for the U.S. presidency when Ross Perot described the "giant sucking sound" that would mark the exit of high-paying jobs from U.S. factories to Mexican facilities, in order to take advantage of Mexico's lower labor costs. In truth, a significant percentage of American manufacturing activity did move across the border following passage of NAFTA, requiring U.S. managers to develop proficiency in interacting with employees working in a national culture differing from than that of the United States (see Table 15-1).

Ten years later, a new round of globalization sent more jobs offshore—this time in areas such as computer chip design, software programming, and financial analysis. At Bank of America, for example, information technology (IT) workers were once in such short supply that the company often found itself paying a premium to outbid rivals and secure the necessary workforce. By 2002, however, Bank of America was in the midst of slashing nearly 5,000 of its 25,000 IT jobs. One-third of these jobs went to India, where work that costs $100 per hour in the United States could be done for $20.

Today, at Infosys Technologies Ltd., the Bangalore, India, company that now handles Bank of America's IT work, staffers also process home loan applications for Greenpoint Mortgage of Novato, California. At nearby Wipro Ltd., radiologists interpret CT scans for Massachusetts General Hospital. Staffers at Wipro are as much as 60 percent cheaper than their U.S. counterparts. Elsewhere, throughout Eastern Europe, Indian and American IT service providers are opening offices to tap an abundant German and English-speaking workforce. New facilities in Hungary, Poland, the Czech Republic, Romania, and Bulgaria are fulfilling service contracts for European multinationals. Boeing, Nortel, Motorola, and Intel have small research and development centers in Russia, to take advantage of an enormous pool of unemployed scientists and mathematicians. And in South Africa, speakers of German, French, and English are staffing call centers that work mainly for European companies.

Clearly, a global migration in office jobs is under way. The good news coming from this shift is that U.S. and European companies will become more profitable and efficient, perhaps fueling another round of growth-generating breakthroughs. The bad news also accompanying this trend concerns the high-paying jobs that will be lost in America and Western Europe, and the economic displacement that will bring pain to high-tech and white-collar workers who once thought that their jobs were immune from such downturns.

All the while, being able to manage organizational behavior across great cultural distance is becoming even more essential to competitive success. Companies whose management accepts the importance of cross-cultural differences and understands the specific effects of these differences will succeed in a world where information technology negates the effects of geographic distance and international laws favor trade over national isolation. Managers who do not learn to recognize cultural tendencies and manage in the context of cultural diversity will find it increasingly difficult to be successful.

Sources: P. Engardio, A. Bernstein, and M. Kripalani, "Is Your Job Next?" *Business Week,* February 3, 2003, pp. 50–60; D. Fairlamb and J. Rossant, "Mega Europe," *Business Week,* November 25, 2002, pp. 62–68.

In Pakistan, however, people focus on external social causes to explain similar outcomes. Giving people rewards for personal performance seems unwarranted because of cultural beliefs that behaviors are strongly influenced by outside forces. How can you explain this difference?

4. *Status and social position.* In India, status is accorded on the basis of family, class, ethnicity, and even accent. High-status people can impose their will on lower-status people, even when both are equally knowledgeable and competent. In New Zealand, status is earned through personal achievement, and shared governance by majority rule or participatory decision making is valued more highly than personal fiat. Expertise outranks social position in determining who will be involved in decision-making procedures. What lies beneath this difference?[15]

TABLE 15-1   A Comparison of Cultural Characteristics

National Culture	Uncertainty Avoidance	Masculinity–Femininity	Individualism–Collectivism	Power Distance	Short-Term/Long-Term Orientation
Argentina	86	56	46	49	—
Australia	51	61	90	36	—
Austria	70	79	55	11	—
Belgium	94	54	75	65	—
Brazil	76	49	38	69	—
Canada	48	52	80	39	—
Chile	86	28	23	63	—
China	60	50	20	80	118
Colombia	80	64	13	67	—
Denmark	23	16	74	18	—
Finland	59	26	63	33	—
France	86	43	71	68	30
Great Britain	35	66	89	35	—
Germany	65	66	67	35	31
Greece	112	57	35	60	—
Hong Kong	29	57	25	68	96
India	40	56	48	77	—
Indonesia	48	46	14	78	25
Iran	59	43	41	58	—
Ireland	35	68	70	28	—
Israel	81	47	54	13	—
Italy	75	70	76	50	—
Japan	92	95	46	54	80
Mexico	82	69	30	81	—
Netherlands	53	14	80	38	44
New Zealand	49	58	79	22	—
Norway	50	8	69	31	—
Pakistan	70	50	14	55	—
Peru	87	42	16	64	—
Philippines	44	64	32	94	—
Portugal	104	31	27	63	—
Russia	90	40	50	95	10
Singapore	8	48	20	74	—
South Africa	49	63	65	49	—
Spain	86	42	51	57	—
Sweden	29	5	71	31	—
Switzerland	58	70	68	34	—
Taiwan	69	45	17	58	—
Thailand	64	34	20	64	—
Turkey	85	45	37	66	—
United States	46	62	91	40	29
Venezuela	76	73	12	81	—
West Africa	54	46	20	77	16
Yugoslavia	88	21	27	76	—

Source: Based on G. Hofstede, "Motivation, Leadership, and Organization: Do American Theories Apply Abroad?" *Organizational Dynamics* 9 (1980), 42–63; and G. Hofstede, "Cultural Constraints in Management Theories," *Academy of Management Executive* 7 (1993), 81–94.

Were you able to explain the first scenario? Differing attitudes toward progress are produced by cross-cultural differences in short-term/long-term orientation. Cultures like that of Russia, which incorporate short-term orientations (10 on short-term/long-term orientation, as indicated in Table 15-1), honor tradition and feel threatened by new ways of doing things. Cultures like that of China, which include long-term orientations (118 on short-term/long-term orientation), more readily embrace modern ways.

The second scenario focuses on conflict avoidance, a cultural tendency that is closely associated with uncertainty avoidance. Conflict creates uncertainty, and cultures that cannot deal with uncertainty, like the Greek culture (112 on uncertainty avoidance), prefer to avoid the competition and aggression that conflict unleashes. In contrast, cultures that can tolerate uncertainty, like the Danish culture (23 on uncertainty avoidance), can cope with conflict as well.

The third scenario concerns locus of control and arises out of cross-cultural differences based on individualism and collectivism. On the one hand, the sense of personal responsibility stimulated by believing that the locus of control for personal behavior lies inside the individual is consistent with the norms and values of an individualistic national culture like that of Australia (90 on individualism–collectivism). On the other hand, the focus on social causes as the source of behaviors that is prompted by an external locus of control is compatible with the cultural collectivism of countries like Pakistan (14 on individualism–collectivism).

The fourth scenario shows how cultural differences in power distance can affect the way in which status and social position are accorded and perceived. Cultures like that of India, in which status and position are seen as birthrights—the special-privilege approach—also tend to be oriented toward large power distance (77 in Table 15-1). In contrast, cultures in countries like New Zealand, in which status and position are awarded according to personal abilities—the equal opportunity approach—are more inclined toward smaller power distance (22 in the table).

Organizational Effects

The four scenarios illustrate how the Hofstede–Bond five-dimensional model can diagnose differences in national culture and help identify some of the cultural roots of everyday customs and behaviors. To understand how these cultural differences can influence organizational behavior, consider first the national culture of the United States and its effects on American theories and practices. As shown in Table 15-1, the U.S. national culture is extremely individualistic (91) and oriented toward larger degrees of power distance (40) than many of the other cultures included in Hofstede's study. If attention is limited to these two cultural characteristics—to simplify the discussion—a few brief examples will suffice to show how the U.S. national culture shapes and affects organizational behavior in American firms.

As indicated in Chapter 5, work behaviors in U.S. companies are influenced most strongly by the receipt of rewards expected to satisfy personal needs, especially when those rewards are distributed in proportion to personal performance. Thus American firms often use piece-rate wages or commission payments tied to personal performance to encourage productivity, and these tactics typically succeed in the United States as motivational devices. As suggested by the Hofstede–Bond model, this tendency is consistent with the strong individualism of the U.S. national culture, and of individualistic proclivities to perceive work as something that people accomplish alone and rewards as allocated fairly when received according to personal—not group—achievements.

In addition, as described in Chapter 10, American models of leadership suggest that leading is largely a process of directing the behaviors and strengthening the motivation of individual employees. Individualism requires that leaders in U.S. firms use direct supervision to coordinate the work of their subordinates, so that success at personal jobs in turn leads to fulfillment of group and organizational goals. The leader is the "glue" that keeps groups of co-workers from falling apart. Large power distance justifies the leader's use of the power necessary to accomplish this feat.

Finally, American organizations often reflect the tenet that large firms should be structured as hierarchies in which rules and procedures govern employee behaviors, in the manner indicated in Chapter 12. The type of direct supervision undertaken as part of the task of being a leader is implemented when rules and procedures fail to provide the necessary guidance. This kind of hierarchical structuring requires workers to agree with the belief that differences in power are a normal part of everyday life. It is made possible by the fact that the U.S. national culture favors norms supportive of a relatively large degree of power distance.

Cross-Cultural Differences

To further understand how the differences highlighted in the Hofstede–Bond model can influence behavior in organizations, consider the various areas of organizational behavior as practiced in organizations throughout the world.

Decision Making On an Israeli **kibbutz**—a self-contained community, often located along Israel's undeveloped border and organized around Zionist religious principles—decision making is shared among the adult membership, being vested in the kibbutz's general assembly rather than in the hands of a small management group. The general assembly, which is the principal governing body of the kibbutz, meets once per week in most kibbutzim. Topics considered in assembly meetings may include the purchase, cleaning, and repair of kibbutznik clothing, as all clothing is collectively owned, or the practices used to raise and educate kibbutz children, as children are raised in communal quarters. Participation in assembly meetings is nearly universal, because all members who are kibbutz-born and age nineteen or older or who have completed a one-year naturalization program can vote on the issues.

The secretariat, an administrative board consisting of elected officials, is empowered only to implement policies approved by the kibbutz assembly. No official is permitted to act outside assembly mandates. Each is elected by the assembly, serves a fixed term of office, and cannot hold the same office for more than one consecutive term. As a result, the ability of any officeholder to amass the power needed to make decisions autonomously is strictly limited.[16]

In a similar vein, Japanese organizations are well known for their use of *ringisei*, a consensus-based process of decision making in which managers circulate proposals among subordinates to gain their approval before implementing decisions. Such a scheme increases commitment, reduces resistance to change, and can minimize the time required to implement the results of decision-making processes. However, the decision-making process itself can consume a considerable amount of time.[17]

In contrast to the Israeli and Japanese approaches, Korean businesses seldom use groups to make decisions. Instead, members of the families that own Korea's *chaebol* conglomerates make all corporate decisions themselves and require subordinates to implement them without question. Although Korean firms sometimes employ an approach that outwardly resembles Japanese consensus decision making, it is actually a process of communicating management decisions already made, because employees are not allowed to suggest significant changes.[18]

In sum, Israeli kibbutz, Japanese, and Korean organizations differ in terms of the extent to which members can influence decisions and decision-making processes. This difference is explained by the contrasting levels of power distance evident in the national cultures of Israel (13), Japan (54), and Korea (Korean power distance was not measured in the Hofstede and Bond studies, but is similar in level to that of Hong Kong [68] and Singapore [74]). Lower power distance, which minimizes hierarchical differences, encourages decentralized decision making among an organization's membership. Higher power distance, which encourages hierarchical differentiation, also favors the retention of decision making at the top of the organization.

Motivation   Japanese motives and motivation are influenced by the relatively strong collectivism that characterizes Japan's national culture (46 in Table 15-1). For the current managers of large Japanese corporations, managing motivation is primarily a matter of stimulating in each employee a sense of loyalty, obligation, and dependence on superiors and co-workers.

The resulting feelings reinforce the collectivism that holds Japanese organizations together. In particular, the practice in larger Japanese firms of offering lifetime employment (to age fifty-six) to their permanent employees greatly encourages workers to display loyalty to the company. Japanese employees find it difficult to behave disloyally toward a firm that is willing to commit itself to them up to their retirement.[19]

Collectivistic loyalty is also encouraged in large Japanese firms by the *nenko* system of wage payment. Under the *nenko* system, the employee's pay consists of a basic wage plus merit supplements and job-level allowances. The basic wage, which constitutes about 55 percent of total pay, includes the employee's starting wage plus yearly increases. Those increases are determined by (in order of importance) seniority or length of service with the company, age, and supervisory ratings on such qualities as seriousness, attendance, performance, and cooperativeness.[20]

Merit supplements account for an additional 15 percent of the employee's pay and are based on supervisory assessments of specific job behaviors. In principle, they are meant to reward exemplary performance. In fact, merit supplements are heavily influenced by seniority because they are calculated as a percentage of the basic wage. Moreover, junior employees' performance is typically rated below senior employees' work regardless of any real differences between the two.[21] Clearly, Japanese merit supplements reward loyalty and longevity with the company.

Job-level allowances, which account for about 30 percent of each Japanese worker's total pay, reflect the importance of each worker's job in relation to the other jobs in the organization. Such allowances may sound similar to the pay increments that result in the United States from job-evaluation procedures. In Japan, however, each employee's position in the hierarchy of jobs—which affects his or her job-level allowance—is more directly influenced by seniority than by skill.[22]

Thus seniority is the single most important factor in determining a Japanese worker's compensation. It affects the basic wage, merit supplements, and job-level allowances. The large Japanese firm resembles an idealized family in the sense that its employees spend their lives in a stable social setting and receive positions of increasing social importance as they grow older.[23] Along with the *nenko* method of financial compensation, this family-like system provides its members with social rewards for emphasizing loyalty to the company over all other concerns. Employees' decisions to attend work and to perform productively grow out of their sense of loyalty and obligation to the collectivistic firm.

Work Design   Jobs in the Swedish automotive industry are organized not around the assembly-line processes commonly found in the United States, Japan, and elsewhere, but instead according to the principles of reflective production. Embodied in these principles are the following ideas:

1. Assembly work must be viewed in a wide context on the shop floor. It includes not only the assembly itself, but also the preceding phases (that is, controlling the materials, structuring the materials and tools) and the subsequent phases (that is, final inspection, and if necessary, adjustment and further inspection). The vertical

division of labor is also affected in that assembly workers assume responsibility for certain administrative tasks. This new concept of assembly work calls for workers' own reflections.

2. In reflective production, the assembly work itself becomes intellectualized and therefore meaningful. Work teams are able to rebalance their own work.

3. Established empirical knowledge of grouping and restructuring work tasks is a basic precondition for the realization of efficient and humane production systems.[24]

Thus, from the perspective of reflective production, employees are encouraged to develop an understanding of the entire manufacturing process and contribute to its design. Reflected are values of work as an intellectual, humane activity; these values are consistent with the extremely high femininity (5 in Table 15-1) demonstrated by the Swedish national culture.

Leadership   Consistent with cultural proclivities favoring low power distance (31 in Table 15-1), managers in Sweden often do not supervise employees directly, nor do they always issue direct orders to coordinate work activities. Instead, they function as boundary spanners who facilitate the flow of work between groups, while allowing employees to handle intragroup coordination responsibilities themselves. Managers also resolve conflicts within groups and help members communicate with one another in the course of participatory decision making. Thus managers act more as facilitators or social catalysts than as direct supervisors.

As shown in Figure 15-1, groups and committees fulfill leadership functions in many Swedish firms.[25] The **works council,** for example, is composed of worker representatives who are elected by their peers and management representatives who are appointed by top management. An organization usually has only one works council, which assumes responsibility for developing the overall organizational policies and procedures. Works councils have little or no direct decision-making power, but they provide a forum in which worker representatives can express their opinions and thereby be instrumental in shaping the mission and strategic direction of the firm. They are usually supported by several general advisory committees located lower in the organization hierarchy, which also provide leadership. These advisory groups may include suggestion committees, personnel-policy committees, or information committees. Their purpose is to contribute advice on general problems or issues lying outside the domains of the special-interest committees (described next).

Special-interest committees, which are also composed of worker and manager representatives, provide the works council with advice on specific issues, such as job design, plant sanitation, personnel practices, and environmental safety. These committees cooperate with middle management to produce yearly reports that assist

FIGURE 15-1   The Structure of Advisory Committees in a Scandinavian Firm

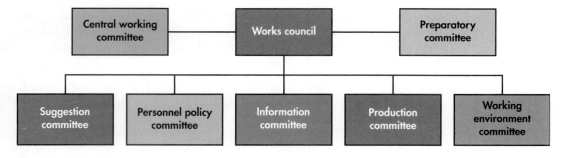

works councils with the task of formulating company policies. Such reports might include an analysis of water and air pollution produced by the company, a set of guidelines for curbing absenteeism, or a proposal on ways to reduce the amount of costly inventory kept on hand. As a whole, then, leadership in Swedish organizations often comes from groups in which employees and management work together to influence company policies and procedures.

Organization Structure   The structures of family businesses in China reflect the ideology of patrimonialism, which brings together the elements of paternalism, hierarchy, mutual obligation, responsibility, and familialism that grow out of the Chinese national culture's high collectivism (20) and power distance (80). Chinese family businesses are typically small in size and take on simple structures that limit them to only a single business function, such as production, sales, or logistics. All employees are expected to help execute this function, resulting in a negligible division of labor. Formalized rules and systems of roles are largely lacking or completely absent. Correspondingly, interpersonal relationships and feelings take priority over concerns with organizational efficiency and effectiveness in determining whether structural arrangements are considered appropriate. Informal groups and personal loyalty replace standardized coordination and formal structuring in such organizations.[26]

Showing the effects of a similar pattern (albeit lesser absolute amounts) of collectivism (46) and power distance (54), the structures of most large Japanese corporations resemble the hierarchical, pyramidal structures of many U.S. companies. In fact, Japanese organization charts often show the same hierarchy of vertical relationships that characterize a U.S. firm's organization chart. In Japanese firms, however, these vertical relationships are often patterned after the parent–child (*oyabun–kobun*) relationships of traditional Japanese families. In the organizational version of this relationship, a subordinate is encouraged to feel loyal and obligated to his or her superior as well as dependent on the superior. This feeling of dependence, in turn, encourages—in fact, requires—acquiescence to the superior's demands.[27]

Another significant feature of Japanese organizational structures relates to communication patterns. In traditionally structured organizations elsewhere in the world, the vertical lines of command that appear in organization charts are meant to serve as the primary formal channels of communication. To communicate with a colleague in another department or division, an employee is expected to pass a message up the hierarchy to a superior, who then sends it downward to the final recipient. In Japanese corporations, however, certain formally designated *horizontal* relationships are accorded the same degree of importance as the vertical relationships depicted in the organization chart. These horizontal relationships, which allow communication to flow across the hierarchy rather than having to go up and down, connect managers who entered the company at the same time. They are encouraged by the group socialization that managers receive on first entering the company—other members of the manager's group become lifetime contacts throughout the company. In addition, such relationships are encouraged by the practice of rotating Japanese managers among the different functional areas of the firm—marketing, accounting, production, finance, and so forth. As a result, each manager becomes more of a generalist than a specialist and can cultivate a collection of horizontal linkages that unites him or her with management peers across functional boundaries.[28]

Together, the kinds of dependence relations and communication patterns formed in Japanese organizations create a **latticework structure** of vertical and horizontal relationships among the company's managers. Continuing relations among management peers from different functional areas, such as marketing and manufacturing, help stimulate harmony and coordination between functional groups. Nonetheless, in large Japanese firms, decision-making authority remains highly centralized. This combination of central control and strong relationships among peers is unique to the latticework structure of large Japanese corporations.

Organizational Change   In general, national cultures that are highly supportive of organizational change tend to have low power distance, high individualism, and low uncertainty avoidance.[29] Consequently, one would expect cultural resistance to organizational change to be quite high in Russia (with measures of 95, 50, and 90 for power distance, individualism–collectivism, and uncertainty avoidance, respectively)—a supposition that has been borne out by recent experience.[30]

Interestingly, however, in Korea, Japan, and Taiwan (three other countries with cultural profiles similar to that of Russia), innovation and change are relatively common. This apparent paradox can be explained by the pronounced long-term orientation in such cultures (80 for Japan), which strongly emphasizes persistence and adaptive growth in the face of challenge and adversity.[31]

MANAGING INTERNATIONAL DIFFERENCES

Diagnosing and understanding the primary features of national cultures—as in the previous examples—are critical to success in the management of international organizational behavior, because this exercise represents the first step toward determining whether familiar management practices must be reconfigured before being used abroad. A glance back at Table 15-1 indicates that the national cultures of the United States and Canada, for example, are approximately equal in terms of power distance, uncertainty avoidance, masculinity, and individualism. Owing to this similarity, U.S. managers can expect to succeed in Canada, and Canadian managers can anticipate working effectively in the United States, without making major adjustments to customary management practices.

According to Hofstede's findings, however, the level of uncertainty avoidance in Denmark (23) is about half that in the United States (46) and Canada (48). As a result, North American managers will likely find it necessary to change their normal way of doing things if they must work in Denmark. More generally, managers working in national cultures characterized by weaker uncertainty avoidance must learn to cope with higher levels of anxiety and stress, while reducing their reliance on planning, rule making, and other familiar ways of absorbing uncertainty. On the other side of the coin, managers working in cultures with stronger uncertainty avoidance must learn not only to accept, but also to participate in, the development of seemingly unnecessary rules and apparently meaningless planning to help other organization members cope with stressful uncertainty. Rituals that at first glance might seem useless or even irrational may, in fact, serve the very important function of diminishing an otherwise intolerable level of uncertainty.

Next, consider the dimension of masculinity–femininity. Female managers working in cultures characterized by more cultural masculinity than in their own culture face the prospect of receiving less respect at work than they feel they deserve. To cope with gender discrimination of this sort, a female manager may want to seek out male mentors in senior management to secure her place in the organization. Conversely, male managers in national cultures marked by more cultural femininity than their own must control their aggressive tendencies and learn to treat members of both sexes with equal dignity and respect. Acting as mentors, female managers can demonstrate that women are as adept at their jobs as men.

The next dimension to be examined is individualism–collectivism. Managers who must work in national cultures that are more individualistic than their own must first learn to cope with the sense of rootlessness that comes from the absence of close-knit group relationships. They must learn not to be embarrassed by personal compliments, despite their belief that success stems from group effort. At work, they must develop an understanding of the importance of rewarding individuals equitably and adjust to the idea that organizational membership is impermanent. Conversely, managers attempting to work in cultures that are more collectivistic than their own must learn to deal with demands for self-sacrifice in support of group well-being. They must also learn to accept equal sharing in lieu of equity and exchange at work. Consequently, they must refrain from paying individual employees compliments and instead praise group performance. In addition, managers adjusting to collectivistic national cultures must understand that belonging to an organization in such cultures means more than just forming a temporary association; it is an important basis of each employee's personal identity.

Managers who work in cultures that favor less power distance may initially feel discomfort stemming from the unfamiliar decentralization of authority and a perceived loss of control. They must learn to be less autocratic and more participatory in their work with others. On the other hand, managers facing cultural tendencies toward more power distance must accept the role that centralization and tall hierarchies play in maintaining what is deemed to be an acceptable level of control. They must adopt a more authoritarian, autocratic style of management. Indeed, they may find that subordinates, if asked to participate in decision making, will refuse on the grounds that decision making is management's rightful job.

Finally, short-term/long-term orientation may have its greatest effect during the planning activities that represent an integral part of management. For managers who are most familiar with a short-term orientation, working in a culture characterized by a long-term orientation will require them to pay less attention to past successes or failures and more attention to future possibilities as they set organizational objectives and define group and individual goals. In contrast, managers from cultures with long-term orientations must accept that colleagues with short-term orientations will spend considerable energy looking backward in time to decide how to approach the future. Traditional approaches will likely be favored over innovation and creativity, and much attention may be paid to avoiding the mistakes of history.

Although the cross-cultural differences just described are readily evident among contemporary national cultures, some have suggested that management practices throughout the world are growing more alike.[32] Consistent with this idea, practices developed in one culture are occasionally borrowed for use in another. For instance, in the United States, teams of co-workers are being formed where employees once worked as individuals, in interventions patterned after Scandinavian work design programs. Quality circles resembling the Japanese groups have become so prevalent that they are now considered part of the U.S. approach to job design. In addition, U.S. business organization structures are becoming flatter and more participatory as downsizing reduces the size of management staffs and as reengineering breaks down barriers separating tasks and task groups. All of these changes are occurring as U.S. companies strive to become more flexible and market-oriented.

Such trends seem to support the **convergence hypothesis**, which suggests that national cultures, organizations, and management practices throughout the world are becoming more homogeneous.[33] In a review of studies that examined this hypothesis, John Child found both evidence for convergence and evidence for divergence (that is, continued cross-cultural differences). Interestingly, studies that supported

CUTTING-EDGE RESEARCH

CONVERTING GLOBAL PRESENCE INTO GLOBAL COMPETITIVE ADVANTAGE

In a recent article, researchers Anil K. Gupta and Vijay Govindarajan suggested that simply creating a global presence does not confer competitive advantage. Instead, such presence makes available opportunities that may or may not produce advantage, depending on how they are managed.

One opportunity involves local market differences. On one hand, companies can offer standardized products that ignore these differences, and increase to some extent the business they are able to do. On the other hand, however, companies can recognize local differences, tailor their products to those differences, and gain huge competitive advantage over local firms and those who choose to standardize.

A second opportunity involves the exploitation of economies of global scale. Growing to become global automatically expands a company's scope of operations. Whether this will lead to competitive advantage depends on the degree to which the firm is able to spread fixed costs over the larger volume of goods or services it produces, pool purchasing power over suppliers, or reduce operating costs through higher-capacity operations.

A third opportunity has to do with tapping the optimal locations for company activities and resources. Some countries have workforces with particular skills not found elsewhere. Others can provide low-cost labor. And others have natural resources found elsewhere only at higher cost. The company that can

identify such prospects and take advantage of them is able to gain advantage over others that cannot.

A fourth opportunity involves economies of global scope offered by multinational growth. Companies that can facilitate the delivery of goods or services across diverse geographic areas will do far better than those that cannot offer similar coordination.

Finally, a fifth opportunity occurs when a company is able to maximize the transfer of knowledge across locations. Subsidiary locations viewed as reservoirs of knowledge, not simply as packages of tangible assets or holders of market position, can provide information about innovations likely to be useful in other global locations. The company that is able to take advantage of such reservoirs is able to innovate without having to absorb the costs of "reinventing the same wheel."

Deriving benefit from these five opportunities requires careful coordination that, in turn, necessitates the development of an organization structure that can overcome the separating effects of geographic distance. It also requires taking stock of the competencies possessed by the firm and its workforce. Many such competencies grow out of the kinds of cultural differences discussed in this chapter. Knowing how to identify and manage these differences is thus an important part of the task of transforming global opportunities into competitive gains.

Source: From "Converting Global Presence into Global Competitive Advantage," by A.K. Gupta and V. Govindarajan in *Academy of Management Executive: The Thinking Manager's Source* 15 (2001), 45–56. Copyright © 2001 by Academy of Management. Reproduced with permission of Academy of Management via copyright clearance center.

convergence typically focused on organizational variables, such as structure and technology, whereas studies that revealed divergence usually dealt with employee attitudes, beliefs, and behaviors.[34] Child concluded that organizations themselves may be becoming more alike throughout the world, but that people in these organizations are maintaining their cultural distinctiveness. Management in a multicultural world currently requires an understanding of cultural differences and will continue to do so for quite some time (see the Cutting-Edge Research box).

In closing, the five dimensions introduced in this chapter form a model that highlights important differences among national cultures. As you use this model in the future, remember that each dimension simplifies the kinds of variations that exist among the world's national cultures. Such simplification is the necessary consequence of the goal of researchers like Hofstede and Bond, who seek to create theories and models that can be readily understood and used in many situations.[35] Realize also that this simplification encourages stereotyping—that is, the perception that all members of a particular culture are alike in some specific way. Always keep in mind the fact that beneath societal similarities like those discussed in this chapter lie subtle differences among people who also vary along the lines identified in the Hofstede–Bond model. For example, although both the U.S. and Canadian national cultures are highly individualistic, a significant number of people in North America are collectivists.[36] For this reason, you should exercise caution when employing the five-dimensional model, lest you overlook relatively less conspicuous, but nonetheless influential cultural complexities and dissimilarities.

SUMMARY

Whether comparisons are made within a single *national culture* or across different national cultures, no two organizations are exactly alike. Likewise, no two people in the world hold exactly the same beliefs and values. Thus the discussions in this chapter necessarily involved generalization. Not every Japanese organization has a fully developed *latticework structure*, and not every kibbutz is completely collectivistic. Nevertheless, firms in a particular national culture tend to be more like each other than they are like organizations in other national cultures. Moreover, people in the same national culture tend to think and act more similarly than do people from different cultures.

Cross-cultural differences exist and can have significant effects on organizational behavior. The most important of these cross-cultural differences are captured by five dimensions: *uncertainty avoidance, masculinity–femininity, individualism–collectivism, power distance,* and *short-term/long-term orientation.* Differences in individualism–collectivism and power distance seem to explain many of the differences that can be detected among management practices throughout the world. Considered together, these five dimensions are helpful in understanding why people in a particular national culture behave as they do and can prove useful to managers as they strive to adapt familiar management practices for use in unfamiliar cultures.

REVIEW QUESTIONS

1. Compared with the national culture of Sweden, what level of uncertainty avoidance characterizes the national culture of the United States? In which country would you expect to find greater evidence of ritualistic behavior? Why? How would your answers to these questions change if you were asked to compare the United States and Greece?

2. Hofstede's findings indicated that the U.S. national culture at the time of his research was more masculine than many of the other national cultures he examined. In your opinion, is the U.S. culture still as masculine as Hofstede's research suggests? Why or why not?

3. According to Hofstede's research, the three most individualistic national cultures are found in the United States, Australia, and Great Britain. Can you think of a reason why these three countries share this cultural characteristic? Does your answer also explain the relatively strong individualism of the Canadian national culture?

4. Would you expect the structures of organizations in Denmark to be taller or flatter than those of organizations in the United States? Why? How are organization structures in Mexico likely to compare with those in Denmark and the United States?

5. Comparing U.S. business firms with businesses in Colombia and Brazil, in which companies are the wages of workers most likely to reflect differences in personal performance? In which are workers more likely to receive similar payments despite differences in personal performance? What explains this difference?

6. If you had to adapt the theories and models described in this book for use in China, what kinds of changes might you make? Explain your answer using the Hofstede–Bond five-dimensional model.

LEARNING THROUGH EXPERIENCE

DIAGNOSTIC QUESTIONS 15-1

International Organizational Behavior

National cultures can have major effects on organizations and the behaviors of their members. Thus it is critical that managers be able to assess the characteristics of surrounding national cultures and understand the effects of those cultures on organizational behavior. The following questions facilitate this process.

1. What are the characteristics of your own national culture? Is it more individualistic or collectivistic? Are its values consistent with more or less power distance? Is it characterized more by masculinity or femininity? Does it favor strong or weak uncertainty avoidance? Is it more consistent with a short-term or long-term orientation?

2. What are the characteristics of the national culture surrounding your organization? How do they compare with the characteristics of your own national culture?

3. Based on your diagnosis of cultural differences, what adjustments should you make to familiar management practices to better fit them to the current cultural situation?

4. Can any colleagues in the organization help you with the necessary adaptation? Should you also ask others outside the organization to help?

5. Might other managers in the future benefit from what you learn as you cope with cultural adjustment in the present? Will informal mentoring provide enough guidance? Should a formal program be designed and implemented instead?

EXERCISE 15-1

Ethical Dilemmas in International Business

Dorothy Marcic, Vanderbilt University

Conducting global business introduces the possibility of ethical conflicts stemming from contrasting cultural values and differing business practices. This exercise asks you to consider and respond to ten such situations individually and then to consider the implications of your answers in groups.

From *International Management Cases and Exercises*, 1st edition, by D. Marcic and S. Puffer © 1994. Reprinted with permission of South-Western Publishing, Mason, OH.

Step One: Pre-Class Preparation

In the upcoming class you will meet in groups to discuss how you would react to the following situations. To prepare for this discussion, read all of the situations now and write a short paragraph for each, indicating what you would do and why you would choose to behave in this way.

1. For several months, you have been trying to privatize a formerly state-owned business. The company has been doing well and will most likely do better in private hands. Unfortunately, the paperwork is proceeding slowly, and it may take many more months to finish. An official that can help with this problem suggests that if you pay expenses for him and his family to visit the parent company in the United States (plus a two-week vacation at Disney World and in New York City), the paperwork can be completed in a week. What do you do? Why?

2. You have been hired as an independent consultant on a U.S. development grant. Part of your job involves working with the Ministry of Health in a developing country. Your assignment is to help standardize some procedures to test for various diseases in the population. After two weeks on the job, a higher-level manager complains to you that money donated by the World Health Organization to the ministry for purchasing vaccines has actually been used to buy expensive computers for top-ranking officials. What do you do? Why?

3. You are driving to a nearby country from your job as a manager of a foreign subsidiary. In your car are a number of rather expensive gifts for family and friends in the country you are visiting. When you cross the border, the customs official tells you that the duty will be the equivalent of $200. Then he smiles, hands back your passport, and quietly suggests that you put a smaller sum— say $20—in the passport and hand it back to him. What do you do? Why?

4. One of your top managers in a Middle Eastern country has been kidnapped by a terrorist group that has demanded a ransom of $2 million, plus food assistance for refugees in a specified camp. If the ransom is not paid, the kidnappers threaten to kill your manager. What do you do? Why?

5. Your company has been trying to get foreign contracts in a developing country for several months. Yesterday, the brother-in-law of the finance minister offered to work as a consultant to help you secure contracts. He charges one and one-half times as much as anyone else in a similar situation. What do you do? Why?

6. You have been asked to join the board of directors of a large telecommunications company that is about to be privatized. The two main organizers of the project, both former government officials, have asked that their names not be publicized until after government approval has been secured, as they are concerned about being accused of using undue influence in other privatization projects. What do you do? Why?

7. As manager of a foreign subsidiary, you recently discovered that your chief of operations has authorized a very convoluted accounting system, most likely to hide many payments going into his pocket. Although you have no proof, rumors have begun circulating to that effect as well. The chief, however, has close ties to government officials who can make or break your company in this country. What do you do? Why?

8. Your new job is to secure contracts with foreign governments in several developing countries. One day, a colleague takes you aside to give you "tips" on how to ensure you win the contracts. He tells you what each nationality likes to hear, to soothe their egos or other psychological needs. For example, people in one country prefer to be told that they will have a better image with the U.S. government if they contract with your company (you know, however, that their image will be unaffected). If you say these things, according to your colleague, they will definitely give you the contracts. If not, someone in another company will tell them similar things and the competitor will get the contracts. What do you do? Why?

9. You have been working as the director of a foreign subsidiary for several months. Recently, you learned that several valued employees have part-time businesses that they run while on the job. One worker exchanges foreign currency for employees and visitors. Another rents a few cars to visitors. You are told that this practice has been acceptable behavior for years. What do you do? Why?

10. You are the manager of a foreign company in a country where bribery is commonplace. You have been told that an important shipment has arrived but will take as long as six months to clear the paperwork. You have also been informed casually that a "tip" of $200 would cut the time to three days. What would you do? Why?

Step Two: Group Discussion

The class should divide into groups of four to six members each (if you have already formed permanent groups, reassemble in those groups). Within these groups, each member should indicate what he or she would do in each situation and why. After everyone in the group has finished, make a note of differences and discrepancies among the answers and arrive at a group consensus for each situation. A group representative should be appointed to report the results of this step to the class.

Step Three: Class Discussion

The class should reconvene, and group representatives should report on the results of Step Two. The class should then discuss these results, using the following questions as guidelines:

1. What differences are evident among the reactions of different groups to each situation? How can these differences be explained?

2. Looking back at your individual answers, would you change any of them after taking part in group and class discussions? How would you change them? Why?

3. How realistic are the situations? Have you ever experienced a similar ethical dilemma? How do considerations about differences among national cultures complicate such dilemmas?

Conclusion

As you have learned in this exercise, conflicting ethical perspectives can complicate the conduct of business relations across cultural boundaries. What is considered appropriate or normal practice in one national culture may be viewed as inappropriate or even illegal in another culture. Simply looking after one's own interests—or the interests of one's company—in such situations often will not resolve ethical questions. Instead, it is the responsibility of multinational companies—and their managers—to explore possible ethical dilemmas beforehand and prepare their employees to deal with them in the appropriate way.

Critical Thinking and the Scientific Process
Ways of Knowing
The Purposes of Science
The Interplay of Theory and Data
Characteristics of Good Theories and Good Data

Causal Inferences
Criteria for Inferring Cause
Designing Observations to Infer Cause

Generalizing Research Results
Sample, Setting, and Time
Facilitating Generalization

Linking Organizational Behavior Science and Practice
Summary
Review Questions

Critical Thinking and Continuous Learning

In Search of Excellence, *published more than twenty years ago, was really the first of its kind—a book about management practices that was written directly for popular consumption. With more than 3 million copies sold, it is the top-selling pop management book of all time, and it virtually launched an industry. Today, pop management books roll off the press constantly, often landing on the best-seller list for nonfiction. However, after a recent confession by Tom Peters, one of the authors of* In Search of Excellence, *this categorization may need to be revised because in Peters's own words, "This is pretty small beer, but for what it's worth, okay I confess: We faked the data."* [1]

Although immensely popular among practicing managers, In Search of Excellence *was never a hit among either academics or writers in the traditional business press. Academics blasted the book because it employed what is widely known to be faulty research design called "selecting on the dependent variable." That is, Peters and co-author Robert Waterman selected the companies they were going to study by asking colleagues at consulting company McKinsey & Co. for the names of firms that, again in Peters's own words, "were doing cool work." They then took the list generated by this not-so-rigorous process and selected out those that seemed to score high on the dependent variable—recent financial performance. Based on some real and, apparently, some imaginary interviews, they looked for common practices among these top performing firms. Close to an important deadline, eight principles were hastily derived based on what the firms seemed to share. However, because they did not include any poorly performing firms in their study design, there is no way of knowing whether the firms actually engaged in these principles more or less than firms that performed poorly. For example, although they did not suggest these as principles, this design would support the principles "the CEO sleeps at night" and the "COO went to high school" because these too are things all the top firms had in common.*

A more rigorous study published by Mike Hitt and Duane Ireland in the academic press corrected this design flaw and directly compared Peters and Waterman's "excellent" companies to a matched set of companies that were in the same industry and were the same size. This more rigorously designed study found that (a) the "excellent" firms were no better performers than the matched control firms, (b) the "excellent" companies did not engage in the eight principles any more than the control firms, and (c) even if one ignores the "excellent" versus "control" categorization, firms that scored higher on the eight principles did not perform any better than firms that ignored them.[2]

Meanwhile, the traditional business world also was highly critical of the book, and Business Week *published a cover story titled "Oops!" in 1984 that documented what, at that time, appeared to be errors in the data. Of course, now we know the source of these errors, in the sense that some of the data was simply being fudged. But even beyond this, the* Business Week *article made it clear that the "excellent" firms were not always very high performers in the years before or after their categorization, but only appeared to have peaked right at the moment when Peters and Waterman were selecting their excellent firms. General Electric, who has had a long history of sustained financial success, had an off year when the "excellent" firms were chosen, and hence was not included in Peters's list, but Atari was.[3] If you have never heard of Atari, ask your parents or grandparents about the video game Pong.*

This is another problem with the practice of "selecting on the dependent variable"; momentary fluctuations are treated as reflecting genuine performance differences when in fact, they are just unstable, one-time, almost random blips in the larger picture. This selection method is just too powerfully impacted by what is called "sampling error." For example, on any given night at the roulette wheel at a casino, eventually one will see a performance distribution where some people lose money, some break even, and some win. To pull aside those who won at this random game and then document their "winning strategies" is really not such a good idea, especially if your plan is to "benchmark" or copy their practices to use yourself.

As we saw in the recent case of Jason Blair at the New York Times, *admitting such a fabrication would end the career of a journalist, but this seems to have no impact on the stature of management gurus; Tom Peters is still in huge demand as a speaker and writer. Unfortunately, many current pop management books emulate the precedent-setting work of Peters and Waterman, in both style and substance, and the practice of selecting on the dependent variable is rampant within these works. Hopefully, these books do not also emulate their predecessors' practice of fabricating the data as well. Unlike the academic press, where articles go through a long, difficult, and contentious process of blind peer review by well-established experts in the field, there is no similar system of checks and balances when it comes to what people can say in unrefereed books. Thus, as was the case with* In Search of Excellence, *one should treat the "nonfiction" categorization of such books with some degree of skepticism.*

W hen I was growing up, managers used to say they hired a hand, and they really meant it. But today they say they hire minds. In a world where minds are hired, learning becomes essential."[4]

This quote comes from Chris Argyris, one of the leading academic management scholars, whose specialty area for the last twenty-five years has been the process of organizational learning. According to Argyris, certain features of organizational contexts often make it difficult for people to learn—especially smart people. Learning often comes out of an error detection and correction process, and in many organizational contexts, admitting to having made an error can get one in trouble, and suggesting that one's supervisor has made an error can result in even more trouble.

Thus, there is a great deal of motivation in these contexts to deny that any error has taken place, and the smarter one is, the better he or she often is at "spinning" the evidence in order to deny the error. Although this type of spinning may have some short-term personal value in terms of promoting one's career, the organization may lose out on an opportunity to prevent that same error from happening somewhere else. In fact, the organization may be able to learn from this one mistake and put policies in place that might ensure that it will never happen again, but of course, this hinges on one's willingness to point out the error in the first place.

Firms that systematically try to avoid this trap are called "learning organizations," and two primary features of learning organizations set them apart from their competitors.

First, such firms critically analyze their experiences and the experiences of others to maximize their capacity to learn from past successes and failures. For example, Boeing's "Project Homework" was a three-year study that compared the development process for the lackluster 737 and 747 plane programs with the development process associated with the 707 and 727 programs, which had produced the company's two most profitable planes. The group studying these processes generated a list of more than 100 "lessons learned," which were subsequently transferred to the startup operations for the 757 and 767 planes. Guided by critically analyzed past experience, these launches proved to be the most error-free and successful in Boeing history.

The second primary feature of learning organizations relates to their penchant for experimentation and their use of the scientific method to promote innovation. For example, Corning Glass continually experiments with different raw materials and processes to increase both the yield and quality of its finished glass. Alleghany Ludlam, a specialty steelmaker, expects every manager to launch at least one experimental program each year. The result of its forward-looking philosophy has been a history of productivity improvements averaging close to 8 percent per year.

Although many readers of this book will be business majors, one fact that should not be overlooked is that many of the most successful CEOs do not hold MBAs. General Electric's Jack Welch and Intel's Andy Grove, for example, were formally trained in the "hard" sciences. Although the specialized skills learned in an MBA program are useful for gaining entry-level positions, managers who rise to the top of the organization are often those who generate, test, and implement new ideas and discoveries.[5] Indeed, some have begun to question whether the convergent thinking skills associated with a traditional MBA degree are the most relevant in a changing world, and many employers now look in nonbusiness programs for successful leaders.[6]

Learning organizations rely on critical thinking and rigorously analyzed data to gain a long-term sustainable competitive edge relative to other members of their industry.[7] Unfortunately, knowledge-creating organizations remain the exceptions, not the rule. Too many U.S. businesses "fall prey to every new management fad promising a painless solution, especially when it is presented in a neat, bright package."[8] Indeed, this tendency has created a veritable cottage industry of "pop" management books, such as *In Search of Excellence,* that often substitute for serious thinking about the best way to manage in specific companies.[9] Indeed, as one commentator on these books has noted, "No advice is too lame to get a polite, respectful hearing from a business audience."[10] The vague, "one-best-way" recommendations in these books can rarely withstand rigorous scientific scrutiny.[11]

To avoid this "quick-fix" mentality, managers need to take several steps. First, they must keep current with the literature in the field of management and pay particular attention to journal articles that translate research findings into practical guidelines. Second, managers must be skeptical when simple solutions are offered and analyze such solutions (and their supposed evidence) thoroughly. Third, they must ensure that the concepts they apply are based on science rather than advocacy, and they should experiment with new solutions themselves whenever possible. In other words, managers need to transform their companies into learning organizations and turn themselves into lifelong learners.

The purpose of this chapter is to help promote the kind of philosophy embodied by knowledge-creating organizations. Whereas previous chapters have focused on *content* and learning what is already known about management, this chapter emphasizes the thinking *process,* which will enable you to learn new and innovative approaches to management that will stand the test of time. Being the first to discover and implement innovative management techniques may give your company a sustainable competitive advantage relative to your rivals who are relying on ineffective and widely copied business fads.

The chapter begins by examining the nature of the scientific process, showing you how to successfully conduct your own experiments. It then discusses ways to draw valid causal inferences; this exercise will allow you to maximize your ability to learn from your own experiences and critically evaluate the claims made by others. Next, the chapter considers how to generalize research results to determine whether the results found in one sample and setting are likely to be repeatable in a different sample and setting. Finally, it describes some of the scientific sources to which you can turn when seeking answers to your managerial questions.

CRITICAL THINKING AND THE SCIENTIFIC PROCESS

Ways of Knowing

To form a learning organization, all employees—but especially managers—must become more disciplined in their thinking and pay more attention to detail. They must continually ask, "How do we know that's true?" and push beyond the symptom level to discover underlying causes of problems. How do we come to know things? For example, when we say that our solar system contains nine planets, how do we know that this statement is true? When we state that providing workers with specific and difficult goals will lead them to perform better than simply telling them to do their best, how do we know that this assertion is true? And when we note that an effective organization's structure must match its technology and its environment, how do we know that this claim is true?

Philosophers of science have explored many ways of arriving at knowledge.[12] The most common source of knowledge for most of us is *personal experience.* Most people tend to believe information they acquire by interacting with other people and the world at large and to conclude that their experience reflects truth. Our own personal experiences may not always be a reliable source of truth, however, for several reasons. First, different people may have different experiences that point to different truths. Second, as we saw in Chapter 4, people's perceptions and memories of their experiences are often biased, inaccurate, or distorted over time. Finally, even if we disregard inaccuracies of perception or memory, the fact remains that any one person can experience only a tiny fraction of all possible situations, and thus the knowledge acquired by personal experience will necessarily be extremely limited.

Despite these shortcomings, a reflective and critical approach to one's past experience can lead to enhanced understanding. This case is especially relevant for "productive failures" that, when critically analyzed, lead to insight, understanding, and ultimately future success. For example, IBM's 360 computer series, one of the most popular and profitable lines ever built, was based on the technology of the failed Stretch computer that preceded it.[13] Productive failures can be even more important to an organization's long-term viability than "unproductive successes," where something goes well but no one understands why.

Earlier, we noted that many managers tend to seek quick-fix remedies to their problems. Sustainable competitive advantage does not come from simple solutions to complex problems. Instead, managers need a method for helping them generate and test new methods of competing. Although critically examined personal experience can be a source of knowledge, several problems and pitfalls arise from simply using personal experience as a means of discerning what is true. In fact, the limits of personal experience in this regard led to the development of the **scientific method.** As Charles Sanders Peirce has stated, "To satisfy our doubts . . . it is necessary that a method should be found by which our beliefs may be determined by nothing human, but by some external permanency. . . . The method must be such that the ultimate conclusion of every man shall be the same. Such is the method of science."[14]

Objectivity, or the degree to which scientific findings are independent of any one person's opinion about them, represents the major difference between the scientific approach to knowledge and the other approaches described so far. For example, as the recent scandals made clear, many who conducted so-called research for Wall Street companies were anything but objective in conducting their analyses. Conflict of interest came about because the analysts in the research arm of the companies were pressured by those in the investment banking arm of the companies to rate certain firms as good investments despite the problems the researchers uncovered. As one analyst noted, "It's hard enough to be right about stocks, even harder to build customer relationships when all your companies blow up, you knew they were going to, and you couldn't say anything."[15]

Science as an enterprise is *public,* in the sense that the methods and results obtained by one scientist are shared with others. It is *self-correcting,* in the sense that erroneous findings can be isolated through the replication of one scientist's work by another scientist. In today's competitive and fast-paced environment, however, the manner in which many scientists go public has in some respects changed, and this has impacted the self-correcting nature of applied research. For example, traditionally scientists who came upon an important discovery would write up their research for peer review in a professional journal, where it would be carefully vetted and edited to ensure accuracy—a process that could take up to two years. The process was slow but sure in the sense that irresponsible or erroneous claims were kept out of the public's attention. Increasingly, however, researchers are bypassing this process and going straight to an unprofessionally reviewed news release when they think they have made an important discovery.

For example, Advanced Cell Technologies, a biotechnology firm, announced in a news release that it had created a human clone embryo. This was a major scientific breakthrough; unfortunately, when other scientists tried to replicate the results it became clear that there were serious flaws in the experiments run by Advanced Cell's scientists, and the claim was essentially bogus. Philip Campbell, editor of *Nature,* the scientific journal where the study should have been submitted first, noted, "It undermines public trust in science if key results are released without peer review."[16]

The public and self-correcting nature of this process when successfully practiced means that the results that are eventually accepted are *cumulative,* in the sense that one scientist's experiment often builds on another's work. These features of the scientific method make it ideal as a means of generating reliable knowledge, and it is no coincidence that the physical, natural, and social sciences receive so much emphasis in today's colleges and universities.

For these reasons, we will explore the nature of the scientific process more closely. We look first at the major goals or purposes of science, then consider how the scientific method is structured to achieve these objectives.

The Purposes of Science

The basic goal of science is to help humans understand the world around us. Science defines the understanding it seeks as the ability to describe, explain, predict, and control the subjects of its inquiry. We will examine each of these objectives in turn.

The purpose of some research is simply *description*—that is, drawing an accurate picture of a particular phenomenon or event. Chapter 2, for example, presented data from Mintzberg's study of managerial roles. The purpose of Mintzberg's research was to find out what managers actually do on the job on a daily basis. Chapter 3 reviewed research that described the major dimensions of personality. Chapter 7 examined descriptive research that sought to delineate the dimensions best suited to describe the nature of jobs. The development of scientific knowledge usually begins with this kind of descriptive work. The ultimate criterion for evaluating all descriptive research is the fidelity with which it reflects the real world.

For other scientific studies, *predicting,* or stating what will happen in the future, is the primary goal. Prediction requires that we know the relationships between certain conditions and outcomes. For example, Chapter 6 described research that attempted to predict who will leave organizations and who will stay. Chapter 10 reviewed studies of leadership that predicted when decisions would be best made by groups and when they would be best left to individuals. Chapter 14 discussed studies that predicted the effects associated with various kinds of organizational cultures. When we cannot accurately predict what will happen in a given situation, we have generally failed to understand it.

Studies that focus on prediction often lead to further research in which the goal is to *control* the situation. Predictive studies often uncover relationships between causes and effects. If one can manipulate the causes, it may be possible to affect some outcome in a desirable manner. Chapter 5, for example, reviewed studies indicating that manipulation of pay practices may allow firms to change how hard individuals work. Chapter 8 discussed research that shows how group performance can be controlled by manipulating patterns of communication. In Chapter 13, changing the characteristics of organizational design was shown to be able to improve the fit between the firm and its environment. It is in the area of control that the interests of scientists and management practitioners most clearly converge.[17]

As we have seen throughout this book, managers are responsible for controlling the behaviors of others in organizations. Thus the more information a study provides on ways to achieve this control, the more useful it is to practicing managers. Indeed, research guided by the other objectives is often perceived by managers as merely academic and not worthwhile. In reality, studies dealing with control often represent the by-products of earlier descriptive or predictive studies. Without good descriptive and predictive research, we would probably do little successful research aimed at control.

The ultimate goal of science is *explanation*—stating why some relationship exists. Some might argue that as long as we can describe, predict, and control things, why go any further? For example, if managers in the insurance business know that people with college degrees sell more life insurance than do people with high school degrees, why find out anything else? Why not just hire college graduates for all sales positions? If researchers can uncover the reason for college graduates' greater success, however, managers might be able to bring about the desired outcome (selling more insurance) in a more efficient or cost-effective way.

For example, suppose that college-educated salespeople outperform their counterparts who lack higher education, not because they have more years of study per se but because on average they are more self-confident. This self-confidence increases persistence on sales calls, which leads to higher sales volume. If this explanation holds true, a manager might be able to hire high school graduates and then train them to become more self-confident and persistent. As suggested by this example, if we know the exact reason why something occurs, we can usually explain and control it much more efficiently.

The Interplay of Theory and Data

Having discussed the different ways of arriving at knowledge and the goals, or purposes, of scientific inquiry, we must now consider precisely what the scientific method entails. Figure 16-1 represents a conception of scientific inquiry, depicting science as a continuous process that links theory, which resides in the world of abstract ideas, with data, which reside in the world of concrete facts. A theory is translated into real-world terms by the process of creating hypotheses, and real-world data are translated back into the realm of ideas through the process of verification.

Kerlinger defines a **theory** as "a set of interrelated constructs, definitions, and propositions that presents a systematic view of a phenomenon by specifying relationships among variables."[18] With an understanding of the purposes of science and this definition of theory, it is easy to see why theory plays such a central role in the scientific process. A good theory, through its constructs and definitions, should clearly describe a part of the real world. Moreover, by specifying relations among variables, a theory facilitates both prediction and control. Finally, a theory's systematic nature

FIGURE 16-1   The Nature of the Scientific Process

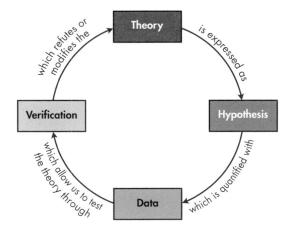

allows us to explain the relationships described. The preceding chapters of this book were filled with theories intended to help you understand how to manage the behavior of people in organizations.

To have any practical utility, theories must prove themselves in the world of data. Through a process of deduction, researchers generate **hypotheses,** or specific predictions about the relationships between certain conditions in the real world. These hypotheses are related to the theory in the following way: If the theory is correct, then the predictions made by the hypotheses should be found in the real world.

Data enter the scientific process at this point. Once hypotheses are formulated, we can collect data and compare the hypothesized results with the actual results. Through the process of **verification,** we then use this comparison to check the accuracy of the theory and to judge the extent to which it holds true. If very little correspondence exists between the hypothesized results and the actual findings, we must reject the theory. At this point, the process begins again with the generation of a new theory. If the projected and actual findings do correspond somewhat, we may need to change the theory in some way so as to be more consistent with the data.

If almost complete correspondence exists between the hypothesized results and the actual findings, we may be tempted to claim that the theory is true. Such a conclusion would not be warranted, however, unless we could establish that all other possible explanations for the results have been eliminated. Because this task is almost never achievable, we usually refer to data that correspond closely with a hypothesis as "supporting" rather than "proving" the theory.

Characteristics of Good Theories and Good Data

You do not have to be a scientist to create a theory. Indeed, in our daily lives, we routinely develop informal or **implicit theories** about the world around us. We arrive at these theories through our personal experience and are often unaware of their existence. Many of these implicit theories can be lumped together under the general heading of common sense. Thus, although some real-world managers claim to be skeptical of "theories," they often fail to realize that they carry around a large number of implicit theories.

In most cases, scientific theories are developed more formally. We will refer to these theories as **explicit theories** to distinguish them from implicit theories. As you have seen, much of this book is intended to persuade managers to replace their implicit theories with explicit theories that have been supported by research. Explicit theories are not always better than implicit theories, however. Moreover, often multiple explicit theories deal with the same subject, and some may be better than others. How do we judge whether a theory is good or bad, or decide which of two competing theories is best?

John B. Miner has offered several criteria for judging the worth of theories in organizational behavior.[19] First and foremost, a theory should contribute to the objectives of science. That is, it should be useful in describing, explaining, predicting, or controlling important things. Most theories, whether implicit or explicit, meet this test.

Second, a theory must be logically consistent within itself. Many implicit theories (and some explicit ones) fall short on this criterion. For example, common sense tells us that "Fortune favors the brave." Conversely, common sense also says that "Fools rush in where angels fear to tread," which has the opposite implication. Similarly, common sense tells us that "Two heads are better than one" as well as that "Too many cooks spoil the broth." Clearly, common sense—and many of the implicit theories on which it is based—does not represent good theory because of its self-contradicting nature.

Third, a theory must be consistent with known facts. For example, many people have an implicit theory that men are better leaders than women, but as we saw in our last chapter, this is inconsistent with known data that shows very weak evidence of sex differences in leadership capacity, which, if anything, supports the superiority of women by a small amount. Thus, any theory that assumed or proposed that men are better than women on this dimension would be a bad theory because it is inconsistent with established facts.

A fourth criterion by which to evaluate a theory is its consistency with respect to future events. The theory must not only predict, but also make *testable* predictions. A prediction is considered testable if it can be refuted by data. A theory that predicts all possible outcomes actually says nothing. For example, if a theory states that a particular leadership style can increase, decrease, or leave employee performance unchanged, it has offered nothing of value about the relationship between that leadership style and worker performance.

Finally, simplicity is a desirable characteristic of a theory. Highly complex and involved theories are not only more difficult to test, but also more difficult to apply. A theory that uses only a few concepts to predict and explain some outcome is preferable to one that accomplishes the same goal with more concepts. Simplicity is surprisingly difficult to maintain, however. By their very nature, theories oversimplify the real world. Thus, for a theory to be consistent with real-world data, we must inevitably push it toward increasing complexity over time. A good theory can walk the fine line between being too simple (when it will fail to predict events with any accuracy) and being too complex (when it is no longer testable or useful for any purpose).

Having established the scientific method as the interplay between explicit theories and data, and having covered the characteristics of a good theory, we must next discuss the characteristics of good data. Experienced managers have long known that "If you can't measure it, you can't manage it." Most data for testing theories are gathered through measurements of the theory's important concepts. Good data are just as important to scientists as is good theory. Several characteristics render some measures, and therefore the data they generate, better than others.

First, the measures must possess **reliability;** that is, they must be free of random errors. Suppose, for example, that the person who was interviewing you for graduate school was interested in your scholastic aptitude because it predicts success in graduate school. Imagine that to assess your aptitude, the interviewer handed you two dice and asked you to toss them, suggesting that a high score would mean high aptitude and a low score would indicate low aptitude. At this point, you would probably start wondering about the aptitude of the interviewer. The unreliability of dice as a measure makes them virtually worthless.

Consider the following, less obvious example of a reliability problem. It was once believed that interviewers, after talking to job applicants in an unstructured way for approximately 30 minutes, could provide ratings reflecting the applicants' suitability for many different jobs. Research showed, however, that these ratings were roughly as reliable as the results of tossing dice.[20] An interviewer would rate the same applicant high one day and low another day. As a consequence, in making important decisions like admitting an applicant to graduate school, most institutions rely heavily on scores on tests such as the Graduate Record Exam (GRE), the Graduate Management Admissions Test (GMAT), and the Law School Admissions Test (LSAT). Although these tests are not perfectly reliable (students taking them repeatedly will not get the exact same score each time), they do exhibit a high degree of consistency.

Second, the measures of a theory's concepts must possess **validity;** that is, they must assess what they were meant to assess. To see whether the GMAT is valid, for example, we might seek to determine whether students who perform better on the test actually perform better in graduate school. This means of testing validity is called **criterion-related validation,** because it studies whether the measure really predicts the criterion (for example, grade-point average) that it is supposed to be able to predict. Criterion-related validation is based on an objective assessment of a measure's ability to predict future events. Alternatively, we can assess validity of a measure subjectively by having experts on the concept examine the measure. These experts can determine the extent to which the content embodied in the measure actually reflects the theoretical concept being studied. This approach is called **content validation,** because it focuses on whether the content of the test is appropriate according to experts on the subject.

Reliability and validity are closely related. Reliability is necessary for validity, but it is not sufficient for proving it, because we could develop highly reliable measures that might not be valid. For example, we could probably measure people's height reliably, but this measure would have little validity as a measure of scholastic aptitude (that is, it could not predict who would do well in graduate school). Reliability is necessary for validity, however, because an unreliable measure cannot pass any of the tests necessary for establishing validity. An unreliable measure does not relate well even to itself.

A third desirable property of the measures of a theory's concepts is **standardization,** which means that everyone who measures the concepts uses the same instrument in the same way. Because it takes time and effort to develop measures that are reliable and valid, we can achieve a great deal of efficiency by using existing standardized measures.[21]

Standardized measures provide two other advantages. First, they are far more likely than other measures to achieve *objectivity*. Because everyone uses the same procedures, the results of measurement are much less likely to be affected by the choice of an investigator. Second, standardized measures make it easy to *communicate* and compare results across situations. Although you could construct a scale to measure job satisfaction in your own company, even if you succeeded in developing a reliable and valid measure (a difficult task), you could not compare the satisfaction level in your company to that in other companies. That is because other companies will not have used (and may not be willing to use) your measure. On the other hand, the Job Descriptive Index (JDI) is a standardized measure of job satisfaction that has been used in hundreds of companies. For most standardized measures, the availability of a great deal of existing data allows you to compare your company with other companies that all have been measured on the same criteria in the same way.

For these and other reasons, managers should rarely try to develop their own measures for every situation. At worst, the measures would lack reliability and validity. At best, managers would "reinvent the wheel." Of course, on some occasion you might need to test new concepts or develop measures that are unique to your situation. Such cases, however, will be the exception, rather than the rule.

CAUSAL INFERENCES

We can use the scientific method to further our understanding of management. To translate this enhanced understanding into more effective practice, however, we must apply this learning. Knowledge is most applicable when it can be expressed in terms of cause-and-effect relationships. After identifying these relationships, we can often manipulate the causes to bring about the desired effects (such as enhanced productivity or job satisfaction). Good theory and good measures take us a long way toward achieving this objective, but they are not sufficient for identifying cause-and-effect relations (that is, making causal inferences). As noted later in this chapter, making causal inferences depends not only on how the data are obtained, but also on when the data are obtained and what is done with them once collected.

Moreover, even if a manager is not engaging in scientific experimentation but just trying to learn from daily experience, rigorously thinking about cause-and-effect relationships can ensure that he or she does not learn the wrong lesson from past experience. True learning can take place only when a person seriously reflects upon past experience and analyzes it critically. For this reason, we will closely examine how to go about making the proper causal inferences.

Criteria for Inferring Cause

One of the foremost authorities on the philosophy of science, John Stuart Mill, argued that to state unequivocally that one thing causes another, we must establish three criteria. First, we must establish *temporal precedence;* that is, the cause must come before—not after—the effect in time. Second, we must document *covariation;* that is, if the cause is varied (for example, turned on or off), the effect must vary as well. Third, we must be able to *eliminate alternative explanations* for the observed results.

The first step in establishing a cause-and-effect relationship is demonstrating **temporal precedence,** which simply means that the cause must precede the effect in time. One common mistake made by people in trying to learn from experience is falsely inferring a causal relationship between two variables just because they are related at one point in time. For example, imagine that you tour a factory and observe that work groups with low absenteeism rates have supervisors who give team members a great deal of latitude and allow them to participate in decision making. In contrast, during the same factory tour, you observe that work groups with the highest absenteeism rates are closely monitored by their supervisors at all times and do not participate in decision making. It would be a mistake to jump to the conclusion that close supervision *causes* high absenteeism. It would be even a greater mistake to act on this unproven conclusion by demanding that all managers of the company "loosen up" their supervision.

In fact, the causal order between these two variables might lie in the opposite direction. That is, perhaps all supervisors started out acting the same. High absenteeism in some groups may have caused supervisors to tighten their control, and low absenteeism in other groups may have led their supervisors to give them more latitude. Failing to consider temporal precedence in this case would lead you to learn the wrong lesson from this factory tour. If you then acted on this misinformation and loosened up the supervision of the managers in the plant, absenteeism might actually worsen rather than improve. Instead of solving a problem, you may make the situation worse.

The second criterion for inferring cause is **covariation,** which simply means that the cause and effect are related. For example, if we believe that providing day care for employees' children causes lower absenteeism, then a relationship should exist between company day-care services and low employee absenteeism.

Several ways to assess covariation are available, all of which rely on statistical methods. As this text is not a statistics book, and given that most readers will also take courses in statistics, we will limit our discussion here to two simple, but widely applicable statistical techniques. Although not perfect for every situation, they are useful in a wide variety of contexts.

The first means of establishing covariation, known as a *test of mean differences,* compares the average scores of two groups on the outcome we wish to change. For

TABLE 16-1
Absence
Data at Two
Hypothetical
Plants

| Employee | Number of Absences | |
	Plant A (With Day Care)	Plant B (Without Day Care)
1	10	12
2	11	11
3	8	13
4	11	8
5	3	16
6	4	14
7	3	10
8	2	4
9	1	2
10	5	3
Average	5.8	9.3

example, Table 16-1 presents data on absenteeism for two groups of workers: 10 work in Plant A, which offers an in-house day-care center, and 10 work in Plant B, which lacks on-site provisions for day care. As shown in Figure 16-2, the level of absenteeism is much higher for Plant B than for Plant A. This simple analysis of mean differences suggests that day-care provision and absenteeism are, in fact, related.

We might also test for mean differences between numbers of absences at Plant A before and after the establishment of the day-care center and generate data like that listed in Table 16-2 and graphed in Figure 16-3. If the average absenteeism rates were higher before the plant installed the day-care center than they were after it was implemented, we might again conclude (before engaging in more rigorous analyses) that a relationship exists between provided day care and lower absenteeism. Both mean differences described here are easy to comprehend when presented as bar charts like those shown in Figures 16-2 and 16-3. Indeed, these kinds of charts are reminiscent of what we observed back in Chapter 6 when we saw how researchers were trying to determine whether dissatisfaction among workers at the Decatur Firestone plant "caused" them to produce faulty and dangerous tires.

FIGURE 16-2 Absenteeism in Two Different Plants Assessed over One Time Period

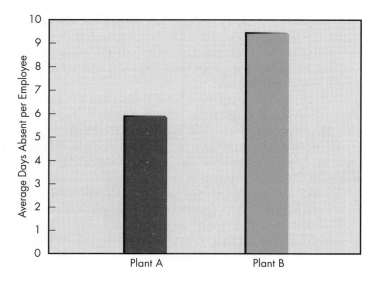

TABLE 16-2
Absence
Data for One
Hypothetical
Plant at Two
Different Times

| Employee | Number of Absences at Plant A | |
	Before Day Care	After Day Care
1	12	10
2	14	11
3	10	8
4	12	11
5	6	3
6	8	4
7	4	3
8	2	2
9	1	1
10	6	5
Average	7.5	5.8

A second means of establishing covariation is through the use of the **correlation coefficient.** This statistic, a number that ranges from $+1.0$ to -1.0, expresses the relationship between two things. A $+1.0$ correlation means that a perfect positive relationship exists between the two measures in question (for example, absenteeism rates and employee age). That is, as the value of one measure increases, the value of the other increases to the same relative degree. A correlation of -1.0 reflects a perfect negative relationship between the two measures. Here, as the value of one variable increases, the value of the other decreases, again to the same relative degree. A correlation of .00 indicates that no relationship links the measures; thus, as the value of one measure increases, the value of the other can be anything—high, medium, or low.

To give you a feeling for other values of the correlation coefficient, Figure 16-4 shows plots of points, where each point represents a person of a given age (specified on the x-axis) and that person's corresponding level of absenteeism (specified on the y-axis). This figure depicts four correlation values: $+1.0$, $+.50$, $.00$, and $-.50$. The sign of the correlation reveals whether the relationship is positive or negative, and the absolute value of the correlation reveals the magnitude of the relationship.

FIGURE 16-3 Absenteeism at One Plant Assessed over Two Different Time Periods

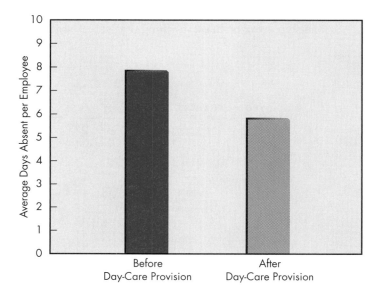

FIGURE 16-4 Plots Depicting Various Levels of Correlation between Variables

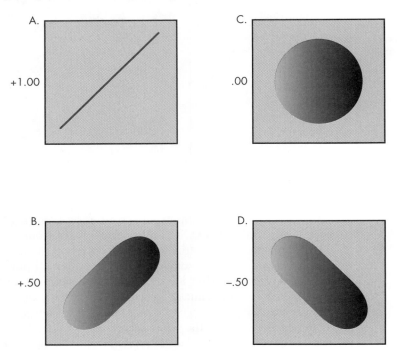

Returning to our employees at Plants A and B, Table 16-3, in addition to providing data on day care and rates of absenteeism, shows the ages of all the workers. We could use the correlation coefficient to determine whether a relationship exists between age and absenteeism. In fact, the correlation between age and absenteeism for these data is −.50, indicating that older workers are absent less often than younger ones. If we plotted these data on a graph, where x is the horizontal axis and y the vertical axis, the result would look like the graph shown in Figure 16-4D. As you can see, graphically depicting the correlation in this fashion makes it easy to understand the strength and nature of the relationship between these two variables.

Once we have established both covariation and temporal precedence, we are only one step away from establishing that something actually caused something else. The

TABLE 16-3
Absence
and Age
Data at Two
Hypothetical
Plants

Employee	Plant A (Day Care) Number of Absences	Age	Plant B (No Day Care) Number of Absences	Age
1	10	27	12	27
2	11	31	11	34
3	8	30	13	31
4	11	26	8	25
5	3	40	16	33
6	4	61	14	35
7	3	52	10	25
8	2	47	4	40
9	1	46	2	52
10	5	41	3	46
Average	5.8	40.1	9.3	34.6

elimination of alternative explanations, Mill's third criterion for establishing cause, entails a major effort, however. In our continuing example, if we are to infer that providing day care caused lower absenteeism, we must show that no other factor caused the low rates. The complexity of most real-world situations makes it very difficult to rule out all other possible explanations. Indeed, this problem, more than any other, complicates the process of conducting research in the applied behavioral social sciences.

In the physical sciences, experimenters can use physical means such as lead shields and vacuum chambers to isolate variables and rule out alternative causes. This kind of tight control is much more difficult to achieve in social science research. In fact, some valid alternative explanations arise so frequently that they have been given special names.

The **selection threat,** for example, involves the danger that the groups we selected for comparison were not the same initially.[22] If we had only the data on absenteeism in the two plants (the data in Table 16-1), the lower mean rate of absenteeism in the plant with day care might have led us to conclude, based on our past experience, that providing day care caused lower absenteeism. Our additional data shows that age is negatively related to absenteeism, however, and workers in Plant A are known to be older than those in Plant B. In fact, if we controlled for age by comparing only workers who were the same age, we would find no differences in absenteeism between the plants.

At this point, you may say, "So what—what difference does it make?" It makes a huge difference if your faulty cause-and-effect judgment prompts your company to invest a large sum of money in providing day-care facilities on a corporation-wide basis. Funding of this benefit would be based on your conclusion that day care would pay for itself through lower absenteeism. Because day care is actually irrelevant to absenteeism, this investment would eventually be lost, and many people would be left wondering what happened. The selection threat is the most common threat to studies that compare two different groups at one point in time.

The **history threat** is the most common problem in studies that observe the same group in a "before-and-after" situation. It occurs when the real cause is not the change you made, but rather something else that happened at the same time. In Figure 16-3, when we compared the mean number of absences for Plant A *before* day care with the mean number of absences *after* day care, we found a lower average rate of absenteeism after the day-care program was implemented. We might be tempted to infer that the day-care center caused lower absenteeism. Suppose, however, that we obtained the "before" measure during the summer months and the "after" measure during the winter months. Perhaps people simply found more reasons to be absent in the summer than in the winter. That is, the weather—rather than the day-care center—may have caused the difference in absenteeism rates. If we extended the day-care program throughout the corporation, we would find that it would not reduce absenteeism and would again be left wondering why.

Designing Observations to Infer Cause

The timing and the frequency of data collection affect our ability to make causal interpretations. Deciding on the timing of measurement is an important part of research design.

Consider the two *faulty designs* shown in Figure 16-5. In the One Group Before-After design (Figure 16-5A), data are collected both before and after some event or treatment. If the after score differs from the before score, we assume that the change in the situation caused the difference. The flaw in this design relates to the history threat, which is an alternative explanation for the results. In our day-care example,

FIGURE 16-5 Two Faulty Research Designs

A. One Group Before-After

| Collect data at Time 1 | Change situation | Collect data at Time 2 |

If Score at Time 2 differs from score at Time 1, it would not be correct to infer that the change in the situation caused the difference

B. After Only with Unequal Groups

Score for Group 1 in Situation A

Score for Group 2 in Situation B

If Score for Group 1 in Situation A differs from the score for Group 2 in Situation B, it would not be correct to infer that Situation A versus B caused the difference

if we collected data from only one plant, once in the summer and once in the winter, we would be using this type of faulty design.

In the After Only with Unequal Groups design (Figure 16-5B), data are collected from two groups, one of which experiences a situation while the other does not. This design is flawed because we do not know for certain that the groups were equal before the treatment or during the treatment; thus the selection threat might explain the results. In our day-care example, we collected data from both Plant A and Plant B without verifying that the people in those plants were similar (for example, were the same age on average); thus our experiment has this kind of faulty design. Such designs constituted the structure underlying many of our day-to-day past experiences, and, if not analyzed critically, they can lead us to learn the wrong lessons from those past experiences.

We can change designs in several ways to help eliminate some of these threats. Consider the One Group Before-After design, where the history threat poses the major problem. We could improve the situation by adding a control group (that is, a group that does not receive the day-care assistance), thereby turning the design into the Two Groups Before-After design (Figure 16-6A). This design allows us to test whether the two groups were equal initially by comparing scores at Time 1. That is, in our day-care example, was the rate of absenteeism in Plants A and B similar before the treatment—the day-care center—was implemented? This design also allows us to test whether some historical factor other than the day-care center could have caused the results. That is, if the real cause was time of the year (summer versus winter), we could expect a decrease in absenteeism in Plant B as we moved from Time 1 to Time 2, even though no day-care center was established there.

The Two Groups After Only model becomes even stronger in terms of causal inferences if people are randomly assigned to the groups. **Random assignment** of

FIGURE 16-6   Two Improved Research Designs

A. Two Groups Before-After

Score at Time 1 for Group 1	Change situation for Group 1	Score at Time 2 for Group 1
Score at Time 1 for Group 2	No change in situation for Group 2	Score at Time 2 for Group 2

B. Two Groups After-Only with Randomization

	Score for Group 1 in Situation A
Randomly Assignment of people to groups A and B	
	Score for Group 2 in Situation B

people to conditions means that each person has an equal chance of being placed in either the experimental or the control group. We can achieve this random arrangement by pulling names out of a hat, flipping coins, tossing dice, or using a random numbers table from a statistics book. In our day-care study, if we could have initially assembled the twenty workers at the two plants and then tossed a coin to see who would get day care and who would not, the odds are that, when we were finished, the two resulting groups would have been equal in age. That is, each group would have included roughly the same number of people of a given age.

In fact, the real value of randomization is that it not only equalizes groups on factors (such as age) expected to influence results, but also equates groups on virtually all factors. Thus, in our day-care study, if we randomized the groups at the outset, we could be fairly confident that they would be equated not only on age, but also on other factors, such as height and weight. You might not think that a person's height or weight would relate to absenteeism, but some research has found such a relationship between absenteeism and weight.[23] Even if we were unaware of this relationship at the outset of the day-care study, it is nice to know that randomization neatly solved a potential problem. In fact, the equalizing effect of random assignment is so powerful that one can often infer cause even in the absence of a before measure. For example, Figure 16-6b shows the Two Groups After-Only design, where two groups are established randomly and then exposed to two different situations. Even though there is no before measure that proves the two groups were equal on other potential causal factors, one can safely presume that randomization made them equal (provided there were enough cases), and infer that any differences between the two situations as actually being caused by the situation and not some external factor. Because of randomization's ability to rule out both anticipated and unanticipated selection threats, people conducting experiments should randomly assign subjects to treatments whenever possible.

Because randomization is not always possible, we must often resort to other tools to rule out selection threats. Suppose that, when we start our day-care experiment, we know that workers at the two plants are not evenly distributed in terms of age, and we know that age affects absenteeism. In the real world, we cannot randomly move people from plant to plant; we must work with existing groups.

How, then, can we rule out age as the alternative explanation for our results? We have several choices. First, we could use *homogeneous* groups, or study groups that do not differ in age. For example, we might compare absenteeism in the two plants, but only among workers who are 25 to 35 years old. As you can see from Table 16-3, we would therefore compare Persons 1, 2, 3, and 4 in Plant A with Persons 1, 2, 3, 4, 5, 6, and 7 in Plant B. With this sample, if we still found lower absenteeism in Plant A than in Plant B, we could not attribute the difference to age, because all subjects were roughly the same age.

Alternatively, we could also equate groups by *matching subjects*. For example, we might study only the subjects in Plant A for whom there are corresponding subjects in Plant B, or subjects who are within two years of one another in terms of age. Thus, looking again at Table 16-3, we could match Subjects 1, 2, 5, 7, and 9 in Plant A with Subjects 1, 3, 8, 9, and 10 in Plant B. If we found lower absenteeism in one plant, we could not attribute this result to age because we equated the groups on this factor.

Finally, we could *build the threat into the design*. That is, we could simply treat age as another possible factor affecting the rate of absenteeism and examine its effect at the same time that we study the effect of day care. One advantage of building alternative explanations into your design is that you can then test for **interactions**. An interaction exists when the relationship between the treatment (the day-care center, in our example) and the outcome (absenteeism) depends on some other variable (age). Figure 16-7 shows a possible result if we built the alternative expla-

FIGURE 16-7 The Effect of Age and Day-Care Facilities on Absenteeism

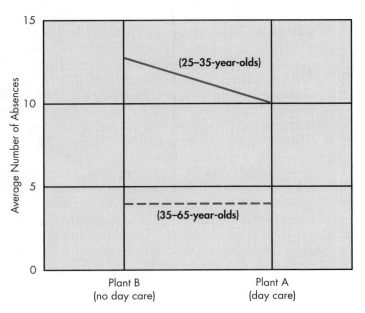

nation of age into our day-care study. As you can see, among the younger group of workers, providing day care does lower absenteeism; among the older group, however, it has no effect. Thus the relationship between day care and absenteeism depends on the factor of age.

Clearly, many factors must be considered in designing studies that will allow us to infer causality. The more variables we can control, the tighter our research design, and the more likely that we can rule out alternative explanations for any relationships discovered.

GENERALIZING RESEARCH RESULTS

Research is usually conducted with one sample, in one setting, at one time period. Often, however, we wish to know the generalizability of results, where **generalizability** is defined as the extent to which results obtained in one sample-setting-time configuration can be repeated in a different sample-setting-time configuration. This ability is sometimes of interest when we are conducting research, but always critical when we evaluate research findings to see whether what worked for the investigators can be applied in a real-world setting.

Sample, Setting, and Time

Our day-care example provides a good illustration of how results might not generalize across all samples. Recall that the results of our study eventually showed that provision of day care reduced absenteeism among workers who were twenty-five to thirty-five years old but not among members of the older group. Astute managers who studied our results would want to apply these lessons only if their company employed a large number of workers in this age category.

Suppose, however, our design homogenized our subjects on age (that is, used only people in the twenty-five to thirty-five bracket). In this case, we would have reported simply that providing day care reduced absenteeism. A manager who read these results, but did not pay enough attention to the details on age, might institute a day-care center in a company where most of the workers were between thirty-five and sixty-five years old. This person would soon discover that the results of our work did not generalize to his or her organization. Thus a major drawback of making groups homogeneous is that it limits our ability to generalize results across other types of samples.

We may also be concerned about generalizing research results across settings. For example, suppose that both of the plants in our original study were located in rural settings. Assume further that it is more difficult to obtain high-quality day care in rural settings than in urban settings. Someone reading the results of our study who manages a plant in an urban area might establish an in-plant day-care center, only to find that the center has no effect on absenteeism, because childcare is not a problem for workers in urban settings. Here again, our results would not generalize to another setting.

Finally, we might worry about whether our results would generalize across time. For example, suppose that we conducted our study during a time characterized by a huge labor shortage; many more jobs were available than there were people to fill them. At such a time, unemployment rates would be low, both parents might well be working, and many people who might in other circumstances serve as day-care providers would very likely be working at different and perhaps higher-paying jobs. Thus, at the time when we conducted our study, demand for day-care services might have been high but only a small supply was available. By providing our own day-care services, we solved a major problem for our workers with small children, which ultimately led to lower absenteeism rates.

Now move forward ten years, to a time characterized by a labor surplus. Unemployment is high, one parent is likely not working, and anyone capable of setting up a day-care center has opened a business. In this situation, because the demand for day care is small and the supply of day-care services large, company-sponsored day care does not provide a needed service to employees. Consequently, no relationship exists between providing day care and lowering absenteeism. In this case, our results do not generalize across time.

Facilitating Generalization

You may wonder whether any findings are generalizable given the many factors that might differ from one unique sample-setting-time to another. From a researcher's perspective, can we take any steps to increase the ability to generalize? The answer is "yes." Technically, we can safely generalize from one sample to another if the original sample of people we study is *randomly selected* from the larger population of people to which we wish to generalize.

As an example of random selection, you may have noticed that in presidential elections the television networks usually declare a winner when less than 10 percent of the actual results are available. As we saw in the 2000 Al Gore–George W. Bush election, when the networks mistakenly called the race in Florida first for Gore, an error in this process can prove highly embarrassing.

The key to successfully predicting the final outcome from the initial, partial results is randomly selecting the people polled from the voting population. This endeavor ensures that the small percentage of people who are polled are, by all odds, exactly the same as the larger group of voters. In fact, the science of polling is so accurate that it is exceedingly rare for these judgment calls to prove to be wrong. Indeed, many believe that the science of polling is more accurate than the science of the voting machines, and some have speculated that the machines, rather than the pollsters, actually made the wrong call in the presidential results from Florida. That is, a large number of people who told the pollsters that they voted for Gore may have failed to punch their ballots correctly (or the machine did not read the ballots accurately). Thus the pollsters may have captured the voters' intentions better than the voting machines did.

Although random selection is the only way to guarantee the ability to generalize results across samples, from a practical perspective it is often very difficult to achieve. Studies that employ random selection are usually huge in scale, requiring the efforts of many investigators and a great deal of money. More often, in the real world of research, the ability to generalize a finding is achieved not by undertaking one large experiment, but rather by conducting many small experiments, using the same measures, in which results are replicated in a host of different sample-setting-time configurations. For example, Chapter 4 discussed research results that generalize very well—that is, the repeated finding that high performance is more likely to result from setting specific and difficult goals than from offering vague goals like "do your best." The generalizability of this finding comes not from one large study that randomly sampled people, settings, and times, but rather from many smaller studies, each of which used different samples, settings, and times but obtained the same result.

Although generalizing results is always of interest in evaluating research, the original researchers may not emphasize this issue. Often research is conducted strictly to test or build theories. In such a case, investigators may be less interested in what *does* happen than in what *can* happen.[24] For example, research on biofeedback shows that people can learn to control some of their own physiological processes, such as heart rate and blood pressure, when hooked up to special devices that give them information on these processes. You might think that few real-world situations correspond to the one faced by subjects in this kind of research. That is not the point of this research, however. Rather, this research is intended to test the theory that humans can voluntarily control supposedly involuntary physiological responses when provided with the appropriate feedback. Nothing inherent in this theory suggests that it would not work with college sophomores in a laboratory setting at some specific time period. Thus, if the results fail to support the theory in this sample-setting-time configuration, we must either reject the theory or modify and retest it. The fact that neither subjects, settings, nor times were randomized is completely irrelevant. With this kind of research, the ultimate aim is not to make the laboratory setting more like the real world, but rather to make the real world more like the laboratory—that is, to change the real world in ways that benefit us all.

LINKING ORGANIZATIONAL BEHAVIOR SCIENCE AND PRACTICE

As noted earlier, people in knowledge-creating companies or learning organizations are encouraged to experiment. As a practicing manager, however, you should recognize that a wealth of research conducted by others is just waiting to be discovered. Some studies might deal directly with an issue that is critical to your company or your career or with a problem you are trying to manage. Rather than conducting your own experiment (a choice that is costly in terms of both time and money), you might be able to generalize these studies' findings to your context. Table 16-4 lists some of the major scientific journals that publish theory and research related to topics covered in this book.

A great deal of the research into this area is performed by people working in university settings. Thus you may be able to uncover research on topics of interest by contacting university faculty who publish frequently on aspects of organizational behavior. Faculty and students at local universities can help with management issues, and these people bring fresh perspectives, unique skills, and diverse experiences to the organization. In return, the internships, case studies, or field research conducted by university personnel provide excellent learning opportunities that the company can use to promote organizational effectiveness.

One company, Chaparral Steel, even sends its first-line supervisors on academic sabbaticals to develop an understanding of new work practices and technologies.

TABLE 16-4
The 10 Most Influential Journals in Organizational Behavior

1. *Administrative Science Quarterly*
2. *Academy of Management Review*
3. *Academy of Management Journal*
4. *Personnel Psychology*
5. *Journal of Management*
6. *Journal of Applied Psychology*
7. *Journal of Vocational Behavior*
8. *Organizational Behavior and Human Decision Processes*
9. *Journal of Occupational Psychology*
10. *Human Relations*

Source: W. Starbuck and J. Mezias, "Journal Impact Ratings," *Industrial Psychologist* (April 1996), pp. 101–105.

ETHICS AND SOCIAL RESPONSIBILITY

LEARNING ETHICS IN GRADUATE SCHOOL: TOO LITTLE, TOO LATE?

Although bashing politicians is a popular sport in the United States, recent polls now document that in terms of social esteem, business executives rank lower than politicians. Outrageous salaries and perks, combined with all the recent scandals regarding corporate misdeeds on the part of executives, have taken their toll, and this is filtered down to business schools. Many are now asking two questions: (1) Are business schools part of the problem, and (2) are business schools part of the solution?

In terms of being a part of the problem, many have accused business schools of creating a hyper-competitive cutthroat environment where intellectual power and ambition are rewarded over all else. This creates a get-ahead-at-any-cost mentality, which is then reinforced by a curriculum that treats ethics as almost an afterthought. As Judith Samuelson notes, "Those big feeder schools accentuate the technical and analytical skill sets that Wall Street looks for and not the ethical side."

This is quickly changing on many campuses, and for the incoming classes of 2005 and 2006, ethics, values, and corporate responsibility are being more heavily weighted in MBA curriculums. This includes the traditional Ethics 101 type of course, but also an emphasis to integrate this kind of material systematically within the content of substantive courses. Thus, as you see in this book, where each chapter has an Ethics and Social Responsibility box related to the substantive material, the expectation in many MBA programs is that professors will use a similar approach in their lectures.

There are limits to what can be accomplished via curriculum, however, and some have noted that by the time students get to graduate school it may be too late to drastically alter the moral values. Michele Rogers, director of student affairs at Northwestern's Kellogg school, alma mater of Enron's Andrew Fastow, defends her institution by insisting that "people's values have been formed by the time they get here." Thomas Donaldson, a professor of ethics at Wharton, acknowledges this, but notes that classes like his can help students appreciate how various practices relate to their values, since, in his words, "your mother didn't teach you about off-balance sheet entities and how to grapple with them."

Those who have low expectations regarding the impact of curriculum changes suggest that business schools could still be part of the solution if they were willing to more closely scrutinize incoming students, with an eye for rejecting those who have questionable ethical standards. For example, Wharton hired the security firm ADP Avert to verify the authenticity of applications in 2002. This is an expensive process, however, and even with Wharton's large endowment and high tuition, it is only attempting to verify the veracity of a random sample of 10 percent of the 800 students it accepts. To verify all 8,400 applicants is even beyond their reach financially.

Other schools have added essays to the application process. These essay questions either present standard ethical dilemmas or ask the applicants to discuss an ethical dilemma they have faced in the past. In either case, the response is analyzed to see how it conforms to the admissions committee's sense of morality. Although these kinds of essays will probably never replace the GMAT when it comes to make final decisions, they do send a message to incoming students that the institution cares about these kinds of issues. It also sends a message to recruiters, who themselves are now placing more weight on issues of integrity when it comes to making hiring decisions. Indeed, many feel that MBA programs will really get serious about ethics when the labor market demands it, and increasingly it looks like that time is now.

Sources: J. Merritt, "For MBAs, Soul-Searching 101," *Business Week*, September 16, 2002, 64–66; L. Browning, "MBA Programs Now Screening for Integrity Too," *New York Times*, September 15, 2002, p. C1; J. Merritt, "Why Ethics Is Also a B-School Business," *Business Week*, January 27, 2002, p. 105.

These workers bring back the lessons learned and apply them to daily operations in the company. Thanks to initiatives such as this one, Chaparral is one of the five lowest-cost steel producers in the world. In light of the recent scandals, some organizations have also turned to universities to help teach business ethics.[25] However, as the Ethics and Social Responsibility box illustrates, some question the degree to which conventional educational curricula can teach people who are old enough to be in graduate

SECURING COMPETITIVE ADVANTAGE

CONSULTANT, HEAL THYSELF

What do the following organizations all have in common: Enron, SwissAir, Kmart, Global Crossing, North-Point Communications, Pets.com, and Exides Technology? If you answered, "They all went bankrupt," give yourself an A. If you answered, "They were all clients of management consulting firm McKinsey & Co. when they went bankrupt," give yourself an A+.

The use of external consultants has exploded in recent years, and in today's complex business environment it is hard to blame managers who seek advice from consulting firms when it comes to extricating themselves from some problem-solving mess. Before taking such a step, however, you had better be sure that the consulting organization you are turning to is not even more messed up than you are. Although McKinsey & Co. is one of the oldest and most prestigious of management consulting firms, a recent set of debacles experienced by its clients has focused an uncomfortable light on the secretive consulting firm's own internal operations. In the process, several managerial problems have surfaced that you might not expect to find at a company that charges most of its clients more than $10 million a year for managerial advice.

First, one of McKinsey's guiding principles was to "hire the best people" and throughout most of its history, it was highly selective of its partners, intentionally staying small in order to safeguard its culture and quality. However, it dramatically expanded its size under the reign of new CEO Rajat Gupta, who in a few years increased the number of branches from fifty-eight to eighty-four and doubled the number of partners from roughly 450 to 900. As one partner notes, "It's a less personal place than it used to be. In the old days you knew everybody and that's not possible anymore." The depersonalized nature of the new culture created more variability in how people behaved, and quality control began to suffer.

Second, one of McKinsey's other guiding principles was to "put the customer first," but increasingly its consultants were signing lucrative book deals, and for many, personal fame became an attractive possibility. This included the *In Search of Excellence* book we mentioned in our opening story, but also included *The War for Talent, Race for the World,* and the ironically titled *Creative Destruction,* which extolled the values of strategies that McKinsey partner Richard Foster was championing at Enron. In the wake of the subsequent Enron disaster, one analyst noted, "McKinsey seems to have partners who develop academic theories and then run clinical trials on their clients."

Third, in addition to selectivity in its hiring, McKinsey was also once very selective with respect to its clientele. However, the firm got caught up in the dot-com craze and increasingly took on small upstarts. While the company was once adamant about not linking its fees to client performance, it relaxed this policy and started accepting stock as payment from companies that could not afford McKinsey's typical fees. One of the partners who opposed this policy stated bluntly, "I was in the room saying, 'you're smoking dope on this dot-com stuff,'" and in fact, most of the stock that the company accepted for this work turned out to be worthless.

Finally, many inside the firm noticed another shift in compensation polices, wherein salaries began to be increasingly based upon the amount of revenue each partner was able to generate, not necessarily the quality or innovativeness of their ideas. As one partner noted, "Earlier, the whole place had this tremendous focus on ideas, but now I think knowledge has taken a backseat to revenue generation."

In fairness, McKinsey has hundreds of clients, and not all of them have gone bankrupt. However, there is no guarantee that a consulting company can provide your firm with competitive advantage, and even if they do, nothing can stop them from giving the exact same advice to your competitors, which many often do. Given your own unique knowledge of your situation, combined with some familiarity of the new ideas published in the scholarly journals, plus your own experimentation and critical examination of your past history, you may come up with better ideas than a consulting firm. Indeed, as long as your ideas are not $10-million-a-year worse, you could still come out ahead.

Sources: D. Faust, "First, Sue All the Consultants," *Business Week,* July 17, 2000, pp. 96–97; J. A. Byrne, "Inside McKinsey," *Business Week,* July 8, 2002, pp. 66–76; D. A. Blackman, "Consultant Issued Almost Identical Advice," *Wall Street Journal,* March 11, 1997, p. A16.

school or executive development classes morality. Some believe that by this stage in life, one's level of moral development is pretty well established.

Specialized expertise in certain management can also be found in some consulting companies. As the Securing Competitive Advantage box notes, however, one should not count on gaining a sustainable competitive advantage from these types of outside sources. Consulting companies do not always have the answer to your question, and many have their own set of organizational problems that make it difficult for them to truly meet the needs of their clients.

People who teach organizational behavior and executive development often lament the inadequate dialogue that takes place between practicing managers and researchers. This kind of dialogue can develop only when managers and researchers understand each other's work and appreciate its value in guiding their own efforts. Practicing managers need to know what organizational behavior researchers do and why they follow certain paths. Researchers, in turn, need to identify practitioners' most pressing problems so that they can study those issues that managers view as significant. Because it is so important to create and encourage this kind of ongoing practitioner–researcher dialogue, we have included this chapter on research methods in this book.

Although you may never conduct formal research yourself, you will undoubtedly find it invaluable to familiarize yourself with the large body of scientific evidence available on topics that will be crucial to you, your employer, and your employees. Although this research may not provide all the answers you need, it will certainly inspire and intrigue you, perhaps promoting the kind of spirit embodied in some of the learning organizations described at the outset of this chapter.

SUMMARY

Traditional ways of acquiring knowledge, such as rationalism, personal experience, and reliance on authorities, have many limitations. The advantage of science relative to these more traditional means of knowledge acquisition is its *objectivity,* and science as an enterprise tends to be public, self-correcting, and cumulative. The major goals of science are the description, explanation, prediction, and control of various phenomena. These goals are achieved through an interplay of *theory* and *data,* whereby ideas contained in theories are expressed in testable *hypotheses,* which are then compared with actual data. The correspondence (or lack thereof) between the hypothesized results and the actual results is then used to verify, refute, or modify the theory.

Good theories are characterized by simplicity, self-consistency, and consistency with known facts; they should also contribute to the objectives of science. To be useful, data for testing theories should be *reliable* and *valid.* In obtaining such data, using established *standardized* measures offers many advantages.

At the core of many theories lies the idea of establishing causes. Cause can be inferred only when we establish *temporal precedence* and *covariation,* and when we eliminate all *alternative explanations.* The last requirement is often the most troublesome aspect of research in the social sciences, and threats such as *selection* and *history* threats can prove especially problematic. We partially avoid these threats by employing research designs that use control groups and make these controls comparable to experimental groups through *randomization, matching,* or *homogenization.*

To *generalize* the findings from one study to another context, it is necessary to randomly select samples, settings, and time periods. This goal is rarely achieved to its fullest extent in the social sciences. Nevertheless, if experimental results are repeatedly confirmed in different samples and settings and at different times, it may be possible to generalize such findings.

REVIEW QUESTIONS

1. Many theories seem to follow a similar pattern. They start out simple, grow increasingly complex as empirical tests on the theory proliferate, and then die out or are replaced by new theories. Review the criteria for a good theory and discuss why this pattern occurs so commonly. In your discussion, specify possible conflicts or inconsistencies among the criteria for a good theory.

2. Although objectivity is a hallmark of scientific inquiry, all scientists have their own subjective beliefs and biases surrounding the phenomena they study. Indeed, some scientists are motivated to do their work precisely because they hold passionate beliefs about these phenomena. Discuss whether this kind of passion is an asset or a liability to the scientist. In addition, discuss how science can be an objective exercise even though the people who practice it demonstrate personal biases. What prevents a passionate scientist from cheating or distorting results in favor of his or her personal beliefs?

3. Experiments in organizations usually involve people other than the experimenters—that is, managers or employees. What are some of the ethical responsibilities of an experimenter with respect to these people? Is it ethical, for example, for an experimenter to use one group of employees as a control group when he or she strongly suspects that the treatment given to the experimental group will enhance the members' chances for success, promotion, or satisfaction? If the experimenter is afraid that explaining the nature of the experiment will cause people to act differently than they would otherwise (and hence ruin the experiment), is it ethical to deceive them about the study's true purpose?

4. Philosopher of science Murray S. Davis once remarked that "The truth of a theory has very little to do with its impact." (See his article, "That's Interesting! Towards a Phenomenology of Sociology and a Sociology of Phenomenology," *Philosophy of the Social Sciences* 1 (1978), 309–344.) History, according to Davis, shows that the legacy of a theory depends more on how interesting the theory is perceived to be by practitioners and scientists than on how much truth it holds. Earlier in this chapter, we listed criteria for good theories; now list what you think are criteria for "interesting" theories. Where do these two lists seem to conflict most, and how can scientists and the practitioners they serve generate theories that are both interesting and truthful?

ENDNOTES

Chapter 1

1. J. Green, and D. Welch, "Jaguar May Find Out It's a Jungle Out There," *Business Week,* March 26, 2001, p. 62; M. J. Mandel, "Big Boom, Weak Profits," *Business Week,* August 12, 2002, pp. 30–33; K. Kerwin, J. Muller, and D. Welch, "Bill Ford's Long, Hard Road," *Business Week,* October 7, 2002, pp. 88–92; R. Miller, P. Coy, R. Hof, P. Burrows, and R. Berner, "Productivity's Second Wind," *Business Week,* February 17, 2003, pp. 36–37; K. Kerwin, "Can Ford Pull Out of Its Skid?" *Business Week,* March 31, 2003, pp. 70–72; J. Porretto, "Ford, GM Step Up Cost Cutting," *Lansing State Journal,* April 8, 2003, p. 1D; D. Welch, "Pick Me as Your Strike Target! No, Me!" *Business Week,* April 21, 2003, pp. 68–69; D. Welch, "Whacking Away at Ford," *Business Week,* April 28, 2003, p. 42.

2. E. A. Locke, D. B. Feren, V. M. McCaleb, K. N. Shaw, and A. T. Denny, "The Relative Effectiveness of Four Methods of Motivating Employee Performance," in K. D. Duncan, M. M. Gruneberg, and D. Wallis, eds., *Changes in Working Life* (Chichester, UK: Wiley, 1980), pp. 363–388.

3. Ibid.

4. Ibid.; J. A. Wagner III, P. A. Rubin, and T. J. Callahan, "Incentive Payment and Nonmanagerial Productivity: An Interrupted Time Series Analysis of Magnitude and Trend," *Organizational Behavior and Human Decision Processes* 42 (1988), 47–74.

5. Locke et al., "The Relative Effectiveness"; J. A. Wagner III and R. Z. Gooding, "Shared Influence and Organizational Behavior: A Meta-Analysis of Situational Variables Expected to Moderate Participation-Outcome Relationships," *Academy of Management Journal* 30 (1987), 524–541; J. A. Wagner III and J. A. LePine, "Participation's Effects on Performance and Satisfaction: Additional Evidence from U.S. Research," *Psychological Reports* 84 (1999), 719–725.

6. B. Nussbaum, "Needed: Human Capital," *Business Week,* September 19, 1988, pp. 100–103; W. Trueman, "Alternative Visions," *Canadian Business,* March 1991, pp. 28–33; D. Brady, "Wanted: Eclectic Visionary with a Sense of Humor," *Business Week,* August 28, 2000, pp. 143–144.

7. J. Barney, "Strategic Market Factors: Expectation, Luck, and Business Strategy," *Management Science* 32 (1986), 1231–1241; I. Dierickx and K. Cool, "Asset Stock Accumulation and Sustainability of Competitive Advantage," *Management Science* 35 (1989), 1504–1511; J. Nahapiet and S. Ghoshal, "Social Capital, Intellectual Capital, and the Organizational Advantage," *Academy of Management Review* 23 (1998), 242–266.

8. J. Pfeffer, "Producing Sustainable Competitive Advantage through the Effective Management of People," *Academy of Management Executive* 9 (1995), 55–69; P. M. Wright and G. C. McMahan, "Theoretical Perspectives for Strategic Human Resources Management," *Journal of Management* 18 (1992), 295–320.

9. L. L. Greiner, "A Recent History of Organizational Behavior," in S. Kerr, ed., *Organizational Behavior* (Columbus, OH: Grid Publishing, 1979), pp. 3–14.

10. L. L. Cummings, "Toward Organizational Behavior," *Academy of Management Review* 3 (1978), 90–98.

11. P. Cappelli and P. D. Sherer, "The Missing Role of Context in OB: The Need for a Meso-Level Approach," in L. L. Cummings and B. M. Staw, eds., *Research in Organizational Behavior* 13 (Greenwich, CT: JAI Press, 1991), pp. 55–110; R. House, D. M. Rousseau, and M. Thomas-Hunt, "The Meso Paradigm: A Framework for the Integration of Micro and Macro Organizational Behavior," in L. L. Cummings and B. M. Staw, eds., *Research in Organizational Behavior* 17 (Greenwich, CT: JAI Press, 1995), pp. 71–114.

12. R. H. Miles, *Macro Organizational Behavior* (Santa Monica, CA: Goodyear, 1980); R. L. Daft and R. M. Steers, *Organizations: A Micro/Macro Approach* (Glenview, IL: Scott, Foresman, 1986).

13. C. Hymowitz, "A Day in the Life of Tomorrow's Manager," *Wall Street Journal,* March 20, 1989, p. B1; J. Dreyfus, "Get Ready for the New Workforce," *Fortune,* April 23, 1990, p. 12.

14. G. E. Ledford, Jr. and E. E. Lawler III, "Research on Employee Participation: Beating a Dead Horse," *Academy of Management Review* 19 (1994), 633–636.

15. M. Hammer and J. Champy, *Reengineering the Corporation: A Manifesto for Business Revolution* (New York: Harper Business, 1993); D. Greising, "Quality: How to Make It Pay," *Business Week,* August 8, 1994, pp. 54–59; J. W. Dean, Jr., and D. E. Bowen, "Management Theory and Total Quality: Improving Research and Practice through Theory Development," *Academy of Management Review* 19 (1994), 392–418.

16. L. Nakarmi, M. DiCicco, G. Edmondson, A. Cortese, and D. Menaker, "Global Hot Spots," *Business Week,* September 25, 1995, pp. 116–126; G. Edmondson, "See the World, Erase Its Borders," *Business Week,* August 28, 2000, pp. 113–114.

17. Our model of problem solving is derived from the action research model presented in W. L. French, "Organization Development Objectives, Assumptions, and Strategies," *California Management Review* 12 (Winter 1969), 23–34.

18. T. J. Peters and R. H. Waterman, Jr., *In Search of Excellence: Lessons from America's Best-Run Companies* (New York: Harper & Row, 1982).

19. J. B. Treece, "A Little Bit of Smarts, a Lot of Hard Work," *Business Week,* November 30, 1992, pp. 70–71.

20. H. Simon, *Administrative Behavior,* 3rd ed. (New York: Free Press, 1976).

21. W. L. French and C. H. Bell, Jr., *Organization Development: Behavioral Science Interventions for Organization Improvement,* 6th ed. (Englewood Cliffs, NJ: Prentice Hall, 1999), pp. 76–77.

Chapter 2

1. M. Hyman, "David Stern Takes His Shots," *Business Week,* May 6, 2002, p. 91; M. Hyman, "Down to Their Last Out," *Business Week,* June 10, 2002, p. 64; M. Hyman, "Salaries Are Slamming the NHL. Who's to Blame?" *Business Week,* December 2, 2002, p. 78; M. Hyman, "The Winning Ways of the NBA's Bad Boy," *Business Week,* December 16, 2002, pp. 66–67; T. Lowry, "The NFL Machine," *Business Week,* January 27, 2003, pp. 86–94.

2. A. Smith, *An Inquiry into the Nature and Causes of the Wealth of Nations,* 5th ed. (Edinburgh: Adam and Charles Black, 1859), p. 3.

3. H. A. Simon, *Administrative Behavior: A Study of Decision Making Processes in Administrative Organizations,* 3rd ed. (New York: Free Press, 1976), pp. 257–278.

4. L. R. Gomez-Mejia, J. E. McCann, and R. C. Page, "The Structure of Managerial Behaviors and Rewards," *Industrial Relations* 24 (1985), 147–154.

5. R. L. Katz, "Skills of an Effective Administrator," *Harvard Business Review* 52 (1974), 90–102.

6. The list of ten roles described in this section is adapted from H. Mintzberg, *The Nature of Managerial Work* (Englewood Cliffs, NJ: Prentice Hall, 1980). Other researchers who have described similar managerial roles include S. Carlson, *Executive Behavior* (Stockholm: Stromsberg, 1951), and R. Stewart, *Managers and Their Jobs* (London: Macmillan, 1967).

7. J. B. Quinn, *Strategies for Change: Logical Incrementalism* (Homewood, IL: Irwin, 1980), p. 18.

8. The truthfulness of Taylor's accounts of his shovel demonstration and similar industrial experiments have been questioned, as described in R. Kanigel, *The One Best Way* (New York: Viking, 1997), and C. D. Wrenge and R. M. Hodgetts, "Frederick W. Taylor's 1899 Pig Iron Observations: Examining Fact, Fiction, and Lessons for the New Millennium," *Academy of Management Journal* 43 (2000), 1283–1291. Nonetheless, Taylor's descriptions of these experiments, published in F. W. Taylor, *The Principles of Scientific Management* (New York: Norton, 1911), and elsewhere had an influence on management that was immediate and continues today.

9. H. L. Gantt, "A Bonus System of Rewarding Labor," *ASME Transactions* 23 (1901), 341–372; H. L. Gantt, *Work, Wages, and Profits* (New York: Engineering Magazine Company, 1910), pp. 18–29.

10. H. L. Gantt, *Organizing for Work* (New York: Harcourt, Brace, & Howe, 1919), pp. 74–97.

11. H. Emerson, *The Twelve Principles of Efficiency* (New York: Engineering Magazine Company, 1912), pp. 359–367.

12. H. Fayol, *General and Industrial Management,* trans. Constance Storrs (London: Pitman & Sons, 1949), pp. 19–43.

13. H. Fayol, *Industrial and General Administration,* trans. J. A. Coubrough (Geneva: International Management Institute, 1930), p. 19.

14. H. H. Gerth and C.W. Mills, trans., *From Max Weber: Essays in Sociology* (New York: Oxford University Press, 1946); N. P. Mouzelis, *Organization and Bureaucracy: An Analysis of Modern Theories* (Chicago: Aldine, 1967); T. Parsons, trans., *Max Weber: The Theory of Social and Economic Organization* (New York: Free Press, 1947).

15. J. D. Mooney and A. C. Redev, *Onward Industry: The Principles of Organization and Their Significance to Modern Industry* (New York: Harper & Brothers, 1931); revised and published as J. D. Mooney, *The Principles of Organization* (New York: Harper & Brothers, 1947).

16. L. Urwick, *The Elements of Administration* (New York: Harper & Brothers, 1944).

17. H. C. Metcalf and L. Urwick, eds., *Dynamic Administration: The Collected Papers of Mary Parker Follett* (New York: Harper & Row, 1940). Also see J. Garwood, "A Review of Dynamic Administration: The Collected Papers of Mary Parker Follett," *New Management* 2 (1984), 61–62.

18. A. Carey, "The Hawthorne Studies: A Radical Criticism," *American Sociological Review* 33 (1967), 403–416.

19. Ibid.; R. H. Franke and J. D. Kaul, "The Hawthorne Experiments: First Statistical Interpretation," *American Sociological Review* 43 (1978), 623–643; A. J. M. Sykes, "Economic Interests and the Hawthorne Researchers," *Human Relations* 18 (1965), 253–263.

20. Examples from the body of research stimulated by the Hawthorne studies include L. Coch and J. R. P. French, Jr., "Overcoming Resistance to Change," *Human Relations* 1 (1948), 512–533; L. Berkowitz, "Group Standards, Cohesiveness, and Productivity," *Human Relations* 7 (1954), 509–514; S. E. Seashore, *Group Cohesiveness in the Industrial Work Group* (Ann Arbor: University of Michigan Survey Research Center, 1954).

21. D. McGregor, "The Human Side of Enterprise," *Management Review* 56 (1957), 22–28, 88–92; D. McGregor, *The Human Side of Enterprise* (New York: McGraw-Hill, 1960).

22. Adapted from McGregor, "The Human Side of Enterprise," p. 23.

23. Adapted from McGregor, "The Human Side of Enterprise," pp. 88–89.

24. D. Katz and R. L. Kahn, *The Social Psychology of Organizations* (New York: Wiley, 1966).

25. F. E. Emery and E. Trist, "The Causal Texture of Organizational Environments," *Human Relations* 18 (1965), 21–32; F. E. Emery and E. Trist, *Towards a Social Ecology* (London: Plenum, 1973).

26. Our classification system is based on research conducted by R. E. Quinn and associates. See, for example, R. E. Quinn and J. Rohrbaugh, "A Spatial Model of Effectiveness Criteria: Towards a Competing Values Approach to Organizational Analysis," *Management Science* 29 (1983), 363–377; R. E. Quinn, *Beyond Rational Management: Mastering the Paradoxes and Competing Demands of High Performance* (San Francisco: Jossey-Bass, 1988), pp. 50–54; R. E. Quinn, S. R. Faerman, M. P. Thompson, and M. R. McGrath, *Becoming a Master Manager: A Competency Framework*, 3rd ed. (New York: Wiley, 2002), pp. 2–12.

27. J. M. Pennings, "Structural Contingency Theory: A Reappraisal," in B. M. Staw and L. L. Cummings, eds., *Research in Organizational Behavior* 14 (Greenwich, CT: JAI Press, 1992), pp. 267–310.

Chapter 3

1. R. Smith, "Contractor Background Checks Recommended," *HRPath Management Bulletin,* May 2001, pp. 2–3.

2. C. Lachnit, "Protecting People and Profits with Background Checks," *Workforce,* February 2002, pp. 50–54.

3. S. Caudron, "Who Are You Really Hiring?" *Workforce,* November 2002, pp. 28–32.

4. P. Magnussan, "Your Jitters Are Their Lifeblood," *Business Week,* April 14, 2003, p. 41.

5. J. Pfeffer, "Producing Sustainable Competitive Advantage through the Effective Management of People," *Academy of Management Executive* 9 (1995), 55–72; J. T. Delaney and M. A. Huselid, "The Impact of Human Resource Management Practices on Perceptions of Organizational Performance," *Academy of Management Journal* 39 (1996), 949–969; M. A. Huselid, "The Impact of Human Resource Management Practices on Turnover, Productivity, and Corporate Financial Performance," *Academy of Management Journal* 38 (1995), 635–672; J. B. Arthur, "Effects of Human Resource Management Systems on Manufacturing Performance and Turnover," *Academy of Management Journal* 38 (1994), 670–687; and A. A. Lado and M. C. Wilson, "Human Resource Systems and Sustained Competitive Advantage," *Academy of Management Review* 19 (1994), 699–727.

6. L. Bossidy, "Execution: The Discipline of Getting Things Done," *Fortune,* June 10, 2002, pp. 149–152.

7. D. Anfuso, "3M's Staffing Strategy Promotes Productivity and Pride," *Personnel Journal,* February 1995, pp. 28–34.

8. J. B. Cooper and K. Madigan, "So Hard to Get Good Help These Days," *Business Week,* January 24, 2000.

9. A. Bernstein, "The Time Bomb in the Workforce: Illiteracy," *Business Week,* February 25, 2002, p. 122.

10. A. Durity, "A Critical Role for Corporate Education," *Personnel* 68 (1992), 5–6.

11. A. Farnham, "Are You Smart Enough to Keep Your Job?" *Fortune,* January 15, 1996, pp. 35–48.

12. G. L. Stewart, K. P. Carson, and R. L. Cardy, "The Joint Effects of Conscientiousness and Self-Leadership Training on Employee Self-Directed Behavior in a Service Setting," *Personnel Psychology* 49 (1996), 143–164.

13. B. McKee, "What You must Do for the Disabled," *Nations Business,* December 1991, pp. 37–39.

14. N. L. Breuer, "Resources Can Relieve ADA Fears," *Personnel Journal,* September 1993, pp. 131–134.

15. J. J. Laabs, "Individuals with Disabilities Augment Marriott's Work Force," *Personnel Journal,* September 1994, pp. 46–50.

16. L. M. Hough, N. K. Eaton, M. D. Dunnette, J. D. Camp, and R. A. McCloy, "Criterion-Related Validities of Personality Constructs and the Effect

of Response Distortion on Those Validities," *Journal of Applied Psychology* 75 (1990), 467–476.

17. M. R. Barrick and M. K. Mount, "The Big Five Personality Dimensions and Job Performance: A Meta-Analysis," *Personnel Psychology* 44 (1991), 1–26.

18. W. F. Wagner, "All Skill, No Finesse," *Workforce*, June 2000, pp. 108–116.

19. R. M. Guion and R. F. Gottier, "Validity of Personality Measures in Personnel Selection," *Personnel Psychology* 18 (1965), 135–164; F. J. Landy, *The Psychology of Work Behavior*, 4th ed. (New York: Free Press, 1985), p. 186.

20. J. J. McHenry, L. M. Hough, J. L. Toquam, M. A. Hanson, and S. Ashworth, "Project A Results: The Relationship between Predictor and Criterion Domains," *Personnel Psychology* 43 (1990), 335–355.

21. H. J. Bernardin and D. K. Cooke, "Validity of an Honesty Test in Predicting Theft among Convenience Store Employees," *Academy of Management Journal* 36 (1993), 1097–1108.

22. J. M. Collins and F. L. Schmidt, "Personality, Integrity, and White-Collar Crime: A Construct Validity Study," *Personnel Psychology* 46 (1993), 295–311.

23. R. P. Tett, D. N. Jackson, and M. Rothstein, "Personality Measures as Predictors of Job Performance: A Meta-Analytic Review," *Personnel Psychology* 44 (1991), 703–742.

24. M. B. Barrick and M. K. Mount, "Autonomy as a Moderator of the Relationships between the Big Five Personality Dimensions and Job Performance," *Journal of Applied Psychology* 78 (1993), 111–118.

25. Farnham, "Are You Smart Enough?"

26. P. M. Wright, K. M. Kacmer, G. C. McMahan, and K. Deleeuw, "$P = f(M \times A)$: Cognitive Ability as a Moderator of the Relationship between Personality and Job Performance," *Journal of Management* 21 (1995), 1129–1139.

27. L. A. Witt, L. A. Burke, M. R. Barrick, and M. K. Mount, "The Interactive Effects of Conscientiousness and Agreeableness on Performance," *Journal of Applied Psychology* 87 (2002), 164–169.

28. A. Raghavan, "How a Bright Star at Andersen Burned Out Along with Enron," *Wall Street Journal Online*, May 15, 2002, pp. 1–4.

29. J. A. Colquitt, J. R. Hollenbeck, D. R. Ilgen, J. A. LePine, and L. Sheppard, "Computer-Assisted Communication and Team Decision-Making Performance: The Moderating Effect of Openness to Experience," *Journal of Applied Psychology* 87 (2002), 402–410.

30. R. A. Posthuma, F. P. Morgeson, M. A. Campion, "Beyond Employment Interview Validity: A Comprehensive Narrative Review of Recent Research and Trends over Time," *Personnel Psychology* 55 (2002), 1–81.

31. J. Merritt, "Improv at the Interview," *Business Week*, February 3, 2003, p. 63.

32. J. C. Nunnally, *Psychometric Theory* (New York: McGraw-Hill, 1978).

33. A. R. Jenson, *Bias in Mental Testing* (New York: Free Press, 1980), p. 313.

34. J. E. Hunter, "Cognitive Ability, Cognitive Aptitudes, Job Knowledge, and Job Performance," *Journal of Vocational Behavior* 29 (1986), 340–362.

35. R. L. Gutenberg, R. D. Arvey, H. G. Osburn, and R. P. Jeanneret, "Moderating Effects of Decision-Making/Information Processing Dimensions on Test Validities," *Journal of Applied Psychology* 68 (1983), 600–708.

36. F. L. Schmidt, J. E. Hunter, A. N. Outerbridge, and S. Goff, "Joint Relation of Experience and Ability with Job Performance: Test of Three Hypotheses," *Journal of Applied Psychology* 73 (1998), 46–57.

37. L. G. Humphreys, D. Lubinski, and G. Yao, "Utility in Predicting Group Membership and the role of Spatial Visualization in Becoming an Engineer, Physical Scientist, or Artist," *Journal of Applied Psychology* 78 (1993), 250–261.

38. E. A. Feishman, *The Structure and Measurement of Physical Fitness* (Englewood Cliffs, NJ: Prentice Hall, 1964).

39. J. Hogan, "Structure of Physical Performance in Occupational Tasks," *Journal of Applied Psychology* 76 (1991), 495–507.

40. R. D. Arvey, T. E. Landon, S. M. Nutting, and S. E. Maxwell, "Development of Physical Ability Tests for Police Officers: A Construct Validation Approach," *Journal of Applied Psychology* 77 (1992), 996–254.

41. D. B. Chaffin, "Human Strength Capability and Low Back Pain," *Journal of Occupational Medicine* 16 (1974), 248–254.

42. W. Johnston, "The Coming Labor Shortage," *Journal of Labor Research* 13 (1992), 68–70.

43. M. Bertrand, "It Helps to Have a 'White' Name," CNN.com, January 14, 2003, p. 1.

44. W. Zellner, "No Way to Treat a Lady," *Business Week*, March 3, 2003, pp. 63–66.

45. C. Farrell, "Is Black Progress Set to Stall?" *Business Week*, November 6, 1995, pp. 71–73.

46. D. Anfuso, "Diversity Keeps Newspapers Up with the Times," *Personnel Journal*, July 1995, pp. 30–32.

47. D. A. Kravitz and S. L. Klineberg, "Reactions to Two Versions of Affirmative Action Among

Whites, Blacks, and Hispanics," *Journal of Applied Psychology* 85 (2000), 597–611.

48. O. C. Richard, "Racial Diversity, Business Strategy, and Firm Performance: A Resource Based View," *Academy of Management Journal* 43 (2000), 164–177.

49. G. Flynn, "Do You Have the Right Approach to Diversity?" *Personnel Journal,* October 1995, pp. 68–75.

50. F. Rice, "How to Make Diversity Pay," *Fortune,* August 8, 1994, pp. 78–86.

51. C. M. Solomon, "What You Need to Know about Affirmative Action," *Personnel Journal,* August 1995, pp. 57–67.

52. R. R. Thompson, "More Diversity in Agriculture: A Hard Row," *Wall Street Journal,* September 19, 1995, p. B1.

53. S. Peters, "*Personnel Journal* Announces Grant Recipients," *Personnel Journal,* October 1993, pp. 34–37.

54. P. Wright, S. P. Ferris, J. S. Hiller, and M. Kroll, "Competitiveness through Management of Diversity: Effects on Stock Price Evaluation," *Academy of Management Journal* 38 (1995), 272–287.

55. R. Crockett, "Memo to the Supreme Court: Diversity Is Good Business," *Business Week,* January 27, 2003, p. 96.

56. M. Galen, "Diversity: Beyond the Numbers Game," *Business Week,* August 14, 1995, pp. 60–61.

57. J. Dreyfus, "Get Ready for the New Workforce," *Fortune,* April 23, 1990, p. 12.

58. S. Mehta, "What Minority Employees Really Want," *Fortune,* July 10, 2000. pp. 181–186.

59. G. F. Dreher and T. H. Cox, "Race, Gender, and Opportunity: A Study of Compensation Attainment and the Establishment of Mentoring Relationships," *Journal of Applied Psychology* 81 (1996), 297–308.

60. G. Bylinsky, "Women Move Up in Manufacturing," *Fortune,* May 15, 2000, pp. 372C–372Z.

61. S. Rynes and B. Rosen, "A Field Survey of Factors Affecting the Adoption and Perceived Success of Diversity Training," *Personnel Psychology* 48 (1995), 247–270.

62. J. Laabs, "Interest in Diversity Training Continues to Grow," *Personnel Journal,* October 1993, p. 18.

63. C. M. Solomon, "Unlock the Potential of Older Workers," *Personnel Journal,* October 1995, pp. 56–66.

64. D. Fandray, "Gray Matters: The Tight Job Market Means That Employers Will Increasingly Rely on Older Workers," *Workforce,* July 2000, p. 32.

65. B. J. Avolio, B. J. Waldman, and D. A. McDaniel, "Age and Work Experience in Nonmanagerial Jobs: The Effects of Experience and Occupational

Type," *Journal of Applied Psychology* 33 (1990), 407–422; M. C. Healy, M. Lehman, and M. A. McDaniel, "Age and Voluntary Turnover: A Quantitative Review," *Personnel Psychology* 48 (1995), 335–345.

66. Farnham, "Are You Smart Enough?"

67. M. G. Morris, "Age Differences in Technology Adoption Decisions: Implications for a Changing Work Force," *Personnel Psychology* 53 (2000), 375–403.

68. J. Lee-Young, "Starbuck's Expansion in China Slated," *Wall Street Journal,* October 5, 1998, p. B13c.

69. Windham International and National Foreign Trade Council, *Global Trends: 1998 Survey Report* (New York: Windham International, 1998).

70. P. M. Claigiuri, "The Big Five Personality Characteristics as Predictors of Expatriates' Desire to Terminate the Assignment and Supervisor-Rated Performance," *Personnel Psychology* 55 (2000), 67–88.

71. L. D. Tyson, "Open the Gates Wide to High Skill Immigrants," *Business Week,* July 9, 2000, p. 16.

72. C. Mellow, "Brain Rush: Why Western Business Is Investing in Russia and R&D," *Fortune,* June 10, 1996, pp. 83–84.

73. W. Zellner, "Keeping the Hive Humming: Immigrants May Prevent the Economy from Overheating," *Business Week,* April 24, 2000, pp. 50–52.

74. R. Sharpe, "Summer Help Wanted: Foreigners Please Apply," *Business Week,* July 24, 2000, p. 32.

75. C. Vinzant, "How Do You Say Labor Shortage," *Fortune,* September 18, 2000, pp. 342–344.

76. A. Davies, "The Welcome Mat Is Out for Nerds," *Business Week,* October 16, 2000, p. 64.

77. R. Horn, "Give Me Your Huddled . . . High Tech Ph.D.s: Are High Skilled Foreigners Displacing U.S. Workers?" *Business Week,* November 6, 1995, pp. 161–162.

78. C. M. Solomon, "Foreign Relations," *Workforce,* November 2000, pp. 51–56.

79. E. D. Pulakos, S. Arad, M. Donovan, and K. E. Plamondon, "Adaptability in the Workplace: Development of a Taxonomy of Adaptive Performance," *Journal of Applied Psychology* 85 (2000), 612–624.

80. J. A. LePine, J. A. Colquitt, and A. Erez, "Adaptability to Changing Task Contexts: Effects of General Cognitive Ability, Conscientiousness, and Openness to Experience," *Personnel Psychology* 53 (2000), 563–593.

Chapter 4

1. R. Smith, "Feds Criticized as Pre-9/11 Clues Are Revealed," CNN.com, May 15, 2002, p. 1.

2. S. Warm, "Bush Briefed on Hijacking Threat before September 11," CNN.com, May 16, 2002, p. 1.

3. J. Cummings and G. Fields, "For Two Tense Days, Bush Team Wrestled with Vague Terror Threat," *Wall Street Journal Online*, May 17, 2002, pp. 1–5.

4. R. L. Priem, A. M. Rasheed, and A. G. Kotulic, "Rationality in Strategic Decision Processes, Environmental Dynamism and Firm Performance," *Journal of Management* 21 (1995), 913–929.

5. R. Smith, "Business as a War Game: A Report from the Battlefront," *Fortune*, September, 30, 1996, pp. 190–193.

6. B. B. Baltes and C. P. Parker, "Reducing the Effects of Performance Expectations on Behavioral Ratings," *Organizational Behavior and Human Decision Processes* 82 (2000), 237–267.

7. O. B. Davidson and D. Eden, "Remedial Self-Fulfilling Prophecy: Two Field Experiments to Prevent Golem Effects among Disadvantaged women," *Journal of Applied Psychology* 85 (2000), 386–398.

8. M. C. Heilman, C. J. Block, and J. A. Lucas, "Presumed Incompetent: Stigmatization and Affirmative Action Efforts," *Journal of Applied Psychology* 77 (1992), 536–544.

9. D. A. Kravitz and S. L. Klineberg, "Reactions to Two Versions of Affirmative Action among Whites, Blacks, and Hispanics," *Journal of Applied Psychology* 85 (2000), 597–611.

10. U. Neisser, *Cognition and Reality* (San Francisco: Freeman, 1976), p. 112.

11. J. E. Mathieu, T. S. Heffner, G. F. Goodwin, E. Salas, and J. A. Cannon-Bowers, "The Influence of Shared Mental Models on Team Process and Performance," *Journal of Applied Psychology* 85 (2000), 273–283.

12. P. Sellers, "These Women Rule," *Fortune*, October 25, 2000, pp. 94–110.

13. G. Bylinsky, "Women Move Up in Manufacturing: Unsung Women behind the Surging Productivity," *Fortune*, May 15, 2000, pp. 372C–372Z.

14. B. Rosen and T. H. Jerdee, "The Influence of Age Stereotypes on Managerial Decisions," *Journal of Applied Psychology* 61 (1976), 428–432.

15. D. Fandray, "Gray Matters," *Workforce*, July 2000, pp. 27–32.

16. C. Ofir, "Ease of Recall versus Recalled Evidence in Judgment: Experts versus Laymen," *Organizational Behavior and Human Decision Processes* 81 (2000), 28–42.

17. T. A. Louie, M. T. Curren, and K. R. Harich, "'I Knew We Would Win': Hindsight Bias for Favorable and Unfavorable Team Decision Outcomes," *Journal of Applied Psychology* 85 (2000), 264–272.

18. W. C. Borman, "Exploring the Upper Limits of Reliability and Validity of Performance Ratings," *Journal of Applied Psychology* 63 (1978), 135–144.

19. J. Rothfeder, M. Galen, and L. Driscoll, "Is Your Boss Spying on You? High Tech Snooping in the Electronic Sweatshop," *Business Week*, January 15, 1990, pp. 74–75.

20. A. D. Hovorka-Mead, W. H. Ross, T. Whipple, and M. B. Renchin, "Watching the Detectives: Seasonal Student Employee Reactions to Electronic Warning with and without Advance Notification," *Personnel Psychology*, 55 (2002), 329–361.

21. L. E. Atwater, D. A. Waldman, D. Atwater, and P. Cartier, "An Upward Feedback Field Experiment: Supervisor's Cynicism, Reactions, and Commitment to Subordinates," *Personnel Psychology* 53 (2000), 275–298.

22. T. DeAngelis, "Why We Overestimate Our Competence," *Monitor on Psychology*, February 2003, pp. 60–61.

23. P. W. B. Atkins and R. E. Wood, "Self-versus Others' Ratings as Predictors of Assessment Center Ratings: Validation Evidence for 360-Degree Feedback Programs," *Personnel Psychology* 55 (2002), 871–904.

24. S. Alper, D. Tjosvold, and K. S. Law, "Conflict Management Efficacy, and Performance in Organizational Teams," *Personnel Psychology* 53 (2000), 625–642.

25. L. T. DeFong and C. J. Ferguson-Hessler, "Information Processing Differences in Experts and Novices," *Journal of Applied Social Psychology* 21 (1987), 19–27.

26. L. Rhee, "Korea's Biggest Firm Teaches Junior Exec Strange Foreign Ways," *Wall Street Journal*, December 30, 1992, pp. A1, A4.

27. A. Tversky and D. Kahneman, "The Framing of Decisions and the Psychology of Choice," *Science* 211 (1981), 453–458.

28. D. Smith, "Psychologist Wins Nobel Prize," *Psychologist* 15 (2002), 596.

29. J. A. Byrne, "Fall from Grace," *Business Week*, August 12, 2002, pp. 50–55.

30. D. Elliott, W. F. Helsen, and R. Chua, "A Century Later: Woodworth's (1899) Two-Component Model of Goal-Directed Aiming," *Psychological Bulletin* 127 (2001), 342–357.

31. B. Beersma, J. R. Hollenbeck, S. E. Humphrey, H. Moon, D. E. Conlon, and D. R. Ilgen, "Cooperation, Competition and Team Performance: Toward a Contingency Approach," *Academy of Management Journal* 47 (2004).

32. L. A. Perlow, G. A. Okhuyson, and N. P. Repenning, "The Speed Trap: Exploring the Relation-

ship between Decision Making and Temporal Context," *Academy of Management Journal* 45 (2002), 931–955.

33. D. B. Boehne and P. W. Paese, "Deciding Whether to Complete or Terminate an Unfinished Product: A Strong Test of the Project Completion Hypothesis," *Organizational Behavior and Human Decision Processes* 81 (2000), 178–194.

34. B. M. Staw and J. Ross, "Behavior in Escalation Situations," in *Research in Organizational Behavior*, B. M. Staw and L. L. Cummings, eds. (Greenwich, CT: JAI Press, 1987), pp. 12–47.

35. J. G. March and H. A. Simon, *Organizations* (New York: Wiley, 1958), p. 10.

36. T. A. Stewart, "A Refreshing Change: Vision Statements That Make Sense," *Fortune*, September 30, 1996, pp. 195–196.

37. T. A. Stewart, "Company Values That Add Value," *Fortune*, July 8, 1996, pp. 145–147.

38. H. Simon, *The New Science of Management Decision* (New York: Harper & Row, 1960).

39. J. L. Lunsford, "Losing Ground to Airbus, Boeing Faces a Key Choice," *Wall Street Journal Online*, April 23, 2003, pp. 1–2.

40. L. Himelstein and B. Elgin, "Tech's Kickback Culture," *Business Week*, February 10, 2003, pp. 74–77.

41. P. Dwyer and D. Carney, "Year of the Whistle-blower," *Business Week*, December 16, 2002, pp. 107–110.

42. B. Brehmer, "Response Consistency in Probabilistic Inference Tasks," *Organizational Behavior and Human Performance* 22 (1978), 103–115.

43. March and Simon, *Organizations*, pp. 10–12.

44. Y. Ganzach, A. N. Kluger, and N. Klayman, "Making Decisions from an Interview: Expert Measurement and Mechanical Combination," *Personnel Psychology* 53 (2000), 1–20.

45. C. Daniels, "To Hire a Lumber Expert, Click Here," *Fortune*, April 3, 2000, pp. 267–270.

46. J.R. Hollenbeck, D. R. Ilgen, J. A. LePine, J. A. Colquitt, and J. Hedlund, "Extending the Multilevel Theory of Team Decision Making: Effects of Feedback and Experience in Hierarchical Teams." *Academy of Management Journal* 21 (1998), 269–282.

47. G. McNamara, H. Moon, and P. Bromily, "Banking on Commitment: Intended and Unintended Consequences of an Organization's Attempt to Attenuate Escalation of Commitment," *Academy of Management Journal* 45 (2002), 443–452.

48. J. V. Anderson, "Weirder Than Fiction: The Reality and Myths of Creativity," *Academy of Management Executive* 6 (1992), 40–47.

49. L. Armstrong, "The Geniuses Who Made VCRs Simple Enough for a 50-Year-Old," *Business Week*, December 31, 1990, p. 54.

50. P. B. Paulus, "Idea Generation in Groups: A Basis for Creativity in Organizations," *Organizational Behavior and Human Decision Processes* 82 (2000), 76–87.

51. F. Meeks, "Whistle Blower," *Forbes*, April 12, 1993, p. 104.

52. J. M. George and J. Zhou, "Understanding When Bad Moods Foster Creativity and Good Ones Don't: The Role of Context and Clarity of Feelings," *Journal of Applied Psychology* 87 (2002), 687–697.

53. T. Rotundi, "Organizational Identification: Issues and Implications," *Organizational Behavior and Human Performance* 13 (1975), 95–109.

54. P. Tierney, and S. M. Farmer, "Creative Self-Efficacy: Its Potential Antecedents and Relationship to Creative Performance," *Academy of Management Journal* 45 (2002), 1137–1148.

55. H. C. Lehman, *Age and Achievement* (Princeton, NJ: Princeton University Press, 1953), pp. 50–61.

56. B. Murray, "A Ticking Clock Means a Creative Drop," *Monitor on Psychology*, November 2002, pp. 24–25.

57. G. Zaltman, R. Duncan, and J. Holbek, *Innovations and Organizations* (New York: Wiley, 1969), p. 191.

58. T. A. Stewart, "3M Fights Back," *Fortune*, February 5, 1996, pp. 94–96.

59. R. Henkoff, "P&G: New and Improved," *Fortune*, October 14, 1996, pp. 151–156.

60. N. Madjar, G. R. Oldham, and M. G. Pratt, "There's No Place Like Home? The Contributions of Work and Nonwork Creativity Support to Employees' Creative Performance," *Academy of Management Journal* 45 (2002), 757–767.

61. G. Hamel, "Reinvent Your Company," *Fortune*, June 12, 2000, pp. 99–118.

62. G. R. Oldham and A. Cummings, "Employee Creativity: Personal and Contextual Factors at Work," *Academy of Management Journal* 39 (1996), 607–634.

63. C. E. Shalley, L. L. Gilson, and T. C. Blum, "Matching Creativity Requirements and the Work Environment: Effects on Satisfaction and Intentions to Leave," *Academy of Management Journal* 43 (2000), 215–223.

64. D. Leonard and W. Swap, "Igniting Creativity," *Workforce*, October 1999, pp. 87–89.

65. W. Guzzardi, "The National Business Hall of Fame," *Fortune*, February 1, 1990, pp. 17–29.

Chapter 5

1. R. D. Hof, "This Reform Won't Kill Silicon Valley," *Business Week,* July 29, 2002, p. 48.
2. L. Lavelle, "How to Halt the Options Express," *Business Week,* September 9, 2002, pp. 74–76.
3. G. S. Becker, "Options Are Useful—but Only If They're Used Right," *Business Week,* August 5, 2002, p. 26.
4. Lavelle, "How to Halt the Options Express."
5. J. Blasi, D. Kruse, and A. Bernstein, "Stock Options: The Right Way to Go," *Business Week,* January 6, 2003, pp. 65–67.
6. Lavelle, "How to Halt the Options Express."
7. A. Bernstein, "Options: Middle Managers Will Take the Hit, *Business Week,* December 9, 2002, p. 120.
8. V. H. Vroom, *Work and Motivation* (New York: Wiley, 1964), pp. 55–71; L. W. Porter and E. E. Lawler, *Managerial Attitudes and Performance* (Homewood, IL: Irwin, 1968), pp. 107–139.
9. T. R. Mitchell, "Expectancy Models of Job Satisfaction, Occupational Choice, and Effort: A Theoretical, Methodological, and Empirical Appraisal," *Psychological Bulletin* 81 (1974), 1053–1077.
10. Vroom, *Work and Motivation,* p. 27.
11. G. F. Dreher and T. H. Cox, "Labor Market Mobility and Cash Compensation: The Moderating Effects of Race and Gender," *Academy of Management Journal* 43 (2000), 890–900.
12. M. Conlin, "Now It Is Getting Personal," *Business Week,* December 18, 2002, pp. 90–92.
13. A. H. Maslow, "Theory of Human Motivation," *Psychological Reports* 50 (1943), 370–396.
14. M. A. Wahba and L. G. Bridwell, "Maslow Reconsidered: A Review of Research on the Need Hierarchy," *Organizational Behavior and Human Performance* 15 (1976), 121–140.
15. H. A. Murray, *Explorations in Personality* (New York: Oxford University Press, 1938).
16. D. C. McClelland, *The Achieving Society* (Princeton, NJ: Van Nostrand Press, 1963).
17. M. Gimein, "Smart Is Not Enough," *Fortune,* January 8, 2001, pp. 124–136.
18. S. Armour, "Higher Pay May Be Layoff Target," *USA Today Online,* June 23, 2003, pp. 1–2.
19. S. E. Markham, K. D. Scott, G. H. McKee, "Recognizing Good Attendance: A Longitudinal, Quasi-Experimental Field Study," *Personnel Psychology* 55 (2002), 639–660.
20. J. Martin, "Are You as Good as You Think You Are?" *Fortune,* September 30, 1996, pp. 142–152.
21. S. M. Gully, S. C. Payne, K. L Keichel Koles, and J. K. Whiteman, "The Impact of Error Training and Individual Differences on Training Outcomes: An Attribute–Treatment Interaction Perspective," *Journal of Applied Psychology* 87 (2002), 143–155.
22. D. Heimbeck, M. Frese, S. Sonnentag, and N. Keith, "Integrating Errors into the Training Process: The Function of Error Management Instructions and the Role of Goal Orientation," *Personnel Psychology* 56 (2003), 333–361.
23. R. L. Solomon, "Punishment," *American Psychologist* 19 (1962), 239–253.
24. R. C. Liden, S. J. Wayne, T. A. Judge, R. S. Sparrowe, M. L. Kraimer, and T. M. Franz, "Management of Poor Performance: A Comparison of Manager, Group Member, and Group Disciplinary Decisions," *Journal of Applied Psychology* 84 (1999), 835–850.
25. W. Kiechel, "Firing Line: Legal Challenges Force Firms to Revamp Ways They Dismiss Workers," *Wall Street Journal,* September 13, 1993, p. B1.
26. R. Charan and J. Useem, "Why Companies Fail," *Fortune,* May 27, 2002, pp. 50–62.
27. A. Bandura, "Self-Reinforcement: Theoretical and Methodological Considerations," *Behaviorism* 4 (1976), 135–155.
28. I. Wallace, "Self-Control Techniques of Famous Novelists," *Journal of Applied Behavioral Analysis* 10 (1977), 515–525.
29. F. H. Kanfer and J. S. Phillips, *Learning Foundations of Behavior Therapy* (New York: John Wiley, 1970), p. 59; F. H. Kanfer, "Self-Regulation: Research, Issues, and Speculation," in C. Neuringer and J. Michael, eds., *Behavior Modification in Clinical Psychology* (New York: Appleton-Century-Crofts, 1974), pp. 178–220; M. J. Mahoney, N. G. Moura, and T. C. Wade, "The Relative Efficacy of Self-Reward, Self-Punishment, and Self-Monitoring Techniques for Weight Loss," *Journal of Consulting and Clinical Psychology* 40 (1973), 404–407; C. S. Richards, "When Self-Control Fails; Selective Bibliography of Research on the Maintenance Problems in Self-Control Treatment Programs," *JSAS: Catalog of Selected Documents in Psychology* 8 (1976), 67–68; E. L. Glynn, "Classroom Applications of Self-Determined Reinforcement," *Journal of Applied Behavioral Analysis* 3 (1970), 123–130; C. A. Frayne and G. P. Latham, "Application of Social Learning Theory to Employee Self-Management of Attendance," *Journal of Applied Psychology* 72 (1987), 387–392.
30. A. Bandura, "Self-Efficacy Mechanism in Human Behavior," *American Psychologist* 37 (1982), 122–147.
31. J. Schaubroeck, S. K. Lam, and J. L. Xie, "Collective Efficacy Versus Self-Efficacy in Coping Responses to Stressors and Control: A Cross-

Cultural Study," *Journal of Applied Psychology* 85 (2000), 512–525.

32. A. A. Nease, B. O. Mudgett, and M. A. Quinones, "Relationships among Feedback Sign, Self-Efficacy, and Acceptance of Performance Feedback," *Journal of Applied Psychology* 84 (1999), 806–814.

33. J. B. Vancouver, C. M. Thompson, E. C. Tischner, and D. J. Putka, "Two Studies Examining the Negative Effect of Self-Efficacy on Performance," *Journal of Applied Psychology* 87 (2002), 506–516.

34. A. Bandura and E. A. Locke, "Negative Self-Efficacy and Goal Effects Revisited," *Journal of Applied Psychology* 88 (2003), 87–99.

35. J. E. Mathieu, J. W. Martinau, and S. I. Tannenbaum, "Individual and Situational Influences on the Development of Self-Efficacy: Implications for Training Effectiveness," *Personnel Psychology* 46 (1993), 125–147.

36. E. A. Locke, "Toward a Theory of Task Motivation and Incentives," *Organizational Behavior and Human Performance* 3 (1968), 145.

37. J. E. Sawyer, W. R. Latham, R. D. Pritchard, and W. R. Bennett, "Analysis of Work Group Productivity in an Applied Setting," *Personnel Psychology* 52 (1999), 927–967.

38. J. M. Phillips, J. R. Hollenbeck, and D. R. Ilgen, "Prevalence and Prediction of Positive Discrepancy Creation: Examining a Discrepancy between Two Self-Regulation Theories," *Journal of Applied Psychology* 81 (1996), 498–511.

39. F. K. Lee, K. M. Sheldon, and D. B. Turban, "Personality and Goal Striving: The Influence of Achievement Goal Patterns, Goal Level, and Mental Focus on Performance and Enjoyment," *Journal of Applied Psychology* 88 (2003), 256–263.

40. J. B. Vancouver and D. J. Putka, "Analyzing Goal Striving Processes and a Test of the Generalizability of Perceptual Control Theory," *Organizational Behavior and Human Decision Processes* 82 (2000), 334–362.

41. D. Henry and L. Lavelle, "Exploring Options," *Business Week*, February 3, 2003, pp. 78–79.

42. Charan and Useem, "Why Companies Fail," pp. 50–62.

43. H. J. Klein, M. J. Wesson, J. R. Hollenbeck, and B. J. Alge, "Goal Commitment and the Goal Setting Process: Conceptual Clarification and Empirical Synthesis," *Journal of Applied Psychology* 84 (1999), 885–896.

44. J. R. Hollenbeck, C. R. Williams, and H. J. Klein, "An Empirical Examination of Antecedents of Commitment to Difficult Goals," *Journal of Applied Psychology* 74 (1989), 18–25.

45. C. Sue-Chan and M. Ong, "Goal Assignment and Performance: Assessing the Mediating Roles of Goal Commitment, Self-Efficacy and the Moderating Role of Power Distance," *Organizational Behavior and Human Decision Processes* 89, (2002), 1140–1161.

46. R. E. Wood, E. A. Locke, and A. J. Mento, "Task Complexity as a Moderator of Goal Effects: A Meta-Analysis," *Journal of Applied Psychology* 72 (1987), 416–425.

47. P. C. Earley and B. C. Perry, "Work Plan Availability and Performance: An Assessment of Task Strategy Priming on Subsequent Task Completion," *Organizational Behavior and Human Decision Processes* 39 (1987), 279–302; P. C. Earley, P. Wajnaroski, and W. Prest, "Task Planning and Energy Expended: Exploration of How Goals Influence Performance," *Journal of Applied Psychology* 74 (1987), 107–114.

48. P. C. Earley, T. Connolly, and G. Ekegren, "Goals, Strategy Development and Task Performance: Some Limits on the Efficacy of Goal Setting," *Journal of Applied Psychology* 74 (1989), 24–33.

49. D. VandeWalle, S. P. Brown, W. L. Cron, and J. W. Slocum, "The Influence of Goal Orientation and Self-Regulation Tactics on Sales Performance: A Longitudinal Field Test," *Journal of Applied Psychology* 84 (1999), 249–259.

50. D. Vandewalle, S. Ganesan, G. N. Challagalla, and S. P. Brown, "An Integrated Model of Feedback-Seeking Behavior: Disposition, Context, and Cognition," *Journal of Applied Psychology* 85 (2000), 996–1003.

51. D. Steele-Johnson, R. S. Beauregard, P. B. Hoover, and A. M. Schmidt, "Goal Orientation and Task Demand Effects on Motivation, Affect, and Performance," *Journal of Applied Psychology* 85 (2000), 724–738.

52. B. S. Bell and S. W. J. Kozlowski, "Goal Orientation and Ability: Interactive Effects on Self-Efficacy, Performance, and Knowledge," *Journal of Applied Psychology* 87 (2002), 497–505.

53. R. Kanfer and P. L. Ackerman, "Motivation and Cognitive Abilities: An Integrative/Aptitude–Treatment Interaction Approach to Skill Acquisition," *Journal of Applied Psychology* 74 (1989), 657–690.

54. L. R. Gomez-Mejia, T. M. Welbourne, and R. M. Wiseman, "The Role of Risk Sharing and Risk Taking under Gainsharing," *Academy of Management Review* 25 (2000), 492–507.

55. T. R. Zenger and C. R. Marshall, "Determinants of Incentive Intensity in Group-Based Rewards," *Academy of Management Journal* 43 (2000), 149–163.

56. M. Bloom, "The Performance Effects of Pay Dispersion on Individuals and Organizations," *Academy of Management Journal* 42 (1999), 25–50.

57. S. Kerr, "Risky Business: The New Pay Game," *Fortune*, July 22, 1996, pp. 94–95.

58. S. Phillips, A. Dunkin, J. B. Treece, and K. H. Hammonds, "King Customer: At Companies That Listen Hard and Respond Fast, Bottom Lines Thrive," *Business Week*, March 12, 1990, pp. 88–94.

59. C. W. Hamner, "How to Ruin Motivation with Pay," *Compensation Review* 21 (1975), 88–98.

60. L. Scism, "Insurers Study Ways of Paying Sales Personnel," *Wall Street Journal*, November 3, 1995, p. A7.

61. P. Nulty, "Incentive Pay Can Be Crippling," *Fortune*, November 13, 1995, p. 235.

62. S. Hays, "Pros and Cons of Pay for Performance," *Workforce*, February 1999, pp. 69–72.

63. Bureau of National Affairs, "Incentive Pay Schemes Seen as a Result of Economic Employee Relation Change," *BNA Daily Report*, October 9, 1984, p. 1.

64. R. McCaffery, *Managing the Employee Benefits Process* (New York: AMACOM, 1983), p. 17.

65. C. Mahoney, "Share the Wealth—and the Headache: Stock Options Are Not All Glory," *Workforce*, June 2000, pp. 119–122.

66. P. K. Zingheim and J. R. Schuster, "Value Is the Goal," *Workforce*, February 2000, pp. 56–61.

Chapter 6

1. R. Stone, "Securicor Warns of Difficult Second Half," *Wall Street Journal Online*, May 29, 2003, pp. 1–2.

2. J. Smitty, "Argenbright Security: Securicor Unit to End Operations on December 14 at Boston's Airport," *Wall Street Journal Online*, December 3, 2001, p. 1.

3. S. Power, "DOT Won't Do Business with Argenbright Security," *Wall Street Journal Online*, February 6, 2002, pp. B2–B3.

4. D. Morse, "Campaign against Terror: Argenbright's New CEO Promises to Reshape Airport-Security Firm," *Wall Street Journal Online*, November 12, 2001, pp. A12–A13.

5. S. Powers and S. Carey, "Uncle Sam Mans the Scanners," *Wall Street Journal Online*, February 8, 2002, p. B1.

6. B. Schneider, S. D. Ashworth, A. C. Higgs, and L. Carr, "Design, Validity, and Use of Strategically-Focused Employee Attitude Surveys," *Personnel Psychology* 49 (1996), 695–705.

7. R. Levering and M. Moskowitz, "The 100 Best Companies to Work For," *Fortune*, January 20, 2003, pp. 127–152.

8. N. Stein, "Winning the War to Keep Top Talent," *Fortune*, May 29, 2000, pp. 132–138.

9. G. Koretz, "Yes, Workers Are Grumpier: Job Satisfaction Falling Sharply," *Business Week*, November 18, 2000, p. 42.

10. E. A. Locke, "The Nature and Causes of Job Dissatisfaction," in M. D. Dunnette, ed., *Handbook of Industrial–Organizational Psychology* (Chicago: Rand McNally, 1976), pp. 901–969.

11. J. E. McGrath, "Stress in Organizations," in M. D. Dunnette, ed., *Handbook of Industrial and Organizational Psychology* (Chicago: Rand McNally, 1977), pp. 1310–1367.

12. J. R. Edwards, "An Examination of Competing Versions of the Person–Environment Fit Approach to Stress," *Academy of Management Journal* 39 (1996), 292–339.

13. D. H. Funkenstein, "The Physiology of Fear and Anger," *Scientific American* 192 (1955), 74–80.

14. H. J. Freudenberger, "Staff Burnout," *Journal of Social Issues* 30 (1974), 159–164.

15. S. G. Rogelberg, A. Luong, M. E. Sederberg, and D. S. Cristol, "Employee Attitude Surveys: Examining the Attitudes of Non-Compliant Employees," *Journal of Applied Psychology* 85 (2000), 284–293.

16. M. A. Donovan, F. D. Drasgow, and T. M. Probst, "Does Computerizing Paper-and-Pencil Job Attitude Scales Make a Difference? New IRT Analyses Offer Insight," *Journal of Applied Psychology* 85 (2000), 305–313.

17. T. A. Judge, C. J. Thoresen, J. E. Bono, and G. K. Patton, "The Job Satisfaction–Job Performance Relationship: A Qualitative and Quantitative Review," *Psychological Bulletin* 127 (2001), 376–407.

18. J. M. Brett and L. K. Stroh, "Working 61 Plus Hours a Week: Why Do Managers Do It?" *Journal of Applied Psychology* 88 (2003), 67–78.

19. A. M. Susskind, K. M. Kacmer, and C. P. Borchgrevink, "Customer Service Providers' Attitudes Relating to Customer Service and Customer Satisfaction in the Customer-Server Exchange," *Journal of Applied Psychology* 88 (2003), 179–187.

20. A. A. Grandey, "When 'the Show Must Go On': Surface Acting and Deep Acting as Determinants of Emotional Exhaustion and Peer-Related Service Delivery," *Academy of Management Journal* 46 (2003), 86–96.

21. R. Suskind, "Humor Has Returned to Southwest Airlines," *Wall Street Journal Online*, January 13, 2003, pp. 1–3.

22. I. S. Fulmer, B. Gerhart, and K. S. Scott, "Are the 100 Best Better? An Empirical Investigation of the Relationship between Being a 'great place to

work' and Firm Performance," *Personnel Psychology* 56 (2004), in press.

23. J. Downes, "2000 Employee Benefits Survey," U.S. Chamber of Commerce, Washington, DC, April 2001.

24. *Analysis of Workers' Compensation Laws* (Washington, DC: U.S. Chamber of Commerce, 1985), p. 3.

25. O. Port, "Does Job Satisfaction Prevent Back Injuries?" *Business Week*, April 1, 1991, p. 82.

26. R. Poe, "Does Your Job Make You Sick?" *Across the Board* 9 (1987), 34–43.

27. S. B. Bacharach, P. A. Bamberger, and W. J. Sonnestuhl, "Driven to Drink: Managerial Control, Work-Related Risk Factors, and Employee Problem Drinking," *Academy of Management Journal* 45 (2002), 637–658.

28. G. E. Hardy, D. Woods, and T. D. Wall, "The Impact of Psychological Distress on Absence from Work," *Journal of Applied Psychology* 88 (2002), 306–314.

29. T. W. Lee, T. R. Mitchell, L. Wise, and S. Fireman, "An Unfolding Model of Voluntary Employee Turnover," *Academy of Management Journal* 39 (1996), 5–36.

30. P. J. Kiger, "Retention on the Brink," *Workforce*, November 2000, pp. 59–65.

31. C. L. Cole, "Building Loyalty," *Workforce*, August 2000, pp. 43–48.

32. J. J. Laabs, "Employee Commitment: New Employment Rules," *Personnel Journal*, August 1996, pp. 58–68.

33. D. W. Organ and M. Konovsky, "Cognitive versus Affective Determinants of Organizational Citizenship Behavior," *Journal of Applied Psychology* 74 (2000), 157–164.

34. J. A. LePine, A. Erez, and D. E. Johnson, "The Nature and Dimensionality of Organizational Citizenship Behavior," *Journal of Applied Psychology* 87 (2002), 52–65.

35. S. J. Lambert, "Added Benefits: The Link between Work–Life Benefits and Organizational Citizenship Behaviors," *Academy of Management Journal* 43 (2000), 801–815.

36. R. Cropanzano, D. E. Rupp, and Z. S. Byrne, "The Relationship of Emotional Exhaustion to Work Attitudes, Job Performance, and Organizational Citizenship Behaviors," *Journal of Applied Psychology* 88 (2003), 160–169.

37. A. Q. Nomani, "Women Likelier to Face Violence in the Workplace," *Wall Street Journal*, October 31, 1995, p. A16.

38. O. M. Kurland, "Workplace Violence," *Risk Management* 40 (1993), 76–77.

39. A. M. O'Leary-Kelly, R. W. Griffin, and D. J. Glew, "Organization-Motivated Aggression: A Research Framework," *Academy of Management Review* 21 (1996), 225–253.

40. D. Anfuso, "The Postal Service Delivers a Violence Prevention Program," *Personnel Journal*, October 1994, p. 69.

41. J. Laabs, "Employee Sabotage," *Workforce*, July, 2000, pp. 33–42.

42. E. Van de Vliert and N. W. Van Yperen, "Why Cross-Cultural Differences in Role Overload? Don't Overlook Ambient Temperature!" *Academy of Management Journal* 39 (1996), 986–1004.

43. G. R. Oldham and N. L. Rotchford, "Relationships between Office Characteristics and Employee Reactions: A Study of the Physical Environment," *Administrative Science Quarterly* 28 (1983), 542–556.

44. E. F. Stone and H. G. Gueutal, "An Empirical Derivation of the Dimensions along Which Characteristics of Jobs Are Perceived," *Academy of Management Journal* 28 (1985), 376–396.

45. M. Conlin, "Is Your Office Killing You? Sick Buildings Are Seething with Molds, Monoxide—and Worse," *Business Week*, June 5, 2000, pp. 114–128.

46. B. J. Tepper, "Consequences of Abusive Supervision," *Academy of Management Journal* 43 (2000), pp. 178–190.

47. J. Laabs, "Will to-Die-for Benefits Really Help Retention?" *Workforce*, July 2000, pp. 62–66.

48. R. E. Mitchell, A. G. Billings, and R. M. Moos, "Social Support and Well-Being: Implications for Prevention Programs," *Journal of Primary Prevention* (1982), 77–98.

49. A. Weintraub, "Nursing: On the Critical List," *Business Week*, June 3, 2002, p. 81.

50. R. I. Sutton and A. Rafaeli, "Characteristics of Work Stations as Potential Occupational Stressors," *Academy of Management Journal* 30 (1987), 260–276.

51. S. Greengard, "Privacy: Entitlement or Illusion?" *Personnel Journal*, May 1996, 74–88.

52. G. R. Oldham and Y. Fried, "Employee Reactions to Workspace Characteristics," *Journal of Applied Psychology* 72 (1987), 75–84.

53. D. Watson, L. A. Clark, and A. Tellegen, "Development and Validation of Brief Measures of Positive and Negative Affect: The PANAS Scales," *Journal of Personality and Social Psychology* 54 (1988), pp. 1063–1070.

54. T. A. Judge, J. E. Bono, and E. A. Locke, "Personality and Job Satisfaction: The Mediating Role of Job Characteristics," *Journal of Applied Psychology* 85 (2000), 237–249.

55. P. E. Spector, P. E. Chen, and B. J. O'Connell, "A Longitudinal Study of Relations between Job

Stressors and Job Strains While Controlling for Prior Negative Affectivity and Strains," *Journal of Applied Psychology* 85 (2000), 211–218.

56. B. M. Staw, N. E. Bell, and J. A. Clausen, "The Dispositional Approach to Job Attitudes: A Lifetime Longitudinal Test," *Administrative Science Quarterly* 31 (1986), pp. 56–78.

57. J. Forster, "When Workers Just Can't Cope: New Rulings Clarify What Employers Should and Shouldn't Do," *Business Week,* October 23, 2000, pp. 100–102.

58. J. Klein and L. Sussman, "An Executive Guide to Workplace Depression," *Academy of Management Executive* 14 (2000), 103–114.

59. J. H. Howard, D. A. Cunningham, and P. A. Rechnitzer, "Health Patterns Associated with Type A Behavior: A Managerial Population," *Journal of Human Stress* 2 (1976), 24–31.

60. K. A. Mathews, "Psychological Perspectives on the Type A Behavior Pattern," *Psychological Bulletin* 91 (1982), 293–323.

61. M. A. Campion and C. L. McClelland, "Follow-Up and Extension of the Interdisciplinary Costs and Benefits of Enlarged Jobs," *Journal of Applied Psychology* 78 (1993), 339–351.

62. J. E. Edwards, J. A. Scully, and M. D. Brtek, "The Nature and Outcomes of Work: A Replication and Extension of Interdisciplinary Work Design Research," *Journal of Applied Psychology* 85 (2000), 860–868.

63. G. R. Oldham, A. Cummings, L. J. Mischel, J. M. Schmidtke, and J. Zhou, "Listen While You Work? Quasi-Experimental Relations between Personal-Stereo Headset Use and Employee Work Responses," *Journal of Applied Psychology* 80 (1995), 547–564.

64. J. R. Hollenbeck, D. R. Illgen, D. B. Tuttle, and D. J. Sego, "Team Performance in Monitoring Tasks: An Examination of Decision Errors in Contexts Requiring Sustained Attention," *Journal of Applied Psychology* 80 (1995), 685–696.

65. M. Der Hovanesian and M. Conlin, "Wall Street's Broken Spirit," *Business Week,* September 2, 2002, pp. 84–85.

66. R. C. Liden, S. J. Wayne, and R. T. Sparrowe, "An Examination of the Mediating Role of Psychological Empowerment on the Relations between the Job, Interpersonal Relationships and Work Outcomes," *Journal of Applied Psychology* 85 (2000), 407–416.

67. N. L. Breuer, "Shelf Life," *Workforce,* August 2000, pp. 29–34.

68. C. Rober, T. M. Probst, J. J. Martocchio, F. Drasgow, and J. L. Lawler, "Empowerment and Continuous Improvement in the United States, Mex-

ico, Poland and India: Predicting Fit on the Basis of the Dimensions of Power Distance and Individualism," *Journal of Applied Psychology* 85 (2000), pp. 643–658.

69. J. Schlosser and J. Sung, "The 100 Best Companies to Work For," *Fortune,* January 8, 2000, pp. 148–168.

70. M. Conlin, "Give a Geek a Break," *Business Week,* July 10, 2000, pp. 102–104.

71. D. Brady, "Rethinking the Rat Trap," *Business Week,* August 26, 2002, pp. 142–143.

72. T. Gray, "A Hospital Takes Action on Employee Survey," *Personnel Journal,* March 1995, pp. 74–77.

73. B. Schneider, S. D. Ashworth, A. C. Higgs, and L. Carr, "Design, Validity and Use of Strategically-Focused Employee Attitude Surveys," *Personnel Psychology* 49 (1996), 695–705.

74. N. S. Bruning and D. R. Frew, "Effects of Exercise, Relaxation, and Management Skills Training on Physiological Stress Indicators: A Field Experiment," *Journal of Applied Psychology* 72 (1987), 515–521.

75. P. E. Spector, "Locus of Control and Well-Being at Work: How Generalizable Are the Findings?" *Academy of Management Journal* 45 (2002), 453–466.

76. K. Park, "A New Frontier: U.S. Electronics Firm Expands in Asia," *Far Eastern Economic Review* 41 (1992), 75–93.

77. L. E. Parker, "When to Fix It and When to Leave: Relationships among Perceived Control, Self Efficacy, Dissent, and Exit," *Journal of Applied Psychology* 78 (1993), 949–959.

78. J. B. Olson-Buchanan, "The Role of Employee Loyalty and Formality in Voicing Discontent," *Journal of Applied Psychology* 87 (2002), 1167–1174.

79. D. G. Spencer, "Employee Voice and Employee Retention," *Academy of Management Journal* 29 (1986), 488–502.

80. S. E. Jackson, "Participation in Decision Making as a Strategy for Reducing Job-Related Strain," *Journal of Applied Psychology* 68 (1983), 3–19.

81. M. Freudenheim, "Assessing the Corporate Fitness Craze," *New York Times,* March 18, 1990, p. D1.

82. D. C. Ganster, B. T. Mayes, W. F. Sime, and G. D. Tharp, "Managing Organizational Stress: A Field Experiment," *Journal of Applied Psychology* 67 (1982), 533–542.

83. J. S. Manuso, "Executive Stress Management," *Personnel Administrator* 24 (1979), 23–26.

84. G. Flynn, "Rhino Foods Is a Workplace of the Future Now," *Personnel Journal,* January 1996, p. 64.

85. B. M. Meglino, A. S. DeNisi, and E. C. Ravlin. "Job Status on the Functioning of a Realistic Job Preview," *Personnel Psychology* 46 (1993), 803–822.

Chapter 7

1. S. Terkel, *Working* (New York: Avon, 1972), pp. 221–223.
2. B. Garson, *All the Livelong Day: The Meaning and Demeaning of Routine Work* (New York: Penguin Books, 1977), p. 171.
3. C. T. Morgan, J. S. Cook, A. Chapanis, and M. W. Lund, *Human Engineering Guide to Equipment Design* (New York: McGraw-Hill, 1963).
4. Adapted from M. E. Mundel, *Motion and Time Study: Improving Productivity,* 7th ed. (Englewood Cliffs, NJ: Prentice Hall, 1993), p. 398.
5. M. A. Campion, "Ability Requirement Implications of Job Design: An Interdisciplinary Perspective," *Personnel Psychology* 42 (1989), 1–24; M. A. Campion and C. L. McClelland, "Interdisciplinary Examination of the Costs and Benefits of Enlarged Jobs: A Job Design Quasi Experiment," *Journal of Applied Psychology* 76 (1991), 186–198; J. R. Edwards, J. A. Scully, and M. D. Brtek, "The Measurement of Work: Hierarchical Representation of the Multimethod Job Design Questionnaire," *Personnel Psychology* 52 (1999), 305–334; J. R. Edwards, J. A. Scully, and M. D. Brtek, "The Nature and Outcomes of Work: A Replication and Extension of Interdisciplinary Work-Design Research," *Journal of Applied Psychology* 85 (2000), 860–868.
6. M. Galen, M. Mallory, S. Siwolop, and S. Garland, "Repetitive Stress: The Pain Has Just Begun," *Business Week,* July 13, 1992, pp. 142–146; "Repetitive Motion Disorders Lead Increase in Job Illnesses," *New York Times,* November 16, 1990, p. D7; "Chrysler Agrees to Curtail Repetitive Tasks for Workers," *Lansing State Journal,* November 3, 1989, p. 4B.
7. L. M. Gilbreth, *The Psychology of Management* (New York: Macmillan, 1921), p. 19.
8. G. R. Salancik and J. Pfeffer, "An Examination of Need-Satisfaction Models of Job Attitudes," *Administrative Science Quarterly* 22 (1977), 427–456.
9. The classic piece on this approach to counteracting oversimplification is C. R. Walker and R. H. Guest, *The Man on the Assembly Line* (Cambridge, MA: Harvard University Press, 1952).
10. J. D. Kilbridge, "Reduced Costs through Job Enlargement: A Case," *Journal of Business* 33 (1960), 357–362; J. F. Biggane and P. A. Stewart, "Job Enlargement: A Case Study," in L. E. Davis and J. C. Taylor, eds., *Design of Jobs* (New York: Penguin, 1972), pp. 264–276; G. E. Susman, "Job Enlargement: Effects of Culture on Worker Responses," *Industrial Relations* 12 (1973), 1–15; S. K. Parker, "Enhancing Role Breadth Self-Efficacy: The Roles of Job Enrichment and Other Organizational Interventions," *Journal of Applied Psychology* 83 (1998), 835–852.
11. P. P. F. M. Kuijer, B. Visser, and H. C. G. Kemper, "Job Rotation as a Factor in Reducing Physical Workload at a Refuse Collecting Department," *Ergonomics* 42 (1999), 1167–1178; C. Gaudart, "Conditions for Maintaining Aging Operators at Work—A Case Study Conducted at an Automobile Manufacturing Plant," *Applied Ergonomics* 31 (2000), 453–462; A. Mikkelsen and P. O. Saksvik, "Impact of a Participatory Organizational Intervention on Job Characteristics and Job Stress," *International Journal of Health Services* 29 (1999), 871–893; R. W. Griffin, *Task Design: An Integrative Approach* (Glenview, IL: Scott, Foresman, 1982), p. 25.
12. F. Herzberg, B. Mausner, and B. B. Snyderman, *The Motivation to Work* (New York: Wiley, 1959).
13. For example, see R. J. House and L. A. Wigdor, "Herzberg's Dual-Factor Theory of Job Satisfaction and Motivation: A Review of the Empirical Evidence and a Criticism," *Personnel Psychology* 20 (1967), 369–389; M. D. Dunnette, J. P. Campbell, and M. D. Hakel, "Factors Contributing to Job Dissatisfaction in Six Occupational Groups," *Organizational Behavior and Human Performance* 2 (1967), 146–164; J. Schneider and E. A. Locke, "A Critique of Herzberg's Classification System and a Suggested Revision," *Organizational Behavior and Human Performance* 6 (1971), 441–458; D. P. Schwab and L. L. Cummings, "Theories of Performance and Satisfaction: A Review," *Industrial Relations* 9 (1970), 408–430; R. J. Caston and R. Braito, "A Specification Issue in Job Satisfaction Research," *Sociological Perspectives* 28 (1985), 175–197.
14. Griffin, *Task Design;* also see J. R. Hackman, "On the Coming Demise of Job Enrichment," in E. L. Cass and F. G. Zimmer, eds., *Man and Work in Society,* (New York: Van Nostrand, 1975), pp. 45–63.
15. J. R. Hackman and G. R. Oldham, *Work Redesign* (Reading, MA: Addison-Wesley, 1980); J. R. Hackman and G. R. Oldham, "Motivation through the Design of Work: Test of a Theory," *Organizational Behavior and Human Performance* 16 (1976), 250–279; K. H. Roberts and W. H. Glick, "The Job Characteristics Approach to

Task Design: A Critical Review," *Journal of Applied Psychology* 86 (1981), 193–217; R. J. Aldag, S. H. Barr, and A. P. Brief, "Measurement of Perceived Task Characteristics," *Psychological Bulletin* 99 (1981), 415–431; Y. Fried and G. R. Ferris, "The Validity of the Job Characteristics Model: A Review and Meta-Analysis," *Personnel Psychology* 40 (1987), 287–322; B. T. Loher, R. A. Noe, N. L. Moeller, and M. P. Fitzgerald, "A Meta-Analysis of the Relation of Job Characteristics to Job Satisfaction," *Journal of Applied Psychology* 70 (1985), 280–289.

16. Hackman and Oldham, "Motivation through the Design of Work," pp. 256–257.

17. R. A. Katzell, P. Bienstock, and P. H. Faerstein, *A Guide to Worker Productivity Experiments in the United States 1971–1975* (New York: New York University Press, 1977), p. 14; E. A. Locke, D. B. Feren, V. M. McCaleb, K. N. Shaw, and A. T. Denny, "The Relative Effectiveness of Four Methods of Motivating Employee Performance," in K. D. Duncan, M. M. Gruneberg, and D. Wallis, eds., *Changes in Working Life* (London: Wiley, 1980), pp. 363–388; and R. E. Kopelman, "Job Redesign and Productivity: A Review of the Evidence," *National Productivity Review* 4 (1985), 237–255.

18. K. Kelly, "The New Soul of John Deere," *Business Week,* January 31, 1994, pp. 64–66.

19. E. L. Trist and K. W. Bamforth, "Some Social and Psychological Consequences of the Longwall Method of Coal-Getting," *Human Relations* 4 (1951), 3–38.

20. Adapted from F. E. Emery and E. Thorsrud, *Democracy at Work: The Report of the Norwegian Industrial Democracy Program* (Leiden, Netherlands: H. E. Stenfert Kroese, 1976), p. 14.

21. D. Jenkins, trans., *Job Reform in Sweden: Conclusions from 500 Shop Floor Projects* (Stockholm: Swedish Employers' Confederation, 1975), pp. 63–64.

22. Apparently, the motivational effects of Hackman–Oldham enrichment grow stronger over time, as a study by Griffin indicated that productivity increased over the course of four years. However, the same study suggested that initial improvements in satisfaction triggered by Hackman–Oldham enrichment may disappear over the same period of time. See R. W. Griffin, "Effects of Work Redesign on Employee Perceptions, Attitudes, and Behaviors: A Long-Term Investigation," *Academy of Management Journal* 34 (1991), 425–435.

23. Studies that have confirmed the existence of five distinct characteristics include R. Katz, "Job Longevity as a Situational Factor in Job Satisfaction," *Administrative Science Quarterly* 23 (1978), 204–223; R. Lee and A. R. Klein, "Structure of the Job Diagnostic Survey for Public Service Organizations," *Journal of Applied Psychology* 67 (1982), 515–519. Studies that have failed to reveal confirmatory evidence include R. B. Dunham, "The Measurement and Dimensionality of Job Characteristics," *Journal of Applied Psychology* 61 (1976), 404–409; J. Gaines and J. M. Jermier, "Functional Exhaustion in a High Stress Organization," *Academy of Management Journal* 26 (1983), 567–586; J. L. Pierce and R. B. Dunham, "The Measurement of Perceived Job Characteristics: The Job Diagnostic Survey vs. the Job Characteristics Inventory," *Academy of Management Journal* 21 (1978), 123–128; D. M. Rousseau, "Technological Differences in Job Characteristics, Job Satisfaction, and Motivation: A Synthesis of Job Design Research and Sociotechnical Systems Theory," *Organizational Behavior and Human Performance* 19 (1977), 18–42.

24. Objectivity is suggested by studies such as R. W. Griffin, "A Longitudinal Investigation of Task Characteristics Relationships," *Academy of Management Journal* 42 (1981), 99–113; E. F. Stone and L. W. Porter, "Job Characteristics and Job Attitudes: A Multivariate Study," *Journal of Applied Psychology* 60 (1975), 57–64; and C. T. Kulik, G. R. Oldham, and P. H. Langner, "Measurement of Job Characteristics: Comparison of the Original and the Revised Job Diagnostic Survey," *Journal of Applied Psychology* 73 (1988), 462–466. Other studies that seem to support the subjectivity side of the argument include A. P. Brief and R. J. Aldag, "The Job Characteristic Inventory: An Examination," *Academy of Management Journal* 21 (1978), 659–670; P. H. Birnbaum, J. L. Farh, and G. Y. Y. Wong, "The Job Characteristics Model in Hong Kong," *Journal of Applied Psychology* 71 (1986), 598–605.

25. G. R. Salancik and J. Pfeffer, "A Social Information Processing Approach to Job Attitudes and Task Design," *Administrative Science Quarterly* 23 (1978), 224–253; C. S. Wong, C. Hui, and K. S. Law, "A Longitudinal Study of the Job Perception–Job Satisfaction Relationship: A Test of the Three Alternative Specifications," *Journal of Occupational and Organizational Psychology* 71 (1998), 127–146.

26. A. P. Brief and R. J. Aldag, "Employee Reactions to Job Characteristics: A Constructive Replication," *Journal of Applied Psychology* 60 (1975), 182–186; and H. P. Sims and A. D. Szilagyi, "Job

Characteristic Relationships: Individual and Structural Moderators," *Organizational Behavior and Human Performance* 17 (1976), 211–230.

27. R. E. Walton, "From Control to Commitment in the Workplace," *Harvard Business Review* 63 (1985), 76–84; J. C. Taylor and D. F. Felten, *Performance by Design: Sociotechnical Systems in North America* (Englewood Cliffs, NJ: Prentice Hall, 1993).

28. A. H. van de Zwaan and J. De Vries, "A Critical Assessment of the Modern Sociotechnical Approach within Production and Operations Management," *International Journal of Production Research* 38 (2000), 1755–1767; C. W. Clegg, "Sociotechnical Principles for System Design," *Applied Ergonomics* 31 (2000), 463–477; J. L. Cordery, W. S. Mueller, and L. M. Smith, "Attitudinal and Behavioral Effects of Autonomous Group Working: A Longitudinal Field Study," *Academy of Management Journal* 34 (1991), 464–476; C. A. Pearson, "Autonomous Work Groups: An Evaluation at an Industrial Site," *Human Relations* 45 (1992), 905–936.

29. T. A. Lowe and J. M. Mazzoo, "Three Preachers, One Religion," *Quality* 25 (1986), 32–37; see also W. E. Deming, *Out of the Crisis* (Cambridge, MA: MIT Center for Advanced Engineering Study, 1986); P. B. Crosby, *Quality Is Free* (New York: McGraw-Hill, 1979); and J. M. Juran, *Juran on Leadership for Quality* (New York: Free Press, 1989).

30. R. J. Schonberger, "Is Strategy Strategic? Impact of Total Quality Management on Strategy," *Academy of Management Executive* 6 (1992), 80–87; J. W. Dean, Jr., and J. R. Evans, *Total Quality: Management, Organization, and Strategy* (St. Paul, MN: West, 1994); J. D. Westphal, R. Gulati, and S. M Shortell, "Customization or Conformity? An Institutional and Network Perspective on the Content and Consequences of TQM Adoption," *Administrative Science Quarterly* 42 (1997), 366–394.

31. R. Blackburn and B. Rosen, "Total Quality and Human Resources Management: Lessons Learned from Baldridge Award–Winning Companies," *Academy of Management Executive* 7 (1993), 49–66.

32. W. L. Mohr and H. Mohr, *Quality Circles: Changing Images of People at Work* (Reading, MA: Addison-Wesley, 1983), p. 13.

33. D. L. Dewar, *The Quality Circle Handbook* (Red Bluff, CA: Quality Circle Institute, 1980), pp. 17–104.

34. G. R. Ferris and J. A. Wagner III, "Quality Circles in the United States: A Conceptual Reevaluation," *Journal of Applied Behavioral Science* 21 (1985), 155–167.

35. B. R. Lee, "Organization Development and Group Perceptions: A Study of Quality Circles," Ph.D. dissertation, University of Minnesota, 1982; and M. Robson, *Quality Circles: A Practical Guide,* 2nd ed. (Hants, UK: Gower, 1988), pp. 47–62.

36. E. Molleman, "Modalities of Self-Managing Teams—The 'Must,' 'May,' 'Can,' and 'Will' of Local Decision Making," *International Journal of Operations and Productivity Management* 20 (2000), 889–910; C. C. Manz and H. P. Sims, "Leading Workers to Lead Themselves," *Administrative Science Quarterly* 32 (1987), 106–128.

37. A. H. van de Zwaan and E. Molleman, "Self-Organizing Groups: Conditions and Constraints in a Sociotechnical Perspective," *International Journal of Manpower* 19 (1998), 301–329; J. R. Barker, "Tightening the Iron Cage: Concertive Control in Self-Managed Organizations," *Administrative Science Quarterly* 38 (1993), 408–437.

38. M. Hammer and J. Champy, *Reengineering the Corporation: A Manifesto for Business Revolution* (New York: Harper Business, 1993).

39. J. M. Hoc, "From Human–Machine Interaction to Human–Machine Cooperation," *Ergonomics* 43 (2000), 833–843; R. Parasuraman, T. B. Sheridan, and C. D. Wickens, "A Model for Types and Levels of Human Interaction with Automation," *IEEE Transactions on Systems, Man, and Cybernetics Part A—Systems and Humans* 30 (2000), 286–297.

40. S. Baker, "A Surgeon Whose Hands Never Shake," *Business Week,* October 4, 1993, pp. 111–114.

41. D. Sharon, J. Harstein, and G. Yantian, *Robotics and Automated Manufacturing* (London: Pitman, 1987).

42. P. T. Kilborn, "Brave New World Seen for Robots Appears Stalled by Quirks and Costs," *New York Times,* July 1, 1990, p. C7.

43. O. Port, "Brave New Factory," *Business Week,* July 23, 2001, pp. 75–76; R. B. Kurtz, *Toward a New Era in U.S. Manufacturing* (Washington, DC: National Academy Press, 1986), p. 3.

44. A. Aston and M. Arndt, "The Flexible Factory," *Business Week,* May 5, 2003, pp. 90–91; R. Jaikumar, "Postindustrial Manufacturing," *Harvard Business Review* 44 (1986), 69–76.

45. P. Senker, *Towards the Automatic Factory: The Need for Training* (New York: Springer-Verlag, 1986), pp. 27–43.

46. R. P. Steel and R. F. Lloyd, "Cognitive, Affective, and Behavioral Outcomes of Participation in

Quality Circles: Conceptual and Empirical Findings," *Journal of Applied Behavioral Science* 24 (1988), 1–17; H. H. Greenbaum, I. T. Kaplan, and W. Metlay, "Evaluation of Problem Solving Groups: The Case of Quality Circle Programs," *Group and Organization Studies* 13 (1988), 133–147; K. Buch and R. Spangler, "The Effects of Quality Circles on Performance and Promotions," *Human Relations* 43 (1990), 573–582; R. P. Steel, K. R. Jennings, and J. T. Lindsey, "Quality Circle Problem Solving and Common Cents: Evaluation Study Findings from a United States Federal Mint," *Journal of Applied Behavioral Science* 26 (1990), 365–381.

47. J. D. Orsburn, L. Moran, E. Musselwhite, and J. H. Zenger, *Self-Directed Work Teams: The New American Challenge* (Homewood, IL: Irwin, 1990); M. J. Zbaracki, "The Rhetoric and Reality of Total Quality Management," *Administrative Science Quarterly* 43 (1998), 602–636.

48. J. R. Hackman and R. Wageman, "Total Quality Management: Empirical, Conceptual, and Practical Issues," *Administrative Science Quarterly* 40 (1995), 309–342; B. Victor, A. Boynton, and T. Stephens-Jahng, "The Effective Design of Work under Total Quality Management," *Organization Science* 11 (2000), 102–117.

49. P. S. Adler, "Workers and Flexible Manufacturing Systems: Three Installations Compared," *Journal of Organizational Behavior* 12 (1991), 447–460; but see J. W. Dean, Jr., and S. A. Snell, "Integrated Manufacturing and Job Design: Moderating Effects of Organizational Inertia," *Academy of Management Journal* 34 (1991), 776–804.

50. J. W. Dean, Jr., and D. E. Bowen, "Management Theory and Total Quality: Improving Research and Theory through Theory Development," *Academy of Management Review* 19 (1994), 392–419; D. A. Waldman, "The Contributions of Total Quality Management to a Theory of Work Performance," *Academy of Management Review* 19 (1994), 510–536; R. Reed, D. J. Lemak, and J. C. Montgomery, "Beyond Process: TQM Content and Firm Performance," *Academy of Management Review* 21 (1996), 173–202.

Chapter 8

1. W. Zellner, "What Was Don Carty Thinking?" *Business Week,* May 5, 2003, p. 32.

2. C. March, "American bonuses cause outrage," *CNN.com,* April 19, 2003, pp. 1–2.

3. E. Brennan, "American Airlines CEO quits," *CNN.com,* April 25, 2003, pp. 1–2.

4. D. Reed, "New AMR chief hopes worst is past for airline," *USA Today,* May 8, 2003, pp. 1–2.

5. W. Zellner, "Coffee, Tea or Bile? Resentful Airline Workers Could Hobble Turnaround Plans," *Business Week,* June 2, 2003, pp. 56–58.

6. K. D. Doerr, T. R. Mitchell, C. A. Schiesheim, T. Freed, and X. Zhou, "Heterogeneity and Variability in the Context of Flow Lines," *Academy of Management Review* 27 (2002), 594–607.

7. R. Wageman, "Interdependence and Group Effectiveness," *Administrative Science Quarterly* 40 (1995), 145–179.

8. B. J. Biddle, *Role Theory: Expectations, Identities and Behaviors* (New York: Academic Press, 1979), p. 20.

9. D. R. Ilgen and J. R. Hollenbeck, "The Structure of Work: Job Design and Roles," in M. Dunnette, ed., *Handbook of Industrial Organizational Psychology,* (Houston: Consulting Psychologist Press, 1993), pp. 165–207.

10. D. Fanning, "Calling on Secretaries to Fill In the Gaps," *New York Times,* March 11, 1990, p. A12.

11. J. L. Levine, E. T. Higgens, and H. Choi, "Development of Strategic Norms in Groups," *Organizational Behavior and Human Decision Processes* 82 (2000), 88–101.

12. J. R. Hackman, "Toward Understanding the Role of Tasks in Behavioral Research," *Acta Psychologica* 31 (1979), 97–128.

13. D. C. Feldman, "The Development and Enforcement of Group Norms," *Academy of Management Review* 9 (1984), 47–53.

14. E. H. Schein, *Organizational Psychology,* 3rd ed. (Englewood Cliffs, NJ: Prentice Hall, 1980), p. 99.

15. B. Johnson, "25 Ideas for a Changing World," *Business Week,* August 26, 2002, pp. 70–72.

16. J. Useem, "From Heroes to Goats and Back Again: How Corporate Leaders Lost Our Trust," *Fortune,* November 18, 2002, pp. 40–48.

17. A. Borrus, "Executive Pay: Labor Strikes Back," *Business Week,* May 26, 2003, p. 46.

18. J. Cummings, J. Schlesinger, and M. Schoeder, "Bush Crackdown on Business Fraud Is Sure Signal That New Era Is Here," *Wall Street Journal Online,* July 10, 2002, pp. 1–5.

19. A. C. Bluedorn, D. B. Turban, and M. S. Love, "The Effects of Stand-Up and Sit-Down Meeting Formats on Meeting Outcomes," *Journal of Applied Psychology* 84 (1999), 277–285.

20. J. Barker, "Tightening the Iron Cage: Concertive Control in Self-Managing Teams," *Administrative Science Quarterly* 38 (1993), 408–437.

21. C. Shannon and W. Weaver, *The Mathematical Theory of Communication* (Urbana: University of Illinois Press, 1948), p. 17.

22. S. Kiesler and L. Sproull, "Group Decision Making and Communication Technology," *Organiza-*

tional Behavior and Human Decision Processes 52 (1992), 96–123.

23. J. Webster and L. K. Trevino, "Rational and Social Theories of Communication Media Choices: Two Policy-Capturing Studies," *Academy of Management Journal* 38 (1995), 1544–1572.

24. S. P. Weisband, S. K. Schneider, and T. Connolly, "Computer-Mediated Communication and Social Information: Status Salience and Status Differences," *Academy of Management Journal* 38 (1995), 1124–1151.

25. B. Ziegler, "Going Wireless," *Business Week,* April 5, 1993, pp. 56–60.

26. H. Mintzberg, *The Nature of Managerial Work* (New York: Harper & Row, 1973), p. 22.

27. S. McGinty, "How You Speak Shows Where You Rank," *Fortune,* February 2, 1998, p. 156.

28. N. Varchaver, "The Perils of Email," *Fortune,* February 17, 2003, pp. 96–102.

29. C. Gasparino, "How a String of E-mail Came to Haunt CSFB, Star Banker," *Wall Street Journal Online,* February 28, 2003, pp. 1–6.

30. C. M. Solomon, "Communicating in a Global Environment," *Workforce,* November 1999, pp. 50–55.

31. J. T. Gullahorn, "District and Friendship as Factors in the Gross Interaction Matrix," *Sociometry* 15 (1952), 123–124.

32. P. Wilson, "White House Acknowledges Iraq Uranium Claim Wrong," *USA Today,* July 8, 2003, p. 1.

33. A. S. Tsui, "A Role Set Analysis of Managerial Reputation," *Organizational Behavior and Human Decision Processes* 34 (1984), 64–96.

34. M. Conlin, "CEO Coaches," *Business Week,* November 11, 2002, pp. 98–104.

35. J. W. Smither, "Can Working with an Executive Coach Improve Multisource Feedback Ratings over Time? A Quasi-Experimental Field Study," *Personnel Psychology,* 56 (2003), 23–44.

36. J. Van Maanen and E. H. Schein, "Toward a Theory of Organizational Socialization," in B. Staw and L. L. Cummings, eds., *Research in Organizational Behavior* (Greenwich, CT: JAI Press, 1979), pp. 209–264.

37. Schein, *Organizational Psychology,* pp. 111–133.

38. S. Davis, "Minority Execs Want an Even Break," *Workforce,* April 2000, pp. 50–55.

39. A. L. Kristof-Brown, "Perceived Applicant Fit: Distinguishing between Recruiters' Perceptions of Person–Job and Person–Organization Fit," *Personnel Psychology* 53 (2000), 643–671.

40. C. E. Lance, R. J. Vandenberg, and R. M. Self, "Latent Growth Models of Individual Change: The Case of Newcomer Adjustment," *Organizational Behavior and Human Decision Processes* 83 (2000), 107–140.

41. G. Blau, "Early-Career Job Factors Influencing the Professional Commitment of Medical Technologists," *Academy of Management Journal* 43 (2000), 687–695.

42. J. W. Verity, "Deconstructing the Computer Industry," *Business Week,* November 23, 1992, pp. 90–100.

43. C. Ostroff and S. W. J. Kozlowski, "Organizational Socialization as a Learning Process: The Role of Information Acquisition," *Personnel Psychology* 45 (1992), 849–874.

44. F. Coleman, "Colonial Grunts No Longer," *U.S. News & World Report,* November 1, 1993, pp. 74–76.

45. D. Porch, *The French Foreign Legion: A Complete History of a Legendary Fighting Force* (New York: Harper Collins, 1991).

46. B. E. Ashforth and A. M. Saks, "Socialization Tactics: Longitudinal Effects on Newcomer Adjustment," *Academy of Management Journal* 39 (1996), 149–178.

47. C. R. Wanberg and J. D. Kammeyer-Mueller, "Predictors and Outcomes of Proactivity in the Socialization Process," *Journal of Applied Psychology* 85 (2000), 373–385.

48. E. W. Morrison, "Newcomers' Relationships: The Role of Social Network Ties during Socialization," *Academy of Management Journal* 45 (2002), 1149–1160.

49. H. J. Klein and N. A. Weaver, "The Effectiveness of an Organizational-Level Orientation Program in the Socialization of New Hires," *Personnel Psychology* 53 (2000), 47–66.

50. D. A. Hofmann and F. P. Morgeson, "Safety Related Behavior as a Social Exchange: The Role of Perceived Organizational Support and Leader–Member Exchange," *Journal of Applied Psychology* 84 (1999), 286–296.

51. D. Faust, "A Battle Royal against Regal Paychecks," *Business Week,* February 24, 2003, p. 127.

52. M. J. Gelfand, "Culture and Egocentric Perceptions of Fairness in Conflict and Negotiation," *Journal of Applied Psychology,* 87 (2002), 833–845.

53. D. P. Skarlicki and R. Folger, "Retaliation in the Workplace: The Roles of Distributive, Procedural, and Interactive Justice," *Journal of Applied Psychology* 82 (1997), 434–443.

54. M. A. Korsgaard, S. E. Brodt, and E. M. Whitener, "Trust in the Face of Conflict: The Role of Managerial Trustworthy Behavior and Organizational Context," *Journal of Applied Psychology* 87 (2002), 312–319.

55. Q. M. Robinson, N. A. Moye, and E. A. Locke, "Identifying a Missing Link between Participation

and Satisfaction: The Mediating Role of Procedural Justice Perceptions," *Journal of Applied Psychology* 84 (1999), 585–593.

56. S. J. Wayne, L. M. Shore, W. H. Bommer, and L. E. Tetrick, "The Role of Fair Treatment and Rewards in Perceptions of Organizational Support and Leader-Member Exchange," *Journal of Applied Psychology* 87 (2002), 590–598.

57. B. J. Tepper and E. C. Taylor, "Relationships among Supervisors' and Subordinates' Procedural Justice Perceptions and Organizational Citizenship Behaviors," *Journal of Applied Psychology* 46 (2003), 97–105.

58. J. A. Colquitt, R. A. Noe, and C. L. Jackson, "Justice in Teams: Antecedents and Consequences of Procedural Justice Climate," *Personnel Psychology* 55 (2002), 83–109.

59. M. Ambrose and M. Schminke, "Organization Structure as a Moderator of the Relationship between Procedural Justice, Interactional Justice, Perceived Organizational Support, and Supervisory Trust," *Journal of Applied Psychology* 88 (2003), 295–305.

60. M. C. Kernan and P. J. Hanges, "Survivor Reactions to Reorganization: Antecedents and Consequences of Procedural, Interpersonal, and Informational Justice," *Journal of Applied Psychology* 87 (2002), 916–928.

61. R. C. Mayer and J. H. Davis, "The Effect of the Performance Appraisal System on Trust for Management: A Quasi-Experiment," *Journal of Applied Psychology* 85 (2000), 123–136.

62. T. A. Stewart, "Whom Can You Trust? It's Not Easy to Tell," *Fortune,* June 12, 2000, pp. 331–334.

63. K. T. Dirks, "The Effects of Interpersonal Trust on Work Group Performance," *Journal of Applied Psychology* 84 (1999), 445–455.

64. S. E. Naumann and N. Bennett, "A Case for Procedural Justice Climate: Development and Test of a Multilevel Model," *Academy of Management Journal* 43 (2000), 81–89.

65. D. P. Skarlicki, R. Folger, and P. Tesluk, "Personality as a Moderator in the Relationship Between Fairness and Retaliation," *Academy of Management Journal* 42 (1999), 100–108.

66. M. A. Korsgaard, D. M. Schweiger, and H. J. Sapienza, "Building Commitment, Attachment, and Trust in Strategic Decision-Making Teams: The Role of Procedural Justice," *Academy of Management Journal* 38 (1995), 60–84.

67. C. Vinzant, "Messing with the Boss's Head," *Fortune,* May 1, 2000, pp. 329–331.

68. M. L. Ambrose, M. A. Seabright, and M. Schminke, "Sabotage in the Workplace: The Role of Organizational Justice," *Organizational Behavior and Human Performance* 89 (2002), 947–965.

69. M. R. Forehand, "Extending Overjustification: The Effect of Perceived Reward-Giver Intention on Responses to Rewards," *Journal of Applied Psychology* 85 (2000), 919–931.

70. M. Borden, "It's the Manager, Stupid," *Fortune,* October 25, 1999, pp. 366–368.

71. S. M. Lilienthal, "What Do Departing Workers Really Think of Your Company," *Workforce,* October 2000, pp. 71–85.

72. M. France, "The Mea Culpa Defense," *Business Week,* August 26, 2002, pp. 76–78.

Chapter 9

1. D. Heymann, "Taiwan, Last SARS Hotspot Is Removed from List by WHO," *Wall Street Journal Online,* July 5, 2003, p. 1.

2. M. Pottinger, E. Cherney, G. Naik, and M. Waldholz, "How a Global Effort Identified SARS Virus in a Matter of Weeks," *Wall Street Journal Online,* April 16, 2003, pp. 1–5.

3. D. Jones, "Affitech, Viventia Plan Research Collaboration," *Wall Street Journal Online,* June 23, 2003, p. 1.

4. F. Keenan and S. Ante, "The New Teamwork," *Business Week,* February 18, 2002, pp. 12–16.

5. K. Kelly, "The Drought Is Over at 3M," *Business Week,* November 7, 1994, pp. 140–141; T. A. Stewart and M. Warner, "3M Fights Back," *Fortune,* February 5, 1996, pp. 94–99.

6. S. Sherman, "Secrets of HP's 'Muddled' Team," *Fortune,* March 18, 1996, pp. 116–120.

7. P. Strozniak, "Small Company Executives Tell How Team Development Improves Productivity and Profits," *Industry Week,* September 18, 2000, pp. 21–23.

8. S. Sherman, "Levi's: As Ye Sew, So Shall Ye Reap," *Fortune,* May 12, 1997, pp. 104–116.

9. R. T. King, "Levi's Factory Workers Are Assigned to Teams, and Morale Takes a Hit," *The Wall Street Journal,* May 20, 1998, pp. A1–A6.

10. G. C. Homans, *The Human Group* (New York: Harcourt, Brace, Jovanovich, 1950), p. 1; M. E. Shaw, *Group Dynamics: The Psychology of Small Group Behavior* (New York: McGraw-Hill, 1981), p. 8; D. L. Gladstein, "Groups in Context: A Model of Task Group Effectiveness," *Administrative Science Quarterly* 29 (1984), 499–517.

11. D. Cartwright and A. Zander, *Group Dynamics: Research and Theory* (New York: Harper & Row, 1968), pp. 46–48.

12. K. L. Bettenhausen, "Five Years of Group Research: What We Have Learned and What

Needs to Be Addressed," *Journal of Management* 17 (1991), 345–381.

13. D. A. Nadler, J. R. Hackman, and E. E. Lawler III, *Managing Organizational Behavior* (Boston: Little, Brown, 1979), pp. 136–137.

14. S. L. Bernman, J. Down, and C. W. Hill, "Tacit Knowledge as a Source of Competitive Advantage in the National Basketball Association," *Academy of Management Journal* 45 (2002), 13–31.

15. H. Mintzberg, *The Structuring of Organizations* (Englewood Cliffs, NJ: Prentice Hall, 1979), pp. 108–129.

16. J. R. Hollenbeck, H. Moon, A. P. Ellis, B. J. West, D. R. Ilgen, L. Sheppard, C. O. Porter, and J. A. Wagner, "Structural Contingency Theory and Individual Differences: Examination of External and Internal Person-Environment Fit," *Journal of Applied Psychology* 87 (2002), 509–606.

17. B. W. Tuckman, "Developmental Sequence in Small Groups," *Psychological Bulletin* 63 (1965), 384–399.

18. M. Booth-Butterfield, S. Booth-Butterfield, and J. Koester, "The Function of Uncertainty Reduction in Alleviating Tension in Small Groups," *Communication Research Reports* 5 (1988), 146–153.

19. K. L. Bettenhausen and J. K. Murnighan, "The Emergence of Norms in Competitive Decision-Making Groups," *Administrative Science Quarterly* 30 (1985), 350–372; C. J. Gersick, "Time and Transition in Work Teams: Toward a New Model of Group Development," *Academy of Management Journal* 31 (1988), 9–41; C. J. Gersick, "Marking Time: Predictable Transitions in Task Groups," *Academy of Management Journal* 32 (1989), 274–309.

20. A. Chang, P. Bordia, and J. Duck, "Punctuated Equilibrium and Linear Progression: Toward a New Understanding of Group Development" *Academy of Management Journal* 46 (2003), 106–117.

21. G. R. Ferris and J. A. Wagner III, "Quality Circles in the United States: A Conceptual Reevaluation," *Journal of Applied Behavioral Science* 21 (1985), 155–167.

22. G. W. Hill, "Group versus Individual Performance: Are N + 1 Heads Better Than One?" *Psychological Bulletin* 9 (1982), 517–539.

23. I. D. Steiner, *Group Processes and Productivity* (New York: Academic Press, 1972). We use the term *process loss* somewhat more broadly than Steiner, applying it to all decrements in group productivity.

24. M. Diehl and W. Stroebe, "Productivity Loss in Brainstorming Groups: Toward the Solution of a Riddle," *Journal of Personality and Social Psychology* 53 (1987), 497–509.

25. K. Benne and P. Sheats, "Functional Roles of Group Members," *Journal of Social Issues* 2 (1948), 42–47.

26. B. Latané, K. Williams, and S. Harkins, "Many Hands Make Light Work: The Causes and Consequences of Social Loafing," *Journal of Personality and Social Psychology* 37 (1979), 822–832; A. Shepperd, "Productivity Loss in Performance Groups: A Motivation Analysis," *Psychological Bulletin* 113 (1993), 67–81.

27. M. Olson, *The Logic of Collective Action* (Cambridge, MA: Harvard University Press, 1965), p. 11. See also R. Albanese and D. D. Van Fleet, "Rational Behavior in Groups: The Free-Riding Tendency," *Academy of Management Review* 10 (1985), 244–255.

28. C. L. Jackson and J. A. LePine, "Peer Responses to a Team's Weakest Link: A Test and Extension of LePine and Van Dyne's Model," *Journal of Applied Psychology* 88 (2003), 459–475.

29. B. Beersma, J. R. Hollenbeck, S. E. Humphrey, H. Moon, D. E. Conlon, and D. R. Ilgen, "Cooperation, Competition, and Team Performance: Towards a Contingency Approach," *Academy of Management Journal*, in press.

30. L. Harrison, "We're All the Boss," *Time*, April 17, 2002, pp. 41–43.

31. G, Khan, "For New Balance, a Surprise: China Partner Became Rival," *Wall Street Journal Online*, December 19, 2002, pp. 1–6.

32. T. Becker, "Telecom Forgers Slip Fakes across Oceans to Store Shelves," *Wall Street Journal Online*, July 3, 2003, pp. 1–4.

33. G. L. Stewart and M. R. Barrick, "Team Structure and Performance: Assessing the Mediating Role of Intrateam Process and the Moderating Role of Task Type," *Academy of Management Journal* 43 (2000), 135–148.

34. J. W. Bishop and K. D. Scott, "An Examination of Organizational and Team Commitment in a Self-Directed Team Environment," *Journal of Applied Psychology* 85 (2000), 439–450.

35. M. Marks, M. J. Sabella, C. S. Burke, and S. J. Zaccaro, "The Impact of Cross-Training on Team Effectiveness," *Journal of Applied Psychology* 87 (2002), 3–13.

36. J. S. Bunderson and K. M. Sutcliffe, "Comparing Alternative Conceptualizations of Functional Diversity in Management Teams: Process and Performance Effects," *Academy of Management Journal*, 45 (2002), 875–893.

37. A. Erez, J. A. LePine, and H. Elms, "Effects of Rotated Leadership and Peer Evaluations on the Functioning and Effectiveness of Self-Managed Teams: A Quasi-Experiment," *Personnel Psychology* 55 (2000), 929–948.

38. I. D. Steiner, *Group Processes and Productivity* (New York: Academic Press, 1972).

39. J. A. LePine, J. R. Hollenbeck, D. R. Ilgen, and J. Hedlund, "Effects of Individual Differences on the Performance of Hierarchical Decision-Making Teams: Much More Than 'g,'" *Journal of Applied Psychology* 82 (1997), 803–811.

40. A. Bavelas and D. Barrett, "An Experimental Approach to Organizational Communication," *Personnel* 27 (1951), 366–371.

41. J. A Wagner III and R. Z. Gooding, "Shared Influence and Organizational Behavior: A Meta-Analysis of Situational Factors Expected to Moderate Participation–Outcome Relationships," *Academy of Management Journal* 30 (1987), 524–541.

42. S. W. Lester, B. M. Meglino, M. A. Korsgaard, "The Antecedents and Consequences of Group Potency: A Longitudinal Investigation of Newly Formed Groups," *Academy of Management Journal* 45 (2002), 352–368.

43. R. Z. Gooding and J. A. Wagner III, "A Meta-Analytic Review of the Relationship between Size and Performance: The Productivity and Efficiency of Organizations and Their Subunits," *Administrative Science Quarterly* 30 (1985), 462–481.

44. J. A. Fleishman, "Collective Action as Helping Behavior: Effects of Responsibility Diffusion on Contributions to a Public Good," *Journal of Personality and Social Psychology* 38 (1980), 629–637; G. R. Jones, "Task Visibility, Free Riding, and Shirking: Explaining the Effect of Structure and Technology on Employee Behavior," *Academy of Management Review* 9 (1984), 684–695.

45. J. George, "Extrinsic and Intrinsic Origins of Perceived Social Loafing in Organizations," *Academy of Management Journal* 43 (2000), 81–92.

46. T. Simons, L. H. Pelled, and K. A. Smith, "Making Use of Difference: Diversity, Debate, and Decision Comprehensiveness in Top Management Teams," *Academy of Management Journal* 42 (1999), 662–673.

47. R. L. Moreland and L. Myaskovsky, "Exploring the Performance Benefits of Group Training: Transactive Memory or Improved Communication," *Organizational Behavior and Human Decision Processes* 82 (2000), 117–133.

48. D. H. Gruenfeld, P. V. Martorana, and E. T. Fan, "What Do Groups Learn from Their Worldliest Members? Direct and Indirect Influence in Dynamic Teams," *Organizational Behavior and Human Decision Processes* 82 (2000), 45–59.

49. M. R. Barrick, G. L. Stewart, M. J. Neubert, and M. K. Mount, "Relating Member Ability and Personality to Work-Team Effectiveness," *Journal of Applied Psychology* 83 (1998), 377–391.

50. C. O. Porter, J. R. Hollenbeck, D. R. Ilgen, A. P. Ellis, B. J. West, and H. Moon, "Backing Up Behaviors in Teams: The Role of Personality and Legitimacy of Need," *Journal of Applied Psychology* 88 (2003), 391–403.

51. D. A. Harrison, K. H. Price, J. H. Gavin, and A. T. Florey, "Time, Teams, and Task Performance; Changing Effects of Surface- and Deep-Level Diversity on Group Functioning," *Academy of Management Journal* 45 (2002), 1029–1045.

52. M. Maynord, "Amid the Turmoil, a Rare Success at DaimlerChrysler," *Fortune*, January 22, 2001, pp. 112C–112P.

53. P. C. Earley and E. Mosakowski, "Creating Hybrid Cultures: An Empirical Test of Transnational Team Functioning," *Academy of Management Journal* 43 (2000), 26–49.

54. J. A. LePine, J. R. Hollenbeck, D. R. Ilgen, and A. Ellis, "Gender Composition, Situational Strength, and Team Decision-Making Accuracy: A Criterion Decomposition Approach," *Organizational Behavior and Human Decision Processes* 88 (2002), 445–475.

55. J. Orasanu and E. Salas, "Team Decision Making in Complex Environments," in G. Klein, J. Orasanu, R. Calderwood, and C. Szambok, eds., *Decision-Making in Action: Models and Methods* (Wildwood, NJ: Ablex, 1993).

56. J. E. Mathieu, T. S. Heffner, G. F. Goodwin, E. Salas, and J. A. Cannon-Bowers, "The Influence of Shared Mental Models on Team Process and Performance," *Journal of Applied Psychology* 85 (2000), 273–283.

57. P. J. Hinds, K. M. Carley, D. Krackhardt, and D. Wholey, "Choosing Work Group Members: Balancing Similarity, Competence, and Familiarity," *Organizational Behavior and Human Decision Processes* 81 (2000), 226–251.

58. E. London, "Scientists: Opposites Don't Attract," *CNN.com,* July 1, 2003, p. 1.

59. B. H. Raven and J. Reitsema, "The Effects of Varied Clarity of Group Goals and Group Path on the Individual and His Relation to the Group," *Human Relations* 10 (1957), 29–44.

60. J. E. Sawyer, W. R. Latham, R. D. Pritchard, and W. R. Bennett, "Analysis of Work Group Productivity in an Applied Setting: Application of a Time Series Panel Design," *Personnel Psychology* 52 (2000), 927–968.

61. K. G. Smith, E. A. Locke, and D. Berry, "Goal Setting, Planning and Organizational Performance: An Experimental Simulation," *Organiza-*

tional Behavior and Human Decision Processes 46 (1990), 118–134.

62. L. R. Weingart, "Impact of Group Goals, Task Component Complexity, Effort, and Planning on Group Performance," *Journal of Applied Psychology* 77 (1992), 682–693.

63. M. J. Waller, M. E. Zellmer-Bruhn, and R. C. Giambatista, "Watching the Clock: Group Pacing Behavior under Dynamic Deadlines," *Academy of Management Journal* 45 (2002), 1046–1055.

64. M. Deutsch, *The Resolution of Conflict: Constructive and Destructive Processes* (New Haven, CT: Yale University Press, 1973), p. 325.

65. R. Wageman, "Interdependence and Group Effectiveness," *Administrative Science Quarterly* 40 (1995), 145–180.

66. Beersma et al., "Cooperation, Competition, and Team Performance."

67. R. A. Henry, J. Kmet, E. Desrosiers, and A. Landa, "Examining the Impact of Interpersonal Cohesiveness on Group Accuracy Interventions: The Importance of Matching versus Buffering," *Organizational Behavior and Human Decision Processes* 87 (2002), 25–43.

68. Shaw, *Group Dynamics*, p. 197; D. Cartwright, "The Nature of Group Cohesiveness," in D. Cartwright and A. Zander, eds., *Group Dynamics*, 3rd ed. (New York: Harper & Row, 1968), pp. 91–109.

69. L. Berkowitz, "Group Standards, Cohesiveness, and Productivity," *Human Relations* 7 (1954), 509–519.

70. P. E. Tesluk and J. E. Mathieu, "Overcoming Roadblocks to Effectiveness: Incorporating Management of Performance Barriers into Models of Work Group Effectiveness," *Journal of Applied Psychology* 84 (1990), 200–217.

71. M. E. Turner and A. R. Pratkanis, "Twenty-Five Years of Groupthink Theory and Research: Lessons from the Evaluation of a Theory," *Organizational Behavior and Human Decision Processes* 73 (1998), 105–115.

72. S. Alper, D. Tjosvold, and K. S. Law, "Conflict Management, Efficacy and Performance in Organizational Teams," *Personnel Psychology* 52 (2000), 625–642.

73. T. L. Simons and R. S. Peterson, "Task Conflict and Relationship Conflict in Top Management Teams: The Pivotal Role of Trust," *Journal of Applied Psychology* 85 (2000), 102–111.

74. R. S. Dooley and G. E. Fryxell, "Attaining Decision Quality and Commitment from Dissent: The Moderating Effects of Loyalty and Competence in Strategic Decision Making Teams," *Academy of Management Journal* 42 (1999), 389–402.

75. S. Schultz-Hardt, M. Jochims, and D. Frey, "Productive Conflict in Group Decision Making: Genuine and Contrived Dissent as Strategies to Counteract Biased Information Seeking," *Organizational Behavior and Human Decision Processes* 88 (2002), 563–586.

Chapter 10

1. A. Gabor, "Challenging a Corporate Addiction to Outsiders," *New York Times*, November 17, 2002, pp. A1–A5.

2. D. Foust, "What Worked at GE Isn't Working at Home Depot," *Business Week*, January 27, 2003, p. 40.

3. D. Morse, "Home Depot Is Struggling to Adjust to New Blueprint," *Wall Street Journal Online*, January 17, 2003, pp. 1–5.

4. S. Caudron, "The Looming Leadership Crisis," *Workforce*, September 1999, pp. 72–79.

5. J. A. Byrne, "Wanted: A Few Good CEOs," *Business Week*, August 11, 1997, p. 97.

6. E. Ahlberg, "Conseco Chairman Says Loan Program Put Turnaround at Risk," *Wall Street Journal Online*, July 9, 2003, pp. 1–2.

7. C. Hymowitz, "How a 3M Leader Managed to Get His Employees to Back Big Changes," *Wall Street Journal Online*, April 23, 2002, pp. 1–2.

8. S. Caudron, "Where Have All the Leaders Gone," *Workforce*, December 2002, pp. 29–31.

9. J. R. Meindl and S. B. Ehrlich, "The Romance of Leadership and the Evaluation of Organizational Performance," *Academy of Management Journal* 30 (1987), 91–109.

10. A. Jago, "Leadership: Perspectives in Theory and Research," *Management Sciences* 28 (1982), 315–336.

11. H. Mintzberg, *The Nature of Managerial Work* (New York: Harper & Row, 1973).

12. E. P. Hollander, *Leadership Dynamics* (New York: Free Press, 1978).

13. H. Donovan, "Managing Your Intellectuals," *Fortune*, October 29, 1989, pp. 177–180.

14. G. Yukl, *Leadership in Organizations* (Englewood Cliffs, NJ: Prentice Hall, 1981), p. 71.

15. A. S. Tsui, S. J. Ashford, L. St. Clair, and K. R. Xin, "Dealing with Discrepant Expectations: Response Strategies and Managerial Effectiveness," *Academy of Management Journal* 38 (1995), 1515–1543.

16. R. Karlgaard, "An Interview with Bill Gates," *Forbes*, December 11, 1992, pp. 63–74.

17. R. M. Stodgill, *Handbook of Leadership* (New York: Free Press, 1974), p. 112.

18. R. Katz, "Skills of an Effective Administrator," *Harvard Business Review* 72 (1974), 90–101.

19. T. A. Judge, J. E. Bono, R. Ilies, and M. W. Gerhart, "Personality and Leadership: A Qualitative and Quantitative Review," *Journal of Applied Psychology* 87 (2002), 765–780.

20. B. J. Avolio, J. M. Howell, and J. J. Sosik, "A Funny Thing Happened on the Way to the Bottom Line: Humor as a Moderator of Leadership Style Effects," *Academy of Management Journal* 42 (1999), 219–227.

21. K. Lewin, R. Lippitt, and R. K. White, "Patterns of Aggressive Behavior in Experimentally Created Social Climates," *Journal of Social Psychology* 10 (1939), 271–301.

22. D. B. Welsh, F. Luthans, and S. M. Summer, "Managing Russian Factory Workers: The Impact of U.S.-Based Behavioral and Participative Techniques," *Academy of Management Journal* 36 (1993), 58–79.

23. R. Buckman, "Microsoft Tries to Outgrow the Bill and Steve Show," *Wall Street Journal Online,* April 8, 2002, pp. 1–3.

24. R. Likert, *New Patterns of Management* (New York: McGraw-Hill, 1961), p. 36.

25. N. C. Morse and E. Reimer, "The Experimental Change of a Major Organizational Variable," *Journal of Abnormal and Social Psychology* 52 (1956), 120–129.

26. R. M. Stodgill and A. E. Coons, *Leader Behavior: Its Description and Measurement* (Columbus: Ohio State University, Bureau of Business Research, 1957), p. 75.

27. P. Weissenberg and M. H. Kavanaugh, "The Independence of Initiating Structure and Consideration: A Review of the Evidence," *Personnel Psychology* 25 (1972), 119–130.

28. R. Blake and J. S. Mouton, *The Managerial Grid III: The Key to Leadership Excellence* (Houston: Gulf, 1985); R. Blake and A. A. McCanse, *Leadership Dilemmas—Grid Solutions* (Houston: Gulf, 1991), pp. 21–31.

29. L. L. Larson, J. G. Hunt, and R. Osburn, "The Great Hi-Hi Leader Myth: A Lesson from Occam's Razor," *Academy of Management Journal* 19 (1976), 628–641.

30. J. M. Burns, *Leadership* (New York: Harper & Row, 1979), p. 2.

31. N. Turner, J. Barling, O. Epitropaki, V. Butcher, and C. Milner, "Transformational Leadership and Moral Reasoning," *Journal of Applied Psychology* 87 (2002), 304–311.

32. S. A. Kirkpatrick and E. A. Locke, "Direct and Indirect Effects of Three Core Charismatic Leadership Components on Performance and Attitudes," *Journal of Applied Psychology* 81 (1996), 36–51.

33. J. J. Hater and B. M. Bass, "Superiors' Evaluations and Subordinates' Perceptions of Transformational Leadership," *Journal of Applied Psychology* 73 (1988), 695–702.

34. J. M. Howell and B. J. Avolio, "Transformational Leadership, Transactional Leadership, Locus of Control, and Support for Innovation: Key Predictors of Consolidated-Business-Unit Performance," *Journal of Applied Psychology* 78 (1993), 891–902.

35. K.T. Dirks and D. L. Ferrin, "Trust in Leadership: Meta-Analytical Findings and Implications for Research and Practice," *Journal of Applied Psychology* 87 (2002), 611–628.

36. R. Kark, B. Shamir, and G. Chen, "The Two Faces of Transformational Leadership: Empowerment and Dependency," *Journal of Applied Psychology* 88 (2003), 246–255.

37. G. Chen and P. D. Bliese, "The Role of Different Levels of Leadership in Predicting Self- and Collective Efficacy: Evidence for Discontinuity," *Journal of Applied Psychology* 87 (2002), 549–556.

38. J. C. Pastor, J. R. Meindl, and M. C. Mayo, "A Network Effects Model of Charisma Attributions," *Academy of Management Journal* 45 (2002), 410–420.

39. B. M. Bass, B. J. Avolio, D. I. Jung, and Y. Berson, "Predicting Unit Performance by Assessing Transformational and Transactive Leadership," *Journal of Applied Psychology* 88 (2003), 207–218.

40. P. Bycio, R. D. Hackett, and J. S. Allen, "Further Assessments of Bass's (1985) Conceptualization of Transactional and Transformational Leadership," *Journal of Applied Psychology* 80 (1995), 468–478.

41. D. I. Jung and B. J. Avolio, "Effects of Leadership Style and Followers' Cultural Orientation on Performance in Group and Individual Task Conditions," *Academy of Management Journal* 42 (1999), 208–218.

42. T. Dvir, D. Eden, B. J. Avolio, and B. Shamir, "Impact of Transformational Leadership on Follower Development and Performance: A Field Experiment," *Academy of Management Journal* 45 (2002), 735–744.

43. C. R. Egri and S. Herman, "Leadership in North American Environmental Sector: Values, Leadership Styles, and Contexts of Environmental Leaders and Their Organizations," *Academy of Management Journal* 43 (2000), 571–604.

44. D. De Cremer & D. van Knippenberg, "How Do Leaders Promote Cooperation," *Journal of Applied Psychology* 87 (2002), 858–866.

45. J. Pfeffer, "The Ambiguity of Leadership," *Academy of Management Review* 2 (1977), 104–112.

46. D. C. McClelland and R. E. Boyatzis, "Leadership Motive Pattern and Long-Term Success in Management," *Journal of Applied Psychology* 67 (1982), 737–743.

47. G. Graen, "Role-Making Processes within Complex Organizations," in M. D. Dunnette, ed., *Handbook of Industrial/Organizational Psychology* (Chicago: Rand McNally, 1976), pp. 1210–1259; R. Katerberg and P. Hom, "Effects of Within–Group and Between–Groups Variation in Leadership," *Journal of Applied Psychology* 66 (1981), 218–223.

48. C. A. Schriesheim, S. L. Castro, and F. J.Yammarino, "Investigating Contingencies: An Examination of the Impact of Span of Supervision and Upward Controllingness on Leader–Member Exchange Using Traditional and Multivariate Within- and Between-Entities Analysis," *Journal of Applied Psychology* 85 (2000), 659–677.

49. D. A. Hoffman, F. P. Morgeson, and S. J. Gerras, "Climate as a Moderator of the Relationship between Leader–Member Exchange and Content-Specific Citizenship: Safety Climate as an Exemplar," *Journal of Applied Psychology* 88 (2003), 170–178.

50. G. Graen, R. Liden, and W. Hoel, "Role of Leadership in the Employee Withdrawal Process," *Journal of Applied Psychology* 67 (1982), 868–872.

51. R. C. Liden, S. J. Wayne, and D. Stilwell, "A Longitudinal Study on the Early Development of Leader–Member Exchanges," *Journal of Applied Psychology* 78 (1993), 662–674.

52. J. R. Hollenbeck, D. R. Ilgen, J. A. Hedlund, J. A. Colquitt, and J. Hedlund, "Extending the Multilevel Theory of Team Decision Making: Effects of Feedback and Experience in Hierarchical Teams," *Academy of Management Journal* 41 (1998) 269–283.

53. P. Hersey and K. Blanchard, *Management of Organizational Behavior* (Englewood Cliffs, NJ: Prentice Hall, 1991).

54. S. K. Lam and J. Schaubroeck, "A Field Experiment Testing Frontline Opinion Leaders as Change Agents," *Journal of Applied Psychology* 85 (2000), 987–995.

55. B. Elgin, "Yahoo: Act Two," *Business Week*, June 2, 2003, pp. 70–76.

56. S. Kerr and J. M. Jermier, "Substitutes for Leadership: Their Meaning and Measurement," *Organizational Behavior and Human Decision Processes* 22 (1978), pp. 375–403.

57. P. M. Podsakoff, S. B. MacKenzie, and W. H. Bommer, "Meta-Analysis of the Relationships between Kerr and Jermier's Substitutes for Leadership and Employee Job Attitudes, Role Perceptions, and Performance," *Journal of Applied Psychology* 81 (1996), 380–399.

58. K. T. Dirks, "Trust in Leadership and Team Performance: Evidence from NCAA Basketball," *Journal of Applied Psychology* 85 (2000), 1004–1012.

59. F. E. Fiedler, *A Theory of Leadership Effectiveness* (New York: McGraw-Hill, 1967), pp. 120–137.

60. C. Cooper and G. Chazan, "Once in Intifada, a Palestinian Now Must Try to Hold It Back," *Wall Street Journal Online*, July 15, 2003, pp. 1–5.

61. F. E. Fiedler, "Engineering the Job to Fit the Manager," *Harvard Business Review* 43 (1965), 115–122.

62. A. K. Korman, "Contingency Approaches to Leadership: An Overview," in J. G. Hunt and L. L. Larson, eds., *Contingency Approaches to Leadership,* (Carbondale: Southern Illinois University Press, 1974), p. 24; C. A. Schriesheim, B. D. Bannister, and W. H. Money, "Psychometric Properties of the LPC Scale: An Extension of Rice's Review," *Academy of Management Review* 4 (1979), 287–290.

63. B. Kabanoff, "A Critique of Leader Match and Its Implications for Leadership Research," *Personnel Psychology* 34 (1981), 749–764.

64. V. H. Vroom, "Leadership," in M. D. Dunnette, ed., *Handbook of Industrial/Organizational Psychology,* (Chicago: Rand McNally, 1976), p. 912.

65. V. H. Vroom and A. G. Jago, "Decision Making as a Social Process: Normative and Descriptive Models of Leader Behavior," *Decision Sciences* 5 (1974), 743–769.

66. V. H. Vroom and P. W. Yetton, *Leadership and Decision Making* (Pittsburgh, PA: University of Pittsburgh Press, 1973), p. 12.

67. Vroom and Yetton, *Leadership and Decision Making,* p. 13.

68. B. Gruley and R. Smith, "Anatomy of a Fall: Keys to Success Left Kenneth Lay Open to Disaster," *Wall Street Journal Online,* April 26, 2002, pp. 1–8.

69. M. G. Evans, "The Effect of Supervisory Behavior on the Path–Goal Relationship," *Organizational Behavior and Human Performance* 5 (1970), 277–298; R. J. House, "A Path–Goal Theory of Leadership Effectiveness," *Administrative Science Quarterly* 16 (1971), 321–338.

70. R. J. House and T. R. Mitchell, "Path–Goal Theory of Leadership," *Journal of Contemporary Business* 3 (1974), 81–97.

71. A. C. Filley, R. J. House, and S. Kerr, *Managerial Processes and Organizational Behavior* (Glenview, IL: Scott, Foresman, 1976), p. 91.

72. R. T. Keller, "A Test of the Path–Goal Theory of Leadership with Need for Clarity as a Moderator in Research and Development Organizations," *Journal of Applied Psychology* 74 (1989), 208–212.

73. Ibid.

74. J. E. Stinson and T. W. Johnson, "A Path–Goal Theory of Leadership: A Partial Test and Suggested Refinements," *Academy of Management Journal* 18 (1975), 242–252.

75. M. Erez and I. Zidon, "Effect of Goal Acceptance on the Relationship between Goal Difficulty and Performance," *Journal of Applied Psychology* 69 (1984), 69–78.

76. L. E. Atwater and F. J.Yammarino, "Does Self–Other Agreement on Leadership Perceptions Moderate the Validity of Leadership and Performance Predictions?" *Personnel Psychology* 45 (1992), 141–164.

77. L. Atwater, P. Roush, and A. Fischthal, "The Influence of Upward Feedback on Self- and Follower Ratings of Leadership," *Personnel Psychology* 48 (1995), 35–39.

Chapter 11

1. A. Bianco and P. L. Moore, "Downfall of Xerox," *Business Week,* March 5, 2001, pp. 82–92; P. L. Moore, "She's Here to Fix Xerox," *Business Week,* August 6, 2001, pp. 47–48.

2. A. Park, "Family Feuds Don't Get Any Nastier Than This," *Business Week,* February 10, 2003, pp. 62–63.

3. B. Morris and P. Sellers, "What Really Happened at Coke," *Fortune,* January 10, 2000, pp. 114–116; A. Taylor III, "Is the World Big Enough for Jurgen Schrempp?" *Fortune,* March 6, 2000, pp. 140–146; T. Lowry, "AOL Has No Future," *Business Week,* January 27, 2003, p. 36.

4. J. A. Byrne, W. Zeller, and S. Ticer, "Caught in the Middle: Six Managers Speak Out on Corporate Life," *Business Week,* September 12, 1988, pp. 80–88.

5. R. A. Dahl, "The Concept of Power," *Behavioral Science* 2 (1957), 201–215; A. Kaplan, "Power in Perspective," in R. L. Kahn and E. Boulding, eds., *Power and Conflict in Organizations* (London: Tavistock, 1964), pp. 11–32; and R. M. Emerson, "Power Dependence Relations," *American Sociological Review* 27 (1962), 31–41.

6. V. V. McMurray, "Some Unanswered Questions on Organizational Conflict," *Organization and Administrative Sciences* 6 (1975), 35–53.

7. D. C. McClelland, *Power: The Inner Experience* (New York: Irvington, 1975), pp. 3–29; D. C. McClelland and D. H. Burnham, "Power Is the Great Motivator," *Harvard Business Review* 54 (1976), 100–110.

8. McClelland and Burnham, "Power Is the Great Motivator."

9. J. R. P. French, Jr., and B. Raven, "The Bases of Social Power," in D. Cartwright, ed., *Studies in Social Power,* (Ann Arbor: Institute for Social Research, University of Michigan, 1959), pp. 150–165; for a recent extension, see N. B. Kurland and L. H. Pelled, "Passing the Word: Toward a Model of Gossip and Power in the Workplace," *Academy of Management Review* 25 (2000), 428–438.

10. H. C. Kelman, "Compliance, Identification, and Internalization: Three Processes of Attitude Change," *Journal of Conflict Resolution* 2 (1958), 51–60.

11. C. N. Greene and P. M. Podsakoff, "Effects of Withdrawal of a Performance-Contingent Reward on Supervisory Influence and Power," *Academy of Management Journal* 24 (1981), 527–542.

12. Another criticism of this model relates to problems with the measures and methods used to study the French and Raven classification scheme. For further information about these problems and their effects on power research, see G. A. Yukl, *Leadership in Organizations* (Englewood Cliffs, NJ: Prentice Hall, 1981), pp. 38–43; P. M. Podsakoff and C. A. Schreisheim, "Field Studies of French and Raven's Bases of Power: Critique, Reanalysis, and Suggestions for Future Research," *Psychological Bulletin* 97 (1985), 387–411.

13. D. J. Hickson, C. R. Hinings, C. A. Lee, R. H. Schneck, and J. M. Pennings, "A Strategic Contingencies Theory of Intraorganizational Power," *Administrative Science Quarterly* 16 (1971), 216–229; J. Pfeffer and G. R. Salancik, *The External Control of Organizations: A Resource Dependence Perspective* (New York: Harper & Row, 1978) p. 231; J. Pfeffer, *Power in Organizations* (Marshfield, MA: Pitman, 1981), pp. 109–122.

14. G. R. Salancik and J. Pfeffer, "Who Gets Power and How They Hold on to It: A Strategic-Contingency Model of Power," *Organizational Dynamics* 5 (1977), 3–4.

15. R. M. Kanter, "Power Failures in Management Circuits," *Harvard Business Review* 57 (1979), 65–75.

16. R. H. Miles, *Macro Organizational Behavior* (Santa Monica, CA: Goodyear, 1980), pp. 171–172.

17. G. A. Crawford, "Information as a Strategic Contingency: Applying the Strategic Contingencies

Theory of Intraorganizational Power to Academic Libraries," *College and Research Libraries* 58 (1997), 145–155; Miles, *Macro Organizational Behavior,* p. 171.

18. G. R. Salancik and J. Pfeffer, "The Bases and Uses of Power in Organizational Decision Making," *Administrative Science Quarterly* 19 (1974), p. 470.

19. Hickson et al., "A Strategic Contingencies Theory," p. 40.

20. D. Krackhardt, "Assessing the Political Landscape: Structure, Cognition, and Power in Organizations," *Administrative Science Quarterly* 35 (1990), 342–369; D. J. Brass and M. E. Burkhardt, "Potential Power and Power Use: An Investigation of Structure and Behavior," *Academy of Management Journal* 36 (1993), 441–470; H. Ibarra, "Network Centrality, Power, and Innovation Involvement: Determinants of Technical and Administrative Roles," *Academy of Management Journal* 36 (1993), 471–501; H. Ibarra and S. B. Andrews, "Power, Social Influence, and Sense Making: Effects of Network Centrality and Proximity on Employee Perceptions," *Administrative Science Quarterly* 38 (1993), 277–303; W. Tsai, "Knowledge Transfer in Intraorganizational Networks: Effects of Network Position and Absorptive Capacity on Business Unit Innovation and Performance," *Academy of Management Journal* 44 (2001), 996–1004.

21. W. G. Astley and E. J. Zajac, "Intraorganizational Power and Organizational Design: Reconciling Rational and Coalitional Models of Organization," *Organization Science* 2 (1991), 399–411.

22. H. A. Landsberger, "A Horizontal Dimension in Bureaucracy," *Administrative Science Quarterly* 6 (1961), 299–332.

23. Salancik and Pfeffer, "The Bases and Uses of Power"; see also J. Pfeffer and G. R. Salancik, "Organizational Decision Making as a Political Process: The Case of a University Budget," *Administrative Science Quarterly* 19 (1974), 135–151.

24. M. Crozier, *The Bureaucratic Phenomenon* (Chicago: University of Chicago Press, 1964), pp. 153–154.

25. D. Mechanic, "Sources of Power of Lower Participants in Complex Organizations," *Administrative Science Quarterly* 7 (1962), 349–364; L. W. Porter, R. W. Allen, and H. L. Angle, "The Politics of Upward Influence in Organizations," in B. M. Staw and L. L. Cummings, eds., *Research in Organizational Behavior,* vol. 3, (Greenwich, CT: JAI Press, 1981), pp. 109–150; R. S. Blackburn, "Lower Participant Power: Toward a Conceptual Integration," *Academy of Management Review* 6 (1981), 127–131; S. M. Farmer and J. M. Maslyn, "Why Are Styles of Upward Influence

Neglected? Making the Case for a Configurational Approach to Influences," *Journal of Management* 25 (1999), 653–682.

26. R. W. Allen, D. L. Madison, L. W. Porter, P. A. Renwick, and B. T. Mayes, "Organizational Politics: Tactics and Characteristics of Its Actors," *California Management Review* 22 (1979), 77–83; B. T. Mayes and R. W. Allen, "Toward a Definition of Organizational Politics," *Academy of Management Review* 2 (1977), 672–678; V. Murray and J. Gandz, "Games Executives Play: Politics at Work," *Business Horizons* 23 (1980), 11–23; Pfeffer, *Power in Organizations*, p. 6.

27. Miles, *Macro Organizational Behavior*, p. 155.

28. M. Valle and P. L. Perrewe, "Do Politics Perceptions Relate to Political Behaviors? Tests of an Implicit Assumption and Expanded Model," *Human Relations* 53 (2000), 359–386; L. A. Witt, M. C. Andrews, and K. M. Kacmar, "The Role of Participation in Decision-Making in the Organizational Politics–Job Satisfaction Relationship," *Human Relations* 53 (2000), 341–358; W. A. Hochwater, P. L. Perrewe, G. R. Ferris, and R. Guercio, "Commitment as an Antidote to the Tension and Turnover Consequences of Organizational Politics," *Journal of Vocational Behavior* 55 (1999), 277–297.

29. D. C. McClelland, "The Two Faces of Power," *Journal of International Affairs* 24 (1970), 32–41; R. Christie and F. L. Geis, *Studies in Machiavellianism* (New York: Academic Press, 1970), pp. 1–9; G. R. Ferris, G. S. Russ, and P. M. Fandt, "Politics in Organizations," in R. A. Giacalone and P. Rosenfeld, eds., *Impression Management in the Organization*, (Hillsdale, NJ: Erlbaum, 1989), pp. 143–170.

30. Pfeffer, *Power in Organizations*; R. L. Daft and R. M. Steers, *Organizations: A Micro/Macro Approach* (Glenview, IL: Scott, Foresman, 1986), pp. 488–489; Allen et al., "Organizational Politics," pp. 77–83.

31. W. B. Stevenson, J. B. Pearce, and L. W. Porter, "The Concept of Coalition in Organization Theory and Research," *Academy of Management Review* 10 (1985), 256–268.

32. M. Gargiulo, "Two-Step Leverage: Managing Constraints in Organizational Politics," *Administrative Science Quarterly* 38 (1993), 1–19.

33. E. E. Jones, *Ingratiation* (New York: Appleton-Century-Crofts, 1964); C. B. Wortman and J. A. W. Linsenmeier, "Interpersonal Attraction and Techniques of Ingratiation in Organizational Settings," in B. M. Staw and G. R. Salancik, eds., *New Directions in Organizational Behavior* (Chicago: St. Clair Press, 1977), pp. 133–178; G. Harrell-Cook, G. R. Ferris, and J. H. Dulebohn, "Political Behaviors as Moderators of the Perceptions of Organizational Politics–Work Outcomes

Relationships," *Journal of Organizational Behavior* 20 (1999), 1093–1105; K. M. Kacmar and D. S. Carlson, "Effectiveness of Impression Management Tactics across Human Resource Situations," *Journal of Applied Social Psychology* 29 (1999), 1293–1315.

34. W. Boeker, "Power and Managerial Dismissal: Scapegoating at the Top," *Administrative Science Quarterly* 37 (1992), 400–421.

35. The political management techniques described in this section are based partly on discussions in R. P. Vecchio, *Organizational Behavior*, 2nd ed. (Chicago: Dryden Press, 1991), pp. 281–282; G. Moorhead and R. W. Griffin, *Organizational Behavior*, 3rd ed. (Boston: Houghton Mifflin, 1992), pp. 306–307.

36. Miles, *Macro Organizational Behavior*, p. 122.

37. R. E. Quinn, *Beyond Rational Management: Mastering the Paradoxes and Competing Demands of High Performance* (San Francisco: Jossey-Bass, 1988), p. 2; A. C. Amason, "Distinguishing the Effects of Functional and Dysfunctional Conflict on Strategic Decision Making: Resolving a Paradox for Top Management Teams," *Academy of Management Journal* 39 (1996), 123–148.

38. L. Coser, *The Functions of Social Conflict* (New York: Free Press, 1956), p. 154; Miles, *Macro Organizational Behavior*, p. 123; J. Wall and R. R. Callister, "Conflict and Its Management," *Journal of Management* 21 (1995), 515–558.

39. Miles, *Macro Organizational Behavior*, p. 131.

40. Miles, *Macro Organizational Behavior*, pp. 132–138; J. M. Ivancevich and M. T. Matteson, *Organizational Behavior and Management*, 3rd ed. (Homewood, IL: Irwin, 1993), pp. 340–344.

41. D. Ulrich and J. B. Barney, "Perspectives on Organizations: Resource Dependence, Efficiency, and Population," *Academy of Management Review* 9 (1984), 471–481.

42. M. Sherif and C. W. Sherif, *Groups in Harmony and Tension* (New York: Harper, 1953), pp. 229–295; A. D. Szilagyi, Jr., and M. J. Wallace, Jr., *Organizational Behavior and Performance*, 4th ed. (Glenview, IL: Scott, Foresman, 1987), p. 301; J. L. Gibson, J. M. Ivancevich, and J. H. Donnelly, Jr., *Organizations: Behavior, Structure, Process*, 7th ed. (Homewood, IL: Irwin, 1991), pp. 308–309; Ivancevich and Matteson, *Organizational Behavior and Management*, pp. 344–347.

43. J. Z. Rubin and B. R. Brown, *The Social Psychology of Bargaining and Negotiation* (New York: Academic Press, 1975), p. 3; R. J. Lewicki and J. R. Litterer, *Negotiation* (Homewood, IL: Irwin, 1985).

44. K. W. Thomas, "Conflict and Conflict Management," in M. D. Dunnette, ed., *Handbook of Industrial and Organizational Psychology*, (Chicago: Rand McNally, 1976), pp. 889–935; also see K.W. Thomas, "Toward Multidimensional Values in Teaching: The Example of Conflict Behaviors," *Academy of Management Review* 2 (1977), 472–489; K. W. Thomas, "Conflict and Conflict Management: Reflections and Update," *Journal of Organizational Behavior* 13 (1992), 265–274.

45. M. Sherif, "Superordinate Goals in the Reduction of Intergroup Conflict," *American Journal of Sociology* 63 (1958), 349–356; J. R. Galbraith, "Organization Design: An Information Processing View," *Interfaces* 4 (1974), 28–36; and Pfeffer, *Power in Organizations*.

46. J. R. Galbraith, *Designing Complex Organizations* (Reading, MA: Addison-Wesley, 1973), pp. 14–18.

47. J. R. Galbraith, *Competing with Flexible Lateral Organizations* (Reading, MA: Addison-Wesley, 1994); T. Smart, "Jack Welch's Cyber-Czar," *Business Week*, August 5, 1996, pp. 82–83; A. L. Sprout, "The Internet inside Your Company," *Fortune*, November 27, 1995, pp. 161–168.

48. D. E. Conlon, P. Carnevale, and W. H. Ross, "The Influence of Third Party Power and Suggestions on Negotiation: The Surface Value of Compromise," *Journal of Applied Social Psychology* 24 (1994), 1084–1113.

49. L. R. Burns and D. R. Wholey, "Adoption and Abandonment of Matrix Management Programs: Effects of Organizational Characteristics and Interorganizational Networks," *Academy of Management Journal* 36 (1993), 106–138.

Chapter 12

1. P. Burrows, "Can Fiorina Reboot HP?" *Business Week*, November 27, 2000, p. 59; P. Burrows, "The Radical: Carly Fiorina's Bold Management Experiment at Hewlett Packard," *Business Week*, February 19, 2001, pp. 70–80; P. Burrows, "Carly's Last Stand?" *Business Week*, December 24, 2001, pp. 62–70; B. Elgin, "HP's Beachhead in High-Tech Services," *Business Week*, April 28, 2003, pp. 40.

2. J. G. March and H. A. Simon, *Organizations* (New York: Wiley, 1958), p. 4; J. D. Thompson, *Organizations in Action* (New York: McGraw-Hill, 1967), p. 51; W. R. Scott, *Organizations: Rational, Natural, and Open Systems*, 3rd ed. (Englewood Cliffs, NJ: Prentice Hall, 1992), p. 15.

3. P. R. Lawrence and J. W. Lorsch, "Differentiation and Integration in Complex Organizations," *Administrative Science Quarterly* 12 (1967), 1–47; P. R. Lawrence and J. W. Lorsch, *Organization and Environment* (Homewood, IL: Irwin, 1967), p. 7.

4. Lawrence and Lorsch,"Differentiation and Integration," pp. 2–3; March and Simon, *Organizations,* p. 160; J. R. Galbraith, *Designing Complex Organizations* (Reading, MA: Addison-Wesley, 1973), p. 4.

5. Thompson, *Organizations in Action,*p.62.

6. E. A. Locke, M. Alavi, and J. A. Wagner III, "Participation in Decision Making: An Information Exchange Perspective," in G. R. Ferris, ed., *Research in Personnel and Human Resources Management,* vol. 15 (Greenwich, CT: JAI Press, 1997), pp. 293–331.

7. H. Mintzberg, *Structuring of Organizations* (Englewood Cliffs, NJ: Prentice Hall, 1979), pp. 3–4.

8. Ibid., p.5.

9. R. H. Hall, "Professionalism and Bureaucratization," *American Sociological Review* 33 (1968), 92–104; J. Hage and M. Aiken, "Relationship of Centralization to Other Structural Properties," *Administrative Science Quarterly* 12 (1967), 72–91.

10. Mintzberg, *Structuring of Organizations,* pp. 7–9; H. Mintzberg,"The Structuring of Organizations," in J. B. Quinn, H. Mintzberg, and R. M. James, eds., *The Strategy Process: Concepts, Contexts, and Cases* (Englewood Cliffs, NJ: Prentice Hall, 1988), pp. 276–304.

11. Mintzberg, *Structuring of Organizations,* p.7.

12. P. N. Khandwalla, *The Design of Organizations* (New York: Harcourt Brace Jovanovich, 1977), pp. 489–497; A. Walker and J. Lorsch,"Organizational Choice: Product Versus Function," *Harvard Business Review* 46 (1968), 129–138.

13. D. S. Pugh, D. J. Hickson, C. R. Hinings, and C. Turner, "Dimensions of Organization Structure," *Administrative Science Quarterly* 13 (1968), 65–91; J. Hage and M. Aiken, "Relationship of Centralization to Other Structural Properties," *Administrative Science Quarterly* 12 (1967), 72–92; P. M. Blau, "Decentralization in Bureaucracies," in M. N. Zald, ed., *Power in Organizations* (Nashville, TN: Vanderbilt University Press, 1970), pp. 42–81; N. M. Carter and J. B. Cullen, "A Comparison of Centralization/Decentralization of Decision Making Concepts and Measures," *Journal of Management* 10 (1984), 259–268; R. Mansfield, "Bureaucracy and Centralization: An Examination of Organizational

Structure," *Administrative Science Quarterly* 18 (1973), 477–478.

14. R. E. Hoskisson, C. W. L. Hill, and H. Kim, "The Multidivisional Structure: Organizational Fossil or Source of Value?" *Journal of Management* 19 (1993), 269–298.

15. R. C. Ford and W. A. Randolph, "Cross Functional Structures: A Review and Integration of Matrix Organization and Project Management," *Journal of Management* 18 (1992), 267–294.

16. L. R. Burns, "Matrix Management in Hospitals: Testing Theories of Matrix Structure and Development," *Administrative Science Quarterly* 34 (1989), 349–368; L. R. Burns and D. R. Wholey,"Adoption and Abandonment of Matrix Management Programs: Effects of Organizational Characteristics and Interorganizational Programs," *Academy of Management Journal* 36 (1993), 106–138.

17. J. A. Wagner III, "Organizations," in A. E. Kasdin, ed., *Encyclopedia of Psychology,* (New York: Oxford Press, 2000), pp. 14–20.

18. M. Hammer and J. Champy, *Reengineering the Corporation:A Manifesto for Business Revolution* (New York: Harper Business, 1993); S. Lubove,"How to Grow Big Yet Stay Small," *Forbes,* December 7, 1992, pp. 64–67; M. Rothschild,"Coming Soon: Internal Markets," *Forbes ASAP,* June 7, 1993, pp. 19–21.

19. M. A. Schilling and H. K. Steensma, "The Use of Modular Organizational Forms: An Industry-Level Analysis," *Academy of Management Journal* 44 (2001), 1149–1168; G. De Sanctis, J. T. Glass, and I. M. Ensing, "Organizational Designs for R&D," *Academy of Management Executive* 16 (2002), 55–66; R. E. Miles and C. C. Snow, "The New Network Firm: A Spherical Structure Built on a Human Investment Philosophy," *Organizational Dynamics* 23 (1995), 5–18; R. E. Miles, C. C. Snow, J. A. Matthews, and H. C. Coleman, Jr., "Organizing in the Knowledge Age: Anticipating the Cellular Form," *Academy of Management Executive* 11 (1997), 7–24.

20. G. DeSanctis and P. Monge,"Communication Processes for Virtual Organizations," *Organization Science* 10 (1999), 693–703; G. G. Dess, A. M. A. Rasheed, K. J. McLaughlin, and R. L. Priem, "The New Corporate Architecture," *Academy of Management Executive* 9 (1995), 7–20; R. E. Miles and C. C. Snow, "Organizations: New Concepts for New Forms," *California Management Review* 28 (1986), 62–73; M. K. Ahuja and K. M. Carley, "Network Structure in Virtual Organizations," *Organization Science* 10 (1999), 741–757.

21. W. H. Davidow and M. S. Malone, *The Virtual Corporation: Structuring and Revitalizing the Corporation for the 21st Century* (New York: Harper Collins, 1992); J. A. Byrne, R. Brandt, and O. Port, "The Virtual Corporation: The Company of the Future Will Be the Ultimate in Adaptability," *Business Week,* February 8, 1993, pp. 99–102; J. A. Byrne, "The Futurists Who Fathered the Ideas," *Business Week,* February 8, 1993, p. 103; M. Malone and W. Davidow, "Virtual Corporation," *Forbes ASAP,* December 7, 1992, pp. 102–107; J. W. Verity, "A Company That's 100% Virtual," *Business Week,* November 21, 1994, p. 85; D. Greising,"The Virtual Olympics," *Business Week,* April 29, 1996, pp. 64–66.

22. D. Tapscott, D. Ticoll, and A. Lowy, "Internet Nirvana," *E-Company,* December 2000, pp. 99–108.

Chapter 13

1. A. Barrett, "Staying on Top," *Business Week,* May 5, 2003, pp. 60–68.

2. R. L. Priem and J. Rosenstein, "Is Organization Theory Obvious to Practitioners? A Test of One Established Theory," *Organization Science* 11 (2000), 509–524; J. Biorkinshaw, R. Nobel, and J. Ridderstråle, "Knowledge as a Contingency Variable: Do the Characteristics of Knowledge Predict Organization Structure?" *Organization Science* 13 (2002), 274–289.

3. J. L. Price, "The Study of Organizational Effectiveness," *Sociological Quarterly* 13 (1972), 3–15; S. Strasser, J. D. Eveland, G. Cummings, O. L. Deniston, and J. H. Romani, "Conceptualizing the Goal and System Models of Organizational Effectiveness—Implications for Comparative Evaluative Research," *Journal of Management Studies* 18 (1981), 321–340; Y. K. Shetty, "New Look at Corporate Goals," *California Management Review* 22 (1979), 71–79.

4. Constituency models of effectiveness and other examples of constituencies and their interests are discussed by P. S. Goodman, J. M. Pennings, and Associates, *New Perspectives on Organizational Effectiveness* (San Francisco: Jossey-Bass, 1977); J. A. Wagner III and B. Schneider, "Legal Regulation and the Constraint of Constituent Satisfaction," *Journal of Management Studies* 24 (1987), 189–200; R. F. Zammuto, "A Comparison of Multiple Constituency Models of Organizational Effectiveness," *Academy of Management Review* 9 (1984), 606–616. Related stakeholder models are discussed by R. E. Freeman, *Strategic Management: A Stakeholder Approach* (Boston: Pitman, 1984); C. W. L. Hill and T. M. Jones,

"Stakeholder-Agency Theory," *Journal of Management Studies* 29 (1992), 131–154; T. Donaldson and L. E. Preston, "A Stakeholder Theory of the Corporation: Concepts, Evidence, and Implications," *Academy of Management Review* 20 (1995), 65–91; T. A. Kochan and S. A. Rubinstein, "A Stakeholder Theory of the Firm: The Saturn Partnership," *Organization Science* 11 (2000), 367–386.

5. R. Z. Gooding and J. A. Wagner III, "A Meta-Analytic Review of the Relationship between Size and Performance: The Productivity and Efficiency of Organizations and Their Subunits," *Administrative Science Quarterly* 30 (1985), 462–481; H. A. Haveman, "Organizational Size and Change: Diversification in the Savings and Loan Industry after Deregulation," *Administrative Science Quarterly* 38 (1993), 20–50; P. Dass, "Relationship of Firm Size, Initial Diversification, and Internationalization with Strategic Change," *Journal of Business Research* 48 (2000), 135–146.

6. Gooding and Wagner, "A Meta-Analytic Review."

7. T. Burns and G. M. Stalker, *The Management of Innovation* (London: Tavistock, 1961), pp. 119–122; J. A. Courtright, G. T. Fairhurst, and L. E. Rogers, "Interaction Patterns in Organic and Mechanistic Systems," *Academy of Management Journal* 32 (1989), 773–802; V. L. Barker and M. A. Mone, "The Mechanistic Structure Shift and Strategic Reorientation in Declining Firms Attempting Turnarounds," *Human Relations* 51 (1998), 1227–1258.

8. L. Greiner, "Evolution and Revolution as Organizations Grow," *Harvard Business Review* 50 (1972), 37–46; J. R. Kimberly, R. H. Miles, and Associates, *The Organizational Life Cycle* (San Francisco: Jossey-Bass, 1980); R. F. Quinn and K. Cameron, "Organizational Life Cycles and Shifting Criteria of Effectiveness: Some Preliminary Evidence," *Management Science* 29 (1983), 29–34.

9. S. M. Davis, *Future Perfect* (Reading, MA: Addison-Wesley, 1987); B. J. Pine II, *Mass Customization: The New Frontier in Business Competition* (Boston: Harvard University Press, 1993).

10. J. R. Kimberly, "Organizational Size and the Structuralist Perspective: A Review, Critique, and Proposal," *Administrative Science Quarterly* 21 (1976), 571–597; P. Y. Martin, "Size in Residential Service Organizations," *Sociological Quarterly* 20 (1979), 569–579; Gooding and Wagner, "A Meta-Analytic Review," p. 463.

11. C. C. Miller, W. H. Glick, Y. Wang, and G. P. Huber, "Understanding Technology–Structure Relationships: Theory Development and Meta-

Analytic Theory Testing," *Academy of Management Journal* 34 (1991), 370–399; D. Miller, "Environmental Fit versus Internal Fit," *Organization Science* 3 (1992), 159–178.

12. C. Perrow, "A Framework for the Comparative Analysis of Organizations," *American Sociological Review* 32 (1967), 194–208; D. Rousseau, "Assessment of Technology in Organizations: Closed versus Open System Approaches," *Academy of Management Review* 4 (1979), 531–542.

13. J. Woodward, *Management and Technology* (London: Her Majesty's Stationery Office, 1958). See also Woodward's *Industrial Organization: Theory and Practice* (London: Oxford University Press, 1975).

14. F. M. Hull and P. D. Collins, "High Technology Batch Production Systems: Woodward's Missing Type," *Academy of Management Journal* 30 (1987), 786–797; R. Parthasarthy and S. P. Sethi, "The Impact of Flexible Automation on Business Strategy and Organizational Structure," *Academy of Management Review* 17 (1992), 86–111.

15. J. D. Thompson, *Organizations in Action* (New York: McGraw-Hill, 1967), pp. 15–18.

16. Perrow, "A Framework for the Comparative Analysis of Organizations"; R. G. Hunt, "Technology and Organization," *Academy of Management Journal* 13 (1970), 235–252; W. H. Starbuck, "Organizational Growth and Development," in J. G. March, ed., *Handbook of Organizations* (New York: Rand McNally, 1965), chapter 11; Courtright, Fairhurst, and Rogers, "Interaction Patterns in Organic and Mechanistic Systems."

17. A. C. Bluedorn, R. A. Johnson, D. K. Cartwright, and B. R. Barringer, "The Interface and Convergence of the Strategic Management and Organizational Environment Domains," *Journal of Management* 20 (1994), 201–262.

18. Burns and Stalker, *The Management of Innovation*; C. R. Hinings, D. J. Hickson, J. M. Pennings, and R. E. Schneck, "Structural Conditions of Intraorganizational Power," *Administrative Science Quarterly* 19 (1974), 22–44; R. B. Duncan, "Multiple Decision-Making Structures in Adapting to Environmental Uncertainty: The Impact of Organizational Effectiveness," *Human Relations* 26 (1973), 273–291.

19. R. B. Duncan, "Characteristics of Organizational Environments and Perceived Environmental Uncertainty," *Administrative Science Quarterly* 17 (1972), 313–327; J. R. Galbraith, *Designing Complex Organizations* (Reading, MA: Addison-Wesley, 1973), pp. 4–6.

20. J. Flint, "Volume Be Damned," *Forbes*, April 12, 1993, pp. 52–53.

21. Galbraith, *Designing Complex Organizations,* p. 4.

22. O. O. Sawyerr, "Environmental Uncertainty and Environmental Scanning Activities of Nigerian Manufacturing Executives: A Comparative Analysis," *Strategic Management Journal* 14 (1993), 287–299.

23. J. S. Adams, "The Structure and Dynamics of Behavior in Organization Boundary Roles," in M. D. Dunnette, ed., *Handbook of Industrial and Organizational Psychology* (Chicago: Rand McNally, 1976), pp. 1175–1199.

24. H. Aldrich and D. Herker, "Boundary Spanning Roles and Organization Structure," *Academy of Management Review* 2 (1977), 217–239; R. H. Miles, *Macro Organizational Behavior* (Santa Monica, CA: Goodyear, 1979), pp. 320–339; R. L. Daft and R. M. Steers, *Organizations: A Micro/Macro Approach* (Glenview, IL: Scott, Foresman, 1986), p. 299.

25. G. J. Castrogiovanni, "Environmental Munificence: A Theoretical Assessment," *Academy of Management Review* 16 (1991), 542–565.

26. D. Greising, L. Himelstein, J. Carey, and L. Bongiorno, "Does Tobacco Pay Its Way," *Business Week*, February 19, 1996, pp. 89–90; J. Carey, L. Bongiorno, and M. France, "The Fire This Time," *Business Week*, August 12, 1996, pp. 66–68; C. Farrell, M. J. Mandel, T. Peterson, A. Borrus, R. W. King, and J. E. Ellis, "The Cold War's Grim Aftermath," *Business Week*, February 24, 1992, pp. 78–80.

27. H. Mintzberg, *Structuring of Organizations* (Englewood Cliffs, NJ: Prentice-Hall, 1979), p. 281; M. Yasi-Ardekani, "Effects of Environmental Scarcity on the Relationship of Context to Organizational Structure," *Academy of Management Journal* 32 (1989), 131–156.

28. Thompson, *Organizations in Action*, pp. 25–38.

29. G. R. Carroll, "The Specialist Strategy," *California Management Review* 26 (1984), 126–137.

30. R. L. Daft and A. Y. Lewin, "Where Are the Theories for the 'New' Organization Forms? An Editorial Essay," *Organization Science* 4 (1993), i–vi.

31. F. E. Emery and E. Trist, "The Causal Texture of Organizational Environments," *Human Relations* 18 (1965), 21–32; R. D'Aveni, *Hypercompetition: Managing the Dynamics of Strategic Maneuvering* (New York: Free Press, 1994); H. W. Volberda, "Toward the Flexible Form: How to Remain Vital in Hypercompetitive Environments," *Organization Science* 7 (1996), 359–374.

32. M. A. Schilling and H. K. Steensma, "The Use of Modular Organization Forms: An Industry-Level Analysis," *Academy of Management Journal*, 44 (2001), 1149–1168; D. C. Galunic and K. M.

Eisenhardt, "Architectural Innovation and Modular Corporate Forms," *Academy of Management Journal* 44 (2001), 1229–1250.

33. J. Pfeffer and G. R. Salancik, *The External Control of Organizations: A Resource Dependence Perspective* (New York: Harper & Row, 1978).

34. R. D. Hof, N. Gross, and I. Sager, "A Computer Maker's Power Move," *Business Week,* March 7, 1994, p. 48.

35. O. Williamson, *Markets and Hierarchies: Analysis and Antitrust Implications* (New York: Free Press, 1975). See also J. R. Commons, *Institutional Economics* (Madison: University of Wisconsin Press, 1934); R. H. Coase, "The Nature of the Firm," *Economica N. S.* 4 (1937), 386–405; A. A. Alchian and H. Demsetz, "Production, Information Costs, and Economic Organization," *American Economic Review* 62 (1972), 777–795.

36. For related discussions, see P. S. Ring and A. H. Van de Ven, "Structuring Cooperative Relationships between Organizations," *Strategic Management Journal* 13 (1992), 483–498; J. T. Mahoney, "The Choice of Organizational Form: Vertical Financial Ownership versus Other Methods of Vertical Integration," *Strategic Management Journal* 13 (1992), 559–584.

Chapter 14

1. S. Levy, "Sony's New Day," *Newsweek,* January 27, 2003, pp. 50–53; "The Best Managers: Ken Kutaragi, Sony Computer Entertainment," *Business Week,* January 13, 2003, p. 64.

2. E. H. Schein, *Organizational Culture and Leadership* (San Francisco: Jossey-Bass, 1985), p. 9.

3. L. Smircich, "Concepts of Culture and Organizational Analysis," *Administrative Science Quarterly* 28 (1983), 339–358; S. G. Harris, "Organizational Culture and Individual Sensemaking: A Schema-Based Perspective," *Organization Science* 5 (1994), 309–321; E. H. Schein, "Organizational Culture," *American Psychologist* 45 (1990), 109–119; A. D. Brown and K. Starkey, "The Effect of Organizational Culture on Communication and Information," *Journal of Management Studies* 31 (1994), 807–828.

4. J. B. Sørensen, "The Strength of Corporate Culture and the Reliability of Firm Performance," *Administrative Science Quarterly* 47 (2002), 70–91; A. Zuckerman, "Strong Corporate Cultures and Firm Performance: Are There Trade-offs?" *Academy of Management Executive* 16 (2002), 158–160.

5. T. E. Deal and A. A. Kennedy, *Corporate Cultures: The Rites and Rituals of Corporate Life* (Reading, MA: Addison-Wesley, 1982), p. 15.

6. H. M. Trice and J. M. Beyer, *The Cultures of Work Organizations* (Englewood Cliffs, NJ: Prentice Hall, 1993), pp. 1–2; E. H. Schein, *Organizational Culture and Leadership,* 2nd ed. (San Francisco: Jossey-Bass, 1992), pp. 3–27.

7. M. J. Hatch, "The Dynamics of Organizational Culture," *Academy of Management Review* 18 (1993), 657–693; L. K. Gundry and D. M. Rousseau, "Critical Incidents in Communicating Culture to Newcomers: The Meaning Is the Message," *Human Relations* 47 (1994), 1063–1088.

8. Deal and Kennedy, *Corporate Cultures,* p. 63.

9. J. M. Beyer and H. M. Trice, "How an Organization's Rites Reveal Its Culture," *Organizational Dynamics* 15 (1987), 3–21; Trice and Beyer, *The Cultures of Work Organizations,* pp. 107–127.

10. J. Martin, "Stories and Scripts in Organizational Settings," in A. Hastorf and A. Isen, eds., *Cognitive Social Psychology* (New York: Elsevier-North Holland, 1982), pp. 225–305; C. D. Hansen and W. M. Kahnweiler, "Storytelling: An Instrument for Understanding the Dynamics of Corporate Relationships," *Human Relations* 46 (1993), 1391–1409; D. M. Boje, "The Storytelling Organization: A Study of Story Performance in an Office- Supply Firm," *Administrative Science Quarterly* 36 (1991), 106–126; D. M. Boje, "Stories of the Storytelling Organization: A Postmodern Analysis of Disney as 'Tamara-Land,'" *Academy of Management Journal* 38 (1995), 997–1035.

11. A. L. Wilkins, "Organizational Stories as Symbols Which Control the Organization," in L. R. Pondy, P. J. Frost, G. Morgan, and T. C. Dandridge, eds., *Organizational Symbolism* (Greenwich, CT: JAI Press, 1983), pp. 81–92.

12. Deal and Kennedy, *Corporate Cultures,* pp. 40–41.

13. D. A. Gioia, "Symbols, Scripts, and Sensemaking," in H. P. Sims, ed., *The Thinking Organization* (San Francisco: Jossey-Bass, 1986), pp. 48–112.

14. J. Pfeffer, *Power in Organizations* (Marshfield, MA: Pitman, 1981), p. 50.

15. G. Morgan, P. J. Frost, and L. R. Pondy, "Organizational Symbolism," in L. R. Pondy, P. J. Frost, G. Morgan, and T. C. Dandridge, eds., *Organizational Symbolism* (Greenwich, CT: JAI Press, 1983), pp. 3–38.

16. Trice and Beyer, *The Cultures of Work Organizations,* p. 90.

17. R. Brandt, "The Billion-Dollar Whiz Kid," *Business Week,* April 13, 1987, pp. 68–76; K. I. Rebello and E. I. Schwartz, "Microsoft: Bill Gates' Baby Is on Top of the World. Can It Stay There?" *Business Week,* February 24, 1992, pp. 60–64.

18. C. A. O'Reilly III, J. Chatman, and D. F. Caldwell, "People and Organizational Culture: A Profile Comparison Approach to Assessing Person–Organization Fit," *Academy of Management Journal* 34 (1991), 487–516; J. E. Sheridan, "Organizational Culture and Employee Retention," *Academy of Management Journal* 35 (1992), 1036–1056.

19. G. R. Salancik and J. Pfeffer, "A Social Information Processing Approach to Job Attitudes and Task Design," *Administrative Science Quarterly* 23 (1978), 224–253; R. E. Rice and C. Aydin, "Attitudes toward New Organizational Technology: Network Proximity as a Mechanism for Social Information Processing," *Administrative Science Quarterly* 36 (1991), 219–244; H. Ibarra and S. B. Andrews, "Power, Social Influence, and Sense Making: Effects of Network Centrality and Proximity on Employee Perceptions," *Administrative Science Quarterly* 38 (1993), 277–303.

20. J. B. Miner, *Organizational Behavior: Performance and Productivity* (New York: Random House, 1988), p. 571; H. M. Trice and J. M. Beyer, "Using Six Organizational Rites to Change Culture," in R. H. Kilmann, M. J. Saxon, and R. Serpa, eds., *Gaining Control of the Corporate Culture* (San Francisco: Jossey-Bass, 1985), pp. 370–399.

21. J. Pfeffer, "Management as Symbolic Action: The Creation and Maintenance of Organizational Paradigms," in L. L. Cummings and B. M. Staw, eds., *Research in Organizational Behavior*, vol. 3 (Greenwich, CT: JAI Press, 1981), pp. 1–52; R. F. Dennehy, "The Executive as Storyteller," *Management Review*, March 1999, pp. 40–43.

22. B. Dumaine, "Creating a New Company Culture," *Fortune*, January 15, 1990, 127–131; S. Fox and Y. Amichai-Hamburger, "The Power of Emotional Appeals in Promoting Organizational Change Programs," *Academy of Management Executive* 15 (2001), 84–93.

23. Miner, *Organizational Behavior*, pp. 574–575; R. H. Kilmann, *Beyond the Quick Fix* (San Francisco: Jossey-Bass, 1984), pp. 105–123.

24. G. L. Lippitt, P. Longseth, and J. Mossop, *Implementing Organizational Change* (San Francisco: Jossey-Bass, 1985), p. 3; E. Fagenson and W.W. Burke, "The Current Activities and Skills of Organization Development Practitioners," *Academy of Management Proceedings*, August 13–16, 1989, p. 251.

25. A. C. Filley, R. J. House, and S. Kerr, *Managerial Process and Organizational Behavior*, 2nd ed. (Glenview, IL: Scott, Foresman, 1976), pp. 488–490; W. L. French and C. H. Bell, Jr., *Organization Development: Behavioral Science Interventions for Organizational Improvement*, 4th ed. (Englewood Cliffs, NJ: Prentice Hall, 1990), pp. 21–22.

26. H. Tsouikas and R. Chia, "On Organizational Becoming: Rethinking Organizational Change," *Organization Science* 13 (2002), 567–582.

27. J. P. Kotter and L. A. Schlesinger, "Choosing Strategies for Change," *Harvard Business Review* 57 (1979), 102–121; J. M. Ivancevich and M. T. Matteson, *Organizational Behavior and Management*, 2nd ed. (Homewood, IL: Irwin, 1990), pp. 621–622; J. A. Wagner III, "Use Participation to Share Information and Distribute Knowledge," in E. A. Locke, ed., *The Blackwell Handbook of Principles of Organizational Behavior* (Oxford, UK: Blackwell, 2000), pp. 304–315; J. E. Dutton, S. J. Ashford, R. M. O'Neill, and K. A. Lawrence, "Moves That Matter: Issue Selling and Organizational Change," *Academy of Management Journal* 44 (2001), 716–736.

28. J. M. Bartunek, "Scholarly Dialogues and Participatory Action Research," *Human Relations* 46 (1993), 1221–1233; F. Heller, "Another Look at Action Research," *Human Relations* 46 (1993), 1235–1242.

29. R. Harrison, "Choosing the Depth of Organizational Intervention," *Journal of Applied Behavioral Science* 6 (1970), 181–202.

30. I. Dayal and J. M. Thomas, "Operation KPE: Developing a New Organization," *Journal of Applied Behavioral Science* 4 (1968), 473–506; V. D. Miller, J. R. Johnson, Z. Hart, and D. L. Peterson, "A Test of Antecedents and Outcomes of Employee Role Negotiation Ability," *Journal of Applied Communication Research* 27 (1999), 24–48; J. Watkins and R. A. Luke, "Role Negotiation: Sorting Out the Nuts and Bolts of Day-to-Day Staff Supervision," *Federal Probation* 55 (1991), 18–23.

31. J. P. Campbell and M. D. Dunnette, "Effectiveness of T-Group Experiences in Managerial Training and Development," *Psychological Bulletin* 65 (1968), 73–104; P. Sachdev, "Cultural Sensitivity Training through Experiential Learning: A Participatory Demonstration Field Education Project," *International Social Work* 40 (1997), 7–36.

32. E. Aronson, "Communication in Sensitivity Training Groups," in W. L. French, C. H. Bell, Jr., and R. A. Zawacki, eds., *Organization Development: Theory, Practice, and Research* (Plano, TX: Business Publications, 1983), pp. 249–253.

33. G. David, "Building Cooperation and Trust," in A. J. Marrow, D. G. Bowers, and S. E. Seashore, eds., *Management by Participation* (New York: Harper & Row, 1967), pp. 99–100.

34. C. A. Bramlette and J. H. Tucker, "Encounter Groups: Positive Change or Deterioration,"

Human Relations 34 (1981), 303–314; S. Satoh, N. Morita, I. Matsuzaki, E. Seno, S. Obata, M. Yashikawa, T. Okada, A. Nishimura, T. Konishi, and A. Yamagimi, "Brief Reaction Psychosis Induced by Sensitivity Training: Similarities between Sensitivity Training and Brainstorming," *Psychiatry and Clinical Neurosciences* 50 (1996), 261–265.

35. E. H. Schein, *Process Consultation* (Reading, MA: Addison-Wesley, 1968), pp. 102–103; C. F. Paul and A. C. Gross, "Increasing Productivity and Morale in a Municipality: Effects of Organization Development," *Journal of Applied Behavioral Science* 17 (1981), 59–78.

36. Schein, *Process Consultation*, p. 135; J. C. Quick and E. H. Schein, "The Next Frontier: Edgar Schein on Organizational Therapy," *Academy of Management Executive* 14 (2000), 32–44; E. H. Schein, "The Concept of 'Client' from a Process Consultation Perspective: A Guide," *Journal of Organizational Change Management* 10 (1997), 22–24; C. C. Hebard, "A Story of Real Change," *Training & Development* 52 (1998), 47–64; R. Weir, L. Stewart, G. Browne, J. Roberts, A. Gafni, S. Easton, and L. Seymour, "The Efficacy and Effectiveness of Process Consultation in Improving Staff Morale and Absenteeism," *Medical Care* 35 (1997), 334–353.

37. R. T. Golembiewski, *Approaches to Planned Change, Part I: Orienting Perspectives and Micro-Level Interventions* (New York: Marcel Dekker, 1979), p. 301; H. Prager, "Cooking Up Effective Team Building," *Training & Development* 53 (1999), 14–15; D. J. Svyantek, S. A. Goodman, L. L. Benz, and J. A. Gard, "The Relationship between Organizational Characteristics and Team Building Success," *Journal of Business and Psychology* 14 (1999), 265–283.

38. G. L. Lippitt, *Organization Renewal* (New York: Appleton-Century-Crofts, 1969), pp. 107–113.

39. A. K. Rice, *Learning for Leadership* (London: Tavistock, 1965), pp. 65–66.

40. P. S. Nugent, "Managing Conflict: Third-Party Interventions for Managers," *Academy of Management Executive* 16 (2002), 139–154.

41. R. E. Walton, *Interpersonal Peacemaking: Confrontation and Third Party Consultation* (Reading, MA: Addison-Wesley, 1969), 94–115.

42. R. R. Blake, H. A. Shepard, and J. S. Mouton, *Managing Intergroup Conflict in Industry* (Houston: Gulf, 1965), pp. 36–100; R. Beckhard, *Organization Development: Strategies and Models* (Reading, MA: Addison-Wesley, 1969), pp. 33–35.

43. F. C. Mann, "Studying and Creating Change," in W. G. Bennis, K. D. Benne, and R. Chin, eds., *The Planning of Change* (New York: Holt, Rinehart & Winston, 1961), pp. 605–613; V. M. C. van Geen, "The Measure and Discussion Intervention: A Procedure for Client Empowerment and Quality Control in Residential Care Homes," *Gerontologist* 37 (1997), 817–822; and M. A. Peter, "Making the Hidden Obvious: Management Education through Survey Feedback," *Journal of Nursing Administration* 24 (1994), 13–19.

44. W. G. Dyer, *Strategies for Managing Change* (Reading, MA: Addison-Wesley, 1984), pp. 149–150; B. H. Kleiner, "Open Systems Planning: Its Theory and Practice," *Behavioral Science* 31 (1986), 189–204.

Chapter 15

1. S. Holmes, D. Bennett, K. Carlise, and C. Dawson, "Planet Starbucks: To Keep Up the Growth It Must Go Global Quickly," *Business Week,* September 9, 2002, pp. 100–110; S. Holmes, I. M. Kunii, J. Ewing, and K. Capell, "For Starbucks, There's No Place Like Home," June 9, 2003, pp. 89–91; G. Khermouch, "The Best Global Brands," *Business Week*, August 5, 2002, pp. 92–94.

2. G. Hofstede, "Motivation, Leadership, and Organization: Do American Theories Apply Abroad?" *Organizational Dynamics* 9 (1980), 42–63; G. Hofstede, *Culture's Consequences: International Differences in Work-Related Values* (Beverly Hills, CA: Sage, 1984), pp. 153–212.

3. G. Hofstede, "Cultural Constraints in Management Theories," *Academy of Management Executive* 7 (1993), 81–94.

4. Hofstede, "Motivation, Leadership, and Organization," p. 47.

5. Ibid.

6. Ibid., p. 49.

7. Ibid.

8. Ibid., p. 48.

9. Ibid.

10. H. C. Triandis, *Individualism and Collectivism* (Boulder, CO: Westview Press, 1995); M. Erez and P. C. Earley, *Culture, Self-Identity, and Work* (New York: Oxford Press, 1993).

11. Hofstede, "Motivation, Leadership, and Organization," p. 46.

12. Ibid.

13. Hofstede, "Cultural Constraints," p. 90.

14. R. Yeh, "Values of American, Japanese, and Taiwanese Managers in Taiwan: A Test of Hofstede's Framework," *Academy of Management Proceedings* (1988), 106–110.

15. For additional examples, see L. Sayles, "A 'Primer' on Cultural Dimensions," *Issues and*

Observations of the Center for Creative Leadership 9 (1989), 8–9.

16. Y. Criden and S. Gelb, *The Kibbutz Experience,* pp. 37–57; J. Blasi, *The Communal Experience of the Kibbutz* (New Brunswick, NJ: Transaction Books, 1986), p. 112.

17. For further discussion on this topic, see S. P. Sethi, N. Namiki, and C. L. Swanson, *The False Promise of the Japanese Miracle: Illusions and Realities of the Japanese Management System* (Boston: Pitman, 1984), pp. 34–41.

18. C. Chang and N. Chang, *The Korean Management System: Cultural, Political, Economic Foundations* (Westport, CT: Quorum, 1994).

19. R. E. Cole, *Japanese Blue Collar* (Berkeley: University of California Press, 1971), pp. 72–100; R. Dore, *British Factory—Japanese Factory* (Berkeley, CA: University of California Press, 1973), pp. 74–113; E. Fingleton, "Jobs for Life," *Fortune,* March 20, 1995, pp. 119–125. Note that *nenko* employment occurs only in large firms and applies to no more than one-third of Japan's labor force; for further information, see T. K. Oh, "Japanese Management: A Critical Review," *Academy of Management Review* 1 (1976), 14–25.

20. Cole, *Japanese Blue Collar,* p. 75.

21. Dore, *British Factory—Japanese Factory,* p. 112.

22. Cole, *Japanese Blue Collar,* p. 79; Dore, *British Factory—Japanese Factory,* p. 390.

23. R. Clark, *The Japanese Company* (New Haven, CT: Yale University Press, 1979), p. 38.

24. K. Ellegard, D. Jonsson, T. Enstrom, M. Johansson, L. Medbo, and B. Johansson, "Reflective Production in the Final Assembly of Motor Vehicles: An Emerging Swedish Challenge," *International Journal of Operations and Production Management* 12 (1992), 117–133; A. M. Francesco and B. A. Gold, *International Organizational Behavior* (Upper Saddle River, NJ: Prentice Hall, 1998).

25. D. E. Zand, "Collateral Organization: A New Change Strategy," *Journal of Applied Behavioral Science* 10 (1974), 63–89; H. Lindestadt and G. Rosander, *The Scan Vast Report* (Stockholm: Swedish Employers' Confederation [SAF], 1977), pp. 3–12; F. E. Emery and E. Thorsrud, *Democracy at Work* (Leiden, Netherlands: Kroese, 1976), pp. 27–32; J. F. Bolweg, *Job Design and Industrial Democracy: The Case of Norway* (Leiden, Netherlands: Martinus Nijhoff, 1976), pp. 98–109.

26. M. Chen, *Asian Management Systems: Chinese, Japanese, and Korean Styles of Business* (New York: Routledge, 1995).

27. Dore, *British Factory—Japanese Factory;* Peter F. Drucker, *Management* (New York: Harper & Row, 1974); N. Hatvany and C. V. Pucik, "Japanese Management Practices and Productivity," *Organizational Dynamics* 9 (1981), 5–21; A. D. Bhappu, "The Japanese Family: An Institutional Logic for Japanese Corporate Networks and Japanese Management," *Academy of Management Review* 25 (2000), 409–415.

28. Cole, *Japanese Blue Collar;* R. J. Samuels, "Looking Behind Japan Inc.," *Technology Review* 83 (1981), 43–46.

29. A. Harzing and G. Hofstede, "Planned Change in Organizations: The Influence of National Culture," in P. Bamberger and M. Erez, eds., *Research in the Sociology of Organizations: Cross-Cultural Analysis of Organizations* (Greenwich, CT: JAI Press, 1996).

30. S. Michailova, "Contrasts in Culture: Russian and Western Perspectives on Organizational Change," *Academy of Management Executive* 14 (2000), 99–112.

31. Harzing and Hofstede, "Planned Change in Organizations."

32. C. Kerr, J. T. Dunlop, F. H. Harbison, and C. A. Meyers, *Industrialism and Industrial Man* (Cambridge, MA: Harvard University Press, 1960), pp. 282–288; J. K. Galbraith, *The New Industrial State* (Boston: Houghton Mifflin, 1967), pp. 11–21; F. Harbison, "Management in Japan," in F. Harbison and C. A. Meyers, eds., *Management in the Industrial World: An International Analysis* (New York: McGraw-Hill, 1959), pp. 249–264.

33. P. J. Dowling and R. S. Schuler, *International Dimensions of Human Resource Management* (Boston: PWS-Kent, 1990), pp. 163–164.

34. J. Child, "Culture, Contingency, and Capitalism in the Cross-National Study of Organizations," in L. L. Cummings and B. M. Staw, eds., *Research in Organizational Behavior* (Greenwich, CT: JAI Press, 1981), pp. 303–356.

35. W. Thorngate, "In 'General' vs. 'It Depends'; Some Comments on the Gergen–Schlenker Debate," *Personality and Social Psychology Bulletin* 2 (1976), 404–410; K. E. Weick, *The Social Psychology of Organizing,* 2nd ed. (Reading, MA: Addison-Wesley, 1979).

36. J. A. Wagner III and M. K. Moch, "Individualism–Collectivism: Concept and Measure," *Group and Organization Studies* 11 (1986), 280–304; J. A. Wagner III, "Studies of Individualism–Collectivism: Effects on Cooperation in Groups," *Academy of Management Journal* 38 (1995), 152–172.

Chapter 16

1. J. A. Byrne, "The Real Confessions of Tom Peters," *Business Week,* December 3, 2001.

2. M. A. Hitt and R. D. Ireland, "Peters and Waters Revisited: The Unending Quest for Excellence," *Academy of Management Executive* 2 (1987), 91–98.

3. T. Peters, "Tom Peters's True Confessions," *Fast Company,* December 2001, pp. 78–85.

4. M. Crossan, "Altering Theories of Learning and Action: An interview with Chris Argyris," *Academy of Management Executive* 17 (2003), 40–46.

5. H. Mintzberg, "Ten Ideas Designed to Rile Everyone Who Cares about Management," *Harvard Business Review,* July–August 1996, pp. 61–67.

6. D. Jones, "Some Say MBAs No Longer Worth the Extra Cash," *USA Today Online,* July 22, 2002, 1–2.

7. M. S. Schilling, "Technology Success and Failure in Winner-Take-All Markets: The Impact of Learning Orientation, Timing, and Network Externalities," *Academy of Management Journal* 45 (2002), 387–398.

8. I. I. Mitroff and S. A. Mohrman, "The Slack Is Gone: How the United States Lost Its Competitive Edge in the World Economy," *Academy of Management Executive* 1 (1987), 69.

9. J. A. Byrne, "Management Theory—or Fad of the Month," *Business Week,* June 23, 1997, p. 47.

10. E. Shapiro, *Fad Surfing in the Boardroom: Reclaiming the Courage to Manage in the Age of Instant Answers* (Boston: Addison-Wesley, 1995), pp. 21–22.

11. A. Farnham, "In Search of Suckers," *Fortune,* October 14, 1996, pp. 119–126.

12. J. Buchler, *Philosophical Writings of Peirce* (New York: Dover, 1955); M. Cohen and E. Nagel, *An Introduction to Logic and the Scientific Method* (New York: Harcourt, 1954); M. Polyani, *Personal Knowledge* (Chicago: University of Chicago Press, 1958); L. B. Christenson, *Experimental Methodology* (Boston: Allyn & Bacon, 1977).

13. D. Nadler, "Even Failure Can Be Productive," *New York Times,* April 23, 1989, p. 3.

14. Buchler, *Philosophical Writings of Peirce,* p. 18.

15. N. Byrnes, "Rot on the Street: Worse Than You Thought," *Business Week,* May 12, 2003, 32–33.

16. G. Naik, "Quick Publishing of Research Breakthroughs Can Lift Stock, but May Undermine Science," *Wall Street Journal Online,* January 28, 2002, 1–2.

17. J. R. Hollenbeck, "Quasi-Experimentation and Applied Psychology: Introduction to a Special Issue of Personnel Psychology," *Personnel Psychology* 55 (2002), 56–57.

18. F. N. Kerlinger, *Foundations of Behavioral Research* (New York: Holt, Rinehart & Winston, 1986), p. 9.

19. J. B. Miner, *Theories of Organizational Behavior* (Hinsdale, IL: Dryden Press, 1980).

20. R. Arvey and M. Campion, "The Employment Interview: A Summary and Review of Recent Research," *Personnel Psychology* 34 (1982), 281–322.

21. J. C. Nunnally, *Psychometric Theory* (New York: McGraw-Hill, 1978), p. 4.

22. T. D. Cook and D. T. Campbell, *Quasi-Experimentation: Design Analysis Issues for Field Settings* (Chicago: Rand McNally, 1979), p. 53.

23. K. R. Parkes, "Relative Weight, Smoking and Mental Health as Predictors of Sickness and Absence from Work," *Journal of Applied Psychology* 72 (1987), 275–287.

24. D. G. Mook, "In Defense of External Invalidity," *American Psychologist* 38 (1983), 379–387.

25. D. Rynecki, "Wall Street Trashes Analysts," *Fortune,* March 3, 2003, 52.

action Stipulating the specific actions needed to implement a prescribed solution and overseeing their execution.

action research model A model of the organization development process that permits the development and assessment of original, innovative interventions.

adaptability The ability of a person to display flexibility and versatility in his or her behavior at different times and in different situations.

additive task A group task where the group's performance equals the sum of the performances of its individual members.

administrative principles perspective The management perspective that deals with streamlining administrative procedures to encourage internal stability and efficiency.

agreeableness One of the Big Five personality traits, it reflects individual differences in terms of being courteous, trusting, good-natured, tolerant, cooperative, and forgiving.

attention stage The stage in the information-processing cycle in which the individual decides what will be processed and what will be ignored.

authoritarian leader A leader who makes almost all decisions by himself or herself, minimizing the input of subordinates.

availability bias The tendency in decision makers to judge the likelihood that something will happen by the ease with which they can recall examples of it.

bargaining A process in which offers, counteroffers, and concessions are exchanged while conflicting groups search for some mutually acceptable resolution.

base rate bias The tendency in decision makers to ignore the underlying objective probability or base rate that a particular outcome will follow a particular course of action.

basic coordination mechanism A mechanism that sustains structural interconnections in and among groups by helping to mesh interdependent task activities.

biofeedback A technique that uses machines to monitor bodily functions thought to be involuntary, such as heartbeat and blood pressure, so that a person can learn to regulate these functions.

boundary spanner A member or unit of an organization that interacts with individuals or firms in the organization's environment.

bounded discretion The fact that the list of alternatives that any decision maker generates is restricted by social, legal, and moral norms.

buffering The notion that certain positive factors in the person's environment can limit the capacity of other factors to create dissatisfaction and stress.

bureaucracy An idealized description of an efficient organization based on clearly defined authority, formal recordkeeping, and standardized procedures.

bureaucratic structure A structure used in a large, complex organization that involves significant standardization.

burnout A condition of emotional, physical, and mental exhaustion resulting from prolonged exposure to intense, job-related stress.

centrality The position of person or group within the flow of work in an organization.

centralization The concentration of authority and decision making at the top of an organization; the opposite of decentralization.

ceremonies Special events in which the members of an organization celebrate the myths, heroes, and symbols of their culture.

change To alter, vary, or modify. Change is both an important impetus and a primary product of the process of organization development.

change agent A person who manages the organization development process, serving both as a catalyst for change and as a source of information about organization development.

charismatic leadership Creating a new vision of an organization and getting group members to commit themselves enthusiastically to the new mission, structure, and culture embodied in the vision. Encouraging members to transcend self-interests on behalf of the organization as a whole.

coalition A group that forms so as to allow its members to combine their political strength and thereby pursue interests they hold in common.

coercive power Interpersonal power based on the ability to control the distribution of undesirable outcomes.

cognitive conflict Conflict among group members who share the same goals and values, but differ in terms of their beliefs about the best way to achieve those goals and values.

cohesiveness A measure of the interpersonal attraction among members of a group and their attraction to the group as a whole.

communication The exchange of information between people through a common set of symbols.

communication structure The pattern of interactions by which group members share information.

competitive group rewards Group rewards distributed in such a way that members receive equitable rewards in exchange for successful performance as individuals in a group.

comprehensive interdependence A type of group interaction in which every group member depends on every other member.

comprehensive job enrichment A type of job design that combines both horizontal and vertical improvements to stimulate employee motivation and satisfaction.

conceptual skills The ability to perceive an organization or organizational unit as a whole, to understand how its labor is divided into tasks and reintegrated by the pursuit of common goals or objectives, and to recognize important relationships between the organization or unit and its environment.

conflict A process of opposition and confrontation that can occur between either individuals or groups.

conformity Loyal but uncreative adherence by group members to both pivotal and peripheral norms.

conjunctive task A group task where the group's performance equals the performance of its worst member.

conscientiousness One of the Big Five personality traits, it reflects individual differences in terms of being dependable, organized, persevering, thorough, and achievement–oriented.

consideration Leadership behavior aimed at meeting the social and emotional needs of workers, such as helping them, doing them favors, looking out for their best interests, and explaining decisions.

constituency groups Groups such as employees, customers, and suppliers upon whom the survival of an organization depends. Constituency groups make demands that they expect will be fulfilled in return for their support of the organization.

content validation Establishing validity by showing that, according to expert judges, the measure samples the appropriate material.

contingency approach The view that no single theory, procedure, or set of rules is useful in every situation.

controlling The management function of evaluating the performance of an organization or organizational unit to determine whether it is progressing in the desired direction.

convergence hypothesis The assertion that organizations and management practices throughout the world are growing more alike.

cooperative group rewards Group rewards distributed in such a way that each member receives an equal reward in exchange for the successful performance of the group.

cooptation Making former adversaries into allies by involving them in planning and decision-making processes.

core job characteristics Job characteristics identified in the Hackman-Oldham model that lead workers to experience certain critical psychological states.

core technology The dominant technology used in performing work at the base of the organization.

correlation coefficient A statistic that assesses the degree of relationship between two variables.

covariation The degree to which two variables are associated with each other; the degree to which changes in one variable are related to changes in the other.

creative individualism Acceptance by group members of pivotal norms but rejection of peripheral ones.

criterion-related validation Establishing validity by showing that a measure predicts some variable that, based on theory, it should predict.

critical contingencies Events, activities, or objects that are required by an organization and its various parts to accomplish organizational goals and to ensure continued survival.

critical psychological states Mental conditions identified in the Hackman-Oldham model as being triggered by the presence of certain core job characteristics.

cultural experience The amount of exposure a person has had working with people from different countries and cultures.

culture The shared attitudes and perceptions in an organization that are based on a set of fundamental norms and values and help members understand the organization.

decentralization   The dispersion of authority and decision making downward and outward through the hierarchy of an organization; the opposite of centralization.

decoupling mechanism   A structural approach to managing conflict in which intergroup relations are eliminated, either by buffering or by self-containment.

democratic leader   A leader who works to ensure that all subordinates have a voice in making decisions.

demographic experience   The amount of exposure a person has had with working with people of a different race, sex, or age.

departmentation   The process of clustering structural groups into larger units, called departments or divisions.

depth   The degree or intensity of change that an organization development intervention is designed to stimulate.

diagnosis   Gathering information about a troublesome situation and analyzing it to develop a problem statement.

differentiation   The second stage of group development, characterized by conflicts that erupt as members seek agreement on the purpose, goals, and objectives of the group and the roles of its members.

direct supervision   A basic coordination mechanism in which one person takes responsibility for the work of a group of others and has the authority to decide which tasks must be performed, who will perform them, and how they will be linked together to produce the desired end result.

directing   The management function of encouraging and guiding employees' efforts toward the attainment of organizational goals and objectives.

disjunctive task   A group task where the group's performance equals the performance of its best member.

distributional justice   The fairness judgment that people make with respect to the input/outcome ratios they experience relative to the same ratios experienced by others with whom they identify (that is, reference person).

division of labor   The process and result of breaking difficult work into smaller tasks.

divisional structure   The type of bureaucratic structure characterized by standardization, divisional departmentation, and moderate decentralization.

efficiency perspective   An approach to job design that focuses on the creation of jobs that economize on time, human energy, raw materials, and other productive resources.

emergent task elements   The components of work roles that are not formally recognized by the organization but arise out of expectations held by others for the role occupant.

emotional adjustment   One of the Big Five personality traits, it reflects individual differences in terms of being stable, content, secure, and nondepressed.

employee-oriented behavior   Leadership behavior designed to meet the social and emotional needs of group members.

entity attraction   Satisfaction with other persons in the workplace that arises because these people share the individual's fundamental values, attitudes, or philosophy.

environment   The context surrounding an organization, consisting of those economic, geographic, and political conditions that impinge on the firm.

environmental change   An environmental characteristic concerning the extent to which conditions in an organization's environment change unpredictably.

environmental complexity   An environmental characteristic referring to the degree to which an organization's environment is complicated and therefore difficult to understand.

environmental diversity   The degree to which an organization's environment is varied or heterogeneous in nature.

environmental receptivity   The degree to which an organization's environment supports the organization's progress toward fulfilling its purpose.

environmental turbulence   The speed and scope of change that occurs in the environment surrounding an organization.

environmental uncertainty   An environmental characteristic formed by the combination of change and complexity that reflects a lack of information about environmental factors, activities, and events.

ergonomics   Another name for human factors engineering; a type of methods engineering that focuses on designing machines to match human capacities and limitations.

escalation of commitment   Investing additional resources in failing courses of action that are not justified by any foreseeable payoff.

established task elements   The components of work roles that are contained in written job descriptions and formally recognized in the organization.

eustress   A particular kind of stress created when an individual is confronted with an opportunity.

evaluation   Measuring the effectiveness of planned actions to determine whether additional action is required.

expectancy   A person's beliefs regarding the link between that individual's efforts and his or her performance.

expert power   Interpersonal power based on the possession of expertise, knowledge, and talent.

explicit theories   Internally consistent, formal theories that are subject to empirical testing.

extinction   The gradual disappearance of response that occurs after the cessation of positive reinforcement.

extroversion   One of the Big Five personality traits, it reflects individual differences in terms of being sociable, gregarious, assertive, talkative, and expressive.

force field analysis   A diagnostic method that depicts the array of forces for and against a particular change in a graphic analysis; often used as a component of the organization development process.

functional attraction   Satisfaction with other people in the workplace that arises because these other people help the individual attain valued work outcomes.

functional grouping   Grouping people into units based on similarities in the functions they perform.

functional structure   The type of bureaucratic structure characterized by standardization, functional departmentation, and centralization.

general adaptation syndrome   The theory developed by Hans Selye stating that the body's response to stress occurs in three distinct stages: alarm, resistance, and exhaustion.

general cognitive ability   The sum of an individual's standing on all facets of mental ability.

generalizability   The degree to which the result of a study conducted in one sample-setting-time configuration can be replicated in other sample-setting-time configurations.

goal orientation   A distinction drawn between people who approach a task with the goal of learning how to improve themselves (learning orientation) from those whose goals are strictly to perform at a certain level (performance orientation).

group effectiveness   An assessment of the extent to which a group is accomplishing its task in the most productive and satisfactory manner.

group formation   The process of grouping the members of an organization into work groups or units.

group maintenance roles   Group roles that help ensure a group's continued existence by building and preserving strong interpersonal relations among its members.

group synergy   A situation in which group productivity exceeds what would be expected based on individual contributions.

hedonism   The belief that human beings generally behave so as to maximize pleasure and minimize pain.

heroes   People who embody the values of an organization's culture and serve as role models for other members in the organization.

hierarchy   The pyramidal differentiation of rank that occurs as authority is assigned to individual organization members according to their organizational status and responsibilities.

hierarchy of authority   A pyramidal distribution of authority in which managers higher in the pyramid can tell managers in lower positions what to do.

hindsight bias   When people feel that they would have predicted the outcome to events better than they actually did or better than they actually would have if they had been asked to make a forecast.

history threat   A threat to data validity created when some important variable other than the one being manipulated experimentally changes during an experiment.

horizontal job enlargement   A type of job design based on the idea that increasing the number of tasks that a jobholder performs will reduce the repetitive nature of the job and thus eliminate worker boredom.

human factors engineering   A type of methods engineering in which experts design machines, operations, and work environments so that they better match human capacities and limitations.

human relations perspective   The management perspective that emphasizes increasing employee growth, development, and satisfaction.

human skills   The ability to work effectively as a group member and to build cooperation among the members of an organization or unit.

hygiene factors   Characteristics of the job that, according to Frederick Herzberg, influence the amount of dissatisfaction experienced at work.

hypothesis   A specific, testable prediction, derived typically from a theory, about the relationship between two variables.

implicit theories   Loose, informal theories about phenomena that people rarely test in a rigorous, empirical fashion.

individualism-collectivism   A cross-cultural dimension that reflects two opposing points of view of the norms and values of a national culture—whether they should place greater emphasis on satisfying personal interests or on looking after group needs.

industrial engineering   A branch of engineering that concerns itself with maximizing the efficiency of the methods, facilities, and materials used to produce commercial products.

industrial robots   Machines that can be programmed to repeat the same sequence of work movements over and over.

information overload   A condition in which a person is presented with more information than he or she can possibly process.

initiating structure   Leadership behaviors aimed at meeting the group's task requirements, such as getting workers to follow rules, monitoring performance standards, clarifying roles, and setting goals.

initiation   The initial stage of group development, characterized by uncertainty and anxiety.

instrumentality   A person's subjective belief about the relationship between performing a behavior and receiving an outcome.

integration   The third stage of group development, which is focused on reestablishing the central purpose of the group in light of the structure of roles developed during differentiation.

interaction   An experimental outcome in which the relationship between two variables changes depending on the presence or absence of some third variable.

interactional justice   The fairness judgment that people make with respect to the interpersonal manner in which decisions are communicated.

intergroup team building   A deep organization development intervention intended to improve communication and interaction between work-related groups.

intervention   A particular organization development technique, such as counseling or team building, that is used to stimulate change in organizations.

jargon   Idiosyncratic use of language that is often useful among specialists but that inhibits their ability to communicate with nonspecialists.

job depth   The amount of discretion that a jobholder has in choosing job activities and outcomes.

Job Diagnostic Survey   A questionnaire that measures workers' perceptions of core job characteristics, critical psychological states, and different moderating factors.

job extension   A type of horizontal job enlargement in which several simplified jobs are combined to form a single new job.

job-oriented behavior   Leadership behavior that focuses on careful supervision of employees' work methods and performance level.

job range   The number of tasks that a jobholder performs to complete the job.

job rotation   A process whereby an individual systematically moves from one job to another over the course of time. A job rotation can also be a type of horizontal job enlargement in which workers are rotated among several jobs in a structured, predefined manner.

job satisfaction   The perception that one's job enables one to fulfill important job values.

kibbutz   A close-knit community of people located in Israel and organized based on the principles of collective ownership and direct participation in self-governance.

laissez-faire leader   A leader who lets a group run itself, with minimal intervention from upper levels of the organizational hierarchy.

language   A system of shared symbols that the members of an organization use to communicate cultural ideas and understandings.

latticework structure   The structure of vertical and horizontal relationships found in many large Japanese corporations.

leader-follower relations   A component of Fiedler's contingency theory that describes the level of trust and respect between leader and follower.

leadership   The use of noncoercive influence to direct and coordinate the activities of the members of an organized group toward the accomplishment of group objectives.

legitimate power   Interpersonal power based on holding a position of formal authority.

loosely coupling   Weakening the effect that one subgroup has on another so that each can plan and operate almost as if the other were nonexistent.

loss-aversion bias   The tendency of most decision makers to give a heavier weight to losses than to gains, even when the absolute value of each is equal.

Machiavellianism   A personality trait characterized by the tendency to seek to control other people through opportunistic, manipulative behaviors.

macro organizational behavior   The subfield of organizational behavior that focuses on understanding the actions of a group or an organization as a whole.

management   A process of planning, organizing, directing, and controlling organizational behaviors so as to accomplish a mission through the division of labor.

manager   A person who is responsible for planning, organizing, directing, and controlling behavior in organizations.

managerial role   Behaviors expected of managers in performing their jobs. Managers promote good interpersonal relations in the **interpersonal** role, receive and send information to others in the **informational** role, and determine the firm's direction in the **decisional** role.

masculinity-femininity   A cross-cultural dimension that reflects the degree to which a culture is founded on values that emphasize independence, aggressiveness, dominance, and physical strength, on the one hand, or interdependence, compassion, empathy, and emotional openness, on the other hand.

matrix structure   The type of bureaucratic organization structure that incorporates both functional and divisional departmentation, along with significant mutual adjustment at the top of the organization.

maturation contingencies   Structural contingency factors associated with an organization's level of maturity that determine whether pre-bureaucratic, bureaucratic, or post-bureaucratic structures are more likely to produce effectiveness.

maturity   The fourth and final stage of group development, in which members begin to fulfill their prescribed roles and work toward attaining group goals.

mechanistic structures   Machine-like organization structures designed to enhance efficiency; characterized by large amounts of formalization, standardization, specialization, and centralization.

meso organizational behavior   The subfield of organizational behavior concerned with behaviors in and of groups and teams.

methods engineering   An area of industrial engineering that attempts to improve the methods used to perform work.

micro organizational behavior   The subfield of organizational behavior concerned with understanding the behaviors of individuals working alone or in small groups.

micromotion analysis   A type of work measurement in which industrial engineers analyze the hand and body movements required to do a job.

mirror image fallacy   The false belief that there is little variation in people and that the whole world is "just like me."

mission   An organization's purpose or reason for being.

mixed motive conflict   Conflict among group members that arises out of their differing goals and values.

modular structure   The type of post-bureaucratic structure consisting of autonomous teams of employees joined together by an intrafirm computer network (intranet).

motivation   The factors that initiate, direct, and sustain human behavior over time.

motivational perspective   An approach to job design that suggests that fitting the characteristics of jobs to the needs and interests of the people who perform them provides the opportunity for satisfaction at work.

motivator factors   Characteristics of the job that, according to Frederick Herzberg, influence the amount of satisfaction experienced at work.

multiunit structure   The type of bureaucratic organization structure that is composed of autonomous, self-managed business units and is characterized by divisional departmentation and extreme decentralization.

mutual adjustment   A basic coordination mechanism in which coordination is accomplished via face-to-face communications among coworkers who occupy positions of similar hierarchical authority.

myth   A story that provides a fictional, but plausible explanation for something that might otherwise seem puzzling.

national culture   The collection of societal norms and values in the environment surrounding an organization.

negative affectivity   A person's tendency to experience feelings of subjective distress such as anger, contempt, disgust, guilt, fear, and nervousness.

negative reinforcement   The increase in response that occurs when engaging in the response leads to the removal of an aversive stimulus.

negotiation   A process in which groups with conflicting interests decide what each will give and take in the exchange between them.

nenko system   A Japanese system of payment in which the pay received by an employee consists of a basic wage plus merit supplements and job-level allowances.

noise A collective term for several factors that can distort a message as it is transmitted from one person to another.

norms A strong set of expectations that members of a role set have for the role occupant.

objectivity In science, the degree to which a set of scientific findings are independent of any one person's opinion about them.

open revolution Rejection by group members of both pivotal and peripheral norms.

open system planning A deep, organization-level intervention that helps the members of an organization devise ways to accomplish the mission of their firm in light of the demands of environmental constituency groups.

open systems perspective The management perspective that characterizes every organization as a system that is open to the influence of the surrounding environment.

openness to experience One of the Big Five personality traits, it reflects individual differences in terms of being curious, imaginative, artistic, broad-minded, sensitive, and playful.

organic structures Organism-like organization structures designed to enhance flexibility and innovation; characterized by large amounts of mutual adjustment and decentralization.

organization An assembly of people and materials brought together to accomplish a purpose that would not be achievable through the efforts of individuals working alone.

organization design The process of diagnosing the situation that confronts a particular organization, then selecting and implementing the organization structure most appropriate for that situation.

organization development A planned approach to interpersonal, group, intergroup, and organization-wide change that is comprehensive, long-term, and under the guidance of a change agent.

organization role The total set of expectations that people who interact with an organizational member have for both that person and his or her job performance.

organization size The number of members in an organization; its volume of sales, clients, or profits; its physical capacity (for example, a hospital's number of beds or a hotel's number of rooms); or the total financial assets that it controls.

organization stage The stage in the information-processing cycle in which many discrete bits of information are chunked into higher-level, abstract concepts.

organization structure The relatively stable network of interconnections or interdependencies among the people and tasks that make up an organization.

organizational behavior A field of study that endeavors to understand, explain, predict, and change human behavior as it occurs in the organizational context.

organizational citizenship behaviors Acts that promote the organization's interest, but are not formally a part of any person's documented job requirements.

organizational commitment Identification with one's employer that includes the willingness to work hard on behalf of the organization and the intention to remain with the organization for an extended period of time.

organizational effectiveness The degree to which an organization is successful in achieving its goals and objectives while simultaneously ensuring its continued survival by satisfying the demands of interested parties, such as suppliers and customers.

organizational efficiency The ratio of outputs produced per unit of inputs consumed; minimizing the raw materials and energy consumed by the production of goods and services.

organizational power Types of interpersonal power (reward, coercive, and legitimate power) that often derive from company policies and procedures.

organizational productivity The amount of goods or services produced by an organization. Higher productivity means that more goods or services are produced.

organizing The management function of developing a structure of interrelated tasks and allocating people and resources within this structure.

peripheral norms Group norms for which adherence is desirable but not essential.

personal power Types of interpersonal power (expert and referent power) that are based on the possession of certain personal traits or characteristics.

pivotal norms Group norms for which adherence is an absolute requirement of continued group membership.

planning The management function of deciding what to do in the future—that is, setting goals and establishing the means to attain those goals.

politics Activities in which individuals or groups acquire power and then use that power to advance their own interests.

pooled interdependence   A type of interaction where individuals draw off a common resource pool but do not interact with one another in any other way.

position power   A component of Fiedler's contingency theory that describes the degree to which the leader can administer significant rewards and punishments to followers.

positive reinforcement   The increase in response that occurs when engaging in the response leads to receipt of a pleasurable stimulus.

post-bureaucratic structure   An extremely flexible structure that substitutes various information-processing mechanisms for hierarchy and incorporates significant mutual adjustment, decentralization, and either functional or divisional departmentation among different autonomous units or allied organizations.

power distance   A cross-cultural dimension that reflects the degree to which the members of a society accept differences in power and status among themselves.

power   The ability to influence the conduct of others and resist unwanted influence in return.

pre-bureaucratic structure   A structure used in a small, simple organization, which lacks standardization.

prepotency   The notion arising from Maslow's theory that higher-order needs can influence motivation only if lower-order needs are largely satisfied.

privacy   The freedom to work unobserved by others and without undue interruption.

procedural justice   The fairness judgment that people make with respect to the methods used to determine the outcomes received.

process consultation   A shallow, group-level organization development intervention in which a change agent meets with a work group and helps its members examine group processes such as communication, leadership and followership, problem solving, and cooperation.

process engineering   A type of methods engineering in which specialists study the sequence of tasks required to produce a particular good or service and examine how these tasks fit together into an integrated job.

process loss   The difference between what is produced by a group of individuals and what would be produced by the same people working alone.

production blocking   The negative effect on productivity caused by people getting in one another's way as they try to perform a group task.

prototype   One type of schema that involves a unified configuration of personal characteristics that are used to classify persons into "types."

punishment   A decrease in response that occurs when engaging in the response leads to receipt of an aversive stimulus.

quality circles   Small groups of employees who meet on company time to identify and resolve job-related problems.

quality perspective   An approach to job design in which elements of the efficiency and satisfaction perspectives are combined to improve the quality of goods or services produced.

quantitative ability   A facet of mental ability that reflects the person's ability to perform all kinds of arithmetic problems.

random assignment   A method of increasing the validity of a study by ensuring that each subject has an equal probability of being assigned to any one experimental condition. Random assignment eliminates the selection threat.

reasoning ability   A facet of mental ability that reflects a person's capacity to invent solutions to many different types of problems.

reciprocal interdependence   A type of interaction characterized by two-way links among individuals.

referent power   Interpersonal power based on the possession of attractive personal characteristics.

reliability   The degree to which a measure of an individual, group, organizational, or environmental attribute is free from random error and thus replicable.

reward power   Interpersonal power based on the ability to control how desirable outcomes are distributed.

rite   A ceremonial activity meant to communicate particular messages or accomplish specific purposes.

ritual   A ceremonial event that occurs repeatedly and continues to reinforce key norms and values.

role   The typical and expected behaviors that characterize an individual's position in some social context.

role ambiguity   Lack of clarity about the expectations of a person's role in an organization.

role conflict   Conflict or incompatibility between the demands facing a person who occupies a particular role.

role custodianship   A product of socialization in which a new group member adopts the means and ends associated with the role unquestioningly.

role innovation   A product of socialization in which a new group member is expected to improve on both the goals for his or her job and the means of achieving them.

role negotiation technique   An interpersonal organization development intervention of moderate depth intended to help people form and maintain effective working relationships by clarifying role expectations.

role occupant   The current incumbent of an existing role.

role scope   The total number of expectations that exist for the person occupying a particular role.

role set   The entire group of individuals who have an interest in and expectations about the way that a role occupant performs his or her job.

satisficing   Settling for the first alternative that meets some minimum level of acceptability, as opposed to searching for an optimal solution.

schema   Cognitive structures that group discrete bits of perceptual information in an organized fashion.

scientific management perspective   The management perspective that focuses on increasing the efficiency of production processes to enhance organizational profitability.

scientific method   An objective method of expanding knowledge characterized by an endless cycle of theory building, hypothesis formation, data collection, empirical hypothesis testing, and theoretical modification.

script   A schema that involves well-known sequences of action.

selection threat   A threat to data validity created when experimental and control groups differ from each other before an experimental manipulation.

self-efficacy   The judgments people make about their ability to execute courses of action required to deal with prospective situations.

self-managing teams   Teams of employees empowered with the authority to determine job procedures, work assignments, membership, and so on.

semiautonomous groups   Groups that must follow the management direction needed to ensure adherence to organizational policies but otherwise manage themselves.

sensitivity training   A deep, interpersonal organization development intervention that focuses on developing greater sensitivity to oneself, to others, and to one's relations with others through an intense, leaderless group experience.

sequential interdependence   A type of interaction in which individuals are arrayed in a chain of one-way links.

shaping   Bringing about a desired behavior by rewarding successive approximations to that behavior.

shared mental model   A set of common schemas, scripts, and prototypes that helps promote a common understanding among group members.

short-term/long-term orientation   A cross-cultural dimension that reflects the degree to which people favor tradition and the present versus innovation and the future.

simple differentiated structure   The type of pre-bureaucratic structure in which coordination is achieved by means of direct supervision.

simple undifferentiated structure   The type of pre-bureaucratic structure in which coordination is achieved solely by means of mutual adjustment.

social density   An index of crowding, typically calculated as the number of people occupying an area divided by the number of square feet in that area.

social facilitation   A situation in which performing in groups increases the motivation and performance of individual members.

social information   Information growing out of cultural norms, values, and shared opinions that shapes the ways that people perceive themselves, their jobs, and the organization.

social loafing   The choice by some group members to take advantage of others by doing less work, working more slowly, or otherwise contributing less to group productivity.

social support   A surrounding environment in which people are sympathetic and caring.

socialization   The process by which a person acquires the social knowledge and skills necessary to assume a role.

sociotechnical enrichment   A type of job design that recognizes the importance of satisfying the needs of employees within the technical requirements of an organization's production system.

solution   Identifying ways to resolve a problem uncovered during diagnosis.

spatial visualization   A facet of mental ability that reflects a person's ability to imagine how an object would look if its position in space were changed.

special-interest committees   Committees in Scandinavian industrial democracies composed of worker and manager representatives; they cooperate with middle management to produce yearly reports that assist works councils with the task of formulating company policies.

standard time analysis   A time-study technique in which an analyst matches the results of micromotion analysis with standard time charts to determine the average time that should be required to perform a job.

standardization   A basic coordination mechanism in which work is coordinated by providing employees with carefully planned standards and procedures that guide the performance of their tasks. In the context of scientific measurement, standardization is the practice of ensuring that all people measure the same variables by applying the same instruments in the same manner.

stereotype   A standardized mental picture that is held in common by members of a group and that represents an oversimplified opinion, prejudiced attitude, or uncritical judgment.

stopwatch time analysis   A time-study technique in which an analyst uses a stopwatch to time the sequence of motions needed to complete a job.

story   An account of past events with which all employees are familiar and that serves as a reminder of cultural understandings.

stress   An unpleasant emotional state resulting from the perception that a situational demand exceeds one's capacity and that it is very important to meet the demand.

structural contingency factors   Characteristics of an organization and its surrounding circumstances that influence whether its structure will contribute to organizational effectiveness.

substitutability   The extent to which other people or groups can grant access to the same critical contingencies provided by the focal person or group.

substitutes for leadership   Someone or something in the leader's environment that affects workers' attitudes, perceptions, or behaviors in such a way as to render the leader's role superfluous.

subversive rebellion   Acceptance by group members of peripheral norms but rejection of pivotal ones.

survey feedback   A shallow, organization-level organization development intervention intended to stimulate information sharing throughout the entire organization.

symbol   An object, action, or event to which people have assigned special meaning.

symbolic management   A process in which managers attempt to influence deep cultural norms and values by shaping the surface cultural elements that organization members use to express and transmit cultural understandings.

target   The specific focus of an organization development intervention's change efforts.

task structure   A component of Fiedler's contingency theory that describes the clarity of goals and of means—end relationships in a group's task.

team   A type of group characterized by tight interdependence, cross-functional expertise, and differential information among members.

team development   A deep, group-level extension of interpersonal sensitivity training in which a group of people who work together on a daily basis meet over an extended period to assess and modify group processes.

technical skills   An understanding of the specific knowledge, procedures, and tools used to make the goods or services produced by an organization or units.

technology   The knowledge, procedures, and equipment used in an organization to transform unprocessed resources into finished goods or services.

temporal precedence   The degree to which any measured cause actually precedes an effect in time.

theory   A set of interrelated constructs, definitions, and propositions that present a systematic view of phenomena by specifying relations among variables.

Theory X   A managerial point of view that assumes that nonmanagerial employees have little interest in attaining organizational goals and must therefore be motivated to satisfy the needs of the organization.

Theory Y   A managerial point of view that assumes that nonmanagerial employees will readily direct their behavior toward organizational goals if they are given the opportunity to do so.

third-party peace making   A shallow organization development intervention in which a change agent seeks to resolve intergroup misunderstandings by encouraging communication between or among groups.

transaction costs   Costs incurred while initiating and conducting business transactions, either within or between organizations.

uncertainty avoidance   A cross-cultural dimension that reflects the degree to which people are comfortable with ambiguous situations and with the inability to predict future events with assurance.

unit-linking mechanism   A structural approach to managing conflict and coordinating intergroup relations in which mutual adjustment is encouraged among interdependent groups.

valence The amount of satisfaction that an individual anticipates receiving from a particular outcome.

validity The degree to which a measure of an individual, group, organizational, or environmental attribute does what it is intended to do.

verbal ability A facet of mental ability that reflects the degree to which a person can understand and use written and spoken language.

verification A stage in the scientific process in which scientists assess the degree to which hypotheses based on theories match empirical data.

vertical dyad Two persons who are related hierarchically, such as a supervisor-subordinate pair.

vertical job enrichment A type of job design based on the idea that giving jobholders the discretion to choose job activities and outcomes will improve their satisfaction.

virtual structure The type of post-bureaucratic structure consisting of multiple companies specializing in different functional tasks and joined together by an interfirm computer network (internet).

voice The formal opportunity to complain to the organization about one's work situation.

work design The process of deciding what specific tasks each jobholder should perform in the context of the overall work that an organization must accomplish.

work flow grouping Grouping people into units based on similarities in the products they make or markets they serve.

work measurement An area of industrial engineering concerned with measuring the amount of work accomplished and developing standards for performing work of an acceptable quantity and quality.

works council A committee of worker representatives who are elected by their peers and management representatives who are appointed by top management; it oversees policy formulation in Scandinavian industrial democracies.

NAME INDEX

Note: The letter "n" refers to notes.

Ackerman, P.L., 123, 566n53
Adams, J.S., 239n, 585n23
Adler, P.S., 572n49
Aguren, S, 202n
Ahlberg, E., 145n, 577n6
Ahuja, M.K., 584n20
Aiken, M., 583n9, 583n13
Alavi, M., 583n6
Albanese, R., 575n27
Alchian, A.A., 586n35
Aldag, R.J., 570n15, 571n24, 571n26
Aldrich, H., 585n24
Alge, B.J., 565n43
Allaire, Paul A., 343
Allen, J.S., 579n40
Allen, R.W., 581n25, 581n26
Alper, S., 562n24, 577n72
Amason, A.C., 582n37
Ambrose, M., 574n59
Ambrose, M.L., 239n, 574n68
Amichai-Hamburger, Y., 587n22
Amos, Karen, 290
Anderson, J.V., 563n48
Ando, Kunitake, 436
Andrews, M.C., 581n28
Andrews, S.B., 581n20, 587n10
Anfuso, D., 559n7, 561n46, 567n40
Angle, H.L., 581n25
Ante, S., 574n4
Ante, S.E., 376n, 427n
Arad, S., 561n78
Armour, S., 564n18
Armstrong, L., 563n49
Arndt, M., 572n44
Aronson, E., 588n32
Arpey, Gerard, 216, 221
Arthur, J.B., 559n5
Arvey, R., 590n20

Arvey, R.D., 560n35, 560n40
Ashcroft, John, 71, 77
Ashford, S.J., 578n15, 587n27
Ashforth, B.E., 573n46
Ashworth, S., 560n20
Ashworth, S.D., 566n6, 568n73
Astley, W.G., 581n21
Aston, A., 572n44
Atkins, P.W.B., 562n23
Atwater, D., 562n21
Atwater, L., 580n77
Atwater, L.E., 562n21, 580n76
Avolio, B.J., 561n65, 578n20, 578n34, 579n39, 579n41, 579n42
Aydin, C., 587n19

Bacharach, S.B., 567n27
Baker, J.R., 571n37
Baker, S., 572n40
Bales, K., 150n
Balfour, F., 57
Ballmer, Steve, 287
Baltes, B.B., 264, 562n6
Bamberger, P., 589n29
Bamberger, P.A., 567n27
Bamforth, K.W., 570n19
Bandura, A., 117–119, 564n27, 565n30, 565n34
Bannister, B.D., 579n62
Barker, J., 573n20
Barker, V.L., 584n7
Barling, J., 578n31
Barnard, Janet, 166
Barney, J., 557n7
Barney, J.B., 582n41
Barr, S.H., 570n15
Barrett, A., 584n1
Barrett, Colleen, 290
Barrett, D., 576n40
Barrick, M.B., 560n24
Barrick, M.R., 49n, 560n17, 560n27, 576n33, 576n49
Barringer, B.R., 585n17

Bartunek, J.M., 587n28
Bass, B.M., 578n33, 579n39
Batt, R., 142n
Bauer, C.C., 264n
Bavelas, A., 576n40
Beauregard, R.S., 565n51
Becker, G.S., 564n3
Becker, T., 576n32
Beckhard, Richard, 444, 445n, 588n42
Beersma, B.Z, 563n31, 575n29, 577n66
Beinstock, P., 570n17
Bell, B.S., 565n52
Bell, C.H. Jr., 456n, 458n, 558n21, 587n25, 588n32
Bell, N.E., 568n56
Bell-Irvine, Richard, 49
Beman, D.R., 355n
Benne, K., 575n25, 588n43
Bennett, D., 588n1
Bennett, N., 574n64
Bennett, W.R., 565n37, 577n60
Bennis, W., 445n
Bennis, W.G., 588n43
Benzz, L.L., 588n37
Berkowitz, L., 239n, 577n69
Bernardin, H.J., 560n21
Berner, R., 557n1
Bernman, S.L., 575n14
Bernstein, A., 6n, 515n, 559n9, 564n5, 564n7
Berry, D., 577n61
Berson, Y., 579n39
Bertrand, M., 560n43
Bettenhausen, K.L., 575n12, 575n19
Bettman, Gary, 15
Beyer, J.M., 586n6, 587n16, 587n20
Bezos, Jeff, 20
Bhappu, A.D., 589n27
Bianco, A., 580n1
Biddle, B.J., 572n8
Biggane, F., 569n10
Billings, A.G., 567n48

bin Laden, Osama, 271
Biorkinshaw, J., 584n2
Birnbaum, P.H., 571n24
Bishop, J.W., 576n34
Black, S., 63
Blackburn, R., 571n31
Blackburn, R.S., 581n25
Blake, R., 287, 578n28
Blake, R.R., 588n42
Blanchard, K., 293, 579n53
Blasi, J., 564n5
Blau, G., 573n41
Blau, P.M., 583n13
Bliese, P.D., 578n37
Block, C.J., 562n8
Blodgett, Henry, 225
Bloom, M., 566n56
Bluedorn, A.C., 573n19, 585n17
Blum, T.C., 564n63
Boeker, W., 582n34
Boje, D.M., 586n10
Bolweg, J.F., 589n25
Bommer, W.H., 574n56, 579n57
Bond, Michael Harris, 510, 514, 517, 518, 524, 525
Bongiorno, L., 585n26
Bono, J.E., 50, 566n17, 568n54, 578n19
Booth-Butterfield, M., 575n18
Booth-Butterfield, S., 575n18
Borchgrevink, C.P., 567n19
Borden, M., 574n70
Bordia, P., 575n20
Borman, W.C., 562n18
Borrus, A., 386n, 573n17, 585n26
Bossidy, L., 45, 559n6
Boulding, E., 580n5
Bowen, D.E., 557n15, 572n50
Bower, Marvin, 12
Bowers, D.G., 588n33
Boyatzis, R.E., 579n46
Boyle, M., 269n
Boynton, A., 572n48
Brady, D., 557n6, 568n71

Braito, R., 570n13
Bramlette, C.A., 588n34
Brandt, R., 584n21, 587n17
Brass, D.J., 581n20
Brehmer, D., 563n42
Brender, Y., 345n
Brennan, E., 572n3
Brett, J.M., 566n18
Breuer, N.L., 560n14, 568n67
Bridwell, L.G., 564n14
Brief, A.P., 570n15, 571n24, 571n26
Brodt, S.E., 574n54
Brown, A.D., 586n3
Brown, B.R., 582n43
Brown, S.P., 565n49, 565n50
Browne, G., 588n36
Brtek, M.D., 568n62, 569n5
Bruke, James, 95
Bruning, N.S., 568n74
Bryne, J.A., 577n5
Buch, K., 572n46
Buchler, J., 590n12, 590n14
Buckman, R., 578n23
Bunderson, J.S., 576n36
Burke, C.S., 576n35
Burke, L.A., 560n27
Burke, W. Warner, 431, 461, 587n24
Burkhardt, M.E., 581n20
Burnham, D.H., 580n7, 580n8
Burnham, Daniel P., 386
Burns, J.M., 578n30
Burns, L.R., 583n16, 583n49
Burns, T., 409n, 584n7
Burrows, P., 557n1, 583n1
Bush, George W., 71, 92, 222, 296
Butcher, V., 578n31
Bycio, P., 579n40
Bylinksy, G., 561n60, 562n13
Byrne, J.A., 12n, 563n29, 580n4, 584n21, 590n1, 590n9
Byrne, Z.S., 567n36
Byrnes, N., 386n, 583n1, 590n15

Calderwood, R., 577n55
Caldwell, D.F., 587n18
Callahan, T.J., 557n4
Callister, J., 582n38
Cameron, K., 585n8
Camp, J.D., 560n16
Campbell, D.T., 590n22
Campbell, J.P., 569n13, 588n31
Campion, M.A., 195, 560n30, 568n61, 569n5, 590n20
Cannon-Bowers, J.A., 562n11, 577n56
Capell, K., 6n, 588n1
Cappelli, P., 557n11
Cardy, R.L., 559n12
Carey, A., 559n18
Carey, J., 585n26
Carey, S., 566n6
Carley, K.M., 577n57, 584n20
Carlise, K., 6n, 588n1
Carlson, D.S., 582n33
Carlson, S.M, 558n6
Carnevale, P., 582n48
Carney, D., 563n41
Carr, L., 566n6, 568n73
Carroll, G.R., 586n29
Carson, K.P., 559n12
Carter, N.M., 583n13
Cartier, P., 562n21
Cartrwright, D., 575n11, 577n68, 580n9, 585n17
Carty, Don, 215–217, 225, 234, 240
Cass, E.L., 570n14
Caston, R.J., 570n13
Castro, S.L., 579n48
Castrogiovanni, G.J., 585n25
Caudron, S., 286n, 559n3, 577n4, 578n8
Cavanagh, G.F., 345n
Chaffin, D.B., 560n41
Challagalla, 565n50
Chambers, Jeff, 112–113
Champy, J., 557n15, 571n38, 583n18
Chang, A., 575n20
Chang, C., 589n18
Chang, N., 589n18
Chapanis, A., 569n3
Charan, R., 564n26, 565n42

Chatman, J., 587n18
Chazan, G., 579n60
Chen, G., 578n36, 578n37
Chen, M., 589n26
Chen, P.E., 568n55
Cherney, E., 574n2
Chia, R., 587n26
Child, J., 523, 524, 590n34
Chin, R., 588n43
Choi, H., 572n11
Christenson, L.B., 590n12
Christie, R., 581n29
Chua, R., 563n30
Churchill, Winston, 344
Claigiuri, P.M., 561n70
Clark, D., 237n
Clark, L.A., 568n53
Clark, R., 589n23
Clausen, J.A., 568n56
Clegg, C.W., 571n28
Clifford, M., 226n
Clinton, Bill, 271, 344
Coase, R.H., 586n35
Coch, L., 559n20
Coghill, Skip, 125
Cohen, M., 590n12
Cole, C.L., 567n31
Cole, R.E., 589n19, 589n20, 589n22, 589n28
Cole, Sheryl, 238–240
Coleman, F., 573n44
Coleman, H.C. Jr., 584n19
Collins, J., 283, 560n 22
Collins, P.D., 585n14
Colquitt, J.A., 239, 560n29, 562n80, 563n46, 574n58, 579n52
Commons, J.R., 586n35
Conlin, M., 63, 113, 125, 564n12, 567n45, 568n65, 568n70, 573n34
Conlon, D.E., 239n, 563n31, 582n48
Connolly, T., 565n48, 573n24
Conolon, D.E., 575n29
Cook, J.S., 569n3
Cook, T.D., 590n22
Cooke, D.K., 560n21
Cool, K., 557n7
Coons, A.E., 578n26

Cooper, C., 579n60
Cooper, J.B., 559n8
Cordery, J.L., 571n28
Corssan, M., 590n4
Cortese, A., 558n16
Coser, L., 582n38
Coubrough, J.A., 558n13
Courtright, J.A., 584n7, 585n16
Cowley, Rowleen, 88, 89
Cox, Robert J., 182
Cox, T.H., 561n59, 564n11
Coy, P., 557n1
Crawford, G.A., 581n17
Criden, Y., 589n16
Cristol, D.S., 566n15
Crockett, R., 427n, 561n55
Cron, W.L., 565n49
Cropanzano, R., 567n36
Crosby, P.B., 203, 571n29
Crozier, M., 352, 581n24
Cuban, Mark, 15
Cullen, J.B., 583n13
Cullison, A., 271n
Cummings, A., 564n62, 568n63
Cummings, G., 584n3
Cummings, J., 562n3, 573n18
Cummings, L.L., 557n10, 557n11, 559n27, 563n34, 570n13, 573n36, 581n25, 587n21, 590n34
Cummins Engine, 203
Cunningham, D.A., 568n59
Curren, M.T., 562n17
Curtice, Harlow, 308

D'Aveni, R., 586n31
Daft, R.L., 557n12, 582n30, 585n24, 586n30
Dahl, R.A., 580n5
Dahlan, Muhammad, 296–297
Dandridge, T.C., 586n11, 587n15
Daniels, C., 89, 563n45
Danner, D.L., 189n, 190n
Dass, P., 584n5
David, G., 588n33

Davidson, O.B., 562n7
Davidow, W.H., 584n21
Davies, A., 561n76
Davis, A., 63
Davis, J.H., 574n61
Davis, L.E., 569n10
Davis, S., 573n38
Davis, S.A., 445n
Davis, S.M., 585n9
Dawson, C., 588n1
Dayal, I., 587n30
Deal, T.E., 586n5, 586n8, 586n12
Dean, J.W. Jr., 557n15, 571n30, 572n49, 572n50, 572
DeAngelis, T., 562n22
Deci, E.L., 115
DeCremer, D., 579n44
DeFong, L.T., 562n25
Delaney, J.T., 559n5
Deleeuw, K., 560n26
Deming, W. Edwards, 203, 571n29
Demsetz, H., 586n35
DeNisi, A.S., 569n85
Deniston, O.L., 584n3
Denn, A.T., 557n2
Denny, A.T., 570n17
Der Hovanesian, M., 568n65
DeSanctis, G., 584n20
DeSimone, L.D., 250–251
Desmaris, P., 237n
Desrosiers, E., 577n67
Dess, G.G., 584n20
Deutsch, M., 577n64
DeVader, D., 77n
DeVries, J., 571n28
Deward, D.L., 571n33
Dhar, R., 85
DiCicco, M., 558n16
Dickson, M.W., 264n
Didwiddle, Tim, 226
Diehl, M., 575n24, 575
Dirks, K.T., 574n63, 579n58
Diuerckx, I., 557n7
Doerr, K.D., 572n6
Donaldson, T., 584n4
Donnelly, J.H. Jr., 582n42
Donovan, H., 578n13
Donovan, M., 561n78, 566n16
Dooley, R.S., 577n74

Dowling, P.J., 590n33
Down, J., 575n14
Downes, J., 567n23
Doyle, Patrick, 156
Drasgow, F.D., 566n16, 568n68
Dreher, G.E., 564n11
Dreher, G.F., 561n59
Drew, Richard A., 439
Dreyfus, J., 557n13, 561n57
Driscoll, L., 562n19
Duck, J., 575n20
Dulebohn, J.H., 582n33
Dumaine, B., 587n22
Duncan, David, 51
Duncan, K.D., 557n2, 570n17
Duncan, R.B., 38, 421n, 563n57, 585n18, 585n19
Dunham, R.B., 570n23, 570
Dunkin, A., 566n58
Dunlop, J.T., 589n32
Dunn, M., 442n
Dunnette, M.D., 26, 560n16, 566n10, 566n11, 569n13, 572n9, 579n47, 582n44, 585n23, 588n31
Durand, Doug, 88–89
Durity, A., 559n10
Dutton, J.E., 587n27
Dutton, Richard E., 329
Dvir, T., 579n42
Dwyer, P., 89, 563n41
Dyer, W.G., 588n44

Eagly, Alice, 286
Earley, P.C., 565n47, 565n48, 576n53, 589n10
Easton, S., 588n36
Eaton, N.K., 560n16
Ebbers, Bernard, 120–121
Echikson, W., 583n1
Eden, D., 562n7, 579n42
Edmondson, G., 558n16
Edwards, J.R., 566n12, 569n5
Edwards, J.E., 568n62
Egri, C.R., 579n43
Ehrlich, S.B., 578n9

Eisenhardt, K.M., 586n32
Eisner, Michael, 18, 19
Ekegren, G., 565n48
Elgin, B., 563n40, 579n55
Ellegard, K., 589n24
Elliott, D., 563n30
Ellis, A.P., 411n, 575n16, 576n50, 576n54
Ellis, J.E., 585n26
Ellison, Larry, 104
Elms, H., 576n37
Emergy, F.E., 37, 38, 586n31, 589n25
Emerson, Harrington, 29–30, 558n11
Emerson, R.M., 580n5
Emery, F.E., 559n25, 570n20
Engardio, P., 515n
Enstrom, T., 589n24
Epitropaki, O., 578n31
Erez, A., 562n80, 567n34, 576n37., 589n10, 589n29
Ericcson, 150, 373
Evans, J.R., 571n30
Evans, M.G., 580n69
Eveland, J.D., 584n3
Ewing, J., 6n, 87, 588n1

Faerman, S.R., 559n26
Faerstein, P.H., 570n17
Fagenson, E., 587n24
Fairhurst, G.T., 584n7
Fairlamb, D., 515n
Fan, E.T., 576n48
Fandray, D., 561n64, 562n15
Fandt, P.M., 354n, 582n29
Fanning, D., 572n10
Farh, J.L., 571n24
Farmer, M., 581n25
Farmer, S.M., 563n54
Farnham, A., 559n11, 560n25, 561n66, 590n11
Farrell, C., 561n45, 585n26
Faust, D., 574n51
Fayol, H., 30–32, 357, 558n12, 558n13
Feguson-Hessler, C.J., 562n25
Feishman, E.A., 560n38
Feldman, D.C., 573n13

Felten, D.F., 571n27
Fenn, Margaret P., 333
Feren, D.B., 557n2, 570n17
Ferrin, D.L., 578n35
Ferris, G.R., 354n, 570n15, 571n34, 575n21, 581n28, 582n29, 582n33
Ferris, S.P., 561n54
Fiedler, F.E., 296–297, 579n59, 579n61
Fields, G., 562n3
Filley, A.C., 580n71, 587n25
Fingleton, E., 589n19
Fiorina, Carleton S., 286, 373–374
Fireman, S., 567n29
Fischthal, A, 580n77
Fitzgerlad, M.P., 570n15
Fleishman, Edwin, 55
Fleishman, J.A., 576n44
Flint, J., 585n20
Florey, A.T., 576n51
Flynn, G., 561n49, 569n84
Foit, R.J., 77n
Folger, R., 574n53, 574n65
Follett, Mary Parker, 32
Ford, David L., 502
Ford, R.C., 583n15
Ford, William Clay (Bill) Jr., 3
Forest, S.A., 583n1
Forster, J., 568n57
Foust, D., 577n2, 583n1
Fox, S., 587n22
Fox, William M., 318
France, M., 574n72, 585n26
Francesco, A.M., 589n24
Franke, R.H., 559n19
Franz, T.M., 564n24
Frayne, C.A., 565n29
Freed, T., 572n6
Freemand, R.E., 584n4
French, J.R.P., 559n20, 580n9, 580
French, John, 345, 347, 348, 349
French, W.L., 447n, 456n, 458n, 558n17, 558n21, 587n25, 588n32
Frese, M., 564n22

Freudenberger, H.J., 566n14
Freudenheim, M., 569n81
Frew, D.R., 568n74
Frey, D., 577n75
Fried, Y., 568n52, 570n15
Frost, P.J., 586n11, 587n15
Fry, Ronald E., 431, 461
Fryxell, G.E., 577n74
Fulmer, I.S., 567n22
Funkenstein, D.H., 566n13

Gabor, A., 577n1
Gafni, A., 588n36
Gaines, J., 570n23
Galbraith, J.R., 582n45, 582n46, 582n47, 585n19
Galbraith, J.K., 589n32
Galbraith, Jay, 38
Galen, M., 60, 561n56, 562n19, 569n6
Galton, Francis, 285
Galunic, D.C., 586n32
Gandhi, Mahatma, 284, 346
Gandz, J., 581n26
Ganesan, S., 565n50
Ganster, D.C., 569n82
Gantt, H.L., 29, 558n9, 558n10
Ganzach, Y., 563n44
Gard, J.A., 588n37
Gargiulo, M., 582n32
Garland, S., 569n6
Garson, B., 569n2
Garwood, J., 558n17
Gasol, Pau, 57
Gasparaino, C., 573n29
Gates, Bill, 285, 287
Gaudart, C., 569n11
Gavin, J.H., 576n51
Geis, F.L., 581n29
Gelb, S., 589n16
Gelfand, M.J., 574n52
George, J., 576n45, 563n52
Gerhardt, M., 50
Gerhart, B., 567n22
Gerhart, M.W., 578n19
Gerras, S.J., 579n49
Gersick, C.J., 575n19
Gerstner, Louis, 59
Gerth, H.H., 32, 558n14

Ghoshal, S., 557n7
Giacalone, R.A., 582n29
Giambatista, R.C., 577n63
Gibson, J.L., 582n42
Gideon, Pia, 150
Giffin, R.W., 570n22
Gilbreth, Frank, 29, 192, 196, 208
Gilbreth, Lillian, 29, 192, 196, 208, 569n7
Gilson, L.L., 564n63
Gimein, M., 564n17
Gioia, D.A., 587n13
Glacalone, R.A., 354n
Gladstein, D.L., 575n10
Glew, D.J., 567n39
Glick, W.H., 570n15, 585n11
Glynn, E.L., 565n29
Goff, S., 55n, 560n36
Gold, B.A., 589n24
Golembiewski, R.T., 588n37
Gomez-Mejia, L., 23, 558n4, 566n54
Goodin, R.Z., 557n5
Gooding, R.Z., 576n41, 576n43, 584n5, 584n6, 585n10
Goodman, P.S., 584n4
Goodman, S.A., 588n37
Goodnight, James, 137
Goodwin, G.F., 562n11, 577n566
Gorsten, E., 145n
Gottier, R.F., 560n19
Govindarajan, Vijay, 524
Graen, G., 579n47, 579n50
Grandey, A.A., 567n20
Gray, T., 568n72
Green, H., 205n, 427n
Green, J., 557n1
Greenbaum, H.H., 572n46
Greene, Charles, 348, 349n, 580n11
Greengard, S., 568n51
Greenwood, Royston, 472
Greiner, L., 557n9, 584n8
Greising, D., 557n15, 584n21, 585n26
Griffin, R.W., 567n39, 569n11, 570n14, 570n24, 582n35
Gross, A.C., 588n35

Gross, N., 586n34
Grossman, C., 283n
Gruenfeld, D.H., 576n48
Gruley, B., 580n68
Gruneberg, M.M., 557n2, 570n17
Guercio, R., 581n28
Guest, R.H., 569n9
Gueutal, H.G., 567n44
Guion, R.M., 560n19
Gulati, R., 571n30
Gullahorn, J.T., 573n31
Gully, S.M., 564n21
Gundry, L.K., 586n7
Gupta, Anil K., 524
Gutenberg, R.L., 560n35
Guzzardi, W., 564n65

Hackett, R.D., 579n40
Hackman J.R., 197–201, 203, 205, 207, 570n14, 570n15, 572n12, 572n48, 575n13
Haddad, C., 89
Hage, J., 583n9, 583n13
Hakel, M.D., 569n13
Hall, R.H., 583n9
Hamel, G., 563n61
Hamidi, Kourish, 237
Hammer, M., 478, 557n15, 571n38, 583n18
Hammonds, K.H., 566n58
Hamner, C.W., 566n59
Hanges, P.J., 574n60
Hansen, C.D., 586n10
Hanson, M.A., 560n20
Harbison, F.H., 589n32
Hardy, G.E., 567n28
Harich, K.R., 562n17
Harkins, S., 575n26
Harrell-Cook, G., 582n33
Harrison, D.A., 576n51
Harrison, L., 575n30
Harrison, R., 587n29
Harstein, J., 572n41
Hart, Z., 587n30
Harter, J.K., 142n
Harzing, A., 589n29, 589n31
Hastorf, A., 586n10
Hatch, M.J., 586n7
Hater, J.J., 578n33
Hatvany, N., 589n27
Haveman, H.A., 584n5

Hayes, T.L., 142n
Hays, S., 566n62
Hebard, C.C., 588n36
Hedlund, J., 563n46, 576n39, 579n52
Heffner, T.S., 562n11, 577n56
Heilman, Madeline, 74–75, 562n8
Heimbeck, D., 564n22
Heisler, William J., 242
Heller, D., 50
Heller, F., 587n28
Helsen, W.F., 563n30
Henkoff, R., 563n59
Henninger, D., 226n
Henry, D., 565n41
Henry, R.A., 577n67
Herkere, D., 585n824
Herman, S., 579n43
Hersey, P., 293, 579n53
Herzberg, Frederick, 36, 194–197, 208, 569n12
Hewlett, Bill, 373
Hewlett, Walter B., 373
Heymann, D., 574n1
Hickson, D.J., 350n, 581n13, 581n19., 583n13, 585n18
Higgens, A., 271n
Higgens, E.T., 572n11
Higgs, A.C., 566n6, 568n73
Hilario, Nene, 57
Hill, C.W., 575n14
Hill, C.W.L., 583n14, 584n4
Hill, G.W., 575n22
Hiller, J.S., 561n54
Himelstein, L., 563n40, 585n26
Hinds, P.J., 577n57
Hingins, C.R., 585n18
Hinings, C.R., 350n, 581n13, 583n13
Hitler, Adolph, 284
Hitt, M.A., 590n2
Hobek, J., 563n57
Hoc, J.M., 571n39
Hochwater, W.A., 581n28
Hodgetts, R.M., 558n8
Hoel, W., 579n50
Hof, R.D., 557n1, 564n1, 586n34
Hoffman, D.A., 574n50, 579n49

Hofstede, G., 67, 510–518, 522, 524, 525, 588n2, 588n3, 589n29, 589n31, 589n4–9, 589n11
Hogan, J., 50, 56n, 560n39
Holland, B., 50
Hollander, E.P., 284, 578n12
Hollenbeck, J.R., 411n, 576n54, 560n29, 563n31, 563n46, 565n38, 565n43, 565n44, 568n64, 572n9, 575n16, 575n29, 576n39, 576n50, 579n52, 590n17
Holmes, S., 427n, 588n1
Homans, G.C., 575n10
Honeywell, 45
Hoover, P.B., 565n51
Horn, P., 579n47
Horn, R., 561n77
Hoskisson, R.E., 583n14
Hough, L.M., 560n16, 560n20
House, R., 557n11
House, R.J., 569n13, 580n69, 580n70, 580n71, 587n25
Hovorka-Mead, A.D., 562
Howard, J.H., 568n59
Howell, J.M., 578n20, 578n34
Huber, G.P., 585n11
Hui, C., 571n25
Hull, F.M., 585n14
Humphrey, S.E., 411n, 563n31, 575n29
Humphreys, L.G., 560n37
Hunt, J.G., 578n29, 579n62
Hunt, R.G., 585n16
Hunter, J.E., 55n, 560n34, 560n36
Huselid, M.A., 559n5
Hussein, Mohammed, 63
Hussein, Saddam, 284
Hyman, M., 558n1
Hymowitz, C., 557n13, 577n7

Ibarra, H., 581n20, 587n19

Idei, Nobukuki, 435
Ilgen, D.R., 411n, 560n29, 563n31, 563n46, 565n38, 572n9, 575n16, 575n29, 576n39, 576n50, 576n54, 579n52
Ilies, R., 50, 578n19
Illgen, D.R., 568n64
Irleand, R.D., 590n2
Isen, A., 586n10
Ivancevich, J.M., 582n42, 587n27

Jackson, C.L., 574n58
Jackson, C.Z.L., 575n28
Jackson, D.N., 560n23
Jackson, S.E., 569n80
Jago, A., 578n10, 580n65
James, George, 251
James, R.M., 583n10
Jeanneret, R.P., 560n35
Jenkins, D., 570n21
Jennings, K.R., 572n46
Jennings, Mark, 59
Jension, A.R., 560n33
Jerdee, T.H., 562n14
Jermier, J.M., 570n23, 579n56
Jimerson, P.D., 502
Jobs, Steve, 20, 104
Jochims, M., 577n75
Johansson, B., 589n24
Johansson, M., 589n24
Johnnesen-Schmidt, M., 286n
Johnson, B., 573n15
Johnson, E., 567n34
Johnson, R.A., 585n17, 587n30
Johnson, T.W., 580n74
Johnston, W., 560n42
Jones, D., 150n, 226n, 574n3, 590n6
Jones, E.E., 582n33
Jones, G.R., 576n44
Jones, John E., 242n
Jones, T.M., 584n4
Jonsson, D., 589n24
Judge, T.A., 50, 564n24, 566n17, 568n54, 578n19
Jung, D.I., 579n39, 579n41
Juran, J.M., 203, 571n29

Kabanoff, B., 580n63
Kacmar, K.M., 560n26, 567n19, 581n28, 582n33
Kahn, R.L., 36–37, 230n, 559n24, 580n5
Kahneman, D., 81, 82n, 562n27
Kahnweiler, W.M., 586n19
Kammeyer-Mueller, J.D., 573n47
Kanfer, F.H., 564n29
Kanfer, R., 566n53
Kanigel, R., 558n8
Kanter, R.M., 581n15
Kaplan, A., 580n5
Kaplan, I.T., 572n46
Kark, R., 578n36
Karlgaard, R., 578n16
Kasdin, A.E., 583n17
Katerberg, R., 579n47
Katz, D., 36–37, 230n, 559n24
Katz, R., 24, 558n5, 570n23, 578n18
Katzell, R.A., 570n17
Kaufman, J., 57
Kaul, J.D., 559n19
Kavanaugh, M.H., 578n27
Keenan, F., 376n, 427n, 574n4
Keichel-Koles, K.I., 564n21
Keillor, Garrison, 269
Keith, N., 564n22
Kelleher, Herb, 290–291
Keller, R.T., 580n72, 580n73
Kelly, K., 63, 570n18, 575n5
Kelman, H.C., 580n10
Kelman, Herbert, 347–349
Kemper, H.C.G., 569n11
Kennedy, A.A., 586n5, 586n8, 586n12
Kennedy, John F., 346
Kerbow, Chris, 51
Kerlinger, F.N., 590n18
Kernan, M.C., 574n60
Kerr, C., 589n32
Kerr, S., 557n9, 566n57, 579n56, 587n25
Kerwin, K., 33, 557n1
Ketelsen, James, 154
Khan, G., 575n31
Khandwalla, P.N., 583n12

Khermouch, G., 588n1
Khurana, Rakesh, 283
Kiechel, W., 564n25
Kiesler, S., 573n22
Kiger, P.J., 567n30
Kilborn, P.T., 572n42
Kilbridge, J.D., 569n10
Kilmann, R.H., 587n20, 587n23
Kilpartick, Kay, 220
Kim, H., 583n14
Kimberly, J.R., 584n8, 585n10
King, Martin Luther, Jr., 284, 346
King, R.T., 575n9
King, R.W., 585n26
Kirilenko, Andre, 57
Kirkpatrick, S.A., 578n32
Kirks, K.T., 578n35
Klayman, N., 563n44
Klein, A.R., 570n23
Klein, H.J., 565n43., 565n44, 574n49
Klein, J., 568n58
Kleiner, B.H., 588n44
Klineberg, S.L., 75n, 561n47, 562n9
Kluger, A.N., 563n44
Kmet, J., 577n67
Knoblach, Jennifer, 87
Kochan, T.A., 584n4
Kodlec, D., 113
Koester, J., 575n18
Kohn, A., 115
Konishi, T., 588n34
Konovsky, M., 567n33
Kopelman, R.E., 570n17
Koretz, G., 566n9
Korman, A.K., 579n62
Korsgaard, M.A., 574n54, 574n66, 576n42
Kotter, J.P., 355n, 587n27
Kotulic, A.G., 562n4
Koys, D.J., 142n
Kozlowski, S.W.J., 565n52, 573n43
Krackhardt, D., 577n57, 581n20
Kraimer, M.L., 564n24
Kraut, A.I., 26
Kravitz, D.A., 75n, 561n 47, 562n9
Kripalani, M., 515n

Kristof-Brown, A.L., 573n39
Kroll, M., 561n54
Kruse, D., 564n5
Kuijer, P.P.F.M., 569n11
Kulik, C.T., 570n24
Kunii, I.M., 588n1
Kurland, N.B., 580n9
Kurland, O.M., 567n38
Kurtz, R.B., 572n43
Kutaragi, Ken, 435
Kwoh, Daniel, 93

Laabs, J.J., 560n15, 561n62, 567n32, 567n41, 567n47
Lachnit, C., 559n2
Lado, A.A., 559n5
LaGanke, J.S., 264n
Lam, S.K., 565n31, 579n54
Lambert, S.J., 567n35
Lancaster, Pat, 128
Lance, C.E., 573n40
Landa, A., 577n67
Landon, T.E., 560n40
Landsberger, H.A., 581n22
Landy, F.J., 560n19
Langner, P.H., 570n24
Lantech, 128
Larson, L.L., 578n29, 579n62
Latane, B., 575n26
Latham, G.P., 565n29
Latham, W.R., 565n37, 577n60
Lavelle, L., 564n2, 564n4, 564n6, 565n41
Law, K.S., 562n24, 571n25, 577n72
Lawler, E.E., 106, 131, 132, 557n14, 564n8, 575n13
Lawler, J.L., 568n68
Lawrence, K.A., 587n27
Lawrence, P.R., 38, 583n3, 583n4
Lay, Ken, 105, 300
Ledford, G.E., 557n14
Lee, B.R., 571n35
Lee, C.A., 350n, 581n13
Lee, F.K., 565n39
Lee, Hak-Chong, 307
Lee, Jerry, 153
Lee, L., 583n1
Lee, R., 570n23

Lee, T.W., 567n29
Lee-Young, J., 561n68
Lehman, H.C., 563n55
Lemak, D.J., 572n50
Lenin, Vladimir, 29
Leonard, D., 564n64
LePine, J.A., 557n5, 562n80, 563n46, 567, 567n34, 575n28, 576n37, 576n39, 576n54
Lester, S.W., 576n42
Levering, R., 566n7
Levi, Ariel S., 98
Levine, J.L., 572n11
Levy, S., 586n1
Lewicki, R.J., 582n43
Lewin, A.Y., 586n30
Lewin, K., 578n21
Lewinsky, Monica, 271
Lewis, P., 264n
Liden, R., 579n50
Liden, R.C., 564n24, 568n66, 579n51
Likert, R., 75n, 578n24
Lilienthal, S.M., 871, 574
Lindestadt, H., 589n25
Lindsey, J.T., 572n46
Linsenmeier, J.A.W., 582n33
Lippitt, G.L., 587n24, 588n38
Lippitt, R., 578n21
Listad, Richard, 46
Litterer, J.R., 582n43
Livermore, Ann M., 373–374
Lloyd, R.F., 572n46
Lochard, Chris, 63
Locke, E.A., 138, 557n2, 557n5, 565n34, 565n36, 565n46, 566n10, 568n54, 569n13, 570n17, 574n55, 577n61, 578n32, 583n6, 587n27
Loher, B.T., 570n15
London, E., 577n58
Longseth, P., 587n24
Lopez, L., 271n
Lord, Robert, 76–77
Loria, Jeffrey, 15
Lorsch, J.W., 583n3, 583n4, 583n12
Louie, T.A., 562n17
Love, M.S., 573n19

Lovelace, Bonnie J., 472
Lowe, T.A., 571n29
Lowry, T., 580n3
Lowy, A., 584n22
Lubove, S., 583n18
Lucas, J.A., 562n8
Luce, M.F., 85
Luke, R.A., 587n30
Lund, M.W., 569n3
Lunsford, J.L., 563n39
Luong, A., 566n15
Luthans, F., 115, 578n22
Lutz, Robert A., 33

Machiavelli, Niccolo, 27
Mack, John J., 386
MacKenzie, S.B., 579n57
Madigan, K., 559n8
Madison, D.L., 581n26
Madjar, N., 563n60
Magnussan, P., 559n4
Mahoney, C., 566n65
Mahoney, J.T., 586n36
Mahoney, M.J., 564n29
Mainstone, Larry E., 98
Mallard, C., 237n
Mallory, M., 569n6
Malone, M.S., 584n21
Mandel, M.J., 557n1, 585n26
Mandela, Nelson, 346
Mann, F.C., 588n43
Mansfield, R., 583n13
Manuso, J.S., 569n83
Manz, C.C., 571n36
March, C., 572n2
March, J.G., 90, 563n35, 563n43, 583n2
Marcic, Dorothy, 526
Marcus, Bernie, 280
Markham, S.E., 564n19
Marks, M., 576n35
Marrone, Janine, 114
Marrow, A.J., 588n33
Marshall, C.R., 566n55
Marshall, Edward, 499
Martin, J., 564n21, 586n10
Martinau, J.W., 565n35
Martocchio, J.J., 568n68
Martorana, P.V., 576n48
Mary Kay, 437, 438
Maslow, A.H., 36, 109–111, 564n13
Maslyn, J.M., 581n25
Mathews, K.A., 568n60

Mathhews, J.A., 584n19
Mathieu, J.E., 562n11, 565n35, 577n56, 577n70
Matsuzaki, I., 588n34
Matteson, M.T., 582n40, 587n27
Mausner, B., 569n12
Maxwell, S.E., 560n40
Mayer, R.C., 574n61
Mayers, B.T., 569n82, 581n26
Maynord, M., 576n52
Mayo, M.C., 578n38
Mazzoo, J.M., 571n29
McBeth, J., 271n
McCaffery, R., 566n64
McCaleb, V.M., 557n2, 570n17
McCann, J.E., 23, 558n4
McCartney, S., 291n
McClelland, C.L., 568n61, 569n5
McClelland, D.C., 110, 291–292, 344, 353, 564n16, 579n46, 580n7, 580n8, 581n29
McCloy, R.A., 560n16
McDaniel, D.A., 561n65
McGinty, S., 573n27
McGrath, J.E., 566n11
McGrath, M.R., 559n26
McGregor, D., 34–36, 559n21
McHenry, J.J., 560n20
McKee, B., 559n13
McKee, G.H., 564n19
McKenna, D.D., 26
McLaughlin, K.J., 584n20
McMahan, G.C., 557n8, 560n26
McMurray, V.V., 580n6
McNamara, G., 563n47
McNamee, M., 386n
McNealy, Scott, 103
McNearney, W. James, 281
McWilliams, G., 113
Mechanic, D., 581n25
Medbo, L., 589n24
Meeks, F., 563n51
Meglino, B.M., 569n85, 576n42
Mehta, S., 561n58
Meindl, J.R., 578n9, 578n38
Meisler, A., 269n

Mellow, C., 561n72
Menaker, D., 558n16
Mento, A.J., 565n46
Merritt, J., 12, 560n31
Metcalf, H.C., 558n17
Metlay, W., 572n46
Meyers, C.A., 589n32
Michael, J., 564n29
Michailova, S., 589n30
Mikkelsen, A., 569n11
Miles, R.E., 584n19, 584n20
Miles, R.H., 557n12, 581n16, 581n17, 581n27, 582n36, 582n38, 582n39, 582n40., 584n8, 585n24
Miller C.C., 585n11
Miller, D., 585n11
Miller, R., 557n1
Miller, Thomas R., 173
Miller, V.D., 587n30
Mills, C.W., 32, 558n14
Milner, C., 578n31
Miner, J.B., 587n29, 590n19
Ming, Yao, 57
Minter, 587n23
Mintzberg, Henry, 25–27, 282–283, 301, 558n6, 573n26, 575n15, 578n11, 583n7, 583n8, 583n10, 583n11, 585n27, 590n5
Mischel, L.J., 568n63
Mitchell, R.E., 567n48
Mitchell, T.R., 564n9, 567n29, 572n6, 580n70
Mitroff, I.I., 590n8
Moberg, D., 345n
Moch, M.K., 590n36
Moeller, N.L., 570n15
Mohr, H., 571n32
Mohr, W.L., 571n32
Mohrman, S.A., 590n8
Molleman, E., 571n36, 571n37
Mone, M.A., 584n7
Money, W.H., 579n62
Monge, P., 584n20
Monsanto, 391
Montgomery, J.C., 572n50
Moo, Park Kwang, 79–80
Mook, D.G., 590n24

Moon, H., 411, 563n31, 563n47, 575n16, 575n29, 576n50
Mooney, J.D., 558n15
Mooney, James, 31–32
Moore, P.L., 580n1
Moorhead, G., 582n35
Mooris, B., 580n3
Moos, R.M., 567n48
Moran, L., 572n47
Moregson, F.P., 579n49
Moreland, R.L., 576n47
Morgan, C.T., 569n3
Morgan, G., 586n11, 587n15
Morgeson, F.P., 195, 560n30, 574n50
Morita, N., 588n34
Morris, M.G., 561n67
Morrison, E.W., 573n48
Morse, D., 566n4, 577n3
Morse, N.C., 578n25
Mosakowski, E., 576n53
Moser, Martin R., 163
Moskowitz, M., 566n7
Mossop, J., 587n24
Mount, M.K., 49n, 50, 560n17, 560n24, 560n27, 576n49
Moura, N.G., 564n29
Mouton, J.S., 287, 578n28, 588n42
Mouzelis, N.P., 558n14
Moye, N., 574n55
Mudgett, B.O., 565n32
Mueller, Robert, 71, 88
Mueller, W.S., 571n28
Muller, J., 557n1
Mundel, M.E., 189n, 190n, 569n4
Murnighan, J.K., 575n19
Murray, B., 563n56
Murray, H.A., 110, 111, 564n15
Murray, V., 581n26
Musselwhite, E., 572n47
Myaskovsky, L., 576n47

Nacchio, Joe, 105
Nadler, D., 575n13, 590n13
Nagel, E., 590n12
Nahapiet, J., 557n7
Naik, G., 574n2, 590n16
Najero, Eduardo, 57
Nakarmi, L., 558n16

Nardelli, Robert, 279–281
Naughton, K., 205n
Naumann, S.E., 574n64
Nease, A.A., 565n32
Neisser, U., 562n10
Neubert, M.J., 576n49
Neuringer, C., 564n29
Ng, K.Y., 239n
Nichols, Pat, 59
Nisberg, J.N., 458n
Nishimura, A., 588n34
Nissan, 10, 17
Nobel, R., 584n2
Noe, R.A., 570n15, 574n58
Nomani, A.Q., 567n37
Norstedt, J.P., 202n
Nortel, 515
Nowitzki, Dirk, 57
Nugent, P.S., 588n40
Nulty, P., 566n61
Nunnally, J.C., 53n, 560n32, 590n21
Nussbaum, B., 557n6
Nutting, S.M., 560n40

O'Connell, B.J., 568n 55
O'Leary-Kelly, A.M., 567n39
O'Neill, Paul, 71, 72
O'Neill, R.M., 587n27
O'Reilly, C.A. III, 587n18
Obata, S., 588n34
Ofir, C., 562n16
Oh, T.K., 589n19
Okada, T., 588n34
Okhuyson, G.A., 563n32
Oldham, G.R., 197–201, 203, 205, 207, 563n60, 564n62, 567n43, 568n52, 568n63, 570n15, 570n16, 570n24
Olson, M., 575n27
Olson-Buchanan, J.B., 568n78
Omar, Muhammad, 271
Ong, M., 565n45
Oracle, 104
Orasanu, J., 576n55
Organ, D.W., 567n33
Orsburn, J.D., 572n47
Osburn, H.G., 560n35
Osburn, R., 578n29
Ostroff, C., 573n43
Outerbridge, A.N., 55n, 560n36

Paese, P.W., 563n33
Page, R.C., 23, 558n4
Panitz, Eric, 396
Parasuraman, R., 571n40
Park, A., 386n, 580n2
Park, K., 568n76
Parker, C.P., 562n6
Parker, James F., 290
Parker, L.E., 568n77
Parker, S.K., 569n10
Parker, Tony, 57
Parkes, K.R., 590n23
Parsons, T., 558n14
Parthasarthy, R., 585n14
Pastor, J.C., 578n38
Patton, G.K., 566n17
Paul, C.F., 588n35
Paulus, P.B., 563n50
Payne, S.C., 564n21
Pearce J.B., 582n31
Pearson, C.A., 571n28
Peden, Mark, 250
Pedigo, P.R., 26
Pelled, L.H., 576n46, 580n9
Pennings, J.M., 350n, 559n27, 581n13, 584n4, 585n18
Pepper, John, 95
Perlman, Lawrence, 60
Perlow, L.A., 563n32
Perot, Ross, 515
Perrewe, P.L., 581n28
Perrow, C., 585n12, 585n16
Perry, B.C., 565n47
Peters, S., 561n53
Peters, T., 590n3
Peters, T.J., 558n 18
Peterson, D.L., 587n30
Peterson, R.S., 577n73
Peterson, Richard, 175
Peterson, T., 585n26
Pewter, M.A., 588n43
Pfeffer, J. William, 156n, 242n, 306n, 350, 440n, 557n8, 559n5, 569n8, 571n25, 579n45, 581n13, 581n14, 581n18, 581n23, 581n26, 582n30, 582n45, 586n33, 587n14, 587n19, 587n21
Phillips, J.M., 565n38
Phillips, J.S., 564n29

Phillips, S., 566n58
Pierce, J.L., 570n23
Pierce, L.L., 584n3
Pine, B.J. II, 585n9
Plamondon, K.E., 561n78
Plovnick, Mark S., 431, 461
Plumley, Michael A., 9–10
Podsakoff, P.M., 348, 349n, 579n57, 580n11, 580n12
Poe, R., 567n26
Polyani, M., 590n12
Pondy, L.R., 586n11, 587n15
Porch, D., 573n45
Porretto, J., 33, 557n1
Port, O., 567n25, 572n43, 584n21
Porter, C.O., 411n, 239n, 575n16, 576n50
Porter, I.W., 564n8
Porter, L.W., 570n24, 581n25, 581n26, 582n31
Posthuma, R.A., 560n30
Pottinger, M., 574n2
Powers, S., 63, 566n3, 566n5
Prager, H., 588n37
Pratkanis, A.R., 577n71
Pratt, M.G., 563n60
Prest, W., 565n47
Preston, L.E., 584n4
Price, K.H., 576n51
Priem, R.L., 562n4, 584n2, 584n20
Pritchard, R.D., 565n37, 577n60
Probst, T.M., 566n16, 568n68
Pruneau, Steven, 125
Pucik, C.V., 589n27
Puffer, S., 526n
Pugh, D.S., 583n13
Pulakos, E.D., 561n78
Purka, D.J., 565n33, 565n40
Putnam, Stephan H., 304

Quick, J.C., 588n36
Quinn, J.B., 558n7, 583n10
Quinn, R.E., 559n26, 582n37
Quinn, R.F., 585n8
Quinones, M.A., 565n32

Rafaeli, A., 567n50
Raghavan, 560n28
Raia, A., 355n
Ralston Purina, 113
Randolph, W.A., 583n15
Raphaely, Tod, 112
Rasheed, A.M., 562n4
Rasheed, A.M.A., 584n20
Rautenberg, Arndt, 87
Raven, Bertram, 345, 347, 348, 577n59, 580n9
Ravlin, E.C., 569n85
Rawe, J., 113
Rebellow, K.I., 587n17
Recer, P., 442n
Rechnitzer, P.A., 568n59
Redev, A.C., 558n15
Reed, D., 572n4
Reed, R., 572n50
Reimer, E., 578n25
Reitsema, J., 577n59
Renchin, M.B., 562n20
Renwick, P.A., 581n26
Repenning, N.P., 563n32
Rhee, L., 562n26
Rice, R.E., 587n19
Rice, A.K., 588n39
Rice, F., 561n50
Richard, O.C., 561n48
Richards, C.S., 564n29
Ridderstrale, J., 584n2
Ridge, Tom, 71, 72
Ring, P.S., 586n36
Ripley, A., 89
Ritchie, J.B., 169, 465, 495
Robarge, Randy, 88, 89
Rober, C., 568n68
Roberts, D., 226n
Roberts, J., 588n36
Roberts, K.H., 570n15
Robinson, Q.M., 574n55
Rodriguez, Marisa, 145
Roehand, M.R., 574n69
Rogelberg, S.G., 566n15
Rogers, L.E., 584n7
Rohrbaugh, J., 559n26
Romani, J.H., 584n3
Rosander, G., 589n25
Rosen, B., 561n61, 562n14, 571n31
Rosenbush, S., 427n
Rosenfeld, P., 354n, 582n29
Rosenstein, J., 584n2
Ross, J., 563n34
Ross, W.H., 562n20, 582n48

Rossant, J., 87., 515n
Rotchford, N.L., 567n43
Rothfeder, J., 562n19
Rothschild, M., 583n18
Rothstein, M., 560n23
Rotundi, T, 563n53
Roush, P., 580n77
Rousseau, D.M., 557n11, 570n23, 585n12, 586n7
Rubin, J.Z., 582n43
Rubinstein, S.A., 584n4
Ruble, T.L., 361n
Rublin, P.A., 557n4
Rupp, D.E., 567n36
Russ, G.S., 354n, 582n29
Rynecki, D., 590n25
Rynes, S., 561n61

Sabella, M.J., 576n35
Sachdev, P., 588n31
Sager, I., 586n34
Saks, A.M., 573n46
Saksvik, P.O., 569n11
Salancik, G.R., 350, 440n, 569n8, 571n25, 581n13, 581n14, 581n18, 581n23, 582n33, 587n19
Salas, E., 562n11, 576n55
Sals, E., 577n56
Samuels, R.J., 589n28
SAP, 87
Sapienza, H.J., 574n66
Satoh, S., 588n34
Sawyer, J.E., 565n37, 577n60
Sawyer, O.O., 585n22
Saxon, M.J., 587n20
Sayles, L., 589n15
Schaubroeck, J., 565n31, 579n54
Schein, E.H., 222n, 573n14, 573n36, 573n37, 586n2, 586n3, 586n6, 588n35, 588n36
Schiesheim, C.A., 572n6
Schilling, M.A., 586n32
Schilling, M.S., 590n7
Schlesinger, J., 573n18
Schlesinger, L.A., 587n27
Schlosser, J., 568n69
Schmidrke, J.M., 568n63
Schmidt, A.M., 565n51
Schmidt, F.L., 55n, 142n, 560n22, 560n36
Schmidt, Joette, 238–240

Schminke, M., 574n59, 574n68
Schneck, R.E., 585n18
Schneck, R.H, 350n, 581n13
Schnedier, B., 566n6, 568n73, 584n4
Schneider, J., 569n13
Schneider, S.K., 573n24
Schoeder, M., 573n18
Schonberger, R.J., 571n30
Schreisheim, C.A., 579n48, 579n62, 580n12
Schuler, R.S., 590n33
Schultz, Howard, 509
Schultz-Hardt, S., 577n75
Schuster, J.R., 566n66
Schwab, D.P., 570n13
Schwartz, E.I., 587n17
Schweiger, D.M., 574n66
Scism, L, 566n60
Scott, K.D., 564n19, 576n34
Scott, K.S., 567n22
Scott, W.R., 583n2
Scully, J.A., 568n62, 569n5
Seabright, M.A., 574n68
Sederberg, M.E., 566n15
Sego, D.J., 568n64
Self, R.M., 573n40
Selig, Bud, 15
Sellers, P., 83, 562n12
Selye, Hans, 139
Semel, Terry, 293–294
Senker, P., 572n45
Seno, E., 588n34
Serpa, R., 587n20
Sethi, S.P., 585n14, 589n17
Seymour, L., 588n36
Shalley, C.E., 564n63
Shamir, B., 578n36, 579n42
Shannon, C., 573n21
Shapiro, B.S., 359n
Shapiro, E., 590n10
Sharkey, T.W., 355n
Sharon, D., 572n41
Sharpe, R., 561n74
Shaw, K.N., 557n2, 570n17
Shaw, M.E., 262n, 575n10
Sheats, P., 575n25
Sheldon, K.M., 565n39
Shepard, H.A., 588n42
Sheppard, L., 560n29, 575n16

Sherer, P.D., 557n11
Sheridan, J.E., 587n19
Sheridan, T.B., 571n40
Sherif, C.W., 582n42
Sherif, M., 582n42, 582n45
Sherman, M.P., 264n
Sherman, Rodney C., 329
Sherman, S., 85, 575n6, 575n8
Shetty, Y.K., 584n3
Shoemake, Robert, 269
Shore, L.M., 574n56
Shortell, S.M., 571n30
Shuman, Nancy, 220
Sieger, M., 89
Sime, W.F., 569n82
Simon, H.A., 83, 86, 90, 91, 558n3, 558n20, 563n35, 563n38, 563n43, 583n2
Simons, T., 576n46, 577n73
Sims, H.P., 571n26, 571n36, 587n13
Siwolop, S., 569n6
Skarlicki, D.P., 574n53, 574n65
Skipp, C., 205n
Sloan, Alfred P., 439
Slocum, J.W., 565n49
Smircich, L., 586n3
Smith, A., 558n2
Smith, D., 563n28
Smith, G., 6n
Smith, K.A., 576n46
Smith, K.G., 577n61
Smith, L.M., 571n28
Smith, R., 559n1, 562n1, 562n5, 580n68
Smith, Raymond, 72–73
Smith, Richard, 220
Smither, J.W., 573n35
Smitty, J, 566n2
Snell, S.A., 572n49
Snodgrass, Sandy, 63
Snow, C.C., 584n19, 584n20
Snyderman, B.B., 569n12
Solomon, C.M., 561n51, 561n63, 561n78, 573n30
Solomon, R.L., 564n23
Sonnefeld, J., 283n
Sonnentag, S., 564n22
Sonnesthul, W.J., 567n27
Sorensen, J.B., 586n4

Sosik, J.J., 578n20
Spangler, R., 572n46
Sparrowe, R.S., 564n24
Sparrowe, R.T., 568n66
Spector, P.E., 568n55, 568n75
Spencer, D.G., 569n79
Spencer, J., 125
Spooner-Dean, Kerry, 43
Sproull, L., 573n22
Sprout, A.L., 582n47
St. Clair, L., 578n15
Stajkovic, A.D., 115
Stalker, G.M., 409n, 584n7, 585n18
Starbuck, W.H., 585n16
Starkey, K., 586n3
Staw, B.M., 557n11, 559n27, 563n34, 568n56, 573n36, 581n25, 582n33, 587n21, 590n34
Steel, R.P., 572n46
Steele-Johnson, D., 565n51
Steensma, H.K., 586n32
Steers, R.M., 557n12, 582n30, 585n24
Stein, N., 150n, 566n8
Steiner, I.D., 575n23, 576n38
Steingraber, Frederick G., 343
Stephens-Jahng, T., 572n48
Stern, David, 15, 16, 57
Stevenson, W.B., 582n31
Stewart, G.L., 559n12, 576n33, 576n49
Stewart, L., 588n36
Stewart, P.A., 569n10
Stewart, T.A., 563n36, 563n37, 563n58, 574n62, 575n5
Stilwell, D., 579n51
Stinson, J.E., 580n74
Stodgill, R.M., 578n17, 578n26
Stohr, Klaus, 249–250
Stojakovic, Peja, 57
Stone, E.F., 567n44, 570n24
Stone, R., 566n1
Straser, S., 584n3
Stroebe, W., 575n24
Stroh, L.K., 566n18
Strozniak, P., 575n7
Sue-Chan, C., 565n45
Summer, S.M., 578n22

Sung, J., 568n69
Suriano, R., 442n
Suskind, R., 291n, 567n21
Susman, G.E., 569n10
Susskind, A.M., 567n19
Sussman, L., 568n58
Sussmann, M., 348n
Sutcliffe, K.M., 576n36
Sutton, R.I., 567n50
Svyantek, D.J., 588n37
Swap, W., 564n64
Sweilan, Osama, 63
Sykes, A.J.M., 559n19
Symond, W., 386n
Symonds, W.C., 583n1
Szambok, C., 577n55
Szilagyi, A.D. Jr., 571n26, 582n42

Tagliabue, Paul, 15, 16
Tannenbaum, R., 445n
Tannenbaum, S.I., 565n35
Tapscott, D., 584n22
Taylor, A. III, 580n3
Taylor, E.C., 574n57
Taylor, Frederick Winslow, 28–30, 188, 192, 196, 208, 357, 558n8
Taylor, J.C., 569n10, 571n27
Tejada, C., 113
Tellegen, A., 568n53
Tepper, B.J., 567n46, 574n57
Tepper, Bennett J., 353
Terkel, S., 569n1
Tesluk, P., 574n65
Tesluk, P.E., 577n70
Tetrick, L.E., 574n56
Tett, R.P., 560n23
Tharenou, Phyllis, 22
Tharp, G.D., 569n82
Thibaut, J., 239n
Thoman, G. Richard, 343
Thomas, C.B., 57
Thomas, J.M., 587n30
Thomas, K., 361n
Thomas, K.W., 363n, 582n44, 582n44
Thomas-Hunt, M., 557n11
Thompson, C.M., 565n33
Thompson, J.D., 417–419, 583n2, 583n5, 585n15
Thompson, M.P., 559n26
Thompson, Paul H., 169, 465, 495
Thompson, R.R., 561n52

Thoresen, C.J., 566n17
Thorngate, W., 590n35
Thornton, E., 386n
Thorsrud, E., 570n20, 589n25
Ticer, S., 580n4
Ticoll, D., 584n22
Tierney, P., 563n54
Tischner, E.C., 565n33
Tjosvold, D., 562n24, 577n72
Toquam, J.L., 560n20
Tower, Spence, 67
Treece, J.B., 558n19, 566n58
Trevino, L.K., 573n23
Triandis, H.C., 589n10
Trice, H.M., 586n6, 586n9, 587n16, 587n20
Trist, E., 37, 38, 559n25, 570n19, 586n31, 586
Trottman, M., 291n
Trueman, W., 557n6
Tsai, W., 581n20
Tsouikas, H., 587n26
Tsui, A.S., 573n33, 578n15
Tucker, J.H., 588n34
Tuckman, B.W., 575n17
Tuner, N., 578n31
Turban, D.B., 565n39, 573n19
Turkoglu, Hedo, 57
Turner, C., 583n13
Turner, M.E., 577n71
Tuttle, D.B., 568n64
Tversky, Amos, 81, 82n, 562n27
Tyson, L.D., 561n71

Ulrich, D., 582n41
Urwick, L., 32, 558n16, 558n17
Useem, 565n42, 565
Useem, J., 283n, 564n26, 565n42, 573n16

Valle, M., 581n28
Van de Vliert, E., 567n42
van de Zwaan, A.H., 571n28, 571n37
Van Fleet, D.D., 575n27
van Geen, V.M.C., 588n43
van Knippenberg, D., 579n44
van Maanen, J., 573n36
Van Yperen, N.W., 567n42

Vancouver, J.B., 565n33, 565n40
Vandenberg, R.J., 573n40
VanDeVen, A.H., 586n36
VandeWalle, D., 565n49, 565n50
Varchaver, N., 573n28, 583n1
Vaughan, D., 442n
Vecchio, R.P., 348n
Velasquez, M., 345n
Verity, J.W., 573n42
Victor, B., 572n48
Vinzant, C., 561n75, 574n67
Visser, B., 569n11
Viventia, 250, 259
Volberda, H.W., 586n31
Volcker, Paul, 81
von Engen, M., 286n
Vrendenburgh, D., 345n
Vroom, V.H., 106, 297, 564n 8, 564n10, 580n64, 580n65, 580n66, 580n67

Wade, T.C., 564n29
Wageman, R., 572n7, 572n48, 577n65
Wagner, J.A. III, 67, 210, 275, 368, 557n4, 557n5, 571n34, 575n16, 575n21, 576n41, 576n43, 583n6, 583n17, 584n4, 584n5, 584n6, 587n27, 590n36
Wagner, W.F., 560n 18
Wagoner, Rick, 33
Wahba, M.A., 564n14
Wahlstrom, Mark, 499
Wajnarooski, P., 565n47
Waldholz, M., 574n2
Waldman, B.J., 561n65
Waldman, D.A., 562n21
Walker, A., 583n12
Walker, C.R., 569n9
Walker, L., 239n
Wall, J., 582n38
Wall, T.D., 567n28
Wallace, I., 564n28
Wallace, M.J. Jr., 582n42
Waller, M.J., 577n63
Wallis, D., 557n2, 570n17
Walton, R.E., 571n27, 588n41
Wanberg, C.R., 573n47
Wang, Y., 585n11
Ward, John, 215
Warm, S, 562n2
Warner, M., 575n5
Waterman, R.H.558n18
Watkins, J., 587n30

Watson, D., 568n53
Watt, James, 27–28
Wayne, S.J., 564n24, 579n51
Waynes, S.J., 568n66, 574n56
Weaver, N.A., 574n49
Weaver, W., 573n21
Weber, J., 583n1
Weber, Max, 30, 385
Webster, J., 573n23
Weick, K.E., 590n35
Weingart, L.R., 577n62
Weintraub, A., 567n49
Weir, R., 588n36
Weisband, P.S., 264n
Weisband, S.P., 573n24
Weiss, Joseph, 499
Weissenberg, P., 578n27
Welbourne, T.M., 566n54
Welch, D., 33, 557n1
Welch, Jack, 269
Weldon, William C., 405–406
Welsh, D.B., 578n22
Wendt, Gary, 281
Wessel, D., 145n
Wesson, M.J., 239n, 565n43
West, B.J., 575n16, 576n50
West, Bradley, 411n
Westphal, J.D., 571n30
Whipple, T., 562n20
White, Donald D., 323
White, R.K., 578n21
Whiteman, J.K, 564n21
Whitener, E.M., 574n54
Whitney, Eli, 28
Whitney, Gary, 478
Wholey, D.R., 577n57, 583n16, 583n49
Wickens, C.D., 571n40
Wigdor, L.A., 569n13
Wilkins, A.L., 586n11
Williams, C.R., 565n44
Williams, David, 62
Williams, K., 575n26
Williamson, O., 427, 586n35
Wilson, Charles, 308
Wilson, M.C., 559n5
Wilson, P., 573n32
Wilson, Samuel M., 467
Winnick, Gary, 105
Wintes, Deborah, 67
Wise, 567n29
Wiseman, R.M., 566n54
Witt, L.A., 560n27, 581n28
Wong, C.S., 571n25
Wong, G.Y.Y., 571n24

Wood, R.E., 112, 562n23, 565n46
Woods, D., 567n28
Woods, Jerrol Glenn, 43
Woodward, Joan, 414–417, 418, 585n13
Woolf, Donald Austin, 314
Wortman, C.B., 582
Wrenge, C.D., 558n8
Wright, Howard, 93–94
Wright, P.M., 557n8, 560n26, 561n54

Xie, J.L., 565n31
Xin, K.R., 578n15

Yamagimi, A., 588n34
Yammarino, F.J., 579n48, 580n76
Yancho, C, 145n
Yantian, G, 572n41
Yao, G., 560n37
Yashikawa, M., 588n34
Yasi-Ardekani, M., 585n27
Yeh, R., 589n14
Yellin, E., 376n
Yetton, P.W., 580n66, 580n67
Ying, Luo, 57
Yuen, Henry, 93
Yukl, G., 578n14, 580n12

Zabayda, Abu, 72, 77
Zaccaro, S.J., 576n35
Zajac, E.J., 581n21
Zald, M.N., 583n13
Zaltman, G., 563n57
Zammuto, R.F., 584n4
Zand, D.E., 589n25
Zander, A., 575n11, 577n68
Zawacki, R.A., 458n, 588n32
Zbaracki, M.J., 572n47
Zeller, W., 580n4
Zellmer-Bruhn, M.E., 577n63
Zellner, W., 291n, 561n44, 561n73, 572n1, 572n5
Zenger, J.H., 572n47
Zenger, T.R., 566n55
Zhou, J., 563n52, 568n63
Zhou, X., 572n6
Zidon, I., 580n75
Ziegler, B., 573n25
Zimmer, F.G., 570n14
Zimmerman, E., 125
Zingheim, P.K., 566n66
Zuckerman, A., 586n4

COMPANY INDEX

Note: The letter "n" refers to notes.

A.T. Kearney Inc., 343, 344
Accenture, 81
Adidas, 346
Aetna Institute for Corporate Education, 46–47
Aetna Life and Casualty Corporation, 46, 193
Affitech, 250
Airbus Industries, 420
al-Aqsa, 296
Alco Standard, 392
All Weather Safety Whistle Company, 94
Allstate, 188
Amazon.com, 20
America West Airlines, 238–240
America's Best Carpet Care Company, 43
American Airlines, 215–217, 219, 221, 225, 234, 240
American Cyanamid, 49
American League Baseball, 15
American Motors, 37
Ameritech, 60
Amway, 437, 438
Apple Computer, 20, 104, 412, 426
Argenbright Security, 135–136, 141, 152
Arthur Andersen, 12, 51, 81, 386
Association of Professional Flight Attendants, 215
AT&T, 194, 203, 291–292, 376, 437
Atlas Industrial Door, 394
Avon, 60–61

Bank of America, 515
Bank of Ireland, 373
Bank One, 60
Beijing Mei Da Coffee Company, 62
Bell Atlantic, 72–73, 79
Bentley College, 499
Best Buy, 112

Bethlehem Steel Company, 29
BMW, 445
Boeing Company, 19, 62, 85–86, 143, 390, 420, 515
Briggs & Stratton, 18
Brigham Young University, 169, 465, 495
British Airways, 125
Buick Division, General Motors, 9–10
Bureau of National Affairs, 566n63
Burger King, 377, 414

Capital One, 21
Career Blazers, 220
Case Western Reserve University, 431, 461
Catholic Relief Services, 150
Center for Ethical Business Practices, 269
Century Pool Management, 62
Ceridian Corporation, 60
Chase Manhattan Bank, 391
Chemical Bank, 47
Chrysler Corporation (See also DaimlerChrysler), 10, 33, 37, 420
Circuit City, 112, 113
Clorox Company, 251
Coca-Cola, 20, 205, 344, 412, 509
Colgate-Palmolive, 61, 218, 230, 365
Columbia University, 431, 461
Commentry-Fourchambault-Decazeville, 30
Compaq Computers, 373
ConEd, 88
Corning, 60, 61
Credit Suisse First Boston (CSFB), 386
Cummins Engine, 203
CuttingEdge Research, 21, 22, 49, 50, 83, 84, 114, 115, 141, 193, 195, 240, 263, 285, 353, 410, 411, 524

Daimler-Benz, 33, 37
DaimlerChrysler (See also Chrysler Corporation), 3, 37, 193, 204, 344, 378, 414, 420–421
Dallas Cowboys, 113
Dallas Mavericks, 15
Dell Computer, 394, 423
Delta Airlines, 78, 141, 216, 234
Deutsche Post, 87
Disney (See Walt Disney Company)
Doctor's Hospital, Manteca, California, 152
Dow Chemicals, 60
DuPont Chemicals, 59, 78, 437, 441

Eastman Kodak, 204
Electronic Data Systems (EDS), 343, 373
Eli Lilly, 63
Enron, 12, 51, 81, 103, 105, 300, 386
Equitable Life Insurance, 154

Federal Express, 63, 376
Fel-Pro, 144
Firestone, 145
Fisher Body, 308–313
Flextronic International, 226, 427
Florida Marlins, 15
Ford Motor Company, 3, 4, 5, 10, 37, 145, 188, 194, 204, 205, 383, 392, 414, 423, 509
Fortune magazine, 137, 141, 151
French Foreign Legion, 232

Gannett News, 59
Gap, The, 150
Gaylord Container Corporation, 59
General Dynamics Corporation, 56
General Electric, 4, 16, 20, 127, 203, 269, 279–280, 281, 289, 291, 392, 423, 425, 426
General Mills Inc., 502

General Motors, 3, 4, 9–10, 31, 33, 37, 49, 60, 204, 206, 307–313, 383, 414, 427, 428, 439, 445, 446
Georgia-Pacific, 427
Global Crossing, 12, 103, 105, 386
Goldman Sachs, 149
Greenpoint Mortgage, 515
GTE, 127

Harcourt General Inc., 220
Hawthorne Plant, Western Electric, 33–34
Hershey Foods, 17
Hewlett-Packard, 143, 286, 373–374, 378
Hollywood Video, 91
Home Depot, 91, 279–281, 282, 289, 291
Home Shopping Network (HSN), 61–62
Honeywell, 45

IBM, 4, 10, 16, 19, 59, 203, 373, 410, 426, 510
Infiniti, 445
Infosys Technologies Ltd., 515
Intel, 237
Internal Revenue Service (IRS), 79
International Management Institute, 32

JCPenney, 49
Jet Blue, 290
John Deere & Company, 199–200
Johnson & Johnson, 95, 405–406

Krispy Kreme, 205

L.L. Bean, 94
Land O'Lakes Inc., 427
Lantech, 128
Levi Strauss, 394
Lexus, 445
Lockheed Aircraft, Lockheed Martin Corporation, 10, 96, 250, 259, 376, 427
Logan International Airport, 135

Lordstown Plant, General Motors, 307–313
Los Angeles County Health Department, 59
Lowe's, 279

Major League Baseball (MLB), 15
Management Recruiters, Inc., 78–79
Marathon Petroleum, 416
Marriott Hotels, 49, 51, 149
Mary Kay, 437, 438
Mastercard, 113
Maybelline, 59
Maytag Appliances, 194, 437
MBNA Company, 113–114
McDonald's Corporation, 61, 422, 439
McDonnell-Douglas, 62, 64, 86
McKinsey & Company, 12
Memphis State University, 173
Mercedes Benz, 439
Merrill Lynch, 225
Metropolitan Life Insurance, 217
Michigan State University, 67, 210, 275, 368
Microsoft Corporation, 60, 109–110, 226, 285, 287, 427
Midvale Steel Works, 28
Monsanto, 391
Motorola, 150, 203, 376, 426, 515

Nabisco, 205
NASA, 390, 442
National Association of Manufacturers, 46
National Basketball Association (NBA), 15, 57, 252
National Football League (NFL), 15
National Hockey League (NHL), 15
National League Baseball, 15
NCR Corporation, 438
New Balance Shoes, 260
New York Presbyterian Hospital, 6

Nike, 346
Nordstrom, 47–48
Norsk Hydro, 203
Nortel, 515
North American Free Trade Agreement (NAFTA), 515

O'Hare Airport, 135
Omega Engineering, 144
Orrefors Glass Works, 203

Palestinian Authority, 296–297
Peace Corps, 149
Philip Morris, 346
Pitney Bowes Inc., 224
Plumley Companies, 9–10
Polaroid, 17n, 60, 203, 437
Pratt and Whitney, 62
Procter & Gamble (P&G), 95, 204, 218, 230, 365, 373
Prudential Insurance, 188, 391
Public Service Commission (PSC) of Canada, 472–478
Publix Supermarkets, 91

Quaker Oats, 61
Qwest Communications, 103, 105

R.J. Reynolds, 422
Ralston Purina, 113
Ralton Electronics, 112
Raytheon, 386
Reebok, 346
Rhino Foods, 154
Rochester Institute of Technology, 166
Rockwell, 62
Rolls-Royce, 62

Saab-Scania, 203
Salt Lake Community College, 182
Samsonite Corporation, 47
Samsung Company, 79–80
SAP, 87
Sapphire Technologies, 125
SAS Institute, 112, 137
Saturn Division, General Motors, 10
Schering, 87

Sears, Roebuck & Company, 43
Singapore Airlines, 249
Sony, 435–436
Southwest Airlines, 141, 290–291
St. Lawrence College, 156
Starbucks Coffee, 62, 509
State Farm Insurance, 137, 188
Steelcase, 60
Sun Microsystems, 103
Sunbeam, 425

Tandem Computers, 438
TAP Pharmaceutical Products, 88–89
Target, 91
Tavistock Institute, 200–201, 206, 208
Temple University, 467
Tenneco, 153–154
Texaco, 60
Texas Instruments, 153, 203
3M, 46, 95, 250–251, 254, 281, 437, 439
Time Warner, 344
Toyota, 188
Trans State Airlines, 63
Transportation Security Administration (TSA), 136
Trusted Health Resources, 44

U.S. Bureau of Labor Statistics, 112, 286n
U.S. Civil Service, 194
U.S. Department of Defense, 96
U.S. Department of Justice, 300
U.S. Department of Labor, 59–60
U.S. Department of Transportation, 135–136
U.S. Environmental Protection Agency, 146
U.S. Fleet, 205
U.S. Government agency case study, 314–318
U.S. Marine Corps, 230
U.S. Postal Service, 144
United Auto Workers (UAW), 309

United Cerebral Palsy Association, 47–48
United Parcel Service, 427
University of Alberta, 472
University of Arkansas, 323
University of Detroit, 396
University of Florida, 318
University of Lowell, 163
University of Michigan, 60
University of North Carolina, Chapel Hill, 304
University of Oklahoma, 314
University of San Diego, 478
University of South Florida, 329
University of Southern California, 131
University of Texas at Dallas, 502
University of the Pacific, 431, 461
University of Washington, 175, 333

Vanderbilt University, 526
Visa, 21, 113
Volkswagen, 188
Volvo, 203, 205

W.L. Gore Company, 260
Wake Forest University, 242
Wal-Mart, 58
Walt Disney Company, 18, 19, 441
Wayne State University, 98
Wendy's, 414
Western Electric, 33–34, 194
Westinghouse, 49, 204
Whirlpool, 19
Windham International and National Foreign Trade Council, 561n69
Wipro Ltd, 515
World Bank, 71, 77
World Health Organization (WHO), 249, 251, 267
WorldCom, 120–121

Xerox, 203, 343, 344, 392

Yahoo Inc., 293–294
Yonsei University, 307

SUBJECT INDEX

A

ability, 123. *see also* cognitive abilities
absenteeism, 143
abusive supervision, 353
accommodation, conflict and, 361, 363
accomplishments, 119
accountability, 198
accuracy
   decision making and, 91–92
   perception and, 78
action, in problem solving, 10
action planning, 457
action research model, 446–448
adaptability, 64–65
additive tasks, 261
administrative decision-making model, 90–91
administrative principles perspective, 30–32, 38–39
age, 94. *see also* diversity
agreeableness, 49–51
alarm stage, of general adaptation syndrome, 139
assessment, 348–349, 351–352
attention, 74–75, 123
authoritarian leaders, 285–287, 297–300
autocratic leaders, 304–306, 360
automation, 206–207
autonomy, 197–200, 201
availability bias, 77
avoidance. *see also* uncertainty avoidance
   conflict and, 362, 363
   in decision making, 84–85

B

bandwidth, 440
bargaining, 360–361, 446
base rate bias, 82
basic coordination mechanisms, 375

behavior. *see also* motivation
   equity and, 238
   of leaders, 287–288, 302
   management, 115
   Type A/B, 148
behavioral standardization, 377–381
biases. *see also* decision making
   availability bias, 77
   base rate bias, 82
   hindsight bias, 77
   judgment and, 98–101
   loss-aversion bias, 81
   suppression of, 235
Big Five personality characteristics, 48–51
biofeedback, 154
boundary spanner, 422
bounded discretion, 86–89
broad banding, 127
buffering, 146
bureaucracy, competition and, 33
bureaucratic organization structures, 387–393, 410–414
bureaucratic prototype, 220
bureaucratic situation, leadership and, 291–292
burnout, 139

C

causal inferences, 540–549
cell phones, 150
centrality, 351
centralization, 383–385
ceremonies, 437
chaebol conglomerates, 518–519
chain structure, 261–262
change, 411, 419, 435–436, 442–448
   culture and, 522
   environmental, 423–425, 442–448
   evaluating, 457–459
   organization development and, 442–448
   resistance to, 443–446
change agents, 443

charisma, 283, 288–289. *see also* referent power
charismatic power, 346
   politics and, 355
chat rooms, 375
chief information officers (CIOs), 364
circle structure, 261–262
clinical depression, 147–148
coalitions, 354–355, 357
coercion, 446
coercive power, 345, 346, 348–349
cognitive abilities
   aspects of, 52–53
   leadership and, 285
   performance and, 123
   tests for, 53–55
cognitive conflict, 282
cognitive distortion, 237–238
collaboration, conflict and, 362, 363
collective bargaining, 355
collective socialization, 230
collectivism. *see* individualism-collectivism
commitment, organizational, 143–144, 436
communication, 216
   chief information officers, 364
   communication campaigns, 226
   conflict and, 360
   culture and, 521
   organization development and, 446
   organization structure and, 375
   politics and, 356
   processes, 223–227
   in teams, 261–263
compensation
   for group rewards, 267–270
   high-performance work systems and, 126–129
   nenko system, 519
   power and assessment, 348–349
   stock option plans, 103–105

competition, 361, 363
competitive group rewards, 268–270
completed connected communication network, 261–262
complexity, environmental, 423–425
compliance, 347
comprehensive interdependence, 217–219, 358
comprehensive theories of leadership, 295–301
   contingency theory (Fiedler), 296–297
   decision tree model (Vroom-Yetton), 297–300
   path-goal theory, 300–301
compromise, conflict and, 362, 363
computer-mediated communication (CMC), 264
conceptual skills, 23
conflict, 343–344, 357–360. *see also* politics; power
   avoidance, 517
   effects of, 360
   negotiation and restructuring, 360–366
   role conflict, 151, 160
conformity, 222
confrontation, 514
conjunctive tasks, 261
conscientiousness, 49–51
consensus, 514
consensus acceptance, 242–247
consideration dimension, of leader behavior, 287, 288
constituency groups, 407, 456, 457
consultants, 553
consultation, 447
consultative leaders, 297–300, 304–306
content, process *vs.*, 534
contingency factors
   organization design and, 405
   transformation, 425–428

contingency theory (Fiedler), 296–297
continuous learning, 531–532, 531–534. *see also* critical thinking
continuous-process production, 416–417, 419
contractual relationships, 428
control
  of information, 350–351
  locus of, 514, 517
  of resources, 350
  science and, 536
controlling function, of managers, 20–21
convergence hypothesis, 523–524
cooperative group rewards, 267–270
cooptation, 355
coordination requirements, in groups, 263
core job characteristics, 197–200
correlation coefficient, 543–544
cost-savings plans, 128–129
covariation, 541–544
creative individualism, 222
creativity, 71–72
  in decision making, 92
  innovativeness and, 95
  process of, 93–94
credibility, 225
criterion-related validation, 540
critical contingencies model, 350–352
critical-incident technique, 197
critical psychological states, 198
critical resources, 362
critical thinking, 531–532. *see also* continuous learning
  causal inferences, 540–545
  designing observations to infer cause, 545–549

facilitating generalization in, 550–551
  organizational behavior and, 551–554
  research results, 549–551
  scientific process and, 534–540
  theory and data, 537–538
cultural diversity, 58
cultural experience, 58, 62–64
culture. *see also* international organizational behavior; organization culture
  characteristics comparison, 516
  creativity and, 95
  cultural heterogeneity, 266
  decision making and, 87
  national cultures, 510
  trends in organizational behavior and, 514–517
cyclical effects, 124–126

D

data, theory and, 537–540. *see also* critical thinking
data gathering and provisional diagnosis, 447, 456
debt bondage, 150
decentralization, 385, 389, 410
decisional roles, of managers, 25–26
decision importance, 354
decision making, 71–72. *see also* groups; leadership; organization design (OD); teams
  administrative decision-making model, 90–91
  avoidance of, 84–85
  creativity in, 92–96
  culture and, 518–519

decision tree model, 297–300
  defined, 72
  leadership and, 285–287
  life-cycle model of leadership, 283–294
  observation and, 79
  rational decision-making model, 80–89
  reducing errors in, 91–92
  whistle blowing and, 88–89
decision tree model (Vroom-Yetton), 297–300
decoupling mechanism, 362–363
deferred payment plans, 128
degradation, rites of, 438
delegating style, 293–294, 297–300, 304–306
democratic leaders, 285–287
demographic diversity, 56–58
demographic experience, 58–60
departmentation, 381–383, 411
depression, 147–148
depth, of OD interventions, 448–449
description, science and, 536
diagnosis, in problem solving, 9–10
differentiation
  of groups, 255
  structural, 374
diffusion of responsibility, 263
directing function, of managers, 20
direct supervision, 376, 379
discipline programs, 116–117
disjunctive socialization, 231–232
disjunctive tasks, 261
dissatisfaction, 94. *see also* job satisfaction; stress

coping with, 152–155
  organizational costs of, 141–145
  sources of, 146–151
distributional justice, 234–236
disturbed reactive environments, 37
divergence, conflict and, 358, 360–362
diversity, 8, 43–44
  adaptability, 64–65
  in cognitive abilities, 52–56
  in experience, 56–58
  mirror image fallacy and, 44–45
  in personality, 48–52
  in physical abilities, 55–56
  reengineering and, 47–48
  selection and placement, 45–46
  training and, 46–47
diversity, environmental, 423–425
divestiture socialization, 232
divisional departmentation, 382–383, 411
divisional objectives, 19
divisional structures, 389–391, 414
division of labor, 16–17, 188
dysfunctional conflict, 357–358

E

economic rationality. *see* rational decision-making model
effectiveness, organizational, 407–408
efficiency, 187–188. *see also* efficiency perspective; motivation; quality perspective
  methods engineering, 188–191

organizational, 407–408
process engineering,
  188–191
efficiency perspective,
  188–193, 194,
  407–408
  industrial engineering
    and, 192–193
  motivation trade-offs
    and, 195
effort-performance linkage,
  107
elaboration contingencies,
  412
electronic bulletin boards
  (EBBs), 375
electronic conferencing,
  375
elimination of alternative
  explanations, 541, 545
e-mail, 224–225, 237, 375
emergent task elements,
  219–220
emotional stability, 49–51
employee retention. see
  retention
employees. see also culture;
  diversity; job
  satisfaction; labor;
  motivation; stress
  creative people as, 94
  employee-oriented
    behavior, 287,
    290–291
  monitoring, 78–80
empowerment, 8, 149
encoding, 223–224
encouragers, 257
endurance, 55–56
enhancement, rites of, 438
enrichment
  model of, 197–200
  programs for, 207
  sociotechnical, 200–202,
    208
  stress and, 152–153
  vertical, 194–197
entrepreneurial situation,
  leadership and,
  291–292
environment, 405–406. see
  also organization
  design (OD)
environmental change,
  419, 423–425

environmental complexity,
  420–421
environmental receptivity,
  422–423
environmental turbulence,
  426
environmental uncertainty,
  421–422
equity theory, 217, 233–240
ergonomics, 190. see also
  human factors
  engineering
escalation of commitment,
  83
established task elements,
  219–220
ethics
  culture and, 526–529
  organization
    development and,
    444–445
  in organizations, 386
  of power, 345
  teaching, 552
evaluation, in problem
  solving, 10, 12
exhaustion stage, of
  general adaptation
  syndrome, 139
expectancy, 107, 118–119
  experience and, 124
  path-goal theory and,
    300–301
expectations, role scope
  and, 151
experience
  analyzing, 533
  cultural, 58, 62–64
  cyclical effects and,
    124–126
  demographic, 58–60
  diversity in, 56–58
  nonmotivational
    determinants of
    performance, 123
  openness to, 49–51
  personal, 534–535
expert power, 345, 346,
  348–349
explanation, science and,
  537
explicit coercion, 446
explicit theories, 538
external environment,
  419–425

external threats, 270, 271
extinction, 114
extroversion, 49–51

F

feedback, 115
  to client organization,
    448
  as core job characteristic,
    197–200
  feedback channels, 200
  goal-setting theory and,
    120–121
  motivation and, 124
  survey feedback,
    455–456
femininity, 510–512. see
  also gender
five-dimensional model of
  international
  organizational
  behavior (Hofstede-
  Bond), 510–518
flat hierarchies, 408, 409
flexibility
  in divisional structures,
    390–391
  electronic manual
    adjustment and, 376
  in matrix structures, 392
flexible-cell production,
  416–417, 419
flexible manufacturing
  cells, 207
followers, 281, 282, 284.
  see also leadership
  characteristics of, 302
  leader-follower relations,
    296
  vertical dyad linkage
    and, 292–293
force field analysis, 443,
  445
force ranking systems, 269
formalization, 377
formalization contingencies
  core technology and,
    414–419
  as stage in organizational
    maturity, 412
formal organization, 436
Fourteen Principles of
  Management (Fayol),
  31

free riding, 257–258. see
  also social loafing
free speech, 237
functional
  departmentation, 382,
    411
functional dimension, of
  socialization, 227–230
functional grouping,
  253–254
functional objectives, 19
functional structure, 388,
  414

G

gender
  leadership and, 286
  masculinity-femininity,
    510–512, 522
general adaptation
  syndrome, 139
general cognitive ability,
  52–53
generalizability, 549
globalization. see also
  international
  organizational
  behavior
  culture and, 510, 515
  global presence, 524
goal orientation, 123
goals, 18–21
  conflict and, 358
  group motivation and,
    267–270, 270
  leadership and, 282
  marketing vs.
    manufacturing, 359
  mixed motive conflict,
    272–273
  power and, 344
  socialization and,
    230–232
  superordinate, 362
goal-setting theory,
  119–123
group-based leadership,
  297–300, 304–306
group maintenance roles,
  257
groups, 249–251. see also
  leadership
  cohesiveness, 270–272,
    360

groups *(continued)*
  composition of, 263–267
  conflict in, 272–273
  defined, 251–252
  development of,
    255–256
  formation of, 252–254
  group effectiveness, 252
  individual productivity
    vs., 256–260
  intergroup mirroring,
    461–463
  intergroup team
    building, 453–455
  motivation in, 267–270
  mutual adjustment and,
    379
  representative, 365
  size of, 263
  sociotechnical
    enrichment of,
    200–202
  synergy of, 258–259
  teams *vs.*, 259–260
groupthink, 271, 272

H

Hackman-Oldham model,
  of job enrichment,
  197–200, 207
harmonizers, 257
Hawthorne Studies, 33–34
health care costs, 142–143
hedonism, 113
heroes, 437, 439
heterogeneity, 265–267
  membership, 354
heuristics, 98–101
hierarchical dimension, of
  socialization, 228–230
  team-based structure *vs.*,
  260
hierarchical level, politics
  and, 354
hierarchy, in organization
  structure, 383–385
hierarchy of authority, 17
high-performance work
  systems, 126–129
hindsight bias, 77
hiring. *see also* employees;
  labor
  diversity and, 59–60
  practices, 553
history threat, 545

HIV (AIDS), 249–250
holding units, 392
homogeneity, 265–267
  for data gathering, 548,
  549
  leader irrelevance and,
  289–291
horizontal job enlargement,
  193–194, 203
hostile environment,
  422–423
human factors engineering,
  190–191
human relations
  perspective, 32–34,
  38–39
human skills, 23
hygiene factors, 196
hypercompetitiveness, 426
hypotheses, 538

I

identification
  organizational identity,
  436
  power and, 347
illness, in workplace, 146
implicit coercion, 446
implicit theories, 538
impression management,
  355
incentives. *see also*
  motivation
  culture and, 519
  power and assessment,
  348–349
  systems, 126–129
inception contingencies,
  411, 413
inclusionary dimension,
  of socialization,
  228–230
incubation, creative
  process, 93
individualism-collectivism,
  510, 512–513, 517,
  519, 521, 523
individuality. *see also*
  diversity
  competitive group
    rewards and, 268–270
  group productivity *vs.*,
    256–260
  norms and individual
    adjustment, 222

individual socialization,
  230–231
industrial engineering, 188,
  192–193
industrial robots, 206–207
inequity, 236–240. *see also*
  equity theory
influence, 282, 304–306
informal organization, 436
informational roles, of
  managers, 24–25
information control,
  350–351
information inputs, 37
information overload, 263
information technology
  (IT), 205, 515
ingratiation, 355
in-group members, 293
initiating structure
  dimension, of leader
  behavior, 287, 288
initiation, of groups, 255
innovation
  creativity and, 72, 95
  scientific method and,
  533
inputs, 36
inspiration, creative
  process, 93–94
instrumentality, 106–107,
  111–118, 124,
  300–301
integrated leadership
  model, 281–284,
  301–302
integrating managers, 365
integration. *see also*
  organization structure
  of groups, 255–256
  rites of, 438
  structural, 374–375
intelligence, 52–53
intensive technology,
  417–419, 419
interactional justice,
  234–236
interactions, 548–549
interdependence, 215–217.
  see also groups; role
  relationships; teams
  communication
    processes and,
    223–227
  conflict and, 358, 360,
    362–366

consensus acceptance,
  242–247
  equity theory and,
    233–240
  norms and role episodes,
    220–223
  role taking/role making
    and, 219–220
  types of, 217–219
intergroup mirroring,
  461–463
intergroup team building,
  453–455
internalization, 347–348
international
  organizational
    behavior, 509–511
  characteristics
    comparison, 516
  cultural trends, 514–517
  effects on, 518–522
  ethics and, 526–529
  global presence and, 524
  growth and
    development, 8–9
  individualism-
    collectivism, 510,
    512–513
  managing differences of,
    522–525
  masculinity-femininity,
    510–512
  offshore jobs, 515
  power distance, 510,
    513
  short-term/long-term
    orientation, 510,
    513–514
  uncertainty avoidance,
    510–511
interpersonal power,
  345–348
  affiliations and, 354–355
  assessment, 348–349
  conformity responses to,
    347–348
  sources of, 345–347
interpersonal roles
  of managers, 24, 25
  quality of, 233–240
interrole conflict, 151, 223
intersender role conflict,
  151, 223
intranets, 375
intrasender role conflict,
  151, 223

investiture socialization, 232
irrelevance, leader, 289–291
isolation, 270
"is" planning, 456

J

jargon, 227
job, standardization by, 377
job analysis, 377
job description, 220, 377
Job Descriptive Index (JDI), 540
Job Diagnostic Survey (JDS), 199–200
job enrichment
    model of, 197–200
    programs, 207
    sociotechnical, 200–202, 208
    stress and, 152–153
    vertical, 194–197
job extension, 193–194
job-oriented behavior, 287
job range, 193
job rotation, 154, 194
job satisfaction, 135–137. see also dissatisfaction; stress
    defined, 138
    measuring, 140–141
    motivational perspective and, 193
    profitability and, 142
    safety and, 145
joint diagnosis and action planning, 448
judgment. see also biases; decision making
    equity, 234–236
justice, 239, 345. see also equity theory
just-in-time (JIT) procedures, 364

K

kibbutzim, 518–519
knowledge of results, 198

L

labor. see also employees

collective bargaining, 355
    cost of, 112–113
    debt bondage of, 150
    offshore jobs, 515
    shortages, 6
laissez-faire leaders, 285–287
language, 437, 440
large-batch production, 415. see also mass production
lateral linkage devices, 364
latticework structure, 521–522
leader-follower relations, 296
leader prototype, 76–77
leaders. see leadership
leadership
    behavior and, 287–288
    characteristics of followers and situations, 291–295
    charisma and, 283, 288–289
    comprehensive theories of, 295–301
    conflict and, 360
    contingency theory (Fiedler), 296–297
    culture and, 517
    decision-making styles, 285–287
    decision tree model, 297–300
    defined, 281–284
    gender and, 286
    integrated leadership model, 281–284, 301–302
    leader irrelevance, 289–291
    leadership motivation pattern, 292
    leader traits, 285
    life-cycle model, 283–294
    path-goal theory of, 300–301
    substitutes for, 294–295, 300
    transformational, 288–289
    universal theories of, 284–291

vertical dyad linkage, 292–293
Leadership Behavior Description Questionnaire (LBDQ), 287, 288
leadership motivation pattern (LMP), 291
leadership traits, 50, 279–281
learning organizations, 533
learning theories, 107. see also continuous learning
    reinforcement theory, 113–117
    social learning theory, 117–118
least preferred co-workers (LPC), 296–297
legitimate power, 345, 346, 348–349
lifecycle contingencies, 410–413
life-cycle model, 283–294
line divisions, 389
local area networks (LANs), 375
locus of control, 514, 517
locus of leadership, 284
logical verification, 119
long-linked technology, 417–419, 419
loose-cannon prototype, 220
loose coupling, of parts, 92
loss-aversion bias, 81

M

Machiavellianism, 353–354
macro organizational behavior, 7–8, 13
management, 15–16
    administrative principles perspective, 30–32, 38–39
    contingency approach to, 39
    defined, 16–21
    goals and objectives, 19–21
    history of, 27–28
    human relations perspective, 32–34, 38–39

managerial
    advancement, 22
    managerial jobs, 21–23
    managerial roles, 24–26
    managerial skills, 23–24
    nature of managerial work, 26–27
    open systems perspective, 36, 38–39
    power and, 344–345
    scientific management perspective, 28–30, 38–39
manufacturing goals, 359
manufacturing technologies (Woodward), 414–419
marketing goals, 359
masculinity-femininity, 510–512, 522
mass customization contingencies, 412
mass production, 415–417, 419
matrix organization structure, 365–366, 391–392, 414
maturity
    organizational, 410
maturity, of groups, 256
meaningfulness, 149, 198
mechanistic structures, 408, 409, 419
media, 223–225
mediating technology, 417–419, 419
membership heterogeneity, 354
merit-pay systems, 127–128
meso organizational behavior, 7, 8, 13. see also efficiency; groups; interdependence; leadership; motivation; quality perspective; role relationships; teams
methods engineering, 188–191
micro organizational behavior, 7, 8, 11. see also creativity; decision making; diversity; job satisfaction; motivation; perception; performance; stress

middle managers, 21–22, 26
mirror image fallacy, 44–45
mirroring, intergroup, 461–463
mission, 16, 456
mixed motive conflict, 272–273
modeling, 117
modular structure, 393
monitoring, of employees, 78–80
moral rights, 345
motion studies, 192
motivation, 103–105, 187–188. *see also* efficiency; motivational perspective; performance; quality perspective
 culture and, 519
 cyclical effects and, 124–126
 defined, 105
 expectancy, 106–107, 118–119
 goal-setting theory, 119–123
 in groups, 267–270
 high-performance work systems and, 126–129
 learning theories of, 111–118
 need theories of, 108–111
motivational perspective
 comprehensive job enrichment, 197–200
 efficiency trade-offs and, 195
 evaluating, 202–203
 horizontal job enlargement, 193–194
 sociotechnical enrichment, 200–202, 208
 vertical job enrichment, 194–197
motivator factors, 196
movement quality, 55–56
multinationalization, 510. *see also* international organizational behavior

multiunit structures, 392–393, 414
muscular strength, 55–56
mutual adjustment, 375–376, 376, 378–381
myths, 437, 439

N

national cultures, 510
need for achievement (nAch), 110–111, 281
need for power (nPow), 344, 353
need theories, 107, 108
 need hierarchy (Maslow), 109–110
 theory of manifest needs (Murray), 110–111
negative affectivity, 147–148
negative feedback, 37
negative politics, 356
negative reinforcement, 114–117
negotiation, 360–366
 defined, 361
 organization development and, 446
 role negotiation technique, 449–450
nenko system, 519
network information systems, 364
noise, 225
norms, 220–223
 groups and, 270
 legitimate power and, 346
 organization development, 441
norm standardization, 378, 379–381

O

objectives, 19–21
objectivity, 535, 540
observation
 accuracy and, 78
 decision making and, 79
 self-efficacy theory and, 119
openness to experience, 49–51
open revolution, 222

open system planning (OSP), 431–433, 456–457
open systems perspective, 36, 38–39
operant learning, 114
operational objectives, 19
oral communication, 224
organic structures, 408–410, 419
organizational adaptability, 8
organizational behavior. *see also* macro organizational behavior; management; meso organizational behavior; micro organizational behavior
 contemporary issues of, 7–9
 definitions of, 5–7
 problem solving and, 9–12
 science and, 551–554
 workplace productivity and, 3–5
organizational citizenship behaviors (OCBs), 143–144, 235
organizational commitment, 143
organizational efficiency, 407–408
organizational identity, 436
organizational power, 348
organizational productivity, 407
organization charts, 18
organization culture, 435–436. *see also* culture; organization development (OD)
 creativity and, 95
 defined, 436–437
 elements of, 437–440
 failures of, 442
 managing, 440–443
 "open-book management," 222
 structure and, 521
organization design (OD), 373–375, 405–406, 428
 alternatives, 408–410

bureaucratic, 387–393
coordination mechanisms, 375–378
departmentation, 381–383
external environment, 419–425
hierarchy and centralization, 383–385
lifecycle contingencies, 410–413
open system planning (OSP), 431–433
organizational effectiveness and, 407–408
organization design and, 406
postbureaucratic, 393–394, 427
prebureaucratic, 385–387, 410–413
selecting mechanisms for, 378–381
transformation contingencies, 425–428
organization development (OD), 435–436
 action research model, 446–448
 change and, 442–448
 evaluating change and, 457–459
 group interventions, 451–453
 intergroup mirroring, 461–463
 interpersonal interventions, 448–451
 interventions, 441–443
 organizational interventions, 455–457
organization roles, 149
organization size, 354, 413
organization structure, 374. *see also* organization design (OD)
organizing function, of managers, 19–20
"ought" planning, 456
outcomes
 pay increases and, 126

in rational decision-making model, 82–83, 89
out-group members, 293
outputs, 36
output standardization, 377, 379–381
oversimplification, 205–206

P

participating style, 293–294
participation in decision making (PDM), 153
path-goal theory of leadership, 300–301
perceived challenge, 139
perception, 71–72
  conflict and, 359–360, 360
  defined, 72
  equity judgments and, 234–236
  of inequity, 236–238
  of job satisfaction, 138–139
  perceptual processes, 73–80
  reducing problems of, 78–80
perceptual processes
  attention stage of, 74–75
  organization stage of, 75–77
  recall stage of, 77–78
performance, 103–105. see also motivation; personality
  cyclical effects and, 124–126
  goal commitment and, 121
  job satisfaction and, 141–142
  nonmotivational determinants of, 123
performance-outcome expectation, 106–107. see also instrumentality
performance-outcome linkage, 107
peripheral norms, 221–223
personality
  Big Five characteristics of, 48–51

homogeneity vs. heterogeneity, 265–267
negative affectivity and, 147–148
politics and, 353–354
tests, 51–52
traits of leaders, 285, 302
personal power, 348
person-role conflict, 223
persuasion, 119, 446
physical abilities, diversity and, 55–56
physical conditioning, 153–154
physical constraints, of groups, 263
physical strain, 148–149
piecework plans, 127–128
pivotal norms, 221–223
placid/clustered random environments, 37
planning, 18–19
political indeterminism, 358
politics, 343–344. see also conflict; power
  decision making and, 87
  defined, 352
  demographic experience and, 58–59
  emergence of, 354
  managing problems of, 356–357
  personality and, 353–354
  power and, 352–354
  tactics, 354–356
polling, 550–551
pooled interdependence, 217–219, 358
position power, 296
positive reinforcement, 114–117
post-action data gathering and evaluation, 448
postbureacratic organization structures, 393–394, 427
power, 343–344. see also conflict; politics
  abusive supervision, 353
  conflict and, 357–360

conformity and, 347–348
critical contingencies model, 351–352
defined, 344–345
interpersonal sources of, 345–347
structural sources of, 349–351
power distance, 510, 513, 517, 521, 523
power imbalance, 227
prebureaucratic organization structure, 385–387
prediction, science and, 536
preparation, in creative process, 93
prepotency, 109
privacy, 63
  productivity and, 125
  stress and, 146
probabilities, 82–83
problem identification, 447
problem solving, 9–12
procedural justice, 234–236
process, content vs., 534
process consultation, 451–452
process engineering, 188–191
process loss, 256–258, 379
production blocking, 256–257
productivity, 3–5, 125. see also motivation
  of groups, 252
  group vs. individual, 256–260
  norms, 270
  organizational, 407
profitability, 142
profit-sharing plans, 128–129
progress, 514, 516–517
prototypes
  bureaucratic vs. loose-cannon, 220
  leader, 76–77
punctuated equilibrium, 256
punishment, 114–117
  position power, 296
  power and, 348–349

Q

Quality Circles (QCs), 204–206
quality perspective, 187–188, 203–208. see also efficiency; motivation
  automation and robotics, 206–207
  evaluating, 207–208
  of interpersonal role relationships, 233–240
  Quality Circles, 204–206
  self-managing teams, 206
quantitative ability, 53, 54

R

race. see culture; diversity
random assignment, 546–548
random sampling, 78, 550–551
random socialization processes, 231
"rate busters," 238
rational decision-making model
  influences on, 83
  limiting factors of, 83–89
  outcomes, 80–82
  probabilities, 82–83
realistic job previews (RJPs), 154–155
reasoning ability, 53, 54
recall, 77–78
receptivity, environmental, 423–425
reciprocal interdependence, 217–219, 358
reengineering, 47–48
referent power, 345, 346, 348–349
reinforcement theory, 113–117
relaxation techniques, 154
reliability, 539, 540
repetitive stress injuries (RSIs), 193
research results, 549–551. see also critical thinking

resistance stage, of general adaptation syndrome, 139
resource allocation, 359
resource control, 350
responsibility, 198, 359
results
    knowledge of, 198
    of research, 549–551
retention
    dissatisfaction and, 143
    diversity and, 60–62
    job satisfaction and, 136–137
reward power, 345–346, 348–349
rewards, 126–129
    conflict and, 359
    culture and, 517
    for groups, 267–270, 270
    position power, 296
ringisei, 518–519
rites, 437–438
rituals, 438
robotics, 206–207
role ambiguity, 149–150
role conflict, 151, 160
role custodianship, 230
role episodes, 220–223
role innovation, 230
role negotiation technique (RNT), 449–450
role perceptions, 119–123
role relationships, 215–217. *see also* interdependence
    equity theory and, 233–240
    managing structural interdependence and, 362
    quality of, 233–240
    socialization, 227–233
role scope, 151
role-sending messages, 223

S

sabotage, 144–145
safety, 145
SARS epidemic, 226
satisfaction. *see* job satisfaction
satisficing solution, 90–91
scapegoating, 356

schemas, 76–77
science, purposes of, 536–537
scientific management perspective, 28–30, 38–39
    efficiency and, 188
scientific method, 533, 535
    causal inferences and, 540
    linking organizational behavior to, 551–554
scripts, 76
security, 63
selection and placement, 45–46
selection threat, 545
self-efficacy theory, 107, 118–119
self-managing teams, 206
self-reinforcement, 117–118
selling style, 293–294
semiautonomous groups, 201
sensitivity training, 450–453
sequential interdependence, 217–219, 358
sequential socialization, 231
serial socialization, 231
service technologies (Thompson), 417–419
sex roles, 511. *see also* gender
shaping, 114
shared mental model, 76
short-term/long-term orientation, 510, 513–514, 523
sick-building syndrome, 146
simple differentiated structure, 387
simple undifferentiated structure, 385–387
simultaneous structures, 391. *see also* matrix organization structure
situations, leadership, 281, 284. *see also* leadership
    characteristics of, 302
    leader irrelevance and, 289–291

leadership motivation pattern and, 291–292
skills
    of managers, 23–24
    standardization of, 377–378, 379–381
    technical, 24, 285
    training, 153
    variety of, 197–200
slack resources, 363–364
small-batch production, 415–417, 419
social density, 146, 147
social distraction, in groups, 263
social facilitation, 258–259
social information, 440–441
social information processing, 203
socialization, 216
    designing programs for, 232–233
    goals and tactics, 230–232
    to new roles, 227–233
    organization structure and, 378
social justice, 345
social learning theory, 117–118
social loafing, 257–259
social recognition, 115
social support, 146
sociotechnical enrichment, 200–202, 208
solution
    in problem solving, 10
    verification, in creative process, 94
spatial ability, 53, 54
special-interest committees, 520–521
stability, 436
staff divisions, 389
standardization
    as coordination mechanism, 376–377, 379
    of theories, 540
standard setters, 257
standard time analysis, 192
standing committees, 365
status, 515
status discrepancies, 359
stereotypes, 77

stock option plans, 103–105, 128–129
stopwatch time analysis, 192
stories, 438
strategic goals, 18, 122–123
stress, 135–137. *see also* job satisfaction
    coping with, 152–155
    defined, 138–139
    measuring, 140–141
    roles as, 156–161
    sources of, 146–151
structural contingency factors, 410
structure. *see also* organization design (OD)
    managing interdependence, 362–366
    power and, 349–351
substitutability, 351
substitutes for leadership theory, 294–295, 300
subversive rebellion, 222
supervisory managers, 22–23, 26
surface elements, 437
survey feedback, 455–456
symbolic management, 441
symbols, 437, 439–440
synergy, 258–259. *see also* groups

T

tall hierarchies, 408–410
target, of OD interventions, 448
task forces, 365
tasks
    complexity, 148–149
    established *vs.* emergent task elements, 219–220
    identity/significance of, 197–200
    strategies, 122–123
    structure, 260–261, 296
team development, 452–453
team productivity, 8
teams, 249–251. *see also* leadership

communication structure for, 261–263
computer-mediated communication and, 264
force ranking systems, 269
groups *vs.*, 259–260
homogeneity *vs.* heterogeneity, 265–267
intergroup team building, 453–455
task structure of, 260–261
team development, 452–453
technical skills, 24, 285
technological contingencies, 418–419
technology, 405–406
    communication and, 224
    core technology, 414–419
    flexibility and, 205
    in postbureaucratic organization, 427
telling style, 293–294
temporal precedence, 541
terrorism, 63, 71–72, 88–89, 135–136
test of mean differences, 541–542
theory, data and, 537–540
theory of moral rights, 345
Theory X, 34, 35
Theory Y, 35
"therblig," 192

third-party peace making, 453–455
threat
    external, 270, 271
    history, 545
    selection, 545
time orientation, 359
time-study techniques, 192
top managers, 21, 26
Total Quality Management (TQM), 203–204
training
    individual differences and, 46–47
    organization structure and, 378
transaction costs, 426–428
transformational leadership, 288–289
transformation contingencies, 412, 425–428
turbulent fields, 37
turnover
    dissatisfaction and, 143
    interdependence and, 219
two-factor theory, 196–197
Type A/B behavior, 148

U

uncertainty
    environmental, 423–425
    politics and, 354, 356–357
    reduction, 350–351
    of resolution, 139

uncertainty avoidance, 510–511, 517, 522
unit-linking mechanisms, 364
unit production, 415. *see also* small-batch production
universal theories of leadership, 284–291
    behavior, 287–288
    decision-making styles, 285–287
    irrelevance, 289–291
    traits, 285
    transformational, 288–289
upper communication, 227
utilitarianism, 345

V

valence, 106, 108–111, 124, 300–301
validity, 539–540
values, 138
    conflict and, 359–360
    importance of, 139
    legitimate power, 346
verbal ability, 52–54
verbal persuasion, 119
verification, 538
vertical dyad linkage (VDL), 292–293
vertical job enrichment, 194–197, 203
vertical loading, 200

violence, in workplace, 144–145
virtual structure, 394, 426

W

wages. *see* compensation
wheel structure, 261–262
whistle blowing, 88–89
wireless technology, 224
work design, 188. *see also* motivation
    culture and, 519–520
    efficiency perspective, 188–193, 195, 407–408
    motivational perspective, 193–203, 208
    quality perspective, 203–208, 233–240
work flow
    grouping, 253–254
    standardization by, 377
workplace. *see also* diversity; productivity
    illness in, 146
    physical and social environment of, 146–147
    violence and sabotage in, 144–145
works council, 520
written communication, 224

Y

Y structure, 261–262